SIMON AND SCHUSTER

WORLD COIN CATALOGUE

1982–1983

TWENTIETH CENTURY

Revised and Expanded Edition

by

Günter Schön

Simon and Schuster · New York

Contents

5

Introduction

Yeoman Numbers

In order to help collectors and dealers, we have added after most Schön numbers the corresponding number assigned by R.S. Yeoman in his well-known works entitled »A Catalog of Modern World Coins« and »Current Coins of the World«.

Hints for Quick Understanding of the Book

The coins described in this catalogue are arranged in the alphabetical order of issuing countries. Certain territories have, however, been classified under those countries with which they are, or were formerly, linked, as for instance the Faroe Islands and Greenland come under Denmark; the Riau Islands and West Irian under Indonesia, etc. In the case of Germany, all the territories linked with it, which have issued their own coinage since the foundation of the German Reich on 18th January 1871, have been grouped together in date order.

The issues are listed systematically in chronological order; coins of the same type are nevertheless given together in the increasing order of their nominal value. The catalogue begins, broadly speaking, with 1900; but care has been taken not to break artificially the series with issues going back to an earlier date; for example, in the case of an issue dated 1874–1906, the listing in the catalogue covers all the coins of the same type struck between those two extreme dates.

In spite of intensive care taken throughout in quest of accuracy, this catalogue cannot pretend to be exhaustive. The compilers will, therefore, be glad to receive any additional information that might contribute to make it more complete and more perfect.

Illustrations and Descriptions

All the coins which are illustrated are reproduced in actual size and are placed above the text which refers to them. Whenever this proved impossible, the relative catalogue numbers are given with the illustrations. These illustrations are intended to help to recognize the coins, and can under no circumstances be used for comparison in the case of an expertise.

In view of the greatly increasing interest in commemorative issues, the author has sought to give a more complete description of them, whilst usually only the bare essentials are offered when ordinary current coins are under consideration.

For the amateurs of »collections with a theme« a very complete documentation can be found in the works by Dieter Fassbender entitled »Gedenkmünzen« (»Commemorative Coins«), and by Anton von Ziegésar entitled »Tiermotivkatalog« (»Thematic Catalogue of Animals on Coins«).

Abbreviations Used for Metal Contents

Acm	=	Acmonital (Italian coinage)	Fe	= Iron
Ag	=	Silver	Mg	= Magnesium
Al	=	Aluminium	Ni	= Nickel
Au	=	Gold	Pb	= Lead
Bi	=	Billon	Pd	= Palladium
Bra	=	Brass	Sn	= Zinc
Br	=	Bronze	St	= Steel
Cu	=	Copper	Ti	= Tin

Abbreviations Used in the Text

EE	= Ethiopian Era	R	= reverse
EF	= Extremely Fine (XF)	Rev.	= reverse
FAO	= Food and Agricultural Organization of the United Nations	S-HC	= Solar-Hidshra Calendar
		Unc	= Uncirculated
		VF	= Very Fine
H-C	= Hidshra Calendar	XF	= Extremely Fine
No.	= number	Y	= Yeoman Numbers

State of Preservation of the Coins

In the case of both buying and selling coins it is all important to know the terms which are used by the numismatists to define the grades of preservation. There are eight main grades, but the first two are best left out as far as coins of the 20th century are concerned.

Good = gut erhalten (German) = bien conservé (French) = mediocre (Italian) = goed (Dutch) = regular (Spanish), and *Very Good* = sehr gut erhalten = très bien conservé = discreto = zeer goed = bien conservada: these grades are less and less in use as dealers and buyers have turned more and more quality conscious; such terms describe coins which have long been in circulation and have suffered much from wear, leaving types and inscriptions rather flat and unrecognizable. Such coins should not be found in good collections.

Fine = schön = beau = bello = fraai = bien conservada: is used to describe coins which, in spite of having been much in circulation, still show clearly the contours of the types in fairly high relief. This is the lowest grade which should be acceptable to collectors.

Very Fine = sehr schön = très beau = bellissimo = zeer fraai = muy bien conservada: the coins in this state show some traces of wear on the portions in high relief and the legends.

Extremely Fine = vorzüglich = superbe = splendido = prachtig = extraordinariamente bien conservada: all the details of the engraving are seen; there is almost no wear at all even on the portions of the type in high relief, and in the deeper parts the original shine is still preserved.

Uncirculated = Stempelglanz = fleur de coin = fior di conio: there is no trace of wear at all, the coin looks fresh from the mint. Coins issued after 1950 must, broadly speaking, be in this state of preservation to be really worth having. It is since about that date that, at the request of the collecting public, the various mints have often made the new coinage available for sale in special containers. It must, however, be pointed out that, as the coins are struck by machines in great quantities, the handling and transport in bags often cause slight scratches or marks on the surface. These coins are sometimes struck on specially prepared flans.

Proof = Spiegelglanz or polierte Platte = flan bruni = fondo specchio = proefslag = flor de cuño: This term defines no longer the state of preservation, but a special form of production. The flans are previously polished and struck with polished dies, and meticulous care is taken.

Valuations

The prices given in the catalogue are, broadly speaking, for coins in the best condition obtainable, generally in an extremely fine state of preservation (EF). Coins in VF (very fine) condition may only be worth half, and those in F (fine) might be worth very little. Top prices are always paid for top quality pieces. Scratched or damaged coins command very low figures.

It should be also said that there is a general tendency for collectors to demand VF-EF condition in the case of coins struck between 1900–1939, and EF-FDC for the more recent issues. Coins which have circulated for years or even decades are seldom to be found in a state of perservation better than VF. The quality of a coin will make its price; so also will its rarity.

It must be evident to all that it is very difficult in a catalogue like this to quote prices; these depend largely on the law of offer and demand and can fluctuate widely over the years and in various parts of the world. It is accepted that US material fetches higher prices in the United States, and British coins are much more in demand in Britain than in the rest of Europe, for instance; prices depend, therefore, largely on the interest attached to the coins by the collecting public. It is a well-known fact that sometimes at an auction sale certain objects fetch exorbitant or unrealistic prices; only two amateurs are needed to send the prices rocketing sky high.

Commemorative coins, or coins issued for a special purpose (patterns, coronation sets, etc.) call for a separate consideration. The state of preservation required here is, as a rule, EF, even better EF-FDC. The reason for this is that commemorative issues are generally preserved with great care and seldom come into circulation.

As coins cannot keep "fresh" indefinitely (even in a box or case), it is necessary to look after them. Much information as to how to do this will be found in the work by Horst Winskowsky entitled "Münzen pflegen" ("How to Look after Your Coins").

All valuations in the SCHÖN are stated in U.S. Dollars.

Where to Secure Coins

When a collector desires to obtain recent issues of coins, he may turn either to an official institution, or to a private firm, as in the case of special issues. A list of official organizations likely to be able to offer coins to collectors is given below. The formalities of sale and delivery vary greatly from country to country, it is therefore advisable to write first for information (return postage can be paid by International Reply Coupons). It will be appreciated that the author cannot guarantee that the information given is always exact; the help of all is sought to correct or complete this list, which is based on documentation kindly supplied by the editor of the HELVETISCHE MÜNZENZEITUNG (HMZ – Swiss Numismatic Gazette).

Afghanistan
1 Afghani = 100 Puls

Royal Afghan Mint, Kabul, Afghanistan

Ajman
1 Riyal = 100 Dirham

Crown Agents Coin Bureau,
St. Nicholas House, Sutton, Surrey/England

Argentina
1 Peso = 100 Centavos

Casa de Moneda,
Avenida Antardida, Buenos Aires

Australia
1 Dollar = 100 Cents

Royal Mint, 280, William St., Melbourne C. 1

Austria
1 Schilling = 100 Groschen

Österreichisches Hauptmünzamt,
A-1031 Wien, Postfach 225
and: Österreichische Nationalbank,
A-1090 Wien, Otto-Wagner-Platz 3
(for ordinary current coins)

Bahamas
1 Dollar = 100 Cents

Treasury Dept., P. O. Box 557, Nassau

Bahrain
1 Dinar = 1000 Fils

Bank of Bahrain, P. O. Box 106, Manama, Bahrain
For FAO issues also:
Eastern Bank Ltd., P. O. Box 29, Manama, Bahrain

Belgium
1 Franc = 100 Centimes

Monnaie Royale de Belgique, Av. De Pacheco, 32,
B-1000 Brussels

Bolivia
1 Peso = 100 Centavos

Casa de la Moneda, Potosi

Brazil
1 Cruzeiro = 100 Centavos

Casa da Moeda, Praca da Republica 173,
Rio de Janeiro

Brunei
1 Dollar = 100 Sen

Crown Agents Coin Bureau, St. Nicholas House,
Sutton, Surrey/England

Bulgaria
1 Lew = 100 Stotinki

HEMUS, Ruski 6, Sofia
and: Numismatic Shop, 29, Vitosha Blvd., Sofia

Burundi
1 Franc = 100 Centimes

For FAO issues:
Banque de la République, Bujumbura

Canada
1 Dollar = 100 Cents

Coins Uncirculated, P. O. Box 470, Ottawa 2,
Ontario

Chile
1 Escudo = 100 Centesimos

Casa de Moneda, Santiago

Colombia
1 Peso = 100 Centavos

Casa de Moneda, Calle 11 No. 4–93, Bogotá

Cyprus £ 1 = 1000 Mils	Central Bank of Cyprus P. O. Box 1087, Nicosia For FAO issues: Crown Agents Coin Bureau, St. Nicholas House, Sutton, Surrey/England
Czechoslovakia 1 Koruna = 100 Halere	Artia, Ve Smečkách 30, Praha 1
Denmark 1 Krone = 100 Øre	Danmarks Nationalbank, Holmens Kanal 17 1060 Kopenhagen K.
Egypt, VAR £ 1 = 100 Piastres = 1000 Millièmes	For FAO issues: Mint House, Abbasia, Kairo
Equatorial Guinea 1 Peseta = 100 Centimos	Banco Central de la Republica, Santa Isabel
Fiji 1 Dollar = 100 Cents	Currency Board, Victoria Parade, Suva/Fiji and: Crown Agents Coin Bureau, St. Nicholas House, Sutton, Surrey/England
Finland 1 Markka = 100 Penniä	Suomen Rahapaja, Katajanokanlaituri 3, Helsinki 16 and: Bank of Finland, P.O. Box 10160, Helsinki 10 (no commemorative issues)
France 1 Franc = 100 Centimes	Monnaie de Paris, 11, Quai de Conti, Paris 6e
Germany, GDR 1 Mark = 100 Pfennig	Deutsche Handelsbank DDR-108 Berlin, Behrenstraße 22
Germany, GFR 1 Deutsche Mark = 100 Pfennig	Verkaufsstelle für Sammlermünzen, D–638 Bad Homburg v.d.H., Bahnhofstraße 16–18
Great Britain £ 1 = 100 New Pence	Royal Mint, London, E.C. 3
Greece 1 Drachma = 100 Lepta	Bank of Greece, Treasury Department, Cash, Delivery, and Dispatch Division, Athens
Guatemala 1 Quetzal = 100 Centavos	Casa Nacional de Moneda, Calle 4–28, Zona 1, Guatemala City
Guyana 1 Dollar = 100 Cents	Bank of Guyana, P.O. Box 658, Georgetown
Hungary 1 Forint = 100 Filler	Hungarian State Mint, Üllöi út 102, Budapest VIII and: Artex, P.O. Box 167, Budapest 62, and: Konsumturist, Népköztársaság útja 27, Budapest VI
Iceland 1 Krone = 100 Aurar	Sedlabanki Islands, Reykjavik
India 1 Rupee = 100 Paisa	Indian Government Mint, Bombay 1
Indonesia 1 Rupiah = 100 Sen	Arthie Vasa, Kabajoran Baru, Djakarta
Iran 1 Rial = 100 Dinars	Imperial Irian Mint, Teheran For FAO issues: Bank Markazi, Teheran
Iraq 1 Dinar = 1000 Fils	For FAO issues: Central Bank of Iraq, Issue Dept., P.O. Box 64, Bagdad
Israel £ 1 = 100 Agorot	Israel Stamp and Coin Gallery, 4, Maze St., Tel Aviv
Italy 1 Lira = 100 Centesimi	La Zecca, Via Principe Umberto 4, Roma

Jamaica 1 Dollar = 100 Cents	Decimal Currency Board Office, P. O. Box 8000, Kingston
Japan 1 Yen = 100 Sen	Mint Bureau, 1, Shinkawasakicho, Kita-ku, Osaka
Jordan 1 Dinar = 1000 Fils	Central Bank of Jordan, Amman For FAO issues: Crown Agents Coin Bureau, St. Nicholas House, Sutton, Surrey/England
Lebanon 1 Lira = 100 Piastres	For FAO issues: 25, King St. West, Toronto 1, Canada For FAO issues also: Banque du Liban, Rue Masraf Loubnan, Beirut
Kuwait 1 Dinar = 1000 Fils	Central Bank, P. O. Box 526, Kuwait
Liberia 1 Dollar = 100 Cents	For proof coins: Treasury Dept., P. O. Box 557, Nassau, Bahamas
Luxembourg 1 Franc = 100 Centimes	Caisse Générale de l'Etat, 5, Rue Goethe, Luxembourg
Madagascar 1 Franc = 100 Centimes	Institut d'Emission Malgache, B. P. 205, Tananarive
Malawi 1 Kwacha = 100 Tambala	Crown Agents Coin Bureau, St. Nicholas House, Sutton, Surrey/England
Malta £ 1 = 100 Cents = 1000 Mills	Central Bank of Malta, Valletta
Mexico 1 Peso = 100 Centavos	Casa de Moneda, Calle del Apartado No. 13, Mexico 1 D. F.
Nepal 1 Rupee = 100 Paisa	Royal Mint, Katmandu and: Nepal Rastra Bank, Katmandu
Netherlands 1 Gulden = 100 Cents	s'Rijks Munt, Leidseweg 90, Utrecht
New Zealand 1 Dollar = 100 Cents	The Treasury, Private Bag, Lambton Quai, Wellington
Nicaragua 1 Córdoba = 100 Centavos	Banco de Nicaragua, Depart. de Tresoreria, Apartado 2252, Managua
Nigeria 1 Naira = 100 Kobo	Minting Company, Victoria Islands, Lagos
Norway 1 Krone = 100 Øre	Norges Bank, Oslo
Oman 1 Rial = 1000 Baiza	British Bank of Middle East, Muscat
Pakistan 1 Rupee = 100 Paisa	Pakistan Mint, Baghban Pura, Lahore
Panama 1 Balboa = 100 Centesimos	For proof coins: Treasury Dept., P. O. Box 557, Nassau, Bahamas
Peru 1 Sol de oro = 100 Centavos	Casa Nacional de Moneda, Junin 791, Lima
Poland 1 Zloty = 100 Groszy	Bank Handlowy w Warszawie Traugutta 7, Warsaw
Portugal 1 Escudo = 100 Centavos	Casa da Moeda, Avenida Dr. Antonio José de Almeida, Lissabon 1
Qatar 1 Riyal = 100 Dirham	Qatar Monetary Agency P. O. Box 1234, Doha

Ras al Khaima 1 Riyal = 100 Dirham	Crown Agents Coin Bureau, St. Nicholas House, Sutton, Surrey/England
Rwanda 1 Franc = 100 Centimes	Banque Nationale du Rwanda, B. P. 351, Kigali
San Marino 1 Lira = 100 Centisimi	Ufficio filatelico di Stato, Sezione numismatica San Marino
Seychelles 1 Rupee = 100 Cents	The Treasury, P.O. Box 59, Victoria and: Crown Agents Coin Bureau, St. Nicholas House, Sutton, Surrey/England
Singapore 1 Dollar = 100 Cents	Chartered Industries Ltd., 249 Jalan Boon Lay, Jurong
Somalia 1 Shilling = 100 Centesimi	For FAO issues: Crown Agents Coin Bureau, St. Nicholas House, Sutton, Surrey/England
South Africa 1 Rand = 100 Cents	South African Mint, P.O. Box 464, Pretoria
South Korea 1 Won = 100 Chon	Government Printing Agency, 93 Bukchang Dong, Chungku, Seoul
South Vietnam 1 Dong (Piastre) = 100 Centimes	National Bank, Saigon. For FAO issues also: Commercial Credit Bank of Vietnam, Saigon
Spain 1 Peseta = 100 Céntimos	Fabrica Nacional de Moneda y Timbre, Jorge Juan 106, Madrid 9
Sri Lanka 1 Rupee = 100 Cents	Bank of Sri Lanka P. O. Box 241, Colombo
Sudan £ 1 = 100 Piastres = 100 Millièmes	Sudan Mint, P.O. Box 43, Khartum
Swaziland 1 Lilangeni = 25 Luhlanga, 1 Luhlanga = 100 Cents	Crown Agents Coin Bureau, St. Nicholas House, Sutton, Surrey/England
Sweden 1 Krona = 100 Øre	Kungelige Mynt, Box 22055, Stockholm
Switzerland 1 Franken = 100 Rappen	Eidgenössische Staatskasse, Bundesgasse 14, CH-3003 Bern
Syria £ 1 = 100 Piastres	Central Bank of Syria, Damascus, S. A. R.
Taiwan (Formosa) 1 New Taiwan Dollar = 100 Cents	Central Mint of China, 44 Chiu Chuan St., Taipeh
Thailand 1 Baht = 100 Stangs	Royal Mint, 4, Chao Fah Road, Bangkok
Tonga 1 Pa'anga = 100 Seniti	Numismatic Section Treasury, Nuku'alofa
Trinidad and Tobago 1 Dollar = 100 Cents	Central Bank of Trinidad & Tobago, P.O. Box 1250, Port of Spain For FAO issues: Treasury Dept., P.O. Box 557, Nassau, Bahamas
Tunisia 1 Dinar = 1000 Millimes	For FAO issues: Banque Central de Tunisie, Tunis
Turkey 1 Lira = 100 Kurus = 4000 Paras	State Mint, Maliye Bakanligi Darphane Mudurlugu, Istanbul
Turks and Caicos Islands £ 1 = 20 Shillings = 240 Pence	Crown Agents Coin Bureau, St. Nicholas House, Sutton, Surrey/England

Uganda	Bank of Uganda, P. O. Box 7120, Kampala
1 Shilling = 100 Cents	and: Crown Agents Coin Bureau,
	St. Nicholas House, Sutton, Surrey/England

| United States of America | Numismatic Service, US Assay Office, |
| 1 Dollar = 100 Cents | 350, Duboce Avenue, San Francisco, 94 102 CA |

| Uruguay | Banco Central del Uruguay, |
| 1 Peso = 100 Centesimos | Cerrito 351, Montevideo |

| USSR | Bank of Foreign Trade, Commercial Department, |
| 1 Rouble = 100 Kopeks | Moscow K 16, Neglinnaja 12 |

| Vatican City | Stato della Città del Vaticano, Governatorato, |
| 1 Lira = 100 Centesimi | Vatican City |

Western Samoa	Numismatic Section, Box 194 G. P. O., Apia
1 Tala = 100 Sene	and: Crown Agents Coin Bureau,
	St. Nicholas House, Sutton, Surrey/England

| Yugoslavia | For FAO issues: |
| 1 Dinar = 100 Para | Bank of Yugoslavia, P. O. Box 1010, Belgrade |

Zambia	For FAO issues:
1 Kwacha = Ngwee	Crown Agents Coin Bureau, St. Nicholas House,
	Sutton, Surrey/England

*

There is the occasional criticism that so-called not-collectable pseudo coins are entered indiscriminately; in this respect it must be mentioned that when listing new coins it depends on the completeness of the information and it is frequently difficult to determine whether the minting in question concerns an authentic current coin. The listing of a coin therefore does not purport anything regarding its essence as a genuine coin in circulation and does not embrace any opinion in the sense of such persons who do not consider the »pseudo coins« as collectable.

FAO COIN PLAN

The FAO COIN PLAN with its subject "Produce More Food" which was commenced by the World Food Council in 1968, is the first issue of coins in the history of money coming under international patronage. The main object of the plan centers around the spreading of the message of the FAO over the greatest possible area; in order that this message will appear on coins in many languages and with many symbols. The only objects which will change hands daily for a generation and more.

Our sincerest thanks are due to:

Dr. Walter Alexander-Katz, Lisbon; Mrs. Myriam Avida, Jerusalem; M. I. Bathia, Muscat; Roland Becker, Avellino; Udo Bläs, Ottweiler; David Boehm, New York; W. Ernst Boehm, Ludwigshafen; Böhringer und Schmuck, Munich; Dr. Lore Börner, Berlin; Professor Dr. Klaus Brehme, Stuttgart; Tim J. Browder, San Marino, California; J. F. Cartier, Chambéry; Peter A. Clayton, Hemel Hempstead; Paul Conrid, Munich; Ernst Debrunner, Zürich; Joachim Düster, Pforzheim; Holger Dombrowski, Münster; Miss Barbara Ernst, Korntal; Dieter Fassbender, Hollerath; G. Ferguson, Ottawa; Enrique Franke, San Salvador; Michel Gebara, Beirut; Herbert S. Halm, Montevideo; Robert E. Herwegh (†), Frankfurt am Main; B. G. Heyne, Berlin; Burt Hobson, New York; Walter Hüsch, Dortmund; Octavian Iliescu, Bukarest; Kurt Jaeger, Korntal; Heinz Jaenicke, Munich; Jørgen Steen Jensen, Copenhagen; Ewald Junge, London; Gerhard Kellberg, Eschen; Willy Kisskalt, Munich; Melvin J. Kohl, Mission Place, California; Hermann Krause, Minneiska, Minn.; Vlastimil von Maly, Wuppertal-Barmen; Dr. Ottfried Neubecker, Wiesbaden; Miss Gerda Paehlke, Ludwigshafen; Bernard Poindessault, Paris; Ralf Ring, Jena; Dr. Bernard Schaaf, Dubuque, Iowa; Peter-M. Schiller, Offenbach; Hans Schlumberger, Stuttgart; Dr. Gregor Schwirtz, Jena; Bohumil Struhala (†), Holešov; Heinz Thormann, Münster; Hermann Webler, Berg; Günter Wehner, Kehrsatz; Arne Wink, Doha; Horst Winskowsky, Langen; Anton Freiherr von Ziegésar, Frankfurt am Main. Artexport, Tirana; Artia, Prague; Arve Uruguay Coins, Montevideo; Banco Nacional de Cuba, Havana; Bank of Ghana, Accra; Bank of Jamaica, Kingston; Banque Centrale du Liban, Beirut; Banque du Maroc, Rabat; Banque Nationale de Yougoslavie, Belgrade; Bernhardt Inc., Geneva; British Bank of Middle East, Muscat; Bundesstelle für Außenhandelsinformation, Cologne; Caisse Générale de l'Etat, Luxembourg; Casa da Moeda, Lisbon; Central Bank of Cyprus, Nicosia; Central Bank of Ireland, Dublin; Central Mint of China, Taipeh; Chase Manhattan Bank, New York; Consulado de la Republica Argentina, Munich; Consulado-Geral do Brasil, Munich; Consulat de Monaco, Munich; Consulate-General of South Africa, Munich; Crown Agents Coin Bureau, Sutton; Currency Board, Suva; Department of Archaeology, Katmandu; Der Bundesminister für Finanzen, Bonn; DESA Foreign Trade Company, Warsaw; Deutsche Bundesbank, Frankfurt am Main; Deutsche Numismatik, Frankfurt am Main; Buchexport, Leipzig; Dresdner Bank AG, Numismatischer Handel, Frankfurt am Main; Eidgenössische Münzstätte, Bern; Embassy of Cyprus, Bonn-Bad Godesberg; Embassy of Ireland, Bonn-Bad Godesberg; Etablissement Evolena, Vaduz; Euronummis, Milan; Financial Secretary Treasury Department, Apia; Hemus, Sofia; Heraldischer Verein "Zum Kleeblatt", Hannover; International Numismatic Promotion, Brussels; Israel Government Coins and Medals Corporation Ltd., Jerusalem; Italcambio, Milan; Karl-May-Verlag, Bamberg; Landsbanki Islands, Reykjavik; Magyar Nemzeti Bank, Budapest; Mecattaf Bank, Beirut; Merkur Bank, Munich; Mint Bureau Ministry of Finance, Osaka; Monnaies Or Agent, Chiasso; Nationalmuseet, Copenhagen; Numismatica Italiana, Milan; Numismatic Section Treasury, Nuku'alofa; Österreichisches Hauptmünzamt, Vienna; Reserve Bank of Rhodesia, Salisbury; Royal Australian Mint, Canberra; Royal Canadian Mint, Ottawa; Services Commerciaux Français en Allemagne, Munich; Staatliche Münzsammlung, Munich; Staatliche Museen (Münzkabinett), Berlin; Suomen Kansallismuseo, Helsinki; The Treasury, Wellington.

Afghanistan

Area: 250,000 sq. mi. Population: 17,600,000.
Emirate; independent kingdom since 1919, constitutional monarchy since 1926; republic since 17th July 1973. Capital: Kabul.
Monetary unit until 1925 the Rupee-Kabuli; since 1926 decimal system, i. e. 100 Puls = 1 Afghani. During the currency conversion of 1926, the factor was 11 Rupees for 10 Afghani.

60 Paisa = 1 Rupee, 5 Paisa = Shahi, 10 Paisa = Senar, 6 Senar = 1 Rupee, 20 Paisa = 1 Abbasi, 3 Abbasi = 1 Rupee, 30 Paisa = 1 Quiran, 2 Quiran = 1 Rupee, 30 Rupees = 1 Habibi, 1 Amani, 1 Tilla

30 Rupees = 1 Habibi, 1 Amani, 1 Tilla. These coins weighed 1 Musqual = 4.6 grams. After the currency conversion to Afghani, the weight system was also changed over to grams. Since 1933 a Tilla possesses a coin weight of only 4 grams. Gold coins are not in circulation and are not being dealt with at any Afghan bank.

HABIB ULLAH KHAN 1901–1919

National arms: mosque flanked by tilted flags and rifles with fixed bayonets, underneath crossed swords, rifles, flags and cannons. In one instance Star of David below mosque in a wreath of light rays. In many instances there are, however, only crossed canons below the mosque.

			VF	XF
1 (15)	1 Abbasi (Ag) H–C 1320 (1902). Toughra and date in wreath. ℞ national arms; mosque with flags on either side; below, crossed sabres, the whole within wreath of corn-ears		30.00	50.00
2 (16)	1 Quiran (Ag) H–C 1320, 1321, 1325 (1902, 1903, 1907)		12.00	20.00
3 (17)	1 Rupee (Ag) H–C 1319–1321, 1325 (1901–1903, 1907)		12.00	20.00
4 (18)	5 Rupees (Ag) H–C 1319 (1901)		60.00	100.00
5 (19)	1 Tilla (Au) H–C 1319–1320 (1901–1902)		140.00	250.00
6 (20)	1 Paisa (Bra) H–C 1329 (1911). Inscription in circle. ℞ national arms.		10.00	18.00
7 (21)	1 Senar (Ag) H–C 1326–1329 (1908–1911). Inscription in wreath, above star. ℞ national arms in wreath.		10.00	18.00
8 (22)	1 Abbasi (Ag) H–C 1324–1329 (1906–1911)		16.00	25.00

				VF	**XF**
9 (23)	1	Quiran (Ag) H–C 1323–1329 (1905–1911)		10.00	15.00
10 (24)	1	Rupee (Ag) H–C 1321–1329 (1903–1911)		10.00	15.00
11 (25)	5	Rupees (Ag) H–C 1322–1329 (1904–1911)		60.00	100.00
12 (26)	1	Paisa (Cu) H–C 1329–1337 (1911–1919). Inscription. ℞ national arms in octagon		5.00	7.00
13 (27)	1	Senar (Ag) H–C 1329–1337 (1911–1919). Inscription in wreath, above star. ℞ national arms in octagon, in wreath		7.00	10.00
14 (28)	1	Abbasi (Ag) H–C 1330–1337 (1912–1919)		7.00	10.00
15 (29)	1	Quiran (Ag) H–C 1329–1337 (1911–1919)		5.00	8.00
16 (30)	1	Rupee (Ag) H–C 1329–1337 (1911–1919)		8.00	10.00
17 (31)	1	Tilla (Au) H–C 1336–1337 (1918–1919)		265.00	320.00

AMAN ULLAH KHAN 1919–1929

National arms: mosque flanked by tilted flags, below crossed swords, all within a partly round or oval wreath of light rays.

18 (32)	1	Paisa (Cu) H–C 1337 (1919)		4.00	6.00
19 (34)	1	Shahi (Cu) H–C 1337 (1919)		8.50	12.00
20 (35)	1	Senar (Cu) H–C 1337 (1919)		8.00	12.00
21 (36)	3	Shahi (Cu) H–C 1337 (1919). With date according to Solar-Hidshra calendar: No. 26		4.50	7.50
22 (39)	½	Rupee (Ag) H–C 1337 (1919). With date according to Solar-Hidshra calendar: No. 29		4.00	7.00
23 (40)	1	Rupee (Ag) H–C 1337 (1919). With date according to Solar-Hidshra calendar: No. 30		8.00	11.00
24 (41)	1	Tilla (Au) H–C 1337 (1919). Star above, Toughra and date below, all within a wreath of leaves. ℞ mosque crossed swords below, wreath of light rays			
24a (41)		surrounded by wreath of leaves. 4.6 grams; 21 mm dia.		115.00	175.00

24a　1 Tilla (Au) H–C 1337 (1919). Type

<table>
<thead>
<tr><th></th><th></th><th></th><th>VF</th><th>XF</th></tr>
</thead>
</table>

| | | similar to No. 24, but Star of David in place of the crossed swords | **VF** 115.00 | **XF** 200.00 |

After the introduction of the Solar-Hidshra calendar (hidshri shamsi) on the strength of a decree of 1920, the dates 1298–1307 given on the coins correspond to the years 1920–1929 of the Christian calendar. Coins of same types, but bearing different dates, are listed separately.

25 (33)	1	Paisa (Cu) S–HC 1299–1303 (1921–1925)	4.00	6.00
26 (36)	3	Shahi (Cu) S–HC 1298–1300 (1920–1922). Type as No. 21	5.00	8.00
27 (37)	1	Abbasi (Bi) S–HC 1298 (1920)	50.00	75.00
28 (38)	1	Abbasi (Bi) S–HC 1299 (1921). Type as No. 27, yet with a diameter now of 25 mm instead of 20 mm	28.00	40.00
29 (39)	½	Rupee (Ag) S–HC 1298–1300 (1920–1922). Type as No. 22	6.00	10.00
30 (40)	1	Rupee (Ag) S–HC 1298–1299 (1920–1921). Type as No. 23	10.00	18.00

31 (42)	2	Tilla (Au) S–HC 1298 (1920). Type as No. 24	215.00	300.00
32 (43)	3	Shahi (Cu) S–HC 1300–1301 (1922–1923). Toughra surrounded by stars. ℞ national arms in octagon, surrounded by stars.	6.00	8.00
33 (44)	1	Abbasi (Cu) S–HC 1299–1303 (1921–1925)	3.00	6.00
34 (45)	½	Rupee (Ag) S–HC 1300–1303 (1922–1925). Toughra in wreath. ℞ national arms in oval, septagon, the whole within wreath	7.00	11.00
35 (46)	1	Rupee (Ag) S–HC 1299–1303 (1921–1925)	13.00	18.00
36 (47)	2½	Rupees (Ag) S–HC 1298–1303 (1920–1925)	30.00	50.00
37 (48)	½	Amani (Au) S–HC 1299 (1921)	115.00	160.00

				VF	**XF**
38 (49)	1	Amani (Au) S–HC 1299 (1921). Toughra, date below, all within a wreath of leaves. ℞ Amani above, mosque below and crossed swords, in an oval wreath of light rays, all within a wreath of leaves. 4.6 grams; 22.5 mm dia.		120.00	190.00
39 (50)	2	Amani (Au) S–HC 1299–1303 (1921–1925)		200.00	350.00

40 (51)	5	Amani (Au) S–HC 1299 (1921). Denomination above, Toughra and date below, all within a wreath of leaves. ℞ Amani above, mosque, crossed swords below, in oval wreath of light rays, all within wreath of leaves. 23 grams, 33.5 mm dia.		900.00	1400.00

40a (51)	5	Amani (Au) S–HC 1299 (1921). Type as No. 40, but in place of the numeral 5, a star; ℞ in place of Amani, a '5'		1000.00	1600.00

NEW VALUE: 100 Puls = 1 Afghani

			VF	XF
41 (52)	2	Puls (Cu) S–C 1304–1305 (1926–1927). Toughra within circle, the whole within wreath. ℞ value in circle, the whole within wreath.	2.00	4.00
42 (53)	5	Puls (Cu) S–HC 1304–1305 (1926–1927)	4.00	7.00
43 (54)	10	Puls (Cu) S–HC 1304–1306 (1926–1928)	3.00	5.00
44 (55)	20	Puls (Ag) S–HC 1304 (1926)	55.00	90.00
45 (56)	½	Afghani (Ag) S–HC 1304–1307 (1926–1929). National arms in wreath. ℞ Toughra within wreath, above value.	2.50	4.00
46 (57)	1	Afghani (Ag) S–HC 1304–1307 (1926–1929)	4.00	7.00
47 (58)	2½	Afghani (Ag) S–HC 1305–1306 (1927–1928)	28.00	50.00
48 (59)	½	Amani (Au) S–HC 1304–1306 (1926–1928)	90.00	150.00

49 (60)	1	Amani (Au) S–HC 1304–1306 (1926–1928). Denomination above, Toughra below, date, all within a wreath of leaves. ℞ Great Mosque without wreath of rays of light. Number of the years of the reign, all within a wreath of leaves. 4.6 grams, 23 mm dia.	95.00	150.00
50 (61)	2½	Amani (Au) S–HC 1306 (1928)	1300.00	1800.00

HABIB ULLAH GHAZI (Bätschä-ji Saqqa) 1929

National arms: mosque flanked by tilted flags in a round wreath of light rays. Pulpit at left.

51 (66)	10	Paisa (Cu) H–C 1348 (1929). Denomination in Pashtu, between two stars. Legend partly arranged in a circle, and date within a wreath of leaves. ℞ denomination in Dari, between two stars. Mosque within wreath of rays of light, pulpit at left	18.00	30.00
52 (62)	20	Paisa (Cu) H–C 1347 (1929). Denomination in Pashtu, between two stars, legend and date within a wreath of		

			VF	XF
		leaves. ℞ denomination in Dari, between two stars. Mosque in a wreath of light rays, pulpit at left	7.00	10.00
53 (67)	1	Quiran (Ag) H–C 1347 (1929). Star above, legend partly arranged in a circle, date below, all within a wreath of leaves. ℞ 1 Quiran, mosque in a wreath of light rays, date below	26.00	40.00
54 (63)	1	Quiran (Ag) H–C 1348 (1929). Similar to No. 53, but legend arranged horizontally	11.00	16.00
55 (68)	1	Rupee (Ag) H–C 1347 (1929). Star above, legend partly arranged in a circle, date below, all within a wreath of leaves. ℞ mosque in a wreath of light rays	70.00	110.00
56 (64)	1	Rupee (Ag) H–C 1348 (1929). Similar to No. 55, but legend arranged horizontally on left in the national arms	20.00	32.00

| 57 (65) | 1 | Habibi (Au) H–C 1347 (1929). Denomination 30 Rupees, legend, date below, surrounded by wreath of leaves. ℞ 1 Habibi, below mosque in a wreath of light rays, pulpit at left. 4.6 grams, 21 mm dia. | 350.00 | 450.00 |
| 57a (65) | 1 | Habibi (Au) H–C 1347 (1929). Type similar to No. 57, but a star in place of the denomination of 30 Rupees | 380.00 | 480.00 |

MOHAMMED NADIR SHAH 1929–1933

National arms: mosque flanked by flags, within a wreath of corn ears or of leaves. Pulpit at left.

58 (69)	1	Pul (Cu) H–C 1349 (1930). Inscription surrounded by stars. ℞ value in circle, the whole surrounded by stars	1.50	2.50
59 (70)	2	Puls (Cu) H–C 1348 (1929). Toughra and date in circle, the whole within wreath	1.50	2.50
60 (71)	5	Puls (Cu) H–C 1349–1350 (1930–1931)	2.50	4.00
61 (72)	10	Puls (Cu) H–C 1348–1349 (1929–1930)	2.50	4.00
62 (73)	20	Puls (Cu) H–C 1348–1349 (1929–1930)	4.00	6.00

			VF	**XF**
63	(74)	25 Puls (Cu) H–C 1349 (1930)	3.00	5.00
64	(75)	½ Afghani (Ag) H–C 1348–1350 (1929–1931)	3.00	5.00

| **65** | (76) | 1 Afghani (Ag) H–C 1348–1350 (1929–1931) | 9.00 | 15.00 |

66 (78) 20 Afghani (Au) H–C 1349–1350 (1930–1931). Toughra, name and title within the wreath of leaves; denomination in brackets above. ℞ mosque and date within wreath of leaves, pulpit at left. 21.8 mm dia.   260.00   360.00

In the type similar to No. 66 there is another 1 Tilla gold coin (H–C 1348–1350). This coin probably weighs 4.6 grams, diameter unknown, and must be described as extremely rare.

67 (80) 2 Puls (Bra) S–HC 1311–1314 (1932–1935). Inscription in dotted circle, within wreath. ℞ value in dotted circle, within wreath   2.00   4.00

68 (81) 5 Puls (Bra) S–HC 1311–1314 (1932–1935)   2.00   4.00

69 (82) 10 Puls (Bra) S–HC 1311–1314 (1932–1935)   2.00   4.00

As can be seen from the dates given, the coins listed under Nos. 67–69 were still issued during the reign of King Mohammed Sahir Shah.

70 (83) ½ Afghani (Ag) S–HC 1310–1312 (1929–1931). Inscription in dotted circle, within wreath. ℞ national arms within wreath   4.00   6.00

71 (84) 1 Afghani (Ag) S–HC 1310 (1929)   55.00   90.00

National arms: mosque between flags, within the wreath of corn ears. Pulpit at left.

			VF	XF
72 (90)	2	Puls (Br) S–HC 1316 (1937). National arms within wreath. ℞ value in circle, within wreath.	0.25	0.50
73 (91)	3	Puls (Br) S–HC 1316 (1937)	0.50	1.00
74 (92)	5	Puls (Br) S–HC 1316 (1937)	0.35	0.70
75 (93)	10	Puls (Cu-Ni) S–HC 1316 (1937)	0.50	0.90
76 (85)	25	Puls (Cu) S–HC 1312–1316 (1933–1937). Inscription in dotted circle, within wreath. ℞ value in dotted circle, within wreath	5.00	10.00
77 (94)	25	Puls (Cu-Ni) S–HC 1316 (1937). National arms in wreath. ℞ inscription in circle, the whole surrounded by legend	0.50	1.00
78 (95)	25	Puls (Br) S–HC 1330–1332 (1951–1953)	0.50	1.00
79 (95a)	25	Puls (Ni–St) S–HC 1331–1334 (1952–1955)	0.50	1.00
80 (95b)	25	Puls (Al) S–HC 1331 (1952). Denomination in Pashtu in the circle. The word Afghanistan in the outer circle. ℞ national arms in the dotted circle, date below. 24 mm dia.	0.40	0.60
81 (86)	1	Quiran (Ag) H–C 1313–1314 (1934–1935). Legend in the dotted circle (60 dots), surrounded by wreath of corn ears; the word Afghanistan above. ℞ denomination 1 Quiran, date below, all within the wreath of ears of corn	3.00	5.00
81a (86)	1	Quiran (Ag) H–C 1315–1316 (1936–1937). Type as No. 81, but dotted circle with 40 dots	3.00	5.00

			VF	XF
82 (97)	50	Puls (Ni–St) S–HC 1331 (1952). National arms within wreath. ℞ value in circle, the whole surrounded by inscription	0.90	1.50

			VF	XF
83 (96)	50	Puls (Br) S–HC 1330 (1951). National arms in wreath. ℞ value in circle, the whole within legend	0.90	1.60
84 (96a)	50	Puls (Ni–St) S–HC 1331–1334 (1952–1955)	0.70	1.20
85 (98)	2	Afghani (Al) S–HC 1337 (1958). National arms in dotted circle, the whole surrounded by stars and legend. ℞ value in dotted circle, the whole surrounded by stars	1.60	3.00
86 (99)	5	Afghani (Al) S–HC 1337 (1958)	2.20	4.00

87 (88)	4	Grami = 1 Tilla (Au) S-HC 1315 (1936). Legend in dottet circle, surrounded by corn ears, the word Afghanistan above. ℞ denomination 4 Grami, national arms and date below, 4 grams, 19 mm dia.	155.00	240.00
88 (87)	6	Grami = 1½ Tilla (Au) S–HC 1313 (1934). Type similar to No. 87, but 6 grams and 22.2 mm dia.	280.00	440.00
89 (89)	8	Grami = 2 Tilla (Au) S–HC 1314–1315 (1935–1936). Type similar to No. 87, but 8 grams and 22.2 mm dia.	300.00	500.00

			XF	Unc
90 (100)	1	Afghani (Ni–St) S–HC 1340 (1961). 3 ears of corn and date. ℞ value surrounded by stars	0.20	0.30

91 (101) 2 Afghani (Ni–St) S–HC 1340 (1961).
Above inscription "Afghanistan", in
the center the fabulous eagle in front
of the sun who is reputed to have
placed a gold crown on the head of
the legendary first King Yamma, below
the date 1340. ℞ numeral of value
below the word "two" and above the
word "Afghani" between an ear of
corn and three stars

	XF	Unc
	0.30	0.40

92 (102) 5 Afghani (Ni–St) S–HC 1340, H–C 1381
(1961). King Mohammed Sahir Shah
(* 1914), in uniform between the dates
1340 and 1381, above the legend "Mohammed Sahir – asterisk – Afghanistan's – asterisk – King". ℞ numeral
of value below the word "five" and
above the word "Afghani" between
two ears of corn

| | 0.70 | 1.20 |

93 (A 102) 4 Grami = 1 Tilla (Au) S–HC 1339, HC
1380 (1960). The king's name in
Thoughra shape, to the right invoca-
tion of God, below: "De Afghanistan
Padshahi Daulat" (= Royal Afghan
Government). ℞ above "four Grami",
below "Kabul", left 1339, right 1380,
in the center an emblem above crossed
ears of corn formed of the mosque of
the national arms and historico-reli-
gious beasts (Eagle of Zarathustra and
the Bull of Mithras). 4 grams

| | Proof | 220.00 |

94 (B 102) 8 Grami = 2 Tilla (Au) S–HC 1339, HC
1380 (1960). Type similar to No. 93,
but 8 grams, 22.2 mm dia.   Proof   450.00

REPUBLIC since 1973

		XF	Unc
95 (103) 25 Puls (Brass-clad steel) S-HC 1352 (1973). Coat of arms. *R* value		0.30	0.50
96 (104) 50 Puls (Cu-clad steel) S-HC 1352 (1973). Type as No. 95		0.40	0.70
97 (105) 5 Afghani (Cu-Ni-clad steel) S-HC 1352 (1973). *R* value between two ears		0.60	1.00

CONSERVATION COMMEMORATIVE (3)

		Unc	Proof
98 (106)	250 Afghani (Ag) 1978	35.00	50.00
99 (107)	500 Afghani (Ag) 1978	45.00	65.00
100 (108)	10000 Afghani (Au) 1978	650.00	750.00

		XF	Unc
101 (109) 25 Puls (Al-Br) S-HC 1357 (1978). Coat of arms. R value		0.20	0.35
102 (110) 50 Puls (Al-Br) S-HC 1357 (1978). Same type as No. 101		0.25	0.45
103 (111) 5 Afghani (Cu-Ni) S-HC 1357 (1978). Same type as No. 101		0.50	0.80

			XF	Unc
104	25	Puls (Al-Br) 1980. New coat of arms. Rev. value, inscription, stars	0.15	0.25
105	50	Puls (Al-Br) 1980. Type as No. 104	0.30	0.40
106	1	Afghani (Cu-Ni) 1980. Type as No. 104	0.40	0.60
107	2	Afghani (Cu-Ni) 1980. Type as No. 104	0.50	0.75
108	5	Afghani (Cu-Ni) 1980. Type as No. 104	0.70	0.90

FOR THE FAO COIN PLAN (2)

			XF	Unc
109 (113)	5	Afghani (Cu-Ni) 1981	0.50	1.00
110 (114)	500	Afghani (Ag) 1981	Proof	25.00

Previous issues, see »Weltmünzkatalog 19. Jahrhundert« (World Coin Catalogue of the 19th Century)

Adschman # Ajman **Ajman**

Area: 96 sq. mi. Population: 5,000.
The sheikdom of Ajman belonged to the seven Trucial States in the Pacified Oman. Ajman also administratively includes the territory of Manama. Since December 2, 1971 Ajman is a member state of the "United Arab Emirates" (UAE). In addition to the Ajman-Riyal, the Qatar and Dubai-Riyal were legal tender. Capital: Ajman.

100 Dirham = 1 Ajman-Riyal

RASHID BIN HUMAID

		Unc	Proof
1	1 Riyal (Ag) 1969. Crossed flags and jambijas, underneath Arabian sandhen or May's partridge (Ammoperdix hayi – Fam. Phasianidae). ℞ value and name of country	3.00	10.00
2	2 Riyals (Ag) 1969. Type as No. 1	5.00	12.00

3	5 Riyals (Ag) 1969. Type as No. 1	12.00	16.00
4	7½ Riyals (Ag) 1970. Bone-fish (or Ladyfish) (Albula vulpes – Albulidae), stylized	25.00	90.00
5	7½ Riyals (Ag) 1970. Berber falcon (or Peregrine falcon) (Falco peregrinoides – Falconidae)	25.00	90.00
6	7½ Riyals (Ag) 1970. Gazelle (Gazella sp. – Bovidae)	25.00	90.00
7	10 Riyals (Ag) 1970. Lenin	28.00	
8	100 Riyals (Au) 1970. Type as No. 7	450.00	
9	1 Riyal (Ag) 1970. Type similar to No. 1	3.00	
10	2 Riyals (Ag) 1970. Type similar to No. 2	5.00	
11	5 Riyals (Ag) 1970. Type similar to No. 3	12.00	

COMMEMORATIVE COINS (4) AT THE DEATH
OF GAMAL ABD EL NASSER

		Unc	Proof
12	5 Riyals (Ag) 1970. Gamal Abd el Nasser (1918–1970), President of the United Arab Republic 1958–1970; head facing left in front of Sphinx and Pyramid. ℞ national emblem, denomination	12.00	

			Unc	
13	7½	Riyals (Ag) 1970. Type similar to No. 12	20.00	
14	25	Riyals (Au) 1970. Type similar to No. 12	100.00	
15	50	Riyals (Au) 1970. Type similar to No. 12	200.00	

COIN COMMEMORATING THE FAO COIN PLAN

16	5 Riyals (Ag) 1970. Ears of corn supported by two hands. ℞ national emblem, denomination (Not recognized by the FAO)	20.00	
A 16	75 Riyals (Au) 1970. Fish	300.00	

COMMEMORATIVE COINS (4)
FOR SAFEGUARDING VENICE

			Unc	Proof
17	5	Riyals (Ag) 1971. Motto: SAVE VENICE and symbolical representation. ℞ national emblem, above denomination in Arabic. Portrait of the sheik	10.00	120.00
18	25	Riyals (Au) 1971. Type as No. 17	60.00	125.00
19	50	Riyals (Au) 1971. Type as No. 17	120.00	200.00
20	100	Riyals (Au) 1971. Type as No. 17	300.00	400.00

21	5	Riyals (Ag) undated. Dag Hammerskjöld	12.00	25.00
22	25	Riyals (Au) undated. Type as No. 21		120.00
23	5	Riyals (Ag) undated. Mahatma Gandhi	12.00	25.00
24	25	Riyals (Au) undated. Type as No. 23		120.00
25	5	Riyals (Ag) undated. Martin Luther King	12.00	25.00
26	25	Riyals (Au) undated. Type as No. 25		120.00

		Unc	Proof
27	5 Riyals (Ag) undated. George C. Marshall	12.00	25.00
28	25 Riyals (Au) undated. Type as No. 27		120.00
29	5 Riyals (Ag) undated. Bertrand A. Russel	12.00	25.00
30	25 Riyals (Au) undated. Type as No. 29		120.00
31	5 Riyals (Ag) undated. Albert Schweitzer	12.00	25.00
32	25 Riyals (Au) undated. Type as No. 31		120.00
33	5 Riyals (Ag) undated. Jan Palac	12.00	25.00
34	25 Riyals (Au) undated. Type as No. 33		120.00
35	5 Riyals (Ag) undated. Albert J. Luthuli	12.00	25.00
36	25 Riyals (Au) undated. Type as No. 35		120.00

Albanien   # Albania   **Albanie**

Shqipëri

Area: 11,057 sq. mi. Population: 2,300,000.
After a long struggle under the leadership of the national hero Prince
Skanderbeg, Albania fell under Turkish domination in the 15th century. The country did not regain its independence until 28th November
1912. As it was occupied by the warring powers, it began its independent political life only after the First World War. In 1925 Ahmet Zogu
founded a dictatorship with himself as President. On 1st September 1928
he proclaimed himself King as Zog I. After the military occupation of
Albania by Italy in April 1939, the country was linked to the Italian
State in a close union. After the War of Liberation, successfully fought
first against the Italian domination, and then from 1943 against the
German occupation, the new People's State was formed on 24th May
1944 with a provisional Government under Enver Hodja, which was
able to exercise full control over the whole country from 29th November
1944 onward. On 11th January 1946 a People's Republic was proclaimed.
Capital: Tirana.

100 Qindarka Leku = 1 Lek, 100 Qindarka Ari = 1 Franka Ari, 5 Lek
= 1 Franka Ari; since 1939–1944: 1 Lek = 1 Lire; since 1947 only Lekë;
since 1964: 100 Qindarka = 1 Lek

			VF	XF
1 (1)	5	Qindarka Leku (Br) 1926. Lion's head. ℞ value above oak leaves	45.00	85.00
2 (2)	10	Qindarka Leku (Br) 1926. Eagle's head to right. ℞ value between olive bran-ches (Olea europaea – Oleaceae)	45.00	85.00
3 (3)	¼	Leku (Ni) 1926–1927. Lion (Panthera leo – Felidae). ℞ oak branch above value	6.00	10.00
4 (4)	½	Lek (Ni) 1926. Double eagle. ℞ Hercu-les fighting the Nemean lion	7.00	12.00
5 (5)	1	Lek (Ni) 1926–1927, 1930–1931. Clas-sical head. ℞ horseman	7.00	12.00

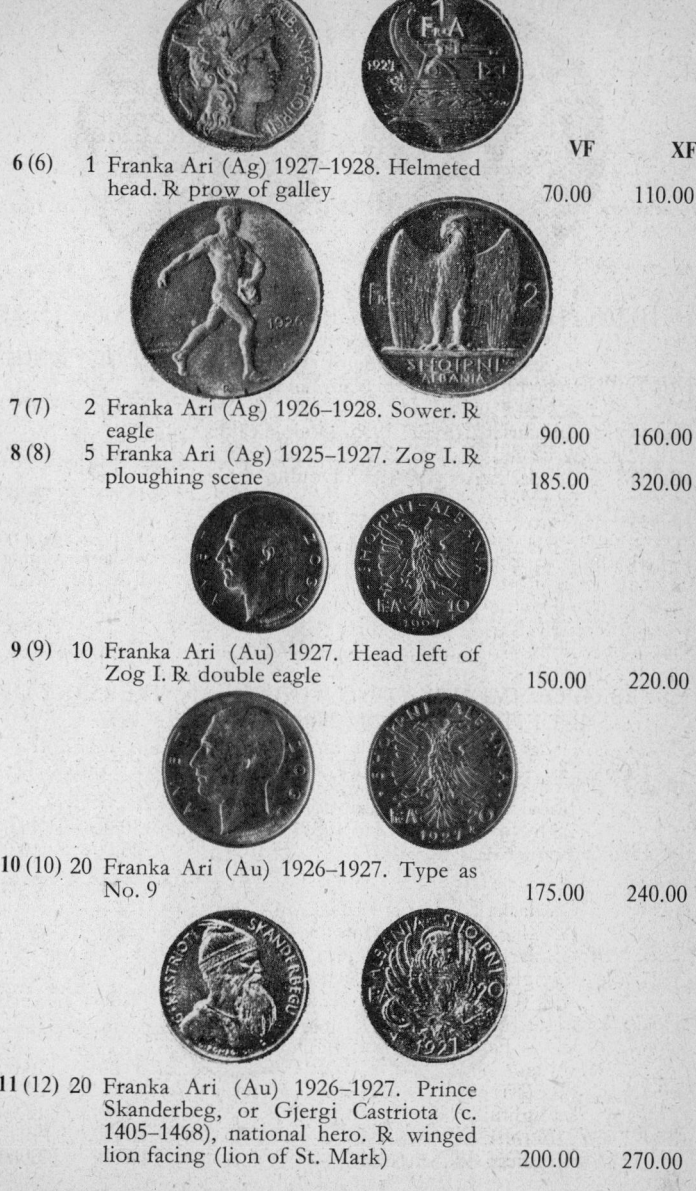

			VF	XF
6 (6)	1	Franka Ari (Ag) 1927–1928. Helmeted head. ℞ prow of galley	70.00	110.00
7 (7)	2	Franka Ari (Ag) 1926–1928. Sower. ℞ eagle	90.00	160.00
8 (8)	5	Franka Ari (Ag) 1925–1927. Zog I. ℞ ploughing scene	185.00	320.00
9 (9)	10	Franka Ari (Au) 1927. Head left of Zog I. ℞ double eagle	150.00	220.00
10 (10)	20	Franka Ari (Au) 1926–1927. Type as No. 9	175.00	240.00
11 (12)	20	Franka Ari (Au) 1926–1927. Prince Skanderbeg, or Gjergi Castriota (c. 1405–1468), national hero. ℞ winged lion facing (lion of St. Mark)	200.00	270.00

			VF	XF
12 (11)	100	Franka Ari (Au) 1926–1927. Zog I. ℞ Biga. Variants: at the cut of the neck, no star; sometimes one or two stars	750.00	1000.00
13 (13)	½	Lek (Ni) 1930–1931. National arms. ℞ as No. 4	5.00	8.00
14 (14)	1	Qindarka Ari (Br) 1935. Double eagle. ℞ value	9.00	15.00
15 (15)	2	Qindarka Ari (Br) 1935. Double eagle. ℞ value	15.00	25.00
16 (16)	1	Franka Ari (Ag) 1935–1937. Zog I. (1895–1961). ℞ national arms	13.00	18.00
17 (17)	2	Franka Ari (Ag) 1935. Type as No. 16	22.00	30.00

ISSUES (4) COMMEMORATING THE 25th ANNIVERSARY OF INDEPENDENCE ON 28th NOVEMBER 1937

18 (18)	1	Franka Ari (Ag) 1937. Zog I. ℞ national arms with inscription and dates 28th November 1912 to 1937	30.00	40.00
19 (19)	2	Franka Ari (Ag) 1937	45.00	60.00

20 (20)	20	Franka Ari (Au) 1937	325.00	410.00
21 (21)	100	Franka Ari (Au) 1937	2000.00	2400.00

ISSUES (2) COMMEMORATING THE MARRIAGE OF KING ZOG TO COUNTESS GERALDINE APPONYI ON 27th APRIL 1938

			VF	XF
22 (22)	20	Franka Ari (Au) 1938. Zog I. ℞ national arms with inscription and date 27th April 1938	325.00	410.00
23 (23)	100	Franka Ari (Au) 1938	2000.00	2400.00

ISSUES (3) COMMEMORATING THE 10th JUBILEE OF THE REIGN OF KING ZOG I ON 1st SEPTEMBER 1938

24 (24)	20	Franka Ari (Au) 1938. Zog I. ℞ national arms with inscription and date 1st September 1928–1938	400.00	600.00
25 (25)	50	Franka Ari (Au) 1938	1350.00	1800.00
26 (26)	100	Franka Ari (Au) 1938	2000.00	2400.00

CLOSE UNION WITH ITALY (ITALIAN DOMINATION) UNDER VICTOR EMMANUEL III 1939–1943

27 (27)	0,05	Lek (Al–Br) 1940–1941, Victor Emmanuel III (1869–1947), King of Italy 1900–1946, Emperor of Ethiopia 1939–1941. King of Albania 1939–1943. ℞ oak branch above value	5.00	8.00

28 (28)	0,10	Lek (Al–Br) 1940–1941. Victor Emmanuel III. ℞ olive branch (Olea europaea – Oleaceae) above value	7.00	12.00
29 (29)	0,20	Lek (Ac) 1939–1941. Helmeted bust to right. ℞ double eagle with fasces	1.50	3.00

			VF	XF
30 (30)	0.50	Lek (Ac) 1939–1941. Helmeted bust to left	2.00	3.50
31 (31)	1	Lek (Ac) 1939–1941. Helmeted bust to right	3.00	5.00
32 (32)	2	Lek (Ac) 1939–1941. Helmeted bust to left	4.00	6.00
33 (33)	5	Lek (Ag) 1939. Head of Victor Emmanuel to left	16.00	22.00
34 (34)	10	Lek (Ag) 1939. Head of Victor Emmanuel to right	55.00	90.00

PEOPLE'S REPUBLIC since 1946

35 (35)	½	Lek (Zi) 1947–1957. National arms of the People's Republic with name of country and stars. ℞ value surrounded by stars	0.50	1.00
36 (36)	1	Lek (Zi) 1947–1957	0.60	1.20

37 (37)	2	Lekë (Zi) 1947–1957	1.00	1.80
38 (38)	5	Lekë (Zi) 1947–1957	1.40	2.40
39 (39)	5	Qindarka (Al) 1964. National arms with name of country, stars and date. ℞ value, ears of corn, stars	0.20	0.40
40 (40)	10	Qindarka (Al) 1964	0.20	0.40
41 (41)	20	Qindarka (Al) 1964	0.40	0.80
42 (42)	50	Qindarka (Al) 1964	0.70	1.20

43 (43)	1	Lek (Al) 1964	0.90	1.60

44   5 Lekë (Ag) 1968-1970. Helmet with ram's horns, arms of the Skanderbeg family (Castriota) with swords in saltire. *R* national arms, value   Proof   40.00

45   10 Lekë (Ag) 1968-1970. Equestrian statue of Skanderbeg in Tirana. *R* as No. 44   Proof   80.00

46   20 Lekë (Au) 1968-1970. Helmet with ram's horns. Oak wreath and sword of the Prince. *R* as No. 44   Proof   100.00

47   25 Lekë (Ag) 1968-1970. Sword dancers with
           mountains in background. *R* as No. 44   Proof   120.00

48   50 Lekë (Au) 1968-1970. View of Argirocas-
           trum. *R* as No. 44   Proof   150.00

49   100 Lekë (Au) 1968-1970. Grape-picking scen-
           ce. Rev. as No. 44   Proof   300.00

50 200 Lekë (Au) 1968. Butrinto (Buthrotum),
in Epirus: the Apollo head of the so-
called "Goddess of Butrinto", in background Odeon theatre. The coin type
refers to Greco-Roman times. It is
reported that in the former city of
Augusta Buthrotum (in Albanian Bu-
trinti, in Italian Butrino) the Romans
had already placed the head of a young
man on top of a headless Greek marble
statue – probably that of a goddess.
When discovered, this archaeological
work of art was therefore described as
"the Apollo-like head of the goddess
of Butrinto"; it is now in the Archaeo-
logical Museum in Tirana. ℞ as No. 44   Proof   600.00

51   500 Lekë (Au) 1968. Prince Skanderbeg,
or Gjergi Castriotá (c. 1405–1468),
national hero. ℞ as No. 44   Proof   1500.00

ISSUES (5) COMMEMORATING THE 25th ANNIVERSARY
OF THE LIBERATION

			VF	XF
52 (44)	5	Qindarka (Al) 1969. National emblem; below, date 1944–1969. ℞ value between ears of corn; above, five stars	0.15	0.30
53 (45)	10	Qindarka (Al) 1969. Same type as No. 52	0.25	0.50
54 (46)	20	Qindarka (Al) 1969. Same type as No. 52	0.50	1.00
55 (47)	50	Qindarka (Al) 1969. Obverse as No. 52. ℞ armed warrior holding torch; below, value	1.00	2.00
56 (48)	1	Lek (Al) 1969. Obverse as No. 52. ℞ battle scene; below, value	1.20	2.40

Algerien   # Algeria   **Algérie**

Area: 916,150 sq. mi. Population: 16,200,000.

In ancient times what is now Algeria was part of the Roman Province of Numidia and Mauretania Caesariensis. In the 5th century A. D. it belonged to the Vandalic Empire and towards the end of the 7th century was conquered by the Arabs. The country was then ruled by the Beys of Algeria who had been chosen as sovereigns by the Turkish Janissaries, until the French conquered Algiers in 1830. Later it became a French Department; then, since 1st July 1962 an indepedent republic and finally a People's Republic since 15th September 1963.
Capital: Algiers.

100 Centimes = 1 France
since 1st April 1964: 100 Centimes = 1 Algerian Dinar

FRENCH DEPARTMENT AS PART OF THE FRENCH STATE

			VF	XF
1 (1)	20	Francs (Cu-Ni) 1949, 1956. Marianne, symbol of the French Republic. ℞ value between ears of corn	3.00	4.00

2 (2)	50	Francs (Cu-Ni) 1949	4.00	5.00
3 (3)	100	Francs (Cu-Ni) 1950, 1952	6.00	8.50

REPUBLIC since 1962

4 (4)	1	Centime (Al) 1964. National arms within wreath. ℞ value	0.05	0.10
5 (5)	2	Centimes (Al) 1964	0.05	0.10
6 (6)	5	Centimes (Al) 1964	0.10	0.15
7 (7)	10	Centimes (Al-Br) 1964	0.15	•0.30
8 (8)	20	Centimes (Al-Br) 1964	0.20	0.40
9 (9)	50	Centimes (Al-Br) 1964	0.25	0.50

	VF	XF
10 (10) 1 Dinar (Cu-Ni) 1964	0.60	1.00

COMMEMORATIVE ISSUE FOR THE FIRST FOUR-YEAR PLAN 1970/73 AND FOR THE FAO COIN PLAN

	VF	XF
11 (11) 5 Centimes (Al-Mg) 1970/1973	0.30	0.40
12 (16) 50 Centimes (Al-Br) 1971, 1973. Motto: Reconstruction, Education, Progress	1.00	1.50

COMMEMORATIVE ISSUE (2) FOR THE AGRICULTURAL REVOLUTION OF 1972 AND FOR THE FAO COIN PLAN

	VF	XF
13 (13) 20 Centimes (Bra) 1972. Horn of Plenty with local fruit, date. ℞ denomination	0.60	1.00

14 (14) 1 Dinar (Cu-Ni) 1972. Tractor between branches. Clasped hands, date. ℞ denomination

	XF	Unc
	1.00	1.60

COMMEMORATIVE ISSUE FOR THE 10th ANNIVERSARY OF INDEPENDENCE

15 (15) 5 Dinar 1972. Ear of corn in front of oil derrick between 10 stars. Symbol for 10 years of independence. Dates. *R* denomination between rosettes

	XF	Unc
a) (Ag)	8.50	12.50
b) (Ni)	7.00	12.50

COMMEMORATIVE ISSUE FOR THE SECOND FOUR-YEAR PLAN 1974/77 AND FOR THE FAO COIN PLAN

16 (12) 5 Centimes (Al-Mg) 1974/1977. Similar to No. 11

	0.20	0.35

20th ANNIVERSARY OF REVOLUTION

17 (17) 5 Dinar (Ni) 1974. Revolutionist. *R* as No. 15   6.00   10.00

30th ANNIVERSARY FRENCH-ALGERIAN CLASH (8.5.1945)

		XF	Unc
18 (18) 50 Centimes (Bra) 1975. Inscription. *R* value		1.20	2.00

19 (19)   20 Centimes (Cu-Ni) 1975. Head of ram. R
value. F.A.O. Issue   0.60   1.00

20 (20)   10 Dinar (Al-Br) 1979. Arabic legend. R
value and date   7.00   12.00

1400th ANNIVERSARY OF MOHAMMED'S FLIGHT

21   50 Centimes (Bra) 1981. Mosque   1.50   2.50

Previous issues, see »Weltmünzkatalog 19. Jahrhundert« (World Coin
Catalogue of the 19th Century)

Andorra   # Andorra   **Andorre**

Area: 175 sq. mi. Population: 20,000.
The tiny republic of Andorra in the Pyrenees is under the mutual
protection (co-principate) of the North Spanish Bishop of Urgel and
the President of the day of the French Republic as legal heir to the
Comte de Foix. Capital: Andorra la Vella.
In Andorra French francs and Spanish pesetas are exclusively legal
tender. The coinage in Diners are not current coins and are also not
in circulation. The designation "Diner" is the Catalan version of the
Spanish Dinero or Denario.

1   25 Diners (Ag) 1960. Bust of Carolus
       Magnus (742–814). ℞ arms   Proof   120.00

2   50 Diners (Ag) 1960   Proof   90.00

3   25 Diners (Ag) 1963. Bust of J. Benlloch
       (1864–1926), Bishop of Urgel. ℞ arms   Proof   80.00

| 4 | 50 Diners (Ag) 1963 | Proof | 125.00 |
| 5 | 25 Diners (Ag) 1964. Napoleon I (1769–1821). ℞ arms | Proof | 80.00 |

| 6 | 50 Diners (Ag) 1964 | Proof | 125.00 |

| 7 | 25 Diners (Ag) 1965. Parliament buildings. ℞ value | Proof | 80.00 |
| 8 | 50 Diners (Ag) 1965 | Proof | 125.00 |

Angola

Area: 481,350 sq. mi. Population: 5,800,000.
In 1483 the Portuguese navigator Diego Cão discovered Angola, in 1485 the estuary of the Congo river and during the years up to 1488 explored the adjacent coastline. By recognizing the local rulers, Portugal organized from here a slave trade to Brazil, founded Luanda (Loanda) in 1576 (the full name: São Paulo de Luanda) and from there extended its rule into the interior which was successfully contested by the Dutch between 1641 and 1648. In the course of the international partitioning of Africa by the European colonial powers (Congo Conference of 1885), the present-day Angola together with Cabinda was awarded to Portugal. The attempt in 1951 of hushing up the colonial regime by redesignating the colonies as (overseas) provinces, eventually miscarried. Three independence movements, hostile among each other, formed in Angola: Frente Nacional de Libertação de Angola (FNLA) (National Liberation Front of Angola), Movimento Popular de Libertação de Angola (People's Movement for the Liberation of Angola), União Nacional de Independencia Total de Angola (UNITA) (National Union for the total independence of Angola). Independence was proclaimed on November 11th 1975. Capital: Luanda.

5 Centavos = 1 Macuta; 100 Centavos = 1 Angola-Escudo
since January 10th 1977: 100 Lwei = 1 Kwanza

There was a legal parity with the escudo of the motherland in respect of the escudos circulating in Angola of 1:1.

		COLONY	VF	XF
1 (12)	1	Centavo (Br) 1921. Arms. ℞ value	10.00	18.00
2 (13)	2	Centavos (Br) 1921	26.00	40.00
3 (14)	5	Centavos (Br) 1921–1924	10.00	15.00
4 (15)	10	Centavos (Cu-Ni) 1921–1923. Liberty head. ℞ arms and value	6.00	10.00
5 (16)	20	Centavos (Cu-Ni) 1921-1922	7.00	11.00
6 (17)	50	Centavos (Ni) 1922–1923	5.00	10.00
7 (18)	5	Centavos = 1 Macuta (Ni-Br) 1927. Liberty head, symbol of the Republic. ℞ arms and value	4.00	8.00
8 (19)	10	Centavos = 2 Macuta (Ni-Br) 1927–1928	4.00	8.00

				VF	XF
9 (20)	20	Centavos = 4 Macuta (Ni-Br) 1927–1928		5.00	9.00
10 (21)	50	Centavos = 10 Macuta (Ni-Br) 1927–1928		5.00	9.00
11 (22)	10	Centavos (Br) 1948–1949. Arms with mural crown. ℞ value		1.00	2.00
12 (23)	20	Centavos (Br) 1948–1949		1.50	3.00

			VF	XF
13 (24)	50	Centavos (Ni-Br) 1948–1950	1.50	2.50

OVERSEAS PROVINCE

			VF	XF
14 (23a)	20	Centavos (Br) 1962	0.10	0.20
15 (25)	50	Centavos (Br) 1953-1955, 1958, 1961	0.20	0.40
16 (26)	1	Escudo (Br) 1953-1974	0.40	0.60
17 (27)	2½	Escudos (Cu-Ni) 1953-1974. Arms and cross in background. Rev. arms with mural crown and value	0.80	1.20
18 (A 28)	5	Escudos (Cu-Ni) 1972, 1974	1.60	3.00

			VF	XF
19 (28)	10	Escudos (Ag) 1952, 1955	4.50	7.00
20 (28a)	10	Escudos (Cu-Ni) 1969–1970	2.00	3.00
21 (29)	20	Escudos (Ag) 1952, 1955	5.00	8.00
22 (30)	20	Escudos (Cu-Ni) 1971, 1972	2.00	4.00

23 (22a)	10	Centavos (Al) 1974	30.00
24 (25a)	50	Centavos (Cu-Ni) 1974. Type as No. 15	150.00

NEW CURRENCY: 100 Lwei = 1 Kwanza

			XF	Unc
25 (31)	50	Lwei (Cu-Ni) 1975. Coat of arms. *R* value	0.25	0.50
26 (32)	1	Kwanza (Cu-Ni) 1975. Type as No. 25	0.35	0.70
27 (33)	2	Kwanzas (Cu-Ni) 1975. Type as No. 25	0.50	1.00
28 (34)	5	Kwanzas (Cu-Ni) 1975. Type as No. 25	1.20	2.00
29 (35)	10	Kwanzas (Cu-Ni) 1975. Type as No. 25	2.00	3.00
30 (36)	20	Kwanzas (Cu-Ni) 1978. Type as No. 25	2.50	3.50

Previous issues, see "Weltmünzkatalog 19. Jahrhundert" (World Coin Catalogue of the 19th Century)

Area: 35 sq. mi. Population: 6,000.
Anguilla, also called Snake Island, belongs to the group of the Leeward
Islands (The Lesser Antilles) and administratively is part of the Federa-
tion formed by St. Christopher (St. Kitts), Nevis and Anguilla. On
30th May 1967 it severed all links with the other islands and British
Naval forces had to intervene in 1969.
Capital: The Valley.

100 Cents = 1 Anguilla Dollar

1	½ Dollar (Ag) 1969–. West End Method- ist Church. ℞ arms and value	Proof	10.00

2	1 Dollar (Ag) 1969–. Topographical map of the island; compass-card, sea-horse (Hippocampus sp. — Syngnathidae), Caribbean silver lobster (Panulirus argus – Panuliridae) and shell of a water-snail or murex (family of the spiny snails = Muricidae). ℞ as No. 1	Proof	12.00
3	2 Dollar (Ag) 1969–. Flags over topo- graphical map. ℞ as No. 1	Proof	20.00

4	4 Dollar (Ag) 1969–. The One-and-a-half-master "Atlantic Star". ℞ as No. 1	Proof	40.00
5	5 Dollar (Au) 1969–. Church of St. Mary. ℞ as No. 1	Proof	50.00
6	10 Dollar (Au) 1969–. Caribbean silver lobster, common dolphin (Delphinus delphis – Delphinidae) and starfish (Asterias sp. – Asteridae). ℞ as No. 1	Proof	90.00

| 7 | 20 Dollar (Au) 1969–. Mermaids, stylized scallop (Pectinidae family), starfish and watersnail shell. ℞ as No. 1 | Proof | 180.00 |

| 8 | 100 Dollar (Au) 1969–. Popular uprising. ℞ as No. 1 | Proof | 1000.00 |

Antigua

Area: 108 sq. mi. Population: 57,000.

Belongs to the Lesser Antilles; a member of the Caribbean Free Trade Area (CARIFTA). Antigua is linked with the other countries of Barbados, Dominica, Grenada, Montserrat, St. Christopher (St. Kitts), Nevis and Anguilla, St. Lucia and St. Vincent in the Monetary Union of the East Caribbean Dollar.

The issuing authority for the whole Monetary Union is the East Caribbean Currency Authority with headquarters in Bridgetown, Barbados. Capital: St. Johns.

100 Cents = 1 East Caribbean Dollar

COMMEMORATIVE ISSUE FOR THE INAUGURATION OF THE CARIBBEAN DEVELOPMENT BANK AND FOR THE FAO COIN PLAN

		Unc	Proof
1 (1*)	4 Dollars (Cu-Ni) 1970. Arms with shields held by two ibexes, and helmet decoration. R bananas, sugar-cane and value	10.00	30.00

*This number refers to Yeoman's East Caribbean Territories listings.

Argentinien # Argentina **Argentine**
República Argentina

Area: 1,554,800 sq. mi. (including the Antarctic possessions). Population: 25,000,000.
The Republic of Argentina consists of 22 provinces, and in addition the federal district of Buenos Aires and the national territory of Tierra del Fuego.
Capital: Buenos Aires.

100 Centavos = 1 Argentine Peso

			VF	XF
1 (7)	5	Centavos (Cu-Ni) 1896–1942. Liberty head facing left (head of Argentina, symbol of the Republic). ℞ value within wreath	0.30	0.50
2 (8)	10	Centavos (Cu-Ni) 1896–1942	0.20	0.40
3 (9)	20	Centavos (Cu-Ni) 1896–1942	0.20	0.40
4 (14)	50	Centavos (Ni) 1941. Of similar description: Nos. 17–21	1.20	2.00
5 (12)	1	Centavo. National arms. ℞ value within wreath		
		a) (Br) 1939–1944	0.20	0.40
		b) (Cu) 1945–1948	0.25	0.50
6 (13)	2	Centavos. National arms. ℞ value within wreath		
		a) (Br) 1939–1947	0.20	0.40
		b) (Cu) 1947–1950	0.25	0.50
7 (15)	5	Centavos (Al-Br) 1942–1950. Head of Argentina, symbol of the Republic, facing right. ℞ value, with ears of corn and ox-head	0.20	0.30
8 (16)	10	Centavos (Al-Br) 1942–1950. Type as No. 7	0.20	0.40
9 (17)	20	Centavos (Al-Br) 1942–1950. Type as No. 7	0.20	0.40
10 (18)	5	Centavos (Cu-Ni) 1950. Bust of General José de San Martin (1778–1850). ℞ value	0.50	1.00

			VF	XF
11 (19)	10	Centavos (Cu-Ni) 1950	0.50	1.00
12 (20)	20	Centavos (Cu-Ni) 1950	0.60	1.20
13 (21)	5	Centavos. Bust of José de San Martin. ℞ value, as No. 10 but without commemorative inscription		
		a) (Cu-Ni) 1951–1953	0.20	0.30
		b) (Cu-Ni-St) 1953–1956	0.10	0.20
14 (22)	10	Centavos		
		a) (Cu-Ni) 1951–1952	0.20	0.35
		b) (Cu-Ni-St) 1952–1956	0.10	0.20
15 (23)	20	Centavos		
		a) (Cu-Ni) 1951–1952	0.20	0.40
		b) (Cu-Ni-St) 1952–1956	0.10	0.20
16 (24)	50	Centavos (Cu-Ni-St) 1952–1956	0.50	0.80
17 (25)	5	Centavos (Ni-St) 1957–1959. Head of Argentina, symbol of the Republic, facing left; below, LIBERTAD. ℞ value within wreath, date	0.10	0.20
18 (26)	10	Centavos (Ni-St) 1957–1959	0.10	0.20
19 (27)	20	Centavos (Ni-St) 1957–1961	0.10	0.20
20 (28)	50	Centavos (Ni-St) 1957–1961	0.20	0.40

21 (29)	1	Peso (Ni-St) 1957–1962	0.30	0.50

COMMEMORATIVE ISSUE FOR THE 150th ANNIVERSARY OF THE REMOVAL OF THE SPANISH VICEROY 25th MAI 1810

22 (30)	1	Peso (St) 1960. The old townhall in Buenos Aires. ℞ national arms and value	0.50	1.00

		VF	XF
23 (31)	5 Pesos (St) 1961–1968. The sail training ship "Presidente Sarmiento". ℞ value	0.30	0.50

| **24** (32) | 10 Pesos (St) 1962–1968. Gaucho. ℞ value | 0.30 | 0.50 |

ISSUE COMMEMORATING THE 1st ISSUE OF NATIONAL COINAGE IN 1813

| **25** (33) | 25 Pesos (St) 1964–1968. Representation of the 8-Reales piece of 1813. ℞ reverse of the same coin | 0.50 | 1.00 |

ISSUE COMMEMORATING THE 150th ANNIVERSARY OF THE DECLARATION OF INDEPENDENCE

| **26** (34) | 10 Pesos (St) 1966. The National Museum in Tucumán. It was in this building that the Declaration of Independence for the United Province of Rio de la Plata was read on 9th July 1816. ℞ value | 0.30 | 0.60 |

ISSUE COMMEMORATING THE 80th ANNIVERSARY OF THE DEATH OF D. F. SARMIENTO

			XF	Unc
27 (35)	25	Pesos (Ni) 1968. Head of Domingo Faustino Sarmiento (1811–1888), politician, writer, pedagogue, President of State 1868–1874. ℞ value (dodecagonal)	0.60	1.00

CURRENCY REFORM:
1st January 1970: 100 old Pesos = 1 new Peso

			XF	Unc
28 (36)	1	Centavo (Al-Mg) 1970–. Head of Argentina, symbol of the Republic, facing left. R laurel branch, value, date	0.05	0.10
29 (37)	5	Centavos (Al-Mg) 1970–. Type as No. 28	0.10	0.20
30 (38)	10	Centavos (Cu-Ni) 1970–. Type as No. 28	0.10	0.20
31 (39)	20	Centavos (Cu-Ni) 1970–. Type as No. 28	0.12	0.25
32 (40)	50	Centavos (Cu-Ni) 1970–. Type as No. 28	0.20	0.40

33 (41)	1	Peso (Bra) 1974–. Sun with rays. R value	0.25	0.50
34 (42)	5	Pesos (Al-Br) 1976. Type as No. 33	0.30	0.60
35 (43)	10	Pesos (Al-Br) 1976. Type as No. 33	0.35	0.70

			XF	Unc
36 (44)	20	Pesos (Ni-Bra) 1977, 1978. World Cup emblem, value. *R* two soccer players	0.80	1.25

37 (45)	50	Pesos (Ni-Bra) 1977, 1978, *R* soccer player. Global grid background	0.90	1.50

38 (46)	100	Pesos (Ni-Bra) 1977, 1978. *R* soccer stadium. Global grid background	1.25	2.00

			Unc	Proof
39 (47)	1000	Pesos (Ag) 1977, 1978. *R* radiant sun face. Legend "ARGENTINA 78, BUENOS AIRES, CORDOBA, MAR DEL PLATA, MENDOZA, ROSARIO"	6.00	50.00
40 (48)	2000	Pesos (Ag) 1977, 1978. *R* large Argentinian coat of arms in center and 5 small coats of arms of cities above	15.00	60.00
41 (49)	3000	Pesos (Ag) 1977, 1978. *R* globe featuring South America in center above laurel sprigs	25.00	95.00

200th BIRTHDAY OF G. BROWN (2)

		XF	Unc
42 (50)	5 Pesos (Al-Br) 1977. Guillermo Brown (1777-1857), admiral	0.25	0.50
43 (51)	10 Pesos (Al-Br) 1977. Type as No. 42	0.40	0.80

200th BIRTHDAY OF GENERAL JOSE DE SAN MARTIN (2)

44 (52)	50 Pesos (Al-Br) 1978. General José de San Martin (1778–1850)	0.50	1.00
45 (53)	100 Pesos (Al-Br) 1978. Type as No. 44	0.80	1.50

46 (54)	50 Pesos (Al-Br) 1979. Type as No. 44, but laurel branch instead of dates behind head	0.50	1.00
47 (55)	100 Pesos (Al-Br) 1979. Type as No. 46	0.80	1.50

CONQUEST OF PATAGONIA CENTENNIAL (2)

48 (56)	50 Pesos (Al-Br) 1979	0.50	1.00

			XF	Unc
49 (57)	100	Pesos (Al-Br) 1979	0.80	1.50
50 (54a)	50	Pesos (Bronze-clad steel) 1980–1981. Type as No. 46	0.50	1.00
51 (55a)	100	Pesos (Bronze-clad steel) 1980. Type as No. 47	0.80	1.50

Area: 38 sq. mi. Population: 1,231.

Ascension Island owes ist name to the same Portuguese explorer, Joao da Nova, who discovered it on Ascension Day, 1501. Exactly two centuries later William Dampier was wrecked on its shore, but it remained uninhabited until 1815 when it was garrisoned by British troops, to forestall any attempts by Bonapartists to rescue Napoleon from St. Helena 700 miles to the south-east. Until 1922 it was transferred to the Colonial Office and became a dependency of St. Helena. In addition to the cable station operated by Cable and Wireless Ltd., it has a BBC relay station and a NASA tracking station.

100 Pence = 1 £; 25 Pence = 1 Crown

25th ANNIVERSARY OF THE CORONATION OF HER MAJESTY QUEEN ELIZABETH II

		Unc	Proof
1 (1)	1 Crown 1978:		
	a) (Ag)	25.00	38.00
	b) (Cu-Ni)	1.50	

WEDDING OF PRINCE CHARLES AND LADY DIANA

2 (2)	25 Pence 1981:		
	a) (Ag)		60.00
	b) (Cu-Ni)	3.00	

Area: 2,574,980 sq. mi. Population: 14,800,000.

First discovered by 17th century Dutch navigators, later claimed for Great Britain by Captain Cook, who first landed south of what is today Sidney (1770). Colonised for the next 50 years mainly as an English penal settlement. The discovery of gold in 1851 led to much more extensive exploration of the continent (population increase during 50 years from 405,000 in 1850 to 3,770,000 by 1900. Today comprises 6 states within the independent Commonwealth of Australia. Until 1927 the capital was Melbourne, since when it has been Canberra.

Until decimalisation of the coinage in Feb. 1966, when the Canberra Mint opened, Australian coins were mainly struck at various English mints, more occasionally at Bombay and Calcutta.

Capital: Canberra.

12 Pence = 1 Shilling. 2 Shillings = 1 Florin. 20 Shillings = 1 £.
Since 14th February 1966: 100 Cents = 1 Australian Dollar.

EDWARD VII 1901–1910

1 (1)	3	Pence (Ag) 1910. Edward VII (1841–1910). Crowned bust of Edward VII to right. ℞ arms supported by great red kangaroo (Macropus = Megaleia rufus – Macropodidae) and emu (Dromaeus novaehollandiae – Dromaiidae or Dromiceidae)		
2 (2)	6	Pence (Ag) 1910. Type as No. 1	18.00	50.00
3 (3)	1	Shilling (Ag) 1910. Type as No. 1	30.00	80.00

4 (4)   1 Florin = 2 Shillings (Ag) 1910. Type   140.00   300.00
             as No. 1

5 (A 5) ½ £ (Au) 1902–1910. Edward VII. ℞   110.00   150.00
             St. George and the Dragon

6 (B 5) 1 £ (Au) 1902–1910. Type as No. 5   150.00   200.00
7   2 £ (Au) 1902. Type as No. 5   –,–   –,–
8   5 £ (Au) 1902. Type as No. 5   –,–   –,–

Coins Nos. 5–8 differ only from similar pieces issued at the same time
in Great Britain because of the mint marks. M = Melbourne, P =
Perth or S = Sydney.

GEORGE V 1910–1936

			VF	**XF**
9 (5)	½ Penny (Br) 1911–1936. Head of George V (1865–1936). ℞ value in circle		1.50	4.00

10 (6)	1	Penny (Br) 1911–1936		0.80	2.00
		a) 1930		3000.00	5000.00
11 (9)	3	Pence (Ag) 1911–1936. Head of George V. ℞ arms		4.00	8.00
12 (10)	6	Pence (Ag) 1911–1936		5.00	12.00
13 (11)	1	Shilling (Ag) 1911–1936		10.00	25.00
14 (12)	1	Florin (Ag) 1911–1936		12.00	30.00
		a) 1932		350.00	2000.00

15 (A 13)	½	£ (Au) 1911–1918. Head of George V. ℞ St. George and the Dragon		160.00	200.00
16 (B 13)	1	£ (Au) 1911–1931		150.00	180.00

Coins Nos. 15 and 16 differ only from similar pieces issued at the same time in Great Britain because of the mint marks. M = Melbourne, P = Perth or S = Sydney. The Sydney mint was closed in 1926. There are no mint marks on silver coins after 1921.

ISSUE COMMEMORATING THE OPENING OF PARLIAMENT IN CANBERRA

17 (7)	1	Florin (Ag) 1927. Bust of George V. ℞ Parliament buildings in Canberra		12.00	25.00

ISSUE COMMEMORATING THE CENTENARY OF
VICTORIA AND MELBOURNE

		VF	XF
18 (8)	1 Florin (Ag) 1934–1935. Bust of George V. ℞ horseman holding torch	200.00	300.00

GEORGE VI 1936–1952

		VF	XF
19 (13)	½ Penny (Br) 1938–1939. Head of George VI (1895–1952). ℞ value in circle	0.60	4.00
20 (14)	½ Penny (Br) 1939–1948. Head of George VI. ℞ great red kangaroo (Macropus = Megaleia rufus – Macropodidae)	0.40	1.00

		VF	XF
21 (15)	1 Penny (Br) 1938–1948. ℞ great red kangaroo	0.40	1.00

In the period 1942–1944 Australian silver coins were struck in the cities of Denver and San Francisco, U.S.A. From this period come the coins which bear on reverse the mintmark "D" or "S".

		VF	XF
22 (16)	3 Pence (Ag) 1938–1948. ℞ ears of wheat	0.50	1.00
23 (17)	6 Pence (Ag) 1938–1948. ℞ arms	1.00	3.00
24 (18)	1 Shilling (Ag) 1938–1948. ℞ head of a Merino ram (Ovis ammon aries – Bovidae)	4.00	7.00
25 (19)	1 Florin (Ag) 1938–1947. ℞ crowned arms	5.00	8.00

		VF	XF
26 (20)	1 Crown (Ag) 1937–1938. ℞ crown	20.00	40.00

After 1948 the inscription IND.IMP. is dropped

		VF	XF
27 (21)	½ Penny (Br) 1949–1952. ℞ great red kangaroo to right	0.50	2.00
28 (22)	1 Penny (Br) 1949–1952	0.40	1.00
29 (24)	3 Pence (Ag) 1949–1952. ℞ ears of wheat	0.50	1.00
30 (25)	6 Pence (Ag) 1950–1952. ℞ arms	1.00	3.00
31 (26)	1 Shilling (Ag) 1950–1952. ℞ head of a Merino ram	1.50	7.00
32 (27)	1 Florin (Ag) 1951–1952. ℞ crowned arms	5.00	8.00

COMMEMORATIVE ISSUE FOR THE 50th ANNIVERSARY OF THE COMMONWEALTH OF AUSTRALIA

		VF	XF
33 (23)	1 Florin (Ag) 1951. Head of George VI to l. ℞ crown above sceptre and sword in saltire, as well as stars in the form of the "Southern Cross"	7.00	10.00

ELIZABETH II since 1952

		VF	XF
34 (28)	½ Penny (Br) 1953–1955. Bust of Elizabeth II (*1926). ℞ great red kangaroo to right	0.30	0.80
35 (29)	1 Penny (Br) 1953. Great red kangaroo to left	0.40	0.90

			VF	XF
36 (30)	3 Pence (Ag) 1953–1954. ℞ ears of wheat		1.50	3.00
37 (31)	6 Pence (Ag) 1953–1954. ℞ arms		1.00	2.00

			VF	XF
38 (32)	1 Shilling (Ag) 1953–1954. ℞ Merino ram		3.00	5.00

			VF	XF
39 (33)	1 Florin (Ag) 1953–1954. ℞ crowned arms		5.00	8.00

ISSUE COMMEMORATING THE VISIT OF THE BRITISH ROYAL COUPLE

			VF	XF
40 (34)	1 Florin (Ag) 1954. Bust of Elizabeth II. ℞ great red kangaroo and lion, animals representative of Australia and Great Britain		6.00	8.00

Coins Nos. 40–46 have the letters F: D: added to the obverse legend.

			VF	XF
41 (35)	½ Penny (Br) 1959–1964		0.15	0.30
42 (36)	1 Penny (Br) 1955–1964		0.15	0.30
43 (37)	3 Pence (Ag) 1955–1964. ℞ ears of weath		0.30	0.60

				VF	XF
44 (38)	6	Pence (Ag) 1955–1963. ℞ arms		1.00	2.00
45 (39)	1	Shilling (Ag) 1955–1963. ℞ head of a Merino ram		2.00	3.00
46 (40)	1	Florin (Ag) 1956–1963. ℞ crowned arms		2.50	5.00

NEW VALUE: 100 Cents = 1 Australian Dollar

			XF	Unc
47 (41)	1	Cent (Br) 1966–. Bust of the Queen right. ℞ Australian ring-tailed opossum or pigmy flying phalanger (Acrobates pygmaeus – Phalangeridae)	0.05	0.10

48 (42)	2	Cent (Br) 1966–. ℞ frilled lizard (Chlamydosaurus kingii – Agamidae)	0.06	0.12

49 (43)	5	Cents (Cu-Ni) 1966–. ℞ Australian short-beaked spiny ant-eater (Tachyglossus aculeatus – Tachyglossidae)	0.10	0.20

50 (44) 10 Cents (Cu-Ni) 1966–. ℞ Superb lyre-

bird (Menura novaehollandiae – Me-
nuridae)   0.15   0.30

51 (45) 20 Cents (Cu-Ni) 1966–. R Duck-billed
platypus (Duckbill) (Ornithorhynchus
anatinus – Ornithorhynchidae)   0.20   0.40

52 (46) 50 Cents (Ag) 1966. Crowned bust of
Elizabeth II facing right. R arms   7.00   9.00

53 (47) 50 Cents (Cu-Ni) 1969, 1971–(dodecagonal)   0.50   1.00

ISSUE COMMEMORATING THE 200th ANNIVERSARY OF COOK'S SEA VOYAGE ALONG THE EAST COAST OF AUSTRALIA

		XF	Unc
54 (48) 50	Cents (Cu-Ni) 1970. James Cook (1728–1779), famous English world sailor; inscription; sketch of Australia and sea route (dodecagonal)	1.50 Proof	2.50 65.00

25th ANNIVERSARY OF THE SILVER JUBILEE OF HER MAJESTY QUEEN ELIZABETH II

55 (49) 50	Cents (Cu-Ni) 1977	1.20 Proof	2.50 28.00

		Unc	Proof
55 (49) 200	Dollars (Au) 1980. Koal Bear, .917 gold, 10.000 g	280.00	550.00

			Unc	Proof
57	50	Cents (Cu-Ni) 1981	2.50	
58	200	Dollars (Au) 1981	300.00	
59	1	Fine Ounce (Au) 1981. Kangaroo		600.00

COMMONWEALTH GAMES (3)

			Unc	Proof
60	50	Cents (Cu-Ni) 1982	2.50	
61	10	Dollars (Ag) 1982		60.00
62	200	Dollars (Au) 1982	300.00	

Österreich   # Austria   **Autriche**

Area: 32,374 sq. mi. Population: 7,500,000.
For centuries the history of Austria and that of Germany as parts of the
Holy Roman Empire were very closely connected. Until the disinte-
gration of the Holy Roman Empire in 1806, the House of Habsburg
provided a long line of remarkable rulers. After the breakdown of the
Danube Monarchy into individual states and the renunciation of the
throne by Emperor Karl, a republic was created.
Capital: Vienna.

100 Heller = 1 Krone, 10 000 Kronen = 1 Schilling,
100 Groschen = 1 Schilling

FRANZ JOSEPH 1848–1916

			VF	**XF**
1 (23c)	1 Ducat (Au) 1872–1915. Laureate bust facing right of Franz Joseph (1830–1916). *R* double eagle:			
	a) 1872-1914		60.00	80.00
	b) 1915. Proof restrike		25.00	30.00
	c) 1951. Mint error for 1915		120.00	150.00

2 (25c)	4 Ducats (Au) 1872-1915. Type as No. 1, but laureate bust:			
	a) 1872-1914		250.00	300.00
	b) 1915. Proof restrike		110.00	120.00

	VF	XF
3 (26) 1 Heller (Cu) 1892–1915. Double eagle with shield. ℞ value	0.40	0.80
4 (28) 2 Heller (Cu) 1892–1915	0.35	0.70

5 (29) 10 Heller (Ni) 1892–1911	0.50	0.80
6 (30) 20 Heller (Ni) 1892–1914	0.80	1.60

7 (35) 1 Krone (Ag) 1892–1907. Laureate bust facing right of Franz Joseph (1830–1916). ℞ crown above value   2.50   3.50

8 (39) 5 Kronen (Ag) 1900, 1907. ℞ eagle within circle, the whole surrounded by crowns and laurel branches	12.50	18.00
9 (42) 10 Kronen (Au) 1892–1906. ℞ double eagle	35.00	42.00
10 (43) 20 Kronen (Au) 1892–1905	62.00	72.00

COMMEMORATIVE ISSUES (5)
FOR THE 60th ANNIVERSARY OF THE ACCESSION
TO THE THRONE

			VF	XF
11 (36)	1 Krone (Ag) 1908. Head of Franz Joseph facing right. R crown above monogram, dates 1848–1908		3.00	5.00

12 (40)	5 Kronen (Ag) 1908. R running figure of Fame, dates 1848–1908		12.50	18.00

13 (44)	10 Kronen (Au) 1908. R double eagle, dates 1848–1908		50.00	60.00
14 (45)	20 Kronen (Au) 1908. Type as No. 13		210.00	240.00

15 (46)	100 Kronen (Au) 1908. R resting figure of Fame with coat of arms		900.00	1000.00
16 (41)	5 Kronen (Ag) 1909		15.00	25.00

Austria   77

				VF	XF
17 (47)	10	Kronen (Au) 1909		35.00	42.00
18 (48)	20	Kronen (Au) 1909		750.00	820.00
19 (37)	1	Krone (Ag) 1912–1916. Head of Franz Joseph facing right, signature: St. Schwartz. ℞ crown above value		1.80	2.40
20 (38)	2	Kronen (Ag) 1912–1913		3.00	5.00
21 (A 41)	5	Kronen (Ag) 1909. Type as No. 16, but smaller head		12.50	20.00

22 (49)	10	Kronen (Au)			
		a) 1909–1911		35.00	42.00
		b) 1912, mostly re-strikes		25.00	30.00
23 (50)	20	Kronen (Au)			
		a) 1909–1916		155.00	180.00
		b) 1915, mostly re-strikes		42.00	50.00

24 (51)	100	Kronen (Au)			
		a) 1909–1916		765.00	840.00
		b) 1915, mostly re-strikes		225.00	240.00

There are official re-strikes of coins Nos. 22–24, which are very difficult to differentiate from the originals.

25 (31)	10	Heller (Cu–Zi) 1915–1916. Double eagle. ℞ value within wreath		0.25	0.50

26 (27)	1	Heller (Cu) 1916. Type as No. 3, but double eagle now with filleted shield		6.00	12.00

				VF	XF

27 (32) 10 Heller (Cu–Zi) 1916. Type as No. 5, but double eagle now with filleted shield — 0.70 — 1.20

28 (52) 20 Kronen (Au) 1916. Type as No. 23, but double eagle now with filleted shield — 500.00 — 700.00

29 (33) 2 Heller (Fe) 1916. Double eagle with filleted shield. ℞ value surrounded by laurel branches — 0.90 — 1.60

For coin No. 29, as first issue of Karl I, see under No. 31

30 (34) 20 Heller (Fe) 1916. Double eagle. ℞ value within wreath — 0.70 — 1.20

For coin No. 30, as first issue of Karl I, see under No. 32

KARL I 1916–1918

31 (33) 2 Heller (Fe) 1917–1918. Type as No. 29 — 0.40 — 0.80
32 (34) 20 Heller (Fe) 1917–1918. Type as No. 30 — 0.40 — 0.80
33 20 Kronen (Au) 1918. Head to right of Karl I (1887–1922). ℞ double eagle with filleted shield — —— — ——

Of No. 33 there is only one known specimen left in existence, which is found in the Münzkabinett in Vienna.

1st REPUBLIC 1918–1938

Austria: Federal Provinces

Burgenland   Carinthia   Lower Austria   Upper Austria   Salzburg

Styria   Tyrol   Vorarlberg   Vienna

		VF	XF
34 (56) 100 Kronen (Br) 1923–1924. Head of eagle. ℞ value and oak leaves		0.70	1.20
35 (57) 200 Kronen (Br) 1924. Kruckenkreuz (similar to the cross of Jerusalem). ℞ value		1:00	1.60
36 (58) 1000 Kronen (Cu–Ni) 1924. Tyrolese woman's head. ℞ value within wreath		2.00	4.00
37 (80) 20 Kronen (Au) 1923–1924. Crowned eagle bearing national arms and holding symbols of agricultural and industrial workers in its claws. ℞ value within wreath		900.00	1000.00
38 (81) 100 Kronen (Au) 1923–1924. Type as No. 37		1550.00	1800.00

			VF	XF
39 (60)	1	Groschen (Br) 1925–1938. Head of eagle. ℞ value	0.40	0.80
40 (61)	2	Groschen (Br) 1925–1938. Kruckenkreuz. *R* value	0.40	0.80

41 (62)	5	Groschen (Cu–Ni) 1931–1938. Krukkenkreuz. ℞ value	0.70	1.20

42 (63)	10	Groschen (Cu–Ni) 1925–1929. Tyrolese woman's head. ℞ value within wreath	1.00	1.60
43 (67)	½	Schilling (Ag) 1925–1926. Arms. ℞ value	6.00	9.00

			VF	XF
44	1	Schilling (Ag) Parliament building in Vienna. ℞ arms with national colours between laurel branches, value		
		a) (Y 59) 1924	4.00	7.20
		b) (Y 68) 1925–1926, 1932; smaller dia.	3.00	4.00

The "value" row for 44 shows: 10.00   25.00

45 (82) 25 Schilling (Au) 1926–1934. Crowned
eagle bearing national arms and holding symbols of agricultural and indus-
trial workers in its claws. ℞ value and
laurel branches

	VF	XF
	100.00	120.00

46 (8) 100 Schilling (Au) 1926–1934. Type as No.
45

	VF	XF
	450.00	550.00

COMMEMORATIVE ISSUE FOR THE CENTENARY OF THE DEATH OF F. SCHUBERT

47 (69) 2 Schilling (Ag) 1928. Bust left of Franz
Schubert (1797–1828), composer. ℞
value within wreath of shields: these
are the armorial shields of the nine
Federal Provinces, surmounted by a
shield with the Austrian national col-
ours

	VF	XF
	9.00	15.00

COMMEMORATIVE ISSUE FOR THE CENTENARY OF THE BIRTH OF BILLROTH

			VF	XF
48 (70)	2 Schilling (Ag) 1929. Bust facing left of Prof. Dr. Theodor Billroth (1829–1894), surgeon. ℞ as No. 47		26.00	42.00

COMMEMORATIVE ISSUE FOR THE 700th ANNIVERSARY OF THE DEATH OF WALTHER VON DER VOGELWEIDE

49 (71)	2 Schilling (Ag) 1903. Walther von der Vogelweide (c. 1170–1230), minstrel. ℞ as No. 47		10.00	16.00

COMMEMORATIVE ISSUE FOR THE 175th ANNIVERSARY OF THE BIRTH OF MOZART

50 (72)	2 Schilling (Ag) 1931. Bust facing right of Wolfgang Amadeus Mozart (1756–1791), composer. ℞ as No. 47		30.00	45.00

COMMEMORATIVE ISSUE FOR THE 200th ANNIVERSARY OF THE BIRTH OF HAYDN

				VF	XF
51 (73)	2	Schilling (Ag) 1932. Bust facing left of Joseph Haydn (1732–1809), composer. ℞ as No. 47		65.00	110.00

COMMEMORATIVE ISSUE FOR THE CENTENARY OF THE DEATH OF DR. SEIPEL

			VF	XF
52 (74)	2	Schilling (Ag) 1933. Bust facing right of Dr. Ignaz Seipel (1876–1932), Federal Chancellor from 1922 to 1924 and from 1926 to 1929. ℞ as No. 47	32.00	50.00

			VF	XF
53 (64)	50	Groschen (Cu-Ni) 1934. Double-headed eagle with haloes and national arms, without symbols in its claws; date. ℞ value within square ("Nacht-schilling")	50.00	90.00

54 (65)   50 Groschen (Cu–Ni) 1935–1936. Double-headed eagle as No. 53, surrounded by name of country. ℞ value

                      VF   **XF**

                      5.00   9.00

55 (66)   1 Schilling (Cu–Ni) 1934–1935. Obverse as No. 53. ℞ value and ears of corn   3.00   5.00

56 (79)   5 Schilling (Ag) 1934–1936. The Madonna of Mariazell. ℞ double-headed eagle, value   35.00   50.00

57 (85) 100 Schilling (Au) 1935–1938. Obverse as No. 56. ℞ similar to No. 56   1000.00   1200.00

Coin No. 57 with date 1938 is very rare.

COMMEMORATIVE ISSUE FOR DR. E. DOLLFUSS

58 (75) 2 Schilling (Ag) 1934. Bust right of Dr. Engelbert Dollfuss (1892–1934), Federal Chancellor from 1932 to 1934. ℞ double-headed eagle with haloes and national arms, without symbols in its claws; value, date

	VF	XF
	20.00	36.00

COMMEMORATIVE ISSUE FOR DR. K. LUEGER

59 (76) 2 Schilling (Ag) 1935. Bust facing right of Dr. Karl Lueger (1844–1910), politician, social reformer. ℞ as No. 58   28.00   48.00

60 (84) 25 Schilling (Au) 1935–1938. Facing bust of St. Leopold. ℞ as No. 57   600.00   800.00

Coin No. 60 with date 1938 is very rare.

COMMEMORATIVE ISSUE FOR THE 200th ANNIVERSARY OF THE DEATH OF PRINCE EUGEN

		VF	XF
61 (77)	2 Schilling (Ag) 1936. Head facing left of Prince Eugen of Savoy (1663–1736), Imperial Austrian Field-Marshal. ℞ as No. 58	22.00	32.00

COMMEMORATIVE ISSUE FOR J. B. FISCHER VON ERLACH

62 (78)	2 Schilling (Ag) 1937. The Karlskirche in Vienna, built by Johann Bernhard Fischer von Erlach (1656–1723), completed in 1737 by his son Joseph Emanuel. ℞ as No. 58	26.00	35.00

2nd REPUBLIC since 1945

63 (86)	1 Groschen (Zi) 1947. Nationals arms. ℞ value	0.25	0.40

64 (89)	2 Groschen (Al) 1950–1952, 1954, 1957, 1962, 1964–1981	0.08	0.16

			VF	XF
65 (87)	5 Groschen (Zi) 1948, 1950, 1951, 1953, 1955, 1957, 1961–1981		0.10	0.20

66 (88) 10 Groschen (Zi) 1947–1949   0.80   2.00

67 (90) 10 Groschen (Al) 1951–1953, 1955, 1957 1959, 1961–1981   0.10   0.20

68 (95) 20 Groschen (Al–Br) 1950, 1951, 1954   0.60   1.20

69 (91) 50 Groschen (Al) 1946, 1947, 1952, 1955   0.70   1.50

		VF	XF
70 (92)	1 Schilling (Al) 1946, 1947, 1952, 1957.		
	℞ peasant sowing	0.80	1.80

		VF	XF
71 (93)	2 Schilling (Al) 1946, 1947, 1952. ℞ grapes and ears of corn:		
	a) 1946, 1947	1.80	3.60
	b) 1952	130.00	200.00
72 (94)	5 Schilling (Al) 1952, 1957.		
	a) 1952	5.00	8.50
	b) 1957	160.00	250.00

COMMEMORATIVE ISSUE FOR THE REOPENING OF THE FEDERAL THEATRES

		XF	Unc
73 (96)	25 Schilling (Ag) 1955. Muse with mask and lyre. The theatre curtain is drawn aside by two attendants. ℞ value within wreath made of the shields of the nine Federal Provinces; below, laurel branches	22.00	32.00

COMMEMORATIVE ISSUE FOR THE 200th ANNIVERSARY OF THE BIRTH OF MOZART

		XF	Unc
74 (97)	25 Schilling (Ag) 1956. Monument to Wolfgang Amadeus Mozart (1756–1791) in the Burggarten in Vienna. ℞ as No. 73	6.00	9.00

COMMEMORATIVE ISSUE FOR THE 8th CENTENNIAL OF MARIAZELL BASILICA

75 (98)	25 Schilling (Ag) 1957. Mariazell. ℞ as No. 73	6.00	9.00
		VF	XF
76 (103)	50 Groschen (Al–Br) 1959–1978. Arms. ℞ value	0.08	0.16

77 (104)	1 Schilling (Al–Br) 1959–. Edelweiss (Leontopodium alpinum - Compositae). ℞ value	0.08	0.16

78 (106) 5 Schilling (Ag) 1960–1968. The Spanish
Riding School in Vienna: rider on
horse in levade. ℞ arms and value

	VF	XF
	1.50	2.50

For coin of similar type, see under No. 98

79 (99) 10 Schilling (Ag) 1957–1959, 1964–1973.
Head of a woman from the Wachau
district with a golden bonnet in profile.
℞ arms

	VF	XF
	2.50	4.00

COMMEMORATIVE ISSUE FOR THE CENTENARY OF THE BIRTH OF AUER VON WELSBACH

80 (100) 25 Schilling (Ag) 1958. Bust facing right
of Carl Freiherr Auer von Welsbach
(1858–1929), chemist. ℞ as No. 73

	XF	Unc
	6.00	9.00

COMMEMORATIVE ISSUE FOR THE LIBERATION OF TYROL

81 (101) 50 Schilling (Ag) 1959. Bust facing of
Andreas Hofer (1767–1810), leader of
the revolt against the occupation of
Tyrol. ℞ Tyrolese eagle surrounded by
shields of the other eight Federal Provinces

	XF	Unc
	11.00	18.00

COMMEMORATIVE ISSUE FOR THE CENTENARY OF THE DEATH OF ARCHDUKE JOHANN

82 (102) 25 Schilling (Ag) 1959. Head facing right
of Archduke Johann (1782–1859), mili-
tary leader in the French Wars, encour-
aged the cultural and economic development, especially of Steiermark;
founder of the Joanneum in Graz. ℞
lion of Styria

	6.00	9.00

COMMEMORATIVE ISSUE FOR THE 40th ANNIVERSARY OF THE CARINTHIAN PLEBISCITE

		XF	Unc
83 (105)	25 Schilling (Ag) 1960. Couple wearing Carinthian traditional costumes standing by voting urn. ℞ as No. 73	7.00	10.00

COMMEMORATIVE ISSUE FOR THE 40th ANNIVERSARY OF BURGENLAND

84 (107)	25 Schilling (Ag) 1961. The Haydn-kirche in Eisenstadt. ℞ as No. 73	17.00	25.00

COMMEMORATIVE ISSUE FOR A. BRUCKNER

85 (108)	25 Schilling (Ag) 1962. Head right of Anton Bruckner (1824–1896), composer. ℞ as No. 73	7.00	10.00

COMMEMORATIVE ISSUE FOR THE 300th ANNIVERSARY OF THE BIRTH OF PRINCE EUGEN

			XF	Unc
86 (109)	25	Schilling (Ag) 1963. Half-length figure of Prince Eugen of Savoy (1663–1736), Imperial Austrian General Field-Marshal. ℞ as No. 73	7.00	10.00

COMMEMORATIVE ISSUE FOR THE 600th ANNIVERSARY OF THE UNION OF TYROL WITH AUSTRIA

87 (110)	50	Schilling (Ag) 1963. The two coats of arms of Austria and Tyrol united by a chain. ℞ as No. 73	10.00	16.00

COMMEMORATIVE ISSUE FOR THE 9th OLYMPIC WINTER GAMES IN INNSBRUCK

				XF	Unc

88 (111) 50 Schilling (Ag) 1964. Ski-jumper with
mountain scenery in background;
above, Olympic rings. ℞ as No. 73   15.00   20.00

COMMEMORATIVE ISSUE FOR F. GRILLPARZER

89 (112) 25 Schilling (Ag) 1964. Bust threequar-
ters facing of Franz Grillparzer (1791–
1872), poet. ℞ value within shield of
arms: these are the arms of the nine
Federal Provinces, surmounted by the
national arms
    a) ℞ of new design   7.00   10.00
    b) ℞ as on Nos. 83–86. **Proof only**   500.00

COMMEMORATIVE ISSUE FOR THE 600th ANNIVERSARY OF THE FOUNDATION OF VIENNA UNIVERSITY

90 (114) 50 Schilling (Ag) 1965. Bust threequar-
ters facing of Rudolf IV, "The Found-
er", Duke of Austria from 1358 to
1365. ℞ as No. 89a   10.00   16.00

COMMEMORATIVE ISSUE FOR THE 150th ANNIVERSARY
OF THE TECHNICAL HIGH SCHOOL

91 (113) 25 Schilling (Ag) 1965. Head facing left
of Joh. Jos. Ritter von Prechtl (1778–
1854), technologist, Director of the
Polytechnic Institute in Vienna. ℞ as
No. 89 a

	XF	Unc
	8.00	12.00

COMMEMORATIVE ISSUE FOR THE 150th ANNIVERSARY
OF THE AUSTRIAN NATIONAL BANK

92 (116) 50 Schilling (Ag) 1966. National Bank
building in Vienna. ℞ as No. 89 a   17.00   22.00

COMMEMORATIVE ISSUE FOR F. RAIMUND

93 (115) 25 Schilling (Ag) 1966. Facing half portrait of Ferdinand Raimund (1790–
1836), poet. ℞ as No. 89a

	XF	Unc
	8.00	12.00

COMMEMORATIVE ISSUE FOR THE 250th ANNIVERSARY OF THE BIRTH OF MARIA THERESIA

94 (117) 25 Schilling (Ag) 1967. Bust facing right
of Maria Theresia (1717–1780), Em-
press, reigned from 1740–1780. ℞ as
No. 89a

8.00   12.00

COMMEMORATIVE ISSUE FOR THE CENTENARY OF THE "BLUE DANUBE" WALTZ

95 (118) 50 Schilling (Ag) 1967. Facing half portrait of Johann Strauss the Younger
(1825–1899), from a bronze statue in
the monument to Strauss (marble arch
of the Muses), unveiled in 1923 in the
Vienna City Park (Park-Ring); the
sculptor was Edmund Hellmer. ℞ as
No. 89a

17.00   22.00

COMMEMORATIVE ISSUE FOR THE 50th ANNIVERSARY OF THE REPUBLIC OF AUSTRIA

96 (120) 50 Schilling (Ag) 1968. Parliament building in Vienna, built by Theophil Han-
sen, Danish architect; in front, the
Pallas-Athena fountain by Karl Kund-
mann. ℞ as No. 89a

	XF	Unc
	17.00	22.00

COMMEMORATIVE ISSUE FOR THE 300th ANNIVERSARY OF THE BIRTH OF LUKAS VON HILDEBRANDT (1668–1745)

97 (119) 25 Schilling (Ag) 1968. Main gateway to
the Belvedere castle in Vienna with
the upper Belvedere gardens. ℞ as No.
89a

	XF	Unc
	16.00	27.00

98 (106a) 5 Schilling (Cu–Ni) 1968–. Type as No.
78, but plain edge

	VF	XF
	0.20	0.40

COMMEMORATIVE ISSUE FOR THE 450th ANNIVERSARY OF THE DEATH OF EMPEROR MAXIMILIAN I

			XF	Unc
99 (122) 50	Schilling (Ag) 1969. Bust right of Maximilian I (1459–1519), Emperor, reigned from 1493 to 1519; reproduction from a contemporary medal. ℞ as No. 89a		11.00	18.00

COMMEMORATIVE ISSUE FOR PETER ROSEGGER

100 (121) 25	Schilling (Ag) 1969. Head facing left of Peter Rosegger (1843–1918), poet and writer; one of his most famous works is entitled "Als ich noch ein Waldbauernbub war." (When I was still a forest lad.) ℞ value within circle of arms		8.00	12.50

COMMEMORATIVE ISSUE FOR THE CENTENARY OF THE BIRTH OF FRANZ LEHÁR

101 (123) 25	Schilling (Ag) 1970. Bust three-quarters facing of Franz Lehár (1870–1948), composer, successful exponent of Viennese operetta. His most famous works are: 'Die lustige Witwe' (The Merry Widow), 'Der Graf von Luxemburg' (The Count of Luxembourg), 'Zarevich', 'Land des Lächelns' (The Land of Smiles)		7.00	11.00

COMMEMORATIVE ISSUE FOR THE 300th ANNIVERSARY OF THE LEOPOLD FRANZENS UNIVERSITY IN INNSBRUCK

102 (124) 50 Schilling (Ag) 1970. The oldest seal of the university dating from 1673, the year of completion of all four Faculties (1669 Philosophy, 1671 Theology and Law, 1673 Medicine). In the centre, the Margrave of Babenberg, Leopold III the Saint, after whom Leopold I, the Founder of the University, was named. In his right hand he holds a model of the monastery Klosterneuburg; in his left, the five-eagle banner half rolled-up. On his right, shield with the eagle of Tyrol, and in front of it the inscription: LEVPOLDO FELICI; on his left, the imperial double eagle in the chain of the Golden Fleece, surmounted by the imperial crown of Rudolf. In the background, canopy on which dove, symbol of the Holy Spirit.

	XF	Unc
	11.00	18.50

COMMEMORATIVE ISSUE FOR THE CENTENARY OF THE BIRTH OF DR. KARL RENNER

103 (125) 50 Schilling (Ag) 1970. Dr. Karl Renner (1870–1950), Federal President 1945 to 1950

	XF	Unc
	10.00	17.00

COMMEMORATIVE ISSUE FOR THE 200th ANNIVERSARY OF THE STOCK EXCHANGE IN VIENNA

	XF	Unc
104 (126) 25 Schilling (Ag) 1971	7.00	11.00

COMMEMORATIVE ISSUE FOR THE 80th BIRTHDAY OF DR. J. RAAB

	XF	Unc
105 (127) 50 Schilling (Ag) 1971. Dr. Julius Raab (1891–1964), Federal Chancellor from 1953 to 1961	10.00	17.00

COMMEMORATIVE ISSUE FOR THE 350th ANNIVERSARY OF THE UNIVERSITY IN SALZBURG

106 (129) 50 Schilling (Ag) 1972. Great Seal of Salzburg University. The pair of letters

"PA" and "SF" refer to the founder
PARIS Lodron, Archbishop (ARCHI-
EPISCOPUS) of Salzburg (SALZ-
BURGENSIS), FUNDATOR. The
left-hand Roman numeral in the seal
signifies the year of its foundation in
1622, the right-hand Roman numeral
1962 indicates the year of its re-esta-
blishment

	XF	Unc
	10.00	17.00

COMMEMORATIVE ISSUE FOR THE 50th ANNIVERSARY
OF THE DEATH OF CARL MICHAEL ZIEHRER

107 (128) 25 Schilling (Ag) 1972. Carl Michael Zieh-
rer (1843–1922). Composer of operet-
tas; also composed dance music and
march tunes. He possessed the Imperial
title of a "Court Ball Music Director"   7.00   11.00

COMMEMORATIVE ISSUE FOR 100 YEARS OF THE
INSTITUTE OF AGRICULTURE IN VIENNA

108 (130) 50 Schilling (Ag) 1972. General view of
the institute building. Coats of arms
are part of the legend, symbolizing the
faculties of "Agriculture", "Forestry
and Timber Management", "Cultivation Technology and Water Manage-

	XF	Unc

ment" and "Food and Fermentation
Technology"   10.00   17.00

COMMEMORATIVE ISSUE FOR THE 500th ANNIVERSARY OF THE BUMMERL HOUSE IN STEYR

109 (132) 50 Schilling (Ag) 1973. A former public
house built in the Gothic style which
was called the "Golden Lion". Since,
however, the figure of a lion located
above the entrance had turned out very
small, and rather resembled a small dog,
called a "Bummerl" in the vernacular,
the house has been traditionally known
as the Bummerl House   10.00   17.00

COMMEMORATIVE ISSUE FOR THE 100th BIRTHDAY OF MAX REINHARDT

110 (131) 25 Schilling (Ag) 1973. Max Reinhardt
(1873–1943), distinguished producer
and theatrical manager   7.00   11.00

COMMEMORATIVE ISSUE FOR THE 100th ANNIVERSARY
OF THE BIRTH OF THEODOR KÖRNER

		XF	Unc
111 (133)	50 Schilling (Ag) 1973. Theodor Körner (1873–1957), Federal President 1951 to 1957	10.00	17.00

		VF	XF
112 (A 99)	10 Schilling (Cu–Ni) 1974–. Head of a woman from the Wachau district with a golden bonnet in profile, denomination, date. ℞ federal arms and legend **"REPUBLIK ÖSTERREICH"**	0.60	1.00

COMMEMORATIVE ISSUE FOR
THE VIENNA INTERNATIONAL FLOWER SHOW
(April 18 to October 14, 1974)

		XF	Unc
113 (134)	50 Schilling (Ag) 1974. Artists impression of plant-life shapes	9.00	12.50

COMMEMORATIVE ISSUE FOR THE 125th ANNIVERSARY OF THE AUSTRIAN POLICE FORCE
(1849 to 1974)

114 (135) 50 Schilling (Ag) 1974. The federal coat of arms with a wreath of oak leaves as an emblem of the police force, above two flaming hand grenades which refer to the corps badge of the police force

	XF	Unc
	9.00	12.50

COMMEMORATIVE ISSUE FOR THE 1200th ANNIVERSARY OF SALZBURG CATHEDRAL

115 (136) 50 Schilling (Ag) 1974   9.00   12.50

COMMEMORATIVE ISSUE FOR THE 50th ANNIVERSARY OF AUSTRIAN BROADCASTING

116 (137) 50 Schilling (Ag) 1974   9.00   12.50

150th ANNIVERSARY OF BIRTH OF JOHANN STRAUSS

			XF	Unc
117 (138)	100	Schilling (Ag) 1975. Johann Strauss the Younger (1825-1899), composer	10.00	15.00

20th ANNIVERSARY OF STATE TREATY

118 (139)	100	Schilling (Ag) 1975.	10.00	15.00

50th ANNIVERSARY OF SCHILLING

119 (140)	100	Schilling (Ag) 1975. A modernistic version of a sower in a plowed field	10.00	15.00

			XF	Unc
120 (141)	100	Schilling (Ag) 1976. Emblem of the Olympic Winter Games 1976	10.50	15.50

			XF	Unc
121 (142)	100	Schilling (Ag) 1976. Buildings with tower against background of 5 Olympic rings. *R* coat of arms and value. A small arms-emblem below, for the mint, in Vienna	10.00	15.00
122 (142)	100	Schilling (Ag) 1976. Type as No. 121, but a small Tyrolian eagle, for the mint, in Hall	10.00	15.00

			XF	Unc
123 (143)	100	Schilling (Ag) 1976.	10.00	15.00

			XF	Unc
124 (143)	100	Schilling (Ag) 1976. Type as No. 123, but a small Tyrolian eagle, for the mint, in Hall	10.00	15.00
125 (144)	100	Schilling (Ag) 1976	10.00	15.00

126 (144)	100	Schilling (Ag) 1976. Type as No. 125, but a small Tyrolian eagle, for the mint, in Hall	10.00	15.00

200th ANNIVERSARY OF BURGTHEATER

127 (145)	100	Schilling (Ag) 1976. General view of the Burgtheater	10.00	15.00

1000th ANNIVERSARY OF CARINTHIA

128 (146)	100	Schilling (Ag) 1976. Herzogstuhl and Carinthian arms	10.00	15.00

1000th ANNIVERSARY OF THE INSTALLATION OF THE BABENBERGER IN AUSTRIA

		XF	Unc
129 (148) 1000 Schilling (Au) 1976. The seal of the Duke Friedrich II			200.00

175th ANNIVERSARY OF BIRTH OF JOHANN NESTROY

130 (147) 100 Schilling (Ag) 1976. Johann Nestroy (1801-1862), singer   10.00   15.00

1200th ANNIVERSARY OF STIFT KREMSMÜNSTER

131 (149) 100 Schilling (Ag) 1977   10.00   15.00

900th ANNIVERSARY OF FORTRESS HOHENSALZBURG

	XF	Unc
132 (150) 100 Schilling (Ag) 1977. View of the fortress Hohensalzburg	10.00	15.00

500th ANNIVERSARY OF THE MINT IN HALL/TYROL

133 (151) 100 Schilling (Ag) 1977	10.00	15.00

700th ANNIVERSARY OF GMUNDEN

134 (153) 100 Schilling (Ag) 1978. Orth, castle in Gmunden	10.00	15.00

700th ANNIVERSARY OF THE BATTLE OF DÜRNKRUT AND JEDENSPEIGEN

		XF	Unc
135 (154)	100 Schilling (Ag) 1978. Bust of Rudolf I, landscape of the Marchfield, battle-scene	10.00	15.00

1100th ANNIVERSARY OF VILLACH

136 (155)	100 Schilling (Ag) 1978. View of the city of Villach and arms	10.00	15.00

150th ANNIVERSARY OF BIRTH OF FRANZ SCHUBERT

137 (152)	50 Schilling (Ag) 1978. Franz Schubert (1797-1828), composer	8.00	12.00

OPENING OF ARLBERG TUNNEL

38 (156)	100 Schilling (Ag) 1978	10.00	15.00

CATHEDRAL OF WIENER NEUSTADT CENTENNIAL

39 (157)	100 Schilling (Ag) 1979	10.00	15.00

200th ANNIVERSARY OF INN DISTRICT

				XF	Unc
140 (158)	100	Schilling (Ag) 1979		10.00	15.00

VIENNA INTERNATIONAL CENTER

141 (159)	100	Schilling (Ag) 1979		10.00	15.00

FESTIVAL AND CONGRESS HALL AT BREGENZ

142 (160)	100	Schilling (Ag) 1979		10.00	15.00

MILLENIUM OF THE CITY OF STEYR

143 (161)	500	Schilling (Ag) 1980		35.00	45.00

25th ANNIVERSARY OF STATE TREATY

144 (162)	500	Schilling (Ag) 1980. Belvedere castle in Vienna		35.00	45.00

BICENTENNIAL OF THE DEATH OF MARIA THERESIA

145 (163)	500	Schilling (Ag) 1980. Maria Theresia (1717–1780), Empress, reigned from 1740–1780		35.00	45.00

CENTENNIAL OF AUSTRIAN RED CROSS

		XF	Unc
146 (164)	500 Schilling (Ag) 1980. Henri Dunant (1828–1910), philanthropist	35.00	45.00

		VF	XF
147 (165)	20 Schilling (Al-Br) 1980–.	1.40	1.70

800th ANNIVERSARY OF THE VERDUN ALTAR

		XF	Unc
148 (166)	500 Schilling (Ag) 1981	35.00	45.00

100th ANNIVERSARY OF THE BIRTH OF ANTON WILDGANS

149	500 Schilling (Ag) 1981. Anton Wildgans (1881–1932), writer	35.00	45.00

100th ANNIVERSARY OF THE BIRTH OF OTTO BAUER

150 500 Schilling (Ag) 1981. Otto Bauer
(1881–1938), Socialdemocrat politician   35.00   45.00

200th ANNIVERSARY OF TOLERANZPATENT

151 500 Schilling (Ag) 1981   35.00   45.00

Previous issues, see »Weltmünzkatalog 19. Jahrhundert« (World Coin
Catalogue of the 19th Century)

Area: 922 sq. mi. Population: 317,400.
The island group in the Atlantic was (re?)-discovered 1432 by the
Portuguese, Cabral, named after the birds found on the islands the
"Hawk Islands", taken possession of in 1445 in the name of Portugal
and since then considered to be an integrated part of the motherland,
on which legitimate and exile governments set up bases and from
where they were able to regain the motherland. The strategically important location of the island group should be able to prevent a fundamental change in this situation also in future.
Capital: Ponte Delgada.

1000 Reis = 1 Milreis

CARLOS I. 1889–1908

		VF	XF
1 (4)	5 Reis (Cu) 1901. Crowned arms. ℞ value in wreath	6.00	11.00
2 (5)	10 Reis (Cu) 1901. Type as No. 1	10.00	20.00

Previous issues, see "Weltmünzkatalog 19. Jahrhundert" (World Coin
Catalogue of the 19th Century)

Bahama-Inseln   # Bahamas   **Bahames**

Area: 4,387 sq. mi. Population: 210,000.
Group of islands in the West Indies including Watlings Island, the former Guanahani or San Salvador. Christopher Columbus landed in Guanahani on 12th October 1492, setting foot for the first time on American soil. Independence 10th July 1973.
Capital: Nassau.

100 Cents = 1 Bahama Dollar

		VF	XF
1 (1)	1 Cent (Ni-Bra) 1966-1970. Head of Queen Elizabeth II to right; inscription around: ELIZABETH II BAHAMA ISLANDS. *R* great netted starfish (Oreaster reticulatus - Oreasteridae):		
	a) 1966, 1969, 22,5 mm dia.	0.15	0.30
	b) 1968, 22,5 mm dia.	0.50	1.00
	c) 1970, 19 mm dia.	0.15	0.30

2   3

		VF	XF
2 (2)	5 Cents (Cu-Ni) 1966-1970. *R* pineapple (Ananas comosus - Bromeliaceae):		
	a) 1966, 1969, 1970	0.15	0.30
	b) 1968	1.00	1.80
3 (3)	10 Cents (Cu-Ni) 1966-1970. *R* king mackerels (Scomberomorus cavalla - Scombridae):		
	a) 1966, 1969, 1970	0.20	0.40
	b) 1968	1.50	3.00

		VF	XF
4 (4)	15 Cents (Cu–Ni) 1966–1970. ℞ Chinese hibiscus (Hibiscus rosa-sinensis – Malvaceae)	0.25	0.50

5 (5)	25 Cents (Ni) 1966–1970. ℞ sloop	0.40	0.70

6 (6)	50 Cents (Ag) 1966–1970. ℞ blue marlin (Makaira indica = Makaira ampla – Istiophoridae)	2.50	6.00

		VF	XF
7 (7)	1 Dollar (Ag) 1966–1970. ℞ queen conch (Strombus gigas – Strombidae)	7.00	9.00

8 (8)   2 Dollars (Ag) 1966–1970. ℞ greater flamingos (Phoenicopterus ruber ruber – Phoenicopteridae)   15.00   20.00

9 (9)   5 Dollars (Ag) 1966–1970. ℞ arms   22.00   28.00

118   **Bahamas**

COMMEMORATIVE ISSUES (4) ON THE OCCASION OF THE 1st GENERAL ELECTION FOR THE ADOPTION OF THE NEW CONSTITUTION

			Unc	Proof
10 (10)	10	Dollars (Au) 1967. Head of Queen Elizabeth II. ℞ fort, two palm branches and value	80.00	120.00
11 (11)	20	Dollars (Au) 1967. ℞ lighthouse and value	150.00	180.00
12 (12)	50	Dollars (Au) 1967. ℞ The "Santa Maria", flagship of Christopher Columbus	350.00	400.00
13 (13)	100	Dollars (Au) 1967. ℞ Christopher Columbus (1451–1506) setting foot on American soil at Guanahani (San Salvador) on 12th October 1492	650.00	750.00
14 (14)	1	Cent (Ni–Bra) 1971–1973. Type as No. 1, but inscription COMMONWEALTH OF THE BAHAMA ISLANDS ELIZABETH II	0.30	0.70
15 (15)	5	Cents (Cu–Ni) 1971–1973. ℞ pineapple	0.30	0.80
16 (16)	10	Cents (Cu–Ni) 1971–1973. ℞ king mackerels	0.50	1.00
17 (17)	15	Cents (Cu–Ni) 1971–1973. ℞ Chinese hibiscus	0.80	1.70
18 (18)	25	Cents (Ni) 1971–1973. ℞ sloop	0.90	2.00
19 (19)	50	Cents (Ag) 1971–1973. Rev. blue marlin	3.00	4.00
20 (20)	1	Dollar (Ag) 1971–1973. Rev. queen conch	5.00	8.00
21 (21)	2	Dollars (Ag) 1971–1973. ℞ greater flamingos	8.00	15.00
22 (22)	5	Dollars (Ag) 1971. ℞ arms	20.00	26.00
23 (23)	10	Dollars (Au) 1971, 1972. Type as No. 10:		
		a) 1971, 3.99 grams	40.00	55.00
		b) 1972, 3.19 grams	35.00	50.00
24 (24)	20	Dollars (Au) 1971, 1972. Type as No. 11:		
		a) 1971, 7.99 grams	150.00	170.00
		b) 1972, 6.38 grams	140.00	160.00
25 (25)	50	Dollars (Au) 1971, 1972. Type as No. 12:		
		a) 1971, 19.97 grams	210.00	260.00
		b) 1972, 15.97 grams	200.00	250.00
26 (26)	100	Dollars (Au) 1971, 1972. Type as No. 9:		
		a) 1971, 39.94 grams	300.00	400.00
		b) 1972, 31.95 grams	280.00	380.00

		Unc	Proof
27 (22a)	5 Dollars (Ag) 1972, 1973. Type as No. 22, but new coat of arms, since December 7, 1971 (rising sun with thirteen rays in the upper field)	20.00	28.00

COMMEMORATIVE ISSUES (6) ON THE OCCASION OF INDEPENDENCE ON 10th JULY 1973

28 (27)	10 Dollars (Ag) 1973. Head of Queen Elizabeth II. R The »Santa Maria«, flagship of Christopher Columbus	40.00	45.00
29 (29)	10 Dollars (Au) 1973. R tobacco dove (Columbigallina passerina – Columbidae)	20.00	30.00
30 (30)	20 Dollars (Au) 1973. R greater flamingos	25.00	35.00
31 (28)	50 Dollars (Au) 1973. R greater flamingos before rising sun	150.00	170.00
32 (31)	50 Dollars (Au) 1973. R lobster (Palinurus argus – Palinuridae)	100.00	120.00
33 (32)	100 Dollars (Au) 1973. R Coat of arms	160.00	185.00

		XF	Unc
A33 (15a)	5 Cents (Cu-Ni) 1973. Type as No. 15, but THE COMMONWEALTH	2.00	4.50
B33 (16a)	10 Cents (Cu-Ni) 1973. Type as No. 16, but THE COMMONWEALTH	2.50	5.00
34 (33)	1 Cent (Bra) 1974-1976. Coat of arms since 7th December 1971. R great netted starfish	0.08	0.16
35 (34)	5 Cents (Cu-Ni) 1974-1976. R pineapple	0.10	0.20
36 (35)	10 Cents (Cu-Ni) 1974-1976. R king mackerels	0.20	0.40
37 (36)	15 Cents (Cu-Ni) 1974-1976. R Chinese hibiscus	0.40	0.80
38 (37)	25 Cents (Ni) 1974-1976. R sloop	0.50	1.00
39 (38)	50 Cents 1974–1976. R blue marlin:		
	a) (Ag) 1974–1980	Proof	8.00
	b) (Cu-Ni) 1974–1978	0.60	1.20
40 (39)	1 Dollar 1974. R queen conch:		
	a) (Ag) 1974–1980	Proof	16.00
	b) (Cu-Ni) 1974–1978	2.50	4.00
41 (40)	2 Dollars 1974–. R greater flamingos:		
	a) (Ag) 1974–1980	Proof	28.00
	b) (Cu-Ni) 1974–1978	5.00	7.00
42 (41)	5 Dollars 1974–. R new national flag since 10th July 1973:		
	a) (Ag) 1974–1980	Proof	32.00
	b) (Cu-Ni) 1974–1978	6.00	11.00

COMMEMORATIVE ISSUES (6)
FOR THE FIRST ANNIVERSARY OF INDEPENDENCE

			XF	Unc
43 (42)	10	Dollars 1974. Sir Milo B. Butler, Governor General:		
		a) (Ag)	Proof	55.00
		b) (Cu-Ni)	16.00	20.00
			Unc	**Proof**
44 (44)	50	Dollars (Au) 1974–1977. R tobacco dove	55.00	65.00
45 (45)	100	Dollars (Au) 1974–1977. R greater flamingos	110.00	150.00
46 (43)	100	Dollars (Au) 1974. R greater flamingos and fully circular inscription; 33 mm dia.	200.00	240.00

47 (46)	150	Dollars (Au) 1974–1977. R lobster	165.00	220.00

48 (47)	200	Dollars (Au) 1974–1977. Rev. coat of	210.00	240.00
49 (57)	2500	Dollars (Au) 1974, 1977. Rev. greater flamingos; 72 mm dia.	Proof	8000.00

2nd ANNIVERSARY OF INDEPENDENCE (2)

50 (48)	10	Dollars 1975–1977. R flower:		
		a) (Ag)		50.00
		b) (Cu-Ni)	20.00	30.00
51 (49)	100	Dollars (Au) 1975–1977. R parrot (Amazona leucocephala - Psittacidae)	200.00	280.00

FIFTH ANNIVERSARY OF INDEPENDENCE (4)

		Unc	Proof
52 (50)	10 Dollars (Ag) 1978. Portrait of H.R.H. Prince Charles		40.00
53 (51)	100 Dollars (Au) 1978		320.00
54 (52)	10 Dollars (Ag) 1978. Sir Milo B. Butler		40.00
55 (53)	100 Dollars (Au) 1978		320.00

250th ANNIVERSARY OF PARLIAMENT (2)

56 (54)	25 Dollars (Ag) 1979		50.00
57 (55)	250 Dollars (Au) 1979		400.00

10th ANNIVERSARY OF CARIBBEAN DEVELOPMENT BANK

58 (56)	10 Dollars (Ag) 1980		40.00

WEDDING OF PRINCE CHARLES AND LADY DIANA (3)

59 (58)	10 Dollars (Ag) 1981		60.00
60 (59)	100 Dollars (Au) 1981		220.00
61 (60)	500 Dollars (Au) 1981		1000.00

Bahrain   **Bahrain**   **(Iles) Bahrain**

Amarat al-Bahrain

Area: 250 sq. mi. Population: 345,000.

Arab Sheikdom on the Persian Gulf; a British Protectorate since 1861; independent since 14th August 1971. The Bahrain Dinar has been legal tender since October 16, 1965; in parallel with it, the socalled Gulf Rupee (1 BD = 10 Gulf Rupees) still remained legal tender until October 25, 1969. The Bahrain Dinar was also temporarily legal tender in Abu Dhabi. The monetary union with Abu Dhabi has been dissolved in the meantime.

Capital: Manama.

1000 Fils = 1 Bahrain Dinar

ISA BEN SULMAN BEN HAMAD AL KHALIFA since 1961

			VF	XF
1 (1)	1	Fils (Br) 1965, 1966. Date palm (Phoenix dactylifera – Palmae). ℞ value	0.05	0.10
2 (2)	5	Fils (Br) 1965	0.10	0.15
3 (3)	10	Fils (Br) 1965	0.10	0.20
4 (4)	25	Fils (Cu–Ni) 1965	0.25	0.50
5 (5)	50	Fils (Cu–Ni) 1965	0.30	0.70

6 (6)	100	Fils (Cu–Ni) 1965	0.50	0.80

COMMEMORATIVE ISSUES (2) FOR THE DEDICATION
OF ISA TOWN ON 6th NOVEMBER 1968

			XF	Unc
7 (7)	500	Fils (Ag) 1968. Bust right of Sheik Isa. R national arms and value	10.00	12.50
8 (8)	10	Dinars (Au) 1968. Type as No. 7	Proof	600.00

ISSUE FOR THE FAO COIN PLAN

			XF	Unc
9 (9)	250	Fils (Cu–Ni) 1969. Date palm with fishing boat, name of country, date. R the FAO emblems and motto FIAT PANIS; value	1.50	3.00

INDEPENDENCE COMMEMORATIVE (14th August 1971)

			Proof
10 (10)	10	Dinars (Au) 1971	700.00
11 (11)	50	Dinars (Au) 1978. Bust of Sheik Isa. R arms	500.00
12 (12)	100	Dinars (Au) 1978	700.00

Bangladesch # Bangladesh **Bangladesh**

Area: 54,501 sq. mi. Population: 85,000,000.
Upon the partition of British India based on the British law of independence, West Bengal came under Indian rule, and East Bengal became a part of the Islamic Republic of Pakistan. With the aid of Indian troops the independence of Bangladesh (Land of the Bengalis), proclaimed on December 17th, 1971 was realized. In December 1971 the »Bank of Bangladesh« was established which took over the function of the Pakistan State Bank in the territory of the former territory of East Pakistan. Capital: Dacca.

100 Paise (Poisha) = 1 Taka

			VF	Unc
1 (A 1)	1	Paisa (Al) 1974. State emblem (National flower Shapla or water lily above wavy lines between ears of padi, crowned by tea leaves and stars). R value, date	0.10	0.20
2 (1)	5	Paise (Al) 1973. Plough, date and denomination within a cogwheel	0.10	0.20

3 (2)	10	Paise (Al) 1973. R leaf, date. Denomination (scalloped edge)	0.15	0.30
4 (3)	25	Paise (St) 1973. R fish	0.20	0.40
5 (4)	50	Paise (Cu-Ni) 1973. R bird	0.50	1.00

ISSUE FOR THE FAO COIN PLAN (7)

6 (5)	5	Paise (Al) 1974–1976. Type similar to No. 2, but motto »Grow More Food«	0.15	0.30

	VF	Unc

7 (6)   10 Paise (Al) 1974–1979. R Rice: grains, jute saplings, plant, tractor; motto: »Green Revolution« (scalloped edge)   0.20   0.40

8 (7)   25 Paise (St) 1974–1978. R carp fish, egg, bananas, pumpkin; motto: »Food for All«   0.25   0.50

9 (8)   1 Taka (Cu-Ni) 1975, 1976. R family   0.50   1.00
10 (9)   5 Paise (Al) 1977, 1978   0.10   0.20

11 (10)   10 Paise (Al) 1977   0.20   0.40

			VF	Unc
12 (11)	25 Paise (Cu-Ni) 1977		0.30	0.60
13 (12)	50 Paise (Cu-Ni) 1977, 1978		0.35	0.70

Barbados

Area: 165 sq. mi. Population: 266,640.

The most eastern of the Lesser Antilles, Barbados was discovered in 1519 by the Spaniards, but has been a British possession since 1625. The colonial status came to an end when independence was proclaimed on 30th November 1966. Barbados is a member of the Caribbean Free Trade Area (CARIFTA) and is linked with the countries of Antigua, Dominica, Grenada, Montserrat, St. Christopher (St. Kitts), Nevis and Anguilla, St. Lucia and St. Vincent to form the Monetary Union of the East Caribbean Dollar. The issuing authority for the whole Monetary Union is the East Caribbean Currency Authority with headquarters in Bridgetown, Barbados.

Capital: Bridgetown.

100 Cents = 1 East Caribbean Dollar;
since 3rd December 1973: 100 Cents = 1 Barbados Dollar

COMMEMORATIVE ISSUE FOR THE INAUGURATION OF THE CARIBBEAN DEVELOPMENT BANK AND FOR THE FAO COIN PLAN

		Unc	Proof
1 (2*)	Dollars (Cu–Ni) 1970. Arms with shield bearers and ornamented helmet. ℞ bananas, sugar-cane and value	10.00	30.00

*This number refers to Yeoman's East Caribbean Territories listings.

			Unc	Proof
2 (1)	1	Cent (Br) 1973–. Coat of arms, name of country, date. R broken trident, symbol of Barbados	0.20	0.80
3 (2)	5	Cents (Bra) 1973–. R South Point light-house, built in 1852	0.20	1.00
4 (3)	10	Cents (Cu-Ni) 1973–. R Bonaparte tern (Larus philadelphia – Laridae)	0.30	1.50
5 (4)	25	Cents (Cu-Ni) 1973–. R Morgan Lewis sugar mill	0.80	2.50
6 (5)	1	Dollar (Cu-Ni) 1973–. R flying fish (Hirundichthys affinis – Exocoëtidae)	2.00	5.00
7 (6)	2	Dollars (Cu-Ni) 1973–. R Staghorn coral (Acropora cervicornis – Madro-poraria)	4.00	8.00
8 (7)	5	Dollars 1973–1980. R shell fountain in Bridgetown's Trafalgar square: a) (Ag) b) (Cu-Ni)	8.00	20.00
9 (8)	10	Dollars 1973–1980. R Neptune, god of the sea with trident a) (Ag) b) (Cu-Ni)	12.00	30.00

350th ANNIVERSARY COMMEMORATIVE

			Unc	Proof
10 (9)	100	Dollars (Au) 1975. Rev. sailing vessel »Olive Blossom«	70.00	80.00

10th ANNIVERSARY OF INDEPENDENCE (8)

			Unc	Proof
11 (10)	1	Cent (Br) 1976	0.20	1.00
12 (11)	5	Cents (Bra) 1976	0.80	2.00
13 (12)	10	Cents (Cu-Ni) 1976	0.90	2.50
14 (13)	25	Cents (Cu-Ni) 1976	1.00	3.00
15 (14)	1	Dollar (Cu-Ni) 1976	5.00	9.00
16 (15)	2	Dollars (Cu-Ni) 1976	9.00	10.00
17 (16)	5	Dollars: a) (Ag) b) (Cu-Ni)	20.00	20.00
18 (17)	10	Dollars 1976: a) (Ag) b) (Cu-Ni)	30.00	35.00

			Unc	Proof

CORONATION JUBILEE

			Unc	Proof
19 (18)	25	Dollars (Ag) 1978		40.00
20 (20)	100	Dollars (Au) 1978. Human Rights:		
		a) .900 gold, dia. 20 mm, 4.06 gm	170.00	
		b) .900 gold, dia. 21 mm, 5.05 gm		210.00

YEAR OF THE CHILD

			Unc	Proof
21 (21)	200	Dollars (Au) 1979. Children, stylized:		
		a) .900 gold, dia. 24 mm, 8.12 gm	300.00	
		b) .900 gold, dia. 27 mm, 10.10 gm		400.00

10th ANNIVERSARY OF CARIBBEAN DEVELOPMENT BANK

			Unc	Proof
22 (19)	25	Dollars (Ag) 1980		40.00

Belgisch-Kongo   # Belgian Congo   **Congo Belge**

This former Belgian Colony in Central Africa was originally the personal property of King Leopold II, under the name of "State of Congo". It secured independence on 30th June 1960.

Capital: Leopoldville, renamed Kinshasa on 1st July 1966.

100 Centimes = 1 Franc

STATE OF CONGO 1885–1908

			VF	XF
1 (9)	5	Centimes (Cu–Ni) 1906–1908. Crown and monogram of King Leopold II repeated five times in the form of a star. ℞ star and value (with central hole)	2.00	4.00
2 (10)	10	Centimes (Cu–Ni) 1906–1908	2.00	4.00
3 (11)	20	Centimes (Cu–Ni) 1906–1908	5.00	9.00

COLONY since 18th October 1908

4 (12)	5	Centimes (Cu–Ni) 1909. Type as No. 1, but with inscription CONGO BELGE – BELGISCH CONGO	4.00	8.50
5 (13)	10	Centimes (Cu–Ni) 1909	5.00	9.00
6 (14)	20	Centimes (Cu–Ni) 1909	6.50	12.00

ALBERT I 1909–1934

7 (15)	1	Centime (Cu) 1910–1919. Crown and monogram of King Albert I repeated five times in the form of a star. ℞ star and value (with central hole)	4.00	7.50
8 (16)	2	Centimes (Cu) 1910–1919	4.00	7.50
9 (17)	5	Centimes (Cu–Ni) 1910–1928	1.00	2.50
10 (18)	10	Centimes (Cu–Ni) 1910–1928	1.50	3.00
11 (19)	20	Centimes (Cu–Ni) 1910–1911	2.00	4.00
12 (20)	50	Centimes (Cu–Ni) 1921–1929. Laureate head l. of King Albert I (1875–1934). ℞ oil palm (Elaeis guineensis – Palmae)		
		a) Belgisch Congo	2.50	4.00
		b) Congo Belge	2.50	4.00

		VF	XF
13 (21)	1 Franc (Cu–Ni) 1920–1930		
	a) Belgisch Congo, 1920–1929	3.00	5.00
	b) Congo Belge, 1920–1930	3.00	5.00

LEOPOLD III 1934–1950

14 (22) 1 Franc (Bra) 1944–1949. African elephant (Loxodonta africana – Elephantidae). ℞ value — 1.50 — 2.50

15 (24) 2 Francs (Bra) 1943 (hexagonal). Issue of the mint of Philadelphia — 9.00 — 16.00

16 (23) 2 Francs (Bra) 1946–1947 — 2.50 — 5.00

17 (26) 5 Francs (Ni–Br) 1936–1937. Head l. of King Leopold III (*1901). ℞ lion — 16.00 — 32.00

18 (25) 5 Francs (Bra) 1947–1948. African elephant. ℞ value — 5.50 — 10.00

19 (27) 50 Francs (Ag) 1944. African elephant. ℞
value

	VF	XF
	50.00	**85.00**

Nos. 14, 16, 17, 18 and 19 were struck at Pretoria, South Africa, because of World War II.

COMBINED ISSUES FOR THE BELGIAN CONGO AND RWANDA-URUNDI

BAUDOUIN 1950–1960

20 (28) 5 Francs (Al–Br) 1952. Oil palm (Elaeis
guineensis – Palmae). ℞ value in star   3.50   7.00
21 (29) 50 Centimes (Al) 1954–1955. Oil palm. ℞
arms   0.40   1.00

22 (30) 1 Franc (Al) 1957–1960   1.00   1.80
23 (31) 5 Francs (Al) 1956–1959   1.50   2.50

For later issues, see under Congo-Kinshasa, Katanga, Burundi, Rwanda and Zaïre.

Belgien   # Belgium   **Belgique**
Belgie

Area: 11,779 sq. mi. Population: 9,800,000.

Since the Congress of Vienna in 1815, the territory of Belgium as we know it today was part of the kingdom of the United Low Countries. Following the revolution of September 1830, the Belgians obtained their independence and elected Prince Leopold of Saxe-Coburg as their king. Since 1921 there is an economic union and the monetary agreement with Luxemburg.

Capital: Brussels.

Most Belgian coins were issued with French as well as Flemish inscriptions. In the case of inscriptions in the two languages, there are usually two varieties, either "Belgie-Belgique" (Flemish = Fl) or "Belgique-Belgie" (French = Fr).

100 Centimes = 1 Belgian Frank (Franc)

LEOPOLD II 1865–1909

			VF	XF
1 (1)	1	Centime (Cu) 1869–1902, 1907. Crown above monogram of King Leopold II. ℞ lion and shield		
		a) Fl., 1882–1907	1.00	2.00
		b) Fr., 1869–1907	0.90	1.80
2 (2)	2	Centimes (Cu) 1869–1876, 1902–1909		
		a) Fl., 1902–1909	1.50	2.50
		b) Fr., 1869–1909	1.50	2.50
3 (3)	5	Centimes (Cu–Ni) 1894–1901. Lion emblem. ℞ value		
		a) Fl., 1894–1901	6.00	10.00
		b) Fr., 1894–1901	6.00	10.00
4 (4)	10	Centimes (Cu–Ni) 1894–1901		
		a) Fl., 1894–1901	5.00	10.00
		b) Fr., 1894–1901	5.00	10.00
5 (12)	5	Centimes (Cu–Ni) 1901–1907. Monogram with crown. ℞ value and laurel branch (with central hole)		
		a) Fl., 1902–1907	0.50	2.00
		b) Fr., 1901–1907	0.50	2.00
6 (13)	10	Centimes (Cu–Ni) 1901–1906		
		a) Fl., 1902–1906	0.40	1.00
		b) Fr., 1901–1906	0.40	1.00

				VF	XF
7 (14)	25	Centimes (Cu–Ni) 1908–1909			
		a) Fl., 1908		2.00	3.50
		b) Fr., 1908–1909		2.00	3.50
8 (15)	50	Centimes (Ag) 1901. Leopold II (1835–1909). ℞ lion and value			
		a) Fl., 1901		5.00	10.00
		b) Fr., 1901		5.00	10.00
9 (16)	50	Centimes (Ag) 1907–1909. Leopold II. ℞ value within wreath			
		a) Fl., 1907–1909		4.50	10.00
		b) Fr., 1907–1909		4.50	10.00

10 (17)	1	Franc (Ag) 1904–1909			
		a) Fl., 1904–1909		5.00	10.00
		b) Fr., 1904–1909		5.00	10.00
11 (18)	2	Francs (Ag) 1904–1909			
		a) Fl., 1904–1909		8.00	12.50
		b) Fr., 1904–1909		8.00	12.50

ALBERT I 1909–1934

			VF	XF
12 (22)	1	Centime (Cu) 1912–1914. Crown above monogram of King Albert I. ℞ lion with shield		
		a) Fl., 1912	1.00	3.00
		b) Fr., 1912–1914	1.00	3.00
13 (23)	2	Centimes (Cu) 1910–1919		
		a) Fl., 1910–1919	1.00	2.50
		b) Fr., 1911–1919	1.00	2.50
14 (24)	5	Centimes (Cu–Ni) 1910–1932. Monogram with crown. ℞ value and branch (with central hole)		
		a) Fl., 1910–1928	0.60	1.00
		b) Fl., 1930 (very rare)	60.00	120.00
		c) Fr., 1910–1928	0.60	1.00
		d) Fr., 1932 (very rare)	60.00	120.00

			VF	**XF**
15 (25)	10	Centimes (Cu–Ni) 1920–1929		
		a) Fl., 1920–1929	0.60	1.20
		b) Fr., 1920–1929	0.60	1.20

Of the same type: Nos. 24 and 25

			VF	XF
16 (26)	25	Centimes (Cu–Ni) 1910–1929		
		a) Fl., 1910–1929	0.60	1.20
		b) Fr., 1913–1929	0.60	1.20
17 (33)	50	Centimes (Ag) 1910–1914. King Albert I (1875–1934). ℞ value within wreath		
		a) Fl., 1910–1912	2.50	4.50
		b) Fr., 1910–1914	2.50	4.50
18 (34)	1	Franc (Ag) 1910–1914		
		a) Fl., 1910–1914	2.50	4.50
		b) Fr., 1910–1914	2.50	4.50
19 (35)	2	Francs (Ag) 1910–1912		
		a) Fl., 1911–1912	7.00	12.50
		b) Fr., 1910–1912	7.00	12.50
20 (37)	20	Francs (Au) 1914. King Albert I in uniform. ℞ national arms		
		a) Fl., 1914	120.00	140.00
		b) Fr., 1914	120.00	140.00

The coins issued during the German Occupation of Belgium in 1915–1918 are listed in the German section of this catalogue.

			VF	XF
21 (27)	50	Centimes (Ni) 1922–1934. Type: female figure representing Belgium, wounded but triumphant. ℞ caduceus		
		a) Fl., 1923–1934	0.40	0.80
		b) Fr., 1922–1934	0.40	0.80
22 (28)	1	Franc (Ni) 1922–1935		
		a) Fl., 1922–1935	0.50	0.90
		b) Fr., 1922–1935	0.50	0.90
23 (29)	2	Francs (Ni) 1923–1930		
		a) Fl., 1923–1930	2.00	4.00
		b) Fr., 1923–1930	2.00	4.00
24 (24a)	5	Centimes (Ni–Bra) 1930–1932. Type as No. 14, but with star		
		a) Fl., 1930–1931	1.20	2.00
		b) Fr., 1932	1.20	2.00
25 (25a)	10	Centimes (Ni–Bra) 1930–1932. Type as No. 15		
		a) Fl., 1930–1931	2.50	4.50
		b) Fr., 1930–1932	2.50	4.50
26 (30)	5	Francs = 1 Belga (Ni) 1930–1934. King Albert I. ℞ value within wreath; above, crown		
		a) Fl., 1930–1933	4.50	9.00
		b) Fr., 1930–1934	4.50	9.00

			VF	XF
27 (31)	10	Francs = 2 Belgas (Ni) 1930. Heads left of Leopold I, reigned 1831–1865, Leopold II, reigned 1865–1909 and Albert I, reigned 1909–1934. ℞ value between laurel branches		
		a) Fl., 1930	110.00	200.00
		b) Fr., 1930	110.00	200.00
28 (32)	20	Francs = 4 Belgas (Ni) 1931–1932. Head left of Albert I. ℞ national arms		
		a) Fl., 1931–1932	95.00	150.00
		b) Fr., 1931–1932	95.00	150.00
29 (36)	20	Francs (Ag) 1933–1934. Type as Nos. 27 and 28. ℞ without the words "Twee Belga", or "Quatre Belgas" respectively		
		a) Fl., 1933–1934	8.00	12.50
		b) Fr., 1933–1934	8.00	12.50

LEOPOLD III 1934–1950

30 (42)	5	Centimes (Ni–Bra) 1938–1940. Crown above monogram of Leopold III. ℞ three shields of arms and value (with central hole)		
		a) Belgie-Belgique, 1939–1940	0.40	1.00
		b) Belgique-Belgie, 1938	0.40	1.00
31 (43)	10	Centimes (Ni–Bra) 1938–1939. Type similar to No. 31, but arms of Namur (Fl. Namen), Antwerp and Hasselt:		
		a) Belgie – Belgique, 1939	0.40	0.90
		b) Belgique – Belgie, 1938–1939	0.40	0.90

32 (44) 25 Centimes (Ni–Bra) 1938–1939. Type

	VF	**XF**
similar to No. 31, but arms of Mons (Fl. Bergen), Brussels and Bruges:		
a) Belgie-Belgique, 1938	0.40	0.90
b) Belgique-Belgie, 1938–1939	0.40	0.90

Of the same type: Nos. 39–41

33 (45) 1 Franc (Ni) 1939–1940. Stylized tree with three shields in foreground. (West Flanders, Namur, Limburg). ℞ lion and value:

a) Belgie-Belgique, 1939–1940	0.40	0.80
b) Belgique-Belgie, 1939	0.40	0.80

34 (46) 5 Francs (Ni) 1938–1939. Type as No. 33, but arms of Ghent, Province of Antwerp and Liege:

a) Belgie-Belgique, 1938–1939	1.60	3.00
b) Belgique-Belgie, 1938	1.60	3.00

35 (47) 5 Francs (Ni) 1936–1937. Leopold III (*1901). ℞ value

a) Fl., 1936	25.00	40.00
b) Fr., 1936–1937	25.00	40.00

36 (49) 20 Francs (Ag) 1934–1935. Leopold III. ℞ crown, value, branches; inscription in two languages

	6.00	10.50

37 (50) 50 Francs (Ag) 1939–1940. Leopold III. ℞ crown above shields of arms of the nine provinces (Antwerp, Brabant, West Flanders, East Flanders, Hennegau, Liege, Limburg, Luxemburg and Namur):

a) Belgie-Belgique, 1939–1940	12.50	21.00
b) Belgique-Belgie, 1939–1940	12.50	21.00

			VF	XF
38 (48)	50	Francs (Ag) 1935. The Exhibition Hall. ℞ St. Michael, patron saint of the city of Brussels, and dragon		
		a) Fl., 1935	260.00	400.00
		b) Fr., 1935	260.00	400.00
39 (51)	5	Centimes (Zi) 1941–1943. As No. 30		
		a) Belgie-Belgique, 1941–1942	0.80	1.50
		b) Belgique-Belgie, 1941–1943	0.80	1.50
40 (52)	10	Centimes (Zi) 1941–1946. As No. 31		
		a) Belgie-Belgique, 1941–1946	0.90	2.00
		b) Belgique-Belgie, 1941–1943	0.90	2.00
41 (53)	25	Centimes (Zi) 1942–1946. As No. 32		
		a) Belgie-Belgique, 1942–1946	0.90	2.00
		b) Belgique-Belgie, 1942–1946	0.90	2.00
42 (54)	1	Franc (Zi) 1941–1947. Crowned shield of arms. ℞ crowned monogram, value, date		
		a) Belgie-Belgique, 1942–1947	0.90	2.00
		b) Belgique-Belgie, 1941–1943	0.90	2.00
43 (55)	5	Francs (Zi) 1941–1947. Head of Leopold III r. ℞ crown above value, and date		
		a) Fl., 1941–1947	1.50	3.50
		b) Fr., 1941–1947	1.50	3.50
44 (56)	2	Francs (zinc-coated steel) 1944. Name of countries in French and Flemish, laurel branches, above star. ℞ value between laurel branches. Philadelphia mint issue	3.00	4.50
45 (57)	1	Franc (Cu–Ni) 1950–. Head of goddess Ceres, cornucopia. ℞ crown over laurel branch, value		
		a) Fl., 1950–	0.10	0.20
		b) Fr., 1950–	0.10	0.20

				VF	XF

46 (58) 5 Francs (Cu–Ni) 1948–
  a) Fl., 1948– — 0.15 — 0.30
  b) Fr., 1948– — 0.15 — 0.30
47 (59) 20 Francs (Ag) 1949–1955. Head r. of Mercury, the messenger of the gods, with caduceus. ℞ lion with shield
  a) Fl., 1949–1955 — 6.00 — 10.00
  b) Fr., 1949–1955 — 6.00 — 10.00
48 (60) 50 Francs (Ag) 1948–1954
  a) Fl , 1948–1954 — 10.00 — 16.00
  b) Fr., 1948–1954 — 10.00 — 16.00

49 (61) 100 Francs (Ag) 1948–1954. Conjoined heads l. of Leopold I, Leopold II, Albert I and Leopold III, facing left. ℞ crowned shield of arms, encircled by the chain of the Order of Leopold:
  a) Fl., 1948–1951 — 14.00 — 19.00
  b) Fr., 1948–1954 — 14.00 — 19.00

BAUDOUIN I since 1950

50 (62) 20 Centimes (Br) 1953–1963. Head of miner. ℞ crown and value
  a) Fl., 1954– — 0.10 — 0.20
  b) Fr., 1953– — 0.10 — 0.20
51 (66) 25 Centimes (Cu–Ni) 1964–. Crown over monogram of Baudouin I. ℞ value
  a) Fl., 1964– — 0.08 — 0.16
  b) Fr., 1964– — 0.08 — 0.16
52 (63) 50 Centimes (Br) 1952–
  a) Fl., 1952– — 0.10 — 0.20
  b) Fr., 1952– — 0.10 — 0.20

COMMEMORATIVE ISSUE FOR THE BRUSSELS WORLD FAIR IN 1958

53 (64) 50 Francs (Ag) 1958. Head of King Baudouin I l. ℞ emblem of "Expo 58"
above the gothic Town Hall of Brussels built in 1402–1454; the tower is
90 m. high.

	VF	XF
a) Fl., 1958	10.00	15.00
b) Fr., 1958	10.00	15.00

COMMEMORATIVE ISSUE FOR THE MARRIAGE OF KING BAUDOUIN I AND DOÑA FABIOLA DE MORA Y ARAGON

54 (65) 50 Francs (Ag) 1960. Conjoined heads l.
of Baudouin I (*1930) and Doña Fa-
biola (*1928), ℞ crown over arms of
Belgium and Aragón; inscriptions in
Latin 10.00   15.00

55 (67) 10 Francs (Ni) 1969. Head l. of Baudouin I.
℞ complete large national arms:

a) Fl., 1969–	0.30	0.60
b) Fr., 1969–	0.30	0.60

25th ANNIVERSARY OF THE SILVER JUBILEE OF
KING BAUDOUIN I

			Unc	Proof
56 (68)	250	Francs (Ag) 1976. Head left of Baudouin I. R crowned monogram:		
		a) Fl.	20.00	
		b) Fl., proof, stars on edge		40.00
		c) Fr.	20.00	
		d) Fr., proof, stars on edge		40.00

			Unc	Proof
57 (A 67)	20	Francs (Cu-Ni-Al) 1980. Head left of Baudouin I. R Laurel branch, value:		
		a) Fl.	0.80	1.00
		b) Fr.	0.80	1.00

150th ANNIVERSARY OF INDEPENDENCE

	XF	Unc

			Unc	Proof
58 (69)	500	Francs (Ag) 1980:		
		a) Fl.	20.00	35.00
		b) Fr.	20.00	35.00

Previous issues, see "Weltmünzkatalog 19. Jahrhundert" (World Coin Catalogue of the 19th Century)

Belize

Area: 8,867 sq. mi. Population: 165,000.
Since 1st June, 1973 when attaining full autonomy, British Honduras
ist now called Belize. The place of the former capital of the same name
is now taken by the newly built capital of Belmopan.

100 Cents = 1 British Honduras Dollar;
100 Cents = 1 Belize Dollar

			XF	Unc
1 (1)	1 Cent (Br) 1973–1976. Elizabeth II, crowned head facing right, R numeral of value in wreath, as legend name of the country BELIZE, denomination in letters, date		0.10	0.20
2 (2)	5 Cents (Ni-Bra) 1973–1976. R denomination in circle of dots, as legend name of the country BELIZE, date		0.10	0.20

			XF	Unc
3 (3)	10 Cents (Cu-Ni) 1974–1976, 1979. Type similar to No. 2		0.20	0.40
4 (4)	25 Cents (Cu-Ni) 1974–1976, 1979. Type similar to No. 2		0.40	0.80
5 (5)	50 Cents (Cu-Ni) 1974–1976, 1979. Type similar to No. 2		1.00	2.00
6 (6)	1 Cent (Br) 1974. Coat of arms. R Swallow-Tailed Kite (Elanoides forficatus – Accipitridae)		0.10	0.20

			XF	Unc
7 (7)	5	Cents (Ni-Bra) 1974. R Fork-Tailed Fly-catcher (Muscivora tyrannus - Tyrannidae)	0.30	0.60
8 (8)	10	Cents (Cu-Ni) 1974. R Long-Tailed Hermit (Phaetornis superciliosus - Trochilidae)	0.40	0.80
9 (9)	25	Cents (Cu-Ni) 1974. R Blue-Crowned Motmot (Momotus momota - Momotidae)	0.70	1.40
10 (10)	50	Cents (Cu-Ni) 1974. R Magnificent Frigate Bird (Fregata magnificens - Fregatidae)	1.40	2.40
11 (11)	1	Dollar (Cu-Ni) 1974-1977. R Scarlet Macaw (Ara macao - Psittacidae)	7.00	10.00
12 (12)	5	Dollars (Cu-Ni) 1974-1977. R Keel-Billed Toucan (Ramphastos sulfuratus - Ramphastidae)	8.00	12.00
13 (13)	10	Dollars (Cu-Ni) 1974-1977. R Great Curassow (Crax rubra - Cracidae)	16.00	20.00

				Proof
14 (6a)	1	Cent (Ag) 1974. Type as No. 6		4.00
15 (7a)	5	Cents (Ag) 1974. Type as No. 7		5.00
16 (8a)	10	Cents (Ag) 1974. Type as No. 8		7.00
17 (9a)	25	Cents (Ag) 1974. Type as No. 9		9.00
18 (10a)	50	Cents (Ag) 1974. Type as No. 10		11.00
19 (11a)	1	Dollar (Ag) 1974-1976. Type as No. 11		16.50
20 (12a)	5	Dollars (Ag) 1974-1976. Type as No. 12		28.00
21 (13a)	10	Dollars (Ag) 1974-1976. Type as No. 13		40.00

			XF	Unc
22 (14)	1	Cent (Br) 1975, 1976. Type as No. 6, but value "1 CENT" (scalloped edge)	0.15	0.40
23 (15)	5	Cents (Ni-Bra) 1975, 1976. Type as No. 7, but value "5 CENTS"	0.20	0.50
24 (16)	10	Cents (Cu-Ni) 1975-1977. Type as No. 8, but value "10 CENTS"	0.50	1.00
25 (17)	25	Cents (Cu-Ni) 1975-1977. Type as No. 9, but value "25 CENTS"	0.80	1.60
26 (18)	50	Cents (Cu-Ni) 1975-1977. Type as No. 10, but value "50 CENTS"	1.20	3.00

				Proof
27 (14a)	1	Cent (Ag) 1975, 1976. Type as No. 22		4.50
28 (15a)	5	Cents (Ag) 1975, 1976. Type as No. 23		5.50
29 (16a)	10	Cents (Ag) 1975, 1976. Type as No. 24		8.00
30 (17a)	25	Cents (Ag) 1975, 1976. Type as No. 25		10.00
31 (18a)	50	Cents (Ag) 1975, 1976. Type as No. 26		12.00

30th ANNIVERSARY OF UNITED NATIONS (24th Oct. 1975)

			XF	Unc
32	100	Dollars (Au) 1975. Coat of arms, date, fineness. R council-room, value	65.00	75.00

			XF	Unc
33 (20)	100	Dollars (Au) 1976. R Mayan number and day heiroglyphs	80.00	90.00
34 (1a)	1	Cent (Al) 1976, 1979, 1980. Type as No. 1	0.10	0.20
35 (14b)	1	Cent (Al) 1977–1980. Type as No. 22	0.10	0.20

36 (2a)	5	Cents (Al) 1976–1980. Type as No. 2	0.20	0.40

37 (15b)	5	Cents (Al) 1977–1980. Type as No. 23	0.25	0.50

			Unc	Proof
38 (21)	100	Dollars (Au) 1977. Carved jade head of the Mayan god Kinich Ahau	300.00	90.00
39 (22)	100	Dollars (Au) 1978. Itzamna, Lord of the Heavens and ruler of all the Mayan gods	200.00	80.00

CORONATION JUBILEE

40 (24)	25	Dollars (Ag) 1978	80.00	60.00
41 (23)	250	Dollars (Au) 1978. Jaguar	250.00	180.00
42 (25)	10	Dollars 1979. Flying Jabirus:		
		a) (Ag)		60.00
		b) (Cu-Ni)	18.00	
43 (26)	100	Dollars (Au) 1979. Queen Angelfish	120.00	100.00

CHRISTMAS 1979

44 (27)	100	Dollars (Au) 1979. Star of Bethlehem	110.00	95.00
45 (28)	10	Dollars 1980. Scarlet Ibis:		
		a) (Ag)		40.00
		b) (Cu-Ni)	20.00	
46 (30)	100	Dollars (Au) 1980. Moorish Idols (fishes)		120.00

47 (31)   100 Dollars (Au) 1980. Orchids   160.00

10th ANNIVERSARY OF CARIBBEAN DEVELOPMENT BANK

48 (29)   25 Dollars (Ag) 1980   100.00

WORLD FOOD DAY

49 (32)   5 Cents (Al) 1981   0.50

INDEPENDENCE COMMEMORATIVE

50   100 Dollars (Au) 1981   260.00

Bermuda-Inseln **Bermuda** Bermudes

Area: 21 sq. mi. Population: 60,000.

The islands of Bermuda were discovered in 1522 by the Spaniard Juan de Bermúdez, then occupied and colonized by the English nearly one hundred years later. This group of islands, which number about 300, is situated about 677 miles south-east of Cape Hatteras, facing the North American Continent; it is the oldest self-governing British Colony (self-goverment granted 1888).

Capital: Hamilton.

12 Pence = 1 Shilling, 5 Shillings = 1 Crown, 20 Shillings = £ 1;
    since 6th February 1970: 100 Cents = 1 Bermuda Dollar

ISSUE COMMEMORATING THE 350th ANNIVERSARY OF THE FOUNDING OF THE COLONY

			XF	Unc
1 (1)	1 Crown (Ag) 1959. Crowned bust r. of Queen Elizabeth II. ℞ map between the sailing ship "Sea Venture" of Sir George Somer and a sailing boat of the Islands' Administration		19.00	26.00

2 (2) 1 Crown (Ag) 1964. Crowned bust r. of   **Unc**   **Proof**
Queen Elizabeth II. ℞ arms of the
Bermuda islands; lion holding shield   11.00   15.00

NEW CURRENCY: 100 Cents = 1 Bermuda Dollar

3 (3) 1 Cent (Br) 1970–. Head of Queen Elizabeth II. R wild boar (Sus scrofa domes-
ticus – Suidae), reproduced from the
reverse of pieces of 2, 3, 6 and 12 pence
called »swine money«, which were   **XF**   **Unc**
current in the years 1616 to 1624, as
the first coins issued in the New World
by the English Colonists   0.05   0.10

4 (4) 5 Cents (Cu-Ni) 1970–. R banded
imperial fish or Queen angel fish
(Holacanthus ciliaris – Chaetodontidae)   0.10   0.20

			XF	Unc
5 (5)	10	Cents (Cu-Ni) 1970–. R Bermuda lily or Easter lily (Lilium longiflorum – Liliaceae)	0.15	0.30
6 (6)	25	Cents (Cu-Ni) 1970–. R white-tailed or yellow-billed tropical bird (Phaëthon lepturus – Phaënthontidae)	0.30	0.60
7 (7)	50	Cents (Cu-Ni) 1970–. R arms of the Bermuda islands; lion holding shield	0.75	1.00
8 (8)	1	Dollar (Ag) 1970. R map between two fishes	Proof	55.00
9 (9)	20	Dollars (Au) 1970. R bird	Proof	1100.00

COMMEMORATIVE ISSUE FOR THE SILVER WEDDING OF THE BRITISH ROYAL COUPLE ON 20th NOVEMBER 1972

			Unc	Proof
10 (10)	1	Dollar (Ag) 1972. R map between crowned monograms:		
		a) .500 fine silver	20.00	
		b) .925 fine silver		30.00

ROYAL VISIT COMMEMORATIVE (2)

11 (11)	25	Dollars 1975. Royal scepter and crowned monograms:		
		a) (Ag)		100.00
		b) (Cu-Ni)	30.00	
12 (12)	100	Dollars (Au) 1975. Type as No. 11	140.00	220.00

25th ANNIVERSARY OF THE SILVER JUBILEE OF HER MAJESTY QUEEN ELIZABETH II (3)

13 (13)	25	Dollars (Ag) 1977. R depicts Bermuda's 18th century "ship penny" sailing vessel	45.00	60.00
14 (14)	50	Dollars (Au) 1977. R Dinghy	120.00	190.00
15 (15)	100	Dollars (Au) 1977. R "Deliverance", the first ship to be built in Bermuda	200.00	250.00

			Unc	Proof
16 (16)	1 Dollar 1981:			
	a) (Ag)			55.00
	b) (Cu-Ni)		3.00	
17	250 Dollars (Au) 1981			550.00

Bhutan   # Bhutan   **Bhoutan**
Druk-jul

Area: 18,077 sq. mi. Population: 1,000,000.
Constitutional monarchy in the eastern Himalayas. Treaty of protection
with British India (8. 1. 1910) and with the Indian Union (8. 8. 1949).
Summer residence: Thimphu, winter residence: Punakha.

64 Pice (Paise) = 1 Rupee; since 1957: 100 Naye Paise = 1 Rupee, 100 Rupees
= 1 Sertum; since 1974: 100 Chetrum (Paise) = 1 Ngultrum (Rupee)

Weight and fineness of the Sertum (gold) correspond to that of the
British Pound Sterling.
The Indian Rupee is commonly used as legal tender.

MAHARAJAH JIGME WANGCHUK 1926-1952

			VF	XF
1 (5)	1	Pice (Cu/Bra) 1875-1930. Inscription on both sides, irregular flan	3.00	6.00

MAHARAJAH JIGME DORJI WANGCHUK 1952–1972

			VF	XF
2 (3)	1	Pice (Br) undated (1951, 1954). Buddhist symbols	1.60	3.00
3 (1)	1	Pice (Br) 1928. Bust l. of Maharajah Jigme Wangchuk. Rev. Buddhist symbols	25.00	40.00

			VF	XF
4 (4)	½ Rupee (Ag) 1928. Type as No. 3		22.00	30.00
5	½ Rupee (Ni) 1928, 1950. Type as No. 4:			
	a) (Y 4a) 1928, 1950; 5.83 gm.		2.50	5.00
	b) (Y 4b) 1950; 5.00 gm.		1.00	2.00

COMMEMORATIVE ISSUES (7) FOR THE 40th ANNIVERSARY OF THE BEGINNING OF THE REIGN OF MAHARAJAH JIGME WANGCHUK

6 (6)	25 Naye Paise (Cu–Ni) 1966. Bust l. of Sir Jigme Wangchuk. ℞ arms	0.30	0.60
7 (7)	50 Naye Paise (Cu–Ni) 1966	0.80	1.60
8 (8)	1 Rupee (Cu–Ni) 1966	1.00	2.00
9 (9)	3 Rupees (Cu–Ni) 1966		
	a) (Cu-Ni)	5.00	8.00
	b) (Ag)	Proof	60.00

		Unc	Proof
10 (40)	1 Sertum (Au) 1966	140.00	200.00
11 (41)	2 Sertum (Au) 1966	260.00	350.00
12 (42)	5 Sertum (Au) 1966	650.00	750.00

There are also off-metal strikes in platinum of Nos. 10-12.

		XF	Unc
13 (43)	1 Sertum (Au) 1970	95.00	110.00

ISSUES (2) FOR THE FAO COIN PLAN

			XF	Unc
14 (10)	20 Chetrum (Bra) 1974. Rice cultivation. R national emblem, name of country, denomination		0.30	0.50

		XF	Unc
15 (11)	15 Ngultrum (Ag) 1974. Type as No. 14	8.50	12.00

		XF	Unc
16 (12)	5 Chetrums (Al) 1974, 1975	0.15	0.30

		XF	Unc
17 (13)	10 Chetrums (Al) 1974	0.20	0.40

		XF	Unc
18 (14)	25 Chetrums (Cu-Ni) 1974, 1975	0.30	0.60

			XF	Unc
19 (15)	1 Ngultrum (Cu-Ni) 1974, 1975		0.60	1.00

INTERNATIONAL WOMAN'S YEAR 1975 (2)

			XF	Unc
20 (16)	10 Chetrums (Al) 1975, 1976		0.25	0.50
21 (17)	30 Ngultrums (Ag) 1975, 1976		10.00	15.00

			Unc	Proof
22 (18)	5 Chetrums (Br) 1979		0.50	
23 (19)	10 Chetrums (Br) 1979		0.50	
24 (20)	25 Chetrums (Cu-Ni) 1979		0.80	
25 (21)	50 Chetrums (Cu-Ni) 1979		1.00	
26 (22)	1 Ngultrum (Cu-Ni) 1979		2.00	
27 (23)	3 Ngultrum 1979:			
	a) (Ag)			40.00
	b) (Cu-Ni)		2.00	
28 (24)	1 Sertum 1979:			
	a) (Au)		200.00	250.00
	b) (Pt)			280.00
29 (25)	2 Sertum 1979:			
	a) (Au)		400.00	450.00
	b) (Pt)			500.00
30 (26)	5 Sertum 1979:			
	a) (Au)		900.00	1100.00
	b) (Pt)			1300.00

Biafra

Area: 29,370 sq. mi. Population: 12,802,000.

On 30th May 1967, on the strength of a request from the Consultative Assembly of the region inhabited predominantly by the Ibos, the Military Governor of the Eastern region of Nigeria proclaimed independence as "The Republic of Biafra". Following a war which lasted 2½ years, and the slow occupation of the country by the Nigerian Federal troops, Biafra surrendered in January 1970. As a result of this the country is again part of Nigeria.

12 Pence = 1 Shilling, 20 Shillings = 1 £

			VF	XF
1 (1)	3	Pence (Al) 1969. Coconut palm (Cocos nucifera – Palmae); in background, rising sun; the whole in a bow of U-shape; inscription around: PEACE. UNITY. FREEDOM. ℞ Name of country: REPUBLIC OF BIAFRA. Mark of value, date	5.00	10.00

			VF	XF
2 (2)	1	Shilling (Al) 1969. ℞ crowned hawk eagle (Stephanoaëtus coronatus – Accipitridae) standing on elephant's tusk. Name of country: REPUBLIC OF BIAFRA. Value, date	4.00	6.00
3 (3)	2½	Shillings (Al) 1969. ℞ lion	10.00	15.00

| 4 | 1 £ (Ag) 1969 | Unc | 70.00 |

COMMEMORATIVE ISSUES (5) FOR THE 2nd ANNIVERSARY OF THE PROCLAMATION OF INDEPENDENCE

| 5 | 1 £ (Au) 1969. National arms. ℞ imperial eagle standing on parchment; in the background, rising sun, value | Proof | 80.00 |
| 6 | 2 £ (Au) 1969. Type as No. 5 | Proof | 150.00 |

7	5 £ (Au) 1969. Type as No. 5	Proof	320.00
8	10 £ (Au) 1969. Type as No. 5	Proof	750.00
9	25 £ (Au) 1969. Type as No. 5	Proof	1600.00

Bolivien   # Bolivia   **Bolivie**

Area: 422,538 sq. mi. Population: 5,500,000.

Bolivia covers mostly the high areas of Ancient Peru, which formerly belonged to the Empire of the Incas and had been part of the Viceroyalty of Peru since the 16th century. In 1825 Bolivia became a Republic.

Capital: La Paz, though according to the Constitution it should be the town of Sucre.

100 Centavos = 1 Boliviano; since 1st January 1963:
100 Centavos = 1 Peso Boliviano

			VF	XF
1 (47a)	5	Centavos (Ag) 1885–1900. National arms. R value	2.50	5.00
2 (48a)	10	Centavos (Ag) 1885–1900	2.50	5.00
3 (49a)	20	Centavos (Ag) 1885–1907	3.50	6.00
4 (51b)	50	Centavos (Ag) 1891–1900	5.50	10.00
5	5	Centavos (Cu-Ni) 1893–1919, 1935. Sun rising over the mount Potosi, vicuña (Lama vicugna – Camelidae). R caduceus and value		
		a) (Y 45) 1893–1919	1.00	2.00
		b) (Y 57) 1935, smaller diameter	0.60	1.20

			VF	XF
6	10	Centavos (Cu-Ni) 1893–1919, 1935–1936		
		a) (Y 46) 1893–1919	1.00	1.60
		b) (Y 58) 1935–1936, smaller diameter	0.90	1.20
7 (55)	20	Centavos (Ag) 1909	3.00	6.00

8 (54)   50 Centavos (Ag) 1900–1908. National

			VF	XF
		arms with Andean condor (Vultur gryphus – Cathartidae). ℞ value in wreath (3 types)	6.00	11.00
9 (60)	10	Centavos (Cu–Ni) 1937. Sun rising over mount Potosi, vicuña. ℞ hand holding torch.	1.20	2.50
10 (61)	50	Centavos (Cu–Ni) 1937	50.00	100.00
11	10	Centavos. Same type as No. 6		
		a) (Y 58) (Cu–Ni) 1939	0.30	0.60
		b) (Y 57a) (Zi) 1942	1.00	2.00
12 (58a)	20	Centavos (Zi) 1942. Same type as No. 7	1.00	2.00
13	50	Centavos. Same type as No. 5		
		a) (Y 59) (Cu–Ni) 1939	1.30	2.50
		b) (Y 59a) (Br) 1942	0.40	0.60

| **14** (62) | 1 | Boliviano (Br) 1951. Sun rising over mount Potosi, vicuña. ℞ value in wreath | 0.30 | 0.60 |

| **15** (63) | 5 | Bolivianos (Br) 1951. National arms. ℞ value in wreath | 0.80 | 1.50 |

| **16** (64) | 10 | Bolivianos (Br) 1951. Head r. of Simón Bolívar (1783–1830), President of the State of Bolivia 1825–1826. ℞ value in wreath | 1.50 | 3.00 |

COMMEMORATIVE ISSUES (4) FOR THE REVOLUTION OF
31st OCTOBER 1952

		VF	XF
17	5 Bolivianos (Au) 1952. Agricultural worker	60.00	75.00

| **18** | 10 Bolivianos (Au) 1952. Miner | 130.00 | 140.00 |

| **19** | 20 Bolivianos (Au) 1952. Head of Germán Busch | 260.00 | 300.00 |

| **20** | 50 Bolivianos (Au) 1952. Head of Gualberto Villarroel | 450.00 | 550.00 |

	CURRENCY REFORM: 1000 old Bolivianos = 1 Peso Boliviano	VF	XF
21 (95)	5 Centavos (Cu-St) 1965–. Sun rising over mount Potosi, vicuña. ℞ value and date between branches	0.08	0.16
22 (96)	10 Centavos (Cu-St) 1965–. Same type as No. 21	0.10	0.20
23 (97)	20 Centavos (Ni-St) 1965–. Same type as No. 21	0.12	0.25

		VF	XF
24 (98)	50 Centavos (Ni-St) 1965–. Same type as No. 21	0.25	0.50
25 (100)	1 Peso Boliviano (Cu-Ni) 1968–. Same type as No. 21	0.40	0.80

COMMEMORATIVE ISSUE FOR THE FAO COIN PLAN AND FOR THE 23rd ANNIVERSARY OF THE FAO
(16th October 1968)

		XF	Unc
26 (99)	1 Peso Boliviano (Ni) 1968. Obverse as No. 25. ℞ under the value: the date 16–10–68 and the legend: GUERRA CONTRA EL HAMBRE	28.00	35.00
27 (101)	25 Centavos (Cu–Ni) 1971, 1972. Type as No. 21 (dodecagonal)	0.15	0.30

150th ANNIVERSARY OF INDEPENDENCE (3)

28 (102)	100 Pesos Bolivianos (Ag) 1975. Coat of arms. ℞ conjoined heads left of Simón Bolívar and Hugo Banzer Suarez	9.00	10.00

			XF	Unc
29 (103)	250	Pesos Bolivianos (Ag) 1975. Type as No. 28	20.00	22.00
30 (104)	500	Pesos Bolivianos (Ag) 1975. Type as No. 28	40.00	42.00

31	5 Pesos Bolivianos (Cu-Ni) 1976, 1978, 1980	2.00	3.00

INTERNATIONAL YEAR OF THE CHILD (2)

32	200	Pesos Bolivianos (Ag) 1979	Proof	45.00
33	4000	Pesos Bolivianos (Au) 1979	Proof	400.00

Previous issues, see "Weltmünzkatalog 19. Jahrhundert" (World Coin Catalogue of the 19th Century)

Area: 221,146 sq. mi. Population: 700,000.
Under the name of Bechuanaland it was a British Protectorate since 1885; it obtained internal autonomy in 1965; since 30th September 1966 it has been an independent Republic with the name of Botswana. Capital: Gaberones.

100 Cents = 1 Rand; since 23th August 1976: 100 Thebe = 1 Pula

Until 30th November 1976 Botswana belongs to the monetary area of the South African Rand.

COMMEMORATIVE ISSUE (2) FOR THE DECLARATION OF INDEPENDENCE ON 30th SEPTEMBER 1966

			Unc	Proof
1 (1)	50	Cents (Ag) 1966. Head l. of Sir Seretse Khama (*1921), Head of State. R national arms supported by Chapman's zebras (Equus quagga chapmani – Equidae)	10.00	
2 (2)	10	Thebes (Au) 1966		220.00

ISSUE FOR THE FAO COIN PLAN (6)

			Unc	Proof
3 (3)	1	Thebe (Al) 1976. Coat of arms, date. R Turako	0.20	2.00
4 (4)	5	Thebe (Br) 1976, 1977. R Toko	0.40	2.00
5 (5)	10	Thebe (Cu-Ni) 1976, 1977. R Buck	0.50	2.00
6 (6)	25	Thebe (Cu-Ni) 1976, 1977. R Zebu	1.00	3.00
7 (7)	50	Thebe (Cu-Ni) 1976, 1977. R African fish eagle	2.00	4.00
8 (8)	1	Pula (Cu-Ni) 1976, 1977. R Zebra (scalloped edge)	3.00	6.00

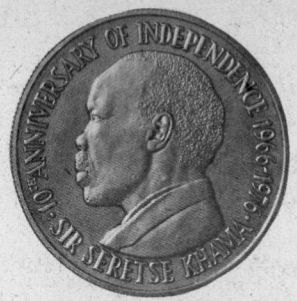 

			Unc	Proof
9 (9)	5	Pula (Ag) 1976. Bust left of Sir Seretse Khama. R The Botswana National Assembly Building, with value above and country name below	15.00	25.00
10 (10)	150	Pula (Au) 1976. Type as No. 9; .916 gold	350.00	400.00

CONSERVATION COMMEMORATIVE (3)

11 (11)	5	Pula (Ag) 1978	35.00	50.00
12 (12)	10	Pula (Ag) 1978	45.00	65.00
13 (13)	150	Pula (Au) 1978	650.00	750.00

WORLD FOOD DAY

14	2	Thebe (Al-Br) 1981	0.50

Brazil

Estados Unidos do Brasil

Area: 3,273,832 sq. mi. Population:: 113,000,000.

The largest country in South America, it was discovered in the year 1500 by Pedro Alvares Cabral who took possession in the name of Portugal. In 1822 Brazil freed itself from the colonial yoke by the Declaration of Independence. First an Empire, it has been a Republic since 15th November 1889.

Capital: Rio de Janeiro; since 21st April 1960: Brasilia.

1000 Reis = 1 Milreis
Since 1942 100 Centavos = 1 Cruzeiro
From 1964 to 1967 only Cruzeiros
Since 1967 100 Centavos = 1 Cruzeiro Novo
Since 15th May 1970: 100 Centavos = 1 Cruzeiro

			VF	XF
1 (1)	20	Reis (Br) 1889–1912. Arms. ℞ value in circle	1.50	3.00
2 (2)	40	Reis (Br) 1889–1912. "Southern Cross" within circle of stars	1.50	3.00
3 (3)	100	Reis (Cu–Ni) 1889–1900	1.50	3.00
4 (4)	200	Reis (Cu–Ni) 1889–1900	2.00	4.00

COMMEMORATIVE ISSUES (4) FOR THE 400th ANNIVERSARY OF THE DISCOVERY OF BRAZIL

			VF	XF
5 (8)	400	Reis (Ag) 1900. Cross within circle. ℞ value in wreath	55.00	90.00
6 (9)	1000	Reis (Ag) 1900. Liberty head between symbols of progress: steamer, railway line and plough. ℞ value in wreath	100.00	180.00
7 (10)	2000	Reis (Ag) 1900. Sailing ship of the time of discovery	140.00	240.00
8 (11)	4000	Reis (Ag) 1900. Pedro Alvares Cabral (c. 1468–1526), explorer and seaman	500.00	850.00
9 (12)	100	Reis (Cu–Ni) 1901. Liberty head r. ℞ arms	0.40	1.20
10 (13)	200	Reis (Cu–Ni) 1901	0.80	1.50
11 (14)	400	Reis (Cu–Ni) 1901	1.50	2.60
12 (15)	500	Reis (Ag) 1906–1912. Liberty head l. ℞ value	5.00	10.00
13 (16)	1000	Reis (Ag) 1906–1912	6.00	12.50
14 (17)	2000	Reis (Ag) 1906–1912	10.50	22.50

			VF	XF
15 (25)	10000	Reis (Au) 1889–1922. Liberty head l. ℞ Southern cross	1000.00	1600.00
16 (26)	20000	Reis (Au) 1889–1922. Liberty head l. ℞ arms	1150.00	1800.00
17 (A14)	400	Reis (Cu–Ni) 1914. Statue of Liberty holding shield with inscription LEX	90.00	160.00
18 (18)	500	Reis (Ag) 1912. Liberty head r. ℞ arms	8.50	12.00
19 (19)	1000	Reis (Ag) 1912–1913	8.50	14.00
20 (20)	2000	Reis (Ag) 1912–1913	14.00	22.00
21 (21)	500	Reis (Ag) 1913. Same type as No. 18. ℞ inscription over arms	6.00	12.00
22 (22)	1000	Reis (Ag) 1913. Same type as No. 19. ℞ inscription over arms	9.00	16.50
23 (23)	2000	Reis (Ag) 1913. Same type as No. 20. ℞ inscription over arms	15.00	20.00
24 (27)	20	Reis (Cu–Ni) 1918–1935. Liberty head r. R value	0.80	1.50
25 (28)	50	Reis (Cu-Ni) 1918–1935	0.80	1.50
26 (29)	100	Reis (Cu-Ni) 1918–1935	0.80	1.80
27 (30)	200	Reis (Cu–Ni) 1918–1935	0.80	1.80
28 (31)	400	Reis (Cu–Ni) 1918–1935	0.80	1.80
29 (32)	500	Reis (Al–Br) 1924–1930. Symbolic figure of the Republic holding horn of plenty. ℞ value in wreath	0.80	1.80
30 (33)	1000	Reis (Al–Br) 1924–1931	1.20	2.00
31 (24)	2000	Reis (Ag) 1924–1934. Liberty head. ℞ value in wreath	5.00	9.00

COMMEMORATIVE ISSUES (3) FOR THE CENTENARY OF INDEPENDENCE

32 (34)	500	Reis (Al–Br) 1922. Conjoined busts of Dom Pedro I (1798–1834), Emperor of Brazil 1822–1831, and Epitácio da Silva Pessôa (1865–1942), President from 1919 to 1922. ℞ torch between crown and Liberty cap	1.50	3.00
33 (35)	1000	Reis (Al–Br) 1922	2.50	5.00

34 (38) 2 Milreis (Ag) 1922. ℞ arms of the Empire and the Republic:

	VF	XF
a) Fine silver content 900	9.50	15.00
b) Fine silver content 500	5.00	10.00

COMMEMORATIVE ISSUES (6) FOR THE 400th ANNIVERSARY OF COLONIZATION 1532–1932

35 (39) 100 Reis (Cu–Ni) 1932. Bust facing of
Kazike Tibiriçá. († 1562). ℞ value   2.60   5.00

36 (40) 200 Reis (Cu–Ni) 1932. Globe. ℞ sailing
ship of the time of discovery   2.60   5.00

37 (41) 400 Reis (Cu–Ni) 1932. Map of South
America. ℞ Lusinian cross   6.00   11.00

38 (42) 500 Reis (Al–Br) 1932. João Ramalho
(1494–1584), a Portuguese colonist and
founder of the town of Santo Andre;
he married the daughter of Kazike
Tibiriçá. ℞ cuirass   7.00   12.00

39 (43) 1000 Reis (Al–Br) 1932. Standing figure
facing of Martim Affonso da Sousa (c.
1500–1571), general, seaman and
colonist. ℞ arms   7.00   12.00

				VF	XF

40 (44) 2000 Reis (Ag) 1932. Bust three-quarters to r. of John III (1502 to 1557), King of Portugal from 1521 to 1557. ℞ arms   7.00   12.00

41 (45) 100 Reis (Cu–Ni) 1936–1938. Bust facing of Admiral Marques Tamandaré (1807 –1897), founder of the Brazilian Navy. ℞ anchor   1.20   2.00

42 (46) 200 Reis (Cu–Ni) 1936–1938. Bust facing of Viscount de Mauá (1813–1889), his family name was Irineu Evangelista de Souza, builder of the first railway line Rio de Janeiro to Queimados. ℞ engine   1.60   3.00

43 (47) 300 Reis (Cu–Ni) 1936–1938. Head facing of Antonio Carlos Gomes (1836– 1896), composer. ℞ lyre   2.00   3.50

| **44 (48)** | 400 | Reis (Cu–Ni) 1936–1938. Head facing of Oswaldo Cruz (1872–1917), microbiologist, well-known for his research into yellow fever. ℞ lamp | **VF** | **XF** |
| | | | 2.00 | 3.60 |

45	500	Reis (Al-Br) 1935–1938. Bust facing of Diego Antônio Feijó (1784–1843), Regent of Brazil 1835–1837. R column		
		a) (Y 49) 1935; 4 gm.	12.50	25.00
		b) (Y 50) 1936–1938; 5 gm.	5.50	10.00

46	1000	Reis (Al-Br) 1935–1938. Fr. José de Anchieta (1534–1597). R open Bible		
		a) (Y 51) 1935, diameter 26 mm	5.00	10.00
		b) (Y 52) 1936–1938, diameter 24 mm	2.00	4.00
47 (55)	2000	Reis (Ag) 1935. Portrait l. of Field-Marshal Luiz Alves de Lima, Duke of Caxias (1803 to 1880), Commanding Officer of the troops of the Emperor of Brazil. ℞ sword		
			5.50	10.00

			VF	XF
48		2000 Reis (Al-Br) 1936–1938. Portrait r. of Duke of Caxias. ℞ sword		
		a) (Y 53) 1936–1938, round	3.60	7.50
		b) (Y 54) 1938, dodecagonal	3.00	6.00

49 (56)	5000 Reis (Ag) 1936–1938. Head l. of Alberto Santos Dumont (1873–1932), pioneer aviator; on 23–10–1906 he flew 60 m. in France. ℞ eagle's wing	5.50	10.00
50 (57)	100 Reis (Cu–Ni) 1938–1942. Dr. Getúlio Dornelles Vargas (1883–1954), President of State from 1930 to 1945 and from 1951 to 1954. ℞ value	0.80	1.80
51 (58)	200 Reis (Cu–Ni) 1938–1942	0.80	1.80
52 (59)	300 Reis (Cu–Ni) 1938–1942	0.80	1.80

53 (60)	400 Reis (Cu–Ni) 1938–1942	1.20	2.80

				VF	XF

54 (61) 500 Reis (Al–Br) 1939. Bust facing of Joaquim Maria Machado de Assis (1839–1908), author and poet. ℞ value in wreath — 1.60 — 3.00

55 (62) 1000 Reis (Al–Br) 1939. Bust facing of Tobias Barreto de Menezes (1839–1889), philosopher and poet. ℞ value in wreath — 2.80 — 5.00

56 (63) 2000 Reis (Al–Br) 1939. Bust facing of Field-Marshal Floriano Peixoto (1842–1895). President of State from 1891 to 1894. ℞ value in wreath — 3.00 — 5.50

57 (64) 10 Centavos (Cu–Ni) 1942–1943. Getúlio D. Vargas. ℞ value — 0.50 — 1.20

58 (64a) 10 Centavos (Al–Br) 1943–1947. Same type as No. 57 — 0.50 — 1.00

59 (65) 20 Centavos (Cu–Ni) 1942–1943 — 0.80 — 1.50

60 (65a) 20 Centavos (Al–Br) 1943–1948. Same type as No. 59 — 0.80 — 1.50

			VF	XF
61 (66)	50	Centavos (Cu–Ni) 1942–1943	0.80	1.60
62 (66a)	50	Centavos (Al–Br) 1943–1947. Same type as No. 61	0.40	0.80
63 (67)	1	Cruzeiro (Al–Br) 1942–1956. Map of Brazil. ℞ value	0.80	1.20
64 (68)	2	Cruzeiros (Al–Br) 1942–1956	0.80	1.50
65 (69)	5	Cruzeiros (Al–Br) 1942–1943	1.80	3.50

66 (73)	10	Centavos (Al–Br) 1947–1955. Bust l. of José Bonifacio de Andrada e Silva (1763 to 1838), fighter for independence, so-called "Patriarch of Independence", Paulistan politician. ℞ value	0.40	0.80

67 (74)	20	Centavos (Al–Br) 1948–1956. Bust l. of Ruy Barbosa (1849–1923), jurist, author, politician. ℞ value	0.50	1.00

68 (75)	50	Centavos (Al–Br) 1948–1956. Bust l. of General Eurico Gaspar Dutra (*1885), President of State from 1946 to 1951. ℞ value	0.70	1.20

			VF	XF
69 (76)	10 Centavos (Al) 1956–1961. National arms. ℞ value		0.10	0.20
70 (77)	20 Centavos (Al) 1956–1961		0.15	0.30
71 (78)	50 Centavos (Al–Br) 1956		0.35	0.70
72 (81)	50 Centavos (Al) 1957–1962		0.25	0.50
73 (79)	1 Cruzeiro (Al–Br) 1956		1.20	2.40
74 (82)	1 Cruzeiro (Al) 1957–1962		0.35	0.70
75 (80)	2 Cruzeiros (Al–Br) 1956		1.40	2.40
76 (83)	2 Cruzeiros (Al) 1957–1962		0.35	0.70
77 (84)	10 Cruzeiros (Al) 1965. Map of Brazil. ℞ value		0.10	0.20

		VF	XF
78 (85)	20 Cruzeiros (Al) 1965	0.25	0.25

		VF	XF
79 (86)	50 Cruzeiros (Cu–Ni) 1965. Liberty head l. ℞ value, branch of a coffee tree, date	0.40	0.80

NEW CURRENCY: 100 Centavos = 1 Cruzeiro Novo

		XF	Unc
80 (87)	1 Centavo (St). Liberty head l. R value, date:		
	a) 1967	0.05	0.10
	b) 1969, 1975; thinner planchet	0.05	0.10

		XF	Unc
81 (88)	2 Centavos (St). Same type as No. 80:		
	a) 1967	0.05	0.10
	b) 1969, 1975; thinner planchet	0.05	0.10

				XF	Unc

82 (89)   5 Centavos (St). Same type as No. 80:

           a) 1967   0.10   0.20

           b) 1969, thinner planchet   0.08   0.16

83 (90)   10 Centavos (Cu-Ni). Factory:

           a) 1967   0.15   0.30

           b) 1970, thinner planchet   0.10   0.20

84 (91)   20 Centavos (Cu-Ni). Oilderrick:

           a) 1967   0.20   0.40

           b) 1970, thinner planchet   0.12   0.24

85 (92)   50 Centavos. Steamship at quay-side:

           a) (Ni) 1967   0.55   1.10

           b) (Cu–Ni) 1970   0.40   0.80

86 (93)   1 Cruzeiro (Ni) 1967–1970. Value, date, branch of a coffee tree:

           a) 1967, pattern   –.–   –.–

           b) 1970   0.60   1.20

COMMEMORATIVE ISSUES (3) FOR THE
150th ANNIVERSARY OF INDEPENDENCE

			XF	Unc
87 (94)	1	Cruzeiro (Ni) 1972	0.80	1.50
88 (95)	20	Cruzeiros (Ag) 1972	14.00	17.50
89 (96)	300	Cruzeiros (Au) 1972	320.00	350.00
90 (90b)	10	Centavos (St) 1974–1979. Type as No. 83; plain edge	0.10	0.20
91 (91b)	20	Centavos (St) 1975–1979. Type as No. 84; plain edge	0.12	0.24
92 (92b)	50	Centavos (St) 1975–1979. Type as No. 85; plain edge	0.40	0.80
93 (93a)	1	Cruzeiro (Cu-Ni) 1974–1978. Type as No. 86	0.60	1.20

10th ANNIVERSARY OF CENTRAL BANK

			XF	Unc
94 (97)	10	Cruzeiros (Ag) 1975. Bust left. R value, emblem		55.00

ISSUES FOR THE FAO COIN PLAN (5)

			XF	Unc
95 (98)	1	Centavo (St) 1975–1979. R sugar-cane	0.12	0.24
96 (99)	2	Centavos (St) 1975–1978. R soja	0.12	0.24
97 (100)	5	Centavos (St) 1975–1978. R zebu	0.15	0.30
98 (101)	1	Centavo (St) 1979. R soja	0.10	0.20

			XF	Unc
99 (102)	1	Cruzeiro (St) 1979. Sugar-cane	0.20	0.35
100 (103)	5	Cruzeiros (St) 1980. Coffee	0.35	0.45
101 (104)	10	Cruzeiros (St) 1980. Map of Brazil	0.45	0.80

| 102 | 20 Cruzeiros (St) 1981. Church | 0.80 | 1.10 |
| 103 | 50 Cruzeiros (St) 1981. Aerial of a harbor | 1.30 | 2.00 |

Previous issues, see "Weltmünzkatalog 19. Jahrhundert" (World Coin Catalogue of the 19th Century)

British Caribbean Territories

Britisch-Karibische Gebiete **Antilles Britanniques**

This economic and monetary area comprised the following territories: Barbados, British Guiana (up to 1962), the Leeward Islands (Antigua, the British Virgin Islands, Montserrat, St. Kitts-Nevis-Anguilla), Trinidad and Tobago (up to 1962), the Windward Islands (Dominica, Grenada, St. Lucia, St. Vincent). On 6th October 1965 the British West Indian Dollar was replaced by the new monetary unit, the East Caribbean Dollar.

100 Cents = 1 British West Indian Dollar

ELIZABETH II since 1952

		XF	Unc
1 (1)	½ Cent (Br) 1955–1958. Crowned bust r. of Queen Elizabeth II. ℞ value	0.60	1.20
2 (2)	1 Cent (Br) 1955–1965	0.15	0.25

3 (3)	2 Cents (Br) 1955–1965. ℞ value in wreath	0.20	0.40
4 (4)	5 Cents (Ni–Bra) 1955–1965. ℞ "The Golden Hind", flagship of Sir Francis Drake	0.25	0.50
5 (5)	10 Cents (Cu–Ni) 1955–1965	0.30	0.60

			XF	Unc
6 (6)	25	Cents (Cu–Ni) 1955–1965	0.70	1.20

			XF	Unc
7 (7)	50	Cents (Cu–Ni) 1955. ℞ arms	1.70	3.00

Area: 82,680 sq. mi. Population: 647,000.
A British Crown Colony since the 17th century on the North-East coast of South America. Since 26th June 1966 the country has been independent under the name of The Republic of Guyana.
Capital: Georgetown.

50 Pence = 1 British Guiana Dollar

EDWARD VII 1901–1910

		VF	XF
1 (2)	4 Pence (Ag) 1903–1910. Crowned bust r. of King Edward VII. ℞ value in wreath; above, crown	11.00	20.00

GEORGE V 1910–1936

2 (3)	4 Pence (Ag) 1911–1916. Crowned bust l. of King George V. ℞ circular legend reading BRITISH GUIANA AND WEST INDIES. Value in wreath; above, crown	11.00	20.00
3 (4)	4 Pence (Ag) 1917–1936. Same type as No. 2, but the legend now reads only BRITISH GUIANA	3.00	6.00

GEORGE VI 1936–1952

4 (5)	4 Pence (Ag) 1938–1945. Crowned bust l. of King George VI. ℞ value in wreath; above, crown	1.50	2.50

Previous issues, see "Weltmünzkatalog 19. Jahrhundert" (World Coin Catalogue of the 19th Century)

Britisch-Honduras **British Honduras** Honduras Britannique

Area: 8,867 sq. mi. Population: 120,000.
This British Colony on the eastern shore of Central America obtained
in 1960 a new Constitution with full internal selfgovernment. Since
1st June 1973, upon attaining full autonomy, the country is called
Belize. The previous capital of the same name is now replaced by the
newly built capital of Belmopan.
The British Honduras Dollar was declared the monetary unit in 1894.

100 Cents = 1 British Honduras Dollar

EDWARD VII 1901–1910

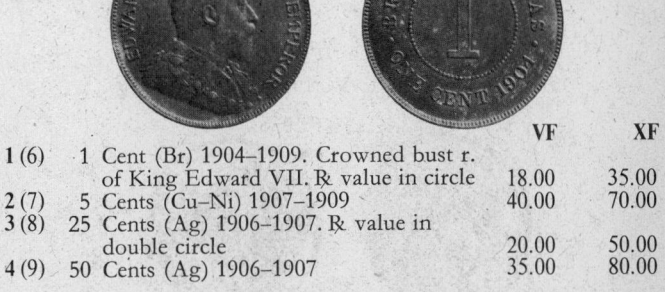

			VF	XF
1 (6)	1	Cent (Br) 1904–1909. Crowned bust r. of King Edward VII. ℞ value in circle	18.00	35.00
2 (7)	5	Cents (Cu–Ni) 1907–1909	40.00	70.00
3 (8)	25	Cents (Ag) 1906–1907. ℞ value in double circle	20.00	50.00
4 (9)	50	Cents (Ag) 1906–1907	35.00	80.00

			VF	XF
5 (10)	1	Cent (Br) 1911–1913. Crowned bust l. of King George V. ℞ value in dotted circle	115.00	200.00
6 (11)	1	Cent (Br) 1914–1936. Same type as No. 5. ℞ value in wreath	8.00	18.00
7 (12)	5	Cents (Cu–Ni) 1911–1936	5.00	10.00
8 (13)	10	Cents (Ag) 1918–1936. ℞ value in double circle	6.00	14.00
9 (14)	25	Cents (Ag) 1911–1919	15.00	40.00

10 (15)	50	Cents (Ag) 1911–1919	20.00	50.00

GEORGE VI 1936–1952

11 (16)	1	Cent (Br) 1937–1947. Crowned head l. of King George VI. ℞ value in wreath	1.50	4.00
12 (17)	5	Cents (Cu-Ni) 1939. ℞ value in dotted circle	5.00	10.00
13 (17a)	5	Cents (Ni-Bra) 1942-1945, 1947. Type as No. 12	5.00	12.00

		VF	XF
14 (18)	10 Cents (Ag) 1939–1946. ℞ value in double circle	4.00	12.50
15 (19)	1 Cent (Br) 1949–1951. Same type as No. 11, but the legend now reads only KING GEORGE THE SIXTH	1.50	3.00
16 (20)	5 Cents (Ni–Bra) 1949–1952	1.20	2.50
17 (21)	25 Cents (Cu–Ni) 1952	4.50	12.00

ELIZABETH II since 1952

18 (22)	1 Cent (Br) 1954. Crowned head r. of Queen Elizabeth II. ℞ value in wreath	0.90	2.00

19 (23)	1 Cent (Br) 1956–1973. Same type as No. 17, but dodecagonal	0.10	0.20
20 (24)	5 Cents (Ni-Bra) 1956–1973. R value in circle	0.20	0.40
21 (25)	10 Cents (Cu-Ni) 1956–1970. R value in double circle	0.30	0.60

22 (26)	25 Cents (Cu-Ni) 1955-1973	0.50	1.00
23 (27)	50 Cents (Cu-Ni) 1954-1971.	1.00	2.00

For later issues, see under Belize.

British North Borneo

Britisch-Nordborneo **Bornéo du Nord Britannique**

The Chartered British North Borneo Company formed with effect of
1st Nov. 1881 administered as the only colonial company existing into
the 20th century the territory of a state in its power until its dissolution
on 15th July 1946. In exercising its rights it was hampered due to the
disastrous consequences of World War II, during the course of which
the real rule was exercised from 1942–1945 by the Japanese and then by
the British military administration. To the now existing Crown Colony
of British North Borneo, the small island of Labuan was added after
the severance of the administrative connection with the Straits Settlements which had existed since the thirties. With the revived name of
"Sabah", North Borneo joined the new state of Malaysia as a founder
member on 16th Sept. 1963 and together with Sarawak constitutes the
territory of East Malaysia.
Capital: Jesselton.

100 Cents = 1 Straits Dollar

			VF	XF
1 (1)	½	Cent (Br) 1885–1907. Coat of arms. ℞ value within wreath	5.00	12.00

2 (2)	1	Cent (Br) 1882–1907. Coat of arms of the North Borneo Company, a privileged company protected by charter. ℞ value within wreath	4.00	10.00
3 (3)	1	Cent (Cu–Ni) 1904–1941. Same type as No. 2. ℞ value in circle, legend: STATE OF NORTH BORNEO	2.50	6.00
4 (4)	2½	Cents (Cu–Ni) 1903–1920	3.00	10.00
5 (5)	5	Cents (Cu–Ni) 1903–1941	2.00	5.00
6 (6)	25	Cents (Ag) 1929	9.00	18.00

British Virgin Islands

Britische Jungferninseln   **Iles de la Vierge Britanniques**

Area: 41 sq. mi. Population: 14,000.
The British Virgin Islands include the islands of Tortola, Virgin Gorda,
Anegada, Jost van Dyke and numerous islets. The British colony of
the "Leeward Islands" (cf. British Caribbean Territories) was dissolved
into the four presidencies, of which it consisted at the time: Antigua,
St. Kitts-Nevis-Anguilla, Montserrat and the Virgin Islands. After the
breakup of the West Indian Federation, which they had joined as individual colonies on 3rd January 1958, the status of these islands was
somewhat obscure; the Virgin Islands reverted to the former status
of a British Colony. Even after the introduction of their own currency
on 30th June 1973, the monetary units of the USA have remained in use.
Capital: Road Town.

100 Cents = 1 East Caribbean Dollar

			Unc	Proof
1 (1)	1	Cent (Br) 1973–. Greenthroated Carib-bean humming bird (Sericotes holo-sericeus) and Antillean crested humming bird (Orthorhynchus crista-tus), both Trochilidae	0.10	1.00
2 (2)	5	Cents (Cu-Ni) 1973–. Zenaida turtle-dove (Zenaida aurita – Columbidae)	0.40	1.00
3 (3)	10	Cents (Cu-Ni) 1973–. Ringed kingsfisher (Ceryle torquata – Alcedinidae)	0.70	1.10
4 (4)	25	Cents (Cu-Ni) 1973–. Mangrove cuckoo (Coccysus minor – Cuculidae)	1.00	1.50
5 (5)	50	Cents (Cu-Ni) 1973–. Brown or sea pelican (Pelecanus occidentalis – Pele-canidae)	1.50	2.50
6 (6)	1	Dollar 1973–. Magnificent frigate bird (Fregata magnificens - Fregatidae): a) (Ag)		20.00
		b) (Cu-Ni)	7.50	
7 (7)	100	Dollars (Au) 1975. Royal Tern (Sterna maxima – Sternidae)	115.00	130.00

50th BIRTHDAY OF HER MAJESTY QUEEN ELIZABETH II

			Unc	Proof
8 (8)	100	Dollars (Au) 1976. R Coat of arms, with crowned monogram above. Commemorative inscription, value	150.00	165.00

25th ANNIVERSARY OF THE SILVER JUBILEE OF HER MAJESTY QUEEN ELIZABETH II (7)

9 (9)	1	Cent (Ag) 1977		3.50
10 (10)	5	Cents (Ag) 1977		4.00
11 (11)	10	Cents (Ag) 1977		6.00
12 (12)	25	Cents (Ag) 1977		9.00
13 (13)	50	Cents (Ag) 1977		15.00
14 (14)	1	Dollar (Ag) 1977		30.00
15 (15)	100	Dollars (Au) 1977. Queen. R crown	1000.00	150.00

25th ANNIVERSARY OF THE CORONATION OF HER MAJESTY QUEEN ELIZABETH II (6)

16 (16)	1	Cent (Ag) 1978		−.−
17 (17)	5	Cents (Ag) 1978		−.−
18 (18)	10	Cents (Ag) 1978		−.−
19 (19)	25	Cents (Ag) 1978		−.−
20 (20)	50	Cents (Ag) 1978		−.−
21 (21)	1	Dollar (Ag) 1978		−.−
		Nos. 16-21		80.00
22 (22)	25	Dollars (Ag) 1978		40.00
23 (23)	100	Dollars (Au) 1978		180.00
24 (24)	5	Dollars 1979. Snowy Egret:		
		a) (Ag)		40.00
		b) (Cu-Ni)	−.−	
25 (25)	100	Dollars (Au) 1979. Sir Francis Drake		200.00
26 (26)	5	Dollars 1980. Great Blue Heron:		
		a) (Ag)		40.00
		b) (Cu-Ni)	10.00	

400th ANNIVERSARY OF DRAKE'S VOYAGE

27 (29)	100	Dollars (Au) 1980		200.00
28 (27)	25	Dollars (Au) 1980. Diving Osprey		52.00
29 (28)	50	Dollars (Au) 1980. Golden Dove of Christmas		85.00

WEDDING OF PRINCE CHARLES AND LADY DIANA

30	10	Dollars 1981:		
		a) (Ag)		−.−
		b) (Cu-Ni)	−.−	

British West Africa

Until they issued their own currencies the territories of the British Cameroons (since 1961 part of the Cameroons), British Togoland (since 1957 linked with Ghana), Gambia, the Gold Coast (since 1957 called Ghana), Nigeria and Sierra Leone formed together an administrative grouping under the name of British West Africa. Coinage now obsolete.

$$12 \text{ Pence} = 1 \text{ Shilling}$$
$$20 \text{ Shillings} = \pounds 1$$

EDWARD VII 1901–1910

				VF	XF
1 (3)	$^1/_{10}$	Penny (Al) 1907–1908. Star within inscription around reading NIGERIA – BRITISH WEST AFRICA. ℞ crown over value (central hole)		2.50	5.00
2 (1)	$^1/_{10}$	Penny (Cu–Ni) 1908–1910		1.00	2.00

3 (2)	1	Penny (Cu–Ni) 1907–1910		2.50	5.50

GEORGE V 1910–1936

4 (4)	$^1/_{10}$	Penny (Cu–Ni) 1911. Star. ℞ crown over value (central hole)		4.00	7.50
5 (5)	$^1/_2$	Penny (Cu–Ni) 1911		12.00	25.00

6 (6)	1	Penny (Cu–Ni) 1911		30.00	55.00
7 (7)	$^1/_{10}$	Penny (Cu–Ni) 1912–1936. Same type as No. 4. ℞ the legend now reads only BRITISH WEST AFRICA (central hole)		0.50	1.00

			VF	XF
8 (8)	$^1/_2$ Penny (Cu–Ni) 1912–1936		2.00	4.00
9 (9)	1 Penny (Cu–Ni) 1912–1936		2.50	4.50
10 (14)	3 Pence (Ag) 1913–1920. ℞ value in wreath		2.50	4.50
11 (15)	6 Pence (Ag) 1913–1920		4.00	8.00
12 (16)	1 Shilling (Ag) 1913–1920. Crowned bust l. of King George V. ℞ oil palm (Elaeis guineensis — Palmae)		5.00	10.00

13 (17)	2 Shillings (Ag) 1913–1920	12.50	18.00
14 (14a)	3 Pence (Bra) 1920–1936	2.00	4.00
15 (15a)	6 Pence (Bra) 1920–1936	3.00	5.50
16 (16a)	1 Shilling (Bra) 1920–1936	4.00	7.50
17 (17a)	2 Shillings (Bra) 1920–1936	5.50	12.00

EDWARD VIII 1936

18 (18)	$^1/_{10}$ Penny (Cu–Ni) 1936. Star. ℞ crown over value (central hole)	1.00	2.00
19 (19)	$^1/_2$ Penny (Cu–Ni) 1936	1.00	2.00

20 (20)	1 Penny (Cu–Ni) 1936	1.20	2.40

GEORGE VI 1936–1952

21 (22)	1/10 Penny (Cu-Ni) 1938–1947. Star. ℞ crown over value (central hole). Legend reading GEORGIUS VI ET IND IMP	0.30	0.60

			VF	XF
22 (23)	$^1/_2$	Penny (Cu–Ni) 1937–1947	0.50	1.00
23 (24)	1	Penny (Cu–Ni) 1937–1947	0.60	1.20

			VF	XF
24 (25)	3	Pence (Cu–Ni) 1938–1948. ℞ value in wreath	0.80	1.60
25 (26)	6	Pence (Bra) 1938–1947	1.00	2.00
26 (27)	1	Shilling (Bra) 1938–1948. ℞ oil palm	1.00	2.50
27 (28)	2	Shillings (Bra) 1938–1948	2.00	4.00
28 (29)	$^1/_{10}$	Penny (Cu–Ni) 1949–1950. Same type as No. 21, but reverse legend reads only GEORGIUS SEXTUS REX (central hole)	1.00	2.00
29 (30)	$^1/_2$	Penny (Cu–Ni) 1949–1951	4.00	8.00
30 (31)	1	Penny (Cu–Ni) 1951	14.00	26.00
31 (29a)	$^1/_{10}$	Penny (Br) 1952	1.60	3.20
32 (30a)	$^1/_2$	Penny (Br) 1952	0.50	1.00
33 (31a)	1	Penny (Br) 1952	0.40	0.80
34 (32)	6	Pence (Ni–Bra) 1952	7.50	15.00
35 (33)	1	Shilling (Ni–Bra) 1949–1952	1.20	2.40
36 (34)	2	Shillings (Ni–Bra) 1949–1952	3.00	6.00

ELIZABETH II since 1952

			VF	XF
37 (38)	1/10	Penny (Br) 1954–1957. Star. R crown over value (central hole)	1.00	2.00
38 (39)	1	Penny (Br) 1956–1958	1.50	3.00

			VF	XF
39 (40)	3	Pence (Cu–Ni) 1957. Elizabeth II. ℞ value in wreath	25.00	45.00

Brunei

Area: 2,217 sq. mi. Population: 144,000.

The Mohammedan sultanate on the north coast of the Island of Borneo was still so powerful in the early 19th century that the Sultan of Brunei was considered as the Sultan of Borneo, resulting in the name of the whole island of Borneo having been formed from the name Brunei. Mineral resources which have become a matter of interest lately, have induced the Sultan of Brunei not to join the Federation of Malaysia, but to allow the protectorate arranged by treaty with Great Britain in 1886 to continue. Capital: Brunei, since 4th October 1970 renamed Bandar Seri Begawan.

The Mexican Piaster was initially the most common trade coin. From 25th June 1903 the Straits Dollar was in circulation and from 1th April 1946 the Malaya Dollar became legal tender. The new currency, the Brunei Dollar, was introduced on 12th June 1967. The Brunei Dollar is on a par with the Malaysia and the Singapore Dollar.

100 Sen = 1 Brunei Dollar

OMAR ALI SAIFUDDIN III 1950–1967

		XF	Unc
1 (2)	1 Sen (Br) 1967. Head l. of Sultan Sir Omar Ali Saifuddin Wasa'dul Khairi Waddin (*1916). ℞ ornamental design	0.16	0.30

		XF	Unc
2 (3)	5 Sen (Cu–Ni) 1967. ℞ ornamental design	0.20	0.40

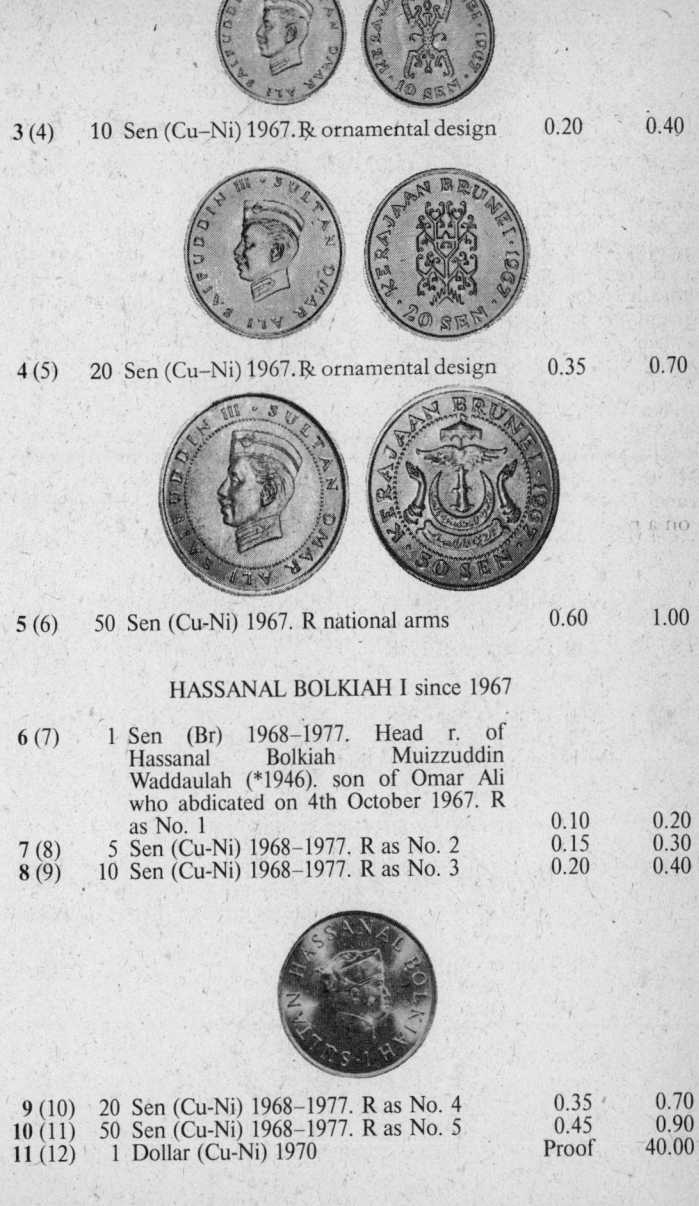

			XF	**Unc**

3 (4)   10 Sen (Cu–Ni) 1967. R ornamental design   0.20   0.40

4 (5)   20 Sen (Cu–Ni) 1967. R ornamental design   0.35   0.70

5 (6)   50 Sen (Cu-Ni) 1967. R national arms   0.60   1.00

HASSANAL BOLKIAH I since 1967

6 (7)   1 Sen (Br) 1968–1977. Head r. of Hassanal Bolkiah Muizzuddin Waddaulah (*1946). son of Omar Ali who abdicated on 4th October 1967. R as No. 1   0.10   0.20

7 (8)   5 Sen (Cu-Ni) 1968–1977. R as No. 2   0.15   0.30

8 (9)   10 Sen (Cu-Ni) 1968–1977. R as No. 3   0.20   0.40

9 (10)   20 Sen (Cu-Ni) 1968–1977. R as No. 4   0.35   0.70

10 (11)   50 Sen (Cu-Ni) 1968–1977. R as No. 5   0.45   0.90

11 (12)   1 Dollar (Cu-Ni) 1970   Proof   40.00

			XF	Unc
12 (7a)	1	Sen (Br) 1977–. Type as No. 6, but without numeral »I« in title	0.10	0.20
13 (8a)	5	Sen (Cu-Ni) 1977–	0.10	0.20
14 (9a)	10	Sen (Cu-Ni) 1977–	0.10	0.20
15 (10a)	20	Sen (Cu-Ni) 1977–	0.20	0.30
16 (11a)	50	Sen (Cu-Ni) 1977–	0.50	0.80

10th ANNIVERSARY OF BRUNEI DOLLAR

			Unc	Proof
17 (13)	10	Dollars (Ag) 1977		40.00

10th ANNIVERSARY OF SULTAN'S CORONATION (2)

18 (14)	10	Dollars (Ag) 1978		42.00
19 (15)	1000	Dollars (Au) 1978		1100.00
20 (12a)	1	Dollar (Cu-Ni) 1979. Type as No. 11, but without numeral »I« in title		12.00

YEAR OF HIJRAH 1400 (2)

21 (16)	50	Dollars (Ag) 1980		30.00
22 (17)	750	Dollars (Au) 1980		400.00

Bulgarien   **Bulgaria**   **Bulgarie**
БЪЛГАРИЯ

Area: 42,823 sq. mi. Population: 8,600,000.
Created in 1879, this principality was declared an independent Kingdom
on 22nd September (5th October) 1908 by Ferdinand I in Tirnowo.
Initially the Julian Calendar continued to be used by the Bulgarian
people, hence the different dates given for example for Independence
Day. A People's Republic since 15th September 1946.
Capital: Sofia.

100 Stotinki (СТОТИНКИ) = 1 Lew (ЛЕВ)

1 (16)   FERDINAND I 1887–1918

			VF	XF
	1 Stotinka (Br) 1901, 1912. National arms. R value in wreath			
	a) 1901 (Paris)		3.00	6.00
	b) 1912 (Vienna)		2.50	5.00
2 (17)	2 Stotinki (Br) 1901, 1912		1.50	3.00
3 (18)	5 Stotinki (Cu-Ni) 1906–1913		0.70	1.20
4 (18a)	5 Stotinki (Zi) 1917		2.50	4.00
5 (19)	10 Stotinki (Cu-Ni) 1906–1913		0.40	0.80
6 (19a)	10 Stotinki (Zi) 1917		1.50	3.00

		VF	XF
7 (20)	20 Stotinki (Cu-Ni) 1906–1913	0.60	1.20
8 (20a)	20 Stotinki (Zi) 1917	2.00	4.00
9 (24)	50 Stotinki (Ag) 1910. Head r. of Ferdinand I. R value in wreath	3.50	6.00
10 (25)	1 Lew (Ag) 1910	4.00	6.50
11 (26)	2 Lewa (Ag) 1910	5.00	11.00

COMMEMORATIVE ISSUES (2) FOR THE DECLARATION OF
INDEPENDENCE AND THE CREATION OF THE KINGDOM
OF BULGARIA ON 22nd SEPTEMBER (5th OCTOBER) 1908

		VF	XF
12 (30)	20 Lewa (Au) 1912. Head l. of Ferdinand of Saxe-Coburg-Gotha (1861–1948), Prince of Bulgaria 1887–1908, as Ferdinand I, 1908–1918 King of Bulgaria	240.00	300.00

		VF	XF
13 (31) 100 Lewa (Au) 1912		1500.00	1800.00

Later restrikes in gold (4 ducats), also with countermark, are medallic
issues for the same occasion.

14 (27) 50 Stotinki (Ag) 1912–1916. Head l. of Ferdinand I			
a) 1912, 1913		4.00	7.00
b) 1916		45.00	60.00
15 (28) 1 Lew (Ag) 1912–1916			
a) 1912, 1913		3.50	6.00
b) 1916		60.00	100.00
16 (29) 2 Lewa (Ag) 1912–1916			
a) 1912, 1913		5.00	9.00
b) 1916		175.00	300.00

BORIS III 1918–1943

17 (32) 1 Lew (Al) 1923. National arms. ℞ value in wreath		6.00	12.50
18 (34) 1 Lew (Cu-Ni) 1925		0.60	1.20
19 (33) 2 Lewa (Al) 1923		14.00	25.00

20 (35) 2 Lewa (Cu-Ni) 1925		0.40	0.80
21 (36) 5 Lewa (Cu-Ni) 1930. Relief figure of Czar Krum (reigned from 802 to 814) as a horseman on the rock at Madara (district of Kolarovgrad, in northeast Bulgaria), dating from the 9th century A. D. ℞ value in wreath		1.70	3.50

				VF	XF
22 (37)	10	Lewa (Cu-Ni) 1930. Same type as No. 21		4.00	8.50
23 (38)	20	Lewa (Ag) 1930. Head l. of Boris III (1894–1943). ℞ value in wreath		2.50	4.00
24 (39)	50	Lewa (Ag) 1930		4.00	8.00
25 (40)	100	Lewa (Ag) 1930		8.00	16.00
26 (41)	50	Stotinki (Al-Br) 1937. National arms. ℞ value in wreath		0.50	0.80
27 (42)	20	Lewa (Cu-Ni) 1940. Same type as No. 23		1.50	2.00
28 (44)	50	Lewa (Ag) 1934. Head l. of Boris III. ℞ value between ears of wheat; below, rose and tobacco plants		4.50	7.50
29 (43)	50	Lewa (Cu-Ni) 1940. Same type as No. 24		1.50	2.50
30 (43a)	50	Lewa (Fe, Ni-St, plated) 1943		2.00	3.50
31 (45)	100	Lewa (Ag) 1934, 1937. Same type as No. 25		4.50	8.50
32 (34a)	1	Lew (Fe) 1941. Same type as No. 18		4.00	8.50
33 (35a)	2	Lewa (Fe) 1941. Same type as No. 20		1.50	2.50

34 (A45)	2	Lewa (Fe) 1943		2.50	4.00
35 (36a)	5	Lewa (Fe) 1941. Same type as No. 21		3.00	5.00
36 (36b)	5	Lewa (Fe, Ni-St, plated) 1943		1.60	3.00
37 (37a)	10	Lewa (Fe) 1941. Same type as No. 22		11.00	20.00
38 (37b)	10	Lewa (Fe, Ni-St, plated) 1943		2.00	4.00

PEOPLE'S REPUBLIC since 1946

39 (46)	1	Stotinka (Bra) 1951. Arms of the People's Republic. ℞ ears of wheat and value		0.10	0.20
40 (47)	3	Stotinki (Bra) 1951		0.15	0.30
41 (48)	5	Stotinki (Bra) 1951		0.20	0.40
42 (49)	10	Stotinki (Cu-Ni) 1951		0.30	0.60

			VF	**XF**
43 (A49)	20	Stotinki (Cu-Ni) 1952–1954		
		a) 1952	10.00	20.00
		b) 1954	0.35	0.70
44 (50)	25	Stotinki (Cu-Ni) 1951	0.40	0.80
45 (51)	50	Stotinki (Cu-Ni) 1959	0.60	1.00

46 (52)	1	Lew (Cu-Ni) 1960. ℞ value in wreath	1.00	1.80

CURRENCY REFORM: 100 old Lewa = 1 new Lew

47 (53)	1	Stotinka (Bra) 1962. National arms. ℞ value between ears of wheat	0.10	0.20

48 (54)	2	Stotinki (Bra) 1962	0.12	0.20
49 (55)	5	Stotinki (Bra) 1962	0.18	0.35
50 (56)	10	Stotinki (Cu-Ni) 1962	0.20	0.45
51 (57)	20	Stotinki (Cu-Ni) 1962	0.30	0.60
52 (58)	50	Stotinki (Cu-Ni) 1962	0.80	1.60
53 (59)	1	Lew (Cu-Ni) 1962	1.20	2.40

COMMEMORATIVE ISSUES (4)
FOR 1100 YEARS OF THE CYRILLIC ALPHABET

			Unc	**Proof**
54 (60)	2	Lewa (Ag) 1963. Cyril (826–869) and Methodios (c. 815–885), Slavic apostles and propagators of the Cyrillic alphabet. ℞ value	9.00	15.00
55 (61)	5	Lewa (Ag) 1963	15.00	25.00

56 (62)	10	Lewa (Au) 1963		120.00
57 (63)	20	Lewa (Au) 1963		280.00

COMMEMORATIVE ISSUES (4) FOR THE 80th BIRTHDAY OF
G. DIMITROV AND FOR THE 20th ANNIVERSARY OF THE
PROCLAMATION OF THE PEOPLE'S REPUBLIC

		Unc	Proof
58 (64)	2 Lewa (Ag) 1964. Georgi Dimitrov (1882–1949), printer and politician, Prime Minister 1946–1949. Ŗ flags over value	6.00	11.00
59 (65)	5 Lewa (Ag) 1964	13.00	18.00
60 (66)	10 Lewa (Au) 1964		130.00

61 (67)	20 Lewa (Au) 1964	270.00

COMMEMORATIVE ISSUE FOR THE 1050th ANNIVERSARY
OF THE DEATH OF KLIMENT OCHRIDSKI

		XF	Unc
62 (68)	2 Lewa (Cu-Ni) 1966. St. Kliment Ochridski († 916), rationalist, he perfected the Bulgarian-Slavonic (Cyrillic) alphabet, and founded the first university in Europe	2.50	4.00

COMMEMORATIVE ISSUES (2) FOR THE 25th ANNIVERSARY OF THE SOCIALIST REVOLUTION OF 9th SEPTEMBER 1944

		XF	Unc
63 (69)	1 Lew (Cu-Ni) 1969. Monument to the fighters of the Resistance. ℞ value between ears of wheat	2.00	3.00
64 (70)	2 Lewa (Cu-Ni) 1969. Monument to the Soviet soldiers in Plovdiv (Philippopolis. ℞ as No. 63	3.00	5.00

COMMEMORATIVE ISSUES (2) FOR THE 90th ANNIVERSARY OF THE LIBERATION OF BULGARIA FROM THE OTTOMAN DOMINATION

65 (71)	1 Lew (Cu-Ni) 1969. Sofia: equestrian statue of Alexander II, Czar of Russia, on a plinth (43 ft high) with effigies from Bulgarian history (1877–1879). Created in the years 1901 to 1907 by the Italian sculptor Arnoldo Zocchi ℞ value in tied laurel wreath	1.50	2.50

66 (72)	2 Lewa (Cu–Ni) 1969. "The Battle on the Orlovo Gnesdo" (Eagle's Nest), by the Russian painter Popov; section of a painting. ℞ as No. 65	2.50	4.50

COMMEMORATIVE ISSUE FOR THE 120th BIRTHDAY OF IVAN VASOV

67 (73)   5 Lewa (Ag) 1970. Ivan Vasov, (1850–1921), poet; his best known work is "Under the Yoke", written in 1889/90. ℞ emblem of state, value

	Unc	Proof
	15.00	22.50

COMMEMORATIVE ISSUE FOR THE 150th BIRTHDAY OF G. RAKOVSKI

68 (74)   5 Lewa (Ag) 1971. Georgi Rakovski (1821–1867), patriot, revolutionary, writer, author of the constitution for the provisional Bulgarian Government. ℞ emblem of state, value   18.50

COMMEMORATIVE ISSUE FOR THE 250th BIRTHDAY
OF PAISSII HILENDARSKI

69 (76) 5 Lewa (Ag) 1972. Paissii Hilendarski, called "Otez Paissii", Bulgarian monk, born 1722 in the town of Bansko, wrote the history of the Bulgarian people and thus roused national consciousness

	Unc	Proof
		18.50

COMMEMORATIVE ISSUE FOR THE 150th BIRTHDAY
OF DOBRI TCHINTULOV

70 (75) 2 Lewa (Cu–Ni) 1972. Dobri Tchintulov (1822–1886), distinguished Bulgarian pioneer of progress

	2.50	4.00

COMMEMORATIVE ISSUE FOR THE 100th ANNIVERSARY
OF THE DEATH OF VASIL LEVSKI

71 (77)   5 Lewa (Ag) 1973. Vasil Levski (1837–
6th February 1873), organizer of the
Bulgarian national freedom movement
against the Turks, founded a revolutio-   **Proof**
nary central committee; executed by the
Turks in Sofia   18.50

COMMEMORATIVE ISSUE FOR THE 50th ANNIVERSARY
OF THE SEPTEMBER RISING (23. 9. 1923) UNDER THE
LEADERSHIP OF G. DIMITROV AND V. KOLAROV

72 (78)   5 Lewa (Ag) 1973   18.50

COMMEMORATIVE ISSUE FOR THE 50th ANNIVERSARY
OF THE DEATH OF ALEXANDER STAMBULIJSKI

73 (79)   5 Lewa (Ag) 1974. Alexander Stambulij-
ski (1879–1923), politician   18.50

COMMEMORATIVE ISSUE FOR THE 30th ANNIVERSARY
OF THE SOCIALIST REVOLUTION OF 9th SEPTEMBER 1944

74 (80)   5 Lewa (Ag) 1974. Two soldiers and factory.
R coat of arms, date, value   18.50

			Unc	Proof

75 (53a) 1 Stotinka (Bra) 1974–1980. Type as No.
47, but new coat of arms, since 14th
May 1971:
  a) 1974   0.20
  b) 1979, 1980   2.00

76 (54a) 2 Stotinki (Bra) 1974–1980. Type as No.
75:
  a) 1974   0.20
  b) 1979, 1980   2.00

77 (55a) 5 Stotinki (Bra) 1974–1980. Type as No.
75:
  a) 1974   0.20
  b) 1979, 1980   3.00

78 (56a) 10 Stotinki (Cu-Ni) 1974–1980. Type as
No. 75:
  a) 1974   0.25
  b) 1979, 1980   3.00

79 (57a) 20 Stotinki (Cu-Ni) 1974–1980. Type as
No. 75:
  a) 1974   0.50
  b) 1979, 1980   4.00

80 (58a) 50 Stotinki (Cu-Ni) 1974–1980. Type as
No. 75:
  a) 1974   1.20
  b) 1979, 1980   5.00

81 (59a) 1 Lew (Cu-Ni) 1979, 1980. Type as No. 75   8.00

82 (81)   10 Lewa (Ag) 1975. Ancient Greek coin with
boxer, and olympic rings below. R coat of **Unc** **Proof**
arms, value, date:
  a) with edge inscription in Cyrillic   35.00
  b) with edge inscription in Latin   35.00

100th ANNIVERSARY OF THE APRIL UPRISING
AGAINST THE TURKS (3)

83 (82)   1 Lew (Cu) 1976   3.00
84 (83)   2 Lewa (Cu-Ni) 1976   6.00
85 (85)   5 Lewa (Ag) 1976   16.00

100th ANNIVERSARY OF THE DEATH OF KHRISTO BOTEV

			Unc	Proof

86 (84)   5 Lewa (Ag) 1976. Khristo Botev (1848-1876), revolutionary and poet   18.50

UNIVERSADE IN SOFIA

87 (86)   50 Stotinki (Cu-Ni) 1977. Runner with torch, commemorative inscription. R coat of arms, value, date   2.00

150th ANNIVERSARY OF THE BIRTH OF P. R. SLAVEYKOV

88 (87)   5 Lewa (Ag) 1977. Petko Racev Slaveykov (1827-1895), poet   15.00

100th ANNIVERSARY OF THE BIRTH OF P. K. YAVOROV

89 (88)   5 Lewa (Ag) 1978. Peijo Yavorov, real name Kracholov, lyric poet and dramatist   15.00

100th ANNIVERSARY OF LIBERATION

90 (89)   10 Lewa (Ag) 1978. Monument   28.00

100th ANNIVERSARY OF NATIONAL LIBRARY

91 (90) 5 Lewa (Ag) 1978. National Library   15.00

100th ANNIVERSARY OF COMMUNICATIONS SYSTEMS

92 (91) 5 Lewa (Ag) 1979   15.00

CENTENNIAL OF SOFIA AS CAPITAL

93 (93) 20 Lewa (Ag) 1979:
    a) .500 silver, dia. 37 mm   85.00
    b) .900 silver, dia. 42 mm   40.00

BULGARIAN-SOVIET COSMONAUT FLIGHT

94 (97) 10 Lewa (Ag) 1979:
    a) .500 silver, dia. 32 mm   60.00
    b) .900 silver, dia. 38 mm   32.00

INTERNATIONAL YEAR OF THE CHILD

95 (92) 10 Lewa (Ag) 1979:
    a) .925 silver, 23.32 gm.   55.00
    b) Piéfort   165.00

		Unc	Proof
96 (94)	1 Lew (Cu-Ni) 1980		5.00
97 (95)	2 Lewa (Cu-Ni) 1980		12.00
98 (96)	5 Lewa (Cu-Ni) 1980		20.00

100th ANNIVERSARY OF THE BIRTH OF YORDAN YOVKOV

99 (98)	2 Lewa (Cu-Ni) 1980. Yordan Yovkov (1880–1937), writer		6.00

1300 YEARS OF BULGARIA (10)

100	1 Stotinka (Bra) 1981. Arms, legend. R value and date between ears	0.40	1.50
101	2 Stotinki (Bra) 1981. Type as No. 100	0.40	1.50

102	5 Stotinki (Bra) 1981. Type as No. 100	0.50	2.00
103	10 Stotinki (Cu-Ni) 1981. Type as No. 100	0.50	2.00
104	20 Stotinki (Cu-Ni) 1981. Type as No. 100	1.20	3.00
105	50 Stotinki (Cu-Ni) 1981. Type as No. 100	2.40	5.50
106	1 Lew (Cu-Ni) 1981. Type as No. 100	4.00	8.50

	Unc	Proof

107 (102) 2 Lewa (Cu-Ni) 1981. Relief figure on the rock at Madara (see also No. 21) — 10.00

108 (103) 50 Lewa (Ag) 1981. Type as No. 107 — — 100.00

109 (104) 50 Lewa (Ag) 1981. Statue of a woman. R portrait of Georgi Dimitrov — — 100.00

WORLD HUNTING EXPOSITION »EXPO 81« (3)

110 (99) 1 Lew (Cu-Ni) 1981. Emblem of »Expo 81« and head of a stag — 6.00 / 10.50

111 (100) 2 Lewa (Cu-Ni) 1981. Falconer

112 (101) 5 Lewa (Cu-Ni) 1981. Large stag skull with horns (Hunting trophy) — 20.00

1300 YEARS OF BULGARIA AND RUSSO-BULGARIAN FRIENDSHIP

113 (105) 1 Lew (Cu-Ni) 1981. Flags above clasped hands — 14.00

1300 YEARS OF BULGARIA

114 2 Lewa (Cu-Ni). Mother and child — 15.00

Birma   # Burma   **Birmanie**

Area: 260,800 sq. mi. Population: 30,000,000.

In historical times several kingdoms have been in control of the territory of the present state, among them the Mon and the Shan Kingdoms, but also the Burmese. In the 19th century Burma was occupied gradually by the English and until 1897 was part of the Union of States of British India. After temporary occupation by the Japanese during World War II, Burma obtained its independence on 4th January 1948 and became an independent Republic.

Capital: Rangoon.

16 Annas = 1 Rupee; since 1st July 1952: 100 Pyas = 1 Kyat

			VF	XF
1 (13)	½ Anna (Cu-Ni) 1949. Lion, mythological guardian figure. ℞ value in wreath (square)		0.60	1.00
2 (14)	1 Anna (Cu-Ni) 1949–1951 (dodecagonal)		0.70	1.20
3 (15)	2 Annas (Cu-Ni) 1949–1951 (square)		1.00	2.00
4 (16)	4 Annas (Ni) 1949–1950 (round)		2.50	4.00

			VF	XF
5 (17)	8 Annas (Ni) 1949–1950 (round)		3.80	7.20

NEW CURRENCY : 100 Pyas = 1 Kyat

			VF	XF
6 (18)	1 Pya (Br) 1952–1966. Lion, mythological guardian figure. R value in wreath (round)		0.10	0.20
7 (19)	5 Pyas (Cu-Ni) 1952–1966 (dodecagonal)		0.10	0.20
8 (20)	10 Pyas (Cu-Ni) 1952–1965 (square)		0.15	0.30
9 (21)	25 Pyas (Cu-Ni) 1952–1965 (hexagonal)		0.25	0.40
10 (22)	50 Pyas (Cu-Ni) 1952–1966 (round)		0.40	0.80
11 (23)	1 Kyat (Cu-Ni) 1952–1965 (round)		1.00	2.00

			VF	**XF**
12 (24)	1 Pya (Al) 1966. General Aung San (1915–1947), liberator and politician; murdered by political enemies. ℞ value in wreath (round)		0.10	0.20
13 (25)	5 Pyas (Al) 1966 (scalloped edge)		0.12	0.25

14 (26)	10 Pyas (Al) 1966 (square)		0.15	0.30

15 (27)	25 Pyas (Al) 1966 (hexagonal)		0.25	0.50

16 (28)	50 Pyas (Al) 1966 (round)		0.50	1.00

ISSUE FOR THE FAO COIN PLAN (3)

17	25 Pyas (Al-Br) 1980. Rice plant		0.30	0.45

18 (33)	50 Pyas (Br) 1975. Type as No. 17		0.90	1.10
19 (34)	1 Kyat (Cu-Ni) 1975. Type as No. 17		1.00	1.40

Previous issues, see "Weltmünzkatalog 19. Jahrhundert" (World Coin Catalogue of the 19th Century)

Burundi

Area: 10,780 sq. mi. Population: 3,700,000.
Belonging at first to German East Africa, it later became part of the
Belgian Trust Territory of Rwanda-Urundi. An independent kingdom
since 1st July 1962, a republic since 1966. Burundi formed an economic
union with Rwanda; the unit of currency was the Rwanda-Burundi
franc; see also Rwanda and Burundi (for joint issues) as well as the
issues dating from before the independence, under Belgian Congo,
years 1952–1960.
Capital: Bujumbura (Usumbura).

100 Centimes = 1 Burundi Franc

MWAMBUTSA IV 1915–1966
COMMEMORATIVE ISSUES (4) FOR INDEPENDENCE

		Proof
1	10 Francs (Au) 1962	70.00
2	25 Francs (Au) 1962	140.00
3	50 Francs (Au) 1962	260.00
4	100 Francs (Au) 1962	500.00

COMMEMORATIVE ISSUES (4)
FOR THE FIFTY YEAR JUBILEE OF THE GOVERNMENT

5	10 Francs (Au) 1965	70.00
6	25 Francs (Au) 1965	140.00
7	50 Francs (Au) 1965	260.00
8	100 Francs (Au) 1965	500.00

		XF	Unc
9 (1)	1 Franc (Bra) 1965. National arms. ℞ value in circle	0.40	1.00
10	500 Francs (Ag) 1966		20.00

NTARE V 1966

A 11	100 Francs (Ag) 1966		50.00
11	500 Francs (Ag) 1966		20.00

COMMEMORATIVE ISSUES (5)
FOR THE FIRST ANNIVERSARY OF THE REPUBLIC

		XF	Unc
12	10 Francs (Au) 1967. Head of Michel Micombero, President of State. ℞ national arms		–,–
13	20 Francs (Au) 1967. Same type as No. 12		–,–
14	25 Francs (Au) 1967. Same type as No. 12		–,–
15	50 Francs (Au) 1967. Same type as No. 12		–,–
16	100 Francs (Au) 1967. Same type as No. 12		–,–

17 (2) 5 Francs (Al) 1968, 1969, 1970, 1971, 1976. National motto: Unity, Work, Progress, in two languages in concentric circles, date. ℞ value between laurel branches — 0.50 — 1.20

ISSUE FOR THE FAO COIN PLAN

18 (3) 10 Francs (Cu–Ni) 1968, 1971. Inscription as No. 17, but arranged differently. ℞ farm produce set in form of a wheel, with value in centre, symbolizing the dynamic improvement of the agrarian structure. — 0.75 — 1.40

19 (A 2) 1 Franc (Al) 1970 — 0.40 — 0.65

20 (4) 1 Franc (Al) 1976. National arms — 0.80 — 1.10

Burundi   209

Kambodscha   # Cambodia (Khmer)   **Cambodge**

Preah Reach Ana Chak Kampuchea

Area: 69,629 sq. mi. Population: 7,000,000.

Cambodia was a constitutional monarchy with a parliamentary form of government. After leaving the French Union, the country achieved full independence in 1955. The Khmer Republic proclaimed on 8th October 1970 removed the reference to the myth of royalty from the existing coat of arms. April 17th 1975, the Khmer Rouge who took control of the government and renamed the country Democratic Cambodia.

Capital: Pnom-Penh.

100 Centimes = 1 Piastre (Franc);
since 1955: 100 Sen = 1 Riel

NORODOM SIHANOUK 1953–1955

			VF	XF
1 (11)	10	Centimes (Al–Mg) 1953. Garuda, mythological bird and mount of the god Vishnu. ℞ value within wreath	1.00	2.50
2 (12)	20	Centimes (Al–Mg) 1953. Goblet. ℞ value within wreath	1.20	2.50
3 (13)	50	Centimes (Al–Mg) 1953. National arms. ℞ value within wreath	1.50	3.00

NORODOM SURAMARIT 1955–1960
NEW CURRENCY: 100 Sen = 1 Riel

4 (11a)	10	Sen (Al–Mg) 1959. Type as No. 1, but with new indication of value	0.50	1.00
5 (12a)	20	Sen (Al–Mg) 1959. Type as No. 2, but with new indication of value	0.60	1.20
6 (13a)	50	Sen (Al–Mg) 1959. Type as No. 3, but with new indication of value	0.70	1.40

			Proof
7	5000	Riels (Ag) 1974. Temple of Angkor-Vath. R new coat of arms	17.00
8	5000	Riels (Ag) 1974. Three Cambodian dancers	17.00
9	10000	Riels (Ag) 1974. Portrait of Marshall Lon Nol	32.00
10	10000	Riels (Ag) 1974. Basrelief of celestial dancer (Apsara)	32.00
11	50000	Riels (Au) 1974. Type as No. 8	160.00

| **12** | 50000 | Riels (Au) 1974. Type as No. 10 | 160.00 |
| **13** | 100000 | Riels (Au) 1974. Type as No. 9 | 320.00 |

Cameroon

Area: 182,863 sq. mi. Population: 6,000,000.

A German protectorate from 14th July 1884; it was enlarged by further acquisitions of territories in the east and south of the country (New Cameroon) on 4th November 1911; it was then occupied by the French and the British in the years 1914–1916. The part of Cameroon which then became French was made a Trust Territory, the English part was joined with Nigeria. The reunification took place only in 1961; the former French part has been a republic since 1960. Like the countries of Gaboon, Congo-Brazzaville, Chad and the Central African Republic, Cameroon is part of the Monetary Union of Equatorial Africa; such joint issues are treated separately under Equatorial Africa.
Capital: Yaoundé.

100 Centimes = 1 CFA Franc

				VF	XF
1 (1)	50	Centimes (Al–Br) 1924–1927. Laureate head of Marianne, symbol of the French Republic. ℞ value between shoots		1.50	3.00
2 (2)	1	Franc (Al–Br) 1924–1927		2.00	4.00
3 (3)	2	Francs (Al–Br) 1924–1925		3.50	6.00
4 (4)	50	Centimes (Br) 1943. Gallic cockerel, inscription CAMEROUN FRANÇAIS. ℞ Croix de Lorraine		2.50	5.50
5 (5)	1	Franc (Br) 1943. Type as No. 4		4.00	7.50
6 (6)	50	Centimes (Br) 1943. Gallic cockerel, inscription now reading CAMEROUN FRANÇAIS LIBRE. ℞ Croix de Lorraine		3.00	6.50

			VF	XF
7 (7)	1	Franc (Br) 1943. Type as No. 6	3.00	6.50

			VF	XF
8 (8)	1	Franc (Al) 1948. Head of Marianne. ℞ head of a slender-horned gazelle (Gazella leptoceros — Bovidae)	0.50	0.90
9 (9)	2	Francs (Al) 1948. Type as No. 8	0.60	1.10
10 (5)	5	Francs (Al–Br) 1958. Addax antelope (Addax nasomaculatus — Bovidae). ℞ value within wreath	0.50	0.90
11 (6)	10	Francs (Al–Br) 1958. Type as No. 10	0.60	1.10
12 (7)	25	Francs (Al–Br) 1958. Type as No. 10	1.20	2.00

COMMEMORATIVE ISSUE FOR THE PROCLAMATION OF INDEPENDENCE ON 1st JANUARY 1960

13 (13)	50	Francs (Cu–Ni) 1960. Addax antelope. Inscription ETAT DU CAMEROUN/ 1er JANVIER 1960/PAIX – TRAVAIL – PATRIE. ℞ value within wreath	3.00	4.50

For coins of 5, 10, and 25 Francs with reproductions of Addax antelopes and inscription ETATS DE L'AFRIQUE EQUATORIALE/CAMEROUN/BANQUE CENTRALE with dates from 1961–1962, ℞ value within wreath, see under Equatorial African States Nos. 1–4.

14 (14)	100	Francs (Ni) 1966–1968. Addax antelope. Inscription ETAT DU CAMEROUN/ BANQUE CENTRALE/PAIX – TRAVAIL – PATRIE/PEACE – WORK – FATHERLAND. R value	2.00	3.50

COMMEMORATIVE ISSUES (5) FOR THE 10th ANNIVERSARY OF INDEPENDENCE

			Proof
15	1000	Francs (Au) 1970. El Haj Ahmadou Ahijo (*1922), politician, leader of the Union Camerounaise since 1958 and President of State since 1960. Motto: Peace – Work – Fatherland. ℞ geometrical design in centre, value	95.00

16 3000 Francs (Au) 1970. ℞ antlers of eland (Taurotragus oryx congolanus — Bovidae), stylized. Value   **Proof**

280.00

17 5000 Francs (Au) 1970. ℞ head of a young native (= national seal), surrounded with branch of the coffee tree (Coffea canephora — Rubiaceae) and five cocoa beans (Theobroma cacao — Sterculiaceae). Value   385.00

18 10000 Francs (Au) 1970. ℞ heads of elands. Value   760.00

19 20000 Francs (Au) 1970. ℞ national arms. Value   1600.00

20 (15) 100 Francs (Ni) 1971, 1972. Mendes antelopes, name of country. R value   1.70   2.50

21 (15a) 100 Francs (Ni) 1972. Type as No. 20, but name of country CAMEROUN - CAMEROON   1.70   2.50

22 (16) 100 Francs (Ni) 1975. Type as No. 21, but inscription "Banque des Etats de l'Afrique Centrale"   1.70   2.50

Canada

Area: 3,836,991 sq. mi. Population: 22,650,000.

The Canadian coast was first explored by John Cabot, who sailed from Bristol in 1797 to discover Newfoundland. The French were next, Champlain colonising Quebec in 1608. Much greater expansion came with the Hudson's Bay Company in 1670; disputes between the British and French became more frequent, and France finally ceded Canada to England in 1763. Nonetheless, 30% of the population remains French to this day, and Montreal is the biggest French-speaking city ouside France. Various divisions (e.g. Upper and Lower Canada) happened from 1791 onwards; certain parts of the country (e.g. Alberta, British Columbia) were not developed until the second half of 19th century. Canada's position as a full member of the Commonwealth was ratified by the Statute of Westminster in 1981; a more independent constitution still was signed in April 1982, with a French minority again dissatisfied.

The Royal Canadian Mint at Ottawa was opened in 1908 and has since then struck the greater part of the country's coins. The mintmark C is, however, by no means always used, and is mentioned in the catalogue where it is to be found.

Canadian gold coins since 1976 are notable for being struck (when .916 fine) in an alloy entirely of silver, with no addition of copper; they are thus paler than others, e.g. the sovereign. The most recent Canadian gold coin, known from its reverse type as the »maple leaf« is a bullion piece struck to the standard of .999 fine, and thus the purest gold coin since medieval times.

Capital: Ottawa.

100 Cents = 1 Canadian Dollar

Mintmarks:
C = Ottawa
H = Heaton

1 (10)　1 Cent (Br) 1902-1910. Crowned bust right
of King Edward VII. R value

	Mintage	Fine	VF	XF
1902	3,000,000	1.50	2.50	4.50
1903	4,000,000	2.00	3.50	5.00
1904	2,500,000	2.50	3.50	6.00
1905	2,000,000	5.00	7.00	9.00
1906	4,100,000	2.00	3.50	5.00
1907	2,400,000	3.00	4.00	7.00
1907 H	800,000	12.00	15.00	26.00
1908	2,401,506	2.00	3.50	5.00
1909	3,973,339	1.50	2.50	4.00
1910	5,146,487	1.50	2.50	4.00

2 (11)　5 Cents (Ag) 1902-1910. Crowned bust right
of King Edward VII. R value within wreath,
above crown:

	Mintage			
1902	2,120,000	3.00	5.00	9.00
1902 H	2,200,000	3.50	6.00	11.00
1903	1,000,000	5.00	9.00	16.00

	Mintage	Fine	VF	XF
1903 H	2,640,000	3.00	6.00	12.00
1904	2,400,000	4.00	6.00	12.00
1905	2,600,000	4.00	6.00	12.00
1906	3,100,000	2.00	5.00	9.00
1907	5,200,000	2.00	5.00	9.00
1908	1,220,524	7.00	12.00	25.00
1909	1,983,725	4.00	7.00	14.00
1910	3,850,325	2.50	5.00	9.00

3 (12)   10 Cents (Ag) 1902-1910. Type as No. 2:

	Mintage			
1902	720,000	8.00	18.00	50.00
1902 H	1,100,000	6.00	12.00	40.00
1903	500,000	12.00	40.00	100.00
1903 H	1,320,000	6.00	12.00	35.00
1904	1,000,000	12.00	40.00	90.00
1905	1,000,000	10.00	30.00	65.00
1906	1,700,000	8.00	15.00	40.00
1907	2,620,000	6.00	12.00	30.00
1908	776,666	10.00	25.00	55.00
1909	1,697,200	8.00	15.00	35.00
1910	4,468,331	4.00	7.00	20.00

4 (13)   25 Cents (Ag) 1902-1910. Type as No. 2:

	Mintage			
1902	464,000	10.00	20.00	55.00
1902 H	800,000	6.00	15.00	45.00
1903	846,150	10.00	18.00	45.00
1904	400,000	40.00	65.00	160.00
1905	800,000	10.00	22.00	55.00
1906	1,237,843	12.00	30.00	60.00
1907	2,088,000	10.00	26.00	50.00
1908	495,016	15.00	40.00	90.00
1909	1,335,929	7.00	25.00	60.00
1910	3,577,569	5.50	20.00	42.00

5 (14) 50 Cents (Ag) 1902-1910. Type as No. 2:

	Mintage			
1902	120,000	50.00	150.00	350.00
1903 H	140,000	65.00	160.00	400.00
1904	60,000	180.00	400.00	1000.00
1905	40,000	190.00	500.00	1250.00
1906	350,000	35.00	90.00	285.00
1907	300,000	35.00	95.00	300.00

	Mintage	Fine	VF	XF
1908	128,119	45.00	100.00	260.00
1909	302,118	38.00	90.00	240.00
1910	649,521	25.00	70.00	200.00

6 (A 14) 1 Sovereign (Au) 1908-1910. Head right of King Edward VII. R St. George and the Dragon:

	Mintage	Proof		
1908 C	636			5500.00
1909 C	16,273	300.00	400.00	500.00
1910 C	28,012	240.00	325.00	420.00

Coin No. 6 can only be distinguished from similar issues made at the same time in Great Britain by the mintmark C for Ottawa.

GEORGE V 1910–1936	VF	XF

7 (15a) 1 Cent (Br) 1911. Crowned bust left of King George V. R value (4,663,486 pieces) — 4.00 8.00

8 (17a) 5 Cents (Ag) 1911. R value within wreath, above crown (3,692,350 pieces) — 8.50 17.00

9 (18a) 10 Cents (Ag) 1911. Type as No. 8 (2,737,584 pieces) — 35.00 85.00

10 (19a) 25 Cents (Ag) 1911. Type as No. 8 (1,721,341 pieces) — 75.00 150.00

11 (20a) 50 Cents (Ag) 1911. Type as No. 8 (209,972 pieces) — 285.00 600.00

12 (15) 1 Cent (Br) 1912-1920. Type as No. 7, but with added inscription DEI GRA:

	Mintage	Fine	VF	XF
1912	5,107,642	1.00	2.00	3.50
1913	5,735,405	1.00	2.00	3.50
1914	3,405,958	1.20	2.50	4.00
1915	4,932,134	1.00	2.00	3.50
1916	11,022,367	0.90	1.80	3.00
1917	11,899,254	0.90	1.80	3.00
1918	12,970,798	0.90	1.80	3.00
1919	11,279,634	0.90	1.80	3.00
1920	6,762,247	1.00	2.00	3.50

13 (17)　　5 Cents (Ag) 1912-1921. Type as No. 12:

	Mintage	Fine	VF	XF
1912	5,863,170	2.00	3.00	5.00
1913	5,488,048	2.00	3.00	5.00
1914	4,202,179	2.50	4.00	6.50
1915	1,172,258	9.00	16.00	32.00
1916	2,481,675	3.00	5.00	9.00
1917	5,521,373	2.00	3.00	6.00
1918	6,052,298	2.00	3.00	6.00
1919	7,835,400	2.00	3.00	6.00
1920	10,649,851	1.50	2.50	5.00
1921	2,582,495	2400.00	3000.00	5000.00

The 5-cent-piece of 1921 had been struck when it was decided to use a nickel coin for this denomination. The silver pieces were then melted down. Approximately 100 pieces known.

14 (18)　10 Cents (Ag) 1912-1936. Type as No. 12:

	Mintage			
1912	3,235,557	3.00	5.00	15.00
1913	3,613,937	2.00	4.00	12.00
1914	2,549,811	3.00	6.00	18.00
1915	688,057	12.00	40.00	140.00
1916	4,218,114	2.50	4.50	11.00
1917	5,011,988	2.00	4.00	10.00
1918	5,133,602	2.00	4.00	10.00
1919	7,877,722	2.00	4.00	10.00
1920	6,305,345	2.00	4.00	10.00
1921	2,469,562	2.50	5.00	11.50
1928	2,458,602	3.00	5.00	9.00
1929	3,253,888	2.50	5.00	11.00
1930	1,831,043	2.50	5.50	12.00
1931	2,067,421	2.50	5.00	11.00
1932	1,154,317	3.00	6.50	15.00
1933	672,368	4.00	8.00	30.00
1934	409,067	4.00	10.00	36.00
1935	384,056	6.00	18.00	45.00
1936	2,460,871	2.00	5.00	12.00

The 10-cent piece of 1936 are also known with raised dot below date (only 4 pieces known).

15 (19)　25 Cents (Ag) 1912-1936. Type as No. 12:

	Mintage			
1912	2,544,199	5.00	10.00	38.00
1913	2,213,595	5.00	9.00	32.00
1914	1,215,397	5.50	12.00	40.00

	Mintage	Fine	VF	XF
1915	242,382	25.00	125.00	300.00
1916	1,462,566	6.00	15.00	35.00
1917	3,365,644	4.00	10.00	30.00
1918	4,175,649	3.50	9.00	25.00
1919	5,852,262	3.50	9.00	25.00
1920	1,975,278	4.00	10.00	30.00
1921	597,337	25.00	50.00	250.00
1927	468,096	35.00	90.00	300.00
1928	2,114,178	4.00	10.00	30.00
1929	2,690,562	4.00	10.00	30.00
1930	968,748	5.00	12.50	40.00
1931	537,815	6.00	15.00	42.00
1932	537,994	7.00	18.00	50.00
1933	421,282	7.00	18.00	50.00
1934	384,350	7.00	18.00	50.00
1935	537,772	6.50	16.00	45.00
1936	972,094	4.00	10.00	30.00
1936 dot	153,322	50.00	180.00	360.00

16 (20) 50 Cents (Ag) 1912-1936. Type as No. 12:

	Mintage			
1912	285,867	22.00	60.00	200.00
1913	265,889	22.00	60.00	200.00
1914	160,128	55.00	150.00	350.00
1916	459,070	18.00	50.00	185.00
1917	752,213	15.00	40.00	125.00
1918	754,989	14.00	35.00	120.00
1919	1,113,429	13.00	30.00	110.00
1920	584,691	15.00	42.00	130.00
1921	206,398	6000.00	9000.00	14000.00
1929	228,328	13.00	30.00	100.00
1931	57,581	20.00	60.00	220.00
1932	19,213	90.00	220.00	400.00
1934	39,539	35.00	90.00	210.00
1936	38,550	25.00	60.00	185.00

Most of the 50-cent-piece of 1921 were melted. Only about 50 pieces known.

			VF	XF
17 (A 22)	1 Dollar (Ag) 1936. Rev. Indian canoe (306,100 pieces)		28.00	35.00

18 (23)   5 Dollars (Au) 1912-1914. Crowned bust left of King George V. Rev. arms:

	Mintage	Fine	VF	XF
1912	165,680	200.00	240.00	260.00
1913	98,832	190.00	200.00	260.00
1914	31,122	400.00	600.00	750.00

19 (24)   10 Dollars (Au) 1912-1914. Type as No. 18:

	Mintage			
1912	74,759	400.00	560.00	600.00
1913	149,232	400.00	550.00	600.00
1914	140,068	450.00	600.00	700.00

20 (25)   1 Sovereign (Au) 1911-1919. Head left of King George V. Rev. St. George and the Dragon:

	Mintage			
1911 C	256,946	100.00	140.00	150.00
1913 C	3,715	450.00	750.00	1000.00
1914 C	14,871	130.00	195.00	250.00

	Mintage	Fine	VF	XF
1916 C	6,111		17000.00	19000.00
1917 C	58,845	130.00	140.00	150.00
1918 C	106,516	120.00	130.00	140.00
1919 C	135,889	115.00	130.00	140.00

Most of the sovereigns of 1916 C were melted. Only about 10 pieces known.

Coin No. 20 can only be distinguished from similar issues made at the same time in Great Britain by the mintmark C for Ottawa.

21 (16)   1 Cent (Br) 1920-1936. Rev. value between maple leaves (Acer saccharum – Aceraceae):

	Mintage			
1920	15,483,923	0.50	1.00	2.50
1921	7,601,627	1.00	2.00	3.00
1922	1,243,635	12.00	20.00	32.00
1923	1,019,002	25.00	30.00	42.00
1924	1,593,195	8.00	11.00	18.50
1925	1,000,622	12.00	22.00	32.00
1926	2,143,372	2.00	3.50	8.00
1927	3,553,928	1.50	3.00	5.00
1928	9,144,860	0.60	1.00	2.50
1929	12,159,840	0.50	1.00	2.00
1930	2,538,613	1.50	2.50	4.00
1931	3,842,776	1.80	3.00	5.00
1932	21,316,190	0.50	1.00	2.00
1933	12,079,310	0.50	1.00	2.00
1934	7,042,358	0.80	1.50	3.00
1935	7,526,400	0.80	1.50	3.00
1936	8,768,769	0.70	0.90	2.50

The 1-cent piece of 1936 are also known with raised dot below date (only 8 pieces known).

22 (21)   5 Cents (Ni) 1922-1936. Rev. value and maple leaves:

	Mintage	Fine	VF	XF
1922	4,794,119	2.50	5.00	7.00
1923	2,502,279	1.80	5.00	9.50
1924	3,105,839	1.30	4.50	9.50
1925	201,921	48.00	110.00	180.00
1926 near 6		6.00	12.50	48.00
1926 far 6	938,162	95.00	160.00	300.00
1927	5,285,627	1.30	3.00	7.50
1928	4,577,712	1.30	3.00	7.50
1929	5,611,911	1.30	3.00	7.50
1930	3,704,673	1.50	3.00	8.00
1931	5,100,830	1.30	2.50	7.00
1932	3,198,566	0.90	2.00	6.00
1933	2,597,867	1.50	4.00	10.00
1934	3,827,304	1.00	3.00	8.00
1935	3,900,000	1.00	3.00	8.00
1936	4,400,450	0.90	2.80	7.00

COMMEMORATIVE ISSUE FOR THE 25th ANNIVERSARY OF REIGN OF KING GEORGE V

			VF	XF
23 (22)	1 Dollar (Ag) 1935. Crowned bust left of King George V, inscription GEORGIUS V. REX IMPERATOR ANNO REGNI XXV. R Indian canoe		28.00	35.00

GEORGE VI 1936-1952

24 (26) 1 Cent (Br) 1937-1947. Head left of King George VI. Rev. maple leaves:

	Mintage	Fine	VF	XF
1937	10,040,231	0.25	0.50	1.00
1938	18,365,608	0.25	0.50	1.00
1939	21,600,319	0.25	0.50	1.00
1940	85,740,532	0.20	0.40	0.70
1941	56,336,011	0.15	0.40	0.70
1942	76,113,708	0.15	0.40	0.60
1943	89,111,969	0.15	0.40	0.60
1944	44,131,216	0.15	0.40	0.60
1945	77,268,591	0.15	0.40	0.60
1946	56,662,071	0.15	0.40	0.60
1947	31,093,901	0.10	0.30	0.50
1947 ML	47,855,448	0.15	0.40	0.60

ML means Maple Leaf. The year 1947 also has a variety with a small maple leaf behind the date.

25 (27) 5 Cents (Ni) 1937-1942. Rev. Canadian
beaver (Castor fiber canadensis – Castoridae):

	Mintage	Fine	VF	XF
1937 dot	4,593,263	0.80	1.60	3.50
1938	3,898,974	1.00	3.50	10.00
1939	5,661,123	0.75	1.50	5.00
1940	13,920,197	0.60	1.00	3.50
1941	8,681,785	0.70	1.40	4.00
1942	6,847,544	0.70	1.60	4.00

26 (28) 5 Cents Rev. Canadian beaver (dodecagonal):

	Mintage			
1942 (Bra)	3,396,234	0.80	1.50	2.00
1946 (Ni)	6,952,684	0.50	1.00	2.50
1947 (Ni)	7,603,724	0.50	1.00	2.50
1947 (Ni) dot	7,603,724	12.00	25.00	50.00
1947 (Ni)	9,595,124	0.50	1.00	2.50

27 (29) 5 Cents. Ṛ large "V" and torch with
Morse characters reading "We shall
win if we work willingly" (dodecagonal)

	Mintage			
1943 (Bra)	24,760,256	0.40	0.80	1.20
1944 (St)	11,532,784	0.30	0.50	1.00
1945 (St)	18,893,216	0.30	0.50	1.00

28 (30) 10 Cents (Ag) 1937-1947. Rev. schooner "Bluenose"

	Mintage	Fine	VF	XF
1937	2,500,095	3.00	5.00	11.00
1938	4,197,323	2.50	4.50	9.00
1939	5,501,748	2.50	4.00	8.00
1940	16,526,470	1.00	2.00	4.00
1941	8,716,386	2.00	4.50	7.00
1942	10,214,011	1.50	3.00	6.00
1943	21,143,229	1.50	3.00	6.00
1944	9,383,582	1.20	3.00	6.00
1945	10,979,570	1.20	3.00	6.00
1946	6,300,066	1.20	3.00	6.00
1947	4,431,926	1.40	3.50	7.00
1947 ML	9,638,793	1.20	3.00	5.50

29 (31) 25 Cents (Ag) 1937-1947. Rev. head of caribou (Rangifer tarandus – Cervidae):

	Mintage			
1937	2,690,176	4.00	5.00	10.00
1938	3,149,245	4.00	5.00	10.00
1939	3,532,495	4.00	5.00	10.00
1940	9,583,650	2.00	4.00	8.00
1941	6,654,672	2.00	4.00	8.00
1942	6,935,871	2.00	4.00	8.00
1943	13,559,575	1.50	3.50	7.00
1944	7,216,237	2.00	4.00	8.00
1945	5,296,495	2.00	4.00	9.00
1946	2,210,810	4.00	6.00	15.00
1947		4.00	7.00	15.00
1947 dot after 7	1,524,554	35.00	80.00	140.00
1947 ML	4,393,938	4.00	7.00	12.00

30 (32) 50 Cents (Ag) 1937-1947. Rev. crowned coat of arms, shield supporters: lion and unicorn:

	Mintage			
1937	192,016	6.00	14.00	30.00
1938	192,018	11.00	25.00	72.00
1939	287,976	6.00	12.00	25.00
1940	1,996,566	5.00	9.00	15.00
1941	1,714,874	5.00	9.00	15.00
1942	1,974,164	5.00	9.00	15.00
1943	3,109,583	4.00	7.00	12.00
1944	2,460,205	4.00	7.00	12.00

	Mintage	Fine	VF	XF
1945	1,959,528	4.00	7.00	12.00
1946	950,235	4.00	7.50	14.00
1946 Hoof in 6		20.00	40.00	100.00
1947 straight 7	424,885	5.00	12.00	20.00
1947 curved 7		5.00	12.00	20.00
1947 ML, straight 7	738,433	20.00	55.00	100.00
1947 ML, curved 7		1250.00	1500.00	2000.00

31 (33) 1 Dollar (Ag) 1937-1947. Rev. Indian canoe:

	Mintage	Fine	VF	XF
1937	241,002	14.00	22.00	30.00
1938	90,304	25.00	38.00	60.00
1945	38,391	100.00	150.00	220.00
1946	93,055	22.00	35.00	55.00
1947 blunt 7	65,595	40.00	60.00	95.00
1947 pointed 7		125.00	175.00	260.00
1947 ML	21,135	90.00	160.00	220.00

COMMEMORATIVE ISSUE FOR THE VISIT OF THE ROYAL COUPLE TO CANADA

	VF	XF
32 (34) 1 Dollar (Ag) 1939. Rev. Parliament building in Ottawa (1,363,816 pieces)	13.00	18.00

33 (35) 1 Cent (Br) 1948-1952. Type as No. 24, but without IND: IMP:

	Mintage	Fine	VF	XF
1948	25,767,779	0.25	0.40	0.50
1949	33,128,933	0.15	0.20	0.30
1950	60,444,992	0.05	0.10	0.20
1951	80,430,379	0.05	0.10	0.20
1952	67,631,736	0.05	0.10	0.20

34 (36) 5 Cents. Rev. Canadian beaver (dodecagonal):

	Mintage	Fine	VF	XF
1948 (Ni)	1,810,789	1.00	2.50	5.00
1949 (Ni)	13,037,090	0.25	0.60	1.00
1950 (Ni)	11,970,521	0.25	0.60	1.00
1951 (St)	4,313,410	0.50	0.80	1.60
1952 (St)	10,891,148	0.30	0.60	1.20

35 (38) 10 Cents (Ag) 1948-1952. Rev. schooner
"Bluenose":

	Mintage	Fine	VF	XF
1948	422,741	5.50	10.00	30.00
1949	11,336,172	1.50	2.00	3.00
1950	17,823,075	1.50	2.00	3.00
1951	15,079,265	1.50	2.00	3.00
1952	10,474,455	1.50	2.00	3.00

36 (39) 25 Cents (Ag) 1948-1952. Rev. head of caribou:

	Mintage			
1948	2,564,424	4.00	7.00	15.00
1949	7,988,830	3.00	4.50	7.00
1950	9,673,335	3.00	4.50	7.00
1951	8,290,719	3.00	4.50	7.00
1952	8,859,642	3.00	4.50	7.00

37 (40) 50 Cents (Ag) 1948-1952. Rev. crowned coat
of arms, shield supporters: lion and
unicorn:

	Mintage			
1948	37,784	45.00	85.00	135.00
1949	858,991	6.00	12.00	20.00
1950	2,384,179	4.00	7.00	15.00
1951	2,421,730	4.00	7.00	15.00
1952	2,596,465	4.00	7.00	15.00

38 (41) 1 Dollar (Ag) 1948-1952. Rev. Indian canoe:

	Mintage			
1948	18,780	300.00	650.00	1000.00
1950	261,002	7.00	12.00	22.00
1951	416,395	4.00	10.00	12.00
1952	406,148	4.00	10.00	12.00

COMMEMORATIVE ISSUE FOR THE ENTRY OF NEW-FOUNDLAND AS A PROVINCE IN THE CANADIAN CONFEDERATION on 11th December 1948

			VF	XF
39 (42)	1	Dollar (Ag) 1949. Rev. The "Matthew", sailing ship of the discoverer John Cabot (672,218 pieces)	25.00	35.00

COMMEMORATIVE ISSUE FOR THE 200th ANNIVERSARY OF THE NICKEL INDUSTRY

40 (37)	5	Cents (Ni) 1951. Rev. nickel preparation plant, maple leaves (dedecagonal) (9,028,507 pieces)	1.60	2.60

ELIZABETH II since 1952

41 (43)   1 Cent (Br) 1953-1964. Head right of Queen Elizabeth II. Rev. maple leaves:

	Mintage	VF	XF	Unc
1953	67,806,016	0.10	0.20	0.60
1954	22,181,760	0.05	0.40	1.60
1955	56,403,193	0.05	0.10	0.60
1956	78,658,535	0.05	0.10	0.50
1957	100,601,792	0.05	0.10	0.20
1958	59,385,679	0.05	0.10	0.20
1959	83,615,343	0.05	0.10	0.20
1960	75,772,775	0.05	0.10	0.20
1961	139,598,404	0.05	0.10	0.15
1962	227,244,069	0.05	0.10	0.15
1963	279,076,334	0.05	0.10	0.15
1964	484,655,322	0.05	0.10	0.10

42   5 Cents 1953–1962. Rev. Canadian beaver
(dodecagonal) (Y 44: St, Y 45: Ni):

	Mintage	VF	XF	Unc
1953 (St)	16,635,552	0.40	1.00	3.60
1954 (St)	6,998,662	0.80	1.50	5.00
1955 (Ni)	5,355,028	0.50	1.00	5.50
1956 (Ni)	9,399,854	0.30	0.60	2.50
1957 (Ni)	7,387,703	0.40	0.80	2.50
1958 (Ni)	7,607,521	0.35	0.70	2.00
1959 (Ni)	11,552,523	0.25	0.50	1.20
1960 (Ni)	37,157,433	0.20	0.40	0.60
1961 (Ni)	47,889,051	0.10	0.30	0.40
1962 (Ni)	46,307,305	0.10	0.30	0.40

43 (45a) 5 Cents (Ni) 1963-1964. Rev. Canadian
beaver (round):

	Mintage			
1963	43,970,320	0.10	0.30	0.40
1964	78,075,068	0.10	0.20	0.30

44 (46) 10 Cents (Ag) 1953-1964. Rev. schooner
"Bluenose":

	Mintage			
1953	17,706,395	0.60	1.00	5.00
1954	4,493,150	0.80	1.50	11.00
1955	12,237,294	0.70	1.20	5.50
1956	16,732,844	0.50	0.80	4.00
1957	16,110,229	0.50	0.60	2.00
1958	10,621,236	0.60	0.70	2.60
1959	19,691,433	0.50	0.60	1.60
1960	45,446,835	0.50	0.60	1.20
1961	26,850,859	0.50	0.60	1.40
1962	41,864,335	0.50	0.60	1.20
1963	41,916,208	0.50	0.60	1.20
1964	49,518,549	0.50	0.60	1.50

45 (47) 25 Cents (Ag) 1953-1964. Rev. head of caribou:

	Mintage			
1953	10,546,769	2.50	4.00	8.00
1954	2,318,891	4.00	10.00	60.00
1955	9,552,505	2.50	4.00	10.00
1956	11,269,353	2.00	3.00	7.00
1957	12,770,190	1.80	2.50	5.00

	Mintage	VF	XF	Unc
1958	9,336,910	1.80	2.50	5.00
1959	13,503,461	1.50	1.80	4.00
1960	22,835,327	1.40	1.60	3.50
1961	18,164,368	1.40	1.60	3.50
1962	29,559,266	1.40	1.60	3.50
1963	21,180,652	1.40	1.60	3.50
1964	36,479,343	1.40	1.60	3.50

46 (48) 50 Cents (Ag) 1965-1958. Rev. crowned coat of arms, shield supporters: lion and unicorn:

	Mintage			
1953	1,630,429	3.00	4.00	15.00
1954	506,305	5.00	10.00	55.00
1955	753,511	4.00	7.00	30.00
1956	1,379,499	3.00	4.00	10.00
1957	2,171,689	2.00	3.00	8.00
1958	2.957,266	2.00	3.00	8.00

47 (51) 50 Cents (Ag) 1959-1964. Type as No. 47, but redesignet revers:

	Mintage			
1959	3,095,535	2.50	3.00	6.00
1960	3,488,897	2.50	3.00	6.00
1961	3,584,417	2.50	3.00	6.00
1962	5,208,030	2.00	2.50	5.00
1963	8,348,871	2.00	2.50	5.00
1964	9,377,676	2.00	2.50	5.00

48 (49) 1 Dollar (Ag) 1953-1963. Rev. Indian canoe:

	Mintage			
1953	1,074,578	10.00	12.00	15.00
1954	246,606	11.00	16.00	22.00
1955	268,105	11.00	16.00	22.00
1956	209,092	12.50	18.00	24.00
1957	496,389	10.00	12.00	15.00
1959	1,443,502	6.00	8.00	10.00
1960	1,420,486	6.00	8.00	10.00
1961	1,262,231	6.00	8.00	10.00
1962	1,884,789	6.00	8.00	10.00
1963	4,179,981	4.00	8.00	10.00

COMMEMORATIVE ISSUE FOR THE CENTENARY OF BRITISH COLUMBIA

		XF	Unc
49 (50)	1 Dollar (Ag) 1958. Rev. totem pole (3,039,630 pieces)	10.00	15.00

COMMEMORATIVE ISSUE FOR THE CONFERENCES AT CHARLOTTETOWN (PRINCE EDWARD ISLAND) AND QUEBEC IN 1864

50 (52)	1 Dollar (Ag) 1964. ℞ lily, cloverleaf, thistle and rose as symbols of the main population groups: the French, Irish, Scottish and English (7,296,832 pieces)	9.00	15.00

51 (53)	1 Cent (Br) 1965–. Rev. maple leaves (reduced size since 1980):

	Mintage	VF	XF	Unc
1965	304,441,082	0.05	0.10	0.20
1966	184,151,087	0.05	0.10	0.40
1968	329,695,772	0.05	0.10	0.20
1969	335,240,929	0.05	0.10	0.20
1970	311,145,010	0.05	0.10	0.20
1971	298,228,936	0.05	0.10	0.20
1972	451,304,591	0.03	0.05	0.10
1973	457,059,852	0.03	0.05	0.10
1974	692,058,489	0.03	0.05	0.10
1975	642,318,000	0.03	0.05	0.10
1976	701,122,890	0.03	0.05	0.10
1977	453,762,670	0.03	0.05	0.10
1978	911,170,647	0.03	0.05	0.10
1979	754,394,064	0.03	0.05	0.10
1980		0.03	0.05	0.10
1981		0.03	0.05	0.10

52 (54) 5 Cents (Ni) 1965-. Rev. Canadian beaver:

	Mintage			
1965	84,876,018	0.08	0.10	0.20
1966	27,976,648	0.08	0.10	0.30
1968	101,930,379	0.08	0.10	0.20
1969	27,830,229	0.08	0.10	0.20
1970	5,726,010	0.15	0.25	0.70
1971	27,312,609	0.08	0.10	0.20
1972	62,417,387	0.08	0.10	0.20
1973	53,507,435	0.08	0.10	0.20
1974	94,704,645	0.08	0.10	0.20
1975	138,882,000	0.08	0.10	0.20
1976	55,140.213	0.08	0.10	0.20
1977	89,120,791	0.08	0.10	0.15
1978	137,079,273	0.07	0.08	0.15
1979	186,706,667	0.07	0.08	0.15
1980		0.07	0.08	0.15
1981		0.07	0.08	0.15

53 (55) 10 Cents (Ag) 1965-1968. Rev. schooner "Bluenose":

	Mintage			
1965	56,965,392	0.50	0.75	1.50
1966	34,567,898	0.60	0.80	1.50
1968	70,460,000	0.40	0.60	1.00

54 (56) 25 Cents (Ag) 1965-1968. Rev. head of caribou:

	Mintage	VF	XF	Unc
1965	44,708,869	0.90	1.80	3.50
1966	25,626,315	0.90	1.80	3.50
1968	71,464,000	0.80	1.50	2.50

55 (57) 50 Cents (Ag)1965-1966. Arms:

	Mintage			
1965	12,629,974	4.00	5.00	7.00
1966	7,920,496	5.00	6.00	9.00

56 (58) 1 Dollar (Ag) 1965-1972. Indian canoe:

	Mintage			
1965	10,768,569	5.00	10.00	18.00
1966	9,912,178	4.00	9.00	17.00
1972	350,109			15.00

COMMEMORATIVE ISSUES (7) FOR THE CENTENARY OF THE EXISTENCE OF THE CANADIAN CONFEDERATION

		XF	Unc
57 (59)	1 Cent (Br) 1967. Rev. common pigeon (Columba livia domestica – Columbidae) (345,140,645 pieces)	0.10	0.20
58 (60)	5 Cents (Ni) 1967. Rev. snoshoe-rabbit or varying hare (Lepus americanus – Leporidae) (36,876,574 pieces)	0.20	0.30
59 (61)	10 Cents (Ag) 1967. Rev. Atlantic mackerel (Scomber scombrus - Scombridae) (63,012,417 pieces)	1.00	1.50

60 (62)	25 Cents (Ag) 1967. Rev. lynx (Lynx lynx – Felidae) (48,855,500 pieces)	2.00	3.50

		XF	Unc
61 (63)	50 Cents (Ag) 1967. Rev. wolf (Canis lupus – Canidae) 4,211,395 pieces)	6.00	9.00

62 (64) 1 Dollar (Ag) 1967. Rev. Canada goose (Branta canadensis – Anatidae) (6,767,496 pieces)   14.00   18.50

63 (65) 20 Dollar (Au) 1967. Rev. arms (337,688 pieces)   Proof   300.00

64 (55) 10 Cents (Ni) 1968-. Type as No. 53:

	Mintage	XF	Unc
1968 Ottawa	87,412,930	0.20	0.30
1968 Philadelphia	85,170,000	0.20	0.30
1969	55,833,929	0.20	0.30
1970	5,249,296	0.40	0.70
1971	41,016,968	0.20	0.30
1972	60,169,387	0.20	0.30
1973	167,715,435	0.15	0.20
1974	201,566,565	0.15	0.20
1975	207,680,000	0.15	0.20
1976	95,018,533	0.15	0.20
1977	128,452,206	0.15	0.20
1978	170,366,431	0.15	0.20

	Mintage	XF	Unc
1979	194,170,000	0.15	0.20
1980		0.12	0.15
1981		0.12	0.15

65 (56a) 25 Cents (Ni) 1968-. Type as No. 54:

	Mintage		
1968	88,686,931	0.40	0.80
1969	133,037,929	0.35	0.70
1970	10,302,010	0.65	1.20
1971	48,170,428	0.40	0.80
1972	43,743,387	0.40	0.80
1974	192,360,598	0.35	0.60
1975	141,148,000	0.35	0.60
1976	86,898,261	0.35	0.60
1977	99,634,555	0.35	0.60
1978	176,475,408	0.35	0.60
1979	112,192,000	0.35	0.60
1980		0.35	0.60
1981		0.35	0.60

66 (57a) 50 Cents (Ni) 1968-. Type as No. 55, but reduced size:

	Mintage		
1968	3,966,932	0.80	1.20
1969	7,113,929	0.80	1.20
1970	2,429,526	1.00	1.60
1971	2,166,444	0.80	1.20
1972	2,515,632	0.80	1.20
1973	2,546,096	0.80	1.20
1974	3,436,650	0.80	1.00
1975	3,710,000	0.80	1.00
1976	2,940,719	0.80	1.00
1977	709,839	2.00	3.50
1978	3,341,892	0.80	1.00
1979	3,835,842	0.80	1.00
1980		0.80	1.00
1981		0.80	1.00

67 (58a) 1 Dollar (Ni) 1968-. Type as No. 56, but reduced size:

	Mintage	XF	Unc
1968	5,579,714	1.50	2.40
1969	4,809,313	2.00	3.00
1972	2,676,041	1.50	2.40
1975	3,256,000	1.40	2.00

	Mintage	XF	Unc
1976	2,498,204	1.40	2.00
1977	1,393,745	1.40	2.00
1978	2,948,488	1.40	2.00
1979	2,954,842	1.40	2.00
1980		1.40	2.00
1981		1.40	2.00

ISSUE FOR THE ENTRY OF
MANITOBA INTO THE CANADIAN CONFEDERATION IN 1870

		XF	Unc
68 (66)	1 Dollar (Ni) 1970. Manitoba pasque flower (Pulsatilla ludoviciana – Ranunculaceae) (4,140,058 pieces)	1.60	2.50

ISSUES (2) FOR THE ENTRY OF
BRITISH COLUMBIA INTO THE CANADIAN CONFEDERATION IN 187

69 (68)	1 Dollar (Ag) 1971. Rev. coat of arms of British Columbia (conferred on 31st March 1906) and shield bearers. Jubilee dates (555,564 pieces)	Proof	15.00
70 (67)	1 Dollar (Ni) 1971. Rev. coat of arms and national flower of British Columbia (4,260,781 pieces)	1.60	2.00

COMMEMORATIVE ISSUE
FOR THE ENTRY OF PRINCE EDWARD ISLAND
IN THE CANADIAN FEDERATION IN 1873

				XF	Unc
71 (69)	1 Dollar (Ni) 1973. ℞ building of the Legislative Assembly in Charlottetown (3,196,452 pieces)			1.60	2.00

COMMEMORATIVE ISSUES (2) CENTENARY
OF THE ROYAL CANADIAN MOUNTED POLICE

		XF	Unc
72 (70)	25 Cents (Ni) 1973. ℞ member of the Royal Canadian Mounted Police in dress uniform on horseback, on a patch of lawn (134,958,587 pieces)	0.50	0.70

73 (71)	1 Dollar (Ag) 1973. ℞ officer of the Northwest Mounties on horseback, on a patch of prairie (904,795 pieces)	Proof	11.00

COMMEMORATIVE ISSUES (4)
FOR THE OLYMPIC GAMES 1976 IN MONTREAL
(1th ISSUE)

74   75

		Unc	Proof
74 (73)	5 Dollars (Ag) 1973. Elisabeth II. head facing right. ℞ map of North America	20.00	22.50
75 (72)	5 Dollars (Ag) 1973. ℞ sailing boats in front of skyline of Kingstone, Ontario	20.00	22.50

76   77

		Unc	Proof
76 (74)	10 Dollars (Ag) 1973. ℞ map of the world	30.00	35.00
	1974 (date error)	600.00	
77 (75)	10 Dollars (Ag) 1973. ℞ city skyline of Montreal	30.00	35.00

COMMEMORATIVE ISSUE (2) FOR THE CENTENARY OF THE FOUNDING OF THE CITY OF WINNIPEG

			Unc	Proof
78 (100)	1 Dollar (Ni) 1974 (2,799,363)		2.00	
79 (100a)	1 Dollar (Ag) 1974 (628,183)			11.00

COMMEMORATIVE ISSUES (4)
FOR THE OLYMPIC GAMES 1976 IN MONTREAL
(2nd ISSUE)

80   82

80 (77)	5 Dollars (Ag) 1974. Rev. athlete and torch	20.00	22.50
81 (76)	5 Dollars (Ag) 1974. Rev. olympic rings	20.00	22.50
82 (78)	10 Dollars (Ag) 1974. Rev. head of Zeus	30.00	35.00
83 (79)	10 Dollars (Ag) 1974. Rev. temple of Zeus	30.00	35.00

COMMEMORATIVE ISSUE (4) FOR THE OLYMPIC GAMES 1976 IN MONTRAL (3rd ISSUE)

84   86

			Unc	Proof
84 (81)	5	Dollars (Ag) 1974. Rev. Indian paddling canoe	20.00	22.50
85 (80)	5	Dollars (Ag) 1974. Rev. olympic rower	20.00	22.50
86 (83)	10	Dollars (Ag) 1974. Rev. Indians playing Lacrosse	30.00	35.00
87 (82)	10	Dollars (Ag) 1974. Rev. high wheel bicycles	30.00	35.00

100th ANNIVERSARY OF CALGARY

88 (101)	1	Dollar (Ag) 1975. Rev. cowboy on horse center with oil weells and city skyline in background (833,095 pieces)	2.00	11.00

COMMEMORATIVE ISSUES (4) FOR THE OLYMPIC GAMES 1976 IN MONTREAL (4th ISSUE)

89   90

		Unc	Proof
89 (85)	5 Dollars (Ag) 1975. Rev. women's javelin	20.00	22.50
90 (84)	5 Dollars (Ag) 1975. Rev. marathon runner	20.00	22.50

91 (86)	10 Dollars (Ag) 1975. Rev. men's high hurdles	30.00	35.00
92 (87)	10 Dollars (Ag) 1975. Rev. women's shot put	30.00	35.00

COMMEMORATIVE ISSUES (4) FOR THE OLYMPIC GAMES 1976 IN MONTREAL (5th ISSUE)

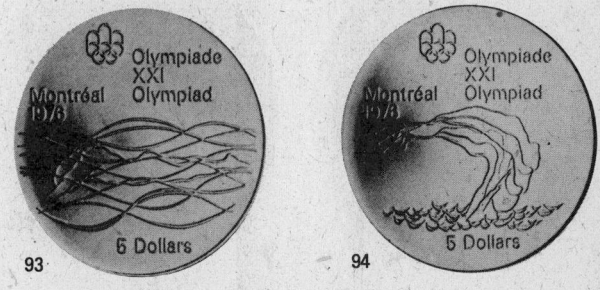

93 (88)	5 Dollars (Ag) 1975. Rev. swimmer	20.00	22.50
94 (89)	5 Dollars (Ag) 1975. Rev. diver	20.00	22.50

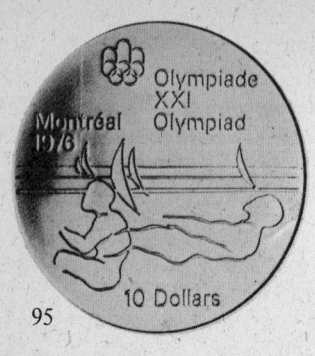

95   96

			Unc	Proof
95	(90)	10 Dollars (Ag) 1975. Rev. sailing	30.00	35.00
96	(91)	10 Dollars (Ag) 1975. Rev. paddler	30.00	35.00

COMMEMORATIVE ISSUES (4) FOR THE OLYMPIC GAMES 1976 IN MONTREAL (6th ISSUE)

97	(92)	5 Dollars (Ag) 1976. Rev. fencing	20.00	22.50
98	(93)	5 Dollars (Ag) 1976. Rev. boxing	20.00	22.50

99   100

99	(94)	10 Dollars (Ag) 1976. Rev. soccer	30.00	35.00
100	(95)	10 Dollars (Ag) 1976. Rev. field hockey	30.00	35.00

COMMEMORATIVE ISSUES (4) FOR THE OLYMPIC GAMES 1976 IN MONTREAL (7th ISSUE)

101	(96)	5 Dollars (Ag) 1976. Rev. olympic village	20.00	22.50

		Unc	Proof
102 (97)	5 Dollars (Ag) 1976. Rev. olympic torch	20.00	22.50
103 (98)	10 Dollars (Ag) 1976. Rev. olympic stadium	30.00	35.00
104 (99)	10 Dollars (Ag) 1976. Rev. olympic velo- drome	30.00	35.00

COMMEMORATIVE ISSUE FOR THE OLYMPIC GAMES 1976 IN MONTREAL (8th ISSUE)

105	100 Dollars (Au) 1976. Rev. Athena, Greek goddes and athlete:		
	a) (Y A 100) .583 gold, dia. 27 mm (650,000)	170.00	
	b) (Y A 100a) .917 gold, dia. 25 mm (350,000)		300.00

100th ANNIVERSARY OF THE LIBRARY OF PARLIAMENT

		Unc	Proof
106 (102)	1 Dollar (Ag) 1976. Rev. Library of Parliament in Ottawa (483,722 pieces)	2.00	12.50

25th ANNIVERSARY OF THE SILVER JUBILEE HER MAJESTY QUEEN ELIZABETH II (2)

107 (103)	1 Dollar (Ag) 1977. Rev. The throne of the Senate (847,194 pieces)	12.50

108 (104)	100 Dollars (Au) 1977. Rev. bouquet of twelve flowers representing the twelve Canadian provinces and territories (180,396 pieces)	360.00

COMMEMORATIVE ISSUE FOR THE 11th COMMONWEALTH GAMES IN EDMONTON (August 3-12, 1978)

			Unc	Proof
109 (106)	1 Dollar (Ag) 1978. Rev. the official symbols of the ten sports which comprise the Commonwealth Games (744,655 pieces)			12.50

110 (105)	100 Dollars (Au) 1978. Twelve flying gooses (180,009 pieces)			360.00

300th ANNIVERSARY OF GRIFFON

Proof

111 (107) 1 Dollar (Ag) 1979. The »Griffon«
(913,818 pieces)   14.00

YEAR OF THE CHILD

112 (108) 100 Dollars (Au) 1979. Children encircling a
globe (273,920 pieces)   360.00

113 (109) 50 Dollars (Au) 1979–. Maple leaf   600.00

ARCTIC TERRITORIES CENTENNIAL (2)

114 (110)   1 Dollar (Ag) 1980. Polar bear   20.00

115 (111)   100 Dollars (Au) 1980   360.00

100th ANNIVERSARY OF TRANS-CANADA RAILROAD

116 (112)   1 Dollar (Ag) 1980   20.00

CANADA NATIONAL ANTHEM »O CANADA«

117 (113)   100 Dollars (Au) 1981. Map and scroll
(250,000 pieces)   360.00

		Unc	Proof
118	1 Dollar (Ag) 1982. Bison's head		20.00

CANADA'S OLD CONFEDERATION (1867) AND NEW CONSTITUTION (1982)

119	1 Dollar (Ni) 1982. »Fathers of Confederation« from a painting by Robert Harris		2.50

Area: 1, 557 sq. mi. Population: 270,000.

The Portuguese navigators, Diego Gomes and Antonio Nola, discovered this island group in 1460; unil then it had been uninhabited and was settled with Negro slaves by Portugal. The colonial status was formally transferred in 1951 to that of an (overseas-) province; this, however, was unable to call a halt to the movements of independence. Mainly on the mainland opposite (Portuguese Guinea) the P(artido) A(fricano) (de) I(ndependencia) (de) G(uiné e) C(abo Verde) (African Party for the Independence of Guinea and the Cape Verde Islands) was operating. After the declaration of independence of Guinea-Bissau (on the mainland) the Cape Verdes became independent on July 5, 1975.

Capital: Praia.

100 Centavos = 1 Escudo; 100 Centavos = 1 Cape Verde Escudo

			VF	XF
1 (1)	5	Centavos (Br) 1930. Allegorical figure of the Republic. ℞ value	3.00	6.00
2 (2)	10	Centavos (Br) 1930. Type as No. 1	2.50	5.00
3 (3)	20	Centavos (Br) 1930. Type as No. 1	2.50	5.00
4 (4)	50	Centavos (Ni–Br) 1930. ℞ arms within wreath above value	6.00	10.00
5 (5)	1	Escudo (Ni–Br) 1930. Type as No. 4	10.00	15.00
6 (6)	50	Centavos (Ni–Br) 1949. Arms with mural crown. ℞ value	4.00	6.00
7 (7)	1	Escudo (Ni–Br) 1949. Type as No. 6	5.00	9.00
8 (A 8)	50	Centavos (Br) 1968. Type as No. 6, but without COLONIA DE in the inscription	0.80	1.40
9 (8)	1	Escudo (Br) 1953, 1968. Type as No. 8	0.80	1.40
10 (9)	2½	Escudos (Cu–Ni) 1953, 1967. Type as No. 8	1.80	2.80
11 (A 10)	5	Escudos (Cu–Ni) 1968. Type as No. 8	2.00	3.50
12 (10)	10	Escudos (Ag) 1953. Type as No. 8	5.50	7.50

1th ANNIVERSARY OF INDEPENDENCE (2)

			Unc	Proof
13 (11)	250	Escudos (Ag) 1976	18.00	
14 (12)	2500	Escudos (Au) 1976		280.00

ISSUE FOR THE FAO COIN PLAN (2)

			VF	XF
15 (15)	1	Escudo (Al-Br) 1977. Rural education	0.40	0.60
16 (16)	2,50	Escudos (Al-Br) 1977. Planting coffee	0.50	0.90

17 (13)	20	Centavos (Al) 1977. Arms. Rev. value	0.40	0.80
18 (14)	50	Centavos (Al) 1977. Type as No. 17	0.50	1.00
19 (17)	10	Escudos (Cu-Ni) 1977. Eduardo Mondlane (1920–1969), patriot	1.50	2.00
20 (18)	20	Escudos (Cu-Ni) 1977. Domingos Ramos (1935–1966), patriot	2.00	2.50
21 (19)	50	Escudos (Cu-Ni) 1977. Amilcar Cabral (1924–1973), patriot	3.00	4.00

Caiman-Inseln   # Cayman Islands   **Caïmanes (Iles)**

Area: 68 sq. mi. Population: 13,000.

The coral islands of Grand Cayman, Little Cayman and Cayman Brac, situated in the Caribbean Ocean, were under the administration of Jamaica until 1959, were under a Governor General from 1959–62 and since 1962 enjoy limited autonomy. Until the introduction of a local currency on 1st May 1972, the Jamaica Dollar was legal tender. Capital: Georgetown.

100 Cents = 1 Cayman Dollar

			Unc	Proof
1 (1)	1	Cent (Bro) 1972–. Queen Elisabeth II. ℞ Great Caiman thrush (Mimocichla ravida – Turtidae), denomination	0.20	1.20
2 (2)	5	Cents (Cu–Ni) 1972–. ℞ Prawn (Penaeus setiferus – Penaeidae) denomination	0.20	2.00
3 (3)	10	Cents (Cu–Ni) 1972–. ℞ green turtle (Chelonia mydas – Cheloniidae) = the heraldic animal of the islands, denomination	0.40	2.50
4 (4)	25	Cents (Cu–Ni) 1972–. ℞ Caiman schooner	0.90	3.00
5 (5)	50	Cents (Ag) 1972–. ℞ Caribbean emperor fish (Holacanthus tricolor – Chaetodontidae), denomination		10.00
6 (6)	1	Dollar (Ag) 1972–. ℞ Flamboyant (Delonix regia – Leguminosae), denomination		12.50

7 (7)   2 Dollars (Ag) 1972–. ℞ Silver Heron

(Casmerodius albus – Ardeidae), de- | | 20.00
nomination |

8 (8)   5 Dollars (Ag) 1972–. ℞ coat of arms,
denomination   30.00

COMMEMORATIVE ISSUES (2) FOR THE SILVER WEDDING OF THE BRITISH ROYAL COUPLE ON 20th NOVEMBER 1972

9 (9)   25 Dollars (Ag) 1972. British Royal Couple, overlapping heads, facing right   70.00   90.00
10 (9a)   25 Dollars (Au) 1972. Type as No. 9   150.00   165.00

COMMEMORATIVE ISSUES (2) FOR THE CENTENARY OF THE BIRTH OF SIR WINSTON CHURCHILL

11 (10)   25 Dollars (Ag) 1974. Bust of Sir Winston
Churchill (1874–1965). ℞ Coat of
arms, value   75.00   95.00
12 (11) 100 Dollars (Au) 1974. Type as No. 11   250.00   280.00

			Unc	Proof
13 (12)	50	Dollars (Ag) 1975-1977. Bust of Queen Elizabeth II. Rev. the Queens Mary I, Elizabeth I, Mary II, Anne, and Victoria. Value in centre	60.00	90.00
14 (13)	100	Dollars (Au) 1975-1977. Type as No. 13	250.00	280.00

25th ANNIVERSARY OF THE SILVER JUBILEE OF HER MAJESTY QUEEN ELIZABETH (12)

15 (14)	25	Dollars (Ag) 1977. Elizabeth II. Rev. Coat of arms	50.00	65.00
16 (15)	100	Dollars (Au) 1977. Type as No. 15	280.00	300.00
17 (16)	25	Dollars (Ag) 1977. Mary I		70.00
18 (17)	25	Dollars (Ag) 1977. Elizabeth I		70.00
19 (18)	25	Dollars (Ag) 1977. Mary II		70.00
20 (19)	25	Dollars (Ag) 1977. Anne		70.00
21 (20)	25	Dollars (Ag) 1977. Victoria		70.00
22 (21)	50	Dollars (Au) 1977. Type as No. 17		200.00
23 (22)	50	Dollars (Au) 1977. Type as No. 18		200.00
24 (23)	50	Dollars (Au) 1977. Type as No. 19		200.00
25 (24)	50	Dollars (Au) 1977. Type as No. 20		200.00
26 (25)	50	Dollars (Au) 1977. Type as No. 21		200.00

25th ANNIVERSARY OF THE CORONATION OF HER MAJESTY QUEEN ELIZABETH II (22)

27 (1a)	1	Cent (Br) 1978. Type as No. 1, but Coronation Anniversary legend	2.50
28 (2a)	5	Cents (Cu-Ni) 1978	4.00
29 (3a)	10	Cents (Cu-Ni) 1978	5.00
30 (4a)	25	Cents (Cu-Ni) 1978	6.00
31 (5a)	50	Cents (Ag) 1978	12.00
32 (6a)	1	Dollar (Ag) 1978	20.00
33 (7a)	2	Dollars (Ag) 1978	30.00
34 (8a)	5	Dollars (Ag) 1978	50.00
35 (38)	50	Dollars (Ag) 1978	150.00
36 (39)	100	Dollars (Au) 1978	300.00

37 (26)	25	Dollars (Ag) 1978. Rev. the Ampulla	70.00
38 (27)	25	Dollars (Ag) 1978. Rev. the Orb	70.00
39 (28)	25	Dollars (Ag) 1978. Rev. St. Edward's crown	70.00
40 (29)	25	Dollars (Ag) 1978. Rev. the Coronation chair	70.00
41 (30)	25	Dollars (Ag) 1978. Rev. the Royal scepter	70.00
42 (31)	25	Dollars (Ag) 1978. Rev. the Spoon	70.00
43 (32)	50	Dollars (Au) 1978. Type as No. 37	145.00
44 (33)	50	Dollars (Au) 1978. Type as No. 38	145.00
45 (34)	50	Dollars (Au) 1978. Type as No. 39	145.00
46 (35)	50	Dollars (Au) 1978. Type as No. 40	145.00
47 (36)	50	Dollars (Au) 1978. Type as No. 41	145.00
48 (37)	50	Dollars (Au) 1978. Type as No. 42	145.00

KINGS OF GREAT BRITAIN (20)

Proof

49 (40)	25 Dollars (Ag) 1980	—,—
50 (41)	25 Dollars (Ag) 1980	—,—
51 (42)	25 Dollars (Ag) 1980	—,—
52 (43)	25 Dollars (Ag) 1980	—,—
53 (44)	25 Dollars (Ag) 1980	—,—
54 (45)	25 Dollars (Ag) 1980	—,—
55 (46)	25 Dollars (Ag) 1980	—,—
56 (47)	25 Dollars (Ag) 1980	—,—
57 (48)	25 Dollars (Ag) 1980	—,—
58 (49)	25 Dollars (Ag) 1980	—,—
59 (50)	50 Dollars (Au) 1980	—,—
60 (51)	50 Dollars (Au) 1980	—,—
61 (52)	50 Dollars (Au) 1980	—,—
62 (53)	50 Dollars (Au) 1980	—,—
63 (54)	50 Dollars (Au) 1980	—,—
64 (55)	50 Dollars (Au) 1980	—,—
65 (66)	50 Dollars (Au) 1980	—,—
66 (57)	50 Dollars (Au) 1980	—,—
67 (58)	50 Dollars (Au) 1980	—,—
68 (59)	50 Dollars (Au) 1980	—,—

Central African Republic

Zentralafrikanische Republik **République Centrafricaine**

Area: 239,609 sq. mi. Population: 2,200,000.
The Central African Republic, part of French Equatorial Africa under
the name of Oubangui-Chari, obtained its autonomy on 1st December
1958 within the French Community; on 12th August 1960 it gained
independence. The Central African Republic belongs to the Monetary
Union of Equatorial Africa; see under this heading for the joint issues
by the Community.
Capital: Bangui.

100 Centimes = 1 CFA Franc

COMMEMORATIVE ISSUES (5) FOR THE 10th ANNIVERSARY OF INDEPENDENCE

1 **1000** Francs (Au) 1970. Jean Bédel Bokassa (*1921), 3rd President of State. Commemorative inscription. Motto: Unity – Honour – Work. ℞ national arms, neck decoration: the national order of service, and legend: Zo Kwe Zo (Man is Man = All men are equal). Value — Proof — 100.00

2 **3000** Francs (Au) 1970. ℞ Dr. Martin Luther King (1929–1968), clergyman, American civil rights campaigner, winner of the Nobel Prize for Peace (1964). Legend in German: "Wir müssen Haß mit tätiger Liebe begegnen" (We must meet hate with active love). Value — 175.00

3 **5000** Francs (Au) 1970. ℞ representation of a wrestler, from an ancient model, a reference to the 1972 Olympic Games in Munich and Kiel. Value — 375.00

4 **10000** Francs (Au) 1970. Emblem for the jubilee of the UN, a reference to the 25th anniversary of the World Organization. Value — 600.00

			VF	XF
5	20000	Francs (Au) 1970. Agricultural and industrial design with the legend "Operation Bokassa". Gearwheels, symbol of industrialisation, and farm produce: wild oat plants (Panicum miliaceum — Gramineae) above; on the right, corn cobs (Zea mays — Gramineae) and cattle horns; on the left, cotton plants (Gossypium sp. — Malvaceae). Value		Proof
				1000.00
6 (1)	100	Francs (Ni) 1971, 1972, 1974. Mendes antelopes (Addax nasomaculatus – Bovidae). Name of country. R inscription: Banque Centrale, value, date	1.20	2.40
7 (2)	100	Francs (Ni) 1975, 1976. Type as No. 6, but inscription »Banque des Etats de l'Afrique Centrale«	1.20	2.40
8	100	Francs (Ni) 1978. Typ as No. 6, but legend EMPIRE CENTRAFRICAINE	4.00	6.00
9	10000	Francs (Au) undated (1979). Bust of Bokassa. Rev. Busts of Caesar, Carolus Magnus and Napoleon		–,–
10	25000	Francs (Au) undated (1979). Rev. eagle and sun		–,–

Central African States

Zentralafrikanische Staaten   **Etats d'Afrique Centrale**

The institution covering the issues of currency for the territories of Central Africa is the Banque des Etats de l'Afrique Centrale. This Monetary Union comprises the states of Gabon, Cameroon, the People's Republic of the Congo, Chad, and the Central African Republic (Central African Empire).

100 Centimes = 1 CFA Franc

			EF	Unc
1 (6)	1	Franc (Al) 1974, 1976. Addax antelopes (Addax nasomaculatus – Bovidae), inscription BANQUE DES ETATS DE L'AFRIQUE CENTRALE. Rev. value within wreath of fruits	0.20	0.30

			EF	Unc
2 (7)	5	Francs (Al-Br) 1973, 1975, 1976. Type as No. 1	0.20	0.40
3 (8)	10	Francs (Al-Br) 1975–1977. Type as No. 1	0.25	0.60
4 (9)	25	Francs (Al-Br) 1976. Type as No. 1	0.40	0.80
5 (10)	50	Francs (Ni) 1976, 1977. Rev. value within a rosette of fruits	0.70	1.30

			EF	Unc
6 (11)	500	Francs (Cu-Ni) 1976	5.00	7.00

Ceylon

Area: 25,384 sq. mi. Population: 13,000,000.

Island in the Indian Ocean off the southern tip of India, Ceylon became a sovereign member of the British Commonwealth on 4th February 1948. As of 22nd May 1972 Ceylon has declared itself a republic and declared its former name, in Singhalese, to be Sri Lanka, the latter also to be used exclusively on an international basis. As of 16th December 1929 the Ceylon Rupee substituted the Indian Rupee, with which it, however, remained at par until 1966. Since 22nd May 1972 the monetary unit is called the Sri Lanka Rupee.
Capital: Colombo.

100 Cents = 1 Rupee

EDWARD VII 1901–1910

			VF	XF
1 (11)	¼	Cent (Br) 1904. Crowned bust r. of Edward VII. ℞ value and coconut palm (Cocos nucifera — Palmae)	4.00	9.00
2 (12)	½	Cent (Br) 1904–1909	1.50	3.00
3 (13)	1	Cent (Br) 1904–1910	1.00	2.00
4 (14)	5	Cents (Cu–Ni) 1909–1910. ℞ value (square)	1.20	2.40
5 (15)	10	Cents (Ag) 1902–1910. ℞ coconut palm between value	4.00	6.00
6 (16)	25	Cents (Ag) 1902–1910	4.00	6.00
7 (17)	50	Cents (Ag) 1902–1910	6.50	10.00

GEORGE V 1910–1936

			VF	XF
8 (18)	½	Cent (Br) 1912–1926. Crowned bust l. of George V. ℞ value and coconut palm	0.80	2.00
9 (19)	1	Cent (Br) 1912–1929	0.60	1.50
10 (20)	5	Cents (Cu–Ni) 1912–1926. ℞ value	1.00	2.00
11 (21)	10	Cents (Ag) 1911–1928. Crowned bust r. of George V. ℞ value and coconut palm	2.50	4.00
12 (22)	25	Cents (Ag) 1911–1926	4.00	6.00
13 (23)	50	Cents (Ag) 1913–1929	6.00	10.00

GEORGE VI 1936–1952

			VF	XF
14 (24)	½	Cent (Br) 1937–1940. Crowned bust l. of George VI. ℞ coconut palm	0.70	2.00

			VF	XF
15 (25)	1	Cent (Br) 1937–1942	1.00	2.60
16 (25a)	1	Cent (Br) 1942–1945. Same as No. 15, but larger type	0.20	0.50
17 (27)	2	Cents (Ni–Bra) 1944 (octagonal)	0.80	1.50
18 (28)	5	Cents (Ni–Bra) 1942–1943 (square)	0.80	1.50

			VF	XF
19 (28a)	5	Cents (Ni–Bra) 1944–1945. Same as No. 18, but lighter in weight and thinner	0.20	0.50
20 (32)	10	Cents (Ag) 1941. ℞ coconut palm and value (round)	2.50	4.00

			VF	XF
21 (29)	10	Cents (Ni–Bra) 1944 (octagonal)	0.30	0.60

			VF	XF
22 (30)	25	Cents (Ni–Bra) 1943–1945. ℞ crown above value (round)	0.40	0.70
23 (33)	50	Cents (Ag) 1942. ℞ coconut palm and value (round)	7.00	10.00
24 (31)	50	Cents (Ni–Bra) 1943–1945 (round)	0.60	1.20
25 (34)	2	Cents (Ni–Bra) 1951. Same type as No. 17, but now inscription reads only: KING GEORGE THE SIXTH	0.15	0.30
26 (35)	5	Cents (Ni–Bra) 1951. Not put into circulation	Proof	20.00
27 36)	10	Cents (Ni–Bra) 1951 (octagonal)	0.20	0.40
28 (37)	25	Cents (Ni–Bra) 1951 (round)	0.30	0.60
29 (38)	50	Cents (Ni–Bra) 1951 (round)	0.70	1.40

ELIZABETH II 1952-1972

			VF	XF
30 (39)	2	Cents (Ni–Bra) 1955–1957. Head r. of Elizabeth II. ℞ value	0.25	0.50

			Unc	Proof
31 (40)	1	Rupee (Cu–Ni) 1957. Stupa (= dome-shaped Buddhist shrine) in front of the dhamachakr (= the Buddhists' wheel of the law). ℞ legend and value	2.50	24.00

| **32** (41) | 5 | Rupees (Ag) 1957. Circular design of elephant, horse, lion, humped bull, each with a symbolic meaning: the elephant representing the East, Indra's steed; the horse, for the North, symbol of strength; the lion, for the South, emblem of the sun; the bull, for the West, Shiva's steed. ℞ legend | 25.00 | 150.00 |

			VF	XF
33 (43)	1	Cent (Al–Mg) 1963–1971. National arms. ℞ value (round)	0.05	0.10
34 (44)	2	Cents (Al–Mg) 1963–1971 (octagonal)	0.05	0.10

| **35** (45) | 5 | Cents (Ni–Bra) 1963–1971 (sqare shape) | 0.10 | 0.20 |

					VF	**XF**
36 (46)	10 Cents (Ni–Bra)	1963–1971	(octagonal)		0.15	0.25
37 (47)	25 Cents (Cu–Ni)	1963–1971	(round)		0.15	0.30
38 (48)	50 Cents (Cu–Ni)	1963–1971	(round)		0.25	0.50

39 (49)	1 Rupee (Cu–Ni) 1963–1971 (round)			0.40	0.80

ISSUE FOR THE FAO COIN PLAN

40 (50) 2 Rupees (Cu–Ni) 1968. Parakramabahu I, The Great, King of Ceylon 1153 to 1186, copied from the statue in Polonnaruva. Under the reign of this Buddhist king, an important system of irrigation was created   1.70   3.00

For later issues, see under Sri Lanka.

Tschad   # Chad   **Tchad**
République du Tchad

Area: 493,849 sq. mi. Population: 4,000,000.
Formerly a part of French Equatorial Africa, Chad became an autonomous republic within the French Community on 28th November 1958, and gained independence. on 11th August 1960.
Capital: N'djamena (formerly, until 4th Sept. 1973 known as Fort Lamy).

100 Centimes = 1 CFA Franc

COMMEMORATIVE ISSUES (5) FOR THE 10th ANNIVERSARY OF INDEPENDENCE

			Proof
1	1000	Francs (Au) 1970. Commandant Lamy (†1900), leader of the French military expedition, defeated the armies of Rabeh near Kuseri in 1900. ℞ a woman of Chad with decorative hair-style; chains; national arms, value	65.00
2	3000	Francs (Au) 1970. Felix Eboué (1885 to 1944), colonial official from Cayenne, Governor of Chad in 1939; on 26th August 1940 he rallied to the side of de Gaulle. ℞ map of the country, national arms, value	180.00
3	5000	Francs (Au) 1970. Leclerc de Haute-cloque (1902–1947), Maréchal de France. Chad became, under Leclerc, in 1941, the basis of operations for the conquest of the Fessan with the goal "From Chad to the Rhine". ℞ coconut palm, Strasbourg cathedral and the Arc de Triomphe in Paris. National arms, value	280.00
4	10000	Francs (Au) 1970. General Charles de Gaulle (1890–1970), French President of State, fought for the independence of Chad. ℞ Croix de Lorraine and sun rays over broken chains. National arms, value	550.00

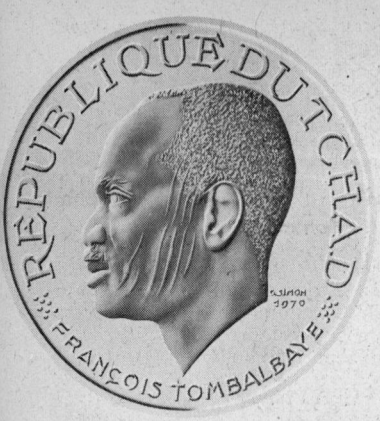

5 20000 Francs (Au) 1970. François Tombal-
baye (1918–1975), Head of State and
Prime Minister. ℞ national arms, commemorative inscription, value

Proof

1100.00

COMMEMORATIVE ISSUES (3) FOR PERSONALITIES
FROM THE UNITED STATES OF AMERICA

6   100 Francs (Ag) 1970. Outline of Africa
with Chad clearly marked. ℞ Robert F.
Kennedy (1925–1968), Attorney-Gen-
eral, candidate for the Presidency in
1968. Value

16.00

7	200	Francs (Ag) 1970. ℞ Dr. Martin Luther King (1929–1968), clergyman, civil rights campaigner, and winner of the Nobel Prize for Peace in 1964. Value		**Proof** 25.00
8	300	Francs (Ag) 1970. ℞ John F. Kennedy (1917–1963), 35th President of the U.S.A. Space capsule over section of the moon. Value		55.00

COMMEMORATIVE ISSUE (2) FOR THE DEATH OF GAMAL ABD EL NASSER

9	200	Francs (Ag) 1970. Gamal Abd el Nasser (1918–70), President of the United Arab Republic 1958–70; head. ℞ outline of Africa with marking of the Chad. Denomination — −,−
10	10000	Francs (Au) 1970. Type as No. 9 — −,−

COMMEMORATIVE ISSUE (2) FOR THE DEATH OF GENERAL CHARLES DE GAULLE

11	200	Francs (Ag) 1970. General Charles de Gaulle (1890–1970), French President; head. ℞ outline of Africa with marking of the Chad. Denomination		−,−
12	10000	Francs (Au) 1970. Type as No. 11		−,−
			VF	**XF**
13 (1)	100	Francs (Ni) 1971, 1972. Mendes antelopes (Addax nasomaculatus – Bovidae). Name of country. R inscription: Banque Centrale, value, date	1.50	2.50

14 (2)	100	Francs (Ni) 1975. Type as No. 13, but inscription »Banques des Etats de l'Afrique Centrale«	1.50	2.50

Chile   # Chile   Chili

Area: 285,295 sq. mi. Population: 10,200,000.
A Republic on the western coastline of South America.
Capital: Santiago de Chile.
N. B.: Because of inflationary tendencies which have been experienced
in this part of the world for decades, size, weight and metal content of
the coins vary for individual pieces of same nominal value.

100 Centavos = 1 Peso
10 Pesos = 1 Condor;
since 1st January 1960: 100 Centesimos = 1 Escudo; since 1975:
100 Centavos = 1 Chilean Peso

			VF	**XF**
1 (38)	5	Pesos (Au) 1898–1925. ℞ national arms: shield with star supported by a Chilean Andes mountain deer or Huëmul (Hippocamelus bisulcus — Cervidae) and an Andean condor (Vultur gryphus — Cathartidae)	125.00	140.00
2 (39)	10	Pesos (Au) 1896–1901. Same type as No. 1	150.00	170.00

3 (40)	20	Pesos (Au) 1896–1917. Same type as No. 1	200.00	250.00
4 (27)		UN (1) Centavo (Cu) 1904–1919. Bust of Liberty l. with cape. ℞ value in wreath	1.80	3.50
5 (28)		DOS (2) Centavos (Cu) 1919	6.00	12.00
6 (29)	2½	Centavos (Cu) 1904–1908	2.00	4.00
7 (30)		CINCO (5) Centavos (Ag) 1899–1919. Andean condor (Vultur gryphus — Cathartidae) on rock to l. ℞ value in wreath	2.00	3.00
8 (41)	5	Centavos (Cu–Ni) 1920–1938	0.40	0.80

			VF	XF
9 (31)		DIEZ (10) Centavos (Ag) 1899–1920	1.00	2.00
10 (42)	10	Centavos (Cu–Ni) 1920–1941	0.25	0.50
11 (32)		VEINTE (20) Centavos (Ag) 1899 to 1920	2.00	3.50
12 (43)	20	Centavos (Cu–Ni) 1920–1941	0.30	0.70
13 (33)	40	Centavos (Ag) 1907–1908		
		a) 1907	12.00	20.00
		b) 1908	2.00	4.00
14 (34)	50	Centavos (Ag) 1902–1906		
		a) 1902–1905	6.50	11.00
		b) 1906	25.00	32.00
15 (35)		UN (1) Peso (Ag) 1902–1932		
		a) 1902–1905, diameter 32 mm	15.00	20.00
		b) 1910, diameter 31.5 mm	7.50	10.00
		c) 1915, 1917, diameter 27.5 mm	6.50	9.00
		d) 1921–1925, diameter 29 mm	4.00	6.00
		e) 1932, diameter 26 mm	6.00	8.00
16 (35e)	1	= UN Peso (Ag) 1927	5.00	7.00

			VF	XF
17 (35)	1	Peso (Cu–Ni) 1933–1940	0.50	1.00
18 (45)	2	= DOS Pesos (Ag) 1927	8.50	12.00
19 (46)	5	= CINCO Pesos (Ag) 1927	35.00	42.00
20 (47)	20	Pesos = DOS Condores (Au) 1926. Date below Liberty head. ℞ national arms	80.00	95.00
21 (48)	50	Pesos = CINCO Condores (Au) 1926	165.00	180.00

			VF	XF
22 (49)	100	Pesos = DIEZ Condores (Au) 1926 to 1960	350.00	365.00
23 (50)	20	Centavos (Cu) 1942–1953. Bust r. of General Bernardo O'Higgins (1778 to 1842), Dictator of Chile 1817–1823. ℞ Copihue flowers (Lapageria rosea — Liliaceae)	0.20	0.40

			VF	XF
24 (51)	50	Centavos (Cu) 1942	0.60	1.20

25 (52)	1	Peso (Cu) 1942–1954	0.40	0.80
26 (52a)	1	Peso (Al) 1954–1958	0.40	0.80
27 (53)	5	Pesos = Medio Condor (Al) 1956. Andean condor flying. ℞ value between ears of wheat	0.60	1.20

| **28** (54) | 10 | Pesos = UN Condor (Al) 1956–1959 | 0.70 | 1.40 |

CURRENCY REFORM: 100 Centesimos = 1 Escudo

29 (55)	½	Centesimo (Al) 1962–1963. Andean condor. ℞ value between ears of wheat	0.10	0.20
30 (56)	1	Centesimo (Al) 1960–1963	0.15	0.30
31 (57)	2	Centesimos (Al–Br) 1964–1970	0.20	0.40
32 (58)	5	Centesimos (Al–Br) 1960–1970	0.25	0.50

| **33** (59) | 10 | Centesimos (Al–Br) 1960–1970 | 0.30 | 0.60 |

COMMEMORATIVE ISSUE FOR 150 YEARS OF THE MILITARY ACADEMY

34   50 Pesos (Au) 1967. Bust r. of General Bernardo O'Higgins (1778 to 1842), founder of the Military Academy. ℞ national arms and value

Proof

150.00

COMMEMORATIVE ISSUE FOR 150 YEARS OF CHILEAN COINAGE

35   100 Pesos (Au) 1967. Laureate bust of Liberty to l.; coin press. ℞ same as No. 34

300.00

COMMEMORATIVE ISSUE FOR THE 150th ANNIVERSARY OF THE CROSSING OF THE ANDES

36   200 Pesos (Au) 1967. "Paso de los Andes" –

"The Crossing of the Andes" from a painting by Vila Prades; the Liberation Army under San Martin and O'Higgins passing across the Andes, February 1817. ℞ same as No. 34

Proof

550.00

COMMEMORATIVE ISSUE FOR 150 YEARS OF THE NATIONAL FLAG

37   500 Pesos (Au) 1967. Laureate head of Liberty to l. In background, national flag. ℞ same as No. 34

1250.00

COMMEMORATIVE ISSUE FOR 150 YEARS OF THE NAVAL SCHOOL

38   5 Pesos (Ag) 1968. Bust facing of Arturo Prat Chacon (1848–1879), Admiral, hero of the naval battle of Iquique. ℞ same as No. 34

35.00

39		10 Pesos (Ag) 1968. Naval squadron under the command of Lord Cochrane. ℞ same as No. 34	**Proof** 50.00	

			VF	**XF**
40 (60)	10	Centesimos (Al–Br) 1971. Bernardo O'Higgins (1778–1842), Dictator of Chile 1817–1823	0.10	0.20
41 (61)	20	Centesimos (Al–Br) 1971. José Manuel Balmaceda (1838–1891), President of State 1886–1891	0.20	0.40
42 (62)	50	Centesimos (Al–Br) 1971. Manuel Rodriguez (1786–1819), advocate and freedom fighter	0.20	0.40
43 (63)	1	Escudo (Cu–Ni) 1971, 1972. José Miguel Carrera (1785–1821), Dictator 1811–1813		
		a) 1971	0.20	0.40
		b) 1972	–,–	–,–
44 (64)	2	Escudos (Cu–Ni) 1971. Caupolicán (died 1558), Chief of the Araucanian Indians, fought together with Lautaro against the Spaniards. Rare. About 190 pieces.		370.00
45 (65)	5	Escudos (Cu–Ni) 1971. Lautaro (1535? to 1557), an Araucanian Indian, served as prisoner under Valdivia, the conqueror of Chile, fled and led an initially		

		successful uprising against the Spaniards; fall in the battle of Mataquito; symbolizes the freedom movement of the Chilean original inhabitants	**VF**	**XF**
			0.50	1.00
46 (65a)	5	Escudos (Al) 1972, 1974, Type as No. 45	0.20	0.40
47 (66)	10	Escudos (Al) 1974. Rising Andean condor. Rev. value, date	0.20	0.40
48 (67)	50	Escudos (Ni-Bra) 1974. Type as No. 47	0.30	0.60
49 (68)	100	Escudos (Ni-Bra) 1974, 1975. Type as No. 47	0.40	0.80

CURRENCY REFORM: 1000 Escudos = 1 Chilean Peso

			XF	**Unc**
50 (69)	1	Centavo (Al) 1975. Rising Andean condor. Rev. value and date between laurel branches	0.10	0.20
51 (70)	5	Centavos (Al-Br) 1975, 1976. Type as No. 50 (twelve-sided)	0.10	0.20
52 (71)	10	Centavos (Al-Br) 1975, 1976. Type as No. 50	0.10	0.20
53 (72)	50	Centavos (Cu-Ni) 1975–1978. Type as No. 55	0.15	0.30

54 (73)	1	Peso (Cu-Ni) 1975. Bust right of Bernardo O'Higgins. In the field BERNARDO/O' Higgins. Rev. value and date between laurel branches	0.25	0.50
55 (70a)	5	Centavos (Al) 1976. Type as No. 51 (twelve-sided)	0.10	0.20
56 (71a)	10	Centavos (Al) 1976–1979. Type as No. 52	0.10	0.20
57 (73a)	1	Peso (Cu-Ni) 1976–1978. Type as No. 54, but in the field LIBERTADOR/B. O'HIGGINS	0.25	0.50

			XF	Unc
58 (74)	5 Pesos (Cu-Ni) 1976–1980. »Chilena« with broken chains		0.50	1.00
59 (75)	10 Pesos (Cu-Ni) 1976–1980. Type as No. 58		0.80	1.50

			Unc	Proof
60 (75a)	10 Pesos (Ag) 1976. Type as No. 58			180.00
61 (76)	50 Pesos (Au) 1976. Type as No. 58			260.00

			Unc	Proof
62 (77)	100 Pesos (Au) 1976. Type similar to No. 58		200.00	*1750.00*
63 (78)	500 Pesos (Au) 1976. Type similar to No. 58			*2600.00*

			XF	Unc
64 (72a)	50 Centavos (Al-Br) 1978–1980. Type as No. 53		0.10	0.20
65 (73b)	1 Peso (Al-Br) 1978, 1979. Type as No. 57		0.25	0.50
66 (79)	1 Onza (Au) 1979–1980. Trade Coin »Pillar Dollar«			*650.00*

67	50 Pesos (Al-Br) 1981		3.00

Chung Kuo 中國

The Chinese Empire, which existed long before our chronology, became the Republic of China in 1912. After the successful operations of the Communist People's Army, the People's Republic of China was proclaimed on 1st October 1949.

During the period of the Empire, and during the time of the Republic, various provinces were temporarily authorized to issue money. For convenience' sake the provincial issues have been listed separately; but in each case they have been coordinated with the issues of both the Empire and the Republic.

Capital: Peking.

10 Cash (Wen 文) = 1 Cent (Fen 分); 10 cents = 1 Chiao (角)

100 Cents = 1 Dollar (Yuan 圓)

10 Li (釐) = 1 Candareen (Fen)

10 Candareens = 1 Mace (Chien 錢)

10 Mace = 1 Tael (Liang 兩)

1 Dollar = 7 Mace and 2 Candareens

EMPIRE (until 1911)

The coins of the Empire bear a description of the Emperor's reign, rather than his name. Dates were reckoned from the beginning of each reign, and these are sometimes indicated, as are the dates according to the Chinese Calendar (sexagenary system – cycles of 60 years). The reigns of the last two Emperors fall within the period covered in this catalogue:

Te Tsung, Kuang Hsü era 光緒 (1875–1908) and

Pu Yih, Hsüan Tung era 宣統 (1909–1911)

			VF	XF
1	5	Candareens (Ag) 1903. Dragon and inscription 29TH YEAR OF KUANG HSÜ. HU POO. ℞ Chinese and Manchu characters, among which denomination and value. Trial piece (pattern)		450.00
2	1	Mace (Ag) 1903. Type as No. 1 Pattern		150.00
3	2	Mace (Ag) 1903. Type as No. 1 Pattern		200.00
4	5	Mace (Ag) 1903. Type as No. 1 Pattern		300.00
5	1	Tael (Ag) 1903. Type as No. 1 Pattern		600.00
6	1	Cash (Cu) 1905 (undated). Dragon. Chinese and Manchu characters, among which denomination and value	1.00	2.00
7	2	Cash (Cu) 1905 (undated). Type as No. 6	2.00	4.00
8	5	Cash (Cu) 1905 (undated). Dragon in dotted circle and inscription HU POO FIVE CASH. ℞ Chinese and Manchu characters, among which denomination, mint, and value	11.00	20.00
9	10	Cash (Cu) 1905 (undated). Type as No. 8, but obverse without dotted circle, and the inscription around giving the value TEN CASH	1.00	2.00
10	20	Cash (Cu) 1905 (undated). Type as No. 8, but in the obverse legend the value 20 CASH	18.00	35.00

| 10a | 20 | Cash (Cu) 1905 (undated). Type as No. 10, but the obverse without dotted circle | 1.00 | 2.00 |

			VF	XF
11	1	Cash (Bra) 1908. Dragon. ℞ Chinese characters, among which denomination, date, and value	2.50	5.00
12	2	Cash (Cu) 1905–1907. Dragon. ℞ Chinese and Manchu characters, among which denomination, date, and value	4.00	8.00
13	5	Cash (Cu) 1905–1908. Dragon in dotted circle and inscription TAI-CHING-TI-KUO COPPER COIN as well as four Chinese characters. ℞ same as No. 12	3.50	7.00
14	10	Cash (Cu) 1905–1908. Type as No. 13	1.50	2.50
15	20	Cash (Cu) 1905–1908. Type as No. 13	18.00	32.00
16	1	Mace (Ag) 1906. Dragon in dotted circle and inscription TAI-CHING-TI-KUO SILVER COIN as well as four Chinese characters. ℞ Chinese and Manchu characters, among which denomination, date, and value	5.00	8.00
17	2	Mace (Ag) 1906. Type as No. 16	9.00	14.00
18	5	Mace (Ag) 1906. Type as No. 16	16.00	22.00
19	1	Tael (Ag) 1906. Type as No. 16, but the reverse with lined triangle border	380.00	700.00
20	1	Tael (Au) 1906, 1907. Dragon. ℞ Chinese characters, among which denomination, date, and value	2000.00	3500.00
21	10	Cents (Ag) 1907. Dragon in dotted circle and inscription TAI-CHING-TI-KUO SILVER COIN as well as four Chinese characters. ℞ Chinese and Manchu characters, among which denomination, date, and value	70.00	115.00
22	20	Cents (Ag) 1907. Type as No. 21	70.00	110.00
23	50	Cents (Ag) 1907. Type as No. 21	175.00	220.00
24	1	Dollar (Ag) 1907, 1908. Type as No. 21, but the reverse with lined triangle border	220.00	360.00
25	10	Cents (Ag) 1908 (undated). Dragon in dotted circle and inscription TAI-CHING-TI-KUO SILVER COIN as well as four Chinese characters. ℞ Chinese characters and, in centre, four Manchu characters, among which denomination and value	22.00	30.00
26	20	Cents (Ag) 1908 (undated). Type as No. 25	40.00	50.00

			VF	XF
27	1	Dollar (Ag) 1908 (undated). Type as No. 25	30.00	45.00
28	1	Cash (Cu) 1909. Type as No. 11, but on the reverse the Chinese characters read Hsüan Tung instead of Kuang Hsü	26.00	50.00
28a	2	Cash (Cu) 1909. Dragon. ℞ Dynasty and coin description in Chinese characters in the circle of dots. In the legend four Manchu characters, including year and denomination in Chinese characters	–.–	–.–
29	5	Cash (Cu) 1909. Type as No. 13, but the obverse inscription has Chinese characters reading Hsüan Tung instead of Kuang Hsü	60.00	90.00

			VF	XF
30	10	Cash (Cu) 1909. Type as No. 29	1.50	2.50
30a	10	Cash (Cu) 1909. Type as No. 30, but with a rosette in the centre on ℞	25.00	40.00
31	20	Cash (Cu) 1909. Type as No. 29	1.20	2.00
32	1	Cash (Cu) (undated). Dragon. ℞ Chinese characters, among which value	1.50	2.50

			VF	XF
33	5	Li (Cu) 1909–1911 (undated). Dragon in dotted circle and inscription of four Chinese characters. ℞ Chinese characters, among which value	–.–	–.–
34	1	Cent (Cu) 1909–1911 (undated). Type as No. 33	–.–	–.–
35	2	Cents (Cu) 1909–1911 (undated). Type as No. 33	–.–	–.–
36	$1/_{10}$	Dollar (Ag) 1910 (undated). Dragon in dotted circle and inscription $1/_{10}$ DOL. as well as four Chinese characters. ℞ Chinese and Manchu characters, among which denomination and value	80.00	140.00
37	¼	Dollar (Ag) 1910 (undated). Type as No. 36, but in the obverse inscription ¼ DOL.	75.00	100.00
38	½	Dollar (Ag) 1910 (undated). Type as No. 36, but in the obverse inscription ½ DOLLAR	50.00	80.00
39	1	Dollar (Ag) 1910 (undated). Type as No. 36, but in the obverse inscription $ 1	185.00	250.00
40	1	Cash (Cu) (undated). Denomination in Chinese characters. ℞ value in Chinese characters. With centre round hole	2.20	4.00
41	5	Cash (Cu) 1911. Dragon in circle and inscription of four Chinese characters. ℞ Chinese characters, among which date and value	160.00	200.00

42	10	Cash (Cu) 1911. Type as No. 41	5.00	8.00
43	20	Cash (Cu) 1911. Type as No. 41	265.00	350.00
44	1	Dollar (Ag) 1911. Dragon, inscription below ONE DOLLAR. ℞ Chinese and Manchu characters, among which denomination, date, and value. Pattern	–.–	–.–

			VF	XF

45 10 Cents (Ag) 1911. Dragon (new design); in the centre, value in Chinese characters. ℞ Chinese characters, among which denomination, date, and value   10.00   15.00

46 20 Cents (Ag) 1911. Type as No. 45   18.00   30.00

47 50 Cents (Ag) 1911. Type as No. 45   170.00   220.00

48 1 Dollar (Ag) 1911. Dragon (again of different design); in the centre, value in Chinese characters, below, ONE DOLLAR. ℞ Chinese and Manchu characters, among which denomination and date   14.00   20.00

49 1 Cash (Bra) 1909–1911 (undated). Four Chinese characters. ℞ on right and left one Manchu character. In the centre, square hole. Cast   6.00   10.00

Anhwei 安 徽 (月完)

			VF	XF
1	5	Cash (Cu) (undated). Dragon in dotted circle, inscription above ANHWEI. Ɍ Chinese characters and two Manchu characters, among which province and denomination as well as value	85.00	150.00
2	10	Cash (Cu) (undated). Dragon in circle of dots and legend AN-HWEI. Ɍ government era and coin description in the way of four Chinese characters in the circle of dots. In the centre a rosette. In the legend name of province and denomination by way of nine Chinese characters. In addition two Manchu characters in the legend	1.50	2.50
2a	10	Cash (Cu) (undated). As type No. 2, but denomination in the legend of Ɍ only by way of six Chinese characters	4.50	9.00
2b	10	Cash (Cu) (undated). Dragon in the circle of dots and legend AN-HWEI TEN CASH. Ɍ government era and coin designation by way of four Chinese characters in the circle of dots. In the centre two Manchu characters. In the legend description of province and denomination by way of eleven Chinese characters	–.–	–.–
2c	10	Cash (Cu) (undated). Dragon (changed design, without circle of dots) and legend AN-HWEI 10 CASH. Ɍ as type No. 2a	4.50	9.00
2d	10	Cash (Cu) (undated). Obverse as type No. 2c, Ɍ as type No. 2	–.–	–.–
3	10	Cash (Cu) (undated). Dragon in the circle of dots and legend AN-HWEI ONE CEN. Ɍ as type No. 2b	35.00	55.00
3a	10	Cash (Cu) (undated). As type No. 3, but legend of the obverse. AN-HWEI ONE SEN	40.00	60.00
4	20	Cash (Cu) (undated). Similar to type No. 1	200.00	300.00
5	10	Cash (Cu) 1906. Dragon in dotted circle and legend TAI-CHING-TI-KUO COPPER COIN, including four Chinese characters	2.00	4.00
6	20	Cash (Cu) 1906. Type as No. 5	65.00	120.00
7	10	Cash (Cu) 1909. Type as No. 5, but in		

the obverse legend the Chinese characters read Hsüan Tung instead of
Kuang Hsü

			VF	XF
			20.00	40.00
8	20	Cash (Cu) 1909. Type as No. 7	25.00	50.00

Chekiang 浙江 (浙)

1	10	Cash (Cu) (undated). Dragon. ℞ Chinese characters, among which province and denomination as well as value	1.20	2.40
1a	10	Cash (Cu) (undated). As type No. 1, in centre of ℞, however, a circle	3.00	6.00
1b	10	Cash (Cu) (undated). As type No. 1, but the centre of ℞ level	–.–	–.–
1c	10	Cash (Cu) (undated). As type No. 1, but in the legend of ℞ instead of six, eight Chinese characters	4.00	8.00
2	20	Cash (Cu) (undated). Type as No. 1	40.00	55.00
3	5	Cents (Ag) 1902 (undated). Dragon and inscription CHE-KIANG PROVINCE 3,2 CANDAREENS. ℞ Chinese characters, among which province and denomination as well as value. In the centre, four Manchu characters	12.00	20.00
3a	5	Cents (Ag) 1902 (undated). Type as No. 3, but now in the legend on obverse with the denomination 3.6 CANDAREENS. Trial strike!	–.–	–.–
4	10	Cents (Ag) 1902 (undated). Type as No. 3, but value in the obverse inscription 7,2 CANDAREENS	30.00	60.00
5	20	Cents (Ag) 1902 (undated). Type as No. 3, but value in the obverse inscription 1 MACE AND 4,4 CANDAREENS	80.00	160.00

			VF	XF
6	50	Cents (Ag) 1902 (undated). Type as No. 3, but the value in the obverse inscription 3 MACE AND 6 CANDA-REENS	130.00	250.00
7	1	Dollar (Ag) 1902 (undated). Type as No. 3, but value in the obverse inscription 7 MACE AND 2 CANDA-REENS		
		Obverse legend:		
		a) CHEH-KIANG PROVINCE		3000.00
		b) CHE-KIANG PROVINCE		3400.00
8	2	Cash (Cu) 1906. Dragon. ℞ Chinese and Manchu characters, among which denomination, date, and value; in the centre, Chinese character for Chekiang	14.00	20.00
9	5	Cash (Cu) 1906. Dragon in dotted circle and inscription TAI-CHING-TI-KUO COPPER COIN as well as four Chinese characters. ℞ as type No. 8	8.50	14.00
10	10	Cash (Cu) 1906. Type as No. 9	5.00	9.00
11	20	Cash (Cu) 1906. Type as No. 9	42.00	75.00

Chihli 智利 (直)

			VF	XF
1	1	Cash (Cu) 1896–1908 (undated). Chinese characters in dotted circle and ornamental border. ℞ name of province and value in Chinese characters	3.50	7.00
2	10	Cash (Cu) 1896–1908 (undated). Dragon in dotted circle and inscription PEI YANG TEN CASH. ℞ Chinese and Manchu characters, among which name of province and denomination as well as value	1.20	2.40
2a	10	Cash (Cu) (undated). Type as No. 2, but in the centre of ℞ additionally a rosette	–.–	–.–
3	20	Cash (Cu) 1896–1908 (undated). Type as No. 2	10.00	20.00
4	5	Cents (Ag) 1900. Dragon and inscription 26th YEAR OF KUANG HSÜ PEI YANG. ℞ Chinese characters, among which name of province and denomination as well as value; in the centre, four Manchu characters	20.00	40.00
5	10	Cents (Ag) 1900. Type as No. 4	–.–	–.–
6	20	Cents (Ag) 1900, 1903. Type as No. 4	30.00	60.00

| 7 | 50 Cents (Ag) 1899. Type as No. 4, but in the obverse inscription 25th YEAR OF KUANG HSÜ PEI YANG | **VF** 40.00 | **XF** 60.00 |

8	1 Dollar (Ag) 1900, 1903, 1907, 1908. Type as No. 4	20.00	30.00
9	5 Cents (Ag) 1900. Dragon and inscription PEKING 3,6 CANDAREENS. ℞ Chinese characters, among which name of province and denomination as well as date and value. In the centre, four Manchu characters. Pattern	200.00	250.00
10	10 Cents (Ag) 1900. Type as No. 9, but in the obverse inscription PEKING 7,2 CANDAREENS	–.–	–.–
11	20 Cents (Ag) 1900. Type as No. 9, but in the obverse inscription PEKING 1 MACE AND 4,4 CANDAREENS. Pattern.	–.–	–.–
12	50 Cents (Ag) 1900. Type as No. 9, but in the obverse inscription PEKING 3 MACE AND 6 CANDAREENS. Pattern.	–.–	–.–
13	1 Dollar (Ag) 1900. Type as No. 9, but in the obverse inscription PEKING 7 MACE AND 2 CANDAREENS. Pattern.	–.–	–.–
14	1 Tael (Ag) 1907. Dragon and inscription 33RD YEAR OF KUANG HSÜ PEI YANG. ℞ Chinese and Manchu characters, among which name of province and denomination as well as value	1500.00	2000.00
15	1 Cash (Cu) 1908. Dragon. ℞ name of province, date, and value in Chinese characters	4.00	8.00

			VF	XF
16	5	Cash (Cu) 1906. Dragon in dotted circle and inscription TAI-CHING-TI-KUO COPPER COIN as well as four Chinese characters. ℞ Chinese and Manchu characters, among which denomination and value, in the centre, Chinese characters for Chihli	5.00	10.00
17	10	Cash (Cu) 1906. Type as No. 16	1.20	2.00
18	20	Cash (Cu) 1906. Type as No. 16	35.00	70.00

Chingkiang or Tsingkiang 淸江 (淮)

			VF	XF
1	10	Cash (Cu) (undated). Dragon and inscription CHING-KIANG. ℞ Chinese characters and two Manchu characters, among which name of province and denomination as well as value	1.50	3.00
1a	10	Cash (Cu) (undated). Type as No. 1, but centre of ℞ level	2.50	5.00
2	10	Cash (Cu) 1905 (undated). Dragon and inscription TSING-KIANG TEN CASH. ℞ Chinese and Manchu characters, among which name of province and denomination as well as value	–.–	–.–
3	10	Cash (Cu) 1906. Dragon in dotted circle and inscription TAI-CHING-TI-KUO COPPER COIN as well as four Chinese characters. ℞ Chinese and Manchu characters, among which denomination, date, and value. In the centre, Chinese characters for Tsing-kiang	1.60	3.20
3a	10	Cash (Cu) (undated). Type as No. 3, but centre of ℞ level	–.–	–.–
4	10	Cash (Cu) 1906. Dragon in dotted circle and inscription TAI-CHING-TI-KUO COPPER COIN as well as four Chinese characters. ℞ Chinese and Manchu characters, among which denomination, date and value. In the centre, a Chinese character for Ching-kiang	1.00	2.00

Fookien (Fukien) 福 建 (閩)

			VF	XF
1	5	Cash (Cu) undated. Dragon in dotted circle and inscription FOO-KIEN as well as value. ℞ name of province and denomination as well as value in Chinese characters	8.00	14.00

			VF	XF
2	10	Cash (Cu) undated. Dragon in dotted circle and inscription FOO-KIEN 10 CASH. ℞ Chinese characters and two Manchu characters, among which name of province and denomination as well as value	1.50	3.00
2a	10	Cash (Cu) (undated). Type as No. 2, but legend of obverse FOO-KIEN 10 CASHES	11.00	20.00
3	20	Cash (Cu) undated. Type as No. 2	24.00	40.00
4	10	Cash (Cu) 1896–1908 (undated). Dragon in dotted circle and inscription F. K. CUSTOM-HOUSE 10 CASH. ℞ name of province and denomination as well as value in Chinese characters and two Manchu characters	1.20	2.50
5	10	Cash (Cu) 1896–1908 (undated). Type as No. 4, but in the obverse inscription FOO-KIEN CUSTOM HOUSE	3.00	3.00
5a	10	Cash (Cu) (undated). Dragon in circle of dots and legend FOO-KIEN CUSTOM 10 CASH. ℞ government era and coin designation by way of four Chinese characters in circle of dots. In the centre two Manchu characters. In the legend Chinese characters, among others province designation and denomination	85.00	150.00
6	5	Cents (Ag) 1902 (undated). Dragon and inscription FOO-KIEN PROVINCE 3,6 CANDAREENS. ℞ name of province and denomination as well as value in Chinese characters. In the centre, four Manchu characters. In the reverse legend, above, four characters instead of the five on the 1898 issue	4.50	6.50
7	10	Cents (Ag) 1902 (undated). Type as No. 6, but in the obverse legend FOO-KIEN PROVINCE 7,2 CANDAREENS	6.50	10.00

			VF	XF
8	20	Cents (Ag) 1902 (undated). Type as No. 6, but in the obverse legend FOO-KIEN PROVINCE 1 MACE AND 4,4 CANDAREENS	6.00	9.00
9	2	Cash (Cu) 1906, 1908. Dragon. ℞ Chinese and Manchu characters, among which denomination, date and value. In the centre, Chinese characters for FOO-KIEN	4.00	9.00
10	5	Cash (Cu) 1906, 1908. Dragon in dotted circle and inscription TAI-CHING-TI-KUO COPPER COIN as well as four Chinese characters. R as type No. 9	6.00	11.00

11	10	Cash (Cu) 1906, 1908. Type as No. 10	1.50	2.50
12	20	Cash (Cu) 1906, 1908. Type as No. 10	3.00	6.50
13	10	Cash (Cu) 1909. Type as No. 10, but in the obverse legend the Chinese characters read Hsüan Tung instead of Kuang Hsü	45.00	90.00
14	1	Cash (Bra) 1909–1911 (undated). Government era and coin designation by way of four Chinese characters. ℞ left and right one Manchu character each. In the centre square hole. Casting	–.–	–.–
15	1	Cash (Bra) 1909–1911 (undated). Type as No. 14, but embossed and in the centre a round hole in a square border	25.00	50.00

			VF	XF
1	10	Cash (Bra) 1903–1906. Dragon and inscription FEN-TIEN PROVINCE TEN CASH. ℞ name of province and denomination as well as date and value in Chinese characters	65.00	120.00
1a	10	Cash (Bra) undated. Dragon and legend FEN-TIEN PROVINCE TEN CASH. ℞ two Chinese characters. Pseudo coin?	–.–	–.–
1b	10	Cash (Cu) undated. Government era and coin designation in four Chinese characters. ℞ sixteen Chinese characters as legend, among others province designation and denomination. With central square hole.	35.00	70.00
2	1	Tael (Cu) 1903. Dragon and inscription FEN-TIEN PROVINCE ONE TAEL. ℞ Chinese characters and, in the centre, four Manchu characters, among which name of province and denomination as well as date and value. Pattern. Only 3 specimens known!	–.–	–.–

			VF	XF
3	10	Cash (Cu) 1904. Dragon and inscription FUNG-TIEN PROVINCE TEN CASH. ℞ as type No. 1	5.50	10.50
4	20	Cash (Cu) 1904, 1905. Dragon and inscription FUNG-TIEN PROVINCE 20 CASH. ℞ as type No. 1	9.00	12.50
5	20	Cents (Ag) 1904. Dragon and inscription FUNG-TIEN PROVINCE 1 MACE AND 4,4 CANDAREENS. ℞ name of province and denomination as well as date and value in Chinese characters. In the centre, two Manchu characters	15.00	20.00

			VF	XF
6	1	Dollar (Ag) 1903. Dragon and inscription FUNG-TIEN PROVINCE 7 MACE AND 2 CANDAREENS. ℞ as type No. 5	70.00	100.00
7	50	Cents (Ag) 1906. Dragon and inscription in Chinese characters (name of province and date). ℞ in the centre, value in Chinese characters; around, inscription in Manchu characters	85.00	120.00
8	10	Cash (Cu) 1905, 1907. Dragon in dotted circle and inscription TAI-CHING-TI-KUO COPPER COIN, as well as four Chinese characters. ℞ Chinese and Manchu characters, among which denomination, date, and value. In the centre, Chinese character for Fungtien	5.50	9.00
9	20	Cash (Cu) 1905, 1907. As type No. 8	8.50	12.50
10	5	Cash (Cu) 1909. As type No. 8, but in the obverse legend the Chinese characters read Hsüan Tung instead of Kuang Hsü	70.00	120.00
11	10	Cash (Cu) 1909. As type No. 10	8.00	15.00
12	20	Cash (Cu) 1909. As type No. 10	42.00	80.00

Heilungkiang 黑龍江

1	50	Cents (Ag) 1903 (undated). Dragon and inscription HEILUNGKIANG PROVINCE 3 MACE AND CANDAREENS 6. ℞ Chinese characters, among which name of province and denomination as well as value. Pattern	–.–	–.–

Honan 河南 (汴)

1	1	Cash (Bra) 1908. Dragon. ℞ government era, date and denomination in Chinese characters. In the Centre a Chinese character for Honan in the circle of dots	15.00	25.00
2	10	Cash (Cu) 1896–1908 (undated). Dragon in dotted circle and inscription HO-NAN TEN CASH. ℞ Chinese characters, among which name of province and denomination as well as value. In the centre, Yin-Yang symbol	1.00	2.00

				VF	XF

3 10 Cash (Cu) 1896–1908 (undated). Dragon and inscription HO-NAN TEN CASH as well as 8 stars. ℞ name of province and denomination as well as value in Chinese characters. In the centre, Yin-Yang symbol — **VF 2.00 / XF 4.00**

3a 10 Cash (Bra) (undated). Dragon and legend HOU-NAN TEN CASH. ℞ government era and coin designation by way of four Chinese characters in the circle of dots. In the centre the Yin-Yang symbol. In the legend province designation and denomination in Chinese characters. In addition in the legend, right and left, one Manchu character each. — **–.– / –.–**

4 20 Cash (Cu) 1896–1908 (?) (undated). Type as No. 3 — **3.00 / 6.00**

5 10 Cash (Cu) 1906. Dragon in dotted circle and inscription TAI-CHING-TI-KUO COPPER COIN as well as four Chinese characters. ℞ Chinese and Manchu characters, among which denomination, date and value. In the centre, Chinese character for Honan — **1.00 / 2.00**

6 10 Cash (Cu) 1909, 1911. Type as No. 5, but in the obverse legend the Chinese characters read Hsüan Tung instead of Kuang Hsü — **5.00 / 10.00**

7 20 Cash (Cu) 1909 (CD). Type as No. 6 — **–.– / –.–**

Hunan 湖 南 (湘)

1 10 Cash (Cu) 1896–1908 (undated). Dragon in dotted circle and inscription HU-NAN TEN CASH. ℞ Chinese characters and, in the centre, two Manchu characters, among which name of province and denomination as well as value — **5.00 / 10.00**

1a 10 Cash (Cu) undated. Type similar to No. 1, but on ℞ the two Manchu characters not in the centre, but in the legend and in centre a rosette — **5.00 / 10.00**

2 10 Cash (Cu) 1896–1908 (undated). Type as No. 1, but different design for the dragon — **3.50 / 7.00**

2a 10 Cash (Cu) 1896–1908 (undated). Type similar to No. 2, but design of the dragon changed once more, as well as — **3.50 / 7.00**

			VF	XF
		in the legend of Ɍ nine instead of eight Chinese characters	2.50	5.00
2b	10	Cash (Cu) (undated). Type similar to No. 2a, but in the legend of Ɍ ten instead of nine Chinese characters	4.50	9.00
2c	10	Cash (Cu) (undated). Type similar to No. 2, but on Ɍ the two Manchu characters in the legend and in the centre a rosette	1.25	2.50
3	5	Cents (Ag) 1902 (undated). Dragon and inscription HU-NAN PROVINCE 3,6 CANDAREENS. Ɍ Chinese characters and, in the centre, four Manchu characters, among which name of province and denomination as well as value	–.–	–.–
4	10	Cents (Ag) 1902 (undated). Type as No. 3, but in the obverse legend HU-NAN PROVINCE 7,2 CANDAREENS	12.50	22.00
5	20	Cents (Ag) 1902 (undated). Type as No. 3, but in the obverse legend HU-NAN PROVINCE 1 MACE 4,4 CANDAREENS	30.00	45.00
6	10	Cash (Cu) 1906. Dragon in dotted circle and inscription TAI-CHING-TI-KUO COPPER COIN as well as four Chinese characters. Ɍ Chinese and Manchu characters, among which denomination, date, and value. In the centre, Chinese character for Hunan	10.00	20.00
7	1	Mace (Ag) 1906 (undated). Two lines each with two Chinese characters, among which name of province. Ɍ value in two Chinese characters. The border of the obverse and the reverse is made up of one dotted circle between two circles of elongated dots. There are three variants due to different arrangement of characters; partial use of new characters	–.–	–.–
8	2	Mace (Ag) 1906 (undated). Type as No. 7, but on the reverse two lines of two Chinese characters each; also two variants	20.00	35.00
9	3	Mace (Ag) 1906 (undated). Type as No. 7, but on the obverse and reverse two horizontal lines of three Chinese characters each; also two variants	20.00	35.00
10	4	Mace (Ag) 1906 (undated). Type as No. 9; also two variants	20.00	35.00

			VF	XF
11	5 Mace (Ag) 1906 (undated). Type as No. 9; also two variants		**20.00**	**35.00**
12	6 Mace (Ag) 1906 (undated). Type as No. 9; also two variants		20.00	35.00
13	7 Mace (Ag) 1906 (undated). Type as No. 9; also two variants		20.00	35.00
14	8 Mace (Ag) 1906 (undated). Type as No. 9; also two variants		20.00	35.00
15	9 Mace (Ag) 1906 (undated). Type as No. 9; also two variants		20.00	35.00
16	1 Tael (Ag) 1906 (undated). Type as No. 9; also two variants		70.00	100.00
16a	1 Tael (Ag) 1906 (undated). Three horizontal rows at four Chinese characters each, among others province designation and denomination. ℞ smooth		–.–	–.–
17	1 Mace (Ag) 1908 (undated). Two lines of two Chinese characters each, among which name of province. ℞ value in two Chinese characters. The border of the obverse and the reverse is made up of one dotted circle between two circles of elongated dots. Similar to type No. 7		–.–	–.–
18	2 Mace (Ag) 1908 (undated). Type as No. 17, but also on the reverse two lines of two Chinese characters each. Similar to type No. 8		–.–	–.–
19	1 Mace (Ag) 1908 (?) (undated). Two horizontal lines of three Chinese characters, each among which name of province. ℞ value in two Chinese characters. The border of the obverse and the reverse is made up of one dotted circle between two circles of elongated dots Coins 19–28 were issued by the mint of Chien-Y in Changsha.		–.–	–.–
20	2 Mace (Ag) 1908 (?) (undated). Type as No. 19, but on the ℞ two lines of two Chinese caracters each		–.–	–.–
21	3 Mace (Ag) 1908 (?) (undated). Type as No. 19, but on the ℞ two horizontal lines of three Chinese characters each		–.–	–.–
22	4 Mace (Ag) 1908 (?) (undated). Type as No. 21		–.–	–.–
23	5 Mace (Ag) 1908 (?) (undated). Type as No. 21		–.–	–.–
24	6 Mace (Ag) 1908 (?) (undated). Type as No. 21		–.–	–.–
25	7 Mace (Ag) 1908 (?) (undated). Type as No. 21		–.–	–.–

			VF	XF
26	8 Mace (Ag) 1908 (?) (undated). Type as No. 21		–.–	–.–
27	9 Mace (Ag) 1908 (?) (undated). Type as No. 21		–.–	–.–
28	1 Tael (Ag) 1908 (?) (undated). Type as No. 21		–.–	–.–
29	1 Mace (Ag) 1909 (undated). Two vertical lines of three Chinese characters each, among which name of province. ℞ two horizontal lines of three Chinese characters each, among which value. The border of the obverse and the reverse is made up of one dotted circle between two circles of elongated dots. (Coins Nos. 29–38 were issued by the Ta Ching Government Bank in Changsha).		–.–	–.–
30	2 Mace (Ag) 1909 (undated). Type as No. 29		–.–	–.–
31	3 Mace (Ag) 1909 (undated). Type as No. 29		–.–	–.–
32	4 Mace (Ag) 1909 (undated). Type as No. 29		–.–	–.–
33	5 Mace (Ag) 1909 (undated). Type as No. 29		–.–	–.–
34	6 Mace (Ag) 1909 (undated). Type as No. 29		–.–	–.–
35	7 Mace (Ag) 1909 (undated). Type as No. 29		–.–	–.–
36	8 Mace (Ag) 1909 (undated). Type as No. 29		–.–	–.–
37	9 Mace (Ag) 1909 (undated). Type as No. 29		–.–	–.–
38	1 Tael (Ag) 1909 (undated). Type as No. 29		95.00	150.00

Hupeh 湖北 (鄂)

1	1 Cash (Cu) 1896–1908 (undated). Dragon and inscription HU-PEH PROVINCE ONE CASH. ℞ name of province and denomination as well as value in Chinese characters		4.00	8.00

2 10 Cash (Cu) 1896–1908 (undated). Dragon and inscription HU-PEH PROVINCE TEN CASH. ℞ name of province and denomination as well as value in Chinese characters and two Manchu characters. In the centre, a rosette (several variants)

2a 10 Cash (Cu) 1896–1908 (undated). Type similar to No. 2, but on ℞ in place of the rosette, a square in a circle

2b 10 Cash (Cu–Bra) undated. Type as No. 2, but changed design of the dragon

2c 10 Cash (Cu) undated. Type similar to No. 2, but dragon in circle of dots

	VF	XF
2	4.00	8.00
2a	2.00	4.00
2b	1.25	2.50
2c	4.50	9.00

3 1 Tael (Ag) 1904. Value in Chinese characters between two dragons and inscription HU-PEH PROVINCE ONE TAEL as well as two Manchu characters. ℞ Chinese characters and, in the centre, four Manchu characters, among which name of province and denomination as well as date and value 120.00   170.00

4 1 Cash (Cu) 1906. Dragon. ℞ Chinese characters 3.00   6.00

5	2	Cash (Cu) 1906. Dragon. ℞ Chinese and Manchu characters, among which denomination, date, and value. In the centre, Chinese character for Hupeh	VF	XF
			45.00	70.00
6	5	Cash (Cu) 1906–1908. Dragon in dotted circle and inscription TAI-CHING-TI-KUO COPPER COIN as well as four Chinese characters. ℞ Chinese and Manchu characters, among which denomination, date, and value. In the centre, Chinese character for Hupeh	4.50	9.00

7	10	Cash (Cu) 1906–1908. Type as No. 6	1.25	2.50
8	20	Cash (Cu) 1906–1908. Type as No. 6	70.00	100.00
9	1	Cash (Bra) 1908. Dragon. ℞ Chinese characters, among which date and value	7.00	12.00
10	5	Cash (Cu) 1909, 1911. Type as No. 6, but in the obverse legend the Chinese characters read Hsüan Tung instead of Kuang Hsü	3.50	7.00
11	10	Cash (Cu) 1909, 1911. Type as No. 10	2.00	4.00
12	20	Cash (Cu) 1909–1911. Type as No. 10	3.50	7.00
13	10	Cents (Ag) 1909 (undated). Dragon and inscription HU-PEH PROVINCE 7,2 CANDAREENS. ℞ Chinese characters and, in the centre, four Manchu characters, among which name of province and denomination as well as value	30.00	40.00
14	20	Cents (Ag) 1909 (undated). Dragon and inscription HU-PEH PROVINCE 1 MACE AND 4,4 CANDAREENS. ℞ as type No. 13	160.00	225.00
15	1	Dollar (Ag) 1909 (undated). Dragon and inscription HU-PEH PROVINCE 7 MACE AND 2 CANDAREENS. ℞ as type No. 13	30.00	40.00
16	10	Cents (Ag) 1911. Dragon. ℞ Chinese characters, among which name of province and denomination as well as date	7.00	10.00

			VF	XF
1	1	Tael (Ag) 1905. Dragon. ℞ Chinese characters, among which name of province and denomination as well as date and value	–.–	–.–

Kiangnan 江 南 (甯)

			VF	XF
1	5	Cents (Ag) 1900, 1901. Dragon and legend KIANG NAN PROVINCE 3,6 CANDAREENS. ℞ Chinese characters and, in centre, four Manchu characters, among which name of province and denomination as well as date and value		
2	10	Cents (Ag) 1900, 1901. Dragon and inscription KIANG NAN PROVINCE, 7,2 CANDAREENS. ℞ as type No. 1	7.00	10.00
			5.00	7.00

			VF	XF
3	20	Cents (Ag) 1900, 1901. Dragon and inscription KIANG NAN PROVINCE 1 MACE AND 4,4 CANDAREENS. ℞ as type No. 1	8.00	12.00
4	50	Cents (Ag) 1900. Dragon and inscription KIANG NAN PROVINCE 3 MACE AND 6 CANDAREENS. ℞ as type No. 1	170.00	250.00
5	1	Dollar (Ag) 1900, 1901. Dragon and inscription KIANG NAN PROVINCE 7 MACE AND 2 CANDAREENS. ℞ as type No. 1	30.00	40.00
6	10	Cents (Ag) 1901–1903. As type No. 2, but the reverse legend has in addition the letters HAH	8.00	10.50
7	20	Cents (Ag) 1901–1903. As type No. 3, but the reverse legend has in addition the letters HAH	6.00	8.50
8	1	Dollar (Ag) 1901–1903. As type No. 5,		

			VF	**XF**

		but the reverse legend has in addition the letters HAH	26.00	38.00
9	10	Cents (Ag) 1904. As type No. 2, but the reverse legend has in addition the letters HAH and TH	4.00	6.00
10	20	Cents (Ag) 1904. As type No. 3, but the reverse legend has in addition the letters HAH and TH	9.00	15.00
11	1	Dollar (Ag) 1904. As type No. 5, but the reverse legend has in addition the letters		
		a) HAH and TH	40.00	50.00
		b) HAH and CH	32.00	40.00
12	10	Cents (Ag) 1905. As type No. 2, but the reverse legend has in addition the letters SY	4.00	6.00
13	20	Cents (Ag) 1905. As type No. 3, but the reverse legend has in addition the letters SY	15.00	20.00
14	1	Dollar (Ag) 1905. As type No. 5, but the reverse legend has in addition the letters SY	30.00	40.00

15	10	Cash (Cu) 1902–1905. Dragon in dotted circle and inscription KIANG-NAN TEN CASH. ℞ Chinese characters and, in centre, two Manchu characters, among which name of province, date, and denomination as well as value	1.25	2.50
15a	10	Cash (Cu) (undated). As type No. 15, but undated	20.00	40.00
16	10	Cash (Cu) 1902–1905. Dragon (new design) and inscription KIANG-NAN TEN CASH; a Manchu character on right and left. ℞ Chinese characters, among which name of province and denomination as well as date and value. In centre, rosette	–.–	–.–
16a	10	Cash (Cu) 1906. Obverse as type No. 16. ℞ Chinese and Manchu characters, among which denomination, date, and value	2.50	5.00

			VF	XF
16 b	10	Cash (Cu) 1905. Dragon (repeated change in design) in the circle of dots and legend KIANG NAN TEN CASH. ℞ Type as No. 16 a	–.–	–.–
17	20	Cash (Cu) 1902–1905. As type No. 16	50.00	90.00
18	1	Cash (Bra) 1908. Dragon. ℞ date and value in Chinese characters. In centre, Chinese character for Kiangnan	5.00	10.00
19	5	Cash (Cu) 1906–1908. Dragon in dotted circle and inscription TAI-CHING-TI-KUO COPPER COIN as well as four Chinese characters. ℞ Chinese and Manchu characters, among which denomination, date, and value. In centre, Chinese character for Kiangnan	55.00	100.00
20	10	Gash (Cu) 1906–1908. As type No. 19	1.00	2.00
21	10	Cash (Cu) 1909. As type No. 20, but the Chinese characters in the obverse inscription read Hsüan Tung instead of Kuang Hsü	2.00	4.00
22	20	Cash (Cu) 1909. As type No. 21	–.–	–.–
23	10	Cents (Ag) 1909 (undated). Dragon and inscription KIANG NAN PROV-INCE 7,2 CANDAREENS. ℞ Chinese characters and, in centre, four Manchu characters, among which name of province and denomination as well as value	12.50	18.00
24	20	Cents (Ag) 1909 (undated). Dragon and inscription KIANG NAN PROV-INCE 1 MACE 4,4 CANDAREENS. ℞ as type No. 23	16.50	25.00

Kiangsee (Kiangsi) 江西 (贛)

1	10	Cash (Cu) 1896–1908 (undated). Drag-on and inscription KIANG SI 10 CASH as well as two stars on right

			VF	XF
		and on left. ℞ Chinese characters and two Manchu characters, among which name of province and denomination as well as value. In centre, rosette	4.00	7.00
2	10	Cash (Cu) (undated). Type similar to No. 1, but dragon of varied type	–.–	–.–
3	10	Cash (Cu) undated. Type similar to No. 2, but in the centre in place of the rosette, two Manchu characters	–.–	–.–
4	10	Cash (Cu) undated. Type similar to No. 1, but on ℞ the two Manchu characters in the centre	–.–	–.–
5	10	Cash (Cu) 1896–1908 (undated). Dragon and legend KIANG-SEE PROVINCE TEN CASH. ℞ Chinese and two Manchu characters, among others province and coin designation as well as denomination. In the centre a rosette	2.00	4.00
6	10	Cash (Cu) undated. Obverse Type as No. 5, but changed design of the dragon. ℞ government era and coin designation by way of four Chinese characters in the circle of dots. In the centre two Manchu and in the legend eight Chinese characters, among others province designation and denomination	–.–	–.–
7	20	Cash (Cu) undated. Type as No. 5	50.00	90.00
8	10	Cash (Cu) 1906. Dragon in dotted circle and legend TAI-CHING TI-KUO COPPER COIN as well as four Chinese characters. ℞ Chinese and Manchu characters, among others coin designation, year and denomination. In the centre Chinese character for Kiang-See	8.00	15.00
9	10	Cash (Cu) undated. Dragon (changed design) and legend KIANG-SI 10 CASH. ℞ province and coin designation as well as denomination in Chinese characters	–.–	–.–

Kiangsoo 江蘇〔蘇〕

			VF	XF
1	2	Cash (Cu) undated. Dragon. ℞ value in Chinese characters	135.00	200.00
2	5	Cash (Cu) undated. Dragon and inscription KIANG-SOO. ℞ name of province and value in Chinese characters	40.00	70.00

			VF	XF
2a	5	Cash (Cu) undated. Type similar to No. 2, but with changed design of the dragon	–.–	–.–
3	10	Cash (Cu) undated. Dragon of varied type and inscription KIANG-SOO as well as value. ℞ name of province and value in Chinese characters	2.50	5.00
3a	10	Cash (Cu) undated. Dragon (new type) in dotted circle and inscription KIANG-SOO TEN CASH. ℞ Chinese characters and two Manchu characters, right and left, among which name of province, denomination, and value. In centre, rosette	0.60	1.20
3b	10	Cash (Cu) undated. Type as No. 3a, but on ℞ the two Manchu characters in the centre in place of the rosette	1.50	3.00
3c	10	Cash (Cu) undated. Type as No. 3a, but the centre of ℞ smooth	–.–	–.–
3d	10	Cash (Cu) 1902, 1903. Type similar to No. 3a, but with two Manchu characters in the centre of ℞ as well as additionally in the legend the date in Chinese characters	–.–	–.–
4	10	Cash (Cu) 1902, 1903, 1905. As type No. 3, but in centre of reverse two Manchu characters instead of rosette. Date in Chinese characters	2.00	4.00
4a	10	Cash (Cu) 1905. Type as No. 4, but on ℞ the two Manchu characters in the legend and a rosette in the centre	–.–	–.–
5	20	Cash (Cu) undated. As type No. 3a	18.00	35.00
6	2	Cash (Cu) 1906. Dragon. ℞ Chinese and Manchu characters, among which denomination, date, and value. In centre, Chinese character for Kiangsoo	70.00	100.00
7	5	Cash (Cu) 1906. Dragon in dotted circle and inscription TAI-CHING-TI-KUO COPPER COIN as well as four Chinese characters. ℞ Chinese and Manchu characters, among which denomination, date, and value. In centre, Chinese character for Kiangsoo	40.00	75.00
8	10	Cash (Cu) 1906. As type No. 7	3.50	7.00
9	20	Cash (Cu) 1906. As type No. 7	25.00	45.00

1 2 Cash (Cu) 1883–1908 (undated). Four Chinese characters, among which denomination. In centre, two Manchu characters. ℞ value in Chinese characters. In centre, Chinese character for Kirin

	VF	XF
	85.00	125.00

2 10 Cash (Cu) 1883–1908 (undated). Dragon in dotted circle and inscription KIRIN 10 CASHES. ℞ Chinese characters and, in centre, two Manchu characters, among which name of province and denomination as well as value. Variants — 5.00 — 9.00

2a 10 Cash (Cu) undated. As type No. 2, but dragon of varied type — –.– — –.–

3 20 Cash (Cu) 1883–1908 (undated). As type No. 2. Variants — 50.00 — 90.00

3a 20 Cash (Cu) 1883–1908 (undated). As type No. 2a — –.– — –.–

4 5 Cents (Ag) 1900, 1906–1908. Dragon and inscription KIRIN-PROVINCE 36 CANDAREENS, one Manchu character to right and left. ℞ Chinese characters, among which name of province and denomination as well as date and value. In centre, bundle of leaves. Variants — 7.00 — 10.00

5 10 Cents (Ag) 1900, 1906–1908. As type No. 4, but value in obverse inscription CANDARINS. 72. Variants — 7.00 — 10.00

6 20 Cents (Ag) 1900, 1906–1908. As type No. 4, but value in obverse inscription 1 MACE AND 44 CANDAREENS. Variants — 16.00 — 24.00

			VF	XF
7	50	Cents (Ag) 1900, 1906–1908. As type No. 4, but value in obverse inscription 3. CANDARINS. 6. Variants	22.00	30.00
8	1	Dollar (Ag) 1900, 1906–1908. As type No. 4, but value in obverse inscription 7. CANDARINS. 2. Variants	45.00	60.00
9	5	Cents (Ag) 1900–1905. As type No. 4, but in centre of reverse the Yin Yang symbol instead of the bundle of leaves. Variants	10.00	15.00
10	10	Cents (Ag) 1900–1905. As type No. 5, but in centre of reverse the Yin Yang symbol instead of the bundle of leaves. Variants	10.00	15.00
11	20	Cents (Ag) 1900–1905. As type No. 6, but in centre of reverse the Yin Yang symbol instead of the bundle of leaves. Variants	12.00	18.00

12	50	Cents (Ag) 1900–1905. As type No. 7, but in centre of reverse the Yin Yang symbol instead of the bundle of leaves. Variants	22.00	30.00
13	1	Dollar (Ag) 1900–1905. As type No. 8, but in centre of reverse the Yin Yang symbol instead of the bundle of leaves. Variants	60.00	80.00

			VF	XF
14	20	Cents (Ag) 1908. Dragon (new design) and inscription KIRIN PROVINCE 1 MACE AND 44 CANDAREENS. ℞ Chinese characters, and, in centre, two Manchu characters, among which name of province and denomination as well as date and value	65.00	90.00
15	50	Cents (Ag) 1908. As type No. 14, but value in obverse inscription 3. CANDARINS. 6	80.00	130.00
16	1	Dollar (Ag) 1908. As type No. 14, but value in obverse inscription. 7. CANDARINS. 2	175.00	240.00
17	10	Cents (Ag) 1908. Dragon and inscription KIRIN-PROVINCE CANDARINS 72. ℞ Chinese characters, among which name of province and denomination as well as date and value. In centre, the figure 1	50.00	70.00
18	20	Cents (Ag) 1908. As type No. 17, but value in obverse inscription 1 MACE AND 44 CANDAREENS and in centre of reverse the figure 2	40.00	60.00
19	1	Dollar (Ag) 1908. As type No. 17, but value in obverse inscription 7. CAINDARINS. 2 and in centre of reverse the figure 11	220.00	320.00
20	1	Tael (Ag) 1908. Dragon and inscription KWANG-SHU KUOPING ONE TAEL. ℞ Chinese and Manchu characters, among which denomination, date, and value. In centre, Chinese character for Kirin	–.–	–.–
21	20	Cents (Ag) 1909. Dragon in dotted circle and inscription TAI-CHING-TI-KUO SILVER COIN as well as four Chinese characters. ℞ Chinese and Manchu characters, among which denomination, date, and value. In centre, Chinese character for Kirin	30.00	50.00
22	10	Cash (Cu) 1909. Dragon in dotted circle and inscription TAI-CHING-TI-KUO COPPER COIN as well as four Chinese characters. ℞ Chinese and Manchu characters, among which denomination, date, and value. In centre, Chinese character for Kirin	12.00	18.00
23	20	Cash (Cu) 1909. As type No. 22	65.00	100.00

			VF	XF
1	10	Cash (Cu) undated. Dragon in dotted circle and inscription KWANG-TUNG TEN CASH. ℞ Chinese characters and, in centre, two Manchu characters, among which name of province and denomination as well as value	1.00	2.00
2	10	Cash (Cu) undated. Dragon in dotted circle and inscription KWANG-TUNG ONE CENT. ℞ Chinese characters, among which value	2.50	4.00
3	1	Tael (Ag) 1904 (undated). Chinese characters in dotted circle. Border formed by two dragons. ℞ Chinese characters, among which name of province and denomination as well as value. In centre, four Manchu characters. Pattern	–.–	–.–
4	10	Cash (Cu) 1906–1908. Dragon in dotted circle and inscription TAI-CHING-TI-KUO COPPER COIN as well as four Chinese characters. ℞ Chinese and Manchu characters, among which denomination as well as date and value. In centre, Chinese character for Kwang-tung	1.00	2.00
5	10	Cash (Cu) 1909. As type No. 4, but the Chinese characters in the obverse inscription read Hsüan Tung instead of Kuang Hsü	1.30	2.50
6	1	Cash (Bra) 1909–1911 (undated). Four Chinese characters. ℞ two Manchu characters. In centre, round hole within square frame	0.60	1.20
7	20	Cents (Ag) 1909 (undated). Dragon and inscription KWANG-TUNG PROVINCE 1 MACE AND 4,4 CANDAREENS. ℞ Chinese characters, among which name of province and denomination as well as value. In centre, four Manchu characters	7.00	11.00

			VF	XF
8	1	Dollar (Ag) 1909 (undated). As type No. 7, but value in the obverse inscription 7 MACE and 2 CANDAREENS	25.00	35.00
9	1	Cash (Bra) 1909–1911 (undated). Government era and coin designation by way of four Chinese characters. ℞ right and left one Manchu characters each. With a square hole. Casting!	–.–	–.–
10	1	Cash (Bra) 1909–1911 (undated). As type No. 9, but embossed!	–.–	–.–

Manchuria 東三省

1	10	Cents (Ag) 1907. Dragon and inscription 33rd YEAR OF KUANG HSU MANCHURIAN PROVINCES. ℞ Chinese characters and, in centre, four Manchu characters, among which name of province and denomination as well as value	11.00	15.00
2	20	Cents (Ag) 1907. As type No. 1	7.00	11.00
3	50	Cents (Ag) 1907. As type No. 1	110.00	165.00
4	1	Dollar (Ag) 1907. As type No. 1	130.00	180.00
5	20	Cents (Ag) 1909 (undated). Dragon and inscription MANCHURIAN PROVICENES 1 MACE AND 44 CANDAREENS. ℞ Chinese characters and, in centre, three Manchu characters, among which name of province and denomination as well as value	5.00	8.50
6	20	Cents (Ag) 1909. As type No. 5, but obverse inscription FIRST YEAR OF HSUEN TUNG MANCHURIAN PROVINCES	5.00	8.50
7	20	Cents (Ag) 1909. As type No. 5, but obverse inscription 1st YEAR OF HSUEN TUNG MANCHURIAN PROVINCES	5.00	8.50
8	20	Cents (Ag) 1910 (undated). Dragon and inscription MANCHURIAN PROVINCES 1 MACE AND 44 CANDAREENS. ℞ Chinese characters, among which name of province and denomination as well as value. In centre, a five-leaved rosette	4.50	8.00
9	20	Cents (Ag) 1910 (undated). As type No. 8, but no rosette in centre of the reverse	6.50	10.00
10	20	Cents (Ag) 1910 (undated). As type No. 9, but in the obverse inscription read PROVIENCES instead of PROVINCES	7.00	10.50

Shansi 山西 (山)

			VF	XF
1	20 Cents (Ag) 1911 (undated). Dragon and inscription NIACEURAN PROVINCES 1 MACE AND 4,4 CINDARRNS (faulty legend). ℞ Chinese characters, among which name of province and denomination as well as value. Variants through other mistakes in the obverse legend		35.00	60.00

Shantung (Shangtung) 山東 (東)

1	10 Cash (Cu) undated. Dragon in dotted circle and inscription SHANG-TUNG TEN CASH. ℞ Chinese characters and, in centre, two Manchu characters, among which name of province and denomination as well as value		2.00	4.00
2	10 Cash (Cu) undated. As type No. 1, but in the obverse inscription read SHAN-TUNG instead of SHANG-TUNG		4.00	8.00
3	10 Cash (Cu) undated. Dragon (new type) and inscription. ℞ Chinese characters		10.00	20.00
4	2 Cash (Cu) 1906. Dragon. ℞ Chinese and Manchu characters, among which denomination as well as date and value. In centre, Chinese character for Shantung		25.00	40.00
5	10 Cash (Cu) 1906. Dragon in dotted circle and inscription TAI-CHING-TI-KUO COPPER COIN as well as four Chinese characters. ℞ as type No. 2		8.00	14.00

Sinkiang (Chinese Turkestan) 新疆

10 Miscals (Mace) = 1 Tael

General issues for Sinkiang:

1	1½ Cents (Cu) (undated). ℞ dragon. Four Chinese characters in dotted circle and legend in Chinese characters, among others province and coin designation as well as denomination. In the centre one and in the legend two fiveleafed rosettes		–.–	–.–
1a	1 Mace (Ag) 1905 (undated). Dragon. ℞ denomination and value in four Chinese characters in dotted circle. Legend in four Arabic characters		170.00	260.00

		VF	XF
2	1 Mace (Ag) 1905 (undated). Dragon and four Arabic characters as legend. ℞ denomination and value in four Chinese characters in dotted circle	170.00	260.00
2a	2 Mace (Ag) 1905 (undated). As type No. 2, but no legend on obverse	–.–	–.–
3	2 Mace (Ag) 1905 (undated). Dragon. ℞ denomination and value in four Chinese characters in dotted circle	40.00	75.00
4	2 Mace (Ag) 1905 (undated). Dragon. Denomination and value in four Chinese characters in dotted circle. Legend in four Arabic characters	40.00	75.00
4a	2 Mace (Ag) 1905 (undated). As type No. 4, but ℞ in the legend, the Arabic characters only in the lower half	30.00	50.00
5	4 Mace (Ag) 1905 (undated). As type No. 4	60.00	100.00
6	5 Mace (Ag) 1905 (undated). As type No. 4	35.00	60.00
6a	5 Mace (Ag) 1905 (undated). Type as No. 6, but dragon within the dotted circle	40.00	70.00
7	1 Tael (Ag) 1905 (undated). Dragon. To left and right, rosette. ℞ denomination and value in four Chinese characters in dotted circle	80.00	140.00
8	1 Tael (Ag) 1905 (undated). As type No. 7, but legend in four Arabic characters and, in centre of reverse, rosette	90.00	170.00
9	1 Tael (Ag) 1905 (undated). Dragon and legend in four Arabic characters. ℞ denomination and value in four Chinese characters in dotted circle	200.00	320.00
9a	1 Tael (Ag) 1905 (undated). Type as No. 9, but dragon within the dotted circle	160.00	220.00
10	1 Mace (Ag) 1907 (undated). Dragon. ℞ denomination and value in four Chinese characters in dotted circle. As legend, above and below, one Chinese character; to right and left, one Arabic character. In centre, six-pointed star	–.–	–.–
11	1 Gold Mace (Au) 1907 (undated). Dragon and inscription in Arabic characters. ℞ value in Chinese characters in dotted circle. (Rate of exchange: 1 Gold Mace = 3 Silver Taels)	500.00	750.00
12	2 Gold Mace (Au) 1907 (undated). As type No. 11	385.00	500.00
13	10 Cash (Cu) 1910–1911 (undated). Dragon and inscription above in Chinese		

				VF	XF
		characters, and below in Arabic characters. ℞ denomination and value in Chinese characters. In centre, five-pointed star in double circle		8.00	15.00
13a	10	Cash (Cu) 1910, 1911. Type as No. 13, but a six-leafed rosette in centre of ℞		70.00	120.00
14	10	Cash (Cu) 1910–1911 (undated). Dragon and inscription below in Arabic characters. ℞ as type No. 11, but in centre, six-pointed star without circle		70.00	120.00

Issues for the Sungarei territory (Tsungarei):

15	1	Mace (Ag) 1906 (undated). Dragon and inscription SUNGAREI 1 MACE. ℞ Chinese characters and, in centre, four Manchu characters, among which name of province and denomination as well as value. Pattern		50.00	80.00
16	2	Mace (Ag) 1906 (undated). As type No. 15, but obverse inscription SUNGAREI 2 MACE. Pattern		50.00	80.00
17	5	Mace (Ag) 1906 (undated). As type No. 15, but the obverse inscription SUNGAREI 5 MACE. Pattern		–.–	–.–
18	1	Dollar (Ag) 1906 (undated). Dragon and inscription SUNGAREI 7 MACE 2 CANDAREENS. ℞ as type No. 15. Pattern		–.–	–.–
19	2	Gold Mace (Au) 1906 (undated). Draggon and inscription SUNGAREI 2 MACE. ℞ Chinese and Manchu characters, among which name of province and denomination as well as value		–.–	–.–

Issues for Kashgar: 喀什

20	1	Mace (Ag) 1904. Eight Chinese characters, among which mint, denomination and value. ℞ Arabic characters within wreath of ten rosettes		80.00	120.00
20a	1	Mace (Ag) 1904. Mint and denomination by way of four Chinese characters. ℞ Arabic characters in the wreath. Top and bottom one rosette each		80.00	120.00

			VF	XF
21	2	Mace (Ag) 1901, 1902. As type No. 20	40.00	70.00
22	3	Mace (Ag) 1900, 1901, 1902. As type No. 20	15.00	20.00
23	5	Mace (Ag) 1900–1902. Obverse as type No. 20. ℞ Arabic characters within wreath of two twigs. Above, rosette	16.50	25.00
24	2	Mace (Ag) 1902–1904. As type No. 20, but some different characters on obverse	12.50	20.00
25	3	Mace (Ag) 1902–1904. As type No. 24	12.50	20.00
26	5	Mace (Ag) 1903, 1904. As type No. 23, but some different characters on obverse	16.00	26.00
27	1	Mace (Ag) 1905. Dragon. ℞ Chinese and Arabic characters, among which value	–.–	–.–
28	2	Mace (Ag) 1905. Dragon. ℞ Four Chinese characters in dotted circle and inscription in Chinese and Arabic characters, among which mint and denomination as well as value	130.00	180.00
29	3	Mace (Ag) 1905. As type No. 28	–.–	–.–
30	5	Mace (Ag) 1905. As type No. 28, but in centre of reverse, in addition, rosette	60.00	100.00
31	5	Mace (Ag) 1907–1910. Dragon in dotted circle, border made of two differing twigs; above, rosette. ℞ Chinese and Arabic characters, among which mint, denomination, and value	40.00	75.00
31a	5	Mace (Ag) 1908 (undated). Type as No. 31, but Arabic characters without year date	45.00	80.00
32	1	Tael (Ag) 1907. Dragon in dotted circle, border made of two differing twigs; above, rosette. ℞ Chinese and Arabic characters, among which mint, denomination and value. In centre, rosette	60.00	100.00
33	2	Mace (Ag) 1907, 1908. As type No. 32, but some different characters	40.00	75.00
34	5	Mace (Ag) 1907. As type No. 33	–.–	–.–
35	1	Tael (Ag) 1907. As type No. 32, but some different characters	65.00	85.00
36	2	Mace (Ag) 1911. Dragon in dotted circle. Outside border of arabesques. In between, ring of 3 mm width. ℞ Chinese and Arabic characters, among which denomination and value	50.00	80.00
37	2	Mace (Ag) 1911. Dragon in wider circle and inscription in Arabic characters. ℞ as type No. 36, but without Arabic characters	–.–	–.–

			VF	XF
38	3	Mace (Ag) 1911. Dragon in wider circle and inscription below in Arabic characters. ℞ four Chinese characters (denomination and value). In centre, rosette	125.00	180.00
39	5	Mace (Ag) 1909–1911. Dragon in dotted circle. Outside border of arabesques. In between, ring of 3 mm width. ℞ Chinese and Arabic characters, among which mint, denomination and value. In centre, five-pointed star	40.00	65.00
39a	5	Mace (Ag) 1910. Type as No. 39, but on ℞ partly different characters	–.–	–.–
40	5	Mace (Ag) 1911–1913. Dragon in wider circle and, as inscription, two Chinese characters above and Arabic characters below. In the legend, three five-pointed stars. ℞ denomination and value in four Chinese characters in dotted circle. In centre, one five-pointed star, in outside border, four five-pointed stars	40.00	65.00
40a	1	Tael (Ag) 1911	–.–	–.–

Issues for Tihwa (Urumchi): 迪化

			VF	XF
41	2	Mace (Ag) 1903–1905. 8 Chinese characters, among which mint, denomination and value. ℞ in border, decoration of 8 rosettes and leaves	40.00	50.00
42	3	Mace (Ag) 1903–1905. As type No. 41	50.00	75.00
43	5	Mace (Ag) 1903, 1904. As type No. 41, but the reverse inscription has a border of two branches, between which rosette above	30.00	40.00
44	2	Mace (Ag) 1905–1907. As type No. 41, but on obverse a different Chinese character for 2	40.00	60.00
45	3	Mace (Ag) 1904–1907. As type No. 42, but on obverse a different Chinese character for 3	48.00	75.00
46	5	Mace (Ag) 1904–1907. As type No. 43, but on obverse a different Chinese character for 5	30.00	45.00

Szechuan (Szeshuan) 四 川 (川)

			VF	XF
1	5	Cash (Cu) undated. Dragon in dotted circle and inscription SZE CHUEN as well as value. ℞ Chinese characters and two Manchu characters, among which name of province and denomination as well as value	35.00	60.00
1a	10	Cash (Cu) (undated). Similar to type No. 1	18.00	30.00
1b	20	Cash (Cu–Bra) undated. As type No. 1, but changed denomination	40.00	80.00
1c	5	Cash (Cu) undated. As type No. 2, but changed denomination	82.00	150.00
2	10	Cash (Cu) undated. Dragon in dotted circle and inscription SZE CHUEN 10 CASH. ℞ Chinese characters and two Manchu characters, among which name of province and denomination as well as value. In centre, circular symbol	5.00	8.00

3	20	Cash (Cu) undated. As type No. 2	12.00	20.00
3a	10	Cash (Cu) undated. As type No. 2, but design of the dragon changed again	95.00	160.00
3b	20	Cash (Cu) undated. As type No. 3a	–.–	–.–
4	30	Cash (Cu) undated. As type No. 2	–.–	–.–
5	5	Cents (Ag) 1902 (undated). Dragon and inscription SZECHUAN PROVINCE 3,6 CANDAREENS. ℞ Chinese characters and, in centre, four Manchu characters, among which name of province and denomination as well as value	10.50	18.00
6	10	Cents (Ag) 1902 (undated). As type No. 5, but obverse legend SZECHUAN PROVINCE 7,2 CANDAREENS	12.50	20.00
7	20	Cents (Ag) 1902 (undated). As type No. 5, but obverse legend SZECHUEN PROVINCE 1 MACE AND 4,4 CANDAREENS	9.00	12.50

			VF	XF
8	50	Cents (Ag) 1901, 1902 (undated). As type No. 5, but obverse legend SZE-CHUEN PROVINCE 3 MACE AND 6 CANDAREENS	28.00	40.00
9	1	Dollar (Ag) 1901, 1902 (undated). As type No. 5, but obverse legend SZE-CHUEN PROVINCE 7 MACE AND 2 CANDAREENS	25.00	32.00
10	10	Cash (Cu) 1906. Dragon in dotted circle and inscription TAI-CHING-TI-KUO COPPER COIN as well as four Chinese characters. ℞ Chinese and Manchu characters, among which de-nomination, date, and value. In centre, Chinese character for Szechuan	1.00	2.00
11	20	Cash (Cu) 1906. As type No. 10	8.50	14.00
12	5	Cash (Cu) 1909. As type No. 10, but the Chinese characters in obverse legend read Hsüan Tung instead of Kuang Hsü	9.00	15.00
13	10	Cash (Cu) 1909. As type No. 12	1.50	3.00
14	20	Cash (Cu) 1909. As type No. 12	17.00	25.00
15	5	Cents (Ag) 1909 (undated). As type No. 5, but the Chinese characters on reverse read Hsüan Tung instead of Kuang Hsü	22.00	35.00
16	10	Cents (Ag) 1909 (undated). As type No. 6, but the Chinese characters on reverse read Hsüan Tung instead of Kuang Hsü	18.00	28.00
17	20	Cents (Ag) 1909 (undated). As type No. 7, but the Chinese characters on reverse read Hsüan Tung instead of Kuang Hsü	8.00	12.50
18	50	Cents (Ag) 1909 (undated). As type No. 8, but the Chinese characters on reverse read Hsüan Tung instead of Kuang Hsü	50.00	80.00
19	1	Dollar (Ag) 1909 (undated). As type No. 9, but the Chinese characters on reverse read Hsüan Tung instead of Kuang Hsü	22.00	35.00

For Szechuan Rupees, see under Tibet.

Yun-Nan or Yunnan 雲 南 (雲 or 滇)

			VF	XF
1	10	Cash (Cu) 1906. Dragon in dotted circle and inscription TAI-CHING-TI-KUO COPPER COIN as well as four Chinese characters. ℞ Chinese and Manchu characters, among which denomination, date, and value. In centre, Chinese character for Yunnan	15.00	25.00
2	20	Cash (Cu) 1906. As type No. 1	45.00	80.00
3	10	Cash (Cu) 1906. As type No. 1, but in centre of reverse, the Chinese characters for Yunnan and Szechuan	3.00	5.00
4	20	Cash (Cu) 1906. As type No. 3	4.00	7.00
4a	10	Cash (Cu) 1906. As type No. 1, but in the centre of ℞ the Chinese character Tien	25.00	40.00
4b	20	Cash (Cu) 1906. As type No. 4a	60.00	110.00
5	20	Cents (Ag) 1907 (undated). Dragon and inscription YUN-NAN-PROVINCE 1 MACE AND 4,4 CANDAREENS. ℞ Chinese characters and, in centre, four Manchu characters, among which name of province and denomination as well as value	15.00	22.00
6	50	Cents (Ag) 1907 (undated). As type No. 5, but obverse legend YUN-NAN-PROVINCE 3 MACE AND 6 CANDAREENS	9.00	12.00
7	1	Dollar (Ag) 1907 (undated). As type No. 5, but obverse legend YUN-NAN PROVINCE 7 MACE AND 2 CANDAREENS	40.00	60.00
7a	1	Rupee (Ag) 1907 (undated). Tsen Yuing, Governor of Yun-Nan Province. Head with cap, facing left, as well as inscription on left YUN-NAN and on right. ℞ the inscription SILVER COIN surrounded by leaf ornamentations. Trial minting or pseudo coin?	–.–	–.–
8	10	Cents (Ag) 1908 (undated). Dragon in dotted circle. To left and right, rosette. ℞ similar to type No. 5	16.00	25.00
9	20	Cents (Ag) 1908 (undated). As type No. 8	16.00	25.00
10	50	Cents (Ag) 1908 (undated). As type No. 8	7.00	10.50
11	1	Dollar (Ag) 1908 (undated). As type No. 8	22.00	30.00

12	50 Cents (Ag) 1909 (undated). As type No. 6, but the Chinese characters on reverse read Hsüan Tung instead of Kuang Hsü	**VF**	**XF**
		8.00	12.50
13	1 Dollar (Ag) 1909 (undated). As type No. 7, but the Chinese characters on reverse read Hsüan Tung instead of Kuang Hsü	24.00	32.00
14	1 Dollar (Ag) 1910. As type No. 13, but in the reverse legend (in the mention of the date) 13 Chinese characters instead of 10	750.00	1200.00
15	1 Cash (Bra) 1909–1911 (undated). Government are and coin designation by way of four Chinese characters. ℞ on left and right one Manchu character each. With square hole. Casting!	3.50	6.00

REPUBLIC (1912–1949)

中華民國

The dates given on the coins of the Republic are reckoned from the foundation of the Republic (1912 = 1st year).

Central Government Issues:

| **1** | 10 Cash (Cu) 1912–1915 (undated). Leaf decoration and rosette in circle and legend THE REPUBLIC OF CHINA TEN CASH. ℞ crossed flags | 0.80 | 1.50 |
| **2** | 10 Cash (Cu) 1912–1915 (undated). Value in Chinese characters in circle between ears of wheat, with legend THE REPUBLIC OF CHINA TEN CASH. ℞ crossed flags (with tassels) and legend in Chinese characters, among which name of country | 1.00 | 2.00 |

| **3** | 10 Cash (Cu) 1912–1915 (undated). Value in Chinese characters in circle between |

			VF	XF
		ears of wheat, with legend THE RE-PUBLIC OF CHINA TEN CASH. ℞ crossed flags (without tassels) in dotted circle and legend in Chinese characters, among which name of country	1.50	2.50
4	10	Cash (Cu) 1912–1915 (undated). Value in Chinese characters in dotted circle between ears of wheat; border of leaf decoration. ℞ crossed flags (with tassels) and legend in Chinese characters, among which name of country	1.50	2.50
4a	10	Cash (Cu) undated. Obv. as type No. 4, ℞ as type No. 3	16.00	30.00
5	10	Cash (Cu) 1912 (undated). Bust l. of Dr. Sun Yat Sen (1866–1925), first President of the Republic of China 1912. ℞ value in Chinese characters in dotted circle between ears of wheat, legend above in Chinese characters, among which name of country, below, TEN CASH. Pattern	–.–	–.–
5a	10	Cash (Cu) 1912 (undated). Bust turned half to l. of Li Yuan Hung (without cap). ℞ value in Chinese characters between ears of wheat in dotted circle; legend. Similar to type No. 13	–.–	–.–
5b	10	Cash (Cu) 1912 (undated). As type No. 5a, but Li Yuan Hung wearing cap. Similar to type No. 14	–.–	–.–
5c	10	Cash (Cu) 1912 (undated). Bust turned half to l. of Yuan Shih Kai in uniform with plumed cap. ℞ value in Chinese characters between rice plants, legend. Similar to type No. 16	–.–	–.–
5d	10	Cash (Cu) 1912–1915 (undated). Value in Chinese characters between rice plants. Below, legend TEN CASH. ℞ crossed flags (new design) and legend in Chinese characters, among which name of country	12.00	20.00
6	20	Cash (Cu) 1912–1915 (undated). Value in Chinese characters between rice plants, below TWENTI CASH. ℞ crossed flags; in the legend THE RE-PUBLIC OF CHINA as well as name of country in Chinese characters. Obv. and ℞ similar to type No. 5a	2.00	4.00
6a	20	Cash (Cu) (undated). As type No. 6, but inscription on obverse TWENTY CASH	22.00	40.00

			VF	XF
7	10	Cash (Cu) 1912–1915, 1919 (undated). Value in Chinese characters between ears of wheat. ℞ crossed flags (ribbons without tassels) in circle; in the legend, name of country and denomination as well as value in Chinese characters	2.00	4.00
8	20	Cash (Cu) 1919. As type No. 7, but in the reverse legend, date instead of value	2.00	4.00
9	10	Cents (Ag) 1912 (undated). Bust l. in circle of Dr. Sun Yat Sen, legend in Chinese characters, among which name of country. ℞ value in Chinese characters in circle between ears of wheat, inscription MEMENTO BIRTH OF REPUBLIC OF CHINA	–.–	–.–
10	20	Cents (Ag) 1912 (undated). Bust l. of Dr. Sun Yat Sen with inscription MEMENTO BIRTH OF REPUBLIC OF CHINA. ℞ crossed flags in dotted circle and inscription in Chinese characters, among which name of country	14.00	18.50
11	1	Dollar (Ag) 1912 (undated). As type No. 9	120.00	175.00

For same type, see No. 45

12   1 Dollar (Ag) 1912 (undated). Bust l. in

circle of Dr. Sun Yat Sen; legend in
Chinese characters, among which name
of country. ℞ value in Chinese characters in circle between ears of wheat,
and legend THE REPUBLIC OF
CHINA ONE DOLLAR

	VF	XF
	45.00	70.00

13   1 Dollar (Ag) 1912 (undated). Bust
(without cap) turned half to l. in dotted
circle of Li Yuan Hung (1864–1930),
Vice-President 1912 – 1916, President
of the Republic of China 1916 – 1918
and 1922 – 1923; legend in Chinese
characters, among which name of country. ℞ value in Chinese characters in
circle between ears of wheat, and legend THE REPUBLIC OF CHINA
ONE DOLLAR. There are also trial
strikes in gold of this coin!   50.00   90.00

14   1 Dollar (Ag) 1912 (undated). As type
No. 13, but Li Yuan Hung wears military cap   105.00   140.00

			VF	XF
14a	1	Dollar (Ag) 1912 (undated). Bearded bust half turned to l. of Chin Teh Chuen, Governor of the province Kiangsoo; legend in Chinese characters, among which name of country. ℞ value in Chinese characters in circle between ears of wheat, and legend THE REPUBLIC OF CHINA ONE DOLLAR. Pattern	–.–	–.–
15	1	Dollar (Ag) 1914. Bust turned half to l. of Yuan Shih Kai (1859–1916), President of the Republic of China 1912 to 1916; above, name of country and date in Chinese characters. ℞ value in Chinese characters between rice plants	–.–	–.–

16	1	Dollar (Ag) 1914 (undated). Bust turned half to l. of Yuan Shih Kai in uniform with plumed cap. ℞ value in Chinese characters in dotted circle between rice plants; in the legend, ONE DOLLAR and Chinese characters, among which name of country	80.00	130.00
17	10	Cents (Ag) 1914, 1916. Bust l. of Yuan Shih Kai in uniform; above, name of country and date in Chinese characters. ℞ value in Chinese characters between, above, rice plants	3.00	4.00
18	20	Cents (Ag) 1914, 1916, 1920. As type No. 17	4.00	5.00
19	50	Cents (Ag) 1914. As type No. 17	9.00	13.00

			VF	XF
20	1	Dollar (Ag) 1914, 1919–1921. Obv. as type No. 17. ℞ as type No. 15	14.00	18.00
20a	5	Cents (Ni) 1914. Bust l. of Yuan Shih Kai; above, name of country and date in Chinese characters. ℞ in centre, value in Chinese characters within wreath opened above; above, inscription in Chinese characters. Pattern	–.–	–.–
21	1	Dollar (Ag) 1916 (undated). Bust turned half to l. of Yuan Shih Kai in uniform with plumed cap. ℞ winged dragon and legend in Chinese characters, among which name of country	210.00	280.00
22	½	Cent (Cu) 1916. Wreath of rice plants and four-pointed star. ℞ within circle, value in Chinese characters, legend in Chinese characters, among which name of country, date, and value. Round hole in centre	11.00	20.00

23	1	Cent (Cu) 1916. As type No. 22		
		a) with round hole in centre	4.00	6.00
		b) without hole	–.–	–.–
24	2	Cents (Cu) 1916. As type No. 22	35.00	60.00

			VF	XF
25	5	Dollars (Au) 1914, 1916. Bust l. of Yuan Shih Kai in uniform. ℞ winged dragon and legend in Chinese characters, among which name of country and date. Pattern	–.–	–.–
26	10	Dollars (Au) 1916. As type No. 25, but not a pattern	2000.00	2400.00
27	10	Dollars (Au) 1919. Bust l. of Yuan Shih Kai in uniform. ℞ name of country, date and value in Chinese characters between, and above, rice plants	1000.00	1200.00
28	20	Dollars (Au) 1919. As type No. 27	1750.00	2000.00
28a	10	Cash (Cu) 1921 (undated). As type No. 7, but new design for flags and ribbons with tassels	2.00	4.00
29	20	Cash (Cu) 1921, 1922. As type No. 8, but new design for flags and ribbons with tassels	3.00	6.00
30	1	Dollar (Ag) 1921. Bust turned half to l. of Hsü Chih Chang (1858–1936) in mufti, President of the Republic of China 1918–1922. ℞ pavilion within circle; name of country, date, and value in Chinese characters, as legend above	300.00	380.00
31	1	Dollar (Ag) 1921. As type No. 30, but the reverse legend is also repeated below the type	300.00	380.00
32	1	Dollar (Ag) 1923 (undated). Bust facing of Tsao Kun (1862–1938) in mufti, President of the Republic of China 1923–1924. ℞ crossed flags; above, legend of six Chinese characters	200.00	280.00
33	1	Dollar (Ag) 1923 (undated). Bust facing of Tsao Kun in uniform. ℞ crossed flags, two Chinese characters in ancient seal-script between the flag-staffs. Six stars within circular border	110.00	160.00
34	10	Cash (Cu) 1924. Name of country, date, and value in Chinese characters between, and above, rice plants. ℞ four Chinese characters in dotted circle. In the legend, THE REPUBLIC OF CHINA as well as four Manchu characters	80.00	150.00
35	20	Cash (Cu) 1924. As type No. 34	7.50	15.00
36	1	Dollar (Ag) 1924 (undated). Bust facing of Tuan Chi Yui (1864–1936) in mufti, General, politician and Minister of the Republic of China; above, nine Chinese characters, among which name of country. ℞ two Chinese char-		

acters in ancient seal-script between rice plants   135.00   180.00

37   1 Dollar (Ag) 1926. Bust facing of Dr. Sun Yat Sen. In the legend, name of country and date in seven Chinese characters. ℞ value in Chinese characters between rice plants. Pattern   –.–   –.–

38   10 Cents (Ag) 1926. Symbol of long life between dragon and phoenix. ℞ value in Chinese characters in dotted circle between rice plants. In the legend, name of country, date, and value in Chinese characters   7.00   9.00

39   20 Cents (Ag) 1926. As type No. 38   7.00   9.00

40   1 Dollar (Ag) 1923. Symbol of long life between dragon and phoenix; above, name of country and date in Chinese characters. ℞ value in Chinese characters between rice plants   290.00   350.00

41   1 Dollar (Ag) 1927. Bust facing of Chu Yu Pu in uniform, Military and Civil Governor of the Hopei province 1926. ℞ crossed flags and legend in Chinese characters, among which name of country and date   750.00   900.00

42   10 Cents (Ag) 1927. Bust facing of Dr. Sun Yat Sen and legend of 13 Chinese characters, among which name of country and date. ℞ crossed flags and value in Chinese characters above, between flag-staffs. Below, value in six Chinese characters   25.00   30.00

43   20 Cents (Ag) 1927. As type No. 42   22.00   30.00

44   20 Cents (Ag) 1927. Head l. of Dr. Sun Yat Sen. Legend comprising name of country and date in Chinese characters.

R crossed flags and value in Chinese
characters between flag-staffs. Below,
value in six Chinese characters

	VF	XF
	–.–	–.–

45	1 Dollar (Ag) 1927 (undated). As type No. 11, but the rosettes in the reverse legend are not round but elliptical	13.00	18.00
46	1 Dollar (Ag) 1927. Head facing of Dr. Sun Yat Sen and legend of eight Chinese characters, among which name of country. R in centre, value in Chinese characters; to right, mausoleum and to left, sun with rays; below, date in Chinese characters	450.00	650.00
47	1 Dollar (Ag) 1926. Bust facing of Chang Tso Lin (1876–1928) in uniform, General and Commander-in-Chief of land and naval forces of the Republic of China 1927. Above, inscription of six Chinese characters. R Chinese characters in dotted circle between ears of wheat; above the characters, sun. In the legend ONE DOLLAR as well as name of country and date in Chinese characters. Pattern	420.00	600.00
48	1 Dollar (Ag) 1927. Bust facing of Chang Tso Lin in uniform; above, name of country and date in Chinese characters. R dragon and phoenix within circle. In the legend ONE DOLLAR as well as Chinese characters. Pattern	550.00	700.00
49	1 Dollar (Ag) 1927 (undated). Obverse as type No. 47. R as type No. 48. Pattern	–.–	–.–
50	1 Dollar (Ag) 1928. Bust facing of Chang Tso Lin in mufti; above, six Chinese characters. R crossed flags. In the leg-		

			VF	XF
		end ONE DOLLAR as well as name of country and value in Chinese characters. Pattern	190.00	250.00
50a	1	Cent (Bra) 1928. 12-rayed sun. ℞ value	250.00	300.00
50b	2	Cents (Bra) 1928. As type No. 50a	265.00	350.00
51	10	Cents (Ag) 1929. Head l. of Dr. Sun Yat Sen; above, name of country and date in Chinese characters. ℞ junk under sail (with three sails) as well as value in Chinese characters to right and left. Pattern	–.–	–.–
52	20	Cents (Ag) 1929. As type No. 51. Pattern	–.–	–.–
53	50	Cents (Ag) 1929. As type No. 51. Pattern	–.–	–.–
54	1	Dollar (Ag) 1929. As type No. 51. Several variants for reverse. Not a pattern	–.–	–.–
55	10	Cents (Cu–Ni) 1929. As type No. 51, but on reverse below, five Chinese characters. Pattern	–.–	–.–
56	20	Cents (Cu–Ni) 1929. As type No. 55. Pattern	–.–	–.–
57	50	Cents (Cu–Ni) 1929. As type No. 55. Pattern	–.–	–.–
58	1	Dollar (Ag) 1929. As type No. 54, but on reverse, junk without eye ornament. Pattern	–.–	–.–
59	1	Dollar (Ag) 1929. Bust facing of Dr. Sun Yat Sen; above, name of country and date in seven Chinese characters. ℞ as type No. 51. Pattern	–.–	–.–
60	20	Cents (Ag) 1929. Bust turned half to l. of Dr. Sun Yat Sen; above, name of country and date in Chinese characters. ℞ value in Chinese characters between, and above, rice plants. Pattern	–.–	–.–
61	1	Dollar (Ag) 1929. Bust turned half to l. of Dr. Sun Yat Sen; above, name of country and date in seven Chinese characters. ℞ crossed flags on globe with legend THE REPUBLIC OF CHINA; below, value in Chinese characters. Pattern	–.–	℣·–
62	1	Dollar (Ag) 1929. Obv. as type No. 61. ℞ value in Chinese characters between rice plants. Pattern	–.–	–.–
63	1	Dollar (Ag) 1929 (undated). Head facing of Dr. Sun Yat Sen. ℞ as type No. 45. Pattern	–.–	–.–
64	1	Dollar (Ag) 1929 (undated). Obv. as		

<table>
<tr><td></td><td></td><td></td><td>VF</td><td>EF</td></tr>
</table>

type No. 63. ℞ value in Chinese characters between rice plants. Pattern — −.− −.−

65 2 Cents (Ni) 1932. Branch in blossom and inscription in Chinese characters, among which value. ℞ sun (national emblem of the Chinese Republic) as well as name of country and date in Chinese characters. Round hole in centre. Pattern — −.− −.−

65a 2 Cents (Ni) 1932. As type No. 65, but without hole in centre. Pattern — −.− −.−

66 5 Cents (Ni) 1932. As type No. 65. Pattern — −.− −.−

66a 5 Cents (Ni) 1932. As type No. 66, but without hole in centre. Pattern — −.− −.−

67 1 Dollar (Ag) 1932. Head l. of Dr. Sun Yat Sen; above, name of country and date in Chinese characters. ℞ junk under sail (only two sails); above, three birds in flight; on r., rising sun; to l. and to r., value in Chinese characters — 70.00 115.00

67a 1 Dollar (Ag) 1932. As type No. 67, but indication of mint in five Chinese characters within circular border — −.− −.−

68 10 Cents ($^1/_{10}$ Sun) (Ag) 1932. Head l. of Dr. Sun Yat Sen; above, name of country and date in Chinese characters. ℞ junk under sail (two sails); on r., rising sun; two birds on the water; above, value in Chinese characters. Diameter 16 mm. Pattern — −.− −.−

A "Sun" is a monetary unit based on gold.

69 20 Cents ($^1/_5$ Sun) (Ag) 1932. As type No. 68. Diameter 26 mm. Pattern — −.− −.−

70 50 Cents ($^1/_2$ Sun) (Ag) 1932. As type No. 68. Diameter 34 mm. Pattern — −.− −.−

			VF	XF
71	1	Dollar (1 Sun) (Ag) 1932. As type No. 68. Diameter 39 mm. Pattern	–.–	–.–
71a	1	Cent (Br) 1933. Similar to No. 22	14.00	22.00
71b	2	Cents (Br) 1933. Similar to No. 22	85.00	120.00

72	1	Dollar (Ag) 1933, 1934. As type No. 67, but reverse without birds and without sun	13.50	17.00
73	50	Cents (Ag) 1935. As type No. 72. Pattern	–.–	–.–
74	50	Cents (Ag) 1935. As type No. 73, but on the reverse, different character on right. Pattern	–.–	–.–
75	1	Dollar (Ag) 1935. As type No. 72. Pattern	–.–	–.–
76	50	Cents (Ag) 1936. As type No. 74, but diameter only 26 mm. Pattern	–.–	–.–
77	1	Dollar (Ag) 1936. As type No. 72, but diameter only 32 mm. Pattern	–.–	–.–
78	50	Cents (Ag) 1936, 1937. Bust l. of Dr. Sun Yat Sen; above, name of country and date in legend of Chinese characters. Meander pattern border. ℞ ancient Pu coin, value to right and left in Chinese characters	–.–	–.–
79	1	Dollar (Ag) 1936, 1937. As type No. 78	–.–	–.–
79a	50	Cents (Ag) 1936. As type No. 78, but obv. and ℞ without the meander pattern border	–.–	–.–
79b	1	Dollar (Ag) 1936. As type No. 79, but obv. and ℞ without the meander pattern border	–.–	–.–
80	1	Dollar (Ag) 1936. Bust l. of Chiang Kai-shek (1886–1975) in uniform with cap, President of the Republic of China 1928–1931 and 1948–1949; President of Nationalist China (Taiwan) since 1950. Border of meander pattern. R ancient Pu coin; above, name of country and		

			date in eight Chinese characters. Meander pattern border. Pattern	–.–	–.–
81	1	Dollar (Ag) 1936. Bust facing of Chiang Kai-shek in uniform without cap. Above, five Chinese characters. Meander pattern border. ℞ ancient Pu coin as well as name of country and date in Chinese characters. Meander pattern border. Pattern	–.–	–.–
82	½	Cent (Br) 1936, 1937, 1939 (?) 1940 (?). In centre, sun (national emblem of the Republic); above, name of country and date in Chinese characters as legend. Meander pattern border. ℞ ancient Pu coin, value to right and left in Chinese characters. Meander pattern border	2.50	5.00

83	1	Cent (Br) 1936–1940. As type No. 82	1.20	2.40
84	1	Cent (Bra) 1939. As type No. 82, but the border on obverse and ℞ is composed of T-shaped elements	22.00	40.00
85	2	Cents (Bra) 1939. As type No. 84	5.50	10.00

86	5	Cents (Ni) 1935–1939, 1941. Bust l. of Dr. Sun Yat Sen; above, name of country and date in Chinese characters. Border of meander pattern. ℞ ancient Pu coin, value in Chinese characters on right and left. Border of meander pattern. The 1935 and 1937 issues are only patterns	0.50	1.00
87	10	Cents (Ni) 1935, 1936, 1938, 1939. As type No. 86. The 1935 issue is a pattern	0.40	0.80
88	20	Cents (Ni) 1935–1939. As type No. 86. The 1935 and 1937 issues are patterns	0.80	1.60
89	5	Cents (Ni) 1936. As type No. 86, but on the obverse, two additional Chinese characters for Tientsin. Pattern	45.00	65.00

			VF	XF
90	5	Cents (Ni) 1936. As type No. 86, but on the obverse, two additional Chinese characters for Peiping. Pattern	45.00	65.00
91	10	Cents (Ni) 1936. As type No. 87, but in the obverse legend another additional Chinese character for Tientsin. Pattern	45.00	65.00
92	10	Cents (Ni) 1936. As type No. 87, but in the obverse legend another additional Chinese character for Peiping. Pattern	55.00	85.00
93	10	Cents (Ni) 1936. As type No. 87, but in the obverse legend, two additional Chinese characters for Tientsin. Pattern	−.−	−.−
94	10	Cents (Ni) 1936. As type No. 87, but in the obverse legend, two additional Chinese characters for Peiping. Pattern	−.−	−.−
95	10	Cents (Ni) 1936. As type No. 87, but on the ℞ an additional Chinese character for Tientsin. Pattern	−.−	−.−
96	10	Cents (Ni) 1936. As type No. 87, but on the ℞ an additional Chinese character for Peiping. Pattern	−.−	−.−
97	10	Cents (Ni) 1936. As type No. 87, but on the obverse, on the robe of Dr. Sun Yat Sen, an additional character for Tientsin. Pattern	−.−	−.−
98	10	Cents (Ni) 1936. As type No. 87, but on the obverse, on the robe of Dr. Sun Yat Sen, an additional character for Peiping. Pattern	−.−	−.−
98a	5	Cents (Ni) 1936. As type No. 86, but on ℞ underneath the Pu coin, additionally the letter A	1.50	3.00
98b	10	Cents (Ni) 1936. As type No. 87, but on ℞ underneath the Pu coin additionally the letter A. Trial strike!	−.−	−.−
98c	20	Cents (Ni) 1936. As type No. 88, but on ℞ underneath the Pu coin additionally the letter A	1.25	2.50
99	5	Cents (Ni) 1940, 1941. As type No. 86, but smaller diameter (17.5 mm)	0.50	1.00
100	10	Cents (Ni) 1940–1942. As type No. 87, but smaller diameter (21 mm)	0.40	0.80
101	20	Cents (Ni) 1941, 1942. As type No. 88, but smaller diameter (24 mm)	0.80	1.50
102	½	Dollar (Ni) 1941–1943. As type No. 101, but diameter of 28 mm. The 1941 issue is a pattern	2.00	4.00

			VF	XF
102a	50	Cents (Ni) 1942. As type No. 102, but on the reverse, beneath the Pu coin, an additional Chinese character for Kweilin	–.–	–.–
103	1	Cent (Ni) 1940. Chinese characters between wings within circle; name of country and date forming circular legend in Chinese characters. R bundle of rice plants; value to right and left in Chinese characters. Hua Shing Bank issue	–.–	–.–
104	5	Cents (Ni) 1940. Obv. as type No. 103. R pagoda and value in Chinese characters. Hua Shing Bank issue	–.–	–.–
105	10	Cents (Ni) 1940. Obv. as type No. 103. R in centre, Chinese characters for long life in ancient seal-script; value to right and left in Chinese characters. Border of meander pattern. Hua Shing Bank issue	5.50	10.50
106	20	Cents (Ni) 1940. Obv. as type No. 103. R junk with three sails, value to right and left in Chinese characters. Hua Shing Bank pattern	–.–	–.–
107	1	Cent (Al) 1939. Value in centre and in the legend, name of country and date in Chinese characters. Dotted border. R ancient Pu coin. Dotted border. Pattern	–.–	–.–
108	5	Cents (Al) 1939. As type No. 107, but on obverse and reverse, meander pattern border. Pattern	–.–	–.–
109	10	Cents (Al) 1940. As type No. 108. Pattern	–.–	–.–
110	1	Cent (Al) 1940. As type No. 107, but not a pattern	0.40	0.60
111	2	Cents (Al) 1940. As type No. 108. Pattern	–.–	–.–
111a	2	Cents (Al) 1940. As type No. 111, but on obverse and reverse, no meander pattern, but only a dotted border. Pattern	–.–	–.–
112	5	Cents (Al) 1940. As type No. 108, but new Chinese character for 5	0.50	1.00
113	10	Cents (Ni) 1941 (undated). Head half turned to left of Chiang Kai-shek. R ancient Pu coin, value to right and left in Chinese characters. Border of meander pattern	–.–	–.–
114	50	Cents (Ni) 1941 (undated). As type No. 113	–.–	–.–

			VF	XF
115	50	Cents (Ag) 1941. Bust facing of Chiang Kai-shek; above, name of country and date in Chinese characters. Border of meander pattern ℞ ancient Pu money, value in Chinese characters to right and left. Meander pattern border. Pattern	–.–	–.–
116	1	Cent (Bra) 1940. In centre, sun (national emblem of the Republic), name of country and date forming legend of Chinese characters. ℞ ancient Pu money, value in Chinese characters to right and left	0.40	0.80
117	2	Cents (Bra) 1940. As type No. 116	0.50	1.00
118	1	Cent (Br) 1948. As type No. 116	11.00	20.00
119	1	Dollar (Ag) 1948. Head l. of Dr. Sun Yat Sen; above, name of country and date forming legend in Chinese characters. ℞ ancient Pu money, value in Chinese characters to right and left	–.–	–.–
120	2	Dollars (Ag) 1948. As type No. 119	–.–	–.–
121	50	Cents (Ag) 1948. Bust r. of Chiang Kai-shek in uniform; above, legend in Chinese characters giving name of country and date. ℞ value in Chinese characters within wreath of rice stalks	–.–	–.–
122	(–)	No face value (Ag?) 1949. Flower with five petals within circle, legend in Chinese characters, among which name of country and date. ℞ above, wreath of rice stalks opened above. No characters	–.–	–.–

For further issues, see under the People's Republic of China and Taiwan (Nationalist China, Formosa).

PROVINCIAL ISSUES DURING THE REPUBLIC

Chekiang 浙江

1	10	Cents (Ag) 1924. Denomination and value in four Chinese characters within circle. Legend CHE-KIANG PROVINCE TEN CENTS. ℞ crossed flags within circle as well as legend in Chinese characters giving names of country and province, and date	7.00	10.50
2	20	Cents (Ag) 1924. As type No. 1, but the obverse legend reads CHE-KIANG PROVINCE TWENTY CENTS	285.00	380.00

			VF	XF
3	20	Cents (Ag) 1924. 20 in dotted circle with legend CHE-KIANG PROVINCE TWENTY CENTS. ℞ denomination and value in four Chinese characters within dotted circle. Circular legend giving names of country and province as well as date in Chinese characters	285.00	380.00

Fookien (Fukien) 福 建

			VF	XF
1	1	Cash (Bra) 1911. Value given by a Chinese character above and below. Flag to right and left. ℞ Chinese characters. Round hole in centre	180.00	275.00
2	2	Cash (Bra) 1911. As type No. 1	20.00	30.00
3	10	Cash (Cu) 1912–1922, 1924. Three flags with ribbons and legend FOO-KIEN COPPER COIN TEN CASH. ℞ Chinese characters, among which denomination and value. In centre, rosette	5.00	9.00
4	20	Cents (Ag) 1912 (undated). Crossed flags in dotted circle and legend THERMEEMEA CBCERO 1 MACE AND 44 CANDAREENS. ℞ denomination in four Chinese characters within dotted circle. Legend in Chinese characters giving name of country and value	–.–	–.–
5	20	Cents (Ag) 1912. In centre, Chinese characters for Fukien in rosette; around, two circles of nine dots each (the dots on the inner and outer circle are connected by straight lines). Legend FOO-KIEN 1 MACE AND 44 CANDAREENS. ℞ Chinese characters, among which name of province and denomination as well as date and value. In centre, Chinese character for Fukien	17.00	26.00
6	20	Cents (Ag) 1912. As type No. 5, but the obverse legend FOO-KIEN GOVERNOR 1 MACE AND 44 CANDAREENS. Pattern	–.–	–.–
7	10	Cents (Ag) 1912 (undated). Three flags with ribbons and legend MADE IN FOO-KIEN MINT 7,2 CANDAREENS. ℞ denomination and name of province as well as value in Chinese characters. In centre, twelve-pointed star	22.00	35.00

			VF	XF
8	20	Cents (Ag) 1912 (undated). As type No. 7, but value in the obverse legend 1 MACE AND 4,4 CANDAREENS	5.00	8.00
9	10	Cents (Ag) 1913 (undated). 10 in dotted circle and legend FOO-KIEN PROVINCE 7,2 CANDAREENS. ℞ names of country and province, and denomination as well as value in Chinese characters	5.00	8.00
10	20	Cents (Ag) 1913 (undated). 20 in dotted circle and legend. FOO-KIEN PROVINCE 1 MACE AND 4 CANDAREENS. ℞ as type No. 9	10.50	15.00
11	20	Cents (Ag) 1923. Three flags with ribbons and legend MADE IN FOO-KIEN MINT 1 MACE AND 44 CANDAREENS. ℞ names of country and province, and denomination as well as date and value in Chinese characters. In centre, twelve-pointed star	8.50	11.00
12	10	Cents (Ag) 1924. As type No. 11, but the value on the obverse 7,2 CANDAREENS and name of country on reverse in different Chinese characters	18.00	25.00
13	20	Cents (Ag) 1924. As type No. 12, but value on the obverse 1 MACE AND 44 CANDAREENS	20.00	28.00
14	20	Cents (Ag) 1924. 20 in dotted circle and legend FOO-KIEN PROVINCE TWENTY CENTS. ℞ Chinese characters, among which name of province and denomination as well as date and value	26.00	40.00
15	20	Cents (Ag) 1927. Two crossed flags within circle and legend in Chinese characters, among which value. ℞ Chinese characters, among which name of country, mint, and date. To right and left a large figure 2; in centre, twelve-pointed star. Issued by the Army	290.00	380.00
16	20	Cents (Ag) 1927. Head l. of Dr. Sun Yat Sen and legend in Chinese characters, among which name of country and date. ℞ two crossed flags and value in Chinese characters. Pattern	—.—	—.—
17	20	Cents (Ag) 1927. Abacus, axe, sickle, gun, and book in the middle; on r. and l. a figure 2; circular inscription in Chinese characters, among which name of country and date as well as legend for National Government. ℞ crossed		

			VF	XF
		flags and legend in Chinese characters, among which value	300.00	380.00
17a	20	Cents (Ag) 1927. As type No. 17, but no figure "2" in the obverse and in the reverse nine instead of thirteen Chinese characters	–.–	–.–
18	10	Cents (Ag) 1928, 1931. Sun with figure 10 in centre; around, dotted circle. Leggend in Chinese characters giving names of country and province as well as date and value. ℞ memorial monument to the Huang Hwa massacre. Above, inscription in Chinese characters	15.00	22.00
19	20	Cents (Ag) 1928, 1931. As type No. 18, but figure 20 within sun	11.50	18.00
20	10	Cents (Ag) 1932. Two crossed flags, value in two Chinese characters between flag-staffs. Legend in Chinese characters. ℞ as type No. 18	120.00	175.00
21	20	Cents (Ag) 1932. As type No. 20	90.00	130.00

Honan 河南

			VF	XF
1	10	Cash (Cu) 1912 (undated). Crossed flags (with tassels) and legend HO-NAN TEN CASH. ℞ value in Chinese characters between ears of corn in dotted circle. Legend in Chinese characters giving names of country and province	2.50	5.00
2	10	Cash (Cu) 1912 (undated). Obv. as type No. 1, but flags different. ℞ rosette between ears of corn in dotted circle. Legend in Chinese characters giving name of country and value	1.00	2.00
3	10	Cash (Cu) 1912 (undated). Obv. as type No. 1. Rev. as type No. 2	–.–	–.–
4	20	Cash (Cu) 1912 (undated). As type No. 2, but value in obverse legend 20 CASH	2.50	5.00
5	20	Cash (Cu) (undated). As type No. 4, but denomination in the legend of R in different Chinese charakters	2.00	4.00
6	50	Cash (Cu) 1912 (undated). As type No. 2, but legend of obverse HO-NAN 50 CASH	5.00	8.00
7	100	Cash (Cu) 1912 (undated)	6.00	9.00
8	200	Cash (Cu) 1912 (undated). Crossed flags (with tassels) and legend HO-NAN 200 CASH	9.00	14.00

			VF	XF
9	20	Cash (Cu) undated. As type No. 4, but in the inscription of the obverse the name of country CHINA instead of the name of province HO-NAN	35.00	60.00
10	50	Cash (Cu) undated. As type No. 9	17.00	32.00
11	50	Cash (Cu) 1931. Similar to No. 12	50.00	65.00
12	100	Cash (Cu) 1931. Value in Chinese characters between ears of corn; above, five-pointed star. ℞ in centre, sun (national emblem of the Republic). Legend in Chinese characters giving names of country and province as well as date	28.00	38.00

Hopei 河北

1	½	Cent (Cu) 1937. Type as No. 2	8.00	14.00
2	1	Cent (Cu) 1937. Starred flags in dotted circle and legend in Chinese characters, among which name of country and date as well as inscription for Chi Tung Government. ℞ value in Chinese characters between ears of corn	4.50	8.00
3	5	Cents (Ni) 1937. As type No. 2	5.50	10.00
4	10	Cents (Ni) 1937. Pagoda in dotted circle and legend in Chinese characters, among which name of country and date as well as inscription for Chi Tung Government. ℞ value in Chinese characters between ears of corn	4.00	7.50
5	20	Cents (Ni) 1937. As type No. 4	7.00	13.00

Hunan 湖南

			VF	XF
1	20	Cash (Cu) 1912–1921 (undated). Ears of corn and leaf decoration within circle. Inscription THE REPUBLIC OF CHINA TWENTY CASH. R crossed flags in circle; above, rosette between flag-staffs. Legend in Chinese characters giving name of country and value. Several variants	2.50	4.00
2	20	Cash (Cu) (undated). As type No. 1, but the reverse legend in different Chinese characters	4.00	7.00
2a	20	Cash (Cu) (undated). As type No. 2, but the obverse legend 20 CASH	55.00	80.00

3	10	Cash (Cu) 1914 (undated). Nine-pointed star in dotted circle and legend HU-NAN TEN CASH. R Chinese characters, among which name of country and value. In centre, rosette	3.50	6.00
4	10	Cash (Cu) 1916 (undated). Ears of corn and leaf decoration within circle. Legend THE FIRST YEAR OF HUNG SHUAN TEN CASH. R Chinese characters, among which name of province and date	11.50	20.00
5	10	Cents (Ag) 1916. Dragon and value in Chinese characters. R Chinese characters, among which name of province and denomination as well as date. Pattern.	–.–	–.–
6	1	Dollar (Ag) 1922. Chinese character (three horizontal lines) between leaf ornaments in dotted circle. Legend in Chinese characters, among which names of country and province as well as date and value. R crossed flags in dotted		

			VF	**XF**

		circle; above, rosette between flag-staffs. Legend THE REPUBLIC OF CHINA ONE DOLLAR	290.00	380.00
7	1	Dollar (Ag) 1922. Head half turned to l. of General Chao Heng Ti between branches in dotted circle. Legend in Chinese characters. ℞ as type No. 6. Pattern	–.–	–.–
8	10	Cash (Cu) 1922. Type similar to No. 6	20.00	30.00
9	20	Cash (Cu) 1922. Type similar to No. 6	25.00	40.00
10	10	Cash (Cu) 1922. Type similar to No. 6, but, above, a five-pointed star between flag-staffs	12.00	20.00
11	20	Cash (Cu) undated. Type as No. 1, but, above, a five-pointed star between flag-staffs	2.50	3.50

Hupeh 湖北 (鄂)

1	5	Cents (Ni) 1915 (undated). Value in Chinese characters within sun (national emblem of the Republic). Border of meander pattern. ℞ name of country in Chinese characters within 16-pointed star. Pattern	–.–	–.–
2	10	Cents (?) 1916. Dragon and value in Chinese characters. ℞ Chinese characters, among which name of province and denomination as well as date. (Issue possibly in white metal?)	–.–	–.–
3	20	Cents (Ag) 1920. Bust l. of Yuan Shih Kai; above, names of country and province as well as date forming inscription in Chinese characters. ℞ value in Chinese characters between, and above, rice stalks	165.00	210.00

			VF	XF
4	50	Cash (Cu–Bra) 1914, 1918. Inscription in ancient Chinese 'seal writing' in the circle, all surrounded by eighteen rings arranged in a circle. Above designation of the country and date as inscription in Chinese characters. ℞ province and coin designation by way of four Chinese characters in the dotted circle. In the centre a stylized flower. In the legend Chinese characters, among others denomination	400.00	650.00
5	20	Cash (Bra) undated. Denomination in four Chinese characters. Rev. value in four Chinese characters. In centre of obverse as well as of reverse a Chinese character in circle	100.00	160.00

Kansu 甘 肅

1	1	Dollar (Ag) 1914. Bust l. of Yuan Shih Kai in uniform. Legend in Chinese characters giving names of country and province as well as date. ℞ value in Chinese characters between rice stalks	300.00	550.00
2	50	Cash (Cu) 1926. Crossed flags. R in centre, Chinese character for Kansu	165.00	240.00
3	100	Cash (Cu) 1926. Crossed flags; above, large rosette between flag-staffs, four small rosettes at the edge. ℞ Chinese characters, among which names of country and province as well as date and value	125.00	160.00
4	1	Dollar (Ag) 1928. Bust facing of Dr. Sun Yat Sen; legend in Chinese characters giving name of country and date. ℞ in centre, sun within dotted circle. Legend in Chinese characters giving name of province and value, as well as two Manchu characters	300.00	480.00

Kiangsee (Kiangsi) 江 西

1	10	Cash (Cu) 1912. Nine-pointed star in dotted circle and legend KIANG-SEE TEN CASH. ℞ names of country, province, and denomination as well as date and value in Chinese characters	2.50	4.00
2	1	Dollar (Ag) 1912. Similar to No. 1, but value in the obverse legend ONE DOLLAR	–.–	–.–

Kwangsea (Kwangsi) 廣西

			VF	XF
1	1	Cent (Bra) 1919. The figure 1 in dotted circle and legend KWANG SEA PROVINCE ONE CENT. ℞ names of country, province, and denomination as well as date and value in Chinese characters	100.00	180.00
2	1	Cent (Bra) 1919. As type No. 1, but in the obverse legend the name of the province reads KWANGSI	35.00	55.00
3	10	Cents (Ag) 1920, 1921. The figure 10 in circle and legend KWANG-SI PROVINCE TEN CENTS. ℞ name of province and denomination as well as date and value. The 1921 issue was only a pattern issue	75.00	110.00
4	20	Cents (Ag) 1919, 1920, 1924. As type No. 3, but on the obverse the figure 20 and the inscription KWANG-SEA PROVINCE TWENTY CENTS	60.00	90.00
5	20	Cents (Ag) 1919–1923. As type No. 4, but in the obverse legend the name of the province KWANG-SI. The 1921 issue was only a pattern issue	30.00	50.00
6	20	Cents (Ag) 1924. As type No. 5, but in addition, in centre of reverse, a Chinese character for Kweilin	65.00	100.00
7	20	Cents (Ag) 1924. As type No. 6, but for the name of the province read KWANG-SEA instead of KWANG-SI	6.00	9.00
8	20	Cents (Ag) 1925. As type No. 5, but in addition, in centre of reverse, the Chinese character Si	–.–	–.–
9	20	Cents (Ag) 1926, 1927. Similar to No. 7, but the figure 20 on obverse is surrounded by ears of corn	14.00	25.00
10	5	Cents (Ni) 1923. Figure 5 within wreath and legend KWANG-SI PROVINCE FIFE CENTS. ℞ name of country and province as well as date and value in Chinese characters. Pattern	–.–	–.–
11	20	Cents (Ag) 1949. Scenery with junk surrounded by 24 rosettes. ℞ Chinese characters, among which names of country and province as well as date and value	120.00	180.00

			VF	XF
1	10	Cents (Ag) 1912. Two crossed flags and five spears in dotted circle. Legend KWANG-TUNG PROVINCE TEN CENTS. ℞ names of country and province as well as date and value in Chinese characters. Pattern	–.–	–.–
2	10	Cents (Ag) 1912. Crossed flags with swords and guns in dotted circle. Legend KWANG-TUNG PROVINCE TEN CENTS. ℞ Chinese characters, among which name of province, date and value. Pattern	–.–	–.–
3	1	Cent (Bra) 1912, 1914–1916, 1918. Figure 1 in dotted circle and legend KWANG-TUNG PROVINCE ONE CENT. ℞ Chinese characters, among which names of country, province, and denomination as well as date and value	2.00	4.00
4	2	Cents (Bra) 1918. Type as No. 3	45.00	80.00
5	10	Cents (Ag) 1913, 1914, 1922. The figure 10 in dotted circle and legend KWANG-TUNG PROVINCE TEN CENTS. ℞ Chinese characters, among which name of province, date and value	4.00	6.00

6	20	Cents (Ag) 1912–1915, 1918–1924. As type No. 5, but value in obverse in form of figure 20 and in the legend TWENTY CENTS	4.00	6.00
7	5	Cents (Ni) 1919. The figure 5 in wreath within dotted circle. Legend KWANG-TUNG PROVINCE FIVE CENTS. R names of country and province as well as date and value in Chinese characters	2.25	4.50
8	5	Cents (Ni) 1923. Type similar to No. 7, but different Chinese characters	4.00	6.00

			VF	XF
9	5	Cents (Ni) 1921. Flags in dotted circle and legend KWANG-TUNG PROVINCE FIVE CENTS. R names of country and province as well as date and value in Chinese characters	4.50	8.00
10	20	Cents (Ag) 1924. Head l. of Dr. Sun Yat Sen. R Chinese characters, among which name of province, date and value	14.00	22.00
11	20	Cents (Ag) 1928–1930. Head l. of Dr. Sun Yat Sen. Value in Chinese characters within wreath and legend in Chinese characters, among which name of province and date. The 1930 issue was only a pattern issue	3.50	6.00
12	10	Cents (Ag) 1929. Head l. of Dr. Sun Yat Sen. R value in Chinese characters in dotted circle as well as names of country, province, and date forming legend in Chinese characters. Twelve-pointed sun to left and right	2.50	4.00
13	1	Cent (Cu) 1936. Landscape with animals, country and province designation as well as the year, as an inscription, above in Chinese characters. R rice panicle as well as denomination in Chinese characters. A round hole in the centre	120.00	220.00

Kweichow 貴州

COMMEMORATIVE ISSUE FOR THE FIRST ROAD IN KWEICHOW

1	1	Dollar (Ag) 1928. Automobile in dotted circle and legend in Chinese characters, among which name of province and value. R Chinese characters,

			VF	XF
		among which name of country, date and value	450.00	750.00
2	10	Cents (Antimony) 1931. Twelve-pointed sun in circle. ℞ four Chinese characters in circle and inscription in Chinese characters, among which names of country and province as well as date and value	650.00	800.00
3	20	Cents (Ag) 1949. The figure 20 within circle made of 28 figures of 20. Meander pattern border. ℞ Chinese characters, among which names of country and province as well as date and value. Meander pattern border. Pattern	200.00	260.00
4	20	Cents (Ag) 1949. Value in old Chinese seal characters within circle made of 30 figures of 20. ℞ similar to No. 2. Pattern	300.00	500.00
5	50	Cents (Ag) 1949. The figure 50 within circle made of 32 figures of 50. Meander pattern border. ℞ similar to No. 2. Pattern	400.00	700.00
6	1	Dollar (Ag) 1949. Bamboo stems (Gramineae family) in dotted circle; value to right and left in Chinese characters. ℞ pavilion within wreath and legend in Chinese characters, among which names of country and province as well as date. Pattern	2600.00	3500.00

Manchuria 東三省

1	1	Cent (Cu) 1929. Sun composed of twelve rays in the floral wreath. ℞ denomination in Chinese characters in dotted circle. Country and province designation in Chinese characters	3.00	5.00
2	1	Tael (Au) 1932 (undated). Chinese character "Fuh". ℞ inscription "24 K 1000"	–.–	–.–
3	1	Teal (Au) 1932 (undated). Chinese character "Hsih". ℞ inscription "24 K 1000"	–.–	–.–
4	1	Tael (Au) 1932 (undated). In the centre the character "Fuh" in ancient Chinese 'seal writing' in square border. Legend by way of four Chinese characters. ℞ "24 K 1000" and four Chinese characters in square border	–.–	–.–
5	1	Tael (Au) 1932 (?) (undated). Chinese character "Shou" in ancient Chinese 'seal writing'. ℞ inscription "24 K 1000"	–.–	–.–

Inner Mongolia 內蒙古

			VF	XF
1	50	Cents (Ni) 1938. Value in Chinese characters between stylized dragons. Above, seven Mongolian characters. ℞ Chinese characters between floral ornaments, among which name of country, mint, and date	10.00	20.00

North China

The provinces of Honan, Hopei, Hupeh, Shansi and Shantung were integrated into the Government territory of North China under the Japanese Occupation.

1	1	Cent (Al) 1941–1943. Sun temple; value to right and left in Chinese characters. ℞ in centre, three interlocking circles within double circle. Inscription in Chinese characters, among which legend reading "The Federal Reserve Bank", and date	0.60	1.20
2	5	Cents (Al) 1941–1943. As type No. 1	2.00	4.00
3	10	Cents (Al) 1941–1943. As type No. 1	1.50	3.00

Shansi 山西

1	10	Cash (Cu) undated. Crossed flags within circle and legend in Chinese characters, among which names of country and province as well as value. ℞ value in Chinese characters between ears of corn	150.00	200.00
2	5	Cents (Ni) 1925. Crossed flags in dotted circle and legend in Chinese characters, among which name of country, date and value. ℞ name of province and denomination in Chinese characters within wreath	–.–	–.–

Shantung (Shangtung) 山東

1	10	Dollars (Au) 1926. Dragon and phoenix. ℞ value in Chinese characters within wreath. Legend in Chinese characters, among which name of country and date. Pattern	3000.00	4000.00

		VF	XF

2 20 Dollars (Au) 1926. As type No. 1.
Pattern .... 4000.00 — 5000.00

3 2 Cents (Ni) 1933. Value in Chinese characters within ring of several rosettes. Above, value in Chinese characters; below, inscription TWO CENTS. ℞ crossed flags and legend in Chinese characters, among which names of country and province as well as date. Pattern .... —.— — —.—

Shensi 陝 西

1 1 Cent (Cu) 1924 (?) (undated). Crossed flags; inscription IMTYPIF .... 140.00 — 200.00

2 2 Cents (Cu) undated. Value in Chinese characters and ears of corn in dotted circle. In centre, dot within circle. Legend in Chinese characters, among which name of province and value. ℞ crossed flags in dotted circle. In centre, dot within circle. Legend above giving name of country in Chinese characters, and below, IMTYPEF .... 60.00 — 100.00

3 2 Cents (Cu) undated. Type as No. 2, but star between flags .... 75.00 — 110.00

Sinkiang (Chinese Turkestan) 新 疆

General issues for Sinkiang:

1 5 Mace (Ag) 1912. Crossed flags, date in Chinese characters between flag-staffs. ℞ Chinese characters, among which name of country and denomination as well as value .... 50.00 — 65.00

2 1 Tael (Ag) 1912. As type No. 1 .... 400.00 — 550.00

2a 5 Mace (Ag) 1912. As type No. 1, but in the flags only two strips with arabesques .... 100.00 — 160.00

2b 1 Tael (Ag) 1912. As type No. 2, but in the flags only two strips with arabesques .... 400.00 — 550.00

2c 20 Cash (Cu) 1912 (undated). Crossed flags. ℞ province and coin designation by way of four Chinese characters in the dotted circle. In the legend, country designation and denomination in Chinese characters .... 130.00 — 180.00

			VF	XF
3	1	Dollar (Ag) 1949. The figure 1 and Arabic characters in dotted circle. In the legend, Arabic characters and date 1949. ℞ value in Chinese characters within wreath of ears of corn. Legend in Chinese characters, among which names of country and province as well as value	–.–	–.–

Issue for Aksu: 阿 城

4	10	Cash (Cu) undated	165.00	240.00

Issues for Kashgar: 喀 什

5	5	Cash (Cu) 1913 (H. C. 1331). Crossed flags, Arabic characters between flag-staffs. ℞ Chinese characters, among which name of country and value	70.00	100.00
6	10	Cash (Cu) 1912–1914	15.00	20.00
7	5	Mace (Ag) 1913, 1914, 1916. Crossed flags, between the flagstaffs Arabic characters. ℞ Chinese characters, among others name of country and province as well as denomination	30.00	50.00
8	10	Cash (Cu) 1918. Coin designation in Chinese characters within sun composed of 12 rays. ℞ name of country in Chinese characters in the dotted circle. In the legend name of province, mint, date and denomination in Chinese characters	–.–	–.–
9	10	Cash (Cu) 1921, 1922. Crossed flags, top and bottom between the flagstaffs Arabic characters. ℞ name of country in Chinese characters in the dotted circle. In the legend name of province, mint, date and denomination in Chinese characters	50.00	80.00
10	10	Cash (Bra) 1930. Crossed flags, above Chinese characters between the flag-staffs. ℞ Chinese characters, among others name of country and province as well as mint and denomination. In the centre a rosette	–.–	–.–

			VF	XF
11	1	Tael (Ag) 1917. Arabic characters in dotted circle and border of leaf decoration and ears of corn. ℞ Chinese and Arabic characters in dotted circle as well as legend in Chinese characters, among which name of country, mint, date, and value	160.00	240.00
12	1	Tael (Ag) 1917. Type as No. 10, but in border decoration of leaves on obverse, in addition a rosette above (several variants through changes in the decoration of leaves)	160.00	240.00
13	1	Tael (Ag) 1918. Type as No. 11, but border decoration of leaves on obverse is of varied type (not in the form of corn-ears)	180.00	260.00

Szechuan 四川

1	5	Cash (Cu or Bra) 1912–1914. Inscription in old Chinese seal characters within circle, the whole surrounded by 18 rings. ℞ Chinese characters, among which name of province and denomination as well as value	65.00	90.00
2	10	Cash (Cu or Bra) 1912–1914. Similar to No. 1	3.00	5.00
3	20	Cash (Cu or Bra) 1912–1914. Similar to No. 1	3.00	5.00
4	50	Cash (Cu or Bra) 1912–1914. Similar to No. 1	4.00	6.00
5	100	Cash (Cu or Bra) 1912–1914. Similar to No. 1	6.00	11.00
6	5	Cash (Cu or Bra) 1912. Crossed flags. ℞ Chinese characters for Szechuan in centre	45.00	70.00

			VF	XF
7	5	Cash (Cu or Bra) 1912. Lion and cloud	55.00	90.00
8	10	Cash (Cu or Bra) 1912	–.–	–.–
9	100	Cash (Cu or Bra) 1913	–.–	–.–
10	200	Cash (Cu or Bra) 1913. Crossed flags within dotted circle and legend THE REPUBLIC OF CHINA 200 CASH. ℞ Value in Chinese characters between ears of corn and flower decoration within dotted circle. Legend in Chinese characters, among which names of country and province	22.00	30.00
11	500	Cash (Cu) undated	–.–	–.–
12	10	Cents (Ag) 1912. In centre, Chinese characters in old Chinese seal characters, surrounded by 18 rings; above, name of country and date in Chinese characters. ℞ Chinese characters, among which name of province and value	20.00	30.00
13	20	Cents (Ag) 1912. Type as No. 12	26.00	40.00
14	50	Cents (Ag) 1912, 1913. Type as No. 12	28.00	45.00
15	1	Dollar (Ag) 1912, 1914. Type as No. 12	32.00	50.00
16	20	Cents (Ag) 1912. Lion above cloud. ℞ crossed flags within dotted circle; name of country and date above in Chinese characters	–.–	–.–
17	10	Cents (Ag) 1912. Value in Chinese characters within wreath of corn-ears. ℞ four Chinese characters with star in centre	–.–	–.–
19	5	Cents (Ni) 1925. Value in Chinese characters within circle; in centre, two circles. Name of country, date, and value forming legend in Chinese characters. ℞ four-pointed star between rice stalks	–.–	–.–
20	10	Cents (Ni) 1926 (undated). Value in Chinese characters surrounded by leaf ornaments. R crossed flags	–.–	–.–
21	10	Cents (Ag) 1926. Type as No. 20	–.–	–.–
22	50	Cash (Cu or Bra) 1926	35.00	55.00
23	100	Cash (Cu or Bra) 1926	10.00	18.00
24	200	Cash (Cu or Bra) 1926. In centre, Chinese character for Szechuan within circle. Legend with name of country, date, and value in Chinese characters. ℞ figure 200 in four-pointed star between rice stalks	10.50	16.00
25	50	Cents (Ag) 1928. Head facing of Dr. Sun Yat Sen within circle. Legend with name of province and date in Chinese characters. ℞ value in Chinese charac-		

			VF	XF
		ters between rice stalks and decoration of leaves	200.00	320.00
26	1	Dollar (Ag) 1928. Type as No. 25	480.00	700.00
27	100	Cash (Bra) 1930. Obverse similar to No. 22. ℞ twelve Chinese characters in four lines	80.00	100.00
28	2	Cents (Cu) 1930. In the centre a sun composed of 12 rays in a wreath of branches of buds, open at the top. Above inscription 2 CENTS. ℞ Chinese characters (partly in ornamental border), among others name of country and province as well as date and denomination	150.00	225.00
29	20	Cents (Ag) 1932. Bust facing of Liu Wen Hwei (*1895), General and Governor of the Szechuan province, in uniform with cap. Legend in Chinese characters, among which name of province. ℞ crossed flags and Chinese characters. Below the flags the date 1932	110.00	160.00

Yunnan 雲南

			VF	XF
1	50	Cash (Bra) 1912 (undated). Bust turned half to l. of T'ang Chi-yao (1882 to 1927), General and Governor of the Yunnan province, within dotted circle. Border of leaf ornaments and, above, four Chinese characters. ℞ crossed flags and legend in Chinese characters, among which name of province and value	40.00	70.00
2	50	Cents (Ag) 1916 (undated). Bust r. of General T'ang Chi-yao; above, legend of seven Chinese characters. ℞ crossed flags in dotted circle; above, star between flag-staffs. Legend in Chinese characters, among which value	18.50	30.00
3	50	Cents (Ag) 1917 (undated). Bust turned half to l. of General T'ang Chi-yao within dotted circle. Border of leaf ornaments and, above, seven Chinese characters. ℞ as No. 2	30.00	55.00
4	5	Dollars (Au) 1917 (undated). Value given by five Chinese characters arranged vertically. To right and left, a group of five dots. ℞ blank	–.–	–.–
5	10	Dollars (Au) 1917 (undated). Type as No. 4	–.–	–.–

			VF	XF
6	5	Dollars (Au) 1919 (undated). Bust turned half to l. of General T'ang Chi-yao; above, legend of Chinese characters. ℞ crossed flags in dotted circle; above, five-pointed star between flag-staffs. Legend in Chinese characters, among which value	–.–	–.–
7	10	Dollars (Au) 1919 (undated). Type as No. 6	800.00	1400.00
8	5	Dollars (Au) 1919 (undated). Type as No. 6, but figure 2 between flag-staffs on the reverse	850.00	1200.00
9	10	Dollars (Au) 1919 (undated). Type as No. 7, but figure 1 between flag-staffs on the reverse	900.00	1500.00
10	5	Cents (Ni) 1923. Flags within dotted circle and legend YUN-NAN PROVINCE FIFE CENTS. ℞ Chinese characters, among which name of country, date, and value	38.00	60.00
11	10	Cents (Ni) 1923. Type as No. 10, but value 10 CENTS in the obverse inscription	3.50	6.00
12	5	Dollars (Au) 1925 (undated). Value in four Chinese characters. In centre, rosette. ℞ Chinese character for Yunnan between ears of corn	750.00	1000.00
13	10	Dollars (Au) 1925 (undated). Type as No. 12, but dot in centre of obverse	850.00	1200.00
14	20	Cents (Ag) 1926. Crossed flags; above, five-pointed star, below, leaf ornament. ℞ Chinese characters, among which name of country and denomination as well as date and value. Pattern	–.–	–.–
14a	2	Cents (Bra) 1932	320.00	400.00
15	5	Cents (Bra) 1932. Crossed flags within dotted circle. In centre, dot surrounded by circle. Above, figure 5 between flag-staffs. Legend in Chinese characters, among which name of country and date. ℞ Chinese characters, among which name of province and value. In centre, dot surrounded by circle	200.00	280.00
16	20	Cents (Ag) 1932. Crossed flags within dotted circle; above, name of country and date in Chinese characters. ℞ Chinese characters, among which name of province and denomination as well as value	12.50	20.00
17	50	Cents (Ag) 1932. Type as No. 16	7.00	12.00
18	20	Cents (Ag) 1949. Building. ℞ names of country and province as well as date		

		VF	XF

and value in Chinese characters. In
centre, rosette   55.00   85.00

Yunnan - Burma

Special coins were issued occasionally during the 2nd World War for
the Chinese troops on the Yunnan-Burma Front. According to more
recent information, this is supposed to concern issues by the troops
of Chiang Kai-shek who had been forced on to Burmese territory by
the Red Army of China.

1   ½ Tael (Ag) 1949? (undated). Denomination in four Chinese characters,
above a semicircle of Burmese characters. ℞ characters in the so-called
small 'seal writing', meaning "Luck"   38.00   72.00

2   1 Tael (Ag) 1949 (undated). Type as No. 1   55.00   84.00

			VF	**XF**
3		1 Tael (Ag) 1943 (undated). Value in Burmese characters (one line) and in Chinese characters (two lines) within circle. ℞ head of stag within circle	45.00	80.00

With the design of type No. 3, a ½ Tael coin has been reported.

Issues of the Communist People's Army

The Red Army of China (Communist People's Army) was established in 1928 during the Chinese civil war until the fall of the Central Government. Under the command of Mao Tse-tung and Chou Teh, this army occupied and governed, at different times, different provinces of China where it issued its own coins between 1931 and 1934. From 1947 to 1949 the Red Army of China occupied the whole of the Chinese mainland, so that the Central Government under General Chiang Kai-shek had to withdraw to Taiwan.

On the mainland, the People's Republic of China was formed in 1949, and in 1950, in Taiwan, the National Republic of China.

Issues for Kiangsee (Kiangsi).

1		1 Cent (Cu) 1932 (undated). Figure 1 in front of hammer and sickle; above, legend in Chinese characters. ℞ value in Chinese characters between ears of corn; above, five-pointed star	10.50	15.00
2		5 Cents (Cu) 1932 (undated). Hammer and sickle; in background, sketch of the land of China in dotted circle. Legend in Chinese characters. ℞ value in Chinese characters between ears of corn; above, five-pointed star	10.50	15.00

			VF	**XF**

3   20 Cents (Ag) 1932, 1933. Hammer and sickle in front of globe placed between ears of corn. Above, five-pointed star and Chinese characters. ℞ value and legend in Chinese characters, among which date   **VF** 55.00   **XF** 90.00

Issues for Hunan:

1   1 Dollar (Ag) 1930 (undated). Head right of Lenin (?) within circle. Above, inscription in Chinese characters. ℞ value in Chinese characters between hammer and sickle in double circle   150.00   200.00

2   1 Dollar (Ag) 1931. Hammer and sickle in front of five-pointed star within circle. Legend in Chinese characters. ℞ value in Chinese characters within wreath   180.00   225.00

Issues for Hupeh, Anhwei and Honan:

1   1 Dollar (Ag) 1932. Hammer and sickle in front of globe and legend in Chinese characters. ℞ value in Chinese characters within circle. Above, date in Chinese characters and, below, legend in pseudo-cyrillic characters   450.00   600.00

2   1 Dollar (Ag) 1932. Hammer and sickle in front of globe within dotted circle. In the legend, twelve Chinese characters. ℞ value in Chinese characters within circle. Legend in Chinese characters, among which date   285.00   400.00

Issues for Szechuan and Shensi:

1   20 Cents (Ag) 1932 (undated). In centre, a linear and a dotted circle. Legend in Chinese characters. ℞ crossed flags within dotted circle. Legend in Chinese characters   –.–   –.–

2   200 Cash (Cu) 1933. Hammer and sickle; above, three five-pointed stars. Chinese characters forming inscription above, and below, CCZC. ℞ figure 200 within wreath and legend in Chinese characters, among which date   50.00   85.00

			VF	EF
3	200	Cash (Cu) 1934. Five-pointed star with hammer and sickle. Four Chinese characters between the points and the date 1934. ℞ figure 200 within circle and legend in Chinese characters, among which value	65.00	100.00
4	500	Cash (Cu) 1934. Hammer and sickle in front of five-pointed star and legend in Chinese characters, among which date. ℞ figure 500 within circle and legend in Chinese characters, among which value	80.00	125.00
5	1	Dollar (Ag) 1934. Hammer and sickle in front of globe. Legend in Chinese characters, among which date. ℞ value in dotted circle and legend in Chinese characters	210.00	280.00

People's Republic of China
Chinesische Volksrepublik   **République populaire du Chine**

Chung Hua Ren Min Gung Ho Kuo

中 華 人 民 共 和 國

Area: 3,700,000 sq. mi. Population: 880,000,000.
The Red Army of China (Communist People's Army) which was
formed in 1928 during the Chinese civil war, occupied the whole of
the Chinese mainland from 1947 to 1949 whilst fighting against the
troops of the Central Government of the Republic of China, so that
the Central Government under General Chiang Kai-shek had to withdraw to Taiwan. On 1st October 1949, the People's Republic of China
was set up in Peking.
Capital: Peking.

100 Fen 分 = 1 Yuan 圓 or 元
since June 1969: 100 Fen = 10 Chiao = 1 Renminbi Yuan

			VF	XF
1 (1)	1 Fen (Al) 1955–. National arms of the People's Republic of China; above, name of country in Chinese charac-ters. ℞ value in Chinese characters between ears of corn; above, value and below, date in Arabic figures		0.25	0.50
2 (2)	2 Fen (Al) 1955–. Type as No. 1		0.30	0.70

3 (3)	5 Fen (Al) 1955–. Type as No. 1		0.50	0.80

			Proof
4 (4)	400 Yuan (Au) 1979. Tian An Men		500.00
5 (5)	400 Yuan (Au) 1979. People's Heroes Monument		500.00
6 (6)	400 Yuan (Au) 1979. Chairman Mao Tse Tung Memorial Hall		500.00
7 (7)	400 Yuan (Au) 1979. Great Hall of the People		500.00

INTERNATIONAL YEAR OF THE CHILD 1979 (2)

8 (8)	35 Yuan (Ag) 1979	55.00
9 (9)	450 Yuan (Au) 1979. Girl and boy:	
	a) 17.2 gm.	900.00
	b) 34,4 gm.; Piéfort	2500.00

13th OLYMPIC WINTER GAMES IN LAKE PLACID (6)

10 (15)	1 Yuan (Bra) 1980. Speed Skating	12.50
11 (14)	1 Yuan (Bra) 1980. Alpine Skiing	12.50
12 (16)	1 Yuan (Bra) 1980. Figure Skating	12.50
13 (17)	1 Yuan (Bra) 1980. Biathlon	12.50
14 (21)	30 Yuan (Ag) 1980. Type as No. 10	65.00
15 (22)	250 Yuan (Au) 1980. Type as No. 11	600.00

			Proof
16 (11)	1 Yuan (Bra) 1980. Wrestling		12.50
17 (12)	1 Yuan (Bra) 1980. Equestrian		12.50
18 (13)	1 Yuan (Bra) 1980. Soccer		12.50
19 (10)	1 Yuan (Bra) 1980. Archery		12.50
20 (18)	20 Yuan (Ag) 1980. Type as No. 16		50.00
21 (19)	30 Yuan (Ag) 1980. Type as No. 17		60.00
22 (20)	30 Yuan (Ag) 1980. Type as No. 18		60.00
23 (23)	300 Yuan (Au) 1980. Type as No. 19		650.00

		VF	XF
24 (24)	1 Chiao (Bra) 1980. Arms. Rev. value		0.50
25 (25)	2 Chiao (Bra) 1980. Type as No. 24		0.60
26 (26)	5 Chiao (Bra) 1980. Type as No. 24		1.00

27 (27)	1 Yuan (Cu-Ni) 1980. Great Wall of China	3.00

CHINESE BRONZE AGE FINDS (4)

		Proof
28 (29)	200 Yuan (Au) 1981. Dragon	500.00
29 (28)	200 Yuan (Au) 1981. Leopard	500.00
30 (30)	400 Yuan (Au) 1981. Rhinocerous	800.00
31 (31)	800 Yuan (Au) 1981. Elephant	1400.00

		Proof
32	30 Yuan (Ag) 1981	75.00
33	250 Yuan (Au) 1981	500.00

WORLD SOCCER CHAMPIONSHIP GAMES 1982 IN SPAIN (4)

34	1 Yuan (Bra) 1982	12.00
35	25 Yuan (Ag) 1982	40.00
36	25 Yuan (Ag) 1982	40.00
37	200 Yuan (Au) 1982	250.00

Kolumbien   # Colombia   **Colombie**

Area: 437,822 sq. mi. Population: 25,000,000.

After the discovery by Hojeda and Vespucci in the year 1499 and the conquest, the kingdom of the Chibcha was made a Spanish Viceroyalty, which also included Ecuador. The Wars of Independence against the Spanish domination began in 1810. The state of Colombia, also known for a long time as New Grenada, also included, temporarily, the countries of Panama and Venezuela as well as Ecuador.

Capital: Bogotá.

100 Centavos = 1 Colombian Peso

REPUBLIC OF COLOMBIA

			VF	XF
1 (23)	2½	Centavos (Cu-Ni) 1900, 1902. Cap of Liberty. R value within circle	80.00	135.00
2 (25)	5	Centavos (Cu-Ni) 1886, 1902. Head of Liberty to left. R value between branches	3.00	6.00
3 (28a)	50	Centavos (Ag) 1889, 1898–1899, 1906 to 1908. Head of Liberty to left. R national arms, value in letters	9.00	15.00
4 (42)	1	Peso (Cu–Ni) 1907–1916. Head of Liberty to right. R value within wreath	1.50	2.20
5 (43)	2	Pesos (Cu–Ni) 1907–1914. Type as No. 4	2.00	3.00
6 (44)	5	Pesos (Cu–Ni) 1907–1914. Type as No. 4	1.50	2.50
7 (45)	5	Centavos (Ag) 1902. Head of Liberty to left. R national arms and value in letters	2.50	4.00
8 (46)	50	Centavos (Ag) 1902. Head of Liberty to left. R national arms and value in letters	25.00	35.00
9 (47)	10	Centavos (Ag) 1911–1942. Simón Bolívar (1783–1830), President of State 1810–1812. R national arms with Andean condor (Vultur gryphus — Cathartidae)	3.00	4.50
10 (48)	20	Centavos (Ag) 1911–1942. Type as No. 9	4.00	6.00
11 (49)	50	Centavos (Ag) 1912–1934. Type as No. 9	10.00	16.00

			VF	XF
12 (50)	2½	Pesos (Au) 1913. Workman cutting stone. ℞ national arms	80.00	105.00
13 (51)	5	Pesos (Au) 1913–1919. Type as No. 12	125.00	150.00
14 (52)	2½	Pesos (Au) 1919–1920. Large head to right of Simón Bolívar, reaching almost to the border above and below. ℞ national arms	85.00	115.00
15 (53)	5	Pesos (Au) 1919–1924. Type as No. 14	150.00	180.00
16 (54)	10	Pesos (Au) 1919–1924. Type as No. 14	250.00	280.00
17 (55)	2½	Pesos (Au) 1924–1928. Smaller head to right of Simón Bolívar. ℞ national arms	85.00	100.00
18 (56)	5	Pesos (Au) 1924–1930. Type as No. 17	155.00	170.00
19 (57)	1	Centavo (Cu–Ni) 1918–1948. Head of Liberty to right. ℞ value within wreath	0.10	0.20
20 (57a)	1	Centavo (Ni–St) 1952–1958. Type as No. 19	0.10	0.20
21 (61)	1	Centavo. Cap of Liberty within wreath. ℞ value between branches		
		a) (Br) 1942–1966	0.20	0.30
		b) (Br–St) 1967–	0.10	0.20
22 (59)	2	Centavos (Cu–Ni) 1918–1947. Head of Liberty to right. ℞ value within wreath	0.30	0.50
23 (62)	2	Centavos (Br) 1948–1950. Cap of Liberty within wreath. ℞ value between branches	0.30	0.50
24 (60)	5	Centavos (Cu-Ni) 1918–1950. Head of Liberty to right. ℞ value within wreath	0.25	0.40
25 (63)	5	Centavos (Br) 1942–1966. Phrygian cap between branches tied below. ℞ branches of the coffee tree, denomination	0.35	0.60
26 (64)	10	Centavos. Head right of Francisco de Paula Santander (1792–1840), President of State of New Grenada (1832–1836). ℞ value within wreath		
		a) (Ag) 1945–1952	0.70	1.20
		b) (Ni–St) 1967–1969	0.20	0.30
27 (65)	20	Centavos		
		a) (Ag) 1945–1952 (1952 very rare)	1.40	2.50
		b) (Ni–St) 1967–1969	0.30	0.50
28 (66)	50	Centavos (Ag) 1947–1948. Head left of Simón Bolívar. ℞ value within wreath	5.00	8.50
29 (A 65)	50	Centavos (Ni–St) 1967–1969. Type as No. 26	0.50	0.80
30 (67)	2	Centavos (Al–Br) 1952–1965. Head of Liberty to left. ℞ value within wreath	0.25	0.40
A30 (67a)	2	Centavos (Al-Br) 1955, 1959, 1961, 1963, 1964, 1965. Type as No. 30, but full circular inscription	0.25	0.40

31 (68)	10	Centavos (Cu–Ni) 1952–1966. National arms. ℞ head right of the Indian Chief Calarcá; value a) 1952, 1953, diameter 18 mm b) 1954–1966, diameter 18.5 mm	**VF** 0.30 0.15	**XF** 0.60 0.30

32 (69)	20	Centavos (Ag) 1953. National arms. ℞ bust left of Simón Bolívar	1.70	3.00
33 (70)	20	Centavos (Cu–Ni) 1956–1966. Head right of Simón Bolívar. ℞ national arms	0.30	0.60
34 (71)	50	Centavos (Cu–Ni) 1958–1966. Type as No. 33	0.70	1.20

COMMEMORATIVE ISSUE FOR THE 200th ANNIVERSARY OF THE EXISTENCE OF THE MINT AT POPAYÁN

35 (72)	1	Peso (Ag) 1956. Mint building surrounded by laurel branches, inscription CASA DE MONEDA 1756–1956. ℞ national arms and value	22.00	30.00

COMMEMORATIVE ISSUES (6) FOR THE 150th ANNIVERSARY OF THE BEGINNING OF THE WARS OF INDEPENDENCE

36 (73)	1	Centavo (Br). Dates 1810–1960	1.60	3.00
37 (74)	2	Centavos (Al–Br). Dates 1810–1960	2.00	3.60
38 (A 74)	5	Centavos (Br). Dates 1810–1960	2.60	4.80
39 (75)	10	Centavos (Cu–Ni). Dates 1810–1960	2.00	3.00
40 (76)	20	Centavos (Cu–Ni). Dates 1810–1960	2.00	3.00
41 (77)	50	Centavos (Cu–Ni) Dates 1810–1960	2.50	4.00

COMMEMORATIVE ISSUES (2) FOR JORGE ELIECER GAITÁN

			VF	XF
42 (78)	20	Centavos (Cu–Ni) 1965. Jorge Eliecer Gaitán (1898–1948), attorney, liberal politician. ℞ national arms	0.60	1.20
43 (79)	50	Centavos (Cu–Ni) 1965. Type as No. 42	1.20	2.40
44 (80)	1	Peso (Cu–Ni) 1967. Simón Bolívar. ℞ value within wreath	0.70	1.50
45 (63a)	5	Centavos (Br–St) 1967. Jacobean cap, or Liberty cap, surrounded by branches. ℞ branches of the coffee tree (Coffea arabica — Rubiaceae) with blossom and fruit; cornucopia	0.10	0.20

COMMEMORATIVE ISSUES (6) FOR THE 39th EUCHARISTIC WORLD CONGRESS IN BOGOTÁ
from 22nd to 24th August 1968

46 (81)	5	Pesos (Cu–Ni) 1968. Emblem of the World Congress, by Dr. Dicken Castro: a cross made of fishes representing the mission work extending to all four corners of the earth. ℞ value within wreath	1.50	2.50
47	100	Pesos (Au) 1968. Pope Paul VI (1897–1978); the cathedral on Plaza de Bolivar in Bogotá; emblem of the World Congress. R national arms, value	Proof	80.00
48	200	Pesos (Au) 1968. Type as No. 47		160.00
49	300	Pesos (Au) 1968. Type as No. 47		240.00
50	500	Pesos (Au) 1968. Type as No. 47		400.00
51	1500	Pesos (Au) 1968. Type as No. 47		1100.00

COMMEMORATIVE ISSUES (5) FOR THE 150th ANNIVERSARY OF THE BATTLE OF BOYACÁ

52	100	Pesos (Au) 1969. Simón Bolívar (1783 to 1830), national hero of Latin Ameri-

		ca. ℞ Joaqín París y Ricaurte (1795 to 1868), Colombian General; national arms, value	Proof
			80.00
53	200	Pesos (Au) 1969. ℞ Carlos Soublette (†1870), Venezuelan General; national arms, value	160.00

54	300	Pesos (Au) 1969. ℞ José Antonio Anzoátegui (1789–1819), Venezuelan General; national arms, value		240.00
55	500	Pesos (Au) 1969. ℞ Juan José Rondón (c. 1780–1822), Colombian General; national arms, value		400.00
56	1500	Pesos (Au) 1969. ℞ Francisco de Paula Santander (1792–1840), General, President of State of New Grenada 1832 to 1836; national arms, value		1100.00
			VF	**XF**
57 (82)	10	Centavos (Ni-clad steel) 1969 1971. Type as No. 26, but legend divided after REPUBLIC DE	0.10	0.20
A57 (82.1)	10	Centavos (Ni-clad steel) 1970, 1971. Type as No. 57, but legend divided after REPUBLICA	0.10	0.20
B57 (82.2)	10	Centavos (Ni-clad steel) 1972–1978. Type as No. 57, but legend continuous	0.10	0.20
58 (83)	20	Centavos (Ni-clad steel) 1969, 1970. Type as No. A 57	0.10	0.20
A58 (83.1)	20	Centavos (Ni-clad steel) 1971. Type as No. 57	0.10	0.20
B58 (83.2)	20	Centavos (Ni-clad steel) 1971–1978. Type as No. B57	0.10	0.20
59 (84)	50	Centavos (Ni-clad steel) 1970–1973, 1975–1979. Type as No. B57	0.15	0.30
60 (84)	50	Centavos (Ni-clad steel) 1974. Type as No. 59, but large date	0.20	0.35

COMMEMORATIVE ISSUES (6) FOR THE VI PANAMERICAN GAMES IN CALI from 28th–30th July 1971

			VF	XF
61 (85)	5 Pesos (Cu–Ni) 1971		1.20	2.00

			Proof
62 (86)	100 Pesos (Au) 1971	100.00
63 (87)	200 Pesos (Au) 1971	200.00
64 (88)	300 Pesos (Au) 1971	260.00
65 (89)	500 Pesos (Au) 1971	500.00
66 (90)	1500 Pesos (Au) 1971	1300.00

COMMEMORATIVE ISSUE FOR THE 50th ANNIVERSARY OF THE GOLD MUSEUM (MUSEO DE ORO) OF THE CENTRAL BANK OF BOGOTÁ

67 (91) 1500 Pesos (Au) 1973. Pre-Columbian urn, rare archeological treasure, made by Chibcha Indians. ℞ value   400.00

100th ANNIVERSARY OF THE BIRTH OF GUILLERMO VALENCIA (3)

68 (92) 1000 Pesos (Au) 1973. Guillermo Valencia (1873-1943), bust right. ℞ coat of arms, value, date   100.00
69 (93) 1500 Pesos (Au) 1973. Type as No. 68   160.00
70 (94) 2000 Pesos (Au) 1973. Type as No. 68   250.00

			XF	Unc
71 (95)	1 Peso (German silver) 1974–1979. Bust of Simón Bolívar (1783–1830), statesman and general, liberator of South America from Spanish rule. ℞ corn cob (Zea mays – Gramineae) and value		0.20	0.40

450th ANNIVERSARY OF THE CITY OF SANTA MARTA (2)

		Proof
72 (96)	1000 Pesos (Au) 1975	100.00
73 (97)	2000 Pesos (Au) 1975	220.00

300th ANNIVERSARY OF MEDELLIN (2)

		Proof
74 (98)	1000 Pesos (Au) 1975	95.00
75 (99)	2000 Pesos (Au) 1975	200.00

		XF	Unc
76 (100)	2 Pesos (Cu-Ni) 1977, 1978	0.35	0.80
77 (100a)	2 Pesos (Br) 1977, 1979	0.35	0.80

CONSERVATION COMMEMORATIVE (3)

		Unc	Proof
78 (101)	300 Pesos (Ag) 1979	25.00	30.00
79 (102)	500 Pesos (Ag) 1979	40.00	50.00
80 (103)	10000 Pesos (Au) 1979	650.00	750.00

		XF	Unc
81 (83.3)	20 Centavos (Cu-Ni) 1979	0.10	0.20

		XF	Unc
82 (104)	25 Centavos (Al-Br) 1979	0.30	0.60

	XF	Unc
83 (105) 5 Pesos (Ni-Al) 1980.	1.00	1.80

DEATH OF SIMON BOLIVAR

	Proof	700.00
84 (106) 30000 Pesos (Au) 1980.	Proof	700.00

Previous issues, see "Weltmünzkatalog 19. Jahrhundert" (World Coin Catalogue of the 19th Century)

Santander

During the revolt, the province of Santander was governed by General Ramon Gonzales Valencia, at whose instigation provisional issues were struck in 1902. (These were made from the brass of old cartridges, and are in relief on one side and intaglio on the other).

			VF	XF
1 (S 1)	10	Centavos (Bra) (1902). Undated. Inscription SANTANDER, value 10/C. ℞ no inscription	20.00	30.00
2 (S 2)	20	Centavos (Bra) 1902. Inscription SANTANDER, the figure 20 within the C of Centavos; below, date	22.00	32.00
3 (S 3)	50	Centavos (Bra) 1902. Type as No. 2	18.00	30.00

Area: 835 sq. mi. Population: 284,000.

The group of islands with the main islands of Anjouan, Great Comoro, Mayotte and Moheli (or Mohilla), situated in the Indian Ocean facing the coast of Africa, East of Mozambique, were governed until 1912 by the four sultans, deposed after this date. The island of Mayotte had been a French protectorate since 1841, the whole group of islands since 1886; since 1912 administered from Madagascar; self-governing since 1925. The autonomy awarded on 9th May 1946 was converted in 1961 to the status of an overseas territory within the framework of the French Community. The franc system was introduced in 1889 on all the islands and the coins brought into circulation were struck in Paris. In 1975 the Comoro Islands became the independent Republic of the Comoros. Mayotte retained the option of determining its future ties.

Capital: Moroni.

$$100 \text{ Centimes} = 1 \text{ Franc}$$

COLONY

			VF	XF
1 (1)	5	Centimes (Br) H. C. 1308, 1319 (1890, 1901). Arabic inscription	12.00	20.00
2 (2)	10	Centimes (Br) H. C. 1308, 1319	13.00	22.00

OVERSEAS TERRITORY

			VF	XF
3 (4)	1	Franc (Al-Mg) 1964. Allegorical figure of the French Republic. ℞ coconut palm (Cocos nucifera – Palmae) and value	0.20	0.30
4 (5)	2	Francs (Al-Mg) 1964	0.25	0.40

			VF	XF
5 (6)	5	Francs (Al-Mg) 1964	0.45	0.80
6 (7)	10	Francs (Ni-Bra) 1964. ℞ Pacific trumpet shell (Charonia tritonis – Cymatiidae or Tritonidae, family of the mantled creatures), fruit and crossopterygii (Latimeria chalumnae – Latimeriidae or Coelacanthidae)	0.45	0.90
7 (8)	20	Francs (Ni-Bra) 1964. Type as No. 6	1.00	1.50

ISSUE FOR THE INDEPENDENCE

			XF	Unc
8 (9)	50	Francs (Ni) 1975	0.90	1.30

			Unc	Proof
9	5000	Francs (Ag) 1975	90.00	110.00
10	10000	Francs (Au) 1975	130.00	150.00
11	20000	Francs (Au) 1975	260.00	300.00

ISSUE FOR THE FAO COIN PLAN

			XF	Unc
12 (10)	100	Francs (Ni) 1977	1.20	2.00

Previous issue, see "Weltmünzkatalog 19. Jahrhundert" (World coin
Catalogue of the 19th Century)

Congo (Brazzaville)

Volksrepublik Kongo **Congo (République populaire du)**
People's Republic of the Congo

Area: 132,000 sq. mi. Population: 1,300,000.
Under the designation of Central Congo, the country was formerly part
of French Equatorial Africa. On 28th November, 1958 the country
received limited autonomy and on 15th August, 1960, Congo-Brazzaville
became independent. Transformation into a People's Republic took
place on 31st December 1969. Congo-Brazzaville belongs to the currency
area of Equatorial Africa; concerning mutual issues, please refer to Equatorial Africa.
Capital: Brazzaville.

100 Centimes = 1 CFA-Franc

			XF	Unc
1 (1)	100	Francs (Ni) 1971, 1972. Mendes antelopes (Addax nasomaculatus – Bovidae). Name of country. R inscription: Banque Centrale, value, date	2.50	4.00

2 (2)	100	Francs (Ni) 1975. Type as No. 1, but inscription "Banque des Etats de l'Afrique Centrale"	1.50	3.00

Republik Saire   # Congo (Kinshasa) République du Zaïre

République du Zaïre

Area: 902,080 sq. mi. Population: 22,600,000.
On 30th June 1960, the colony of the Belgian Congo became independent under the name of Congo (Leopoldville). The temporary secession of the Katanga province was brought to an end by a United Nations police operation in the interests of the unity of the Congo.
Capital: Leopoldville, renamed Kinshasa since 1st July 1966.

100 Centimes = 1 Congo Franc. Since 24th June 1967:
100 Sengi = 1 Likuta, 100 Makuta = 1 Zaïre
(Makuta = plural of Likuta)

		XF	Unc
1 (1)	10 Francs (Al) 1965. Head of a lion (Panthera leo – Felidae). ℞ value	1.20	2.00

COMMEMORATIVE ISSUES (5) FOR THE 5th ANNIVERSARY OF THE REPUBLIC

		Proof
2	10 Francs (Au) 1965. Joseph Kasavubu (1913–1968), Head of State from 1960 to 1965. ℞ African elephant (Loxodonta africana – Elephantidae)	60.00
3	20 Francs (Au) 1965. Type as No. 2	120.00
4	25 Francs (Au) 1965. Type as No. 2	150.00
5	50 Francs (Au) 1965. Type as No. 2	300.00
6	100 Francs (Au) 1965. Type as No. 2	600.00

		XF	Unc
7 (2)	10 Sengi (Al) 1967. Leopard (Panthera pardus – Felidae)	0.40	0.75
8 (3)	1 Likuta (Al) 1967–1969. National arms. ℞ value	0.70	1.00

9 (4) 5 Makuta (Cu–Ni) 1967–1969. Bust left   **XF**   **Unc**
of Joseph Désiré Mobutu (*1930),
Head of State since 1965. ℞ value   1.20   2.00

Area: 90 sq. mi. Population: 21,000.

The Cook Islands, discovered by James Cook in 1773 during his second voyage and named after him, comprise the following 15 islands: Aitutaki, Atiu, Mangaia, Manuae, Manihiki, Mauke, Mitiaro, Nassau, Palmerston Atoll (Avarau), Penrhyn (Tongareva), Pukapuka, Rakahanga, Rarotonga, Suwarrow and Te Au O Tu (Hervey Island). On 16th September 1965, the islands obtained complete internal autonomy as a dependency of New Zealand.

100 Cents = 1 New Zealand Dollar

COMMEMORATIVE ISSUE FOR THE 200th ANNIVERSARY OF THE VOYAGE OF JAMES COOK AND THE VISIT OF THE BRITISH ROYAL COUPLE TO AUSTRALIA AND NEW ZEALAND IN 1970

			Unc	Proof
1 (46*)	1 Dollar (Cu-Ni) 1970. Bust right of Queen Elizabeth II; legend ELIZABETH II – NEW ZEALAND, and date. ℞ bust of the English explorer James Cook (1728–1779) and his ship, H. M. S. "Endeavour"; legend COOK ISLANDS – ONE DOLLAR		35.00	140.00

*This number refers to Yeoman's New Zealand listing.

2 (1)	1 Cent (Br) 1972–. Elizabeth II facing right. ℞ Taro (Colocasia sp. – Araceae)		0.30	1.00
3 (2)	2 Cents (Br) 1972–. ℞ pineapple (Ananas comosus – Bromeliaceae)		0.40	1.00

4 (3)   5 Cents (Cu–Ni) 1972–. ℞ Chinese rose marsh-mallow (Hibiscus rosa-sinensis – Malvaceae)

	Unc	Proof
	0.50	1.00

5 (4)   10 Cents (Cu–Ni) 1972–. ℞ orange (Citrus sinensis – Ritaceae)   0.60   1.80

6 (5)   20 Cents (Cu–Ni) 1972-1975. R Fairylake swallow (Gygis alba - Sternidae)   1.00   3.00

7 (6)   50 Cents (Cu–Ni) 1972–. ℞ bonito (Katsuwonus pelamis – Scombridae)   2.00   5.00

8 (7)   1 Dollar (Cu–Ni) 1972–. ℞ Tangaroa, ancient Polynesian deity surrounded by fifteen stars, symbolizing the number of islands which are also displayed in the flag   10.00   18.00

COMMEMORATIVE ISSUE FOR THE 25th ANNIVERSARY OF THE CORONATION OF QUEEN ELIZABETH II
(2nd June 1953)

		Unc	Proof
9 (8)	2 Dollars (Ag) 1973. ℞ Elizabeth II in coronation robes. Commemorative legend, denomination	18.00	22.00

COMMEMORATIVE ISSUES (2) FOR THE 2nd WORLD CIRCUMNAVIGATION BY JAMES COOK AND THE DISCOVERY OF THE ISLANDS OF MANUAE AND TE AU O TU (23. 9. 1773)

10   11

10 (9)	2½ Dollars (Ag) 1973, 1974	25.00	32.00
11 (10)	7½ Dollars (Ag) 1973, 1974	36.00	50.00

COMMEMORATIVE ISSUES (3) FOR THE CENTENARY OF BIRTH OF SIR WINSTON CHURCHILL

12 (11)	50 Dollars (Ag) 1974	170.00	180.00
13 (11a)	50 Dollars (Ag, gold-plated) 1974		290.00
14 (12)	100 Dollars (Au) 1974	400.00	800.00

ANNIVERSARY OF COOK'S 2nd VOYAGE

15 (13)	100 Dollars (Au) 1975	180.00	200.00

U.S. BICENTENNIAL COMMEMORATIVE

16 (14)	100 Dollars (Au) 1976. Conjoined heads left of Benjamin Franklin and James Cook	180.00	200.00
17 (15)	20 Cents (Cu-Ni) 1976–1979. Rev. Triton seashell	1.00	3.50
18 (16)	5 Dollars (Ag) 1976. Rev. Mangaia Mangaia Kingsfisher	30.00	60.00

25th ANNIVERSARY OF THE SILVER JUBILEE OF HER MAYESTY QUEEN ELIZABETH II (2)

19 (17)	25 Dollars (Ag) 1977	75.00	100.00
20 (18)	100 Dollars (Au) 1977	165.00	180.00
21 (19)	5 Dollars (Ag) 1977. Flying birds	16.00	22.00

200th ANNIVERSARY OF REDISCOVERY OF HAWAII BY CAPTAIN JAMES COOK

22 (22)	Dollars (Au) 1978	250.00	300.00

CORONATION JUBILEE

23 (21)	10 Dollars (Ag) 1978	35.00	40.00
24 (20)	5 Dollars (Ag) 1978. Wildlife Conservation	28.00	40.00

250th ANNIVERSARY OF THE BIRD OF JAMES COOK

25 (23)	250 Dollars (Au) 1978	350.00	400.00

LEGACY OF CAPTAIN COOK

		Unc	Proof
26 (24)	200 Dollars (Au) 1979	400.00	500.00

COOK ISLAND CONSERVATION DAY

27 (25)	5 Dollars (Ag) 1979. Rev. pigeons	25.00	35.00

MEMBERSHIP IN THE COMMONWEALTH OF NATIONS

28 (26)	100 Dollars (Au) 1979	200.00	225.00

FOR THE FAO COIN PLAN (2)

		Unc	Proof
29 (4a)	10 Cents (Cu-Ni 1979. Type as No. 5, but »FAO« added	2.00	3.00
30 (6a)	50 Cents (Cu-Ni) 1979. Type as No. 7, but »FAO« added	3.00	6.00

WEDDING OF PRINCE CHARLES AND LADY DIANA

31 (27)	50 Dollars (Au) 1981. Crown and plumes above a monogram of the letters C and D		125.00

Costa Rica

Area: 19,500 sq. mi. Population: 1,900,000.
An independent Republic since 1821, part of the Central American Confederation from 1824 to 1838.
Capital: San José.

100 Centavos or Centimos = 1 Colon

			VF	XF
1 (46)	2	Centimos (Cu-Ni) 1903. Value. ℞ value and wreath	2.00	4.00
		For No. 1 with countermark, see under No. 23.		
2 (39)	5	Centimos (Ag) 1905–1914. National arms. ℞ value within wreath	3.00	4.00
3 (40)	10	Centimos (Ag) 1905–1914. Type as No. 2. Fine silver content 900	6.00	10.00
4 (42)	10	Centavos (Ag) 1917. Type as No. 2. Fine silver content 500	5.00	7.00
5 (41)	50	Centimos (Ag) 1902–1903, 1914. Type as No. 2. Fine silver content 900	28.00	35.00
6 (A 42)	50	Centimos (Ag) 1917–1918. Type as No. 5. Fine silver content 500. Very rare	300.00	500.00
		No. 6 was almost exclusively countermarked: see No. 19		
7 (35)		DOS (2) Colones (Au) 1897–1928. Head of Christopher Columbus (1451–1506). ℞ national arms	110.00	140.00

8 (36)		Cinco (5) Colones (Au) 1899–1900. Type as No. 7	165.00	190.00
9 (37)		Diez (10) Colones (Au) 1897–1900. Type as No. 7	185.00	220.00
10 (38)		Veinte (20) Colones (Au) 1897–1900. Type as No. 7	475.00	550.00
11 (47)	5	Centavos (Bra) 1917–1919. National arms. ℞ value within wreath, but without the inscription AMERICA CENTRAL	1.60	3.20

			VF	XF
12 (49)	5	Centimos (Bra) 1920–1941. National arms. ℞ value within wreath; inscription G. C. R. = Gobierno Costa Rica	0.70	1.20
13 (51)	5	Centimos (Br) 1929. Type as No. 12	1.25	2.00
14 (48)	10	Centavos (Bra) 1917–1919. Similar to No. 12	1.60	3.00
15 (50)	10	Centimos (Bra) 1920–1922.Type No.12	0.60	1.00
16 (52)	10	Centimos (Br) 1929. Type as No. 12	0.90	1.60
17 (45)	25	Centavos (Ag) 1924. Type as No. 12	7.00	10.00
18 (43)	50	Centavos on 25 C. 1923. Countermarked on various 25 Centavos coins of previous issues	5.00	8.00
19 (44)	1	Colon on 50 Centimos 1923. Countermarked on No. 6 and various previous issues	6.50	13.00
A19 (54)	10	Centimos (Bra) 1936, 1941. Type as No. 16	0.40	0.70
20 (55)	25	Centimos (Cu-Ni) 1935. National arms. ℞ value within wreath; inscription B. I. C. R. = Banco Internacional de Costa Rica	0.60	1.10
21 (56)	50	Centimos (Cu-Ni) 1935. Type as No. 20	0.80	1.40
22 (57)	1	Colon (Cu-Ni) 1935. Type as No. 20	1.50	2.60
23 (58)	5	Centimos on 2 C. 1942. Countermarked on No. 1	3.50	7.00
24 (A 58)	5	Centimos (Bra) 1942–1947. National arms. ℞ value within wreath; inscription B. N./C. R. = Banco Nacional de Costa Rica	0.40	0.80
25 (B 58)	10	Centimos (Bra) 1942–1947. Type as No. 24	0.70	1.25
26 (59)	25	Centimos (Cu-Ni) 1937–1967	0.50	0.80
27 (63)	25	Centimos (Bra) 1944–1946	0.85	1.70
28 (63a)	25	Centimos (Br) 1945	1.30	2.60
29 (60)	50	Centimos (Cu-Ni)		
		a) 1937	1.20	2.00
		b) 1948	0.50	1.20

30 (61)	1	Colon (Cu-Ni) 1937–1948	0.60	1.30
31 (62)	2	Colones (Cu-Ni) 1948	1.00	2.20
32 (A 64)	5	Centimos (Cu-Ni) 1951. National arms. ℞ value within wreath; inscrip-		

			VF	XF

tion B. C./C. R. = Banco Central de Costa Rica — 0.50 / 1.10

33 (64) 5 Centimos (Cu-Ni) 1951, 1969, 1972, 1973, 1976, 1977. Type as No. 32, but the letters B. C. C. R. are close together — 0.20 / 0.35

34 (66) 5 Centavos (St) 1953, 1958, 1967. Type No. 32 — 0.10 / 0.20

35 (65) 10 Centimos (Cu-Ni) 1951. Type as No. 33 — 0.20 / 0.40

36 (67) 10 Centimos (St) 1953, 1958, 1967, 1979. Type as No. 32 — 0.10 / 0.25

37 (65a) 10 Centimos (Cu-Ni) 1969–. Type as No. 32:
a) 1969, 1975, 1976 (small ship) — 0.15 / 0.30
b) 1972, 1975, 1976 (large ship) — 0.15 / 0.30

No.			VF	XF
38 (70)	25	Centimos (Cu-Ni) 1967–1977	0.20	0.40
39 (71)	50	Centimos (Cu-Ni) 1965–1978	0.35	0.60
40 (68)	1	Colon (St) 1954	0.60	1.20
41 (68a)	1	Colon (Cu-Ni) 1961–1977	0.50	0.90
42 (69)	2	Colones (St) 1954	1.50	3.00

43 (69a) 2 Colones (Cu-Ni) 1961, 1968, 1970, 1972, 1978. In national arms seven stars now instead of five as previously — 0.50 / 1.00

Proof

44 2 Colones (Ag) 1970. National arms. R building in San José of the Central Bank founded in 1950 — 9.00

45 5 Colones (Ag) 1970. Similar obverse to No. 44. R head of Juan Vazquez de Coronado, founder of the city of Cartago in Costa Rica (1564) — 17.00

46   10 Colones (Ag) 1970–. Similar obverse   **Proof**
      to No. 44. ℞ kapok tree (Ceiba pen-
      tandra – Bombaceae) in front of 5
      volcanoes, symbol of the efforts for
      reunification of the five states of
      Guatemala, Honduras, Salvador, Ni-   30.00
      caragua and Costa Rica

47   20 Colones (Ag) 1970–. Similar obverse
      to No. 44. ℞ marble statue of the
      "Venus of Milo", made in 150 B.C.,
      the Greek Aphrodite of the island of
      Melos (found in 1820). It is now in
      the Louvre, Paris (symbol of universal
      art)   50.00

48   25 Colones (Ag) 1970–. Similar obverse
      to No. 44. ℞ "Motherhood", a sculp-
      ture by F. Zuñiga (25 years of social
      legislation – law of 15th September 1943)   60.00

49   50 Colones (Au) 1970–. Similar obverse
      to No. 44. ℞ Allegorical representation
      of human rights – Inter-American Con-
      vention   90.00

50   100 Colones (Au) 1970–. ℞ Pendant in the

			Unc	Proof
		form of a vulture, repoussé work in gold of the Chibcha people, according to an original in the San José National Museum	180.00	
51	200	Colones (Au) 1970–. Similar obverse to No. 44. ℞ Head of Juan Santamaria, national hero	350.00	
52	500	Colones (Au) 1970–. Similar obverse to No. 44. ℞ head of Jesús Jiménez (1823–1897), politician, introduced general compulsory education into Costa Rica in 1869	800.00	
53	1000	Colones (Au) 1970–. Similar obverse to No. 44. ℞ national arms with volcanoes, Central American symbol for the efforts for reunification of the five Republics (see No. 46), combined with a geographical sketch of the 5 countries. The national arms refer back to the date of 15th September 1821 and therefore to the "Provincias Unidas del Centro de Américo"	1700.00	

SPECIAL ISSUE (3) CONSERVATION COIN COLLECTION

			Unc	Proof
54 (82)	50	Colones (Ag) 1974. Coat of arms, name of country, date. ℞ green turtle (Chelonia mydas – Cheloniidae)	30.00	35.00
55 (83)	100	Colones (Ag) 1974. ℞ manatee (Trichechus manatus – Trichechidae)	40.00	60.00
56 (84)	1500	Colones (Au) 1974. ℞ great anteater (Myrmecophága tridactyla – Myrmecophagidae)	650.00	750.00

25th ANNIVERSARY OF THE CENTRAL BANK (3)

57 (85)	5	Colones (Ni) 1975	1.50	3.00
58 (86)	10	Colones (Ni) 1975	2.50	6.00
59 (87)	20	Colones (Ni) 1975	5.00	10.00

INTERNATIONAL YEAR OF THE CHILD

			Unc	Proof
60 (88)	100	Colones (Ag) 1979	35.00	70.00

			XF	Unc
61 (64.3)	5	Centimos (Bra) 1979	0.20	0.40
62 (70.1)	25	Centimos (St) 1980	0.25	0.50

125th ANNIVERSARY OF THE DEATH OF JUAN SANTAMARIA (2)

			Proof
63 (89)	300	Colones (Ag) 1981. Juan Santamaria, patriot	60.00
64 (90)	5000	Colones (Au) 1981. Type as No. 63	900.00

Previous issues, see »Weltmünzkatalog 19. Jahrhundert« (World Coin Catalogue of the 19th Century)

Kreta   **Crete**   Crète
КРНТН

Area: 3,220 sq. mi. Population: 483,000.
This island, which had been under Turkish domination since 1669, obtained self-government in 1898 under the aegis of Greece, and was reunited with the motherland on 30th May 1913, after a previous resolution in the Cretan National Assembly.
Capital: Canea.

100 Lepta = 1 Drachma

			VF	XF
1 (1)	1 Lepton (Br) 1900–1901. Crown. ℞ value within wreath			
	a) 1900		25.00	60.00
	b) 1901		16.00	30.00

			VF	XF
2 (2)	2 Lepta (Br) 1900–1901			
	a) 1900		15.00	30.00
	b) 1901		26.00	50.00
3 (3)	5 Lepta (Cu–Ni) 1900		5.00	11.00
4 (4)	10 Lepta (Cu–Ni) 1900		5.00	9.00
5 (5)	20 Lepta (Cu–Ni) 1900		7.00	12.00
6 (6)	50 Lepta (Ag) 1901. Head right of Prince George of Greece (1869–1957) 1st High Commissioner of Crete 1898–1906. ℞ arms with crown on drapery		12.00	22.00
7 (7)	1 Drachma (Ag) 1901		18.00	30.00
8 (8)	2 Drachmai (Ag) 1901		40.00	75.00
9 (9)	5 Drachmai (Ag) 1901		80.00	125.00

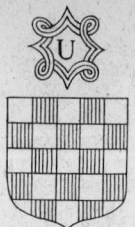

Kroatien # Croatia Croatie

Area: 21,726 sq. mi. Population: 4,250,000.
From 1867 until November 1918 Croatia formed a united kingdom
with Hungary, and later was part of the kingdom of the Serbians,
Croatians and Slovaks, later known as Yugoslavia. After the occupation
of Yugoslavia by German troops, Croatia declared its independence on
10th April 1941. Since 1945 Croatia has been an integral part of the
Republic of Yugoslavia.
Capital: Zagreb (Agram).

100 Banica = 1 Kuna

			VF	XF
1 (1)	2 Kune (Zi) 1941. National arms. ℞ value		5.00	10.00

2	500 Kune (Au) 1941. Ante Pavelić (1889 to 1959), Head of State 1941–1945. ℞ national arms and value	2600.00

3	500 Kune (Ag) 1941. Kneeling female figure with corn ears, personifying Croatia. ℞ as No. 2	3500.00

Cuba

Area: 44,048 sq. mi. Population: 10,000,000.

Discovered by Christopher Columbus on 28th October 1492 and taken possession of by Spain in 1511, under the name of Fernandina. When the various continental Latin-American states obtained their independence at the beginning of the 19th century, the West Indian island of Cuba remained the most important colony of Spain. After several revolts and the formation of a provisional government, and after the end of the Spanish-American War in 1898, Cuba was at first occupied by the United States, and later in 1902 gained independence as a republic, but it remained under the aegis of the United States of America until 1934 (the U. S. dollar was the official currency). As a result of the revolution from 1956 to 1959, Dr. Fidel Castro became Prime Minister on 13th February 1959.

Capital: Havana.

100 Centavos = 1 Peso

PROVISIONAL GOVERNMENT

			VF	XF
1 (1)		Souvenir Peso (Ag) 1897. Liberty head to right, inscription PATRIA Y LIBERTAD and SOUVENIR. ℞ national arms. Several variants	100.00	180.00

WAR OF INDEPENDENCE

2 (2)	1	Peso (Ag) 1898. Type as No. 1, but date below head instead of "SOUVENIR". ℞ national arms and value	380.00	750.00

CIVIL GOVERNMENT AS A REPUBLIC

3 (3)	1	Centavo (Cu–Ni) 1915–1938. National arms, value in letters. ℞ five-pointed star with value in Roman figures; indication of weight "2.5 G" *For coins of same or slightly different description, see Nos. 16, 17 and 29*	0.50	1.20
4 (4)	2	Centavos (Cu–Ni) 1915–1916. Type as No. 3	0.60	1.50

				VF	XF
5 (5)	5	Centavos (Cu–Ni) 1915–1920. Type as No. 3; indication of weight "5.0 G" *For coins of same or slightly different description, see Nos. 18, 19 and 30*		0.70	1.80
6 (6)	10	Centavos (Ag) 1915–1949. Five-pointed star with rays. ℞ national arms and value in letters		2.50	5.00
7 (7)	20	Centavos (Ag) 1915–1949. Type as No. 6			
		a) 1915–1920, 1948–1949		3.50	6.50
		b) 1932		38.00	80.00

			VF	XF
8 (8)	40	Centavos (Ag) 1915–1920. Type as No. 6	8.00	15.00
9 (9)	1	Peso (Ag) 1915–1934. Type as No. 6	20.00	40.00
10 (10)	1	Peso (Au) 1915–1916. Head right of José Julián Marti y Perez (1853–1895), patriot and writer. ℞ national arms and value in letters	220.00	320.00
11 (11)	2	Pesos (Au) 1915–1916. Type as No. 10	100.00	125.00
12 (12)	4	Pesos (Au) 1915–1916. Type as No. 10	180.00	250.00
13 (13)	5	Pesos (Au) 1915–1916. Type as No. 10	190.00	260.00
14 (14)	10	Pesos (Au) 1915–1916. Type as No. 10	300.00	350.00
15 (15)	20	Pesos (Au) 1915–1916. Type as No. 10	700.00	800.00

No. 15 with the date 1916: price according to the demand.

			VF	XF
16 (3a)	1	Centavo (Bra) 1943. Type as No. 3	0.40	0.80
17 (3b)	1	Centavo (Cu–Ni) 1946–1961. Type as No. 3, but indication of weight "2.5 GR"	0.40	0.90

The last year, 1961, is to be considered as a Castro issue.

			VF	XF
18 (5a)	5	Centavos (Bra) 1943. Type as No. 5	1.50	4.00
19 (5b)	5	Centavos (Cu–Ni) 1946–1961. Type as No. 5, but indication of weight "5.0 GR"	0.40	0.80

The last year, 1961, is to be considered as a Castro issue.

			VF	XF
20 (16)	1	Peso (Ag) 1934–1939. Head of Liberty with laureate cap of Liberty, five-pointed star with rays, legend: PATRIA Y LIBERTAD. ℞ national arms and value	75.00	100.00

COMMEMORATIVE ISSUES (3) FOR THE 50th ANNIVERSARY OF THE REPUBLIC

21 (17)	10	Centavos (Ag) 1952. Tree rising from wheel of chariot. ℞ flags in front of the fortress "El Morro" in Havana	3.00	5.00
22 (18)	20	Centavos (Ag) 1952. Type as No. 21	4.50	7.50
23 (19)	40	Centavos (Ag) 1952. Type as No. 21	11.00	15.00

COMMEMORATIVE ISSUES (4) FOR THE CENTENARY OF THE BIRTH OF J. J. MARTI

24 (20)	1	Centavo (Bra) 1953. José Julián Marti y Perez (1853–1895), patriot and writer, inscription CENTENARIO DE MARTI. ℞ star of Cuba on triangle, value	0.30	0.80
		For coin of similar design, see No. 28		
25 (21)	25	Centavos (Ag) 1953. Type as No. 24. ℞ cap of Liberty and value	4.00	6.00
26 (22)	50	Centavos (Ag) 1953. Type as No. 24. ℞ inscribed scroll and value	8.00	12.50
27 (23)	1	Peso (Ag) 1953. Type as No. 24. ℞ key with rising sun in background – part of the national arms	22.00	30.00
28 (24)	1	Centavo (Cu–Ni) 1958. José J. Marti; type as No. 24, but without commemorative inscription. ℞ star of Cuba on triangle, and value	0.30	0.50

SOCIALIST REPUBLIC

			XF	Unc
29 (27)	1	Centavo (Al) 1963, 1966, 1969–1972. Type as No. 3	0.30	0.50

			XF	Unc
30 (28)	5	Centavos (Al) 1963–. Type as No. 5	0.40	0.80

| **31** (25) | 20 | Centavos (Cu–Ni) 1962, 1968. Bust left of José J. Marti, legend: PATRIA O MUERTE. R national arms | 0.90 | 1.60 |

| **32** (26) | 40 | Centavos (Cu–Ni) 1962. Bust right of Camilo Cienfuegos y Gorriarian (1933–1959), revolutionary hero, legend: PATRIA O MUERTE. R national arms | 2.20 | 4.00 |

| **33** (29) | 20 | Centavos (Al) 1969, 1970, 1971, 1972. Type as No. 29 | 0.50 | 1.00 |

			Proof
34 (30)	5 Pesos (Ag) 1975		30.00
35 (31)	10 Pesos (Ag) 1975		40.00
36 (32)	20 Pesos (Ag) 1977. Ignacio Agramonte		40.00
37 (33)	20 Pesos (Ag) 1977. Máximo Gomez		40.00
38 (34)	20 Pesos (Ag) 1977. Antonio Maceo		40.00
39 (35)	100 Pesos (Au) 1977. Carlos Manuel de Céspedes		280.00

60th ANNIVERSARY OF THE OCTOBER REVOLUTION

40	20 Pesos (Ag) 1977. Lenin (1870–1924), Russian politician	40.00

NONALIGNED NATIONS CONFERENCE (2)

41 (36)	20 Pesos (Ag) 1979	40.00
42 (37)	100 Pesos (Au) 1979	280.00

FIRST SOVIET-CUBAN SPACE FLIGHT (3)

43 (38)	5 Pesos (Ag) 1980	25.00
44 (39)	10 Pesos (Ag) 1980	40.00
45 (40)	100 Pesos (Au) 1980	600.00

OLYMPIC GAMES 1980 IN MOSCOW (2)

		Proof
46 (41)	5 Pesos (Ag) 1980	25.00
47 (42)	10 Pesos (Ag) 1980	40.00

CUBAN FLOWERS (3)

		Proof
48 (43)	5 Pesos (Ag) 1981. Mariposa	20.00
49 (44)	5 Pesos (Ag) 1981. Azahar	20.00
50 (45)	5 Pesos (Ag) 1981. Orquidea	20.00

DISCOVERY OF AMERICA (9)

		Unc	Proof
51	10 Pesos (Ni) 1981. »Nina«	6.50	
52	10 Pesos (Ni) 1981. »Pinta«	6.50	
53	10 Pesos (Ni) 1981. »Santa Maria«	6.50	
54	10 Pesos (Ag) 1981	12.00	35.00
55	10 Pesos (Ag) 1981	12.00	35.00
56	10 Pesos (Ag) 1981	12.00	35.00
57	100 Pesos (Au) 1981	250.00	
58	100 Pesos (Au) 1981	250.00	
59	100 Pesos (Au) 1981	250.00	

WORLD SOCCER CHAMPIONSHIP GAMES (2)

		Unc	Proof
60	1 Peso (Ni) 1982	8.00	
61	5 Pesos (Ag) 1982		60.00

Area: 172 sq. mi. Population: 127,900.
Curaçao was discovered in 1499 and first occupied by the Spaniards, then in 1634 by the Dutch. Since 1952 the island forms part of the Dutch East Indies (Netherlands Antilles).
Capital: Willemstad.

100 Cents = 1 Gulden

WILHELMINA 1890–1948

			VF	XF
1 (1)	$^1/_{10}$	Gulden (Ag) 1901. Head left of Wilhelmina (1880–1962), Queen of the Netherlands. ℞ crowned arms and value	20.00	40.00
2 (2)	$^1/_4$	Gulden (Ag) 1900. Type as No. 1	20.00	40.00
3 (3)	1	Cent (Br) 1944–1947. National arms (lion). ℞ value within wreath	0.80	1.80

4 (4)	2½	Cents (Br) 1944–1948. Type as No. 3	1.20	3.50

5 (9)	5	Cents (Cu–Ni) 1948. Flower. ℞ value	0.80	3.00
6 (5)	$^1/_{10}$	Gulden (Ag) 1944–1947. Head of Queen Wilhelmina. ℞ value	1.20	2.50
7 (8)	$^1/_{10}$	Gulden (Ag) 1948. Diademed head left of Queen Wilhelmina	1.20	2.50

8 (6)	$^1/_4$	Gulden (Ag) 1944–1947. Type as No. 6	1.20	5.00

			VF	**XF**
9 (7)	1 Gulden (Ag) 1944. Head left of Queen Wilhemina. ℞ crowned arms		8.00	20.00

10 (10)	2½ Gulden (Ag) 1944. Type as No. 9		9.00	12.00

For other issues, see under NETHERLANDS ANTILLES.

Area: 3,558 sq. mi. Population: 658,000.
Cyprus became a British possession in 1878 and in 1925 obtained the
status of a Crown Colony; it has been an independent republic since
16th August 1960.
Capital: Nicosia.

9 Piastres = 1 Shilling; since 1st August 1955: 1000 Millièmes = £ 1

EDWARD VII 1901–1910

			VF	XF
1 (8)	¼	Piastre (Br) 1902–1908. Crowned bust right of King Edward VII. ℞ value within circle		
		a) 1902, 1905	18.00	30.00
		b) 1908	35.00	60.00
2 (9)	½	Piastre (Br) 1908	140.00	180.00
3 (10)	1	Piastre (Br) 1908	165.00	220.00
4 (11)	9	Piastres (Ag) 1907. ℞ crowned arms	40.00	70.00
5 (12)	18	Piastres (Ag) 1907	90.00	140.00

GEORGE V 1910–1936

6 (13)	¼	Piastre (Br) 1922–1926. Crowned bust left of King George V. ℞ value within circle	10.00	20.00
7 (14)	½	Piastre (Br) 1922-1931. Type as No. 6:		
		a) 1922	22.00	40.00
		b) 1927, 1930, 1931	18.00	30.00
8 (15)	1	Piastre (Br) 1922-1931	40.00	65.00
9 (18)	4½	Piastres (Ag) 1921. R crowned arms	12.00	20.00
10 (19)	9	Piastres (Ag) 1913-1921:		
		a) 1913	22.00	40.00
		b) 1919,1921	15.00	25.00
11 (20)	18	Piastres (Ag) 1913-1921:		
		a) 1913	45.00	90.00
		b) 1921	28.00	45.00

COMMEMORATIVE ISSUE FOR THE 50th ANNIVERSARY OF BRITISH OCCUPATION

				VF	XF
12 (21)	45	Piastres (Ag) 1928. Crowned bust left of King George V. ℞ arms of Cyprus		60.00	85.00
13 (16)	½	Piastre (Cu–Ni) 1934. Crowned bust left of King George V. ℞ value (scalloped edge)		4.00	6.00
14 (17)	1	Piastre (Cu–Ni) 1934		3.00	5.50

GEORGE VI 1936–1952

15 (22)	½	Piastre (Cu–Ni) 1938. Crowned head left of King George VI (scalloped edge)	3.00	4.00
16 (23)	1	Piastre (Cu–Ni) 1938. Type as No. 15	2.50	4.00
17 (28)	4½	Piastres (Ag) 1938	12.00	20.00
18 (29)	9	Piastres (Ag) 1938-1940	12.00	20.00
19 (30)	18	Piastres (Ag) 1938-1940	26.00	40.00
20 (22a)	½	Piastre (Br)1942-1945. Type as No. 15	2.00	4.00
21 (23a)	1	Piastre (Br) 1942-1946. Type as No. 16	1.80	3.00

22 (26)	1	Shilling (Cu–Ni) 1947	3.50	6.00
23 (27)	2	Shillings (Cu–Ni) 1947	5.50	11.00
24 (31)	½	Piastre (Br) 1949. Type as No. 15, but inscription now GEORGIUS SEXTUS DEI GRATIA REX	0.80	1.50
25 (32)	1	Piastre (Br) 1949	0.80	1.20
26 (33)	1	Shilling (Cu–Ni) 1949	4.00	6.50
27 (34)	2	Shillings (Cu–Ni) 1949	8.00	13.00

28 (35)   3 Mils (Br) 1955. Crowned head right of
Queen Elizabeth II. ℞ flying fish in
two-tone style, dating from the Cypriot
archaic period (Iron Age II), 7th cen-
tury B. C.   0.15   0.30

29 (36)   5 Mils (Br) 1955–1956. ℞ "Male figure
carrying copper bar", from a bronze
group from Curium, dating back to the
late Bronze Age, c. 1200 B. C.; the
original is in the British Museum,
London   0.20   0.40

30 (37)   25 Mils (Cu–Ni) 1955. ℞ head of bull l.   0.25   0.50
31 (38)   50 Mils (Cu–Ni) 1955. ℞ fern leaves   0.60   1.20

32 (39)	100 Mils (Cu-Ni) 1955-1957. R merchant ship, c. 6th century B. C.:	**VF**	**XF**
	a) 1955	2.00	4.00
	b) 1957	50.00	100.00

REPUBLIC

33 (41)	1 Mil (Al–Mg) 1963–. National arms of the Republic. R value in figure within wreath	**XF**	**Unc**
		0.10	0.20
34 (42)	5 Mils (Br) 1963–. R merchant ship, c. 6th century B. C.	0.10	0.20
35 (43)	25 Mils (Cu–Ni) 1963–. R cedar of Lebanon (Cedrus libani – Pinaceae)	0.15	0.30

36 (44)	50 Mils (Cu-Ni) 1963–. Bunch of grapes (Vitis vinifera – Vitaceae)	0.30	0.50

37 (45)	100 Mils (Cu-Ni) 1963–. R Cyprus mouflon (Ovis ammon ophion – Bovidae)	0.50	1.00

COMMEMORATIVE MEDALS FOR ARCHBISHOP MAKARIOS III. (3)

38	½ £ (Au) 1966. Head left of Makarios III. (1913-1977), President of State 1959-1977. R double eagle	250.00
39	1 £ (Au) 1966. Type as No. 38	300.00
40	5 £ (Au) 1966. Type as No. 38	3700.00

COMMEMORATIVE MEDALS FOR ARCHBISHOP MAKARIOS III. (3)

41	½ £ (Ag) 1974. Type as No. 38	12.00
42	1 £ (Ag) 1974. Type as No. 38	35.00
43	5 £ (Ag) 1974. Type as No. 38	70.00

		Unc	Proof
44 (46) 500 Mils 1970. Double cornucopia, from a coin of Ptolemy II Philadelphus (271–246 B.C.). R youth with basket of fruit, from a 2nd century mosaic found in Lamboussa, North Cyprus			
a) (Ag)			160.00
b) (Cu-Ni)		6.00	
45 (47) 500 Mils 1975. Hercules:			
a) (Ag)			80.00
b) (Cu-Ni)		4.00	

	Unc	Proof
46 (48) 500 Mils 1976. Mother and child:		
a) (Ag)		30.00
b) (Cu-Ni)	4.00	
47 (49) 1 £ 1976. Type as No. 46:		
a) (Ag)		60.00
b) (Cu-Ni)	6.00	

COMMEMORATIVE ISSUE FOR ARCHBISHOP MAKARIOS III

		Unc	Proof
48 (50)	50 £ (Au) 1977	300.00	400.00

HUMAN RIGHTS COMMEMORATIVE

49 (51)	500 Mils 1978:		
	a) (Ag)		180.00
	b) (Cu-Ni)	4.00	

OLYMPIC GAMES 1980 IN MOSCOW

50 (52)	500 Mils 1980:		
	a) (Ag)		90.00
	b) (Cu-Ni)	4.00	

WORLD FOOD DAY (2)

51 (53)	5 Mils (Al) 1981. Arms. Rev. merchant ship, c. 6th century B.C.	0.20	
52 (54)	500 Mils 1981. Rev. sword fish and ear of wheat:		
	a) (Ag)		50.00
	b) (Cu-Ni)	4.00	

Republika Ceskoslovenská

since 11th July 1960:

Ceskoslovenská socialistická republika

Area: 49,370 sq. mi. Population: 14,600,000.

On 28th October 1918 a republic was proclaimed in the states of Bohemia, Moravia, and Slovakia, which had previously been part of the joint kingdom of Austria-Hungary; the independent state of Czechoslovakia was founded. After the creation of the protectorates of Bohemia and Moravia (Čechy a Morava) on 15th March 1939, Slovakia obtained temporarily the status of an independent state and started issuing its own currency. In May 1945 the Republic of Czechoslovakia was re-established; in 1960 it was made a Socialist Republic.

Capital: Prague.

100 Halere = 1 Koruna

			VF	XF
1 (1)	2	Halere (Zi) 1923–1925. Lion coat of arms. ℞ the Karlsbrücke in Prague	5.00	12.00

2 (2)	5	Halere (Br) 1923–1932, 1938. Type as No. 1	0.30	0.60
3 (3)	10	Halere (Br) 1922–1938. Type as No. 1	0.40	0.80
4 (4)	20	Halere (Cu–Ni) 1921–1922, 1924–1931, 1933, 1937–1938. Lion coat of arms. ℞ sheaf of wheat	0.50	1.00
5 (5)	25	Halere (Cu–Ni) 1933. Lion coat of arms. ℞ value in figures	1.20	2.20
6 (6)	50	Halere (Cu–Ni) 1921–1922, 1924–1927, 1931. Lion coat of arms. ℞ value over linden branch and sheaf of wheat	0.40	0.90
7 (7)	1	Koruna (Cu–Ni) 1922–1925, 1929–1930, 1937–1938. Lion coat of arms. ℞ harvest scene: female agricultural worker kneeling, holding sheaf and sickle	1.00	1.80

			VF	XF
8 (8)	5	Korun (Cu-Ni) 1925-1927. Lion coat of arms. R factory, value; diameter 30 mm	5.50	9.00
9 (8a)	5	Korun (Ag) 1928-1932. Type as No. 8; diameter 27 mm	3.00	6.00
10 (12)	10	Korun (Ag) 1930–1933. National arms. ℞ allegorical figure of the Republic holding linden shoot	7.50	10.50
11 (13)	20	Korun (Ag) 1933–1934. National arms. ℞ three standing figures	9.50	12.50

COMMEMORATIVE ISSUES (2) FOR THE 5th ANNIVERSARY OF THE REPUBLIC

12 (15)	1	Ducat (Au) 1923–1939. National arms. ℞ facing half figure of St. Wenceslas (907–929), national hero and national saint	95.00	120.00

13 (16)	2	Ducats (Au) 1923-1938, 1951. Type as No. 12	300.00	360.00

COMMEMORATIVE ISSUES (3) FOR THE 10th ANNIVERSARY OF THE REPUBLIC

			VF	XF

14 (11) 10 Korun (Ag) 1928. Bust right of Tomás Garrigue Masaryk (1850–1937), 1st President of State. R national arms: Bohemian lion in centre of coat of arms of heart shape; in upper field left, the emblem of Slovakia; in upper field right, the emblem of Carpathian Ukraine (Russian Carpathian mountains); below, Moravian eagle on left, Silesian eagle on right 6.00   11.00

15   2 Ducats (Au) 1928. St. Wenceslas guiding plough drawn by demon   290.00   350.00

16   4 Ducats (Au) 1928. Type as No. 15   400.00   500.00

17 (17)   5 Ducats (Au) 1929-1938, 1951. St. Wenceslas on horseback. R lion within coat of arms; linden shoot on right   800.00   1000.00

18 (18) 10 Ducats (Au) 1929-1938, 1951. Type as No. 17   1550.00   1800.00

COMMEMORATIVE ISSUES (3) FOR THE 1000th ANNIVERSARY OF THE CHRISTIANISATION OF BOHEMIA AND THE MURDER OF ST. WENCESLAS IN ALTBUNZLAU

		VF	XF
19	1 Ducat (Au) 1929. St. Wenceslas holding banner and sword. ℞ St. Wenceslas on horseback; angel		350.00
20	3 Ducats (Au) 1929. Type as No. 19		840.00
21	5 Ducats (Au) 1929. Type as No. 19		1300.00

COMMEMORATIVE ISSUE FOR THE 100th ANNIVERSARY THE BIRTH OF TYRŠ

22	1 Ducat (Au) 1932. Dr. Miroslav Tyrš (1832–1884), founder of the Sokol movement	360.00

COMMEMORATIVE ISSUE FOR ANTONIN ŠVEHLA

23	1 Ducat (Au) 1933. Bust left of Dr. Antonin Švehla (1873–1933), politician and statesman. ℞ peasant sowing	360.00

COMMEMORATIVE ISSUES (4) FOR THE REOPENING OF THE MINT IN KREMNITZ (KREMNICE)

24	1 Ducat (Au) 1934. St. Elizabeth. ℞ mining scene	900.00
25	2 Ducats (Au) 1934. Type as No. 24	1800.00
26	5 Ducats (Au) 1934. Type as No. 24	3600.00
27	10 Ducats (Au) 1934. Type as No. 24	7200.00

COMMEMORATIVE MEDALS (2) FOR THE 300th ANNIVERSARY OF THE DEATH OF ALBRECHT VON WALLENSTEIN

28	5 Ducats (Au) 1934. Albrecht Eusebius Wenceslas von Wallenstein, known as Waldstein (1583–1634), Imperial Generalissimo in the Thirty Years' War. ℞ crowned arms	–.–	–.–

			VF	XF
29		10 Ducats (Au) 1934. Type as No. 28	–.–	–.–
30 (8b)		5 Korun (Ni) 1937, 1938. Type as No. 8; diameter 27 mm	2.00	4.00

COMMEMORATIVE ISSUE FOR THE DEATH OF PRESIDENT MASARYK

			VF	XF
31 (14)	20 Korun (Ag) 1937. Bust right of T. Garrigue Masaryk (1850–1937), 1st President of State. ℞ national arms		9.00	12.00

For the coins of the protectorates of Bohemia and Moravia, which were current from 1939 to 1945 (and even later), see under German Occupation in the 2nd World War.

The Slovakian coins issued between 1939 and 1944 are dealt with separately under Slovakia.

			VF	XF
32 (33)	20 Halere (Br) 1947–1950. Lion coat of arms. ℞ sheaf and sickle; diameter 18 mm		0.30	0.60
33 (35)	50 Halere (Br) 1947–1950. Lion coat of arms. ℞ value above linden branch and sheaf; diameter 20 mm		0.40	0.80
34 (37)	1 Koruna (Cu-Ni) 1946, 1947. Lion coat of arms. ℞ harvest scene: female agricultural worker kneeling, holding sheaf of wheat and sickle		0.50	1.00

			VF	XF
35 (39)	2 Korun (Cu–Ni) 1947–1948. Lion coat of arms. ℞ bust right of Juraj Jánošik (1688–1713), Slovakian national hero		0.80	1.50

COMMEMORATIVE ISSUE FOR THE 3rd ANNIVERSARY OF THE SLOVAKIAN UPRISING ON 29th AUGUST 1944

			VF	XF
36 (40)	50 Korun (Ag) 1947. National arms. ℞ Female fighter holding gun and linden branch		5.00	6.00
37 (34)	20 Halere (Al) 1951, 1952. Type as No. 32; diameter 16 mm		0.30	0.70
38 (36)	50 Halere (Al) 1951-1953. Type as No. 33; diameter 18 mm		0.40	0.80

			VF	**XF**

39 (38)   1 Korun (Al) 1947-1953. Type as No. 34:
                  a) 1947, pattern   –.–   –.–
                  b) 1950-1953   0.40   0.80
40 (A 39) 5 Korun (Al) 1952. Type as No. 8; diameter
                  24 mm   18.00   32.00

No. 40 did not come into circulation. The coins were melted down again; only very few of them came into collectors' hands.

COMMEMORATIVE ISSUE FOR THE 3rd ANNIVERSARY OF THE MAY REVOLUTION

41 (41)   50 Korun (Ag) 1948. Lion coat of arms.
            ℞ male figure holding sword and laurel
            branch   5.00   6.50

COMMEMORATIVE ISSUE FOR 600 YEARS OF THE KARL UNIVERSITY IN PRAGUE

42 (42) 100 Korun (Ag) 1948. Lion coat of arms.
            ℞ St. Wenceslas (907–929) holding
            banner and sword; kneeling in front of
            him, Karl I (1316–1378), Count of
            Luxembourg, from 1346 Karl IV,
            King of Bohemia, from 1347 also Em-
            peror of the Holy Roman Empire,
            founder of the first German-speaking
            university, holding foundation docu-
            ments; on left, coats of arms: Bohe-
            mian lion and eagle of St. Wenceslas   7.00   8.50

COMMEMORATIVE ISSUE FOR THE 30th ANNIVERSARY OF LIBERATION FROM AUSTRIA

	VF	XF
43 (43) 100 Korun (Ag) 1948. Lion coat of arms. R. male figure holding laurel branch	6.50	9.00

COMMEMORATIVE ISSUE FOR 700 YEARS OF THE CODE OF MINING RIGHTS OF JIHLAVA (IGLAU)

44 (44) 100 Korun (Ag) 1949. Lion coat of arms. R. coal miner in traditional costume emerging from pit. The Jihlava code of mining rights goes back to King Wenceslas I (he reigned from 1230 to 1253) and is applied in the regions of the Sudetenland and the Carpathian mountains, as well as in Upper Hungary .... 6.50 ... 9.00

COMMEMORATIVE ISSUES (2) FOR THE 70th ANNIVERSARY OF THE BIRTH OF STALIN

45 (45) 50 Korun (Ag) 1949. Lion coat of arms. R. Generalissimo J. V. Stalin (1879–1953), Soviet statesman	5.00	9.00
46 (46) 100 Korun (Ag) 1949. Type as No. 45	7.00	12.00

COMMEMORATIVE ISSUE FOR THE 30th ANNIVERSARY OF THE CZECHOSLOVAKIAN COMMUNIST PARTY

			VF	XF
47 (47)	100	Korun (Ag) 1951. Lion coat of arms. ℞ Klement Gottwald (1896–1953), President of State 1948–1953	5.00	9.00
48 (48)	1	Haleru (Al) 1953–1960. Lion coat of arms. ℞ value within wreath	0.10	0.20
49 (49)	3	Halere (Al) 1953–1954, 1958. Type as No. 44	0.10	0.20
50 (50)	5	Halere (Al) 1953–1955. Type as No. 44	0.20	0.40
51 (51)	10	Halere (Al) 1953–1956, 1958. Type as No. 44	0.20	0.35
52 (52)	25	Halere (Al) 1953–1954. Type as No. 44	0.40	0.80
53 (61)	1	Koruna (Al–Br) 1957–1960. Lion coat of arms. ℞ female agricultural worker holding plant	0.60	1.20

COMMEMORATIVE ISSUES (2) FOR THE 10th ANNIVERSARY OF THE SLOVAKIAN UPRISING

54 (53)	10	Korun (Ag) 1954. Lion coat of arms. ℞ partisan with factory and railway in background	6.00	7.50
55 (54)	25	Korun (Ag) 1954. Type as No. 54	7.50	10.00

COMMEMORATIVE ISSUES (4) FOR THE 10th ANNIVERSARY OF LIBERATION ON 9th MAY 1945

56 (55)	10	Korun (Ag) 1955. Lion coat of arms. ℞ soldier kneeling to left, holding child	6.00	7.50

			VF	XF
57 (56)	25	Korun (Ag) 1955. Lion coat of arms. ℞ "The return of the soldier": scene with mother holding child in arms, and soldier	8.00	10.50
58 (57)	50	Korun (Ag) 1955. Lion coat of arms. ℞ Soviet soldier	17.00	22.00
59 (58)	100	Korun (Ag) 1955. Lion coat of arms. ℞ scenes of rejoicing at barricade in May 1945	28.00	35.00

COMMEMORATIVE ISSUE FOR THE 300th ANNIVERSARY OF THE PUBLICATION OF THE BOOK "OPERA DIDACTICA OMNIA"

60 (60)	10	Korun (Ag) 1957. Bust right of Jan Amos Komenský, called Comenius (1592–1670), preacher and Bishop of the Moravian Brotherhood, educational reformer and theologian	6.00	9.00

COMMEMORATIVE ISSUE FOR THE 250th ANNIVERSARY OF THE EXISTENCE OF THE TECHNICAL HIGH SCHOOL IN PRAGUE

61 (59)	10	Korun (Ag) 1957. Lion coat of arms. ℞ bust left of Christian Josef Willenberg (1676–1731), founder of the School of Engineering; in background, the Slapy dam near Prague	11.00	15.00

CZECHOSLOVAKIAN SOCIALIST REPUBLIC – ČSSR
Československá socialistická republika

				VF	XF
62 (62)	1	Haleru (Al) 1962–1963. Coat of arms. ℞ value within wreath		0.10	0.20
63 (63)	3	Halere (Al) 1962, 1963. Type as No. 62			
		a) 1962		–.–	–.–
		b) 1963		0.15	0.25
64 (64)	5	Halere (Al) 1962–1963, 1966–1967. 1970–1977. Type as No. 62		0.15	0.25
65 (65)	10	Halere (Al) 1961–1971. Type as No. 62		0.20	0.35
66 (66)	25	Halere (Al) 1962–1965. Type as No. 62		0.20	0.40

			VF	XF
67 (67)	50	Halere (Br) 1963–1965, 1969–1974. Type as No. 62	0.25	0.50

			VF	XF
68 (68)	1	Koruna (Al-Br) 1961–1980. Coat of arms. ℞ female agricultural worker holding plant	0.25	0.50

COMMEMORATIVE ISSUE FOR THE 20th ANNIVERSARY OF THE SLOVAKIAN UPRISING

			VF	XF
69 (69)	10	Korun (Ag) 1964. Coat of arms. ℞ three hands raised holding the symbols of industry, agriculture and science	6.00	7.50

COMMEMORATIVE ISSUE FOR THE 20th ANNIVERSARY OF LIBERATION

			VF	XF
70 (70)	25	Korun (Ag) 1965. Coat of arms. ℞ girl's head to left, with dove of peace holding linden branch; in background, the Karlsbrücke in Prague	7.50	10.00

COMMEMORATIVE ISSUE FOR THE 550th ANNIVERSARY OF THE DEATH OF JAN HUS

			VF	XF
71 (71)	10	Korun (Ag) 1965. Coat of arms. ℞ Jan Hus (1369–1415), rector of the Karl university, religious reformer and martyr	25.00	32.00
72 (72)	3	Korun (Cu–Ni) 1965–1969. Coat of arms. ℞ stylized flower surrounded with ribbons, symbol of liberty and progress	0.50	0.80
73 (73)	5	Korun (Cu–Ni) 1966–1973. Coat of arms. ℞ representation of cranes with star and flower, symbol of reconstruction	0.80	1.40

COMMEMORATIVE ISSUE FOR THE 1100th ANNIVERSARY OF THE FOUNDING OF GREATER MORAVIA

74 (74)	10	Korun (Ag) 1966. Coat of arms. ℞ hawking scene: falconer on horseback; silversmith work of the 9th century found at Staré Mesto in Moravia	7.00	9.00

COMMEMORATIVE ISSUE FOR THE 500th ANNIVERSARY OF THE FOUNDING OF PRESSBURG UNIVERSITY

75 (75)	10	Korun (Ag) 1967. Coat of arms above the spurs of the Carpathian mountains with the castle of Pressburg (Bratislava) and the Danube river, stylized, symbol of the City. ℞ university buildings, and seal of the city, with inscription SIGILLUM CIVITATIS BRATISLAVENSIS	20.00	25.00

COMMEMORATIVE ISSUE FOR THE CENTENARY OF THE LAYING OF THE FOUNDATION STONE OF THE PRAGUE NATIONAL THEATRE

		VF	XF
76 (76)	10 Korun (Ag) 1968. Triga. ℞ coat of arms	25.00	40.00

COMMEMORATIVE ISSUE FOR THE 150th ANNIVERSARY OF THE EXISTENCE OF THE NATIONAL MUSEUM

77 (77)	25 Korun (Ag) 1968. Coat of arms. ℞ the National Museum building in Prague	12.00	17.00

COMMEMORATIVE ISSUE FOR THE 50th ANNIVERSARY OF THE REPUBLIC AND THE 20th ANNIVERSARY OF THE PEOPLE'S REPUBLIC

78 (78)	50 Korun (Ag) 1968. Head left of the Republic crowned with linden leaves, a project by Jiri Harcuba. Around, dates 1918, 1968. ℞ coat of arms, dates 1948, 1968. Name of country and value	60.00	70.00

COMMEMORATIVE ISSUE FOR THE CENTENARY OF THE DEATH OF J. E. PURKINJE

79 (79)	25 Korun (Ag) 1969. Bust right of Jan Evangelista, Knight of Purkinje (1787–

	VF	XF
1869), professor of physiology and pathology. ℞ national arms and value	10.00	13.00

Medal upon the same occasion with the use of the obverse die, approx. 25.3 g fine gold   480.00

COMMEMORATIVE ISSUE FOR THE 25th ANNIVERSARY OF THE SLOVAKIAN UPRISING

80 (80) 25 Korun (Ag) 1969. Allegorical representation with letters S N P (= Slovenské národni povstáni) 1944/1969 ℞ coat of arms, name of country and value   50.00   60.00

COMMEMORATIVE ISSUE FOR THE 50th ANNIVERSARY OF THE SLOVAKIAN NATIONAL THEATRE IN PRESSBURG

81 (81) 25 Korun (Ag) 1970. Facing head of muse crowned with laurel leaves. ℞ coat of arms and value   10.00   12.50

COMMEMORATIVE ISSUE FOR THE 25th ANNIVERSARY OF LIBERATION

		VF	**XF**
82 (82)	25 Korun (Ag) 1970. Coat of arms. ℞ star above landscape. Dates, value	6.00	9.00

COMMEMORATIVE ISSUE FOR THE CENTENARY OF THE BIRTH OF LENIN

83 (83)	50 Korun (Ag) 1970. Vladimir Ilyich Lenin (1870–1924), real name Ulyanov; Soviet-Russian statesman, leader of the world proletariat	8.00	11.00

COMMEMORATIVE ISSUE FOR THE 50th ANNIVERSARY OF THE CZECHOSLOVAKIAN COMMUNIST PARTY

84 (84)	50 Korun (Ag) 1971. Hammer and sickle in front of people, above star	8.00	12.00

COMMEMORATIVE ISSUE FOR THE 50th ANNIVERSARY OF THE DEATH OF P. O. HVIEZDOSLAV

85 (85)	50 Korun (Ag) 1971. Pavel Országh Hviezdoslav (1849–1921), poet and writer	9.00	12.50

COMMEMORATIVE ISSUE FOR THE CENTENARY OF THE DEATH OF J. MÁNES

86 (86)	100 Korun (Ag) 1971. Josef Mánes (1820–1871), painter	12.00	17.00

COMMEMORATIVE ISSUE FOR THE CENTENARY
OF THE DEATH OF A. SLÁDKOVIČ

		VF	XF
87 (87)	20 Korun (Ag) 1972. Andrej Sládkovič, Slovakian poet	5.00	7.50

COMMEMORATIVE ISSUE FOR THE 50th ANNIVERSARY
OF THE DEATH OF J. V. MYSLBEK

88 (88)	50 Korun (Ag) 1972. J. V. Myslbek (1848 to 1922), Czechoslovakian sculptor	9.00	12.00

89 (91)	20 Halere (Al–Br) 1972–	0.10	0.20

90 (94)	2 Korun (Cu-Ni) 1972–1980	0.30	0.60

COMMEMORATIVE ISSUE FOR THE 25th ANNIVERSARY
OF THE PEOPLE'S REPUBLIC

91 (96)   50 Korun (Ag) 1973. Soldier and factory   8.00   10.50

COMMEMORATIVE ISSUE FOR THE 200th ANNIVERSARY
OF THE BIRTH OF J. JUNGMANN

92 (97)   50 Korun (Ag) 1973. Josef Jungmann,
writer and philologist   9.00   12.00

COMMEMORATIVE ISSUE FOR THE 150th BIRTHDAY
OF FRIEDRICH SMETANA

93 (99)   100 Korun (Ag) 1974. Friedrich Smetana
(1824–1884), composer   13.00   17.00

COMMEMORATIVE ISSUE FOR THE 100th BIRTHDAY
OF JANKO JESENSKY

94 (98)   50 Korun (Ag) 1974. Janko Jesensky (30.
12. 1874 to 27. 12. 1945), Slovakian
writer of the people   9.00   12.00
95 (90)   10 Halere (Al) 1974–1980. Type as No. 89   0.10   0.20

100th ANNIVERSARY OF THE BIRTH OF S. K. NEUMANN

			VF	XF
96 (100)	50	Korun (Ag) 1975. Stanislav Kostka Neumann (1875-1947), Czech poet	10.00	12.50

100th ANNIVERSARY OF THE DEATH OF JANKO KRAL

| **97** (101) | 100 | Korun (Ag) 1976. Janko Král (1822-1876), Slovakian poet | 15.00 | 18.00 |

100th ANNIVERSARY OF THE BIRTH OF VIKTOR KAPLAN

| **98** (102) | 100 | Korun (Ag) 1976. Viktor Kaplan (1876-1934), engineer, inventor of the Kaplan-turbine | 15.00 | 18.00 |

125th ANNIVERSARY OF THE DEATH OF JAN KOLLÁR

			VF	XF
99 (103)	50 Korun (Ag) 1977. Jan Kollár (1793-1852), Slovakian poet		9.00	12.00

300th ANNIVERSARY OF THE DEATH OF WENZEL HOLLAR

100 (104)	100 Korun (Ag) 1977. Wenzel Hollar (1607–1677),	12.00	18.00

101 (89)	5 Halere (Al) 1977–1980. Type as No. 89	0.10	0.20

100th ANNIVERSARY OF THE BIRTH OF ZDENĚK NEJEDLÝ

102 (105)	50 Korun (Ag) 1978. Dr. Zdeněk Nejedlý	9.00	12.00

75th ANNIVERSARY OF THE BIRTH OF JULIUS FUČIK

	VF	XF
103 (107) 100 Korun (Ag) 1978. Julius Fučik (1903–1943), journalist	11.00	14.00

650th ANNIVERSARY OF THE MINT OF KREMNICA

104 (106) 50 Korun (Ag) 1978. Coins strack at Kremnica Mint	9.00	11.50

600th ANNIVERSARY OF THE DEATH OF KARL IV (5)

105 (108) 100 Korun (Ag) 1978. Karl IV (1316–1378), Count of Luxembourg, from 1346 King of Bohemia, from 1347 also Emperor of the Holy Roman Empire	11.50	15.00

106 (110) 1 Ducat (Au) 1978–1982	160.00	180.00

		VF	XF
107 (111)	2 Ducats (Au) 1978	280.00	300.00
108 (112)	5 Ducats (Au) 1978	650.00	700.00
109 (113)	10 Ducats (Au) 1978	1200.00	1350.00

			VF	XF
110 (92)	50 Halere (Cu-Ni) 1978–1980. Type as No. 89		0.40	0.80

150th ANNIVERSARY OF THE BIRTH OF JAN BOTTO

111 (109)	100 Korun (Ag) 1979. Ján Botto (1829–1881), Slovakian poet	11.00	14.50

30th ANNIVERSARY OF THE 9th CONGRESS

112 (114)	50 Korun (Ag) 1979. Hammer and sickle as well as gear-wheel	9.00	11.50

650th ANNIVERSARY OF THE BIRTH OF PETER PARLER

113 (115)	100 Korun (Ag) 1980. Peter Parler (1330–1399), architect	11.00	14.50

100th ANNIVERSARY OF THE BIRTH OF B. SMERAL

114 (117)	100 Korun (Ag) 1980. Dr. Bohumir Smeral (1880–1941), writer and politician	11.00	14.50

SPARTAKIADE GAMES 1980	VF	XF
115 (116) 100 Korun (Ag) 1980	11.00	14.50

100th ANNIVERSARY OF THE BIRTH OF O. SPANIEL

	VF	XF
116 (120) 100 Korun (Ag) 1981. Otakar Spaniel (1881–1955), sculptor and medallist	10.50	14.00

125th ANNIVERSARY OF THE DEATH OF L. STUR

117 (118)   500 Korun   (Ag)   1981.   Ludovit   Stur (1815–1856),   Slovakian   poet   and politician   36.00   45.00

20th ANNIVERSARY OF MANNED SPACES FLIGHT

118 (119)   100 Korun (Ag) 1981. Juri A. Gagarin (1934–1968), Soviet cosmonaut   10.50   14.00

100th ANNIVERSARY OF THE BIRTH OF I. OLBRACHT

119   100 Korun (Ag) 1982.   Ivan   Olbracht (1882–1952), writer   10.50   14.00

150th ANNIVERSARY OF HORSE DRAWN TRAM (BUDWEIS – LINZ)

120   100 Korun (Ag) 1982   10.50   14.00

Dahomey

Area: 44,524 sq. mi. Population: 3,800,000.
In the 17th century the powerful kingdom of Dahomey existed in the territory of the present state of Dahomey. One after another, neighbouring tribes were subjected to rigidly organised military power, either through conquest or through voluntary submission. After occupation by, and submission to the French, and the inclusion of Abomey (1894), the country became a colony and part of French West Africa. In 1957 it obtained further internal autonomy within the framework of the Communauté Française. On 4th December 1958 the Republic was proclaimed. Since 1st August 1960 Dahomey has been independent. Dahomey joined up with the countries of the Ivory Coast, Mauretania, Nigeria, Upper Volta, Senegal and Togo in order to form the Union Monétaire Ouest-Africaine; the issuing authority for the whole of the monetary union is the Banque Centrale des Etats de l'Afrique de l'Ouest. See also under the heading "West African States". In 1974, the republic began a transition to a socialist society with Marxism-Leninism as its revolutionary philosophy. On November 30, 1975 the name of the Republic Dahomey was changed to the People's Republic of Benin.
Capital: Porto Novo.

100 Centimes = 1 CFA Franc

COMMEMORATIVE ISSUES (8) FOR THE 10th ANNIVERSARY
OF INDEPENDENCE ON 1st AUGUST 1970

1	100 Francs (Ag) 1971–. Buildings on stilts on Lake Ganvié. ℞ national arms, name of country, commemorative inscription, value	**Proof**	20.00

2   200 Francs (Ag) 1971–. Abomey woman.
Ɽ same as No. 1   30.00

3   500 Francs (Ag) 1971–. Ouémé woman.
Ɽ same as No. 1   60.00

4 1000 Francs (Ag) 1971–. Somba woman.
Ɽ same as No. 1   100.00

5 2500 Francs (Au) 1971–. Group of religious
dancers. Ɽ same as No. 1   300.00

6 5000 Francs (Au) 1971–. African buffaloes
(Syncerus caffer – Bovidae). Ɽ same as
No. 1   600.00

7 10000 Francs (Au) 1971–. Hippopotami (Hip-
popotamus amphibius – Hippopotami-
dae). Ɽ same as No. 1   1200.00

8 25000 Francs (Au) 1971–. Busts of Sourou-
Migan Apithy (*1913), Prime Minister
1957–1959, President of State from
1964 to 1965, Justin Ahomadegbé-
Tometin (*1917) and Hubert Maga
(*1916), Prime Minister 1959–1961,
President of State 1961–1963; present
President of State. Ɽ same as No. 1   2500.00

Danish West Indies

Dänisch-Westindien   **Antilles Danoises**

This group of about 50 islands in the West Indies became a Danish possession in the 17th century and was sold to the United States of America on 31st March 1971 for $ 25,000,000. Since then, these islands have been known as the U. S. Virgin Islands.
Capital: Charlotte Amalie.

5 Bit = 1 Cent, 20 Cents = 1 Franc, 5 Francs = 1 Daler

	CHRISTIAN IX 1863–1906	VF	XF
1 (5)	½ Cent = 2½ Bit (Br) 1905. Crown above monogram. ℞ sickle, herald's staff and trident	16.00	30.00
2 (6)	1 Cent = 5 Bit (Br) 1905. Same type as No. 1	15.00	25.00

		VF	XF
3 (7)	2 Cents = 10 Bit (Br) 1905. Same type as No. 1	20.00	35.00

		VF	XF
4 (8)	5 Cents = 25 Bit (Ni) 1905. Same type as No. 1	10.00	20.00

		VF	XF
5 (9)	10 Cents = 50 Bit (Ag) 1905. Head l. of Christian IX. ℞ value and laurel branch	16.00	25.00

				VF	XF

6 (10) 20 Cents = 1 Franc (Ag) 1905. Bust l. of Christian IX. ℞ 3 female figures — 35.00 — 60.00

7 (11) 40 Cents = 2 Francs (Ag) 1905. Same type as No. 6 — 100.00 — 180.00

8 (12) 4 Daler = 20 Francs (Au) 1904, 1905. Head l. of Christian IX. ℞ seated female figure — 750.00 — 900.00

9 (13) 10 Daler = 50 Francs (Au) 1904. Same type as No. 8 — 6000.00 — 7000.00

FREDERIK VIII 1906–1912

10 (14) 20 Cents = 1 Franc (Ag) 1907. Head l. of Frederik VIII. ℞ three female figures — 40.00 — 80.00

11 (15) 40 Cents = 2 Francs (Ag) 1907. Same type as No. 10 — 130.00 — 210.00

CHRISTIAN X 1912–1917

12 (16) 1 Cent = 5 Bit (Br) 1913. Crown above monogram. ℞ sickle, herald's staff and trident — 22.00 — 40.00

Previous issues, see "Weltmünzkatalog 19. Jahrhundert" (World Coin Catalogue of the 19th Century)

Denmark

Danmark

Area: 16,629 sq. mi. Population: 5,000,000.
The kingdom of Denmark includes the Jutland peninsula and about
50 islands between the Baltic and the North Sea. The Faroe Islands
in the Atlantic Ocean are administered by Denmark, but enjoy limited
autonomy.
Capital: Copenhagen.
Greenland, on the other hand, has been an integral part of the kingdom since 1953, with equal rights, under a governor.

100 Øre = 1 Krone

		CHRISTIAN IX 1863–1906	VF	XF
1 (8)	1	Øre (Br) 1874–1904. Monogram. ℞ common dolphin (Delphinus delphis – Delphinidae), ear of wheat and value	4.00	7.50
2 (9)	2	Øre (Br) 1874–1904. Same type as No. 1	5.00	8.00
3 (10)	5	Øre (Br) 1874–1906. Same type as No. 1	10.50	17.00

			VF	XF
4 (11)	10	Øre (Ag) 1874–1905. Head r. of Christian IX. (1818–1906). ℞ common dolphin, ear of wheat, star and value	6.00	11.00
5 (12)	25	Øre (Ag) 1874–1905. Same type as No. 4	10.50	18.50
6 (13)	1	Krone (Ag) 1875–1898. Head of Christian IX. ℞ crowned arms between common dolphin and ear of wheat	20.00	36.00
7 (14)	2	Kroner (Ag) 1875–1899. Same type as No. 6	20.00	38.00
8 (18)	10	Kroner (Au) 1873–1900. Head of Christian IX. ℞ allegorical representation of Denmark	140.00	175.00
9 (19)	20	Kroner (Au) 1873–1900. Head of Christian IX. ℞ allegorical figure	165.00	200.00

		VF	XF
10 (17)	2 Kroner (Ag) 1903. Bust r. of King Christian IX. ℞ allegorical figure, inscription, value	38.00	60.00

FREDERIK VIII 1906–1912

COMMEMORATIVE ISSUE FOR THE DEATH OF CHRISTIAN IX AND THE ACCESSION TO THE THRONE OF FREDERIK VIII

11 (25)	2 Kroner (Ag) 1906. Bust l. of Frederik VIII (1843–1912). ℞ Bust l. of Christian IX	30.00	40.00
12 (20)	1 Øre (Br) 1907–1912. Monogram. ℞ value	4.00	5.00
13 (21)	2 Øre (Br) 1907–1912. Monogram. ℞ value	4.00	6.00
14 (22)	5 Øre (Br) 1907–1912. Monogram. ℞ value	8.00	14.00
15 (23)	10 Øre (Ag) 1907–1912. Head of Frederik VIII. ℞ value	8.00	14.00
16 (24)	25 Øre (Ag) 1907, 1911. Head of Frederik VIII. ℞ value	7.50	12.50
17 (26)	10 Kroner (Au) 1908–1909. Head of Frederik VIII. ℞ crowned arms and value	140.00	175.00

				VF	XF
18 (27)	20	Kroner (Au) 1908–1912. Same type as No. 17		130.00	165.00

CHRISTIAN X 1912–1947

COMMEMORATIVE ISSUE FOR THE DEATH OF FREDERIK VIII AND THE ACCESSION TO THE THRONE OF CHRISTIAN X

19 (40)	5	Kroner (Ag) 1912. Head of Christian X. ℞ head of Frederik VIII	40.00	55.00
20 (28)	1	Øre (Br) 1913-1923. Monogramm CX with crown, date. R value	1.50	3.00
21 (29)	2	Øre (Br) 1913-1923. Type as No. 20	2.00	4.00

22 (30)	5	Øre (Br) 1913-1923. Type as No. 20	5.00	10.00
23 (36)	10	Øre (Ag) 1914-1919. Type similar to No. 20	4.00	6.00

24 (37)	25	Øre (Ag) 1913-1919. Type as No. 23	4.50	7.50

25 (38)   1 Krone (Ag) 1915–1916. Head r. of **VF**   **XF**
Christian X. ℞ crowned arms between
common dolphin and ear of wheat   7.00   12.00

			VF	XF
26 (39)	2	Kroner (Ag) 1915-1916. Type as No. 25	14.00	22.00
27 (44)	10	Kroner (Au) 1913, 1917. Head of Christian X. R crowned arms	125.00	145.00
28 (45)	20	Kroner (Au) 1913-1931. Type No. 27	135.00	160.00
29 (28a)	1	Øre (Fe) 1918, 1919. Type as No. 20	3.50	7.00
30 (29a)	2	Øre (Fe) 1918, 1919. Type as No. 21	3.50	7.00
31 (30a)	5	Øre (Fe) 1918, 1919. Type as No. 22	10.00	20.00
32 (31)	10	Øre (Cu-Ni) 1920-1923. Type as No. 23	4.00	8.00
33 (32)	25	Øre (Cu-Ni) 1920-1922. Type as No. 24	3.50	7.00

COMMEMORATIVE ISSUE FOR THE SILVER WEDDING OF THE ROYAL COUPLE

34 (41)   2 Kroner (Ag) 1923. Conjoined busts r.
of Christian X and Queen Alexandrine
(1879–1952). ℞ crowned arms   16.50   24.00

			VF	XF
35 (46)	1 Øre (Br) 1926–1940. Monogram CX with crown. ℞ value (with central hole)		0.60	1.10

			VF	XF
36 (47)	2 Øre (Br) 1926–1940. Same type as No. 35		0.60	1.10
37 (48)	5 Øre (Br) 1927–1941. Same type as No. 35		0.80	1.50
38 (49)	10 Øre (Cu-Ni) 1924-1947. Monogramm CX and R above, crown. R value (central hole)		1.60	3.20
39 (50)	25 Øre (Cu-Ni) 1924-1927. Type as No. 38		2.00	4.00

For similar coins to Nos. 35–39, but without any mintmark, see under Faroe Islands.

			VF	XF
40 (33)	½ Krone (Al-Br) 1924-1940. Monogramm CX with crown dividing date. R crown and value		6.00	11.00
41 (34)	1 Krone (Al-Br) 1924-1941. Type as No. 40		3.00	6.00

			VF	XF
42 (35)	2 Kroner (Al-Br) 1924-1941. Same type as No. 40		3.00	6.00

COMMEMORATIVE ISSUE FOR THE 60th BIRTHDAY OF THE KING

43 (42)　2 Kroner (Ag) 1930. Head r. of Christian X (1870–1947). ℞ crowned arms and shield supported by two figures

		VF	XF
		14.00	20.00

COMMEMORATIVE ISSUE FOR 25 YEARS' REIGN

			VF	XF
44 (43)	2	Kroner (Ag) 1937. Head r. of Christian X. ℞ crowned arms, value and inscription 15 Mai 1912–1937	14.00	20.00
45 (51)	1	Øre (Zi) 1941–1946. Monogram CX with crown. ℞ value in wreath	0.70	2.00
46 (52a)	2	Øre (Zi) 1942-1947. Type as No. 45	0.80	1.60
47 (53a)	5	Øre (Zi) 1942-1945. Type as No. 45	1.20	2.50
48 (49a)	10	Øre (Zi) 1941-1945. Type as No. 38	1.50	3.50
49 (50a)	25	Øre (Zi) 1941-1945. Type as No. 39	.4.00	8.00
50	1	Øre (Al) 1941. Type as No. 45. Trial strike!	–.–	–.–
51 (52)	2	Øre (Al) 1941. Type as No. 46	1.20	2.50
52 (53)	5	Øre (Al) 1941. Type as No. 47	2.00	5.00

			VF	XF
53 (54)	1	Krone (Al-Br) 1942–1947. Head r. of Christian X. ℞ value and ears of wheat in saltire	1.50	3.00

COMMEMORATIVE ISSUE FOR THE 75th BIRTHDAY OF THE KING

			VF	XF
54 (55)	2	Kroner (Ag) 1945. Head r. of Christian X. ℞ dates 1870–1945 within wreath	28.00	36.00

			VF	XF
55 (56)	1 Øre (Zi) 1948–1972. Monogram FR; crown above. R value		0.10	0.20
56 (57)	2 Øre (Zi) 1948–1972. Same type as No. 55		0.10	0.20

57 (58)	5 Øre (Zi) 1950–1964. Same type as No. 55		0.40	0.80
58 (59)	10 Øre (Cu-Ni) 1948–1960. Monogram FR; crown above. R value		0.40	0.80
59 (60)	25 Øre (Cu-Ni) 1948–1960. Same type as No. 50		0.50	0.80

60 (61)	1 Krone (Al-Br) 1947-1960. Head r. of Frederik IX. (1899-1972). R crowned arms:			
	a) 1947-1959		1.50	3.00
	b) 1960		–.–	–.–
61 (62)	2 Kroner (Al-Br) 1947-1959. Same type as No. 60		3.00	5.00

COMMEMORATIVE ISSUE FOR GREENLAND FOR THE ANTI-TUBERCULOSIS CAMPAIGN

62 (63)	2 Kroner (Ag) 1953. Conjoined heads r. of Frederik IX and Queen Ingrid (*1910). R map of Greenland		38.00	58.00

COMMEMORATIVE ISSUE FOR THE 18th BIRTHDAY OF PRINCESS MARGRETHE ON 16th APRIL 1958

			VF	**XF**
63 (64)	2 Kroner (Ag) 1958. Head r. of Frederik IX. ℞ Head l. of Princess Margrethe (*1940), Queen since 1972		15.00	20.00

COMMEMORATIVE ISSUE FOR THE SILVER WEDDING OF THE ROYAL COUPLE

64 (65)	5 Kroner (Ag) 1960. Conjoinded heads r. of Frederik IX and Queen Ingrid	12.50	18.00

65 (66)	1 Øre (Br) 1960–1964. Crowned monogram. ℞ value between ears		4.00
66 (67)	2 Øre (Br) 1960–1966. Same type as No. 65		3.50
67 (68)	5 Øre (Br) 1960–1972. Same type as No. 65	0.10	0.20

			VF	XF
68 (69)	10 Øre (Cu–Ni) 1960–1972. ℞ value between oak leaves		0.10	0.20
69 (70)	25 Øre (Cu–Ni) 1960–1967. Same type as No. 60		0.40	0.60
70 (71)	1 Krone (Cu–Ni) 1960–1972. Head r. of Frederik IX. ℞ crowned arms		0.40	0.80

71 (72)	5 Kroner (Cu-Ni) 1960-1972. Type as No. 70, but coat of arms between oak leaves	1.80	2.50

COMMEMORATIVE ISSUE FOR THE WEDDING OF PRINCESS ANNE-MARIE ON 18th SEPTEMBER 1964

72 (73)	5 Kroner (Ag) 1964. Head r. of Frederik IX. ℞ head l. of Princess Anne-Marie (*1947)	14.00	18.00

73 (76) 25 Øre (Cu–Ni) 1966–1972. Monogram   **VF**   **XF**
FR; above, crown; and twig of horn-
beam (Carpinus bétulus). ℞ value and
ears of barley (Hordeum sp. – Grami-
nae)   0.15   0.25

COMMEMORATIVE ISSUE FOR THE WEDDING OF PRINCESS MARGRETHE ON 10th JUNE 1967

74 (74) 10 Kroner (Ag) 1967. Head r. of Frederik
IX. ℞ heads r. of Crown Princess
Margrethe and Count Henry de
Montpezat   12.50   18.00

COMMEMORATIVE ISSUE FOR THE WEDDING OF PRINCESS BENEDIKTE ON 3th FEBRUARY 1968

75 (75) 10 Kroner (Ag) 1968. Head r. of Frederik
IX. ℞ head l. of Princess Benedikte
(*1944)   12.50   18.00

COMMEMORATIVE ISSUE ON THE DEATH
OF FREDERIK IX AND ON THE ACCESSION
TO THE THRONE OF MARGRETHE II

			VF	XF
76 (77)	10	Kroner (Ag) 1972. Margrethe II. R Frederik IX	12.50	18.00

77 (78)	5	Øre (St, Br-plated) 1973-. Crowned monogramm, year date. R value	0.05	0.10

78 (79)	10	Øre (Cu-Ni) 1973–. Type similar to No. 69	0.05	0.10
79 (80)	25	Øre (Cu-Ni) 1973–. Crowned monogram, oak branch, year date. R denomination (with hole)	0.10	0.20
80 (81)	1	Krone (Cu-Ni) 1973–. Margrethe II, bust with legend, facing right. R crowned coat of arms (introduced 16. 11.1972), year date, denomination	0.15	0.30
81 (82)	5	Kroner (Cu-Ni) 1973–. R crowned coat of arms between oak leaves, year date, denomination	0.90	1.50
82 (83)	10	Kroner (Cu-Ni) 1979–	1.20	2.00

Previous issues, see "Weltmünzkatalog 19. Jahrhundert" (World Coin Catalogue of the 19th Century)

Faroe Islands (Faerøerne)

Area: 538 sq. mi. Population: 34,500.
All the coins were struck in London and, unlike Nos. 35–39 of Denmark, show no mintmark.
Capital: Thorshavn.

100 Øre = 1 Krone

			VF	XF
1 (1)	1 Øre (Br) 1941. Monogram CX with crown. ℞ value (with central hole)		38.00 / 7.50	60.00 / 12.50
2 (2)	2 Øre (Br) 1941. Same type as No. 1		8.00	13.50
3 (3)	5 Øre (Br) 1941. Same type as No. 1			
4 (4)	10 Øre (Cu-Ni) 1941. Monogram CX and R, above which, crown. ℞ value (with central hole)		12.00	16.50
5 (5)	25 Øre (Cu-Ni) 1941. Same type as No. 4		12.50	18.00

Greenland (Grønland)

Area: 836,538 sq. mi. Population: 48,000.
According to the Danish Constitution of 5th June 1953, Greenland is an
integral part of the kingdom of Denmark, with equal rights.
Capital: Godthaab.

100 Øre = 1 Krone

		VF	XF
1 (5)	25 Øre (Cu-Ni) 1926. Crowned arms. R polar bear (Thalarctos maritimus– Ursidae)	4.00	7.50
2 (6)	25 Øre (Cu-Ni) 1926. Type as No. 1 (central hole)	18.00	30.00
3 (7)	50 Øre (Al-Br) 1926. Type as No. 1	6.00	11.00
4 (8)	1 Krone (Al-Br) 1926. Typ as No. 1	7.50	12.50
5 (9)	5 Kroner (Bra) 1944. Typ as No. 1	42.00	75.00
6 (10)	1 Krone (Al-Br) 1957. Crown over shields of Denmark and Greenland. R value within wreath	12.50	25.00
7 (10a)	1 Krone (Cu-Ni) 1960, 1964. Type as No. 6	4.00	7.50

Djibouti

Area: 8,462 sq. mi. Population: 125,000.
The former French Territory of the Afars and Issas was renamed Djibouti
and became independent on Juni 27, 1977.
Capital: Djibouti.

100 Centimes = 1 Djibouti Franc

			VF	XF
1	1	Franc (Al) 1977. National arms. Rev. lyre antelope	0.50	1.00
2	2	Francs (Al) 1977. Type as No. 1	0.50	1.00
3	5	Francs (Al) 1977. Type as No. 1	0.50	1.00
4	10	Francs (Al-Br) 1977. Rev. Arab dhow	0.50	1.00
5	20	Francs (Al-Br) 1977. Type as No. 4	0.50	1.00
6	50	Francs (Cu-Ni) 1977. Rev. dromedaries	1.00	1.50
7	100	Francs (Cu-Ni) 1977. Type as No. 6	1.80	3.00

Dominica

Area: 304 sq. mi. Population: 87,000.

Dominica, the largest island of the Lesser Antilles, was discovered by Christopher Columbus on 3rd November 1493. British since 1783, it became in 1968 an associate member of the United Kingdom of Great Britain. Dominica is a member of the Caribbean Free Trade Area (CARIFTA) and is linked with the countries of Antigua, Barbados, Grenada, Montserrat, St. Christopher- (Kitts-) Nevis-Anguilla, St. Lucia and St. Vincent to form the monetary union of the East Caribbean Dollar. The issuing authority for the whole monetary union is the East Caribbean Currency Authority with headquarters in Bridgetown, Barbados. Full independence was attained on 3rd November 1978.

Capital: Roseau.

100 Cents = 1 East Caribbean Dollar

COMMEMORATIVE ISSUE FOR THE INAUGURATION OF THE CARIBBEAN DEVELOPMENT BANK AND THE FAO COIN PLAN

		Unc	Proof
1 (4*)	4 Dollars (Cu-Ni) 1970. Arms with eagles holding shield, and lion as helmet decoration. ℞ bananas, sugar-cane and value	10.00	30.00

*This number refers to Yeoman's East Caribbean Territories listings.

INDEPENDENCE COMMEMORATIVE (4)

		Unc	Proof
2	10 Dollars (Ag) 1978. History of Carnival	30.00	40.00
3	20 Dollars (Ag) 1978. 50th Anniversary Graf Zeppelin	80.00	100.00
4	150 Dollars (Au) 1978. Parrot and map	280.00	350.00
5	300 Dollars (Au) 1978. Arms	500.00	600.00

VISIT OF POPE JOHN PAUL II (2)

6	10 Dollars (Ag) 1979. Portrait of Pope John Paul II	30.00	40.00
7	300 Dollars (Au) 1979	500.00	600.00

ISRAEL AND EGYPT PEACE TREATY (2)

8	20 Dollars (Ag) 1979	80.00	90.00
9	150 Dollars (Au) 1979	350.00	400.00

Dominican Republic

Dominikanische Republik   **Dominicaine**

Area: 18,744 sq. mi. Population: 4,700,000.
State on the east side of the island of Haiti. After the discovery of the island in 1492 the eastern part became a Spanish colony under the name of Santo Domingo; it was ceded to the French in 1795, but was returned to Spain in 1808 with the help of Britain. It was declared independent in 1844.
Capital: Santo Domingo, renamed Ciudad Trujillo during the Trujillo regime.

100 Centavos = 1 Peso

			VF	XF
1 (15)	1	Centavo (Br) 1937–1961. Coconut palm (Cocos nucifera – Palmae). R national arms	0.40	0.80
2 (16)	5	Centavos (Cu–Ni) 1937–1972. Taino Indian with feather headdress. R national arms	0.30	0.60
3 (16a)	5	Centavos (Bi) 1944. Type as No. 2, but oblique stroke through the C of the denomination	4.00	7.50
4 (17)	10	Centavos (Ag) 1937–1961	1.20	2.50
5 (18)	25	Centavos (Ag) 1937–1961	3.00	5.00
6 (19)	½	Peso (Ag) 1937–1961	6.00	8.00
7 (20)	1	Peso (Ag) 1939, 1952:		
		a) 1939	25.00	40.00
		b) 1952	16.00	25.00

COMMEMORATIVE ISSUES (2) FOR THE 25th YEAR OF THE TRUJILLO REGIME

8 (21)	1	Peso (Ag) 1955. Bust right of Dr. Rafael Leonidas Trujillo y Molina (1891–1961), Head of State and Dictator 1930–1961. R national arms	28.00	40.00

			VF	XF
9 (22)	30	Pesos (Au) 1955. Head left of Dr. Rafael L. Trujillo. ℞ national arms	400.00	500.00
10 (23)	1	Centavo (Br) 1963. Type as No. 2. ℞ national arms and commemorative inscription CENTENARIO DE LA RESTAURACION DE LA REPUBLICA 1863–1963	0.20	0.40
11 (24)	5	Centavos (Bi) 1963. Type as No. 10	0.50	0.80
12 (25)	10	Centavos (Ag) 1963. Type as No. 10	1.20	1.70
13 (26)	25	Centavos (Ag) 1963. Type as No. 10	3.00	4.00

			VF	XF
14 (27)	½	Peso (Ag) 1963. Type as No. 10	6.00	9.00
15 (28)	1	Peso (Ag) 1963. Type as No. 10	12.50	17.50
16 (A 16)	1	Centavo (Br) 1968, 1971, 1972, 1975. National arms. R Taino Indian with feather headdress, value, date	0.10	0.20
17 (17a)	10	Centavos (Cu-Ni) 1967, 1973, 1975. Type as No. 16	0.10	0.20
18	25	Centavos (Cu-Ni) 1967–1974. Type as No. 16:		
		a) (Y 18a) 1967, 1972; plain edge	0.50	1.00
		b) (Y 18b) 1974; reeded edge	0.40	0.80

			VF	XF
19	½	Peso (Cu-Ni) 1967–1975. Type as No. 16:		
		a) (Y 19a) 1967, 1968; plain edge	1.00	2.00
		b) (Y 19b) 1973, 1975; reeded edge	0.60	1.20

ISSUE FOR THE FAO COIN PLAN

		XF	Unc
20 (29)	1 Centavo (Br) 1969. Inscription: PRO-DUZCAMOS MAS ALIMENTOS	0.30	0.60

COMMEMORATIVE ISSUE FOR THE 125th ANNIVERSARY OF THE REPUBLIC

21 (30)	1 Peso (Cu–Ni) 1969. National arms, commemorative inscription. ℞ old fort	5.00	8.00

COMMEMORATIVE ISSUE FOR THE 25th ANNIVERSARY OF THE EXISTENCE OF THE CENTRAL BANK OF THE DOMINICAN REPUBLIC

		Unc	Proof
22 (31)	1 Peso (Ag) 1972. State coat of arms, commemorative legend, year dates 1947–1972. ℞ main portal of the Mint (Casa de la Moneda); denomination	20.00	45.00

COMMEMORATIVE ISSUES (2) FOR THE XII CENTRAL AMERICAN AND CARIBBEAN SPORTS GAMES IN SANTO DOMINGO (27. 2. – 13. 3. 1974)

23 (32)	1 Peso (Ag) 1974. State arms. Coat of arms of the city of Santo Domingo on a map outline of the Dominican Republic and 23 rays, symbolizing the participatin nations	20.00	50.00

			Unc	Proof
24 (33)	30	Pesos (Au) 1974. ℞ emblem of the Sports Games, functional legend, denomination, year date	250.00	300.00

INTERNATIONAL BANKER'S CONFERENCE

25 (34)	10	Pesos (Ag) 1975. Reproduction of an old coin. R coat of arms, value, commemorative inscription	25.00	35.00

PUEBLO VIEJO MINE COMMEMORATIVE (2)

26 (35)	10	Pesos (Ag) 1975. Coat of arms, date, inscription PLATA INICIAL EXPLOTACION MINA PUEBLO VIEJO. R Taino-work of art	25.00	35.00
27 (36)	100	Pesos (Au) 1975. Coat of arms, date, inscription ORO INICIAL EXPLOTATION MINA PUEBLO VIEJO. R Taino-work of art	250.00	300.00

100th ANNIVERSARY OF THE DEATH OF JUAN PABLO DUARTE (7)

28 (37)	1	Centavo (Br) 1976. Bust of Juan Pablo Duarte (1813-1876), national hero, date. R coat of arms, memorial legend.	0.40	1.00
29 (38)	5	Centavos (Cu-Ni) 1976. Type as No. 28	0.50	2.00
30 (39)	10	Centavos (Cu-Ni) 1976. Type as No. 28	0.80	2.00
31 (40)	25	Centavos (Cu-Ni) 1976. Type as No. 28	1.25	2.50
32 (41)	½	Peso (Cu-Ni) 1976. Type as No. 28	2.25	3.00
33 (42)	1	Peso (Cu-Ni) 1976. Type as No. 28	5.00	9.00
34 (44)	200	Pesos (Au) 1977. Head of Juan Pablo Duarte	500.00	650.00

30th ANNIVERSARY OF FOUNDATION OF THE CENTRAL BANK OF THE DOMINICAN REPUBLIK

			Unc	Proof
35 (43)	30 Pesos (Ag) 1977. The new building of the Banco Central in Santo Domingo		80.00	100.00

			XF	Unc
36 (45)	1 Centavo (Br) 1978–. Type as No. 28, but without commemorative inscription		0.10	0.20
37 (46)	5 Centavos (Cu-Ni) 1978–. Type as No. 36		0.20	0.40
38 (47)	10 Centavos (Cu-Ni) 1978–. Type as No. 36		0.25	0.50
39 (48)	25 Centavos (Cu-Ni) 1978–. Type as No. 36		0.40	0.75
40 (49)	½ Peso (Cu-Ni) 1978–. Type as No. 36		1.00	2.50
41 (50)	1 Peso (Cu-Ni) 1978–. Type as No. 36		3.00	4.00

VISIT OF POPE JOHN PAUL II (3)

			Unc	Proof
42 (51)	25 Pesos (Ag) 1979. Pope John Paul II and cathedral		70.00	80.00
43 (52)	100 Pesos (Au) 1979. Type as No. 42		300.00	350.00
44 (53)	250 Pesos (Au) 1979. Type as No. 42		700.00	750.00

Previous issues, see "Weltmünzkatalog 19. Jahrhundert" (World Coin Catalogue of the 19th Century)

The East African Monetary Union comprising the now independent states of Kenya (gained independence in 1963), Uganda (1962) and Tanzania (formed by the union of Tanganyika and Zanzibar in 1964) included also British Somaliland until the Republic of Somalia was set up in 1960. The coins issued between 1907 and 1919 have the inscription EAST AFRICA & UGANDA PROTECTORATES.

100 Cents = 1 Rupee (Florin);
since 1921: 100 Cents = 1 Shilling

EDWARD VII 1901–1910

			VF	XF
1 (2)	½	Cent (Al) 1908. Crown above value. Ornamental decoration. ℞ elephants' tusks (central hole)	30.00	60.00
2 (3)	1	Cent (Al) 1907–1908	4.00	8.00
3 (2a)	½	Cent (Cu–Ni) 1909	20.00	40.00
4 (3a)	1	Cent (Cu–Ni) 1907–1910	1.50	3.00
5	5	Cents (Cu–Ni) 1908, pattern!	60.00	110.00
6 (6)	10	Cents (Cu–Ni) 1907–1910	3.50	7.00
7 (7)	25	Cents (Ag) 1906–1910. Crowned bust right of King Edward VII. ℞ lion (Panthera leo – Felidae) with mountains in background	8.00	18.00
8 (8)	50	Cents (Ag) 1906–1910. Type as No. 7	12.00	28.00

GEORGE V 1910–1936

9 (9)	1	Cent (Cu–Ni) 1911–1918. Crown above value, ornamental decoration. ℞ elephants' tusks (central hole)	1.50	3.00
10 (10)	5	Cents (Cu–Ni) 1913–1919	2.50	6.00
11 (11)	10	Cents (Cu–Ni) 1911–1918	3.00	8.00
12 (12)	25	Cents (Ag) 1912–1918. Crowned bust left of King George V. ℞ lion with mountains in background	8.00	15.00
13 (13)	50	Cents (Ag) 1911–1919	12.50	25.00
14 (14)	1	Cent (Cu–Ni) 1920–1921. Type as No. 9, but inscription now reads only EAST AFRICA	50.00	90.00
15 (15)	5	Cents (Cu–Ni) 1920. Type as No. 10, but inscription now reads only EAST AFRICA	50.00	100.00
16 (16)	10	Cents (Cu–Ni) 1920	110.00	185.00
17 (17)	25	Cents (Ag) 1920–1921	35.00	55.00
18 (18)	50	Cents = 1 Shilling (Ag) 1920	500.00	850.00

			VF	**XF**
19 (19)	1	Florin (Ag) 1920–1921	25.00	50.00
20 (20)	1	Cent (Br) 1922–1935. Type as No. 14, but smaller diameter	0.40	1.00
21 (21)	5	Cents (Br) 1921–1936. Type as No. 15, but smaller diameter	0.80	2.00
22 (22)	10	Cents (Br) 1921–1936. Type as No. 16, but smaller diameter	1.00	3.00
23 (23)	50	Cents = ½ Shilling (Ag) 1921–1924. Type as No. 18, but smaller diameter	2.50	6.00

24 (24)	1	Shilling (Ag) 1921–1925. Lion with mountains in background	2.50	4.00

EDWARD VIII 1936

25 (25)	5	Cents (Br) 1936. Crown above value, ornamental decoration. ℞ elephants' tusks	1.00	2.00
26 (26)	10	Cents (Br) 1936. Type as No. 25	1.60	3.20

GEORGE VI 1936–1952

27 (27)	1	Cent (Br) 1942. Crown above value, ornamental decoration. ℞ elephants' tusks	0.25	0.50
28 (28)	5	Cents (Br) 1937–1943	0.80	2.00
29 (29)	10	Cents (Br) 1937–1945	0.50	2.00
30 (30)	50	Cents (Ag) 1937–1944. Crowned head left of King George VI. ℞ lion with mountains in background	2.00	4.00
31 (31)	1	Shilling (Ag) 1937–1946	2.50	5.00
32 (32)	1	Cent (Br) 1949–1952. Type as No. 27, but inscription now reads GEORGIUS SEXTUS REX	0.20	0.40
33 (33)	5	Cents (Br) 1949–1952. Type as No. 28, but inscription now reads GEORGIUS SEXTUS REX	0.30	0.50
34 (34)	10	Cents (Br) 1949–1952. Type as No. 29, but inscription now reads GEORGIUS SEXTUS REX	0.50	1.00
35 (35)	50	Cents (Cu–Ni) 1948–1952. Type as No. 30, but inscription now reads GEORGIUS SEXTUS REX	0.60	1.20

			VF	XF
36 (36)	1	Shilling (Cu–Ni) 1948–1952. Type as No. 31, but inscription now reads GEORGIUS SEXTUS REX	1.00	2.00

ELIZABETH II 1952–1963

37 (37)	1	Cent (Br) 1954–1962. Crown above value, ornamental decoration. ℞ elephants' tusks (central hole)	0.20	0.40

38 (38)	5	Cents (Br) 1955–1963	0.25	0.50
39 (39)	10	Cents (Br) 1956	0.80	2.00
40 (40)	50	Cents (Cu–Ni) 1954–1963. Crowned head right of Queen Elizabeth II	0.40	0.80

JOINT ISSUES OF THE INDEPENDENT STATES

41 (41)	5	Cents (Br) 1964. Ornamental decoration, value also in Swahili. ℞ elephants' tusks	0.10	0.30
42 (42)	10	Cents (Br) 1964	0.20	0.40

East Caribbean States

Westindische Assoziierte Staaten   **Antilles Britanniques**

The East Caribbean Territories, renamed East Caribbean States, comprises the territories of Montserrat, Antigua, St. Christopher-Nevis-Anguilla as well as the independent States of Dominica, Grenada, St. Lucia and St. Vincent.

100 Cents = 1 East Caribbean Dollar

10th ANNIVERSARY OF THE CARIBBEAN DEVELOPMENT BANK

		Unc	Proof
1	10 Dollars (Ag) 1980. »The Golden Hind«. Rev. map and commemorative legend		50.00

ROYAL WEDDING

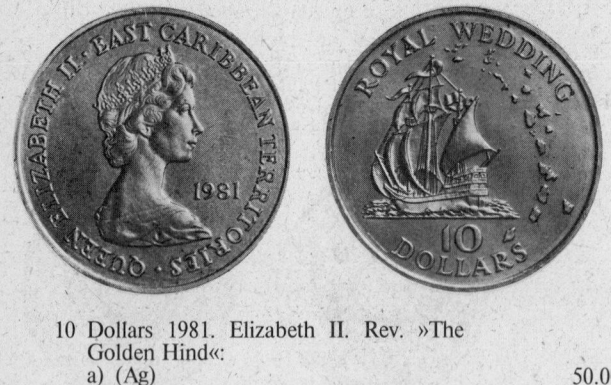

		Unc	Proof
2	10 Dollars 1981. Elizabeth II. Rev. »The Golden Hind«:		
	a) (Ag)		50.00
	b) (Cu-Ni)	8.00	

WORLD FOOD DAY

		Unc	
3	10 Dollars (Cu-Ni) 1981	12.00	

Ecuador

Area: 104,306 sq. mi. Population: 6,500,000.
Formerly part of the Inca Empire. After the conquest by the Spaniards, the country became first a part of the Vice-Kingdom of Peru and later a part of the Vice-Kingdom of New Granada. It belonged to Great Colombia from the time of the revolt against Spain until 1830, when it became an independent republic.
Capital: Quito.

10 Centavos = 1 Decimo
100 Centavos or 10 Decimos = 1 Sucre (Peso)
25 Sucres = 1 Condor

			VF	XF
1 (27)	½	Decimo (Ag) 1893–1915. Head left of Antonio José de Sucre (1795–1830), Grand Marshal of Ayacucho, Mayor of Quito, President of the State of Bolivia 1826–1828, President of the Congress which gave its constitution to Colombia in 1830. ℞ national arms	2.50	4.00
2 (28)	1	Decimo (Ag) 1884–1916	3.00	5.00

			VF	XF
3 (29)	2	Decimos (Ag) 1884–1916. ℞ national arms with Andean condor (Vultur gryphus — Cathartidae)	4.00	6.00
4 (32)	10	Sucres (Au) 1899–1900	225.00	280.00
5 (33)	½	Centavo (Cu–Ni) 1909. National arms. ℞ value within wreath	3.60	7.00
6 (34)	1	Centavo (Cu–Ni) 1909	4.00	8.00
7 (35)	2	Centavos (Cu–Ni) 1909	4.00	8.00
8 (36)	2½	Centavos (Cu–Ni) 1917	9.00	18.00
9 (37)	5	Centavos (Cu–Ni)		
		a) 1909	4.00	8.00
		b) 1917–1918	1.50	3.00
A9 (38)	5	Centavos (Cu–Ni) 1919. Type as No. 9, but smaller diameter and denomination 5 CENTAVOS	1.00	2.00

			VF	XF
10 (39)	10	Centavos (Cu–Ni) 1918. Value in letters	9.00	15.00
11 (40)	10	Centavos (Cu–Ni) 1919	1.25	2.50
12 (41)	5	Centavos (Cu–Ni) 1924. Bust left of Simón Bolívar (1783–1830), President of the State of Colombia 1810–1821. ℞ national arms	1.50	3.00
13 (42)	10	Centavos (Cu–Ni) 1924	1.00	2.50
14 (44)	1	Centavo (Br) 1928. National arms. ℞ value within wreath	1.00	2.00
15 (45)	2½	Centavos (Ni) 1928. Type as No. 14	1.50	3.50
16 (46)	5	Centavos (Ni) 1928. National arms. ℞ bust right in wreath of A. J. de Sucre	0.80	1.60
17 (47)	10	Centavos (Ni) 1928. Type as No. 16	0.80	1.60
18 (48)	50	Centavos (Ag) 1928, 1930. Head left of A. J. de Sucre. ℞ national arms and value	3.00	5.00
19 (49)	1	Sucre (Ag) 1928–1934	4.00	6.00
20 (50)	2	Sucres (Ag) 1928, 1930	6.00	10.00
21 (43)	1	Condor (Au) 1928	375.00	460.00
22 (51)	5	Centavos. National arms. ℞ value within wreath		
		a) (Ni) 1937	0.40	0.80
		b) (Bra) 1942–1944	1.80	2.50
		c) (Cu–Ni) 1946	0.15	0.20
		d) (Ni-St) 1970	0.10	0.20
23 (52)	10	Centavos. Type as No. 22		
		a) (Ni) 1937	0.60	1.20
		b) (Bra) 1942	1.25	2.50
		c) (Cu–Ni) 1946	0.20	0.40
		d) (Ni–St) 1964–	0.10	0.20
24 (53)	20	Centavos. Type as No. 22		
		a) (Ni) 1937	0.80	2.00
		b) (Bra) 1942–1944	1.25	2.50
		c) (Cu–Ni) 1946	0.20	0.40
		d) (Ni-St) 1959, 1962, 1966, 1969, 1971, 1972	0.30	0.80
		e) (Cu-Ni) 1974, 1975	0.10	0.20
25 (57)	50	Centavos (Ni-St) 1963, 1971. Type as No. 22	0.25	0.50
26 (54)	1	Sucre. National arms. ℞ A. J. de Sucre		
		a) (Ni) 1937	0.90	1.80
		b) (Ni) 1946	0.60	1.20
		c) (Cu-Ni) 1959	0.40	0.80
		d) (Ni-St) 1964, 1970, 1971, 1974, 1975	0.25	0.50
27 (55)	2	Sucres (Ag) 1944. A. J. de Sucre. ℞ national arms and value	6.00	9.00
28 (56)	5	Sucres (Ag) 1943–1944. Type as No. 27	8.50	12.00

Previous issues, see "Weltmünzkatalog 19. Jahrhundert" (World Coin Catalogue of the 19th Century)

Ägypten   # Egypt   **Égypte**

Misr

Governed by a Turkish viceroy from 8th July 1867. On 18th December 1914 it became a British Protectorate, but from 15th March 1922 Egypt was recognized as a kingdom independent of Great Britain. On 18th June 1953 it was proclaimed a Republic. Since 1st March 1958 Egypt has been called The United Arab Republic. This official description was maintained even after Syria had left the Union in 1961. Capital: Cairo.

40 Para = 1 Guerche (Piastre)
1000 Millièmes = 100 Piastres
100 Piastres = 1 Egyptian £

ABD UL-HAMID II (1876–1909)

			VF	XF
1 (12)	1	Para (Br) 1885–1908. Toughra. R inscription with star on either side	1.50	3.00
2 (13)	2	Para (Br) 1885–1909	1.50	3.50
3 (14)	4	Para (Cu–Ni) 1885–1909. Toughra in wreath. R value surrounded by inscription	0.40	1.00
4 (15)	8	Para (Cu–Ni) 1885–1909	0.80	1.80
5 (16)	20	Para (Cu–Ni) 1885–1909. Of same type: Nos. 13 to 17	0.80	2.50
6 (18)	1	Guerche (Ag) 1885–1908. Toughra in wreath. R inscription within wreath	4.00	7.50
7 (19)	2	Guerche (Ag) 1885–1908	4.50	8.00
8 (20)	5	Guerche (Ag) 1885–1908	6.50	10.00
9 (21)	10	Guerche (Ag) 1885–1908	10.50	20.00
10 (22)	20	Guerche (Ag) 1885–1908 Of same type: Nos. 18 to 22	25.00	40.00
	5	Guerche (Au) 1880–1909. Toughra. R inscription	45.00	60.00

Other gold coins of the same type were exclusively minted before 1900.

12 (17)	1	Guerche (Cu–Ni) 1898–1908. Toughra in wreath. R inscription surrounded by stars. Of same type: No. 23	1.60	3.50

MOHAMMED V 1909–1915

			VF	XF
13 (23)	1	Para (Br) 1910–1914. Toughra. ℞ inscription with star on either side	2.00	4.00
14 (24)	2	Para (Br) 1910–1914	1.50	3.00
15 (25)	4	Para (Cu–Ni) 1910–1914	1.20	2.00
16 (26)	8	Para (Cu–Ni) 1910–1914	2.00	4.00
17 (27)	20	Para (Cu–Ni) 1910–1914	1.20	2.50
18 (29)	1	Guerche (Ag) 1910–1911	6.00	10.00
19 (30)	2	Guerche (Ag) 1910–1911	9.00	14.00
20 (31)	5	Guerche (Ag) 1911–1914	5.00	9.00
21 (32)	10	Guerche (Ag) 1911–1914	10.50	20.00
22 (33)	20	Guerche (Ag) 1911–1914	22.00	40.00
23 (28)	1	Guerche (Cu–Ni) 1912–1914. Toughra in wreath. ℞ inscription surrounded by stars	4.50	9.00

SULTAN HUSSEIN KAMIL (1915–1917)

			VF	XF
24 (34)	½	Millième (Br) 1917. Inscription. ℞ value	8.00	12.00
25 (35)	1	Millième (Cu–Ni) 1917. Inscription. ℞ value (with hole)	3.50	6.00
26 (36)	2	Millièmes (Cu–Ni) 1916–1917. As No. 25	2.00	4.00
27 (37)	5	Millièmes (Cu–Ni) 1916–1917. As No. 25	1.60	3.00
28 (38)	10	Millièmes (Cu–Ni) 1916–1917. As No. 25	1.60	3.00
29 (39)	2	Piastres (Ag) 1916–1917. Inscription in wreath. ℞ value within wreath	4.00	6.00
30 (40)	5	Piastres (Ag) 1916–1917	3.50	7.50
31 (41)	10	Piastres (Ag) 1916–1917	5.00	18.00
32 (42)	20	Piastres (Ag) 1916–1917	22.00	40.00

			VF	XF
33 (43)	100	Piastres (Au) 1916	140.00	165.00

SULTAN FUAD I (1917–1922)

			VF	XF
34 (44)	2	Piastres (Ag) 1920. Inscription. ℞ inscription and value	65.00	130.00
35 (45)	5	Piastres (Ag) 1920	45.00	100.00
36 (46)	10	Piastres (Ag) 1920	35.00	80.00

KING FUAD I (1922–1936)

			VF	XF
37 (47)	½	Millième (Br) 1924–1925. Portrait of Fuad I (1868–1936). ℞ value with inscription	4.00	7.00
38 (48)	1	Millième (Br) 1924–1925	1.50	3.00
39 (49)	2	Millièmes (Cu–Ni) 1924–1929	2.00	4.00
40 (50)	5	Millièmes (Cu–Ni) 1924	2.00	4.00
41 (51)	10	Millièmes (Cu–Ni) 1924	2.50	4.00
42 (52)	2	Piastres (Ag) 1923–1924. ℞ inscription in circle	4.00	7.00
43 (53)	5	Piastres (Ag) 1923–1926	6.00	10.00
44 (54)	10	Piastres (Ag) 1923–1926	11.50	16.00

45 (55)	20	Piastres (Ag) 1923–1925	45.00	80.00
46 (56)	20	Piastres (Au) 1923–1929	75.00	90.00
47 (57)	50	Piastres (Au) 1923–1929	95.00	120.00

48 (58)	100	Piastres (Au) 1922		
		a) White gold	120.00	150.00
		b) Red gold	130.00	160.00

			VF	XF
49 (59)	500	Piastres (Au) 1922		
		a) White gold	1200.00	1400.00
		b) Red gold	1200.00	1400.00
50 (60)	½	Millième (Br) 1929–1932. Portrait of		
		Fuad I in uniform, to left. ℞ value	1.50	4.00
51 (61)	1	Millième (Br) 1929–1935	1.00	3.00
52 (62)	2	Millièmes (Cu–Ni) 1929	1.00	3.00

53 (63)	2½	Millièmes (Cu–Ni) 1933 (octagonal)	2.00	4.00
54 (64)	5	Millièmes (Cu–Ni) 1929–1935	0.70	1.50
55 (65)	10	Millièmes (Cu–Ni) 1929–1935	1.50	3.00
56 (66)	2	Piastres (Ag) 1929	3.00	6.00
57 (67)	5	Piastres (Ag) 1929–1933	7.00	12.50
58 (68)	10	Piastres (Ag) 1929–1933	11.00	18.50

59 (69)	20	Piastres (Ag) 1929–1933	40.00	65.00
60 (70)	20	Piastres (Au) 1929–1930	60.00	75.00
61 (71)	50	Piastres (Au) 1929–1930	95.00	110.00

62 (72)	100	Piastres (Au) 1929–1930	135.00	150.00
63 (73)	500	Piastres (Au) 1929–1930	1400.00	1500.00

			VF	XF
64 (74)	½	Millième (Br) 1938. Portrait to l. of Faruk I (1920 - 1965). Ŗ value	1.50	4.00
65 (75)	1	Millième (Br) 1938–1950	1.50	4.00

66 (79)	1	Millième (Cu–Ni) 1938 (with hole)	1.50	4.50
67 (80)	2	Millièmes (Cu–Ni) 1938	2.00	3.00
68 (77)	5	Millièmes (Br) 1938–1943	1.50	3.00
69 (81)	5	Millièmes (Cu–Ni) 1938–1941	2.00	2.50

70 (78)	10	Millièmes (Br) 1938–1943 (scalloped)	0.80	2.50

71 (82)	10	Millièmes (Cu-Ni) 1938–1943	1.50	3.50
72 (83)	2	Piastres (Ag) 1937–1948	3.00	6.00
73 (87)	2	Piastres (Ag) 1942–1944 (hexagonal)	2.50	5.50
74 (84)	5	Piastres (Ag) 1937–1939	6.00	10.00
75 (85)	10	Piastres (Ag) 1937–1939	11.00	15.00
76 (86)	20	Piastres (Ag) 1937–1939	45.00	75.00
77 (88)	20	Piastres (Au) 1938	60.00	75.00
78 (89)	50	Piastres (Au) 1938	135.00	150.00

79 (90)	100	Piastres (Au) 1938	140.00	160.00
80 (91)	500	Piastres (Au) 1938	800.00	900.00

REPUBLIC (1953–1958)

			VF	XF
81 (92)	1 Millième (Al-Br) 1954–1958. Head of the Sphinx of Chephren, 4th Dynasty, about 2620 BC, in Gizeh, near Cairo. R value:			
	a) 1954–1956, small sphinx		0.40	2.00
	b) 1957–1958, large sphinx		0.25	0.80

82 (93)	5 Millièmes (Al-Br) 1954–1958:			
	a) 1954–1956, small sphinx		2.00	5.00
	b) 1957–1958, large sphinx		0.40	2.00
83 (94)	10 Millièmes (Al-Br) 1954–1958:			
	a) 1954–1955, small sphinx		2.50	8.00
	b) 1956–1958, large sphinx		0.80	2.00

84 (95)	5 Piastres (Ag) 1955–1959. Sphinx. R sun winged and value		3.00	6.50
85 (96)	10 Piastres (Ag) 1955–1957. Type as No. 84. Varieties exist.		4.50	10.50
86 (97)	20 Piastres (Ag) 1956. Type as No. 84		10.50	18.00

ISSUES (2) COMMEMORATING THE 3rd ANNIVERSARY OF THE REVOLUTION

87 (103)	1 £ (Au) 1955. The Pharaoh Rameses II in war-chariot. R sun winged and inscription		135.00	150.00

88 (104)   5 £ (Au) 1955   700.00   800.00
         Of similar type: Nos. 92 and 93

ISSUE COMMEMORATING THE EVACUATION OF THE BRITISH TROOPS

89 (99)   50 Piastres (Ag) 1956. Pharaoh holding
         torch of liberty and broken chains. ℞
         sun winged and value   17.00   25.00

ISSUE COMMEMORATING THE NATIONALIZATION OF THE SUEZ CANAL

				VF	**XF**
90 (98)	25	Piastres (Ag) 1956. The Headquarters of the Suez Canal Company in Port Said. ℞ sun winged and value		13.00	19.00

ISSUES (2) COMMEMORATING THE 5th ANNIVERSARY OF THE REVOLUTION

91 (102)	25	Piastres (Ag) 1957. National Assembly buildings	13.00	19.00

͜ES (2) COMMEMORATING THE 5th ANNIVERSARY OF THE REVOLUTION

92 (103)	1	£ (Au) 1957. Type as No. 87, but red gold	135.00	150.00
93 (104)	5	£ (Au) 1957. Type as No. 88, but red gold	700.00	800.00

UNITED ARAB REPUBLIC (1958-1971)

ISSUE COMMEMORATING THE 1st INDUSTRIAL AND AGRICULTURAL FAIR IN CAIRO, 1958

94 (105)	20	Millièmes (Al–Br) 1958. Gear-wheel and land produce. ℞ value	1.60	3.00

ISSUE COMMEMORATING THE FOUNDATION OF THE UNITED ARAB REPUBLIC

		VF	XF
95 (106)	½ £ (Au) 1958. Pharaoh Rameses II in war-chariot. ℞ sun winged and inscription	90.00	110.00

ISSUE COMMEMORATING THE 1st ANNIVERSARY OF THE UNITED ARAB REPUBLIC

96 (107)	10 Piastres (Ag) 1959. Emblem of State. R value	12.00	18.00
97 (111)	1 Millième (Al-Br) 1960, 1966. Emblem of State. R value	0.10	0.20
98 (112)	2 Millièmes (Al-Br) 1962, 1966	0.20	0.40
99 (113)	5 Millièmes (Al-Br) 1960, 1966	0.25	0.80
100 (113a)	5 Millièmes (Al) 1967	0.20	0.40
101 (A 113)	10 Millièmes (Al-Br) 1960, 1966	0.50	1.20
102 (A 113a)	10 Millièmes (Al) 1967	0.50	1.20
103 (114)	5 Piastres (Ag) 1960, 1966	3.00	5.00
104 (115)	10 Piastres (Ag) 1960, 1966	5.00	8.00
105 (116)	20 Piastres (Ag) 1960, 1966	8.50	15.00

ISSUES (2) COMMEMORATING THE BEGINNING OF THE BUILDING OF THE ASWAN DAM

106 (108) 1 £ (Au) 1960. Reproduction of the projected Aswan Dam Sadd el-Ali; agricultural produce, rising sun. ℞ sun winged and inscription

		VF	XF
106 (108)	1 £ (Au) 1960. Reproduction of the projected Aswan Dam Sadd el-Ali; agricultural produce, rising sun. ℞ sun winged and inscription	120.00	135.00
107 (109)	5 £ (Au) 1960	600.00	750.00

ISSUE COMMEMORATING THE 3rd YEAR OF THE NATIONAL ASSEMBLY

108 (110)	25 Piastres (Ag) 1960. National Assembly buildings	12.00	16.00

ISSUES (6) COMMEMORATING THE END OF THE FIRST STAGE OF CONSTRUCTION OF THE SADD EL-ALI DAM

109 (117)	5 Piastres (Ag) 1964. Sadd el-Ali Dam, high voltage pylons and rising sun	3.00	3.50
110 (118)	10 Piastres (Ag) 1964	4.00	6.00
111 (119)	25 Piastres (Ag) 1964	7.50	10.00

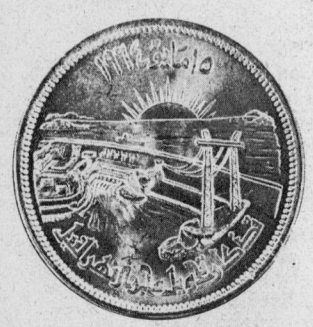 

112 (120)	50 Piastres (Ag) 1964	12.50	19.00

			VF	XF
113 (121)	5	£ (Au) 1964. Type as No. 109. ℞ inscription	350.00	400.00
114 (122)	10	£ (Au) 1964	600.00	750.00
115 (123)	5	Piastres (Cu–Ni) 1967. Emblem of State. ℞ value	0.50	1.20
116 (124)	10	Piastres (Cu–Ni) 1967. Type as No. 115	1.10	1.80

ISSUE COMMEMORATING THE INTERNATIONAL INDUSTRIAL FAIR IN CAIRO

117 (125)	5	Piastres (Cu–Ni) 1968. Globe and inscription in Arabic. ℞ value	1.50	2.50

ISSUE COMMEMORATING THE INAUGURATION OF THE POWER STATION FOR THE ASWAN DAM

118 (126)	1	£ (Ag) 1968. View of the power station. ℞ inscription and dates in Arabic	12.50	17.50

ISSUE COMMEMORATING THE 1400th ANNIVERSARY OF THE KORAN

119 (127)	5	£ (Au) 1968. The Holy Book of Islam, the Koran, open; in background rising sun; globe between arabesques	300.00	350.00

COMMEMORATIVE ISSUE FOR THE FAO COIN PLAN

		VF	**XF**
120	10 Piastres (Cu-Ni) 1968. Agricultural scene copied from an old Egyptian bas-relief. R value, date inscription. Not released for circulation. Of similar type: No. 132	–.–	–.–

ISSUE COMMEMORATING THE INTERNATIONAL AGRICULTURAL FAIR IN CAIRO 1969

121 (139)	10 Piastres (Cu–Ni) 1969. Ears of corn over stylized globe, and the word CAIRO; on right, inscription. R value surrounded by circular inscription	1.70	2.50

ISSUE COMMEMORATING THE 50th ANNIVERSARY OF THE INTERNATIONAL LABOUR ORGANIZATION (ILO)

122 (131)	5 Piastres (Cu–Ni) 1969. Two hands holding screw wrench (emblem of the ILO). R value	1.20	1.80

ISSUES (2) COMMEMORATING THE JUBILEE OF THE EL AZHAR UNIVERSITY IN CAIRO

			VF	XF
123 (130)	1 £ (Ag) 1970. University building		12.50	16.00
124	5 £ (Au) 1979		265.00	300.00

ISSUE COMMEMORATING THE HANDICRAFTS FAIR

			VF	XF
125 (133)	10 Piastres (Cu–Ni) 1970. Emblem. ℞ value		1.90	2.60

ISSUE COMMEMORATING 50 YEARS OF BANK MISR

			VF	XF
126 (132)	10 Piastres (Cu–Ni) 1970. Sun rising over Bank building. ℞ emblem and value		1.90	2.60

ISSUES (5) COMMEMORATING THE DEATH OF GAMAL ABD EL NASSER

			VF	XF
127 (134)	25 Piastres (Ag) 1970. Head to right of Gamal Abd el Nasser (1918–1970), President of the United Arab Republic 1958–1970. ℞ Arabic inscription and date		4.00	6.00
128 (135)	50 Piastres (Ag) 1970. Type as No. 127		7.00	11.00

			VF	XF
129 (136)	1 £ (Ag) 1970. Type as No. 127		7.50	14.00
130 (137)	1 £ (Au) 1970. Type as No. 127		160.00	180.00
131 (138)	5 £ (Au) 1970. Type as No. 127		320.00	380.00

COMMEMORATIVE ISSUE FOR THE FAO COIN PLAN
AND THE 18th ANNIVERSARY
OF THE AGRICULTURAL REFORM

			VF	XF
132 (128)	10	Piastres (Cu–Ni) 1970. Type as No. 120, but above the old Egyptian bas-relief now the state emblem	2.60	4.00

COMMEMORATIVE ISSUE FOR THE CAIRO FAIR 1971

133 (133a)	10	Piastres (Cu–Ni) 1971. Emblem of Cairo Fair 71 (type similar to No. 125)	1.40	2.60

ARAB REPUBLIC OF EGYPT since 1971/72

			XF	Unc
134 (157)	1	Millième (Al) 1972. Type as No. 103, but without stars in the breast plate of the redesigned arms falcon and with new inscription (translated: Federation of Arab Republics and Arab Republic Egypt)	0.20	0.60
135 (141a)	5	Millièmes (Al) 1972. Type as No. 134	0.25	0.80
136 (142a)	10	Millièmes (Al) 1972. Type as No. 134	0.30	0.80
137 (158)	5	Piastres (Cu–Ni) 1972. Type as No. 134	0.90	1.80
138 (159)	10	Piastres (Cu–Ni) 1972. Type as No. 134	1.20	2.40

25th ANNIVERSARY OF UNICEF

			XF	Unc
139 (139)	5 Piastres (Cu-Ni) 1972. Mother and child		1.20	2.50

ISSUE FOR THE CAIRO FAIR 1972

140 (140)	10 Piastres (Cu-Ni) 1972. Type similar to No. 133	1.40	2.50

COMMEMORATIVE ISSUES (2) FOR THE COMPLETION OF THE HIGH DAM SADD EL-ALI ON 15th JANUARY 1971 AND FOR THE FAO COIN PLAN

141 (144)	5 Millièmes (Al) 1973. High Dam Sadd el-Ali between ears of wheat	0.25	0.50
142 (145)	1 £ (Ag) 1973. Type as No. 141	9.00	12.00

ISSUE FOR THE CAIRO FAIR 1973

			XF	Unc
143 (143)	5	Piastres (Cu-Ni) 1973. Emblem of Cairo Fair 1973. R name of country, value	1.10	2.00

75th ANNIVERSARY OF THE EGYPTIAN NATIONAL BANK (4)

			XF	Unc
144 (146)	5	Piastres (Cu-Ni) 1973. Building of the Egyptian National Bank and globe. R inscription, value	1.20	2.00
145 (147)	25	Piastres (Ag) 1973. Type as No. 144	6.00	7.50
146 (148)	1	£ (Au) 1973. Type as No. 144	110.00	130.00
147 (149)	5	£ (Au) 1973. Type as No. 144	350.00	365.00

148 (141)	5	Millièmes (Al-Br) 1973. Type as No. 136	0.30	0.60
149 (142)	10	Millièmes (Al-Br) 1973. Type as No. 148	0.50	1.20

1th ANNIVERSARY OF YOM KIPPUR WAR (4)

			XF	Unc
150 (150)	5	Piastres (Cu-Ni) 1974. Soldier, laurel branch. R value, dates	0.80	1.20
151 (151)	10	Piastres (Cu-Ni) 1974. Type as No. 150	1.20	2.00
152 (152)	1	£ (Ag) 1974. Type as No. 150	10.00	19.00
153 (A 152)	5	£ (Au) 1974. Type as No. 150	650.00	750.00

INTERNATIONAL WOMEN'S YEAR 1975 (2)

154 (153)	5	Millièmes (Al-Br) 1975. Bust right of Nefertiti. R name of country, value	0.25	0.50

155 (155)	5	Piastres (Cu-Ni) 1975. Type as No. 154	0.80	1.80

ISSUE FOR THE FAO COIN PLAN (2)

156 (154)	10	Millièmes (Bra) 1975. Classical Egyptian family	0.40	1.00
157 (156)	10	Piastres (Cu-Ni) 1975. Type as No. 156	1.00	2.00

ISSUE FOR THE CAIRO FAIR 1976

			XF	Unc
158 (162)	5	Piastres (Cu-Ni) 1976. Emblem of Cairo Fair 1976	0.80	1.30

ISSUE FOR THE FAO COIN PLAN (2)

159 (160)	10	Millièmes (Bra) 1976. The god Osiris seated facing an enlarged ear of grain	0.20	0.50
160 (161)	1	£ (Ag) 1976. Type as No. 159	11.00	17.00

RE-OPENING OF THE SUEZ CANAL (4)

161 (163)	10	Piastres (Cu-Ni) 1976. Ships bow at right with two wheat ears and world globe sailing left in Suez Canal towards large building and laurel leaves. All under radiant sun	1.20	2.00
162 (164)	1	£ (Ag) 1976. Type as No. 161	9.00	13.00
163	1	£ (Au) 1976. Type as No. 161	–.–	–.–
164 (165)	5	£ (Au) 1976. Type as No. 161	–.–	–.–

FIRST ANNIVERSARY OF THE DEATH OF KING FAISAL (3)

165 (166)	1	£ (Ag) 1976. King Faisal of Saudi Arabia	9.00	14.00
166 (167)	1	£ (Au) 1976. Type as No. 165		320.00
167 (168)	5	£ (Au) 1976. Type as No. 165		750.00

FIRST ANNIVERSARY OF THE DEATH OF OM KALSOUM (3)

			XF	Unc
168 (169)	1 £ (Ag) 1976. Om Kalsoum (1898–1975), singer		9.00	14.00
169 (170)	1 £ (Au) 1976. Type as No. 168			340.00
A 169 (171)	5 £ (Au) 1976. Type as No. 168			750.00

50th ANNIVERSARY OF THE EGYPTIAN TEXTILE INDUSTRY

170 (184)	5 Piastres (Cu-Ni) 1977. Classical Egyptian figure holding spindle. R emblem and value	0.80	1.40

FOR THE FAO COIN PLAN (2)

171 (179)	5 Millièmes (Bra) 1977. Classical Egyptian rural scene	0.20	0.40

172 (181)	5 Piastres (Cu-Ni) 1977. Type as No. 171	0.80	1.10

			XF	Unc
173 (172)	5	Millièmes (Al-Br) 1977, 1979. Egyptian god	0.30	0.60
174 (173)	10	Millièmes (Al-Br) 1977, 1979. Type as No. 173	0.30	0.60
175 (174)	5	Piastres (Cu-Ni) 1977, 1979. Type as No. 173	0.60	0.80
176 (175)	10	Piastres (Cu-Ni) 1977, 1979. Type as No. 173	0.85	1.20
177 (176)	1	£ (Ag) 1977, 1979. Type as No. 173	9.00	14.00

FOR THE FAO COIN PLAN (3)

178 (180)	10	Millièmes (Bra) 1977. Classical Egyptian professions	0.30	0.60
179 (182)	10	Piastres (Cu-Ni) 1977. Type as No. 178	0.80	1.30
180 (183)	1	£ (Ag) 1977. Type as No. 178	9.00	14.00

20th ANNIVERSARY OF ARABIC ECONOMIC UNION (3)

181 (177)	10	Piastres (Cu-Ni) 1977. Clasped hands	0.80	1.30
182 (178)	1	£ (Ag) 1977. Type as No. 181	9.00	14.00
183 (178a)	1	£ (Au) 1977. Type as No. 181		350.00

SADAT'S PEACE INITIATIVE (4)

			Proof
184	5	£ (Ag) 1977. Bust of President Sadat, rock cathedral of Jerusalem	–.–
185	10	£ (Ag) 1977. Type as No. 184	–.–
186	50	£ (Au) 1977. Type as No. 184	–.–
187	100	£ (Au) 1977. Type as No. 184	–.–

50th ANNIVERSARY OF PORTLAND CEMENT (2)

		XF	Unc
188 (187)	5 Piastres (Cu-Ni) 1978. Industrial district	0.60	0.80
189 (188)	1 £ (Ag) 1978. Type as No. 188	9.00	14.00

CAIRO FAIR 1978

190 (185)	10 Piastres (Cu-Ni) 1978. Emblem of Cairo Fair 1978	0.80	1.10

25th ANNIVERSARY OF AIN SHAMS UNIVERSITY

191 (186)	1 £ (Ag) 1978. Obelisk and falcons	8.50	13.50

FOR THE FAO COIN PLAN (3)

192 (189)	10 Millièmes (Al-Br) 1978. Assistant with microscop	0.30	0.40
193 (190)	5 Piastres (Cu-Ni) 1978. Type as No. 192	0.60	0.80

194 (191)	1 £ (Ag) 1978. Type as No. 192	8.50	13.50

		Unc	Proof
195 (192)	10 Piastres (Cu-Ni) 1979. Mint building	1.10	
196 (193)	1 £ (Ag) 1979. Type as No. 195	14.00	60.00

INTERNATIONAL YEAR OF THE CHILD AND FAO COIN PLAN (3)

197 (194)	10 Millièmes (Al-Br) 1979. Mother and child	0.40
198 (195)	5 Piastres (Cu-Ni) 1979. Type as No. 197	0.80

199 (196)	1 £ (Ag) 1979. Type as No. 197	14.00	60.00

NATIONAL EDUCATION DAY (2)

			Unc	Proof
200 (197)	10 Piastres (Cu-Ni) 1979. Classroom		0.80	

201 (198)	1 £ (Ag) 1979. Type as No. 200		14.00	60.00

100th ANNIVERSARY OF THE BANK OF LAND REFORM (3)

202 (199)	1 £ (Ag) 1979. Writer and rural scene	14.00	60.00
203 (200)	1 £ (Au) 1979. Type as No. 202		600.00
204 (201)	5 £ (Au) 1979. Type as No. 202		1500.00

1400th ANNIVERSARY OF MOHAMMED'S FLIGHT (3)

205 (202)	1 £ (Ag) 1979. Two birds in their nest	14.00	60.00
206 (203)	1 £ (Au) 1979. Type as No. 205		600.00
207 (204)	5 £ (Au) 1979. Type as No. 205		1250.00

FOR THE FAO COIN PLAN (3)

208 (222)	10 Millièmes (Al-Br) 1980. Girl and rural district		0.40

209 (223)	10 Piastres (Cu-Ni) 1980. Type as No. 208	1.20	

			Unc	Proof
210 (224)	1 £ (Ag) 1980. Type as No. 208		14.00	60.00

EGYPTIAN–ISRAELI PEACE TREATY (5)

211 (217)	10 Piastres (Cu-Ni) 1980. Head of President Sadat, dove, palm branch	1.20	

			Unc	Proof
212 (218)	1 £ (Ag) 1980. Type as No. 211		15.00	60.00
213 (219)	1 £ (Au) 1980. Type as No. 211			650.00
214 (220)	5 £ (Au) 1980. Type as No. 211			1600.00
215 (221)	10 £ (Au) 1980. Type as No. 211			2200.00

DOCTER'S DAY (3)

			Unc	Proof
216 (213)	10 Piastres (Cu-Ni) 1980.		1.30	
217 (214)	1 £ (Ag) 1980.		14.00	50.00
218 (215)	1 £ (Au) 1980.		–.–	

HANDICRAFT IN CLASSICAL EGYPT (3)

			Unc	Proof
219 (210)	5 Piastres (Cu-Ni) 1980. Applied professions		0.80	
220 (221)	1 £ (Ag) 1980. Type as No. 219		14.00	50.00
221 (212)	1 £ (Au) 1980. Type as No. 219		–.–	

SADAT'S CORRECTIVE REVOLUTION OF MAY, 15 1971 (5)

			Unc
222 (205)	5 Millièmes (Al-Br) 1980. Sadat's hand holding palm branch		0.50
223 (206)	10 Millièmes (Al-Br) 1980. Type as No. 222		0.50
224 (207)	5 Piastres (Cu-Ni) 1980. Type as No. 222		0.80

225 (208)   10 Piastres (Cu-Ni) 1980. Type as No. 222   1.20

226 (209)   1 £ (Ag) 1980. Type as No. 222   14.00   50.00

FACULTY OF LAW (2)

227 (225)   1 £ (Ag) 1980   14.00   50.00
228 (226)   1 £ (Au) 1980   —.—

WORLD FOOD DAY

229   1 £ (Ag) 1981   14.00

SCIENTIST'S DAY (2)

		Unc
230	10 Piastres (Cu-Ni) 1981	2.00

| 231 (227) | 1 £ (Ag) 1981 | 14.00 |

RE-OPENING OF THE SUEZ CANAL

| 232 | 1 £ (Ag) 1981 | 14.00 |

INDUSTRY MINISTERY

| 233 | 1 £ (Ag) 1981 | 14.00 |

25th ANNIVERSARY OF TRADE-UNION (2)

| 234 | 10 Piastres (Cu-Ni) 1981 | 2.00 |
| 235 | 1 £ (Ag) 1981 | 14.00 |

Previous issues, see »Weltmünzkatalog 19. Jahrhundert« (World Coin Catalogue of the 19th Century)

Equatorial African States

Äquatorialafrikanische Staaten   **Afrique Equatoriale**

The institution covering the issue of currency for the territories of
Equatorial Africa is the Banque Centrale des Etats de l'Afrique Equa-
toriale. This Monetary Union comprises the states of Gabon, Cameroon,
Congo-Brazzaville, Chad and the Central African Republic.

100 Centimes = 1 CFA Franc

			VF	XF
1 (A 1)	1 Franc (Al) 1969–. Addax antelopes (Addax nasomaculatus – Bovidae), inscription ETATS DE L'AFRIQUE EQUATORIALE / CAMEROUN / BANQUE CENTRALE. ℞ value within wreath of fruits		0.20	0.40
2 (1)	5 Francs (Al–Br) 1961–. Type as No. 1		0.40	0.60
3 (2)	10 Francs (Al–Br) 1961–. Type as No. 1		0.50	0.80
4 (3)	25 Francs (Al–Br) 1962–. Type as No. 1		1.00	1.50

		VF	XF
5 (4)	50 Francs (Cu–Ni) 1961, 1963. Antelopes, names of states: Gabon, Congo (Brazzaville), Chad and Central African Republic. ℞ value within wreath of fruits	3.50	4.50

		VF	XF
6 (5)	100 Francs (Ni) 1966-1968. Antelopes without mention of the participating countries. ℞ value	2.00	3.00

For later issues, see under Central
African States.

Äquatorialguinea **Equatorial Guinea** Guinée Equatoriale

Area: 10,789 sq. mi. Population: 300,000.

The Republic of Equatorial Guinea, the only Spanish-speaking state in Africa, obtained its independence on 10th October 1968. The territory covers the mainland strip of Rio Muni and the islands Fernando Poo, Elobey, Annobón and Corisco. On 10th October 1969 the country secured its own currency with parity with the Spanish peseta. Until the issue of the separate currency Spanish coins were exclusively in use. Capital: Santa Isabel.

100 Centimos = 1 Guinea Peseta; since 1975:
100 Céntimos = 1 Ekuele, new currency: Epkwele, plural Bipkwele

			VF	XF
1 (1)	1	Peseta (Al–Br) 1969	0.80	2.00
2 (2)	5	Pesetas (Cu–Ni) 1969	2.25	4.00
3 (3)	25	Pesetas (Cu–Ni) 1969	3.50	6.00
4 (4)	50	Pesetas (Cu–Ni) 1969	5.00	10.00

			Proof
5	25	Pesetas (Ag) 1970–. Emblem of the United Nations. ℞ national arms, value	9.00
6	25	Pesetas (Ag) 1970–. Emblem of the World Bank	9.00

7	50	Pesetas (Ag) 1970–. "Hands joined of an Apostle praying", from a drawing by Albrecht Dürer (1471–1528)	15.00

8	75	Pesetas (Ag) 1970–. Pope John XXIII, Roncalli (1881–1963)	20.00
9	75	Pesetas (Ag) 1970–. Abraham Lincoln (1809–1865), 16th President of the United States of America	20.00
10	75	Pesetas (Ag) 1970–. Mohandas Karamchand Gandhi (1869–1948), called Mahatma ("Sublime Soul"), advocator of the non-violent resistance movement "Satyagraha"	20.00
11	75	Pesetas (Ag) 1970–. Vladimir Ilyich Lenin (1870–1924), real name Ulyanov; Soviet statesman, leader of the world proletariat, name	20.00
12	100	Pesetas (Ag) 1970–. "The Nude Maya", from the painting by Francisco José Goya y Lucientes (1746–1828), Prado Museum, Madrid	30.00
13	100	Pesetas (Ag) 1970–. Type as No. 7	30.00
14	150	Pesetas (Ag) 1970–. Roma Aeterna – (centenary of Rome as capital of Italy)	35.00
15	150	Pesetas (Ag) 1970–. Forum (centenary of Rome as capital of Italy)	35.00

16	150	Pesetas (Ag) 1970–. Caput Mundi (centenary of Rome as capital of Italy)	35.00
17	150	Pesetas (Ag) 1970–. Dea Roma (centenary of Rome as capital of Italy)	35.00
18	200	Pesetas (Ag) 1970–. The Jules Rimet Trophy (World Cup) surrounded by names of places of presentation, indication of dates and names of winners of all the world football championships	40.00
19	200	Pesetas (Ag) 1970–. Francisco Macias Nguema, 1st Head of State	40.00
20	250	Pesetas (Au) 1970–. Type as No. 12	70.00

21	250 Pesetas (Au) 1970. Type as No. 7		70.00
22	500 Pesetas (Au) 1970. Type as No. 8		140.00
23	500 Pesetas (Au) 1970. Type as No. 9		140.00
24	500 Pesetas (Au) 1970. Type as No. 10		140.00
25	500 Pesetas (Au) 1970. Type as No. 11		140.00
26	750 Pesetas (Au) 1970. Type as No. 14		210.00
27	750 Pesetas (Au) 1970. Type as No. 15		210.00
28	750 Pesetas (Au) 1970. Type as No. 16		210.00
29	750 Pesetas (Au) 1970. Type as No. 17		210.00
30	1000 Pesetas (Au) 1970. Type as No. 18		280.00
31	5000 Pesetas (Au) 1970. Type as No. 19		1400.00

NEW CURRENCY: 100 Céntimos = 1 Ekuele

		XF	Unc
32 (5)	1 Ekuele (Al-Br) 1975	0.50	1.00

		XF	Unc
33 (6)	5 Ekuele (Cu-Ni) 1975	1.00	2.00

		XF	Unc
34 (7)	10 Ekuele (Cu-Ni) 1975	1.50	3.00

WORLD SOCCER CHAMPIONSHIP IN ARGENTINA (2)

			Proof
35	2000	Ekuele (Ag) 1978	75.00
36	10000	Ekuele (Au) 1978	550.00

10th ANNIVERSARY OF REIGN OF PRESIDENT NGUEMA (4)

			Proof
37	1000	Ekuele (Ag) 1978. Central Bank	35.00
38	2000	Ekuele (Ag) 1978. President Nguema. Rev. arms	75.00
39	5000	Ekuele (Au) 1978. Central Bank	200.00
40	10000	Ekuele (Au) 1978. Type as No. 38	350.00

OLYMPIC GAMES 1980 IN MOSCOW

			Proof
41	2000	Ekuele (Ag) undated (1979). Man throwing a discus	60.00

NEW CURRENCY: Epkwele, plural Bipkwele

VISIT OF THE ROYAL COUPLE OF SPAIN TO EQUATORIAL GUINEA (4)

42 (12)	1000	Bipkwele (Ag) 1979	30.00	35.00
43 (13)	2000	Bipkwele (Ag) 1979	50.00	55.00
44 (14)	5000	Bipkwele (Au) 1979	180.00	200.00
45 (15)	10000	Bipkwele (Au) 1979	350.00	400.00

VISIT OF KING JUAN CARLOS I TO EQUATORIAL GUINEA (4)

46 (16)	1000	Bipkwele (Ag) 1979	30.00	35.00
47 (17)	2000	Bipkwele (Ag) 1979	50.00	55.00
48 (18)	5000	Bipkwele (Au) 1979	180.00	200.00
49 (19)	10000	Bipkwele (Au) 1979	350.00	400.00

			VF	XF
50	1	Epkwele (Al-Br) 1980	0.30	0.50
51	5	Bipkwele (Cu-Ni) 1980	0.30	0.50
52	25	Bipkwele (Cu-Ni) 1980	1.00	1.50
53	50	Bipkwele (Cu-Ni) 1980	2.00	3.00

This former Italian colony on the coast of the Red Sea was part of
Italian East Africa from 1936 to 1941, and was occupied by the British
in 1941. On 15th September 1952 Eritrea was federated with Ethiopia as an autonomous territory and later in 1960 became an Ethiopian
province.
Capital: Asmara.

100 Centesimi = 1 Lira, 5 Lire = 1 Tallero

VICTOR EMMANUEL III

			VF	XF
1 (5)	1 Tallero (Ag) 1918. Diademed bust right of Italia. ℞ crowned eagle with breast shield with arms of Savoy		60.00	80.00

Estland   # Estonia
                               ### Eesti
                                                          Estonie

At the beginning of the 13th century the Estonians were converted to Christianity by the Germans and the Danes. In the year 1346 the northern part of the territory, hitherto Danish, was sold to a German crusading Order called the Knights of the Sword. Estonia became Swedish in 1561, and a Russian province in 1721. On 24th February 1918 the Estonian Republic was proclaimed, but it was occupied by Russian troops in June 1940 and since then, apart from a short period of time (1941–1944), it has belonged to the Confederation of States of the Soviet Union.
Capital: Reval (Tallinn).

100 Penni = 1 Estonian Mark; from 1st January 1928:
100 Senti = 1 Kroon (Crown)

			VF	XF
1 (4)	1	Mark (Cu-Ni) 1922. Arms: three leopards left dividing date. R Value	4.00	7.00
2 (5)	3	Marka (Cu-Ni) 1922. Type as No. 1	4.50	9.00
3 (6)	5	Marka (Cu-Ni) 1922. Type as No. 1	5.00	10.00
4 (4a)	1	Mark (Ni-Br) 1924. Type as No. 1	6.00	11.00

			VF	XF
5 (5a)	3	Marka (Ni-Br) 1925. Type as No. 2	6.00	11.00
6 (6a)	5	Marka (Ni-Br) 1924. Type as No. 3	7.00	12.00
7 (7)	10	Marka (Ni-Br) 1925. Type as No. 1	11.00	20.00
8 (8)	1	Mark (Ni-Br) 1926. Arms with three leopards (national arms), within wreath. R value	10.00	18.00
9 (9)	3	Marka (Ni-Br) 1926. Type as No. 7	40.00	80.00
10 (10)	5	Marka (Ni-Br) 1926. Type as No. 7	200.00	300.00
11 (A 10)	10	Marka (Ni-Br) 1926. Type as No. 7	2000.00	4000.00
12 (B 10)	25	Marka (Ni-Br) 1926. Type as No. 7. Not released for circulation. Very rare!	–.–	–.–

NEW CURRENCY: 100 Senti = 1 Kroon (Crown)

			VF	XF
13 (1)	1 Sent (Br) 1929. National arms. R Value over oak leaves		2.00	4.00

14 (1a)	1 Sent (Br) 1939. National arms. R figure 1 with legend EESTI VABARIIK and value in letters		20.00	40.00
15 (2)	2 Senti (Br) 1934. Type as No. 13		3.00	6.00
16 (3)	5 Senti (Br) 1931. Type as No. 13		4.00	7.00

17 (11)	10 Senti (Ni-Br) 1931. National arms. R value		3.00	5.00
18 (12)	20 Senti (Ni-Br) 1935. Type as No. 17		4.00	6.00

19 (13)	25 Senti (Ni-Br) 1928. National arms within wreath. R value		7.50	12.50
20 (14)	50 Senti (Ni-Br) 1936. Coat of arms dividing date. R value		7.50	12.00

		VF	XF
21 (15)	1 Kroon (Al–Br) 1934. National arms within wreath. ℞ Viking ship	8.50	15.00

		VF	XF
22 (16)	2 Krooni (Ag) 1930. National arms. ℞ castle of Reval (Tallinn) originally built in 1227, renovated many times	9.00	17.00

COMMEMORATIVE ISSUE FOR THE TERCENTENARY OF THE UNIVERSITY OF DORPAT

		VF	XF
23 (17)	2 Krooni (Ag) 1932. National arms within wreath. ℞ middle section of University buildings of Dorpat (Tartu)	20.00	40.00

COMMEMORATIVE ISSUE FOR THE TENTH SINGING FESTIVAL FROM 23rd – 25th JUNE 1933 IN REVAL

			VF	XF
24 (18)	1 Kroon (Ag) 1933. National arms within crossed oak branches. ℞ lyre with view of open-air staircase		35.00	60.00

Äthiopien   # Ethiopia   **Éthiopie**

Area: 455,538 sq. mi. Population: 28,000,000.
A Christian empire in North Africa. Apart from the ruling Amharen people, among others living in Ethiopia are the predominantly Mohammedan tribes of the Galla, Danakil and Somali. During the years 1936-1941 Ethiopia formed part of the Italian Empire. The emperor was deposed by a military committee in 1974. As of July 1976, Ethiopia's present rule is by a military provisional government which refers to the country as Socialist Ethiopia.

Capital: Addis Ababa.

16 Gersh = 1 Talari = 100 Matoñas (Cents) = 1 Talari (Dollar; since 1945: 100 Cents = 1 Ethiopian Dollar; since 1976: new currency was named Birr

EMPEROR MENELIK II 1889–1913

			VF	XF
1 (1)	¹/₁₀₀	Talari (Cu) Ethiopian Era (EE) 1889 (1897). Bust of Menelik II. ℞ inscription in dotted circle. 25.5 mm dia.	15.00	25.00

2 (5)	1	Gersh (Ag) EE 1889–1895 (1897 to 1903). Crowned head of Menelik II (1844–1913) to right. ℞ lion of Judah (= national arms), its left foreleg raised. 16.5 mm dia.:		
		a) EE 1889, 1891 (1897, 1898)	9.00	12.00
		b) EE 1895 (1903)	6.00	8.50

3 (6) $\frac{1}{8}$ Talari (Ag) EE 1887, 1888 (1894, 1896).   **VF**   **XF**
Type as No. 2. 20 mm dia.:
a) EE 1887 (1894)   35.00   60.00
b) EE 1888 (1896) (200 pieces)   –.–   –.–

4 (7) $\frac{1}{4}$ Talari (Ag) EE 1887–1895 (1894–1903).
Type as No. 2. 25 mm dia.:
a) EE 1887 (1894)   26.00   50.00
b) EE 1888 (1896) (200 pieces)   –.–   –.–
c) EE 1889, 1895 (1897, 1903)   12.50   18.00

5 (8) $\frac{1}{2}$ Talari (Ag) EE 1887–1889 (1894–1897).
Type as No. 2. 30.5 mm dia.:
a) EE 1887 (1894)   40.00   60.00
b) EE 1888 (1896) (200 pieces)   –.–   –.–
c) EE 1889 (1897)   25.00   35.00

				VF	XF
6 (9)	1	Talari (Ag) EE 1887–1889 (1894–1897).			
		Type as No. 2. 40 mm dia.:			
		a) EE 1887 (1894)		45.00	65.00
		b) EE 1888 (1896) (200 pieces)		–.–	–.–
		c) EE 1889 (1897)		30.00	50.00

			VF	XF
7 (17)	1	Besa (Cu) EE 1889 (1897). ℞ lion of Judah, its right foreleg raised. 20 mm dia.	15.00	20.00

			VF	XF
8 (18)	1	Gersh (Ag) EE 1889 (1897). Type as as No. 7. 17 mm dia.	22.00	40.00

			VF	XF
9 (19)	¼	Talari (Ag) EE 1889 (1897). Type as No. 7. 25.5 mm dia.	25.00	35.00

		VF	XF
10 (20)	½ Talari (Ag) EE 1889 (1897). Type as No. 7. 30.2 mm dia.	55.00	80.00

11 (10)	1 Talari (Ag) EE 1892, 1895 (1899, 1903). Type as No. 7. 40 mm dia.	35.00	45.00
12	⅛ Wark (Au) undated	110.00	140.00

13 (11)	¼ Wark (Au) undated	260.00	300.00
14 (12)	½ Wark (Au) undated	320.00	360.00
15 (13)	1 Wark (Au) undated	550.00	600.00
16	2 Wark (Au) undated	600.00	700.00

Coins Nos. 12–16 were first issued in 1916

EMPRESS ZAUDITU 1917–1930

17	1 Wark (Au). Bust, crowned and veiled, to left of Empress Zauditu = Judith, also called Woisero, (1876–1930). Ŗ national arms. Diameter 20 mm	350.00	400.00
18	2 Wark (Au). Diameter 25 mm	1000.00	1250.00
19	4 Wark (Au). Diameter 31 mm	1350.00	1500.00

			VF	XF
20		4 Wark (Au) 1930. Bust of Haile Selassie I (1892–1975), crowned, to right. ℞ national arms, lion to right	350.00	400.00

21 (23)	1	Matoña (Cu) 1931. Crowned bust of Haile Selassie to right. ℞ national arms, lion to right	4.00	6.00
22 (24)	5	Matoñas (Cu) 1931	5.00	8.00
23 (25)	10	Matoñas (Ni) 1931	4.00	6.00
24 (26)	25	Matoñas (Ni) 1931	3.00	4.50
25 (27)	50	Matoñas (Ni) 1931	6.00	9.00
26 (28)	½	Wark (Au) 1931. Crowned bust of Haile Selassie to left. ℞ St. George and the Dragon	270.00	320.00
27 (29)	1	Wark (Au) 1931. Type as No. 26	400.00	450.00

28 (30)	1	Cent (Br) 1944. Bust of Haile Selassie to left. ℞ national arms	0.10	0.30
29 (31)	5	Cents (Br) 1944	0.20	0.40
30 (32)	10	Cents (Br) 1944	0.25	0.50
31 (33)	25	Cents (Br) 1944	22.00	35.00

32 (35)	25	Cents (Br) 1952. Shape of edge scalloped	0.70	1.10

	VF	XF
33 (34) 50 Cents (Ag) 1944	3.50	6.00

COMMEMORATIVE ISSUES (5) FOR THE 75th ANNIVERSARY OF THE BIRTH AND THE 50th JUBILEE OF THE REIGN OF EMPEROR HAILE SELASSIE I

		Unc	Proof
34	10 Dollars (Au) 1966. Bust of Haile Selassie almost facing, between Imperial crown and monogram, commemorative inscription. ℞ national arms and value		120.00
35	20 Dollars (Au) 1966. Type as No. 34		160.00
36	50 Dollars (Au) 1966. Type as No. 34		360.00
37	100 Dollars (Au) 1966. Type as No. 34		720.00
38	200 Dollars (Au) 1966. Type as No. 34		1450.00

39	5 Dollars (Ag) 1972. Theodoros II	18.00	28.00
40	5 Dollars (Ag) 1972. John IV	18.00	28.00

		Unc	Proof
41	5 Dollars (Ag) 1972. Menelik II	18.00	28.00
42	5 Dollars (Ag) 1972. Zewditu	18.00	28.00
43	10 Dollars (Ag) 1972. Haile Selassie	35.00	50.00
44	50 Dollars (Au) 1972. Type as No. 39		360.00
45	50 Dollars (Au) 1972. Type as No. 40		360.00
46	50 Dollars (Au) 1972. Type as No. 41		360.00
47	50 Dollars (Au) 1972. Type as No. 42		360.00
48	100 Dollars (Au) 1972. Type as No. 43		750.00
49 (41)	5 Dollars (Ag) 1972. Haile Selassie		25.00

NEW CURRENCY: 100 Cent = Birr

ISSUE FOR THE FAO COIN PLAN

		Unc	Proof
50 (36)	1 Cent (Al) 1976–1978. Head of a lion. Rev. ploughing	1.20	3.00
51 (37)	5 Cents (Br) 1976–1978	1.50	4.00
52 (38)	10 Cents (Br) 1976–1978	2.00	5.00
53 (39)	25 Cents (Cu-Ni) 1976–1978	3.50	6.00
54 (40)	50 Cents (Cu-Ni) 1976, 1977	4.00	12.00

CONSERVATION COMMEMORATIVE (3)

		Unc	Proof
55 (42)	10 Birr (Ag) 1979	35.00	50.00
56 (43)	25 Birr (Ag) 1979	50.00	65.00
57 (44)	500 Birr (Au) 1979	700.00	800.00

INTERNATIONAL YEAR OF THE CHILD (2)

		Unc	Proof
58 (45)	20 Birr (Ag) 1980		65.00
59 (46)	400 Birr (Au) 1980		500.00

		Unc	Proof
60	20 Birr (Ag) 1981		50.00
61	200 Birr (Au) 1981		250.00

EMERGENCY ISSUE OF DIRE DAOUA

Issued by a commercial syndicate in Dire Daoua.

		VF	XF
1	1 Piastre 16 au Taler (Al) 1922	35.00	65.00

EMERGENCY ISSUE OF ADDIS ABABA
Issued by P. P. Trohalis in Addis Ababa.

		VF	XF
1	1 Piastre 16 au Thaler (Al) undated	40.00	70.00

Falkland Islands

Area: 6,430 sq. mi. Population: 2,260.
Group of islands in the South Atlantic, east of the Straits of Magellan.
Discovered 1592, British since 1833.
Capital: Stanley.

100 Pence = 1 Falkland Pound

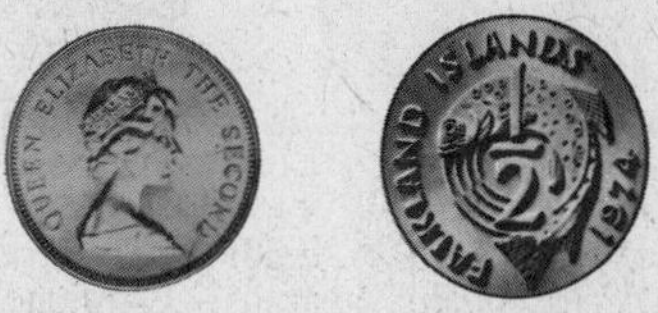

		Unc	Proof
1 (1)	½ Penny (Br) 1974, 1980. Rev. salmon trutta-Salmonidae)	0.20	1.50
2 (2)	1 Penny (Br) 1974, 1980. Rev. Gentoo penguins (Pygoscelis papua – Spheniscidae)	0.25	2.00
3 (3)	2 Pence (Br) 1974, 1980. Rev. Upland goose (Chloephaga picta leucoptera – Anatidae)	0.40	2.50

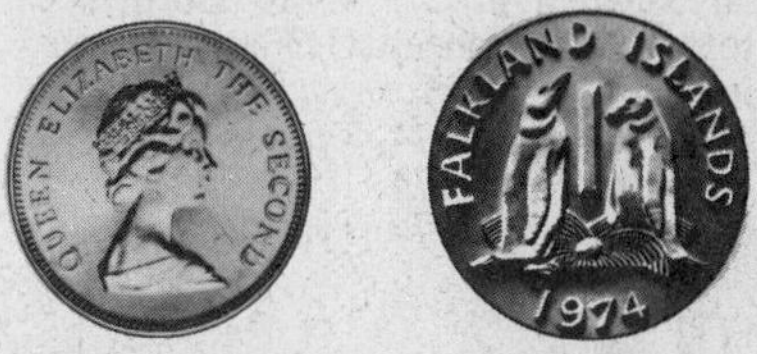

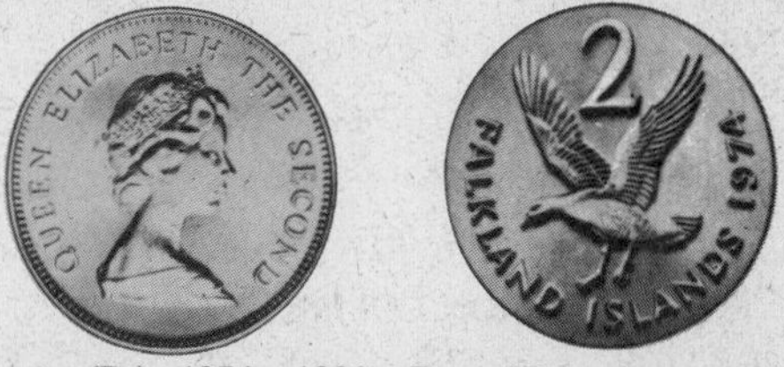

			Unc	Proof
4 (4)	5 Pence (Cu-Ni) 1974, 1980. Rev. black-browed albatross (Diomedea melanophris – Diomedeidae)		0.60	4.00

5 (5)	10 Pence (Cu-Ni) 1974, 1980. Rev. ursine seal (Arctocephalus australis – Otariidae)		1.00	6.00
6 (6)	½ Sovereign (Au) 1974. R Corriedale/Romney marsh sheep (Ovis ammon aries - Bovidae)			150.00
7 (7)	1 Sovereign (Au) 1974. Type as No. 6			225.00
8 (8)	2 Sovereign (Au) 1974. Type as No. 6			400.00
9 (9)	5 Sovereign (Au) 1974. Type as No. 6			950.00

25th ANNIVERSARY OF THE SILVER JUBILEE OF HER MAJESTY QUEEN ELIZABETH II

| **10** (10) | 50 Pence 1977:
a) (Ag)
b) (Cu-Ni) | |

2.00 |
35.00 |

CONSERVATION COMMEMORATIVE (3)

11 (11)	5 £ (Ag) 1979	35.00	50.00
12 (12)	10 £ (Au) 1979	60.00	80.00
13 (13)	150 £ (Au) 1979	800.00	900.00

14 (14)   50 Pence (Cu-Ni) 1980   2.50   11.00

80th ANNIVERSARY OF BIRTH OF QUEEN MOTHER

15 (15)   50 Pence 1980:
      a) (Ag)   70.00
      b) (Cu-Ni)   3.00

WEDDING OF PRINCE CHARLES AND LADY DIANA

16 (16)   50 Pence 1981:
      a) (Ag)   70.00
      b) (Cu-Ni)   4.00

Fidschi-Inseln # Fiji Islands **Fidji (Iles)**

Area: 7,039 sq. mi. Population: 630,000.
A group of islands in the Pacific Ocean. It was discovered in 1643 by
Abel Janszoon Tasman, visited in 1774 by James Cook and explored
in 1827 by Dumont d'Urville. After the abdication of King Cakobau
on 10th October 1874 it became a British possession. The islands have
had a large measure of internal autonomy since 1965.
Capital: Suva.

12 Pence = 1 Shilling, 2 Shillings = 1 Florin, 20 Shillings = £ 1;
since 13th January 1969: 100 Cents = 1 Fiji Dollar

GEORGE V 1910–1936

			VF	XF
1 (1)	½	Penny (Cu–Ni) 1934. Crown above inscription GEORGE V · KING · EMPEROR. ℞ value in letters (with central hole)	4.00	9.00
2 (2)	1	Penny (Cu–Ni) 1934–1936. Type as No. 1	2.00	6.00
3 (3)	6	Pence (Ag) 1934–1936. Crowned bust left of King George V. ℞ sea turtle, stylized (family of the Cheloniidae)	4.00	15.00
4 (4)	1	Shilling (Ag) 1934–1936. ℞ native boat	10.00	25.00
5 (5)	1	Florin (Ag) 1934–1936. ℞ coat of arms	15.00	35.00

EDWARD VIII 1936

6 (6)	1	Penny (Cu–Ni) 1936. Crown above inscription EDWARD VIII · KING · EMPEROR. ℞ value in letters (with central hole)	2.50	5.00

			VF	XF
7 (7)	½	Penny (Cu–Ni) 1940–1941. Crown above inscription GEORGE VI · KING · EMPEROR. ℞ value in letters	3.00	6.00
8 (7a)	½	Penny (Bra) 1942–1943. Type as No. 7	1.50	2.50
9 (8)	1	Penny (Cu–Ni) 1937, 1940, 1941, 1945. Type as No. 7	1.50	3.00
10 (8a)	1	Penny (Bra) 1942–1943. Type as No. 9	2.00	4.50
11 (11)	6	Pence (Ag) 1937. Crowned head of King George VI to left; to the right of the portrait the inscription EMPEROR. ℞ sea turtle	10.00	25.00
12 (12)	1	Shilling (Ag) 1937. ℞ outrigger	8.00	20.00
13 (13)	1	Florin (Ag) 1937. ℞ coat of arms	20.00	35.00
14 (17)	3	Pence (Ni–Bra) 1947. Crowned head of King George VI to left; to the right of the portrait the inscription KING · EMPEROR (scalloped). ℞ native hut	2.00	5.00
15 (11a)	6	Pence (Ag) 1938–1943. Type as No. 11, but to the right of the portrait the inscription KING · EMPEROR	1.50	2.50
16 (12a)	1	Shilling (Ag) 1938–1943. Type as No. 12, but to the right of the portrait the inscription KING · EMPEROR	3.00	5.00
17 (13a)	1	Florin (Ag) 1938–1945. Type as No. 13, but with inscription KING · EMPEROR	6.00	12.00
18 (18)	½	Penny (Cu–Ni) 1949–1952. Crown above inscription KING GEORGE THE SIXTH. ℞ value in letters (with hole)	0.50	1.00
19 (19)	1	Penny (Cu–Ni) 1949–1952. Type as No. 18	0.50	1.20
20 (20)	3	Pence (Ni–Bra) 1950–1952. Type as No. 14, but with inscription KING GEORGE THE SIXTH	1.00	2.00

ELIZABETH II since 1952

			VF	XF
21 (21)	½	Penny (Cu–Ni) 1954. Crown above inscription QUEEN ELIZABETH THE SECOND. ℞ value in letters (with hole)	0.30	0.70
22 (22)	1	Penny (Cu–Ni) 1954–1968. Type as No. 21	0.20	0.40
23 (23)	3	Pence (Ni–Bra) 1955–1967. Head right of Queen Elizabeth II. ℞ native hut	0.20	0.50
24 (24)	6	Pence (Cu–Ni) 1953–1967. ℞ sea-turtle	0.25	0.60

			VF	XF
25 (25)	1	Shilling (Cu–Ni) 1957–1965. ℞ outrigger	0.40	0.90
26 (26)	1	Florin (Cu–Ni) 1957–1965. ℞ coat of arms	0.60	1.20

CURRENCY REFORM: 100 Cents = 1 Fiji Dollar

27 (27)	1	Cent (Br) 1969, 1973, 1975, 1976. R kava dish	0.10	0.20

28 (28)	2	Cents (Br) 1969, 1973–1978, 1980	0.10	0.20

29 (29)	5	Cents (Cu-Ni) 1969, 1973–1980	0.10	0.25

30 (30)	10	Cents (Cu-Ni) 1969, 1973, 1975–1978, 1980	0.15	0.40

31 (31) 20 Cents (Cu-Ni) 1969, 1973–1980. Rev.
ceremonial chain   0.30   0.50

32 (32)   1 Dollar (Cu-Ni) 1969, 1976. R arms and
value   2.50   5.00

COMMEMORATIVE ISSUE TO MARK INDEPENDENCE

33 (33)   1 Dollar 1970. Bust r. of Queen Elizabeth   **Unc**   **Proof**
II. R large seal of state

     a) (Ag)   350.00
     b) (Cu-Ni)   35.00

1ooth ANNIVERSARY OF CESSION TO GREAT BRITAIN

34 (34) 25 Dollars (Ag) 1974. Elizabeth II. R Cakobau, King of the Fiji Islands up the
1874; 45 mm dia   50.00   65.00

		Unc	Proof
35 (35)	100 Dollars (Au) 1974. Type as No. 34; 38 mm dia.	400.00	450.00
36 (A 32)	50 Cents Elizabeth II. R outrigger: a) (Cu-Ni) 1975–1978, 1980 b) (Ag) 1976	2.50	30.00
37 (36)	25 Dollars (Ag) 1975. Type similar to No. 34	150.00	70.00
38 (37)	100 Dollars (Au) 1975. Type similar to No. 35	360.00	380.00

25th ANNIVERSARY OF THE SILVER JUBILEE OF HER MAJESTY QUEEN ELIZABETH II

39 (39)	10 Dollars (Ag) 1977. R coat of arms, value, memorial legend		75.00

ISSUE FOR THE FAO COIN PLAN

40 (38)	1 Cent (Br) 1977, 1978, 1980. Rev. rice	0.20	3.00

CONSERVATION COMMEMORATIVE (3)

41 (40)	10 Dollars (Ag) 1978	30.00	35.00
42 (41)	20 Dollars (Ag) 1978	40.00	45.00
43 (42)	250 Dollars (Au) 1978	600.00	750.00

FOR THE FAO COIN PLAN

		Unc	Proof
44 (43)	50 Cents (Cu-Ni) 1979. Rev. sugar-cane	3.00	15.00

10th ANNIVERSARY OF INDEPENDENCE (3)

		Unc	Proof
45 (44)	50 Cents (Cu-Ni) 1980. Prince Charles	4.00	
46 (45)	10 Dollars (Ag) 1980	55.00	75.00
47 (46)	200 Dollars (Au) 1980	450.00	600.00

WEDDING OF PRINCE CHARLES AND LADY DIANA

48	10 Dollars (Ag) 1981	60.00

Finnland   # Finland   **Finlande**
                       Suomi

Area: 130,160 sq. mi. Population: 4,800,000.
Made a duchy in 1284 and a principality in 1581, Finland was part of the
Swedish kingdom until 1809. Later it became an autonomous principality
within the Russian Union of States. On 6th December 1917 the country
declared its independence and on 17th July 1919 it was granted a
Republican constitution.
Capital: Helsinki.

100 Penniä = 1 Markka

PRINCIPALITY

			VF	XF
1 (13)	1	Penni (Cu) 1895–1916. Filleted crown over monogram of Czar Nicolas II. ℞ value within wreath	1.50	4.00
2 (14)	5	Penniä (Cu) 1896–1917. Type as No. 1	2.00	4.00

3 (15)	10	Penniä (Cu) 1895–1917. Type as No. 1	3.50	7.50
4 (1a)	25	Penniä (Ag) 1897–1917. Crowned double eagle. ℞ value within wreath	2.50	4.50
5 (2a)	50	Penniä (Ag) 1907–1917. Type as No. 4	3.00	6.00
6 (3a)	1	Markka (Ag) 1907–1915. Crowned double eagle and inscription. ℞ value within wreath	6.00	11.00
7 (4a)	2	Markkaa (Ag) 1905–1908. Type as No. 6	18.00	35.00

			VF	**XF**
8 (5)	10	Markkaa (Au) 1904–1913. Crowned double eagle, inscription FINLAND/ SUOMI. ℞ value and date, inscription	420.00	500.00
9 (6)	20	Markkaa (Au) 1903–1913. Type as No. 8	400.00	490.00

INDEPENDENCE

10 (16)	1	Penni (Cu) 1917. Double eagle without crown. ℞ value within wreath	3.00	6.00
11 (17)	5	Penniä (Cu) 1917–1918. Type as No. 10	4.00	8.00
12 (18)	10	Penniä (Cu) 1917. Type as No. 10	6.00	11.00
13 (19)	25	Penniä (Ag) 1917. Double eagle without crown. ℞ value within wreath	3.00	6.00
14 (20)	50	Penniä (Ag) 1917. Type as No. 13	4.00	9.00

RED GOVERNMENT IN SOUTHERN FINLAND

15 (21)	5	Penniä (Cu) 1918. Three trumpets with banner within wreath and inscription. ℞ value	60.00	95.00

REPUBLIC since 1918

16 (22)	1	Penni (Cu) 1919–1924. Arms (lion). ℞ value	1.60	3.00
17 (23a)	5	Penniä (Fe) 1918. Type as No. 16	2000.00	3500.00
18 (23)	5	Penniä (Cu) 1918-1940. Type as No. 17	1.50	3.00

19 (24)	10	Penniä(Cu) 1919-1940.Type as No. 16	1.50	3.00
20 (25)	25	Penniä (Ni) 1921-1940. Arms (lion) dividing date. Rev. value between ears	2.00	6.00
21 (26)	50	Penniä (Ni) 1921-1940. Type as No. 20	2.50	6.00
22 (27)	1	Markka (Ni) 1921-1924. Arms (lion). R value within wreath, diameter 24 mm	3.00	6.00
23 (27a)	1	Markka (Ni) 1928-1940. Type as No. 22; diameter 21 mm	2.00	4.00
24 (28)	5	Markkaa (Al-Br) 1928-1942. Coat of arms within wreath, date. R value within wreath, inscription	2.50	4.00

				VF	XF
25 (29)	10	Markkaa (Al-Br) 1928-1939. Type as No. 24		3.00	5.00
26 (30)	20	Markkaa (Al-Br) 1931-1939. Type as No. 24		4.00	9.00
27 (31)	100	Markkaa (Au) 1926. Arms (lion) dividing date. R value between branches		1000.00	1700.00

28 (32)	200	Markkaa (Au) 1926. Type as No. 27		1500.00	1900.00
29 (33)	5	Penniä (Cu) 1941-1943. Fir-branches, divided date. R value (with center hole)		1.00	2.00
30 (34)	10	Penniä (Cu) 1941-1943. Type as No. 29		1.50	2.50

Nos. 29 and 30 are also know without punched hole (rare)

31 (25a)	25	Penniä (Cu) 1940-1943. Type as No. 20		2.00	3.50
32 (26a)	50	Penniä (Cu) 1940-1943. Type as No. 21		2.50	4.00
33 (27b)	1	Markkaa (Cu) 1940-1951. Type as No. 22:			
		a) 1940-1943, 1950, 1951		2.00	4.00
		b) 1949 (about 250 pieces)		1000.00	1300.00
34 (34b)	10	Penniä (Fe) 1943-1945. Type as No. 30, but smaller diameter		2.00	4.00

No. 34 are also known without punched hole (rare)

35 (25b)	25	Penniä (Fe) 1943–1945. Type as No. 20		1.50	3.50
36 (26b)	50	Penniä (Fe) 1943–1948. Type as No. 21		3.00	6.00
37 (27c)	1	Markka (Fe) 1943-1952. Type as No. 22		2.50	4.00
38 (28a)	5	Markkaa (Bra) 1946-1952. Type as No. 24:			
		a) 1946-1951		2.00	3.50
		b) 1952		8.00	11.00
39 (36)	1	Markkaa 1952-1962. Ornamental pattern. R value, two clasped hands, a subject from the national saga "The Kalevala"			
		a) (Fe) 1952–1953		2.00	4.00
		b) (Fe, nickel-plated) 1953–1962		0.20	0.40

40 (37)	5	Markkaa 1952-1962. Type as No. 39			
		a) (Fe) 1952-1953		3.00	6.00
		b) (Fe, nickel-plated) 1953-1962		0.70	1.50

			VF	**XF**
41 (38)	10	Markkaa (Al–Br) 1952–1962. Arms (lion) and inscription. ℞ fir-tree and value	1.20	3.00
42 (39)	20	Markkaa (Al–Br) 1952–1962. Type as No. 41	1.50	8.00
43 (40)	50	Markkaa (Al–Br) 1952–1962. Type as No. 41	2.50	7.00
44 (41)	100	Markkaa (Ag) 1956–1960. Coat of arms. ℞ value	3.50	6.00
45 (42)	200	Markkaa (Ag) 1956–1959. Type as No. No. 44	4.00	9.00

COMMEMORATIVE ISSUE FOR THE 15th OLYMPIC SUMMER GAMES IN HELSINKI FROM 19. 7. – 3. 8. 1952

46 (35)	500	Markkaa (Ag) 1951, 1952. Olympic rings. ℞ value within wreath		
		a) 1951	320.00	550.00
		b) 1952	45.00	65.00

COMMEMORATIVE ISSUE FOR THE CURRENCY REFORM FROM ROUBLE TO MARKKA AS PER DECREE OF 12th JUNE 1860

47 (43)	1000	Markkaa (Ag) 1960. Head left of Johan Vilhelm Snellman (1806–1881), philosopher, statesman, Finance Minister in 1860. ℞ value within wreath	26.00	32.00

CURRENCY REFORM 1st January 1963:
100 old Markkaa = 1 new Markka

			VF	**XF**
48	(44)	1 Penni (Cu) 1963-1969. Typ as No. 39	0.15	0.35
49	(45)	5 Penniä (Cu) 1963-1977. Type as No. 48	0.12	0.25
50	(46)	10 Penniä (Al-Br) 1963-. Arms (lion).	0.12	0.30
51	(47)	20 Penniä (Al-Br) 1963-. Type as No. 50	0.18	0.35

52	(48)	50 Penniä (Al–Br) 1963–. Arms (lion). R fir-tree and value	0.20	0.40
53	(49)	1 Markka (Bi) 1964–1968. R value in front of stylized trees	1.20	3.00

COMMEMORATIVE ISSUE FOR 50 YEARS OF
INDEPENDENCE

54	(51)	10 Markkaa (Ag) 1967. Five whooper swans in flight (Cygnus cygnus — Anatidae). R buildings and bridges in course of construction, symbol of recovery; value	12.00	16.00
55	(44a)	1 Penni (Al) 1969-. Type as No. 48	0.05	0.10
56	(49a)	1 Markka (Cu-Ni) 1969-. Type as No. 53	0.30	0.50

57 (50)	5 Markkaa (Cu-Ni) 1972–1978. Ice-breaker. R value:	**VF**	**XF**
	a) 1972	3.00	5.00
	b) 1973–1978	1.80	2.50

COMMEMORATIVE ISSUE FOR THE CENTENARY OF THE BIRTH OF JUHO KUSTI PAASIKIVI

58 (52)	10 Markkaa (Ag) 1970. Head facing of Juho Kusti Paasikivi (1870–1956), Head of State 1946–1956. R date, value, names of country on brick wall background	**XF**	**Unc**
		9.00	13.00

COMMEMORATIVE ISSUE FOR THE 10th EUROPEAN ATHLETICS CHAMPIONSHIPS IN HELSINKI
(10th to 15th August 1971)

59 (53)	10 Markkaa (Ag) 1971	7.50	12.00

75th ANNIVERSARY OF THE BIRTH OF URHO KEKKONEN

			XF	Unc
60 (54)	10 Markkaa (Ag) 1975. Urho Kekkonen (*1900), President of State since 1956		7.50	12.00
61 (45a)	5 Penniä (Al) 1977-. Type as No. 49		0.10	0.20

60th ANNIVERSARY OF INDEPENDENCE

		XF	Unc
62 (55)	10 Markkaa (Ag) 1977	11.00	15.00

ISSUE FOR THE SKI CHAMPIONSHIPS IN LAHTI

		XF	Unc
63 (56)	25 Markkaa (Ag) 1978	10.00	15.00

750th ANNIVERSARY OF TURKU

		XF	Unc
64 (58)	25 Markkaa (Ag) 1979	10.00	12.00

65 (57)	5 Markkaa (Al-Br) 1979–. Ice-breaker	1.50	2.00

80th ANNIVERSARY OF THE BIRTH OF URHO KEKKONEN

66 (59)	50 Markkaa (Ag) 1981. President Urho Kekkonen	15.00	18.00

WORLD ICE-HOCKEY CHAMPIONSHIP GAMES

67 (60)	50 Markkaa (Ag) 1982. Ice-hockey player	15.00	18.00

Area: 212,974 sq. mi. Population: 53,000,000.

After the fall of Emperor Napoleon III in 1870 the Third Republic was created, which lasted until 1940. After the Armistice of 22nd June 1940, the Government was in the hands of Marshal Pétain in Vichy, in the part of France which was not occupied by German troops. After the referendum of 13th October 1946 a new Constitution was formulated which established the Fourth Republic. The constitution of the Fifth Republic was granted by popular vote in 1958.

Capital: Paris.

Since 1879, in general no mintmarks appear on French coins, although there are a few exceptions: the mintmark B indicates the striking of coins in Brussels in 1939, and during the years 1943–1958 it refers to issues made by the mint at Beaumont le Roger in the Eure department. The mintmark C indicates special circumstances resulting from the two World Wars, when the mint at Castelsarrasin (Tarn et Garonne) issued coins in 1914 as well as in 1943–1946.

100 Centimes = 1 Franc

THE THIRD REPUBLIC 1870–1940

		VF	XF
1 (58)	1 Centime (Br) 1898–1904, 1908–1914, 1916, 1919–1920. Head of Marianne wearing cap of liberty, symbol of the Republic. ℞ value and date between olive branches	3.00	6.00
2 (59)	2 Centimes (Br) 1898–1904, 1907–1914, 1916, 1919–1920. Type as No. 1	4.00	6.00
3 (60)	5 Centimes (Br) 1898–1917, 1920–1921. ℞ allegorical representation: the Republic protecting her child; value and date	2.00	5.00

			VF	XF
4 (61)	10	Centimes (Br) 1898–1917, 1920 to 1921. Type as No. 3	3.00	7.00
5 (69)	25	Centimes (Ni) 1903. Head left of Marianne. ℞ value within square frame	3.00	6.00
6 (70)	25	Centimes (Ni) 1904–1905. ℞ fasces, oak leaves (Quercus sp. – Fagaceae), value	1.50	4.00
7 (62)	50	Centimes (Ag) 1897–1920. Female figure sowing with rising sun in background. ℞ value and olive branch (Olea europea — Oleaceae)	2.50	3.00
8 (63)	1	Franc (Ag) 1898–1920. Type as No. 7		
		a) 1898–1920	4.00	6.00
		b) 1914, mintmark C	350.00	500.00

			VF	XF
9 (64)	2	Francs (Ag) 1898–1920. Type as No. 7		
		a) 1898–1902, 1904–1905, 1908–1910, 1912–1920	7.00	10.00
		b) 1914, mintmark C	20.00	40.00

			VF	XF
10 (65)	10	Francs (Au) 1899–1901, 1905–1912, 1914. Head right of Marianne. ℞ Gallic cockerel	65.00	75.00

11 (66) 20 Francs (Au) 1899–1914. Type as No. 10 **VF** **XF**
a) 1899–1906, circular inscription
DIEU PROTÈGE LA FRANCE 110.00 125.00
b) 1907–1914, circular inscription
LIBERTÉ ÉGALITÉ FRATERNITÉ 110.00 125.00

12 (56) 50 Francs (Au) 1878–1904. Standing genius writing the Constitution on tablet; on left, fasces; on right, Gallic cockerel. ℞ value and date within oak wreath
a) 1878, 1904 1400.00 2000.00
b) 1887, 1889, 1896, 1900 3000.00 4000.00
13 (57) 100 Francs (Au) 1878–1914. Type as No. 12
a) 1878–1906, circular inscription
DIEU PROTÈGE LA FRANCE 650.00 840.00
b) 1907–1913, circular inscription LIBERTÉ ÉGALITÉ FRATERNITÉ 650.00 840.00
c) 1914, as 13b (1281 pieces issued) 7000.00 9000.00
14 (71) 5 Centimes (Cu–Ni) 1917–1920. Initials RF below cap of liberty and between oak branches. ℞ olive branch between value; no line under CMES. Diameter 19 mm (with central hole) 1.00 2.00
15 (72) 5 Centimes. Type as No. 14, but diameter 17 mm
a) (Cu–Ni) 1920–1927, 1930–1938 0.40 0.80
b) (Cu–Ni) 1929 –.– –.–
c) (Ni–Br) 1938–1939 1.20 2.50
16 (73) 10 Centimes (with hole)
a) (Ni) 1914, CMES with line 1800.00
b) (Cu–Ni) 1917–1938. CMES without line 0.20 0.40
c) (Ni–Br) 1938–1939, as 16b 0.60 1.20
17 (76) 25 Centimes (with hole)
a) (Ni) 1914–1915. CMES with line 5.00 10.00
b) (Ni) 1916–1917, as 17a 35.00 60.00
c) (Cu–Ni) 1917–1938. CMES without line 0.30 0.60
d) (Ni–Br) 1938–1940. CMES without line 1.00 2.00

18 (77)   50 Centimes (Al–Br) 1921–1929. Mercury, the messenger of the gods, seated to left. Inscription COMMERCE IN-DUSTRIE. ℞ value with indication BON POUR. Inscription around: CHAMBRES DE COMMERCE DE FRANCE (token issued by the Chamber of Commerce)   1.00   2.00

19 (78)   1 Franc (Al–Br) 1920–1928. Type as No. 18   1.00   2.00

20 (79)   2 Francs (Al–Br) 1920–1927. Type as No. 18   1.60   4.00

21 (80)   50 Centimes. Head left of Marianne. ℞ value and date between horns of plenty
a) (Al–Br) 1931–1941   0.80   3.00
b) (Al–Br) 1939, mintmark B   6.00   12.50
c) (Al) 1941-1947   0.60   1.20

22 (81)   1 Franc. Type as No. 21
a) (Al–Br) 1931–1941   0.30   0.60
b) (Al) 1941, 1944–1950, 1957–1959   0.40   0.60
c) (Al) 1943, struck in Algiers   1500.00
d) (Zi) 1943, struck in Algiers   1600.00

23 (82)   2 Francs. Type as No. 21
a) (Al–Br) 1931–1941   0.80   1.60
b) (Al) 1941, 1944–1950, 1958–1959   0.30   0.60

24 (83)   5 Francs (Ni) 1933. Head right of Marianne. ℞ ears of corn (Triticum sativum — Gramineae), laurel branch, oak twig and bunch of grapes (Vitis vinifera — Vitaceae); value   6.00   9.00

		VF	XF
25 (84)	5 Francs. Laureate head of Marianne to left. ℞ value within wreath, above which initials RF		
	a) (Ni) 1933, 1935	2.40	5.00
	b) (Ni) 1936	−.−	−.−
	c) (Ni) 1937, 1938	40.00	55.00
	d) (Al-Br) 1938-1940, 1945-1946	7.00	15.00
	e) (Al) 1945-1950, 1952	0.60	1.00
26 (86)	10 Francs. Laureate head of Marianne to right. ℞ value between ears of corn		
	a) (Ag) 1929–1934, 1938–1939; diameter 28 mm	5.00	7.00
	b) (Ag) 1937; diameter 28 mm	90.00	170.00
	c) (Cu–Ni) 1945–1947; diameter 26 mm	2.50	4.00
27 (86b)	10 Francs (Cu–Ni) 1947–1949. Type as No. 26, but with smaller head of Marianne	1.00	4.00
28 (87)	20 Francs (Ag) 1929–1938. Type as No. 26		
	a) 1929, 1933–1934, 1937–1938	12.50	15.00
	b) 1936	300.00	400.00

		VF	XF
29 (88)	100 Francs (Au) 1929, 1933, 1935–1936. Winged head. ℞ ears of corn between laurel and oak branches, value	1000.00	1200.00

Coins of type 29 with dates 1929 and 1933 are patterns, of which only very few specimens came on the market.

		VF	XF
30 (73b)	10 Centimes (Zi) 1941. Type as No. 16	0.50	1.50
31 (74)	10 Centimes (Zi) 1945–1946. Type as No. 16, but diameter 17.5 mm	2.50	4.00

32 (75) 20 Centimes (Zi) 1945–1946. Type as No.   **VF**   **XF**
17, but diameter 24.5 mm
  a) 1945–1946   8.50   18.00
  b) 1945, mintmark B   75.00   140.00

ISSUES OF THE VICHY GOVERNMENT
Legend: ÉTAT FRANÇAIS

			VF	XF
33 (V 91)	10	Centimes (Zi) 1941–1943. Ears of wheat. ℞ oak leaves, value (with hole)		
		a) 1941–1942, diameter 21.5 mm	0.60	3.50
		b) 1943, diameter 21.2 mm	0.60	3.50
34 (V 93)	10	Centimes (Zi) 1943–1944. Type as No. 33, but diameter 17.2 mm	2.00	4.50
35 (V 90)		VINGT (20) Centimes (Zi) 1941. Value in letters (with hole)	3.00	6.00
36 (V 92)	20	Centimes		
		a) (Zi) 1941–1944	1.10	3.50
		b) (Fe) 1944	90.00	125.00
37 (V.94)	50	Centimes (Al) 1942–1944. Battle axe between ears of corn. ℞ value between oak twigs	0.80	2.50
38 (V 95)	1	Franc (Al) 1942–1944. As No. 37	0.80	3.00

39 (V 96) 2 Francs (Al) 1943–1944. As No. 37   0.60   1.80

40 (V 97) 5 Francs (Ni–Br) 1941. Head left of Marshal Henri Philippe Pétain (1856 to 1951), Head of State 1940–1944. ℞ battle axe and value (not put into circulation)   240.00

		VF	**XF**
41 (89)	2 Francs (Bra) 1944. FRANCE within circle. ℞ value, date and legend LIBERTÉ – ÉGALITÉ – FRATER- NITÉ (struck at Philadelphia; circu- lated mostly in Algeria and Southern France as Allied Occupation money)	8.00	12.00

THE FOURTH REPUBLIC 1947–1958

Many issues of the period of the Third Republic still appear with dates until 1959.

42 (98)	10 Francs (Al–Br) 1950–1958. Head left of Marianne. ℞ Gallic cockerel, laurel branch, value	0.30	0.60

43 (99)	20 Francs (Al–Br). Type as No. 42		
	a) 1950. Name of the designer in two lines: Georges/Guiraud	3.50	6.00
	b) 1950–1954. Name of the designer in one line: G. Guiraud	0.40	0.80
44 (100)	50 Francs (Al–Br) 1950–1954, 1958. Type as No. 42	0.70	1.40

45 (101)	100 Francs (Cu–Ni) 1954–1958. Head of Marianne to right with hand holding torch. ℞ value and olive branches	1.20	2.20

			XF	Unc
46 (102)	1	Centime (St) 1962–. Ear of wheat. ℞ value	0.10	0.40

47 (103)	5	Centimes (St) 1961–1964. Type as No. 46	0.20	0.35
48 (A 104)	5	Centimes (Al–Br) 1965–. Head of Marianne to left. ℞ value, olive branch and ear of wheat	0.05	0.10

49 (104)	10	Centimes (Al–Br) 1962–. Type as No. 48	0.10	0.20
50 (105)	20	Centimes (Al–Br) 1962–. Type as No. 48	0.15	0.25

51 (106)	50	Centimes (Al–Br) 1962–1964. Type as No. 48	1.00	2.00

52 (107)	½	Franc (Ni) 1965–. Female figure sowing with rising sun in background. ℞ olive branch and value	0.20	0.30
53 (108)	1	Franc (Ni) 1960–1962, 1964–. Type as No. 52	0.25	0.50

			XF	Unc
54 (110)	5 Francs (Ag) 1960–1969. Type as No. 52		7.00	10.00
55 (110a)	5 Francs (Cu–Ni) 1970–. Type as No. 54		1.50	2.00

56 (111) 10 Francs (Ag) 1964, 1965–1973. Group of three, standing, comprising Hercules and two female figures. ℞ value within wreath. The issue of 1964 is a very rare proof. — 20.00 — 22.00

57 (A 112) 10 Francs (Cu–Ni) 1974– — 2.50 — 4.00
58 (112) 50 Francs (Ag) 1974–. Type as No. 56 — 25.00

59 (109) 2 Francs (Ni) 1979– — 0.40 — 0.80

French Equatorial Africa

Französisch-Äquatorial-Afrika   Afrique Equatoriale Française

On 15th January 1910 the French colonies of Gaboon, Central Congo and Ubangi-Chari-Chad were united to form the administration territory of French Equatorial Africa. Gaboon and Central Congo (renamed Congo Brazzaville) became independent in 1960, so also Chad and the Central African Republic (formerly Ubangi-Chari). The individual states remained as self-governing republics within the Communauté Française.

Capital: Brazzaville.

100 Centimes = 1 Franc

		VF	XF
1 (1)	50 Centimes (Bra) 1942. Gallic cockerel.		
	℞ Lorraine cross	2.00	4.00

		VF	XF
2 (1a)	50 Centimes (Br) 1943. Type as No. 1	2.00	4.00
3 (2)	1 Franc (Bra) 1942. Type as No. 1	3.00	5.00
4 (2a)	1 Franc (Br) 1943. Type as No. 1	2.50	4.50
5 (3)	1 Franc (Al) 1948. Head of Marianne.		
	℞ head of a Loder's gazelle (Gazella leptoceros — Bovidae) and value	0.20	0.40

		VF	XF
6 (4)	2 Francs (Al) 1948. Type as No. 5	0.40	0.80

French Indo-China

Französisch-Indochina   **Indo-Chine Française**

Area: 272,355 sq. mi. Population: 30,000,000.
The French colonies and protectorates of Annam, Cochinchina, Cambodia and Tonkin were originally joined to form this colonial territory. Laos was added to it in 1893 and Kouang-Tchéou-Wan in 1898.

5 Sapek = 1 Centième, 100 Centièmes = 1 Piastre

			VF	XF
1 (1)	2	Sapek (Br) 1887–1902. Name of country, date. ℞ value (with square hole in centre)	3.00	6.00
2 (2)	1	Centième (Br) 1895–1908. Allegorical figure of the French Republic, value. ℞ value in Chinese. Diameter 27.5 mm (with hole)	2.50	3.50
3 (4)	1	Centième (Br) 1908–1939. Type as No. 2, but diameter now 26 mm (with hole)	0.40	0.60

			VF	XF
4 (5)	5	Centièmes. Marianne. ℞ ears of rice and value		
		a) (Cu–Ni) 1923–1938	0.60	0.80
		b) (Ni–Br) 1938–1939	0.60	0.80
5 (14)	10	Centièmes (Ag). Allegorical figure of the French Republic, fasces. ℞ value within wreath		
		a) 1898–1922. Fine silver content 835	3.50	5.50
		b) 1923–1937. Fine silver content 630	2.00	3.50
6 (15)	20	Centièmes (Ag). Type as No. 5		
		a) 1898–1922. Fine silver content 835	4.00	7.50
		b) 1923–1937. Fine silver content 630	2.00	4.00

Coins 5a and 6a dated 1920 also exist without mention of the fine silver content and weight.

			VF	XF
7 (8a)	50	Centièmes (Ag) 1896–1936. Type as No. 5	4.00	8.00
8 (9a)	1	Piastre (Ag) 1895–1928. Type as No. 5	16.00	25.00
9 (18)	1	Piastre (Ag) 1931, 1932. Crowned head of the Republic to left. ℞ value within ornamented oval centre	12.50	22.00

			VF	XF
10 (20)	½	Centième. Cap of Liberty, initials RF and oak wreath. ℞ value and ears of rice (with hole)		
		a) (Br) 1936–1939	0.60	0.80
		b) (Zi) 1940	16.00	25.00
11 (21)	10	Centièmes. Laureate bust of Marianne. ℞ rice plants (Oryza sativa — Gramineae) and value (with hole)		
		a) (Ni) 1939	0.40	0.60
		b) (Cu–Ni) 1939–1941	0.40	0.60

No. 11b with date 1941 and mintmark S was struck in San Francisco.

12 (22)	20	Centièmes. Type as No. 11		
		a) (Ni) 1939	11.00	18.00
		b) (Cu–Ni) 1939–1941. Scalloped border	0.40	0.80

ISSUES OF THE VICHY GOVERNMENT

13 (V 30)	1	Centiéme (Zi) 1940, 1941. Cap of Liberty, laurel, value. R ears of corn, value (with hole):		
		a) 1940; with circles on Phrygian cap	8.00	14.00
		b) 1940, 1941; with rosette on Phrygian cap	1.25	2.50
14 (V 31)	¼	Centième (Zi) 1942. Name of country ÉTAT FRANÇAIS/INDOCHINE. ℞ value (with hole)	9.00	12.50
15 (V 32)	1	Centième (Al) 1943. Name of country ÉTAT FRANÇAIS. ℞ name of country INDOCHINE, value	0.40	1.20
16 (V 33)	5	Centimes (Al) 1943. Type as No. 15	0.40	0.80

ISSUES OF THE FRENCH REPUBLIC

17 (26)	5	Centièmes (Al) 1945–1946. Type as No. 11	0.35	0.50

18 (27)	10	Centièmes (Al) 1945–1946. Type as No. 17	0.40	0.60
19 (28)	20	Centièmes (Al) 1945–1946. Type as No. 17	0.50	0.80
20 (23)	50	Centièmes (Cu–Ni) 1946–1947. Type as No. 7, but in addition the inscription BRONZE DE NICKEL	3.50	5.50

21 (24) 1 Piastre (Cu-Ni). Type as No. 19, but **VF** **XF**
with inscription UNION FRANÇAISE
instead of REPUBLIQUE FRANÇAISE
a) 1946–1947 8.00 12.50
b) 1947. Reeded edge 2.00 4.00

ISSUES FOR THE TERRITORY OF ANNAM
(CENTRAL VIETNAM)

5 Sapek = 1 Centièmes, 100 Centièmes = 1 Piastre,
600 Sapek = 1 Quan-qui

1 1 Sapek (Br) 1889–1907 (Emperor
Thanh–Thai). Four hieroglyphs. ℞ no
inscription, but square hole in centre 6.00 11.00
2 10 Sapek 1889–1907. Four hieroglyphs.
℞ two hieroglyphs (square hole)
a) (Cu) 3.50 5.00
b) (Br) 4.00 6.00

3 10 Sapek (Br) 1907–1916 (Emperor Duy-
Tan). Four hieroglyphs. ℞ two hieroglyphs (square hole) 5.00 8.00
4 1 Sapek 1916–1925 (Emperor Khai-
Dinh). Four hieroglyphs. ℞ no inscription (square hole)
a) (Cu) 10.00 12.50
b) (Br) 11.00 15.00
5 1 Sapek (Br) 1926–1945 (Emperor Bao-
Dai). Four hieroglyphs. ℞ no inscription (square hole); diameter 23 mm 2.50 4.00
6 1 Sapek (Br) 1926–1945. Type as No. 5,
but diameter 17.5 mm 5.00 8.00
7 10 Sapek (Br) 1926–1945. Four hieroglyphs. ℞ two hieroglyphs (square
hole) 6.50 9.00

ISSUES FOR THE TERRITORY OF TONKIN

1 (1) 1 Sapek (Sn–Pb) 1905. Five small hieroglyphs (three above, two below) and
two large hieroglyphs. ℞ inscription
PROTECTORAT DU TONKIN and
date (square hole) 5.00 8.00

A French colony in the Pacific Ocean comprising the Society, Marquesas, Tuamotu, Tubuai, Gambier, Austral, Leeward, and Rapa islands and Clipperton island. Renamed French Polynesia in 1958. For further issues see under this name.
Capital: Papeete.

100 Centimes = 1 Franc

			VF	XF
1 (1)	50	Centimes (Al) 1949. Allegorical figure of the French Republic. ℞ harbour scenery	0.50	1.00
2 (2)	1	Franc (Al) 1949. Type as No. 1	0.50	1.00

3 (3)	2	Francs (Al) 1949. Type as No. 1	1.00	2.00
4 (4)	5	Francs (Al) 1952. Type as No. 1	1.50	3.50

French Polynesia

Französisch-Polynesien   **Polynésie Française**

Area: 1560 sq. mi. Population: 88,000.
A French overseas territory with limited self-government. First known
as French Oceania, but renamed French Polynesia in 1958.
Capital: Papeete.

100 Centimes = 1 Franc

			VF	XF
1 (1)	50	Centimes (Al–Bra) 1965. Allegorical figure of the French Republic. ℞ harbour scenery	0.30	1.00
2 (2)	1	Franc (Al–Bra) 1965. Type as No. 1	0.20	0.50
3 (3)	2	Francs (Al–Bra) 1965. Type as No. 1	0.40	0.70
4 (4)	5	Francs (Al–Bra) 1965. Type as No. 1	0.70	1.50

5 (5)	10	Francs (Ni) 1967. Head of Marianne to left. ℞ upper part of a ceremonial pole	0.80	1.60
6 (6)	20	Francs (Ni) 1967. ℞ breadfruit (Artocarpus communis — Moraceae); Frangipani flowers (Plumeria sp. — Apocynaceae); vanilla shoots (Vanilla planifolia — Orchidaceae)	1.50	3.00
7 (7)	50	Francs (Ni) 1967. ℞ view of Mooréa, an island of the Society group near Tahiti; outrigger canoes, huts and coconut palms (Cocos nucifera — Palmae)	2.50	4.00
8 (2a)	1	Franc (Al) 1975, 1977, 1979. Type as No. 2, but I.E.O.M. added	0.20	0.40
9 (3a)	2	Francs (Al) 1973, 1975, 1977, 1979. Type as No. 8	0.20	0.40
10 (4a)	5	Francs (Al) 1975, 1977, 1979. Type as No. 8	0.60	1.20
11 (5a)	10	Francs (Ni) 1972, 1973, 1975, 1979. Type as No. 5, but I.E.O.M. added	0.80	1.10
12 (6a)	20	Francs (Ni) 1972, 1973, 1975, 1977, 1979. Type as No. 6, but I.E.O.M. added	1.20	1.50
13 (7a)	50	Francs (Ni) 1975, 1979. Type as No. 7, but I.E.O.M. added	2.00	2.50
14 (8)	100	Francs (Ni) 1976, 1979. Type as No. 13	3.00	4.00

French Somaliland

Französisch-Somaliland **Côte Française des Somalis**

Area: 8,900 sq. mi. Population: 81,000.
A French overseas territory with limited self-government on the Gulf of Aden in North East Africa. Renamed Afar and Issar Territories on 19th March 1967.
Capital: Djibouti.

100 Centimes = 1 Franc

			VF	XF
1 (1)	1 Franc (Al) 1949. Head of Marianne to left. ℞ lyre antelope (Damaliscus lunatus — Bovidae)		0.60	1.10
2 (2)	2 Francs (Al) 1949. Type as No. 1		0.80	1.50
3 (3)	5 Francs (Al) 1948. Type as No. 1		1.80	2.50

4 (4)	20 Francs (Al–Br) 1952. Head of Marianne to left. ℞ Arabian dhow and trans-atlantic liner, value		2.50	5.00
5 (5)	1 Franc (Al) 1959. Type as No. 1, but inscription reads only RÉPUBLIQUE FRANÇAISE instead of RÉPUBLI-QUE FRANÇAISE/UNION FRAN-ÇAISE		0.40	0.80
6 (6)	2 Francs (Al) 1959–1965. Type as No. 5		0.40	0.80
7 (7)	5 Francs (Al) 1959–1965. Type as No. 5		0.80	1.60
8 (8)	10 Francs (Al–Br) 1965. Head of Marian-ne to left. ℞ Arabian dhow and trans-atlantic liner, value		0.50	0.80
9 (9)	20 Francs (Al–Br) 1965. Type as No. 8		0.90	2.00

French Territory of the Afars and Issas

Afar- und Issagebiet Territoire Français des Afars et des Issas

Area: 8,462 sq. mi. Population: 125,000.

On 19th March 1967, on the strength of a referendum, the name of French Somaliland was changed into French Territory of the Afars and Issas. The new name was derived from the locally predominant population of the Afars (Danakil) and the Issas. The former French Territory was renamed Djibouti and became independent on June 27, 1977.

Capital: Djibouti.

100 Centimes = 1 Djibouti Franc

			VF	XF
1 (1)	1	Franc (Al) 1969, 1971, 1975. Marianne, design by L. Bazor. R. lyre antelope (Damaliscus lunatus – Bovidae), denomination	0.50	2.00
2 (2)	2	Francs (Al) 1968, 1975. Type as No. 1	3.00	15.00
3 (3)	5	Francs (Al) 1968, 1975. Type as No. 1	0.50	2.00
4 (4)	10	Francs (Al-Br) 1969, 1970, 1975. R Arab dhow in front of a ocean liner, denomination	0.50	2.00
5 (5)	20	Francs (Al-Br) 1968, 1975. Type as No. 4	0.50	2.00
6 (6)	50	Francs (Cu-Ni) 1970, 1975. Marianne, design by L. Joly. R dromedaries (Camelus dromedarius – Camelidae), denomination	1.50	2.50

7 (7)	100	Francs (Cu-Ni) 1970, 1975. Type as No. 6	2.50	3.50

French West Africa

Area: 1,753,100 sq. mi. Population: 17,375,000.
French West Africa comprises the territories of Dahomey, the Ivory
Coast, French Guinea, French Sudan, Mauritania, Niger, Upper Volta
and Senegal. French West Africa was reorganized in 1946 as part of the
Union Française, and at the end of 1958 the individual territories, apart
from French Guinea, became autonomous republics within the Communauté Française, and in 1960, fully independent. French Sudan took the
name of Mali. Since 1957 Togoland is also part of the Monetary Territory of French West Africa.
Capital: Dakar.

100 Centimes = 1 Franc

			VF	XF
1 (1)	50	Centimes (Al–Br) 1944. Head of Marianne to left. ℞ value between horns of plenty	6.00	9.00
2 (2)	1	Franc (Al–Br) 1944	6.00	9.00
3 (3)	1	Franc (Al) 1948–1955. Head of Marianne to left. ℞ head of a Loder's gazelle (Gazella leptoceros — Bovidae) and value	0.20	0.40

4 (4)	2	Francs (Al) 1948–1955. Type as No. 3	0.30	0.70
5 (5)	5	Francs (Al–Br) 1956	0.40	0.80
6 (6)	10	Francs (Al–Br) 1956	0.50	1.10
7 (7)	25	Francs (Al–Br) 1956	1.00	2.00

INTEGRATED COINAGE FOR FRENCH WEST AFRICA AND TOGOLAND

8 (8)	10	Francs (Al–Br) 1957. Head of a Loder's gazelle. ℞ Ashanti gold weight, and inscription INSTITUT D'ÉMISSION AFRIQUE OCCIDENTALE FRAN-ÇAISE – TOGO	0.50	1.20
9 (9)	25	Francs (Al–Br) 1957. Type as No. 8	1.00	2.00

Fudschairah   # Fujairah   **Fujeira**

Area: 454 sq. mi. Population: 10,000.
This Sheikdom situated on the Gulf of Oman was one of the seven Trucial States in the Pacified Oman. Since 2nd December 1971 Fujairah is a member state of the United Arab Emirates (UAE).
Capital: Fujairah.

100 Dirham = 1 Fujairah Ryal

MOHAMMED BIN HAMAD AL SHARQI since 1952

		Proof
1	1 Ryal (Ag) 1969–. Desert fort; in exergue, national arms between olive branches. ℞ national arms, date, value and name of country	9.00
2	2 Ryals (Ag) 1969–. Head of Richard M. Nixon (*1913), 37th President of the U.S.A. ℞ as No. 1	12.00

3   4

3	5 Ryals (Ag) 1969–. Distant view of Munich with flaming torch; Olympic rings, within which arms of city and Olympic medal. Inscription: OLYMPIA MÜNCHEN 1972. ℞ as No. 1	30.00
4	10 Ryals (Ag) 1969–. United States moon research programme, third stage "Manned Landing". Apollo programme. Astronauts: M. Collins, N. Armstrong and E. Aldrin in front of lunar globe	45.00
5	10 Ryals (Ag) 1969–. Astronauts Charles Conrad, Richard Gordon, Alan Bean. Apollo XIII. ℞ as No. 1	45.00
6	10 Ryals (Ag) 1969–. Three winged	

horses ascending before sun with rays.
Apollo XIII. ℞ as No. 1 — 45.00

			Proof
7	25	Ryals (Au) 1969. Type as No. 2	80.00
8	50	Ryals (Au) 1969–. Type as No. 3	160.00
9	100	Ryals (Au) 1969–. Type as No. 4	320.00
10	100	Ryals (Au) 1969–. Type as No. 5	320.00
11	100	Ryals (Au) 1969–. Type as No. 6	320.00
12	200	Ryals (Au) 1969–. Sheikh Mohammed Bin Hamad Al Sharqi. ℞ as No. 1	650.00

COMMEMORATIVE ISSUES (4) FOR THE VISIT OF POPE PAUL VI TO THE PHILIPPINES AND AUSTRALIA

13	10	Ryals (Ag) 1969. Head of Pope Paul VI wearing pileolus (cap). Above, St. Peter's Cathedral, Rome. Below, Manila Cathedral, dedicated in 1958. ℞ as No. 1

45.00

14	10	Ryals (Ag) 1969. Pope Paul VI wearing pileolus; papal arms and coastal outline of Australia with giant red kangaroo. ℞ as No. 1

45.00

15	100	Ryals (Au) 1969. Type as No. 13	320.00
16	100	Ryals (Au) 1969. Type as No. 14	320.00

COMMEMORATIVE ISSUES (2) FOR THE MOON LANDING OF APOLLO 14 ON 4th FEBRUARY 1971

17	10	Ryals (Ag) 1970–. Representation of the flight of the space-ship "Apollo 14" from the earth to the moon. In field, stars	**Proof** 45.00
18	100	Ryals (Au) 1970–. Type as No. 17	320.00

Gabun   # Gaboon   **Gabon**

Area: 102,290 sq. mi. Population: 700,000.
After the French had founded their first settlement in 1839 by the River Gaboon, the whole territory came under French domination and was governed as a part of French Equatorial Africa. In 1958 the country obtained limited autonomy, and became independent on 17th August 1960. Gaboon belongs to the Monetary Territory of Equatorial Africa; for the community coins issues, see under this name. Capital: Libreville.

100 Centimes = 1 CFA Franc

COMMEMORATIVE ISSUES (4) FOR INDEPENDENCE

1	10	Francs (Au) 1960. Head of Léon M'Ba (*1902), Head of State 1960–1967. ℞ national arms, value	**Proof** 80.00
2	25	Francs (Au) 1960. Type as No. 1	200.00
3	50	Francs (Au) 1960. Type as No. 1	400.00
4	100	Francs (Au) 1960. Type as No. 1	800.00

COMMEMORATIVE ISSUES (5) FOR THE FIRST MANNED MOON LANDING ON 20th JULY 1969

5	1000	Francs (Au) 1969. Head left of Albert Bernard Bongo, Head of State since 1967. ℞ Gaboon scenery with stump of okume tree, above which national arms; value	200.00
6	3000	Francs (Au) 1969. ℞ national arms and legend: UNION – TRAVAIL – JUSTICE; value	300.00

7	5000	Francs (Au) 1969. ℞ three-headed reliquary figure of the Bakota (Kota

tribe of Gaboon). The Kota tribe places this "spirit of the dead", known as mbulu-ngulu, on the reliquary basket, the family body, which contains the ancestral skulls, as a symbol of vigilance and meditation. It is two-dimensional and made of wood, mainly brass or copper-plated. Value

8 10000 Francs (Au) 1969. ℞ American space programme, third stage: "manned landing". Apollo programme. Lunar module and astronaut in lunar landscape – 20th July 1969; terrestrial globe, above which national arms; value

500.00

850.00

9 20000 Francs (Au) 1969. ℞ view of Cape Kennedy: departure of "Apollo 11" on 16th July 1969; value

1800.00

			VF	XF
10 (1)	100	Francs (Ni) 1971, 1972	1.50	3.00
11 (2)	100	Francs (Ni) 1975. Type similar to No. 10	1.50	3.00

The Gambia

Area: 4,003 sq. mi. Population: 390,000.

Since 1843 Gambia was first a British possession, then a Crown Colony, and at one time was part of the British West Africa Currency Board. Since 18th February 1965 it has been an independent republic within the British Commonwealth.

Capital: Banjul (formerly named Bathurst).

12 Pence = 1 Shilling, 20 Shillings = £ 1;
since 1st July 1971: 100 Bututs = 1 Dalasi

			VF	XF
1 (1)	1	Penny (Br) 1966. Head right of Queen Elizabeth II. ℞ sailing boat	0.15	0.30

			VF	XF
2 (2)	3	Pence (Bra) 1966. ℞ double-spurred francolin (Francolinus bicalcaratus — Phasianidae)	0.15	0.30
3 (3)	6	Pence (Cu-Ni) 1966. ℞ ground nuts (Arachis hypogaea — Leguminosae)	0.25	0.50
4 (4)	1	Shilling (Cu–Ni) 1966. ℞ oil palm (Elaeis guineensis — Palmae)	0.40	0.80
5 (5)	2	Shillings (Cu–Ni) 1966. ℞ African domestic ox (Bos primigenius taurus — Bovidae)	0.70	1.40
6 (6)	4	Shillings (Cu–Ni) 1966. ℞ slender-snouted crocodile (Crocodilus cataphractus — Crocodilidae)	1.20	2.40

		Unc	Proof
7 (7)	8 Shillings 1970. ℞ hippopotamus (Hippopotamus amphibius — Hippopotamidae)		
	a) (Ag)		60.00
	b) (Cu-Ni)	10.00	

CURRENCY REFORM: 100 Bututs = 1 Dalasi

		VF	XF
8 (8)	1 Butut (Br) 1971, 1973–1975	0.10	0.30
9 (9)	5 Bututs (Bra) 1971	0.10	0.20
10 (10)	10 Bututs (Cu-Ni) 1971	0.15	0.30

11 (11)	25 Bututs (Cu–Ni) 1971	0.40	0.90

12 (12)	50 Bututs (Cu–Ni) 1971	0.60	1.50
13 (13)	1 Dalasi (Cu–Ni) 1971	1.60	3.00

ISSUE FOR THE FAO COIN PLAN

			VF	XF
14 (14)	1	Butut (Br) 1974. Type as No. 8, but inscription FOOD FOR MANKIND added	0.20	0.40

10th ANNIVERSARY OF INDEPENDENCE

			Unc	Proof
15 (15)	10	Dalasis (Ag) 1975. Rev. coat of arms, commemorative inscription, value	11.00	20.00

CONSERVATION COMMEMORATIVE (3)

16 (16)	20	Dalasis (Ag) 1977	30.00	40.00
17 (17)	40	Dalasis (Ag) 1977	40.00	60.00
18 (18)	500	Dalasis (Au) 1977	550.00	750.00

Deutschland   Germany   Allemagne

The great variety of German coins which have appeared since the foundation of the Reich on 18th January 1871 is a clear reflection of most recent German history. The issues of provinces and cities are placed before the small denominations of the Empire and arranged in alphabetical order, each with its own numbering. The coins of the German principalities, Duchies, Grand Duchies and Kingdoms, as well as of the Free Cities and Hanseatic States of Bremen, Hamburg and Lübeck are plainly recognizable as coins of the Reich by the representation of the imperial eagle and by the inscription DEUTSCHES REICH. After the small denominations of the Empire follows the listing in chronological order of the issues of the Weimar Republic, those of the Third Reich, those of the Allied Occupation, of the Bank Deutscher Länder and of the German Federal Republic, simply divided under corresponding headings.

The coins of the GDR are catalogued under yet another system of numbering. It is evident that Danzig and the Saar enjoyed temporary autonomy. German New Guinea, German East Africa and Kiaochow remind us of the short-lived German colonial period. The Occupation issues of the First and Second World War form the close of the German section.

100 Pfennig = 1 Mark (Reichsmark, Rentenmark, Deutsche Mark)

Anhalt (Duchy)

FRIEDRICH I 1871–1904

		VF	XF
1 (1)	2 Mark (Ag) 1876. Head right of Friedrich I (1831–1904). ℞ imperial eagle	190.00	800.00

		VF	XF
2 (2)	20 Mark (Au) 1875. Type as No. 1	750.00	1500.00

COMMEMORATIVE ISSUES (4) FOR THE 25th YEAR OF REIGN

3 (3)	2 Mark (Ag) 1896. Head right of Friedrich I	200.00	350.00
4 (4)	5 Mark (Ag) 1896. Type as No. 3	650.00	1200.00

5 (5)	10 Mark (Au) 1896. Type as No. 3	680.00	1100.00
6 (6)	20 Mark (Au) 1896. Type as No. 3	800.00	1200.00

COMMEMORATIVE ISSUES (2) FOR THE 70th BIRTHDAY OF THE DUKE on 29th April 1901

7 (5)	10 Mark (Au) 1901. Type as No. 5	680.00	1100.00
8 (6)	20 Mark (Au) 1901. Type as No. 6	800.00	1200.00

FRIEDRICH II 1904–1918

9 (7)	2 Mark (Ag) 1904. Head left of Friedrich II (1856–1918). ℞ imperial eagle	200.00	360.00
10 (8)	3 Mark (Ag) 1909, 1911	42.00	100.00
11 (9)	20 Mark (Au) 1904	600.00	1250.00

COMMEMORATIVE ISSUES (2) FOR THE SILVER WEDDING OF THE DUKE AND THE DUCHESS

12 (10)	3 Mark (Ag) 1914. Conjoined heads of Friedrich II and Marie, Duchess of Anhalt, née Princess of Baden	35.00	60.00
13 (11)	5 Mark (Ag) 1914. Type as No. 12	130.00	220.00

Baden (Grand Duchy)

FRIEDRICH I 1852–1907

			VF	XF
1 (15)	10 Mark (Au) 1872–1873. Head left of Friedrich I (1826–1907). ℞ imperial eagle		175.00	260.00

			VF	XF
2 (16)	20 Mark (Au) 1872–1873		175.00	260.00
3 (12)	2 Mark (Ag) 1876–1888		100.00	400.00
4 (13)	5 Mark (Ag) 1874–1888. Type as No. 3		75.00	600.00
5 (14)	5 Mark (Au) 1877		200.00	360.00
6 (15a)	10 Mark (Au) 1875–1888		150.00	300.00
7 (16a)	20 Mark (Au) 1874		400.00	560.00
8 (12a)	2 Mark (Ag) 1892–1902		50.00	165.00
9 (13)	5 Mark (Ag)			
	a) 1891–1902		55.00	250.00
	b) BADEN (A = without crossline)		350.00	700.00

			VF	XF
10 (15b)	10 Mark (Au) 1890–1901		160.00	265.00
11 (16b)	20 Mark (Au) 1894–1895		165.00	285.00

COMMEMORATIVE ISSUES (2) FOR THE 50th YEAR OF REIGN

			VF	XF
12 (20)	2 Mark (Ag) 1902. Head right with laurel branch below		20.00	30.00

Germany 533

		VF	XF
13 (21)	5 Mark (Ag) 1902. As type No. 12	100.00	180.00

| 14 (17) | 2 Mark (Ag) 1902–1907. Similar to No. 12, but without laurel branch | 26.00 | 65.00 |
| 15 (18) | 5 Mark (Ag) 1902–1907. Similar to No. 13, but without laurel branch | 50.00 | 140.00 |

| 16 (19) | 10 Mark (Au) 1902–1907 | 190.00 | 265.00 |

COMMEMORATIVE ISSUES (2) FOR THE GOLDEN WEDDING

| 17 (22) | 2 Mark (Ag) 1906 | 16.00 | 30.00 |
| 18 (23) | 5 Mark (Ag) 1906 | 95.00 | 160.00 |

COMMEMORATIVE ISSUES (2) FOR THE DEATH OF THE GRAND DUKE

| 19 (24) | 2 Mark (Ag) 1907 | 30.00 | 60.00 |
| 20 (25) | 5 Mark (Ag) 1907 | 110.00 | 190.00 |

			VF	XF
21 (26)	2 Mark (Ag) 1911–1913		155.00	280.00
22 (27)	3 Mark (Ag) 1908–1915		17.00	30.00
23 (28)	5 Mark (Ag) 1908–1913		50.00	125.00

		VF	XF
24 (29)	10 Mark (Au) 1909–1913	320.00	600.00
25 (30)	20 Mark (Au) 1911–1914	160.00	250.00

Bavaria (Kingdom)

LUDWIG II 1864–1886

			VF	XF
1 (34)	10 Mark (Au) 1872–1873. Head right of Ludwig II (1845–1886). ℞ imperial eagle		130.00	220.00
2 (35)	20 Mark (Au) 1872–1873. Type as No. 1		140.00	250.00
3 (31)	2 Mark (Ag) 1876–1883		80.00	300.00
4 (32)	5 Mark (Ag) 1874–1876		60.00	200.00
5 (33)	5 Mark (Au) 1877–1878		200.00	360.00
6 (34a)	10 Mark (Au) 1874–1881		130.00	200.00
7 (35a)	20 Mark (Au) 1874–1878		160.00	260.00

OTTO III 1886–1913. Under Regency of Prince Regent Luitpold

			VF	XF
8 (36)	2 Mark (Ag) 1888. Head left of Otto (1848–1916). ℞ imperial eagle		250.00	450.00

			VF	XF
9 (38)	5 Mark (Ag) 1888. Type as No. 8	300.00	600.00

10 (39)	10 Mark (Au) 1888. Type as No. 8	200.00	350.00
11 (36a)	2 Mark (Ag) 1891–1913	16.00	40.00
12 (37)	3 Mark (Ag) 1908–1913	12.00	22.00
13 (38a)	5 Mark (Ag) 1891–1913	25.00	50.00
14 (39a)	10 Mark (Au) 1890–1900	120.00	200.00
15 (40)	20 Mark (Au) 1895–1913	130.00	200.00

| **16** (39b) | 10 Mark (Au) 1900–1912 | 130.00 | 175.00 |

COMMEMORATIVE ISSUES (3) FOR THE 90th BIRTHDAY OF PRINCE REGENT LUITPOLD

17 (41)	2 Mark (Ag) 1911. Head right of Prince Regent Luitpold (1821–1912). ℞ imperial eagle	15.00	30.00
18 (42)	3 Mark (Ag) 1911	15.00	30.00
19 (43)	5 Mark (Ag) 1911	75.00	150.00

		VF	XF
20 (44)	2 Mark (Ag) 1914. Head left of Ludwig III (1845–1921). ℞ imperial eagle	50.00	90.00
21 (45)	3 Mark (Ag) 1914	25.00	40.00

22 (46)	5 Mark (Ag) 1914	110.00	200.00

23 (47)	20 Mark (Au) 1914	2200.00	3200.00

COMMEMORATIVE ISSUE FOR THE GOLDEN WEDDING

24 (48)	3 Mark (Ag) 1918. Conjoined heads of Ludwig III and Marie Therese of Bavaria	17000.00	25000.00

Of No. 24 electrotypes are also on the market.

Bremen (Free Hanseatic City)

		VF	XF
1 (49)	2 Mark (Ag) 1904. Arms of the city. ℞ imperial eagle	50.00	105.00
2 (50)	5 Mark (Ag) 1906	140.00	260.00

3 (51)	10 Mark (Au) 1907	650.00	900.00
4 (52)	20 Mark (Au) 1906	700.00	1050.00

Brunswick (Duchy)

WILHELM 1831–1884

1 (53)	20 Mark (Au) 1875–1876. Head left of Wilhelm (1806–1884). ℞ imperial eagle	650.00	1100.00

ERNST AUGUST 1913–1918

COMMEMORATIVE ISSUES (4) FOR THE ACCESSION AND WEDDING OF THE DUKE

2 (54)	3 Mark (Ag) 1915. Conjoined heads to r. of Ernst August and Viktoria Luise	900.00	1500.00
3 (55)	5 Mark (Ag) 1915. Type as No. 2	1150.00	1700.00
4 (54a)	3 Mark (Ag) 1915. Type as No. 2, but with additional inscription U. LÜNEB	115.00	180.00
5 (55a)	5 Mark (Ag) 1915. Type as No. 4	250.00	500.00

		VF	XF
1 (56)	10 Mark (Au) 1873. Arms of the city. R imperial eagle	1100.00	1500.00

2 (56a)	10 Mark (Au) 1874	900.00	1200.00
3 (57)	2 Mark (Ag) 1876–1888	45.00	190.00
4 (59)	5 Mark (Ag) 1875–1888. Type as No. 3	50.00	300.00
5 (60)	5 Mark (Au) 1877	300.00	350.00
6 (61)	10 Mark (Au) 1875–1888	135.00	200.00
7 (62)	20 Mark (Au) 1875–1889	130.00	165.00

8 (57a)	2 Mark (Ag) 1892–1914. Arms of the city. R imperial eagle	26.00	55.00
9 (58)	3 Mark (Ag) 1908–1914	18.00	30.00
10 (59a)	5 Mark (Ag) 1891–1913	35.00	75.00
11 (61a)	10 Mark (Au) 1890–1913	130.00	160.00
12 (62a)	20 Mark (Au) 1893–1913	120.00	140.00

Hessen (Grand Duchy)

LUDWIG III 1848–1877

		VF	XF
1 (66)	10 Mark (Au) 1872–1873. Head right of Ludwig III (1806–1877). ℞ imperial eagle	280.00	600.00
2 (67)	20 Mark (Au) 1872–1873. Type as No. 1	280.00	600.00
3 (63)	2 Mark (Ag) 1876–1877	250.00	1600.00
4 (64)	5 Mark (Ag) 1875–1876	190.00	800.00
5 (65)	5 Mark (Au) 1877	580.00	900.00

6 (66a)	10 Mark (Au) 1875–1877	175.00	280.00
7 (67a)	20 Mark (Au) 1874	500.00	800.00

LUDWIG IV 1877–1892

8 (68)	2 Mark (Ag) 1888. Head right of Ludwig IV (1837–1892). ℞ imperial eagle	750.00	1600.00
9 (69)	5 Mark (Ag) 1888	900.00	1700.00
10 (70)	5 Mark (Au) 1877	600.00	950.00
11 (71)	10 Mark (Au) 1878–1888	400.00	600.00
12 (68a)	2 Mark (Ag) 1891	420.00	800.00
13 (69a)	5 Mark (Ag) 1891	550.00	1100.00
14 (71a)	10 Mark (Au) 1890	700.00	1200.00
15 (72)	20 Mark (Au) 1892	1200.00	1400.00

ERNST LUDWIG 1892–1918

			VF	**XF**
16 (73)	10 Mark (Au) 1893. Head left of Ernst Ludwig (1866–1937). ℞ imperial eagle		550.00	900.00
17 (74)	20 Mark (Au) 1893. Type as No. 16		700.00	1150.00
18 (75)	2 Mark (Ag) 1895–1900. Head of the Grand Duke to left		200.00	550.00
19 (79)	3 Mark (Ag) 1910		60.00	95.00
20 (76)	5 Mark (Ag) 1895–1900		125.00	350.00
21 (77)	10 Mark (Au) 1896–1898		550.00	800.00

22 (78)	20 Mark (Au) 1896–1903	285.00	400.00

23 (78a)	20 Mark (Au) 1905–1911	285.00	400.00

COMMEMORATIVE ISSUES (2) FOR THE 400th ANNIVERSARY OF THE BIRTH OF PHILIP I, THE MAGNANIMOUS (1504–1567)

24 (80)	2 Mark (Ag) 1904. Conjoined heads to l. of Philip, Landgrave of Hessen, and Ernst Ludwig	35.00	60.00
25 (81)	5 Mark (Ag) 1904	110.00	200.00

26 (82)   3 Mark (Ag) 1917. Head left of the
Grand Duke; laurel branch below   Proof   2500.00

Lippe (Principality)

LEOPOLD IV 1905–1918

		VF	XF
1 (83)	2 Mark (Ag) 1906. Head left of the Prince	185.00	320.00
2 (84)	3 Mark (Ag) 1913	200.00	380.00

Lübeck (Free Hanseatic City)

1 (85)	2 Mark (Ag) 1901. Arms of the city	140.00	250.00
2 (85a)	2 Mark (Ag) 1904–1912	75.00	110.00
3 (86)	3 Mark (Ag) 1908–1914	60.00	105.00
4 (87)	5 Mark (Ag) 1904–1913	225.00	360.00

5 (88)   10 Mark (Au) 1901–1904   550.00   850.00

		VF	XF
6 (88a)	10 Mark (Au) 1905–1910	500.00	800.00

Mecklenburg-Schwerin (Grand Duchy)

FRIEDRICH FRANZ II 1842–1883

1 (90) 10 Mark (Au) 1872. Head right of
Friedrich Franz II (1823–1883) ℞
imperial eagle   1200.00   2000.00

2 (91) 20 Mark (Au) 1872. Type as No. 1   900.00   1200.00

3 (89) 2 Mark (Ag) 1876   210.00   600.00
4 (90a) 10 Mark (Au) 1878   650.00   900.00

FRIEDRICH FRANZ III 1883–1897

5 (92) 10 Mark (Au) 1890. Head right of
Friedrich Franz III (1851–1897). ℞
imperial eagle   420.00   600.00

FRIEDRICH FRANZ IV 1897–1918

COMMEMORATIVE ISSUES (3) FOR THE COMING OF AGE
OF THE GRAND DUKE ON 9th APRIL 1901

6 (93) 2 Mark (Ag) 1901   250.00   400.00
7 (94) 10 Mark (Au) 1901   1200.00   1600.00
8 (95) 20 Mark (Au) 1901   1700.00   2500.00

COMMEMORATIVE ISSUES (2) FOR THE WEDDING OF THE GRAND DUKE, 7th JUNE 1904

		VF	XF
9 (96)	2 Mark (Ag) 1904. Conjoined heads to l. of Friedrich Franz IV (*1884) and Alexandra	40.00	75.00
10 (97)	5 Mark (Ag) 1904. Type as No. 9	110.00	180.00

COMMEMORATIVE ISSUES (2) FOR THE CENTENARY OF THE GRAND DUCHY AND THE ACCESSION TO THE TITLE OF GRAND DUKE OF FRIEDRICH FRANZ ON 9th JUNE 1815

11 (98)	3 Mark (Ag) 1915. Conjoined busts left of Friedrich Franz I (1765–1837) and Friedrich Franz IV	125.00	200.00
12 (99)	5 Mark (Ag) 1915. Type as No. 11	300.00	580.00

Mecklenburg-Strelitz (Grand Duchy)

FRIEDRICH WILHELM 1860–1904

1 (101)	10 Mark (Au) 1873. Head left of Friedrich Wilhelm (1819–1904). ℞ imperial eagle	5000.00	7000.00

2 (102)   20 Mark (Au) 1873. Type as No. 1   4000.00   5000.00

3 (100)   2 Mark (Ag) 1877   350.00   900.00
4 (101a)   10 Mark (Au) 1874, 1880   3200.00   5000.00
5 (102a)   20 Mark (Au) 1874   2750.00   4200.00

ADOLF FRIEDRICH V 1904–1914

6 (103)   2 Mark (Ag) 1905. Head left of the
Grand Duke (1848–1914)   300.00   400.00
7 (106)   3 Mark (Ag) 1913   350.00   600.00
8 (104)   10 Mark (Au) 1905   5000.00   6500.00

9 (105)   20 Mark (Au) 1905   5000.00   6500.00

Oldenburg (Grand Duchy)

NICOLAUS FRIEDRICH PETER 1853–1900

1 (107)   10 Mark (Au) 1874. Head left of Nicolaus Friedrich Peter (1827–1900).
℞ imperial eagle   3500.00   4500.00

2 (108)   2 Mark (Ag) 1891. Head right of
Nicolaus Friedrich Peter   180.00   350.00

FRIEDRICH AUGUST 1900–1918

			VF	XF
3 (109)	2	Mark (Ag) 1900–1901. Head of the Grand Duke to left	160.00	300.00
4 (110)	5	Mark (Ag) 1900–1901	350.00	900.00

Prussia (Kingdom)

WILHELM I 1861–1888

1 (114)	10	Mark (Au) 1872–1873. Head right of Wilhelm I (1797–1888). ℞ imperial eagle	120.00	140.00
2 (115)	20	Mark (Au) 1871–1873. Type as No. 1	130.00	160.00
3 (111)	2	Mark (Ag) 1876–1884	28.00	160.00
4 (112)	5	Mark (Ag) 1874–1876	35.00	200.00
5 (113)	5	Mark (Au) 1877–1878	240.00	300.00
6 (114a)	10	Mark (Au) 1874–1888	125.00	160.00
7 (115a)	20	Mark (Au) 1874–1888	130.00	160.00

FRIEDRICH 1888

8 (116)	2	Mark (Ag) 1888. Head right of Friedrich (1831–1888). ℞ imperial eagle	30.00	60.00
9 (117)	5	Mark (Ag) 1888	65.00	120.00

		VF	XF
10 (118)	10 Mark (Au) 1888	120.00	160.00
11 (119)	20 Mark (Au) 1888	125.00	160.00

WILHELM II 1888–1918

12 (120)	2 Mark (Ag) 1888. Head right of Wilhelm II (1859–1941). ℞ imperial eagle	175.00	400.00
13 (122)	5 Mark (Ag) 1888	300.00	600.00
14 (123)	10 Mark (Au) 1889	2000.00	3000.00
15 (124)	20 Mark (Au) 1888, 1889	130.00	160.00
16 (120a)	2 Mark (Ag) 1891–1912	15.00	38.00
17 (121)	3 Mark (Ag) 1908–1912	12.00	16.00
18 (122a)	5 Mark (Ag) 1891–1908	25.00	45.00

19 (123a)	10 Mark (Au) 1890–1912	130.00	165.00
20 (124a)	20 Mark (Au) 1890–1913	135.00	165.00

COMMEMORATIVE ISSUES (2) FOR THE 2nd CENTENARY OF THE PRUSSIAN KINGDOM

		VF	XF
21 (128)	2 Mark (Ag) 1901. Conjoined busts left of Friedrich I and Wilhelm II	12.00	16.00

| **22** (129) | 5 Mark (Ag) 1901. Type as No. 21 | 45.00 | 75.00 |

COMMEMORATIVE ISSUE FOR THE CENTENARY OF BERLIN UNIVERSITY.

| **23** (130) | 3 Mark (Ag) 1910. Conjoined heads left of Friedrich Wilhelm III and Wilhelm II | 50.00 | 90.00 |

COMMEMORATIVE ISSUE FOR THE CENTENARY OF BRESLAU UNIVERSITY

		VF	XF
24 (131)	3 Mark (Ag) 1911. Conjoined heads of Friedrich Wilhelm III and Wilhelm II	38.00	70.00

COMMEMORATIVE ISSUES (2) FOR THE CENTENARY OF THE WAR OF LIBERATION

25 (132)	2 Mark (Ag) 1913. Friedrich Wilhelm III on horseback surrounded by a rejoicing crowd. ℞ eagle holding serpent in its claws	12.00	16.00
26 (133)	3 Mark (Ag) 1913. Type as No. 25	13.00	22.00

COMMEMORATIVE ISSUES (2) FOR THE 25th YEAR OF REIGN

27 (134)	2 Mark (Ag) 1913. Wilhelm II in the uniform of a cuirassier with the

			VF	XF
		chain of the Order of the Black Eagle; laurel branch	11.00	16.00
28	(135)	3 Mark (Ag) 1913. Type as No. 27	12.00	18.00

29	(125)	3 Mark (Ag) 1914. Type as No. 28, but without laurel branch	13.00	22.00
30	(126)	5 Mark (Ag) 1913, 1914. Type as No. 29	22.00	40.00
31	(127)	20 Mark (Au) 1913-1915. Type as No. 29:		
		a) 1913, 1914	135.00	160.00
		b) 1915	3000.00	3500.00

COMMEMORATIVE ISSUE FOR THE CENTENARY OF THE UNITING OF THE EARLDOM OF MANSFELD TO PRUSSIA

32	(136)	3 Mark (Ag) 1915. St. George to r. fighting the dragon; on the saddle-cloth of his horse the arms of Mansfeld	180.00	350.00

Reuss, elder branch (Principality)

HEINRICH XXII 1859–1902

1	(137)	2 Mark (Ag) 1877. Head right of Heinrich XXII (1846–1902). ℞ imperial eagle	380.00	900.00

			VF	XF
2 (138)	20	Mark (Au) 1875	12000.00	14000.00
3 (137a)	2	Mark (Ag) 1892	280.00	600.00

4 (139)	2	Mark (Ag) 1899, 1901. Head of the Prince to right	180.00	300.00

HEINRICH XXIV 1902–1918

5 (140)	3	Mark (Ag) 1909. Head of the Prince to right	240.00	400.00

Reuss, younger branch (Principality)

HEINRICH XIV 1867–1913

1 (141)	2	Mark (Ag) 1884. Head left of Heinrich XIV (1832–1913). ℞ imperial eagle	240.00	600.00
2 (142)	10	Mark (Au) 1882	4000.00	6000.00

		VF	XF
3 (143)	20 Mark (Au) 1881	1800.00	3000.00

Saxony (Kingdom)

JOHANN 1854–1873

		VF	XF
1 (178)	10 Mark (Au) 1872, 1873. Head left of Johann (1801–1873). ℞ imperial eagle	135.00	220.00
2 (179)	20 Mark (Au) 1872, 1873. Type as No. 1	160.00	250.00

ALBERT 1873–1902

		VF	XF
3 (180)	2 Mark (Ag) 1876–1888. Head right of Albert (1828–1902). ℞ imperial eagle	100.00	380.00
4 (181)	5 Mark (Ag) 1875–1889	45.00	300.00
5 (182)	5 Mark (Au) 1877	265.00	310.00
6 (183)	10 Mark (Au) 1874–1888	130.00	175.00
7 (184)	20 Mark (Au) 1874–1878	200.00	300.00

COMMEMORATIVE MEDAL FOR THE 8th CENTENARY OF THE HOUSE OF WETTIN IN 1889

			VF	XF
8	(–)	1889. Head to right of Albert. ℞ Saxonia seated on throne surrounded by a crowd		
		a) (Ag)	2000.00	2500.00
		b) (Cu)	285.00	420.00
9 (180a)	2	Mark (Ag) 1891–1902	35.00	160.00
10 (181a)	5	Mark (Ag) 1891–1902	40.00	120.00
11 (183a)	10	Mark (Au) 1891–1902	130.00	180.00
12 (184a)	20	Mark (Au) 1894, 1895	180.00	250.00

COMMEMORATIVE MEDAL FOR THE VISIT OF THE KING TO THE MINT AT MULDNER HÜTTE ON 16th JULY 1892

13	(–)	(Ag) 1892. Head of the King to right. ℞ commemorative inscription	650.00	900.00

GEORG 1902–1904

COMMEMORATIVE ISSUES (2) FOR THE DEATH OF KING ALBERT ON 19th JUNE 1902

14 (185)	2	Mark (Ag) 1902	30.00	60.00
15 (186)	5	Mark (Ag) 1902	65.00	130.00
16 (187)	2	Mark (Ag) 1903, 1904	40.00	130.00
17 (188)	5	Mark (Ag) 1903, 1904	45.00	160.00

18 (189)	10	Mark (Au) 1903–1904	160.00	240.00
19 (190)	20	Mark (Au) 1903	220.00	300.00

COMMEMORATIVE MEDAL FOR THE VISIT OF THE KING TO THE MINT AT MULDNER HÜTTE ON 7th MAY 1903

		VF	XF
20	(–) (Ag) 1903. Head of the King to right. ℞ commemorative inscription	650.00	850.00

FRIEDRICH AUGUST III 1904–1918

COMMEMORATIVE ISSUES (2) FOR THE DEATH OF KING GEORG ON 15th OCTOBER 1904

21 (191)	2 Mark (Ag) 1904	30.00	55.00
22 (192)	5 Mark (Ag) 1904	120.00	200.00
23 (193)	2 Mark (Ag) 1905–1914	30.00	60.00
24 (194)	3 Mark (Ag) 1908–1913	12.00	22.00
25 (195)	5 Mark (Ag) 1907–1914	22.00	60.00
26 (196)	10 Mark (Au) 1905–1912	160.00	200.00

27 (197)	20 Mark (Au) 1905–1914	180.00	250.00

COMMEMORATIVE MEDAL FOR THE VISIT OF THE KING TO THE MINT AT MULDNER HÜTTE ON 6th APRIL 1905

28	(–) (Ag) 1905. Head of the King to right. ℞ commemorative inscription	650.00	850.00

COMMEMORATIVE ISSUES (2) FOR THE 5th CENTENARY OF LEIPZIG UNIVERSITY

29 (198)	2 Mark (Ag) 1909. Conjoined heads left of Crown Prince Friedrich the Pugnacious (1370–1428) and Friedrich August III	30.00	65.00
30 (199)	5 Mark (Ag) 1909	110.00	170.00

COMMEMORATIVE ISSUE FOR THE CENTENARY OF THE BATTLE OF LEIPZIG

		VF	XF
31 (200)	3 Mark (Ag) 1913. National battle monument at Leipzig	16.00	28.00

COMMEMORATIVE ISSUE FOR THE 4th CENTENARY OF THE REFORMATION

32 (201) 3 Mark (Ag) 1917. Bust right of Friedrich the Wise (1463–1525) with close-fitting cap and mantle; advocator of the imperial reform, protected Luther who taught at the University of Wittenberg which had been founded by the former in 1502, and granted him asylum at the Wartburg after the Reichstag at Worms 45000.00

Modern copies of No. 32 in the shape of Klippen are known to exist, as well as electrotypes.

Saxe-Altenburg (Duchy)

ERNST 1853–1908

			VF	XF
1 (146)	20 Mark (Au) 1887. Head right of Ernst (1826–1908). ℞ imperial eagle		1200.00	1600.00

COMMEMORATIVE ISSUES (2) FOR THE 75th BIRTHDAY OF THE DUKE ON 16th SEPTEMBER 1901

		VF	XF
2 (144)	2 Mark (Ag) 1901	250.00	400.00
3 (145)	5 Mark (Ag) 1901	450.00	580.00

COMMEMORATIVE ISSUE FOR THE 50th YEAR OF REIGN ON 3rd AUGUST 1903

4 (147)	5 Mark 1903	175.00	300.00

Saxe-Coburg and Gotha (Duchy)

ERNST II 1844–1893

		VF	XF
1 (148)	20 Mark (Au) 1872. Head left of Ernst II (1818–1893). ℞ imperial eagle	12000.00	15000.00
2 (148a)	20 Mark (Au) 1886	1100.00	1400.00

ALFRED 1893–1900

		VF	XF
3 (149)	2 Mark (Ag) 1895. Head right of Alfred (1844–1900). ℞ imperial eagle	300.00	700.00
4 (150)	5 Mark (Ag) 1895	1300.00	2000.00
5 (151)	20 Mark (Au) 1895	1400.00	2200.00

CARL EDUARD 1900–1918

		VF	XF
6 (152)	2 Mark (Ag)		
	a) 1905	280.00	500.00
	b) 1911	4000.00	5500.00

7 (153) 5 Mark (Ag) 1907   620.00   1000.00
8 (154) 10 Mark (Au) 1905   850.00   1400.00

9 (155) 20 Mark (Au) 1905   1050.00   1400.00

Saxe-Meiningen (Duchy)

GEORG II 1866–1914

1 (156) 20 Mark (Au) 1872. Head right of
Georg II (1826–1914). ℞ imperial
eagle   7000.00   10000.00
2 (156a) 20 Mark (Au) 1882   5000.00   6600.00
3 (158) 20 Mark (Au) 1889   4000.00   6800.00

COMMEMORATIVE ISSUES (2) FOR THE 75th BIRTHDAY OF THE DUKE

4 (159) 2 Mark (Ag) 1901   170.00   300.00
5 (160) 5 Mark (Ag) 1901   180.00   320.00
6 (157) 10 Mark (Au) 1890–1898   2000.00   3200.00
7 (158a) 20 Mark (Au) 1900–1905   5000.00   7000.00
8 (161) 2 Mark (Ag) 1902–1913   160.00   300.00
9 (162) 3 Mark (Ag) 1908–1913   70.00   125.00
10 (163) 5 Mark (Ag) 1902–1908   130.00   250.00

11 (164) 10 Mark (Au) 1902–1914   2000.00   3000.00
12 (165) 20 Mark (Au) 1910–1914   5000.00   6600.00

BERNHARD III 1914–1918
COMMEMORATIVE ISSUES (2) FOR THE FIRST ANNIVERSARY OF THE DEATH OF DUKE GEORG II ON 25th JUNE 1915

		VF	XF
13 (166)	2 Mark (Ag) 1915	90.00	140.00
14 (167)	3 Mark (Ag) 1915	95.00	145.00

Saxe-Weimar (Grand Duchy)

CARL ALEXANDER 1853–1901
COMMEMORATIVE ISSUES (2) FOR THE GOLDEN WEDDING

1 (168)	2 Mark (Ag) 1892. Head left of Carl Alexander (1818–1901). ℞ imperial eagle	140.00	300.00
2 (169)	20 Mark (Au) 1892. Type as No. 1	1300.00	2000.00
3 (169)	20 Mark (Au) 1896. Type as No. 2	1100.00	1500.00

COMMEMORATIVE ISSUE FOR THE 80th BIRTHDAY OF THE GRAND DUKE ON 24th JUNE 1898

4 (168)	2 Mark (Ag) 1898	140.00	250.00

WILHELM ERNST 1901–1918

5 (170)	2 Mark (Ag) 1901	210.00	380.00

6 (171)	20 Mark (Au) 1901	1400.00	2500.00

COMMEMORATIVE ISSUES (2) FOR THE FIRST MARRIAGE ON 30th APRIL 1903

		VF	XF
7 (172)	2 Mark (Ag) 1903. Conjoined heads left of Wilhelm Ernst and the Grand Duchess Caroline	52.00	100.00
8 (173)	5 Mark (Ag) 1903	110.00	200.00

COMMEMORATIVE ISSUES (2) FOR 350 YEARS OF THE UNIVERSITY OF JENA

9 (174)	2 Mark (Ag) 1908. Bust facing of Johann Friedrich I the Magnanimous (1503–1554), founder of the University of Jena in 1547 which was ratified by Emperor Ferdinand I in 1558	52.00	100.00
10 (175)	5 Mark (Ag) 1908	110.00	200.00

COMMEMORATIVE ISSUE FOR THE SECOND MARRIAGE OF WILHELM ERNST ON 4th JANUARY 1910

11 (176)	3 Mark (Ag) 1910. Conjoined heads left of Wilhelm Ernst and the Grand Duchess Feodora	40.00	60.00

COMMEMORATIVE ISSUE FOR THE CENTENARY OF THE GRAND DUCHY

12 (177)	3 Mark (Ag) 1915. Conjoined busts right of Wilhelm Ernst and Carl August (1757–1828), Duke until his coming of age in 1758 under his mother, Duchess Anna Amalia, also his guardian; he called Goethe and Herder to Weimar, and also Schiller to Jena	90.00	150.00

Schaumburg-Lippe (Principality)

ADOLF GEORG 1860–1893

			VF	XF
1 (202)	20 Mark (Au) 1874. Head left of Adolf Georg (1817–1893). ℞ imperial eagle		5500.00	9000.00

GEORG 1893–1911

2 (203)	2 Mark (Ag) 1898–1904	320.00	550.00
3 (204)	5 Mark (Ag) 1898–1904	800.00	1300.00
4 (205)	20 Mark (Au) 1898–1904	1350.00	1800.00

COMMEMORATIVE ISSUE FOR THE DEATH OF THE PRINCE

5 (206)	3 Mark (Ag) 1911	75.00	125.00

Schwarzburg-Rudolstadt (Principality)

GÜNTHER VIKTOR 1890–1918

1 (207)	2 Mark (Ag) 1898. Head left of Günther Viktor. ℞ imperial eagle	180.00	350.00

2 (208)	10 Mark (Au) 1898	1200.00	1800.00

Schwarzburg-Sondershausen (Principality)

KARL GÜNTHER 1880–1909

1 (209)	2 Mark (Ag) 1896. Head right of Karl Günther (1830–1909). ℞ imperial eagle	270.00	400.00
2 (210)	20 Mark (Au) 1896	1500.00	2000.00

COMMEMORATIVE ISSUE FOR THE 25th YEAR OF REIGN ON 17th JULY 1905

3 (211)	2 Mark (Ag) 1905. Head of the Prince to right; laurel branch.		
	a) thin rim	45.00	80.00
	b) wide rim	115.00	170.00

COMMEMORATIVE ISSUE FOR THE DEATH OF THE PRINCE ON 28th MARCH 1909

4 (212)	3 Mark (Ag) 1909	60.00	115.00

Waldeck and Pyrmont (Principality)

FRIEDRICH ADOLPH 1893–1918

		VF	XF
1 (213)	5 Mark (Ag) 1903	1300.00	1900.00

2 (214)	20 Mark (Au) 1903	2100.00	2500.00

Württemberg (Kingdom)

KARL 1864–1891

		VF	XF
1 (218)	10 Mark (Au) 1872–1873. Head right of Karl (1823–1891). ℞ imperial eagle	130.00	280.00
2 (219)	20 Mark (Au) 1872–1873	135.00	300.00
3 (215)	2 Mark (Ag) 1876–1888	80.00	400.00
4 (216)	5 Mark (Ag) 1874–1888	55.00	400.00
5 (217)	5 Mark (Au) 1877–1878	280.00	360.00
6 (218a)	10 Mark (Au) 1874–1888	140.00	200.00
7 (219a)	20 Mark (Au) 1874–1876	200.00	300.00
8 (218b)	10 Mark (Au) 1890–1891	180.00	280.00

WILHELM II 1891–1918

		VF	XF
9 (220)	2 Mark (Ag) 1892–1914	18.00	40.00
10 (221)	3 Mark (Ag) 1908–1914	11.00	20.00
11 (222)	5 Mark (Ag) 1892–1913	25.00	40.00

12 (223)	10 Mark (Au) 1893–1913	140.00	180.00
13 (224)	20 Mark (Au) 1894–1914	150.00	200.00

			VF	XF
14 (225)		3 Mark (Ag) 1911		
		a) normal H in Charlotte	20.00	38.00
		b) the bar of the H is placed higher than normal	265.00	480.00

COMMEMORATIVE ISSUE FOR THE 25th YEAR OF REIGN

15 (226)		3 Mark (Ag) 1916	2000.00	3500.00

Of No. 15 electrotypes are also on the market.

German Empire

Small-denomination coins were also in general circulation throughout the Empire.

			VF	XF
1 (1)		1 Pfennig (Cu) 1873–1889. Imperial eagle. ℞ value	3.50	12.00
2 (2)		2 Pfennig (Cu) 1873–1877. Type as No. 1	2.00	14.00
3 (5)		5 Pfennig (Cu-Ni) 1874–1889. Type as No. 1	1.60	9.00
4 (6)		10 Pfennig (Cu-Ni) 1873–1889. Type as No. 1	2.00	9.00
5 (12)		20 Pfennig (Ag) 1873–1877. Type as No. 1	6.00	15.00
6 (13)		50 Pfennig (Ag) 1875–1877. Type as No. 1	16.00	28.00
7 (17)		1 Mark (Ag) 1873–1887	4.00	18.00
8 (7)		20 Pfennig (Cu-Ni) 1887–1888	14.00	30.00
9 (14)		50 Pfennig (Ag) 1877–1878	32.00	75.00

10 (3)		1 Pfennig (Cu) 1890–1916. Large		

		VF	XF
	imperial eagle with small breast-shield	0.40	1.30
11 (4)	2 Pfennig (Cu) 1904–1908, 1910–1916. Large imperial eagle with small breast-shield	0.40	1.30
12 (8)	5 Pfennig (Cu-Ni) 1890–1915. Large imperial eagle with small breast-shield	0.40	0.80
13 (9)	10 Pfennig (Cu-Ni) 1890–1894, 1896–1916. Large imperial eagle with small breast-shield	0.30	0.80
14 (10)	20 Pfennig (Cu-Ni) 1890, 1892. Large imperial eagle with small breast-shield within oak wreath. ℞ value in large figures	25.00	55.00

| **15** (11) | 25 Pfennig (Ni) 1909–1912 | 5.00 | 12.00 |

| **16** (15) | 50 Pfennig (Ag) 1896, 1898, 1900–1903. Large imperial eagle with small breast-shield within oak wreath | 145.00 | 300.00 |
| **17** (16) | ½ Mark (Ag) 1905–1909, 1911–1919. | 2.50 | 3.20 |

| **18** (18) | 1 Mark (Ag) 1891–1894, 1896, 1898–1916. Large imperial eagle with small breast-shield. ℞ value within oak wreath | 4.00 | 6.00 |

In the years 1916–1924 various states, municipalities and provinces issued numerous emergency coins (Notgeld) of very pleasing and widely varied design and finish. An exhaustive study of this very popular sideline of numismatics must, however, remain outside the scope of this catalogue. There is a special catalogue by Funck entitled »Die Notmünzen der deutschen Städte, Gemeinden, Kreise, Länder etc.« (The Emergency Issues of the German States, Minicipalities, Districts and Provinces etc.)

			VF	XF
19 (19)	1	Pfennig (Al) 1916–1918. Small imperial eagle with large breast-shield		
			0.40	0.80
20 (21)	5	Pfennig (Fe) 1915–1922. Large imperial eagle with small breast-shield. ℞ date below denomination	0.30	0.80
21 (22)	10	Pfennig (Fe) 1915–1918, 1921–1922. Large imperial eagle with small breast-shield within dotted circle. ℞ date below denomination. The 1915 issue is a pattern	0.40	1.10
22 (22a)	10	Pfennig (Zi) 1917. Imperial eagle within dotted circle. ℞ date below denomination	120.00	185.00
23 (22.1)	10	Pfennig (Zi) 1917–1922. Imperial eagle similar to No. 13, but without mark of value. ℞ date below denomination	0.40	0.80

WEIMAR REPUBLIC 1919–1933

24 (26)	50	Pfennig (Al) 1919–1922. Wheat sheaf with legend in 2 lines. ℞ value	0.40	0.80

25 (28)	3	Mark (Al) 1922–1923. Imperial eagle with legend VERFAS-SUNGSTAG 11. AUGUST 1922 (date of promulgation of the Weimar Constitution). ℞ value	1.20	2.50
26 (29)	3	Mark (Al) 1922. Imperial eagle. ℞ value	5.00	15.00
27 (30)	200	Mark (Al) 1923	0.60	1.30
28 (31)	500	Mark (Al) 1923	0.80	1.60
29 (32)	1	Rentenpfennig (Br) 1923–1925, 1929. Sheaf between date. ℞ value in large figures within circle		

		VF	XF
	a) 1923, 1924	1.10	4.00
	b) 1925, 1929	260.00	400.00

In the case of No. 29b, these are errors in striking.

30 (33)	2 Rentenpfennig (Br) 1923–1924. Type as No. 29	1.30	4.00
31 (34)	5 Rentenpfennig (Al-Br) 1923–1924. Crossed ears of corn. ℞ value within square surrounded by oak leaves	0.65	2.50
32 (35)	10 Rentenpfennig (Al-Br) 1923–1925. Type as No. 31:		
	a) 1923–1924	1.10	4.00
	b) 1925, mis-strike	420.00	700.00
33 (36)	50 Rentenpfennig (Al-Br) 1923–1924. Type as No. 31	13.00	26.00

100 Reichspfennig = 1 Reichsmark

34 (37)	1 Reichspfennig (Br) 1924–1925, 1927–1936. Sheaf between date. ℞ value in large figures within circle	0.40	1.30
35 (38)	2 Reichspfennig (Br) 1923–1925, 1936. Type as No. 34		
	a) 1923	550.00	1300.00
	b) 1924, 1925, 1936	0.80	2.50

36 (39)	4 Reichspfennig (Cu) 1932. Imperial eagle. ℞ value in large figures within circle	7.00	12.50
37 (40)	5 Reichspfennig (Al-Br) 1924–1926, 1930, 1935, 1936. Crossed ears of corn. ℞ value within square surrounded by oak leaves	0.60	2.00
38 (41)	10 Reichspfennig (Al-Br) 1924–1926, 1928–1936. Type as No. 37	1.20	4.80
39 (42)	50 Reichspfennig (Al-Br) 1924–1925. Type as No. 37	650.00	1100.00
40 (43)	50 Reichspfennig (Ni) 1927–1933, 1935–1938. Imperial eagle within circle. ℞ value in large figures	2.40	4.80
41 (44)	1 Mark (Ag) 1924–1925. Imperial eagle. ℞ value	11.00	22.00
42 (47)	3 Mark (Ag) 1924–1925. Imperial eagle. ℞ value	38.00	75.00

				VF	XF

43 (45)   1 R-Mark (Ag) 1925–1927. Imperial eagle, legend DEUTSCHES REICH and date. ℞ value within oak wreath   12.50   28.00

44 (46)   2 R-Mark (Ag) 1925–1927, 1931. Imperial eagle. ℞ value within oak wreath   13.50   36.00

45 (49)   5 R-Mark (Ag) 1927–1933. Oak tree. ℞ imperial eagle and value   52.00   90.00

COMMEMORATIVE ISSUES (2) FOR THE THOUSANDTH YEAR OF THE RHINELAND

46 (50)   3 R-Mark (Ag) 1925. Knight with right arm raised in oath, holding shield on which imperial eagle. ℞ value within oak wreath   28.00   48.00

47 (51)   5 R-Mark (Ag) 1925   65.00   125.00

COMMEMORATIVE ISSUE FOR THE 700th YEAR OF THE GRANTING OF IMPERIAL FREEDOM TO LÜBECK

48 (52)   3 R-Mark (Ag) 1926. On a Gothic shield, the double eagle of Lübeck with divided breast-shield. Commemorative legend. ℞ value   115.00   180.00

COMMEMORATIVE ISSUES (2) FOR THE HUNDREDTH ANNIVERSARY OF BREMERHAVEN

				VF	XF
49 (53)		3 R-Mark (Ag) 1927. Three-master and arms of Bremen. ℞ eagle on shield, eight-sided scrollwork in background		130.00	200.00
50 (54)		5 R-Mark (Ag) 1927		375.00	550.00

COMMEMORATIVE ISSUE FOR THE THOUSANDTH ANNIVERSARY OF THE FOUNDING OF NORDHAUSEN

51 (55)	3 R-Mark (Ag) 1927. The Emperor Heinrich I (876–936), reigned 919–936, and his wife Mathilde, great granddaughter of Widukind	125.00	185.00

COMMEMORATIVE ISSUES (2) FOR THE 450th ANNIVERSARY OF THE UNIVERSITY OF TÜBINGEN

		VF	XF
52 (57)	3 R-Mark (Ag) 1927. Count Eberhard The Bearded (1445–1496); he founded the University of Tübingen in 1477 and endowed it with a library. ℞ imperial eagle	300.00	500.00
53 (58)	5 R-Mark (Ag) 1927	320.00	550.00

COMMEMORATIVE ISSUE FOR THE 400th ANNIVERSARY OF THE PHILIP UNIVERSITY IN MARBURG

54 (56)	3 R-Mark (Ag) 1927. Arms of Philip I the Magnanimous (1504–1567), Landgrave of Hessen; in 1527 he founded the university in his home town. On the centre shield, the Hessian lion. ℞ imperial eagle	110.00	160.00

COMMEMORATIVE ISSUE FOR THE 400th ANNIVERSARY OF THE DEATH OF ALBRECHT DÜRER

55 (59)	3 R-Mark (Ag) 1928. Bust left of Albrecht Dürer (1471–1528), painter, engraver and writer on art subjects. ℞ imperial eagle	285.00	500.00

COMMEMORATIVE ISSUE FOR THE 900th ANNIVERSARY OF THE FOUNDING OF NAUMBURG/SAALE

		VF	XF
56 (60)	3 R-Mark (Ag) 1928. Margrave Hermann, founder of the city, holding shield with the arms of Naumburg. ℞ imperial eagle	120.00	180.00

COMMEMORATIVE ISSUE FOR THE THOUSANDTH ANNIVERSARY OF THE FOUNDING OF DINKELSBÜHL

57 (61)	3 R-Mark (Ag) 1928. Half figure holding sickle and sheaf of wheat between two towers; below, arms of Dinkelsbühl. ℞ imperial eagle	460.00	750.00

COMMEMORATIVE ISSUES (2) FOR THE 200th ANNIVERSARY OF THE BIRTH OF LESSING

58 (62)	3 R-Mark (Ag) 1929. Gotthold Ephraim Lessing (1729–1781), poet. ℞ imperial eagle	40.00	70.00
59 (63)	5 R-Mark (Ag) 1929	80.00	145.00

COMMEMORATIVE ISSUE FOR THE UNION OF WALDECK WITH PRUSSIA

60 (64)   3 R-Mark (Ag) 1929. Prussian eagle with arms of Waldeck. ℞ imperial eagle

VF   **XF**

115.00   185.00

COMMEMORATIVE ISSUES (2) FOR THE THOUSANDTH ANNIVERSARY OF THE CASTLE AND CITY OF MEISSEN

61 (67)   3 R-Mark (Ag) 1929. Armed figure holding the triangular shields of the Margrave and of the Burgrave of Meissen. ℞ imperial eagle   50.00   80.00

62 (68)   5 R-Mark (Ag) 1929   350.00   520.00

COMMEMORATIVE ISSUES (2) FOR THE 10th ANNIVERSARY OF THE WEIMAR CONSTITUTION

63 (65)   3 R-Mark (Ag) 1929. Hand raised in

oath. ℞ Paul von Beneckendorff
und von Hindenburg (1847–1934),
President of the German Reich
from 1925–1934

		VF	XF
		25.00	40.00
64 (66)	5 R-Mark (Ag) 1929	85.00	150.00

COMMEMORATIVE ISSUES (2) FOR THE ROUND-THE-WORLD FLIGHT OF THE AIRSHIP "GRAF ZEPPELIN" IN 1929

65 (69)	3 R-Mark (Ag) 1930. The airship in front of globe. ℞ imperial eagle	52.00	95.00
66 (70)	5 R-Mark (Ag) 1930	125.00	200.00

COMMEMORATIVE ISSUE FOR THE 700th ANNIVERSARY OF THE DEATH OF VON DER VOGELWEIDE

67 (71)	3 R-Mark (Ag) 1930. Walther von der Vogelweide (c. 1170–1230), minnesinger. ℞ eagle on shield on three-sided scrolled background	60.00	100.00

COMMEMORATIVE ISSUES (2) FOR THE EVACUATION OF THE RHINELAND BY THE ALLIES IN 1930

			VF	XF
68 (72)	3 R-Mark (Ag) 1930. Eagle standing on bridge. ℞ eagle on shield on three-sided scrolled background		30.00	50.00
69 (73)	5 R-Mark (Ag) 1930		125.00	185.00

COMMEMORATIVE ISSUE FOR THE 300th ANNIVERSARY OF THE BURNING OF MAGDEBURG

70 (74)	3 R-Mark (Ag) 1931. Arms of the city over view of the old city. ℞ eagle on shield on eight-sided scrolled background	150.00	255.00

COMMEMORATIVE ISSUE FOR THE CENTENARY OF THE DEATH OF VON STEIN

71 (75)	3 R-Mark (Ag) 1931. Karl Reichsfreiherr vom und zum Stein (1757–1831), statesman. ℞ imperial eagle	130.00	190.00

			VF	XF
72 (48)	3 R-Mark 1931–1933. Imperial eagle, legend DEUTSCHES REICH and date. ℞ value within oak wreath:			
	a) 1931–1932		210.00	360.00
	b) 1933		1300.00	1850.00

COMMEMORATIVE ISSUES (2) FOR THE CENTENARY OF THE DEATH OF GOETHE

		VF	XF
73 (76)	3 R-Mark (Ag) 1932. Johann Wolfgang von Goethe (1749–1832), poet and writer.	65.00	110.00
74 (77)	5 R-Mark (Ag) 1932	1800.00	2500.00

THIRD REICH 1933–1945

COMMEMORATIVE ISSUES (2) FOR THE 450th ANNIVERSARY OF THE BIRTH OF MARTIN LUTHER

		VF	XF
75 (78)	2 R-Mark (Ag) 1933. Head left of Dr. Martin Luther (1483–1546), reformer. ℞ imperial eagle. Edge inscription: EIN FESTE BURG IST UNSER GOTT (a mighty fortress is our God) and date.	13.00	25.00

76 (79) 5 R-Mark (Ag) 1933. Type as No. 75   80.00   125.00

77 (81) 1 R-Mark (Ni) 1933–1939. Imperial
eagle. ℞ value within oak wreath   2.00   4.00

COMMEMORATIVE ISSUES (2) FOR THE FIRST ANNIVERSARY OF THE OPENING OF THE REICHSTAG

78 (83) 2 R-Mark (Ag) 1934. Potsdam Military Church and date 21 March
1933. ℞ imperial eagle, edge inscription: GEMEINNUTZ GEHT
VOR EIGENNUTZ (the common
good comes before personal interest)   8.00   24.00

79 (84) 5 R-Mark (Ag) 1934. Type as No. 78   11.00   32.00
80 (85) 5 R-Mark (Ag) 1934–1935. Type as
No. 79, but no date   7.00   13.00

COMMEMORATIVE ISSUES (2) FOR THE 175th ANNIVERSARY OF THE BIRTH OF FRIEDRICH VON SCHILLER

81 (86) 2 R-Mark (Ag) 1934. Head of Friedrich von Schiller (1759–1805),
poet. ℞ imperial eagle, edge inscription: ANS VATERLAND
ANS TEURE SCHLIESS DICH
AN (cling to the fatherland, the
precious fatherland)   35.00   60.00

			VF	XF
82 (87)	5	R-Mark (Ag) 1934. Type as No. 81	130.00	265.00

83 (82)	5	R-Mark (Ag) 1935–1936. Head right of Paul von Beneckendorff und von Hindenburg. ℞ imperial eagle	6.00	12.50
84 (88)	1	Reichspfennig (Br) 1936–1940. Imperial eagle with swastika	0.40	1.20
85 (89)	2	Reichspfennig (Br) 1936–1940. Imperial eagle with swastika	0.60	2.00
86 (90)	5	Reichspfennig (Al-Br) 1936–1939. Imperial eagle with swastika	0.50	1.30
87 (91)	10	Reichspfennig (Al-Br) 1936–1939. Imperial eagle with swastika	0.70	1.60

88 (93)	50	Reichspfennig (Ni) 1938–1939. Imperial eagle with swastika within circle. ℞ value in large figures within circle	26.00	48.00
89 (96)	2	R-Mark (Ag) 1936–1939. Paul von Beneckendorff und von Hindenburg, head r. ℞ imperial eagle with swastika	3.00	6.50
90 (97)	5	R-Mark (Ag) 1936–1939. Type as No. 89	6.00	12.00

			VF	XF
91 (A 92)	1	Reichspfennig (Zi) 1940–1945. Imperial eagle with swastika. R value	0.40	0.80
92 (B 92)	5	Reichspfennig (Zi) 1940–1944	0.50	1.20
93 (C 92)	10	Reichspfennig (Zi) 1940–1945	0.50	1.20

94 (80)	50	Reichspfennig (Al) (issued 1939) 1935. Imperial eagle. R value. This coin was only put into circulation in 1939	1.10	4.00
95 (92)	50	Reichspfennig (Al) 1939–1944. Type as No. 94, but imperial eagle with swastika	0.80	3.00

ALLIED OCCUPATION 1945–1948

96 (98)	1	Reichspfennig (Zi) 1944–1946. Eagle R value.		
		a) (issued 1945) 1944. Imperial eagle (swastika omitted); only with mintmark D for Munich	–.–	–.–
		b) 1945–1946. New style imperial eagle (without swastika)	12.00	25.00
97 (99)	5	Reichspfennig (Zi) 1947–1948	5.00	12.00

98 (100)	10	Reichspfennig (Zi)	4.00	11.00

		VF	XF
a) 1945–1948			
b) 1947 with "slavonic cross-line" (little line crossing the stem of the seven)		1300.00	1800.00

BANK DEUTSCHER LÄNDER

99 (101)	1 Pfennig (Bronze-clad steel) 1948–1949. Oak twig. ℞ value	0.40	4.00
100 (102)	5 Pfennig (Brass-clad steel) 1949	0.60	4.00

101 (103)	10 Pfennig (Brass-clad steel) 1949	0.40	4.00

102 (104) 50 Pfennig (Cu-Ni) 1949–1950. Girl holding sapling

a) 1949	2.50	15.00
b) 1950	125.00	250.00

No. 102b is available only with the G mintmark and is often a forgery.

Federal Republic of Germany

		XF	Unc
103 (105)	1 Pfennig (Bronze-clad steel) 1950–	0.05	0.10
104 (106)	2 Pfennig		
	a) (Br) 1950–1968	0.15	0.25
	b) (Bronze-clad steel) 1968–	0.05	0.10
105 (107)	5 Pfennig (Brass-clad steel) 1950–	0.05	0.10
106 (108)	10 Pfennig (Brass-clad steel) 1950–	0.05	0.10

		XF	Unc
107 (109)	50 Pfennig (Cu-Ni) 1950-:		
	a) 1950, 1966-1971; reeded edge	0.25	0.40
	b) 1972 -; plain edge	0.20	0.30

108 (110)	1 D-Mark (Cu-Ni) 1950–	0.40	0.60

109 (111)	2 D-Mark (Cu-Ni) 1951. Value between wheat ears, grapes and vine leaves	22.00	45.00

110 (112)	5 D-Mark (Ag) 1951–1974. On the edge, legend reading:		
	a) EINIGKEIT UND RECHT UND FREIHEIT (Unity and Right and Freedom)	3.20	4.00
	b) GRÜSS DICH DEUTSCHLAND AUS HERZENSGRUND (Greetings to Germany with deepest feelings) (1957 J)	1200.00	1800.00

COMMEMORATIVE ISSUE FOR THE CENTENARY OF THE GERMAN NATIONAL MUSEUM IN NÜRNBERG

111 (113) 5 D-Mark (Ag) 1952. Representation of an Ostro-Gothic fibula in the form of an eagle from North Italy, gold cloisonné work dating from the 5th century A. D. Length 4.7 inches. Now in the German National Museum

	XF	Unc
	600.00	780.00

COMMEMORATIVE ISSUE FOR THE 150th ANNIVERSARY OF THE DEATH OF FRIEDRICH VON SCHILLER

112 (114) 5 D-Mark (Ag) 1955. Head right of Friedrich von Schiller (1759–1805), poet. Edge inscription: SEID EINIG EINIG EINIG (Be united, united, united)

480.00	650.00

COMMEMORATIVE ISSUE FOR THE 300th ANNIVERSARY OF THE BIRTH OF THE MARGRAVE VON BADEN

				XF	Unc
113 (115)	5 D-Mark (Ag) 1955. Bust right of Ludwig Wilhelm I von Baden (1655–1707), Margrave since 1677, Imperial Field-Marshal, won the battle over the Turks at Novi Slankamen in 1691; known as the Turkish Louis			420.00	600.00

COMMEMORATIVE ISSUE FOR THE CENTENARY OF THE DEATH OF EICHENDORFF

114 (116)	5 D-Mark (Ag) 1957. Head left of Joseph Freiherr von Eichendorff (1788–1857), poet	380.00	600.00

115 (117)	2 D-Mark (Cu–Ni) 1957–1971. Head left of Max Planck (1858–1947), physicist, creator of the Quantum Theory, Nobel prize winner in 1918	1.00	1.40

COMMEMORATIVE ISSUE FOR THE 150th ANNIVERSARY
OF THE DEATH OF FICHTE

		XF	Unc
116 (118)	5 D-Mark (Ag) 1964. Head left of Johann Gottlieb Fichte (1762–1814), philosopher	140.00	200.00

COMMEMORATIVE ISSUE FOR THE 250th ANNIVERSARY
OF THE DEATH OF LEIBNIZ

| **117** (119) | 5 D-Mark (Ag) 1966. Gottfried Wilhelm Leibniz (1646–1716), philosopher and savant | 28.00 | 40.00 |

COMMEMORATIVE ISSUE FOR WILHELM AND ALEXANDER
VON HUMBOLDT

| **118** (120) | 5 D-Mark (Ag) 1967. Heads of Wilhelm von Humboldt (1767–1835), statesman and philologist, and Alexander von Humboldt (1769–1859), natural philosopher | 32.00 | 40.00 |

COMMEMORATIVE ISSUE FOR THE 150th ANNIVERSARY OF THE BIRTH OF RAIFFEISEN

			XF	Unc
119 (121)	5	D-Mark (Ag) 1968. Bust facing of Friedrich Wilhelm Raiffeisen (1818–1888), society founder and social reformer	7.00	11.00

COMMEMORATIVE ISSUE FOR THE 500th ANNIVERSARY OF THE DEATH OF GUTENBERG

120 (122)	5	D-Mark (Ag) 1968. Bust to r. of Johannes Gutenberg, actually Gensfleisch (c.1400–1468), he introduced printing with movable letters	12.00	16.00

COMMEMORATIVE ISSUE FOR THE 150th ANNIVERSARY OF THE BIRTH OF PETTENKOFER

121 (123)	5	D-Mark (Ag) 1968. Bust l. of Max von Pettenkofer (1818–1901), hygienist and natural scientist	8.00	11.00

COMMEMORATIVE ISSUE FOR THE 150th ANNIVERSARY OF THE BIRTH OF THEODOR FONTANE

			XF	Unc
122 (124)	5 D-Mark (Ag) 1969. Bust l. of Theodor Fontane (1819–1898), writer and poet		12.00	18.00

COMMEMORATIVE ISSUE FOR THE 375th ANNIVERSARY OF THE DEATH OF GERHARD MERCATOR

123 (125) 5 D-Mark (Ag) 1969. Bust facing of Gerhard Mercator, actually Kremer (1512–1594), cartographer and geographer, in front of a map projection; on the orders of Emperor Charles V he made a terrestrial globe and a celestial globe
a) on the edge: TERRAE DESCRIPTIO AD USUM NAVIGANTIUM (description of the earth for the use of navigators) .... 6.50 ... 8.00
b) on the edge: EINIGKEIT UND RECHT UND FREIHEIT (Unity and Right and Freedom) ... –.– ... 800.00
c) no inscription on edge ... –.– ... –.–

124 (A 117) 2 D-Mark (Cu–Ni) 1969–. Head left
of Dr. Konrad Adenauer (1876–
1967), first German Federal Chancellor

	XF	Unc
	1.10	1.40

125 (B 117) 2 D-Mark (Cu–Ni) 1970–. Head left
of Prof. Dr. Theodor Heuss (1884–
1963), first German Federal President

1.10	1.40

COMMEMORATIVE ISSUE FOR THE 200th ANNIVERSARY OF THE BIRTH OF LUDWIG VAN BEETHOVEN

126 (131) 5 D-Mark (Ag) 1970. Head left of
Ludwig van Beethoven (1770–
1827), composer

6.50	8.00

COMMEMORATIVE ISSUE FOR THE FOUNDATION OF THE REICH ON 18th JANUARY 1871

		XF	Unc
127 (132)	5 D-Mark (Ag) 1971. Reichstag building in Berlin	6.50	8.00

COMMEMORATIVE ISSUE FOR THE 500th ANNIVERSARY OF THE BIRTH OF ALBRECHT DÜRER

128 (133)	5 D-Mark (Ag) 1971. Monogram of Albrecht Dürer (1471 – 1528), painter, engraver and writer on art subjects	6.00	7.50

COMMEMORATIVE ISSUES (6)
FOR THE 1972 OLYMPIC GAMES HELD IN MUNICH
(26th August to 11th September 1972)

129 (126)	10 D-Mark (Ag) 1972. Spiral of rays (Emblem of the 1972 Olympic Games)	8.50	12.00

			XF	Unc
130 (127)	10	D-Mark (Ag) 1972. Entwined arms in front of a fan-like background as a symbolical representation of the Olympic theme	7.00	8.00

131 (128)	10	D-Mark (Ag) 1972. Delicately drawn group of a youth and a girl	7.00	8.00

132 (129)	10	D-Mark (Ag) 1972. Representation of buildings put up for the Olympic Games in Munich	7.00	8.00
133 (126a)	10	D-Mark (Ag) 1972. Type as No. 129, but inscription SPIELE DER XX. OLYMPIADE 1972 IN MÜNCHEN	7.50	9.00
134 (130)	10	D-Mark (Ag) 1972. Olympic flame, spiral of rays and 5 interlocking rings	7.00	8.00

COMMEMORATIVE ISSUE FOR THE 500th BIRTHDAY OF NIKOLAUS COPERNICUS (1473–1543)

		XF	Unc
135 (134)	5 D-Mark (Ag) 1973. Representation of the fundamental idea of the Copernican Theory, the Earth and other planets revolving around the central celestial body, the Sun	5.50	6.50

COMMEMORATIVE ISSUE FOR THE 125th RETURN OF THE MEETING OF THE FRANKFURT NATIONAL ASSEMBLY IN THE CHURCH OF PAUL

136 (135)	5 D-Mark (Ag) 1973. Considerably simplified representation of the interior of the Church of Paul, in the centre the year 1848; inscription FRANKFURTER NATIO-NALVERSAMMLUNG	5.50	6.50

COMMEMORATIVE ISSUE FOR THE 25th ANNIVERSARY OF THE CONSTITUTIONAL LAW

137 (136)	5 D-Mark (Ag) 1974	5.50	6.50

COMMEMORATIVE ISSUE FOR THE 250th BIRTHDAY OF IMMANUEL KANT

138 (137)	5 D-Mark (Ag) 1974. Immanuel Kant (1724–1804), philosopher	5.50	6.50

COMMEMORATIVE ISSUE FOR THE 50th ANNIVERSARY
OF THE DEATH OF FRIEDRICH EBERT

			XF	Unc
139 (138)	5 D-Mark (Ag) 1975. Friedrich Ebert (1871–1925), President of the German Reich from 1919 to 1925		5.00	6.00

140 (139)	5 D-Mark (Cu–Ni) 1975-. Federal eagle, year date, mintmark. ℞ name of country, denomination		2.50	3.00

COMMEMORATIVE ISSUE FOR THE CENTENARY OF BIRTH
OF ALBERT SCHWEITZER

141 (141)	5 D-Mark (Ag) 1975. Albert Schweitzer (1875-1965), philosopher and Doctor of Medicine		5.00	6.00

EUROPEAN MONUMENT PROTECTION YEAR 1975

	XF	Unc
142 (140) 5 D-Mark (Ag) 1975	5.00	6.00

300th ANNIVERSARY OF THE DEATH OF HANS JACOB CHRISTOPH VON GRIMMELSHAUSEN

143 (142) 5 D-Mark (Ag) 1976. Hans Jacob Christoph von Grimmelshausen (1621–1676), poet; his best known work is »Der abenteuerliche Simplicissimus Teutsch«   5.00   6.00

200th ANNIVERSARY OF THE BIRTH OF CARL FRIEDRICH GAUSS

144 (143) 5 D-Mark (Ag) 1977. Carl Friedrich Gauss (1777-1855), mathematician and astronomer   5.00   6.00

200th ANNIVERSARY OF THE BIRTH OF HEINRICH VON KLEIST

	XF	Unc
145 (144) 5 D-Mark (Ag) 1977. Heinrich von Kleist (1777-1811), poet	5.00	6.00

100th ANNIVERSARY OF THE BIRTH OF GUSTAV STRESEMANN

146 (145) 5 D-Mark (Ag) 1978. Gustav Stresemann (1878-1929), politician and Nobel Prize winner for peace	5.00	6.00

225th ANNIVERSARY OF THE DEATH OF BALTHASAR NEUMANN

147 (146) 5 D-Mark (Ag) 1978. Balthasar Neumann (1687-1753), architect	5.00	6.00
148 (148) 2 D-Mark (Cu-Ni) 1979-. Dr. Kurt Schumacher (1895-1952), politician	1.10	1.40

150th ANNIVERSARY OF GERMAN ARCHEOLOGICAL INSTITUTE

		XF	Unc
149 (147)	5 D-Mark (Ag) 1979	5.00	6.00

100th ANNIVERSARY OF THE BIRTH OF OTTO HAHN

150 (149)	5 D-Mark (Cu-Ni) 1979	5.00	6.00

750th ANNIVERSARY OF THE DEATH OF WALTHER VON DER VOGELWEIDE

151 (150)	5 D-Mark (Cu-Ni) 1980. Walther von der Vogelweide (c. 1170–1230), minnesinger	5.00	6.00

100th ANNIVERSARY OF COLOGNE CATHEDRAL

		XF	Unc
152 (151)	5 D-Mark (Cu-Ni) 1980. Cologne cathedral	4.00	5.00

200th ANNIVERSARY OF THE DEATH OF G.E. LESSING

| **153** (152) | 5 D-Mark (Cu-Ni) 1981. Gotthold Ephraim Lessing (1729–1781), poet | 4.00 | 5.00 |

150th ANNIVERSARY OF THE DEATH OF VON STEIN

| **154** (153) | 5 D-Mark (Cu-Ni) 1981. Carl Reichsfreiherr vom und zum Stein (1757–1831), statesman | 4.00 | 5.00 |

150th ANNIVERSARY OF THE DEATH OF GOETHE

| **155** (154) | 5 D-Mark (Cu-Ni) 1982. Johann Wolfgang von Goethe (1749–1832), poet and writer | 4.00 | 5.00 |

ENVIRONMENT PROTECTION

| **156** (154) | 5 D-Mark (Cu-Ni) 1982. Emblem | 4.00 | 5.00 |

German Democratic Republic

			VF	XF
1 (1)	1 Pfennig (Al) 1948–1950. Ear of corn with cog wheel. ℞ value		1.10	2.00

| **2** (2) | 5 Pfennig (Al) 1948–1950. Ear of corn with cog wheel. ℞ value | | 0.60 | 2.00 |

| **3** (3) | 10 Pfennig (Al) 1948–1950. Ear of corn with cog wheel. ℞ value | | 1.10 | 3.00 |

4 (4) 50 Pfennig (Al-Br) 1949, 1950. Plough and factory in background. R value:
a) 1949, rare —.— —.—
b) 1950 3.50 7.50

		VF	XF
5 (5)	1 Pfennig (Al) 1952–1953. Hammer and compasses between ears of corn. ℞ value	0.80	2.00
6 (6)	5 Pfennig (Al) 1952–1953. Hammer and compasses between ears of corn. ℞ value	0.80	2.00
7 (7)	10 Pfennig (Al) 1952–1953. Hammer and compasses between ears of corn. ℞ value	0.80	2.50
8 (8)	1 Pfennig (Al) 1960–1965, 1968, 1972, 1973, 1975, 1977–1981. Hammer and compasses within wreath of corn ears. ℞ value between oak leaves	0.10	0.20
9 (9)	5 Pfennig (Al) 1968, 1972, 1975, 1978–1981	0.10	0.20

			VF	XF

10 (10)   10 Pfennig (Al) 1963, 1965, 1967, 1968, 1970–1973, 1978–1981. Rev. oak leaf above value   0.15   0.25

11 (A 11)   20 Pfennig (Bra) 1969–:
     a) without mintmark: 1969, 1971   0.25   0.40
     b) with mintmark A: 1972–1974, 1978–1981   0.20   0.30

12 (11)   50 Pfennig (Al) 1958, 1968, 1971–1973, 1979–1981   0.25   0.40

13 (12)   1 D-Mark (Al) 1956, 1962, 1963. ℞ value between oak leaves   0.40   1.00

14 (13)   2 D-Mark (Al) 1957   0.80   1.50

COMMEMORATIVE ISSUE FOR THE 250th ANNIVERSARY OF THE DEATH OF LEIBNIZ

                                                             Unc

15 (15)   20 MDN (Ag) 1966. Bust right of Gottfried Wilhelm Leibniz (1646–1716), philosopher and savant   60.00

COMMEMORATIVE ISSUE FOR THE 125th ANNIVERSARY OF THE DEATH OF SCHINKEL

16 (14) 10 MDN (S) 1966. Head right of Karl Friedrich Schinkel (1781–1841), architect and painter.
Of No. 16 there is also a pattern in aluminium. No. 16 also has a variety with no inscription on edge.

Unc

58.00

COMMEMORATIVE ISSUE FOR THE 200th ANNIVERSARY OF THE BIRTH OF HUMBOLDT

17 (17) 20 MDN (Ag) 1967. Bust left of Wilhelm von Humboldt (1767–1835), statesman and philologist
a) on the edge: * 20 MARK DER DEUTSCHEN NOTENBANK (20 Marks issued by the Deutschen Notenbank)
b) on the edge: * 20 MARK * 20 MARK * 20 MARK

32.00

150.00

COMMEMORATIVE ISSUE FOR THE 100th ANNIVERSARY OF THE BIRTH OF K. KOLLWITZ

18 (16)   10 MDN (Ag) 1967. Head left of
Käthe Kollwitz (1867 – 1945),
etcher, painter and sculptor

    a) on the edge: * 10 MARK DER
DEUTENBANK
(10 Marks issued by the Deutschen Notenbank)

    b) on the edge: * 10 MARK *
10 MARK * 10 MARK

                  Unc

24.00

110.00

COMMEMORATIVE ISSUE FOR THE 150th ANNIVERSARY OF THE BIRTH OF KARL MARX

19 (20)   20 Mark (Ag) 1968. Head left of Karl
Marx (1818–1883), social ideologist

35.00

COMMEMORATIVE ISSUE FOR THE 500th ANNIVERSARY OF THE DEATH OF GUTENBERG

20 (19)   10 Mark (Ag) 1968. Monogram for Johannes Gutenberg, actually Gensfleisch (c. 1400–1468); he introduced printing with movable letters

	XF	Unc
		20.00

COMMEMORATIVE ISSUE FOR THE 125th ANNIVERSARY OF THE BIRTH OF KOCH

21 (18)   5 Mark (German silver) 1968. Bust left of Dr. Robert Koch (1843 to 1910), physician, bacteriologist; he discovered the tubercule bacillus (1882)   25.00

COMMEMORATIVE ISSUE FOR 20 YEARS OF THE GERMAN DEMOCRATIC REPUBLIC

22 (21)   5 Mark 1969. National arms. ℞ commemorative inscription, value and date
  a) (Cu–Ni)   1.60   2.50
  b) (Ni) Pattern (12,741 pieces)   60.00

COMMEMORATIVE ISSUE FOR THE 220th ANNIVERSARY OF THE BIRTH OF GOETHE

23 (24)   20 Mark (Ag) 1969. Bust left of Johann Wolfgang von Goethe (1749–1832), poet and writer   **Unc**

32.00

COMMEMORATIVE ISSUE FOR THE 75th ANNIVERSARY OF THE DEATH OF HEINRICH HERTZ

24 (22)   5 Mark (German silver) 1969. Head right of Heinrich Hertz (1857 to 1894), physicist; the Hertzian waves, named after him, form the basis of modern radio

12.00

COMMEMORATIVE ISSUE FOR THE 250th ANNIVERSARY OF THE DEATH OF JOHANN FRIEDRICH BÖTTGER (1682–1719)

25 (23)   10 Mark (Ag) 1969. Porcelain jug; the curved swords in saltire are the trademark of the porcelain works,

founded and directed in Meissen
by Böttger (also known as Bötti-
ger)

18.00

COMMEMORATIVE ISSUE FOR THE 125th ANNIVERSARY OF THE BIRTH OF WILHELM CONRAD RÖNTGEN

26 (25) 5 Mark (German silver) 1970. Prof.
Wilhelm Conrad Röntgen (1845 to
1923), physicist; in 1895 he discovered X-rays, which are named
after him; in 1901 he won the first
Nobel prize for physics   11.00

COMMEMORATIVE ISSUE FOR THE 200th ANNIVERSARY OF THE BIRTH OF LUDWIG VAN BEETHOVEN

27 (26) 10 Mark (Ag) 1970. Bust left of Ludwig van Beethoven (1770–1827),
composer   18.00

COMMEMORATIVE ISSUE FOR THE 150th ANNIVERSARY OF THE BIRTH OF FRIEDRICH ENGELS

		XF	Unc

28 (27) 20 Mark (Ag) 1970. Head left of Friedrich Engels (1820–1895), politician and socialist theoretician — — 27.00

29 (31) 20 Mark (German silver) 1971. Heinrich Mann (1871–1950), writer — 5.50 7.50

COMMEMORATIVE ISSUE FOR KEPLER

30 (28) 5 Mark (German silver) 1971. Johannes Kepler (1571–1630), imperial mathematician and court astronomer; in 1596 he published his writings on "Mysterium cosmographicum"; his pricipal work was "Astronomia nova", in 1611 — — 9.00

COMMEMORATIVE ISSUE FOR DÜRER

31 (29) 10 Mark (Ag) 1971. Albrecht Dürer

(1471–1528), painter, engraver and writer on art subjects. Monogram of Albrecht Dürer

	XF	Unc
		20.00

COMMEMORATIVE ISSUE FOR ROSA LUXEMBURG AND KARL LIEBKNECHT

32 (30)   20 Mark (Ag) 1971. Rosa Luxemburg (1870–1919), Socialist politician, and Karl Liebknecht (1871–1919), politician, founder of the Spartacus Association   27.00

COMMEMORATIVE ISSUE FOR THE 85th BIRTHDAY OF ERNST THÄLMANN

33 (32)   20 Mark (German silver) 1971. Ernst Thälmann (1886–1944), politician   5.00   6.00

COMMEMORATIVE ISSUE BRANDENBURG GATE

34 (A 29)   5 Mark (German silver) 1971, 1979, 1980. Brandenburg Gate   1.40   3.00

COMMEMORATIVE ISSUE FOR FRIEDRICH VON SCHILLER

35 (38)   20 Mark (German silver) 1972. Friedrich von Schiller (1759–1805), poet   5.00   6.00

COMMEMORATIVE ISSUE
FOR THE BUCHENWALD MEMORIAL

			XF	Unc
36 (35)	10 Mark (German silver) 1972. Group of figures taken from Buchenwald memorial, near Weimar		2.70	4.00

COMMEMORATIVE ISSUE FOR THE 500th BIRTHDAY OF
LUCAS CRANACH

37 (37)   20 Mark (Ag) 1972. Lucas Cranach the Elder (1472–1553), painter and graphic artist. Having received his patent for bearing arms from the Elector Friedrich the Wise in 1508, Cranach exclusively used as his signature the serpent with raised wings and the crown as well as the ring   30.00

COMMEMORATIVE ISSUE FOR THE 75th ANNIVERSARY
OF THE DEATH OF JOHANNES BRAHMS (1833–1897)

38 (33)   5 Mark (German silver) 1972. Quotation of score from the 4th movement of Symphony No. 1 by Brahms. The third note must be "c" instead of "b".   25.00

COMMEMORATIVE ISSUE FOR WILHELM PIECK

		XF	**Unc**
39 (39)	20 Mark (German silver) 1972. Wilhelm Pieck (1876–1960), President of the GDR	5.00	7.00

COMMEMORATIVE ISSUE FOR THE 175th BIRTHDAY OF HEINRICH HEINE

40 (36)   10 Mark (Ag) 1972. Heinrich Heine (1797 to 1856), lyric poet and satirist   20.00

COMMEMORATIVE ISSUE FOR MEISSEN

41 (34)   5 Mark (German silver) 1972. View of the Meissen castle hill with cathedral (Gothic hall church of the 13th/14th century) and Albrechtsburg (built 1471–1485)   1.30   2.50

42 (67)   1 Mark (Al) 1972, 1973, 1975, 1977–1981. Type as No. 13, but MARK instead of DEUTSCHE MARK   0.40   0.80

43 (68)   2 Mark (Al) 1974, 1975, 1977–1981. Type as No. 42   0.80   1.20

COMMEMORATIVE ISSUE FOR THE 75th BIRTHDAY OF BERTOLT BRECHT

44 (42)   10 Mark (Ag) 1973. Bertolt Brecht (1898–1956), eminent Socialist lyric poet, epic poet and theatrical director   18.00

COMMEMORATIVE ISSUE FOR THE 10th WORLD FESTIVAL OF YOUTH AND STUDENTS IN BERLIN

		XF	Unc
45 (41)	10 Mark (German silver) 1973. Emblem of the World Festival Games, surrounded by functional inscription. ℞ denomination, national emblem	3.00	5.00

COMMEMORATIVE ISSUE FOR THE 125th BIRTHDAY OF OTTO LILIENTHAL

46 (40)	5 Mark (German silver) 1973. Otto Lilienthal (1848–1896), pioneer of German aviation, since 1891 performed flights with selfconstructed gliders over distances of several hundred meters.		9.00

COMMEMORATIVE ISSUE FOR THE 60th ANNIVERSARY OF THE DEATH OF A. BEBEL

47 (43)	20 Mark (Ag) 1973. August Bebel (1840–1913), Socialdemocrat politician and member of the German parliament		30.00
48 (44)	20 Mark (German silver) 1973. Otto Grotewohl (1894–1964), Socialdemocrat politician, took a decisive part in the amalgamation of the Communist Party of Germany and the Socialist Party of Germany forming the "SED" (Socialist Unity Party)	5.00	6.00

COMMEMORATIVE ISSUE FOR THE 250th BIRTHDAY OF IMMANUEL KANT

		Unc	Proof
49 (49)	20 Mark (Ag) 1974. Immanuel Kant (1724–1804), philosopher	30.00	110.00

COMMEMORATIVE ISSUE FOR THE CENTENARY OF THE DEATH OF PHILIPP REIS

50 (45)	5 Mark (German silver) 1974. Philipp Reis (1834–1874), physicist, inventor of the first telephone	9.00	

COMMEMORATIVE ISSUE (2) 25 YEARS GDR

51 (46)	10 Mark 1974: a) German silver b) .500 silver (1,500 pieces)	5.00	*1100.00*
52 (47)	10 Mark (Ag) 1974. For the same occasion as No. 51, but with a different coin design	20.00	*2400.00*

COMMEMORATIVE ISSUE FOR THE 200th BIRTHDAY OF C. D. FRIEDRICH

<table>
<tr><td></td><td></td><td>Unc</td></tr>
</table>

		Unc
53 (48)	10 Mark (Ag) 1974. Caspar David Friedrich (1774–1840), painter	30.00

COMMEMORATIVE ISSUE FOR THE CENTENARY OF BIRTH OF ALBERT SCHWEITZER

54 (52)	10 Mark (Ag) 1975. Albert Schweitzer (1875-1965), philosopher and Doctor of Medicine:	
	a) silver (100,000 pieces)	20.00
	b) .500 silver; proof (1,040 pieces)	1100.00
	c) pattern; .500 silver; reverse like No. 56 (6,614 pieces)	100.00

225th ANNIVERSARY OF THE DEATH OF J. S. BACH

		XF	Unc
55 (54)	20 Mark (Ag) 1975. Johann Sebastian Bach (1685-1750), composer:		
	a) raised notes		30.00
	b) incused notes (pattern)		110.00

20th ANNIVERSARY OF THE WARSAW PACT

56 (53)	10 Mark (German silver) 1975.	3.00	4.50

100th ANNIVERSARY OF THE BIRTH OF THOMAS MANN

57 (50)	5 Mark (German silver) 1975. Thomas Mann (1875-1955), writer		7.50

INTERNATIONAL WOMEN'S YEAR 1975

58 (51)	5 Mark (German silver) 1975. Conjoined women heads, emblem, commemorative legend	3.50	6.00

200th ANNIVERSARY OF THE BIRTH OF FERDINAND VON SCHILL

59 (55)	5 Mark (German silver) 1976. Ferdinand von Schill (1776-1809), Prussian officer		8.50

20th ANNIVERSARY OF NATIONAL PEOPLE'S ARMY

		XF	Unc
60 (56)	10 Mark (German silver) 1976. Bust of a soldier	4.00	8.00

150th ANNIVERSARY OF THE BIRTH OF WILHELM LIEBKNECHT

		Unc	Proof
61 (58)	20 Mark (Ag) 1976. Wilhelm Liebknecht 1826–1900), Socialdemocrat politician	30.00	140.00

150th ANNIVERSARY OF THE DEATH OF CARL MARIA VON WEBER

62 (57)	10 Mark (Ag) 1976. Carl Maria von Weber (1786–1826), composer; one of his most famous works is entitled »Der Freischütz«	24.00	80.00

200th ANNIVERSARY OF THE BIRTH OF CARL FRIEDRICH GAUSS

63 (61)	20 Mark (Ag) 1977. Carl Friedrich Gauss (1777-1855), mathematician and astronomer	30.00

375th ANNIVERSARY OF THE BIRTH OF OTTO VON GUERICKE

	Unc	Proof
64 (60) 10 Mark (Ag) 1977. Otto von Guericke (1602–1686), burgomaster of the city of Magdeburg, inventor:	24.00	95.00
a) pattern; with horses	100.00	

125th ANNIVERSARY OF THE DEATH OF FRIEDRICH LUDWIG JAHN

	Unc	Proof
65 (59) 5 Mark (German silver) 1977. Friedrich Ludwig Jahn (1778–1852), founder of the gymnastics movement in Germany, know as »Turnvater Jahn« (father of the gymnastics)	8.50	38.00

175th ANNIVERSARY OF THE DEATH OF G. F. KLOPSTOCK

		Unc	Proof
66 (62)	5 Mark (German silver) 1978. Friedrich Gottlieb Klopstock (1724-1803), poet:	6.50	90.00

175th ANNIVERSARY OF THE BIRTH OF J. VON LIEBIG

67 (64)	10 Mark (Ag) 1978. Justus von Liebig (1803-1873), chemist:	22.00	80.00

175th ANNIVERSARY OF THE DEATH OF J. G. HERDER

68 (66)	20 Mark (Ag) 1978. Johann Gottfried Herder (1744-1803), philosopher:	30.00	100.00

SOVIET-GERMAN SPACE FLIGHT

			Unc	Proof
69 (65)	10 Mark (German silver) 1978		7.50	550.00

ANTI-APARTHEID YEAR

70 (63)	5 Mark (German silver) 1978		5.00	110.00

100th ANNIVERSARY OF THE BIRTH OF ALBERT EINSTEIN

71 (69)	5 Mark (German silver) 1979. Albert Einstein (1879-1955), physicist		6.50	85.00

175th ANNIVERSARY OF THE BIRTH OF L. FEUERBACH

72 (70)	10 Mark (Ag) 1979. Ludwig Feuerbach (1804-1872), philosopher		20.00	70.00

250th ANNIVERSARY OF THE BIRTH OF G. E. LESSING

		Unc	Proof
73 (71)	20 Mark (Ag) 1979. Gotthold Ephraim Lessing (1729-1781), poet	30.00	110.00

30th ANNIVERSARY OF THE GDR

74 (72)	20 Mark (German silver) 1979	12.00

225th ANNIVERSARY OF THE BIRTH OF J.D. SCHARNHORST

75 (74)	10 Mark (German silver) 1980. Gerhard J.D. von Scharnhorst (1755–1813), general and military theoretician	22.00	60.00

75th ANNIVERSARY OF THE DEATH OF ADOLPH VON MENZEL

76 (73)	5 Mark (German silver) 1980. Adolph von Menzel (1815–1905), engraver and drawer	6.50	30.00

75th ANNIVERSARY OF THE DEATH OF ERNST ABBE

		Unc	Proof
77 (75)	20 Mark (Ag) 1980. Ernst Abbe (1840–1905), physicist	30.00	65.00

25th ANNIVERSARY OF NATIONAL PEOPLE'S ARMY

78 (77)	10 Mark (German silver) 1981	7.50	50.00

150th ANNIVERSARY OF THE DEATH OF VON STEIN

79 (76)	20 Mark (Ag) 1981. Carl Reichsfreiherr vom und zum Stein (1757–1831), statesman	30.00	110.00

150th ANNIVERSARY OF THE DEATH OF G.W. HEGEL

80	10 Mark (Ag) 1981. Georg Wilhelm Hegel (1770–1831), philosopher	20.00	55.00

450th ANNIVERSARY OF THE DEATH OF RIEMENSCHNEIDER

		Unc	Proof
81 (78)	5 Mark (German silver) 1981. Tilman Riemenschneider (c. 1455–1531), sculptor and wood-carver	6.50	28.00

700th ANNIVERSARY OF THE BERLIN MINT

| **82** (80) | 10 Mark (German silver) 1981. Old bear pfennig design | 15.00 | 65.00 |

NEUES GEWANDHAUS LEIPZIG

| **83** | 10 Mark (Ag) 1982 | 20.00 | 60.00 |

200th ANNIVERSARY OF THE BIRTH OF FRIEDRICH FRÖBEL (1782–1852)

		Unc	Proof
84	5 Mark (German silver) 1982. Three nude children with large building blocks and balls	7.50	35.00

125th ANNIVERSARY OF THE BIRTH OF C. ZETKIN

85	20 Mark (Ag) 1982. Clara Zetkin (1857–1933), politician	30.00	60.00

PATTERNS

(Illustrations after the dies of the Neubauer Medal)

P 1	10 Mark (Ag) (1966 or 1967). Head of Theodor Neubauer (1890–1945) over laurel branch. ℞ national arms of somewhat smaller size than on the normal special issues with the inscription DEUTSCHE DE-MOKRATISCHE REPUBLIK forming a fully circular inscription, but no indication either of value or date. Edge inscription: ZEHN MARK DER DEUTSCHEN NOTENBANK	–.–	–.–

Danzig

100 Pfennig(e) = 1 Gulden; since 1923: 100 Pfennig(e) = 1 Danzig Gulden

			VF	XF
1 (1)	10	Pfennig (Zi) 1920. Arms of the city and date. ℞ value on panel	30.00	50.00
2 (2)	10	Pfennig (Zi) 1920. Arms of the city and date. ℞ value in large figures	220.00	380.00

3 (3)	1	Pfennig (Br) 1923–1937. Arms of the city. ℞ value	3.50	6.00
4 (4)	2	Pfennige (Br) 1923–1937	4.00	8.00
5 (5)	5	Pfennige (Cu–Ni) 1923–1928	5.00	9.00

6 (6)	10	Pfennige (Cu–Ni) 1923	6.00	10.00

7 (7)	½	Gulden (Ag) 1923–1927. Small galley	17.00	35.00
8 (8)	1	Gulden (Ag) 1923	25.00	50.00

		VF	XF
9 (9)	2 Gulden (Ag) 1923	55.00	90.00

| **10** (10) | 5 Gulden (Ag) 1923–1927. The Marienkirche in Danzig | 120.00 | 180.00 |

| **11** (11) | 25 Gulden (Au) 1923. Neptune brandishing trident, from the famous Neptune fountain in Danzig | 2500.00 | 3200.00 |

| **12** (13) | 5 Pfennig (Al–Br) 1932. East Atlantic flounder or turbot (Bothus = Rhombus ⇋ Scophthalmus maximus – Bothidae). ℞ value | 3.00 | 6.00 |

			VF	XF
13 (14)	10	Pfennig (Al–Br) 1932. Atlantic codfish (Gadus morrhua – Gadidae). ℞ value	3.00	7.00
14 (15)	½	Gulden (Ni) 1932	22.00	35.00
15 (16)	1	Gulden (Ni) 1932	20.00	32.00
16 (17)	2	Gulden (Ag) 1932	165.00	400.00
17 (18)	5	Gulden (Ag) 1932. The Marienkirche	300.00	550.00

18 (19)	5 Gulden (Ag) 1932. Grain elevator	400.00	700.00

19 (20)	5 Gulden (Ni) 1935. Small galley	220.00	400.00

20 (21)	10 Gulden (Ni) 1935. The Town Hall	550.00	820.00

		XF	Unc
21 (12)	25 Gulden (Au) 1930. Neptune brandishing trident, from the famous Neptune fountain	9000.00	12000.00

Saarland

100 Centimen = 1 Franken

1 (1)	10 Franken (Al–Br) 1954. Pit head and arms	1.60	4.00
2 (2)	20 Franken (Al–Br) 1954	2.50	5.00
3 (3)	50 Franken (Al–Br) 1954	12.00	20.00
4 (4)	100 Franken (Cu–Ni) 1955	5.00	8.00

German New Guinea

1 (1)	1 New Guinea Pfennig (Cu) 1894	25.00	45.00
2 (2)	2 New Guinea Pfennig (Cu) 1894. Type as No. 1	35.00	60.00

3 (3)　10 New Guinea Pfennig (Cu) 1894. Great bird of paradise (Paradisea

			VF	XF

		apoda – Paradisaeidae). ℞ value between palm branches	35.00	60.00
4 (4)	½ New Guinea Mark (Ag) 1894. Type as No. 3		100.00	150.00
5 (5)	1 New Guinea Mark (Ag) 1894. Type as No. 3		80.00	155.00
6 (6)	2 New Guinea Mark (Ag) 1894. Type as No. 3		155.00	220.00
7 (7)	5 New Guinea Mark (Ag) 1894. Type as No. 3		550.00	1400.00
8 (8)	10 New Guinea Mark (Au) 1895. Type as No. 3		3500.00	5500.00
9 (9)	20 New Guinea Mark (Au) 1895. Type as No. 3		4500.00	6400.00

German East Africa

ISSUES OF THE GERMAN EAST AFRICA COMPANY
64 Pesa = 1 Rupie, 100 Heller = 1 Rupie

1 (1)	1 Pesa (Cu) 1890–1892. Imperial eagle, inscription DEUTSCH-OSTAFRIKANISCHE GESELL-SCHAFT. ℞ inscription in Swahili	4.00	7.00
2 (2)	¼ Rupie (Ag) 1891–1901. Bust left of Kaiser Wilhelm II (1859–1941) wearing helmet surmounted by eagle. ℞ arms with palm tree and lion walking to left	18.00	40.00
3 (3)	½ Rupie (Ag) 1891–1901. Type as No. 2	35.00	55.00

| **4 (4)** | 1 Rupie (Ag) 1890–1902. Type as No. 2 | 25.00 | 40.00 |

			VF	XF
5 (5)	2 Rupien (Ag) 1893–1894. Type as No. 2	320.00	440.00

ISSUES OF THE MINISTRY OF FOREIGN AFFAIRS

			VF	XF
6 (6)	½ Heller (Br) 1904–1906. Crown	6.00	12.00
7 (7)	1 Heller (Br) 1904–1913	2.00	4.00
8 (8)	5 Heller (Br) 1908–1909	20.00	45.00
9 (11)	5 Heller (Cu–Ni) 1913–1914 (with hole)	12.50	20.00

		VF	XF
10 (12)	10 Heller (Cu–Ni) 1908–1914	12.00	18.00

		VF	XF
11 (13)	¼ Rupie (Ag) 1904–1914. Bust left of Kaiser Wilhelm II wearing helmet surmounted by eagle	12.50	20.00
12 (14)	½ Rupie (Ag) 1904–1914	30.00	50.00
13 (15)	1 Rupie (Ag) 1904–1914	17.00	30.00

EMERGENCY ISSUES

			VF	**XF**
14 (16)	15	Rupien (Au) 1916. African elephant (Loxodonta africana — Elephantidae)	900.00	1200.00

15 (9)	5	Heller (Bra) 1916. Filleted crown, date and abbreviation D. O. A. for Deutsch-Ostafrika. ℞ value between crossed branches	5.00	12.00
16 (10)	20	Heller 1916. Type as No. 15. Filleted crown of large type		
		a) (Cu)	160.00	190.00
		b) (Bra)	8.00	18.00
17 (10)	20	Heller 1916. Type as No. 16, but only one leaf on each branch below HELLER		
		a) (Cu)	160.00	280.00
		b) (Bra)	8.00	12.00
18 (10)	20	Heller 1916. Type as No. 16, but filleted crown of small type		
		a) (Cu)	110.00	160.00
		b) (Bra)	11.00	18.00
19 (10)	20	Heller 1916. Type as No. 18, but only one leaf on each branch below HELLER		
		a) (Cu)	6.00	10.00
		b) (Bra)	4.00	8.00

Kiaochow

1 (1)	5	Cents (Cu–Ni) 1909. Imperial eagle standing on anchor. ℞ Chinese characters	35.00	50.00

2 (2)	10	Cents (Cu–Ni) 1909	30.00	50.00

GERMAN OCCUPATION ISSUES IN THE OCCUPIED TERRITORIES 1914–1918

Belgium

100 Centimes = 1 Franc

		VF	XF
1 (38)	5 Centimes (Zi) 1915–1916. Arms (lion). ℞ value	2.50	4.00
2 (39)	10 Centimes (Zi) 1915–1917	2.50	4.00
3 (40)	25 Centimes (Zi) 1915–1918	3.50	6.50
4 (41)	50 Centimes (Zi) 1918 (with hole)	11.00	20.00

Territory of the Eastern Kommandantur

100 Kopeks = 1 Rouble

		VF	XF
1 (A 18)	1 Kopek (Fe) 1916. Inscription: GEBIET DES OBERBEFEHLSHABERS OST, oak twigs. ℞ value and date in iron cross	2.00	4.00
2 (B 18)	2 Kopeks (Fe) 1916	2.50	5.00
3 (C 18)	3 Kopeks (Fe) 1916	3.50	6.00

GERMAN OCCUPATION ISSUES IN THE OCCUPIED TERRITORIES 1939–1945

General Issues

		VF	XF
1 (94)	5 Pfennig (Zi) 1940–1941. Swastika. ℞ imperial eagle, value (with hole)	17.00	27.00
2 (95)	10 Pfennig (Zi) 1940–1941 (with hole)	18.00	30.00

Bohemia and Moravia

		VF	XF
1 (B 29)	10 Heller (Zi) 1940–1944. Arms (lion). ℞ the Karl bridge in Prague	2.00	4.00

				VF	**XF**

2 (B 30)   20 Heller (Zi) 1940–1944. Arms (lion).
     ℞ sheaf of wheat   1.10   2.00

3 (B 31)   50 Heller (Zi) 1940–1944. Arms (lion).
     ℞ lime-tree branches and ears of wheat   3.00   5.00

4 (B 32)   1 Krone (Zi) 1941–1944. Arms (lion).
     ℞ lime-tree branches   2.00   3.00

Government General

1 (34)   1 Grosz (Zi) 1939. Polish eagle. ℞ value   3.00   5.00

There exists a zinc pattern piece from 1939 of identical design and denomination.

2 (35)   5 Groszy (Zi) 1939 (with hole) (also known without hole)   6.50   12.50

There exists a zinc pattern piece with hole from 1939 of identical design and denomination.

3 (36)   10 Groszy (Zi) dated 1923 but issued in 1939–45   1.00   1.80

4 (37)   20 Groszy (Zi) dated 1923 but issued in 1939–45   1.00   1.80

5 (38)   50 Groszy (Fe–Ni) 1938. Polish eagle.
     ℞ value within wreath   5.00   8.00

These coins exist in nickel-plated iron with and without mint mark, as well as an iron without mint mark. Three pattern pieces from 1938 exist, two of which are in nickel-plated iron, and one in aluminium, all of identical design and denomination.

A further pattern piece from 1938 exists in nickel-plated iron, of different design, but of identical denomination.

Issues for the Lodz Ghetto
(Litzmannstadt)

Coins were issued by the Jewish camp authorities in the ghetto of Lodz during 1942–1943 for their own use.

Owing to lack of technical facilities at the time of striking, numerous varieties of dies and legends are encountered. There is also a difference in the thickness of the flans. Since hardly any survivors were left at the time of the closing of the ghetto very little is known about the history of the production of these coins, so that many questions – especially as to patterns – still remain unanswered.

1   10 Pfennig (Al–Mg) 1942. Star of David with ears of corn surrounded by in-

scription: Litzmannstadt-Getto · 1942.
℞ value and inscription DER ÄLTE-
STE DER JUDEN (the elder of the
Jews); also oak leaves with small star
of David. Diameter 21 mm.

	VF	XF
	90.00	120.00

These coins were withdrawn because the authorities of the Government General took offence at the reverse side, which resembled the German 10 Pfennig piece.

2 10 Pfennig (Al–Mg) 1942. Star of David with date within circle; around, inscription as No. 1. ℞ value and circular inscription QUITTUNG ÜBER · PFEN-NIG (payment for · Pfennig). Diameter 19 mm — 50.00 — 75.00

3 5 Mark. Large star of David over circular decoration; next to it inscription GETTO 1943. ℞ value on which inscription reading QUITTUNG ÜBER (denomination); circular inscription DER ÄLTESTE DER JUDEN · IN LITZMANNSTADT ·
a) 1943 (Al–Mg) — 7.50 — 15.00
b) 1943 (Al) — 10.00 — 20.00

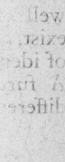

4 10 Mark. Type as No. 3, but of larger diameter
a) 1943 (Al–Mg) — 12.00 — 25.00
b) 1943 (Al) — 12.00 — 25.00

5 20 Mark (Al) 1943. Type as No. 3, but of even larger diameter — 42.00 — 80.00

There is a specimen pattern of No. 3 in silver as well as a trial piece of a 5-Pfennig.

Ghana

Area: 29,100 sq. mi. Population: 9,200,000.

The West African country of Ghana was formed by an Act of Independence of 7th February 1957 passed by the British Parliament from the former British Crown Colony of the Gold Coast and the League of Nations mandate territory of Togoland (West Togo). Independence was proclaimed on 6th March 1957. Though a republic since 1st July 1960, Ghana is a member of the British Commonwealth and previously formed part of the British West Africa Currency Board. Capital: Accra.

12 Pence = 1 Shilling, 20 Shillings = £ 1; since 19th July 1965: 100 Pesewas = 1 Cedi

			VF	XF
1 (1)	½ Penny (Br) 1958. Head right of Dr. Kwame Nkrumah (1909–1972), Prime Minister 1957–1960, Head of State 1960–1966. ℞ star (emblem of state)		0.20	0.30
2 (2)	1 Penny (Br) 1958. Type as No. 1		0.25	0.40
3 (3)	3 Pence (Cu–Ni) 1958 (scalloped edge)		0.30	0.50
4 (4)	6 Pence (Cu–Ni) 1958		0.35	0.60
5 (5)	1 Shilling (Cu–Ni) 1958		0.40	1.00
6 (6)	2 Shillings (Cu–Ni) 1958		0.80	2.00

		Proof
7 (7)	10 Shillings (Ag) 1958	50.00

COMMEMORATIVE ISSUE FOR REPUBLIC DAY ON 1st JULY 1960

				Proof
8		2 £ (Au) 1960. Head right of Dr. Kwame Nkrumah. ℞ national arms, inscription 1st JULY 1960/REPUBLIC DAY		220.00

CURRENCY REFORM: 100 Pesewas = 1 Cedi

			VF	XF
9 (8)	5	Pesewas (Cu–Ni) 1965. Head right of Dr. Kwame Nkrumah. ℞ national emblem (scalloped edge)	0.20	0.40
10 (9)	10	Pesewas (Cu–Ni) 1965. Type as No. 9	0.30	0.60
11 (10)	25	Pesewas (Cu–Ni) 1965. Type as No. 10	0.80	1.20
12 (11)	50	Pesewas (Cu–Ni) 1965. Type as No. 10	1.10	2.00
13 (12)	½	Pesewa (Br) 1967. Bush drums. ℞ emblem of state	0.10	0.20

			VF	XF
14 (13)	1	Pesewa (Br) 1967. Type as No. 13	0.10	0.25
15 (14)	2½	Pesewas (Cu–Ni) 1967. Cocoa beans on stem (Theobroma cacao — Sterculiaceae). ℞ arms (scalloped edge)	0.20	0.40
16 (15)	5	Pesewas (Cu–Ni) 1967. Type as No. 15 (round)	0.20	0.50
17 (16)	10	Pesewas (Cu–Ni) 1967. Type as No. 16	0.35	0.60
18 (17)	20	Pesewas (Cu–Ni) 1967. Type as No. 16	0.80	1.20

20th ANNIVERSARY OF INDEPENDENCE (2)

			Proof
19		2 £ (Au) 1977	–.–
20		4 £ (Au) 1977	–.–

FOR THE FAO COIN PLAN (3)

			XF	Unc
21 (18)	50	Pesewas (Bra) 1979	1.20	1.50
22 (19)	1	Cedi (Bra) 1979	2.00	2.50
23		2 Cedi (Ni) 1979	–.–	–.–

A town sheikhdom called itself the Ghurfah sheikhdom after the town of Al-Ghuraf situated in the wadi Hadramaut slightly to the West of Tarim (in Arabic: Ghurfah). The town is situated near the border between the two parts of the Sultanate of Kathiri, the territory of Seiwun (Seyyun) and that of Tarim, that is on the Tarim side. The fate of the Sultanate of Kathiri was that also of Ghuraf; the Sultanate of Kathiri first belonged to the Aden Protectorate, then to the eastern Protectorate of Aden and was then conquered by the South Yemen rebels without appreciable resistance on 2nd October 1967. On 27th November the People's Republic was proclaimed which in the meantime has been renamed the Democratic People's Republic Yemen.

120 Shomsih = 1 Riyal

			VF	XF
1 (4)	4	Shomsih (Ag) A. H. 1344 (1925). Arabic inscription and date in circle, the whole surrounded by ears of corn crossed below. ℞ numeral of value in the circle, the whole surrounded by ears of corn crossed below.	25.00	35.00
2 (6)	8	Shomsih (Ag) A. H. 1344 (1925). Type as No. 1	25.00	35.00
3 (8)	15	Shomsih (Ag) A. H. 1344 (1925). Type as No. 1	12.00	20.00
4 (10)	30	Shomsih (Ag) A. H. 1344 (1925). Type as No. 1	12.50	22.00
5 (11)	45	Shomsih (Ag) A. H. 1344 (1925). Type as No. 1	65.00	120.00
6 (12)	60	Shomsih (Ag) A. H. 1344 (1925). Type as No. 1	28.00	45.00

Area: 440 acres. Population: 30,000 (without the garrison).
In 1704 siege and capture by the British. Since 1830 a British Crown Colony, since 1964 limited self-government; extended autonomy since 1st June 1969.

12 Pence = 1 Shilling, 5 Shillings = 1 Crown, 20 Shillings = 1 £;
since February 15th, 1971: 100 New Pence = 1 Gibraltar Pound

ELIZABETH II since 1952

			Unc	Proof
1 (1)	1 Crown 1967. Head right of Queen Elizabeth II. R arms (castle and key)			
	a) (Ag) 1967			50.00
	b) (Cu-Ni) 1967–1970		4.00	

NEW CURRENCY (Decimal System): 100 New Pence = 1 £

2 (2)	25 New Pence 1971. R Magot (Macaca sylvana-Cercophitecidae):			
	a) (Ag)			32.00
	b) (Cu-Ni)		4.00	

COMMEMORATIVE ISSUE FOR THE SILVER WEDDING OF THE BRITISH ROYAL COUPLE ON 20th NOVEMBER 1972

3 (3)	25 New Pence 1972. R coats of arms of the alliance:			
	a) (Ag)			32.00
	b) (Cu-Ni)		4.00	

250th ANNIVERSARY OF INTRODUCTION OF THE BRITISH STERLING IN THE COLONY (3)

	Unc	Proof
4 (4) 25 £ (Au) 1975. Rev. lion with key	140.00	200.00

5 (5)   50 £ (Au) 1975. Rev. "Our Lady of Europa"   320.00   400.00

6 (6)   100 £ (Au) 1975. Rev. coat of arms   650.00   800.00

25th ANNIVERSARY OF THE SILVER JUBILEE OF HER MAJESTY QUEEN ELIZABETH II

7 (7)   25 Pence 1977:
    a) (Ag)   30.00
    b) (Cu-Ni)   2.00

80th ANNIVERSARY OF THE BIRTHDAY OF QUEEN MOTHER

8 (8)   1 Crown 1980:
    a) (Ag)   55.00
    b) (Cu-Ni)   2.00

		Unc	Proof
9 (9)	1 Crown 1980:		
	a) (Ag)		55.00
	b) (Cu-Ni)	2.00	
10 (10)	50 £ (Au) 1980	420.00	520.00

WEDDING OF PRINCE CHARLES AND LADY DIANA (2)

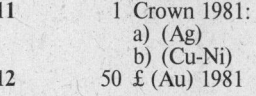

11	1 Crown 1981:		
	a) (Ag)		60.00
	b) (Cu-Ni)	3.00	
12	50 £ (Au) 1981		650.00

Area: 94,284 sq. mi. Population: 56,000,000
The United Kingdom of Great Britain and Northern Ireland comprises
England, Wales, Scotland, the northern part of Ireland and the adjacent
islands. Capital: London.

> 4 Farthings = 1 Penny, 12 Pence = 1 Shilling,
> 2 Shillings = 1 Florin, 5 Shillings = 1 Crown,
> 20 Shillings = £ 1 or 1 Sovereign (Gold);
> **since 15th February 1971: 100 (New) Pence = £ 1**

Mintmarks: H-Heaton;   KN – King's Norton

When no mint-mark is shown, coins were struck by the Royal Mint (London,
or since 1970 at Llantrisant in Wales).

EDWARD VII 1901–1910

1 (46)   1 Farthing (Br) 1902–1910. Head right
of King Edward VII (1841–1910).
℞ Britannia seated:

	Mintage	Fine	VF	XF
1902	5,125,120	0.90	1.20	5.00
1903	5,331,200	1.00	1.50	7.00
1904	3,628,800	2.00	4.00	12.00
1905	4,076,800	1.00	2.00	8.00
1906	5,340,160	0.80	1.50	6.00
1907	4,399,360	0.80	1.20	7.00
1908	4,264,960	1.00	1.80	8.50
1909	8,852,480	0.80	1.20	5.00
1910	2,298,400	3.00	6.00	12.00

2 (47)   ½ Penny (Br) 1902–1910:

	Mintage	Fine	VF	XF
1902	13,672,960	0.80	1.80	6.00
1903	11,450,880	1.00	2.50	14.00
1904	8,131,200	2.00	4.00	20.00
1905	10,124,800	1.00	2.50	12.00
1906	11,101,440	1.00	2.50	12.00
1907	16,849,280	0.80	2.50	11.00
1908	16,620,800	0.80	2.00	11.00
1909	8,279,040	1.00	4.00	15.00
1910	10,769,920	1.00	2.00	11.00

3 (48)   1 Penny (Br) 1902–1910:

	Mintage	Fine	VF	XF
1902	26,976,768	0.90	2.00	6.00
1903	21,415,296	0.80	3.00	15.00
1904	12,913,152	1.00	4.00	20.00
1905	17,783,808	0.80	2.50	18.00
1906	37,989,504	0.80	2.00	12.00
1907	47,322,240	0.50	2.00	12.00
1908	31,506,048	0.60	2.00	11.00
1909	19,617,024	0.80	2.00	12.00
1910	29,549,184	0.70	1.60	10.00

4 (49)   3 Pence (Ag) 1902–1910. ℞ value
within wreath:

	Mintage	Fine	VF	XF
1902	8,283,603	1.20	2.00	7.00
1903	5,227,200	1.50	4.00	16.00
1904	3,627,360	3.00	10.00	30.00
1905	3,548,160	3.00	10.00	32.00
1906	3,152,160	2.00	10.00	26.00
1907	4,831,200	1.00	3.00	12.00
1908	8,157,600	0.90	2.50	10.00
1909	4,055,040	1.00	3.00	12.00
1910	4,563,380	1.00	3.00	12.00

5 (50)   6 Pence (Ag) 1902–1910. ℞ value
within wreath:

	Mintage	Fine	VF	XF
1902	6,382,501	2.50	4.00	18.00
1903	5,410,096	4.00	10.00	35.00
1904	4,487,098	5.00	12.00	55.00
1905	4,235,556	4.00	12.00	40.00
1906	7,641,146	3.00	8.00	26.00
1907	8,733,673	3.00	8.00	30.00
1908	6,739,491	5.00	12.00	50.00
1909	6,584,017	4.00	10.00	40.00
1910	12,490,724	2.00	4.00	20.00

6 (51)   1 Shilling (Ag) 1902–1910. ℞ arms with
lion on crown:

	Mintage	Fine	VF	XF
1902	7,822,604	5.00	7.00	25.00
1903	2,061,823	8.00	20.00	85.00
1904	2,040,161	6.00	20.00	70.00
1905	488,390	50.00	150.00	500.00
1906	10,791,025	7.00	10.00	30.00
1907	14,083,418	4.00	10.00	30.00
1908	3,806,969	8.00	18.00	65.00
1909	5,664,982	5.00	12.00	50.00
1910	26,547,236	4.00	9.00	24.00

7 (52)   1 Florin (Ag) 1902–1910. ℞ Britannia standing:

	Mintage	Fine	VF	XF
1902	2,204,698	10.00	20.00	60.00
1903	1,995,298	15.00	30.00	90.00
1904	2,769,932	12.00	25.00	100.00
1905	1,187,596	25.00	80.00	300.00
1906	6,910,128	10.00	25.00	70.00
1907	5,947,895	10.00	28.00	90.00
1908	3,280,010	12.00	30.00	100.00
1909	3,482,829	12.00	30.00	100.00
1910	5,650,713	10.00	18.00	60.00

8 (53)   ½ Crown (Ag) 1902–1910. ℞ crowned shield:

	Mintage	Fine	VF	XF
1902	1,331,131	10.00	22.00	80.00
1903	274,840	60.00	200.00	500.00
1904	709,652	28.00	90.00	380.00
1905	166,008	140.00	280.00	1000.00
1906	2,886,206	10.00	30.00	110.00
1907	3,693,930	10.00	25.00	90.00
1908	1,758,889	12.00	30.00	150.00
1909	3,051,592	10.00	20.00	100.00
1910	2,557,685	11.00	25.00	105.00

		VF	XF
9 (54)	1 Crown (Ag) 1902. Rev. St. George and the Dragon (271,143 pieces)	85.00	160.00

A 9 Maundy money: 1 Penny, 2 Pence, 3 Pence and 4 Pence (1 Groat), 1902 to 1910. These sets of silver coins are not intended for circulation. Such coins have been issued in Britain since 1660 for the Sovereign to perform the age-old ceremony of making a gift of money to the poor on Maundy Thursday (Y A 55–D 55):

	Mintage	VF	XF	Unc
1902	8,976	20.00	50.00	100.00
1903	8,976	20.00	50.00	100.00
1904	8,976	20.00	50.00	100.00
1905	8,976	20.00	50.00	100.00
1906	8,800	20.00	50.00	100.00
1907	8,760	20.00	50.00	100.00
1908	8,760	20.00	50.00	100.00
1909	1,983	30.00	80.00	150.00
1910	1,440	30.00	85.00	170.00

10 (56) ½ Sovereign (Au) 1902-1910. Rev. St. George and the Dragon:

	Mintage	Fine	VF	XF
1902	4,259,580	60.00	80.00	100.00
1903	2,522,057	60.00	80.00	100.00
1904	1,717,440	70.00	90.00	120.00
1905	3,023,993	60.00	80.00	100.00
1906	4,245,437	60.00	80.00	100.00
1907	4,233,421	60.00	80.00	100.00
1908	3,996,992	60.00	80.00	100.00
1909	4,010,715	60.00	80.00	100.00
1910	5,023,881	60.00	80.00	100.00

11 (57) 1 Sovereign (Au) 1902-1910. Type as No. 10:

	Mintage	Fine	VF	XF
1902	4,752,919	125.00	150.00	180.00
1903	8,888,627	125.00	150.00	180.00
1904	10,041,369	125.00	150.00	180.00
1905	5,910,403	125.00	150.00	180.00
1906	10,466,981	125.00	150.00	180.00
1907	18,458,663	125.00	150.00	180.00

	Mintage	Fine	XF	Unc
1908	11,729,006	125.00	150.00	180.00
1909	12,157,099	125.00	150.00	180.00
1910	22,379,624	125.00	150.00	180.00

	VF	XF
12 (58) 2 £ (Au) 1902. Type as No. 10 (53,873 pieces)	600.00	900.00

	VF	XF
13 (59) 5 £ (Au) 1902. Type as No. 10 (42,977 pieces)	900.00	1700.00

Branches of the Royal Mint were set up in Australia at Sydney (mintmark S), Melbourne (mintmark M), and Perth (mintmark P), as well as in Canada at Ottawa (mintmark C), for coining gold of imperial type. These coins are listed in the Australian and Canadian section of this catalogue.

GEORGE V 1910-1936

14 (60) 1 Farthing (Br) 1911-1936. Head left of King George V (1865-1936). Rev. Britannia seated:

	Mintage	Fine	VF	XF
1911	5,196,800	1.00	1.50	4.00
1912	7,669,760	0.40	1.00	3.00
1913	4,184,320	0.60	1.20	3.50
1914	6,126,988	0.40	1.00	2.50
1915	7,129,254	0.90	2.50	6.00
1916	10,993,325	0.40	0.80	3.00
1917	21,434,844	0.20	0.50	1.50
1918	19,362,818	0.30	0.60	2.00
1919	15,089,425	0.30	0.80	2.50
1920	11,480,536	0.30	0.60	2.00
1921	9,469,097	0.30	0.60	1.80
1922	9,956,983	0.30	0.60	1.80
1923	8,034,457	0.40	0.80	1.80
1924	8,733,414	0.40	0.80	1.80
1925	12,634,697	0.30	0.70	1.50
1926	9,792,397	0.30	0.60	1.50
1927	7,868,355	0.30	0.60	1.50
1928	11,625,600	0.25	0.50	1.50
1929	8,419,200	0.30	0.60	1.80
1930	4,195,200	0.30	0.60	1.80
1931	6,595,200	0.25	0.50	1.50
1932	9,292,800	0.25	0.40	1.00
1933	4,560,000	0.25	0.50	1.20
1934	3,052,800	0.50	1.00	1.80
1935	2,227,200	1.00	2.00	4.00
1936	9,734,400	0.25	0.50	1.00

15 ½ Penny (Br) 1911–1936. Type as No. 14. Since 1925 the portrait has been slightly modified (Y 61,62):

	Mintage	Fine	VF	XF
1911	12,570,880	1.00	1.50	8.00
1912	21,185,920	0.80	1.50	7.00
1913	17,476,480	0.80	2.40	11.00
1914	20,289,111	0.80	1.60	9.00
1915	21,563,040	0,80	1.60	9.00
1916	39,386,143	0.80	1.20	8.00
1917	38,245,436	0.80	1.20	8.00
1918	22,321,072	0.80	1.20	8.00
1919	28,104,001	0.60	1.20	7.00

	Mintage	Fine	VF	XF
1920	35,146,793	0.60	1.20	7.00
1921	28,027,293	0.80	1.20	7.00
1922	10,734,964	0.60	2.50	12.00
1923	12,266,282	0.60	1.50	10.00
1924	13,971,038	0.60	1.50	8.00
1925	12,216,123	0.60	1.50	9.00
1926	6,172,306	1.00	2.00	12.00
1927	15,589,622	0.60	1.50	7.00
1928	20,935,200	0.60	1.00	5.00
1929	25,680,000	0.60	1.00	5.00
1930	12,532,800	0.60	1.20	5.50
1931	16,137,600	0.50	1.00	5.00
1932	14,448,000	0.50	1.00	5.00
1933	10,560,000	0.50	1.00	5.00
1934	7,704,000	0.80	1.50	8.00
1935	12,180,000	0.50	1.00	5.00
1936	23,008,800	0.50	1.00	5.00

16   1 Penny (Br) 1911–1936. Type as No. 14
Since 1926 the portrait has been slightly
modified (Y 63, 64):

	Mintage	Fine	VF	XF
1911	23,079,168	0.50	1.80	7.00
1912	48,306,048	0.50	1.80	8.00
1912H	16,800,000	1.00	6.00	26.00
1913	65,497,812	0.50	1.00	9.00
1914	50,820,997	0.50	1.00	9.00
1915	47,310,807	0.50	1.50	10.00
1916	86,411,165	0.50	1.00	8.00
1917	107,905,436	0.50	0.80	7.00
1918	84,227,372	0.50	1.00	8.00
1918H	3,660,800	5.00	30.00	160.00
1918KN	3,660,800	6.00	35.00	180.00
1919	113,761,090	0.50	1.00	6.00
1919H	5,209,600	5.00	15.00	100.00
1919KN	5,209,600	8.00	40.00	240.00
1920	24,693,485	0.50	1.00	6.00

	Mintage	Fine	VF	XF
1921	29,717,693	0.50	1.00	5.00
1922	16,346,711	1.00	3.00	18.00
1926	4,498,519	1.50	4.00	22.00
1927	60,989,561	0.50	1.00	5.00
1928	50,178,000	0.40	1.00	3.00
1929	49,132,800	0.40	1.00	2.50
1930	29,097,600	0.50	1.00	5.50
1931	19,843,200	0.50	1.50	5.50
1932	8,277,600	0.80	2.00	18.00
1934	13,965,600	0.50	1.00	12.50
1935	56,070,000	0.50	0.80	2.00
1936	154,296,000	0.40	0.80	2.00

17 (65) 3 Pence (Ag) 1911-1926. Since 1926 the portrait has been slightly modified:

	Mintage	Fine	VF	XF
1911	5,847,091	1.00	2.00	5.00
1912	8,932,825	1.00	2.00	5.50
1913	7,143,242	1.00	2.00	5.00
1914	6,733,584	1.00	2.00	5.00
1915	5,450,617	1.00	2.00	5.00
1916	18,555,201	1.00	1.60	4.00
1917	21,662,490	1.00	1.60	4.00
1918	20,630,909	1.00	1.60	4.00
1919	16,845,687	1.00	2.00	5.00
1920	16,703,597	1.00	2.00	5.00
1921	8,749,301	1.00	2.00	5.50
1922	7,979,998	1.00	2.50	6.00
1925	3,731,859	2.00	5.00	12.00
1926	4,107,910	2.00	6.00	16.00

18 (66) 6 Pence (Ag) 1911-1927. Since 1926 the portrait has been slightly modified:

	Mintage	Fine	VF	XF
1911	9,161,317	2.00	4.00	12.50
1912	10,984,129	2.00	5.00	15.00
1913	7,499,833	2.00	6.00	25.00
1914	22,714,602	2.00	4.00	12.00

	Mintage	Fine	VF	XF
1915	15,694,597	2.00	4.00	12.00
1916	22,207,178	2.00	4.00	9.00
1917	7,725,475	2.50	6.00	20.00
1918	27,553,743	2.00	4.00	9.00
1919	13,375,447	2.00	4.00	11.00
1920	14,136,287	2.00	4.00	12.00
1921	30,339,741	2.00	3.00	10.00
1922	16,878,890	2.00	4.00	11.00
1923	6,382,793	4.00	10.00	30.00
1924	17,444,218	2.00	4.00	10.00
1925	12,720,558	2.00	3.50	11.00
1926	21,809,621	2.00	3.00	9.00
1927	8,924,873	2.00	4.00	12.00

19 (67)   1 Shilling (Ag) 1911-1927. Since 1926 the portrait has been slightly modified:

	Mintage	Fine	VF	XF
1911	20,071,908	5.00	8.00	18.00
1912	15,594,009	5.00	9.00	20.00
1913	9,011,509	6.00	10.00	45.00
1914	23,415,843	4.00	6.00	12.00
1915	39,279,024	4.00	5.50	11.00
1916	35,862,015	4.00	5.50	11.00
1917	22,202,608	4.50	6.00	12.00
1918	34,915,934	4.50	6.00	10.00
1919	10,823,824	5.00	8.00	20.00
1920	22,825,142	3.00	5.00	25.00
1921	22,648,763	3.00	5.00	25.00
1922	27,215,738	2.50	5.00	25.00
1923	14,575,243	2.50	5.00	20.00
1924	9,250,095	3.00	6.00	26.00
1925	5,418,764	4.00	8.00	40.00
1926	22,516,453	2.50	6.00	20.00
1927	9,247,344	2.50	6.00	22.00

20 (68) 1 Florin (Ag) 1911–1926. ℞ the four
crowned shields of the United King-
dom in cross pattern with sceptres in saltire:

	Mintage	Fine	VF	XF
1911	5,957,291	9.00	15.00	50.00
1912	8,571,731	8.00	14.00	48.00
1913	4,545,278	9.00	16.00	55.00
1914	21,252,701	6.00	10.00	18.00
1915	12,367,939	6.00	10.00	20.00
1916	21,064,337	6.00	10.00	18.00
1917	11,181,617	7.00	11.00	25.00
1918	29,211,792	6.00	10.00	20.00
1919	9,469,292	8.00	11.00	26.00
1920	15,387,833	3.00	7.00	38.00
1921	34,863,895	3.00	7.00	35.00
1922	23,861,044	3.00	6.00	30.00
1923	21,546,533	3.00	6.00	25.00
1924	4,582,372	6.00	15.00	50.00
1925	1,404,136	9.00	30.00	200.00
1926	5,125,410	6.00	10.00	50.00

21 (69) ½ Crown (Ag) 1911-1927. Rev. crowned
shield:

	Mintage	Fine	VF	XF
1911	2,920,580	9.00	12.00	60.00
1912	4,700,789	7.00	10.00	50.00
1913	4,090,169	10.00	12.50	55.00

	Mintage	Fine	VF	XF
1914	18,333,003	6.00	9.00	18.00
1915	32,433,066	5.50	8.00	15.00
1916	29,530,020	5.50	8.00	18.00
1917	11,172,052	6.00	8.00	15.00
1918	29,079,592	6.00	8.00	15.00
1919	10,266,737	8.00	11.00	25.00
1920	17,982,077	4.00	8.00	25.00
1921	23,677,889	4.00	8.00	28.00
1922	16,396,724	4.00	8.00	30.00
1923	26,308,526	4.00	7.00	22.00
1924	5,866,294	5.00	10.00	35.00
1925	1,413,461	10.00	25.00	200.00
1926	4,473,516	4.00	10.00	40.00
1927	6,837,872	4.00	9.00	22.00

22 (77) ½ Sovereign (Au) 1911-1915. Rev. St. George and the Dragon:

	Mintage	Fine	VF	XF
1911	6,107,870	85.00	95.00	110.00
1912	6,224,316	85.00	95.00	110.00
1913	6,094,290	85.00	95.00	110.00
1914	7,251,124	85.00	95.00	110.00
1915	2,042,747	85.00	95.00	110.00

23 (78) 1 Sovereign (Au) 1911-1925. Type as No. 22:

	Mintage	Fine	VF	XF
1911	30,047,869	130.00	150.00	160.00
1912	30,317,921	130.00	150.00	160.00
1913	24,539,672	130.00	150.00	160.00
1914	11,501,117	130.00	150.00	160.00

	Mintage	Fine	VF	XF
1915	20,295,280	130.00	150.00	160.00
1916	1,554,120	200.00	250.00	275.00
1917	1,014,714	Rare. Beware of numerous counterfeits.		
1925	4,406,431	130.00	150.00	160.00

Coins of imperial type (Nos. 22 and 23) with mintmark C (Ottawa), I (Bombay), M (Melbourne), P (Perth), S (Sydney) or SA (South Africa) are listed in the Australian, Canadian, Indian and South African Section of this catalogue.

Proof

24 (79) 2 £ (Au) 1911. Type as No. 22 (2,812 pieces) 1800.00

25 (80) 5 £ (Au) 1911. Type as No. 22 (2,812 pieces)

26 (70) 3 Pence (Ag) 1927–1936. Rev. three acorns with oak-leaves: 4000.00

	Mintage	Fine	VF	XF
1927	15,022	Proof only		100.00
1928	1,302,106	1.50	3.00	12.00
1930	1,319,412	1.00	2.00	10.00
1931	6,251,936	0.80	1.50	2.50
1932	5,887,325	0.80	1.50	2.50
1933	5,578,541	0.80	1.50	2.50
1934	7,405,954	0.80	1.50	2.50
1935	7,027,654	0.80	1.50	2.50
1936	3,328,670	0.80	1.50	2.50

27 (71) 6 Pence (Ag) 1927–1936. ℞ six-acorn design

	Mintage	Fine	VF	XF
1927	15,000	Proof only		30.00
1928	23,123,384	0.80	2.00	8.00
1929	28,319,326	0.80	2.00	7.00
1930	16,990,289	0.90	2.50	9.00
1931	16,873,268	1.00	3.00	10.00
1932	9,406,117	1.00	3.00	12.00
1933	22,185,083	1.00	2.50	10.00
1934	9,304,009	1.00	2.50	11.00
1935	13,995,621	1.00	2.00	9.00
1936	24,380,171	0.80	1.50	6.00

28 (72) 1 Shilling (Ag) 1927-1936. Rev. lion standing over crown:

	Mintage	Fine	VF	XF
1927	15,000	Proof only		40.00
1928	18,136,778	1.50	2.50	10.00
1929	19,343,006	1.50	2.50	10.00
1930	3,172,092	3.00	8.00	30.00
1931	6,993,926	2.00	4.00	16.00
1932	12,168,101	1.50	3.00	14.00
1933	11,511,624	1.50	3.00	14.00
1934	6,138,463	2.00	4.00	18.00
1935	9,183,462	1.50	3.00	12.00
1936	11,910,613	1.50	3.00	11.00

29 (73) 1 Florin (Ag) 1927–1936. ℞ the four crowned shields of the United Kingdom in cross pattern with sceptres in saltire

	Mintage	Fine	VF	XF
1927	101,497	Proof only		110.00
1928	11,087,186	3.00	4.50	15.00
1929	16,397,279	3.00	4.00	14.00
1930	5,753,568	3.00	4.50	18.00
1931	6,556,331	3.00	4.50	18.00
1932	717,041	12.00	45.00	160.00

	Mintage	Fine	VF	XF
1933	8,685,303	4.00	7.00	15.00
1935	7,540,546	4.00	7.00	15.00
1936	9,897,448	3.50	6.00	10.00

29   30

30 (74) ½ Crown (Ag) 1927-1936. Rev. arms:

	Mintage	Fine	VF	XF
1927	15,000	Proof only		60.00
1928	18,762,727	2.50	4.00	12.00
1929	17,632,636	2.50	4.00	12.00
1930	809,051	8.00	35.00	185.00
1931	11,264,468	2.50	4.00	15.00
1932	4,793,643	6.00	8.00	40.00
1933	10,311,494	2.50	4.00	12.00
1934	2,422,399	6.00	8.00	45.00
1935	7,022,216	2.50	5.00	12.50
1936	7,039,423	2.50	5.00	10.50

31 (75) 1 Crown (Ag) 1927-1936. Rev. crown:

	Mintage	Fine	VF	XF
1927	15,030	Proof only		260.00
1928	9,034	50.00	120.00	200.00
1929	4,994	55.00	150.00	230.00
1930	4,847	50.00	140.00	220.00
1931	4,056	60.00	150.00	260.00
1932	2,395	75.00	200.00	380.00
1933	7,132	50.00	110.00	210.00
1934	932	300.00	750.00	1700.00
1936	2,473	80.00	185.00	380.00

| A31 | Maundy money: 1 Penny, 2 Pence, 3 Pence and 4 Pence, 1911–1936 (Y A81–H81): |

	Mintage	VF	XF	Unc
1911	1.786	35.00	80.00	130.00
1912	1,246	35.00	65.00	120.00
1913	1,228	35.00	65.00	120.00
1914	982	35.00	65.00	120.00
1915	1,293	35.00	65.00	120.00
1916	1.128	35.00	65.00	120.00
1917	1,237	35.00	65.00	120.00
1918	1,375	35.00	65.00	120.00
1919	1,258	35.00	65.00	120.00
1920	1,399	35.00	65.00	120.00
1921	1,386	35.00	65.00	120.00
1922	1,373	35.00	65.00	120.00
1923	1,430	35.00	65.00	120.00
1924	1,515	35.00	65.00	120.00
1925	1,438	35.00	65.00	120.00
1926	1,504	35.00	65.00	120.00
1927	1.647	35.00	65.00	120.00
1928	1,642	35.00	65.00	120.00
1929	1,761	35.00	65.00	120.00
1930	1,724	35.00	65.00	120.00
1931	1,759	35.00	65.00	120.00
1932	1,835	35.00	65.00	120.00
1933	1,872	35.00	65.00	120.00
1934	1,887	35.00	65.00	120.00
1935	1,928	65.00	90.00	150.00
1936	1,323	90.00	110.00	180.00

COMMEMORATIVE ISSUE FOR THE SILVER JUBILEE OF KING GEORGE V

		Unc	Proof
32 (76)	1 Crown (Ag) 1935. Rev. St. George and the Dragon:		
	a) incuse edge (714,769)	25.00	60.00
	b) raised edge (2,500)		600.00

GEORGE VI 1936-1952

33 (82) 1 Farthing (Br) 1937–1948. Head left of King George VI (1895–1952). Ɍ wren (Troglodytes troglodytes — Troglodydidae):

	Mintage	Fine	VF	XF
1937	8,157,602	0.30	0.60	1.00
1938	7,449,600	0.40	0.80	1.50
1939	31,440,000	0.10	0.20	0.60
1940	18,360,000	0.10	0.40	0.80
1941	27,312,000	0.10	0.20	0.60
1942	28,857,600	0.10	0.20	0.60
1943	33,345,600	0.10	0.20	0.60
1944	25,137,600	0.10	0.20	0.60
1945	23,736,000	0.10	0.20	0.60
1946	24,364,800	0.10	0.20	0.60
1947	14,745,600	0.10	0.20	0.60
1948	16,622,400	0.10	0.20	0.60

34 (83) ½ Penny (Br) 1937–1948. ℞ "The Golden
Hind", flagship of Sir Francis Drake:

	Mintage	Fine	VF	XF
1937	24,530,402	0.20	0.50	1.50
1938	40,320,000	0.25	0.60	1.60
1939	28,924,800	0.20	0.80	3.00
1940	32,162,400	0.20	0.80	3.50
1941	45,120,000	0.20	0.60	2.00
1942	71,908,800	0.20	0.50	1.00
1943	76,200,000	0.20	0.50	1.20
1944	81,840,000	0.20	0.40	1.00
1945	57,000,000	0.25	0.40	1.00
1946	22,725,600	0.20	0.60	4.00
1947	21,266,400	0.20	0.40	1.60
1948	26,947,200	0.20	0.40	1.00

35 (84) 1 Penny (Br) 1937–1948. ℞ Britannia
seated:

	Mintage	Fine	VF	XF
1937	88,922,402	0.30	0.60	1.20
1938	121,560,000	0.25	0.50	1.20
1939	55,560,000	0.25	0.50	2.50
1940	42,284,400	0.50	1.00	5.50
1944	42,600,000	0.30	1.00	3.50
1945	79,531,200	0.20	0.80	3.00
1946	66,855,600	0.20	0.60	1.60
1947	52,220,400	0.20	0.60	1.20
1948	63,961,200	0.20	0.40	1.20

36 (85)   3 Pence (Ni–Bra) 1937–1948. ℞ thrift
plant (Allium porrum – Liliaceae) –
emblem of Wales (twelve-sided):

	Mintage	Fine	VF	XF
1937	45,734,359	0.50	0.90	1.50
1938	14,532,332	0.60	1.20	5.00
1939	5,603,021	0.50	3.00	9.00
1940	12,636,018	0.30	1.00	3.60
1941	60,239,489	0.20	0.60	1.00
1942	103,214,400	0.20	0.40	1.00
1943	101,702,400	0.20	0.40	1.20
1944	69,760,000	0.20	0.60	2.50
1945	33,942,466	0.20	0.80	2.60
1946	620,734	3.00	10.00	60.00
1948	4,230,400	0.60	1.50	9.00

37 (86)   3 Pence (Ag) 1937–1944. ℞ shield on
rose:

	Mintage	Fine	VF	XF
1937	8,174,558	0.30	0.50	1.20
1938	6,402,473	0.30	0.60	2.00
1939	1,355,860	0.40	1.60	5.00
1940	7,914,401	0.30	0.60	1.60
1941	7,979,411	0.30	0.60	1.20
1942	4,144,051	1.60	4.00	10.00
1943	1,397,220	2.00	5.00	12.00
1944	2,005,533	3.50	10.00	20.00

38   6 Pence 1937–1948. Rev. crown above monogram (Y 87, 95):

	Mintage	Fine	VF	XF
1937 (Ag)	22,328,926	1.00	1.50	2.50
1938 (Ag)	13,402,701	1.50	2.50	4.50
1939 (Ag)	28,670,304	0.90	1.80	3.50
1940 (Ag)	20,875,196	0.90	1.80	3.50
1941 (Ag)	23,086,616	0.90	1.80	3.50
	44,942,785	0.80	1.20	2.00
1943 (Ag)	46,927,111	0.50	1.00	1.80
1944 (Ag)	36,952,600	0.50	1.10	2.00
1945 (Ag)	39,939,259	0.50	1.00	1.50
1946 (Ag)	43,466,407	0.50	1.00	1.50
1947 (Cu-Ni)	29,993,263	0.20	0.40	1.20
1948 (Cu-Ni)	88,323,540	0.20	0.40	1.00

39   1 Shilling 1937–1948. Rev. arms of England (Y 88, 96):

	Mintage	Fine	VF	XF
1937 (Ag)	8,385,524	1.80	2.50	4.00
1938 (Ag)	4,833,436	2.50	4.00	8.00
1939 (Ag)	11,052,677	1.20	2.00	5.00
1940 (Ag)	11,099,126	1.20	1.80	4.50
1941 (Ag)	11,391,883	1.20	1.80	4.50
1942 (Ag)	17,453,643	1.20	1.80	4.00
1943 (Ag)	11,404,213	1.20	1.80	4.00
1944 (Ag)	11,586,751	0.80	1.50	3.00
1945 (Ag)	15,143,404	0.80	1.50	3.00
1946 (Ag)	18,663,797	0.80	1.50	3.00
1947 (Cu-Ni)	12,120,611	0.30	0.60	1.40
1948 (Cu-Ni)	45,576,923	0.30	0.60	1.20

40   1 Shilling 1937–1948. Rev. arms of
             Scotland (Y 89, 97):

	Mintage	Fine	VF	XF
1937 (Ag)	6,775,277	1.60	2.50	4.00
1938 (Ag)	4,797,852	1.80	4.00	9.00
1939 (Ag)	10,263,892	1.60	3.00	5.00
1940 (Ag)	9,913,089	1.00	2.00	4.00
1941 (Ag)	8,086,030	1.00	2.00	6.00
1942 (Ag)	13,676,759	1.00	2.00	4.00
1943 (Ag)	9,824,214	1.00	2.00	5.00
1944 (Ag)	10,990,167	1.00	2.00	4.00
1945 (Ag)	15,106,270	0.80	1.80	3.00
1946 (Ag)	16,381,501	0.80	1.80	3.00
1947 (Cu-Ni)	12,283,223	0.25	0.50	1.50
1948 (Cu-Ni)	45,351,937	0.20	0.40	1.20

41   2 Shillings 1937–1948. Rev. crown above
             rose, thistle and shamrock (Y 90, 98):

	Mintage	Fine	VF	XF
1937 (Ag)	13,033,183	3.00	6.00	12.00
1938 (Ag)	7,909,388	4.00	6.50	13.00
1939 (Ag)	20,850,607	3.50	6.00	12.00
1940 (Ag)	18,700,338	2.00	5.00	9.00
1941 (Ag)	24,451,079	2.00	5.00	9.00
1942 (Ag)	39,895,243	2.00	5.00	9.00
1943 (Ag)	26,711,987	2.00	5.00	9.00
1944 (Ag)	27,560,005	2.00	5.00	9.00
1945 (Ag)	25,858,049	2.00	5.00	9.00
1946 (Ag)	22,300,254			

	Mintage	Fine	VF	XF
1947 (Cu-Ni)	22,910,085	1.00	1.80	3.00
1948 (Cu-Ni)	67,553,636	1.00	1.50	2.80

42   ½ Crown 1937–1948. Rev. shield (Y 91, 99):

	Mintage			
1937 (Ag)	9,132,842	1.50	4.00	7.00
1938 (Ag)	6,426,478	1.80	4.50	9.00
1939 (Ag)	15,478,635	1.00	3.00	6.00
1940 (Ag)	17,948,439	1.00	3.00	5.00
1941 (Ag)	15,773,984	1.00	3.00	5.00
1942 (Ag)	31,220,090	1.00	3.00	5.00
1943 (Ag)	15,462,875	1.00	3.00	5.00
1944 (Ag)	15,255,165	1.00	3.00	5.00
1945 (Ag)	19,849,242	1.00	3.00	5.00
1946 (Ag)	22,724,873	1.00	3.00	5.00
1947 (Cu-Ni)	21,911,484	0.40	1.00	2.00
1948 (Cu-Ni)	71,164,703	0.30	0.70	2.00

		VF	XF
43 (92)	1 Crown (Ag) 1937. Crowned shield supported by lion for England and unicorn for Scotland (445,101 pieces)	20.00	35.00

A43   Maundy money: 1 Penny, 2 Pence,
3 Pence and 4 Pence, 1937–1948
(Y A93–D93):

	Mintage	VF	XF	Unc
1937	1,325	30.00	50.00	100.00
1938	1,275	30.00	50.00	100.00
1939	1,234	30.00	50.00	100.00
1940	1,277	30.00	50.00	100.00
1941	1,253	30.00	50.00	100.00
1942	1,231	30.00	50.00	100.00
1943	1,239	30.00	50.00	100.00
1944	1,259	30.00	50.00	100.00
1945	1,355	30.00	50.00	100.00
1946	1,365	30.00	50.00	100.00
1947	1,375	30.00	50.00	100.00
1948	1,385	30.00	50.00	100.00

44 (100)   ½ Sovereign (Au) 1937. St. George and
the Dragon (5,501 pieces)   Proof   500.00

45 (101)   1 Sovereign (Au) 1937. Type as No. 44
(5,501 pieces)   Proof   1200.00

Proof

46 (102) 2 £ (Au) 1937. Type as No. 44 (5,501 pieces)   1300.00

47 (103) 5 £ (Au) 1937. Type as No. 44 (5,501 pieces)   2500.00

48 (104) 1 Farthing (Br) 1949-1952. Type as No. 33,
            but shorter inscription:

	Mintage	Fine	VF	XF
1949	8,424,000	0.10	0.25	0.40
1950	10,342,313	0.10	0.25	0.40
1951	14,036,000	0.10	0.25	0.40
1952	5,251,200	0.15	0.30	0.60

49 (105) ½ Penny (Br) 1949–1952. Type as No. 34,
but shorter inscription:

	Mintage	Fine	VF	XF
1949	24,744,000	0.10	0.30	2.00
1950	524,171,113	0.10	0.30	1.50
1951	14,888,000	0.60	1.20	2.50
1952	33,278,400	0.10	0.30	1.00

50 (106) 1 Penny (Br) 1949–1951. Type as No. 35,
but shorter inscription:

	Mintage	Fine	VF	XF
1949	14,324,400	0.20	0.60	1.20
1950	257,513	5.00	8.00	15.00
1951	140,000	9.00	15.00	20.00

51 (107) 3 Pence (Ni–Bra) 1949–1952. Type as
No. 36, but shorter inscription (twelve-
sided):

	Mintage	Fine	VF	XF
1949	464,000	6.00	16.00	70.00
1950	1,617,513	1.00	3.00	15.00
1951	1,204,000	0.80	2.00	16.00
1952	25,494,400	0.30	0.70	2.00

52 (108) 6 Pence (Cu-Ni) 1949-1952. Type similar to
No. 38; shorter inscription:

	Mintage	Fine	VF	XF
1949	41,335,515	0.15	0.30	1.00
1950	32,759,468	0.20	0.40	1.20
1951	40,419,491	0.20	0.50	1.50
1952	1,013,477	3.00	6.00	20.00

53 (109) 1 Shilling (Cu–Ni) 1949–1951. Type as
No. 39, but shorter inscription:

	Mintage	Fine	VF	XF
1949	19,328,405	0.20	0.30	2.00
1950	19,261,385	0.20	0.30	2.50
1951	9,976,930	0.25	0.50	3.00

54 (110) 1 Shilling (Cu–Ni) 1949–1951. Type as
No. 40, but shorter inscription:

	Mintage	Fine	VF	XF
1949	21,243,074	0.20	0.40	3.00
1950	14,317,114	0.15	0.30	2.00
1951	10,981,174	0.15	0.30	2.00

55 (111) 2 Shillings (Cu-Ni) 1949-1951. Type as No. 41, but shorter inscription:

	Mintage	Fine	VF	XF
1949	28,614,939	0.60	1.50	4.50
1950	24,375,003	0.60	1.50	6.00
1951	27,431,747	0.60	1.00	2.00

56 (112) ½ Crown (Cu–Ni) 1949–1952. Type as No. 42, but shorter inscription:

	Mintage	Fine	VF	XF
1949	28,272,512	0.40	1.00	1.50
1950	28,353,013	0.40	1.00	1.60
1951	9,023,520	0.50	1.20	2.00

1952, extremely rare (1 specimen known).

COMMEMMORATIVE ISSUE FESTIVAL OF BRITAIN

57 (114) 1 Crown (Cu-Ni) 1951. Type as No. 44, but shorter inscription (1,983,540 pieces;   Proof   16.00

A57   Maundy money: 1 Penny, 2 Pence, 3 Pence and 4 Pence, 1949–1952 (Y A113–D113):

	Mintage	VF	XF	Unc
1949	1,395	35.00	60.00	130.00
1950	1,405	35.00	60.00	130.00
1951	1,468	35.00	60.00	130.00
1952	1,012	50.00	80.00	150.00

ELIZABETH II since 1952

				XF	Unc
58	(116)	1	Farthing (Br) 1953. Head right of Queen Elizabeth II(*1926). Rev. wren (6,171,037 pieces)	0.60	1.50
59	(117)	½	Penny (Br) 1953. Rev. "The Golden Hind" (8,966,366 pieces)	1.00	3.00

60	(118)	1	Penny (Br) 1953. Rev. Britannia seated (1,348,400 pieces)	3.00	6.00
61	(119)	3	Pence (Ni-Bra) 1953. Rev. portcullis with chains (30,658,000 pieces)	1.00	3.00
62	(120)	6	Pence (Cu–Ni) 1953. ℞ rose (Rosa gallica — Rosaceae), emblem of England; thistle (Cirsium vulgare — Compositae), emblem of Scotland; shamrock (Trifolium repens — Leguminosae), emblem of Northern Ireland; thrift plant (Allium porrum — Liliaceae), emblem of Wales (70,363,876 pieces)	1.00	3.50

		XF	Unc
63 (121) 1	Shilling (Cu-Ni) 1953. Rev. arms of England (41,982,894 pieces)	0.60	2.00

64 (122) 1	Shilling (Cu-Ni) 1953. Rev. arms of Scotland (20,703,528 pieces)	0.80	2.20
65 (123) 2	Shillings (Cu-Ni) 1953. Rev. rose within circle, the border made of horse-thistle, white clover leaves and thrift plant (11,998,710 pieces)	3.00	10.00
66 (124) ½	Crown (Cu-Ni) 1953. Rev. crowned arms (4,373,214 pieces)	2.00	5.00

COMMEMORATIVE ISSUE FOR THE CORONATION OF QUEEN ELIZABETH II

67 (125) 1	Crown (Cu–Ni) 1953. Queen Elizabeth II on horseback. ℞ crown surrounded by the arms and emblems of England, Scotland, Northern Ireland and Wales (6,002,621 pieces)	4.50	10.00
A67	Maundy money: 1 Penny, 2 Pence, 3 Pence and 4 Pence, 1953 (1,025 sets) (Y A126–D126):	150.00	460.00

68 (127)   1 Farthing (Br) 1954-1956. Type as No.
58, but shorter inscription:

	Mintage	VF	XF	Unc
1954	6,566,400	0.20	0.40	1.20
1955	5,779,200	0.20	0.40	1.20
1956	1,996,800	0.80	1.20	3.00

69 (128)   ½ Penny (Br) 1954–1967. Type as No. 59,
but shorter inscription:

	Mintage	VF	XF	Unc
1954	19,375,000	0.60	2.00	6.00
1955	18,799,200	0.30	1.60	5.00
1956	21,799,200	0.30	1.60	5.00
1957	43,684,888	0.20	0.50	2.00
1958	62,318,400	0.20	0.50	1.00
1959	79,176,000	0.10	0.30	0.50
1960	41,340,000	0.10	0.30	0.50
1962	41,779,200	0.10	0.30	0.50
1963	45,036,000	0.10	0.20	0.30
1964	78,583,200	0.05	0.10	0.30
1965	98,083,200	0.05	0.10	0.30
1966	95,289,600	0.05	0.10	0.30
1967	146,491,200	0.05	0.10	0.30

70 (A 128)   1 Penny (Br) 1961-1967. Type as No. 60,
but shorter inscription:

	Mintage	VF	XF	Unc
1961	48,313,400	0.40	0.60	1.20
1962	143,308,600	0.25	0.50	0.80
1963	125,235,600	0.10	0.25	0.50
1964	153,294,000	0.10	0.25	0.50
1965	121,310,400	0.10	0.25	0.50
1966	165,739,200	0.10	0.25	0.50
1967	654,564,000	0.10	0.20	0.50

71 (129) 3 Pence (Ni–Bra) 1954–1967. Type as
No. 61, but shorter inscription:

	Mintage	VF	XF	Unc
1954	41,720,000	0.50	1.70	5.00
1955	41,075,200	0.50	2.00	6.00
1956	36,801,600	0.50	2.40	6.50
1957	24,294,500	0.50	1.20	6.00
1958	20,504,000	0.80	4.00	10.00
1959	28,499,200	0.50	1.20	5.00
1960	83,078,400	0.60	1.00	4.50
1961	41,102,400	0.50	0.60	1.00
1962	51,545,600	0.30	0.50	0.90
1963	39,482,866	0.20	0.40	0.90
1964	44,867,200	0.20	0.40	0.60
1965	27,160,000	0.20	0.40	0.60
1966	53,160,000	0.20	0.40	0.60
1967	151,780,800	0.10	0.20	0.40

72 (130) 6 Pence (Cu–Ni) 1954–1967. Type as
No. 62, but shorter inscription:

	Mintage	VF	XF	Unc
1954	105,241,150	0.40	1.00	5.00
1955	109,929,554	0.30	0.50	3.00
1956	109,841,555	0.30	0.80	3.00
1957	105,654,290	0.30	0.50	1.00
1958	123,518,527	0.40	0.80	6.00
1959	93,089,441	0.30	0.60	1.00
1960	103,283,346	0.30	1.00	6.00
1961	115,052,017	0.30	1.00	5.00
1962	166,483,637	0.30	0.40	2.00
1963	120,056,000	0.30	0.40	2.00
1964	152,336,000	0.30	0.40	1.00
1965	129,644,000	0.30	0.40	1.00

	Mintage	VF	XF	Unc
1966	175,676,000	0.30	0.40	1.00
1967	240,788,000	0.25	0.40	1.00

73 (131) 1 Shilling (Cu–Ni) 1954–1966. Type as
No. 63, but shorter inscription:

	Mintage	VF	XF	Unc
1954	30,262,032	0.40	1.00	4.00
1955	45,259,908	0.40	0.60	3.00
1956	44,907,008	0.60	2.00	12.00
1957	42,774,217	0.30	0.50	2.00
1958	14,392,305	1.50	8.00	30.00
1959	19,442,778	0.30	0.50	1.50
1960	27,027,914	0.30	0.50	1.50
1961	39,816,907	0.30	0.50	1.50
1962	36,704,379	0.30	0.50	1.00
1963	49,433,607	0.30	0.50	1.00
1964	8,590,900	0.40	0.80	2.00
1965	9,216,000	0.40	0.80	2.00
1966	15,002,000	0.30	0.50	1.00

74 (132) 1 Shilling (Cu–Ni) 1954–1966. Type as
No. 64, but shorter inscription:

	Mintage	VF	XF	Unc
1954	26,771,735	0.40	0.60	4.00
1955	27,950,906	0.40	0.60	4.00
1956	42,853,639	0.60	3.00	12.00
1957	17,959,988	1.00	6.00	26.00
1958	40,822,557	0.40	0.60	2.00
1959	1,012,988	2.50	5.00	30.00
1960	14,376,932	0.40	0.60	2.00
1961	2,762,558	0.70	1.60	10.00
1962	17,475,310	0.40	0.50	1.00
1963	32,300,000	0.40	0.50	1.00
1964	5,239,100	0.40	1.00	1.50
1965	2,774,000	0.50	1.20	2.00
1966	15,604,000	0.40	0.50	1.00

75 (133) 2 Shillings (Cu–Ni) 1954–1967. Type as
No. 65, but shorter inscription:

	Mintage	VF	XF	Unc
1954	13,085,422	1.50	12.00	50.00
1955	25,887,253	0.60	1.00	5.00
1956	47,824,500	0.60	1.00	5.00
1957	33,071,282	0.80	7.00	30.00
1958	9,564,580	1.50	10.00	40.00
1959	14,080,319	1.00	8.00	45.00
1960	13,831,782	0.50	1.00	5.00
1961	37,735,315	0.50	0.70	3.00
1962	35,147,903	0.50	0.70	3.00
1963	26,471,000	0.50	0.70	3.00
1964	16,539,000	0.60	1.00	4.00
1965	48,163,000	0.50	0.70	3.00
1966	83,999,000	0.50	0.60	3.00
1967	39,718,000	0.50	0.70	3.00

76 (134) ½ Crown (Cu–Ni) 1954–1967. Type as
No. 66, but shorter inscription:

	Mintage	VF	XF	Unc
1954	11,614,953	0.90	4.00	20.00
1955	23,628,726	0.60	1.60	9.00
1956	33,934,909	0.60	2.00	9.00
1957	34,200,563	0.60	1.40	5.00
1958	15,745,668	1.50	3.00	20.00

	Mintage	VF	XF	Unc
1959	9,028,844	2.00	8.00	22.00
1960	19,929,191	0.60	1.00	8.00
1961	25,887,897	0.60	1.00	4.00
1962	24,013,312	0.60	1.00	4.00
1963	17,625,200	0.60	1.00	4.00
1964	5,973,600	0.80	2.00	8.00
1965	9,778,440	0.60	1.00	5.00
1966	13,375,200	0.60	1.00	4.00
1967	33,058,400	0.60	1.00	4.00

		Unc	Proof
77 (136) 5 Shillings (Cu–Ni) 1960. Head right of Queen Elizabeth II. ℞ crown surrounded by the arms and emblems of England, Scotland, Northern Ireland and Wales (1,094,038 pieces)		14.00	40.00

A77   Maundy money: 1 Penny, 2 Pence, 3 Pence and 4 Pence, 1954– (Y A135–D135):

	Mintage	VF	XF	Unc
1954	1,020	35.00	60.00	130.00
1955	1,036	35.00	60.00	130.00

	Mintage	VF	XF	Unc
1956	1,088	35.00	60.00	130.00
1957	1,094	35.00	60.00	130.00
1958	1,100	35.00	60.00	130.00
1959	1,106	35.00	60.00	130.00
1960	1,112	35.00	60.00	130.00
1961	1,118	35.00	60.00	130.00
1962	1,125	35.00	60.00	130.00
1963	1,131	35.00	60.00	130.00
1964	1,137	35.00	60.00	130.00
1965	1,143	35.00	60.00	130.00
1966	1,206	35.00	60.00	130.00
1967	986	50.00	70.00	145.00
1968	964	50.00	70.00	145.00
1969	1,002	35.00	60.00	130.00
1970	980	40.00	65.00	140.00
1971	1,018	35.00	60.00	130.00
1972	1,026	35.00	60.00	130.00
1973	1,004	35.00	60.00	130.00
1974	1,042	35.00	60.00	130.00
1975	1,050	35.00	60.00	130.00
1976	1,158	35.00	60.00	130.00
1977	1,138	40.00	70.00	150.00
1978	1,138	40.00	65.00	140.00
1979	1,188	40.00	65.00	145.00
1980	1,198	45.00	70.00	150.00
1981		45.00	70.00	150.00

78 (137) 1 Sovereign (Au) 1957-1959, 1962-1968.
Head right of Queen Elizabeth II. Rev.
St. George and the Dragon:

	Mintage	XF	Unc
1957	2,072,000	145.00	160.00
1958	8,700,140	145.00	160.00
1959	1,358,228	145.00	160.00
1962	3,000,000	145.00	160.00
1963	7,400,000	145.00	160.00
1964	3,000,000	145.00	160.00
1965	3.800.000	145.00	160.00
1966	7,050,000	145.00	160.00
1967	5,000,000	145.00	160.00
1968	4,203,000	145.00	160.00

Gold coins of nominal value £ ½, 1, 2 and 5 with date 1953 were
issued as sets in very limited quantities for special purposes.

79 (138) 1 Crown (Cu–Ni) 1965. Head right of Queen Elizabeth II. ℞ Head of Sir Winston Churchill (1874–1965), statesman (19,640,000 pieces)

	XF	Unc
	1.20	2.00

NEW CURRENCY (Decimal System): 100 New Pence = £ 1

80 (139) ½ New Penny (Br) 1971–1981. Bust right of Queen Elizabeth II by Arnold Machin. Rev. the Tudor crown, crown of King Henry VII, founder of the House of Tudor:

	Mintage	XF	Unc	Proof
1971	1,394,188,250	0.05	0.20	3.00
1972	127,000	Proof only		3.00
1973	365,680,000	0.05	0.20	2.50
1974	365,448,000	0.05	0.20	2.50
1975	209,200,000	0.05	0.20	2.50
1976	402,330,000	0.05	0.20	2.50
1977	103,420,000	0.05	0.20	2.50
1978	33,318,000	0.05	0.20	2.50
1979		0.05	0.20	2.50
1980		0.05	0.20	2.50
1981		0.05	0.20	2.50

81 (140) 1 New Penny (Br) 1971–1981. Rev. portcullis with chains surmounted by royal crown, from the badge of King Henry VII (1457–1509):

	Mintage	XF	Unc	Proof
1971	1,521,666,250	0.10	0.30	3.50
1972	127,000	Proof only		3.00
1973	280,196,000	0.10	0.30	3.00
1974	330,892,000	0.10	0.20	3.00
1975	241,900,000	0.10	0.20	3.00
1976	252,466,000	0.10	0.15	3.00
1977	544,512,000	0.10	0.15	3.00
1978	241,318,000	0.10	0.15	3.00
1979		0.10	0.15	3.00
1980		0.10	0.15	3.00
1981		0.10	0.15	3.00

82 (141) 2 New Pence (Br) 1971–1981. Rev. three ostrich feathers over Prince's crown with fillets inscribed with motto »Ich dien«, badge of the Prince of Wales:

	Mintage	XF	Unc	Proof
1971	1,406,203,250	0.20	0.50	4.00
1972	127,000	Proof only		4.00
1973	102,000	Proof only		4.00
1974	104,000	Proof only		4.00
1975	150,458,000	0.20	0.50	4.00
1976	225,549,000	0.15	0.40	4.00
1977	109,533,000	0.20	0.40	4.00
1978	148,518,000	0.15	0.30	4.00
1979		0.10	0.20	4.00
1980		0.10	0.20	4.00
1981		0.10	0.20	4.00

83 (142)   5 New Pence (Cu-Ni) 1968–1981. Rev. horse-thistle, emblem of Scotland, surmounted by royal crown:

	Mintage	XF	Unc	Proof
1968	98,868,250	0.20	0.80	
1969	119,270,000	0.20	0.80	
1970	225,948,525	0.20	0.60	
1971	72,333,475	0.20	0.70	6.00
1972	231,000	Proof only		5.00
1973	102,000	Proof only		5.00
1974	104,000	Proof only		5.00
1975	138,452,000	0.20	0.50	4.50
1976	108,000	Proof only		4.00
1977	24,366,000	0.20	0.50	4.00
1978	37,918,000	0.20	0.50	4.00
1979		0.15	0.40	4.00
1980		0.15	0.40	4.00
1981		0.15	0.40	4.00

84 (143)   10 New Pence (Cu-Ni) 1968–1981. Rev. lion regardant walking to left wearing royal crown, part of the English arms:

	Mintage	XF	Unc	Proof
1968	336,143,250	0.30	0.80	
1969	314,008,000	0.30	1.50	
1970	133,571,000	0.30	1.50	
1971	63,205,000	0.35	2.00	6.00
1972	65,000	Proof only		6.00
1973	152,174,000	0.35	0.70	5.00
1974	92,741,000	0.35	0.70	5.00
1975	181,596,000	0.40	1.00	5.00
1976	267,654,000	0.35	0.80	5.00
1977		0.30	0.70	5.00

	XF	Unc	Proof
1978	0.30	0.70	5.00
1979	0.30	0.60	5.00
1980	0.30	0.60	5.00
1981	0.30	0.60	5.00

85 (144) 50 New Pence (Cu-Ni) 1969–1981. Rev. Britannia seated (seven-sided):

	Mintage	XF	Unc	Proof
1969	188,400,000	1.50	3.50	
1970	19,461,000	2.00	6.00	
1971	191,000	Proof only		8.00
1972	65,000	Proof only		8.00
1973	42,000	Proof only		9.00
1974	41,000	Proof only		8.00
1975	37,000	Proof only		8.00
1976	51,396,000	1.50	3.00	7.00
1977	49,788,000	1.50	3.00	7.00
1978	53,658,000	1.50	3.00	7.00
1979		1.20	2.50	7.00
1980		1.20	2.50	7.00
1981		1.20	2.50	7.00

COMMEMORATIVE ISSUE FOR THE SILVER WEDDING
OF THE BRITISH ROYAL COUPLE
ON 20th NOVEMBER 1972

			Unc	**Proof**
86 (145)	25	New Pence 1972. R Crowned monogram:		
		a) (Ag); (100,000 pieces)		50.00
		b) (Cu-Ni); (7,452,100 pieces)	1.80	

ACCESSION TO EUROPEAN ECONOMIC COMMUNITY

87 (146)	50	New Pence (Cu-Ni) 1973. Rev. value and clasped hands (80,306,000 pieces)	2.00	7.00

88 (A 137) 1 Sovereign (Au) 1974–1980. Type similar
to No. 78:

	Mintage		
1974	5,002,566	150.00	
1976	4,045,056	150.00	
1978		150.00	
1979		150.00	300.00
1980		150.00	290.00

25th ANNIVERSARY OF THE SILVER JUBILEE OF HER MAJESTY QUEEN ELIZABETH II

			Unc	Proof
89 (147)	25 Pence 1977:			
	a) (Ag)			50.00
	b) (Cu-Ni)		1.80	

80th BIRTHDAY OF QUEEN MOTHER

			Unc	Proof
90 (148)	25 Pence 1980:			
	a) (Ag)			45.00
	b) (Cu-Ni)		1.50	

			Unc	Proof
91 (B 137)	½ Sovereign (Au) 1980. Type as No. 88			150.00
92 (C 137)	2 Sovereign (Au) 1980. Type as No. 88			800.00
93 (D 137)	5 Sovereign (Au) 1980. Type as No. 88			2000.00

			Unc	Proof
94 (149)	25	Pence 1981:		
		a) (Ag)		60.00
		b) (Cu-Ni)	1.80	
95	½	Penny (Br) 1982–. Type as No. 80	0.20	2.50
96	1	Penny (Br) 1982–. Type as No. 81	0.20	3.00
97	2	Pence (Br) 1982–. Type as No. 82	0.20	4.00
98	5	Pence (Cu-Ni) 1982–. Type as No. 83	0.40	4.00
99	10	Pence (Cu-Ni) 1982–. Type as No. 84	0.60	5.00
100	20	Pence (Cu-Ni) 1982–. Rev. rose, emblem of England, surmounted by royal crown	1.10	8.00
101	50	Pence (Cu-Ni) 1982–. Type as No. 85	2.50	8.00
102	1	£ (Cu-Ni) 1983–	–.–	–.–

BRITISH TRADE DOLLAR

The Trade Dollar was destined for the Far East. The issues were made mostly in Bombay and Calcutta, less frequently by the Royal Mint in London.

			VF	XF
T 1	1	Dollar (Ag) 1895–1935. Standing Britannia with spear and shield, date and value. ℞ value in Chinese and Malay	16.50	28.00

Guernsey

Area: 31 sq. mi. Population: 54,000.
The Bailiwick of Guernsey also comprises, in addition to the more
important island bearing this name, the islands of Alderney, Brechon,
Herm, Jethou, Lihou and Sark (Sercq).
Capital: St. Peter Port.

8 Doubles = 1 Penny, 12 Pence = 1 Shilling,
20 Shillings = 1 £; 100 New Pence = 1 £

EDWARD VII 1901–1910

			VF	XF
1 (1)	1 Double (Br) 1902, 1903. Three leaves of the Guernsey lily above shield. ℞ value		1.00	2.00
2 (2)	2 Doubles (Br) 1902, 1903, 1906, 1908. Type as No. 1		12.00	20.00
3 (3)	4 Doubles (Br) 1902, 1903, 1906, 1908, 1910. Type as No. 1		3.50	7.00
4 (4)	8 Doubles (Br) 1902, 1903, 1910. Type similar to No. 1		3.00	6.00

GEORGE V 1910–1936

5 (1)	1 Double (Br) 1911. Type as No. 1		2.00	4.50
6 (2)	2 Doubles (Br) 1911. Type as No. 2		10.00	20.00
7 (3)	4 Doubles (Br) 1911. Type as No. 3		7.50	15.00
8 (4)	8 Doubles (Br) 1911. Type as No. 4		10.00	22.00

9 (1a)	1 Double (Br) 1911, 1914, 1929, 1933. Type similar to No. 5		1.00	2.00
10 (2a)	2 Doubles (Br) 1914, 1917, 1918, 1920, 1929. Type as No. 9		3.00	6.00
11 (3a)	4 Doubles (Br) 1914, 1918, 1920. Type as No. 9		2.00	4.00
12 (5)	8 Doubles (Br) 1914, 1918, 1920, 1934. Type similar to No. 8		2.00	4.50

GEORGE VI 1936–1952

13 (1a)	1 Double (Br) 1938. Type as No. 9		1.00	2.00
14 (3a)	4 Doubles (Br) 1945, 1949. Type as No. 11		1.50	3.00
15 (5)	8 Doubles (Br) 1938, 1945, 1947, 1949. Type as No. 12		1.00	2.50

ELIZABETH II since 1952

16 (6)	4 Doubles (Br) 1956–1966. Arms, inscription for the first time BALLIVIE			

	VF	XF
(BAILIWICK) INSULE DE GERNE-REVE. ℞ Guernsey lily, value in letters	1.00	2.00

17 (7)   8 Doubles (Br) 1956–1966. Arms. ℞ three flowers of the Guernsey lily (Nerine sarniensis – Amaryllidaceae)   0.50   1.00

18 (8)   3 Pence (Cu–Ni) 1956. Arms. ℞ Guernsey cow (Bos primigenius taurus – Bovidae)   0.50   1.00

19 (8a)   3 Pence (Cu–Ni) 1959–1966. Type as No. 18, but thicker flan   0.25   0.50

COMMEMORATIVE ISSUE FOR THE 900th ANNIVERSARY OF THE BATTLE OF HASTINGS

20 (9)   10 Shillings (Cu–Ni) 1966. Head of Queen Elizabeth II. ℞ head of William the Conqueror (1027–1087), Duke of Normandy, as William I, King of England 1066–1087   1.00   2.00

NEW CURRENCY (Decimal System): 100 New Pence = 1 £

	XF	Unc
21 (10) ½ New Penny (Br) 1971. Arms. ℞ value, date	0.10	0.20
22 (11) 1 New Penny (Br) 1971. Gannet	0.10	0.20
23 (12) 2 New Pence (Br) 1971. Old windmill (1571) from the island of Sark	0.10	0.20

		XF	Unc

24 (13) 5 New Pence (Cu-Ni) 1968, 1971. Arms. Rev.
value, date; flower of the Guernsey lily   0.15   0.30

25 (14) 10 New Pence (Cu-Ni) 1968, 1970, 1971.
Obverse as No. 24. Rev. value, date; Guern-
sey cow   0.30   0.50

26 (15) 50 New Pence (Cu-Ni) 1969, 1970, 1971.
Obverse as No. 24. Rev. hat, value and
date (sevensided)   1.20   1.80

COMMEMORATIVE ISSUE FOR THE SILVER WEDDDING
OF THE BRITISH ROYAL COUPLE
ON 20th NOVEMBER 1972   **Unc**   **Proof**

27 (16) 25 New Pence 1972:
a) (Ag)   30.00
b) (Cu-Ni)   8.50

25th ANNIVERSARY OF THE SILVER JUBILEE OF HER MAJESTY
QUEEN ELIZABETH II

28 (17) 25 Pence 1977:
a) (Ag)   32.00
b) (Cu-Ni)   1.80

			XF	Unc
29 (18)	½ Penny (Br) 1979. Type as No. 21	0.10	0.20
30 (19)	1 Penny (Br) 1977, 1979. Type as No. 22	0.15	0.25

			XF	Unc
31 (20)	2 Pence (Br) 1977, 1979. Type as No. 23	0.15	0.25
32 (21)	5 Pence (Cu-Ni) 1977, 1979. Type as No. 24	0.25	0.40
33 (22)	10 Pence (Cu-Ni) 1977, 1979. Type as No. 25	0.40	0.70
34 (23)	50 Pence (Cu-Ni) 1979, 1981. Type as No. 26	1.20	1.80

ROYAL VISIT

			Unc	Proof
35 (24)	25 Pence 1978:			
	a) (Ag)			30.00
	b) (Cu-Ni)		1:80	

80th BIRTHDAY OF QUEEN MOTHER

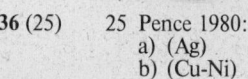

			Unc	Proof
36 (25)	25 Pence 1980:			
	a) (Ag)			30.00
	b) (Cu-Ni)		1.80	

			Unc	Proof
37 (26)	1 £ (Cu-Ni) 1981. Arms. Rev. Guernsey lily		3.00	
38 (26)	1 £ (Au) 1981. Type as No. 37:			
	a) 8.00 gm.			320.00
	b) 16.00 gm. (Pièfort)			800.00

WEDDING OF PRINCE CHARLES AND LADY DIANA

39 (27)	25 Pence 1981:		
	a) (Ag)		55.00
	b) (Cu-Ni)	2.50	

Jersey

Area: 45 sq. mi. Population: 74,000.

The Bailiwick of Jersey also comprises, in addition to the main island of the same name, the islands of Les Boeuftins, Les Dironilles, Les Ecrehos and Les Minquiers. The group of islands of Jersey, like those of Guernsey, has an autonomous government with its own Constitution. It is a dependency of the British Crown, but does not form part of the United Kingdom.

Capital: St. Hélier.

12 Pence = 1 Shilling, 20 Shillings = 1 £;
100 New Pence = 1 £

EDWARD VII 1901–1910

			VF	XF
1 (9)	$^1/_{24}$	Shilling (Br) 1909. Crowned bust right of King Edward VII. ℞ arms	5.00	10.00
2 (10)	$^1/_{12}$	Shilling (Br) 1909. Type as No. 1	4.50	9.00

GEORGE V 1910–1936

			VF	XF
3 (11)	$^1/_{24}$	Shilling (Br) 1911–1923. Crowned bust left of King George V. ℞ pointed shield	5.00	10.00
4 (12)	$^1/_{12}$	Shilling (Br) 1911–1923. Type as No. 3	2.50	5.00
5 (13)	$^1/_{24}$	Shilling (Br) 1923–1926. ℞ blunter shield	3.00	6.00
6 (14)	$^1/_{12}$	Shilling (Br) 1923–1926. Type as No. 5	2.00	4.00
7 (15)	$^1/_{24}$	Shilling (Br) 1931–1935	2.50	5.00
8 (16)	$^1/_{12}$	Shilling (Br) 1931–1935	1.50	3.00

GEORGE VI 1936–1952

			VF	XF
9 (17)	$^1/_{24}$	Shilling (Br) 1937–1947. Crowned head left of King George VI. ℞ arms	2.50	5.00
10 (18)	$^1/_{12}$	Shilling (Br) 1937–1947	1.00	2.00
11 (19)	$^1/_{12}$	Shilling (Br) 1949–1952. Type as No. 11, but with inscription LIBERATED 1945	0.40	0.80

ELIZABETH II since 1952

			VF	XF
12 (20)	$\frac{1}{12}$	Shilling (Br) 1954. Crowned head right of Queen Elizabeth II. ℞ arms, inscription LIBERATED 1945	0.40	0.80
13 (21)	$\frac{1}{12}$	Shilling (Br) 1957–1964. ℞ arms, inscription for the first time BAILIWICK OF JERSEY	0.20	0.40
14 (22)	$\frac{1}{4}$	Shilling (Ni–Bra) 1957–1960	0.20	0.40

COMMEMORATIVE ISSUE FOR KING CHARLES II
(reigned 1660–1685)

15 (23)	$\frac{1}{12}$	Shilling (Br) 1960. Crowned head r. of Queen Elizabeth II. ℞ arms and date 1660–1960	0.20	0.50
16 (24)	$\frac{1}{4}$	Shilling (Ni–Br) 1964 (octagonal)	0.20	0.50

COMMEMORATIVE ISSUES (3) FOR THE 900th ANNIVERSARY OF THE BATTLE OF HASTINGS

17 (25)	$\frac{1}{12}$	Shilling (Br) 1966. ℞ arms and date 1066–1966	0.20	0.50
18 (26)	$\frac{1}{4}$	Shilling (Ni–Bra) 1966. Type similar to No. 16, but with date 1066–1966	0.20	0.50
19 (27)	5	Shillings (Cu–Ni) 1966. ℞ arms and date 1066–1966	1.00	2.00

NEW CURRENCY (Decimal System): 100 New Pence = 1 £

			XF	Unc
20 (28)	½	New Penny (Br) 1971	0.10	0.20
21 (29)	1	New Penny (Br) 1971	0.10	0.20
22 (30)	2	New Pence (Br) 1971, 1975, 1980	0.10	0.20

23 (31)	5	New Pence (Cu-Ni) 1968. Head of Queen Elizabeth II. ℞ arms, value and date	0.15	0.25

				XF	Unc

24 (32) 10 New Pence (Cu-Ni) 1968, 1975. Type as
No. 23 — 0.30 — 0.70

25 (33) 50 New Pence (Cu-Ni) 1969. Type as
No. 23, but seven-sided — 1.00 — 2.00

COMMEMORATIVE ISSUES (9) FOR THE SILVER WEDDING
OF THE BRITISH ROYAL COUPLE

26 (34) 50 Pence (Ag) 1972. ℞ Royal Mace and
map — 8.00

27 (35) 1 £ (Ag) 1972. ℞ Belladonna lily (Amaryllis belladonna – Amaryllidaceae) — 16.00

28 (36) 2 £ (Ag) 1972. ℞ the sailing ship
Alexandra — 40.00

29 (37) 2½ £ (Ag) 1972. ℞ lobster (Homarus
gammarus – Homaridae) — 50.00

30 (38) 5 £ (Au) 1972. ℞ garden shrew (Crocidura suaveolens – Soricidae) — 60.00

31 (39) 10 £ (Au) 1972. ℞ a magnificent Gold
Torque weighing 746 gms used as
jewelry ab. 1500 B.C. was excavated
1889 in St. Hélier, Jersey — 90.00

32 (40) 20 £ (Au) 1972. ℞ the Ormer Shell (Haliotis tuberculata – Haliotidae) — 190.00

			Unc
33 (41)	25	£ (Au) 1972. ℞ the Royal Arms of England 1593, are cut in granite above the Main Gate of Elizabeth Castle, where King Charles II found refuge	220.00
34 (42)	50	£ (Au) 1972. ℞ the Arms of Jersey, Three Golden Lions, are derived from the Arms of King Edward I through a Seal granted to Jersey in 1279	440.00

25th ANNIVERSARY OF THE SILVER JUBILEE OF HER MAJESTY QUEEN ELIZABETH II

			Unc	Proof
35 (43)	25	Pence 1977:		
		a) (Ag)		30.00
		b) (Cu-Ni)	2.00	

BICENTENNIAL BATTLE OF JERSEY (2)

			Unc	Proof
36 (50)	1	£ 1981:		
		a) (Ag)		35.00
		b) (Cu-Ni)	3.00	
37	1	£ (Au) 1981		650.00
38 (44)	½	Penny (Br) 1981. Type as No. 20	0.20	
39 (45)	1	Penny (Br) 1981. Type as No. 21	0.20	
40 (46)	2	Pence (Br) 1981. Type as No. 22	0.20	
41 (47)	5	Pence (Cu-Ni) 1981. Type as No. 23	0.25	
42 (48)	10	Pence (Cu-Ni) 1981. Type as No. 24	0.70	
43 (49)	50	Pence (Cu-Ni) 1981. Type as No. 25	2.00	

WEDDING OF PRINCE CHARLES AND LADY DIANA

			Unc	Proof
44 (51)	2 £ 1981:			
	a) (Ag)			65.00
	b) (Cu-Ni)		8.00	
45	2 £ (Au) 1981			600.00

Isle of Man

Area: 227 sq. mi. Population: 68,000.
Since the 14th century this island in the Irish Sea has belonged to England. It has had its own constitution and judical system since 1866. The PM mintmark is that of the Pobjoy Mint in Sutton, England. Capital: Douglas.

12 Pence = 1 Shilling, 20 Shillings = 1 £;
100 New Pence = 1 £

200th ANNIVERSARY OF THE REVESTMENT ACT (3)

		Unc	Proof
1	½ £ (Au) 1965. Crowned head right of Queen Elizabeth II. ℞ triskelion (three legs joined in centre), emblem of the Isle of Man with circular motto QUOCUMQUE JEGERIS STABIT (how ever you throw him he will stand):		
	a) .917 gold	140.00	
	b) .980 gold		200.00

		Unc	Proof
2	1 £ (Au) 1965. Type as No. 1:		
	a) .917 gold	175.00	
	b) .980 gold		250.00
3	5 £ (Au) 1965. Type as No. 1:		
	a) .917 gold	800.00	
	b) .980 gold		1150.00

4 (1) 1 Crown 1970. Crowned bust right of Queen Elizabeth II. ℞ manx cat, in exergue value and date:

	Unc	Proof
a) (Ag)		45.00
b) (Cu-Ni)	5.00	

NEW CURRENCY (Decimal System): 100 New Pence = 1 £

5 (2) ½ New Penny (Br) 1971. Elizabeth II, head right. ℞ St. James's weed (Senecio jacobaea – Compositae). National flower (Cushag). This medicinal herb blossoms around St. James's Day (25th July), key date for the second mowing

	Unc	Proof
a) 1971	0.50	2.00
b) 1972 PM - 1975 PM	0.50	

6 (3) 1 New Penny (Br) 1971. ℞ Celtic cross (chain cross)

	Unc	Proof
a) 1971	0.50	2.00
b) 1972 PM - 1975 PM	0.50	

7 (4) 2 New Pence (Br) 1971. ℞ falcon (Falco rusticolus – Falconidae) originally given to a feudal lord on the occasion of his coronation

	Unc	Proof
a) 1971	0.80	2.00
b) 1972 PM - 1975 PM	0.40	

8 (5) 5 New Pence (Cu-Ni) 1971. ℞ "Tower of Refuge" at the harbour entrance of the capital Douglas, on the east side of the island. The tower was built in 1832, by the founder of the "Royal National Lifeboat Institution", Sir William Hillary. (1771–1847)

	Unc	Proof
a) 1971	1.00	3.00
b) 1972 PM -1975 PM	0.60	

9 (6) 10 New Pence (Cu–Ni) 1971. ℞ triskelion,
emblem of the Isle of Man. Originating
in Sicily, this old emblem appeared for
the first time on the arms of Henry
de Bello Monte in 1310, and on those of
the Earl of Moray in 1313

	Unc	Proof
a) 1971	1.00	3.50
b) 1972 PM - 1975 PM	0.80	

10 (7) 50 New Pence (Cu–Ni) 1971. ℞ Viking
ship. Vikings on the Isle of Man: two
Viking periods are to be distinguished:
a) around 800 to the battle of Hastings
(1066) and b) 1079 to 1266. The
Viking ship under full sails is document-
ed on 12th and 13th century seals

a) 1971	3.00	8.00
b) 1972 PM - 1975 PM	3.00	
11 (2a) ½ New Penny (Ag) 1975 PM. Type as No. 5	16.00	
12 (3a) 1 New Penny (Ag) 1975 PM. Type as No. 6	20.00	
13 (4a) 2 New Pence (Ag) 1975 PM. Type as No. 7	25.00	
14 (5a) 5 New Pence (Ag) 1975 PM. Type as No. 8	30.00	
15 (6a) 10 New Pence (Ag) 1975 PM. Type as No. 9	35.00	
16 (7a) 50 New Pence (Ag) 1975 PM. Type as No. 10	50.00	
17 (2b) ½ New Penny (Paltinum) 1975 PM. Type as No. 5		200.00
18 (3b) 1 New Penny (Platinum) 1975 PM. Type as No. 6		250.00
19 (4b) 2 New Pence (Platinum) 1975 PM. Type as No. 7		270.00

			Unc	Proof
20 (5b)	5 New Pence (Platinum) 1975 PM. Type as No. 8			*300.00*
21 (6b)	10 New Pence (Platinum) 1975 PM. Type as No. 9			*400.00*
22 (7b)	50 New Pence (Platinum) 1975 PM. Type as No. 10			*500.00*

COMMEMORATIVE ISSUE FOR THE SILVER WEDDING OF THE BRITISH ROYAL COUPLE

			Unc	Proof
23 (8)	25 New Pence 1972:			
	a) (Ag)			35.00
	b) (Cu-Ni)		6.00	

			Unc	Proof
24 (9)	½ £ (Au) 1973–1978, 1980–. Head right. Rev. Viking warrior on horseback:			
	a) 1973–1980 A		120.00	140.00
	b) 1974–1980 B		120.00	140.00
25 (10)	1 £ (Au) 1973–1978, 1980–. Type as No. 24			
	a) 1973–1980 A		160.00	180.00
	b) 1973–1980 B		135.00	180.00
	c) 1973–1980 C		160.00	180.00
26 (11)	2 £ (Au) 1973–1978, 1980–. Type as No. 24			
	a) 1973–1980 A		370.00	400.00
	b) 1974–1980 B		370.00	400.00
27 (12)	5 £ (Au) 1973–1978, 1980–. Type as No. 24			
	a) 1973–1980 A		700.00	750.00
	b) 1973–1980 B		700.00	750.00
	c) 1973 C		690.00	750.00
	d) 1973 D		685.00	750.00
	e) 1973 E (33 pieces)		*1200.00*	

COMMEMORATIVE ISSUE FOR THE CENTENARY OF BIRTH
OF SIR WINSTON CHURCHILL

			Unc	Proof
28 (13)	1 Crown 1974. Full-face portrait of Sir Winston Churchill, after Yousef Karsh:			
		a) (Ag)	25.00	32.00
		b) (Cu-Ni)	3.00	
29 (14)	25 Pence 1975. Manx cat:			
		a) (Ag)	25.00	35.00
		b) (Cu-Ni)	3.00	

BICENTENARY OF AMERICAN INDEPENDENCE

			Unc	Proof
30 (21)	1 Crown 1976. Profile of George Washington (1732-1799), 1st President of the United States of America, after Jean-Antoine Houdon:			
		a) (Ag)	25.00	35.00
		b) (Cu-Ni)	3.00	

CENTENARY OF THE HORSE-DRAWN TRAMS

			Unc	Proof
31 (22)	1 Crown 1976. Horse-drawn Tram, Douglas Promenade:			
	a) (Ag)		25.00	35.00
	b) (Cu-Ni)		2.80	
32 (15)	½ Penny (Br) 1976. Atlantic herring (Clupes harengus - Clupeidae)		0.20	
33 (16)	1 Penny (Br) 1976. Loaghtyn sheep (Capra aegagrus hircus - Bovidae)		0.20	
34 (17)	2 Pence (Br) 1976. Manx shearwater (Puffinus puffinus - Procellariidae)		0.30	
35 (18)	5 Pence (Cu-Ni) 1976. Laxey Wheel		0.50	
36 (19)	10 Pence (Cu-Ni) 1976. Triskelion		1.00	
37 (20)	50 Pence (Cu-Ni) 1976. Viking longship		2.20	
38 (18.1)	5 Pence (Cu-Ni) 1976. Type as No. 35, but mintmark PM on obverse		0.80	
39 (19.2)	10 Pence (Cu-Ni) 1976. Type as No. 36, but mintmark PM on obverse		1.10	
40 (15a)	½ Penny (Ag) 1976. Type as No. 32			18.00
41 (16a)	1 Penny (Ag) 1976. Type as No. 33			22.00
42 (17a)	2 Pence (Ag) 1976. Type as No. 34			28.00
43 (18a)	5 Pence (Ag) 1976. Type as No. 35			30.00
44 (19)	10 Pence (Ag) 1976. Type as No. 36			38.00
45 (20a)	50 Pence (Ag) 1976. Type as No. 37			50.00
46 (15b)	½ Penny (Platinum) 1976. Type as No. 32			*200.00*
47 (16b)	1 Penny (Platinum) 1976. Type as No. 33			*250.00*
48 (17b)	2 Pence (Platinum) 1976. Type as No. 34			*270.00*
49 (18b)	5 Pence (Platinum) 1976. Type as No. 35			*320.00*
50 (19b)	10 Pence (Platinum) 1976. Type as No. 36			*400.00*
51 (20b)	50 Pence (Platinum) 1976. Type as No. 37			*500.00*

25th ANNIVERSARY OF THE SILVER JUBILEE OF HER MAJESTY QUEEN ELIZABETH II(2)

52 (23) 1 Crown 1977. Triskelion surrounded by three St. Edward's crowns and cushag; commemorative legend: **Unc**   **Proof**

	Unc	Proof
a) (Ag)	28.00	50.00
b) (Cu-Ni)	2.80	

53 (25) 1 Crown 1977. Crowned monogram and coat of arms between laurel branches:

	Unc	Proof
a) (Ag)	27.50	35.00
b) (Cu-Ni)	2.50	

ISSUE FOR THE FAO COIN PLAN

54 (24) ½ Penny (Br) 1977, 1981. Type as No. 32, but mintmark PM on reverse and inscription F.A.O./FOOD FOR ALL added:

a) map with mintmark PM	0.20	
b) map without mintmark	0.20	

55 (24a) ½ Penny (Ag) 1977. Type as No. 54a   18.00

25th ANNIVERSARY OF THE CORONATION OF HER MAJESTY QUEEN ELIZABETH II

			Unc	Proof
56 (26)	1 Crown 1978. Rev. falcons:			
	a) (Ag)		26.00	35.00
	b) (Cu-Ni)		2.00	
57 (27)	1 £ (Virenium) 1978–1980. Rev. triskelion and map:			
	a) 1978, 1979 AA		3.50	12.00
	b) 1978, 1979 AB		3.50	12.00
	c) 1978, 1979 AC		3.50	12.00
	d) 1978 AD (3,780 pieces)		20.00	
	e) 1980		3.50	12.00
58 (27a)	1 £ (Ag) 1978–1980. Type as No. 57			*60.00*
A58 (27c)	1 £ (Au) 1980. Type as No. 57, .917 gold, 8 gm.			*400.00*
59 (27b)	1 £ (Platinum) 1978, 1980. Type as No. 57			*500.00*

300th ANNIVERSARY OF MANX COINAGE

			Unc	Proof
60 (28)	1 Crown 1979. Rev. different coins:			
	a) (Ag)		27.00	35.00
	b) (Cu-Ni)		2.00	

MILLENIUM OF TYNWALD (43)
(different coins with Millenium symbol)

			Unc	Proof
61 (15.1)		½ Penny (Br) 1979. Type as No. 32, but with Millenium symbol (circle containing stylized triskelion)	0.20	
62 (16.1)		1 Penny (Br) 1979. Type as No. 33	0.20	
63 (17.1)		2 Pence (Br) 1979. Type as No. 34	0.25	
64 (18.2)		5 Pence (Cu-Ni) 1979. Type as No. 35	0.50	
65 (19.3)		10 Pence (Cu-Ni) 1979. Type as No. 36	1.00	
66 (20.1)		50 Pence (Cu-Ni) 1979. Type as No. 37	3.50	
67 (27.1)		1 £ (Virenium) 1979. Type as No. 57	4.00	
68		½ Penny (Ag) 1979. Type as No. 40		20.00
69		1 Penny (Ag) 1979. Type as No. 41		22.00
70		2 Pence (Ag) 1979. Type as No. 42		26.00
71		5 Pence (Ag) 1979. Type as No. 43		30.00
72		10 Pence (Ag) 1979. Type as No. 44		36.00
73		50 Pence (Ag) 1979. Type as No. 45		50.00
74		1 £ (Ag) 1979. Type as 58		65.00
75		1 £ (Au) 1979. Type as No. 74	–.–	–.–
76		½ Penny (Platinum) 1979. Type as No. 46		*200.00*
77		1 Penny (Platinum) 1979. Type as No. 47		*250.00*
78		2 Pence (Platinum) 1979. Type as No. 48		*280.00*
79		5 Pence (Platinum) 1979. Type as No. 49		*350.00*
80		10 Pence (Platinum) 1979. Type as No. 50		*400.00*
81		50 Pence (Platinum) 1979. Type as No. 51		*500.00*
82		1 £ (Platinum) 1979. Type as No. 59		–.–
83		½ £ (Au) 1979. Type as No. 24		*170.00*
84		1 £ (Au) 1979. Type as No. 25		*250.00*
85		1 £ (Au) 1979. Type as No. 26		*400.00*
86		5 £ (Au) 1979. Type as No. 27		*800.00*
87 (34.2)		50 Pence 1979. Viking ship »Odin's Raven« with Millenium symbol and inscription »DAY OF TYNWALD/JULY 5th«; plain edge:		
		a) (Ag)	50.00	60.00
		b) (Cu-Ni)	4.00	

88 (34b) 50 Pence (Platinum) 1979. Type as No. 87   1200.00

89 (29) 1 Crown 1979. Viking warrior and Viking longship:

      a) (Ag)   55.00   75.00

      b) (Cu-Ni)   3.00   8.00

90 (30) 1 Crown 1979. English cog:

      a) (Ag)   55.00   75.00

      b) (Cu-Ni)   3.00   8.00

91 (31) 1 Crown 1979. Flemish carrack:

      a) (Ag)   55.00   75.00

      b) (Cu-Ni)   3.00   8.00

92 (32) 1 Crown 1979. Loyalist and English Man-of-War:

      a) (Ag)   55.00   75.00

      b) (Cu-Ni)   3.00   8.00

93 (33) 1 Crown 1979. Lifeboat and Sir William Hillary portrait:

      a) (Ag)   55.00   75.00

      b) (Cu-Ni)   3.00   8.00

	Unc	Proof

94 (29b) 1 Crown (Au) 1979. Type as No. 89   *1500.00*

95 (30b) 1 Crown (Au) 1979. Type as No. 90   *1500.00*

96 (31b) 1 Crown (Au) 1979. Type as No. 91   *1500.00*

97 (32b) 1 Crown (Au) 1979. Type as No. 92   *1500.00*

98 (33b) 1 Crown (Au) 1979. Type as No. 93   *1500.00*

99 (29c) 1 Crown (Platinum) 1979. Type as No. 89   *1800.00*

100 (30c) 1 Crown (Platinum) 1979. Type as No. 90   *1800.00*

101 (31c) 1 Crown (Platinum) 1979. Type as No. 91   *1800.00*

			Unc	Proof
102 (32c)	1	Crown (Platinum) 1979. Type as No. 92		*1800.00*
103 (33c)	1	Crown (Platinum) 1979. Type as No. 93		*1800.00*

ROYAL VISIT (2)

			Unc	Proof
104 (34)	50	Pence 1979. Type as No. 87, but edge inscription: »H.M.Q.E. II/ROYAL/ VISIT/I.O.M./JULY 1979«:		
		a) (Ag)	30.00	40.00
		b) (Cu-Ni)	3.00	
105	50	Pence (Platinum) 1979. Type as No. 104		*1200.00*

HENLEY REGATTA

			Unc	Proof
106	1	£ 1979. Type as No. 57, but with crossed rudders:		
		a) (Ag)	–.–	–.–
		b) (Virenium)	11.00	

13th OLYMPIC WINTER GAMES IN LAKE PLACID (3)

			Unc	Proof
107 (40)	1	Crown 1980. Triskelion and different athletes:		
		a) (Ag), without dot between OLYMPICS and LAKE	60.00	105.00
		b) (Ag), with dot between OLYMPICS and LAKE	60.00	105.00
		c) (Cu-Ni), without dot between OLYMPICS and LAKE	2.50	
		d) (Cu-Ni), with dot between OLYMPICS and LAKE	2.50	

				Unc	Proof
108 (40b)	1 Crown (Au) 1980. Type as No. 107b				*1600.00*
109 (40c)	1 Crown (Platinum) 1980. Type as No. 107b				*2200.00*

22nd OLYMPIC GAMES 1980 IN MOSCOW (9)

110 (43) 1 Crown 1980. Triskelion and different athletes: Judo match at top:

	Unc	Proof
a) (Ag)		52.00
b) (Cu-Ni)	4.50	

111 (41) 1 Crown 1980. Triskelion and different athletes: Runner at top:

a) (Ag), without dot between OLYMPIAD and MOSCOW and without dots to right and left of ONE CROWN (see illustration) — 52.00

b) (Ag), without dot between OLYMPIAD and MOSCOW and with dots to right and left of ONE CROWN — 52.00

c) (Ag), with dot between OLYMPIAD and MOSCOW and with dots to right and left of ONE CROWN — 52.00

d) (Cu-Ni), Type as No. 111a — 4.50

e) (Cu-Ni), Type as No. 111b — 4.50

f) (Cu-Ni), Type as No. 111c — 4.50

			Unc	Proof
112 (42)	1 Crown 1980. Triskelion and different athletes: Javelin thrower at top:			
	a) (Ag)			52.00
	b) (Cu-Ni)		4.50	
113 (43b)	1 Crown (Au) 1980. Type as No. 110			*1300.00*
114 (41b)	1 Crown (Au) 1980. Type as No. 111c			*1300.00*
115 42b)	1 Crown (Au) 1980. Type as No. 112			*1300.00*
116 (43c)	1 Crown (Platinum) 1980. Type as No. 110			*1800.00*
117 (41c)	1 Crown (Platinum) 1980. Type as No. 111c			*1800.00*
118 (42c)	1 Crown (Platinum) 1980. Type as No. 112			*1800.00*
119 (44)	½ Penny (Br) 1980–. Atlantic herring		0.15	

120 (45)	1 Penny (Br) 1980–. Manx cat	0.15	
121 (46)	2 Pence (Br) 1980–. Manx shearwater	0.20	
122 (47)	5 Pence (Cu-Ni) 1980–. Loagthyn sheep	0.40	
123 (48)	10 Pence (Cu-Ni) 1980–. Falcon	0.80	

			Unc	Proof
124 (49)	50 Pence (Cu-Ni) 1980–. Viking longship		2.50	

125 (44a)	½ Penny (Ag) 1980. Type as No. 119			20.00
126 (45a)	1 Penny (Ag) 1980. Type as No. 120			22.00
127 (46a)	2 Pence (Ag) 1980. Type as No. 121			26.00
128 (47a)	5 Pence (Ag) 1980. Type as No. 122			30.00
129 (48a)	10 Pence (Ag) 1980. Type as No. 123			36.00
130 (49a)	50 Pence (Ag) 1980. Type as No. 124			50.00

131 (44b)	½ Penny (Au) 1980. Type as No. 119			–.–
132 (45b)	1 Penny (Au) 1980. Type as No. 120			–.–
133 (46b)	2 Pence (Au) 1980. Type as No. 121			–.–
134 (47b)	5 Pence (Au) 1980. Type as No. 122			–.–
135 (48b)	10 Pence (Au) 1980. Type as No. 123			–.–
136 (49b)	50 Pence (Au) 1980. Type as No. 124			–.–

137 (44c)	½ Penny (Platinum) 1980. Type as No. 119			*200.00*
138 (45c)	1 Penny (Platinum) 1980. Type as No. 120			*250.00*
139 (46c)	2 Pence (Platinum) 1980. Type as No. 121			*280.00*
140 (47c)	5 Pence (Platinum) 1980. Type as No. 122			*350.00*
141 (48c)	10 Pence (Platinum) 1980. Type as No. 123			*400.00*
142 (49c)	50 Pence (Platinum) 1980. Type as No. 124			*500.00*

DAILY MAIL IDEAL HOME EXHIBITION, LONDON

143 (27.2)	1 £ 1980. Type as No. 57, but inscription D.M.I.H.E:			
	a) (Ag)			50.00
	b) (Virenium)		5.00	

BICENTENARY OF THE DERBY (3)

			Unc	Proof
144 (39)	1	Crown 1980:		
		a) (Ag)	30.00	40.00
		b) (Cu-Ni)	2.00	
145	1	Crown (Au) 1980. Type as No. 144		–.–
146	1	Crown (Platinum) 1980. Type as No. 144		–.–

80th BIRTHDAY OF QUEEN MOTHER (6)

147 (50)	1	Crown 1980. Queen Elizabeth the Queen Mother:		
		a) (Ag) .925 silver		50.00
		b) (Ag) .500 silver	40.00	
		c) (Cu-Ni)	2.50	
148	1	Crown (Au) 1980. Type as No. 147:		
		a) 22 carat, 7.28 gm.		–.–
		b) 9 carat, 5.00 gm.		–.–

		Unc	Proof

149 (9a) ½ Sovereign (Au) 1980. Viking warrior on horseback, Queen Mother's portrait at top (countermark) | | | −.−
150 (10a) 1 Sovereign (Au) 1980. Type as No. 149 | | | −.−
151 (11a) 2 Sovereign (Au) 1980. Type as No. 149 | | | −.−
152 (12a) 5 Sovereign (Au) 1980. Type as No. 149 (250 pieces) | | | −.−

TOURIST TROPHY 1980

153 (27.4) 1 £ 1980. Type as No. 57, but inscription T.T.:
  a) (Ag) | | | −.−
  b) (Virenium) | | 5.00 |

VIKING EXHIBITION, NEW YORK (3)

154 50 Pence 1980. Type as No. 87, but edge inscription »ODINS/RAVEN/VIKING/ EXHIBN/NEW/YORK/1980«:
  a) (Ag) | | | 80.00
  b) (Cu-Ni) | | 10.00 |
155 50 Pence (Au) 1980. Type as No. 154 | | | −.−
156 50 Pence (Platinum) 1980. Type as No. 154 | | | −.−

CHRISTMAS 1980 (3)

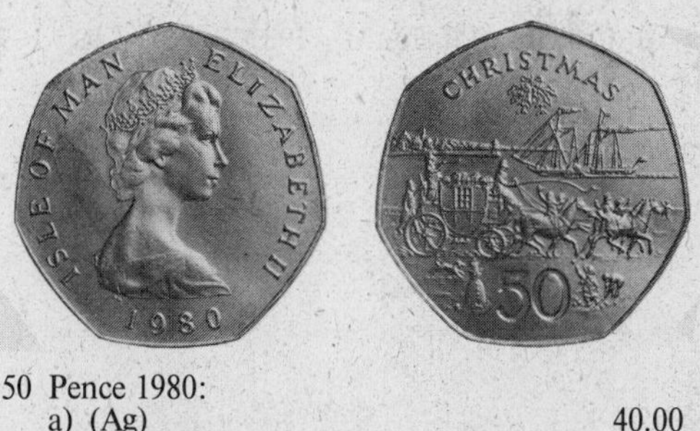

157 (51) 50 Pence 1980:
  a) (Ag) | | 40.00 | 60.00
  b) (Cu-Ni) | | 2.50 | 10.00
158 (51b) 50 Pence (Au) 1980. Type as No. 157 | | | 900.00

			Unc	Proof

159 (51 c)   50 Pence (Platinum) 1980. Type as No. 157 — Proof 1250.00

DUKE OF EDINBURGH AWARD SCHEME (12)

			Unc	Proof
160 (53)	1 Crown 1981:			
	a) (Ag)			36.00
	b) (Cu-Ni)		2.00	
161 (54)	1 Crown 1981:			
	a) (Ag)			36.00
	b) (Cu-Ni)		2.00	
162 (55)	1 Crown 1981:			
	a) (Ag)			36.00
	b) (Cu-Ni)		2.00	
163 (56)	1 Crown 1981:			
	a) (Ag)			36.00
	b) (Cu-Ni)		2.00	
164	1 Crown (Au) 1981. Type as No. 160:			
	a) .916 gold, 7.96 gm.			–.–
	b) .375 gold, 5.1 gm.			–.–
165	1 Crown (Au) 1981. Type as No. 161:			
	a) .916 gold, 7.96 gm.			–.–
	b) .375 gold, 5.1 gm.			–.–
166	1 Crown (Au) 1981. Type as No. 162:			
	a) .916 gold, 7.96 gm.			–.–
	b) .375 gold, 5.1 gm.			–.–
167	1 Crown (Au) 1981. Type as No. 163:			
	a) .916 gold, 7.96 gm.			–.–
	b) .375 gold, 5.1 gm.			–.–
168	1 Crown (Platinum) 1981. Type as No. 160			–.–
169	1 Crown (Platinum) 1981. Type as No. 161			–.–
170	1 Crown (Platinum) 1981. Type as No. 162			–.–
171	1 Crown (Platinum) 1981. Type as No. 163			–.–

			Unc	Proof
172 (63)	1	Crown 1981. Conjoined busts:		
		a) (Ag)		45.00
		b) (Cu-Ni)	2.50	
173	1	Crown (Platinum) 1981. Type as No. 172		2000.00
174	1	Crown 1981. Two arms:		
		a) (Ag)		45.00
		b) (Cu-Ni)	2.50	
175	1	Crown (Platinum) 1981. Type as No. 174		2000.00
176	½	Sovereign (Au) 1981. Conjoined busts and two arms		150.00
177	1	Sovereign (Au) 1981. Type as No. 176		250.00
178	2	Sovereign Au 1981. Type as No. 176		500.00
179	5	Sovereign (Au) 1981. Type as No. 176		1300.00

INTERNATIONAL YEAR OF THE DISABLED (12)

			Unc	Proof
180 (58)	1	Crown 1981. Louis Braille, inventor of the reading system for the blind:		
		a) (Ag)		36.00
		b) (Cu-Ni)	2.00	

			Unc	Proof

181 (59)   1 Crown 1981. Ludwig van Beethoven, composer:
    a) (Ag) — 36.00
    b) (Cu-Ni) — 2.00

182 (60)   1 Crown 1981. Sir Douglas Bader, aviator:
    a) (Ag) — 36.00
    b) (Cu-Ni) — 2.00

183 (61)   1 Crown 1981. Sir Francis Chichester, sailor:
    a) (Ag) — 36.00
    b) (Cu-Ni) — 2.00

184   1 Crown (Au) 1981. Type as No. 180:
    a) .375 gold — –.–
    b) .916 gold — –.–

185   1 Crown (Au) 1981. Type as No. 181:
    a) .375 gold — –.–
    b) .916 gold — –.–

186   1 Crown (Au) 1981. Type as No. 182:
    a) .375 gold — –.–
    b) .916 gold — –.–

187   1 Crown (Au) 1981. Type as No. 183:
    a) .375 gold — –.–
    b) .916 gold — –.–

188   1 Crown (Platinum) 1981. Type as No. 180 — –.–

189   1 Crown (Platinum) 1981. Type as No. 181 — –.–

190   1 Crown (Platinum) 1981. Type as No. 182 — –.–

191   1 Crown (Platinum) 1981. Type as No. 183 — –.–

TOURIST TROPHY 1981 (3)

			Unc	**Proof**
192 (57)	50	Pence 1981. Joey Dunlop, winner of Tourist Trophy, TT at top:		
		a) (Ag)		55.00
		b) (Cu-Ni)	2.00	
193	50	Pence (Au) 1981. Type as No. 192		1200.00
194	50	Pence (Platinum) 1981. Type as No. 192		1350.00
195 (52)	5	£ (Virenium) 1981. Rev. triskelion superimposed on island map	16.00	
196	5	£ (Ag) 1981. Type as No. 195		–.–
197	5	£ (Au) 1981. Type as No. 195		–.–
198	5	£ (Platinum) 1981. Type as No. 195		–.–

CHRISTMAS 1981 (3)

			Unc	**Proof**
199	50	Pence 1981:		
		a) (Ag)		40.00
		b) (Cu-Ni)	2.00	11.00
200	50	Pence (Au) 1981. Type as No. 199		900.00
201	50	Pence (Platinum) 1981. Type as No. 199		1100.00

202	20	Pence (Cu-Ni) 1982	1.20	
203	20	Pence (Ag) 1982		45.00

		Unc	Proof
204	1 Crown 1982. Passarella holding aloft the World Cup:		
	a) (Ag)		45.00
	b) (Cu-Ni)	2.00	
205	1 Crown 1982. A coccer ball covered by the national arms of the championship winners:		
	a) (Ag)		45.00
	b) (Cu-Ni)	2.00	
206	1 Crown 1982. Dramatic actions:		
	a) (Ag)		45.00
	b) (Cu-Ni)	2.00	
207	1 Crown 1982. Dramatic actions:		
	a) (Ag)		45.00
	b) (Cu-Ni)	2.00	
208	1 Crown (Au) 1982. Type as No. 204		–.–
209	1 Crown (Au) 1982. Type as No. 205		–.–
210	1 Crown (Au) 1982. Type as No. 206		–.–
211	1 Crown (Au) 1982. Type as No. 207		–.–

		Unc	Proof
212	1 Crown (Platinum) 1982. Type as No. 204		–.–
213	1 Crown (Platinum) 1982. Type as No. 205		–.–
214	1 Crown (Platinum) 1982. Type as No. 206		–.–
215	1 Crown (Platinum) 1982. Type as No. 207		–.–

Griechenland **Greece** **Grèce**

Hellas, ΕΛΛΑΣ

Area: 50,547 sq. mi. Population: 9,000,000.

The Greek War of Liberation in the years 1821–1830 brought to an end the Turkish domination which had existed since the 15th century. On gaining independence the country became a kingdom, and in the years 1924–1935 was ruled as a republic. After the successful National Revolution of 21st April 1967, King Constantine left the country; republic since 1973.

Capital: Athens.

100 Lepta = 1 Drachma

GEORGE I 1863–1913

			VF	XF
1 (19)	5	Lepta (Ni) 1912. Crown, date. ℞ screech owl (Athene noctua — Strigidae) and value (with hole in centre)	1.50	3.00

2 (20)	10	Lepta (Ni) 1912. Type as No. 1	1.25	2.50
3 (21)	20	Lepta (Ni) 1912. National arms, date. ℞ Athena and olive branch (Olea europea — Oleaceae)	2.00	4.50
4 (22)	1	Drachma (Ag) 1910–1911. Head left of King George I (1845–1913). ℞ Thetis, goddess of the sea, seated on sea-horse	8.00	12.50
5 (23)	2	Drachmai (Ag) 1911. Type as No. 4	12.00	20.00

Under King Constantine I 1913–1917, King Alexander 1917–1920 and King Constantine I 1920–1922 there was no issue of coinage.

GEORGE II 1922–1923

6 (29)	10	Lepta (Al) 1922. Crown, date. ℞ olive branch and value	2.50	4.00
7 (30)	50	Lepta (Ni–Br) 1921. Inscription, arms, date. ℞ olive branch		
		a) mintmark H (Heaton)		1100.00
		b) mintmark KN (King's Norton)		4000.00

REPUBLIC 1924–1935

8 (31) 20 Lepta (Cu–Ni) 1926. Helmeted head left of Athena, patroness of heroes, cities, agriculture, science and the arts. ℞ inscription and value

	VF	XF
	1.60	4.00

9 (32) 50 Lepta (Cu–Ni) 1926. Type as No. 8   1.50   3.00
10 (33) 1 Drachma (Cu–Ni) 1926. Type as No. 8   1.50   4.00
11 (34) 2 Drachmai (Cu–Ni) 1926. Type as No. 8   2.00   4.50

12 (35) 5 Drachmai (Ni) 1930. Phoenix, above High Cross next to rays of light. ℞ value between laurel branches tied underneath   2.00   6.00

13 (36) 10 Drachmai (Ag) 1930. Head left of Demeter. Greek goddess of the earth and all its fruits. ℞ ears of wheat   9.00   30.00
14 (37) 20 Drachmai (Ag) 1930. Head of Poseidon, god of the sea. ℞ prow of galley   11.00   32.00

GEORGE II 1935–1947

COMMEMORATIVE ISSUES (3) FOR THE RESTORATION OF THE MONARCHY

15 (B 37) 20 Drachmai (Au) 1935. Head left of King George II (1890–1947). Inscription. ℞ value within wreath; above, crown

	Proof
	7000.00

710   Greece

			Proof
A 15 (A 37)	100	Drachmai (Ag) 1935. Type as No. 15	2000.00
16 (C 37)	100	Drachmai (Au) 1935. Type as No. 15	10000.00

PAUL I 1947–1964

			VF	XF
17 (38)	5	Lepta (Al) 1954. Olive branches; above, crown. ℞ ears of corn and value	0.20	0.35
18 (39)	10	Lepta (Al) 1954–1969. ℞ bunches of grapes and value	0.20	0.35
19 (40)	20	Lepta (Al) 1954–1959. ℞ olive branch and date	0.25	0.40

			VF	XF
20 (41)	50	Lepta (Cu–Ni) 1954–1965. Head left of Paul I (1901–1964). ℞ national arms. Occurring with different mint marks!	0.80	1.50
21 (42)	1	Drachma (Cu–Ni) 1954–1965. Type as No. 20. Occurring with different mint marks!	0.60	1.50
22 (43)	2	Drachmai (Cu–Ni) 1954–1965. Type as No. 20. Occurring with different mint marks!	1.10	1.80
23 (44)	5	Drachmai (Cu–Ni) 1954, 1965. Type as No. 20	1.30	2.00
24 (45)	10	Drachmai (Ni) 1959, 1965. Type as No. 20	1.80	2.60
25 (46)	20	Drachmai (Ag) 1960–1965. ℞ Selene, the moon goddess, rising from the sea	4.50	8.00

COMMEMORATIVE ISSUE FOR THE CENTENARY OF THE ROYAL GREEK DYNASTY

26 (47)	30	Drachmai (Ag) 1963. Heads of George I, reigned 1863–1913; Con-

stantine I, reigned 1913–1917, 1920 to
1922; Alexander, reigned 1917–1920;
George II, reigned 1922–1923, 1935 to
1947; Paul I, reigned 1947–1964. ℞
map representing the Kingdom of
Greece; value

	VF	XF
	10.50	18.00

CONSTANTINE II 1964–1973
COMMEMORATIVE ISSUE FOR THE WEDDING OF KING CONSTANTINE II AND PRINCESS ANNE-MARIE OF DENMARK

			VF	XF
27 (48)	30	Drachmai (Ag) 1964. Conjoined heads of the Royal couple. ℞ double eagle and value	8.00	12.00
28 (49)	50	Lepta (Cu–Ni) 1966–1970. Head left of King Constantine II (*1940). ℞ national arms and value	0.20	0.40
29 (50)	1	Drachma (Cu–Ni) 1966–1970. Type as No. 28	0.40	0.80
30 (51)	2	Drachmai (Cu–Ni) 1966–1970. Type as No. 28	0.60	1.20

31 (52)	5	Drachmai (Cu–Ni) 1966–1970. Type as No. 28	1.00	2.00
32 (53)	10	Drachmai (Cu–Ni) 1968. Type as No. 28	1.80	2.50

COMMEMORATIVE ISSUES (4) FOR THE NATIONAL REVOLUTION OF 21st APRIL 1967

			Unc
33 (56)	20	Drachmai (Au) 1967. Soldier standing in front of a phoenix rising from flames, emblem of the military régime. ℞ national arms and value	320.00

34 (54)	50	Drachmai (Ag) 1967. Type as No. 33	50.00

				Unc
35 (55)	100	Drachmai (Ag) 1967. Type as No. 33		70.00
36 (57)	100	Drachmai (Au) 1967. Type as No. 33		1000.00

			VF	**XF**
37 (38)	5	Lepta (Al) 1971. Type as No. 17, but hole with smaller diameter	0.10	0.20

			VF	**XF**
38 (39)	10	Lepta (Al) 1971. Type as No. 18, but hole with smaller diameter	0.10	0.20
39 (40)	20	Lepta (Al) 1971. Type as No. 19, but hole with smaller diameter	0.20	0.40

40 (58)	50	Lepta (Cu–Ni) 1971. Constantine II, bust facing left. ℞ emblem of the military government, value	0.30	0.60
41 (59)	1	Drachma (Cu–Ni) 1971, 1973. Type as No. 40	0.50	0.80
42 (60)	2	Drachmai (Cu–Ni) 1971, 1973. Type as No. 40	0.60	1.20
43 (61)	5	Drachmai (Cu–Ni) 1971, 1973. Type as No. 40	0.80	1.50
44 (62)	10	Drachmai (Cu–Ni) 1971, 1973. Type as No. 40	1.00	2.50
45 (A 58)	10	Lepta (Al) 1973. Emblem of the military government, name of country (translated: Kingdom of Greece), date. ℞ trident between two dolphins, value	0.20	0.70
46 (B 58)	20	Lepta (Al) 1973. ℞ fruit branch, value	0.20	0.70

				VF	XF
47 (63)	20	Drachmai (Cu–Ni) 1973. Selene (moon-goddess), rising from the sea. ℞ emblem of the military government		2.50	3.50

REPUBLIC since 1973

48 (64)	10	Lepta (Al) 1973. Phoenix rising from the flames, above rays of light (arms of the Republic), name of country, date. ℞ trident between two dolphins, value		0.10	0.20
49 (65)	20	Lepta (Al) 1973. ℞ fruit branch, value		0.10	0.20
50 (66)	50	Lepta (Br) 1973. ℞ ornament, value		0.10	0.20
51 (67)	1	Drachma (Al–Br) 1973. ℞ screech-owl (Athene noctua – Strigidae), value		0.15	0.25
52 (68)	2	Drachmai (Al–Br) 1973. Type as No. 51		0.20	0.40
53 (69)	5	Drachmai (Cu–Ni) 1973. ℞ Pegasus, value		0.50	1.00

54 (70)	10	Drachmai (Cu–Ni) 1973. Type as No. 53		1.20	1.80
55 (71)	20	Drachmai (Cu–Ni) 1973. ℞ Athene		1.50	2.50

56 (72)	10	Lepta (Al) 1976. Coat of arms. Rev. bull, value		0.10	0.20

			VF	XF
57 (73)	20 Lepta (Al) 1976. Rev. head of a horse, value		0.10	0.20
58 (74)	50 Lepta (Al-Br) 1976, 1978. Markos Botsaris. Rev. value, date		0.10	0.20

59 (75)	1 Drachma (Al-Br) 1976, 1978, 1980. Konstantinos Kanaris. Rev. sailing ship, value, date		0.20	0.40
60 (76)	2 Drachmai (Al-Br) 1976, 1978. Georgios Karaiskakes. Rev. crossed rifles, value, date		0.25	0.50

61 (77)	5 Drachmai (Cu-Ni) 1976, 1978, 1980. Head left of Aristotle. Rev. value, date		0.40	0.90

62 (78)	10 Drachmai (Cu-Ni) 1976, 1978. Head left of Democritos. Rev. symbolic representation of an atom; value, date		0.80	1.40

63 (79) 20 Drachmai (Cu-Ni) 1976, 1978. Head left   **VF**   **XF**
of Pericles. Rev. temple in the Acropolis;
value, date   1.20   2.00

50th ANNIVERSARY OF BANK OF GREECE

                                                 Proof

64 (82) 100 Drachmai (Ag) 1978   80.00

COMMON MARKET MEMBERSHIP (2)

65 (80)   500 Drachmai (Ag) 1979   100.00
66 (81) 10000 Drachmai (Au) 1979   900.00

                                      VF   **XF**

67 (83) 50 Drachmai (Cu-Ni) 1980. Portrait left of
Solon (c. 640–560 B.C.), statesman and
poet of Athens   1.80   2.00

Area: 133 sq. mi. Population: 110,000.
Part of the Lesser Antilles; a member of the Caribbean Free Trade
Area (CARIFTA). Since 1967 an associate member of the United King-
dom of Great Britain. Together with the countries of Antigua, Barba-
dos, Dominica, Montserrat, St. Christopher- (St. Kitts-) Nevis-Anguilla,
St. Lucia and St. Vincent, Grenada forms part of the Monetary Union
of the East Caribbean Dollar. The issuing authority for the whole
Monetary Union is the East Caribbean Currency Authority with head-
quarters in Bridgetown, Barbados.
Capital: St. George's.

100 Cents = 1 East Caribbean Dollar

COMMEMORATIVE ISSUE FOR THE INAUGURATION OF THE CARIBBEAN DEVELOPMENT BANK AND FOR THE FAO COIN PLAN

		Unc	Proof
1 (5*)	4 Dollars (Cu–Ni) 1970. Emblem of state. ℞ bananas, sugar-cane and value	10.00	30.00

*This number refers to Yeoman's East Caribbean Territories listing.

Guadeloupe

Area: 812 sq. mi. Population: 306,000.

Guadeloupe has been a French possession since 1635. Merely in the years 1759–63, 1794, 1810–13 and 1815/16 the island was in British hands. The Overseas Department formed in 1958 comprising the islands of Marie Galante, Désirade, two-thirds of of Saint Martin (the remaining part of Saint Martin belongs to the Netherlands Antilles) and Saint Barthélémy has since then been a part of the French motherland.
Capital: Basse-Terre.

100 Centimes = 1 Franc

				VF	XF
1 (1)	50	Centimes (Cu–Ni) 1903–1921. Head of native to left. ℞ palm branch		8.00	15.00
2 (2)	1	Franc (Cu–Ni) 1903–1921		12.00	24.00

Guatemala

Area: 42,045 sq. mi. Population: 6,500,000.

The Maya tribes were brought under submission in 1524 by the Spaniard Pedro de Alvaredo and their country absorbed into the Captaincy-General of Guatemala. After independence in 1821 Guatemala came temporarily under Mexican domination. In 1823 the country joined up with the other states of Central America to form the "Provincias Unidas del Centro de Américo". After the break-up of the Confederation and warlike conflicts, Guatemala became independent again in 1839. Capital: Guatemala City.

100 Centavos or 8 Reales = 1 Peso
100 Centavos = 1 Quetzal

			VF	XF
1 (85)	¼	Real (Cu–Ni) 1900–1901. Mountain range. ℞ value within wreath	0.80	1.60
2 (86)	½	Real (Cu–Ni) 1900–1901. National arms. ℞ seated allegorical figure of the Republic and value	1.50	3.00
3 (81)	1	Real (Ag) 1899–1900	3.50	6.00
4 (87)	1	Real (Cu–Ni) 1900–1912	2.00	3.50
5 (89)	12½	Centavos (Br) 1915. Name of country, date and inscription PROVISIONAL. ℞ value within circle	3.50	6.00
6 (90)	25	Centavos (Br) 1915. Type as No. 5	5.00	7.00
7 (91)	50	Centavos (Al–Br) 1922. Stylized sun. ℞ value within circle	2.50	5.00
8 (92)	1	Peso (Al–Br) 1923. Bust left of Miguel Garcia Gránados (1809–1878), provisional Head of State 1871–1873. ℞ value	3.00	6.50

9 (93)   5 Pesos (Al–Br) 1923. Bust right of Justo

			VF	XF
		Rufino Barrios (1835–1885), Head of State 1873–1885	5.00	9.00

CURRENCY REFORM on 16th November 1924

			VF	XF
10 (94)	½	Centavo (Bra) 1932, 1946. National arms. ℞ value	0.80	1.60
11 (95)	1	Centavo (Br) 1925. Type as No. 10	4.00	7.00
12 (96)	1	Centavo (Br) 1929. Type as No. 11, but arms larger	2.50	4.00
13 (97)	1	Centavo (Bra) 1932, 1939, 1946–1949	0.40	1.20
14 (98)	2	Centavos (Bra) 1932	0.80	1.60
15 (99)	5	Centavos (Ag) 1925, 1944–1949. National arms with long-tailed quetzal. ℞ quetzal (Pharomachrus mocinno – Trogonidae) on column, value	1.50	2.50
16 (99a)	5	Centavos (Ag) 1928–1943. Type as No. 15, but national arms with short-tailed quetzal	1.50	2.50
17 (100)	10	Centavos (Ag) 1925, 1944–1949. Type as No. 15	1.00	2.00
18 (100a)	10	Centavos (Ag) 1928–1947. Type as No. 16	2.00	3.00
19 (101)	¼	Quetzal (Ag) 1925. With lettered edge	6.00	11.00
20 (102)	¼	Quetzal (Ag) 1926–1929	3.50	5.00
21 (102a)	¼	Quetzal (Ag) 1946–1949. Reeded edge	3.50	5.00
22 (103)	½	Quetzal (Ag) 1925	20.00	30.00
23 (104)	1	Quetzal (Ag) 1925	500.00	800.00
24 (105)	5	Quetzales (Au) 1926	280.00	350.00
25 (106)	10	Quetzales (Au) 1926	450.00	520.00

			VF	XF
26 (107)	20	Quetzales (Au) 1926	600.00	800.00
27 (108)	1	Centavo (Bra) 1943–1944. Quetzal with outstretched wings. ℞ value in letters	1.50	2.50
28 (109)	2	Centavos (Bra) 1943–1944	0.80	1.60
29 (110)	25	Centavos (Ag) 1943. Quetzal and map of Guatemala. ℞ Parliament buildings in Guatemala City	6.50	11.00

			VF	XF
30 (111)	1	Centavo (Bra) 1949–1954. National arms. ℞ Bust left of Bartolomé de las Casas (1474–1566), Missionary to the Indians, value in letters	0.40	0.80
31 (112)	1	Centavo (Bra) 1954–1958. Type as No. 30, but head of Bartolomé de las Casas larger and close to the circular inscription	0.40	0.80
32 (113)	1	Centavo (Bra) 1958–1964. ℞ head of Bartolomé de las Casas, slimmer portrait	0.10	0.20
33 (114)	5	Centavos (Ag) 1949. National arms. ℞ kapok tree (Ceiba pentandra – Bombaceae) and value	4.00	8.00
34 (115)	5	Centavos (Ag) 1950–1959. ℞ kapok tree with bare crown. Heavy figure 5	0.80	1.60
35 (116)	5	Centavos (Ag) 1960–1964. ℞ kapok tree with somewhat lighter foliage; low relief, smaller figures and inscription	0.70	1.20

			VF	XF
36 (117)	10	Centavos (Ag) 1949–1959. National arms. ℞ the monolith at Quiriguà, stele with figures and calendar dates from the Maya culture, c. 750–800; value	2.00	5.00
37 (117a)	10	Centavos (Ag) 1957–1958. ℞ monolith of larger size	3.00	6.00
38 (118)	10	Centavos (Ag) 1960–1964. ℞ monolith even larger	2.00	3.50

			VF	XF
39 (119)	25	Centavos (Ag) 1950–1959. National arms. ℞ bust of an Indian woman wearing costume of Santiago Atitlan; value	3.50	7.00
40 (120)	25	Centavos (Ag) 1960–1964. Type similar to No. 39	2.00	3.50

			VF	**XF**
41 (121)	50	Centavos (Ag) 1962–1963. National arms. ℞ "White Nun" orchid (Lycaste skinneri var. alba – Orchidaceae), the national emblem	4.50	8.00

42 (122)	1	Centavo (Bra) 1965–1970. Type similar to No. 32, but diameter 9 mm instead of 11 mm	0.10	0.15

43 (123)	5	Centavos (Ni–Bra) 1965–1970. Type similar to No. 35	0.10	0.20
44 (124)	10	Centavos (Ni–Bra) 1965–1970. Type similar to No. 38	0.20	0.40
45 (125)	25	Centavos (Ni–Bra) 1965–1969. Type similar to No. 40	0.60	0.90

46 (122a)	1	Centavo (Bra) 1972, 1973	0.10	0.15
47 (123a)	5	Centavos (Ni-Bra) 1971, 1974–1977	0.10	0.20
48 (124a)	10	Centavos (Ni-Bra) 1971	0.20	0.40

			VF	XF
49 (125b)	25	Centavos (Ni-Bra) 1971, 1975, 1976	0.50	0.80
50 (122b)	1	Centavo (Bra) 1974–1979	0.10	0.20
51 (124b)	10	Centavos (Cu-Ni) 1973–1976. Type similar to No. 48	0.20	0.40

			VF	XF
52 (123b)	5	Centavos (Cu-Ni) 1977–1979. Type as No. 47, but fully circular inscription on the obverse	0.10	0.20
53 (124c)	10	Centavos (Cu-Ni) 1977–1979	0.15	0.25
54 (125c)	25	Centavos (Cu-Ni) 1977–1979	0.50	0.80

Guinea   # Guinea   **Guinée**

Area: 98,344 sq. mi. Population: 5,100,000.

From 1904 onwards Guinea was part of French West Africa. The inhabitants voted against joining the French Community in a referendum of 28th September 1958, and as a result independence was declared as soon afterwards as 2nd October 1958.

Capital: Conakry.

100 Centimes = 1 Guinea Franc; since 2nd October 1972:
100 Cauris = 1 Syli

			VF	XF
1 (1)	5	Francs (Al–Br) 1959. Head right of Ahmed Sékou Touré (*1922), Head of State and Prime Minister since 1958. ℞ value between coconut palms	2.00	3.50
2 (2)	10	Francs (Al–Br) 1959. Head left of Ahmed Sekou Touré	2.50	4.00
3 (3)	25	Francs (Al–Br) 1959	3.50	6.00
4 (4)	1	Franc (Cu–Ni) 1962. ℞ value between palm branches	1.00	1.80

			VF	XF
5 (5)	5	Francs (Cu–Ni) 1962. ℞ value between palm branches and coconuts	1.20	2.00
6 (6)	10	Francs (Cu–Ni) 1962. ℞ value within wreath	2.00	3.50
7 (7)	25	Francs (Cu–Ni) 1962. ℞ value within wreath	2.50	5.00
8 (8)	50	Francs (Cu–Ni) 1969. Type as No. 6		110.00
9 (9)	100	Francs (Cu–Ni) 1971. Type similar to No. 7		350.00

COMMEMORATIVE ISSUES (11)
FOR THE 10th ANNIVERSARY OF INDEPENDENCE

10 100 Francs (Ag) 1968–. Head of Dr. Martin
Luther King (1929–1968), evangelist,
American Civil Rights Leader and winner of the Nobel prize for peace in
1964. ℞ national arms, value

Proof

20.00

11 200 Francs (Ag) 1968–. Head of John F.
Kennedy (1917–1963), 35th President
of the United States of America, and
Robert F. Kennedy (1925–1968), Minister of Justice, Presidential Candidate
in 1968. Rev. as No. 10

30.00

12 200 Francs (Ag) 1968–. Head of Almamy
Samory Touré (1830–1900), Chief of
the Bisandugu and leader of the struggle against the French. ℞ as No. 10

30.00

13 250 Francs (Ag) 1968–. U.S. moon research
programme, third stage "Manned Land-
ing". Apollo programme. Lunar module and lunarnauts carrying out stud-
ies of the moon surface; in background, moon scenery; diagram of the
lunar orbits showing the Apollo cap-
sule; on left, terrestrial globe. R as No. 10

40.00

14 250 Francs (Ag) 1968–. Bust facing of
Alpha Yaya Diallo (1850–1912), local
ruler. R as No. 10

40.00

15 500 Francs (Ag) 1968–. Masked bird-man **Proof**
dancer from the Macenta district (South
Guinea). R as No. 10 50.00

16 500 Francs (Ag) 1968–. Distant view of the
city of Munich; medals of the Olympic
Games in Helsinki 1952, Melbourne
1956, Rome 1960, Tokyo 1964 and
Mexico 1968, each set in one of the five
Olympic rings; below, flaming torch.
R as No. 10 50.00
17 1000 Francs (Au) 1968–. John F. Kennedy
and Robert F. Kennedy. R as **No. 10** 70.00
18 2000 Francs (Au) 1968–. Type as **No. 13** 140.00
19 5000 Francs (Au) 1968–. Type as **No. 16** 280.00

20 10 000 Francs (Au) 1968–. Head left of Ahmed
Sékou Touré. ℞ as No. 10 550.00

COMMEMORATIVE ISSUES (4) FOR SPACE RESEARCH

21 250 Francs (Ag) 1969–. Three winged horses
ascending before sun with rays in
background. Apollo XIII, and part of
moon surface. ℞ as No. 10 40.00

22 250 Francs (Ag) 1969–. "Soyuz", the Soviet
space-ship. ℞ as No. 10 40.00
23 2000 Francs (Au) 1969–. Type as No. 21 120.00
24 2000 Francs (Au) 1969–. Type as No. 22 120.00

25   31

			Proof
25	500	Francs (Ag) 1970–. Rameses III (1198–1167 B. C.), Pharaoh of the 20th Dynasty. ℞ as No. 10	50.00
26	500	Francs (Ag) 1970–. Chephren, Pharaoh of the 4th Dynasty; he built the second highest pyramid near Gizeh, which is today still 136.5 metres high	50.00
27	500	Francs (Ag) 1970–. Ikhnaton (Amenophis IV), Pharaoh of the 18th Dynasty; he introduced the sun-worship as the State religion	50.00
28	500	Francs (Ag) 1970–. Tutankhamen, Pharaoh of the 18th Dynasty	50.00
29	500	Francs (Ag) 1970–. Queen Nefertiti	50.00
30	500	Francs (Ag) 1970–. Queen Teyi	50.00
31	500	Francs (Ag) 1970–. Queen Cleopatra	50.00
32	500	Francs (Ag) 1970–. Gamal Abd al Nasser (1918–1970), Egyptian Head of State 1956–1970	50.00
33	5000	Francs (Au) 1970–. Type as No. 23	260.00
34	5000	Francs (Au) 1970–. Type as No. 24	260.00
35	5000	Francs (Au) 1970–. Type as No. 25	260.00
36	5000	Francs (Au) 1970–. Type as No. 26	260.00
37	5000	Francs (Au) 1970–. Type as No. 27	260.00
38	5000	Francs (Au) 1970–. Type as No. 28	260.00
39	5000	Francs (Au) 1970–. Type as No. 29	260.00
40	5000	Francs (Au) 1970–. Type as No. 30	260.00

NEW CURRENCY: 100 Cauris = 1 Syli

			XF	Unc
41 (10)	50	Cauris (Al) 1971.	3.00	10.00
42 (11)	1	Syli (Al) 1971	3.00	10.00
43 (12)	2	Sylis (Al) 1971	3.00	10.00
44 (13)	5	Sylis (Al) 1971	3.00	10.00

				Unc	Proof
45	500	Sylis (Ag) 1977. Miriam Makeba		40.00	50.00
46	500	Sylis (Ag) 1977. Patrice Lumumba		40.00	50.00
47	1000	Sylis (Au) 1977. Miriam Makeba		60.00	75.00
48	1000	Sylis (Au) 1977. Nkrumah		60.00	75.00
49	2000	Sylis (Au) 1977. Sekou Touré		125.00	150.00
50	2000	Sylis (Au) 1977. Mao Tse Tung		125.00	150.00

Guinea-Bissau

Area: 13,948 sq. mi. Population: 600,000.
The former Portuguese colony and overseas territory Portuguese Guinea became independent on Sept. 10th 1974. The new republik took the name of Guinea-Bissau.
Capital: Bissau.

100 Centavos = 1 Guinea Peso

ISSUES FOR THE FAO COIN PLAN (5)

				XF	Unc
1 (1)	50	Centavos (Al) 1977, 1978. Coconuts		0.10	0.20
2 (2)	1	Peso (Ni-Bra) 1977, 1978. Oil palm		0.20	0.30
3 (3)					
3 (3)	2,50	Pesos (Ni-Bra) 1977, 1978. Cassava		0.25	0.50
4 (4)	5	Pesos (Cu-Ni) 1977, 1978. Groundnuts		0.25	0.50
5 (5)	20	Pesos (Cu-Ni) 1977, 1978. Rice		1.00	2.00

Area: 83,00 sq. mi. Population: 850,000.

The former British Crown Colony of British Guiana, situated in the north-eastern part of South America, has considerable deposits of diamonds and aluminium. The country became independent under the name of Guyana on 26th June 1966, but remained within the British Commonwealth; since 23rd February 1970 the country has been a republic.

Capital: Georgetown.

100 Cents = 1 Guyana Dollar

			VF	EF
1 (1)	1	Cent (Bra) 1967–. Stylized lotus flowers (Nelumbo sp. – Nymphaeaceae). ℞ value within circle, date between two hoatzins (Opisthocomus hoazin – Opisthocomidae)	0.05	0.10

2 (2)	5	Cents (Bra) 1967–. Type as No. 1	0.10	0.20
3 (3)	10	Cents (Cu-Ni) 1967. National arms with jaguars ((Panthera onca – Felidae) as supporters and hoatzin as emblem. ℞ as No. 1	0.15	0.30
4 (4)	25	Cents (Cu-Ni) 1967–. Type as No. 3	0.20	0.40
5 (5)	50	Cents (Cu-Ni) 1967. Type as No. 3	0.40	0.80

COMMEMORATIVE ISSUE FOR THE PROCLAMATION OF THE REPUBLIC ON 23rd FEBRUARY 1970 AND FOR THE FAO COIN PLAN

			Unc	Proof
6 (6)	1 Dollar (Cu–Ni) 1970. Cuffy, an African slave who organized a revolt on 23rd February 1763 and captured from the Dutch governor a territory bordering the Berbice river. The Revolutionary Government, subsequently set up, was defeated after initial successes. The "Berbice Revolt" was the first step towards independence. ℞ motto FOOD FOR ALL above figure 1, with head of cow and ears of corn on either side		4.00	10.00

10th ANNIVERSARY OF INDEPENDENCE (10)

		Unc	Proof
7 (7)	1 Cent (Br) 1976–1980	0.25	1.00
8 (8)	5 Cents (Bra) 1976–1980.	0.30	1.20
9 (9)	10 Cents (Cu–Ni) 1976–1980.	0.50	1.50
10 (10)	25 Cents (Cu–Ni) 1976–1980.	1.00	2.50
11 (11)	50 Cents (Cu–Ni) 1976–1980.	2.00	3.00
12 (12)	1 Dollar (Cu–Ni) 1976–1980.	4.00	6.00
13 (13)	5 Dollars 1976–1980		
	a) (Ag)		18.00
	b) (Cu-Ni)	10.00	
14 (14)	10 Dollars 1976–1978:		
	a) (Ag)		40.00
	b) (Cu-Ni)	30.00	
15 (15)	50 Dollars (Ag) 1976		100.00
16 (16)	100 Dollars (Au) 1976. Arawak Indian	110.00	100.00
17 (17)	100 Dollars (Au) 1977. Legendary Golden Man	105.00	95.00

Area: 10,714 sq. mi. together with the islands La Tortuga and Gonave.
Population: 5,000,000.
Haiti (Indian: mountain) was discovered in 1492 by Columbus, and
called Hispaniola, in some parts also San(to) Domingo. The Republic
of Haiti comprises the western part of the Island of Haiti.
Capital: Port-au-Prince.

100 Centimes = 1 Gourde

The medium of exchange of the United States is also used as legal tender.

			VF	XF
1 (14)	5	Centimes (Cu–Ni) 1904. Coat of arms. ℞ value and date	5.00	10.00
2 (10)	5	Centimes (Cu–Ni) 1904–1906. General Pedro Nord-Alexis (1820–1910), president 1902–1908. ℞ coat of arms and value	0.80	1.50
3 (11)	10	Centimes (Cu–Ni) 1905, 1906	1.00	1.80
4 (12)	20	Centimes (Cu–Ni) 1907, 1908	1.50	2.50
5 (13)	50	Centimes (Cu–Ni) 1907–1908	3.00	5.00
6 (15)	5	Centimes (Cu–Ni) 1949. Dumarsais Estimé (1900–1953), President 1946–1950. ℞ coat of arms and value	0.30	0.60
7 (16)	10	Centimes (Cu–Ni) 1949	0.50	0.90
8 (17)	5	Centimes (Ni–St) 1953. Paul E. Magloire (*1907), President 1951–1956. ℞ coat of arms and value	0.25	0.50
9 (18)	10	Centimes (Ni–St) 1953	0.40	0.70
10 (19)	20	Centimes (Ni–St) 1956	0.50	0.90
11 (20)	5	Centimes (Ni–St) 1958, 1970. François Duvalier (1909–1971), President 1957–1971	0.10	0.20

12 (21)	10	Centimes (Ni–St) 1958, 1970	0.16	0.30
13 (22)	20	Centimes (Ni–St) 1970	0.30	0.60

14	5	Gourdes (Ag) 1967–. Map of the Haiti Island (Hispaniola) and Columbus' fleet: "Nina", "Santa Maria", and "Pinta"	**Proof** 35.00
15	10	Gourdes (Ag) 1967–. François Dominique Toussaint-Louverture (1745–1803), descendant of the kings of Allada (Dahomey), Haitian general and politician	40.00
16	25	Gourdes (Ag) 1967–. Art objects	90.00
17	20	Gourdes (Au) 1967–. Mackandal, one of the first revolutionaries of Haiti, with machete	80.00
18	50	Gourdes (Au) 1967–. Voodoo dancer, surrounded by symbols	160.00

19	100	Gourdes (Au) 1967–. Marie Jeanne, wife of General Lamatinière, fought at his side in 1803 for the liberation of Haiti	400.00
20	200	Gourdes (Au) 1967–. Revolt of Santo Domingo during the years 1791–1803 against French domination. Design: liberated slave with machete and torch	800.00
21	1000	Gourdes (Au) 1967–. Dr. François Duvalier, President. ℞ coat of arms	4200.00

COMMEMORATIVE ISSUES (5) FOR THE 10th ANNIVERSARY OF THE REVOLUTION (2nd part)

Proof

22   30 Gourdes (Au) 1967–. Citadel of St. Christopher   100.00

23   40 Gourdes (Au) 1967–. Jean Jacques Dessalines (1758–1806), who overthrew the republic in December 1804, had himself crowned emperor of Haiti, with the title of Jacob I   160.00

24   60 Gourdes (Au) 1967–. Alexander Sabès Pétion (1770–1818), President of Southern Haiti 1808–1818   250.00

25   250 Gourdes 1967–. Henri Christophe (1767–1820), President of Northern Haiti 1808–1810, emperor of Haiti, with the title of Henry I, 1811–1820. Citadel of St. Christopher   1000.00

26   500 Gourdes (Au) 1967–. Handicraft   1850.00

27   5 Gourdes (Ag) 1970. Vacation land Haiti: beach scene   40.00

28   10 Gourdes (Ag) 1970. Billy Bowlegs, deputy chief of the Seminoles. During the Indian War of 1812, he fought with the chieftain King Paine near the border of Georgia, against American troops commanded by Andrew Jackson, who was later to become president. He was wounded in combat   55.00

29   10 Gourdes (Ag) 1970. Geronimo (Goy-

athlay = "One who yawns") (January 1829–17th February 1909), a dreaded warrior, medicine man, and prophet of the Chiricahua Apaches. In 1875, when Cochise (whose image inspired Karl May's creation of "Winnetou") made peace with the Americans, he left his tribe. Together with devoted warriors and some younger Indian chiefs he terrorized Mexican territory. He died as a prisoner in Fort Hill, Oklahoma.

55.00

30	10	Gourdes (Ag) 1970. Sitting Bull (Tatanka Yotanka) (c. 1834–15th December 1890), one of the most important personalities of the Dakota (Sioux) tribe. The last Indian massacre at Little Big Horn in the Black Hills perpetuated his fame: during this battle (1876) General Custer (the Indians called him Long Hair) and his troops were wiped out to the last man. Sitting Bull died from a bullet shot by an Indian sheriff near his birthplace on the Grand River in South Dakota.	55.00
31	10	Gourdes (Ag) 1970. Chief Joseph (Hinmaton-Yalatkit = "The-thunder-that-rushes-over-the-hills") (1840–21st September 1904), impressive, peace-loving character, from the Nez Perzé tribe, who owes his occidental name to his teacher, a white missionary. He died in the Colville Reservation of Nespelem, in the federated state of Washington.	55.00
32	10	Gourdes (Ag) 1970. War Eagle, chief of the Yankton Sioux	55.00
33	10	Gourdes (Ag) 1970. Red Cloud (Machpiya-Luta) (c. 1822–8th October 1909),	

			Proof

important Dakota chief from the Ogläla tribe, who tried by force to prevent the start of road construction at Fort Laramie in 1865. The road was intended to provide an easy approach to the gold fields of Montana. In 1868 he abandoned his warlike activities and did not even take part in the Sioux War of 1876 (battle at Little Big Horn). He died in the Indian Reservation of Pine Ridge in South Dakota. ... 55.00

34   10 Gourdes (Ag) 1970. Stalking Turkey, chief of the Cherokee ... 55.00

35   10 Gourdes (Ag) 1970. Osceola (As-se-he-ho-lar) (1804–30th January 1838), famous chief of the Seminoles, outstanding strategist. Successfully fought the American troops during the Seminole War. During a peace conference he was unjustly arrested, and taken prisoner to Fort Moultrie in South Carolina, where he died. ... 55.00

36   10 Gourdes (Ag) 1970. Playing Fox, chief of the Fox (also Sauk or Sac) ... 55.00

37   25 Gourdes (Ag) 1970. International air port "François Duvalier", main building ... 120.00

38   50 Gourdes (Au) 1970. Héros de Vertières ... 150.00

39   100 Gourdes (Au) 1970. Same type as No. 28 ... 250.00

40   100 Gourdes (Au) 1970. Same type as No. 29 ... 250.00

41   100 Gourdes (Au) 1970. Same type as No. 30 ... 250.00

42   100 Gourdes (Au) 1970. Same type as No. 31 ... 250.00

43   100 Gourdes (Au) 1970. Same type as No. 32 ... 250.00

44   100 Gourdes (Au) 1970. Same type as No. 33 ... 250.00

45   100 Gourdes (Au) 1970. Same type as No. 34 ... 250.00

46   100 Gourdes (Au) 1970. Same type as No. 35 ... 250.00

47   100 Gourdes (Au) 1970. Same type as No. 36 ... 250.00

48   200 Gourdes (Au) 1970. "Le Marron inconnu", the unkonwn rebel of San Domingo ... 550.00

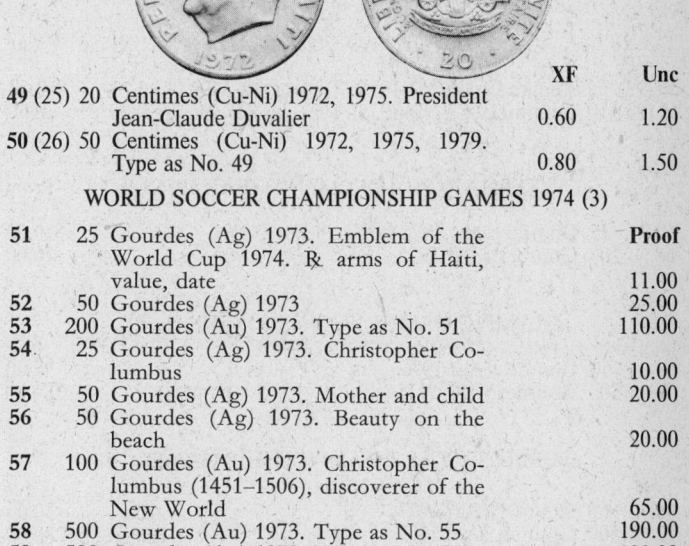

			XF	Unc
49 (25)	20	Centimes (Cu-Ni) 1972, 1975. President Jean-Claude Duvalier	0.60	1.20
50 (26)	50	Centimes (Cu-Ni) 1972, 1975, 1979. Type as No. 49	0.80	1.50

WORLD SOCCER CHAMPIONSHIP GAMES 1974 (3)

			Proof
51	25	Gourdes (Ag) 1973. Emblem of the World Cup 1974. ℞ arms of Haiti, value, date	11.00
52	50	Gourdes (Ag) 1973	25.00
53	200	Gourdes (Au) 1973. Type as No. 51	110.00
54	25	Gourdes (Ag) 1973. Christopher Columbus	10.00
55	50	Gourdes (Ag) 1973. Mother and child	20.00
56	50	Gourdes (Ag) 1973. Beauty on the beach	20.00
57	100	Gourdes (Au) 1973. Christopher Columbus (1451–1506), discoverer of the New World	65.00
58	500	Gourdes (Au) 1973. Type as No. 55	190.00
59	500	Gourdes (Au) 1973. Type as No. 56	190.00
60	1000	Gourdes (Au) 1973. President Jean-Claude Duvalier	1000.00

HOLY YEAR 1975 (2)

61	50	Gourdes (Ag) 1974. 1975-Holy Year	18.00
62	200	Gourdes (Au) 1974. 1975-Holy Year	70.00

BICENTENARY OF AMERICAN INDEPENDENCE (2)

			Unc	Proof
63	25	Gourdes (Ag) 1974. U. S. Bicentennial/ Savannah		20.00
64	1000	Gourdes (Au) 1974. U. S. Bicentennial/ Savannah		400.00

FOR THE FAO COIN PLAN (2)

			XF	Unc
65 (23)	5	Centimes (Cu-Ni) 1975. Type as No. 49	0.25	0.50
66 (24)	10	Centimes (Cu-Ni) 1975. Type as No. 49	0.30	0.60

INTERNATIONAL WOMEN'S YEAR 1975 (2)

			Proof
67	25	Gourdes (Ag) 1975	10.00
68	200	Gourdes (Au) 1975	70.00

OLYMPIC GAMES 1976 IN MONTREAL (2)

69	50	Gourdes (Ag) 1976	25.00
70	500	Gourdes (Au) 1976	280.00

WORLD SOCCER CHAMPIONSHIP GAMES (2)

71	50	Gourdes (Ag) 1977	20.00	30.00
72	500	Gourdes (Au) 1977	220.00	280.00

OLYMPIC GAMES 1980 IN MOSCOW (2)

73	50	Gourdes (Ag) 1977	20.00	30.00
74	500	Gourdes (Au) 1977	250.00	300.00

HUMAN RIGHTS (2)

75	50	Gourdes (Ag) 1977	25.00	32.00
76	250	Gourdes (Au) 1977	150.00	170.00

LINDBERGH'S NEW YORK TO PARIS FLIGHT 1927 (2)

77	100	Gourdes (Ag) 1977	40.00	50.00
78	250	Gourdes (Au) 1977	100.00	120.00

STATUE OF LIBERTY

		Unc	Proof
79	100 Gourdes (Ag) 1977. Statue of Liberty and city skyline of New York	40.00	50.00

20th ANNIVERSARY OF EUROPEAN MARKET (3)

80	50 Gourdes (Ag) 1977. Map of Europe	20.00	30.00
81	100 Gourdes (Ag) 1977	40.00	50.00
82	500 Gourdes (Au) 1977	300.00	350.00

ECONOMIC CONNECTIONS (2)

83	50 Gourdes (Ag) 1977	20.00	30.00
84	500 Gourdes (Au) 1977	280.00	325.00

DUVALIER 1957–1977

85	500 Gourdes (Au) 1977	280.00	325.00

PEACE INITIATIVE (2)

86	100 Gourdes (Ag) 1977. Facing portraits of Sadat and Begin	70.00	85.00
87	250 Gourdes (Au) 1977	150.00	185.00

WORLD CIRCUMNAVIGATION (2)

		Unc	Proof
88	100 Gourdes (Ag) 1978	70.00	80.00
89	250 Gourdes (Au) 1978	150.00	185.00

QUEEN OF THE SUGAR

90	50 Gourdes (Ag) 1978	35.00	45.00

Hedschas   # Hejaz   **Hedjaz**

Area: 180,000 sq. mi. Population: 3,000,000.
This kingdom, situated on the west of the Arabian peninsula, declared
its independence on 30th May 1916. It has been part of the sultanate of
Nejd since 1925, and of Saudi Arabia since 1932.
Capital: Mecca.

40 Paras = 1 Gersh, 20 Gersh = 1 Rial,
100 Gersh = 1 Dinar

HUSEIN IBN ALI 1916–1924

			VF	XF
1 (16)	5 Paras (Br) 1923. (Solar Calendar dating 1334). Arabic inscription in five oval patterns. ℞ similar		16.00	25.00
2 (17)	10 Paras (Br) 1923. (S. C. 1334)		8.00	16.00
3 (18)	20 Paras (Br) 1923 (S. C. 1334)		9.00	18.00
4 (19)	40 Paras (Br) 1923 (S. C. 1334)		12.00	25.00
5 (20)	¼ Gersh (Br) 1923 (S. C. 1334)		8.00	15.00
6 (22)	1 Gersh (Br) 1923 (S. C. 1334)		10.00	18.00
7 (23)	¼ Rial (Ag) 1923 (S. C. 1334)		30.00	50.00
8 (24)	½ Rial (Ag) 1923 (S. C. 1334)		100.00	150.00

9 (25)	1 Rial (Ag) 1923 (S. C. 1334)	55.00	75.00
10 (26)	1 Dinar (Au) 1923 (S. C. 1334)	300.00	400.00

Honduras

Area: 44,836 sq. mi. Population: 2,800,000.
Honduras is a democratic republic with a President. After leaving the Confederation of Central American States (Provincias Unidas del Centro de América) the country declared its independence in 1838.
Capital: Tegucigalpa.

100 Centavos or 8 Reales = 1 Peso;
since 1926: 100 Centavos = 1 Lempira

			VF	XF
1 (14)	1	Centavo (Br) 1881–1907. National arms within circle. ℞ value within wreath	9.00	15.00
2 (15)	1	Centavo (Br) 1890–1908. National arms. ℞ value within circle, inscription PROGRESO * LIBERTAD * PAZ	5.00	10.00
3 (17)	1	Centavo (Br) 1890–1908. National arms within wreath. ℞ value within circle, inscription PROGRESO * LIBER-TAD * PAZ	8.00	15.00
4 (19)	5	Centavos (Ag) 1883–1902. National arms within wreath. R value within circle	20.00	30.00
5 (21)	10	Centavos (Ag) 1883–1900. National arms within circle, the whole within wreath. ℞ value within circle, inscription PROGRESO * LIBERTAD * PAZ	22.50	32.00
6 (23)	25	Centavos (Ag) 1898–1913. National arms within wreath. ℞ allegorical figure of Liberty	8.00	11.00
7 (24a)	50	Centavos (Ag) 1908	45.00	65.00
8 (25a)		UN (1) Peso (Ag) 1881–1914	45.00	85.00
9 (27)	1	Peso (Au) 1887–1922. Head of Liberty. ℞ national arms	580.00	750.00
		Coin No. 9 with date 1912 commands a very high price		
10 (28)	5	Pesos (Au) 1883–1913. Type as No. 9	700.00	900.00
11 (32)	1	Centavo (Br) 1910–1911	20.00	30.00
12 (37)	1	Centavo (Br) 1919–1920. National arms within circle. ℞ value within wreath; but 'Centavo' not mentioned	2.50	4.50
13 (31)	2	Centavos (Br) 1907–1908. National arms within circle. ℞ value within wreath	60.00	85.00
14 (33)	2	Centavos (Br) 1910–1913	3.00	5.00

			VF	**XF**
15 (38)	2	Centavos (Br) 1919–1920. National arms within circle. ℞ value within wreath; but 'Centavos' not mentioned		
			2.00	3.50

CURRENCY REFORM: 100 Centavos = 1 Lempira

16 (39)	1	Centavo (Br) 1935–1957. National arms. ℞ value within circle, the whole within wreath	0.15	0.25
17 (40)	2	Centavos (Br) 1939–1956. Type as No. 16	0.20	0.30
18 (41)	5	Centavos (Cu-Ni) 1931, 1932, 1949, 1954, 1956, 1972. Type as No. 16	0.20	0.40
19 (42)	10	Centavos (Cu-Ni) 1932–1956, 1967. Type as No. 16	0.30	0.60
20 (43)	20	Centavos (Ag) 1931–1958. Lempira, Indian Chieftain (1497–1537), resisted occupation by the first Spanish conquerors. The unit of currency was named after him by an act of Parliament of 3rd April 1926	3.00	5.00
21 (44)	50	Centavos (Ag) 1931–1951. Type as No. 20	5.00	8.00

22 (45)	1	Lempira (Ag) 1931–1937. Type as No. 20	9.00	15.00
23 (46)	20	Centavos (Cu-Ni) 1967, 1973. Type as No. 20	0.20	0.30
24 (47)	50	Centavos (Cu-Ni) 1967, 1978. Type as No. 21	0.30	0.60

ISSUE FOR THE FAO COIN PLAN

25 (48)	50	Centavos (Cu–Ni) 1973	1.20	2.00

				XF	Unc
26 (39a)	1	Centavo (Bronze-clad steel) 1974. Type as No. 16		0.15	0.25
27 (41a)	5	Centavos (Brass-clad steel) 1975. Type as No. 18		0.15	0.25
28 (42a)	10	Centavos (Brass-clad steel) 1976. Type as No. 19		0.20	0.40
29 (49)	20	Centavos (Cu-Ni) 1978		0.30	0.60

Hong Kong

Area: 392 sq. mi. Population: 4,800,000.
This British possession on the south coast of China comprises the island of Hong Kong, the Kowloon peninsula and a small part of the mainland. Since 1956 Hong Kong has been self-governing.
Capital: Victoria.

100 Cents = 1 Hong Kong Dollar

EDWARD VII 1901–1910

			VF	XF
.1 (9)	1 Cent (Br) 1902–1905. Crowned bust right of King Edward VII. ℞ value		1.50	3.00

2 (10)	5 Cents (Ag) 1903–1905	1.50	2.50
3 (11)	10 Cents (Ag) 1902–1905	2.00	4.00
4 (12)	20 Cents (Ag) 1902–1905	45.00	65.00
5 (13)	50 Cents (Ag) 1902–1905	22.00	35.00

GEORGE V 1910–1936

6 (14)	1 Cent (Br) 1919–1926. Crowned bust left of King George V. ℞ value	1.00	2.00

				VF	XF
7 (15)	1	Cent (Br) 1931–1934. Type as No. 6, but diameter 22 mm instead of 28 mm		0.40	1.00
8 (18)	5	Cents (Ag) 1932–1933		1.00	2.00
9 (16)	5	Cents (Cu–Ni) 1935		3.00	6.00
10 (17)	10	Cents (Cu–Ni) 1935–1936		0.50	1.00

GEORGE VI 1936–1952

			VF	XF
11 (19)	1	Cent (Br) 1941	900.00	1500.00
12 (20)	5	Cents (Ni) 1937	1.00	1.60
13 (22)	5	Cents (Ni) 1938–1941. Type as No. 12, but head larger	0.40	0.90
14 (21)	10	Cents (Ni) 1937	0.60	1.20
15 (23)	10	Cents (Ni) 1938–1939. Type as No. 14, but head larger	0.30	0.60
16 (24)	5	Cents (Ni–Bra) 1949–1950. Inscription now KING GEORGE THE SIXTH	0.15	0.25
17 (25)	10	Cents (Ni–Bra) 1948–1951. Inscription now KING GEORGE THE SIXTH	0.20	0.40

			VF	XF
18 (26)	50	Cents (Cu–Ni) 1951. Inscription now KING GEORGE THE SIXTH	1.50	3.00

ELIZABETH II since 1952

			VF	XF
19 (27)	5	Cents (Ni-Bra) 1958–. Crowned head right of Queen Elizabeth II:		
		a) 1958–1968, security edge	0.10	0.20
		b) 1971–, reeded edge	0.08	0.15
20 (28)	10	Cents (Ni–Bra) 1955–		
		a) 1955–1968, security edge	0.12	0.25
		b) 1971–, reeded edge	0.10	0.20
21 (29)	50	Cents (Cu–Ni) 1958–		
		a) 1958–1970, security edge	0.20	0.40
		b) 1971–, reeded edge	0.20	0.35

			VF	XF
22 (30)	1	Dollar (Cu–Ni) 1960–		
		a) 1960–1970, security edge	0.40	0.80
		b) 1971–, reeded edge	0.30	0.60
23 (33)	20	Cents (Ni-Bra) 1975–1979. Portrait of the Queen and legend. Rev. value, date (scalloped)	0.15	0.30
24 (34)	50	Cents (Bra) 1977–1979. Typ as No. 23 (round)	0.30	0.60
25 (36)	2	Dollars (Cu–Ni) 1975, 1978, 1979. Type as No. 23 (scalloped)	0.70	1.20
26 (37)	5	Dollars (Cu–Ni) 1976, 1978. Type as No. 23 (decagon)	1.25	2.00

ROYAL VISIT 1975

			Unc	Proof
27 (31)	1000	Dollars (Au) 1975. Rev. coat of arms	450.00	1000.00

YEAR OF THE DRAGON

28 (32)	1000	Dollars (Au) 1976. Rev. dragon	800.00	1000.00

YEAR OF THE SNAKE

29 (38)	1000	Dollars (Au) 1977. Rev. snake	500.00	800.00

YEAR OF THE HORSE

30 (39)	1000	Dollars (Au) 1978. Rev. horse	500.00	800.00

			XF	Unc
31 (35)	1	Dollar (Cu-Ni) 1978–. Type as No. 22, but diameter 25 mm	0.40	0.80

			Unc	Proof
		YEAR OF THE GOAT		
32 (40)	1000	Dollars (Au) 1979	500.00	800.00
		YEAR OF THE MONKEY		
33 (42)	1000	Dollars (Au) 1980	500.00	800.00

			XF	Unc
34 (41)	5	Dollars (Cu-Ni) 1980–	1.25	2.00

			Unc	Proof
		YEAR OF THE COCKEREL		
35 (43)	1000	Dollars (Au) 1981	500.00	800.00

Ungarn **Hungary** Hongrie
Magyarország

Area: 35,918 sq. mi. Population: 10,400,000.
From 1867 to 1918 the country was one of the two component states of
the Austro-Hungarian Empire. In 1918 it was declared a republic, and
on 21st March 1919 the Republic of Revolutionary Councils was created,
which only had a short existence. The National Assembly, which was
called together at the beginning of 1920, decided in favour of the re-
institution of the kingdom, and elected Admiral Horthy as Regent on 1st
March 1920. At the end of the Second World War Hungary again
became a republic, which was changed into a People's Republic by
parliamentary resolution on 20th August 1949.
Capital: Budapest.

100 Filler = 1 Korona, from 1925 to 1945: 100 Filler = 1 Pengö,
since 1946: 100 Filler = 1 Forint

			VF	XF
1 (23)	1	Filler (Br) 1892–1914. Crown of St. Stephen. ℞ value within wreath:		
		a) 1892–1903, 1906	0.80	2.00
		b) 1914	–.–	–.–
2 (24)	2	Filler (Br) 1892–1915. Type as No. 1	0.50	1.00
3 (25)	10	Filler (Ni) 1892–1909. Type as No. 1:		
		a) 1892–1894, 1908, 1909	0.50	0.80
		b) 1895, 1906	12.00	20.00
4 (27)	20	Filler (Ni) 1892–1914. Type as No. 1:		
		a) 1892–1894, 1907, 1908	5.00	8.00
		b) 1906, 1914	1.60	3.60
5 (32)	1	Korona (Ag) 1892–1916. Head right of Emperor Franz Joseph (1830–1916.) ℞ crown of St. Stephen above value:		
		a) large head, 1892–1896	4.00	6.00
		b) large head, 1906	8.00	12.00
		c) small head, 1912, 1914–1916	3.50	5.50
		d) small head, 1913	5.00	8.00
6 (33)	2	Korona (Ag) 1912–1914. Crown of St. Stephen held by angels:		
		a) 1912, 1913	6.00	7.50
		b) 1914	6.50	11.00

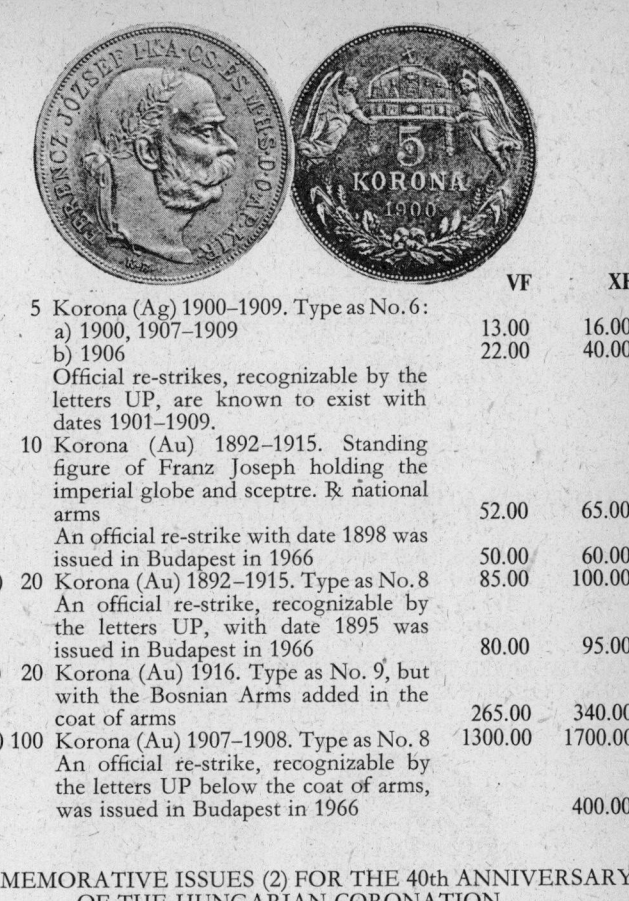

			VF	XF
7 (34)	5	Korona (Ag) 1900–1909. Type as No. 6:		
		a) 1900, 1907–1909	13.00	16.00
		b) 1906	22.00	40.00
		Official re-strikes, recognizable by the letters UP, are known to exist with dates 1901–1909.		
8 (36)	10	Korona (Au) 1892–1915. Standing figure of Franz Joseph holding the imperial globe and sceptre. ℞ national arms	52.00	65.00
		An official re-strike with date 1898 was issued in Budapest in 1966	50.00	60.00
9 (A 36)	20	Korona (Au) 1892–1915. Type as No. 8	85.00	100.00
		An official re-strike, recognizable by the letters UP, with date 1895 was issued in Budapest in 1966	80.00	95.00
10 (B 36)	20	Korona (Au) 1916. Type as No. 9, but with the Bosnian Arms added in the coat of arms	265.00	340.00
11 (D 36)	100	Korona (Au) 1907–1908. Type as No. 8	1300.00	1700.00
		An official re-strike, recognizable by the letters UP below the coat of arms, was issued in Budapest in 1966		400.00

COMMEMORATIVE ISSUES (2) FOR THE 40th ANNIVERSARY OF THE HUNGARIAN CORONATION

			VF	XF
12 (35)	5	Korona (Ag) 1907. Head right of Franz Joseph. ℞ coronation scene	20.00	30.00
13 (C 36)	100	Korona (Au) 1907	1000.00	1200.00
		An official re-strike, recognizable by the letters UP, was issued in Budapest in 1966		480.00
14 (28)	2	Filler (Fe) 1916–1918	2.00	3.00
15	10	Filler. Crown of St. Stephen. R value and laurel branch		
		a) (Y 26) (German Silver) 1915–1916	0.40	0.60
		b) (Y 29) (Fe) 1915, 1918, 1920	12.00	16.00
16 (30)	20	Filler (Fe) 1916–1921. Type as No. 15	0.80	1.00

NEW CURRENCY: 100 Filler = 1 Pengö

			VF	**XF**
17 (37)	1	Filler (Br) 1926–1939. Crown of St. Stephen. ℞ value:		
		a) 1926–1936, 1938, 1939	0.40	0.70
		b) 1929	2.50	5.00
18 (38)	2	Filler (Br) 1926–1940:		
		a) 1926–1931, 1934–1940	0.40	0.70
		b) 1932, 1933	2.50	4.00
19 (39)	10	Filler (Cu–Ni) 1926–1940	0.40	0.70
20 (40)	20	Filler (Cu–Ni) 1926–1940	0.80	1.20
21 (41)	50	Filler (Cu–Ni) 1926–1940	1.20	1.80
22 (42)	1	Pengö (Ag) 1926–1939. Crowned arms within wreath. ℞ value in wreath	3.50	5.00
23 (43)	2	Pengö (Ag) 1929–1939. Madonna, patroness of Hungary. ℞ crowned arms:		
		a) 1929, 1933, 1936–1939	4.00	6.00
		b) 1931	25.00	40.00
		c) 1932	6.00	9.00
		d) 1935	10.00	15.00

COMMEMORATIVE ISSUE FOR THE 10th ANNIVERSARY OF THE REGENCY OF ADMIRAL HORTHY

24 (44)	5	Pengö (Ag) 1930. Bust to right of Miklós Horthy von Nagybánya (1868–1957), admiral and statesman. ℞ national arms	12.00	16.00

COMMEMORATIVE ISSUE FOR THE 300th ANNIVERSARY OF THE FOUNDING OF THE PETER PÁZMÁNY UNIVERSITY IN BUDAPEST

25 (45)	2	Pengö (Ag) 1935. Standing figure of Cardinal Peter Pázmány (1570–1637), founder of the university. ℞ national arms	15.00	26.00

COMMEMORATIVE ISSUE FOR THE 200th ANNIVERSARY OF THE DEATH OF RÁKOCZI

26 (46)	2	Pengö (Ag) 1935. Bust to right of Francis II Rákóczi (1676–1735), Prince of Hungary and Transylvania 1694–1711;

	VF	XF

leader of the War of Independence
1703–1711. ℞ national arms 8.50 12.00

COMMEMORATIVE ISSUE FOR THE 50th ANNIVERSARY OF THE DEATH OF LISZT

27 (47) 2 Pengö (Ag) 1936. Head right of Franz
von Liszt (1811–1886), pianist and
composer. ℞ national arms 7.50 11.20

COMMEMORATIVE ISSUE FOR THE 900th ANNIVERSARY OF THE DEATH OF ST. STEPHEN

28 (48) 5 Pengö (Ag) 1938. Bust to right with
halo of Stephen I the Saint (969–1038),
King of Hungary 995–1038. ℞ national
arms 12.00 16.00

COMMEMORATIVE ISSUE FOR ADMIRAL HORTHY

29 (49) 5 Pengö (Ag) 1939. Bust to left of Miklós
Horthy von Nagybánya. ℞ national
arms 11.00 12.50

30 (50) 2 Filler (St). Type as No. 18
  a) 1940, plain edge 1.80 4.00
  b) 1940–1942, reeded edge 0.40 0.80

31 (51) 2 Filler (Zi) 1943–1944 0.30 0.50

32 (52) 10 Filler (St) 1940–1942. Type as No. 19 0.80 1.20

			VF	XF
33 (53)	20	Filler (St) 1941–1944. Crown of St. Stephen. ℞ value (central hole)	1.00	1.60
34 (54)	1	Pengö (Al) 1941–1944. National arms. ℞ value within wreath	0.40	0.80
35 (55)	2	Pengö (Al) 1941–1943. National arms within circle. ℞ value in circle	0.60	1.10

COMMEMORATIVE ISSUE FOR THE 75th ANNIVERSARY OF THE BIRTH OF ADMIRAL HORTHY

			VF	XF
36 (57)	5	Pengö (Al) 1943. Bust to left of Miklós Horthy von Nagybánya. ℞ national arms	2.00	4.80
37 (56)	5	Pengö (Al) 1945. Parliament building in Budapest. ℞ national arms, bunch of grapes, ears of corn	1.10	3.00

MAGYAR KÖZTÁRSASÁG
Republic since 2nd February 1946

Various gold coins issued after 1946 never came into circulation, but were exchanged for convertible currencies by the Hungarian official services.

			VF	XF
38 (58)	2	Filler (Br) 1946–1947. Arms of the Republic, inscription MAGYAR ÁLLAMI VÁLTOPÉNZ (small coin of the Hungarian state). ℞ value and ear of corn	0.20	0.30
39 (59)	5	Filler (Al) 1948–1951. Head left of Hungaria. ℞ value with leaf decoration on border	0.40	0.60

			VF	XF
40 (60)	10	Filler (Al–Br) 1946–1950. Dove, inscription MAGYAR ÁLLAMI VÁLTOPÉNZ (small coin of the Hungarian state). ℞ value	0.40	0.60
41 (61)	20	Filler (Al–Br) 1946–1950. Three ears of corn, inscription MAGYAR ÁLLAMI VÁLTOPÉNZ (small coin of the Hungarian state). ℞ value	0.45	0.80
42 (62)	50	Filler (Al) 1948. Blacksmith seated at his anvil. ℞ value within oak wreath	1.00	1.60

			VF	XF
43 (63)	1	Forint (Al) 1946–1949. National arms, inscription MAGYAR ÁLLAMI VÁL-TOPÉNZ (small coin of the Hungarian state). ℞ value	0.80	1.60
44 (64)	2	Forint (Al) 1946–1947. National arms. ℞ value	1.00	2.00

45	5	Forint (Ag). Head right of Lajós Kossuth (1802–1894), Governor of Hungary 1848–1849, President of the Hungarian Republic in 1849. R national arms		
	a)	(Y 65) 1946, thick flan with edge inscription MUNKA A NEMZETI JOLET ALAPJA (Work – the basis of national prosperity)	12.00	18.00
	b)	(Y 66) 1947, thinner flan without inscription	3.50	5.50

Of same design: Nos. 77 and 95

COMMEMORATIVE ISSUES (3) FOR THE CENTENARY OF THE 1848 REVOLUTION

46 (67)	5	Forint (Ag) 1948. Head left of Alexander Petöfi (1823–1849), poet (among other works he wrote the National Anthem); he died on 31st July 1849 as a Major in the Revolutionary Army. ℞ value	6.00	11.00
47 (68)	10	Forint (Ag) 1948. Head left of Stephen, Count of Szécheny (1791–1860), liberal political reformer, founder of the Hungarian Academy, Minister of Transport in 1848. ℞ value	9.00	12.00

48 (69)   20 Forint (Ag) 1948. Head left of Michael Táncsics (1799–1884), revolutionary writer, Member of Parliament 1848–1849. ℞ national arms and value

	VF	**XF**
	20.00	26.00

MAGYAR NÉPKÖZTÁRSASÁG – People's Republic

49 (70)   2 Filler (Al) 1950–1979. Name of state. ℞ value and wreath (central hole) — 0.06 / 0.15

50 (71)   5 Filler (Al) 1953–. Type as No. 39, but with new name of state — 0.08 / 0.20

51 (72)   10 Filler. Type as No. 40, but with new name of state
     a) (Al) 1950, milled edge, diameter 19 mm — 1.60 / 3.00
     b) (Al) 1951, 1955, 1957–1966, milled edge, diameter 19 mm — 0.16 / 0.35
     c) (Al–Mg) 1967, plain edge, diameter 18 mm — 1.20 / 2.00
     d) (Al–Mg) 1968–1971, plain edge, diameter 18 mm — 0.10 / 0.20

52 (73)   20 Filler. Type as No. 41, but with new name of state
     a) (Al) 1953–1966, plain edge, diameter 21 mm — 0.25 / 0.40
     b) (Al–Mg) 1967–1974, milled edge, diameter 20 mm — 0.15 / 0.30

53 (74)   50 Filler (Al) 1953–1966. Type as No. 42, but with new name of state — 0.30 / 0.50

54 (75)   1 Forint (Al) 1949–1952. Arms of the People's Republic. ℞ value — 0.35 / 0.60

55 (76)   2 Forint (Cu–Ni) 1950–1952. Arms of the People's Republic. ℞ value — 0.50 / 0.80

COMMEMORATIVE ISSUES (3) FOR THE 10th ANNIVERSARY OF THE FORINT CURRENCY

			VF	XF
56 (77)	10	Forint (Ag) 1956. The National Museum in Budapest. ℞ value	10.00	12.50

57 (78)	20	Forint (Ag) 1956. The Szechenyi suspension bridge in Budapest. ℞ arms of the People's Republic	16.00	20.00
58 (79)	25	Forint (Ag) 1956. The Parliament building in Budapest. ℞ arms of the People's Republic over cog-wheel	20.00	25.00
59 (80)	1	Forint. New arms of the People's Republic. ℞ value	0.40	0.80
		a) (Al) 1957–1966, diameter 24 mm		
		b) (Al–Mg) 1967–1970, diameter 22.5 mm	0.30	0.70
60 (81)	2	Forint. New arms of the People's Republic. ℞ value		
		a) (Cu–Ni) 1957–1962	0.80	1.50
		b) (Cu–Ni–Zi) 1963–1966	0.60	1.20

COMMEMORATIVE ISSUES (5) FOR THE 150th ANNIVERSARY OF FRANZ VON LISZT

			Proof
61 (82)	25	Forint (Ag) 1961. Head right of Franz von Liszt (1811–1886), pianist and composer. ℞ value and lyre	25.00

62 (83)	50	Forint (Ag) 1961. Type as No. 61	26.00
63 (84)	50	Forint (Au) 1961. Type as No. 61	120.00
64 (85)	100	Forint (Au) 1961. Type as No. 61	200.00
65 (86)	500	Forint (Au) 1961. Type as No. 61	700.00

COMMEMORATIVE ISSUES (5) FOR THE 80th ANNIVERSARY OF THE BIRTH OF BÉLA BARTÓK

66 (87)	25 Forint (Ag) 1961. Head left of Béla Bartók (1881–1945), composer and pioneer of the New Music. ℞ lyre above value	25.00
67 (88)	50 Forint (Ag) 1961. Type as No. 66	28.00
68 (89)	50 Forint (Au) 1961. Type as No. 66	120.00
69 (90)	100 Forint (Au) 1961. Type as No. 66	200.00
70 (91)	500 Forint (Au) 1961. Type as No. 66	700.00

COMMEMORATIVE ISSUES (5) FOR THE 400th ANNIVERSARY OF THE DEATH OF MIKLOS ZRINYI

71 (92)   25 Forint (Ag) 1966. Facing head of Count Miklos Zrinyi (1508–1566), defender of the fortress of Sigeth (Szigetvár), which was besieged and conquered in 1566 by the Turks under Sultan Sulei-

man II (1494–1566). ℞ scene showing
soldiers trying to break out from the
fortress; family arms

				Proof
				25.00
72 (93)	50	Forint (Ag) 1966. Type as No. 71		40.00
73 (94)	100	Forint (Au) 1966. Type as No. 71		200.00
74 (95)	500	Forint (Au) 1966. Type as No. 71		700.00
75 (96)	1000	Forint (Au) 1966. Type as No. 71		1600.00

Nos. 71–75 were issued on polished flans only (proofs).

			XF	Unc
76 (97)	50	Filler (Al–Mg) 1967–. The Elizabeth Bridge in Budapest. ℞ value	0.15	0.30

77 (98)	5	Forint (Cu–Ni–Zi) 1967, 1968. Type as No. 45, but diameter only 27.5 mm, milled edge	1.00	2.00

COMMEMORATIVE ISSUES (5) FOR THE 85th
ANNIVERSARY OF THE BIRTH OF ZOLTAN KODÁLY

78 (99) 25 Forint (Ag) 1967. Bust three-quarters
to left of Zoltán Kodály (1882–1967),
composer of modern national Hungar-

				Unc	Proof
		ian music; he collected and systematized the folk music of Hungary. Ⱳ blue peacock (Pavo cristatus – Phasianidae)		10.00	
79	(100)	50	Forint (Ag) 1967. Type as No. 78	14.00	
80	(101)	100	Forint (Ag) 1967. Type as No. 78	40.00	
81	(102)	500	Forint (Au) 1967. Type as No. 78		700.00
82	(103)	1000	Forint (Au) 1967. Type as No. 78		1200.00

COMMEMORATIVE ISSUES (7) FOR THE 150th ANNIVERSARY OF THE BIRTH OF SEMMELWEIS

83	(104)	50	Forint (Ag) 1968. Head right of Dr. Ignatius Philip Semmelweis (1818 to 1865), who discovered the origin of puerperal fever	12.00	16.00
84	(106)	50	Forint (Au) 1968. Type as No. 83		90.00
85	(105)	100	Forint (Ag) 1968. Type as No. 83	25.00	35.00
86	(107)	100	Forint (Au) 1968. Type as No. 83		160.00
87	(108)	200	Forint (Au) 1968. Type as No. 83		320.00
88	(109)	500	Forint (Au) 1968. Type as No. 83		800.00
89	(110)	1000	Forint (Au) 1968. Type as No. 83		1300.00

COMMEMORATIVE ISSUES (2) FOR THE PROCLAMATION OF THE REPUBLIC OF REVOLUTIONARY COUNCILS ON 21st MAY 1919

90 (111) 50 Forint (Ag) 1969. "Revolutionary hold-

ing flag", from a contemporary poster.
R emblem of state, value — 12.50 — 18.00

91 (112) 100 Forint (Ag) 1969. Type as No. 90 — 28.00 — 35.00

COMMEMORATIVE ISSUES (2) FOR THE 25th ANNIVERSARY OF THE LIBERATION

92 (113) 50 Forint (Ag) 1970. "Allegorical figure of Liberty", the Strobl Monument in Budapest — 8.00 — 12.50

93 (114) 100 Forint (Ag) 1970. Type as No. 92 — 16.00 — 25.00

			XF	Unc

94 (115) 2 Forint (Bra) 1970–. Emblem of state and name of country in semi-circular legend above. R value, date — 0.40 — 0.75

95 (116) 5 Forint (Ni) 1971–. Lajos Kossuth (1802–1894), Governor of Hungary 1848–1849, President of the Hungarian Republic in 1849. R emblem of state, date and value — 0.80 — 1.50

96 (117) 10 Forint (Ni) 1971–. "Allegorical figure of Liberty", the Strobl Monument in Budapest. R value, emblem of state and date — 0.80 — 2.00

COMMEMORATIVE ISSUES (2) FOR THE 1000th BIRTHDAY OF ST. STEPHEN

97 (118) 50 Forint (Ag) 1972. Equestrian portrait

of Stephen I, the Saint, King of Hungary 955–1038. ℞ contemporary silver denarius. Value, date

	Unc	Proof
	8.00	15.00

98 (119) 100 Forint (Ag) 1972. Portrait of the King. ℞ monogram of the King. Value, date 16.00 30.00

COMMEMORATIVE ISSUE FOR THE CENTENARY OF BUDAPEST BY THE AMALGAMATION OF THE TOWNS OF BUDA (OFEN) AND PEST

99 (120) 100 Forint (Ag) 1972. Clamped parts of cornices as symbol of the union. ℞ value, national emblem, date 12.00 22.00

COMMEMORATIVE ISSUES (2) FOR THE 150th BIRTHDAY OF SANDOR PETÖFI

100 (121) 50 Forint (Ag) 1973. Sandor (Alexander) Petöfi (1823–1849), poet, among others of the National Anthem, fell as a major in the Revolutionary Army on 31st July 1849. ℞ rosette, date, year 8.00 12.00

101 (122) 100 Forint (Ag) 1973. Head similar to No. 100 and quotation from his poem "March Youth", translated: "We have dared to act for the fatherland", including his signature. ℞ national emblem, value, date 16.00 28.00

COMMEMORATIVE ISSUE FOR THE 25th ANNIVERSARY OF THE FOUNDING OF THE COUNCIL FOR MUTUAL ECONOMIC AID (25. 1. 1974)

102 (123) 100 Forint (Ag) 1974. National arms, name of country, value. ℞ the letters KGST

	Unc	Proof
and figures relating to the anniversary, surrounded by coins of the member states of Hungary, the Soviet Union, Rumania, the German Democratic Republic, People's Republic of Mongolia, Poland, Cuba, Czechoslovakia and Bulgaria (arranged clockwise)	16.00	32.00

50th ANNIVERSARY OF HUNGARIAN NATIONAL BANK (2)

			Unc	Proof
103 (124)	50 Forint (Ag) 1974. Building of Hungarian National Bank		8.00	16.00

			Unc	Proof
104 (125)	100 Forint (Ag) 1974		17.00	32.00

		Unc	Proof

30th ANNIVERSARY OF THE LIBERATION

105 (126) 200 Forint (Ag) 1975   25.00   32.00

150th ANNIVERSARY OF THE ACADEMY OF SCIENCE

106 (127) 200 Forint (Ag) 1975   25.00   32.00

300th ANNIVERSARY OF THE BIRTH OF RAKOCZI

107 (128) 200 Forint (Ag) 1976. Scene of Francis II Rákóczi on horseback surrounded by serveral followers   25.00   32.00

HUNGARIAN PAINTERS (3)

108 (129) 200 Forint (Ag) 1976. Mihaly Munkácsy   24.00   26.00
109 (130) 200 Forint (Ag) 1976. Pál Szinyei Merse   24.00   26.00
110 (131) 200 Forint (Ag) 1976. Gyula Derkovits   24.00   26.00

			Unc	Proof
111 (132)	200 Forint (Ag) 1977. Adám Mányoki		24.00	26.00
112 (134)	200 Forint (Ag) 1977. Rónai Rippl		24.00	26.00
113 (133)	200 Forint (Ag) 1977. Kosztka Csontváry		24.00	26.00

175th ANNIVERSARY OF THE HUNGARIAN NATIONAL MUSEUM

114 (135)	200 Forint (Ag) 1977	20.00	25.00

FIRST GOLD FORINT

115 (136)	200 Forint (Ag) 1978	18.00	24.00

INTERNATIONAL YEAR OF THE CHILD 1979

116 (137)	200 Forint (Ag) 1979:		
	a) 28 gm., dia. 37 mm	40.00	60.00
	b) 56 gm., dia. 37 mm; Piéfort		185.00

350th ANNIVERSARY OF THE DEATH OF GABOR BETHLEN

	Unc	Proof

117 (138)   200 Forint (Ag) 1979:

    a) 28 gm., dia. 37 mm   25.00   35.00
    b) 56 gm., dia. 37 mm; Piéfort   160.00

13th OLYMPIC WINTER GAMES IN LAKE PLACID (2)

118 (140)   200 Forint (Ag) 1980:
    a) 16 gm., dia. 36 mm   38.00
    b) 32 gm., dia. 36 mm; Piéfort   150.00
119 (141)   500 Forint (Ag) 1980:
    a) 39 gm., dia. 46 mm   55.00
    b) 78 gm., dia. 46 mm; Piéfort   225.00

1st SOVIET-HUNGARIAN SPACE FLIGHT

120 (139)   100 Forint (Ni) 1980   6.00

100th ANNIVERSARY OF THE BIRTH OF B. BARTOK

121 (143)   500 Forint (Ag) 1981. Béla Bartók (1881–
            1945), composer   35.00   42.00

122   10 Forint (Ni) 1981   2.50

123   100 Forint (Ni) 1981   8.00   12.50

WORLD SOCCER CHAMPIONSHIP GAMES 1982 IN SPAIN (2)

 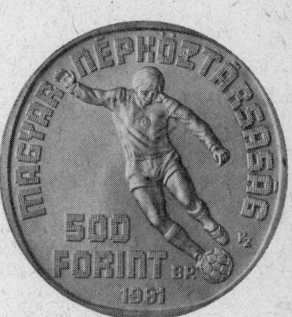

124   500 Forint (Ag) 1981   45.00
125   500 Forint (Ag) 1981   45.00

1300 YEARS OF BULGARIA

126   100 Forint (Ni) 1981. Portraits of Alexander
                 Petőfi (1823–1849), Hungarian poet and
                 Khristo Botev (1848–1876), Bulgarian
                 poet   11.00

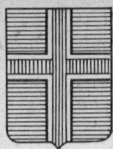

Island **Iceland** Islande

Area: 39,760 sq. mi. Population: 210,000.
This island in the North Atlantic Ocean was colonized in 874 mainly by
the Norwegian Vikings. Iceland became the point of departure for
voyages of discovery to Greenland and North America. In 1262 it came
under the rule of the Norwegian kings. In 1380 Iceland fell to Denmark
at the same time as Norway. On 1st December 1918 it became a sovereign state closely united with Denmark under the King. In 1944, following a referendum, the republic was proclaimed.
Capital: Reykjavik.

100 Aurar = 1 Icelandic Krona

CHRISTIAN X 1912–1944

			VF	XF
1 (1)	1	Eyrir (Br) 1926–1942. Monogram CX, above which crown. R value	1.10	1.50
2 (2)	2	Aurar (Br) 1926–1942. Type as No. 1	1.00	1.50
3 (3)	5	Aurar (Br) 1926–1942. Type as No. 1	1.30	2.00
4 (4)	10	Aurar (Cu-Ni) 1922–1940. Crowned arms, monogram, divided date. Rev. value	2.00	4.00
5 (5)	25	Aurar (Cu-Ni) 1922–1940. Type as No. 4	1.80	3.00
6 (6)	1	Krona (Al-Br) 1925, 1929, 1940. Type similar to No. 4	2.00	3.00

7 (7)	2 Kronur (Al–Br) 1925–1940. Type as No. 6	2.60	4.00

			VF	XF
8 (8)	2	Kronur (Br) 1930. Seated figure. ℞ Icelandic cross, representation of animals and hunting scene		65.00
9 (9)	5	Kronur (Ag) 1930. Ulfliot, the lawgiver. ℞ decoration: intertwined dragons		160.00

10 (10)	10	Kronur (Ag) 1930. The King of Thule. National arms		200.00
11 (4a)	10	Aurar (Zi) 1942. Type as No. 4	3.00	8.00
12 (5a)	25	Aurar (Zi) 1942. Type as No. 5	4.00	9.00

REPUBLIC since 1944

13 (11)	1	Eyrir (Br) 1946–1966. Coat of arms within wreath. ℞ value	0.15	0.30

14 (12)	5	Aurar (Br) 1946-1966. Type as No. 13	0.20	0.35
15 (13)	10	Aurar (Cu-Ni) 1946-1969. Type as No. 13	0.15	0.30

			VF	**XF**
16 (13a)	10	Aurar (Al) 1970-. Type as No. 13	0.05	0.10
17 (14)	25	Aurar (Cu-Ni) 1946-1967. Type as No. 13	0.15	0.30

			VF	**XF**
18 (A 15)	50	Aurar (Ni-Bra) 1969-. Coat of arms within wreath. R value	0.12	0.25
19 (15)	1	Krona (Al-Br) 1946. Coat of arms. Rev. value	0.80	1.80

			VF	**XF**
20 (15a)	1	Krona (Ni-Bra) 1957-1975. Type as No. 19	0.20	0.40
21 (15b)	1	Krona (Al) 1976-. Type as No. 20; 17 mm dia.	0.05	0.10
22 (16)	2	Kronur (Al-Br) 1946. Type as No. 19	2.50	4.50
23 (16a)	2	Kronur (Ni-Bra) 1958, 1962, 1963, 1966. Type as No. 19	0.50	0.80
24 (18)	5	Kronur (Cu-Ni) 1969-. Type as No. 19	0.20	0.30
25 (19)	10	Kronur (Cu-Ni) 1967-. Type as No. 19	0.35	0.60

			VF	**XF**
26 (21)	50	Kronur (Cu-Ni) 1970-. Parliament building in Reykjavik. R value	0.80	2.00

150th ANNIVERSARY OF THE BIRTH OF SIGURDSSON

		VF	Unc
27 (17) 500 Kronur (Au) 1961. Jón Sigurdsson (1811–1879), philologist, historian and politician; advocate of Icelandic independence. ℞ national arms		250.00	300.00

COMMEMORATIVE ISSUE FOR THE 50th ANNIVERSARY OF INDEPENDENCE

28 (20) 50 Kronur (Cu–Ni) 1968. Parliament building in Reykjavik; commemorative inscription. ℞ value		1.60	2.50

COMMEMORATIVE ISSUES (3)
FOR THE 100th ANNIVERSARY OF THE SETTLEMENT BY NORWEGIAN VIKINGS

29 (22) 500 Kronur (Ag) 1974. Viking woman with cow. ℞ sea eagle, dragon, bull and

giant in quartered circle, the so-called
protectors of the land who in accordance with the legend are reputed to
have protected Iceland against an in-
vasion of the Danish King Harald
Blatand, value, name of country

	Unc	Proof
	10.00	20.00

30 (23) 1000 Kronur (Ag) 1974. Two vikings, in the
background a blazing fire which was
lit when taking possession of the country as a boundary of occupation. ℞ as
No. 29 — 20.00 — 30.00

31 (24) 10000 Kronur (Au) 1974. Ingulfur (Ingólfr)
Arnason from Firdafylke in Norway
in his boat, proceeding to toss the two
posts of his subsequent raised domicile
on to the beach when landing (legend
of the foundation of Reykjavik). ℞ as
with No. 29 — 250.00 — 280.00

CURRENCY REFORM: 1 new Kronur = 100 old Kronur

			XF	Unc
32 (25)	5	Aurar (Br) 1981–	0.10	0.20
33 (26)	10	Aurar (Br) 1981–	0.10	0.20
34 (27)	50	Aurar (Br) 1981–	0.10	0.20
35 (28)	1	Kronur (Cu-Ni) 1981–	0.25	0.40
36 (29)	5	Kronur (Cu-Ni) 1981–	1.00	1.30

Indien **Inde**

India

Area: 1,259,797 sq. mi. Population: 631,000,000.
On the basis of the Act of Independence passed by the British Parliament, British India was divided in 1947 into an almost exclusively Mohammedan state (Pakistan) and a predominantly Hindu state (India). On 15th August 1947 India obtained the status of an independent dominion, and since 26th January 1950 it has been a republic within the British Commonwealth.
Capital: New Delhi.

3 Pies = 1 Pice (Paisa), 12 Pies = 1 Anna; 16 Annas = 1 Rupee,
15 Rupees = 1 Mohur; since 1st April 1957: 100 Naye Paise =
1 Rupee; since 1st April 1964: 100 Paise = 1 Rupee

EDWARD VII 1901–1910

			VF	XF
1 (27)	$^1/_{12}$	Anna (Cu) 1903–1910. Head right of King Edward VII. ℞ value within dotted circle, the whole surrounded by leaf decoration	0.25	0.50
2 (28)	½	Pice (Cu) 1903–1910	0.30	0.60
3 (29)	¼	Anna (Cu) 1903–1910	0.30	0.60
4 (30)	1	Anna (Cu–Ni) 1907–1910. ℞ value within scroll (scalloped edge)	0.50	1.50
5 (31)	2	Annas (Ag) 1903–1910. ℞ crown above value	1.00	2.00
6 (32)	¼	Rupee (Ag) 1903–1910	1.20	3.00
7 (33)	½	Rupee (Ag) 1903–1910	3.00	5.00
8 (34)	1	Rupee (Ag) 1903–1910	4.00	6.50

KING GEORGE V 1910–1936

9 (35)	$^1/_{12}$	Anna (Br) 1911–1936. Crowned bust to left of King George V	0.15	0.25
10 (36)	½	Pice (Br) 1911–1936	0.30	0.50
11 (37)	¼	Anna (Br) 1911–1936	0.30	0.50

			VF	XF
12 (38)	1	Anna (Cu–Ni) 1912–1936. ℞ value within scroll (scalloped edge)	0.30	0.60
13 (42)	2	Annas (Ag) 1911–1917. ℞ value within circle, the whole surrounded by floral decoration	1.00	1.50
14 (43)	¼	Rupee (Ag) 1911–1936	1.50	2.50
15 (44)	½	Rupee (Ag) 1911–1936	2.50	4.00

			VF	XF
16 (45)	1	Rupee (Ag) 1911–1922. Value also given in Persian	5.00	6.50
17 (39)	2	Annas (Cu–Ni) 1918–1936. ℞ large "2" within square (square shape)	0.60	1.20
18 (40)	4	Annas (Cu–Ni) 1919–1921. ℞ large "4" within square (octagonal)	1.00	2.00
19 (41)	8	Annas (Cu–Ni) 1919–1920. Large "8"; value also given in Nagpuri, Persian, Bengali and Tamili	3.00	7.00
20 (46)	15	Rupees (1 Mohur) (Au) 1918. Crowned bust to left of King George V. ℞ value within dotted circle, the whole surrounded by border decoration	130.00	160.00

			VF	XF
21 (A 46)	1	£ (Au) 1918. King George V. ℞ St. George and the Dragon	120.00	150.00

Coin No. 21 can only be distinguished from the other similar coins issued at the same time in Great Britain by the mintmark "I".

KING GEORGE VI 1936–1952

			VF	XF
22 (47)	$^1/_{12}$	Anna (Br) 1938–1939. Crowned head left of King George VI. ℞ value within dotted circle, the whole surrounded by border decoration	0.15	0.25
23 (47a)	$^1/_{12}$	Anna (Br) 1939–1942. Type as No. 22, but low-relief head (second head)	0.15	0.30

			VF	XF
24 (49)		½ Pice (Br) 1938–1940	0.20	0.40
25 (49a)		½ Pice (Br) 1940–1942. Type as No. 22, second head	0.30	0.50
26 (50)		¼ Anna (Br) 1938–1940	0.30	0.50
27 (50a)		¼ Anna (Br) 1940–1942. Type as No. 26, second head	0.30	0.60
28 (51)		1 Pice (Br) 1943–1947. Border decoration. ℞ crown and date (central hole); value also given in Devanagari and Persian	0.15	0.30
29 (52)		½ Anna. ℞ value within scroll		
		a) (Ni-Bra) 1942–1945	0.10	0.25
		b) (Cu-Ni) 1946–1947	0.10	0.25
30 (53)		1 Anna (Cu-Ni) 1938–1940, ℞ value within scroll	0.10	0.20
31 (53)		1 Anna. Type as No. 30, second head		
		a) (Cu-Ni) 1940–1947	0.10	0.20
		b) (Ni-Bra) 1942–1945	0.10	0.20
32 (54)		2 Annas (Cu-Ni) 1939. ℞ large »2« within scroll (square shape)	0.15	0.30
33 (54)		2 Annas. Type as No. 32, second head		
		a) (Cu-Ni) 1939–1947	0.15	0.30
		b) (Ni-Bra) 1942–1945	0.15	0.30
34 (55)		¼ Rupee (Ag) 1939–1940	2.00	3.00
35 (55)		¼ Rupee (Ag) 1939–1945. Type as No. 34, second head	1.60	2.50
36 (56)		½ Rupee (Ag) 1938–1939	4.00	6.00
37 (56)		½ Rupee (Ag) 1939–1945. Type as No. 36, second head	1.80	2.50
38 (57)		1 Rupee (Ag) 1938–1945	3.50	7.00
39 (58)		¼ Rupee (Ni) 1946–1947. ℞ tiger (Panthera tigris – Felidae)	1.00	1.60
40 (59)		½ Rupee (Ni) 1946–1947. Type as No. 39	1.10	1.80

41 (60)		1 Rupee (Ni) 1947. Type as No. 39	1.50	2.60

42 (61) 1 Pice (Br). Capital of the Ashoka column (Edict column) from Sarnat surmounted by three lions with the "Wheel of the Law", today in the National Museum in New Delhi; emblem of the national coat of arms. ℞ horse (Equus caballus caballus — Equidae)

	VF	XF
a) 1950, thick flan	0.15	0.30
b) 1951–1955, thin flan	0.05	0.10

43 (62) ½ Anna (Cu–Ni) 1950–1955. ℞ Zebu (square shape) — 0.10 — 0.20

44 (63) 1 Anna (Cu–Ni) 1950–1955. ℞ Zebu (scalloped edge) — 0.20 — 0.40

45 (64) 2 Annas (Cu–Ni) 1950–1954. ℞ Zebu (square shape) — 0.20 — 0.40

46 (65) ¼ Rupee (Ni) 1950–1956. ℞ value with ear of corn on either side — 0.25 — 0.50

47 (66) ½ Rupee (Ni) 1950–1956 — 0.30 — 0.60

48 (67) 1 Rupee (Ni) 1950–1954 — 1.00 — 1.80

NEW CURRENCY (Decimal System): 100 Naye Paise = 1 Rupee

			VF	XF
49 (68)	1	Naya Paisa. R value		
		a) (Br) 1957–1962	0.10	0.15
		b) (Ni-Bra) 1962–1963	0.10	0.15
50 (69)	2	Naye Paise (Cu-Ni) 1957–1963. R value (scalloped edge)	0.10	0.15
51 (70)	5	Naye Paise (Cu-Ni) 1957–1963 (square shape)	0.10	0.20
52 (71)	10	Naye Paise (Cu-Ni) 1957–1963 (scalloped edge)	0.10	0.20
53 (72)	25	Naye Paise (Ni) 1957–1963	0.20	0.50
54 (73)	50	Naye Paise (Ni) 1960–1963	0.40	0.70
55 (74)	1	Rupee (Ni) 1962–1974; 10 gm.:		
		a) 1962, 1970	0.80	1.60
		b) 1971–1974, proof only		3.50

NEW CURRENCY: 100 Paise = 1 Rupee

			VF	XF
56 (75)	1	Paisa (Ni–Bra) 1964. Type as No. 49	0.10	0.20
57 (76)	2	Paise (Cu–Ni) 1964. Type as No. 50	0.10	0.20

			VF	XF
58 (77)	3	Paise (Al) 1964–1971 (hexagonal)	0.08	0.15
59 (78)	5	Paise (Cu-Ni) 1964–1966. Type as No. 51	0.10	0.16
60 (79)	10	Paise (Cu-Ni) 1964–1967. Type as No. 52	0.10	0.20
61 (80)	25	Paise (Ni) 1964–1968. Type as No. 53	0.12	0.25
62 (81)	50	Paise (Ni) 1964–1971. Type as No. 54	0.15	0.30

COMMEMORATIVE ISSUES (2) FOR THE DEATH OF JAWAHARLAL NEHRU

			VF	XF
63 (82)	50	Paise (Ni) 1964. Head left of Jawaharlal Nehru (1889–1964), politican, Prime Minister 1947–1964. R capital of the Ashoka column from Sarnat surmounted by three lions, and value also given in Devanagari	0.40	1.00
64 (82.1)	50	Paise (Ni) 1964. Type as No. 63, but Hindi obverse	0.35	0.80

				VF	XF
65 (83)	1	Rupee (Ni) 1964. Type as No. 63		1.00	2.00
66 (84)	1	Paisa (Al) 1965–. ℞ value (square shape)		0.05	0.10
67 (85)	2	Paise (Al) 1965–. ℞ value (scalloped edge)		0.05	0.10
68 (78)	5	Paise (Al) 1967–1971. Rev. value (square shape)		0.05	0.10

				VF	XF
69 (79a)	10	Paise (Ni-Bra) 1968–1971. Type as No. 60		0.10	0.20

				VF	XF
70 (86)	20	Paise (Ni-Bra) 1968–1971. Rev. lotus flower, value and date		0.15	0.25

COMMEMORATIVE ISSUES (4) FOR THE CENTENARY OF THE BIRTH OF MAHATMA GANDHI

				XF	Unc
71 (87)	20	Paise (Al–Br) 1969. Head left of Mohandas Karamchand Gandhi (1869–1948), known as Mahatma ("Sublime Soul"), advocate of the non-violent resistance advocator of the non-violent resistance movement "Satyagraha". ℞ emblem of state and value		0.30	0.50
72 (88)	50	Paise (Ni) 1969. Type as No. 71		0.35	0.70
73 (89)	1	Rupee (Ni) 1969. Type as No. 71		0.60	1.00

			XF	Unc
74 (90)	10	Rupees (Ag) 1969. Type as No. 71	8.00	12.50

COMMEMORATIVE ISSUES (2) FOR THE FAO COIN PLAN

75 (91)	20	Paise (Al-Br) 1970, 1971. Lotus flower between ears of corn; above stylized sun	7.00	12.00
76 (92)	10	Rupees (Ag) 1970, 1971. Type as No. 75	7.00	12.00
77 (A 93)	3	Paise (Al) 1972–. Coat of arms. Rev. value, date; proof		2.00

78 (B 93)	5	Paise (Al) 1972–. Type as No. 77	0.06	0.12
79 (93)	10	Paise (Al) 1971–. National emblem in dotted circle, the whole in wreath of leaf ornaments. R value (rounded serrated edge)	0.08	0.15
80 (94)	25	Paise (Ni-Al) 1972–. National emblem. Value, date, crossed branches	0.15	0.30
81 (95)	50	Paise (Ni-Al) 1972–. Type as No. 78	0.20	0.40

FOR THE 25th ANNIVERSARY OF INDEPENDENCE
(15th August 1972)

		XF	Unc
82 (96)	50 Paise (Cu–Ni) 1972	0.30	0.70

		XF	Unc
83 (97)	10 Rupees (Ag) 1972	7.50	12.00

COMMEMORATIVE ISSUES (3) FOR THE FAO COIN PLAN

		XF	Unc
84 (98)	50 Paise (Cu–Ni) 1973. Lettering in square between ears of wheat, date. & national arms, value	0.30	0.70
85 (99)	10 Rupees (Ag) 1973. Type as No. 84	7.00	11.00
86 (100)	20 Rupees (Ag) 1973. Type as No. 84	10.00	16.50

ISSUE FOR THE FAO COIN PLAN (3)

		XF	Unc
87 (101)	10 Paise (Al) 1974	0.20	0.30
88 (102)	10 Rupees (Cu–Ni) 1974	2.50	4.00
89 (103)	50 Rupees (Ag) 1974	12.50	20.00

			XF	Unc
90 (104)	10	Paise (Al) 1975	0.20	0.30
91 (105)	10	Rupees (Cu-Ni) 1975	1.80	3.60
92 (106)	50	Rupees (Ag) 1975	12.50	20.00
93 (74a)	1	Rupee (Cu-Ni) 1975–1978. Type as No. 55; 8 gm.	0.30	0.60

ISSUES FOR THE FAO COIN PLAN (4)

94 (107)	5	Paise (Al) 1976. Farm Mechanization	0.20	0.30
95 (108)	10	Paise (Al) 1976. Type as No. 94	0.20	0.30
96 (109)	10	Rupees (Cu-Ni) 1976. Type as No. 94	1.80	3.60
97 (110)	50	Rupees (Ag) 1976. Type as No. 94	12.50	20.00

ISSUES FOR THE FAO COIN PLAN (4)

98 (111)	5	Paise (Al) 1977	0.20	0.30
99 (112)	10	Paise (Al) 1977	0.20	0.30
100 (113)	10	Rupees (Cu-Ni) 1977	1.80	3.60
101 (114)	50	Rupees (Ag) 1977	12.50	20.00

FOR THE FAO COIN PLAN (4)	XF	Unc
102 (115) 5 Paise (Al) 1978	0.20	0.30
103 (116) 10 Paise (Al) 1978	0.20	0.30
104 (117) 10 Rupees (Cu-Ni) 1978	1.80	3.60

105 (118) 50 Rupees (Ag) 1978	12.50	20.00

INTERNATIONAL YEAR OF THE CHILD (4)

106 (119) 5 Paise (Al) 1979	0.15	0.25
107 (120) 10 Paise (Al) 1979	0.15	0.25
108 (121) 10 Rupees (Cu-Ni) 1979	1.80	3.60
109 (122) 50 Rupees (Ag) 1979	12.50	20.00

RURAL WOMEN'S ADVANCEMENT (4)

110 (123) 10 Paise (Al) 1980	0.15	0.25
111 (124) 25 Paise (Cu-Ni) 1980	0.20	0.40
112 (125) 10 Rupees (Cu-Ni) 1980	1.80	3.60
113 (126) 100 Rupees (Ag) 1980	22.00	30.00

Bahawalpur

The emirate of Bahawalpur belonged to British India until 1947 when it became part of Pakistan. Its integration into the state of West Pakistan followed on 14th October 1955.

SADIQ MOHAMMED KHAN V 1907–1947

			VF	XF
1 (8)	1	Paisa (Br) 1924 (Hegira Calendar dating 1342). Toughra. ℞ three stylized ears of corn, above which four stars (square shape)	9.00	12.00
2 (9)	1	Paisa (Br) 1925 (H. C. 1343). Toughra within double linear square. ℞ three stylized ears of corn, above which four stars, the whole within double linear square	10.00	15.00
3 (10)	1	Rupee (Ag) 1925 (H. C. 1343). Bust left of Emir Sadiq Mohammed Khan V. ℞ arms	40.00	60.00
4 (11)	1	Mohur (1 Ashrafi) (Au) 1925 (H. C. 1343). Type as No. 3	250.00	300.00
5 (12)	½	Pice (Cu) 1940. Bust left of Emir Sadiq Mohammed Khan V (1904 to 1966) wearing fez. ℞ toughra surrounded by stars	1.00	2.00
6 (13)	¼	Anna (Cu) 1940. Type as No. 5	2.00	4.00

Bikanir

The dating of the coins corresponds to the Samvat calendar.

SRI GANGA SINGHJI 1887–1943
COMMEMORATIVE ISSUE FOR THE 50th YEAR OF REIGN

1 (19)	1	Rupee (Ag) 1937 (S. C. 1994). Bust facing of Maharajah Sri Ganga Singhji. ℞ monogram within wreath, the whole surrounded by inscription and symbols	12.50	20.00
2 (20)	½	Mohur (Au) 1937. ℞ inscription within circle broken by emblems	120.00	140.00
3 (21)	1	Mohur (Au) 1937. Type as No. 2	220.00	300.00

Bundi

State in Rajasthan. The dating of the coins corresponds to the Samvat calendar. The coins were issued in the name of the reigning British monarch.

MAHARAO RAJAH RAGHUBIR SINGH 1889–1927

			VF	XF
1 (9)	1	Rupee (Ag) 1889–1900 (S. C. 1946 to 1957). Kunjar (Indian dagger) and inscription QUEEN VICTORIA. ℞ inscription in Devanagari	3.50	7.00
2 (10)	1	Rupee (Ag) 1901 (S. C. 1958). Bust of a Yaksha and inscription QUEEN VICTORIA. ℞ inscription in Devanagari	5.00	10.00
3 (12)	¼	Rupee (Ag) 1907–1909 (S. C. 1964 to 1966). Kunjar and inscription EDWARD VII. ℞ inscription in Devanagari	2.50	5.00
4 (13)	½	Rupee (Ag) 1909 (S. C. 1966). Type as No. 3	5.00	8.00
5 (11)	1	Rupee (Ag) 1901–1905 (S. C. 1958 to 1962). Bust of a Yaksha	7.00	10.00
6 (14)	1	Rupee (Ag) 1906–1911 (S. C. 1963 to 1968). Type as No. 3 (the coin can be round or square)	8.00	12.00
7 (15)	¼	Paisa (Cu) 1916–1929 (S. C. 1973 to 1986). Kunjar and inscription GEORGE V. ℞ inscription (square shape)	3.00	5.00
8 (16)	¼	Rupee (Ag) 1916–1924 (S. C. 1973 to 1981). Kunjar	4.50	6.00
9 (17)	½	Rupee (Ag) 1923–1926 (S. C. 1980 to 1983). Type as No. 8	5.00	8.00
10 (18)	1	Rupee (Ag) 1922–1926 (S. C. 1979 to 1983). Type as No. 8 (the coin can be round or square)	7.50	10.00
11 (19)	½	Rupee (Ag) 1925. Date and inscription	17.50	25.00
12 (20)	1	Rupee (Ag) 1925. Type as No. 11	26.00	35.00

Datia

State in the Bundelkhand territory.

MAHARAJAH GOVIND SINGH 1907–1955

1 (1)	½	Mohur (Au) undated. Portrait of the Maharajah. ℞ arms		260.00	300.00

Dungarpur

The dating of the coins corresponds to the Samvat calendar.

LAKSHMAN SINGH 1918–1948

			VF	XF
1 (1)	1	Paisa (Br) 1944 (S. C. 2001). Emblem of state. ℞ inscription (square shape)	15.00	30.00

Gwalior

State in the Malwa territory. The dating of the coins corresponds to the Samvat calendar.

MAHARAJAH MADHAO RAO SINDIA II
1886–1925

1 (45)   ½ Pice (Cu) 1901. Cobra (Naja naja — Elapidae or Elaphidae) (in Sanskrit: naga), trident (attribute of the god Shiva) and sceptre, the whole within dotted circle; inscription reading Sri Madhava Rao ma Sinde Alijabahadar in Devanagari. ℞ value and date within floral decoration   1.60   2.50

2 (46)	¼ Anna (Cu) 1901. Type as No. 1	2.00	4.00
3 (48)	¼ Anna (Cu) 1913–1917 (S. C. 1970 to 1974). Bust of the Maharajah wearing turban. ℞ arms of the state	2.00	3.00
4 (47)	⅓ Mohur (Au) 1902 (S. C. 1959). Type similar to No. 3	200.00	240.00

MAHARAJAH GEORGE JIVAJI RAO SINDIA
1925–1961

5 (49)	¼ Anna (Cu) 1929 (S. C. 1986). Bust of the Maharajah. ℞ arms of the state	1.00	1.50
6 (50)	¼ Anna (Cu) 1942. Type as No. 5, but diameter only 19 mm instead of 22 mm	0.80	1.20
7 (51)	½ Anna (Bra) 1942	0.90	1.50

State in Upper Deccan. In 1948 Hyderabad was integrated into the
Dominion of India and in November 1956 was divided into the Union
States of Andhra Pradesh, Maisur and Bombay.

NAWAB MIR MAHBUB ALI KHAN BAHADUR, ASAFJAH VI, NIZAM OF HYDERABAD 1869–1911

			VF	XF
1 (37)	$^1/_8$ Rupee (Ag) 1905 (H. C. 1323). The Char Minar in Hyderabad. ℞ inscription		1.50	3.00
2 (38)	$^1/_4$ Rupee (Ag) 1905–1911 (H. C. 1323 to 1329)		1.50	3.00
3 (39)	$^1/_2$ Rupee (Ag) 1910–1911 (H. C. 1328 to 1329)		3.50	6.50

			VF	XF
4 (40)	1 Rupee (Ag) 1903–1911 (H. C. 1321 to 1329)		6.00	8.00
5 (41)	$^1/_8$ Mohur (Au) 1903–1911 (H. C. 1321 to 1329). Type as No. 1		26.00	35.00
6 (42)	$^1/_4$ Mohur (Au) 1903–1911 (H. C. 1321 to 1329)		38.00	45.00
7 (43)	$^1/_2$ Mohur (Au) 1903–1911 (H. C. 1321 to 1329)		60.00	75.00

			VF	XF
8 (44)	1 Mohur (Au) 1903–1911 (H. C. 1321 to 1329)		85.00	100.00

NAWAB MIR USMAN ALI KHAN, ASAF JAH VII, NIZAM OF HYDERABAD & BERAR 1911–1948

			VF	XF
9 (45)	1 Pai (Br) 1920–1935 (H. C. 1338–1353). Toughra. ℞ inscription		0.70	1.00

			VF	XF
10 (46a)	2	Pai (Br) 1912–1932 (H. C. 1330–1349)	1.00	1.50
11 (47)	½	Anna (Br) 1914–1930 (H. C. 1332 to 1348)	1.50	3.00
12 (48)	1	Anna (Cu–Ni) 1920–1936 (H. C. 1338 to 1354). Toughra. ℞ three sections, the central one with value, the other two with inscription surrounded by meander pattern	1.00	2.00
13	1	Anna. Toughra. R value within scroll (square shape)		
		a) (Y 49) (Cu-Ni) 1938–1941 (H. C. 1356 to 1359)	1.00	1.50
		b) (Y 59) (Br) 1943–1950 (H. C. 1361 to 1368)	0.40	0.60
14 (50)	⅛	Rupee (Ag) 1912–1929 (H. C. 1330 to 1347). The Char minaret in Hyderabad. ℞ inscription	1.10	1.60
15 (51)	¼	Rupee (Ag) 1912–1936 (H. C. 1330 to 1354)	1.80	3.00
16 (52)	½	Rupee (Ag) 1912–1924 (H. C. 1330 to 1342)	4.00	7.00
17 (53)	1	Rupee (Ag) 1912–1925 (H. C. 1330 to 1343)	6.00	8.00
18 (54)	⅛	Mohur (Au) 1919–1925 (H. C. 1337 to 1343)	35.00	45.00
19 (55)	¼	Mohur (Au) 1919 (H. C. 1337)	50.00	65.00

			VF	XF
20 (56)	½	Mohur (Au) 1919–1935 (H. C. 1337 to 1353)	70.00	85.00
21 (57a)	1	Mohur (Au) 1925–1926 (H. C. 1343 to 1344)	100.00	120.00
22 (60)	⅛	Rupee (Ag) 1944–1946 (H. C. 1362 to 1364). ℞ value within circle	1.00	2.00
23 (61)	¼	Rupee (Ag) 1944–1946 (H. C. 1362 to 1364). Type as No. 22	1.00	1.50
24 (62)	½	Rupee (Ag) 1945 (H. C. 1363). Type as No. 22	2.00	3.00
25 (63)	1	Rupee (Ag) 1943–1947 (H. C. 1361 to 1365)	6.00	9.00

				VF	**XF**
26 (58)	2	Pai (Br) 1944–1950. Inscription (central hole)		0.50	1.00
27 (64)	1/8	Rupee (Ni) 1947–1950 (H. C. 1365 to 1368)		0.30	0.60
28 (65)	1/4	Rupee (Ni) 1947–1950 (H. C. 1365 to 1368)		0.50	0.90
29 (66)	1/2	Rupee (Ni) 1948 (H. C. 1366)		1.50	3.00

Indore

State in the Malwa territory. The dating of the coins corresponds to the Samvat calendar.

MAHARAJAH SHIVAJI RAO HOLKAR
1886–1903

1 (10a)	1/4	Anna (Cu) 1886–1902 (S. C. 1943 to 1959). Zebu, inscription reading Sri-mant Maharaja Holkar Sirkar Indore in Devanagari. ℞ value and date within dotted circle, the whole surrounded by leaf decoration	1.00	1.80
2 (11a)	1/2	Anna (Cu) 1886–1902 (S. C. 1943 to 1959). Type as No. 1	1.20	2.50
3 (19)	1	Rupee (Ag) 1899–1901 (S. C. 1956 to 1958). Facing bust of the Maharajah wearing turban. ℞ emblem of state	110.00	150.00
4 (18)	1	Rupee (Ag) 1904–1911 (S. C. 1961 to 1968). Sun surrounded by inscription		

in Devanagari. ℞ inscription within
wreath   7.50   10.00

MAHARAJAH YESHVANT RAO HOLKAR II
1926–1961

			VF	XF
5 (20)	¼	Anna (Cu) 1935 (S. C. 1992). Facing bust of the Maharajah within dotted circle. ℞ value and date in dotted circle, the whole surrounded by leaf decoration	0.50	1.00
6 (21)	½	Anna (Cu) 1935 (S. C. 1992). Type as No. 5	1.00	1.80

Jaipur

State in Rajasthan. The dating of the coins corresponds to the year of
reign of the ruling monarch.

MAHARAJAH SAWAI MADHO SINGH II
1880–1922

			VF	XF
1 (8)	1	Paisa (Br) 5–37 (1880–1916). Inscription in Hindi	1.20	2.50
2 (10)	⅛	Rupee (Ag) 1–29 (1880–1908). Inscription in Hindi	3.00	5.00
3 (11)	¼	Rupee (Ag) 1–43 (1880–1922). Inscription in Hindi surrounded by border decoration	4.00	7.00
4 (12)	½	Rupee (Ag) 1–28 (1880–1907). Type as No. 3	6.00	10.00
5 (13)	1	Rupee (Ag) 1–42 (1880–1921). Type as No. 3	8.00	12.50

MAHARAJAH SAWAI MAN SINGH II
1922–1949

			VF	XF
6 (18)	1	Anna (Bra) 1943–1944. Emblem of state within circle. ℞ value in circle	1.00	2.50

			VF	XF
7 (19)	1	Anna (Bra) 1944. Bust to right of the Maharajah. ℞ emblem of state	1.00	2.50

		VF	XF
8 (20)	2 Annas (Bra) 21 (1942). Inscription in Hindi (square shape)	2.00	4.00
9 (21)	1 Rupee (Ag) 17–28 (1938–1949)	12.50	20.00

Kutch

Until 1947 the coins were issued in the name of the reigning British monarch.

24 Dokda = 1 Kori

KHENGARJI III 1876–1942

		VF	XF
1 (71)	3 Dokda (Cu) 1936. Trident and inscription in Devanagari. ℞ kunjar (Indian dagger)	8.00	12.00
2 (73)	1 Kori (Ag) 1936. Inscriptions	4.00	6.00
3 (74)	2½ Kori (Ag) 1936	30.00	48.00

		VF	XF
4 (75)	5 Kori (Ag) 1936	8.00	12.50

VIJAYAARIJI 1942–1947

		VF	XF
5 (77)	¹⁄₁₆ Kori (Cu) 1943–1947. Wreath surrounded by circle and inscription. ℞ trident, half-moon and kunjar surrounded by inscription (central hole)	0.40	0.80
6 (78)	⅛ Kori (Cu) 1943–1944 (central hole)	1.00	2.00
7 (79)	¼ Kori (Cu) 1943–1947 (central hole)	1.20	2.50
8 (80)	½ Kori (Cu) 1943–1946 (central hole)	2.50	4.00

MADANASINHJI 1947

		VF	XF
9 (84)	1 Kori (Ag) 1947. Castle with towers and pinnacles, surrounded by double circle and leaf decoration. ℞ trident, half-moon and kunjar, inscription	11.00	15.00
10 (85)	5 Kori (Ag) 1947	80.00	100.00

Mewar Udaipur

BHUPAL SINGH 1930–1948

			VF	XF
1 (18)	1	Anna (Ag) 1932. The hills of Mewar and inscription within floral border ℞ inscription in four lines with floral border	1.20	2.00
2 (19)	2	Annas (Ag) 1932	1.50	2.50
3 (20)	¼	Rupee (Ag) 1932	3.00	4.50
4 (21)	½	Rupee (Ag) 1932	4.00	6.00
5 (22)	1	Rupee (Ag) 1932	7.00	10.00

Sailana

YESHVANT SINGH 1895–1919

			VF	XF
1 (5)	¼	Anna (Cu) 1908. Crowned bust left of King Edward VII. ℞ value and date within dotted circle, inscription giving name of state in English and Devanagari	7.00	15.00
2 (6)	¼	Anna (Cu) 1912. Type as No. 1, but with bust of King George V	16.00	25.00

Travancore

State on the south-west coast of the Indian sub-continent. The dating of the coins corresponds in part to the Malabar calendar.

16 Cash = 1 Chuckram, 4 Chuckrams = 1 Fanam,
8 Fanams = 1 Rupee

MAHARAJAH RAMA VARMA IX 1885–1924

			VF	XF
1 (29)	1	Cash (Cu) undated (1901). Chank snail (Xancus pyrum – Xancidae), symbol of the Indian god Vishnu. Rev. monogram RV	4.00	8.00
2 (30)	4	Cash (Cu) undated. Type as No. 1	1.50	3.00
3 (31)	8	Cash (Cu) undated. Type as No. 1	1.00	2.00
4 (32)	1	Chuckram (Cu) undated (1901–1903). Type as No. 1, legend »CHUCKRAM ONE«	3.00	6.00
5 (32a)	1	Chuckram (Cu) undated (1924). Type as No. 4, but legend »ONE CHUCKRAM«	1.50	3.00
6 (33)	2	Chuckrams (Ag) 1885–1930	3.00	5.00
7 (34)	1	Fanam (Ag) 1911–1930 (M. C. 1087 to 1106)	4.00	6.00
8 (35)	¼	Rupee (Ag) 1906–1930 (M. C. 1082 to 1106)	6.50	9.00
9 (36)	½	Rupee (Ag) 1910–1931 (M. C. 1086 to 1107)	8.50	12.00

As can be seen from the dates, coins Nos. 1–3 and 6–9 continued to be issued under the era of Maharajah Bala Rama Varma.

			VF	XF
10 (4)	¼	Pagoda (Au) 1885–1924. Chank snail within wreath. ℞ inscription in wreath	80.00	100.00
11 (5)	½	Pagoda (Au) 1885–1924. Type as No. 10	110.00	130.00
12 (6)	1	Pagoda (Au) 1885–1924. Type as No. 10	255.00	280.00
13 (7)	2	Pagoda (Au) 1885–1924. Type as No. 10	375.00	420.00

MAHARAJAH SIR BALA RAMA VARMA X
1924–1949

			VF	XF
14 (41)	1	Cash (Br) undated (1938–1945). Chank snail surrounded by circle and wreath. ℞ monogram BRV and value	0.50	1.00
15 (42)	4	Cash (Br) undated (1938–1945)	0.50	1.00
16 (43)	8	Cash (Br) undated (1938–1945)	1.00	2.00
17 (44)	1	Chuckram (Br) undated (1938–1945). Bust to right of the Maharajah wearing plumed hat. ℞ Chank snail within wreath, value	2.00	4.00
18 (45)	1	Fanam (Ag) 1936–1945 (M. C. 1112 to 1121). Chank snail surrounded by circle and wreath. ℞ value and date	2.00	4.00
19 (46)	¼	Rupee (Ag) 1936–1945 (M. C. 1112 to 1121)	5.00	8.00
20 (47)	½	Rupee (Ag) 1936–1945 (M. C. 1112 to 1121)	5.00	8.00

Indonesien   # Indonesia   **Indonésie**

Area: 735,268 sq. mi. Population: 136,000,000.
The proclamation of the Indonesian Republic within the realm of the
former Dutch East Indies took place on 17th August 1945 under the
leadership of Sukarno and Hatta. It was only after the end of the Dutch
police action to restore the old order, and the Conference of The Hague
on 28th December 1949, that Indonesia obtained full sovereignty over
all the islands, with the exception of Dutch New Guinea (since 1963
Irian Barat or West Irian). This territory passed to Indonesia only after
an interim period.
Capital: Djakarta (formerly Batavia).

100 Sen = 1 Rupiah

			XF	Unc
1 (1)	1	Sen (Al) 1952. Malay inscription. ℞ name of country INDONESIA, rice plant and value (central hole)	0.50	0.80

2 (2)	5	Sen (Al) 1951–1954. Type as No. 1	0.50	0.70
3 (3)	10	Sen (Al) 1951–1954. Garuda bird holding symbolic representation of the Pantjasila (national emblem) over Malay inscription. ℞ value	0.30	0.50
4 (4)	25	Sen (Al) 1952. Type as No. 3	0.40	0.60
5 (5)	50	Sen (Cu-Ni) 1952–1954. Head left of Dipanegara, national hero. ℞ value	0.30	0.60
6 (3a)	10	Sen (Al) 1957. Type as No. 3, but also on the obverse the inscription INDONESIA now in English	0.80	1.50
7 (6)	25	Sen (Al) 1955–1957. Type as No. 4, but also on the obverse the inscription INDONESIA now in English	0.30	0.60
8 (5a)	50	Sen (Cu-Ni) 1954–1957. Type as No. 5, but without Malay inscription:		
		a) 1954	3.00	6.00
		b) 1955, 1957	0.50	1.00

		XF	Unc
9 (7)	50 Sen (Al) 1958–1961. National arms. ℞ value	0.20	0.30

COMMEMORATIVE ISSUES (10) FOR THE 25th ANNIVERSARY OF INDEPENDENCE ON 17th AUGUST 1970

		Proof
10	200 Rupiah (Ag) 1970. Great bird of paradise (Paradisea apoda — Paradisaeidae). ℞ national arms, above which dates 1945–1970. Initials of the Bank of Indonesia, date and value	18.00
11	250 Rupiah (Ag) 1970. Mandjusjri statue in stone, from the temple of Tumpang	20.00

12	500 Rupiah (Ag) 1970. Wajang dancer	30.00

				Proof
13	750	Rupiah (Ag) 1970. Garuda, mythological bird, Balinese chisel work	40.00
14	1000	Rupiah (Ag) 1970. General Sudirman (1912–1950), leader of the revolt against Dutch domination	60.00
15	2000	Rupiah (Au) 1970. Type as No. 10	75.00
16	5000	Rupiah (Au) 1970. Type as No. 11	200.00
17	10000	Rupiah (Au) 1970. Type as No. 12	400.00
18	20000	Rupiah (Au) 1970. Type as No. 13	800.00
19	25000	Rupiah (Au) 1970. Type as No. 14	1000.00

				XF	Unc
20 (13)	1	Rupiah (Al) 1970	0.10	0.20
21 (14)	2	Rupiah (Al) 1970	0.15	0.30
22 (15)	5	Rupiah (Al) 1970	0.20	0.40
23 (16)	25	Rupiah (Cu–Ni) 1971	0.25	0.60
24 (17)	50	Rupiah (Cu–Ni) 1971	0.40	0.90

COMMEMORATIVE ISSUE FOR THE FAO COIN PLAN

				XF	Unc
25 (18)	10	Rupiah (Cu-Ni) 1971, 1973. Value surrounded by rice plant (Oryza sativa – Gramineae) and cotton plant Gossypium sp. – Malvaceae). R inscription reading Bank Indonesia, value and date	0.20	0.40
26 (19)	100	Rupiah (Cu–Ni) 1973. House with sagging gable roof in the style of the Menangkabau	0.70	1.00

ISSUE FOR THE FAO COIN PLAN

			XF	Unc
27 (20)	5	Rupiah (Al) 1974. Family planning	0.20	0.40

SPECIAL ISSUE (3) CONSERVATION COIN COLLECTION

			Unc	Proof
28 (22)	2000	Rupiah (Ag) 1974. Coat of arms, date. ℞ Javan Tiger (Panthera tigris – Felidae)	30.00	35.00
29 (23)	5000	Rupiah (Ag) 1974. ℞ Orang-Utan (Pongo pygmaeus – Pongidae)	45.00	60.00
30 (24)	100000	Rupiah (Au) 1974. ℞ Komodo Dragon (Varanus komodensis – Varanidae)	600.00	650.00

ISSUE FOR THE FAO COIN PLAN (4)

31 (21)	10	Rupiah (Brass-clad steel) 1974	0.25	0.50
32 (25)	100	Rupiah (Cu-Ni) 1978	1.10	1.60
33 (26)	5	Rupiah (Al) 1979	0.20	0.40
34 (27)	10	Rupiah (Al) 1979	0.30	0.50

Riau Archipelago

Group of islands between Sumatra and Singapore under Indonesian rule.

			XF	Unc
1 (8)	1 Sen (Al) 1962. Bust left of President Mohammed Ahmad Sukarno (1901 to 1970), known simply as Sukarno. ℞ value within wreath, border inscription: KEPULAUAN RIAU		0.80	1.20

			XF	Unc
2 (9)	5	Sen (Al) 1962	0.80	1.20
3 (10)	10	Sen (Al) 1962	0.80	1.20
4 (11)	25	Sen (Al) 1962	1.10	1.50
5 (12)	50	Sen (Al) 1962	1.60	2.00

West Irian (Irian Barat)

The former territory of Dutch New Guinea, renamed Irian Barat in 1963, was only added to Indonesia after an interim period. From 1st October 1962 to 1st March 1963, following negotiations, Dutch New Guinea was by treaty placed under the supervision of the United Nations. Since 1963 Irian Barat has been under Indonesian rule.

100 Sen = 1 Irian Barat Rupiah

1 (8a)	1	Sen (Al) 1962. Bust left of President Mohammed Ahmad Sukarno (1901 to 1970). ℞ value within wreath	1.20	1.60
2 (9a)	5	Sen (Al) 1962	1.60	2.00
3 (10a)	10	Sen (Al) 1962	1.80	2.20
4 (11a)	25	Sen (Al) 1962	2.00	2.60
5 (12a)	50	Sen (Al) 1962	2.20	3.00

Area: 630,000 sq. mi. Population: 34,000,000.

Located between the Arrarat highland and the Persian Gulf, this country once produced the powerful empires of the Persians and Medes. This second large Persian empire was created by the Sassanids in 226.

Due to its geographical location and its enormous oil recources, present-day Persia, since 1935 officially called Iran, holds a tremendous interest for the Great Powers.

Capital: Teheran.

50 Dinars = 1 Chahi, 20 Chahis = 1 Kran,
10 Krans = 1 Toman, 100 Dinars = 1 Rial, 20 Rials = 1 Pahlevi,
since 1937: 100 Rials = 1 Pahlevi
20 Rials = 1 Pahlevi, since 1937: 100 Rials = 1 Pahlevi

MUZAFFAR-ED-DIN SHAHINSHAH 1896–1907

			VF	XF
1 (23)	1 Chahi (Cu–Ni) H-C 1318–1323 (1900–1905). Coat of arms (=lion with sword in front of sun). ℞ legend in wreath, with crown above		0.80	1.20
2 (24)	2 Chahis (Cu–Ni) H-C 1318–1324 (1900–1906)		1.20	1.60
3 (25)	1 Chahi (Ag) H-C 1318 (1900). ℞ legend in wreath, with crown above		4.00	7.00
4 (26)	¼ Kran (Ag) H-C 1319 (1901)		7.00	11.00
5 (27)	½ Kran (Ag) H-C 1316–1323 (1898–1905)		8.00	12.00
6 (A 27)	1 Kran (Ag) H-C 1317–1318 (1899–1900)		12.50	20.00
7 (28)	2 Krans (Ag) H-C 1315–1322 (1897–1904)		10.00	16.00
8 (29)	5 Krans (Ag) H-C 1320 (1902)		15.00	25.00
9 (30)	½ Kran (Ag) H-C 1323 (1905). Muzaffar-ed-Din Shahinshah (1853–1907), portrait in wreath. ℞ coat of arms		7.00	12.00
10 (31)	1 Kran (Ag) H-C 1319–1324 (1901–1906)		10.00	16.00
11 (32)	2 Krans (Ag) H-C 1319–1324 (1901–1906)		12.00	20.00
12 (33)	5 Krans (Ag) H-C 1322–1324 (1904–1906)		120.00	170.00

			VF	XF
13 (34)	¼	Toman (Au) H-C 1314–1325 (1896–1907). Muzaffar-ed-Din Shahinshah, portrait right. ℞ legend in wreath	32.00	40.00
14 (35)	½	Toman (Au) H-C 1314–1325 (1896–1907)	38.00	45.00
15 (36)	1	Toman (Au) H-C 1314–1325 (1896–1907)	60.00	70.00
16 (37)	2	Tomans (Au) H-C 1314–1325 (1896–1907)	100.00	120.00
17	5	Tomans (Au) H-C 1314–1325 (1896–1907)	–.–	–.–
18	10	Tomans (Au) H-C 1314–1325 (1896–1907)	–.–	–.–

COMMEMORATIVE ISSUES (2) FOR THE BIRTHDAY OF THE SHAHINSHAH

19 (40)	1	Toman (Au) H-C 1322 (1904). Muzaffar-ed-Din Shahinshah, portrait left. ℞ in wreath	80.00	100.00
20 (41)	2	Tomans (Au) H-C 1322 (1904)	100.00	125.00
21 (A 38)	⅕	Toman (Au) H-C 1316–1324 (1898–1906). Coat of arms. ℞ legend in wreath	–.–	–.–
22 (38)	½	Toman (Au) H-C 1316–1324 (1898–1906)	60.00	70.00
23 (39)	1	Toman (Au) H-C 1316–1325 (1898–1907)	90.00	110.00
24	5	Tomans (Au) H-C 1316–1325 (1898–1907)	–.–	–.–
25	10	Tomans (Au) H-C 1316–1325 (1898–1907)	–.–	–.–

MOHAMMED ALI 1907–1909

26 (23)	1	Chahi (Cu–Ni) H-C 1326–1327 (1908–1909). Coat of arms. ℞ legend in wreath	0.80	1.20
27 (24)	2	Chahis (Cu–Ni) H-C 1326–1327 (1908–1909)	1.20	1.60
28 (44)	1	Chahi (Ag) undated	4.50	8.00
29 (45)	¼	Kran (Ag) H-C 1326–1327 (1908–1909)	6.00	10.00
30 (46)	½	Kran (Ag) H-C 1326–1327 (1908–1909)	8.00	12.00
31 (47)	2	Krans (Ag) H-C 1325–1327 (1907–1909)	10.00	16.00
32 (48)	½	Kran (Ag) H-C 1326–1327 (1908–1909). Mohammed Ali Shahinshah (1872–1930), portrait left. ℞ coat of arms	10.00	16.00

				VF	XF
33 (49)	1	Kran (Ag) H-C 1326–1327 (1908–1909)		12.50	20.00
34 (50)	2	Krans (Ag) H-C 1326 (1908)		100.00	150.00
35 (A 50)	5	Krans (Ag) H-C 1327 (1909)		300.00	500.00
36 (56)	½	Toman (Au) H-C 1325 (1907). Coat of arms. Ⱥ legend in wreath		18.00	25.00
37 (A 56)	1	Toman (Au) H-C 1325 (1907)		55.00	70.00
38	⅕	Toman (Au) H-C 1326 (1908). Mohammed Ali Shahinshah, portrait. Ⱥ legend in wreath		–.–	–.–
39 (53)	½	Toman (Au) H-C 1326 (1908)		50.00	60.00
40 (54)	1	Toman (Au) H-C 1326 (1908)		50.00	60.00
41 (55)	2	Tomans (Au) H-C 1326 (1908)		–.–	–.–
42	5	Tomans (Au) H-C 1325–1327 (1907–1909). Mohammed Ali Shahinshah, portrait. Ⱥ coat of arms		–.–	–.–

AHMED SHAH 1909–1925

				VF	XF
43 (64)	1	Chahi Sefid (Ag) H-C 1328–1330. Coat of arms date at bottom. Rev. legend in wreath		2.00	4.00
44 (A 64)	1	Chahi Sefid (Ag) H-C 1332. Type as No. 43, but date in lion's legs		4.00	7.00
45 (65)	¼	Kran (Ag) H-C 1327–1331. Type as No. 43; dia. 15 mm		5.00	8.00
46 (66)	500	Dinars (Ag) H-C 1327–1330; dia. 18 mm		4.00	7.00
47 (67)	1000	Dinars (Ag) H-C 1327–1330; dia. 23 mm		5.00	8.00
48 (68)	2	Krans (Ag) H-C 1327–1329; dia. 28 mm		8.00	12.00
49 (68a)	2000	Dinars (Ag) H-C 1330; dia. 28 mm		8.00	12.00
50 (68b)	2000	Dinars (Ag) H-C 1330–1331. Type as No. 49, but date in lion's legs		8.00	12.00
51 (75)	⅕	Toman (Au) H-C 1329. .900 gold, 0.57 gm.		55.00	70.00
52 (76)	½	Toman (Au) H-C 1328–1329. .900 gold, 1.43 gm.		60.00	80.00
53 (77)	1	Toman (Au) H-C 1329		–.–	–.–
54 (A 70)	1	Chahi Sefid (Ag) H-C 1333–1342		2.50	4.00
55 (B 70)	1	Chahi Sefid (Ag) H-C 1332–1342. Type as No. 54, but date in lion's legs		2.50	4.00
56 (C 70)	¼	Kran (Ag) H-C 1332–1343		3.50	6.00
57 (C 70a)	¼	Kran (Ag) H-C 1334. Typ as No. 56, but date at bottom		10.00	16.00
58 (70)	500	Dinars (Ag) H-C 1331–1343		6.00	10.00
59 (71)	1000	Dinars (Ag) H-C 1331–1344		5.50	8.00
60 (72)	2000	Dinars (Ag) H-C 1330–1344		7.50	9.50
61 (69)	5000	Dinars (Ag) H-C 1331–1344		16.00	30.00

			VF	XF
62 (79)	1/5	Toman (Au) H-C 1332–1341. Ahmed Shah, portrait. Rev. legend	40.00	50.00
63 (80)	½	Toman (Au) H-C (1332–1343)	50.00	60.00

64 (81)	1	Toman (Au) H-C 1333–1343 (1915–1925)	65.00	85.00
65	2	Tomans (Au) H-C 1333–1343 (1915–1925)	125.00	160.00
66 (83)	10	Tomans (Au) H-C 1333–1343 (1915–1925)	–.–	–.–

COMMEMORATIVE ISSUES (6) FOR THE 10th REGNAL ANNIVERSARY

67 (73)	1	Kran (Ag) H-C 1337 (1919). Ahmed Shah, portrait. ℞ coat of arms	16.00	20.00

68 (74)	2	Krans (Ag) H-C 1337 (1919)	18.00	25.00
69	1	Toman (Au) H-C 1337 (1919)	120.00	150.00
70	2	Tomans (Au) H-C 1337 (1919)	185.00	250.00
71	5	Tomans (Au) H-C 1337 (1919)	420.00	500.00
72	10	Tomans (Au) H-C 1337 (1919)	850.00	1000.00

RIZA SHAH PAHLEVI 1925–1941

Upon the introduction of the Solar-Hidshra-calendar (hidshri shamsi) the following dates, 1305–1349, correspond with the years 1924–1971, of the Christian calendar.

			VF	XF
73 (95)	50	Dinars (Cu-Ni) SH 1305–1307. Coat of arms. Rev. legend in wreath	0.80	1.20
74 (96)	100	Dinars (Cu-Ni) SH 1305–1307. Type as No. 73	1.20	2.00
75 (100)	¼	Kran (Ag) SH 1304. Coat of arms. Rev. legend; dia. 15 mm	8.50	12.00
76 (A101)	500	Dinars (Ag) SH 1304	130.00	200.00
77 (101)	1000	Dinars (Ag) SH 1304–1305	5.00	8.00
78 (102)	2000	Dinars (Ag) SH 1304–1305	8.50	12.50
79 (103)	5000	Dinars (Ag) SH 1304–1305	25.00	40.00
80 (119)	1	Toman (Au) SH 1305, .900 gold, 2.87 gm.	200.00	250.00
81 (105)	500	Dinars (Ag) SH 1305	65.00	90.00
82 (106)	1000	Dinars (Ag) SH 1305–1306	6.50	10.00
83 (107)	2000	Dinars (Ag) SH 1305–1306	9.00	12.00
84 (108)	5000	Dinars (Ag) SH 1305–1306	22.00	30.00
85 (116)	1	Pahlevi (Au) SH· 1305, .900 gold, 1.91 gm.	120.00	140.00
86 (117)	2	Pahlevis (Au) SH 1305, .900 gold, 3.83 gm.	175.00	200.00
87 (118)	5	Pahlavi (Au) SH 1305, .900 gold, 9.59 gm.	350.00	400.00
88 (A109)	500	Dinars (Ag) SH 1306–1308. Bust of the Shah. Rev. coat of arms	8.50	12.00
89 (109)	1000	Dinars (Ag) SH 1306–1308. Type as No. 88	6.50	9.00
90 (110)	2000	Dinars (Ag) SH 1306–1308. Type as No. 88	8.00	12.00
91 (111)	5000	Dinars (Ag) SH 1306–1308	20.00	32.00
92 (120)	1	Pahlevi (Au) SH 1306–1308. Bust of the Shah. Rev. legend within dotted circle, .900 gold, 1.91 gm.	65.00	90.00
93 (121)	2	Pahlevis (Au) SH 1306–1308. Type as No. 92, .900 gold, 3.83 gm.	70.00	95.00
94 (122)	5	Pahlevis (Au) SH 1306–1308. Type as No. 92, .900 gold, 9.59 gm.	220.00	250.00
95 (93)	1	Dinar (Br) SH 1310. Coat of arms. Rev. value	1.20	2.50
96 (94)	2	Dinars (Br) SH 1310. Type as No. 95	1.20	2.50

			VF	XF
97 (97)	5	Dinars:		
		a) (Cu-Ni) SH 1310	2.50	5.50
		b) (Br) SH 1314	11.50	18.00
98 (98)	10	Dinars:		
		a) (Cu-Ni) SH 1310	3.50	6.00
		b) (Br) SH 1314	6.00	11.50
99 (99)	25	Dinars:		
		a) (Cu-Ni) SH 1310	12.50	20.00
		b) (Br) SH 1314	20.00	32.00
100 (92)	10	Chahis (Br) SH 1314	6.00	11.50
101 (104)	¼	Rial (Ag) SH 1315	2.00	3.20
102 (112)	½	Rial (Ag) SH 1310–1315	3.50	5.50
103 (113)	1	Rial (Ag) SH 1310–1313	4.00	6.50
104 (114)	2	Rials (Ag) SH 1310–1313	6.00	10.00
105 (115)	5	Rials (Ag) SH 1310–1313	16.00	20.00
106 (123)	½	Pahlevi (Au) SH 1310–1315	80.00	95.00
107 (124)	1	Pahlevi (Au) SH 1310	280.00	325.00
108 (125)	5	Dinars (Al-Br) SH 1315–1320	0.80	1.20
109 (126)	10	Dinars (Al-Br) SH 1315–1320	0.80	1.20
110 (128)	50	Dinars (Al-Br) SH 1315–1320	0.80	1.20

MOHAMMED RIZA PAHLEVI 1941–1978

			VF	XF
111 (125)	5	Dinars (Al–Br) S-HC 1320–1321 (1942–1943). Coat of arms. ℞ value in wreath	0.80	1.20
112 (126)	10	Dinars (Al–Br) S-HC 1320–1321 (1942–1943)	0.80	1.20
113 (127)	25	Dinars (Al–Br) S-HC 1324–1329 (1946–1951)	4.00	6.50
114 (128)	50	Dinars		
		a) (Al–Br) S-HC 1321–1332 (1942–1954)	0.80	1.20
		b) (Cu) S-HC 1322 (1943)	2.50	4.00
115 (129)	1	Rial (Ag) S-HC 1322–1328 (1944–1950)	0.80	1.20
116 (130)	2	Rials (Ag) S-HC 1322–1338 (1944–1960)	1.20	2.00
117 (131)	5	Rials (Ag) S-HC 1322–1331 (1944–1953)	4.00	6.00
118 (132)	10	Rials (Ag) S-HC 1322–1325 (1944–1947)	8.00	12.00

				VF	XF
119 (133)	½	Pahlevi (Au) S-HC 1322–1327 (1944–1949)		80.00	90.00
120 (134)	1	Pahlevi (Au) S-HC 1320–1327 (1942–1949)		150.00	165.00
121 (137)	50	Dinars (Al–Br) S-HC 1333– (1955–)		0.25	0.40
122 (138)	1	Rial (Cu–Ni) S-HC 1331–1339 (1953–1961). Coat of arms. ℞ value		0.60	1.00
123 (139)	2	Rials (Cu–Ni) S-HC 1331–1336 (1953–1958)		0.60	1.00
124 (140)	5	Rials (Cu–Ni) S-HC 1331–1332 (1953–1954)		1.00	1.80
125 (141)	¼	Pahlevi (Au) S-HC 1333 (1955). Mohammed Riza Pahlevi (1919–1980), head left. R coat of arms		32.00	40.00

				VF	XF
126 (142)	½	Pahlevi (Au) S-HC 1333 (1955)		65.00	85.00
127 (143)	1	Pahlevi (Au) S-HC 1333 (1955)		125.00	135.00
128 (144)	2½	Pahlevis (Au) S-HC 1339 (1961)		250.00	270.00
129 (145)	5	Pahlevis (Au) S-HC 1339 (1961)		450.00	500.00
130 (A140)	1	Rial (Cu–Ni) S-HC 1337– (1959–). Coat of arms. ℞ value		0.25	0.40
131 (B140)	2	Rials (Cu–Ni) S-HC 1338– (1960–)		0.20	0.35
132 (C140)	5	Rials (Cu–Ni) S-HC 1337– (1959–)		0.25	0.50
133 (D140)	10	Rials (Cu–Ni) S-HC 1334– (1956–)		0.80	1.20

				VF	XF
134 (149)	10	Rials (Cu-Ni) S-HC 1345–1352 (1967–1972). Mohammed Riza Pahlevi, head left. R coat of arms		0.80	1.20
135 (151)	20	Rials (Cu-Ni) S-HC 1350–1352. Same type as No. 134		1.00	2.00

			VF	XF
136 (152)	1	Rial (Cu-Ni) S-HC 1350–1354. Similar to No. 137	0.25	0.40
137 (150)	10	Rials (Cu–Ni) S-HC 1348 (1969). Head of the shah, left. ℞ coat of arms, letters "FAO" and dates, surrounded by ears of rice, and a quotation from the Holy Avesta, "sow wheat, and harvest the truth"	1.20	2.00

COMMEMORATIVE COINS (9) FOR THE 2500th ANNIVERSARY OF THE PERSIAN EMPIRE

			Proof
138	25	Rials (Ag) 1971. Column head with averted steer heads above double volutes from the Artaxerxes palace in Susa. Now in the Louvre, Paris (Achaemenidian). ℞ State emblem, with name and title of Mohammed Riza Pahlevi above, value, dates. Wreath of 25 stylized Pahlevi crowns symbolising 25 centuries of monarchy	20.00
139	50	Rials (Ag) 1971. Walking griffin with ram's antlers, glazed brick tile relief, Susa; now in the Louvre, Paris (Achaemenidian). ℞ like No. 138	30.00
140	75	Rials (Ag) 1971. Stone of Cyrus II, the original is in the British Museum, London. Wreath of stylized Pahlevi crowns, imperial emblem. ℞ like No. 138	40.00
141	100	Rials (Ag) 1971. Tatshara (= palace) of Darius I and pillars of the Apadana (= reception hall) in Persepolis (Achaemenidian). ℞ like No. 138	55.00

142	200 Rials (Ag) 1971. Imperial couple. ℞ like No. 138		100.00
143	500 Rials (Au) 1971. Same type as No. 139		125.00
144	750 Rials (Au) 1971. Same type as No. 140		200.00
145	1000 Rials (Au) 1971. Same type as No. 141		250.00
146	2000 Rials (Au) 1971. Same type as No. 142		500.00

			XF	Unc
147 (149a)	10 Rials (Cu-Ni) S-HC 1352-1354 (1973-1975). Type as No. 134, but value in numerals (below lion)		0.40	0.80

| **148** (151a) | 20 Rials (Cu-Ni) S-HC 1352-1354 (1973-1975). Type as No. 147 | 0.60 | 1.20 |

			XF	Unc
149 (153)	20	Rials (Cu-Ni) S-HC 1353 (1974). Emblem of the games, Motto: EVER ONWARD	1.50	2.50
150	5	Pahlevis (Au) S-HS 1353	–.–	

The new monarchial calender system was adopted in 1976 = MS 2535.

50th ANNIVERSARY OF THE PAHLEVI RULE (6)

151 (154)	1	Rial (Cu-Ni) MS 2535 (1976). Coat of arms. Rev. value, inscription, crown	0.30	0.50
152 (155)	2	Rials (Cu-Ni) MS 2535 (1976). Type as No. 151	0.30	0.50
153 (156)	5	Rials (Cu-Ni) MS 2535 (1976). Type as No. 151	0.50	0.90
154 (157)	10	Rials (Cu-Ni) MS 2535 (1976). Head left, inscription above, date below. Rev. coat of arms, value	0.70	1.00
155 (158)	20	Rials (Cu-Ni) MS 2535 (1976). Type as No. 154	1.10	2.00
156 (159)	5	Pahlevi (Au) MS 3535 (1976).	–.–	

ISSUE FOR THE FAO COIN PLAN

157 (160)	20	Rials (Cu-Ni) MS 2535–2536. Type as No. 137	1.00	2.00
158 (137a)	50	Dinars (Brass-coated steel) MS 2535–2537. Type as No. 121	0.40	0.80
159 (A140a)	1	Rial (Cu-Ni) MS 2536. Type as No. 130	0.25	0.50
160 (B140)	2	Rials (Cu-Ni) MS 2536. Type as No. 131	0.40	0.80

				XF	Unc
161 (C140b)	5	Rials (Cu-Ni) MS 2536–2537. Type as No. 132		0.80	1.20
162 (149a)	10	Rials (Cu-Ni) MS 2536–2537. Type as No. 147		1.00	1.60
163 (151a)	20	Rials (Cu-Ni) MS 2536–2537. Type as No. 148		1.20	2.00
164 (141b)	¼	Pahlevi (Au) MS 2536–2538. Type as No. 125		32.00	40.00
165 (142a)	½	Pahlevi (Au) MS 2536–2538. Type as No. 126		65.00	80.00
166 (143a)	1	Pahlevi (Au) MS 2536–2538. Type as No. 127		120.00	140.00
167 (144a)	2½	Pahlevis (Au) MS 2536–2538. Type as No. 128		265.00	300.00
168 (145a)	5	Pahlevis (Au) MS 2536–2538. Type as No. 129		650.00	700.00

50th ANNIVERSARY OF BANK MELLI

			XF	Unc
169 (162)	20	Rials (Cu-Ni) SH 1357	3.50	4.50

FOR THE FAO COIN PLAN

			XF	Unc
170 (163)	20	Rials (Cu-Ni) SH 1357	1.00	2.00

ISLAMIC REPUBLIC OF IRAN

			XF	Unc
171 (164)	1	Rial (Cu-Ni) SH 1358–1359	0.25	0.50
172 (165)	2	Rials (Cu-Ni) SH 1358–1359	0.40	0.80
173 (166)	5	Rials (Cu-Ni) SH 1358–1359	0.60	1.20
174 (167)	10	Rials (Cu-Ni) SH 1358–1359	1.00	2.00
175 (168)	20	Rials (Cu-Ni) SH 1358–1359	1.50	3.00

1st ANNIVERSARY OF REVOLUTION

			XF	Unc
176 (169)	10	Rials (Cu-Ni) SH 1358	2.00	3.00

			VF	XF
177 (170)	20	Rials (Cu-Ni) SH 1358	3.00	4.00
178	1	Dinar (Bra) SH 1359. Jerusalem	2.00	2.50
179	20	Rials (Cu-Ni) SH 1360. Agriculture	4.00	5.00

Iraq

Area: 171,599 sq. mi. Population: 9,800,000.
The territory, which was once the centre of the Sassanian Empire, was conquered by the Mongolians in 1258. Then, before the country came under Turkish domination, it was ruled temporarily by Persia. In the years 1915–1917 the British Army of India conquered the Wilayets of Mesopotamia. On 2nd March 1921 Iraq became a British mandate under the League of Nations, and in the same year Faisal I was made King. It has been a republic since 14th July 1958.
Capital: Baghdad.

50 Fils = 1 Dirham, 200 Fils = 1 Ryal, 1000 Fils = 1 Dinar

FAISAL I 1921–1933

			VF	XF
1 (1)	1	Fils (Br) 1931–1933. Head right of King Faisal I (1883–1933). ℞ value, date and inscription in Arabic	1.20	2.00
2 (2)	2	Fils (Br) 1931–1933	2.00	4.00
3 (3)	4	Fils (Ni) 1931–1933 (scalloped)	1.20	2.50
4 (4)	10	Fils (Ni) 1931–1933 (scalloped)	2.00	4.00
5 (5)	20	Fils (Ag) 1931–1933	3.00	4.00
6 (6)	50	Fils = 1 Dirham (Ag) 1931–1933	16.00	10.00
7 (7)	200	Fils = 1 Ryal (Ag) 1932	22.00	35.00

GHAZI I 1933–1939

8 (8)	1	Fils (Br) 1936–1938. Head left of King Ghazi I (1912–1939). ℞ value, date and inscription in Arabic	0.40	0.80
9 (9)	4	Fils. Type as No. 8, but scalloped		
		a) (Ni) 1938–1939	1.20	2.00
		b) (Cu–Ni) 1938	0.80	1.80
		c) (Br) 1938	0.90	1.80
10 (10)	10	Fils. Type as No. 8, but scalloped		
		a) (Ni) 1937–1938	5.00	8.00
		b) (Cu–Ni) 1938	0.80	1.20
		c) (Br) 1938	0.80	1.20
11 (11)	20	Fils (Ag) 1938	3.00	4.00

			VF	XF
12 (12)	50 Fils (Ag) 1937–1938		5.00	8.00

FAISAL II 1939–1958

13 (13) 4 Fils (Br) 1943. Young head right of King Faisal II (1935–1958). ℞ value, date and inscription in Arabic (scalloped)   2.50   5.00

14 (14) 10 Fils (Br) 1943. Type as No. 13   3.50   7.00

15 (15) 1 Fils (Br) 1953. Head right of King Faisal II   0.25   0.50

16 (16) 2 Fils (Br) 1953   1.40   2.50

		VF	XF
17 (17)	4 Fils (Cu–Ni) 1953 (scalloped)	0.60	1.20
18 (18)	10 Fils (Cu–Ni) 1953 (scalloped)	0.80	1.50
19 (19)	20 Fils (Ag) 1953	6.50	10.00
20 (20)	50 Fils (Ag) 1953	20.00	28.00
21 (21)	100 Fils (Ag) 1953–1955	20.00	26.00
22 (22)	20 Fils (Ag) 1955. Type as No. 19, but smaller diameter	4.50	7.50
23 (23)	50 Fils (Ag) 1955. Type as No. 20, but smaller diameter	7.50	11.00

REPUBLIC since 1958

24 (24) 1 Fils (Br) 1959. National emblem of the Republic. ℞ value within circle (decagonal)   0.25   0.50

25 (25)	5 Fils (Cu–Ni) 1959 (scalloped)	0.30	0.60
26 (26)	10 Fils (Cu–Ni) 1959 (scalloped)	0.50	1.00
27 (27)	25 Fils (Ag) 1959	1.80	2.50
28 (28)	50 Fils (Ag) 1959	3.00	4.00

		VF	**XF**
29 (29)	100 Fils (Ag) 1959	5.50	7.50
30	500 Fils (Ag) 1959. Bust in uniform of General Abdul Karim Kassem (1914–1963). ℞ national emblem (medallic issue)	26.00	32.00

31 (31)	5 Fils (Cu-Ni) 1967, 1971. Date palms (Phoenix dactylifera – Palmae). Rev. value within circle surrounded by Arabic inscription; below, ear of corn and tobacco leaf (scalloped)	0.30	0.50
32 (32)	10 Fils (Cu-Ni) 1967, 1971. Type as No. 31	0.50	0.90
33 (33)	25 Fils (Cu-Ni) 1969, 1979, 1972, 1975. Type as No. 31, but round	0.60	1.20
34 (34)	50 Fils (Cu-Ni) 1969, 1970, 1972, 1975. Type as No. 33	1.20	1.80
35 (35)	100 Fils (Cu-Ni) 1970, 1972, 1975. Type as No. 34	1.20	2.00

COMMEMORATIVE ISSUE FOR THE FAO COIN PLAN AND FOR THE AGRARIAN REFORM DAY
(September 30, 1970)

		XF	**Unc**
36 (36)	250 Fils (Ni) 1970. Date Palms. ℞ Same as No. 33	4.00	7.50

COMMEMORATIVE ISSUE FOR THE PEACE TREATY WITH THE KURDS (March 3, 1970)

		XF	Unc
37 (40) 250 Fils (Ni) 1971. Allegory of Peace (with flying dove)		4.00	7.50

COMMEMORATIVE ISSUES (3) FOR THE GOLDEN JUBILEE OF THE IRAQI ARMY

		XF	Unc
38 (37) 500 Fils (Ni) 1971. Busts of two soldiers. ℞ value		6.00	8.50
39 (38) 1 Dinar (Ag) 1971. Same type as No. 38		15.00	20.00
40 (39) 5 Dinars (Au) 1971. Same type as No. 38		265.00	300.00

COMMEMORATIVE ISSUE FOR THE SILVER JUBILEE OF THE ARAB SOCIALIST BAATH PARTY (7. 4. 1972)

		XF	Unc
41 (41) 250 Fils (Ni) 1972. Date palm grove. ℞ value in circle, below date 7. 4. 1972; legend "Iraqi Republic" (above) and "Silver Jubilee of the Baath Party (= ABSP)" (below)		4.50	8.00

COMMEMORATIVE ISSUES (2) FOR THE SILVER JUBILEE OF THE IRAQI CENTRAL BANK

42 (42) 250 Fils (Ni) 1972. Date palm grove. ℞ value in circle, below dates; legend "Iraqi Republic" (above) and "Silver

Jubilee of the Central Bank of Iraq"
(below)   4.00   6.00

43 (43)   1 Dinar (Ag) 1972. Type as No. 42   20.00   25.00

COMMEMORATIVE ISSUES (3)
FOR THE NATIONALIZATION OF OIL

44 (44)   250 Fils (Ni) 1973   3.00   4.00

45 (45)   500 Fils (Ni) 1973   6.00   8.00

46 (46)   1 Dinar (Ag) 1973   20.00   25.00

ISSUES FOR THE FAO COIN PLAN (2)

		XF	Unc
47 (47)	5 Fils (St) 1975. Type similar to No. 31	0.25	0.40
48 (48)	10 Fils (St) 1975. Type as No. 47	0.30	0.60

INAUGURATION OF THE THATHAR EUPHRATES CANAL

		Unc	Proof
49 (49)	1 Dinar (Ag) 1977		35.00

INTERNATIONAL YEAR OF THE CHILD (2)

		Unc	Proof
50 (50)	250 Fils (Ni) 1979	6.00	10.00
51 (51)	1 Dinar (Ag) 1979		25.00

		Unc	Proof
52 (52)	250 Fils (Ni) 1979. President Saddam Hussein	4.00	

15th CENTURY OF HEGIRA

		Unc	Proof
53 (53)	1 Dinar (Ag) 1980		30.00

Ireland
Eire

Area: 26,600 sq. mi. Population: 4,254,000.
Until the conquest by the Normans there were many Celtic kingdoms in this island. Later Ireland came under British domination. On 16th January 1922, as a result of the Anglo-Irish Treaty, Southern Ireland became a free state with the status of a dominion (Saorstát Eireann). When the Constitution came into force on 29th December 1937, the independent state of Eire was created.
Capital: Dublin.

4 Farthings = 1 Penny, 12 Pence = 1 Shilling,
2 Shillings = 1 Florin, 5 Shillings = 1 Crown, 20 Shillings = 1 £
since 15th February 1971: 100 New Pence = 1 £

Gaelic Legend: SAORSTÁT EIREANN

			VF	XF
1 (1)	1	Farthing (Br) 1928–1937. Harp (national emblem). ℞ European woodcock (Scolopax rusticola – Scolopacidae)	1.60	3.00
2 (2)	½	Penny (Br) 1928–1937. ℞ sow (Sus scrofa domestica – Suidae) with piglets	1.80	4.00
3 (3)	1	Penny (Br) 1928–1937. ℞ hen (Gallus gallus domesticus – Phasianidae) with chicks	1.60	4.00
4 (4)	3	Pence (Ni) 1928–1935. ℞ blue hare (Lepus timidus – Leporidae)	2.00	4.00
5 (5)	6	Pence (Ni) 1928–1935. ℞ Irish wolfhound (Canis familiaris leineri – Canidae)	2.50	5.00
6 (6)	1	Shilling (Ag) 1928–1937. ℞ bull	5.00	8.00
7 (7)	1	Florin (Ag) 1928–1937. ℞ Atlantic salmon (Salmo salar – Salmonidae)	10.00	15.00
8 (8)	½	Crown (Ag) 1928–1937. ℞ Irish hunter	15.00	20.00

EIRE

9 (9)	1	Farthing (Br) 1939–1966. Harp (national emblem), name of country now EIRE. ℞ woodcock	0.60	2.00

				VF	XF
10 (10)	½	Penny (Br) 1939–1967. ℞ sow with piglets		0.40	1.60
11 (11)	1	Penny (Br) 1940–1968. ℞ hen with chicks		0.20	0.40
12 (12)	3	Pence (Ni) 1939, 1940. Blue hare		3.00	7.00
13 (13)	6	Pence (Ni) 1939, 1940. Irish wolfhound		2.50	5.00
14 (14)	1	Shilling (Ag) 1939–1942. Bull		8.00	12.50

15 (15)	1	Florin (Ag) 1939-1943. Atlantic salmon:			
		a) 1939-1942		8.00	12.50
		b) 1943 (about 30 specimens known)		3000.00	5000.00
16 (16)	½	Crown (Ag) 1939-1943. Irish hunter:			
		a) 1939-1942		7.50	12.00
		b) 1943		300.00	500.00
17 (12a)	3	Pence (Cu-Ni) 1942-1968. Type as No. 12		0.25	0.40
18 (13a)	6	Pence (Cu-Ni) 1942-1969. Type as No. 13		0.25	0.50
19 (14a)	1	Shilling (Cu-Ni) 1951-1968. Type as No. 14		0.40	0.60
20 (15a)	1	Florin (Cu-Ni) 1951-1968. Type as No. 15		0.60	1.00
21 (16a)	½	Crown (Cu-Ni) 1951-1967. Type as No. 16		1.00	2.00

COMMEMORATIVE ISSUE FOR THE 50th ANNIVERSARY OF THE EASTER UPRISING OF 1916

			XF	Unc

22 (17)　10 Shillings (Ag) 1966. Padraig (Patrik) Henry Pearse (1879–1916), author, educator, politician, and fighter for independence; executed 1916. ℞ the dying hero Cuchulainn, Irish legendary hero, with a raven (Corvus corax – Corvidae) on his shoulder　　10.00　15.00

CURRENCY REFORM (Decimal System): 100 New Pence = 1 £

23 (18)　½ New Penny (Br) 1971–. Har (= state emblem). R fabulous creature according to an old Irish manuscript　0.05　0.10

24 (19)　1 New Penny (Br) 1971–. R fabulous creature according to an old Irish manuscript　0.10　0.15

25 (20)　2 New Pence (Br) 1971–. R fabulous creature according to an old Irish manuscript　0.16

sript ·　0.15　0.25

26 (21)　5 New Pence (Cu-Ni) 1969–. ℞ bull　0.25　0.40

27 (22)　10 New Pence (Cu-Ni) 1969–. ℞ Atlantic salmon　0.60　1.00

28 (23)　50 New Pence (Cu-Ni) 1970–. ℞ European woodcock; seven-sided　1.50　2.00

Usually the commemorative coins of Israel reflect the events of current history. Since 1958, the 10th anniversary of independent Israel, the majority of coins depict the nation's economic, cultural and political accomplishments, but occasionally they contain references to Old Testament times.

Additional commemorative issues, known as Chanukah (Hanukkah) coins, appeared between 1959 and 1963, to celebrate Chanukah, the festival celebrating the lighting of the Menorah for eight days, which lasts from the end of December to the beginning of January. To this day, the nine candles of the candelabra are lighted in increasing numbers on the eight successive days of Chanukah. The coins therefore display symbols of light, such as the Menorah, stars, etc.

A third category of commemorative coins comprises irregular issues, celebrating special events such as the anniverseries of celebrities, institutions, etc.

Since the Israeliate calendar starts with August/September, its conversion into Christian chronology necessarily produces differences whenever the dates are given.

1000 Mils = 1 Lira (£), 1000 Prutot = 1 Lira (£),
100 Agorot = 1 Israel £

1 (1)   25 Mils (Al) 1948–1949 = 5708–5709.
Bunch of grapes (Vitus vinifera – Vitaceae) with vine leaf, in beaded border.
This design is modelled after a bronze Prutot originating in the time of Herod

Antipas (about the time of the birth of
Christ), similar to the later bronze and
silver coins from the time of the Second
Revolt (132–135 A. D., also called the
Bar Kokhba War); compare with No. 7.
In the Bible, grapes are one of the
seven fruits of the Promised Land. ℞
25 Mils – 5708–5709 in wreath of two
olive branches

	VF	XF
	14.00	28.00

NEW CURRENCY: 1000 Prutot = 1 Israel £

General characteristics of circulating Prutot coins: usually beaded
border on obverse and reverse. On reverse, value, numerals of value,
date, in Hebrew, in wreath of olive branches. Already on ancient Jewish
coins the beaded border was in use. The two olive branches occur for
the first time on the coins of the Hasmonean Dynasty, starting with
Yohanan Hyrkanos I (135–104 B. C.). Other coins of the Hasmonean
period display also names such as "Yehuda", "Yehonathan", or "Mat-
tathiahu" in wreath of two olive branches.

2 (2)   1   Pruta (Al) 1949 = 5709. Anchor. Design
modelled after the coins from the time
of King Alexander Yannaeus (103–76
B. C.). The anchor symbolized the Hebrew sovereignty over the coastal
towns, and is repeated on the later
coins of the Herod Dynasty. ℞ 1 Pruta
in wreath of two olive branches   0.80   2.00

3 (3)   5   Prutot (Br) 1949 = 5709. Four-stringed
large lyre. This design comes from a
vessel of the temple, and was first used

			VF	XF

on coins at the time of the Second Revolt (Bar Kokhba War, 132–135 A.D.). ℞ 5 Prutot – 5709 in wreath of two olive branches — **1.50** / **3.00**

4 (4) 10 Prutot (Br) 1949 = 5709. Amphora with two handles. Design modelled after a copper coin from the time of the Second Revolt (132–135 A.D.). This ceremonial object was to symbolize the rebuilding of the destroyed temple. ℞ 10 Prutot – 5709 in wreath of two olive branches — **1.00** / **2.00**

5 (5) 10 Prutot (Al) 1952 = 5712. Jug with one handle between two palm branches. Originally a ceremonial object, the design is borrowed from a silver denar from the time of the Second Revolt (132–135 A.D.). The jug itself was probably used to store oil for the temple lamps. This supposition is reinforced by the palm branch, even though on antique coins it occurs only once, on the right of the jug. ℞ 10 Prutot – 5712 in wreath of olive branches, scalloped — **0.60** / **1.50**

6 (5) 10 Prutot 1957 = 5717. The design varies only slightly from that on No. 5. Round
a) (Al-Cu-plated) 1957 = 5717 — **0.70** / **1.40**
b) (Al-Br) 1957 = 5717 — **0.70** / **1.40**

7 (6) 25 Prutot (Cu–Ni) 1949 = 5709. Bunch of grapes with vine tendrils. The design is modelled after the coins from the time of the Second Revolt (132–135 A.D.). Golden grapes used to decorate the entrance to the inner holy temple, a fact that emphasizes the symbolic significance of the design. The only difference between this coin and No. 1 is that here the grapes are displayed with the tendrils instead of the leaf. ℞ 25 Prutot – 5709 in wreath of two olive branches — **1.00** / **2.00**

8 (6a) 25 Prutot (Ni–St) 1954 = 5714. Same type as No. 7, but different date — **1.00** / **2.00**

9 (8) 50 Prutot (Cu–Ni) 1949–1954 = 5709–5714. Vine leaf. Design modelled after a bronze Prutot from the time of the First Revolt against the Romans (66–70 A.D.) and the 3rd year (68 A.D.) of the revolt. ℞ 50 Prutot – 5709 in wreath of two olive branches. With reeded edge — **1.50** / **3.00**

10 (8a) 50 Prutot (Cu–Ni) 1954 = 5714. Same type as No. 9, but plain edge — **1.00** / **2.00**

		VF	**XF**
11 (8b) 50	Prutot (Ni–St) 1954 = 5714. Same type as No. 9, but plain edge	0.80	1.60
12 (10) 100	Prutot (Cu–Ni) 1949 = 5709. Seven-branched date palm (Phoenix dactylifera-Palmae) with two date clusters. In Jewish history the date palm is the most commonly recurring symbol and was equally popular with the Romans during their provincial period. On coinage, the date palm first appeared on the issues of King Herod Antipas (4 B.C. – 37 A.D.), and later on those of the Second Revolt (132–135 A.D.). On coins from this time of the so-called Bar Kokhba War, the date palm is the most commonly used symbol. ℞ 100 Prutot – 5709 in wreath of two olive branches	1.20	2.80
13 (10a) 100	Prutot (Ni–St) 1954 = 5714. Same design as No. 12, but diameter 25.6 mm instead of 28.5 mm	2.00	4.00

		VF	**XF**
14 (12) 250	Prutot (Cu–Ni) 1949 = 5709. Three ears of barley. Design modelled after a silver quarter shekel from the 4th year of the First Revolt against the Romans (69 A.D.). The only coin of this type is owned by the British Museum, London. For similar design compare No. 23. ℞ 250 Prutot – 5709 in wreath of two olive branches	1.80	3.50
15 (12a) 250	Prutot (Ag) 1949 = 5709. Same type as No. 14, but with mint mark H below the two olive branches	8.00	15.00

		VF	XF
16 (14)	500 Prutot (Ag) 1949 = 5709. Three pomegranates (Punica granatum – Punicaceae). Designed after a Jewish shekel from the time of the First Revolt against the Romans (66–70 A.D.). ℞ 500 Prutot – 5709 in wreath of two olive branches. Pomegranates are one of the seven fruits of the Promised Land. During the time of the second temple, as well as in the following periods, this fruit was often used as a decoration	15.00	30.00

COMMEMORATIVE ISSUE FOR THE 10th ANNIVERSARY OF INDEPENDENT ISRAEL

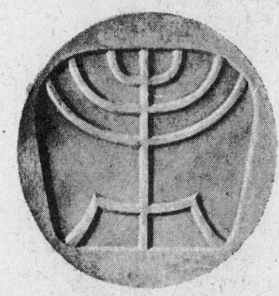 

		Unc	Proof
17 (16)	5 £ (Ag) 1958 = 5718. Menorah (= seven-branched candelabrum), old Jewish symbol, now state emblem. This candelabrum with three feet and seven branches symbolizes the number 10 and stems from the time of King Mattathias Antigonus (40–37 B.C., Hasmonean Dynasty)	25.00	450.00

COMMEMORATIVE ISSUE FOR THE CHANUKAH FESTIVAL (5718)

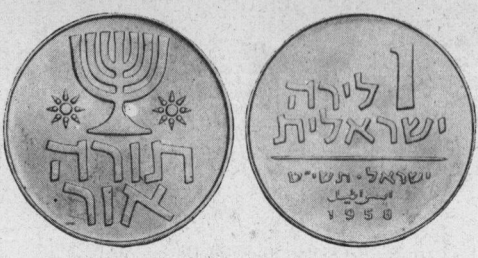

		Unc	Proof
18(17)	1 £ (Cu–Ni) 1958 = 5718. Menorah between two eight-pointed stars, design modelled after a coin from the time of King Mattathias Antigonus (Hasmonean Dynasty). Legend: "The Law (Torah) is Light". ℞ 1 Lira Israelit, underneath ISRAEL and 5718	6.00	50.00

COMMEMORATIVE ISSUE FOR THE 11th ANNIVERSARY OF INDEPENDENT ISRAEL AND THE INGATHERING OF THE EXILES

		Unc	Proof
19(18)	5 £ (Ag) 1959 = 5719. Eleven immigrants (symbol of 11 years) dancing around the biblical legend, "Thy children shall return home" – Jer. 31, 17. ℞ value and dates 5708–5719 (= 1948–1959)	50.00	185.00

COMMEMORATIVE ISSUE FOR THE CHANUKAH FESTIVAL (5720) AND THE 50th ANNIVERSARY OF DEGANIA

				Unc	Proof
20 (19)	1 £ (Cu–Ni) 1959 = 5719. View of the first Kibbutz of Degania. This oldest collective settlement, located on lake Genezareth, was founded by Russian immigrants in 1909. ℞ 1 Lira Israelit – 5720			9.00	130.00

COMMEMORATIVE ISSUE FOR THE 12th ANNIVERSARY OF INDEPENDENT ISRAEL AND THE 100th BIRTHDAY OF DR. THEODOR HERZL

21 (20)	5 £ .(Ag) 1960 = 5720. Dr. Theodor Zeev Herzl (1860–1904), author, lawyer, and co-founder of the Zionist Movement. In the lower left Herzl's famous words: "[If you will it] it is not a legend", next to coat of arms. ℞ 5 Lirot Israeliot			45.00	185.00

COMMEMORATIVE ISSUE FOR THE 100th BIRTHDAY OF DR. THEODOR HERZL

22 (21) 20 £ (Au) 1960 = 5720. Obverse similar to No. 21. ℞ Menorah (= seven-branched

candelabrum), state emblem, between
two olive branches with name of country
ISRAEL. This Menorah was made after
a relief detail from the Arc of Titus in
Rome, with the caption "The loot
from Israel". Legends surrounded by
two circles: Twenty Israel pounds
(above), the anniversary years 5620–
5720 = 1860–1960 (below)

	XF	Unc
		600.00

NEW CURRENCY: 100 Agorot = 1 Israel £

The new decimal coins utilize an asymmetric design. On the denominations up to 25 Agorot basket-like arches alternate with beaded border
and olive branches giving the edge the almost dynamic appearance of
a perpetual band. On the obverse are partially new designs with
ISRAEL written in Hebrew and Arabic. On the obverse of the high
denominations (designated £), Israel is written in Latin in addition to
the two other languages. The reverse carries the value in numerals as
well as in letters, with the date of coinage underneath.

23 (22) 1 Agora (Al) 1960 = 5720–. Three ears
of barley, design modelled after a bronze
Prutot from the 6th year of the reign
Agrippa I (42/43 B.C.). Barley is one
of the seven fruits of the Promised
Land. ℞ 1 Agora – 5720 in basket-like
arches. Scalloped edge   0.10   0.20

24 (24) 5 Agorot (Al–Br) 1960 = 5720–. Three
ripe pomegranates (Punica granatum –
Punicaceae). On old Hebrew shekels

the pomegranate is shown in different form, see No. 16, but not as mature as on this modern version. ℞ 5 Agorot – 5720 in basket-like arches

	XF	Unc
	0.15	0.30

25 (25) 10 Agorot (Al–Br) 1960 = 5720–. Seven-branched date palm with two date clusters. For further details see No. 12. ℞ 10 Agorot – 5720 in basket-like arches — 0.15 — 0.30

26 (26) 25 Agorot (Al–Br) 1960 = 5720–. Three-stringed kithara. Design modelled after silver dinars and bronze coins from the time of the Second Revolt (132–135 A.D.). See No. 3. ℞ 25 Agorot – 5720 in basket-like arches — 0.25 — 0.50

27 (36) ½ £ (Cu–Ni) 1963 = 5723–. State emblem in olive branches and ISRAEL, see No. 22. On the obverse ISRAEL, for the first time on Israeli coins also in Latin. ℞ ½ Lira Israelit – 5723 — 0.40 — 0.80

28 (37)   1   £ (Cu–Ni) 1963 = 5723 – 1967 = 5727, same as No. 27. ℞ 1 Lira Israelit – 5723   1.00   2.00

XF	Unc

29 (46)   1   £ (Cu–Ni) 1967 = 5727–. Three pomegranates, coat of arms in lower left. For text see No. 16 or No. 24. ℞ "1" between eight-pointed stars (coins from the time of Alexander Yannaeus, 103 B.C.), underneath: 1 Lira Israelit – 5727   0.40   0.80

COMMEMORATIVE ISSUE FOR THE CHANUKAH FESTIVAL (5721) AND THE 100th BIRTHDAY OF HENRIETTA SZOLD

30 (27)   1   £ (Cu–Ni) 1960 = 5721. Seated woman to left holding a lamb in her arms. Legend: Henrietta Szold 5621–5721. HADASSAH – ALIYAT HANOAR (=youth immigration), since the honoured had founded the American Women's Aid Association "Hadassah" and the "Aliyat Hanoar". ℞ Hadassah Medical Centre, located on Mount Scopus west of Jerusalem, opened in 1961, financed by the Zionist Women's organization "Hadassah" in America; architect: Joseph Neufeld, USA. Legend: 1 Lira Israelit – 5721

Unc	Proof
120.00	850.00

COMMEMORATIVE ISSUE FOR THE 13th ANNIVERSARY OF INDEPENDENT ISRAEL AND FOR "BAR MITZVAH" OF ISRAEL

31 (28)   5 £ (Ag) 1961 = 5721. Ark of the Law with six Torah (= law) scrolls. The design is borrowed from a golden goblet of the third century, now owned by the Vatican. The term "BAR MITZVAH" refers to the commencing of the 13th year of a Jewish boy, when he comes of age for religious duty and responsibility, and was therefore chosen for the celebration of the 13th anniversary of the independence. ℞ olive branch with ten leaves and three olives = 13, also a symbolic implication. Legend: "13th year of the State of Israel" 5721–1961, underneath 5 Lirot Israeliot

	Unc	Proof
	125.00	250.00

COMMEMORATIVE ISSUE FOR THE CHANUKAH FESTIVAL 5722 (1961) AND FOR THE DEATH OF A HASMONEAN HERO

32 (30)   1 £ (Cu–Ni) 5722 (1961). Combat elephant in asymmetrical pentagon, from the time of the Hasmonean war when Elazar (Mattathias), Judas Maccabeus' brother, fought with his sword against

a heavily armed combat elephant of the
Seleucids. ℞ torch with legend "...and
he gave up his soul in battle", and:
1 Lira Israelit – 5722 = 1961

	Unc	Proof
	40.00	75.00

COMMEMORATIVE ISSUE FOR
THE HALF SHEKEL TEMPLE SACRIFICE

33 (29) ½ £ (Cu–Ni) 1961–1962 = 5721–5722.
Old half shekel coin with chalice. Design modelled after a half shekel silver
coin from the third year (= 68 A.D.)
of the First Revolt against the Romans.
Commemorates the half shekel due
which every male Jew above 20 years
of age had to pay yearly to the temple.
℞ legend "Half Israel Pound (Chazi
Lira Israelit)", left 5721 or 5722   22.00   50.00

COMMEMORATIVE ISSUES (2) FOR THE 10th ANNIVERSARY
OF THE DEATH OF ISRAEL'S PRESIDENT

34 (32) 50 £ (Au) 1962 = 5723. Dr. Chaim Weiz-
mann (1874–1952), President from
1948 to 1952, in basket-like arches. ℞
state emblem with legend "Fifty
Israel Pounds – 5713–5723" = 1952–
1962. Diameter 27 mm   350.00   600.00

35 (33)   100 £ (Au) 1962 = 5723. Same type as No.   **Unc**   **Proof**
34. ℞ but on top "One hundred Israel
Pounds". Diameter 33 mm   800.00

COMMEMORATIVE ISSUE FOR THE 14th ANNIVERSARY
OF INDEPENDENT ISRAEL
UNDER THE MOTTO "DEVELOPMENT"

36 (31)   5 £ (Ag) 1962 = 5722. Stylized bulldozer,
used in canal construction, in front of
landscape of the Negev desert. Legend:
"...and Israel shall blossom" – Isaiah
27, 6. ℞ stylized equipment of petro-
chemical industry; legend: 5 Israel
Pounds, Israel, 5722–1962   150.00   200.00

COMMEMORATIVE ISSUE FOR THE
CHANUKAH FESTIVAL (5723)

37 (34)   1 £ (Cu–Ni) 1962 = 5723. Chanukah
lamp with eight compartments in triangular, basket-like pattern. These Chanukah lamps in the style of the baroque
era originated in seventeenth century
Italian workshops, today owned by the
Jerusalem Museum, therefore legend:
"Chanukia from Italy — 17th century".
℞ 1 Lira Israelit 1962–5723   100.00   185.00

COMMEMORATIVE ISSUE FOR THE 15th ANNIVERSARY
OF INDEPENDENT ISRAEL
UNDER THE MOTTO "SEAFARING"

		Unc	Proof
38 (35)	5 £ (Ag) 1963 = 5723. Ancient galley, designed after a Hasmonean drawing discovered in a tomb. Legend "15th year of Israel's independence". ℞ funnel of a modern Israel ship, in front of the port of Haifa with Mount Carmel, and "5 Lirot Israeliot" 5723–1963	600.00	800.00

COMMEMORATIVE ISSUE FOR THE
CHANUKAH FESTIVAL (5724)

| **39** (38) | 1 £ (Cu–Ni) 1963 = 5724. Chanukah lamp with eight compartments and side wings, accommodating the Islamic style. The original was manufactured during the 18th century in North Africa, and is now owned by the Jerusalem Museum. ℞ 1 Lira Israelit – 1963–5724 | 90.00 | 125.00 |

COMMEMORATIVE ISSUE FOR THE 16th ANNIVERSARY
OF INDEPENDENT ISRAEL
WITH THE MOTTO "ISRAEL MUSEUM"

		Unc	Proof
40 (39)	5 £ (Ag) 1964 = 5724. Israel Museum in Jerusalem opened in 1964. ℞ capital of an ancient pillar, legends "5 Lirot Israeliot" – 1964–5724	125.00	200.00

COMMEMORATIVE ISSUE: 10 YEARS BANK OF ISRAEL

41 (40)	50 £ (Au) 1964 = 5724. Legend "Ten years Bank of Israel"; pomegranate, surrounded by cornucopias. ℞ state emblem. In circle: "Fifty Lirot Israeliot" 1964–5724	700.00	3500.00

COMMEMORATIVE ISSUE FOR THE 17th ANNIVERSARY
OF INDEPENDENT ISRAEL
WITH THE MOTTO "THE KNESSET"

42 (41)   5 £ (Ag) 1965 = 5725. Parliament build-   **Unc**   **Proof**
ing in Jerusalem, located opposite from
the Israel Museum, shown on No. 40,
opened in 1965, seat of the legislative
assembly of Israel. ℞ state emblem.
1965–5725 and 5 Lirot Israeliot   35.00   80.00

COMMEMORATIVE ISSUE FOR THE 18th ANNIVERSARY
OF INDEPENDENT ISRAEL
WITH THE MOTTO "ISRAEL LIVES ON"

43 (42)   5 £ (Ag) 1966 = 5726. Design of the
Hebrew words "Am Israel Hai" = The
people of Israel lives on. ℞ 5 Lirot
Israeliot 1966–5726   30.00   75.00

COMMEMORATIVE ISSUE FOR THE 19th ANNIVERSARY
OF INDEPENDENT ISRAEL
WITH THE MOTTO "PORT OF EILAT"

44 (43)   5 £ (Ag) 1967 = 5727. The letters of the
word EILAT stylized to represent har-
bour scene with lighthouse. The gateway to Africa and Asia, the port of
Eilat celebrated its 10th year of existence in 1967. ℞ 5 Lirot Israeliot –1967–
5727   35.00   80.00

COMMEMORATIVE ISSUES (2) FOR THE VICTORIES OF THE DEFENCE FORCES DURING THE SIX DAY WAR

			Unc	Proof
45 (44)	10 £ (Ag) 1967 = 5727. Westermost part of the Wailing Wall (once the surrounding wall of the old temple, in Jerusalem), destroyed by Titus in 70 A.D. ℞ emblem of the defence forces in front of a star formed of "arrows", symbol of the widely and successfully executed military operations. 10 Lirot Israeliot		25.00	30.00
46 (45)	100 £ (Au) 1967 = 5727. Same type as No. 45, but with smaller diameter and "100 Lirot Israeliot"			500.00

COMMEMORATIVE ISSUES (2) FOR THE 20th ANNIVERSARY OF INDEPENDENT ISRAEL WITH THE MOTTO "JERUSALEM'S RE-UNIFICATION"

47 (47)   10 £ (Ag) 1968 = 5728. Allegory of Mount Zion (Jerusalem) with striking buildings of the modern Jerusalem, state emblem. ℞ facade of the temple of Solomon, designed after a silver sela from the time of the Second Revolt (132–135 A.D.) and "10 Lirot Israeliot" – 1968–5728. Diameter 37 mm

	Unc	Proof
	28.00	

48 (48) 100 £ (Au) 1968 = 5728. Same type as No. 47, but with diameter 33 mm, and "100 Lirot Israeliot" on reverse 600.00

COMMEMORATIVE ISSUES (2) FOR THE 21st ANNIVERSARY OF INDEPENDENT ISRAEL WITH THE MOTTO "SHALOM"

49 (49) 10 £ (Ag) 1969 = 5729. Allegory of Mount Zion in the form of a memorial for a soldier fallen in combat, shaped in the words "...and no man knoweth the place of his burial" – Deuteronomy 34, 6. Helmet and olive plant in foreground. ℞ letters of the word "Shalom" (= peace) in shape of the seven-branched candelabrum, 10 Lirot Israeliot – 1969–5729 .... 28.00 45.00

50 (50) 100 £ (Au) 1969 = 5729. Same type as No. 49, but with diameter of 33 mm, and "100 Lirot Israeliot" on reverse 550.00

COMMEMORATIVE ISSUE PIDYON HABEN –
FOR THE REDEMPTION OF THE FIRST-BORN

	Unc	Proof
10 £ (Ag) 1970 = 5730. Above the quotation "All the first-born of thy sons thou shalt redeem" – Exodus 34, 20: stylized imitation of the Tables of the Law. On the lower edge: Pidyon Haben – Coin. The redemption of the first-born carried out by the father dates back to the time of the Old Testament. According to the law every first-born son has to be redeemed to the payment of 5 silver pieces. ℞ coat of arms, 10 Lirot Israeliot – 1970–5730	26.00	32.50

COMMEMORATIVE ISSUE FOR THE 22nd ANNIVERSARY
OF INDEPENDENT ISRAEL
WITH THE MOTTO "100 YEARS MIKVEH ISRAEL"

52 (52) 10 £ (Ag) 1970 = 5730. Plough. Upper left, four lines of writing "One hundred years Mikveh Israel"; underneath the plough: Kol Israel Haverim = Israeli World Alliance. ℞ ear of wheat and "10 Lirot Israeliot" with main building of the Mikveh school, an agricultural educational and experimental institute near Jaffa, founded by Charles Netter one hundred years ago. Underneath the centennial dates 5630–5730 = 1870–1970

	Unc	Proof
	26.00	30.00

COMMEMORATIVE ISSUE PIDYON HABEN – FOR THE REDEMPTION OF THE FIRST-BORN

53 (51a) 10 £ ·(Ag) 1971 = 5731. Similar type as No. 51

25.00	45.00

COMMEMORATIVE ISSUE FOR THE 23rd ANNIVERSARY OF INDEPENDENT ISRAEL WITH THE MOTTO "SCIENCE IN THE SERVICE OF INDUSTRY"

54 (53) 10 £ (Ag) 1971 = 5731. Molecule, driving cog-wheel. ℞ Nahal Sorek: stylized atomic reactor

25.00	42.00

COMMEMORATIVE ISSUES (2) FOR THE FIGHT FOR FREEDOM WITH THE MOTTO "LET MY PEOPLE GO"

55 (54) 10 £ (Ag) 1971–5731. Sun behind bars. Motto in Hebrew and in English. ℞ coat of arms, 10 Lirot Israeliot – 5731–1971   **Unc** 25.00   **Proof** 45.00

56 (55) 100 £ (Au) 1971–5731. Same type as No. 55, but diameter 30 mm, and "100 Lirot Israeliot" on reverse   600.00

COMMEMORATIVE ISSUE PIDYON HABEN – FOR THE REDEMPTION OF THE FIRST-BORN

57 (51b) 10 £ (Ag) 1972–5732. Similar to No. 53, but the arms again altered   20.00   40.00

COMMEMORATIVE ISSUE FOR THE 24th ANNIVERSARY OF INDEPENDENT ISRAEL WITH THE MOTTO "ISRAEL AVIATION"

58 (56) 10 £ (Ag) 1971–5732. Stylized jet. ℞ numeral 1 in shape of a rocket, blasting off   25.00   60.00

			Unc	Proof
59 (57)	5 £ (Ag) 1972 = 5732. Russian Chanukah candelabra, 20th century. ℞ national arms, 5 Loriot Israeliot		12.50	20.00

COMMEMORATIVE ISSUE PIDYON HABEN –
FOR THE REDEMPTION OF THE FIRST-BORN

60 (58)	10 £ (Ag) 1973 = 5733. Surrounded by five silver shekels, the quotation from the Bible: "All the first-born of thy sons thou shalt redeem" – Exodus 34, 20; the whole within an oval		25.00	30.00

COMMEMORATIVE ISSUES (10)
FOR THE 25th ANNIVERSARY OF THE INDEPENDENCE
OF THE STATE OF ISRAEL

61 (59)	1 Agora (Al) 1973. Type as No. 23, but with additional commemorative inscription "25th Anniversary of the State"		2.50	
62 (60)	5 Agorot (Cu–Ni) 1973. Type as No. 24, but with additional inscription as with No. 61		2.50	

				Unc	Proof
63 (61)	10	Agorot (Cu–Ni) 1973. Type as No. 25, but with additional inscription as with No. 61			2.50	
64 (62)	25	Agorot (Cu–Ni) 1973. Type as No. 26, but with additional inscription as with No. 61			2.50	
65 (63)	½	£ (Cu–Ni) 1973. Type as No. 27, but with additional inscription as with No. 61			2.50	
66 (64)	1	£ (Cu–Ni) 1973. Type as No. 29, but with additional inscription as with No. 61			2.50	

				Unc	Proof
67 (65)	10	£ (Ag) 1973		25.00	30.00
68 (66)	50	£ (Au) 1973			150.00
69 (67)	100	£ (Au) 1973			300.00
70 (68)	200	£ (Au) 1973			600.00

COMMEMORATIVE ISSUE FOR THE CHANUKAH FESTIVAL

			Unc	Proof
71 (69)	5	£ (Ag) 1973 = 5734. Chanukah candelabra from Mesopotamia, 18th entury, now in the Israel Museum in Jerusalem. ℞ value, name of country, date	12.00	18.50

COMMEMORATIVE ISSUE PIDYON HABEN –
FOR THE REDEMPTION OF THE FIRST-BORN

		Unc	**Proof**
72 (58a) 10 £ (Ag) 1974 = 5734. Type similar to No. 60		25.00	30.00

COMMEMORATIVE ISSUE FOR THE 26th ANNIVERSARY
OF THE INDEPENDENCE OF THE STATE OF ISRAEL

73 (70)   10 £ (Ag) 1974 = 5734   25.00   32.00

COMMEMORATIVE ISSUES (2) FOR THE 1th ANNIVERSARY
OF THE DEATH OF DAVID BEN GURION

74 (71)   25 £ (Ag) 1974 = 5734   25.00   28.00

75 (72)   500 £ (Au) 1974 = 5734   600.00

CHANUKAH FESTIVAL

			Unc	Proof
76 (73)	10	£(Ag)1974 = 5735. Chanukah candelabra from Damascus, 18th century	12.00	18.00
77 (24a)	5	Agorot (Cu-Ni) 1974 = 5735 – 1976 = 5736. Type as No. 24	1.00	
78 (25a)	10	Agorot (Cu-Ni) 1974 = 5735 – 1976 = 5736. Type as No. 25	1.00	
79 (26a)	25	Agorot (Cu-Ni) 1974 = 5735 –. Type as No. 26	1.00	

PIDYON HABEN – FOR THE REDEMPTION OF THE FIRST-BORN

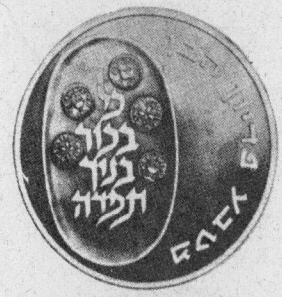

			Unc	Proof
80 (74)	25	£ (Ag) 1975 = 5735. Type similar to No. 60	25.00	30.00

25th ANNIVERSARY OF ISRAEL BOND PROGRAM (2)

			Unc	Proof
81 (75)	25	£(Ag) 1975 = 5735. Multiple image of the Star of David	25.00	30.00
82 (76)	500	£ (Au) 1975 = 5735. Type as No. 81		400.00

CHANUKAH FESTIVAL 5736

		Unc	Proof
83 (77)	10 £ (Ag) 1975 =5736. Holland Chanukah candelabra, 18th century	16.50	22.50

PIDYON HABEN – FOR THE REDEMPTION OF THE FIRST-BORN

84 (79)	25 £ (Ag) 1976 = 5736. Five pomegranate flowers around a five-pointed star	25.00	40.00

28th ANNIVERSARY OF THE INDEPENDENCE OF THE STATE OF ISRAEL

				Unc	Proof

85 (78)   25 £ (Ag) 1976 = 5736. The words "Strength for Israel" in Hebrew and a stylized Star of David — 25.00 / 40.00

86 (24b)   5 Agorot (Al) 1976 = 5736. Type as No. 24 or 77 — 1.00

87 (25b)   10 Agorot (Al) 1977 = 5737. Type as No. 25 or 78 — 1.00

CHANUKAH FESTIVAL 5735 AND BICENTENARY OF AMERICAN INDEPENDENCE

88 (80)   10 £ (Ag) 1976 = 5737. An early American Chanukah candelabra from the Jewish Museum in New York — 55.00 / 65.00

29th ANNIVERSARY OF THE INDEPENDENCE OF THE STATE OF ISRAEL

89 (81)   25 £ (Ag) 1977 = 5737 — 20.00 / 40.00

PIDYON HABEN – FOR THE REDEMPTION OF THE FIRST-BORN

90 (82)   25 £ (Ag) 1977 = 5738. Type similar to No. 84 — 22.00 / 35.00

CHANUKAH FESTIVAL 5738

91 (83) 10 £ (Cu-Ni) 1977 = 5738. An early 20th century Chanukah candelabra from Jerusalem, now in the Ha'aretz Museum in Ramat Aviv

	Unc	Proof
	9.00	22.00

30th ANNIVERSARY OF THE INDEPENDENCE OF THE STATE OF ISRAEL (2)

92 (84) 50 £ (Ag) 1978 = 5738. Olive tree with the Hebrew words "ISRAEL'S THIRTY YEARS" 22.00 35.00

93 (85) 1000 £ (Au) 1978 = 5738. Type as No. 92 350.00

CHANUKAH FESTIVAL 5739

94 (87) 25 £ (Cu-Ni) 1978 = 5739 7.50 12.50
95 (86) 5 £ (Cu-Ni) 1978 = 5739 1.20

31th ANNIVERSARY OF THE INDEPENDENCE OF THE STATE OF ISRAEL – MOTHERHOOD

96 (88) 50 £ (Ag) 1979 = 5740. Mother and child 20.00 30.00

CHANUKAH FESTIVAL 5740

97 (89) 100 £ (Ag) 1979 = 5740 20.00 35.00

32th ANNIVERSARY OF THE INDEPENDENCE OF THE STATE OF ISRAEL AND ISRAEL – EGYPT PEACE TREATY (2)

		Unc	Proof
98 (90)	200 £ (Ag) 1980	35.00	50.00
99 (91)	5000 £ (Au) 1980		450.00

25th ANNIVERSARY OF THE BANK OF ISRAEL (7)

		Unc	Proof
100 (92)	1 Agora (Ni) 1980 = 5740	1.00	1.50
101 (93)	5 Agora (Ni) 1980 = 5740	1.00	1.50
102 (94)	10 Agora (Ni) 1980 = 5740	1.00	1.50
103 (95)	25 Agora (Ni) 1980 = 5740	1.50	2.00
104 (96)	½ £ (Ni) 1980 = 5740	2.00	2.50
105 (97)	1 £ (Ni) 1980 = 5740	2.00	3.00
106 (98)	5 £ (Ni) 1980 = 5740	4.00	6.00

MONETARY REFORM: 10 Agorot = 1 New Agorot, 1 Lira (£) = 10 New Agorot, 5 Lira = ½ Shekel (Shequalim)

		XF	Unc
107 (99)	1 New Agora (Al) 1980–	0.05	0.10

108 (100)	5 New Agorot (Al) 1980–	0.05	0.10

			XF	Unc

109 (101) 10 New Agorot (Br) 1980–   0.10   0.15

110 (102) ½ Shekel (Cu-Ni) 1980–   0.15   0.30
111 (106) 1 Shekel (Cu-Ni) 1981–   0.40   0.80

112 5 Shekel (Cu-Ni) 1981–   1.80   3.60

113 10 Shekel (Cu-Ni) 1982–   3.50   6.80

100th ANNIVERSARY OF THE BIRTH OF ZEEV JABOTINSKY (2)

		Unc	Proof
114 (103)	'25 Shekel (Ag) 1980 = 5740. Zeev Jabotinsky (1880–1940), patriot	35.00	52.00
115 (104)	500 Shekel (Au) 1980 = 5740. Type as No. 114		400.00

CHANUKAH FESTIVAL 5741

		Unc	Proof
116 (105)	1 Shekel (Ag) 1980 = 5740	18.00	40.00

33th ANNIVERSARY OF THE INDEPENDENCE OF THE STATE OF ISRAEL (2)

117 (107)	2 Shekel (Ag) 1981 = 5741	35.00	50.00
118 (108)	10 Shekel (Au) 1981 = 5741	370.00	425.00

CHANUKAH FESTIVAL 5742

119 (109)	1 Shekel (Ag) 1981	17.50	35.00

34th ANNIVERSARY OF THE INDEPENDENCE OF THE STATE OF ISRAEL (2)

		Unc	Proof
120	2 Shekel (Ag) 1982 = 5742. Baron Edmond de Rothschild (1845–1934)	35.00	60.00
121	10 Shekel (Au) 1982 = 5742. Type as No. 120		

Italian Somaliland

Italienisch-Somaliland   **Somalie Italienne**

Having been administered by the Benadir Company, this territory came under Italian jurisdiction in 1905. Since 1960 the former Italian Colony is united with British Somaliland, and thus forming the Republic of Somalia.
Capital: Mogadishu.

100 Bese = 1 Rupia, 100 Centesimi = 1 Lira

VICTOR EMMANUEL III 1905–1944

			VF	XF
1 (1)	1	Besa (Br) 1909–1921. Victor Emmanuel III, head left. ℞ value	18.50	28.00
2 (2)	2	Bese (Br) 1909–1924	22.00	35.00

3 (3)	4	Bese (Br) 1909–1924	28.00	50.00
4 (4)	¼	Rupia (Ag) 1910–1913. Victor Emmanuel III, head right. ℞ crown above value	35.00	70.00
5 (5)	½	Rupia (Ag) 1910–1919	65.00	115.00
6 (6)	1	Rupia (Ag) 1910–1921	80.00	125.00

NEW COINAGE STANDARD: 100 Centesimi = 1 Lira

7 (7)	5	Lire (Ag) 1925. Victor Emmanuel III, crowned portrait right. ℞ crowned coat of arms	90.00	180.00
8 (8)	10	Lire (Ag) 1925	120.00	250.00

Italy

Italien   **Italie**

Area: 116,286 sq. mi. Population: 55,000,000.
After Italy had been united, the Sardinian king, Victor Emmanuel II
acquired the title of "King of Italy". Following the abdication of
Humbert II, the kingdom became a republic in 1946.
Capital: Rome.

100 Centesimi = 1 Lira

VICTOR EMMANUEL III 1900–1946

			VF	XF
1 (35)	1	Centesimo (Br) 1902–1908. Victor Emmanuel III (1869–1947), head left. ℞ value in wreath	0.40	2.50
2 (36)	2	Centesimi (Br) 1903–1908	0.40	2.50
3 (37)	25	Centesimi (Ni) 1902–1903	25.00	60.00
4 (38)	1	Lira (Ag) 1901–1907. Victor Emmanuel III, head right. ℞ crowned heraldic eagle	10.00	32.00
5 (39)	2	Lire (Ag) 1901–1907	25.00	60.00
6 (40)	5	Lire (Ag) 1901 (114 pieces)		*6500.00*
7 (41)	20	Lire (Au). Victor Emmanuel III, head left. ℞ crowned heraldic eagle		
		a) 1902		5000.00
		b) 1902; small anchor – Eritrea gold		6000.00
		c) 1903, 1905	400.00	650.00
		d) 1908, 1910		–.–

8 (42)	100	Lire (Au) 1903, 1905. Same type as No. 7	3500.00	5800.00
A8	100	Lire (Au) 1903. Victor Emmanuel III,		

			VF	XF
		head facing right. ℞ two female figures, representing the "Italia" and Agriculture. Date MCMIII, value. Rare!	–.–	–.–
9 (43)	1	Centesimo (Br) 1908–1918. ℞ Italia standing	0.80	2.50
10 (44)	2	Centesimi (Br) 1908–1917	0.80	2.50
11 (45)	5	Centesimi (Br) 1908–1918	2.50	6.00
12 (46)	10	Centesimi (Br) 1908	–.–	–.–
13 (47)	20	Centesimi (Ni) 1908–1935. Classical head. ℞ Italia floating in the air, with torch. Coins struck after 1922 were never put into circulation	0.80	1.80
14 (48)	1	Lira (Ag) 1908–1913. Victor Emmanuel III, head right. ℞ Italia riding in quadriga	7.50	15.00
15 (49)	2	Lire (Ag) 1908–1912	8.00	20.00
16 (50)	1	Lira (Ag) 1915–1917. Similar type as No. 14	6.00	25.00
17 (51)	2	Lire (Ag) 1914–1917. Same type as No. 16	7.50	15.00
18 (52)	5	Lire (Ag) 1914. Same type as No. 16		2750.00
19 (53)	10	Lire (Au) 1910–1927. Victor Emmanuel III, head left. ℞ Italia with plough:		
		a) 1910	–.–	–.–
		b) 1912	1200.00	1600.00
		c) 1926, 1927	–.–	–.–
20 (54)	20	Lire (Au) 1910–1927. Same type as No. 19:		
		a) 1910	–.–	–.–
		b) 1912	650.00	800.00
		c) 1926, 1927		–.–

			VF	XF
21 (55)	50	Lire (Au) 1910, 1912, 1926, 1927. Same type as No. 19:		
		a) 1910		–.–
		b) 1912	600.00	850.00
		c) 1926, 1927		–.–
22 (56)	100	Lire (Au) 1910, 1912, 1926, 1927. Same type as No. 19:		
		a) 1910		–.–
		b) 1912	1600.00	2000.00
		c) 1926, 1927		–.–

COMMEMORATIVE COINS (4) FOR THE 50th ANNIVERSARY OF THE KINGDOM OF ITALY

			VF	XF
23 (57)	10	Centesimi (Br) 1911. Victor Emmanuel III, head left. ℞ allegory of the unification; industrial plants, bow of a ship, plough	3.50	8.00
24 (58)	2	Lire (Ag) 1911. Same type as No. 23	26.00	45.00

			VF	XF
25 (59)	5	Lire (Ag) 1911. Same type as No. 23	400.00	620.00
26 (60)	50	Lire (Au) 1911. Same type as No. 23	780.00	1100.00
27 (61)	5	Centesimi (Br) 1919–1937. Victor Emmanuel III, head left. ℞ ear of wheat	0.40	1.00
28 (62)	10	Centesimi (Br) 1919–1937. ℞ honey bee (Apis mellifica – Apidae)	0.80	2.00
29 (63)	20	Centesimi (Cu–Ni) 1918–1920. Crowned coat of arms. ℞ value in hexagon	2.00	4.00
30 (64)	50	Centesimi (Ni). ℞ Victor Emmanuel III, head left. ℞ Justitia riding in quadriga, drawn by lions. Coins struck after 1925 were never put into circulation		
		a) 1919–1928. Plain edge	8.00	11.50
		b) 1919–1935. Milled edge	1.60	4.50
31 (65)	1	Lira (Ni) 1922–1935. Seated Italia. ℞ value and coat of arms in wreath. Coins struck after 1928 were never put into circulation	2.00	4.50
32 (66)	2	Lire (Ni) 1923–1935. Victor Emmanuel III, head right. ℞ fasces. Coins struck after 1927 were never put into circulation	4.00	9.00
33 (67)	5	Lire (Ag) 1926–1935. Victor Emmanuel III, head left. ℞ heraldic eagle with fasces. Coins struck after 1930 were never put into circulation	4.50	8.00
34 (68)	10	Lire (Ag) 1926–1934. ℞ biga. Coins struck after 1930 were never put into circulation:		

	a) 1926	30.00	170.00
	b) 1927	12.50	20.00
	c) 1928, 1929, 1930	20.00	45.00

35 (69) 20 Lire (Ag) 1927–1934. Coins struck after 1928 were never put into circulation   60.00   120.00

36 (72) 20 Lire (Au) 1923. Victor Emmanuel III, head left. ℞ fasces and date October 1922 (first anniversary of the March on Rome)   400.00   600.00

37 (73) 100 Lire (Au) 1923. Same type as No. 36   800.00   1200.00

COMMEMORATIVE COIN FOR THE 25th YEAR OF REIGN AND 10th ANNIVERSARY OF ENTERING WORLD WAR I

38 (74) 100 Lire (Au) 1925. Victor Emmanuel III, head left. ℞ male figure with flag holding statue of Victory   1600.00   2500.00

39 (70) 50 Lire (Au) 1931–1933. Victor Emmanuel III, head left. ℞ male figure carrying fasces   200.00   250.00

40 (71) 100 Lire (Au) 1931–1933. ℞ Italia standing at bow of galley   320.00   400.00

COMMEMORATIVE COIN FOR THE 10th ANNIVERSARY OF THE END OF WORLD WAR I

41 (75) 20 Lire (Ag) 1928. Victor Emmanuel III, with steel helmet. ℞ fasces, lion head, legend and value   80.00   160.00

			VF	XF
42 (77)	5	Centesimi (Cu) 1936-1939. Victor Emmanuel III, head right, legend now RE. E. IMP. instead of RE. D. ITALIA. Rev. eagle with spread wings and fasces	0.40	1.60
43 (78)	10	Centesimi (Cu) 1936-1939. Rev. fasces, ear of wheat and oak leaves	0.80	2.00
44 (79)	20	Centesimi (Ni) 1936-1938. Rev. fasces, in front of profiled head. Issues dated 1937 and 1938 were never put into circulation	45.00	105.00
45 (80)	50	Centesimi (Ni) 1936-1938. Rev. eagle with spread wings in front of fasces. Issues dated 1937 and 1938 were never put into circulation	25.00	50.00
46 (81)	1	Lira (Ni) 1936-1938. Rev. eagle with spread wings in front of fasces. Issues dated 1937 and 1938 were never put into circulation	18.50	38.00

			VF	XF
47 (82)	2	Lire (Ni) 1936-1938. Rev. eagle in wreath. Issues dated 1937 and 1938 were never put into circulation:		
		a) 1936	22.00	40.00
		b) 1937, 1938	–.–	–.–
48 (89)	5	Lire (Ag) 1936–1941. ℞ mother with children. Coins struck after 1937 were never put into circulation	25.00	48.00
49 (90)	10	Lire (Ag) 1936–1941. ℞ Italia standing at bow of galley. Coins struck after 1936 were never put into circulation	20.00	38.00
50 (91)	20	Lire (Ag) 1936–1941. ℞ quadriga. Coins struck after 1936 were never put into circulation	600.00	800.00
51 (92)	50	Lire (Au) 1936. ℞ Italian eagle over emblems of Italy and Ethiopia, resembling Roman field badge	2600.00	3200.00

				VF	XF

			VF	XF
52 (93)	100	Lire (Au) 1936. R̶ male figure carrying fasces; diameter: 25 mm		3200.00	4000.00
53 (93a)	100	Lire (Au) 1937. Same type as No. 52, but; diameter: 20 mm		4800.00	6000.00

Forgeries are known to exist of Nos. 50-53.

			VF	XF
54 (77a)	5	Centesimi (Al-Br) 1939-1943. Type as No. 42	0.40	1.00
55 (78a)	10	Centesimi (Al-Br) 1939-1943. Type as No. 43	0.40	1.00
56 (79a)	20	Centesimi (St) 1939-1943. Type as No. 44	0.40	0.80
57 (80a)	50	Centesimi (St) 1939-1943. Type as No. 45	0.40	1.60
58 (81a)	1	Lira (St) 1939-1943. Type as No. 46	0.80	1.60
59 (82a)	2	Lire (St) 1939-1943. Type as No. 47	1.00	2.00

REPUBLIC since 1946

			VF	XF
60 (95)	1	Lira (Al) 1946–1950. Head of goddess Ceres. R̶ orange:		
		a) 1946	6.00	25.00
		b) 1947	12.00	100.00
		c) 1948–1950	1.50	2.50
61 (96)	2	Lire (Al) 1946–1950. Ploughman. R̶ ear of wheat:		
		a) 1946	16.00	40.00
		b) 1947	20.00	90.00
		c) 1948–1950	1.00	4.00
62 (97)	5	Lire (Al) 1946–1950. Head of liberty with torch. R̶ grape (Vitis vinifera – Vitaceae):		
		a) 1946	40.00	165.00
		b) 1947	28.00	60.00
		c) 1948–1950	1.00	3.00

			VF	XF
63 (98)	10	Lire (Al) 1946–1950. Pegasus. R̶ olive branch (Olea europea – Oleaceae):		
		a) 1946	16.00	40.00
		b) 1947	160.00	260.00
		c) 1948–1950	2.00	4.00

			VF	XF
64 (99)	1	Lira (Al) 1951–1970. Scale. R cornu-copia:		
		a) 1951–1953	0.50	2.50
		b) 1954–1959	0.25	0.80
		c) 1968–1970; in mint sets only		5.00
65 (100)	2	Lire (Al) 1953–1970. Honey bee (Apis mellifica – Apidae). R olive branch:		
		a) 1953–1957, 1959	0.30	0.80
		b) 1958	25.00	60.00
		c) 1968–1970; in mint sets only		3.00
66 (101)	5	Lire (Al) 1951–1973. Oar. R common dolphin (Delphinus delphis – Delphini-dae):		
		a) 1951–1955, 1966–1979	0.15	0.30
		b) 1956	20.00	50.00
67 (102)	10	Lire (Al) 1951–. Plough. ℞ ears of wheat:		
		a) 1951–1953	0.80	4.00
		b) 1954	2.00	7.00
		c) 1955–1956, 1965–	0.15	0.30
68 (A102)	20	Lire (Al-Br) 1955–1959, 1968–. Head of Italia. Rev. oak leaves:		
		a) 1955, 1956, 1968; reeded edge	–.–	–.–
		b) 1957-1959; reeded edge	1.50	3.00
		c) 1969–; plain edge	0.15	0.30
69 (103)	50	Lire (St) 1954–. Head of Italia. Rev. black-smith with anvil:		
		a) 1954-1957, 1959-	0.20	0.40
		b) 1958	3.50	10.00
70 (104)	100	Lire (St) 1955–. Head of Italia. Rev. goddess Ceres with sprig	0.25	0.50

			VF	XF
71 (105)	500	Lire (Ag) 1958–. Portrait of young girl. ℞ fleet of Columbus: Santa Maria, Nina, Pinta:		
		a) 1958–1960	6.00	9.00
		b) 1961	6.50	12.00
		c) 1964, 1965	6.00	9.00
		d) 1966, 1967	6.00	8.50
		e) 1968	28.00	40.00
		f) 1969, 1970	6.00	9.00

COMMEMORATIVE COIN FOR THE CENTENNIAL
OF ITALY'S UNIFICATION

			XF	Unc

2 (106) 500 Lire (Ag) 1961. Seated Italia. ℞ quad-
riga   6.50   8.00

COMMEMORATIVE COIN FOR THE 700th BIRTHDAY
OF DANTE ALIGHIERI

73 (107) 500 Lire (Ag) 1965. Dante Alighieri (1265–
1321), poet. ℞ scene from "Inferno"   7.00   10.00

COMMEMORATIVE COIN FOR THE CENTENNIAL OF ROME
AS ITALY'S CAPITAL

4 (108) 1000 Lire (Ag) 1970. Concordia, divine per-
sonification of civic unity – here symbol
of Italy's national unity. ℞ design
Michel Angelo's (1538) for the multi-
coloured stone pattern of the Capitol
plaza paving   11.50   16.50

	XF	Unc
75 (109) 100 Lire (St) 1974. Guglielmo Marconi (1874–1937), physicist	0.40	0.60

	XF	Unc
76 (110) 500 Lire (Ag) 1974. Bust left. Rev. map of Italy and surrounding areas under four sets of concentric circles	28.00	35.00

500th ANNIVERSARY OF THE BIRTH OF MICHELANGELO BUONARROTI

77 (111) 500 Lire (Ag) 1975. Michelangelo Buonarroti (1475–1564), bust facing left   60.00

		XF	Unc
78 (112) 200 Lire (Ni) 1977–		0.80	1.20

FOR THE FAO COIN PLAN

	XF	Unc
79 (113) 100 Lire (St) 1979	0.30	0.50

PARLIAMENT OF EUROPE

80 100 Lire (St) 1979	0.30	0.50

INTERNATIONAL WOMEN'S YEAR

81 (116) 200 Lire (Al-Br) 1980	0.60	1.00

100th ANNIVERSARY OF NAVAL ACADEMY

	XF	Unc
82 100 Lire (St) 1981	0.30	0.50

FOR THE FAO COIN PLAN

83 (118) 200 Lire (Br) 1981. Girl with cornucopia	0.40	0.80
84 500 Lire (Ni) 1981	2.00	2.50

Elfenbeinküste   # Ivory Coast   Côte d'Ivoire

Area: 128,364 sq. mi. Population: 5,000,000.
From the end of the last century the Ivory Coast belonged as a French colony to the Union of French West Africa; in 1957 it obtained a high degree of internal autonomy within the structure of the Communauté Française. On 7th August 1960 the Republic was proclaimed. The Ivory Coast is linked with the states of Dahomey, Mauretania, Niger, Upper Volta, Senegal and Togo in the Union Monétaire Ouest-Africaine; the issuing authority for the whole Monetary Union is the Banque Centrale des Etats de l'Afrique de l'Ouest; see also under West Africa.
Capital: Abidjan.

100 Centimes = 1 CFA Franc

		Proof
1	10 Francs (Ag) 1966. Head right of Dr. Félix Houphouét-Boigny (*1905), Head of State since 1960. ℞ African elephant (Loxodonta africana — Elephantidae) = national arms, within wreath	20.00
2	10 Francs (Au) 1966. Type as No. 1	75.00
3	25 Francs (Au) 1966. Type as No. 1	150.00
4	50 Francs (Au) 1966. Type as No. 1	300.00
5	100 Francs (Au) 1966. Type as No. 1	600.00

Jamaika   # Jamaica   Jamaïque

Area: 4,411 sq. mi. Population: 2,000,000.
Discovered by Christopher Columbus in 1494, this island became British Territory in 1670. Following the temporary membership of the West Indian Federation, Jamaica declared her independence on August 6th, 1962. Jamaica is a member of the British Commonwealth.
Capital: Kingston.

4 Farthings = 1 Penny, 12 Pence = 1 Shilling, 20 Shillings= 1 £;
since September 8th, 1969: 100 Cents = 1 Jamaica Dollar

EDWARD VII 1901–1910

			VF	XF
1	1	Farthing (Cu-Ni) Edward VII (1841–1910), crowned head right		
		a) (Y 4) 1902–1903; shading in coat of arms horizontal	5.50	11.00
		b) (Y 7) 1904–1910; shading in coat of arms vertical	3.50	8.00
2	½	Penny (Cu-Ni). Same type as No. 1		
		a) (Y 5) 1902–1904; shading in coat of arms horizontal	5.50	12.00
		b) (Y 8) 1904–1910; shading in coat of arms vertical	3.50	6.00
3	1	Penny (Cu-Ni). Same type as No. 1		
		a) (Y 6) 1902–1904; shading in coat of arms horizontal	6.50	12.00
		b) (Y 9) 1904–1910; shading in coat of arms vertical	3.50	8.00

GEORGE V 1910–1936

			VF	XF
4 (10)	1	Farthing (Cu-Ni) 1914–1934. George V (1865–1936), crowned head left. R coat of arms with American crocodile (Crocodylus acutus – Crocodylidae)	4.00	8.00

				VF	**XF**

5 (11) ½ Penny (Cu–Ni) 1914–1928. Same type
as No. 4 .... 3.50 6.00

6 (12) 1 Penny (Cu–Ni) 1914–1928. Same type
as No. 4 .... 3.50 6.00

GEORGE VI 1936–1952

7 (13) 1 Farthing (Ni–Bra) 1937. George VI
(1895–1952), crowned head left. ℞ coat
of arms 2.00 3.50

8 (14) ½ Penny (Ni–Bra) 1937. Same type as
No. 7 .... 2.50 4.00

9 (15) 1 Penny (Ni–Bra) 1937. Same type as
No. 7 .... 2.80 4.50

10 (16) 1 Farthing (Ni–Bra) 1938–1947. Same
type as No. 7, but larger head 0.50 0.80

11 (17) ½ Penny (Ni–Bra) 1938–1947. Same type
as No. 8, but larger head 0.70 1.50

12 (18) 1 Penny (Ni–Bra) 1938–1947. Same type
as No. 8, but larger head 0.80 1.50

13 (19) 1 Farthing (Ni–Bra) 1950–1952. Same
type as No. 10, but with new legend
KING GEORGE THE SIXTH 0.20 0.40

14 (20) ½ Penny (Ni–Bra) 1950–1952. Same type
as No. 11, but with new legend KING
GEORGE THE SIXTH 0.25 0.50

15 (21) 1 Penny (Ni–Bra) 1950–1952. Same type
as No. 12, but with new legend KING
GEORGE THE SIXTH 0.40 1.00

ELIZABETH II since 1952

16 (22) ½ Penny (Ni–Bra) 1955–1963. Elizabeth II
(*1926), crowned head right. ℞ coat of
arms 0.20 0.40

17 (23) 1 Penny (Ni–Bra) 1953–1963. Same type
as No. 16 .... 0.25 0.55

18 (24) ½ Penny (Ni–Bra) 1964–1966. Elizabeth
II, crowned head right. ℞ coat of arms ... 0.15 0.30

19 (25) 1 Penny (Ni–Bra) 1964–1967. Same type
as No. 18 .... 0.25 0.60

COMMEMORATIVE ISSUE FOR THE 8th BRITISH EMPIRE AND COMMONWEALTH GAMES IN KINGSTON ON JAMAICA

			XF	Unc
20 (26)	5 Shillings (Cu–Ni) 1966. Crown between dates, legend surrounded by chain with 10 links. ℞ coat of arms		1.80	3.60

COMMEMORATIVE ISSUES (2) FOR JAMAICA'S 100th YEAR OF COINAGE

			XF	Unc
21 (27)	½ Penny (Br) 1969. Elizabeth II, crowned head right. ℞ coat of arms, dates 1869–1969, value		0.40	0.90
22 (28)	1 Penny (Br) 1969. Same type as No. 21		0.40	0.90

NEW CURRENCY: 100 Cents = 1 Jamaica Dollar

			XF	Unc
23 (29)	1 Cent (Br) 1969–. Coat of arms. ℞ ackee (Blighia sapida – Sapindaceae)		0.10	0.20

			XF	Unc
24 (30)	5 Cents (Cu–Ni) 1969–. ℞ American crocodile (Crocodylus acutus – Crocodylidae)		0.10	0.20

		XF	**Unc**

25 (31) 10 Cents (Cu–Ni) 1969. ℞ butterfly (Papilio sp. – Papilionidae) on lignum vitae tree, branch with blossoms (Guaiacum officinale – Zygophyllaceae) — 0.20 / 0.40

26 (32) 20 Cents (Cu–Ni) 1969. ℞ blue mahoe (Hibiscus elatus – Malvaceae) — 0.40 / 0.90

27 (33) 25 Cents (Cu–Ni) 1969. ℞ Jamaica humming bird (Trochilus polytmus – Trochilidae) — 0.50 / 1.00

28 (34) 1 Dollar (Cu-Ni) 1969–. Sir William Alexander Bustamante (*1884), Prime Minister 1962–1967. R coat of arms, value — 4.00 / 7.00

COMMEMORATIVE ISSUE FOR THE FAO COIN PLAN

29 (36) 1 Cent (Br) 1971–1974. Coat of arms. R ackee (Blighia sapida – Sapindaceae), motto: »Let us produce more food«, value — 0.15 / 0.30

			Unc	Proof
30 (35)	5 Dollars (Ag) 1971. Norman W. Manley, Prime Minister 1959-1962. Rev. coat of arms, value		20.00	30.00
31 (A36)	5 Dollars (Ag) 1972–1976. Norman W. Manley, head left:			
	a) .925 silver; 1972, 1973		25.00	30.00
	b) (Cu-Ni), 42 mm dia.; 1974–1979		7.00	
	c) .500 silver; 1974–1979;			15.00

10th ANNIVERSARY OF INDEPENDENCE(2)

32 (37)	10 Dollars (Ag) 1972. Alexander Busta-mante and Norman W. Manley, map of the island. ℞ coat of arms, new memorial legend, value		30.00	40.00

33 (38)	20 Dollars (Au) 1972. Map of the island. Sail boats: "Cardera", "San Juan" and "Nina". ℞ like No. 32		100.00	150.00

34 (39)	10 Dollars 1974. Sir Henry Morgan (1635–1688), Lieutenant Governor of Jamaica 1674:			
	a) (Ag)			40.00
	b) (Cu-Ni)		16.00	

				Unc	Proof
35 (40)	10	Dollars 1975. Christopher Columbus (1451–1506), discoverer of the New World. Rev. coat of arms, value:			
		a) (Ag)			40.00
		b) (Cu-Ni)		15.00	
36 (41)	100	Dollars (Au) 1975. Type similar to No. 35		125.00	185.00

ISSUE FOR THE FAO COIN PLAN

				XF	Unc
37 (36a)	1	Cent (Al) 1975–1980. Type as No. 29	0.10	0.30
38 (43)	50	Cents (Cu-Ni) 1975–1980. Marcus Garvey (1887–1940), politician	0.80	1.50

				Unc	Proof
39 (44)	10	Dollars 1976. Admiral Horatio Nelson:			
		a) (Ag)			40.00
		b) (Cu-Ni)		20.00	
40 (45)	100	Dollars (Au) 1976. Admiral Horatio Nelson			200.00

ISSUE FOR THE FAO COIN PLAN

				XF	Unc
41 (42)	20	Cents (Cu-Ni) 1976–1980. Type as No. 26, but inscription FORESTRY FOR DEVELOPMENT	0.75	1.20

				Unc	Proof
42 (46)	10	Dollars 1977. Admiral George Rodney:			
		a) (Ag)			35.00
		b) (Cu-Ni)		20.00	
43 (47)	10	Dollars (Ag) 1978 »Out of many, one people«			40.00

25th ANNIVERSARY OF THE CORONATION OF HER MAJESTY QUEEN ELIZABETH II (3)

		Unc	Proof
44 (48)	25 Dollars (Ag) 1978. The Queen seated on the Throne in full coronation regalia	140.00	160.00
45 (49)	100 Dollars (Au) 1978. Type as No. 44		250.00
46 (50)	250 Dollars (Au) 1978. Type as No. 44		750.00

10th ANNIVERSARY OF INVESTITURE OF PRINCE CHARLES (3)

47 (52)	25 Dollars (Ag) 1979	160.00	140.00
48 (53)	100 Dollars (Au) 1979		220.00
49 (54)	250 Dollars (Au) 1979		750.00

 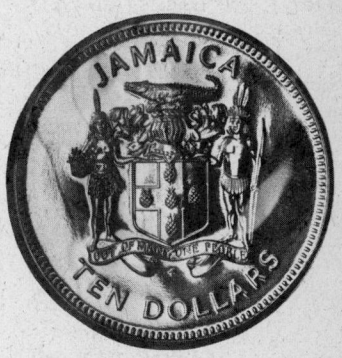

50 (51)	10 Dollars 1979:		
	a) (Ag)		40.00
	b) (Cu-Ni)	20.00	

INTERNATIONAL YEAR OF THE CHILD

51 (55)	10 Dollars (Ag) 1979		65.00

OLYMPIC GAMES (2)

52 (58)	25 Dollars (Ag) 1980		100.00
53 (59)	250 Dollars (Au) 1980		350.00

		Unc	Proof

54 (56)   10 Dollars   1980.   Trochilus   polytmus
Hummingbirds:
a) (Ag)   50.00
b) (Cu-Ni)   18.00

10th ANNIVERSARY OF CARIBBEAN DEVELOPMENT BANK

55 (57)   10 Dollars (Ag) 1980.   55.00

WEDDING OF PRINCE CHARLES AND LADY DIANA (3)

56 (60)   10 Dollars (Ag) 1981   50.00
57 (61)   25 Dollars (Ag) 1981   120.00
58 (62)   250 Dollars (Au) 1981   380.00

WORLD SOCCER CHAMPIONSHIP GAMES (2)

59   10 Dollars (Ag) 1982   50.00
60   100 Dollars (Au) 1982   250.00

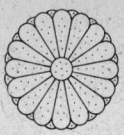

Japan

Nippon, also Nihon

Area: 142,720 sq. mi. Population: 115,000,000.
The Japanese empire has existed since about 660 B. C. until the present
day. After the rigid isolation towards the outer world had been given
up by the middle of the last century, industrialization also began in
Japan which was especially forced very strongly after World War II
and allowed Japan to rise to be an economic world power. Capital:
Tokyo. The first coins were issued in Japan, patterned on the Cast
Chinese cash coins, at the beginning of the 7th Century. Subsequently
also silver and gold coins were put into circulation. These old coin
shapes were substituted around 1870 by the introduction of modern
minted round coins. The dates quoted on the modern coins refer to
the era of the reign (Japanese: nengo) of the respective ruling emperor
(Japanese: tenno), at the beginning of which the years are once more
counted from one. The periods of reign of the emperors mentioned
below fall into the period covered by this catalog.

Mutsuhito, Meiji Era	明治	1868–1912
Yoshihito, Taisho Era	大正	1912–1926
Hirohito, Showa Era	昭禾口	1926–.

Upon the introduction of the modern coins the following nominal
values and value ratios were laid down:

10 Rin (厘) = 1 Sen (金菱);
100 Sen = 1 Yen (圓 or 円).

During the period covered by this catalog, the following country
designations are used on the Japanese coins:

–1945: 大 日 本
1945–1947:
1947– :日 本 國 or 日 本 国

Emperor: Mutsuhito (1868–1912)

Era: Meiji 明氵台

1 (20) 1 Sen (Br) 1898–1902, 1906. Sun with
rays in dotted circle. In the legend
1 SEN including name of country, era
and date in Japanese characters. ℞
value in Japanese characters in a wreath
of rice panicles. The issue of 1906 is a
trial strike

	VF	XF
	2.50	11.00

2 (21) 5 Sen (Cu–Ni) 1895–1905. Similar to
type No. 1, but changed value. The
issues of 1895 and 1896 are trial strikes

3.00 9.00

3 (23) 10 Sen (Ag) 1873–1902, 1904–1906. Dragon in dotted circle. In the legend: 10
SEN including name of country, era
and date in Japanese characters in a
wreath of branches. Above the national
emblem

5.00 8.00

4 (24) 20 Sen (Ag) 1873–1901, 1904, 1905. As
type No. 3, but with changed value

7.00 11.00

			VF	**XF**

5 (25) 50 Sen (Ag) 1873–1905. As type No. 3, but with changed value 16.00 25.00

6 (A25) 1 Yen (Ag) 1874–1906, 1908, 1912. As type No. 3, but with changed value (in the legend on the obverse 416. ONE YEN. 900) 40.00 75.00

6a 1 Yen (Ag) 1901. Sun with rays in double circle. In the legend 1 YEN including name of country, era and date in Japanese characters. ℞ as type No. 6. Trial strike! –.– –.–

7 (29) 10 Sen (Ag) 1906–1912. Sun with rays in a circle of rosettes. In the legend 10 SEN including name of country, era and date in Japanese characters in a wreath of two branches. Above the state emblem. (℞ similar to type No. 3). The issue of 1906 was not put in circulation. 4.00 6.00

		VF	XF
8 (30)	20 Sen (Ag) 1906–1911. As type No. 7, but with changed value	5.00	8.00

| **9** (31) | 50 Sen (Ag) 1906–1912. As type No. 7, but with changed value | 9.00 | 15.00 |

| **10** (32) | 5 Yen (Au) 1897, 1898, 1903, 1911, 1912. Sun with rays in octagonal surround. In the legend name of country, era and date in Japanese characters. ℞ value in Japanese characters in a wreath of two branches. Above the state emblem. (℞ similar to type No. 3) | 800.00 | 900.00 |

| **11** (33) | 10 Yen (Au) 1897–1904, 1907–1910. As type No. 10, but with changed value | 1000.00 | 1250.00 |

					VF	**XF**

12 (34) 20 Yen (Au) 1897, 1903–1912. As type
No. 10, but with changed value 2000.00 2500.00

Emperor: Yoshihito (1912–1926)

Era: Taisho 大 正

13 (35) 1 Sen (Bro) 1913–1915. As type No. 1,
but now with the Japanese characters
for the Taisho Era 2.50 6.00

14 (36) 10 Sen (Ag) 1912–1917. As type No. 7,
but now with the Japanese characters
for the Taisho Era 5.00 7.00

15 (37) 50 Sen (Ag) 1912–1917. As type No. 9,
but now with the Japanese characters
for the Taisho Era 10.00 16.00

16 (38) 1 Yen (Ag) 1914. Similar to type No. 6,
but with the Japanese characters for
the Taisho Era 35.00 60.00

17 (39) 5 Yen (Au) 1912 (?), 1913, 1924. Similar
to type No. 10, but now with the
Japanese characters for the Taisho Era 800.00 900.00

18 (40) 20 Yen (Au) 1912–1920. Similar to type
No. 12, but now with the Japanese
characters for the Taisho Era 1900.00 2400.00

19 (41) 5 Rin (Br) 1916–1919. Kiri-mon (Paul-

ownia imperiales) = Imperial arms. In
the legend: era and date in Japanese
characters. ℞ value Japanese characters
in the double circle, border in the way
of arabesques and two rosettes

	VF	XF
	1.60	3.50

20 (42) 1 Sen (Br) 1916–1924. Similar to type
No. 19, but with changed value 0.60 2.00

21 (43) 5 Sen (Cu–Ni) 1916–1920. Central hole
in octagonal border. In the legend:
name of country, era and date in Japanese characters. ℞ value in Japanese
characters above leaf decoration. With
central round hole. 21 mm dia. The
issue of 1916 is a trial strike. 4.00 8.00

21a (44) 5 Sen (Cu–Ni) 1920–1923. Similar to
type No. 21, but diameter only 18.5 mm 0.60 2.00

22 (45) 10 Sen (Cu–Ni) 1920–1923, 1925, 1926.
Similar to type No. 21, but with chang-
ed value 0.80 2.00

22a 10 Sen (Ag) 1918, 1919. Sun with rays
with a dove in the centre. In the legend:
10 SEN including name of country in

			VF	**XF**
		Japanese characters. ℞ value in Japanese characters between two phoenixes. Above the state emblem. Both issues were not put in circulation	–.–	–.–
22 b	20	Sen (Ag) 1918, 1919, 1921. Similar to type No. 22 a, but with changed value. Trial strikes	–.–	–.–

22 c	50	Sen (Ag) 1918, 1919. Similar to type No. 22 a, but with changed value. Both issues were not put in circulation	–.–	–.–

23 (46)	50	Sen (Ag) 1922–1926. Sun with rays in the centre (changed design in respect of type No. 22 a). In the legend: name of country, era and date in Japanese characters. ℞ similar to type No. 22 a	3.50	6.00

Emperor: Hirohito (1926–)

Era: Showa 昭和

24 (47)	1	Sen (Br) 1927, 1929–1938. As type No. 20, but changed value and now with the Japanese characters for the Showa Era	0.80	1.60
25 (48)	5	Sen (Cu–Ni) 1932. As type No. 21 a, but now with the Japanese characters for the Showa Era	1.20	2.00
26 (49)	10	Sen (Cu–Ni) 1927–1929, 1931, 1932. As type No. 22, but now with the Japanese characters for the Showa Era	0.80	1.80

			VF	**XF**
27 (50)	50	Sen (Ag) 1928–1938. As type No. 23, but now with the Japanese characters for the Showa Era	4.50	8.00
28 (51)	5	Yen (Au) 1930. As type No. 10, but now with the Japanese characters for the Showa Era	1500.00	1800.00
29 (52)	20	Yen (Au) 1930–1932. As type No. 12, but now with the Japanese characters for the Showa Era	3000.00	3500.00

30 (55)	1	Sen (Bra) 1938. In the centre a bird. Name of country, era and date as legend in Japanese characters. ℞ value in Japanese characters in ornamental border. Above the state emblem, below Kiri-mon (Imperial arms). 23 mm dia.	0.80	2.50
	1	Sen (Al) 1938. As type No. 30. Trial strike!	–.–	–.–

31 (56)	1	Sen (Al) 1938–1940. As type No. 30, but 18 mm dia.	0.60	1.30
31a	5	Sen (Cu–Ni) 1933. Name of country, era and date as legend in Japanese characters, right and left with ornamental background. ℞ value in Japanese characters. Above the state emblem, below Kiri-mon (Imperial arms). With central round hole. Trial strike!	–.–	–.–

			VF	XF

32 (53) 5 Sen (Cu–Ni) 1933–1938. Central round hole inside border with eight-curved design. Name of country, era and date as legend in Japanese characters. ℞ value in Japanese characters. Above the state emblem, below a stylized bird. The issue of 1938 was not put in circulation — **1.20** / **2.50**

32a 10 Sen (Ni) 1933. As type No. 32, but with changed value. Trial strike! — –.– / –.–

33 (57) 5 Sen (Al–Br) 1938–1940. Name of country, era and date as legend in Japanese characters. Left and right a flower. ℞ value in Japanese characters. Above the state emblem, below Kiri-mon (Imperial arms). With central round hole — **0.80** / **2.00**

34 (54) 10 Sen (Ni) 1933–1937. As type No. 31a, but with changed value and no trial strike — **1.20** / **2.50**

35 (58) 10 Sen (Al–Br) 1938–1940. Name of country, era and date as legend in Japanese characters. ℞ value in Japanese char-

acters. Above the state emblem, below
wavy decoration in front of ray-like
background. With central round hole

	VF	XF
	0.80	1.60

36 (59) 1 Sen (Al) 1941–1943. Name of country,
era and date as legend in Japanese
characters. ℞ Fujiyama (volcano,
12,390 ft., national shrine). Above
state emblem, below value in Japanese
characters. Weight 0.65 gram 0.60 1.10

36a (59a) 1 Sen (Al) 1943. As type No. 36, but
weight only 0.55 gram (thinner planch-
et) 0.80 1.60

37 (60) 5 Sen (Al) 1940, 1941. Peregrine (Falco
peregrinus callidus – Falconidae) (stylized) including name of country, era
and date in Japanese characters. ℞ in
the centre the state emblem. Above
and below value in Japanese characters.
Weight 1.2 gram 0.40 1.50

37a (60a) 5 Sen (Al) 1941, 1942. As type No. 37,
but weight only 1.0 gram (thinner
planchet) 0.80 2.00

37b (60b) 5 Sen (Al) 1943. As type No. 37, but
weight only 0.8 gram (thinner planchet) 0.90 2.00

38 (61) 10 Sen (Al) 1940, 1941. In the centre a
stylized flower, name of the country,
era and date as legend in Japanese
characters. ℞ in the centre the state
emblem. Above value in Japanese
characters, below leaf decoration.
Weight 1.5 gram 0.40 1.50

			VF	XF
38a (61a)	10	Sen (Al) 1941, 1942. As type No. 38, but weight 1.2 gram (thinner planchet)	0.60	2.00
38b (61b)	10	Sen (Al) 1943. As type No. 38, but weight 1.0 gram (thinner planchet)	0.60	2.00
39 (62)	1	Sen (Zn) 1944, 1945. Name of country, era and date in Japanese characters. ℞ in the centre the state emblem. Above and below value in Japanese characters	0.40	1.10
40 (63)	5	Sen (Zn) 1944. Name of country, era and date as legend in Japanese characters. ℞ right and left value in Japanese characters. Above the state emblem and below Kiri-mon (Imperial arms). With central round hole	0.80	1.60

			VF	XF
41 (64)	10	Sen (Zn) 1944. As type No. 40, but with changed value	0.80	1.80
41a	1	Sen (fiber) undated (1945?). In the centre a stylized flower. Name of country as legend in Japanese characters. ℞ Fujiyama including value in Japanese characters. This issue was not put into circulation	–.–	–.–
41b	5	Sen (fiber) 1945. In the centre a stylized flower (changed design in respect of No. 41a). Name of country and date as legend in Japanese characters. ℞ state emblem and value in Japanese characters. This issue was not put into circulation	–.–	–.–
41c	10	Sen (fiber) 1945. In the centre the Imperial arms (Kiri-mon). Name of country, era and date as legend in Japanese characters. In the centre the state emblem. This issue was not put into circulation	–.–	–.–

From No. 42 changed name of country!

| **42** (65) | 5 | Sen (Zn) 1945, 1946. In the centre the |

numeral '5'. Name of country, era and
date as legend in Japanese characters.
℞ in the centre a flying dove (Columba
livi adomestica – Columbidae). Above
the state emblem, below value in Japanese characters

			VF	XF
			1.00	2.00

43 (68) 10 Sen (Al) 1945, 1946. The numeral '10'
in front of a stylized flower. Name of
country, era and date as legend in
Japanese characters. ℞ rice panicles
(Oryza sativa – Gramineae). Above the
state emblem, below value in Japanese
characters. 22 mm dia. 0.80 2.00

43a 10 Sen (Bra) 1946. As type No. 43, but
diameter only 18.5 mm. This issue was
not put into circulation .... –.– –.–

44 (67) 50 Sen (Bra) 1946, 1947. In the centre the
value 50 SEN in front of a sheaf of
corn. Name of country, era and date
as legend in Japanese characters. ℞ in
the centre the Bird Phoenix. Above the
state emblem, below value in Japanese
characters. The issue of 1947 was not
put into circulation 1.00 5.00

As from No. 45 name of country changed once more.

45 (69) 50 Sen (Bra) 1947, 1948. In the centre the
numeral '50' in a circle. Name of coun-
try, era and date as legend in Japanese
characters. ℞ value in Japanese characters in an open wreath of blooms.
Above the state emblem 0.40 1.50

As from No. 46: method of reading the Japanese characters is from
left to right!

46 (70) 1 Yen (Bra) 1948–1950. Value 1 YEN in circle. Name of country, era and date as legend in Japanese characters. ℞ value in Japanese characters between branches of blooms

	VF	XF
	0.70	1.80

47 (74) 1 Yen (Al) 1955–. Sapling with branches and leaves. In the legend: name of country and value in Japanese characters. ℞ in the centre the numeral '1' in the circle. Below era and date in Japanese characters

| 0.10 | 0.15 |

48 (71) 5 Yen (Bra) 1948, 1949. Dove and plum blossoms in the circle. Name of country, era and date as legend in Japanese characters. ℞ Parliament Buildings in Tokyo in the circle. Ornamental border. Value in Japanese characters

| 0.60 | 4.80 |

49 (72) 5 Yen (Bra) 1949–1958. Name of country, era and date as legend in Japanese

characters around a central hole. ℞ above rice panicles (Agriculture). In the centre a cogwheel (Industry). Below stylized waves (Fisheries) and value in Japanese characters

	VF	XF
	0.40	2.00

50 (72a) 5 Yen (Bra) 1959–. As type No. 49, but with slightly changed design 　　　0.10　　0.15

50a　　10 Yen (German silver) 1950, 1951. Name of the country, era and date as legend in Japanese characters around a central round hole. ℞ above and below value in Japanese characters. Left and right leaf decorations. Both issues were not put into circulation 　　　–.–　　–.–

51 (73)　10 Yen (Br) 1951–1958. Phoenix Hall of the Byodo-in Temple in Uji near Kyoto. Name of the country and value as legend in Japanese characters. ℞ the numeral '10' including the era and date in Japanese characters in a wreath open at the top. Edge reeded 　　0.40　　1.00

51a (73a) 10 Yen (Br) 1959–. As type No. 51, but with plain edge 　　　　　　0.10　　0.20

52 (75) 50 Yen (Ni) 1955–1958. In the centre a
chrysanthemum (Chrysanthemum sp. –
Compositae). Name of country and
value in Japanese characters. ℞ in the
centre the numeral '50'. Era and date
as legend in Japanese characters

	VF	**XF**
	0.50	1.00

53 (76) 50 Yen (Ni) 1959–1966. Chrysanthemum,
surrounding a central round hole. Na-
me of country and value as legend in
Japanese characters. ℞ at the top the
numeral '50'. Underneath era and date
in Japanese characters

	0.80	2.50

54 (77) 100 Yen (Ag) 1957, 1958. In the centre the
Bird Phoenix. Name of country and
date as legend in Japanese characters.
℞ ornamental decoration in the form
of blooms. The value of 100 YEN as
well as era and date in Japanese characters as legend

	2.00	5.00

55 (78) 100 Yen (Ag) 1959–1966. Rice panicles. Name of country and value as legend in Japanese characters. ℞ in the centre the numeral '100'. Era and date as legend in Japanese characters

	VF	XF
	2.00	4.00

COMMEMORATIVE ISSUES (2)
FOR THE 18th OLYMPIC SUMMER GAMES 1964 IN TOKYO

56 (79) 100 Yen (Ag) 1964. Olympic rings in front of Olympic flame. Name of country and date as legend in Japanese characters. ℞ in the centre the numeral '100'. In the legend at the top TOKYO 1964 and underneath the era in Japanese characters as well as the numeral '39' (date)

	XF	Unc
	2.50	4.00

57 (80) 1000 Yen (Ag) 1964. Fujiyama between cherry blossoms. Name of country and value as legend in Japanese characters. ℞ the value of 1000 YEN above the Olympic rings. In the legend

above 1964 TOKYO and below the
era in Japanese characters as well as
the numeral '39' (date). To the right
and left cherry blossoms

	XF	Unc
	30.00	50.00

Forgeries are known to exist of No. 57.

58 (81) 50 Yen (Cu–Ni) 1967–. Above name of
country and below value in Japanese
characters. Right and left chrysanthe-
mums. ℞ above the numeral '50' and
the date in Arabic figures. With central
round hole   0.25   0.35

59 (82) 100 Yen (Cu–Ni) 1967–. In the centre
cherry blossoms. Name of country and
value as legend in Japanese characters.
℞ in the centre the numeral '100',
below the era in Japanese characters
as well as the date in Arabic figures   0.50   0.70

COMMEMORATIVE ISSUE FOR THE EXPO 70 FROM 15th MARCH TO 13th SEPTEMBER 1970 IN OSAKA

 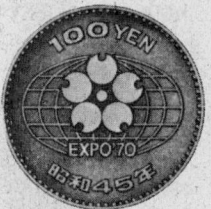

60 (83) 100 Yen (Cu–Ni) 1970. Fujiyama (after a
coloured woodcut by Hokusai [1760–
1849]). Above name of country and
below value in Japanese characters. ℞

symbol of the Expo 70. In the legend above 100 YEN and below the era in Japanese characters as well as the numeral '45' (date)

	XF	Unc
	1.50	4.00

COMMEMORATIVE ISSUE
FOR THE 11th OLYMPIC WINTER GAMES FROM
3rd TO 13th FEBRUARY 1972 IN SAPPORO

61 (84) 100 Yen (Cu–Ni) 1972. Olympic Flame and value in Japanese characters. As legend the name of country in Japanese characters as well as the place name: SAPPORO. ℞ the numeral '100' above Olympic rings. In the legend the date 1972, the era in Japanese characters and the numeral '47' (date). At right and left a stylized ice crystal

3.00   5.00

COMMEMORATIVE ISSUE FOR THE EXPO 75 IN OKINAWA

62 (85) 100 Yen (Cu–Ni) 1975

1.00   2.00

			VF	XF
63 (86)	100 Yen (Cu-Ni) 1976. Imperial Palace and Niju bridge		1.20	2.00

JAPANESE OCCUPIED TERRITORIES DURING WORLD WAR II
NETHERLANDS EAST INDIES

The dates on the coins correspond with the Japanese calendar.

			VF	XF
1 (22)	1	Sen (Al) 2603–2604 (1943–1944). Dragon. ℞ value	60.00	85.00
2	5	Sen (Zn) 2603 (1943)	–.–	–.–
3 (24)	10	Sen (Zn) 2603–2604 (1943–1944). Sculpture of a dancer. ℞ value	40.00	70.00

No. 2 is not recorded in official documents.

Kingdom in the Near East.
Capital: Amman.

10 Fils = 1 Piaster, 100 Fils = 1 Dirham, 1000 Fils = 1 Jordan Dinar

ABDALLAH IBN AL HUSSEIN 1946–1951

			VF	XF
1 (1)	1	Fil (Br) 1949. Value in circle, surrounded by ears of wheat with crown above. ℞ value and legend THE HASHEMITE KINGDOM OF THE JORDAN	2.00	4.00
2 (2)	1	Fils (Br) 1949. Same type as No. 1	0.40	0.60
3 (3)	5	Fils (Br) 1949. Same type as No. 1	0.50	0.70
4 (4)	10	Fils (Br) 1949. Same type as No. 1	0.60	0.80
5 (5)	20	Fils (Cu–Ni) 1949. Same type as No. 1	0.60	1.10
6 (6)	50	Fils (Cu–Ni) 1949. Same type as No. 1	1.20	2.50
7 (7)	100	Fils (Cu–Ni) 1949. Same type as No. 1	1.60	3.50

HUSSEIN II since 1952

			VF	XF
8 (8)	1	Fils (Br) 1955–1966. Value in circle, surrounded by ears of wheat with crown above. ℞ value and legend THE HASHEMITE KINGDOM OF JORDAN	0.20	0.40
9 (9)	5	Fils (Br) 1955–1967. Same type as No. 8	0.20	0.40
10 (10)	10	Fils (Br) 1955–1967. Same type as No. 8	0.30	0.60
11 (A10)	20	Fils (Cu–Ni) 1964, 1965. Same type as No. 8	3.00	5.00
12 (11)	50	Fils (Cu–Ni) 1955–1966. Same type as No. 8	0.80	1.50
13 (12)	100	Fils (Cu–Ni) 1955–1966. Same type as No. 8	1.20	2.50
14 (13)	1	Fils (Br) 1968–. Hussein II (*1935), head right. ℞ value in Arabic and English, dates, surrounded by olive branches between circles; name of country in English	0.15	0.30

				VF	XF

15 (14)   5   Fils (Br) 1968–. Same type as No. 14   0.10   0.20
16 (15)   10   Fils (Br) 1968–. Same type as No. 14   0.15   0.30
17 (16)   25   Fils (Cu–Ni) 1968–. Same type as No. 14   0.25   0.50
18 (17)   50   Fils (Cu–Ni) 1968–. Same type as No. 14   0.30   0.60
19 (18) 100   Fils (Cu–Ni) 1968–. Same type as No. 14   0.60   1.20

Proof

20   ½   Dinar (Ag) 1969. Hussein II (*1935).
          ℞ Al Harraneh (also Qasr el-Kharaneh),
          desert castle from the Omajjada Era,
          located 40 miles west of Amman   40.00

21   ¾   Dinar (Ag) 1969. ℞ birth place of
          Christ under the Church of Nativity,
          Bethlehem   45.00

22   1   Dinar (Ag) 1969. ℞ old part of Jerusa-
          lem with rock cathedral on Temple
          Hill (Haram esh-Sharif)   65.00

23   2   Dinars (Au) 1969. ℞ forum in Jerash
          (Roman Gerasa). Remainder of the
          oval-shaped main meeting place, sur-
          rounded by Ionic pillars from the time
          of Roman sovereignty, originated du-
          ring 1st–2nd century A.D.   85.00

24   5   Dinars (Au) 1969. ℞ treasury (Arabic:

			Proof

Khaznet Firaoun) in Petra. Memorial
temple cut from pink sandstone, probably dedicated to a Nabatean king. Nabatean architecture with Greek-Roman
influence in the style of Sassanidian
rock tombs 200.00

25	10 Dinars (Au) 1969. ℞ portrait of Pope Paul VI, visit to Jerusalem on January 5, 1964; Garden of Gethsemane with Mount of Olives and Church of Gethsemane (church of peace among nations, built in 1924)	400.00
26	25 Dinars (Au) 1969. ℞ Jerusalem: rock cathedral with chain cathedral, southern entrance to the temple square	1000.00

ISSUE FOR THE FAO COIN PLAN

			XF	**Unc**
27 (19)	250 Fils (Cu–Ni) 1969. Hussein II, head right. ℞ olive tree and dates in circle; name of country, value Quarter Dinar and letters FAO		3.00	5.00
28 (20)	250 Fils (Cu–Ni) 1970, 1974, 1978. Same type as No. 27, but without FAO		2.00	3.50

CONSERVATION COMMEMORATIVE (3)

			Unc	Proof
29 (23)	2½	Dinars (Ag) 1977	30.00	35.00
30 (24)	3	Dinars (Ag) 1977	45.00	60.00
31 (25)	50	Dinars (Au) 1977	600.00	750.00

25th ANNIVERSARY OF THE REIGN OF KING HUSSEIN II (2)

32 (21)	¼ Dinar (Cu-Ni) 1977. King's portrait in center of a crowned wing shield, dates, commemorative inscription. Rev. Petra Temple	5.00	
33 (22)	25 Dinars (Au) 1977		300.00
34 (31)	¼ Dinar (Cu-Ni) 1978	3.00	

1400th ANNIVERSARY OF ISLAM

35 (32)	½ Dinar (Cu-Ni) 1980	7.50

INTERNATIONAL YEAR OF THE CHILD (2)

36	3 Dinars (Ag) 1980	55.00
37	60 Dinars (Au) 1981	500.00

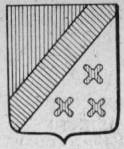

Katanga

When the Belgian Congo declared its independence on 30th June 1960, the province of Katanga detached herself from the Congo, and, under Moise Tshombé also became independent. A military intervention, supported by the UN, put à stop to this secession in January 1963. In 1972 the country was renamed Shaba.

Capital: Elisabethville (now: Lubumbashi).

100 Centimes = 1 Franc

			XF	Unc
1 (2)	1	Franc (Br) 1961. Bananas. (Musa x paradisiaca – Musaceae). ℞ Baluba cross or Katanga cross (in Katanga, rich in copper, such Katanga crosses some time possessed monetary character, e. g. also a bride price); value	1.00	2.00

			XF	Unc
2 (3)		5 Francs (Br) 1961. Same type as No. 1	1.50	3.00
3 (1)		5 Francs (Au) 1961. Same type as No. 1	280.00	320.00

Keeling-Cocos Islands

Group of coral islands located in the Indian Ocean 1,300 miles northwest of
Australia. The islands were placed under the administration of Australia in
1955 with the Australian headquarter on West Island. There the Australian
currency is accepted as legal tender only. The seat of the Clunies Ross family
and the currency area of the rupee is Home Island. The rupee coinage is on a
par with the Singapore Dollar. Seventeen different plastic "ivory" tokens and
modern plastic tokens of 1913 and 1968 on rupee scale are also known.

100 Cents = 1 Rupee

			XF	Unc
1	5	Cents (Br) 1977. Portrait of John Clunies Ross facing left. Rev. coconut tree, value, date	0.10	0.20
2	10	Cents (Br) 1977. Type as No. 1	0.15	0.30
3	25	Cents (Br) 1977. Type as No. 1	0.20	0.50
4	50	Cents (Br) 1977. Type as No. 1	0.40	0.80
5	1	Rupee (Cu-Ni) 1977. Type as No. 1	1.00	1.50
6	2	Rupees (Cu-Ni) 1977. Type as No. 1	2.00	3.00
7	5	Rupees (Cu-Ni) 1977. Type as No. 1	4.00	7.50

150th ANNIVERSARY KEELING-COCOS ISLANDS (3)

			XF	Proof
8	10	Rupees (Ag) 1977. Type as No. 1, but with commemorative inscription	9.00	10.00
9	25	Rupees (Ag) 1977. Type as No. 8	16.00	22.00
10	150	Rupees (Au) 1977. Type as No. 8	165.00	180.00

Area: 224,960 sq. mi. Population: 12,000,000.

Formerly a British Colony and Protectorate, Kenya became independent on 12th December 1963. Following the Constitution of December 12, 1964, the country was proclaimed a Republic, and became a member of the British Commonwealth.

Capital: Nairobi.

100 Cents = 1 Kenya Shilling, 20 Kenya Shillings = 1 Kenya Pound

			XF	Unc
1 (1)	5	Cents (Ni-Bra) 1966-1968. Jomo Kenyatta (1893-1978), sociologist and president. Rev. coat of arms	0.10	0.50
2 (2)	10	Cents (Ni–Bra) 1966–1968. Syme type as No. 1	0.15	0.50
3 (3)	25	Cents (Cu–Ni) 1966–1967. Same type as No. 1	0.25	0.50
4 (4)	50	Cents (Cu–Ni) 1966–1968. Same type as No. 1.	0.30	0.60
5 (5)	1	Shilling (Cu–Ni) 1966–1968. Same type as No. 1	0.40	0.80

6 (6)	2	Shillings (Cu–Ni) 1966–1968. Same type as No. 1	1.00	2.00

			Unc	Proof
7	100	Shillings (Au) 1966	160.00	180.00
8	250	Shillings (Au) 1966	400.00	450.00
9	500	Shillings (Au) 1966	800.00	1000.00

			XF	Unc
10 (7)	5	Cents (Ni-Bra) 1969–1978. Same type as No. 1, but on the obverse THE FIRST PRESIDENT OF KENYA – MZEE JOMO KENYATTA	0.10	0.20

			XF	Unc
11 (8)	10	Cents (Ni-Bra) 1969–1978. Same type as No. 10	0.10	0.25
12 (9)	25	Cents (Cu-Ni) 1969–1973. Same type as No. 10	0.25	0.50
13 (10)	50	Cents (Cu-Ni) 1969–1977. Same type as No. 10	0.30	0.60
14 (11)	1	Shilling (Cu-Ni) 1969–1975. Same type as No. 10	0.40	0.70
15 (12)	2	Shillings (Cu-Ni) 1969–1973. Same type as No. 10	0.90	1.30

COMMEMORATIVE ISSUE FOR THE 10th ANNIVERSARY OF INDEPENDENCE

			XF	Unc
16 (13)	5	Shillings (Al-Br) 1973. Type as No. 15, but commemorative inscription	6.00	8.00
17 (14)	5	Cents (Ni-Bra) 1980. President Moi		0.25
18 (17)	50	Cents (Cu-Ni) 1980. Type as No. 17		0.50
19 (18)	1	Shilling (Cu-Ni) 1980. Type as No. 17		3.00

Kiribati

Area: 290 sq. mi. Population: 50,000.
Kiribati (formerly a part of the Gilbert and Ellice Islands) attained independence on July 12, 1979.
Capital: Bairiki.

100 Cents = 1 Dollar

		Unc	Proof
1 (1)	1 Cent (Br) 1979	0.20	3.00
2 (2)	2 Cents (Br) 1979	0.20	3.00

3 (3)	5 Cents (Cu-Ni) 1979	0.40	4.00
4 (4)	10 Cents (Cu-Ni) 1979	0.60	5.00

		Unc	Proof
5 (5)	20 Cents (Cu-Ni) 1979	1.00	6.00

		Unc	Proof
6 (6)	50 Cents (Cu-Ni) 1979	1.60	6.00
7 (7)	1 Dollar (Cu-Ni) 1979	3.00	8.00

8 (8)	5 Dollars (Ag) 1979	20.00	36.00
9 (9)	150 Dollars (Au) 1979		350.00

WEDDING OF PRINCE CHARLES AND LADY DIANA

10	5 Dollars 1981:		
	b) (Ag)		55.00
	b) (Cu-Ni)	9.00	

Area: 85,266 sq. mi. Population: 40,453,000.

In 668 the various separate empires were united by Silla, located in the South East. During the years between 1640 and 1885 Korea cut herself off the remaining world, but soon China, Japan, and Russia gained a continuously growing influence in Korea. Finally the territory became a Japanese Protectorate in 1905, but from 1910 to 1945 it held the position of Japanese Province.

Capital: Seoul.

100 Fun = 1 Yang, since 1912: 100 Chon = 1 Won

KUANG-MU ERA 1897–1907

			VF	XF
1 (A10)	5	Fun (Cu) 1898–1902. Dragon in dotted circle. ℞ value in wreath	3.00	5.00
2 (B10)	¼	Yang (Cu–Ni) 1897–1901	2.50	4.00
3 (C10)	1	Yang (Ag) 1898	11.00	15.00

NEW CURRENCY: 100 Chon = 1 Won

4 (10)	1	Chon (Br) 1902. Heraldic eagle in dotted circle	750.00	1000.00
5 (11)	5	Chon (Cu–Ni) 1902. Same type as No. 4	750.00	1000.00
6 (12)	½	Won (Ag) 1901. Same type as No. 4	800.00	1200.00
7	½	Dollar (Ag) 1899. Same type as No. 4. Not circulated	–.–	–.–
8	10	Won (Cu) 1901, 1903. Same type as No. 4. Pattern	–.–	–.–
9	20	Won (Cu) 1900, 1902. Same type as No. 4. Pattern	–.–	–.–

Nos. 4–9 are so-called "Russian" issues.

10 (13)	½	Chon (Br) 1906. Phoenix; diameter: 22 mm	3.50	4.50
11 (14)	1	Chon (Br) 1905–1906. Phoenix; diameter: 28 mm	2.50	4.00
12 (B22)	1	Chon (Br) 1907. Same type as No. 11; diameter: 23.5 mm	2.50	4.00

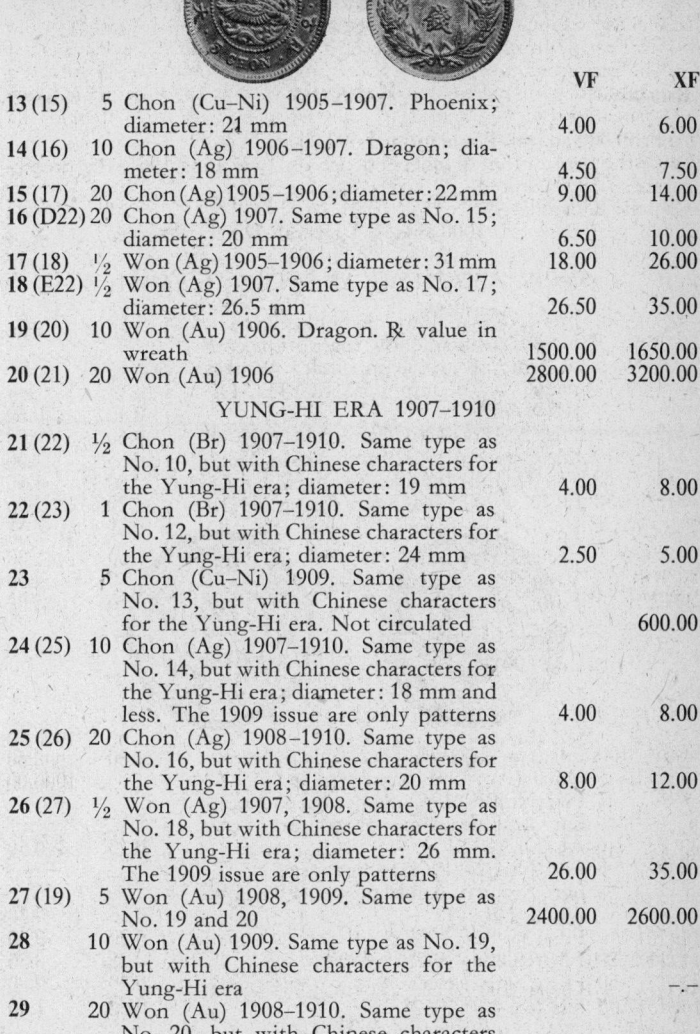

				VF	**XF**
13 (15)	5	Chon (Cu–Ni) 1905–1907. Phoenix; diameter: 21 mm		4.00	6.00
14 (16)	10	Chon (Ag) 1906–1907. Dragon; diameter: 18 mm		4.50	7.50
15 (17)	20	Chon (Ag) 1905–1906; diameter: 22 mm		9.00	14.00
16 (D22)	20	Chon (Ag) 1907. Same type as No. 15; diameter: 20 mm		6.50	10.00
17 (18)	½	Won (Ag) 1905–1906; diameter: 31 mm		18.00	26.00
18 (E22)	½	Won (Ag) 1907. Same type as No. 17; diameter: 26.5 mm		26.50	35.00
19 (20)	10	Won (Au) 1906. Dragon. ℞ value in wreath		1500.00	1650.00
20 (21)	20	Won (Au) 1906		2800.00	3200.00

YUNG-HI ERA 1907–1910

				VF	**XF**
21 (22)	½	Chon (Br) 1907–1910. Same type as No. 10, but with Chinese characters for the Yung-Hi era; diameter: 19 mm		4.00	8.00
22 (23)	1	Chon (Br) 1907–1910. Same type as No. 12, but with Chinese characters for the Yung-Hi era; diameter: 24 mm		2.50	5.00
23	5	Chon (Cu–Ni) 1909. Same type as No. 13, but with Chinese characters for the Yung-Hi era. Not circulated			600.00
24 (25)	10	Chon (Ag) 1907–1910. Same type as No. 14, but with Chinese characters for the Yung-Hi era; diameter: 18 mm and less. The 1909 issue are only patterns		4.00	8.00
25 (26)	20	Chon (Ag) 1908–1910. Same type as No. 16, but with Chinese characters for the Yung-Hi era; diameter: 20 mm		8.00	12.00
26 (27)	½	Won (Ag) 1907, 1908. Same type as No. 18, but with Chinese characters for the Yung-Hi era; diameter: 26 mm. The 1909 issue are only patterns		26.00	35.00
27 (19)	5	Won (Au) 1908, 1909. Same type as No. 19 and 20		2400.00	2600.00
28	10	Won (Au) 1909. Same type as No. 19, but with Chinese characters for the Yung-Hi era			–.–
29	20	Won (Au) 1908–1910. Same type as No. 20, but with Chinese characters for the Yung-Hi era			–.–

For further issues see *North Korea* or *South Korea*.

Area: 5,000 sq. mi. Population: 1,400,000.
With the declaration of independence on 19th June 1961, the protectorate of 1899 expired.
Capital: Kuwait.

1000 Fils = 1 Kuwait Dinar

SHEIK ABDULLAH AL-SALIM AL SABAH

			XF	Unc
1 (1)	1	Fils (Ni–Bra) 1961. Sambuke = two-masted Arabian dhow (part of the coat of arms). ℞ value in circle, Arabian name of country EMIRATE OF KUWAIT	0.40	0.60
2 (2)	5	Fils (Ni–Bra) 1961. Same type as No. 1	0.60	0.90
3 (3)	10	Fils (Ni–Bra) 1961. Same type as No. 1	0.65	1.00
4 (4)	20	Fils (Cu–Ni) 1961. Same type as No. 1	0.80	1.50
5 (5)	50	Fils (Cu–Ni) 1961. Same type as No. 1	1.20	2.00

6 (6)	100	Fils (Cu–Ni) 1961. Same type as No. 1	1.80	2.50
7 (7)	5	Dinar (Au) 1961. Same type as No. 1		1000.00
8 (8)	1	Fils (Ni–Bra) 1962. Same type as No. 1, but Arabian name of country now AL-KUWAIT	0.25	0.50
9 (9)	5	Fils (Ni–Bra) 1962. Same type as No. 2, but Arabian name of country now AL-KUWAIT	0.15	0.30
10 (10)	10	Fils (Ni–Bra) 1962	0.20	0.40
11 (11)	20	Fils (Cu–Ni) 1962	0.25	0.50
12 (12)	50	Fils (Cu–Ni) 1962	0.40	0.80
13 (13)	100	Fils (Cu–Ni) 1962	0.75	1.50

15th ANNIVERSARY OF INDEPENDENCE

			Unc	Proof
14 (14)	2	Dinars (Ag) 1976	50.00	65.00

			Proof
	15th CENTURY OF HEGIRA		
15	5 Dinars (Ag) 1981		70.00
	20th ANNIVERSARY OF INDEPENDENCE		
16	5 Dinars (Ag) 1981		70.00

Laos

Area: 91,428 sq. mi. Population: 3,000,000.
On 7th December 1959, this state, formerly under French protection, became an independent kingdom.
Capital: Vientiane.

100 Centimes = 1 Kip

			XF	Unc
1 (1)	10	Centimes (Al–Mg) 1952. Woman from Laos. ℞ value (center hole)	0.30	0.50
2 (2)	20	Centimes (Al–Mg) 1952. (Center hole)	0.30	0.60
3 (3)	50	Centimes (Al–Mg) 1952. Book of constitution (center hole)	0.80	1.60

COMMEMORATIVE ISSUES (9) FOR THE CORONATION OF HIS MAJESTY THE KING OF LAOS OF NOVEMBER 13, 1971

			Proof
4	1000	Kip (Ag) 1971. Boromo Setha Khatia Suria Vongsa Phra Maha Sri Savang Vatthana (*1907), King since 1959. ℞ state emblem, name of country, value	12.00
5	2500	Kip (Ag) 1971. Same type as No. 4	20.00

6	4000	Kip (Au) 1971. Same type as No. 4	75.00
7	5000	Kip (Ag) 1971. Same type as No. 4	60.00
8	8000	Kip (Au) 1971. Same type as No. 4	150.00
9	10000	Kip (Au) 1971. Same type as No. 4	100.00
10	20000	Kip (Au) 1971. Same type as No. 4	350.00
11	40000	Kip (Au) 1971. Same type as No. 4	750.00
12	80000	Kip (Au) 1971. Same type as No. 4	1500.00
13	5000	Kip (Ag) 1975. His Majesty the King of Laos and the royal coat of arms. ℞ Wat Phra Kio Museum, Vientiane	15.00

			Proof
14	5000	Kip (Ag) 1975. ℞ young Laotian girl	15.00
15	10000	Kip (Ag) 1975. ℞ Wat Xieng-Thong Sanctuaty (1560) Luang Prabang	30.00
16	50000	Kip (Au) 1975. ℞ That Luang Sanctuary (XVI Century) Vientiane	150.00
17	50000	Kip (Au) 1975. ℞ young Laotian girl	150.00

18	100000	Kip (Au) 1975. ℞ statue of Laotian Buddha	280.00

NEW MONETARY SYSTEM: 100 Att = 1 Kip

			XF	Unc
19 (4)	10	Att (Al) 1980	0.30	0.50
20 (5)	20	Att (Al) 1980	0.50	0.80
21 (6)	50	Att (Al) 1980	1.10	1.50

Lettland # Latvia **Lettonie**

Latvija

Area: 24,600 sq. mi. Population: 2,000,000 (1939).

In the 18th century Latvia and the Baltic Provinces were annexed by Russia. On 18th November 1918, the independent Democratic Republic was proclaimed, and in June of 1940 occupied by Russian troops. With occasional interruptions, Latvia has since been a member state of the Soviet Union.

Capital: Riga.

		100 Santimu = 1 Lats	VF	XF
1 (1)	1	Santims (Br) 1922–1935. Coat of arms. ℞ value	2.50	4.00
2 (2)	2	Santimi (Br) 1922–1932	2.50	4.00
3 (3)	5	Santimi (Br) 1922	3.00	5.00
4 (4)	10	Santimu (Ni) 1922	2.50	4.00
5 (5)	20	Santimu (Ni) 1922	3.50	6.00
6 (6)	50	Santimu (Ni) 1922. Coat of arms. ℞ Latvija, symbol of the Latvian Republic, at the oar of a boat. Value	6.00	11.00
7 (7)	1	Lats (Ag) 1924. Coat of arms. ℞ value in wreath	3.50	6.50
8 (8)	2	Lati (Ag) 1925–1926	5.00	7.50

			VF	XF
9 (9)	5	Lati (Ag) 1929–1932. Head of Latvija. ℞ coat of arms and value	11.00	15.00
10 (10)	1	Santims (Br) 1937–1939. Coat of arms. ℞ value, flanked by ears of wheat	4.00	6.00
11 (11)	2	Santimi (Br)		
		a) 1937, diameter: 19 mm	60.00	100.00
		b) 1938–1939, diameter: 19.5 mm	4.00	6.00

Libanon   # Lebanon   **Liban**

Area: 3,400 sq. mi. Population: 2,900,000.
Until 1918 this South West Asian country, located at the eastern end of the Mediterranean, was part of the Turkish Empire. Constituting a French Mandate until 1924, Lebanon and Syria were governed separately between 1924 and 1941. In 1927 the French Confederation created the Republic of Lebanon. The independence was declared on November 26, 1941, the mandatory privileges however, were not transferred to the Lebanese government until 1944. The last occupational forces left the country in 1946.
Capital: Beirut.

100 Piastres = 1 Lebanese Pound (Livre)

ÉTAT DU GRAND LIBAN

			VF	XF
1 (1)	2	Piastres (Al–Br) 1924. Lebanon cedar (Cedrus libani - Pinaceae). ℞ value	2.00	4.00
2 (2)	5	Piastres (Al–Br) 1924	1.60	3.00
3 (3)	2	Piastres (Al–Br) 1925. Lebanon cedar. ℞ galley	2.50	5.00
4 (4)	5	Piastres (Al–Br) 1925–1940	1.20	2.50
5 (6)	1	Piastre (Cu-Ni) 1925–1936. Legend. ℞ lion heads, value (center hole)	0.80	1.60

REPUBLIQUE LIBANAISE

			VF	XF
6 (5)	½	Piastre (Cu-Ni) 1934–1936	1.20	2.00
7 (8)	10	Piastres(Ag) 1929. Lebanon cedar, new name of country. ℞ cornucopias	6.00	9.00
8 (9)	25	Piastres (Ag) 1929–1936	6.50	10.00
9 (10)	50	Piastres (Ag) 1929–1937	8.00	12.00
10 (5a)	½	Piastre (Sn) 1940–1941. Same type as No. 6	1.20	2.50
11 (6a)	1	Piastre (Sn) 1940–1941. Same type as No. 5	2.00	4.00
12 (7)	2½	Piastres (Al–Br) 1940. Legend. ℞ value (center hole)	0.80	1.60
13 (11)	½	Piastre (Bra) without date (1941–1945). Legend. ℞ value, name of country LIBAN (center hole)	2.00	3.50
14 (12)	1	Piastre (Bra) without date (1941–1945)	2.00	3.50
15 (13)	2½	Piastres (Al) without date (1941–1945)	2.00	3.50
16 (14)	5	Piastres (Al) 1952. Lebanon cedar. ℞ galley	2.00	4.00

			VF	XF
17 (15)	10	Piastres (Al) 1952	2.50	5.00

			VF	XF
18 (16)	25	Piastres (Al-Br) 1952, 1961	1.20	2.00
19 (17)	50	Piastres (Ag) 1952	4.00	6.00
20 (18)	1	Piastre (Al-Br) 1955. Legend. R value (center hole)	0.10	0.25
21 (19)	2½	Piastres (Al-Br) 1955. Legend. R value (center hole)	0.30	0.50
22 (20)	5	Piastres (Al) 1954. R value	0.35	0.50
23 (21)	10	Piastres (Al-Br) 1955. Galley. R Lebanon cedar, value	0.60	1.20
24 (22)	5	Piastres (Al-Br) 1955–1961. Lebanon cedar. R lion head, value	0.20	0.35
25 (23)	10	Piastres (Al-Br) 1955. Lebanon cedar. R galley	0.60	1.10
26 (24)	10	Piastres (Cu-Ni) 1961. Lebanon cedar. R galley	0.35	0.50

ISSUE FOR THE FAO COIN PLAN

			VF	XF
27 (29)	1	Livre = Pound (Ni) 1968. Lebanon cedar. R fruit typical of the country, value	1.20	2.00
28 (25)	5	Piastres (Al–Br) 1968–1972. Lebanon cedar, new legend: BANQUE DU LIBAN. R value in laurel wreath	0.12	0.20

			VF	XF
29 (26)	10	Piastres (Al–Br) 1968–1972. Same type as No. 28	0.20	0.30
30 (27)	25	Piastres (Al–Br) 1968–1972. Same type as No. 28	0.40	0.60

			VF	XF
31 (28)	50	Piastres (Ni) 1968–1971, 1975, 1978. Type similar to Nos. 28–30	0.50	1.00
32 (30)	1	Livre (Ni) 1975, 1977. Lebanon cedar, date. Rev. value in laurel wreath	0.90	1.50

ISSUE FOR THE FAO COIN PLAN

			VF	XF
33 (31)	5	Livres (Ni) 1977	2.50	4.00

13th OLYMPIC WINTER GAMES IN LAKE PLACID (3)

			Unc	Proof
34 (32)	1	Livre (Cu-Ni) 1980		12.00
35 (33)	10	Livres (Ag) 1980		35.00
36 (34)	400	Livres (Au) 1980		450.00

Lesotho

Area: 11,716 sq. mi. Population: 1,000,000.
The former Basutoland, an enclave in the Eastern Republic of South Africa, was a British High Commission Territory, until it received its independence on 4th October, 1966. Adopting the name of Lesotho, the kingdom became a member of the British Commonwealth.
Capital: Maseru.

100 Cents = 1 Rand, 100 Licente = 1 Maloti

Besides the South African Rand, the Licente coins are legal tender.

			Proof
1	5	Licente (Ag) 1966	8.00
2	10	Licente (Ag) 1966	8.00
3	20	Licente (Ag) 1966	10.00

4	50	Licente (Ag) 1966. Moshoeshoe I (deceased 1870). King and founder of the Basuto Nation. Rev. coat of arms	22.00
5	1	Maloti (Au) 1966	120.00
6	2	Maloti (Au) 1966	200.00
7	4	Maloti (Au) 1966	350.00

ISSUES (5) FOR THE FAO COIN PLAN

8	1	Maloti (Au) 1969	80.00
9	2	Maloti (Au) 1969	125.00

			Unc	Proof
10	4	Maloti (Au) 1969		250.00
11	10	Maloti (Au) 1969		600.00
12	20	Maloti (Au) 1969		1200.00

10th ANNIVERSARY OF INDEPENDENCE (2)

			Unc	Proof
13	10	Maloti (Ag) 1976. King Moshoeshoe II in military uniform. Rev. native woman, wearing a traditional wide hat and robe	22.00	28.00
14	100	Maloti (Au) 1976	350.00	400.00

10th ANNIVERSARY OF INDEPENDENCE AND 45th ANNIVERSARY OF THE COMMONWEALTH

			Unc	Proof
15	50	Maloti (Au) 1976. Coat of arms. Rev. Queen Elizabeth II, value	150.00	180.00

			XF	Unc
16 (1)	1	Sente (Ni-Bra) 1979–	0.15	0.20
17 (2)	2	Lisente (Ni-Bra) 1979–	0.15	0.20
18 (3)	5	Lisente (Ni-Bra) 1979–	0.20	0.40
19 (4)	10	Lisente (Cu-Ni) 1979–	0.40	0.80
20 (5)	25	Lisente (Cu-Ni) 1979–	0.50	1.00
21 (6)	50	Lisente (Cu-Ni) 1979–	0.60	1.20
22 (7)	1	Loti (Cu-Ni) 1979–	1.00	1.80

			Unc	Proof
23 (8)	10	Maloti (Ag) 1979–1980	25.00	35.00

INTERNATIONAL YEAR OF THE CHILD (2)

24 (9)	15	Maloti (Ag) 1979	40.00	50.00
25 (10)	250	Maloti (Au) 1979	900.00	1000.00

110th ANNIVERSARY OF THE DEATH OF KING MOSHOESHOE I (3)

26 (11)	50	Maloti (Ag) 1980	60.00	80.00
27 (12)	250	Maloti (Au) 1980	400.00	450.00
28 (13)	500	Maloti (Au) 1980	700.00	800.00

Liberia

Area: 43,000 sq. mi. Population: 1,900,000.
Since 1822 small settlements grew up along the African West Coast, housing former United States slaves, liberated by the American Colonization Society, and other organizations. Following the announcement of the constitution, the actual state was founded in 1847.
Capital: Monrovia.

100 Cents = 1 Liberian Dollar

			VF	XF
1 (4)	1 Cent (Br) 1896–1906. Head of liberty, left. ℞ palm tree (Elaeis guineensis – Palmae), rising sun, value:			
	a) 1896		10.00	20.00
	b) 1906		15.00	30.00
2 (5)	2 Cents (Br) 1896–1906		5.00	10.00
3 (6)	10 Cents (Ag) 1896–1906. ℞ value in wreath		8.00	15.00
4 (7)	25 Cents (Ag) 1896–1906		10.00	25.00

		VF	XF
5 (8)	50 Cents (Ag) 1896–1906	18.00	40.00

			VF	**XF**
6 (9)	½ Cent. African elephant (Loxodonta africana – Elephantidae). ℞ palm tree			
	a) (Bra) 1937		0.40	0.80
	b) (Cu–Ni) 1941		0.30	0.60
7 (10)	1 Cent. Same type as No. 6			
	a) (Bra) 1937		1.20	2.40
	b) (Cu–Ni) 1941		2.00	5.00
8 (11)	2 Cents. Same type as No. 6			
	a) (Bra) 1937		1.60	3.20
	b) (Cu–Ni) 1941		1.00	2.00
9 (12)	1 Cent (Br) 1960–. African elephant. ℞ palm tree, sailing vessel		0.10	0.20

10 (13)	5 Cents (Cu–Ni) 1960–. Same type as No. 9		0.25	0.50
11 (14)	10 Cents. Liberian woman. ℞ value in wreath			
	a) (Ag) 1960–1961		1.00	2.00
	b) (Cu–Ni) 1966–		0.30	0.50
12 (15)	25 Cents. Same type as No. 11			
	a) (Ag) 1960–1961		3.00	4.00
	b) (Cu–Ni) 1966–		0.40	0.80

13 (16)	50 Cents. Same type as No. 11			
	a) (Ag) 1960–1961		6.00	10.00
	b) (Cu–Ni) 1966–		0.80	1.25

		VF	XF
14 (17)	1 Dollar. Same type as No. 11		
	a) (Ag) 1961–1962	10.00	15.00
	b) (Cu–Ni) 1966–	1.50	3.00

		Unc	Proof
15 (27)	20 Dollars (Au) 1964. William Jacanarat Shadrach Tubman (1895–1971), head of government from 1943 to 1971. ℞ coat of arms		
	a) mintmark B below date	350.00	
	b) mintmark L above date		500.00

70th ANNIVERSARY OF THE BIRTH OF PRESIDENT TUBMAN (3)

16	12 Dollars (Au) 1965. Bust of President Tubman. Rev. coat of arms and value		225.00
17	25 Dollars (Au) 1965. Head of President Tubman. Rev. Providence Island		450.00
18	30 Dollars (Au) 1965. Type as No. 16		600.00

COMMEMORATIVE ISSUES (4)
FOR THE INAUGURATION INTO OFFICE
OF PRESIDENT TOLBERT ON 3rd JAN. 1972

19	2½ Dollars (Au) 1972. The Capitol in Monrovia	100.00
20	5 Dollars (Au) 1972. Sailing boat, motif from the national coat of arms and as legend the national motto	200.00
21	10 Dollars (Au) 1972. Head of Freedom with crown of rays	400.00
22	20 Dollars (Au) 1972. President Tolbert, head facing left. Factual legend. ℞ national coat of arms, name of country, value	800.00

SESQUICENTENNIAL OF FOUNDING OF LIBERIA

23 (A38)	25 Dollars (Au) 1972	600.00

			Unc	Proof
24 (18)	5	Dollars (Ag) 1973–. African elephant and national coat of arms as with No. 15	20.00	30.00

ISSUE FOR THE FAO COIN PLAN

			XF	Unc
25 (38)	25	Cents (Cu-Ni) 1976–1979. Portrait of President Tolbert. Rev. a woman carrying a basket of food stuffs on her head	1.00	2.00
26 (39)	50	Cents (Cu-Ni) 1976–1979. Rev. coat of arms, value, date		3.00
27 (40)	1	Dollar (Cu-Ni) 1976–1979. Rev. map of Liberia		5.00

				Proof
28 (35)	100	Dollars (Au) 1976		300.00
29 (36)	200	Dollars (Au) 1976		600.00
30 (37)	400	Dollars (Au) 1976		1200.00
31 (41)	100	Dollars (Au) 1977	200.00	300.00

ORGANIZATION OF AFRICAN UNITY SUMMIT CONFERENCE IN MONROVIA

32 (42)	100	Dollars (Au) 1979		200.00

Libyen **Libya** Libye

Area: 674,358 sq. mi. Population: 2,300,000.
Formerly under Turkish sovereignty, this North African country came
to be governed by Italy in 1911. In 1934, following several military
campaigns against the Senussi (1914–1932), Italy succeeded in uniting
Cyrenaica and Tripolitania with Fezzan, thus creating the Colony of
Libya. On October 7, 1951, the territory became an independent king-
dom, and on September 1, 1969 the Libyan Arab Republic.
Capital: Tripolis, future capital: Beida.

10 Millièmes= 1 Piastre, 100 Piastres = 1 £;
since 28th August 1971: 1000 Dirham = 1 Libyan Dinar

IDRIS I 1951–1969

			VF	XF
1 (1)	1 Millième (Br) 1952. Idris I (*1890), head right. Value in wreath, with crown above		0.20	0.50
2 (2)	2 Millièmes (Br) 1952		0.20	0.50
3 (3)	5 Millièmes (Br) 1952		0.30	0.70
4 (4)	1 Piastre (Cu–Ni) 1952		0.50	1.00
5 (5)	2 Piastres (Cu–Ni) 1952		0.60	1.40
6 (6)	1 Millième (Ni–Bra) 1965. Coat of arms. ℞ value in wreath		0.10	0.30
7 (7)	5 Millièmes (Ni–Bra) 1965 (scalloped)		0.20	0.60
8 (8)	10 Millièmes (Cu–Ni) 1965		0.25	0.70
9 (9)	20 Millièmes (Cu–Ni) 1965		0.50	1.50
10 (10)	50 Millièmes (Cu–Ni) 1965 (scalloped)		0.60	2.00

11 (11)	100 Millièmes (Cu–Ni) 1965		0.80	2.50

NEW CURRENCY: 1000 Dirham = 1 Libyan Dinar

			XF	Unc
12 (12)	1	Dirham (Brass-clad steel) 1975. Coat of arms, date. Rev. value within ornament	3.00	5.00
13 (13)	5	Dirhams (Brass-clad steel) 1975. Type as No. 12	2.50	4.00
14 (14)	10	Dirhams (Cu-Ni-clad steel) 1975. Type as No. 12	2.00	3.50
15 (15)	20	Dirhams (Cu-Ni-clad steel) 1975. Type as No. 12	3.00	6.00
16 (16)	50	Dirhams (Cu-Ni) 1975. Type as No. 12 (scalloped)	4.00	6.50
17 (17)	100	Dirhams (Cu-Ni) 1975. Type as No. 12	4.50	7.00

SOCIALIST LIBYAN ARAB PEOPLE'S REPUBLIC since 1977

18	1	Dirham (Brass-clad steel) 1979	–.–	–.–
19	5	Dirhams (Brass-clad steel) 1979	–.–	–.–
20	10	Dirhams (Brass-clad steel) 1979	–.–	–.–
21	20	Dirhams (Brass-clad steel) 1979	–.–	–.–
22	50	Dirhams (Cu-Ni) 1979	–.–	–.–
23	100	Dirhams (Cu-Ni) 1979	–.–	–.–

Area: 61 sq. mi. Population: 23,000.
On January 23, 1719, Karl VI combined the immediate states of the empire, Schellenberg, and Vaduz, thus creating the principality of Liechtenstein. A member of the German Confederation (Deutscher Bund) from 1815 to 1866, Liechtenstein formed a customs and tax district with the Austrian Vorarlberg in 1852 (to 1919), and finally entered into the Customs and Monetary Union of Switzerland in 1924.
Capital: Vaduz.

150 Kreuzer = 1½ Gulden = 1 Vereinstaler (Konventionstaler)
100 Heller = 1 Krone; since 1924: 100 Rappen = 1 Franken

JOHANN II 1858–1929

			VF	XF
1 (1)	1	Vereinstaler (Ag) 1862. Johann II, head right. ℞ mantled coat of arms with crown	1050.00	1700.00
		Modern special issue in gold, with mint mark "M"		450.00
2 (2)	1	Krone (Ag) 1900–1915	12.00	20.00
3 (3)	2	Kronen (Ag) 1912–1915	25.00	40.00

4 (4)	5	Kronen (Ag) 1900–1915	170.00	260.00
5 (5)	10	Kronen (Au) 1900. Johann II (1840–1929), head left. ℞ coat of arms	2600.00	3000.00

			VF	XF
6 (6)	20	Kronen (Au) 1898. Same type as No. 5	2500.00	3200.00
7 (7)	½	Franken (Ag) 1924	45.00	65.00
8 (8)	1	Franken (Ag) 1924	30.00	42.00
9 (9)	2	Franken (Ag) 1924	45.00	65.00
10 (10)	5	Franken (Ag) 1924	270.00	380.00

FRANZ I 1929–1938

11 (11)	10	Franken (Au) 1930. Franz I (1853–1938), head right. ℞ coat of arms	800.00	1000.00
12 (12)	20	Franken (Au) 1930	850.00	1100.00

FRANZ JOSEPH II since 1938

13 (13)	10	Franken (Au) 1946. Franz Joseph II (*1906), head left. ℞ coat of arms	150.00	175.00
14 (14)	20	Franken (Au) 1946	180.00	250.00
15 (15)	25	Franken (Au) 1956. Franz Joseph II and Princess Georgina (Gina) of Wilczek (*1921). ℞ coat of arms	170.00	260.00
16 (16)	50	Franken (Au) 1956. Same type as No. 15	250.00	285.00

17 (17)	100	Franken (Au) 1952. Same type as No. 15	1800.00	2400.00

COMMEMORATIVE ISSUES (2) FOR THE CENTENNIAL OF THE BANK OF LIECHTENSTEIN

18 (18)	25	Franken (Au) 1961	–.–	–.–
19 (19)	50	Franken (Au) 1961	–.–	–.–

Nos. 18 and 19 have not been in circulation yet.

Litauen   # Lithuania   **Lithuanie**
Lietuva

Area: 25,200 sq. mi. Population: 2,550,000 (1938).

Having succeeded in uniting the Lithuanian tribes of the upper Memel and Duna, Grand Duke Gedimin created the large Lithuanian Empire during the 14th century. In 1386 Jagaila accepted as Jagiello the Polish royal dignity, thus creating a basis for unity throughout the empire. Following the dismemberment of Poland (1772, 1793, 1795), the entire Lithuanian territory fell to Russia. The independent Republic was proclaimed on November 2, 1918. The Soviet Republic was created on July 21, 1940. Since August 3rd of that year, Lithuania has been, with occasional interruptions, a member state of the Soviet Union.

Capital: Kaunas (Kovno), 1920–1940, provisional capital instead of Vilna.

100 Centu = 1 Litas

		VF	XF
1 (1)	1 Centas (Al–Br) 1925. Rider on horseback, "Vytis", principal design of the state of arms. ℞ value	6.00	12.00
2 (2)	5 Centai (Al–Br) 1925	3.50	6.00

3 (3)	10 Centu (Al–Br) 1925	4.00	6.50
4 (4)	20 Centu (Al–Br) 1925	4.50	7.50
5 (5)	50 Centu (Al–Br) 1925	6.50	11.50
6 (6)	1 Litas (Ag) 1925	6.00	9.00
7 (7)	2 Litu (Ag) 1925	8.00	12.00
8 (8)	5 Litai (Ag) 1925	16.00	36.00
9 (9)	1 Centas (Br) 1936	2.50	5.00

10 (10)	2 Centai (Br) 1936	5.00	10.50

		VF	XF
11 (11)	5 Centai (Br) 1936	4.50	7.50
12 (12)	5 Litai (Ag) 1936. Dr. Jonas Basanavicius (1851–1927), doctor of medicine, politician and co-founder of "Auštra", the first newspaper appearing in Lithuanian, in 1883. ℞ rider on horse-back, "Vytis"	7.50	12.00

13 (13)	10 Litu (Ag) 1936. Witold, also Witowt or Vytautas Didysis (c. 1350–1430), Grand Duke of Lithuania 1392–1430. ℞ rider on horse-back, "Vytis"	16.00	26.00

COMMEMORATIVE COIN FOR
THE 20th ANNIVERSARY OF THE REPUBLIC

14 (14)	10 Litu (Ag) 1938. "The three pillars of Grand Duke Gediminas", also found on Lithuanian seals of the 15th century. Name of country, anniversary numerals, commemorative legend. ℞ Anton Smetona (1874 to 1944), President of Lithuania 1919–1921 and 1926–1940	38.00	50.00

Luxemburg   # Luxembourg   **Luxembourg**

Letzeburg

Area: 998 sq. mi. Population: 340,000.

The Duchy of Luxembourg was declared a Grand Duchy in 1815 by a resolution of the Congress of Vienna and in personal union with the Dutch crown and with membership of the Deutsche Bund (German Confederation). At the London Conference of 1839 the great powers decided that the Walloon part as well as a part of the German-speaking territories be detached from Luxembourg. This territorial section was attached to the Belgian Kingdom as "Province de Luxembourg". From 1839 Luxembourg exists as a recognized independent state in its present form.

In 1842 Luxembourg joined the German Customs Union and thus also accepted the responsibilities of the Dresden Monetary Convention of 1838. Upon the restoration of the Customs Union in 1847, Luxembourg left the Dresden Monetary Union. Taking the difficulties into consideration with which the introduction of a new monetary, weights and measures system is connected, the states in the Customs Union declared their willingness to allow the Grand Duchy of Luxembourg to retain the decimal system introduced, as well as the French monetary standard for the duration of the treaty. With the dissolution of the German Confederation in 1867, Luxembourg remeined in the German Customs Union until 1918.

Luxembourg was connected with the Netherlands in a personal union until 1890. When the male line died out of the Dutch royal house, the House of Nassau took over the offices of state in accordance with the right of succession.

The economic union as well as the currency agreement with Belgium were concluded in 1921. The duration of the agreement was initially for 50 years and in 1971 was extended for a further 10 years after previous negotiations.

Capital: Luxembourg.

The gold strikes issued in the Grand Duchy of Luxembourg in the years 1953, 1963 and 1964, weighing 20 francs as well as in 1964 weighing 40 francs must be looked upon as commemorative medallions.

100 Centimes = 1 Luxembourg Franc (Frang)

ADOLPHE 1890–1905

			VF	XF
1 (1)	2½	Centimes (Cu) 1901. Crowned coat of arms. ℞ value in wreath	3.00	6.00
2 (10)	5	Centimes (Cu–Ni) 1901. Adolphe (1817–1905), head right. ℞ value in wreath	1.60	3.20
3 (11)	10	Centimes (Cu–Ni) 1901. Same type as No. 2	1.20	2.50

WILLIAM IV 1905-1912

4 (1)	2½	Centimes (Cu) 1908. Same type as No. 1	3.00	4.50

5 (12)	5	Centimes (Cu–Ni) 1908. William IV (1852-1912), head right. Rev. value in wreath	1.20	2.50

MARIE ADELAIDE 1912–1919

6 (4)	5	Centimes (Z) 1915. Name of country and date. Value (center hole)		
7 (5)	10	Centimes (Z) 1915. Same type as No. 6	4.50	9.00
8 (6)	25	Centimes (Z) 1916. Same type as No. 6	4.00	8.00
9 (7)	5	Centimes (Fe) 1918. Coat of arms. ℞ value in wreath	7.50	13.00
10 (8)	10	Centimes (Fe) 1918. Same type as No. 9	4.50	9.00
			3.50	6.50

CHARLOTTE 1919–1964

11 (7)	5	Centimes (Fe) 1921, 1922. Same type as No. 9	9.00	12.50
12 (8)	10	Centimes (Fe) 1921, 1923. Same type as No. 10	16.00	30.00

			VF	XF
13 (9)	25	Centimes (Fe) 1919–1922	6.00	12.00
14 (13)	5	Centimes (Cu–Ni) 1924. Crowned monogram. ℞ value in wreath	0.40	0.80
15 (14)	10	Centimes (Cu–Ni) 1924	0.60	1.20
16 (15)	25	Centimes (Cu–Ni) 1927. Crowned coat of arms. ℞ value and oak branch	1.20	2.00
17 (17)	1	Franc (Ni) 1924–1935. Steel worker	1.20	1.80
18 (18)	2	Francs (Ni) 1924. Same type as No. 17	2.50	4.50
19 (19)	5	Francs (Ag) 1929. Charlotte (*1896), head left. ℞ coat of arms	6.50	11.00
20 (20)	10	Francs (Ag) 1929. Same type as No. 19	9.00	15.00

			VF	XF
21 (21)	5	Centimes (Br) 1930. Charlotte, head left. ℞ value	0.40	0.80
22 (22)	10	Centimes (Br) 1930. Charlotte, head left. ℞ value	0.40	0.80
23 (15b)	25	Centimes (Br) 1930. Crowned coat of arms. Rev. value and oak branch	1.60	3.00
24 (15a)	25	Centimes (Cu–Ni) 1938. Type as No. 23	2.00	3.50
25 (16)	50	Centimes (Ni) 1930. Steel worker. ℞ value and ears of wheat	1.60	2.50
26 (24)	1	Franc (Cu–Ni) 1939. Crowned monogram. ℞ standing figure, allegory of agriculture	0.80	1.20

COMMEMORATIVE COINS (3)
FOR THE 600th ANNIVERSARY OF THE BATTLE OF CRECY AND IN MEMORY OF THE HEROIC DEATH IN ACTION OF JOHN THE BLIND

			VF	XF
27 (28)	20	Francs (Ag) 1946. Prince Jean, head facing left. Escutcheons: Bourbon/Parma and Luxembourg. ℞ John the Blind (1296 to 26th Aug. 1346), Duke of Luxembourg and King of Bohemia 1310–1346	8.00	16.00
28 (29)	50	Francs (Ag) 1946. Same type as No. 27	15.00	25.00

			VF	XF
29 (30)	100	Francs (Ag) 1946. Same type as No. 27		
		a) with name of engraver	35.00	50.00
		b) without name of engraver (restrike 1964)	70.00	100.00
30 (25)	25	Centimes (Br) 1946, 1947. Crowned coat of arms. Rev. value and oak branch	0.25	0.50
31 (26)	1	Franc (Cu–Ni) 1946–1947. Steel worker. ℞ crowned monogram, value	0.40	0.60
32 (26)	1	Franc (Cu–Ni). Same type as No. 30, but size reduced		
		a) 1952	1.00	1.80
		b) 1953–1964	0.15	0.25
33 (27)	5	Francs (Cu–Ni) 1949. Charlotte, head left. ℞ value between roses, crown above	1.00	1.60
34 (25a)	25	Centimes (Al) 1954-1957, 1960, 1963. Type as No. 30	0.20	0.50
35 (31)	5	Francs (Cu–Ni) 1962. Charlotte, head right. ℞ crowned coat of arms	0.60	1.00
36 (32)	100	Francs (Ag) 1963. Charlotte, head right. ℞ crowned coat of arms	18.00	30.00

COMMEMORATIVE COIN FOR THE MILLENARY OF LUXEMBOURG CITY

			VF	XF
37 (33)	250	Francs (Ag) 1963. Charlotte, head right, memorial legend. ℞ medieval fortress and value	110.00	160.00

JEAN since 1964

			XF	Unc
38 (25a)	25	Centimes (Al) 1965, 1967, 1968, 1970, 1972. Type as No. 34	0.10	0.20
39 (34)	1	Franc (Cu-Ni) 1965, 1966, 1968, 1970, 1972, 1973, 1976-1978. Jean (*1921), head left. Rev. crown, value	0.12	0.25

40 (35) 5 Franc (Cu-Ni) 1971, 1976, 1981. Head of Grand Duke Jean. R value, date, flanked by two oak branches

	XF	Unc
	0.20	0.40

41 (36) 10 Francs (Ni) 1971, 1972, 1974, 1976, 1977–1980, 1982. Head of Grand Duke Jean. Rev. value between oak leaves, crown above, date — 0.30 — 0.60

42 (38) 100 Francs (Ag) 1964. Jean, head left. Rev. crowned coat of arms — 8.00 — 12.00

43 (37) 20 Francs (Ni) 1980–1982. Rev. value between oak leaves — 0.70 — 1.00

Area: 6 sq. mi. Population: 280,000.
An island in the Canton river delta in South China; Macao has been
Portuguese Territory since 1557. Maintaining the status of an Overseas
Province for centuries, it was only during the years of 1930 to 1951,
that Macao held the position of a colony.
Capital: Macao.

100 Avos = 1 Pataca

			VF	XF
1 (1)	5	Avos (Br) 1952. Coat of arms with mural crown. ℞ value	1.20	2.00
2 (2)	10	Avos (Br) 1952	0.60	1.20
3 (3)	50	Avos (Cu-Ni) 1952-1973		
		a) 1952, 20 mm dia.	1.20	2.00
		b) 1972, 1973, 23 mm dia.	0.70	1.20
4 (4)	1	Pataca (Ag) 1952	3.00	4.00

			VF	XF
5 (5)	5	Patacas (Ag) 1952, 1971:		
		a) 1952. Fine silver content 720	6.00	9.00
		b) 1971. Fine silver content 650	3.80	5.50
6 (1a)	5	Avos (Ni–Bra) 1967	0.20	0.40
7 (2a)	10	Avos (Ni–Bra) 1967, 1968	0.30	0.50
8 (6)	1	Pataca (Ni) 1968–	0.70	2.00

OPENING OF MACAO-TAIPA BRIDGE

			Unc
9 (7)	20	Patacas (Ag) 1974. Junk and Macao-Taipa bridge	10.00

25th ANNIVERSARY OF GRAND PRIX (4)

Proof

10 (8) 100 Patacas (Ag) 1978. With inscriptions on
race car   125.00
11 (9) 500 Patacas (Au) 1978. Type as No. 10   280.00

12 (8a) 100 Patacas (Ag) 1978. Type as 10, but
without inscriptions on race car   45.00
13 (9a) 500 Patacas (Au) 1978. Type as No. 12   175.00

YEAR OF THE GOAT (2)

14 (10) 100 Patacas (Ag) 1979   60.00
15 (11) 500 Patacas (Au) 1979   180.00

YEAR OF THE MONKEY (2)

16 (12)   100 Patacas (Ag) 1980   55.00
17 (13) 1000 Patacas (Au) 1980   550.00

YEAR OF THE COCKEREL (2)

18 (14)   100 Patacas (Ag) 1981   55.00

19 (15) 1000 Patacas (Au) 1981   550.00

Madagaskar

Madagascar

Madagaskar

Area: 228,000 sq. mi. Population: 8,100,000.
The world's fourth largest island, off the southeast coast of Africa, in the Indian Ocean. In 1885 France succeeded in establishing a protectorate, and in 1896 Madagascar became a French Colony. After holding the status of an autonomous republic of the French Community, independence was declared on June 26, 1960. The Republic of Madagascar remained a member of the French Community; its name was recently changed to "Repoblika Malagasy".
Capital: Tananarive.

100 Centimes = 1 Franc

		FRENCH COLONY	VF	XF
1 (1)	50	Centimes (Br) 1943. Gallic rooster. ℞ cross of Lorraine	3.00	7.00
2 (2)	1	Franc (Br) 1943. Same type as No. 1	4.00	7.50
3 (3)	1	Franc (Al) 1948–1958. Marianne, allegory of the French Republic. ℞ heads of zebus	0.60	1.50

4 (4)	2	Francs (Al) 1948. Same type as No. 3	0.40	1.00
5 (5)	5	Francs (Al) 1953. Same type as No. 3	0.60	1.50
6 (6)	10	Francs (Al–Br) 1953. Marianne, head left. ℞ map of Madagascar, zebu horns, value	1.00	2.00
7 (7)	20	Francs (Al–Br) 1953	1.50	3.00

REPUBLIC

8 (8)	1	Franc (St) 1965, 1966, 1970, 1974. Poinsetta (Euphorbia pulcherrima – Euphorbiaceae). R head of zebu, laurel branches, value	0.30	0.50

			VF	XF
9 (9)	2 Francs (St) 1965, 1970, 1974. Same type as No. 8		0.40	0.80

			VF	XF
10 (10)	5 Francs (St) 1966–1968, 1970, 1972. Same type as No. 8		0.60	1.50

ISSUES (2) FOR THE FAO COIN PLAN AND THE 10th ANNIVERSARY OF INDEPENDENCE

			VF	XF
11 (11)	10 Francs (Al-Br) 1970–1976. Genuine vanilla (Vanilla planifolia – Orchidaceae)		0.60	1.00
12 (12)	20 Francs (Al-Br) 1970–1976. Cotton plant (Gossypium sp. – Malvaceae). R like No. 11		1.00	1.80

FOR THE FAO COIN PLAN (2)

			VF	XF
13 (13)	10 Ariary 1978:			
	a) (Ag)			15.00
	b) (Cu-Ni)		5.00	
14 (14)	20 Ariary 1978:			
	a) (Ag)			30.00
	b) (Cu-Ni)		10.00	

Area: 49,177 sq. mi. Population: 5,000,000.
The former British Protectorate of Nyasaland was renamed Malawi.
Between 1953 and 1963 the Central African Federation consisted of
Northern Rhodesia, Southern Rhodesia and Nyasaland (called Rhodesia
and Nyasaland), but on July 6, 1964, Malawi became independent. On
July 6, 1966 Malawi attained the position of a republic within the
British Commonwealth.
Capital: Zomba (to be replaced by Lilongwe).

12 Pence = 1 Shilling, 2 Shillings = 1 Florin,
5 Shillings = 1 Crown, 20 Shillings = 1 Malawi Pound;
since February 15, 1971: 100 Tambala = 1 Malawi Kwacha

			VF	XF
1 (1)	6	Pence (Ni–Bra) 1964. Dr. Hastings Kamuzu Banda (*1906), prime minister. ℞ domestic cock (Gallus gallus domesticus – Phasianidae), emblem of the Malawi Congress Party	0.80	1.60

2 (2)	1	Shilling (Ni–Bra) 1964. ℞ corn cob (Zea mays – Gramineae)	0.80	2.00
3 (3)	1	Florin (Ni–Bra) 1964. ℞ African elephant (Loxodonta africana – Elephantidae)	1.50	4.00
4 (4)	½	Crown (Ni–Bra) 1964. ℞ coat of arms	3.00	6.00

COMMEMORATIVE COIN FOR THE DAY OF THE REPUBLIC ON JULY 6, 1966

5 (5)	1	Crown (Cu-Ni) 1966	Proof	16.00
6 (6)	1	Penny (Br) 1967, 1968. Value and date. Rev. value	0.50	1.00

			XF	Unc
7 (7)	1	Tambala (Br) 1971–. Dr. Hastings Kamuzu Banda. R domestic cock (Emblem of the Malawi Congress Party)	0.15	0.25

			XF	Unc
8 (8)	2	Tambala (Br) 1971–. R blue crane (Steganura paradisaea, family of weaver birds – Ploceidae)	0.15	0.30

			XF	Unc
9 (9)	5	Tambala (Cu–Ni) 1971. R purple heron. (Ardea purpurea – Ardeidae)	0.20	0.40
10 (10)	10	Tambala (Cu–Ni) 1971. R corn cob	0.30	0.60
11 (11)	20	Tambala (Cu–Ni) 1971. R African elephant	0.60	1.20
12 (12)	1	Kwacha (Cu–Ni) 1971. R coat of arms	2.00	5.00

10th ANNIVERSARY OF INDEPENDENCE

			XF	Unc
13 (13	10	Kwacha (Ag) 1974. Head right of President Banda. Rev. map, value and independence date between chain, above coat of arms	25.00	35.00

10th ANNIVERSARY OF THE RESERVE BANK OF MALAWI

			XF	Unc
14 (14)	10	Kwacha (Ag) 1975. Obv. like No. 13. Rev. emblem. commemorative inscription, value	25.00	35.00

CONSERVATION COMMEMORATIVE (3)

			Unc	Proof
15 (15)	5	Kwacha (Ag) 1978	35.00	50.00
16 (16)	10	Kwacha (Ag) 1978	45.00	65.00
17 (17)	250	Kwacha (Au) 1978	650.00	750.00

Malaya

Formerly known as Straits Settlements, the Malay States were jointly administered until 1946.
Capital: Kuala Lumpur.
The Straits Dollar, simultaneously valid also in British North Borneo, Brunei and Sarawak, was substituted on 1st April 1946 by the new currency unit, the Malaya Dollar.

100 Cents = 1 Dollar

GEORGE VI 1936–1952

			VF	XF
1 (1)	½	Cent (Br) 1940. George VI, crowned head left. ℞ value and new legend COMMISSIONERS OF MALAYA, date (square)	0.80	1.50
2 (2)	1	Cent (Br) 1939–1941 (square)	0.20	0.60
3 (3)	5	Cents (Cu–Ni) 1939–1945 (round)	0.70	1.50
4 (4)	10	Cents (Cu–Ni) 1939–1945 (round)	1.00	2.00
5 (5)	20	Cents (Cu–Ni) 1939–1945 (round)	2.00	4.00
6 (2a)	1	Cent (Br) 1943–1945 (square; reduced size)	0.20	0.40
7 (7)	5	Cents (Cu–Ni) 1948–1950. George VI, crowned head left; new legend KING GEORGE THE SIXTH (round)	0.30	0.80
8 (8)	10	Cents (Cu–Ni) 1948–1950 (round)	0.40	0.90
9 (9)	20	Cents (Cu–Ni) 1948–1950 (round)	0.60	1.20

For further issues, see under Malaya and British Borneo, Malaysia, Brunei and Singapore.

Malaya and British Borneo
Malaya und Britisch-Borneo   Malaisie et Bornéo Britannique

Joint issues of Malaya, Singapore, the British territories on Borneo (Kalimantan) such as Brunei, North Borneo (in 1963 renamed Sabah), and Sarawak.

100 Cents = 1 Dollar

ELIZABETH II 1952–1963

			VF	XF
1 (A1)	1	Cent (Br) 1956–1961. Elizabeth II, head right. ℞ value in circle (square)	0.15	0.30
2 (1)	5	Cents (Cu–Ni) 1953–1961. ℞ value in dotted circle	0.20	0.40
3 (2)	10	Cents (Cu–Ni) 1953–1961. Same type as No. 2	0.40	0.80
4 (3)	20	Cents (Cu–Ni) 1954–1961. Same type as No. 2	0.40	0.80
5 (4)	50	Cents (Cu–Ni) 1954–1961. Same type as No. 2	1.00	2.00
6 (5)	1	Cent (Br) 1962. Crossed Malayan daggers (Kris). ℞ value	0.20	0.30

For further issues see *Brunei*, *Malaysia* and *Singapore*.

Area: 127,334 sq. mi. Population: 13,000,000.

The monarchical, federated State of Malaysia was created on September 16, 1963. Malaysia includes the territories of Malaya (Johor, Kedah, Kelantan, Malakka, Negri Sembilan, Pahang, Penang, Perak, Perlis, Selangor, and Trengganu), as well as Sabah and Sarawak on Borneo or Kalimantan. Independent by now, Singapore withdrew from the federation on August 9, 1965.

Capital: Kuala Lumpur.   100 Sen = 1 Malaysian Dollar (Ringgit)

			XF	Unc
1 (1)	1 Sen 1967–. Parliament building in Kuala Lumpur and state emblem. Rev. value:			
	a) (Br) 1967, 1968, 1970, 1971, 1973		0.10	0.20
	b) (Cu-clad steel) 1973, 1976–1979		0.10	0.20
2 (2)	5 Sen (Cu–Ni) 1967–. Same type as No. 1		0.10	0.20
3 (3)	10 Sen (Cu–Ni) 1967–. Same type as No. 1		0.12	0.25
4 (4)	20 Sen (Cu–Ni) 1967–. Same type as No. 1		0.20	0.30

5 (5)	50 Sen (Cu–Ni) 1967–. Same type as No. 1			
	a) 1967–1969; reeded edge		0.50	1.00
	b) 1971–; lettered edge		0.40	0.70

COMMEMORATIVE ISSUE FOR THE 10th ANNIVERSARY OF THE CENTRAL BANK (BANK NEGARA MALAYSIA)

6 (6)   1 Dollar 1969. Ismail Nasirud-

			XF	Unc
		din (*1907), Sultan (Tuanku) of Trenganu and 4th king (Yang di-Pertuan Agong) of Malaysia. ℞ value in wreath of hibiscus blossoms (Hibiscus rosa-sinensis – Malvaceae), with state emblem above		
		a) (Cu–Ni)	0.90	2.00
		b) (Ag); proof		360.00
7 (7)	1	Dollar (Cu–Ni) 1971. Type similar to No. 5	0.70	1.70

8 (8)	5	Ringgit (= Dollar) (Cu–Ni) 1971. Sultan (Tuanku) Abdul Rahman Putra Al-Haj. ℞ similar to No. 7	2.50	4.80
9 (9)	100	Ringgit (Au) 1971. Same type as No. 8		285.00

KUALA LUMPUR ANNIVERSARY

10 (10)	1	Dollar (Cu–Ni) 1972. Emblem, inscription. Rev. value, date	1.00	2.00

CONSERVATION COMMEMORATIVE (3) '

			Unc	Proof
11 (11)	15	Ringgit (Ag) 1976. Coat of arms, date. Rev. banteng	25.00	35.00
12 (12)	25	Ringgit (Ag) 1976. Rev. rhinoceros hornbill	40.00	60.00
13 (13)	500	Ringgit (Au) 1976. Rev. tapir	600.00	800.00

25th ANNIVERSARY OF THE EMPLOYEE PROVIDENT FUND (3)

		Unc	Proof
14 (17)	1 Ringgit (Cu-Ni) 1976	1.25	
15 (18)	25 Ringgit (Ag) 1976	25.00	
16 (19)	250 Ringgit (Au) 1976	200.00	250.00

FIVE-YEAR PLAN 1976/1980 (3)

17 (14)	1 Ringgit (Cu-Ni) 1976	1.25	
18 (15)	10 Ringgit (Ag) 1976	20.00	
19 (16)	200 Ringgit (Au) 1976	200.00	250.00

9th SOUTHEAST ASIA GAMES

20 (20)	1 Ringgit (Cu-Ni) 1977	1.25	12.50
21 (21)	25 Ringgit (Ag) 1977	32.00	120.00
22 (22)	200 Ringgit (Au) 1977	350.00	450.00

20th ANNIVERSARY OF INDEPENDENCE

		Unc	Proof
23 (23)	1 Ringgit 1977	1.00	16.00

100th ANNIVERSARY OF NATURAL RUBBER PRODUCTION

24 (24)	1 Ringgit (Ni) 1977	1.00

20th ANNIVERSARY OF BANK NEGARA MALAYSIA

25 (25) 1 Ringgit 1979. Building of the Bank
Negara Malaysia:
a) (Ag) — 18.00
b) (Cu-Ni) — 1.00

Malediven　　　　**Maldive Islands**　　　**Maldives (Iles)**

Area: 115 sq. mi. Population: 150,000.
Group of 12 atolls in the Indian Ocean, approximately 600 miles west
of Ceylon. British Protectorate since 1887, administrated by Ceylon.
Sultanate, but republic from January 1953 to February 1954. On July 26,
1965 the Maldives attained full sovereignty, and withdrew from the
British Commonwealth. On November 11, 1968 the Maldives were
again proclaimed a republic.
Capital: Malé.

100 Lari = 1 Rupee

MOHAMMED IMAD-EDIN 1900-1904

		VF	XF
1 (38)	1 Larin A.H. 1318–1319 (1900–1901). Legend in Arabic only; diameter: 11 mm		
	a) (Cu)	3.50	6.00
	b) (Bra)	10.00	15.00
2 (39)	2 Lari A.H. 1319 (1900). Legend in Arabic only; diameter: 13 mm		
	a) (Cu)	3.50	6.00
	b) (Bra)	12.50	24.00
3 (40)	4 Lari A.H. 1320 (1902). Legend in Arabic only; diameter: 17.5 mm		
	a) (Cu)	3.50	6.00
	b) (Bra)	16.00	30.00

4	1 Rupee (Ag) A.H. 1320 (1902). Legend in Arabic only	–.–	–.–

MOHAMMED SHAMS-EDIN 1904-1936

5 (41)	1 Larin (Cu) A.H. 1331 (1913). Legend in Arabic only	3.00	6.00
6 (42)	4 Lari (Cu) A.H. 1331 (1913). Legend in Arabic only	4.00	8.00

MOHAMMED FARID DIDI 1954–1968

			XF	Unc
7 (43)	1	Larin (Br) 1960. Coat of arms. ℞ value (round)	0.30	0.50

| | | | | |
| **8** (44) | 2 | Lari (Br) 1960 (square) | 0.40 | 0.60 |

9 (45)	5	Lari (Ni–Bra) 1960 (scalloped)	0.40	0.70
10 (46)	10	Lari (Ni–Bra) 1960 (scalloped)	0.60	1.20

11 (47)	25	Lari (Ni–Bra) 1960 (round)	0.70	1.50
12 (48)	50	Lari (Ni–Bra) 1960 (round)	1.00	2.50

| | | | | |
| **13** (49) | 1 | Larin (Al) 1970. Same type as No. 7 | 0.20 | 0.40 |

| | | | | |
| **14** (50) | 2 | Lari (Al) 1970. Same type as No. 8 | 0.30 | 0.50 |

ISSUES FOR THE FAO COIN PLAN (2)

15 (55)	5	Rupees (Cu-Ni) 1977. Coat of arms, date. Rs. bonito (fish), value	3.50	5.00
16 (56)	20	Rupees (Ag) 1977. Rev. value between two fishes, one a bonito and the other a blue-fin tuna	12.00	18.00

938 **Maldive Islands**

FOR THE FAO COIN PLAN (4)

			Unc	Proof
17 (57)	5	Rupees 1978. Lobster:		
		a) (Ag)		45.00
		b) (Cu-Ni)	5.00	
18	5	Rupees (Au) 1978. Type as No. 17		–.–
19 (58)	25	Rupees (Ag) 1978. Dhow (sailing ship)	20.00	50.00
20	25	Rupees (Au) 1978. Type as No. 19		–.–

FOR THE FAO COIN PLAN (2)

			Unc	Proof
21 (59)	10	Rupees (Cu-Ni) 1979	10.00	
22 (60)	100	Rupees (Ag) 1979		40.00

INTERNATIONAL YEAR OF THE CHILD

23 (61)	20	Rupees (Ag) 1979		55.00

Mali

Area: 464,872 sq. mi. Population: 6,300,000.

Known as French Sudan, this territory belonged to French West Africa until 1958. With Senegal as a temporary member, the Mali Federation was founded in 1959. In 1960 Mali was proclaimed a republic. Capital: Bamako.

100 Centimes = 1 CFA Franc;
since 2nd July 1962: 100 Centimes = 1 Mali Franc

COMMEMORATIVE ISSUE FOR INDEPENDENCE

			XF	Unc
1	10	Francs (Ag) 1960. Modibo Keita (*1915), President. Appropriate legend INDEPENDANCE 22 SEPT. 1960. ℞ state emblem, name of country, value, motto		9.00
2 (1)	5	Francs (Al) 1961. Hippopotamus' head (Hippopotamus amphibius – Hippopotamidae). ℞ value	0.80	1.60
3 (2)	10	Francs (Al) 1961. Horse's head. ℞ value	1.20	2.50
4 (3)	25	Francs (Al) 1961. Lion's head (Panthera leo – Felidae)	1.60	3.20

COMMEMORATIVE ISSUES (4) FOR MODIBO KEITA

			Proof
5	10	Francs (Au) 1967. Modibo Keita (*1915), President. ℞ coat of arms	60.00
6	25	Francs (Au) 1967. Same type as No. 5	150.00
7	50	Francs (Au) 1967. Same type as No. 5	300.00
8	100	Francs (Au) 1967. Same type as No. 5	600.00

ISSUES FOR THE FAO COIN PLAN (2)

			XF	Unc
9 (4)	50	Francs (Ni-Bra) 1975, 1977. Millet	0.40	0.80
10 (5)	100	Francs (Ni-Bra) 1975. Maize	0.80	1.50
11 (6)	10	Francs (Al) 1976. Rice plant	0.30	0.50
12 (7)	25	Francs (Al) 1976. Type as No. 11	0.40	0.60

Malta

State Malta; Stat ta' Malta

Area: 122 sq. mi. Population: 360,000.
Group of islands in the Mediterranean, in British possession since 1800.
On 21st September 1964, Malta became an independent member of the
British Commonwealth. The Parliament of Malta decided on 13th De-
cember 1974 with 49 to 6 votes that Malta should become a republic,
that is with immediate effect. The former Governor-General (since 1971)
will be the first president of the republic.
Capital: Valletta (il-Belt Valletta).

4 Farthings = 1 Penny, 12 Pence = 1 Shilling, 20 Shillings = 1 £;
since 16th May 1972: 1000 Mils = 100 Cents = 1 Malta-Pound
Except for the $\frac{1}{3}$ Farthing, British coins were legal tender.
Decimal System since 16th May, 1972.

EDWARD VII 1901–1910

		VF	XF
1 (3)	$\frac{1}{3}$ Farthing (Br) 1902. Edward VII, head right. ℞ value in wreath, with crown above	4.00	10.00

GEORGE V 1910–1936

2 (4)	$\frac{1}{3}$ Farthing (Br) 1913. Georg V, head left. R value in wreath with crown above	3.00	9.00

NEW CURRENCY (Decimal System):
10 Mils = 1 Cent, 100 Cents = 1 Maltese £

3 (5)	2 Mils (Al) 1972–	0.05	0.10
4 (6)	3 Mils (Al) 1972–	0.05	0.10

5 (7)	5 Mils (Al) 1972–	0.05	0.10
6 (8)	1 Cent (Br) 1972–	0.10	0.20

			XF	Unc
7 (9)	2 Cents (Cu-Ni) 1972–		0.10	0.20
8 (10)	5 Cents (Cu-Ni) 1972–		0.20	0.40
9 (11)	10 Cents (Cu-Ni) 1972–		0.40	0.90
10 (12)	50 Cents (Cu-Ni) 1972–		1.40	2.80
11 (13)	1 £ (Ag) 1972. National arms. ℞ Manwel Dimech (1860–1921), politician			12.00
12 (14)	2 £ (Ag) 1972. ℞ Fort St. Angelo			18.00

13 (15) 5 £ (Au) 1972. ℞ Hand holding torch and outline of the islands of Malta and Gozo (Ghawdex)   40.00

14 (16) 10 £ (Au) 1972. ℞ Kenur, a typical Maltese stone charcoal oven   80.00

15 (17) 20 £ (Au) 1972. ℞ blue thrush (Monticola solitarius – Turtidae), national bird; rising sun   160.00

16 (18) 50 £ (Au) 1972. ℞ Neptune, statue in front of the Governor General's Palace in Valletta   400.00

17 (19) 1 £ (Ag) 1973. Coat of arms. Rev. Sir Temi Zammit (1864-1935), historian   12.00

18 (20) 2 £ (Ag) 1973. Rev. Mdina gate   25.00

19 (21)   10 £ (Au) 1973. Rev. watch-tower   50.00

20 (22)   20 £ (Au) 1973. Rev. dolphin fountain   100.00

21 (23)   50 £ (Au) 1973. Rev. castle   260.00

22 (24)   2 £ (Ag) 1974. Coat of arms. Rev. Giov.
             Francesco Abela (1582-1655), historian   12.00
23 (25)   4 £ (Ag) 1974. Rev. Cottonera gate   20.00
24 (26)   10 £ (Au) 1974. Rev. National flower   40.00
25 (27)   20 £ (Au) 1974. Rev. boat   80.00

					Unc
26 (28)	50	£ (Au) 1974. Rev. first Maltese coin			200.00
27 (29)	2	£ (Ag) 1975. Coat of arms. Rev. Alfonso Maria Galea (1861-1941), writer and philantropist			11.00
28 (30)	4	£ (Ag) 1975. Rev. St. Agatha fortress			18.00
29 (31)	10	£ (Au) 1975. Rev. Maltese falcon			100.00
30 (32)	20	£ (Au) 1975. Rev. fresh water crab			160.00
31 (33)	50	£ (Au) 1975. Rev. ornamental stone balcony			350.00

1st ANNIVERSARY OF REPUBLIC OF MALTA

			Unc	Proof
32 (39)	25	Cents 1975–. New coat of arms (since July 11, 1975), date. Rev. value:		
		a) (Br) 1975		16.00
		b) (Al-Br) 1975	2.00	
		c) (Cu-Ni) 1976	200.00	20.00
		d) (Cu-Ni) 1977–	20.00	8.00
				Unc
33 (34)	2	£ (Ag) 1975. Type as No. 27, but new coat of arms		11.00
34 (35)	4	£ (Ag) 1975. Type as No. 28, but new coat of arms		18.00
35 (36)	10	£ (Au) 1975. Type as No. 29, but new coat of arms		60.00
36 (37)	20	£ (Au) 1975. Type as No. 30, but new coat of arms		110.00
37 (38)	50	£ (Au) 1975. Type as No. 31, but new coat of arms		220.00
38 (40)	2	£ (Ag) 1976. Coat of arms. Rev. Guze' Ellul Mercer (1897-1961), politician and writer		11.00
39 (41)	4	£ (Ag) 1976. Rev. fort Manoel gate		16.00
40 (42)	10	£ (Au) 1976. Rev. swallow-tail butterfly		60.00
41 (43)	20	£ (Au) 1976. Rev. storm petrel		110.00
42 (44)	50	£ (Au) 1976. Rev. ornamental Maltese door knocker		220.00

			Unc	Proof
43 (45)	1	£ (Ag) 1977	6.00	12.00
44 (46)	2	£ (Ag) 1977	12.00	20.00
45 (47)	5	£ (Ag) 1977	30.00	45.00

		Unc	Proof
46 (48)	25 £ (Au) 1977	120.00	200.00
47 (49)	50 £ (Au) 1977	220.00	400.00
48 (50)	100 £ (Au) 1977	450.00	750.00

DEPARTURE OF FOREIGN FORCES

| **49** (51) | 1 £ (Ag) 1979 | 12.00 | 55.00 |

FOR THE FAO COIN PLAN

| **50** | 2 £ (Ag) 1981 | 11.00 | |

INTERNATIONAL YEAR OF THE CHILD

| **51** | 5 £ (Ag) 1981 | | 55.00 |

Mandschukuo **Manchukuo** **Mandchoukouo**
Ta Man Zhou Kuo

大 滿 洲 國

Area: 521,360 sq. mi. Population: 43,200,000.
Under the lax central government of the Republic of China Manchuria
attained a relatively large measure of independence. This occurred in
1917, under the leadership of Marshal Tschang Tso-lin and his son
Tshang Hue-liang. Following the Japanese occupation the State of
Manchukuo was established on February 18, 1932, with the annexation
of the Chinese Province of Jehol. Under Japanese auspices, Manchukuo
is ruled by Pu Yi, the last emperor of the Manchu (Ching) Dynasty,
that renounced the Chinese throne in 1911. In 1934 Manchukuo was
declared an empire, and Pu Yi proclaimed the emperor.
The empire was dissolved when Soviet troups occupied the territory in
August of 1945. Following the Soviet evacuation, Manchukuo was
re-incorporated into China.
Capital: Hsinking.
Coin dates are referring to the two reigns:

Ta Tung 大 同 1932–1934

Kang Teh 康 德 1934–1945

The dates were always reckoned from the beginning of the reign.

10 Li 釐 = 1 Fen 分 ; 10 Fen = 1 Chiao 角 ;

100 Fen = 1 Yuan 圓

			VF	XF
1 (1)	5 Li (Cu) 1933, 1934. National flag in dotted circle, name of country, date, and reign in Chinese. On right and left of legend a five-pointed star. ℞ value in Chinese lettering between flower ornament		5.00	9.00
2 (2)	1 Fen (Cu) 1933, 1934. Same type as No. 1		2.00	4.00
3 (3)	5 Fen (Ni) 1933, 1934. Chrysanthemum in center. Name of country, date, and reign in Chinese legend. On left and			

right of legend a five-pointed star. ℞
value in Chinese lettering between two
dragons

		VF	XF
			1.20	2.00

4 (4)   1 Chiao (Ni) 1933, 1934. Same type as
           No. 3 .... 1.50   3.00
5 (5)   5 Li (Cu) 1934–1939. Same type as No. 1,
           but new legend on obverse: Chinese
           letters for the reign of Kang Teh
           instead of Ta Tung 4.00   8.00

6 (6)   1 Fen (Cu) 1934–1939. Same type as No. 2,
           but new legend on obverse: Chinese
           letters for the reign of Kang Teh
           instead of Ta Tung 2.00   4.00
7 (7)   5 Fen (Ni) 1934–1939. Same type as No. 3,
           but new legend on obverse: Chinese
           letters for the reign of Kang Teh
           instead of Ta Tung 2.00   4.00
8 (8)   1 Chiao (Ni) 1934–1939. Same type as
           No. 4, but new legend on obverse:
           Chinese letters for the reign of Kang
           Teh instead of Ta Tung 2.50   4.50

9 (9)   1 Fen (Al) 1939–1943. Stylized flower in

center. Name of country, date, and
reign on new legend in Chinese. ℞
value in Chinese letters between rice
panicles

	VF	XF
	2.00	3.50

10 (11) 5 Fen (Al) 1940–1943. Number 5 in
circle. Name of country, date, and
reign on new legend in Chinese letters
between flowers 2.00 3.50

11 (12) 1 Chiao (Al) 1940–1942. Number 10 in
center. Name of country, date, and
reign on new legend in Chinese letters.
℞ value in Chinese letters between
flowers 2.00 3.50

12 (10) 1 Chiao (Ni) 1940. Two winged horses
in centre. Name of country, date, and
reign on new legend in Chinese letters.
℞ value in Chinese letters in circle (sun)
surrounded by rays and clouds. On top,
a stylized flower 2.50 4.50

13 (13) 1 Fen (Al) 1943–1944 .... 1.60 3.00

14 (A13) 5 Fen (Al) 1943–1944. Number 5 in center. Name of country, date, and reign
on new legend in Chinese letters 0.80 1.60

15 (14) 1 Chiao (Al) 1943. Number 10 in center. Name of country, date, and reign on new legend in Chinese letters. ℞ on right and left value in Chinese letters, on top and bottom ornaments

	VF	XF
	0.80	1.50

16 (13a) 1 Fen (red fiber) 1945 — 20.00 — 40.00

17 (A13a) 5 Fen (red fiber) 1944 — 12.50 — 25.00

Martinique

Martinique

Martinique

Area: 421 sq. mi. Population: 290,000.
A French possession since 1635, this island in the Lesser Antilles has been a French Overseas Department since 1946.
Capital: Fort-de-France.

100 Centimes = 1 Franc

	VF	XF
1 (1) 50 Centimes (Cu–Ni) 1897–1922. Bust left. ℞ value within wreath	6.50	12.00

2 (2) 1 Franc (Cu–Ni) 1897–1922 — 12.00 — 22.00

Mauretanien # **Mauritania** **Mauritanie**

Area: 419,000 sq. mi. Population: 1,400,000.

Mauritania, formerly a part of French West Africa, became a French Overseas Territory in 1946 and in 1957 received limited self-government. On 28th Nov. 1958 the establishment of the Islamic Republic of Mauritania took place within the French Community. The country received full independence on 28th Nov. 1960. Initially belonging to the French West African Monetary Area, Mauritania in 1962 became a member of the West African Monetary Union (UMOA) within the Franc zone. The introduction of its own currency took place after leaving the Franc zone on 29th June 1973. The exchange of the new media of exchange was effected in the ratio of 5 CFA-Francs to 1 Ouguiya. Issuing institute is the Banque Centrale de Mauritanie. Thus the CFA-Franc lost its validity in this country.

Capital: Nouakchott.

5 Khoums = 1 Ouguiya

			VF	XF
1 (1)	¹/₅	Ouguiya (Al–Bra) 1973. National emblem, value, date, name of issuing institution. ℞ Arabic inscriptions	*12.00*	*25.00*
2 (2)	1	Ouguiya (Al–Br) 1973. Type as No. 1	*7.00*	*12.00*
3 (3)	5	Ouguiya (Al–Br) 1973. Type as No. 1	*7.00*	*12.00*
4 (4)	10	Ouguiya (Cu–Ni) 1973. Type as No. 1	*7.00*	*12.00*
5 (5)	20	Ouguiya (Cu–Ni) 1973. Type as No. 1	*7.00*	*12.00*

15th ANNIVERSARY OF INDEPENDENCE

6 (6)	500 Ouguiya (Au) 1975	400.00

Mauritius   **Mauritius**   **Maurice**

Area: 808 sq. mi. Population: 900,000.
Island in the Indian Ocean, east of Madagascar, belonging to the group of the Mascarenes. Mauritius was discovered in the 16th century by the Portuguese navigator Mascarenhas, and became Dutch Territory in 1598. The island was named after Prince Maurits of Orange. A British crown colony since 1810, Mauritius attained its independence on 12th March 1968.
Capital: Port Louis.

100 Cents = 1 Rupee

GEORGE V 1910–1936

			VF	XF
1 (6)	1	Cent (Br) 1911–1924. Crowned portrait of George V, left. ℞ value	2.50	5.00
2 (7)	2	Cents (Br) 1911–1924	3.00	6.00
3 (8)	5	Cents (Br) 1917–1924	6.00	10.00
4 (9)	¼	Rupee (Ag) 1934–1936. ℞ crown above clover, lily, and lotus blossom	4.00	8.00

			VF	XF
5 (10)	½	Rupee (Ag) 1934. Sunda-Sambar (Cervus timorensis – Cervidae)	8.00	14.00
6 (11)	1	Rupee (Ag) 1934. ℞ coat of arms	16.00	28.00

GEORGE VI 1936–1952

			VF	XF
7 (12)	1	Cent (Br) 1943–1947. Crowned head of George VI, left. ℞ value	1.20	2.50
8 (13)	2	Cents (Br) 1943–1947	1.20	2.50
9 (14)	5	Cents (Br) 1942–1945	1.00	2.00
10 (15)	10	Cents (Cu–Ni) 1947 (scalloped)	1.50	3.00
11 (16)	¼	Rupee (Ag) 1938–1946. ℞ crown above clover, lily, and lotus blossom	5.00	8.00
12 (17)	½	Rupee (Ag) 1946. ℞ Sundar-Sambar	10.00	18.00

		VF	XF
13 (18)	1 Rupee (Ag) 1938. ℞ coat of arms	12.00	25.00
14 (23)	1 Cent (Br) 1949–1952. Same type as No. 7, but with legend KING GEORGE THE SIXTH	0.50	1.00
15 (24)	2 Cents (Br) 1949–1952. Same type as No. 8, but with legend KING GEORGE THE SIXTH	0.90	1.70
16 (19)	10 Cents (Cu–Ni) 1952. Same type as No. 10, but with legend KING GEORGE THE SIXTH	1.00	2.00
17 (20)	¼ Rupee (Cu–Ni) 1950–1951. Same type as No. 11, but with legend KING GEORGE THE SIXTH	1.00	2.00
18 (21)	½ Rupee (Cu–Ni) 1950–1951. Same type as No. 12, but with legend KING GEORGE THE SIXTH	1.50	3.50
19 (22)	1 Rupee (Cu–Ni) 1950–1951. Same type as No. 13, but with legend KING GEORGE THE SIXTH	3.50	5.00

ELIZABETH II since 1952

		XF	Unc
20 (25)	1 Cent (Br) 1953–. Elizabeth II, crowned head, right. ℞ value	0.10	0.20
21 (26)	2 Cents (Br) 1953–	0.12	0.25
22 (27)	5 Cents (Br) 1956–	0.25	0.50
23 (28)	10 Cents (Cu–Ni) 1954– (scalloped)	0.30	0.60
24 (30)	¼ Rupee (Cu–Ni) 1960–. R crown above clover, lily, and lotus blossom	0.50	1.00
25 (31)	½ Rupee (Cu–Ni) 1965–. ℞ Sunda-Sambar	0.50	1.00
26 (29)	1 Rupee (Cu–Ni) 1956–. ℞ coat of arms	1.00	2.00

COMMEMORATIVE ISSUES (2) FOR THE THIRD ANNIVERSARY OF INDEPENDENCE

	Unc	Proof
27 (32) 10 Rupees 1971. ℞ dodo (Raphus cucullatus – Raphidae), extinct		
a) (Ag) 20 g		400.00
b) (Cu–Ni) 17.4 g	4.00	

	Unc	Proof
28 (33) 200 Rupees (Au) 1971. Scene from love-story "Paul et Virginie" (1788) by Bernardin de St.-Pierre	400.00	1000.00

CONSERVATION COMMEMORATIVE (3)

	Unc	Proof
29 (34) 25 Rupees (Ag) 1975	20.00	25.00
30 (35) 50 Rupees (Ag) 1975	40.00	50.00
31 (36) 1000 Rupees (Au) 1975	600.00	850.00

25th ANNIVERSARY OF THE SILVER JUBILEE OF HER MAJESTY QUEEN ELIZABETH II

	Unc	Proof
32 (37) 25 Rupees (Ag) 1977	15.00	35.00

10th ANNIVERSARY OF INDEPENDENCE (2)

		Unc	Proof
33 (38)	25 Rupees (Ag) 1978	12.50	30.00
34 (39) 1000	Rupees (Au) 1978	300.00	450.00

WEDDING OF PRINCE CHARLES AND LADY DIANA

		Unc	Proof
35	10 Rupees 1981:		
	a) (Ag)		60.00
	b) (Cu-Ni)	4.00	

Mexiko **Mexico** Mexique

Estados Unidos Mexicanos

Area: 763,944 sq. mi. Population: 64,000,000.
Before the conquest of the Aztec empire by the Spaniards under Ferdinand Cortés, there existed on Mexican soil, among others, the high cultures of the Maya, Mixtecs, Olmekes and Toltecs. Mexico later became part of the Spanish colonial empire, from the beginning of the 16th century until it obtained its independence in 1821. In the 19th century Mexico lost over one-third of its old territory to the United States of America. The revolution which broke out in 1910 unleashed a civil war of many years duration, and led in 1917 to fundamental changes in the constitution and social reforms.
Capital: Mexico City.

100 Centavos = 1 Peso

REPUBLIC

			VF	XF
1 (3)	1	Centavo (Cu) 1899–1905. Coat of arms: carancho or crested caracara (Polyborus plancus – Falconidae), nopal cactus (Nopalea coccinellifera – Cactaceae), and snake. ℞ number above value		
		a) 1899	150.00	270.00
		b) 1900–1905	1.80	3.60
2 (16)	5	Centavos (Ag) 1898–1905. Coat of arms. ℞ value	3.00	6.00
3 (17)	10	Centavos (Ag) 1898–1905	4.00	7.00
4 (18)	20	Centavos (Ag) 1898–1905	5.50	8.00
5 (20)	1	Peso (Ag) 1898–1909. Coat of arms. ℞ liberty cap in sunburst	12.00	20.00
6 (21)	1	Peso (Au) 1870–1905. Coat of arms. ℞ value in wreath	120.00	150.00
7 (22)	2½	Pesos (Au) 1870–1893	160.00	180.00
8 (23)	5	Pesos (Au) 1870–1905. Coat of arms. ℞ scale of justice, law scroll, with liberty cap above	450.00	500.00
9 (24)	10	Pesos (Au) 1870–1905	600.00	750.00
10 (25)	20	Pesos (Au) 1870–1905	1000.00	1150.00

				VF	XF
11 (27)	1	Centavo (Br) 1905–1949. Coat of arms. Ṛ value; diameter: 20 mm			
		a) 1905–1914, 1920–1949		0.15	0.25
		b)1915, 1916		25.00	40.00
12 (28)	1	Centavo (Br) 1915. Same type as No. 11, but with diameter: 16 mm		11.00	20.00
13 (29)	2	Centavos (Br) 1905–1941. Diameter: 25 mm			
		a) 1905		55.00	100.00
		b) 1906		8.00	16.00
		c) 1920, 1921, 1924–1941		1.20	2.50
		d) 1922		300.00	600.00
14 (30)	2	Centavos (Br) 1915. Diameter: 20 mm		5.50	10.00

During the years of the revolution, between 1913 and 1916, some states and other authorities issued revolutionary coins.

				VF	XF
15 (31)	5	Centavos (Ni) 1905–1914. Coat of arms. Ṛ value in circle		2.00	4.00
16 (39)	10	Centavos (Ag) 1905–1914		2.00	4.00
17 (40)	20	Centavos (Ag) 1905–1914		2.50	4.50
18 (41)	50	Centavos (Ag) 1905–1918		6.00	8.00
19 (42)	1	Peso (Ag) 1910–1914. Liberty on horseback, rising sun. Ṛ coat of arms and value			
		a) 1910–1913		25.00	35.00
		b) 1944		300.00	500.00
20 (32)	5	Centavos (Br) 1914–1935. Coat of arms. Ṛ value in wreath		2.50	4.00
21 (33)	10	Centavos (Br) 1919–1935. Same type as No. 20:			
		a) 1919–1921		12.50	30.00
		b) 1935		9.00	20.00
22 (34)	20	Centavos (Br) 1920, 1935:			
		a) 1920		18.00	40.00
		b) 1935		4.00	8.00
23	2	Pesos (Au) 1919-1948. Coat of arms. Rev. value in wreath:			
		a) 1919, 1920, 1944, 1946,1947		30.00	35.00
		b) 1945, official restrike			25.00
		c) 1948			–.–
24 (56)	2½	Pesos (Au) 1918-1948. Coat of arms. Rev. Miguel Hidalgo y Costilla (1753-1811), priest and fighter for independence:			
		a) 1918-1920, 1944, 1946, 1948		35.00	42.00
		b) 1945, official restrike			30.00
		c) 1947		350.00	420.00
25 (57)	5	Pesos (Au) 1905-1955. Same type as No. 24:			
		a) 1905		160.00	250.00
		b) 1906, 1907, 1910, 1918-1920		60.00	70.00
		c) 1955, official restrike			60.00

				VF	XF
26 (58)	10	Pesos (Au) 1905-1959. Same type as No. 24:			
		a) 1905-1908, 1910, 1916, 1917, 1919		120.00	150.00
		b) 1920		320.00	450.00
		1959, official restrike			120.00

			VF	XF
27 (59)	20	Pesos (Au) 1917-1959. Coat of arms. Rev. Aztec calendar stone, 15th century:		
		a) 1917-1921	230.00	260.00
		b) 1959, official restrike		220.00
28	10	Centavos (Ag) 1919-1935. Coat of arms. Rev. value, date, above liberty cap in sunburst:		
		a) (Y 43) 1919	16.00	30.00
		b) (Y 47) 1925–1928, 1930, 1933–1935	4.00	6.00
29	20	Centavos (Ag) 1919–1943. Type as No. 28:		
		a) (Y 44) 1919	20.00	40.00
		b) (Y 48) 1920, 1921, 1925–1928, 1930, 1933–1935, 1937, 1939–1943	1.50	2.50
30	50	Centavos (Ag) 1918–1945. Type as No. 28:		
		a) (Y 45) 1918; .800 silver	10.00	20.00
		b) (Y 45) 1919; .800 silver	6.00	10.00
		c) (Y 49) 1919–1921, 1925; .720 silver	4.00	7.00
		d) (Y 49) 1935; .420 silver	3.00	5.00
		e) (Y 49) 1937, 1939, 1942–1945; .720 silver	3.00	5.00
		f) (Y 49) 1938; .720 silver	12.50	22.00
31	1	Peso (Ag) 1918–1945. Type as No. 28:		
		a) (Y 46) 1918; .800 silver	35.00	60.00
		b) (Y 46) 1919; .800 silver	14.00	25.00
		c) (Y 50) 1920; .720 silver	6.00	10.00
		d) (Y 50) 1921–1945; .720 silver	5.00	7.00

			VF	XF
32 (51)	2	Pesos (Ag) 1921. Coat of arms. ℞ goddess of victory	32.00	45.00

			VF	XF
33 (60)	50	Pesos (Au) 1921–1947. Same type as No. 32:		
		a) 1921-1931, 1944-1946	450.00	550.00
		b) 1943. No value, in its place 37.5 Gr./ORO/PURO twice (see illustration)	450.00	550.00
		c) 1947, official restrike		400.00
34 (52)	50	Centavos (Ag) 1935. Coat of arms. ℞ value with liberty cap above	2.50	4.00
35 (35)	5	Centavos (Cu–Ni) 1936–1942. Coat of arms. ℞ value in circle of pre-Columbian ornaments	0.40	0.80
36 (36)	10	Centavos (Cu–Ni) 1936–1946. Same type as No. 35	0.40	0.80
37 (37)	5	Centavos (Br) 1942–1946, 1951–1955. Coat of arms. ℞ Josefa Ortiz de Dominguez (1773–1829), fighter for independence, facing left	0.20	0.40

Similar design: Nos. 42, 49 and 65.

			VF	XF
38 (38)	20	Centavos (Br) 1943–1955. Coat of arms. ℞ Sun Pyramid of Teotihuacán	0.40	0.80

Similar design: No. 51.

			VF	XF
39 (53)	1	Peso (Ag) 1947–1949. ℞ José Maria Teclo Morelos y Pavón (1765–1815), priest and fighter for independence		
		a) 1947, 1948	3.00	5.00
		b) 1949 (Beware of counterfeits)	200.00	275.00

			VF	XF
40 (54)	5	Pesos (Ag) 1947–1948. ℞ Cuautémoc († 1525), Huetlatoani (= ruler) of Tenochtitlan, 1520–1525	12.50	18.00

41 (61)	1	Centavo (Bra) 1950–1969. ℞ ear of wheat	0.10	0.15
42 (62)	5	Centavos (Cu–Ni) 1950. ℞ Josefa Ortiz de Dominguez	1.50	3.00
43 (63)	25	Centavos (Ag) 1950–1953. ℞ scale of justice, law scroll, with liberty cap above	0.60	0.80
44 (64)	50	Centavos (Ag) 1950–1951. Cuautémoc. ℞ coat of arms	1.10	1.50
45 (65)	1	Peso (Bi) 1950. Coat of arms. ℞ José Maria Teclo Morelos y Pavón	2.00	2.60

COMMEMORATIVE COIN FOR THE OPENING OF THE SOUTHERN RAILWAY BETWEEN MEXICO CITY AND YUCATAN

46 (66)	5	Pesos (Ag) 1950. Engine, rising sun and palm trees. ℞ coat of arms and value	30.00	50.00
47 (67)	5	Pesos (Ag) 1951–1954. Miguel Hidalgo y Costilla, facing left, in wreath. ℞ coat of arms		
		a) 1951-1953	11.00	15.00
		b) 1954	40.00	60.00

Similar design: No. 54.

COMMEMORATIVE ISSUE FOR THE 200th BIRTHDAY OF HIDALGO

48 (68) 5 Pesos (Ag) 1953. Miguel Hidalgo y Costilla (1753–1811), priest and fighter for independence in front of church in Dolores, Guanajuato. ℞ coat of arms and value

	VF	XF
	11.00	15.00

		VF	XF
49 (69)	5 Centavos (Bra) 1954–1969. Coat of arms. ℞ Josefa Ortiz de Dominguez	0.10	0.15
50 (70)	10 Centavos (Br) 1955–1967. Coat of arms. ℞ Benito Juarez	0.10	0.20
51 (71)	20 Centavos (Br) 1955-1971. Coat of arms. ℞ sun pyramid of Teotihuacán	0.15	0.30
52 (72)	50 Centavos (Bra) 1955–1959. Coat of arms. ℞ Cuautémoc	0.30	0.70

53 (A72) 1 Peso (Ag) 1957–1967. José Maria Teclo Morelos y Pavón. ℞ coat of arms   0.90   2.00

			VF	**XF**
54 (73)	5	Pesos (Ag) 1955–1957. Miguel Hidalgo y Costilla and new legend INDEPENDENCIA Y LIBERTAD-HIDALGO. ℞ Coat of arms	7.00	10.00
55 (74)	10	Pesos (Ag) 1955–1956. Same type as No. 54	11.00	15.00

COMMEMORATIVE ISSUES (3) FOR 100 YEARS MEXICAN CONSTITUTION

56 (75)	1	Peso (Ag) 1957. Benito Juarez (1806–1872), President 1861–1872. ℞ coat of arms	4.00	8.00
57 (76)	5	Pesos (Ag) 1957. Same type as No. 56	8.00	15.00
58 (77)	10	Pesos (Ag) 1957. Same type as No. 56	26.00	42.00

COMMEMORATIVE ISSUE FOR THE 100th BIRTHDAY OF CARRANZA

59 (78)	5	Pesos (Ag) 1959. Venustiano Carranza (1859–1920). ℞ coat of arms	8.00	11.50

COMMEMORATIVE ISSUE FOR THE 150th ANNIVERSARY OF THE WAR OF INDEPENDENCE AND THE 50th ANNIVERSARY OF THE REVOLUTION

60 (79)	10	Pesos (Ag) 1960. Miguel Hidalgo y Costilla and Francisco Indalecio Madero (1873–1913), President 1911–1913. ℞ coat of arms	11.00	20.00
61 (80)	25	Centavos (Cu–Ni) 1964, 1966. Coat of arms. ℞ Francisco Indalecio Madero	0.10	0.20
62 (81)	50	Centavos (Cu–Ni) 1964–1969. Coat of arms. ℞ Cuautémoc	0.10	0.20

COMMEMORATIVE ISSUE FOR THE 19th OLYMPIC SUMMER GAMES OF 1968 IN MEXICO CITY

63 (82) 25 Pesos (Ag) 1968. Maya ball player in

		front of I-shaped ball court. ℞ coat of arms	XF	Unc

			XF	Unc
		a) Type I, see illustration	9.00	12.00
		b) Type II, center ring lowered	15.00	20.00
		c) Type III, center ring lowered and snake's tongue curved	16.00	22.50
64 (83)	1	Centavo (Br) 1970–1973. Similar type as No. 41, but changed coat of arms	0.10	0.50

65 (84)	5	Centavos (Al-Br) 1970–1976. Similar type as No. 49, but changed coat of arms	0.05	0.10

66 (91)	10	Centavos (Cu-Ni) 1974–1980. Coat of arms. Rev. corn cob	0.10	0.20
67 (86)	20	Centavos (Br) 1970–1974. Similar type as No. 51, but changed coat of arms	0.15	0.30

68 (92)	20	Centavos (Cu-Ni) 1974–1980. Rev. portrait of President Francisco Indalecio Madero	0.05	0.10

69 (87)	50	Centavos (Cu-Ni) 1970–1980. Same		

	XF	Unc

type as No. 62, but changed coat of arms — 0.10 — 0.25

70 (88) 1 Peso (Cu-Ni) 1970–1980. New coat of arms, like No. 66. R José Maria Teclo Morelos Pavón — 0.10 — 0.30

71 (89) 5 Pesos (Cu-Ni) 1971–1974, 1976–1978. Vicente Guerrero, General during the War of Independence against Spain

	XF	Unc
a) 1971, 1972	0.40	0.80
b) 1973, 1974	0.60	1.20
c) 1976, small date	0.80	2.00
d) 1976, large date	0.40	0.80
e) 1977, 1978	0.40	0.80

72 (A90) 10 Pesos (Cu-Ni) 1974–1980. Rev. Miguel Hidalgo y Costilla

	XF	Unc
a) 1974	2.00	5.00
b) 1975	2.50	6.50
c) 1976, 1977, 1978, 1980	0.60	1.20
d) 1979	2.00	4.50

73 (90) 25 Pesos (Ag) 1972. Benito Juárez (1806 to 1972), statesman, Indian by birth — 10.00 — 12.00

		XF	**Unc**
74	100 Pesos (Ag) 1977–1979. Rev. facing portrait of Morelos	12.50	18.00
75	5 Pesos (Cu-Ni) 1980–	0.50	1.00

76	20 Pesos (Cu-Ni) 1980	1.10	1.80

Monaco

Area: 368 acres. Population: 26,000.
Principality under French protection.
Capital: Monte Carlo.

100 Centimes = 1 Franc

ALBERT I 1889–1922

				VF	XF
1 (1)	100	Francs (Au) 1891–1904. Albert I (1848–1922), head left. ℞ coat of arms		600.00	840.00

LOUIS II 1922–1949

			VF	XF
2 (2)	50	Centimes (Al–Br) 1924. Archer. ℞ value, coat of arms and legend in circle	11.00	25.00
3 (3)	1	Franc (Al–Br) 1924. Same type as No. 2	10.00	20.00
4 (4)	2	Francs (Al–Br) 1924. Same type as No. 2	15.00	26.00
5 (5)	50	Centimes (Al–Br) 1926. Archer. ℞ value and coat of arms in circle	15.00	26.00
6 (6)	1	Franc (Al–Br) 1926. Same type as No. 5	12.00	25.00
7 (7)	2	Francs (Al–Br) 1926. Same type as No. 5	16.00	28.00
8 (8)	1	Franc. Louis II (1870–1949), head left. ℞ coat of arms		
		a) (Al) undated (1943)	1.20	2.80
		b) (Al–Br) undated (1945)	1.60	2.50
9 (9)	2	Francs. Same type as No. 8		
		a) (Al) undated (1943)	3.50	6.00
		b) (Al–Br) undated (1945)	2.50	4.00
10 (10)	5	Francs (Al) 1945. Same type as No. 8	2.50	4.50

Gold coins with design as Nos. 8–10 are pattern pieces. See at the end of listing.

			VF	XF
11 (11)	10	Francs (Cu–Ni) 1946. Louis II in uniform, portrait left. ℞ coat of arms	3.00	6.00
12 (12)	20	Francs (Cu–Ni) 1947. Same type as No. 11	4.00	7.00

Gold coins with design as Nos. 11 and 12 are pattern pieces. See at the end of listing.

RAINIER III since 1949

		VF	XF
13 (13)	10 Francs (Al–Br) 1950–1951. Rainier III (*1923), head left. ℞ coat of arms	2.00	3.00

		VF	XF
14 (14)	20 Francs (Al–Br) 1950–1951. Same type as No. 13	1.50	2.50

Gold coins with design as Nos. 13 and 14 are pattern pieces. See at the end of listing.

		VF	XF
15 (15)	50 Francs (Al–Br) 1950. ℞ rider on horseback with sword and Grimaldi shield	4.00	7.00
16 (16)	100 Francs (Cu–Ni) 1950. Same type as No. 15	9.00	14.00

Gold coins with design as Nos. 15 and 16 are pattern pieces. See at the end of listing.

		VF	XF
17 (17)	100 Francs (Cu–Ni) 1956. Rainier III, head left. ℞ coat of arms	4.00	8.00

Gold coin with design as No. 17 is a pattern piece. See at the end of listing.

CURRENCY REFORM: 100 Old Francs = 1 New Franc

		VF	XF
18 (20)	10 Centimes (Al–Br) 1962–. Rainier III, head right. ℞ St. Rainier, patron saint of Monaco, crown above arms, value	0.20	0.40
19 (21)	20 Centimes (Al–Br) 1962–. Same type as No. 18	0.50	1.00

		VF	XF
20 (22)	50 Centimes (Al–Br) 1962. Same type as No. 18	2.00	3.20

			VF	XF
21 (A18)	½ Franc (Ni) 1965–. R crown in front of arms		0.60	1.20
22 (18)	1 Franc (Ni) 1960–. Same type as No. 21		1.00	1.60
23 (19)	5 Franc (Ag) 1960–. Rainier III, head left. R coat of arms		10.00	12.50

COMMEMORATIVE ISSUES (2) FOR THE 10th WEDDING ANNIVERSARY OF THE PRINCE AND THE PRINCESS

			Unc	Proof
24 (23)	10 Francs (Ag) 1966. Prince Rainier III and Princess Gracia Patricia (*1929), former film actress Grace Kelly. R crowned coat of arms		40.00	
25 (24)	200 Francs (Au) 1966. Same type as No. 24		600.00	800.00

COMMEMORATIVE COIN FOR THE CENTENNIAL OF THE FOUNDING OF MONTE CARLO

			XF	Unc
26 (25)	10 Francs (Ag) 1966. Charles III (1818–1889), reigned 1856–1889. R crowned coat of arms			40.00
27 (26)	5 Francs (Ni) 1971–. Rainier III, head left. R monogram and crown		2.00	3.00

25th ANNIVERSARY OF REIGN (6)

			Unc	Proof
28 (27)	10 Francs (Cu-Ni) 1974. Head left. Rev. coat of arms, value, date		10.00	
29 (28)	50 Francs (Ag) 1974. Head right. Rev. crowned monograms. Commemorative edge inscription		50.00	
30 (29)	100 Francs (Ag) 1974. Head left. Rev. coat of arms		65.00	
31	1000 Francs (Platinum) 1974. Type as No. 30			*300.00*
32	2000 Francs (Platinum) 1974. Type as No. 30			*600.00*
33	3000 Francs (Au) 1974. Type as No. 30			*900.00*

			XF	Unc
34 (33)	10	Francs (Cu-Ni) 1975–1978. Head left. Rev. Coat of arms, value, date	4.00	6.00
35	50	Francs (Ag) 1975, 1976. Type as No. 29, but plain edge		60.00

36 (34)	1	Centime (St) 1977–	1.50	3.00
37 (35)	5	Centimes (Al-Br) 1977–	1.80	3.60
38 (36)	2	Francs (Ni) 1979	1.80	2.50

MONTE CARLO CASINO CENTENNIAL

39 (37)	1000	Francs (Au) 1979	300.00

PATTERN PIECES
LOUIS II 1922–1949

			Unc
P 1	500	Francs (Au) 1934. Head left. ℞ Coat of arms, value, date	3000.00
P 2	1	Franc (Au) no date (1943). Same type as No. 8:	
		a) normal thickness	700.00
		b) double thickness	800.00
P 3	2	Francs (Au) no date (1943). Same type as No. 9:	
		a) normal thickness	900.00
		b) double thickness	1200.00
P 4	5	Francs (Au) 1945. Same type as No. 10:	
		a) normal thickness	1000.00
		b) double thickness	1400.00
P 5	10	Francs (Au) 1946. Same type as No. 11:	
		a) normal thickness	600.00
		b) double thickness	1000.00
P 6	20	Francs (Au) 1947. Same type as No. 12:	
		a) normal thickness	750.00
		b) double thickness	1100.00

			Unc
P 7	10	Francs (Au) 1950. Same type as No. 13:	
		a) normal thickness	600.00
		b) double thickness	750.00
P 8	20	Francs (Au) 1950. Same type as No. 14:	
		a) normal thickness	600.00
		b) double thickness	840.00
P 9	50	Francs (Au) 1950. Same type as No. 15:	
		a) normal thickness	800.00
		b) double thickness	1100.00
P 10	100	Francs (Au) 1950. Same type as No. 16:	
		a) normal thickness	900.00
		b) double thickness	1200.00
P 11	100	Francs (Au) 1956. Same type as No. 17:	
		a) normal thickness	720.00
		b) double thickness	1500.00
P 12	10	Centimes (Au) 1962. Same type as No. 18:	
		a) normal thickness	160.00
		b) double thickness	250.00
P 13	20	Centimes (Au) 1962. Same type as No. 19:	
		a) normal thickness	220.00
		b) double thickness	350.00
P 14	50	Centimes (Au) 1962. Same type as No. 20:	
		a) normal thickness	350.00
		b) double thickness	550.00
P 15	½	Franc (Au) 1965. Same type as No. 21	180.00
P 16	1	Franc (Au) 1960. Same type as No. 22:	
		a) normal thickness	300.00
		b) double thickness	550.00
P 17	5	Francs (Au) 1960, 1966. Same type as No. 23:	
		a) 1960, 1966; normal thickness	600.00
		b) 1960; double thickness	1100.00
P 18	10	Francs (Au) 1966. Same type as No. 26	620.00
P 19	5	Francs (Au) 1971. Same type as No. 27:	
		a) normal thickness	320.00
		b) double thickness	600.00
P 20	10	Francs (Au) 1974:	
		a) normal thickness	300.00
		b) double thickness	550.00
P 21	50	Francs (Au) 1974:	
		a) normal thickness	1100.00
		b) double thickness	1600.00

Mongolian People's Republic

Mongolische Volksrepublik **Mongolie**

Bugd Nairamdach Mongol Ard Uls

Area: 625,783 sq. mi. Population: 1,300,000.
At the time of the Chinese revolution, self-government was instituted
in Outer Mongolia with the aid of the Kalkha princes. On 10th July
1921 the country declared its independence, and the Mongolian People's
Republic was proclaimed on 26th November 1924.
Capital: Ulan Bator.

100 Mongo = 1 Tugrik

Note: The year dates shown on the coins up to and including 1945 refer to
the New-Mongolian calendar, beginning with the year 1911.

			VF	XF
1 (1)	1 Mongo (Cu) 1925. Soyombo-emblem (old coat of arms) and old Mongolian legends; year date 15. ℞ value in Mongolian; wreath of wheat ears		10.00	20.00

2 (2)	2 Mongo (Cu) 1925		7.00	12.00

3 (3)	5 Mongo			
	a) (Cu) 1925		10.00	20.00
	b) (Cu) 1925. Variety		30.00	40.00

Coin No. 3 b can be recognized by the lack of one ornament in the lower left Mongolian word of the legend on each side of Soyombo-emblem (old coat of arms). The origin of this type is uncertain; according to some sources it is a forgery manufactured in a convent.

			VF	XF
4 (4)	10 Mongo (Ag) 1925		8.00	12.00
5 (5)	15 Mongo (Ag) 1925		8.00	12.00
6 (6)	20 Mongo (Ag) 1925		9.00	13.00

			VF	XF
7 (7)	50 Mongo (Ag) 1925		12.00	22.00

			VF	XF
8 (8)	1 Tugrik (Ag) 1925		25.00	38.00

		VF	XF
9 (10)	1 Mongo (Al–Br) 1937. Same type as No. 1, but year date 27	6.00	10.00

		VF	XF
10 (11)	2 Mongo (Al–Br) 1937	6.00	8.00

			VF	XF
11 (12)	5	Mongo (Al–Br) 1937	6.00	9.00

| **12** (13) | 10 | Mongo (Cu–Ni) 1937 | 6.00 | 9.00 |

| **13** (14) | 15 | Mongo (Cu–Ni) 1937 | 6.00 | 9.00 |

14 (15)	20	Mongo (Cu–Ni) 1937	8.00	12.00
15 (16)	1	Mongo (Al–Br) 1945. Coat of arms of Mongolia. Name of country now in Mongolian-Cyrillic lettering, year date 35. ℞ value in wreath	4.50	8.00
16 (17)	2	Mongo (Al–Br) 1945	4.50	8.00

17 (18)	5	Mongo (Al–Br) 1945	4.50	8.00
18 (19)	10	Mongo (Cu–Ni) 1945	4.50	8.00
19 (20)	15	Mongo (Cu–Ni) 1945	4.50	8.00
20 (21)	20	Mongo (Cu–Ni) 1945	4.50	8.00
21 (22)	1	Mongo (Al) 1959. Name of country in Mongolian-Cyrillic lettering. ℞ value in wreath (center hole)	2.50	4.00
22 (23)	2	Mongo (Al) 1959 (center hole)	2.50	4.00

			VF	XF
23 (24)	5	Mongo (Al) 1959 (center hole)	3.00	4.50
24 (25)	10	Mongo (Al) 1959. Coat of arms, name of country now in Mongolian-Cyrillic lettering. ℞ value in wreath	4.00	5.00
25 (26)	15	Mongo (Al) 1959. Same type as No. 24	4.00	6.00
26 (27)	20	Mongo (Al) 1959. Same type as No. 24	4.50	8.00

			XF	Unc
27 (28)	1	Mongo (Al) 1970. Coat of arms and abbreviation of country name, BNMAU, in Mongolian-Cyrillic letters, year date. ℞ value and ornament	0.80	1.60
28 (29)	2	Mongo (Al) 1970. Same type as No. 27	0.80	1.80
29 (30)	5	Mongo (Al) 1970. Same type as No. 27	1.20	2.60
30 (31)	10	Mongo (Al) 1970. Coat of arms, country name spelt out, year date. ℞ value and leaf ornament	1.60	3.00

31 (32)	15	Mongo (Al) 1970. Same type as No. 30	2.00	3.20
32 (33)	20	Mongo (Cu–Ni) 1970. Same type as No. 30	2.40	4.00
33 (34)	50	Mongo (Cu–Ni) 1970. Same type as No. 30	2.80	4.50

COMMEMORATIVE ISSUE FOR 50 YEARS
PEOPLE'S REPUBLIC OF MONGOLIA

			Unc	
34 (35)	1 Tugrik (Br, gilded) 1971. Equestrian statue of Suche-Bator (1893–1923) and legend 50 Years People's Republic of Mongolia. ℞ coat of arms, country name spelt out, value in words (NEG TOGROG). Trial strikes in silver (proof) and gold (9 Ex.) are known:			
	a) (Al–Br)		10.00	
	b) (Cu–Ni)		22.00	

50th ANNIVERSARY OF MONGOLIAN STATE BANK

35 (36)	10 Tugrik (Cu-Ni) 1974. Building of the State Bank	35.00

CONSERVATION COMMEMORATIVE (3)

			Unc	Proof
36 (37)	25 Tugrik (Ag) 1976. Coat of arms. Argali sheep		20.00	30.00
37 (38)	50 Tugrik (Ag) 1976. Rev. camel		40.00	50.00
38 (39)	750 Tugrik (Au) 1976. Rev. Przewalski horse		500.00	800.00

INTERNATIONAL YEAR OF THE CHILD (2)

				Proof
39 (40)	25 Tugrik (Ag) 1980			45.00
40 (41)	750 Tugrik (Au) 1980			500.00

Montenegro

Monténégro

ЦРНА ГОРА

Area: 5,330 sq. mi. Population: 471,800.

The principality of Montenegro was raised to the status of a kingdom in 1910. The National Assembly then decided in favor of uniting with the state of the Serbs, Croats and Slovenes on November 26, 1918. During World War II, the state of Montenegro (1941-1944) was created, initially under Italian domination, later under German. Subsequently the country again became part of Yugoslavia.

Capital: Cetinje.

100 Para = 1 Perper

PRINCIPALITY
NICHOLAS I 1860–1918

			VF	XF
1 (1)	1	Para (Br) 1906. Crowned heraldic eagle. ℞ value	16.00	35.00
2 (2)	2	Pare (Br) 1906–1908	6.00	12.00
3 (3)	10	Para (Ni) 1906–1908	2.00	4.00
4 (4)	20	Para (Ni) 1906–1908	4.00	7.00
5 (5)	1	Perper (Ag) 1909	8.00	16.00
6 (6)	2	Perpera (Ag) 1910	16.00	30.00
7 (7)	5	Perpera (Ag) 1909	110.00	180.00
8 (8)	10	Perpera (Au) 1910. Nicholas I (1841–1921), Prince of Montenegro, also known as poet and dramatist. ℞ heraldic eagle on mantled arms	360.00	500.00

			VF	XF
9 (9)	20	Perpera (Au) 1910	400.00	600.00
10 (10)	100	Perpera (Au) 1910	6500.00	10000.00

KINGDOM

COMMEMORATIVE ISSUES (3) FOR THE 50th ANNIVERSARY OF THE GOVERNMENT

			VF	XF
11 (18)	10	Perpera (Au) 1910. Nicholas I, head with laurel wreath. ℞ heraldic eagle on mantled arms	360.00	500.00

			VF	**XF**
12 (19)	20	Perpera (Au) 1910	420.00	600.00

13 (20)	100	Perpera (Au) 1910	850.00	1200.00
14 (11)	1	Para (Br) 1913–1914	11.00	25.00
15 (12)	2	Pare (Br) 1913–1914	6.00	12.00
16 (13)	10	Para (Ni) 1913–1914	2.80	5.00

17 (14)	20	Para (Ni) 1913–1914	5.00	10.00
18 (15)	1	Perper (Ag) 1912–1914	15.00	20.00

19 (16)	2	Perpera (Ag) 1914	16.00	22.00
20 (17)	5	Perpera (Ag) 1912–1914	105.00	160.00

Area: 32.5 sq. mi. Population: 18,500.

One of the Leeward Islands and a member of the Caribbean Free Trade Area (CARIFTA). Montserrat has united with the countries of Antigua, Barbados, Dominica, Grenada, St. Christopher-(Kitts-) Nevis-Anguilla, St. Lucia and St. Vincent to form the currency area of the East Caribbean Dollar. The issuing authority for the whole of the currency area is the East Caribbean Currency Authority with its seat in Bridgetown on the island of Barbados.

Capital: Plymouth.

100 Cents = 1 East Caribbean Dollar

COMMEMORATIVE ISSUE FOR THE INAUGURATION OF THE CARIBBEAN DEVELOPMENT BANK AND THE FAO COIN PLAN

			Unc	Proof
1 (6*)	4 Dollars (Cu–Ni) 1970. Coat of arms. ℞ bananas, sugar cane, value		10.00	30.00

*This number refers to Yeoman's East Caribbean Territories listing.

Morocco

Al Mamlakah al Maghrebia

Area: c. 174,000 sq. mi. Population: 18,500,000.
After decades as an European protectorate, this North African country was restored to independence in 1956. Based upon the constitution of 1962, Morocco is a constitutional democratic and social monarchy. Capital: Rabat.

50 Mazunas = 1 Dirham, 10 Dirhams = 1 Rial, 100 Centimes =
1 Franc; since 17th October 1959: 100 Francs = 1 Dirham
100 Centimes = 1 Dirham

ABD AL AZIZ IV 1894–1908

			VF	XF
1 (14)	1 Mazuna (Br) H-C 1319–1321 (1901–1903). Arabic legend and date in circle, meander ornament. ℞ value in circle; meander ornament		6.00	9.00
2 (15)	2 Mazunas (Br) H-C 1320–1323 (1902–1905)		4.00	8.00
3 (16)	5 Mazunas (Br) H-C 1320–1322 (1902–1904)		1.50	3.00
4 (17)	10 Mazunas (Br) H-C 1320–1323 (1902–1905)		1.00	1.60
5 (9)	½ Dirham (Ag) H-C 1313–1319 (1896–1901)		5.00	8.00
6 (10)	1 Dirham (Ag) H-C 1313–1318 (1896–1900)		6.50	11.00
7 (11)	2½ Dirhams (Ag) H-C 1313–1318 (1896–1900)		12.50	18.00
8 (12)	5 Dirhams (Ag) H-C 1313–1318 (1896–1900)		15.00	30.00
9 (13)	10 Dirhams (Ag) H-C 1313 (1896)		130.00	200.00
10 (18)	1/20 Rial (Ag) H-C 1320–1321 (1902–1904)		4.00	6.00
11 (19)	1/10 Rial (Ag) H-C 1320–1321 (1902–1904)		4.00	7.00
12 (20)	¼ Rial (Ag) H-C 1320–1321 (1902–1904)		6.00	11.00
13 (21)	½ Rial (Ag) H-C 1320–1323 (1902–1906)		8.00	15.00
14 (22)	1 Rial (Ag) H-C 1320–1321 (1902–1904)		35.00	65.00

ABD AL HAFIZ 1908-1912

				VF	XF
15 (23)	¼	Rial (Ag) H-C 1329 (1911)		8.00	12.00
16 (24)	½	Rial (Ag) H-C 1329 (1911)		12.00	20.00
17 (25)	1	Rial (Ag) H-C 1329 (1911)		20.00	35.00

JOUSSEF 1912–1927

				VF	XF
18 (26)	1	Mazuna (Br) H-C 1330 (1912). Overlapping triangle with date. ℞ pentagram with value		12.50	25.00
19 (27)	2	Mazunas (Br) H-C 1330 (1912)		2.50	4.50
20 (28)	5	Mazunas (Br) H-C 1330–1340 (1912–1922)		0.80	1.60
21 (29)	10	Mazunas (Br) H-C 1330–1340 (1912–1922)		1.20	2.00
22 (30)	¹⁄₁₀	Rial (Ag) H-C 1331 (1913). Legend in circle, all in star. ℞ date in circle, legend		30.00	45.00
23 (31)	¼	Rial (Ag) H-C 1331 (1913)		10.50	20.00
24 (32)	½	Rial (Ag) H-C 1331–1336 (1913–1918)		15.00	20.00
25 (33)	1	Rial (Ag) H-C 1331–1336 (1913–1918)		25.00	35.00

NEW CURRENCY: 100 Centimes = 1 Franc

				VF	XF
26 (34)	25	Centimes (Cu–Ni) undated (1922–1927). Star, Moorish ornament. ℞ value (center hole)		0.80	1.60
27 (35)	50	Centimes (Ni) undated (1921–1926)		0.80	1.60

				VF	XF
28 (36)	1	Franc (Ni) undated (1922–1925)		1.20	2.00

MOHAMMED BEN JOUSSEF 1927–1956

				VF	XF
29 (37)	5	Francs (Ag) H-C 1347–1352 (1929–1934)		4.50	7.50
30 (38)	10	Francs (Ag) H-C 1347–1352 (1929–1934)		7.50	12.00
31 (39)	20	Francs (Ag) H-C 1347–1352 (1929–1934)		16.00	28.00
32 (40)	50	Centimes (Al–Br) H-C 1364 (1945). Pentagram. ℞ value, dates		0.50	1.50
33 (41)	1	Franc (Al–Br) H-C 1364 (1945)		1.00	2.00
34 (42)	2	Francs (Al–Br) H-C 1364 (1945)		0.60	1.50

			VF	XF
35 (43)	5	Francs (Al–Br) H-C 1365 (1946)	1.00	2.00
36 (44)	10	Francs (Cu–Ni) H-C 1366 (1947)	1.00	2.00
37 (45)	20	Francs (Cu–Ni) H-C 1366 (1947)	1.50	3.00
38 (46)	1	Franc (Al) H-C 1370 (1951)	0.10	0.20

39 (47)	2	Francs (Al) H-C 1370 (1951)	0.20	0.40
40 (48)	5	Francs (Al) H-C 1370 (1951)	0.25	0.50
41 (49)	10	Francs (Al–Br) H-C 1371 (1952)	0.40	0.80
42 (50)	20	Francs (Al–Br) H-C 1371 (1952)	0.50	1.00
43 (51)	50	Francs (Al–Br) H-C 1371 (1952)	0.90	1.50
44 (52)	100	Francs (Ag) H-C 1372 (1953)	4.00	6.00

| 45 (53) | 200 | Francs (Ag) H-C 1372 (1953) | 6.00 | 8.00 |

MOHAMMED V 1956–1961

46 (54) 500 Francs (Ag) H-C 1376 (1956). Mohammed V (1911–1961), sultan of Morocco 1927–1956, King 1956–1961, bust left. ℞ crown in pentagram — 15.00 / 22.50

NEW CURRENCY: 100 Francs = 1 Dirham

47 (55) 1 Dirham (Ag) H-C 1380 (1960). Mohammed V. ℞ coat of arms — 2.50 / 4.00

HASSAN II since 1961

48 (56) 1 Dirham (Ni) 1965, 1968, 1969. Hassan II (*1930), head left. Rev. coat of arms — 0.80 / 1.50

49 (57) 5 Dirhams (Ag) 1965 — 5.00 / 8.00

			XF	Unc
50 (58)	1	Centime (Al) 1974, 1975	0.25	0.50

FOR THE FAO COIN PLAN

			XF	Unc
51 (59)	5	Centimes (Bra) 1974–. Fishery	0.15	0.30
52 (60)	10	Centimes (Bra) 1974–. Cultivation of sunflowers	0.20	0.40
53 (61)	20	Centimes (Bra) 1974–. Head left. Rev. coat of arms, value, date	0.25	0.50
54 (62)	50	Centimes (Cu-Ni) 1974–. Type as No. 53	0.25	0.50
55 (63)	1	Dirham (Cu-Ni) 1974–. Type as No. 53	0.45	0.90

45th ANNIVERSARY OF THE BIRTH OF KING HASSAN II (2)

			Unc
56 (65)	50	Dirhams (Ag) 1975. Rev. coat of arms, value, date	40.00
57 (66)	250	Dirhams (Au) 1975, 1977. Type as No. 56	150.00

INTERNATIONAL WOMEN'S YEAR 1975

			Unc
58 (67)	50	Dirhams (Ag) 1975	60.00

FOR THE WORLD FOOD CONFERENCE AND FOR THE FAO COIN PLAN

			Unc
59 (64)	5	Dirhams (Cu-Ni) 1975. Rev. dam, sugar-beet, value, date	5.00

1st ANNIVERSARY OF THE GREEN MARCH (2)

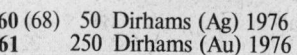

			Unc
60 (68)	50	Dirhams (Ag) 1976	40.00
61	250	Dirhams (Au) 1976	*300.00*

Mosambik   # Mozambique   **Mozambique**

Moçambique

Area: 297,729 sq. mi. Population: 9,000,000.

Since the early years of the 16th Century the Portuguese consolidated their economic influence on the East Coast (cf. Mombasa in the World Coin Catalog of the 19th Century and Zanzibar) in the coastal strip (south of Beira) and the island of Mozambique in the form of fortified settlements and at the same time also penetrated the interior along the path of the Zambesi. The British and Dutch interests in the colonization of Africa adversely affected the already slack Portuguese colonial policy which defended itself by declaring the overseas possessions as overseas provinces. Mozambique and the dependencies were already administered in the early 19th century by a Governor General, in 1891 declared as the "State of East Africa", mainly, however, continued to be described under the usual name. The designation "Portuguese Colony" returned in use, was substituted in 1951 by "Overseas Territory" (Province of Mozambique), in place of which even "Portuguese State of Mozambique" (Estado português de Moçambique) was used. After fighting which extended over more than a decade, one of the indigenous independence movements (Frelimo = Frente de Libertação de Moçambique) (Mozambique Freedom Front) has had the power of government transferred, following upon the fall of the government in the motherland (25th April 1974). On June 25, 1975, Mozambique became full independence. Capital: Lourenco Marques, now Maputo.

100 Centavos = 1 Escudo; 100 Centavos = 1 Mozambique Escudo; 100 Centavos = 1 Metica

For the Escudos circulating in Mozambique there was a legal parity with the Escudo of Portugal of 1:1

			VF	XF
1 (1)	10	Centavos (Br) 1936. Coat of arms. ℞ value	4.00	7.00
2 (2)	20	Centavos (Br) 1936	4.50	8.00
3 (3)	50	Centavos (Cu–Ni) 1936	6.00	9.00
4 (4)	1	Escudo (Cu–Ni) 1936	8.00	10.50
5 (5)	2½	Escudos (Ag) 1935	9.00	12.00
6 (6)	5	Escudos (Ag) 1935	8.00	12.00
7 (7)	10	Escudos (Ag) 1936	18.00	35.00
8 (8)	2½	Escudos (Ag) 1938–1951. ℞ coat of arms with mural crown	5.00	8.00
9 (9)	5	Escudos (Ag) 1938–1949	15.00	22.00

			VF	XF
10 (10)	10	Escudos (Ag) 1938	25.00	45.00
11 (11)	10	Centavos (Br) 1942	3.00	6.00
12 (12)	20	Centavos (Br) 1941	3.00	6.00
13 (13)	50	Centavos (Br) 1945	3.00	6.00
14 (14)	1	Escudo (Br) 1945	3.50	6.00
15 (15)	20	Centavos (Br) 1949–1950	2.00	3.50
16 (16)	50	Centavos (Ni–Br) 1950–1951	2.00	4.00
17 (17)	1	Escudo (Ni–Br) 1950–1951	2.00	4.00
18 (24)	10	Centavos (Br) 1960, 1961	0.20	0.40
19 (25)	20	Centavos (Br) 1961	0.30	0.60
20 (18)	50	Centavos (Br) 1953–1957	0.30	0.50
21 (19)	1	Escudo (Br) 1953–1974	0.30	0.60
22 (20)	2½	Escudos (Cu-Ni) 1952–1973	0.60	1.00

23 (21)	5	Escudos (Ag) 1951, 1960	1.50	2.50
24 (22)	10	Escudos (Ag) 1952–1966	2.50	5.00
25 (23)	20	Escudos (Ag) 1952–1966	6.50	12.00
26 (21a)	5	Escudos (Cu-Ni) 1971, 1973. Same type as No. 23	0.80	1.20
27 (22a)	10	Escudos (Cu-Ni) 1968, 1970, 1974. Same type as No. 24	1.20	2.50
28 (26)	20	Escudos (Ni) 1971–1973. Same type as No. 25	2.50	4.00
29 (25a)	20	Centavos (Br) 1973, 1974. Type as 19, but reduced size	0.20	0.40
30 (18a)	50	Centavos (Br) 1973, 1974. Type as No. 20, but changed diameter and weight	0.25	0.50
31 (27)	1	Metica (Cu-Ni) 1975. Head right of Samora Machel	–.–	–.–

MONETARY REFORM: 100 Centavos = 1 Metical
(Meticais = plural of Metical)

			Unc
32 (28)	50	Centavos (Al) 1980	0.80
33 (29)	1	Metical (Me) 1980	0.80
34 (30)	2½	Meticais (Cu-Ni) 1980	1.20
35 (31)	5	Meticais (Al) 1980	2.50
36 (32)	10	Meticais (Cu-Ni) 1980	4.00
37 (33)	20	Meticais (Cu-Ni) 1980	7.50
38	500	Meticais (Ag) 1980	*150.00*
39	5000	Meticais (Au) 1980	*1200.00*

Oman   **Muscat and Oman**   **Sultanat d'Oman**
Sultanate of Oman

Area: 82,000 sq. mi. Population: 750,000.
Sultanate in the south-east of the Arabian Peninsula.
Capital: Muscat.

4 Baiza = 1 Anna, 64 Baiza = 1 Rupee;
200 Baiza = 1 Muscat Rial.
Since May 7, 1970: 1000 Baiza = 1 Rial Saidi

The Indian Rupee, which had been in circulation for some considerable
time, lost its validity on May 20, 1970. The Maria Theresa Taler (= 450
Baiza, fluctuating rate of exchange) is recognized, together with the
Rial Saidi and its sub-divisions, for private transactions.

FAISAL BIN TURKEE 1888–1913

			VF	XF
1 (1)	$^{1}/_{12}$	Anna (Cu) H-C 1311 (1894). View of the harbour. ℞ lines of lettering in wreath of branches	28.00	50.00
2 (2)	$^{1}/_{4}$	Anna (Cu) H-C 1311 (1894). Same type as No. 1	20.00	45.00
3 (3)	$^{1}/_{4}$	Anna (Cu or Bra) H-C 1312–1319 (1895–1902). Value, legend and date in circle. ℞ legend in wreath	2.00	3.50

SAID BEN TAIMUR 1932–1970

4 (7)	2	Baiza (Cu–Ni) H-C 1365 (1946). jambija and crossed sabers (state emblem), value. ℞ legend and date. Square	1.20	2.00

			VF	XF
5 (8)	5	Baiza (Cu–Ni) H-C 1365 (1946). Scalloped	1.60	2.50
6 (10)	20	Baiza (Cu–Ni) H-C 1365 (1946). Square	2.00	3.50
7 (14)	3	Baiza (Br) H-C 1380 (1961). Diameter: 18 mm	1.20	2.00

8 (16)	5	Baiza (Cu–Ni) H-C 1381 (1962). State emblem, legend. ℞ dhow and date in circle, value	2.00	3.00

ISSUES FOR DHUFAR

9 (4)	10	Baiza (Cu–Ni) H-C 1359 (1940). State emblem. ℞ legend	4.50	6.50

10 (5)	20	Baiza (Cu–Ni) H-C 1359 (1940). Square	6.50	9.00
11 (6)	50	Baiza (Cu–Ni) H-C 1359 (1940). Octagonal	8.00	11.00

			VF	XF
12 (11)	½	Rial (Ag) H-C 1367 (1948). State emblem in wreath. ℞ legend in circle, all surrounded by leaves	20.00	30.00
13 (12)	1	Rial (Ag) H-C 1378 (1959). State emblem surrounded by legend and circle; edge decoration: dhow and palm tree, alternating. ℞ value and date	25.00	35.00
14 (13)	3	Baiza (Br) H-C 1378 (1959). Diameter 20 mm	3.00	4.50
15 (15)	½	Rial (Ag) H-C 1380–1381 (1961–1962)	5.50	8.00
16 (17)	15	Rials (Au) H-C 1381 (1962). State emblem, surrounded by new legend and circle; edge decoration: dhow and palm tree, alternating. ℞ value and date	175.00	220.00

NEW CURRENCY: 1000 Baiza = 1 Rial Saidi

In the Sultanate of Muscat and Oman, as well as in the Province of Dhufar, the Rial Saidi is now the only legal tender.

			XF	Unc
17 (18)	2	Baiza (Br) H-C 1390 (1970). State emblem. ℞ value, date	0.10	0.20
18 (19)	5	Baiza (Br) H-C 1390. Same type as No. 17	0.10	0.20
19 (20)	10	Baiza (Br) H-C 1390. Same type as No. 17	0.12	0.25
20 (21)	25	Baiza (Cu–Ni) H-C 1390. Same type as No. 17	0.15	0.30

21 (22)	50	Baiza (Cu–Ni) H-C 1390. Same type as No. 17	0.20	0.30
22 (23)	100	Baiza (Cu–Ni) H-C 1390. Same type as No. 17	0.35	0.50
23	25	Baiza (Au) H-C 1390. Same type as No. 20		*100.00*
24	50	Baiza (Au) H-C 1390. Same type as No. 21		*100.00*
25	100	Baiza (Au) H-C 1390. Same type as No. 22		*100.00*
26	½	Rial (Au) H-C 1390		*200.00*
27	1	Rial (Au) H-C 1390		*320.00*

Area: c. 800,000 sq. mi. Population: 4,000,000.
The Sultanate in central Arabia, independent until 1932, now forms the
core of Saudi Arabia.
Capital: Riyadh.

$$20 \text{ Guerche} = 1 \text{ Riyal}$$

ABDUL AZIZ ABDUR RAHMAN IBN SAUD

There is no evidence of any coins struck for the sultanate. Egyptian or
Turkish silver coins, and even Maria Theresa Talers, were counter-
marked with the Arab name of Nejd.

			VF	XF
1 (1)	¼ Riyal		25.00	35.00
2 (2)	½ Riyal		35.00	40.00

3 (3a)	1 Riyal		65.00	85.00

Nepal   # Nepal   **Népal**

Sri Nepála Sarkár

Area: 54,000 sq. mi. Population: 14,000,000.

Kingdom on the south side of the Himalayas, situated between Tibet and India.

Capital: Katmandu.

32 Paise = 16 Dak = 1 Mohar, 100 Paise = 1 Nepalese Rupee

Dates on coins correspond with the Samwat (A. S.) or the Saka Calendar.

PRITHVI BIR BIKRAM SHAH DEV 1881–1911

			VF	XF
1 (1)	¼	Paisa (Cu) 1907–1911 (A. S. 1964–1968). Nepalese inscription around lotus flower, within eight-pointed star, formed of two squares. ℞ trident in center, otherwise similar to obverse	9.00	12.00
2 (A3)	1	Paisa (Cu) 1892–1907 (A.S. 1949–1964). Same type as No. 1	8.00	11.50
3 (B3)	1	Paisa (Cu) 1902–1911 (A.S. 1959–1968). Same type as No. 1	6.50	9.00
4 (4)	1	Dak (Cu) 1891–1911 (A. S. 1948–1968). Same type as No. 1	7.50	10.50
5	8	Dak (Br) 1902 (A. Saka 1824). Same type as No. 1, but with center hole	–.–	–.–
6 (9)	¹⁄₆₄	Mohar (Ag) undated	4.00	6.00
7 (10)	¹⁄₃₂	Mohar (Ag) undated	4.00	6.00
8 (11)	¹⁄₁₆	Mohar (Ag) undated	6.00	8.00
9 (12)	⅛	Mohar (Ag) undated	6.50	9.00
10 (13)	¼	Mohar (Ag) 1881–1911 (A. Saka 1803–1833). Lettering around small circle of arms. ℞ lettering in three lines with central symbol	8.00	10.50
11 (14)	½	Mohar (Ag) 1881–1911 (A. Saka 1803–1833). Same type as No. 10	8.50	12.00
12 (15)	1	Mohar (Ag) 1881–1911 (A. Saka 1803–1833). Lettering in swastika ornament. ℞ lettering in stylized lotus flower	12.00	16.00
13 (16)	2	Mohar (Ag) 1889–1911 (A. Saka 1811–1833). Same type as No. 12, diameter: 25.5 mm	28.00	40.00
14 (17)	4	Mohar (Ag) 1895–1911 (A. Saka 1817–1833). Same type as No. 12, diameter: 29 mm	55.00	75.00

			VF	XF
15 (18)	$^1/_{64}$	Mohar (Au) no date	30.00	40.00
16 (19)	$^1/_{32}$	Mohar (Au) no date	35.00	48.00
17 (20)	$^1/_{16}$	Mohar (Au) no date	40.00	60.00
18 (21)	$^1/_8$	Mohar (Au) no date	45.00	72.00
19 (22)	$^1/_4$	Mohar (Au) 1886–1911 (A. Saka 1808–1833). Lettering in quadrangular arrangement around small circle of arms, date below. ℞ lettering in lotus flower	65.00	85.00
20 (23)	$^1/_2$	Mohar (Au) 1901–1911 (A. Saka 1823–1833). Same type as No. 19	90.00	100.00
21 (24)	1	Mohar (Au) 1899–1911 (A. Saka 1821–1833). Same type as No. 19	100.00	120.00
22 (25)	2	Mohar (Au) 1904–1911 (A. Saka 1826–1833). Same type as No. 19	150.00	170.00
23	4	Mohar (Au) 1911 (A. Saka 1833). Same type as No. 19	–.–	–.–

PATTERN PIECES

The Mohar coinages of 1911 (A. Saka 1833) can also be considered pattern pieces.

			VF	XF
P 1 (5)	$^1/_4$	Paisa (Cu) 1911 (A.S. 1968). Nine letters in square. ℞ twelve letters in square. Date below. Diameter: 16 mm	8.00	12.00
P 2 (6)	$^1/_2$	Paisa (Cu) 1911 (A.S. 1968). Same type as P 1, but diameter: 19 mm	8.00	12.00
P 3 (7)	1	Paisa (Cu) 1911. (A.S. 1968). Same type as P 1, but diameter: 23 mm	9.00	12.50
P 4 (8)	1	Dak (Cu) 1911 (A.S. 1968). Same type as P 1, but diameter: 26.6 mm	10.50	15.00

QUEEN LAKSHMI DEVJESBARI Sovereign in 1914

			VF	XF
24 (A26)	$^1/_4$	Mohar (Ag) 1914 (A.S. 1971). Same type as No. 10	10.50	15.00
25 (B26)	1	Mohar (Ag) 1914 (A.S. 1971). Same type as No. 12	12.50	18.50
26 (C26)	1	Mohar (Au) 1914 (A.S. 1971). Same type as No. 12	120.00	150.00

TRIBHUVANA BIR BIKRAM SHAH DEV 1911–1955

			VF	XF
27 (27)	1	Paisa (Cu) 1911–1914 (A.S. 1968–1971). Same type as No. 3, but crude design. Change in name and date	4.50	6.00
28 (28)	$^1/_2$	Paisa (Cu) 1921–1928 (A.S. 1978–1985). Circle of lettering around crossed kukris (daggers). ℞ circle of lettering around lines of lettering	5.00	8.00

			VF	XF
29 (29)	1	Paisa (Cu) 1918–1929 (A.S. 1975–1986). Same type as No. 28	2.50	4.00
30 (30)	2	Paise (Cu) 1921–1928 (A.S. 1978–1985). Same type as No. 28	3.50	5.00
31 (31)	5	Paise (Cu) 1919–1927 (A.S. 1976–1984). Same type as No. 28	6.00	8.00
32 (32)	¼	Mohar (Ag) 1912–1913 (A.S. 1969–1970). Same type as No. 10	2.50	3.50
33 (33)	½	Mohar (Ag) 1913 (A.S. 1970). Same type as No. 10	3.50	5.00
34 (34)	1	Mohar (Ag) 1912 (A.S. 1969). Same type as No. 12	6.00	8.00
35 (35)	2	Mohar (Ag) 1912–1932 (A.S. 1969–1989). Same type as No. 12	12.00	16.00
36 (36)	4	Mohar (Ag) 1912 (A.S. 1969). Same type as No. 12	28.00	40.00
37 (37)	½	Mohar (Au) 1938 (A.S. 1995). Same type as No. 19	70.00	85.00
38 (38)	1	Mohar (Au) 1912–1937 (A.S. 1969–1994). Same type as No. 19	150.00	170.00

| **39** (39) | 2 | Mohar (Au) 1918 (A.S. 1975). Same type as No. 19 | 265.00 | 300.00 |

NEW CURRENCY: 100 Paise = 1 Rupee

40 (40)	1	Paisa (Cu) 1933–1939 (A.S. 1990–1996). Type similar to No. 28, but two ears of wheat above kukris	2.50	4.00
41 (41)	2	Paise (Cu) 1935–1939 (A.S. 1992–1996). Same type as No. 40	4.00	6.00
42 (42)	5	Paise (Cu) 1934–1939 (A.S. 1991–1996). Same type as No. 40	5.00	7.00
43 (A42)	¼	Paisa (Cu–Br) 1947 (A.S. 2004)	12.00	16.00
44 (B42)	½	Paisa (Cu–Br) 1947 (A.S. 2004)	12.00	16.00
45 (43a)	1	Paisa (Cu–Br) 1943–1951 (A.S. 2000–2008). Type similar to No. 40, but ℞ with sun, sword and crescent in center	1.50	2.00
46 (44)	2	Paise (Cu–Br) 1935–1953 (A.S. 1992–2010). Same type as No. 45 a) (Cu) 1935–1936, diameter: 27 mm	3.50	5.00

			VF	**XF**
		b) (Cu) 1937–1941, diameter: 25 mm	1.50	2.50
		c) (Cu–Br) 1943–1953, diameter: 23 mm	1.50	2.50
47	4	Paise (Ag) 1939	–.–	–.–
48	5	Paise (Cu) 1941 (A. S. 1998). Same type as No. 45	–.–	–.–
49 (45)	5	Paise (Cu–Ni) 1943, 1953 (A. S. 2000, 2010). Obverse similar to No. 48, but hoe instead of kukris. ℞ without inner circle, sword instead of trident	1.20	2.00
50 (46)	20	Paise (Ag) 1935–1953 (A. S. 1992–2010). Trident and legend. ℞ small sword and ears of wheat in stylized lotus flower, with lettering	1.50	2.50
51 (47)	50	Paise (Ag) 1938–1948 (A. S. 1995–2005). Trident in center of swastika ornament with lettering. ℞ same as No. 50	3.00	4.00
52 (54)	50	Paise (Ag) 1950 (A. S. 2007). Same type as No. 51, but name of ruler INANENDRA	250.00	300.00

53 (48)	1	Rupee (Ag) 1932–1943 (A. S. 1989–2000). Same type as No. 51	10.00	16.00
54 (55)	1	Rupee (Ag) 1944–1951 (A. S. 2001–2008). Same type as No. 52	16.00	20.00
55 (50)	¼	Rupee (Au) 1937	45.00	60.00
56 (51)	½	Rupee (Au) 1915–1948	70.00	80.00
57 (52)	1	Rupee (Au) 1918–1948	150.00	180.00
58 (53)	2	Rupees (Au) 1948	310.00	360.00
59 (59)	2	Paise (Bra) 1954	1.00	2.00
60	5	Paise (Cu–Ni) 1953. Similar to No. 49	1.20	2.00

61 (62)	5	Paise (Bra) 1954 (A. S. 2011). Mountains with rising sun and ears of wheat. ℞ Buddha's hand raised to teach	1.00	1.50

			VF	XF
62 (63)	10	Paise (Br) 1954 (A. S. 2011). Obverse like No. 61. ℞ kukri (dagger) in front of mountains in circle of ornamental lettering	1.20	1.60
63 (64)	20	Paise (Cu–Ni) 1953–1954	3.00	4.50

64 (65)	25	Paise (Cu–Ni) A. S. 2011 (1954). Same type as No. 62	1.50	2.50
65 (56)	50	Paise (Cu–Ni) A. S. 2010–2011 (1953–1954). Tribhuvana Bir Bikram (1906–1955), head in pentagram. ℞ mountains and rising sun, between ears of wheat	2.00	3.50

66 (57)	1	Rupee (Cu–Ni) A. S. 2010–2011 (1953–1954). Same type as No. 65	5.00	7.50

MAHENDRA BIR BIKRAM 1955–1972

67 (58)	1	Paisa (Bra) A. S. 2012 (1955). Kukri in front of mountains. ℞ mountains and rising sun, between ears of wheat. Date	1.50	2.50
68 (59)	2	Paise (Bra) A. S. 2012–2013 (1955–1956). Same type as No. 67	0.40	0.60

69 (61)	4	Paise (Bra) A. S. 2012 (1955). Center hole	1.20	2.50

			VF	XF
70 (62)	5	Paise (Br) A. S. 2012-2014 (1955-1957). Buddha's hand raised to teach. Rev. mountains and rising sun, between ears of wheat; 3,89 grams	0.80	1.20
71 (62a)	5	Paise (Cu-Ni) A. S. 2014 (1957). Type as No. 70; 4,04 grams	–.–	–.–
72 (63)	10	Paise (Br) A. S. 2012 (1955). Kukri in front of mountains. ℞ mountains and rising sun, between ears of wheat. Date	1.00	1.50
73 (65)	25	Paise (Cu–Ni) A. S. 2012–2014 (1955–1957). Same type as No. 72	1.20	1.80
74 (82)	25	Paise (Cu-Ni) A. S. 2015-2023 (1958-1966). Trident in circle, all within a tablet. Four characters in line above trident	1.00	1.50
75 (83)	50	Paise (Cu-Ni) A. S. 2012-2023 (1955-1966). Type as No. 74; 25 mm dia.	1.50	3.00
76 (83a)	50	Paise (Cu-Ni) A. S. 2023 (1966). Type as No. 75; 23,5 mm dia.	1.50	3.00
77 (84)	1	Rupee (Cu-Ni) A. S. 2012 (1955). Type as No. 74; 29,6 mm dia.	3.00	5.00
78 (84a)	1	Rupee (Cu-Ni) A. S. 2023 (1966). Type as No. 77; 27 mm dia.	3.00	5.00
79 (82a)	25	Paise (Cu-Ni) A. S. 2024-2028 (1967-1971). Type as No. 74, but five characters in line above trident	1.20	2.00
80 (83a)	50	Paise (Cu-Ni) A. S. 2025-2028 (1968-1971). Type as No. 76, but five characters in line above trident:		
		a) A. S. 2025-2026 (1968-1969)	1.50	2.80
		b) A. S. 2027-2028 (1970-1971); proof only		10.00
81 (84b)	1	Rupee (Cu-Ni) A. S. 2025-2028 (1968-1971). Type as No. 78, but five characters in line above trident:		
		a) A. S. 2025-2026 (1968-1969)	3.00	5.00
		b) A. S. 2027-2028 (1970-1971); proof only		14.00
82 (85)	1/5	Asarfi (Au) A. S. 2012 (1955); 2.33 grams	28.00	36.00
83 (86)	¼	Asarfi (Au) A. S. 2012 (1955); 2.91 grams	30.00	40.00
84 (87)	½	Asarfi (Au) A. S. 2012-2019 (1955-1962)	40.00	50.00
85 (88)	1	Asarfi (Au) A. S. 2012-2019 (1955-1962)	80.00	96.00
86 (89)	2	Asarfi (Au) A. S. 2012 (1955)	185.00	240.00

COMMEMORATIVE COINS (10) FOR THE CORONATION OF THE KING AND QUEEN OF NEPAL

			VF	XF
87 (66)	1	Paisa (Bra) A. S. 2013 (1956). Royal crown of the Shah dev Dynasty. Rev. value in circle	2.50	3.50
88 (67)	2	Paise (Bra) A. S. 2013. Type similar to No. 87	2.50	4.00
89 (68)	5	Paise (Br) A. S. 2013. Type similar to No. 87	3.50	5.00

				VF	XF
90 (69)	10	Paise (Br) A. S. 2013. Type similar to No. 87		3.50	6.00
91 (70)	25	Paise (Cu-Ni) A. S. 2013. Type similar to No. 87		2.50	4.00
92 (71)	50	Paise (Cu-Ni) A. S. 2013. Type similar to No. 87		2.50	4.00
93 (72)	1	Rupee (Cu-Ni) A. S. 2013. Type similar to No. 87		4.00	6.00
94 (73)	1/6	Asarfi (Au) A. S. 2013. Type similar to No. 87		35.00	48.00
95 (76)	½	Asarfi (Au) A. S. 2013. Type similar to No. 87		80.00	90.00
96 (77)	1	Asarfi (Au) A. S. 2013. Type similar to No. 87		300.00	360.00
97 (78)	1	Paisa (Bra) A. S. 2014-2020 (1957-1963). Trident between moon and sun. Rev. value between branches. Denomination with shading		0.25	0.40
98 (79)	2	Paise (Bra) A. S. 2014-2020 (1957-1963). Rev. value in rhombiodal ornament. Denomination with shading		0.40	0.60
99 (80)	5	Paise (Br) A. S. 2014-2020 (1957-1963). Rev. value on lotus flower with eight leaves. Denomination with shading; 22 mm dia.		0.40	0.60
100 (81)	10	Paise (Br) A. S. 2014-2020 (1975-1963). Rev. value on lotus flower with four leaves		0.50	0.80
101 (78a)	1	Paisa (Bra) A. S. 2021-2022 (1964-1965). Type as No. 97, but large sun with short rays. Denomination without shading		0.25	0.40
102 (79a)	2	Paise (Bra) A. S. 2021-2023 (1964-1966). Type as No. 98, but large sun with short rays. Denomination without shading		0.40	0.60
103 (80a)	5	Paise (Al-Br) A. S. 2021 (1964). Type as No. 99, but large sun with short rays. Denomination without shading		2.50	4.00

				VF	XF
104 (81a)	10	Paise (Al-Br) A. S. 2021 (1964). Type as No. 100, but large sun with short rays; 24.5 mm dia.		3.00	4.00

			VF	XF
105 (80b)	5	Paise (Br) A. S. 2021-2023 (1964-1966). Type as No. 103, but 20.5 mm dia.	0.40	0.60
106 (81b)	10	Paise (Br) A. S. 2021-2023 (1964-1966). Type similar to No. 104. Modified design; 24 mm dia.	0.50	0.80

107 (90)	1	Paisa (Al) A. S. 2023-2028 (1966-1971). Mountains. Rev. national flower	0.15	0.30

108 (91)	2	Paise (Al) A. S. 2023-2028 (1966-1971). Rev. Himalayan Monal (Lophophorus impejanus – Phasianidae)	0.25	0.40
109 (92)	5	Paise (Al) A. S. 2023-2028 (1966-1971). Rev. cow	0.30	0.60

110 (93)	10	Paise (Bra) A. S. 2023-2028 (1966-1971). Type as No. 109	0.50	1.00

			XF	Unc
111 (98)	10 Paise (Bra) A. S. 2028 (1971). Ear of wheat. Rev. cow		0.25	0.50

		XF	Unc
112 (97)	10 Rupees (Ag) A. S. 2025 (1968). King Mahendra with crown of the Shah Dev Dynasty. Rev. trident and Symbols of progress. Motto: FOOD FOR ALL	10.00	15.00

BIRENDRA BIR BIKRAM since 1972

		XF	Unc
113 (99)	1 Paisa (Al) A. S. 2028– (1972–)	0.10	0.20
114 (100)	2 Paise (Al) A. S. 2028– (1972–)	0.15	0.25
115 (101)	5 Paise (Al) A. S. 2028– (1972–)	0.15	0.35
116 (102)	10 Paise (Bra) A. S. 2028 (1972)	1.50	3.00
117 (103)	25 Paise (Cu–Ni) A. S. 2028– (1972–)	0.40	0.75
118 (104)	50 Paise (Cu–Ni) A. S. 2028– (1972–)	0.50	1.00
119 (105)	1 Rupee (Cu–Ni) A. S. 2028– (1972–)	1.00	2.00
120 (106)	10 Paise (Bra) A. S. 2029– (1973–)	0.20	0.40

ISSUES (2) FOR THE FAO COIN PLAN

		XF	Unc
121 (107)	5 Paise (Al) A. S. 2031 (1974)	0.20	0.40

				XF	Unc
122 (108)	10	Rupees (Ag) A. S. 2031 (1974)		5.00	8.00

BIRENDRA CORONATION COMMEMORATIVE (10)

				XF	Unc
123 (109)	1	Paisa (Al) A. S. 2031 (1974). Royal crown of the Shah Dev Dynasty. Rev. sword with garland and value in Devanagari		0.10	0.20
124 (110)	5	Paise (Al) A. S. 2031 (1974). Type as No. 123		0.15	0.30
125 (111)	10	Paise (Al) A. S. 2031 (1974). Type as No. 123		0.20	0.40
126 (112)	25	Paise (Cu-Ni) A. S. 2031 (1974). Type as No. 123		0.40	0.80
127 (113)	50	Paise (Cu-Ni) A. S. 2031 (1974). Type as No. 123		0.60	1.20
128 (114)	1	Rupee (Cu-Ni) A. S. 2031 (1974). Type as No. 123		1.10	2.50
129 (115)	25	Rupees (Ag) A. S. 2031 (1974). Type as No. 123		11.00	15.00
130 (116)	¼	Asarfi (Au) A. S. 2031 (1974). Type as No. 123			125.00
131 (117)	½	Asarfi (Au) A. S. 2031 (1974). Type as No. 123			180.00
132 (118)	1	Asarfi (Au) A. S. 2031 (1974). Type as No. 123			360.00

CONSERVATION COMMEMORATIVE (3)

				Unc	Proof
133 (119)	25	Rupees (Ag) A. S. 2031 (1974). Bust right of King Birendra. Rev. Himalayan Monal		25.00	30.00
134 (120)	50	Rupees (Ag) A. S. 2031 (1974). Rev. Himalayan Panda		40.00	50.00
135 (121)	1	Asarfi (Au) A. S. 2031 (1974). rev. Indian One-horned Rhinoceros		650.00	850.00

			XF	Unc
136 (122)	10	Paise (Bra) A. S. 2032 (1975). Conjoined busts of the royal couple, date. Rev. value between ears	0.25	0.50
137 (123)	1	Rupee (Cu-Ni) A. S. 2032 (1975). Type as No. 136	1.20	2.00
138 (124)	20	Rupees (Ag) A. S. 2032 (1975). Type as No. 136	10.00	15.00

ISSUE FOR THE FAO COIN PLAN (2)

139 (125)	10	Paise (Bra) A. S. 2033 (1976). Head of a Barwal sheep. Rev. value, date	0.25	0.50

140 (126)	20	Paise (Bra) A. S. 2035 (1978)	0.40	0.80

5th ANNIVERSARY OF CORONATION

			Proof
141 (127)	1000	Asarfi (Au) 1979	350.00

RURAL WOMEN'S ADVANCEMENT (2)

142 (128)	5	Paise (Al) A. S. 2036 (1979)	0.25	0.50
143 (130)	5	Rupees (Cu-Ni) A. S. 2037 (1980)	3.00	4.00

Niederlande   # Netherlands   **Pays-Bas**

Koninkrijk der Nederlanden

Area: 15,780 sq. mi. Population: 13,200,000.
The country is subdivided into the provinces of Drente, Friesland,
Gelderland, Groningen, Limburg, North Brabant, North Holland,
Overijsel, Zealand, South Holland, and Utrecht.
Capital: Amsterdam, seat of government: Den Haag (The Hague).

100 Cents = 1 Gulden

WILHELMINA 1890–1948

			VF	XF
1 (15)	1	Ducat (Au) 1894–1937. Knight with sword and bundle of arrows. ℞ latin	80.00	90.00
2 (23)	10	Cents (Ag) 1898, 1901	60.00	90.00
3 (23a)	10	Cents (Ag) 1903	25.00	45.00
4 (23b)	10	Cents (Ag) 1904–1906	20.00	55.00
5 (24)	25	Cents (Ag) 1898–1906:		
		a) 1898	285.00	650.00
		b) 1901–1906	28.00	55.00
6 (25a)	½	Gulden (Ag) 1904–1909	30.00	60.00

			VF	XF
7 (26)	1	Gulden (Ag) 1898, 1901. With mark »100 C« underneath coat of arms	65.00	120.00
8 (26a)	1	Gulden (Ag) 1904–1909. Same type as No. 7, but without mark »100 C«	38.00	80.00
9 (33)	5	Cents (Cu-Ni) 1907–1909. Crown in wreath. R value in wreath	16.00	32.00

			VF	XF
10 (35)	½	Cent (Br) 1909–1940. Heraldic lion. R value in wreath	3.00	8.00
11 (36)	1	Cent (Br) 1913–1941. Type as No. 10	1.20	6.00
12 (37)	2½	Cents (Br) 1912–1941. Type similar to No. 10	2.00	8.00
13 (34)	5	Cents (Cu-Ni) 1913–1940. Orange branch in wreath. Rev. value	4.50	12.00

			VF	XF
14 (39)	10	Cents (Ag) 1910–1925	4.00	16.00
15 (40)	25	Cents (Ag) 1910–1925	10.00	32.00
16 (41)	½	Gulden (Ag) 1910–1919	20.00	40.00

			VF	XF
17 (42)	1	Gulden (Ag) 1910–1917	28.00	45.00

			VF	XF
18 (31)	5	Gulden (Au) 1912. Wilhelmina, head right. R crowned coat of arms	225.00	350.00
19 (30)	10	Gulden (Au) 1911–1913, 1917	100.00	120.00
20 (43)	10	Cents (Ag) 1926–1945	1.20	4.00
21 (44)	25	Cents (Ag) 1926–1945	2.00	8.00
22 (45)	½	Gulden (Ag) 1921–1930	3.50	8.00
23 (46)	1	Gulden (Ag) 1922–1945	6.00	12.00
24 (47)	2½	Gulden (Ag) 1929–1943	16.00	25.00

			VF	XF
25 (32)	10	Gulden (Au) 1925–1933	100.00	120.00

			VF	XF
26 (48)	1	Cent (Z) 1941–1944. Cross. ℞ value and ears of wheat	0.40	1.20
27 (49)	2½	Cents (Z) 1941–1942. Ornamentation. ℞ value and ears of wheat	6.00	12.00
28 (50)	5	Cents (Z) 1941–1943. Crossed horse's heads. ℞ value	3.50	11.00
29 (51)	10	Cents (Z) 1941–1943. Stylized tulips. ℞ value	1.20	3.50
30 (52)	25	Cents (Z) 1941–1943. Vessel. ℞ value	4.00	7.50
31 (53)	1	Cent (Br) 1948. Wilhelmina, head left. ℞ value	0.40	0.80
32 (54)	5	Cents (Br) 1948. ℞ value	0.40	1.50
33 (55)	10	Cents (Ni) 1948. ℞ crown above value	0.40	1.20
34 (56)	25	Cents (Ni) 1948	0.40	2.00

JULIANA 1948–1980

			XF	Unc
35 (57)	1	Cent (Br) 1950–1980. Juliana, head right. R value	0.10	0.20
36 (58)	5	Cents (Br) 1950–1980.	0.10	0.20
37 (59)	10	Cents (Ni) 1950–1980.	0.10	0.20

38 (60)	25	Cents (Ni) 1950–1980	0.15	0.25

39 (61)	1	Gulden (Ag) 1954–1967	4.00	7.00
40 (61a)	1	Gulden (Ni) 1967–1980. Same type as No. 39	0.50	0.80
41 (62)	2½	Gulden (Ag) 1959–1966	9.00	12.50
42 (62a)	2½	Gulden (Ni) 1969–1980. Same type as No. 41 but smaller diameter	1.20	2.00
43 (15)	1	Ducat (Au) 1960–1978. Same type as No. 1:		
		a) 1960		1000.00
		b) 1972		150.00
		c) 1974–1976, 1978		80.00

COMMEMORATIVE ISSUE FOR THE 25th ANNIVERSARY OF THE END OF WORLD WAR II

			XF	Unc
44 (64)	10 Gulden (Ag) 1970		15.00	18.00

COMMEMORATIVE ISSUE FOR THE 25th ANNIVERSARY OF THE REIGN ON 4th SEPT. 1973

45 (65)	10 Gulden (Ag) 1973. Juliana, head facing right. ℞ crowned armorial shield, date, value	16.00	22.00

400th ANNIVERSARY OF THE UNION OF UTRECHT

46 (66)	2½ Gulden (Cu-Ni) 1979	1.25	2.00

BEATRIX since 1980

47 (67)	1 Gulden (Cu-Ni) 1980	0.80	1.00
48 (68)	2½ Gulden (Cu-Ni) 1980	1.25	2.00

Netherlands Antilles

Niederländische Antillen　　　　　**Antilles Néerlandaises**

Nederlandse Antillen

Area: 336 sq. mi. Population: 225,000.

Group of islands, comprising the islands of Curaçao, Aruba, Bonaire, Saint Martin, Saint Eustatius, and Saba. After the statute of 1954, this group constitutes part of the kingdom of the Netherlands.

Capital: Willemstad.

100 Cents = 1 Gulden

JULIANA since 1948

			VF	XF
1 (1)	1 Cent (Br) 1952–1970. Heraldic lion. ℞ value within wreath		0.40	1.20

			VF	XF
2 (2)	2½ Cents (Br) 1956–1965		0.40	1.20

			VF	XF
3 (3)	5 Cents (Cu-Ni) 1957–1970. Orange branch (Citrus sinensis – Rutaceae) within circle. R value		0.50	1.20
4 (4)	1/10 Gulden (Ag) 1954–1970		1.20	2.80
5 (5)	¼ Gulden (Ag) 1954–1970		2.50	6.00
6 (6)	1 Gulden (Ag) 1952–1970		6.50	10.50
7 (7)	2½ Gulden (Ag) 1964		11.50	18.00

			XF	Unc
8 (8)	1	Cent (Br) 1970–1978. Crowned coat of arms, name of country, date. R value	0.10	0.20
9 (9)	2½	Cents (Br) 1970–1978. Same type as No. 8	0.15	0.25
10 (10)	5	Cents (Cu-Ni) 1971–1980. Same type as No. 8 (Square with rounded corners)	0.20	0.30
11 (11)	10	Cents (Cu-Ni) 1970–1980. Same type as No. 8	0.25	0.40

12 (12)	25	Cents (Ni) 1970–1980. Same type as No. 8	0.30	0.60
13 (13)	1	Gulden (Ni) 1970–1980. Juliana, Queen of the Netherlands, head right. R crowned coat of arms, value	1.00	2.00

COMMEMORATIVE ISSUE FOR THE 25th ANNIVERSARY OF THE REIGN ON 4th SEPT. 1973

			Unc	Proof
14 (14)	25	Gulden (Ag) 1973. Juliana, head facing right. R Juliana and Prince Consort Bernhard in the State Coach upon the occasion of their visit to the island of Curacao while crossing the "Queen Emma Bridge"; legend in papiamento, the local vernacular; names of the individual islands. Edge inscription DIOS KU NOS	40.00	60.00

BICENTENARY OF AMERICAN INDEPENDENCE (2)

15 (15)	25	Gulden (Ag) 1976. Head right of Queen Juliana. Rev. the ship "Andrew Doria"; 45 mm dia.	50.00	65.00
16 (16)	200	Gulden (Au) 1976. Type as No. 16	180.00	260.00
17 (17)	25	Gulden (Ag) 1977. Peter Stuyvesant	60.00	
18 (18)	200	Gulden (Au) 1977. Peter Stuyvesant		270.00

			XF	Unc
19 (19)	2½	Gulden (Cu-Ni) 1978–1980	1.60	2.50

BANK COMMEMORATIVE (2)

			Unc	Proof
20 (20)	10	Gulden (Ag) 1978	20.00	40.00
21 (21)	100	Gulden (Au) 1978	150.00	180.00

INTERNATIONAL YEAR OF THE CHILD

		Unc	Proof
22 (22) 25 Gulden (Ag) 1979:			
a)			80.00
b) Piéfort			200.00

		XF	Unc
23 (8a) 1 Cent (Al) 1979–. Type as No. 8		0.10	0.20
24 (9a) 2½ Cents (Al) 1979–. Type as No. 9		0.20	0.30

25th ANNIVERSARY OF THE ROYAL STATUTE

		Unc	Proof
25 (23) 50 Gulden (Au) 1979			80.00
26 (24) 300 Gulden (Au) 1980		135.00	160.00

Netherlands East Indies

Niederländisch-Indien   **Indes Néerlandaises**
Nederlandsch Indië

The establishment of the Netherlands East Indian Company in 1602 resulted in the first trading posts in the area of today's Indonesia. From 1942 to 1945 the entire territory was occupied by the Japanese.

Dutch administration, limited since 1945 to only part of the island state, ended completely with the establishment of the Indonesian Republic, and the Conference of The Hague on December 28, 1949.

Capital: Djakarta (Dutch: Batavia).

100 Cents = 1 Gulden

			VF	XF
1 (1)	½	Cent (Cu) 1856–1909. Crowned coat of arms. ℞ legend in Malayan and Javanese	1.20	2.00
2 (2)	1	Cent (Cu) 1855–1912	0.80	1.20
3 (3)	2½	Cents (Cu) 1856–1913	1.20	2.00
4 (5)	¹⁄₁₀	Gulden (Ag) 1854–1901	3.00	4.50
5 (6)	¼	Gulden (Ag) 1854–1901	4.00	6.50
6 (7)	¹⁄₁₀	Gulden (Ag) 1903–1909	3.50	5.50
7 (8)	¼	Gulden (Ag) 1903–1909	3.50	5.50
8 (14)	¹⁄₁₀	Gulden (Ag) 1910–1945	1.60	2.00
9 (15)	¼	Gulden (Ag) 1910–1945	1.60	2.00

			VF	XF
10 (17)	5	Cents (Cu–Ni) 1913–1922. Crown above rice panicles. ℞ garudas, mythological birds (center hole)	0.80	1.20
11 (18)	½	Cent (Br) 1914–1945	0.40	0.60
12 (19)	1	Cent (Br) 1914–1929	0.50	0.80
13 (20)	2½	Cents (Br) 1914–1945	0.60	0.80
14 (21)	1	Cent (Br) 1936–1945. Rice panicles. ℞ legends (center hole)	0.25	0.40

For Japanese Occupation issues see at the end of the section for Japan.

Neukaledonien   # New Caledonia   **Nouvelle Calédonie**

Area: 9,401 sq. mi. Population: 112,000.
Located in the Pacific, north of New Zealand, this island has been
French territory since 1854. Together with the Loyalties, and other
small island groups, it constitutes a French Overseas Department.
Capital: Nouméa.

100 Centimes = 1 CFP Franc

		VF	**XF**
1 (1)	50 Centimes (Al) 1949. Marianne, sitting, allegory of the Republic of France. ℞ Kagu (Rhynochetos jubatus – Rhynochetidae)	0.60	1.00
2 (2)	1 Franc (Al) 1949. Same type as No. 1	0.70	1.20
3 (3)	2 Francs (Al) 1949. Same type as No. 1	0.80	1.50
4 (4)	5 Francs (Al) 1952. Same type as No. 1	1.50	2.00

5 (5)	10 Francs (Ni) 1967, 1970. Head of Marianne, allegory of the Republic of France. ℞ Melanesian pirogue	1.20	1.80

6 (6)	20 Francs (Ni) 1967, 1970. ℞ zebus	1.60	2.50

	VF	XF

7 (7) 50 Francs (Ni) 1967. Rev. vative's hut, surrounded by trees 3.00 5.00

8 (A5) 1 Franc (Al) 1971. Type as No. 1, but
inscription REPUBLIQUE FRANÇAISE 0.50 1.00
9 (B5) 2 Francs (Al) 1971. Type as No. 8 ..... 0.50 1.00

10 (A5a) 1 Franc (Al) 1972, 1973. Type as No. 8,
but I.E.O.M. added 0.20 0.40
11 (B5a) 2 Francs (Al) 1973. Type as No. 9, but
I.E.O.M. added 0.40 0.70
12 (5a) 10 Francs (Ni) 1972, 1973. Type as No. 5,
but I.E.O.M. added 0.80 1.30
13 (6a) 20 Francs (Ni) 1972. Type as No. 6, but
I.E.O.M. added 1.50 2.00
14 (7a) 50 Francs (Ni) 1972. Type as No. 7, but
I.E.O.M. added 2.00 3.60
15 (8) 100 Francs (Ni) 1976. Type as No. 14 ..... 2.50 4.50

Newfoundland

Area: 152,734 sq. mi. Population: 515,000.
Newfoundland was discovered by John Cabot in 1497, and adjudicated
to England in 1713. In 1855 Newfoundland attained the status of a
dominion, and joined the Canadian Confederacy on 11th December
1948.
Capital: St. John's.

100 Cents = 1 Dollar

EDWARD VII 1901–1910

			VF	XF
1 (7)	1	Cent (Br) 1904–1909. Crowned portrait of Edward VII, right. ℞ value in letters, crown and date in circle	6.00	10.00
2 (8)	5	Cents (Ag) 1903–1908. ℞ value and date in circle	8.00	15.00
3 (9)	10	Cents (Ag) 1903–1904	12.00	18.00
4 (10)	20	Cents (Ag) 1904	16.00	30.00
5 (11)	50	Cents (Ag) 1904–1909	16.00	30.00

GEORGE V 1910–1936

6 (12)	1	Cent (Br) 1913–1936. Crowned portrait of George V, left. ℞ value in letters and date in circle	3.00	4.50
7 (13)	5	Cents (Ag) 1912–1929. ℞ value and date in circle	5.00	8.00
8 (14)	10	Cents (Ag) 1912–1919	7.50	16.00
9 (15)	20	Cents (Ag) 1912	8.00	18.00
10 (16)	25	Cents (Ag) 1917–1919	6.00	11.00

			VF	XF
11 (17)	50	Cents (Ag) 1911–1919	12.00	20.00

GEORGE VI 1936–1952

			VF	XF
12 (18)	1	Cent (Br) 1938–1947. Crowned portrait of George VI, left. ℞ red sarracenia (Sarracenia purpurea – Sarraceniaceae)	0.80	1.60
13 (19)	5	Cents (Ag) 1938–1947. ℞ value and date in circle	2.00	4.00
14 (20)	10	Cents (Ag) 1938–1947	2.00	4.00

This former German protectorate was under mandate after 1921. Its status was changed in 1946, when it became an Australian Trust Territory.

12 Pence = 1 Shilling, 20 Shillings = £ 1

GEORGE V 1921–1936

			VF	XF
1 (1)	½	Penny (Cu–Ni) 1929. Crown and crossed maces. ℞ ornamentation in cross (center hole)	350.00	450.00

2 (2)	1	Penny (Cu–Ni) 1929. Crown and crossed maces. ℞ ornamentation in cross (center hole)	350.00	450.00
3 (3)	3	Pence (Cu–Ni) 1935. Crown, monogram. ℞ square above a quadrangle, standing on its tip (center hole)	6.00	10.50
4 (4)	6	Pence (Cu–Ni) 1935. Crown, monogram. ℞ rosette (center hole)	4.00	8.00
5 (5)	1	Shilling (Ag) 1935–1936. Crown and crossed maces. ℞ ornamentation in cross (center hole)	4.00	6.00

EDWARD VIII 1936

6 (6)	1	Penny (Br) 1936. Crown above native carving, monogram. ℞ idol of the native ancestor worship (center hole)	3.50	6.00

			VF	**XF**
7 (7)	1	Penny (Br) 1938–1944. Same type as No. 6, but with monogram of George VI	2.50	4.00
8 (8)	3	Pence (Cu–Ni) 1944. Same type as No. 3 but with monogram of George VI	3.00	4.50

9 (9)	6	Pence (Cu–Ni) 1943. Same type as No. 4 but with monogram of George VI	4.00	7.50
10 (10)	1	Shilling (Ag) 1938–1945. Same type as No. 5 but with monogram of George VI	2.00	3.00

New Hebrides

Neue Hebriden   Nouvelles Hébrides

Area: 5,700 sq. mi. Population: 80,000.
Melanese island group in the South West Pacific, including the Banks and Torres Islands, and, since the treaties of 1906 and 1914 to 1922, constituting an Anglo-French Condominium.
Capital: Port Vila.

100 Centimes = 1 New Hebrides Franc

In addition to the N. H. Franc, the Australian Dollar is also in circulation as common legal tender.

			VF	XF
1 (1)	10	Francs (Ni) 1967, 1970. Head of Marianne, allegory of the French Republic. ℞ native mask, flanked by cowry, taken from the shells of a giant clam (Tridacna gigas - Tridacnidae)	1.20	1.60
2 (2)	20	Francs (Ni) 1967, 1970. Same type as No. 1	1.80	2.00

			VF	XF
3 (3)	100	Francs (Ag) 1966. ℞ carved ceremonial staff of natives	15.00	20.00
4 (4)	1	Franc (Ni-Bra) 1970. Head of Marianne, date. Rev. Frigate Bird (Fregata minor – Fregatidae), value	0.25	0.50
5 (5)	2	Francs (Ni-Bra) 1970. Type as No. 4	0.25	0.50
6 (6)	5	Francs (Ni-Bra) 1970. Type as No. 5	0.50	1.00

			VF	XF
7 (4a)	1	Franc (Ni-Bra) 1975. Type as No. 4, but I.E.O.M. added	0.30	0.40

				VF	XF
8 (5a)	2	Francs (Ni-Bra) 1973, 1975. Type as No. 5, but I.E.O.M. added		0.35	0.50
9 (6a)	5	Francs (Ni-Bra) 1975. Type as No. 6, but I.E.O.M. added		0.40	0.80
10 (1a)	10	Francs (Ni) 1973, 1975. Type as No. 1, but I.E.O.M. added		1.00	1.50
11 (2a)	20	Francs (Ni) 1973, 1975. Type as No. 2, but I.E.O.M. added		2.00	2.50
12 (7)	50	Francs (Ni) 1972. Type as No. 3, but I.E.O.M. added		2.50	3.50

INTERNATIONAL YEAR OF THE CHILD

				Unc
13 (8)	500	Francs (Ag) 1979		35.00

Area: 103,738 sq. mi. Population: 3,400,000.
British crown colony 1840–1907, dominion 1907–1953, monarchist
state in the British Commonwealth since 1953 with a parliamentary constitution. The Crown is represented by a Governor General. Administratively the Cook Islands, Niue and the Tokelau Islands also belong
to New Zealand. In the Antarctic the Ross Dependency comes under
the jurisdiction of New Zealand.
Capital: Wellington.

12 Pence = 1 Shilling, 2 Shillings = 1 Florin, 5 Shillings =
1 Crown, 20 Shillings = 1 Pound (£)
since 10th July 1967: 100 Cents = 1 New Zealand Dollar ($)

GEORGE V 1910–1936

			VF	XF
1 (1)	3 Pence (Ag) 1933–1936. Georg V, crowned bust, facing left. R Maori war clubs			
	a) 1933, 1934, 1936		5.00	10.00
	b) 1935		140.00	250.00

		VF	XF
2 (2)	6 Pence (Ag) 1933–1936. R huia bird (Heteralocha acutirostris – Callaeidae): sacred bird of the Maoris (extinct!)	4.00	6.00
3 (3)	1 Shilling (Ag) 1933–1935. R Maori warrior	4.50	8.00

		VF	XF
4 (4)	1 Florin (Ag) 1933–1936. ℞ kiwi bird (Apteryx australis – Apterygidae)	9.00	15.00
5 (5)	½ Crown (Ag) 1933–1935. ℞ arms	12.00	18.00

COMMEMORATIVE ISSUE FOR THE 25th JUBILEE OF REIGN OF KING GEORGE V AND THE TREATY OF WAITANGI IN THE YEAR 1840

6 (6) 1 Crown (Ag) 1935. ℞ Maori chief and William Hobson († 1842), Captain in the Royal Navy and plenipotentiary of the British Crown 2000.00 2500.00

GEORGE VI 1936–1952

7 (7) ½ Penny (Br) 1940–1947. George VI, head towards left. ℞ tiki, demigod and idol of the Maoris 1.00 2.00

			VF	XF
8 (8)	1	Penny (Br) 1940–1947. ℞ parson bird or tui (Prosthemadura novaeseelandiae – Meliphagidae)	1.00	2.00
9 (9)	3	Pence (Ag) 1936–1946. ℞ Maori war clubs	2.00	4.00
10 (10)	6	Pence (Ag) 1937–1946. ℞ huia bird	2.00	4.00
11 (11)	1	Shilling (Ag) 1937–1946. ℞ Maori warrior	3.50	6.00
12 (12)	1	Florin (Ag) 1937–1946. ℞ kiwi bird	6.50	9.00
13 (13)	½	Crown (Ag) 1937–1946. ℞ arms	8.50	12.00

COMMEMORATIVE ISSUE FOR THE CENTENARY OF THE FOUNDING OF THE BRITISH COLONY ON THE BASIS OF THE TREATY OF WAITANGI

			VF	XF
14 (14)	½	Crown (Ag) 1940. ℞ Maori woman against background of a city	26.00	48.00
15 (9a)	3	Pence (Cu–Ni) 1947. Type as No. 9	0.80	2.00
16 (10a)	6	Pence (Cu–Ni) 1947. Type as No. 10	1.25	2.50
17 (11a)	1	Shilling (Cu–Ni) 1947. Type as No. 11	1.60	2.50
18 (12a)	1	Florin (Cu–Ni) 1947. Type as No. 12	3.00	5.00
19 (13a)	½	Crown (Cu–Ni) 1947. Type as No. 13	5.00	9.00
20 (20)	½	Penny (Br) 1949–1952. Type as No. 7, but inscription KING GEORGE THE SIXTH	0.60	1.20
21 (21)	1	Penny (Br) 1949–1952. Type as No. 8, but inscription KING GEORGE THE SIXTH	0.80	1.20
22 (22)	3	Pence (Cu–Ni) 1948–1952. Type as No. 15, but inscription KING GEORGE THE SIXTH	0.60	1.20
23 (23)	6	Pence (Cu–Ni) 1948–1952. Type as No. 16, but inscription KING GEORGE THE SIXTH	0.80	1.60
24 (24)	1	Shilling (Cu–Ni) 1948–1952. Type as No 17, but inscription KING GEORGE THE SIXTH	1.60	2.50
25 (25)	1	Florin (Cu–Ni) 1948–1951. Type as No 18, but inscription KING GEORGE THE SIXTH	2.00	4.00

				VF	**XF**
26 (26)	½	Crown (Cu–Ni) 1948–1951. Type as No 19, but inscription KING GEORGE THE SIXTH			
				4.00	7.00

COMMEMORATIVE ISSUE FOR THE PROPOSED ROYAL VISIT

27 (27)	1	Crown (Ag) 1949. ℞ fern leaf	18.50	35.00

ELIZABETH II since 1952

28 (28)	½	Penny (Br) 1953–1965. Queen Elizabeth II, head towards right. ℞ tiki	0.20	0.40
29 (29)	1	Penny (Br) 1953–1965. ℞ parson bird or tui	0.30	0.60
30 (30)	3	Pence (Cu–Ni) 1953–1965. ℞ Maori war clubs	0.40	0.70
31 (31)	6	Pence (Cu–Ni) 1953–1965. ℞ huia bird	0.50	1.00
32 (32)	1	Shilling (Cu–Ni) 1953–1965. ℞ Maori warrior	1.00	2.00
33 (33)	1	Florin (Cu–Ni) 1953–1965. ℞ kiwi	1.60	2.80
34 (34)	½	Crown (Cu–Ni) 1953–1965. ℞ arms	2.00	3.50
35 (35)	1	Crown (Cu–Ni) 1953. ℞ Royal monogram and crown above a Maori design	15.00	28.00

NEW CURRENCY: 100 Cents = 1 New Zealand Dollar

36 (36)	1	Cent (Br) 1967–. ℞ stylized fern leaf	0.15	0.20
37 (37)	2	Cents (Br) 1967–. ℞ kowhai (Sophora microphylla – Leguminosae)		
		a) Obverse with date	0.20	0.40
		b) without date: muled with obverse of Bahamas No. 2		30.00
38 (38)	5	Cents (Cu–Ni) 1967–. ℞ tuatara (Sphenodon punctatus – Sphenodontidae or Rhynchocephalidae)	0.30	0.60

39 (39)	10	Cents (Cu–Ni) 1967-1969. Rev. a Maori carved head or koruru	0.50	1.00

			VF	XF
40 (40)	20	Cents (Cu–Ni) 1967–. ℞ kiwi (Apteryx australis – Apterygidae)	0.60	1.20
41 (41)	50	Cents (Cu–Ni) 1967–. ℞ H. M. S. "Endeavour", sailing ship of the English circumnavigator James Cook (1728–1779)	0.80	1.50
42 (42)	1	Dollar (Cu–Ni). Rev. arms:		
		a) 1967, lettered edge	3.00	6.00
		b) 1971 –, reeded edge	1.80	3.50

COMMEMORATIVE ISSUES (2) OF THE BI-CENTENARY OF THE DISCOVERY OF NEW ZEALAND BY CAPTAIN JAMES COOK ON 7th OCTOBER 1769

			VF	XF
43 (43)	50	Cents (Cu–Ni) 1969. Type as No. 41, but edge inscription COOK BI-CENTENARY 1769–1969	3.50	4.50
44 (44)	1	Dollar (Cu–Ni) 1969. James Cook (1728 to 1779), English circumnavigator, map of New Zealand of 1769 and H. M. S. "Endeavour". Variants	3.00	5.50

COMMEMORATIVE ISSUE FOR THE VISIT OF THE ROYAL FAMILY

			VF	XF
45 (45)	1	Dollar (Cu–Ni) 1970. Elizabeth II. ℞ Mt. Cook or Aorangi, 12,346 feet	3.00	5.50

			VF	XF
46 (39a)	10	Cents (Cu–Ni) 1970–. Type as No. 39, but without inscription ONE SHILLING	0.20	0.40

COMMEMORATIVE ISSUE FOR THE 10th BRITISH EMPIRE AND COMMONWEALTH GAMES IN CHRISTCHURCH (24. 1. – 2. 2. 1974)

			Unc	Proof
47 (47)	1	Dollar 1974:		
		a) (Ag)		100.00
		b) (Cu–Ni)	5.00	

NEW ZEALAND DAY

			Unc	Proof
48 (48)	1 Dollar 1974:			
	a) (Ag)			300.00
	b) (Cu-Ni)		5.00	

25th ANNIVERSARY OF THE SILVER JUBILEE OF HER MAJESTY QUEEN ELIZABETH II AND WAITANGI DAY

49 (49)	1 Dollar 1977:		
	a) (Ag)		80.00
	b) (Cu-Ni)	5.00	

25th ANNIVERSARY OF CORONATION

50 (50)	1 Dollar 1978. Parliament building:		
	a) (Ag)		40.00
	b) (Cu-Ni)	3.50	
51 (51)	1 Dollar 1979:		
	a) (Ag)		35.00
	b) (Cu-Ni)	3.50	

52 (52)	1 Dollar 1980:		
	a) (Ag)		35.00
	b) (Cu-Ni)	3.50	

		Unc	Proof
53	1 Dollar 1981:		
	a) (Ag)		35.00
	b) (Cu-Ni)	3.50	

Nicaragua

Area: 57,100 sq. mi. Population: 2,000,000.
Republic in Central America. From 1823 to 1839 it was a member of the
Confederacy of the Central American States.
Capital: Managua.

100 Centavos = 1 Córdoba

				VF	XF
1 (10)	½	Centavo (Br) 1912–1937. Coat of arms. R value within wreath		1.50	2.50
2 (11)	1	Centavo (Br) 1912–1940		1.20	2.00
3 (12)	5	Centavos (Cu–Ni) 1912–1940		1.00	1.60
4 (13)	10	Centavos (Ag) 1912–1936. Francisco Hernández de Córdoba (1476–1526), Spanish conqueror, governor. R sunburst over crests of hills		2.00	3.00
5 (14)	25	Centavos (Ag) 1912–1936		2.50	4.50
6 (15)	50	Centavos (Ag) 1912, 1929		10.50	16.00
7 (16)	1	Córdoba (Ag) 1912		80.00	110.00
8 (17)	5	Centavos (Cu–Ni) 1946–1956. Edge inscription: B. N. N. (Banco Nacional de Nicaragua)		0.25	0.40
9 (18)	10	Centavos (Cu–Ni) 1939–1956		0.40	0.60
10 (19)	25	Centavos (Cu–Ni) 1939–1956		0.50	0.80

11 (20)	50	Centavos (Cu–Ni) 1939–1956		0.80	1.20
12 (21)	1	Centavo (Bra) 1943. Coat of arms. R value within wreath		1.00	1.60
13 (22)	5	Centavos (Bra) 1943. Same type as No. 8, but with reeded edge		1.10	1.50
14 (23)	10	Centavos (Bra) 1943. Same type as No. 9, but with reeded edge		1.50	2.50
15 (24)	25	Centavos (Bra) 1943. Same type as No. 10, but with reeded edge		1.60	2.80

			VF	XF
16 (17a)	5	Centavos (Cu–Ni) 1962, 1964, 1965. Same type as No. 8, but with edge inscription: B. C. N. (Banco Central de Nicaragua)	0.10	0.20
17 (18a)	10	Centavos (Cu–Ni) 1962, 1964, 1965. Same type as No. 16	0.25	0.40
18 (19a)	25	Centavos (Cu–Ni) 1964, 1965. Same type as No. 16	0.40	0.60
19 (20a)	50	Centavos (Cu–Ni) 1965. Same type as No. 16	0.60	1.10

100th ANNIVERSARY OF THE BIRTH OF RUBÉN DARÍO

20 (29)	50	Córdobas (Au) 1967. Rubén Darío (1867-1916), poet. Rev. coat of arms, value	Proof	400.00
21 (17b)	5	Centavos (Cu–Ni) 1972. Same type as No. 16, but reeded edge	0.10	0.20
22 (18b)	10	Centavos (Cu–Ni) 1972. Same type as No. 21	0.20	0.40
23 (19b)	25	Centavos (Cu–Ni) 1972. Same type as No. 21	0.50	0.70
24 (20b)	50	Centavos (Cu–Ni) 1972. Same type as No. 21	0.80	2.00
25 (25)	1	Córdoba (Cu–Ni) 1972. Same type as No. 21	1.20	2.50

ISSUES FOR THE FAO COIN PLAN (2)

26 (27)	5	Centavos (Al) 1974. Coat of arms, below PRODUZCAMOS MAS ALIMENTOS	0.10	0.25
27 (28)	10	Centavos (Al) 1974. Map of Nicaragua, below PRODUZCAMOS MAS ALIMENTOS	0.30	0.50
28 (26)	5	Centavos (Al) 1974. Type as No. 26, but without PRODUZCAMOS MAS ALIMENTOS	0.10	0.25

29 (A26)	10	Centavos (Al) 1974. Type as No. 27, but without PRODUZCAMOS MAS ALIMENTOS	0.40	0.80
			Unc	Proof
30 (30)	20	Córdobas (Ag) 1975. Peace and Progress	12.00	18.00

				Unc	Proof
31 (A31)	50	Córdobas (Ag) 1975. "The Bud" painting by Annigoni (Rebirth of Managua)		20.00	30.00
32 (31)	50	Córdobas (Ag) 1975. Liberty Bell (U. S. Bicentennial)		20.00	30.00

33 (A32)	100	Córdobas (Ag) 1975. Globe with flags (Tribute to world for help received)	35.00	50.00
34 (32)	100	Córdobas (Ag) 1975. Woman and Astronaut (U. S. Bicentennial)	35.00	50.00
35 (33)	200	Córdobas (Au) 1975. The "Pieta" by Michelangelo	70.00	80.00
36 (34)	500	Córdobas (Au) 1975. Colonial church "La Merced"	150.00	160.00
37 (A34)	500	Córdobas (Au) 1975. "The Bud" painting by Annigoni (Rebirth of Managua)	150.00	160.00

38 (35)	1000	Córdobas (Au) 1975. Liberty Bell (U.S. Bicentennial)	300.00	350.00

			Unc	Proof
39 (36)	2000 Córdobas (Au) 1975. Woman and Astronaut (U.S. Bicentennial)		400.00	450.00

			XF	Unc
40 (37)	5 Córdobas (Cu-Ni) 1980		1.20	2.00

Area: 458,976 sq. mi. Population: 4,500,000.

Formerly a part of French West Africa, Niger became an autonomous republic in 1958, and independent on August 3, 1960.
Capital: Niamey.

100 Centimes = 1 CFA Franc

COMMEMORATIVE ISSUES (6) FOR INDEPENDENCE

			Proof
1	10	Francs (Au) 1960	75.00
2	25	Francs (Au) 1960	160.00
3	50	Francs (Au) 1960	300.00
4	100	Francs (Au) 1960	600.00
5	500	Francs (Ag) 1960. Diori Hamani (*1916), Head of State and Prime Minister. ℞ coat of arms and flags, value	20.00
6	1000	Francs (Ag) 1960. Same type as No. 5	40.00

7	10	Francs (Ag) 1968. Lion (Panthera leo – Felidae). ℞ coat of arms and flags, motto, value, date	
		a) normal thickness	20.00
		b) double thickness. Pattern	80.00
8	10	Francs (Au) 1968	70.00
9	25	Francs (Au) 1968	150.00
10	50	Francs (Au) 1968	280.00
11	100	Francs (Au) 1968	550.00

Area: 339,168 sq. mi. Population: 79,760,000.
As a crown colony, Nigeria used the coins of British West Africa until 1959. On October 1, 1960, Nigeria became an independent state and a member of the Commonwealth.
Capital: Lagos.

12 Pence = 1 Shilling, 20 Shillings = £ 1;
since January 1, 1973: 100 Kobo = 1 Naira

ELIZABETH II since 1952

			VF	XF
1 (1)	½ Penny (Br) 1959. Star, name of country. ℞ crown, legend, value (center hole)		0.15	0.40
2 (2)	1 Penny (Br) 1959–1961. Same type as No. 1		0.20	0.40

3 (3)	3 Pence (Ni–Bra) 1959. Elizabeth II, crowned head, right. ℞ cotton plant (Gossypium sp. – Malvaceae) (dodecagonal)		0.50	1.00
4 (4)	6 Pence (Cu–Ni) 1959. ℞ cocoa beans (Theobroma cacao – Sterculiaceae)		0.50	1.00

5 (5)	1 Shilling (Cu–Ni) 1959, 1961, 1962. ℞ palm branches (Elaeis guineensis – Palmae)		0.60	1.00
6 (6)	2 Shillings (Cu–Ni) 1959. ℞ flowers		0.70	1.50

			XF	Unc
		New currency: 100 Kobo = 1 Naira		
7 (7)	½ Kobo (Br) 1973. State arms, name of country, date. R cotton plants, value	0.15	0.25
8 (8)	1 Kobo (Br) 1973, 1974. R two oil derricks	0.20	0.30
9 (9)	5 Kobo (Cu-Ni) 1973, 1974, 1976. Cocoa fruit (Theobroma cacao – Sterculiaceae)	0.40	0.60
10 (10)	10 Kobo (Cu-Ni) 1973, 1974, 1976. R two oil palms	0.60	1.00
11 (11)	25 Kobo (Cu-Ni) 1973, 1975. R groundnuts (Arachis hypogaea – Leguminosae) and seco (groundnuts packed in bags for export and heaped into a pyramid)	1.20	2.00

Nordkorea   # North Korea   **Corée du Nord**
Tschoson Minds hudshuy Inmin Konghwaguk

Area: 46,812 sq. mi. Population: 15,000,000.
Under Japanese administration until 1945. The northern part of the
country was proclaimed as the People's Republic of North Korea on
September 12, 1948. The border between North and South Korea falls
approximately on the 38th degree of latitude.
Capital: Pyongyang.

100 Chon = 1 Won

		VF	XF
1 (1)	1 Chon (Al) 1959, 1970. Coat of arms of the People's Republic. R value	1.00	2.00
2 (2)	5 Chon (Al) 1959, 1974. Same type as No. 1	1.10	2.50

3 (3)	10 Chon (Al) 1959. Same type as No. 1	1.50	3.00

4 (4)	50 Chon (Al) 1978	–.–	–.–

Nordvietnam **North Vietnam** **Vietnam du Nord**

Viet-nam Dan-chu Cong-hoa

Area: 63,344 sq. mi. Population: 21,900,000.

Annam, Tongking, and Cochinchina were parts of former French Indochina. Following a plesbiscite, these territories merged into the Republic of Vietnam, under President Ho Chi Minh, recognized by France within the frame-work of the Indochina Federation, and the Union Française. However, instead of constructive collaboration, severe discrepancies developed, leading to a break with France, and ultimately to the Indochina war. Ho Chi Minh's political power was limited to the North, and a few southern territories, areas not yet reoccupied by the French after the defeat of Japan. After the Geneva Indochina agreement effected an armistice in Vietnam, the 17th parallel became the demarcation line between North and South Vietnam.

Capital: Hanoi.

$$100 \text{ Xu} = 1 \text{ Hao} = 1 \text{ Dong}$$

			VF	XF
1 (1)	20	Xu (Al) 1945. Star, surrounded by name of country. ℞ value	18.00	35.00
2 (2)	5	Hao (Al) 1946. Copper censer, surrounded by name of country. ℞ value in star		
		a) value incused	8.00	20.00
		b) value raised	7.00	18.00
3 (3)	1	Dong (Al) 1946. Ho Chi Minh (1890–1969), president from 1945–1969. ℞ value	60.00	110.00
4 (4)		HAI (2) Dong (Br) 1946. Ho Chi Minh. ℞ value in letters and star in wreath	40.00	65.00
5 (5)	1	Xu (Al) 1958. Coat of arms. ℞ value (center hole)	1.00	2.00

			VF	XF
6 (6)	2	Xu (Al) 1958. Same type as No. 5	1.20	2.50
7 (7)	5	Xu (Al) 1958. Same type as No. 5	1.20	2.50

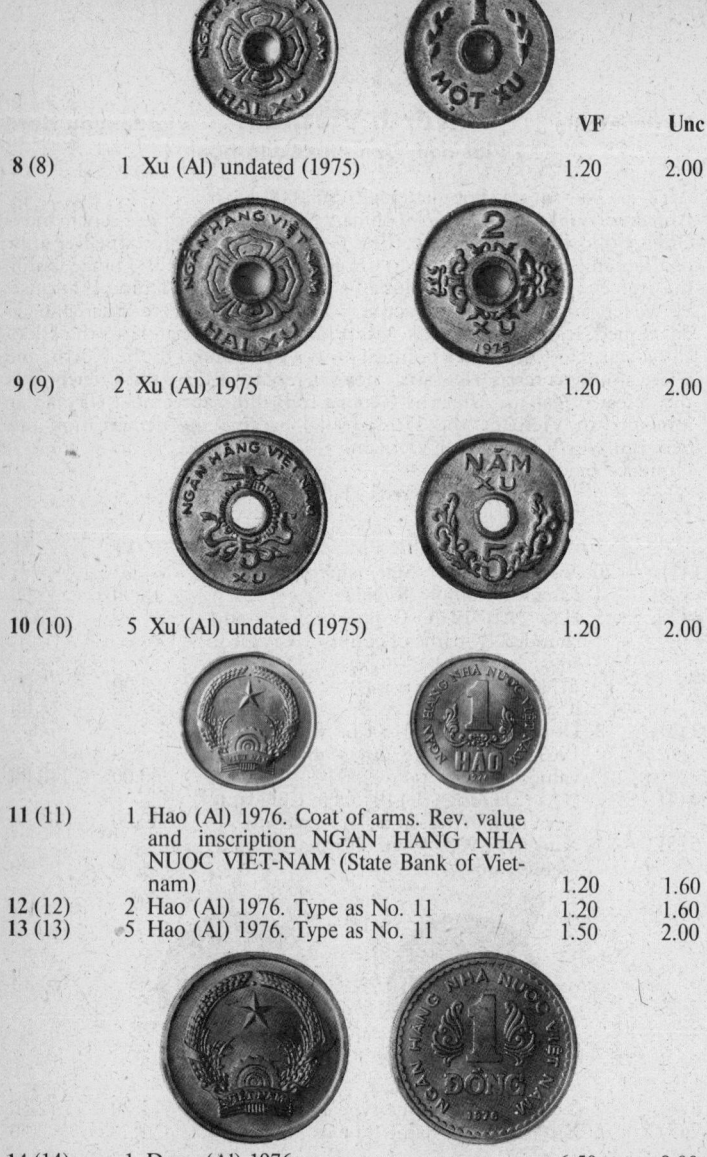

		VF	Unc
8 (8)	1 Xu (Al) undated (1975)	1.20	2.00
9 (9)	2 Xu (Al) 1975	1.20	2.00
10 (10)	5 Xu (Al) undated (1975)	1.20	2.00
11 (11)	1 Hao (Al) 1976. Coat of arms. Rev. value and inscription NGAN HANG NHA NUOC VIET-NAM (State Bank of Vietnam)	1.20	1.60
12 (12)	2 Hao (Al) 1976. Type as No. 11	1.20	1.60
13 (13)	5 Hao (Al) 1976. Type as No. 11	1.50	2.00
14 (14)	1 Dong (Al) 1976	6.50	8.00

1032   **North Vietnam**

Norway
Norge, Noreg

Area: 125,068 sq. mi. Population: 4,000,000.
From 1387 to 1814 Norway was united with Denmark. The subsequent union with Sweden continued until June 7, 1905, when the kingdom became independent.
Capital: Oslo.

100 Øre = 1 Krone

OSCAR II 1872–1905

		VF	XF
1 (19)	1 Øre (Br) 1876–1902. Crowned arms. ℞ value in wreath	4.00	8.00
2 (20)	2 Øre (Br) 1876–1902	4.50	9.00
3 (21)	5 Øre (Br) 1875–1902	5.00	10.00
4 (22)	10 Øre (Ag) 1875–1903. Monogram. ℞ crowned arms	11.00	18.00
5 (24)	25 Øre (Ag) 1896–1904. Arms	8.00	14.00
6 (25)	50 Øre (Ag) 1877–1904. Oscar II (1829–1907), head left. ℞ arms in wreath	12.00	25.00
7 (26)	1 Krone (Ag) 1877–1904	12.00	22.00
8 (27)	2 Kroner (Ag) 1878–1904	20.00	40.00
9 (28)	10 Kroner (Au) 1877–1902. Oscar II, head right. ℞ arms in wreath	500.00	600.00

10 (29)	20 Kroner (Au) 1876–1902	310.00	360.00

HAAKON VII 1905–1957

11 (30)	1 Øre (Br) 1906–1907. Crowned shield, monogram. ℞ value in wreath	4.00	7.50

		VF	**XF**
12 (31)	2 Øre (Br) 1906–1907	4.50	10.50
13 (32)	5 Øre (Br) 1907	7.50	15.00

COMMEMORATIVE ISSUES (3) FOR INDE

		VF	**XF**
14 (33)	2 Kroner (Ag) 1906. Memorial legend. ℞ shield with mantle and crown (civil issue)	90.00	125.00
15 (33a)	2 Kroner (Ag) 1907. Same type as No. 14, but smaller shield (civil issue)	160.00	220.00
16 (34)	2 Kroner (Ag) 1907. Same type as No. 15, but crossed rifles under legend, symbol of defence vigilance (military issue)	300.00	400.00
17 (35)	1 Øre (Br) 1908–1952. Crown above monogram. ℞ value	0.40	0.80
18 (36)	2 Øre (Br) 1909–1952	0.40	0.80
19 (37)	5 Øre (Br) 1908–1952	0.80	1.20
20 (38)	10 Øre (Ag) 1909–1919	4.00	6.50
21 (39)	25 Øre (Ag) 1909–1919. Crowned monogram in shape of cross. ℞ heraldic lion	10.50	16.00
22 (40)	50 Øre (Ag) 1909–1919. Haakon VII, head right. ℞ shield	8.00	12.00
23 (41)	1 Krone (Ag) 1908–1917. ℞ order of Saint Olaf	16.00	25.00

		VF	**XF**
24 (42)	2 Kroner (Ag) 1908–1917. ℞ crowned shield with order of Saint Olaf, surrounded by arms	30.00	52.00

		VF	**XF**
25 (43)	10 Kroner (Ag) 1910. Haakon VII (1872–1957), crowned head right. ℞ Olaf II Haraldson, the Saint (995–1030), King of Norway 1016–1030	255.00	280.00
26 (44)	20 Kroner (Au) 1910. Same type as No. 25	350.00	400.00

COMMEMORATIVE ISSUE FOR THE CENTENNIAL
OF THE CONSTITUTION OF NORWAY

			VF	XF
27 (45)	2 Kroner (Ag) 1914. Standing Norwegia. R crowned shield		40.00	65.00
28 (35a)	1 Øre (E) 1918–1921. Crowned monogram and crown. R value		7.50	12.00
29 (36a)	2 Øre (E) 1917–1920		8.00	13.00
30 (37a)	5 Øre (E) 1917–1920		18.00	30.00
31 (46)	10 Øre (Cu–Ni) 1920–1923. Crowned monogram		8.00	13.00
32 (49)	10 Øre (Cu–Ni) 1924–1951. Crown. R value (center hole)		0.30	0.50
33 (47)	25 Øre (Cu–Ni) 1921–1923. Crowned monogram. R heraldic lion		13.00	22.00
34 (47a)	25 Øre (Cu–Ni) 1921–1923 (center hole)		2.00	4.50
35 (50)	25 Øre (Cu–Ni) 1924–1950. Crowned monogram in shape of cross. R crown		0.40	0.80
36 (48)	50 Øre (Cu–Ni) 1920–1923. Crowned monogram in shape of cross. R crowned shield		12.00	22.00
37 (48a)	50 Øre (Cu–Ni) 1920–1923 (center hole)		4.00	8.00
38 (51)	50 Øre (Cu–Ni) 1926–1949. Crowned monogram in shape of cross. R crown (center hole)		0.90	2.00
39 (52)	1 Krone (Cu–Ni) 1925–1951. Crowned monogram in shape of cross. R crown with order of Saint Olaf (center hole)		1.00	2.00
40 (53)	1 Øre (E) 1941–1945. Shield. R value		0.80	1.60
41 (54)	2 Øre (E) 1943–1945		1.20	2.00
42 (55)	5 Øre (E) 1941–1945		1.20	2.00
43 (56)	10 Øre (Z) 1941–1945		1.50	3.20
44 (57)	25 Øre (Z) 1943–1945		3.00	6.00
45 (58)	50 Øre (Z) 1941–1945		3.00	7.50
46 (49a)	10 Øre (Ni–Bra) 1942		30.00	70.00
47 (50a)	25 Øre (Ni–Bra) 1942		30.00	70.00
48 (51a)	50 Øre (Ni–Bra) 1942		60.00	100.00

The coins Nos. 46–48 were issued by the Government in exile, in London.

			VF	XF
49 (59)	1	Øre (Br) 1952–1957	0.10	0.40
50 (60)	2	Øre (Br) 1952–1957	0.10	0.40
51 (61)	5	Øre (Br) 1952–1957	0.10	0.40
52 (62)	10	Øre (Cu–Ni) 1951–1957	0.20	0.40
53 (63)	25	Øre (Cu–Ni) 1952–1957	0.40	0.80

54 (64)	50	Øre (Cu–Ni) 1953–1957	0.60	1.00
55 (65)	1	Krone (Cu–Ni) 1951–1957	0.80	1.60

OLAF V since 1957

56a   56b

56 (66)   1 Øre (Br) 1958–1972. Crown above monogram OV. R squirrel (Sciurus vulgaris – Sciuridae)

	VF	XF
a) 1958. Legend small (pattern)	–.–	–.–
b) 1958–1972. Legend larger	0.20	0.40

57a   57b

57 (67)   2 Øre (Br). Moor hen (Lyrurus tetrix – Tetraonidae)

	VF	XF
a) 1958. Legend small	2.00	3.50
b) 1959-1967, 1969-1972. Legend larger	0.20	0.40
c) 1968 (3,467 pieces)	180.00	300.00

			VF	XF

58 (68) 5 Øre (Br) 1958–1973. Olaf V (*1903), head left. ℞ elk (Alces alces – Cervidae) — 0.20 0.40

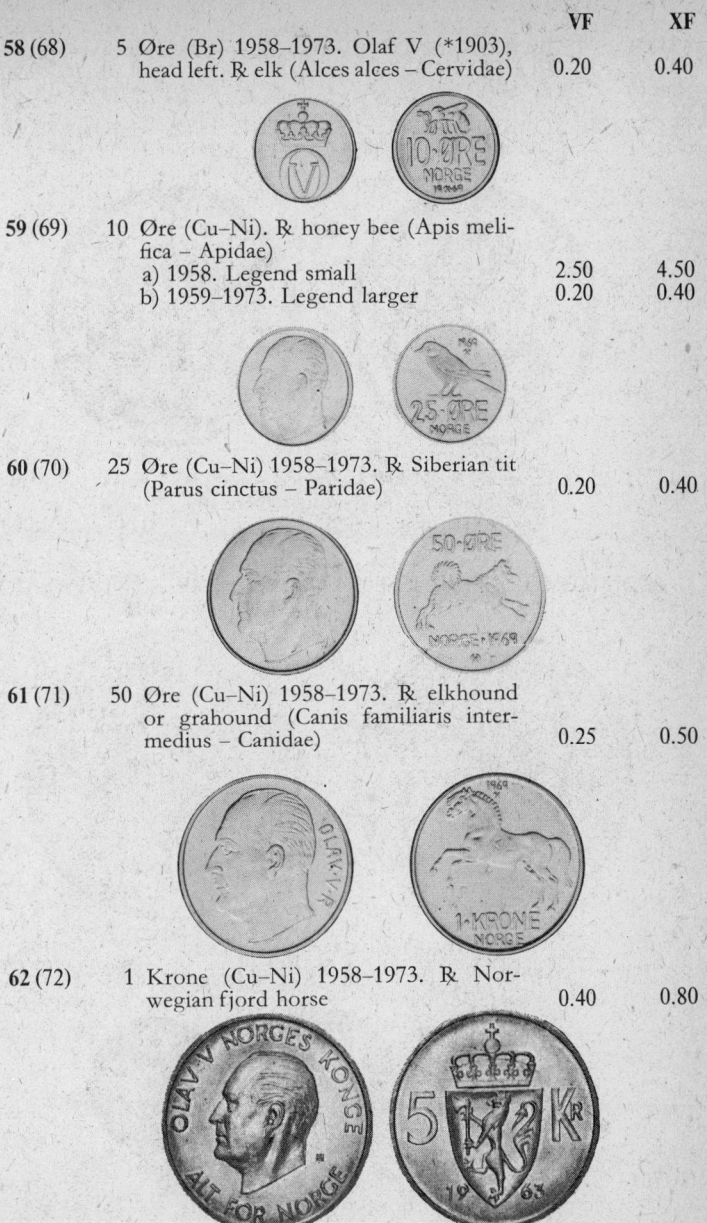

59 (69) 10 Øre (Cu–Ni). ℞ honey bee (Apis melifica – Apidae)
  a) 1958. Legend small 2.50 4.50
  b) 1959–1973. Legend larger 0.20 0.40

60 (70) 25 Øre (Cu–Ni) 1958–1973. ℞ Siberian tit (Parus cinctus – Paridae) 0.20 0.40

61 (71) 50 Øre (Cu–Ni) 1958–1973. ℞ elkhound or grahound (Canis familiaris intermedius – Canidae) 0.25 0.50

62 (72) 1 Krone (Cu–Ni) 1958–1973. ℞ Norwegian fjord horse 0.40 0.80

			VF	XF
63 (73)	5 Kroner (Cu–Ni) 1963–1973. ℞ crowned arms		1.20	2.50

COMMEMORATIVE ISSUE FOR THE 150th ANNIVERSARY OF NORWAY SIGNING THE CONSTITUTION

		XF	Unc
64 (74)	10 Kroner (Ag) 1964. Crowned shield. ℞ farm house in Eidsvoll, where the constitution was signed	11.00	18.00

COMMEMORATIVE ISSUE FOR THE 25th ANNIVERSARY OF THE END OF WORLD WAR II

65 (75)	25 Kroner (Ag) 1970. Haakon VII and Olaf V, heads right. ℞ legend, value	15.00	22.00

66a   66b

66 (76)	5 Øre (Br) 1973–. Norwegian armorial lion with axe. ℞ value, name of coun-

	XF	Unc
try, date, mint mark:		
a) 1973	0.20	0.40
b) 1974–. Design variety	0.05	0.10

67 (77) 10 Øre (Cu–Ni) 1974. Crowned monogram

	0.10	0.20

68 (78) 25 Øre (Cu–Ni) 1974. Crowned monograms placed in the shape of a cross 0.10 0.20

69 (79) 50 Øre (Cu–Ni) 1974. Crowned shield 0.15 0.30

70 (80) 1 Krone (Cu–Ni) 1974. Olaf V, head facing left, motto. ℞ crown, value 0.25 0.50

71 (81) 5 Kroner (Cu–Ni) 1974. ℞ crowned shield, value, date 0.70 1.40

100th ANNIVERSARY OF KRONE SYSTEM

72 (82)   5 Kroner (Cu-Ni) 1975. Crowned coat of arms, value. Rev. sitting mintmaker superimposed on a lever balance

	XF	Unc
	1.00	2.00

150th ANNIVERSARY OF NORWEGIAN EMMIGRATION TO AMERICA

73 (83)   5 Kroner (Cu-Ni) 1975. Norwegian lion with axe, value. Rev. The imagined likeness of the sloop "Restauration". In the lower segment the words VEIEN MOT VEST (the road westward)

	1.00	2.00

350th ANNIVERSARY OF THE NORWEGIAN ARMY

74 (84)   5 Kroner (Cu-Ni) 1978. Sword dividing crowned monograms of Kings Christian IV and Olaf V; above the word HÆREN. Norwegian lion with axe, value

	1.00	2.00

75th ANNIVERSARY OF THE BIRTH OF KING OLAV V

		XF	Unc
75 (85)	50 Kroner (Ag) 1978. Head left of the King. Rev. King's signature, stylized flower, value	16.50	24.00

35th ANNIVERSARY OF THE END OF WORLD WAR II

76 (86) 200 Kroner (Ag) 1980. View of the Norwegian castle Akershus   40.00

Oman

Sultanate of Oman

Sultanat Oman   Sultanat d'Oman

Area: 82,000 sq. mi. Population: 750,000.
Sultanate in the south-east of the Arabian Peninsula (formerly Muscat and Oman).
Capital: Muscat.

1000 Baiza = 1 Rial Omani

QABUS SA'ID since 1970

			Proof
1 (7)	15 Rials Omani (Au) H-C 1391 (1971). .917 gold, 7.99 gm.		–.–
2 (2)	25 Baiza (Au) H-C 1394 (1974). National arms. Rs. value and date; .917 gold, 5.96 gm.		–.–
3 (3)	50 Baiza (Au) H-C 1394 (1974). Type as No. 2; .917 gold, 12.89 gm.		–.–
4 (4)	100 Baiza (Au) H-C 1394, 1395 (1974, 1975). Type as No. 2; .917 gold, 22.74 gm.		–.–
5 (5)	½ Rial Omani (Au) H-C 1394, 1397 (1974, 1977). Type similar as No. 2; .917 gold, 25.6 gm.		–.–
6 (6)	1 Rial Omani (Au) H-C 1394, 1397 (1974, 1977). Type as No. 5; .917 gold, 46.65 gm.		*1000.00*

ISSUE FOR THE FAO COIN PLAN

		XF	Unc
7 (1)	10 Baiza (Br) H-C 1395 (1975). Date palms (Phoenix dactylifera – Palmae). Rev. value, date	0.25	0.50

			XF	Unc
8 (8)	5 Baiza (Br) H-C 1395 (1975). National arms. Rs. value and date		0.10	0.20
9 (9)	10 Baiza (Br) H-C 1395 (1975). Type as No. 8		0.15	0.30
10 (10)	25 Baiza (Cu-Ni) H-C 1395 (1975). Type as No. 8		0.30	0.70
11 (12)	50 Baiza (Cu-Ni) H-C 1395 (1975). Type as No. 8		0.50	0.90

			Unc	Proof
12 (11)	25 Baiza (Au) H-C 1395 (1975). Type as No. 10			–.–
13 (13)	50 Baiza (Au) H-C 1395, 1397 (1975, 1977). Type as No. 11			– –

CONSERVATION COMMEMORATIVE (3)

		XF	Proof
14 (14)	2½ Rials (Ag) 1977	30.00	40.00
15 (15)	5 Rials (Ag) 1977	40.00	50.00
16 (16)	75 Rials (Au) 1977	600.00	850.00

FAO COIN ISSUES (2)

		XF	Unc
17 (17)	½ Rial (Cu-Ni) 1978	2.50	4.00
18 (18)	1 Rial (Cu-Ni) 1978	8.50	12.00
19	¼ Rial (Al-Br) 1980	–.–	–.–
20	½ Rial (Al-Br) 1980	–.–	–.–

Pakistan

Area: 310,236 sq. mi. Population: 71,000,000.
Republic in the western part of the Indian subcontinent, consisting to
1971 of the provinces of West and East Pakistan (now Bangladesh).
Capital: Rawalpindi, the future capital: Islamabad.

3 Pies = 1 Pice, 4 Pice = 1 Anna, 16 Annas = 1 Rupee;
since January 1st, 1961: 100 Paisa = 1 Pakistan Rupee

			VF	XF
1 (1)	1	Pice (Br) 1948–1952. Legend with name of country. ℞ value (center hole)	0.15	0.40
2 (2)	½	Anna (Cu–Ni) 1948–1951. Toughra. ℞ state emblem (crescent and star)	0.15	0.30
3 (3)	1	Anna (Cu–Ni) 1948–1952. Toughra. ℞ crescent, facing right (scalloped)	0.30	0.80
4 (3a)	1	Anna (Cu–Ni) 1950. ℞ crescent, facing left (scalloped)	9.00	16.00
5 (4)	2	Anna (Cu–Ni) 1948–1951. ℞ crescent, facing right (square)	0.25	0.50
6 (4a)	2	Anna (Cu–Ni) 1950. ℞ crescent, facing left (square)	12.00	20.00
7 (5)	¼	Rupee (Ni) 1948–1951. ℞ crescent, facing right	0.40	0.60
8 (5a)	¼	Rupee (Ni) 1950. ℞ crescent, facing left	18.00	28.00
9 (6)	½	Rupee (Ni) 1948–1951. Type as No. 7	0.80	1.20
10 (7)	1	Rupee (Ni) 1948–1949. Type as No. 7	1.50	2.50
11 (8)	1	Pie (Br) 1951–1957. Toughra and state emblem. ℞ value	0.15	0.25

12 (9)	1	Pice (Ni–Bra) 1953–1959. Toughra and state emblem. ℞ value between ears of wheat	0.10	0.25

			VF	**XF**
13 (10)	½	Anna (Ni–Bra) 1953–1958 (square)	0.10	0.25

			VF	**XF**
14 (11)	1	Anna (Cu–Ni) 1953–1958 (scalloped)	0.20	0.30
15 (12)	2	Annas (Cu–Ni) 1953–1959. ℞ value in wreath (square)	0.40	0.75

NEW CURRENCY: 100 Paisa = 1 Rupee

			VF	**XF**
16 (13)	1	Pice (Br) 1961. Toughra and state emblem. ℞ value	0.10	0.20
17 (13a)	1	Paisa (Br) 1961–1963. Type as No. 16	0.10	0.20
18 (14)	5	Pice (Ni–Bra) 1961. ℞ sailing boat (pallar) with value on sail (square)	0.20	0.40

			VF	**XF**
19 (14a)	5	Paise (Ni–Bra) 1961–1963. ℞ pallar with value on sail (square)	0.10	0.20
20 (15)	10	Pice (Cu–Ni) 1961. ℞ value in wreath (scalloped)	0.30	0.60

			VF	**XF**
21 (15a)	10	Paisa (Cu–Ni) 1961-1963. Rev. value in wreath (scalloped)	0.40	0.60
22 (18)	1	Paisa (Br) 1964-1965. Rev. value between ears of wheat (round)	0.25	0.50
23 (18a)	1	Paisa (Ni–Bra) 1965-1966. Type as No. 22	0.10	0.20
24 (19)	2	Paisa (Br) 1964-1966 (scalloped)	0.10	0.25
25 (23)	2	Paisa (Al) 1966-1968 (round)	0.10	0.20

				VF	**XF**
26 (20)	5	Paisa	(Ni-Bra) 1964-1974 (square)	0.10	0.25
27 (21)	10	Paisa	(Cu-Ni) 1964-1968 (scalloped)	0.15	0.40
28 (16)	25	Paisa	(Ni) 1963-1967 (round)	0.15	0.40

| **29** (17) | 50 | Paisa | (Ni) 1963-1966, 1968, 1969 | 0.40 | 0.80 |
| **30** (22) | 1 | Paisa | (Al) 1967-1972 (round) | 0.10 | 0.20 |

31 (19a)	2	Paisa	(Al) 1968-1974. Type as No. 25, but scalloped	0.10	0.20
32 (21a)	10	Paisa	(Cu-Ni) 1969-1974	0.10	0.25
33 (24)	25	Paisa	(Cu-Ni) 1967-1974. Obverse like No. 28. Rev. value in Persian on right and left flower; below "25"	0.20	0.40
34 (25)	50	Paisa	(Cu-Ni) 1969-1974. Same type as No. 33	0.30	0.60

ISSUE FOR THE FAO COIN PLAN (4)

				XF	**Unc**
35 (26)	1	Paisa	(Al) 1974–1979. Cotton	0.10	0.25
36 (27)	2	Paisa	(Al) 1974–1976. Rice	0.10	0.25
37 (28)	5	Paisa	(Al) 1974–1979. Sugar-cane	0.15	0.30
38 (29)	10	Paisa	(Al) 1974–1979. Ears	0.15	0.30

| **39** (30) | 25 | Paise | (Cu-Ni) 1975–1979 | 0.15 | 0.30 |
| **40** (31) | 50 | Paisa | (Cu-Ni) 1975–1979 | 0.25 | 0.50 |

			Unc	Proof

CONSERVATION COMMEMORATIVE (3)

			Unc	Proof
41 (32)	100	Rupees (Ag) 1976	30.00	40.00
42 (33)	150	Rupees (Ag) 1976	40.00	50.00
43 (34)	3000	Rupees (Au) 1976	550.00	800.00

100th ANNIVERSARY OF THE BIRTH OF MOHAMMAD ALI JINNAH (3)

44 (35)	50	Paisa (Cu-Ni) 1976	0.60	
45 (36)	100	Rupees (Ag) 1976	30.00	40.00
46 (37)	500	Rupees (Au) 1976	140.00	160.00

ISLAMIC SUMMIT CONFERENCE (4)

47 (38)	1	Rupee (Cu-Ni) 1977	0.80	
48 (39)	100	Rupees (Ag) 1977	28.00	35.00
49	500	Rupees (Au) 1977		80.00
50 (40)	1000	Rupees (Au) 1977	120.00	160.00

100th ANNIVERSARY OF THE BIRTH OF MOHAMMAD IQBAL (3)

51 (41)	1	Rupee (Cu-Ni) 1977	0.80	
52 (42)	100	Rupees (Ag) 1977	15.00	20.00
53 (43)	500	Rupees (Au) 1977	70.00	90.00

WORLD FOOD DAY

			XF	Unc
54	1	Rupee (Cu-Ni) 1981	0.70	1.10

1400th ANNIVERSARY OF MOHAMMED'S FLIGHT

			XF	Unc
55	1	Rupee (Cu-Ni) 1981	0.70	1.10

Between 1918 and 1948 Palestine was under British mandate. After the repeal of the mandate, and the withdrawal of the troops, the State of Israel was proclaimed on May 14, 1948.

1000 Mils = £ 1

			VF	XF
1 (1)	1	Mil (Br) 1927–1947. A'rab name of country, also English and Hebrew name. ℞ olive branch, and value	0.80	1.60
2 (2)	2	Mils (Br) 1927–1947	0.60	2.00

3 (3)	5	Mils (center hole)		
		a) (Cu–Ni) 1927–1941, 1946, 1947	0.90	2.00
		b) (Br) 1942–1944	1.60	3.00
4 (4)	10	Mils (center hole)		
		a) (Cu–Ni) 1927–1941, 1946, 1947	1.60	2.50
		b) (Br) 1942–1943	5.50	9.00
5 (5)	20	Mils (center hole)		
		a) (Cu–Ni) 1927–1941	6.00	10.00
		b) (Br) 1942–1944	9.00	16.00
6 (6)	50	Mils (Ag) 1927–1942. Olive branch. ℞ value	4.50	8.00
7 (7)	100	Mils (Ag) 1927–1942. Olive branch. ℞ value in circle	7.50	16.00

Panama

Area: 28,575 sq. mi. Population: 2,000,000.
Formerly a member of the Columbian Confederacy, the country declared
its independence in 1903.
Capital: Panama City.

100 Centesimos = 1 Balboa

			VF	XF
1 (5)	2½	Centesimos (Ag) 1904. Vasco Núñez de Balboa (ca. 1475–1517), Spanish conqueror, reached the Gulf of San Miguel in the Pacific on September 29, 1513. ℞ coat of arms. So-called Panama pill.	16.00	28.00
2 (6)	5	Centesimos (Ag) 1904–1916:		
		a) 1904	8.00	12.00
		b) 1916	140.00	200.00
3 (7)	10	Centesimos (Ag) 1904	10.00	22.00
4 (8)	25	Centesimos (Ag) 1904	15.00	30.00
5 (9)	50	Centesimos (Ag) 1904–1905	40.00	70.00
6 (1)	½	Centesimo (Cu–Ni) 1907. ℞ value in letters	1.50	3.00
7 (2)	2½	Centesimos (Cu–Ni) 1907. Coat of arms. ℞ value in letters: DOS Y MEDIOS CENTESIMOS	3.00	7.00
8 (2a)	2½	Centesimos (Cu–Ni) 1916. Same type as No. 7, value in letters, but this time: DOS Y MEDIO CENTESIMOS	4.00	8.00

9 (3)	2½	Centesimos (Cu–Ni) 1929. Balboa, bust left. ℞ value in letters	5.50	12.00
10 (4)	5	Centesimos (Cu–Ni) 1929–1932. Coat of arms. ℞ value	4.00	7.00

			VF	XF
11 (10)	1 Centesimo (Cu) 1935–1937. Urraca, cazique (Indian chief) of Burica (Costa Rica); portrait left. R value in letters		2.00	4.00
12 (11)	1¼ Centesimos (Cu) 1940. Balbao, portrait left. R. value in letters		1.50	2.50
13 (12)	2½ Centesimos (Cu-Ni) 1940		1.20	2.50
14 (13)	1/10 Balboa. Balboa, portrait left. Rs coat of arms:		3.50	6.00
	a) Y 13 (Ag) 1930–1934		1.00	1.50
	b) Y 13 (Ag) 1947–1962		0.15	0.25
	c) Y 13a (Cu-Ni) 1966–1972		8.00	18.00
15 (14)	¼ Balboa. Type as No. 14:		4.00	7.00
	a) Y 14 (Ag) 1930–1934		0.30	0.50
	b) Y 14 (Ag) 1947–1962			
	c) Y 14a (Cu-Ni) 1966–1972			
16 (15)	½ Balboa. Type as No. 14:			
	a) Y 15 (Ag) 1930–1934		8.00	12.00
	b) Y 15 (Ag) 1947–1962		4.00	8.00
	c) Y 15a (Cu-Ni) 1966–1972		1.50	3.00
17 (16)	1 Balboa (Ag) 1931–1947. R allegory of the Republic and coat of arms		15.00	20.00

COMMEMORATIVE ISSUES (5) FOR THE 50th ANNIVERSARY OF THE REPUBLIC

18 (17)	1 Centesimo (Cu) 1953. Same type as No. 11, but with addition of CIN-CUENTENARIO. R date and value		0.30	0.60
19 (18)	1/10 Balboa (Ag) 1953. Same type as No. 14, but with addition of CINCUENTE-NARIO		1.00	2.50
20 (19)	¼ Balboa (Ag) 1953. Same type as No. 15, but with addition of CINCUENTE-NARIO		3.00	5.50
21 (20)	½ Balboa (Ag) 1953. Same type as No. 16, but with addition of CINCUENTE-NARIO		5.00	8.00

			XF	Unc
22 (21)	1	Balboa (Ag) 1953. Same type as No. 17, but with addition of CINCUENTENARIO	18.00	25.00
23 (22)	1	Centesimo (Cu) 1961–1977. Same type as No. 18, but without CINCUENTENARIO	0.10	0.20
24 (23)	5	Centesimos (Cu-Ni) 1961. Coat of arms. R value	0.60	1.20
25 (23a)	5	Centesimos (Cu-Ni) 1962–1975. Same type as No. 24, but with coat of arms narrower, and number smaller	0.15	0.30
26 (24)	1/10	Balboa (Ag) 1961. Same type as No. 19, but with laurel branches in place of CINCUENTENARIO	1.20	2.00
27 (25)	¼	Balboa (Ag) 1961. Same type as No. 20, but with laurel branches in place of CINCUENTENARIO	3.50	5.00
28 (26)	½	Balboa (Ag) 1961, 1962, 1970. Same type as No. 21, but with laurel branches in place of CINCUENTENARIO	5.50	8.00
29 (27)	1	Balboa (Ag) 1966–1974. Type as No. 14: a) 1966	15.00	18.00
		b) 1966–1972, Proof only		20.00

COMMEMORATIVE ISSUE FOR THE 11th CENTRAL AMERICAN AND CARIBBEAN ATHLETIC GAMES OF 1970, IN PANAMA

		Unc	Proof
30 (28)	5 Balboas (Ag) 1970. Man throwing a discus, memorial legend. ℞ coat of arms, value	25.00	32.00

COMMEMORATIVE ISSUE FOR THE 150th ANNIVERSARY OF INDEPENDENCE FROM SPAIN

		Unc	Proof
31 (29)	20 Balboas (Ag) 1971. Simón Bolívar (1783–1830), statesman and general, liberator of South America from Spanish rule. ℞ national coat of arms and value	90.00	140.00

			Unc	Proof
32 (30)	20	Balboas (Ag) 1972–1976. Type as No. 33, but legend reads on the obverse SIMON BOLIVAR 1783–1830	90.00	110.00

ISSUES (2) FOR THE FAO COIN PLAN

33 (31)	2½	Centesimos (Br) 1973, 1975. Coat of arms, value. Rev. rice (Oryza sativa – Gramineae)	0.30	
34 (32)	5	Balboas (Ag) 1972. Type as No. 33	28.00	100.00

500th ANNIVERSARY OF THE BIRTH OF VASCO NUNEZ DE BALBOA (2)

35 (41)	100	Balboas (Au) 1975–1977. Coat of arms. Rev. Head of Vasco Nunez de Balboa	150.00	175.00

36 (42)	500	Balboas (Au) 1975–1977. Balboa kneeling holding sword	750.00	800.00

			XF	Unc
37 (33)	1	Centesimo (Br) 1975–. Head of Urraca, Indian chief of Burica	0.40	1.00
38 (34)	2½	Centesimos (Cu-Ni) 1975–. Head of Victoriano Lorenzo, Indian chief	0.60	1.50
39 (35)	5	Centesimos (Cu-Ni) 1975–. Head of Carlos J. Finlay	1.00	2.00
40 (36)	10	Centesimos (Cu-Ni) 1975–. Head of Manuel E. Amador	1.10	2.20
41 (37)	25	Centesimos (Cu-Ni) 1975–. Head of Justo Arosemena	1.25	2.40

			XF	Unc
42 (38)	50	Centesimos (Cu-Ni) 1975–. Head of Fernando de Lesseps	1.50	2.70
43 (39)	1	Balboa 1975–. Vasco Nunez de Balboa:		
		a) (Cu-Ni) 1975–	4.00	8.00
		b) (Ag) 1975–; proof only		20.00
44 (40)	5	Balboas 1975–. Head of Belisario Porras:		
		a) (Cu-Ni) 1975–	10.00	17.50
		b) (Ag) 1975–; proof only		28.00
45 (39b)	1	Balboa (Cu-Ni) 1975, 1976. Type as No. 43b (with .925 silver fineness on reverse)		30.00
46 (40b)	5	Balboas (Cu-Ni) 1975, 1976. Type as No. 44 b (with .925 silver fineness on reverse)		40.00

150th ANNIVERSARY OF THE PAN-AMERICAN CONGRESS

			XF	Unc
47 (43)	150	Balboas (Platinum) 1976. Bust left of Simon Bolivar	400.00	300.00
48 (44)	20	Balboas (Ag) 1977, 1979. Vasco Nuñez de Balboa	90.00	110.00

75th ANNIVERSARY OF INDEPENDENCE (10)

			Unc	Proof
49 (45)	1	Centesimo (Br) 1978	0.60	2.00
50 (46)	2½	Centesimos (Cu-Ni) 1978	0.80	2.00
51 (47)	5	Centesimos (Cu-Ni) 1978	1.00	2.00
52 (48)	10	Centesimos (Cu-Ni) 1978	1.10	2.00
53 (49)	25	Centesimos (Cu-Ni) 1978	1.25	2.50
54 (50)	50	Centesimos (Cu-Ni) 1978	1.60	4.00
55 (51)	1	Balboa 1978:		
		a) (Cu-Ni)	10.00	
		b) (Ag)		22.00
56 (52)	5	Balboas 1978:		
		a) (Cu-Ni)	40.00	
		b) (Ag)		25.00
57 (53)	20	Balboas (Ag) 1978	100.00	120.00
58 (54)	75	Balboas (Au) 1978. Rev. flag	140.00	120.00
59 (56)	100	Balboas (Au) 1978. Dove-Orchid	300.00	180.00

30th ANNIVERSARY OF THE ORGANIZATION OF AMERICAN STATE

			XF	Unc
60 (57)	500	Balboas (Au) 1978. Rev. Globe with North and South America	850.00	800.00

PANAMA CANAL TREATY RATIFICATION

			Unc	Proof
61 (55)	10	Balboas 1978:		
		a) (Cu-Ni)	12.50	
		b) (Ag)		40.00

PANAMA CANAL TREATY IMPLEMENTATION

			Unc	Proof
62 (59)	5	Balboas (Ag) 1979		40.00
63 (60)	10	Balboas (Ag) 1979		80.00
64 (58)	500	Balboas (Au) 1979. Golden Jaguar		850.00
65 (61)	200	Balboas (Platinum) 1979. Panama Canal Treaties		400.00
66 (62)	100	Balboas (Au) 1979. Golden Turtle	300.00	280.00
67 (63)	20	Balboas (Ag) 1980. Simon Bolivar on horseback		220.00
68 (64)	100	Balboas (Au) 1980. Golden Condor	400.00	380.00
69 (67)	500	Balboas (Au) 1980. White herons		1400.00

PANAMA CANAL CENTENNIAL

			Unc	Proof
70 (65)	100	Balboas (Au) 1980. Fernando de Lesseps	150.00	185.00

SIMON BOLIVAR SESQUICENTENARIUM

			Unc	Proof
71 (66)	100	Balboas (Au) 1980. Simon Bolivar	200.00	225.00
72	500	Balboas (Au) 1981. Rev. Sailfish		420.00

CHRISTMAS 1981

			Unc	Proof
73	50	Balboas (Au) 1981. Rev. Dove		200.00

Papua New Guinea

Papua-Neuguinea   Papoua Nouvelle Guinée

Area: 183,540 sq. mi. Population: 2,600,000
The largest island in the world after Greenland has been known geographically since the 16th century, but was hardly developed up to the 19th century and also later on only slightly opened up. Partycularly Dutch interests on the western half fluctuated between commercial and political activities. In the 19th century the Netherlands declared their claims regarding the western half, whereupon a British man-of-war proclaimed British rule over the Southeast; Germany followed soon after (cf. New Guinea). The island was partly named Papua according to the inhabitants, partly New Guinea due to its supposed similarity with West African coastlines. In Port Moresby, after British New Guinea had been declared a Crown Colony in 1888, an administrator under the control of the Governor of Queensland was appointed; after the formation of the Australian Federation, the latter were also entrusted with the administration of the territory now called "Papua" on 1st Sept. 1906. The Territory of Papua was united with the Territory of New Guinea (see New Guinea) in 1949 to form a new Territory of Papua and New Guinea which, since 24th June 1971 is called Papua New Guinea (without the word "Territory" and without „and"), was permitted to elect in March 1972 a House of Deputies received internal autonomy in December 1973 and was to receive full independence at the end of 1974.
Capital: Port Moresby.

100 Toea = 1 Kina

			Unc	Proof
1 (1)	1	Toea (Br) 1975-	0.10	1.00
2 (2)	2	Toea (Br) 1975-	0.15	1.20
3 (3)	5	Toea (Cu-Ni) 1975-	0.25	1.50
4 (4)	10	Toea (Cu-Ni) 1975-	0.45	2.00
5 (5)	20	Toea (Cu-Ni) 1975-	1.00	3.00
6 (6)	1	Kina (Cu-Ni) 1975-	3.00	4.50
7 (7)	5	Kina 1975-		
		a) (Cu-Ni)	12.00	
		b) (Ag)		35.00
8 (8)	10	Kina 1975-		
		a) (Cu-Ni)	22.00	
		b) (Ag)		50.00

INDEPENDENCE COMMEMORATIVE

			Unc	Proof
9 (9)	100	Kina (Au) 1975. Prime Minister Michael T. Somare. Rev. bird of Paradise	190.00	200.00

1st ANNIVERSARY OF INDEPENDENCE

		Unc	Proof
10 (10) 100 Kina (Au) 1976		190.00	200.00

25th ANNIVERSARY OF THE SILVER JUBILEE OF HER MAJESTY QUEEN ELIZABETH II

		Unc	Proof
11 (11) 10 Kina 1977:			
a) (Cu-Ni)		60.00	
b) (Ag)			105.00
12 (12) 100 Kina (Au) 1977		250.00	220.00
13 (13) 100 Kina (Au) 1978		200.00	180.00
14 (14) 100 Kina (Au) 1979		200.00	220.00

SOUTH PACIFIC FESTIVAL OF ARTS (2)

15 (15) 50 Toea (Cu-Ni) 1980		1.50	–.–
16 (16) 100 Kina (Au) 1980			200.00

5th ANNIVERSARY OF INDEPENDENCE

17 (17) 100 Kina Au) 1980			300.00

Paraguay
Republica del Paraguay

Area: 157,000 sq. mi. Population: 3,000,000.

The town of Asunción, founded on August 15, 1537, soon became the center of colonization of the upper La Plata territory and later the center of the Jesuit state. After the uprising against Spain, Paraguay became a republic on May 14, 1811.

Capital: Asunción.

100 Centavos = 1 Peso,
since 5th October 1943: 100 Centimos = 1 Guarani

			VF	XF
1 (6)	5	Centavos (Cu–Ni) 1900–1903. Coat of arms showing lion with liberty cap (= state emblem). ℞ value within wreath	3.20	6.00
2 (7)	10	Centavos (Cu–Ni) 1900–1903	4.50	7.50
3 (8)	20	Centavos (Cu–Ni) 1900–1903	5.00	8.00
4 (9)	5	Centavos (Cu–Ni) 1908. Star within wreath. ℞ value	10.00	25.00
5 (10)	10	Centavos (Cu–Ni) 1908	15.00	25.00
6 (11)	20	Centavos (Cu–Ni) 1908	5.00	11.50
7 (12)	50	Centavos (Cu–Ni) 1925	2.00	3.00
8 (13)	1	Peso (Cu–Ni) 1925	2.50	4.50
9 (14)	2	Pesos (Cu–Ni) 1925	3.50	5.50
10 (15)	5	Pesos (Cu–Ni) 1939	3.50	5.50

11 (16)	10	Pesos (Cu–Ni) 1939	4.50	6.50
12 (17)	50	Centavos (Al) 1938	1.00	2.00
13 (18)	1	Peso (Al) 1938	2.00	3.00
14 (19)	2	Pesos (Al) 1938	3.00	5.00

			VF	XF
15 (20)	1 Centimo (Al–Br) 1944–1950. Flower. ℞ value within wreath		0.40	0.60
16 (21)	5 Centimos (Al–Br) 1944–1947. Passion-flower (Passiflora sp. – Passifloraceae). ℞ value within wreath		0.50	0.80

			VF	XF
17 (22)	10 Centimos (Al–Br) 1944–1947. Orchid. ℞ value within wreath		0.25	0.50
18 (23)	25 Centimos (Al–Br) 1944–1951. Orchid. ℞ value within wreath		0.60	1.00
19 (24)	50 Centimos (Al–Br) 1944–1951. Coat of arms. ℞ value within wreath		0.80	1.50
20 (25)	10 Centimos (Al–Br) 1953 (scalloped)		0.20	0.30
21 (26)	15 Centimos (Al–Br) 1953		0.25	0.40
22 (27)	25 Centimos (Al–Br) 1953		0.25	0.50

			VF	XF
23 (28)	50 Centimos (Al–Br) 1953		0.40	0.80

COMMEMORATIVE COINS (2) FOR PRESIDENT STROESSNER'S 4th TERM IN OFFICE 1968–1973

			XF	Unc
24 (29)	300 Guaranies (Ag) 1968. Alfredo Stroessner (*1912), military officer and politician, President since 1954. ℞ state emblem and motto; name of country, value. Edge inscription: CENTENARIO DE LA EPOPEYA NACIONAL		16.00	25.00
25 (30)	10000 Guaranies (Au) 1968. Same type as No. 24		–.–	–.–

26	150	Guaranies (Ag) 1972. President Stroessner	30.00
27	1500	Guaranies (Au) 1972. Type as No. 26	200.00
28	3000	Guaranies (Au) 1972. Type as No. 26	400.00
29	4500	Guaranies (Au) 1972. Type as No. 26	600.00
30	150	Guaranies (Ag) 1972. Munich Olympics 1972 – sprinter	30.00

31	1500	Guaranies (Au) 1972. Type as No. 30	200.00
32	3000	Guaranies (Au) 1972. Type as No. 30	400.00
33	4500	Guaranies (Au) 1972. Type as No. 30	600.00
34	150	Guaranies (Ag) 1972. Munich Olympics 1972 – footballer	30.00
35	1500	Guaranies (Au) 1972. Type as No. 34	200.00
36	3000	Guaranies (Au) 1972. Type as No. 34	400.00
37	4500	Guaranies (Au) 1972. Type as No. 34	600.00
38	150	Guaranies (Ag) 1972. Munich Olympics 1952 – long-jumper	30.00
39	1500	Guaranies (Au) 1972. Type as No. 38	200.00
40	3000	Guaranies (Au) 1972. Type as No. 38	400.00
41	4500	Guaranies (Au) 1972. Type as No. 38	600.00
42	150	Guaranies (Ag) 1972. Munich Olympics 1972 – high-jumper	30.00
43	1500	Guaranies (Au) 1972. Type as No. 42	200.00
44	3000	Guaranies (Au) 1972. Type as No. 42	400.00
45	4500	Guaranies (Au) 1972. Type as No. 42	600.00
46	150	Guaranies (Ag) 1972. Munich Olympics 1972 – hurdler	30.00
47	1500	Guaranies (Au) 1972. Type as No. 46	200.00
48	3000	Guaranies (Au) 1972. Type as No. 46	400.00
49	4500	Guaranies (Au) 1972. Type as No. 46	600.00
50	150	Guaranies (Ag) 1973. Munich Olympics 1972 – boxer	30.00
51	1500	Guaranies (Au) 1973. Type as No. 50	200.00
52	3000	Guaranies (Au) 1973. Type as No. 50	400.00
53	4500	Guaranies (Au) 1973. Type as No. 50	600.00
54	150	Guaranies (Ag) 1973. Marshal José F. Estigarribia (1888–1940), president 1939–1940	30.00
55	1500	Guaranies (Au) 1973. Type as No. 54	200.00
56	3000	Guaranies (Au) 1973. Type as No. 54	400.00
57	4500	Guaranies (Au) 1973. Type as No. 54	600.00

			Proof
58	150	Guaranies (Ag) 1973. Marshal Solano López (1827–1870), president 1862 to 1870	30.00
59	1500	Guaranies (Au) 1973. Type as No. 58	200.00
60	3000	Guaranies (Au) 1973. Type as No. 58	400.00
61	4500	Guaranies (Au) 1973. Type as No. 58	600.00
62	150	Guaranies (Ag) 1973. General José E. Diaz	30.00
63	1500	Guaranies (Au) 1973. Type as No. 62	200.00
64	3000	Guaranies (Au) 1973. Type as No. 62	400.00
65	4500	Guaranies (Au) 1973. Type as No. 62	600.00
66	150	Guaranies (Ag) 1973. General Bernardino Caballero (1831–1885), president 1880–1885	30.00
67	1500	Guaranies (Au) 1973. Type as No. 66	200.00
68	3000	Guaranies (Au) 1973. Type as No. 66	400.00
69	4500	Guaranies (Au) 1973. Type as No. 66	600.00
70	150	Guaranies (Ag) 1973. Seated woman, Teotihuacán culture, highland of Mexico, c. 100 B. C. – 400 A. D.	30.00
71	1500	Guaranies (Au) 1973. Type as No. 70	200.00
72	3000	Guaranies (Au) 1973. Type as No. 70	400.00
73	4500	Guaranies (Au) 1973. Type as No. 70	600.00
74	150	Guaranies (Ag) 1973. Vessel, polychrome decoration, Huaxtec culture of the northern Gulf coast of Mexico	30.00
75	1500	Guaranies (Au) 1973. Type as No. 74	200.00
76	3000	Guaranies (Au) 1973. Type as No. 74	400.00
77	4500	Guaranies (Au) 1973. Type as No. 74	600.00
78	150	Guaranies (Ag) 1973. Four-legged earthenware vessel in the shape of a jaguar, polychrome decoration, Mixtec cuture, c. 900–1494 A. D.	30.00

79	1500	Guaranies (Au) 1973. Type as No. 78	200.00
80	3000	Guaranies (Au) 1973. Type as No. 78	400.00
81	4500	Guaranies (Au) 1973. Type as No. 78	600.00
82	150	Guaranies (Ag) 1973. Vessel, Tolul style of Veracruz	30.00
83	1500	Guaranies (Au) 1973. Type as No. 82	200.00
84	3000	Guaranies (Au) 1973. Type as No. 82	400.00
85	4500	Guaranies (Au) 1973. Type as No. 82	600.00

			Proof
86	150	Guaranies (Ag) 1973. "Smiling face", culture of Veracruz	30.00
87	1500	Guaranies (Au) 1973. Type as No. 86	200.00
88	3000	Guaranies (Au) 1973. Type as No. 86	400.00
89	4500	Guaranies (Au) 1973. Type as No. 86	600.00
90	150	Guaranies (Ag) 1973. Albrecht Dürer (1471–1528), painter, graphic artist, author on the arts	30.00
91	1500	Guaranies (Au) 1973. Type as No. 90	200.00
92	3000	Guaranies (Au) 1973. Type as No. 90	400.00
93	4500	Guaranies (Au) 1973. Type as No. 90	600.00
94	150	Guaranies (Ag) 1973. Johann Wolfgang von Goethe (1749–1832), poet	30.00
95	1500	Guaranies (Au) 1973. Type as No. 94	200.00
96	3000	Guaranies (Au) 1973. Type as No. 94	400.00
97	4500	Guaranies (Au) 1973. Type as No. 94	600.00
98	150	Guaranies (Ag) 1973. Abraham Lincoln (1809–1865), 16th President of the United States of America	30.00
99	1500	Guaranies (Au) 1974. Type as No. 98	200.00
100	3000	Guaranies (Au) 1974. Type as No. 98	400.00
101	4500	Guaranies (Au) 1974. Type as No. 98	600.00
102	150	Guaranies (Ag) 1974. Ludwig van Beethoven (1770–1827), composer	30.00
103	1500	Guaranies (Au) 1974. Type as No. 102	200.00
104	3000	Guaranies (Au) 1974. Type as No. 102	400.00
105	4500	Guaranies (Au) 1974. Type as No. 102	600.00
106	150	Guaranies (Ag) 1974. Otto von Bismarck (1815–1898), founder of the second German Reich	30.00
107	1500	Guaranies (Au) 1974. Type as No. 106	200.00
108	3000	Guaranies (Au) 1974. Type as No. 106	400.00
109	4500	Guaranies (Au) 1974. Type as No. 106	600.00
110	150	Guaranies (Ag) 1974. Albert Einstein (1879–1955), physicist	30.00
111	1500	Guaranies (Au) 1974. Type as No. 110	200.00
112	3000	Guaranies (Au) 1974. Type as No. 110	400.00
113	4500	Guaranies (Au) 1974. Type as No. 110	600.00
114	150	Guaranies (Ag) 1974. Giuseppe Garibaldi (1807–1882), Italian hero in the struggle for freedom	30.00
115	1500	Guaranies (Au) 1974. Type as No. 114	200.00
116	3000	Guaranies (Au) 1974. Type as No. 114	400.00
117	4500	Guaranies (Au) 1974. Type as No. 114	600.00
118	150	Guaranies (Ag) 1974. Alessandro Manzoni (1785–1873), Italian poet	30.00
119	1500	Guaranies (Au) 1974. Type as No. 118	200.00
120	3000	Guaranies (Au) 1974. Type as No. 118	400.00
121	4500	Guaranies (Au) 1974. Type as No. 118	600.00
122	150	Guaranies (Ag) 1974. William Tell, the hero of the well-kown Swiss legend	30.00

123	1500	Guaranies (Au) 1974. Type as No. 122	200.00
124	3000	Guaranies (Au) 1974. Type as No. 122	400.00
125	4500	Guaranies (Au) 1974. Type as No. 122	600.00
126	150	Guaranies (Ag) 1974. John F. Kennedy (1917–1963), 35th President of the United States of America	30.00
127	1500	Guaranies (Au) 1974. Type as No. 126	200.00
128	3000	Guaranies (Au) 1974. Type as No. 126	400.00
129	4500	Guaranies (Au) 1974. Type as No. 126	600.00
130	150	Guaranies (Ag) 1974. Konrad Adenauer (1876–1967), first German Federal chancellor	30.00
131	1500	Guaranies (Au) 1974. Type as No. 130	200.00
132	3000	Guaranies (Au) 1974. Type as No. 130	400.00
133	4500	Guaranies (Au) 1974. Type as No. 130	600.00
134	150	Guaranies (Ag) 1974. Winston Churchill (1874–1965), British statesman	30.00
135	1500	Guaranies (Au) 1974. Type as No. 134	200.00
136	3000	Guaranies (Au) 1974. Type as No. 134	400.00
137	4500	Guaranies (Au) 1974. Type as No. 134	600.00
138	150	Guaranies (Ag) 1974. Pope John XXIII, Roncalli (1881–1963)	30.00
139	1500	Guaranies (Au) 1974. Type as No. 138	200.00
140	3000	Guaranies (Au) 1974. Type as No. 138	400.00
141	4500	Guaranies (Au) 1974. Type as No. 138	600.00
142	150	Guaranies (Ag) 1975. Pope Paul VI, Montini (1897-1978)	30.00
143	1500	Guaranies (Au) 1975. Type as No. 142	200.00
144	3000	Guaranies (Au) 1975. Type as No. 142	400.00
145	4500	Guaranies (Au) 1975. Type as No. 142	600.00
146	150	Guaranies (Ag) 1975. Bridge of Friendship	30.00
147	1500	Guaranies (Au) 1975. Type as No. 146	200.00
148	3000	Guaranies (Au) 1975. Type as No. 146	400.00
149	4500	Guaranies (Au) 1975. Type as No. 146	600.00
150	150	Guaranies (Ag) 1975. Parliament building in Asunción	30.00

151	1500	Guaranies (Au) 1975. Type as No. 150	200.00
152	3000	Guaranies (Au) 1975. Type as No. 150	400.00

153	4500	Guaranies (Au) 1975. Type as No. 150	600.00
154	150	Guaranies (Ag) 1975. Church of San Roque in Yaguaron	30.00
155	1500	Guaranies (Au) 1975. Type as No. 154	200.00
156	3000	Guaranies (Au) 1975. Type as No. 154	400.00
157	4500	Guaranies (Au) 1975. Type as No. 154	600.00
158	150	Guaranies (Ag) 1975. Ruin of the church of Humaitá	30.00
159	1500	Guaranies (Au) 1975. Type as No. 158	200.00
160	3000	Guaranies (Au) 1975. Type as No. 158	400.00
161	4500	Guaranies (Au) 1975. Type as No. 158	600.00
162	150	Guaranies (Ag) 1975. US research program ,,Apollo 11"	30.00
163	1500	Guaranies (Au) 1975. Type as No. 162	200.00
164	3000	Guaranies (Au) 1975. Type as No. 162	400.00
165	4500	Guaranies (Au) 1975. Type as No. 162	600.00
166	150	Guaranies (Ag) 1975. US research program "Apollo 15"	30.00
167	1500	Guaranies (Ag) 1975. Type as No. 166	200.00
168	3000	Guaranies (Au) 1975. Type as No. 166	400.00
169	4500	Guaranies (Au) 1975. Type as No. 166	600.00

			XF	Unc
170 (31)	1	Guarani (St) 1975. Soldier. Rev. tobacco plant	0.05	0.10
171 (32)	5	Guaranies (St) 1975. A young woman holding a vessel in her right arm. Rev. cotton	0.10	0.15
172 (33)	10	Guaranies (St) 1975. Portrait of General Garay. Rev. cow's head	0.20	0.30
173 (34)	50	Guaranies (St) 1975	0.60	0.90

FOR THE FAO COIN PLAN (3)

174 (35)	1	Guarani (St) 1978	0.05	0.10
175 (36)	5	Guaranies (St) 1978	0.10	0.15
176 (37)	10	Guaranies (St) 1978	0.20	0.30

Peru

Peru   **Peru**   Pérou

Area: 514,060 sq. mi. Population: 18,000,000.
Before the conquest by the Spaniards under Francisco Pizarro (1531-1534),
Peru was the central province of the Inca empire. The province created
in 1542, and governed by a viceroy of Peru, comprised initially almost
the whole of Spanish South America. The provinces of New Granada
and Rio de la Plata were only detached in the 18th century. During the
early years of the battles of independence in South America, Peru was
the focal point of Spanish domination. The Republic was proclaimed on
28th July 1821, after the entry of General José de San Martín into Lima.
Capital: Lima.

10 Centavos = 1 Dinero,
100 Centavos = 10 Dineros = 1 Sol de Oro

			VF	XF
1 (9a)	1	Centavo (Br) 1975–1878, 1919. Date above sunburst. R value in wreath	1.20	2.00
2 (11)	1	Centavo (Br) 1901–1941. Date at bottom	1.00	1.50
3 (12)	1	Centavo (Br) 1876–1937. Date at bottom CENTAVO curved	1.00	2.00
4 (11a)	1	Centavo (Br) 1941–1944. Date at bottom CENTAVO straight	0.80	1.60
5 (12a)	1	Centavo (Br) 1941–1949. Date at bottom CENTAVO curved	0.40	0.80

			VF	XF
6 (10a)	2	Centavos (Br) 1876–1895, 1919. Date above sunburst. R value in wreath	1.00	1.60
7 (13)	2	Centavos (Br) 1917–1941. Date at bottom, CENTAVOS curved	0.50	0.80
8 (13a)	2	Centavos (Br) 1941–1949. Date at bottom, CENTAVOS curved. Same type as No. 7, but thinner planchet	0.40	0.60
9 (14)	½	Dinero (Ag) 1863–1917. Figure of Liberty, seated. R coat of arms	1.50	2.50

			VF	XF
10 (15)	1	Dinero (Ag) 1864–1916	2.50	3.50
11 (16)	1/5	Sol (Ag) 1863–1967	3.50	5.00
12 (17)	½	Sol (Ag) 1864–1917	8.00	12.00
13 (18)	1	Sol (Ag) 1864–1916	16.00	28.00
14 (20)	1/5	Libra (Au) 1906–1969. Head right of Manco Capac, founder of the Inca empire. R coat of arms	26.00	30.00
15 (21)	½	Libra (Au) 1902–1969. Same type as No. 14	65.00	75.00
A15 (22)	1	Libra (Au) 1898–1969. Same type as No. 14	125.00	150.00
B15 (23)	1	Sol (Ag) 1910	40.00	60.00
16 (24)	5	Soles (Au) 1910. Coat of arms. R motto and value	100.00	130.00
17 (31)	5	Centavos. Head of Liberty, right; date spelled out. R value and branch		
		a) (Cu-Ni) 1918–1941	0.25	0.40
		b) (Bra) 1942–1944	0.25	0.40
18 (32)	10	Centavos. Same type as No. 17		
		a) (Cu-Ni) 1918–1941	0.40	0.60
		b) (Bra) 1942–1944	0.50	0.80
19 (33)	20	Centavos. Same type as No. 17		
		a) (Cu-Ni) 1918–1941	0.40	0.80
		b) (Bra) 1942–1944	1.00	2.00
20 (34)	½	Sol (Ag) 1922–1935	5.00	8.00
21 (36)	1	Sol (Ag) 1923–1935. Coat of arms, new legend: REPUBLICA PERUANA LIMA 5 DECIMOS FINO, date. R allegory of the Liberty, UN SOL in exergue	7.50	11.00

			VF	XF
21a (35)	1	Sol (Ag) 1923. Same type as No. 21, but no Fineness	60.00	75.00

22 (37) 50 Soles (Au) 1930–1931, 1967–1969.
Manco Capac, founder of the Inca
empire in the 11th century. R Inca ornament:

	XF	Unc
a) 1930–1931	900.00	1100.00
b) 1967–1969	450.00	600.00

			VF	XF
23 (43)	½	Sol (Bra) 1935–1965. Coat of arms. R value in circle, new legend: EL BANCO CENTRAL DE RESERVA DEL PERU	0.30	0.50
24 (44)	1	Sol (Bra) 1943–1965	0.50	0.70
25 (41)	1	Centavo (Sn) 1950–1965. Sunburst. R value in wreath	0.30	0.60
26 (42)	2	Centavos (Sn) 1950–1956	0.30	0.60
27 (38)	5	Centavos (Bra). Head of Liberty, right. Name of country, date. R value and branch		
		a) 1945–1951	0.20	0.40
		b) 1951–1965, thinner planchet	0.15	0.25
28 (39)	10	Centavos (Bra). Same type as No. 27		
		a) 1945–1950	0.25	0.40
		b) 1951–1965, thinner planchet	0.15	0.25
29 (40)	20	Centavos (Bra). Same type as No. 27		
		a) 1942–1951	0.40	0.60
		b) 1951–1965	0.10	0.20
30 (48)	5	Soles (Au) 1956–1969. Coat of arms. R Liberty seated	35.00	45.00
31 (49)	10	Soles (Au) 1956–1969	52.00	60.00
32 (50)	20	Soles (Au) 1950–1969	115.00	140.00
33 (51)	50	Soles (Au) 1950–1969	300.00	325.00
34 (52)	100	Soles (Au) 1950–1969	525.00	600.00

			VF	XF
35 (45)	5	Centavos (Al–Br) 1954. Ramón Castilla (1797–1867), president 1845–1851 and 1855–1862. ℞ value in wreath, and torch	2.50	5.00
36 (46)	10	Centavos (Al–Br) 1954. Same type as No. 35	2.50	5.00

			VF	XF
37 (47)	20	Centavos (Al–Br) 1954. Same type as No. 35	4.00	8.00

COMMEMORATIVE COINS (8) FOR THE 400th ANNIVERSARY OF THE LIMA MINT

			XF	Unc
38 (53)	5	Centavos (Bra) 1965. 8-Reales-coin of 1565	0.10	0.20
39 (54)	10	Centavos (Bra) 1965. Same type as No. 38	0.25	0.50
40 (55)	25	Centavos (Bra) 1965. Same type as No. 38	0.30	0.60
41 (56)	½	Sol (Bra) 1965. Same type as No. 38	0.40	0.70
42 (57)	1	Sol (Bra) 1965. Same type as No. 38	0.50	0.80
43 (58)	20	Soles (Ag) 1965. Same type as No. 38	6.50	9.00
44 (59)	50	Soles (Au) 1965. Same type as No. 38	320.00	400.00
45 (60)	100	Soles (Au) 1965. Same type as No. 38	650.00	800.00

COMMEMORATIVE COINS (3) FOR THE CENTENNIAL OF THE UNSUCCESSFUL SIEGE OF CALLAO BY THE SPANISH FLEET ON 2nd MAY 1866

46 (61)	20	Soles (Ag) 1966. Victoria, from the Victory Monument in Lima. ℞ coat of arms	10.00	16.00
47 (62)	50	Soles (Au) 1966	380.00	420.00
48 (63)	100	Soles (Au) 1966	700.00	800.00

			XF	Unc

49 (64) 5 Centavos (Bra) 1966–. Coat of arms. R flowers of the chinabark tree (Chinchona sp. – Rubiaceae)
    a) 1966–1968, reeded edge   0.15   0.25
    b) 1969–1975, plain edge   0.10   0.20

50 (65) 10 Centavos (Bra) 1966-1975. Type as No. 49:
    a) 1966-1968, reeded edge   0.20   0.30
    b) 1969-1975, plain edge   0.15   0.25

51 (66) 25 Centavos (Bra) 1966-1975. Type as No. 49:
    a) 1966-1968, reeded edge   0.25   0.40
    b) 1969-1975, plain edge   0.20   0.35

52 (67) ½ Sol (Bra) 1966–1975. R vicugna (Lama vicugna – Camelidae)   0.30   0.50

53 (68) 1 Sol (Bra) 1966–1975. Type as No. 52   0.30   0.70

54 (69) 5 Soles (Cu-Ni) 1969. Coat of arms. R cup (Keru) of the Inca era   0.50   1.00

			XF	**Unc**
55 (70)	10 Soles (Cu–Ni) 1969. R stylized fish from pre-Columbian design		1.00	2.00

COMMEMORATIVE ISSUE (3) FOR THE 150th ANNIVERSARY OF INDEPENDENCE

56 (71)	5 Soles (Cu–Ni) 1971. Coat of arms. R Tupác Amarú (c. 1740–1781), descendent of the Inca rulers, leader of the great Indian rebellion (1780/81); executed in 1781 for treason	1.00	2.00
57 (72)	10 Soles (Cu–Ni) 1971. Same type as No. 56	2.00	3.00
58 (73)	50 Soles (Ag) 1971. Same type as No. 56	12.50	20.00

59 (74)	5 Soles (Cu–Ni) 1972–1975. Type similar to No. 57, but without legend	0.50	0.75
60 (75)	10 Soles (Cu–Ni) 1972–1975. Same type as No. 59	1.00	1.50

COMMEMORATIVE ISSUE FOR THE 100th ANNIVERSARY OF THE PERUVIAN-JAPANESE TRADE AGREEMENT

61 (76)	100 Soles (Ag) 1973. National coat of arms and anniversary dates. R chrysanthemum (Chrysanthemum sp. – Compositae), value, functional legend	12.00	16.00

AVIATION HEROES

			XF	Unc
62 (77)	200	Soles (Ag) 1974–1977. Conjoined heads left of Jorge Chavez and José Quinones	12.00	16.00

			XF	Unc
63 (78)	10	Centavos (Bra) 1975. Coat of arms. Rev. value	0.10	0.20
64 (79)	20	Centavos (Bra) 1975. Type as No. 63	0.10	0.20
65 (80)	½	Sol (Bra) 1975–1977. Type as No. 63	0.20	0.30

			XF	Unc
66 (81)	1	Sol (Bra) 1975, 1976. Type similar to No. 63	0.20	0.40
67 (82)	5	Soles (Cu-Ni) 1975, 1976. Type similar to No. 59	0.30	0.60

150th ANNIVERSARY OF THE BATTLE OF AYACUCHO (3)

			XF	Unc
68 (84)	½	Sol (Au) 1976. Ayacucho monument; 9.35 grams		150.00
69 (85)	1	Sol (Au) 1976. Type as No. 68; 23.4 grams		360.00
70 (83)	400	Soles (Ag) 1976. Type as No. 68		40.00
71 (81a)	1	Sol (Bra) 1978, 1980. Type as No. 66, but dia. 17 mm	0.20	0.30

			XF	Unc
72 (86)	5	Soles (Bra) 1978–1980. Coat of arms. Rev. value	0.30	0.50

			XF	Unc
73 (75a)	10	Soles (Bra) 1978–1980. Similar to No. 59	0.70	1.20

NATIONAL CONGRESS

74 (95)	1000	Soles (Ag) 1979	8.50	12.00

100th ANNIVERSARY OF THE BATTLE OF IQUIQUE (2)

			XF	Unc
75 (87)	1000	Soles (Ag) 1979	8.00	10.00
76 (88)	5000	Soles (Ag) 1979	30.00	35.00
77 (89)	50000	Soles (Au) 1979. Alfonso Urgarte		400.00
78 (90)	50000	Soles (Au) 1979. Elias Aguirre		400.00
79 (91)	50000	Soles (Au) 1979. F. Garcia Calderon		400.00
80 (92)	100000	Soles (Au) 1979. Francisco Bolognese		750.00
81 (93)	100000	Soles (Au) 1979. Andres A. Caceras		750.00
82 (94)	100000	Soles (Au) 1979. Miguel Grau		750.00
83 (96)	50	Soles (Al-Br) 1980	0.70	1.00

84 (97)	100	Soles (Cu-Ni) 1980	1.00	1.50

Area: 115,700 sq. mi. Population: 50,000,000.
The Philippines were discovered by Magellan in 1521. The group of
islands, situated in the Malayan archipelago, was a Spanish possession
until 1898 when it was ceded to the United States of America after the
Peace of Paris. In 1916 the Philippines obtained limited self-government
and, in 1935, were awarded dominion status with the designation of
Commonwealth of the Philippines. The island nation became independent on 4th July 1946.
Capital: Manila.

100 Centavos = 1 Peso, since 1967: 100 Sentimos = 1 Piso

UNDER AMERICAN SOVEREIGNTY

			VF	XF
1 (14)	½	Centavo (Br) 1903–1908. Blacksmith with anvil, Mt. Mayon, 7,926 feet, volcano on Luzon. R coat of arms	1.50	4.00
2 (15)	1	Centavo (Br) 1903–1936	1.50	4.50

3 (16)	5	Centavos (Cu–Ni) 1903–1928	1.00	2.50
4 (17)	5	Centavos (Cu–Ni) 1930–1935. Same type as No. 3, but smaller diameter	2.00	5.00
5	10	Centavos (Ag). Walking Philippina		
		a) (Y 18) 1903–1906	4.00	8.00
		b) (Y 22) 1907–1935	2.00	3.00
6	20	Centavos (Ag). Same type as No. 5		
		a) (Y 19) 1903–1906	4.00	6.00
		b) (Y 23) 1907–1929	3.00	4.00
7	50	Centavos (Ag). Same type as No. 5		
		a) (Y 20) 1903–1906	10.00	18.00
		b) (Y 24) 1907–1921	7.00	9.00

			VF	XF
8	1	Peso (Ag). Same type as No. 5		
		a) (Y 21) 1903–1906	20.00	26.00
		b) (Y 25) 1907–1912	15.00	20.00

COMMONWEALTH OF THE PHILIPPINES 1935–1946

COMMEMORATIVE ISSUES (3) FOR THE ESTABLISHMENT OF THE COMMONWEALTH OF THE PHILIPPINES ON NOVEMBER 15th, 1935

9 (26)   50 Centavos (Ag) 1936. Frank Murphy (1890–1949), American civil governor and ambassador, Manuel L. Quezón (1878–1944), lawyer and politician; 1st President of the Commonwealth. ℞ coat of arms   32.00   55.00

10 (27)	1 Peso (Ag) 1936. Franklin D. Roosevelt (1882–1945) and President Quezón	60.00	100.00
11 (28)	1 Peso (Ag) 1936. F. Murphy and President Quezón	60.00	100.00
12 (29)	1 Centavo (Br) 1937–1944. Blacksmith with anvil, Mt. Mayon, 7,926 feet, volcano on Luzon. ℞ coat of arms	0.10	0.20
13 (30)	5 Centavos. Same type as No. 12		
	a) (Y 30) (Cu-Ni) 1937–1941	1.20	2.50
	b) (Y 30a) (Ni-St) 1944–1945	0.10	0.20

				VF	**XF**
14 (31)	10	Centavos (Ag) 1937–1945		0.80	1.20
15 (32)	20	Centavos (Ag) 1937–1945		1.20	2.00
16 (33)	50	Centavos (Ag) 1944–1945		3.00	5.00

REPUBLIC since 1946
COMMEMORATIVE ISSUES (2) FOR GENERAL MACARTHUR

17 (34)	50	Centavos (Ag) 1947. General Douglas MacArthur (1888–1964), commander-in-chief of the American Forces in the Pacific during World War II. ℞ coat of arms		5.00	8.00
18 (35)	1	Peso (Ag) 1947. Same type as No. 17		10.00	15.00
19 (36)	1	Centavo (Br) 1958–1963. Blacksmith with anvil, Mt. Mayon, 7,926 feet, volcano on Luzon. R coat of arms		0.10	0.20
20 (37)	5	Centavos (Bra) 1958–1966		0.20	0.30
21 (38)	10	Centavos (Cu–Ni–Sn) 1958–1966. Walking Philippina		0.25	0.40
22 (39)	25	Centavos (Cu–Ni–Sn) 1958–1966		0.40	0.60
23 (40)	50	Centavos (Cu–Ni–Sn) 1958–1964		0.80	1.20

COMMEMORATIVE ISSUES (2) FOR THE 100th BIRTHDAY OF DR. JOSÉ RIZAL

24 (41)	½	Peso (Ag) 1961. José Rizal, Doctor of Medicine (1861–1896), national hero; executed as a rebel; head left. ℞ coat of arms		5.50	8.50

25 (42)	1	Peso (Ag) 1961. José Rizal, portrait		10.00	16.00

COMMEMORATIVE ISSUE FOR THE 100th BIRTHDAY OF ANDRES BONIFACIO

			VF	XF
26 (43)	1 Peso (Ag) 1963. Andres Bonifacio (1863–1897), national hero		10.00	16.00

COMMEMORATIVE ISSUE FOR THE 100th BIRTHDAY OF APOLINARIO MABINI

27 (44)	1 Peso (Ag) 1964. Apolinario Mabini (1864–1903), national hero		10.00	16.00

COMMEMORATIVE ISSUE FOR THE 25th ANNIVERSARY OF THE BATTLE OF BATAAN

28 (45)	1 Peso (Ag) 1967. Sword in flames surrounded by laurel wreath. ℞ coat of arms		10.00	16.00

NEW CURRENCY: 100 Sentimos = 1 Piso

			XF	Unc
29 (46)	1 Sentimo (Al) 1967–1974. King Lapu-Lapu. R coat of arms, legend in Tagalog		0.05	0.10
30 (47)	5 Sentimos (Bra) 1967–1974. Melchora Aquino (1812–1919), patriot. R same as No. 29		0.05	0.10

31 (48) 10 Sentimos (Cu-Ni-Sn) 1967–1974. Francisco

				XF	Unc
			Baltazar (1788–1862), poet. R same as No. 29	0.10	0.20
32	(49)	25	Sentimos (Cu-Ni-Sn) 1967–1975. Juan Luna (1857–1899), painter. R same as No. 29	0.20	0.30
33	(50)	50	Sentimos (Cu-Ni-Sn) 1967–1975. Marcelo H. del Pilar (1850–1886), lawyer and journalist. R same as No. 29	0.30	0.60

COMMEMORATIVE ISSUE FOR THE 100th BIRTHDAY OF EMILIO AGUINALDO

34	(51)	1	Piso (Ag) 1969. Emilio Aguinaldo (1869–1964), General and leader of the rebellious Philippinos from 1898 to 1901. R coat of arms, name of country, value PISO	12.00	16.00

COMMEMORATIVE ISSUES (3) FOR THE VISIT OF POPE PAUL VI

35	(52)	1	Piso (Ni) 1970. Pope Paul VI, portrait right. R Ferdinand E. Marcos, portrait left. Value	1.20	2.50
36	(52a)	1	Piso (Ag) 1970. Type as No. 35, but plain edge	12.00	16.00
37	(52b)	1	Piso (Au) 1970. Same type as No. 35		800.00
38	(53)	1	Piso (Cu-Ni) 1972, 1974. José Rizal, Doctor of Medicine. Rev. coat of arms	0.60	1.20

COMMEMORATIVE ISSUE 25 YEARS OF NATIONAL BANK

				XF	Unc
39 (54)	25	Piso (Ag) 1974		12.00	16.00

3rd ANNIVERSARY OF THE NEW SOCIETY (2)

40 (62)	50	Piso (Ag) 1975. Head left of President Ferdinand E. Marcos. Rev. coat of arms, value		24.00	32.00

41 (63)	1000	Piso (Au) 1975. Type as No. 40		185.00	225.00
42 (55)	1	Sentimo (Al) 1975-. King Lapulapu		0.05	0.10
43 (56)	5	Sentimos (Bra) 1975-. Melchora Aquino (scalloped)		0.05	0.10
44 (57)	10	Sentimos (Cu-Ni) 1975-. Francisco Baltasar		0.10	0.20
45 (58)	25	Sentimos (Cu-Ni) 1975-. Juan Luna		0.15	0.30
46 (59)	1	Piso (Cu-Ni) 1975-. José Rizal		0.50	1.00
				Unc	**Proof**
47 (60)	5	Piso (Ni) 1975–. Head left of President Ferdinand E. Marcos		1.00	16.00
48 (61)	25	Piso (Ag) 1975. Emilio Aguinaldo		20.00	22.00

ISSUE FOR THE FAO COIN PLAN

49 (64)	25	Piso (Ag) 1976. Rice harvest		18.00	30.00

I.M.F. MEETING IN MANILA (2)

		Unc	Proof
50 (65)	50 Piso (Ag) 1976	28.00	30.00
51 (66)	1500 Piso (Au) 1976	280.00	400.00

NEW SOCIETY

52 (69)	5000 Piso (Au) 1977	1500.00	1100.00

RICE CULTIVATION

53 (67)	25 Piso (Ag) 1977	27.50	30.00

NEW MINT

54 (68)	50 Piso (Ag) 1977	35.00	40.00

SECURITY PRINTING AND MINT

55 (72)	1500 Piso (Au) 1977	400.00	420.00

100th ANNIVERSARY OF THE BIRTH OF MANUEL L. QUEZON (2)

56 (70)	25 Piso (Ag) 1978	28.00	30.00
57 (71)	50 Piso (Ag) 1978	35.00	50.00

UN CONFERENCE ON TRADE AND DEVELOPMENT

58 (73)	25 Piso (Ag) 1979	28.00	30.00

INTERNATIONAL YEAR OF THE CHILD

59 (74)	50 Piso (Ag) 1979	35.00	55.00

100th ANNIVERSARY OF THE BIRTH OF GENERAL MACARTHUR (2)

		Unc	Proof
60 (75)	25 Piso (Ag) 1980	35.00	60.00
61 (76)	2500 Piso (Au) 1980		450.00

VISIT OF POPE JOHN PAUL II

62	50 Piso (Ag) 1981	50.00

WORLD FOOD DAY

63	25 Piso (Ag) 1981	25.00

Polen   # Poland   **Pologne**
Polska

Area: 120,330 sq. mi. Population: 34,000,000.

The first historical ruler of Poland was Duke Mieszko of the House of Piasts. The eventful history comprises the greatness and decline of the Polish state. The Piasts were superseded at the end of the 14th century by the Jagiello dynasty; after the Jagiellos became extinct, the Polish aristocracy elected foreign princes as their kings. In the more recent past, the rule of Jan III Sobieski (1674–1696) can be described as a glorious climax in Polish history, who by virtue of his victory over the Turks before the gates of Vienna was acclaimed as the hero of the occident. The years 1772, 1793 and 1795 brought the partition of Poland and thus the temporary ceasing of the independent state. The Duchy of Warsaw created in 1807, the later Congress Poland, must be considered as a transition stage up to the foundation of the republic. Although the Central Powers had supported the creation of a kingdom in 1916, the republic was proclaimed on November 11, 1918. During 1939 to 1944 Central Poland came under the German State as a government of occupation. After the end of the Second World War, the People's Republic was created.

Capital: Warsaw.

100 Fenigów = 1 Marka, since 1923: 100 Groszy = 1 Zloty

INTERIM 1917–1918

			VF	XF
1 (4)	1	Fenig (Fe) 1918. Polish eagle, with crown above. ℞ value and legend KROLESTWO POLSKIE	6.00	16.00
2 (5)	5	Fenigów (Fe) 1917–1918. Same type as No. 1	1.50	3.50
3 (6)	10	Fenigów. Same type as No. 1		
		a) (Fe) 1917, 1918	1.50	3.50
		b) (Sn) 1917	50.00	75.00
4 (7)	20	Fenigów. Same type as No. 1		
		a) (Fe) 1917, 1918	3.50	6.50
		b) (Sn) 1917	55.00	80.00

			VF	XF
5 (8)	1 Grosz (Br) 1923–1939. Heraldic eagle.			
	℞ value		0.40	0.60
6 (9)	2 Grosze (Br) 1923–1939		0.60	1.00

Of practically all Polish coins, struck since 1923, pattern pieces exist as counterparts, distributed by the Bank of Poland. These coins usually bear the word PROBA, and are distinguished by more or less changed designs. Besides these pattern pieces, another group of issues was struck but for several reasons never officially distributed; these include numbers 15–17 from 1925, and the 10 Zlotych and 20 Zlotych coins struck for the 20th anniversary of the People's Republic of Poland, in 1964.

7 (10)	5 Groszy (Br) 1923–1939		0.30	0.60
8 (11)	10 Groszy (Ni) 1923. ℞ value in wreath		0.25	0.40
9 (12)	20 Groszy (Ni) 1923		0.40	0.60

10 (13)	50 Groszy (Ni) 1923		0.50	0.80
11 (14)	1 Zloty (Ni) 1929. ℞ value in ornament		1.50	2.00

12 (15)	1 Zloty (Ag) 1924–1925. ℞ peasant girl, ears of wheat			
	a) 1924, Hôtel des Monnaies, Paris: low relief strike, torches right and left of date		16.00	25.00
	b) 1925, Royal Mint, London: high relief strike, dot behind date		15.00	20.00

Three official silver pattern pieces are dated 1924, all of identical design and denomination.

13 (16) 2 Zlote (Ag) 1924–1925. Same type as   **VF**   **XF**
No. 12
  a) 1924, Hôtel des Monnaies, Paris:
     low relief strike, torches right and
     left of date   35.00   45.00
  b) 1924, Royal Mint, London: low
     relief strike, mint mark: small H in-
     stead of torches   40.00   75.00
  c) 1924, United States Mint, Philadel-
     phia: without mint mark, but invert-
     ed reverse   35.00   55.00
  d) 1925, Royal Mint, London: dot
     behind date   28.00   36.00
  e) 1925, United States Mint, Philadel-
     phia: without mint mark   55.00   70.00

Six official pattern pieces were struck in 1924, five in silver, and one in
brass. Except for one silver strike all bear identical designs, denominations are identical. There is one official silver pattern piece from 1925,
of identical design and denomination. Further official pattern pieces
are two silver and one bronze coin from 1927, all bearing identical
design and denomination.

14 (18) 5 Zlotych (Ag) 1928, 1930–1932. Nike.
R heraldic eagle and value
  a) 1928, Munt Belgie: without mint
     mark   65.00   90.00
  b) 1928, 1930–1932, Warsaw: dot left
     of Nike's foot   190.00   280.00

Three official pattern pieces are dated 1927, two in silver and one in
bronze, only slightly differing in design, but of identical denomination. There is one official silver pattern piece in high relief strike, of
identical design and denomination, issued in 1928.

COMMEMORATIVE ISSUE FOR THE ADOPTION OF THE CONSTITUTION

				VF	XF
15 (17)	5	Zlotych (Ag) 1925. Heraldic eagle. ℞ allegory by S. Lewandowski; "Mother Polonia, right hand on eagle shield, receives constitution from an elected representative"		700.00	800.00

No. 15 did not circulate. There are eight types, all of identical design and denomination: in high relief two pieces of gold, two pieces of silver and one of brass, in low relief two pieces of silver and one of tombac.

			VF	XF
16 (32)	10	Zlotych (Au) 1925. Boleslaw I. Chrobry (967–1025), duke since 992, first king of Poland 1024/25	70.00	80.00

One official pattern piece from 1925 was struck in bronze of identical design and denomination.

			VF	XF
17 (33)	20	Zlotych (Au) 1925	120.00	140.00

Two offical pattern pieces were struck in 1925, one in bronze and one in nickel, both bear identical designs and denomination.
Coins No. 16 and 17 never circulated, but could be purchased until 1939 from the Bank Polski by furnishing the gold and paying the cost of coinage.

COMMEMORATIVE COIN FOR THE CENTENNIAL OF THE POLISH UPRISING OF 1830

			VF	XF
18 (19)	5	Zlotych (Ag) 1930. Flag, memorial legend, dates. ℞ heraldic eagle and value	70.00	100.00

Two strikes are to be distinguished: one low and one high relief.
An official bronze pattern piece from 1930, with high relief, identical design and denomination, was struck for the same event.

		VF	XF
19 (20) 2 Zlote (Ag) 1932–1934. Woman's head with wreath of clover, allegory of the republic. ℞ heraldic eagle and value		2.50	5.00

Two official pattern pieces date from 1933, one each in silver and in bronze, both of identical design and denomination.

20 (21) 5 Zlotych (Ag) 1932–1934. Same type as No. 19		5.50	10.50

The coins of 1932 were struck in Warsaw with a mint mark in the left claw of the eagle, London strikes are without mint mark.
Two official pattern pieces are dated 1933, one each in silver and in bronze, both of identical design and denomination.

21 (22) 10 Zlotych (Ag) 1932–1933. Same type as No. 19		9.00	16.00

The coins of 1932 were struck in Warsaw with the mint mark in the left claw of the eagle, London strikes are without mintmark.
Two offical pattern pieces are dated 1932, one each in silver and in bronze, also one official bronze pattern piece dated 1933, all are of identical design and face denomination.

COMMEMORATIVE COIN FOR THE 250th ANNIVERSARY OF THE LIBERATION OF VIENNA

22 (23) 10 Zlotych (Ag) 1933. Jan III Sobieski
         (1624–1696), king from 1674 to 1696,   **VF**   **XF**
         liberated Vienna from the Turkish siege
         in 1683. ℞ heraldic eagle and value   22.00   45.00

Three official silver pattern pieces from 1933, one on square planchet
(klippe), all of identical design and denomination, commemorate the
same event.

COMMEMORATIVE COIN FOR THE 70th ANNIVERSARY OF THE JANUARY REBELLION OF 1863

23 (24) 10 Zlotych (Ag) 1933. Romuald Traugutt
         (1826–1864), patriot and leader of the
         rebellion. ℞ heraldic eagle and value   22.00   40.00

Three official silver pattern pieces from 1933, one on square planchet, all
of identical design and denomination, commemorate the same event.

COMMEMORATIVE COINS (2) FOR THE FOUNDING OF THE POLISH LEGION

			VF	XF
24 (25)	5	Zlotych (Ag) 1934. Jósef Pilsudski (1867–1935), marshal and statesman. ℞ heraldic eagle, with emblem below	**VF** 9.00	**XF** 15.00

Three official pattern pieces from 1934, two of silver and one of bronze, all of identical design and denomination, commemorate the same event.

25 (26) 10 Zlotych (Ag) 1934. Same type as No. 24   18.00   28.00

Four official pattern pieces from 1934, three of silver, one square planchet, and one of bronze, all of identical design and denomination, commemorate the same event.

26 (27) 2 Zlote (Ag) 1934, 1936. J. Pilsudski. ℞ heraldic eagle   4.00   6.50

27 (28) 5 Zlotych (Ag) 1934–1936, 1938. Same type as No. 26   6.00   9.00

28 (29) 10 Zlotych (Ag) 1934–1939. Same type as No. 26   10.00   20.00

29 (30) 2 Zlote (Ag) 1936. Heraldic eagle. ℞ three-masted sailing vessel "Dar Pomorza", value   4.50   8.00

There are two official silver pattern pieces dated 1936 of identical design and denomination.

An additional official pattern piece was struck from the original dies at the Warsaw mint, in 1958, in aluminum.

30 (31) 5 Zlotych (Ag) 1936. Same type as No. 29   11.00   16.00

Four official pattern pieces were struck in 1936, two in silver, one square planchet (klippe), also of silver and one square planchet of bronze, all of identical design and denomination.

For coins of the military government (Generalgouvernement), circulating between 1939 and 1944, see under German Occupations of World War II.

				VF	XF
31 (39)	1	Grosz (Al) 1949. Heraldic eagle. R value		0.10	0.25
32 (40)	2	Grosze (Al) 1949		0.40	0.80
33 (41)	5	Groszy 1949			
		a) (Br)		1.00	2.00
		b) (Al)		1.00	2.50
34 (42)	10	Groszy 1949			
		a) (Cu–Ni)		1.50	3.00
		b) (Al)		0.80	1.50
35 (43)	20	Groszy 1949			
		a) (Cu–Ni)		2.00	4.00
		b) (Al)		0.80	1.50
36 (44)	50	Groszy 1949			
		a) (Cu–Ni)		1.50	3.00
		b) (Al)		1.00	2.00
37 (45)	1	Zloty 1949			
		a) (Cu–Ni)		2.50	5.00
		b) (Al)		1.50	2.50

Since 1965 some regular coins as well as commemorative coins, bear the Warsaw mintmark MW.

			VF	XF
38 (A46)	5	Groszy (Al) 1958–. Same type as No. 33, but with new legend POLSKA RZECZPOSPOLITA LUDOWA	0.10	0.20
39 (AA47)	10	Groszy (Al) 1961–. Heraldic eagle. R value and laurel branch	0.15	0.30
40 (A47)	20	Groszy (Al) 1957–	0.20	0.30
41 (48)	50	Groszy (Al) 1957–	0.25	0.40

			VF	XF
42 (49)	1	Zloty (Al) 1957–	0.40	0.60
43 (46)	2	Zlote (Al) 1958–1974. Heraldic eagle. R fruits and ears of wheat	0.60	1.00

44 (47) 5 Zlotych (Al) 1958–1960, 1971–1976.

	VF	XF
Rev. fisherman	0.60	1.10

45 (50) 10 Zlotych (Cu-Ni) 1959–1973. Heraldic eagle. R Tadeusz Kosciuszko (1746–1817), General and fighter for independence

	VF	XF
a) 1959, 1960, 1966, diameter: 31 mm	1.00	2.00
b) 1969–1973, diameter: 28 mm	0.80	1.25

Of No. 45a exist two official nickel pattern pieces, one from 1958 with a slightly different design and one from 1959 with identical design, both of identical denomination.

46 (51) 10 Zlotych (Cu-Ni). Nikolaus Kopernikus (1473–1543). theologian and astronomer

	VF	XF
a) 1959, 1965, diameter: 31 mm	2.00	3.00
b) 1967–1969, diameter: 28 mm	1.00	1.50

Of No. 46a exist one official nickel pattern piece from 1959 of identical design and denomination.

COMMEMORATIVE COIN FOR THE 600th ANNIVERSARY OF THE JAGIELLO UNIVERSITY IN CRACOW

47 (52) 10 Zlotych (Cu-Ni) 1964. Kasimir the Great (1309–1370), founder of the Cra-

cow University. ℞ heraldic eagle and value	**VF**	**XF**
a) raised memorial legend	1.00	2.00
b) incused memorial legend	1.00	2.00

Two official nickel pattern pieces, dated 1964, one each with raised and incused memorial legend, both of same design and denomination, commemorate the same event. Two more official nickel pattern pieces of 1964, one each with crowned and uncrowned heraldic eagle, are of identical denomination.

COMMEMORATIVE COINS (2): 700 YEARS WARSAW

48 (54) 10 Zlotych (Cu–Ni) 1965. Nike of Warsaw, modern large monument for the liberation of Warsaw in 1945. ℞ heraldic eagle and value 1.00 1.80

Four official nickel pattern pieces from 1965, one of identical and three of different design, but all of identical denomination, commemorate the same event.

49 (55) 10 Zlotych (Cu–Ni) 1965. Eagle. ℞ Sigismund (Zygmunt) pillar in Warsaw and value 1.00 1.80

One official nickel pattern piece of 1965, with identical design and denomination, commemorates the same event.

				VF	XF
50 (56)	10	Zlotych (Cu–Ni) 1966. Same type as and egde inscription W DWUSETNA ROCZNICE MENNICY WARSZAWSKIEJ		1.60	4.00

One official nickel pattern piece, dated 1966, of identical design and denomination, commemorates the same event.

COMMEMORATIVE COIN FOR THE MILLENIUM OF POLAND

51 (57)	100	Zlotych (Ag) 1966. Heraldic eagle, city arms arranged in circle. ℞ Mieszko I and his Bohemian wife Dabrówka; value		15.00	25.00

Two official silver pattern pieces, dated 1966, of different design but identical denomination commemorate the same event. Eight additional nickel pattern pieces were struck in 1966, one of identical and seven of different design, but all of identical denomination.

COMMEMORATIVE COIN FOR THE 20th ANNIVERSARY OF SWIERCZEWSKI'S DEATH

52 (58)	10	Zlotych (Cu–Ni) 1967. Karol Swierczewski, called General Walter (1896–1947), politician, Deputy Defense Minister 1943–1947. ℞ heraldic eagle		1.00	2.00

COMMEMORATIVE COIN FOR THE 100th BIRTHDAY
OF MARIE CURIE

53 (59) 10 Zlotych (Cu–Ni) 1967. Heraldic eagle. **VF** **XF**
Ŗ Marie Curie, former Sklodowska
(1867–1934), 1903 Nobel Prize winner
for physics (discovery of polonium and
radium) and for chemistry 1911   0.90   1.80

COMMEMORATIVE COIN FOR THE 25th ANNIVERSARY
OF THE POLISH PEOPLE'S ARMY

54 (60) 10 Zlotych (Cu–Ni) 1968. Polish eagle as
army emblem. Ŗ profiled head of sol-
dier; memorial legend, value   0.80   1.50

COMMEMORATIVE COIN:
25 YEARS PEOPLE'S REPUBLIC OF POLAND

55 (61) 10 Zlotych (Cu–Ni) 1969. Heraldic eagle
in circle, surrounded by legend. Ŗ sheaf
of wheat in circle, surrounded by legend; value   0.80   1.50

COMMEMORATIVE ISSUE FOR THE 25th ANNIVERSARY
OF THE END OF WORLD WAR II

				VF	XF
56 (62)	10	Zlotych (Cu–Ni) 1970. City arms of the seven district capitals in the Northern and Western areas with border marker, and dates below: 1945–1970. ℞ heraldic eagle with breast shield; value		**VF**	**XF**
				0.80	1.50

ISSUE FOR THE FAO COIN PLAN

57 (63)	10	Zlotych (Cu–Ni) 1971. Ear of barley (Hordeum sp. – Gramineae) in front of East Atlantic turbot (Bothus maximus – Bothidae). ℞ heraldic shield, value	0.80	1.50

Two official cupro-nickel pattern pieces, dated 1971, of different design but identical denomination commemorate the same event.

COMMEMORATIVE ISSUE FOR THE 50th ANNIVERSARY
OF THE THIRD SILESIAN UPRISING

58 (64)	10	Zlotych (Cu–Ni) 1971. Detail from insurrection monument in Katowice, cross of insurgents, date and inscription. ℞ heraldic eagle, date, value	0.80	1.50

COMMEMORATIVE ISSUE FOR FRÉDÉRIC CHOPIN

Proof

59 (66)   50 Zlotych (Ag) 1972, 1974. Frédéric
Chopin (1810–1849), famous pianist   15.00

For the same event there is an official pattern piece of 1972 in silver
with a changed design and the same face value.

COMMEMORATIVE ISSUE FOR THE 50 YEARS
CELEBRATION OF THE PORT OF GDYNIA (GDINGEN)

		XF	Unc
60 (65)	10 Zlotych (Cu–Ni) 1972. City coat of arms above outline of the coastline.		
	℞ heraldic eagle, legend, date, value	1.00	1.60

COMMEMORATIVE ISSUE FOR THE 500th BIRTHDAY
OF NIKOLAUS KOPERNIKUS

Proof

61 (68)   100 Zlotych (Ag) 1973, 1974. Nikolaus Kopernikus (1473–1543), theologian and
astronomer   15.00

62 (67) 20 Zlotych (Cu-Ni) 1973; 1974, 1976. **XF** **Unc**
Heraldic eagle, legend, date. R corn-
field in front of skyscraper under con-
struction   0.80   1.20

COMMEMORATIVE ISSUE
30 YEARS POLISH PEOPLE'S REPUBLIC

63 (72) 200 Zlotych (Ag) 1974. Outline of the
Polish frontier and functional legend.
R heraldic eagle, name of country,
value, date   10.00   18.00

COMMEMORATIVE ISSUE FOR M. NOWOTKO

64 (69) 20 Zlotych (Cu-Ni) 1974–1976. Marceli **XF** **Unc**
Nowotko (1893–1942), leading activist
of the revolutionary movement, First
Secretary of the Central Committee of
the Polish Labour Party   0.80   1.20

25th ANNIVERSARY OF THE COMECON

65 (70) 20 Zlotych (Cu-Ni) 1974. In a circle formed
of sun-flower leaves and one half of cog-
wheel, inscription. Rev. heraldic eagle,
value

	XF	Unc
	1.00	1.60

40th ANNIVERSARY OF THE DEATH OF MARIE CURIE

66 (71) 100 Zlotych (Ag) 1974. Marie Curie, former
Sklodowska (1867-1934). Head left with
radiation running from the symbol of the
element Ra

	Proof
	22.00

RECONSTRUCTION OF THE ROYAL CASTLE IN WARSAW

67 (76) 100 Zlotych (Ag) 1974. The frontal view of the
royal castle in Warsaw, Sigismund III's
column in front of it   14.00

			XF	Unc

68 (73)　10　Zlotych　(Cu-Ni)　1975-1977.　Boleslaw
Prus (1847-1912), writer　　　0.60　　0.90

69 (74)　10　Zlotych　(Cu-Ni)　1975,　1976.　Adam
Mickiewicz (1798-1855), poet　0.60　　0.90

Proof

70 (77)　100　Zlotych (Ag) 1975. Jgnacy Jan Paderewski
(1860-1941), pianist, composer, politician　　16.00

71 (78)　100　Zlotych (Ag) 1975. Helena Modrzejewska
(1840-1909), actress　　　16.00

30th ANNIVERSARY OF THE END OF WORLD WAR II

			Unc	Proof
72 (79)	200	Zlotych (Ag) 1975. Coinjoined heads left	10.00	16.00

INTERNATIONAL WOMEN'S YEAR 1975

			XF	Unc
73 (75)	20	Zlotych (Cu-Ni) 1975. A woman's profile, in her hair the emblem of a stylized dove of peace	1.00	2.00

| **74** (80) | 2 | Zlote (Bra) 1975–1979. Heraldic eagle. Rev. value and stylized corn-ears | 0.35 | 0.60 |

| **75** (81) | 5 | Zlotych (Bra) 1975–1977, 1981. Rev. value | 0.45 | 0.80 |

76 (82) 100 Zlotych (Ag) 1976. Tadeusz Kościuszko **Proof**
(1746-1817), General and fighter for
independence 16.00
77 (83) 500 Zlotych (Au) 1976, 1977. Type as No. 76 550.00

78 (84) 100 Zlotych (Ag) 1976. Kazimierz Pulaski
(1747-1779), fighter for independence 16.00
79 (85) 500 Zlotych (Au) 1976, 1977. Type as No. 78 550.00

FOR THE OLYMPIC GAMES 1976 IN MONTREAL

80 (86) 200 Zlotych (Ag) 1976. Olympic rings and
torch 16.00

NATURAL PROTECTION

81 (87) 100 Zlotych (Ag) 1977. Bison 16.00

82 (88)   100 Zlotych (Ag) 1977. Henryk Sienkiewicz   **Proof**
                (1846-1916), writer, 1905 Nobel Prize
                winner   16.00

83 (89)   100 Zlotych (Ag) 1977 Wladyslaw Reymont
                (1867-1925), story-teller, 1924 Nobel
                Prize winner   16.00

84 (90)   2000 Zlotych (Au) 1977. Frédéric Chopin
                (1810-1849), pianist   180.00
85 (91)   100 Zlotych (Ag) 1977. Royal castle in Crakow   16.00
86 (92)   100 Zlotych (Ag) 1978. Adam Mickiewicz
                (1798-1855), poet   16.00

NATURAL PROTECTION

		Proof
87 (93)	100 Zlotych (Ag) 1978. Elk	16.00

		XF	Unc
88 (95)	20 Zlotych (Cu-Ni) 1978. Maria Konopnicka (1842–1910)	1.50	2.50

100th ANNIVERSARY OF THE BIRTH OF JANUSZ KORCZAK

		Proof
89 (94)	100 Zlotych (Ag) 1978	16.00

FIRST POLISH COSMONAUT

		XF	Unc
90 (97)	20 Zlotych (Cu-Ni) 1978	1.50	2.50

NATURAL PROTECTION

		Proof
91 (96)	100 Zlotych (Ag) 1978. Beaver	16.00
92 (98)	100 Zlotych (Ag) 1979. Henryk Wieniawski (1835–1880), composer	16.00

INTERNATIONAL YEAR OF THE CHILD

		XF	Unc
93 (99)	20 Zlotych (Cu-Ni) 1979	1.50	2.50

		Unc	Proof
94 (106)	2000 Zlotych (Au) 1979. Nikolaus Koperni-kus (1473–1543), theologian and astro-nomer		180.00
95 (103)	100 Zlotych (Ag) 1979. Dr. Ludwig Zamen-hof (1859–1917)		16.00

NATURAL PROTECTION (2)

96 (104)	100 Zlotych (Ag) 1979. Lynx		16.00

		Unc	Proof
97 (105)	100 Zlotych (Ag) 1979. Chamois		16.00

DUKE MIESZKO (3)

98 (100)	50 Zlotych (Cu-Ni) 1979. Duke Mieszko (960–992)	4.00	
99 (101)	200 Zlotych (Ag) 1979		28.00

		Unc	Proof
100 (102) 2000 Zlotych (Au) 1979			300.00
101 (107) 2000 Zlotych (Au) 1979. Marie Curie			300.00

13th OLYMPIC WINTER GAMES 1980 IN LAKE PLACID (3)

102 (110)   200 Zlotych (Ag) 1980. Ski-jumper   25.00

103   200 Zlotych (Ag) 1980. Type as No. 102,
                but torch added   25.00
104 (111) 2000 Zlotych (Au) 1980   350.00

22nd OLYMPIC GAMES 1980 IN MOSCOW (3)

105 (108)   20 Zlotych (Cu-Ni) 1980. Runner and
                olympic rings   6.00   15.00
106 (109) 100 Zlotych (Ag) 1980   22.00
107   2000 Zlotych (Au) 1980   400.00
108 (112)   20 Zlotych (Cu-Ni) 1980   2.00

450th ANNIVERSARY OF THE BIRTH OF JAN KOCHANOWSKI

109 (120) 100 Zlotych (Ag) 1980. Jan Kochanowski
                (1530–1584), poet   16.00

			Unc	Proof
110 (114)	50	Zlotych (Cu-Ni) 1980. King Boleslaw I Chrobry	6.00	
111 (115)	200	Zlotych (Ag) 1980. Type as No. 110		20.00
112 (116)	2000	Zlotych (Au) 1980. Type as No. 110		380.00

NATURAL PROTECTION

113 (121)	100	Zlotych (Ag) 1980. Heath cock		20.00
114 (117)	50	Zlotych (Cu-Ni) 1980. King Kazimierz	2.50	
115 (118)	200	Zlotych (Ag) 1980. Type as No. 114		20.00
116	20	Zlotych (Cu-Ni) 1981. Crakow	8.00	
117 (122)	50	Zlotych (Cu-Ni) 1981. General Sikorski	3.00	
118 (123)	100	Zlotych (Ag) 1981		30.00
119	50	Zlotych (Cu-Ni) 1981. King Boleslaw II	3.00	
120	200	Zlotych (Ag) 1971. Type as No. 119		20.00

WORLD SOCCER CHAMPIONSHIP GAMES 1982 IN SPAIN

121	200	Zlotych (Ag) 1981		28.00

NATURAL PROTECTION

122	200	Zlotych (Ag) 1981. Horse		16.00

WORLD FOOD DAY

			Unc	Proof
123	50	Zlotych (Cu-Ni) 1981	3.00	

Area: 35,490 sq. mi. Population: 9,800,000.
In the Age of Discoveries, the kingdom of Portugal was one of the leading seafaring nations. Since 1910 the country situated on the Iberian Peninsula has a republican form of government.
Capital: Lisbon.

1000 Reis = 1 Milreis, 100 Centavos = 1 Escudo

CARLOS I 1889–1908

			VF	XF
1 (15)	5	Reis (Br) 1890–1906. Carlos I (1863–1908), head right. ℞ value in wreath	2.50	5.00
2 (16)	10	Reis (Br) 1891–1892	2.50	4.00
3 (17)	20	Reis (Br) 1891–1892	2.00	4.00
4 (18)	50	Reis (Cu–Ni) 1900. Crowned arms. ℞ value	2.50	4.00
5 (19)	100	Reis (Cu–Ni) 1900	2.00	3.00
6 (21)	100	Reis (Ag) 1890–1898. Carlos I, head right. ℞ value in wreath	20.00	35.00
7 (22)	200	Reis (Ag) 1891–1903. Same type as No. 6	22.00	38.00
8 (23)	500	Reis (Ag) 1891–1908. ℞ crowned arms	18.00	28.00
9 (24)	1000	Reis (Ag) 1899–1900. ℞ Shield on crowned ermine mantle:		
		a) 1899	40.00	65.00
		b) 1900	1500.00	1800.00

MANUEL II 1908–1910

10 (28)	5	Reis (Br) 1910. Manuel II (1888–1932), head left. ℞ value in wreath	2.50	4.50
11 (29)	100	Reis (Ag) 1909–1910. ℞ crown above value, all in wreath	4.00	6.50
12 (30)	200	Reis (Ag) 1909	10.00	16.00
13 (31)	500	Reis (Ag) 1908–1909	20.00	32.00

COMMEMORATIVE ISSUES (2) FOR THE CENTENNIAL OF THE WAR AGAINST NAPOLEON

14 (32)	500	Reis (Ag) 1910. Manuel II. ℞ crowned arms	90.00	120.00
15 (33)	1000	Reis (Ag) 1910	100.00	130.00

COMMEMORATIVE ISSUE FOR MARQUIS DE POMBAL

			VF	**XF**
16 (34)	500	Reis (Ag) 1910. Manuel II. ℞ Goddess of Victory with crowned shield and monument of Marquis de Pombal (1699–1782), rebuilder of Lisbon after the earthquake of 1755	35.00	55.00

REPUBLIC since 1910

			VF	**XF**
17 (48)	10	Centavos (Ag) 1915. Head of Liberty. ℞ coat of arms, surrounded by laurel branches	2.50	4.00
18 (49)	20	Centavos (Ag) 1913–1916	15.00	25.00
19 (50)	50	Centavos (Ag) 1912–1916	9.00	16.00

20 (51)	1 Escudo (Ag) 1915–1916	26.00	40.00

COMMEMORATIVE ISSUE FOR THE FOUNDING OF THE REPUBLIC, ON OCTOBER 5, 1910

			VF	XF
21 (47)	1	Escudo (Ag) undated (1914). Allegory of the Republic with torch. ℞ coat of arms in wreath	40.00	52.00
22 (36)	1	Centavo (Br) 1917–1922. Coat of arms. ℞ value	0.80	2.00
23 (35)	2	Centavos (Fe) 1918. Same type as No. 22	75.00	110.00
24 (37)	2	Centavos (Br) 1918–1921. Same type as No. 22	2.00	3.50
25 (42)	4	Centavos (Cu–Ni) 1917–1919. Head of Liberty, left. ℞ value	0.80	1.60
26 (38)	5	Centavos (Br) 1920–1922. Same type as No. 22	2.50	4.00
27 (39)	5	Centavos (Br) 1924–1927. Same type as No. 25	0.80	1.60
28 (43)	10	Centavos (Cu–Ni) 1920–1921. Same type as No. 25	4.00	6.50
29 (40)	10	Centavos (Br) 1924–1940. Same type as No. 25	1.50	4.00

			VF	XF
30 (44)	20	Centavos (Cu–Ni) 1920–1922. Same type as No. 25	3.00	4.50
31 (41)	20	Centavos (Br) 1924–1925. Same type as No. 25	2.50	4.00
32 (45)	50	Centavos (Al–Br) 1924–1926. Allegory of the Republic. ℞ coat of arms in wreath	8.00	12.00
33 (46)	1	Escudo (Al–Br) 1924–1926	12.00	20.00
34	5	Escudos (Au) 1920. Allegory of the Republic. ℞ coat of arms and value Coin No. 34 is a pattern piece and did not circulate.	–.–	–.–

35 (54)	50	Centavos (Ni–Bra) 1927–1968. Head of Liberty, right. ℞ coat of arms in wreath	0.15	0.25
36 (55)	1	Escudo (Ni–Bra) 1927–1968	0.25	0.50

COMMEMORATIVE ISSUE FOR THE BATTLE OF OURIQUE 1139

37 (56)	10	Escudos (Ag) 1928. Knight on horse-back. ℞ coat of arms	22.00	35.00
38 (57)	2.50	Escudos (Ag) 1932–1951. Sailing vessel, 15th century. ℞ coat of arms	1.50	2.00
39 (58)	5	Escudos (Ag) 1932–1951	3.00	4.00

			VF	XF
40 (59)	10	Escudos (Ag) 1932–1948	8.00	16.00
41 (60)	X	(10) Centavos (Br) 1942–1969. Quinas cross. ℞ value	0.10	0.20
42 (61)	XX	(20) Centavos (Br) 1942–1969	0.15	0.25

COMMEMORATIVE ISSUE FOR THE 25th ANNIVERSARY OF THE FINANCE REFORM

43 (62)	20	Escudos (Ag) 1953. Sitting figure. ℞ shield with Quinas cross above globe	12.00	18.00
44 (63)	10	Escudos (Ag) 1954–1955. Sailing vessel, 15th century. ℞ shield with Quinas cross above globe	7.50	12.00

COMMEMORATIVE ISSUES (3) FOR THE 500th ANNIVERSARY OF THE DEATH OF HENRY THE NAVIGATOR

45 (64)	5	Escudos (Ag) 1960. Henry the Navigator (Dom Enrique el Navegador) 1394–1460, promoter of Portuguese seafaring and discoverer of West Africa. ℞ coat of arms	2.50	4.00
46 (65)	10	Escudos (Ag) 1960	15.00	20.00
47 (66)	20	Escudos (Ag) 1960	28.00	40.00

			VF	XF
48 (67)	2.50	Escudos (Cu–Ni) 1963–. Sailing vessel, 15th century. ℞ coat of arms	0.15	0.40
49 (68)	5	Escudos (Cu–Ni) 1963–1981. Type as No. 48	0.30	0.60

COMMEMORATIVE ISSUE FOR THE OPENING OF THE SALAZAR-BRIDGE

			XF	Unc
50 (69)	20	Escudos (Ag) 1966. Salazar-Bridge crossing the Tejo near Lisbon. ℞ coat of arms	4.00	7.50

COMMEMORATIVE ISSUE FOR THE 500th BIRTHDAY OF PEDRO ALVARES CABRAL

51 (70)	50	Escudos (Ag) 1968. Pedro Alvares Cabral (c. 1468–1526), navigator, discoverer of Brazil. ℞ crowned coat of arms, value	8.00	10.00

52 (72)	20	Centavos (Br) 1969–. Quinas Cross, name of country, date. ℞ value, olive branches	0.05	0.10

			VF	XF
53 (73)	50	Centavos (Br) 1969–. Obverse as No. 52. ℞ value, ears of wheat	0.06	0.12
54 (74)	1	Escudo (Br) 1969–. Same type as No. 53	0.08	0.16

COMMEMORATIVE ISSUE FOR THE 500th BIRTHDAY OF VASCO DA GAMA

			VF	XF
55 (75)	50	Escudos (Ag) 1969. Vasco da Gama (1469–1524), navigator, discovered the sea route to India in 1497/98. ℞ coat of arms, value	9.00	12.00

COMMEMORATIVE ISSUE FOR THE 100th BIRTHDAY OF MARSHAL CARMONA

			VF	XF
56 (76)	50	Escudos (Ag) 1969. Marshal Oscar Fragoso de Carmona (1869–1951), politician, president 1928–1951. ℞ coat of arms, value	8.50	11.00
57 (71)	10	Centavos (Al) 1971–. Same type as No. 52	0.05	0.10
58 (A68)	10	Escudos (Cu–Ni) 1971–. Same type as No. 48 to 49	0.40	0.80

COMMEMORATIVE ISSUE 125 YEARS BANK OF PORTUGAL

			VF	XF
59 (77)	50	Escudos (Ag) 1971. Stylized tree, date 1846 · 1971. ℞ arms, value	8.50	11.00

			XF	Unc
60 (78)	50 Escudos (Ag) 1972. Angel with quill pen and laurel wreath in front of lyre. ℞ Quinas cross, bearing the book "Os Lusiadas", decorated with the sign of the cross of the crusaders			
			8.50	11.00

1974 REVOLUTION COMMEMORATIVE (2)

			Unc	Proof
61 (79)	100 Escudos (Ag) 1974		10.00	12.00
62 (80)	250 Escudos (Ag) 1974		20.00	25.00

		XF	Unc
63 (81)	25 Escudos (Cu-Ni) 1977–. Classical head. Rev. coat of arms, value:		
	a) 1977–1979, 9.5 gm. dia. 26.25 mm	0.70	1.50
	b) 1980–, 11 gm., dia. 28.5 mm	0.60	1.20

100th ANNIVERSARY OF THE DEATH OF
ALEXANDRE HERCULANO (3)

		Unc	Proof
64 (82)	2½ Escudos (Cu-Ni) 1977. Alexandre Herculano (1810–1877), poet	0.40	2.00
65 (83)	5 Escudos (Cu-Ni) 1977. Type as No. 64	0.90	4.50
66 (84)	25 Escudos (Cu-Ni) 1977. Type as No. 64	1.20	6.50

		XF	Unc
67 (85)	1 Escudo (Ni-Bra) 1981–.	0.20	0.40

Portuguese Guinea

Portugiesisch-Guinea   **Guineé Portugaise**

Area: 13,948 sq. mi. Population: 530,000.
The territory until 1879 administratively dependent on the Cape Verde Islands, then became an individual colony, but in 1951 – the same as the other Portuguese colonies – was reorganized as an (overseas) province. It is the first Portuguese overseas territory which has succeeded – after the proclamation of the Republic on 23rd Sept. 1973 – in being given complete independence and sovereignty from 10th Sept. 1974 as Guinea-Bissau together with membership of the United Nations. Champion of the movement was and is the P(artido) A(fricano da) I(ndependencia de) G (uiné e) C(abo Verde).
Capital: Bissau.

100 Centavos = 1 Escudo

			VF	XF
1 (1)	5	Centavos (Br) 1933. Head of liberty, left. ℞ value	30.00	60.00
2 (2)	10	Centavos (Br) 1933	6.00	15.00
3 (3)	20	Centavos (Br) 1933	3.50	8.00
4 (4)	50	Centavos (Ni–Br) 1933. Head of liberty, right. ℞ coat of arms	15.00	26.00
5 (5)	1	Escudo (Ni–Br) 1933	5.00	9.00

COMMEMORATIVE ISSUES (2) FOR THE 500th ANNIVERSARY OF DISCOVERY

			VF	XF
6 (6)	50	Centavos (Br) 1946. Coat of arms with mural crown of the colonies and commemorative legend. ℞ value and dates 1446–1946	2.50	5.00

			VF	XF
7 (7)	1	Escudo (Cu–Ni) 1946	2.50	5.00
8 (8)	50	Centavos (Br) 1952. Coat of arms with mural crown. ℞ value	0.80	1.40
9 (9)	2.50	Escudos (Cu–Ni) 1952	1.20	2.00
10 (10)	10	Escudos (Ag) 1952	6.50	9.00
11 (11)	20	Escudos (Ag) 1952	10.00	15.00

			Unc
12 (12)	10	Centavos (Al) 1973	2.00
13 (13)	20	Centavos (Br) 1973	3.00
14 (8a)	50	Centavos (Br) 1973	–.–
15 (14)	1	Escudo (Br) 1973	5.00
16 (15)	5	Escudos (Cu-Ni) 1973	6.00
17 (10a)	10	Escudos (Cu-Ni) 1973	7.50

Portuguese India

Portugiesisch-Indien   **Indes Portugaises**

Area: 1426 sq. mi. Population: 720,000 (1966).
Around 1500 the Portuguese captured several economically interesting
places in eastern India within the scope of their overseas activities,
where they installed viceroys. The second in this line, Alfonso de
Albuquerque, captured the city of Goa on the west coast on 25th Nov.
1510 and made it the centre of the dispersed Portuguese acquisitions.
Of these colonial possessions, the so-called Estado da India, there
remeined in the 19th century apart from Goa only the towns of Daman
(Damão in Portuguese, captured 1559) and Diu (captured 1536), situated
five degrees of latitude to the north on both sides of the Gulf of Cambay.
Goa was the seat of the viceroy since 1559, the residence, however,
being transferred from this city in 1759 for climatic reasons to the
nearby Pangim (also called Nova Goa). The widespread autonomy
conferred in 1951 and its own constitution (of 1955) did not save
Portuguese India from the capture by Indian troops on the 17th/18th
Dec. 1961. A plesbiscite legalized the integration in India retrospectively
for the 20th Dec. 1961, but was only recognized by treaty on 31st Dec.
1974. The three widely dispersed territories since then form a territory
of the Indian Union under the names of Goa, Daman and Diu.
Capital: Pangim (Nova Goa).

16 Tangas = 1 Rupia, 100 Centavos = 1 Escudo

CARLOS I 1889–1908

			VF	XF
1 (15)	$1/_{12}$	Tanga (Br) 1901–1903. Carlos I (1863–1908), head right. ℞ crowned arms	3.00	4.50
2 (16)	$1/_{8}$	Tanga (Br) 1901–1903	2.50	4.00
3 (17)	$1/_{4}$	Tanga (Br) 1901–1903	1.50	2.50
4 (18)	$1/_{2}$	Tanga (Br) 1901–1903	2.00	3.50
5 (19)	1	Rupia (Ag) 1903–1905	12.00	18.00

ISSUES OF THE PORTUGUESE REPUBLIC

		VF	XF
6 (20)	1 Rupia (Ag) 1912. Head of Republic, left. ℞ value in wreath	35.00	52.00

			VF	XF
7 (21)	1	Tanga (Br) 1934. Provisional coat of arms above date. ℞ coat of arms above value	3.00	6.00
8 (22)	2	Tangas (Cu–Ni) 1934	4.00	6.50
9 (23)	4	Tangas (Cu–Ni) 1934	5.00	8.00
10 (24)	½	Rupia (Ag) 1936. Coat of arms over cross. ℞ coat of arms (Old Portugal)	12.00	17.50
11 (25)	1	Rupia (Ag) 1935	12.00	16.00
12 (26)	1	Tanga (Br) 1947. Coat of arms with mural crown of the colonies. ℞ value	1.00	1.50
13 (27)	¼	Rupia (Cu–Ni) 1947, 1952	1.50	2.00
14 (28)	½	Rupia (Cu–Ni) 1947, 1952	2.00	3.00
15 (29)	1	Rupia (Ag) 1947. Coat of arms over cross. ℞ coat of arms with mural crown	7.50	10.00
16 (26a)	1	Tanga (Br) 1952. Same type as No. 12, but smaller diameter	1.20	2.00
17 (29a)	1	Rupia (Cu–Ni) 1952	4.50	7.50

NEW CURRENCY: 100 Centavos = 1 Escudo

18 (34)	10	Centavos (Br) 1958–1961. Coat of arms with mural crown. ℞ value	0.60	0.80

19 (35)	30	Centavos (Br) 1958–1959	0.80	1.20
20 (36)	60	Centavos (Cu–Ni) 1958–1959	1.20	1.80
21 (37)	1	Escudo (Cu–Ni) 1958–1959	1.50	2.00
22 (38)	3	Escudos (Cu–Ni) 1958–1959	2.00	3.50
23 (39)	6	Escudos (Cu–Ni) 1959	3.50	5.00

Area: c. 8000 sq. mi. Population: 140,000.

The emirate of Qatar, situated on a peninsula in the Persian Gulf, placed itself under British protection since 1896 and on 3rd Nov. 1916 concluded an exclusive treaty of protection with Great Britain. The Emir declared the independence of the "State of Qatar" on 1st Sept. 1971 and on 3rd Sept. 1971 concluded a new treaty of friendship with Great Britain. Until 1959 the Indian rupee was also in circulation in Qatar, but was then substituted by the Gulf-Rupee. From June 1966 until the introduction of the Qatar and Dubai Riyal (QDR) in September 1966, the Saudi-Riyal was legal tender. Due to the participation of Dubai in the founding of the United Arab Emirates on 2nd Dec. 1971 Dubai left the monetary union with Qatar; the latter's legal tender were legally valid until 18th Aug. 1973, being exchanged at the rate of 1 QDR to 1 QR.

Capital: Doha.

100 Dirham = 1 Qatar-Riyal

			XF	Unc
1 (1)	1	Dirham (Br) 1973. Arab dhow and two palms, dates. ℞ value and name of country STATE OF QATAR	0.10	0.20
2 (2)	5	Dirham (Br) 1973. Type as No. 1	0.15	0.30
3 (3)	10	Dirham (Br) 1973. Type as No. 1	0.30	0.50
4 (4)	25	Dirham (Cu–Ni) 1973. Type as No. 1	0.35	0.70
5 (5)	50	Dirham (Cu–Ni) 1973. Type as No. 1	0.70	1.10

Katar und Dubai **Qatar and Dubai** **Qatar et Dubai**

Despite of the fact that the emirate of Qatar and the sheikdom of Dubai have merged under a Monetary Union, the two territories are governed independently from each other.
Qatar: Under British patronage since 1916, this sultanate, located on the Persian Gulf, declared its independence on 1st Sept. 1971.
Capital: Doha.
Dubai: The sheikdom is situated on the south shore of the Persian Gulf and represents one of the seven Trucial States.
Capital: Dubai.

100 Dirhams = 1 Qatar and Dubai Riyal

			XF	Unc
1 (1)	1	Dirham (Br) 1966. Slender horned gazelle (Gazella leptoceros – Bovidae). R value and name of country	0.20	0.30
2 (2)	5	Dirhams (Br) 1966	0.25	0.60
3 (3)	10	Dirhams (Br) 1966	0.30	0.60
4 (4)	25	Dirhams (Cu–Ni) 1966	0.50	1.20

5 (5)	50	Dirhams (Cu–Ni) 1966	0.90	1.50

Ras El Khaimah   **Ras Al Khaima**   Ras Al Khaima

Area: 642 sq. mi. Population: 34,000.
The sheikdom of Ras Al Khaima is one of the seven Trucial States on the
Persian Gulf and the Gulf of Oman. Since February 1972 Ras Al Khaima
is a member state of the "United Arab Emirates" (UAE).
Capital: Ras Al Khaima.

100 Dirham = 1 Rial or Riyal

SAKER BEN MOHAMMED AL KAISIMI

			Unc	Proof
1	1	Rial (Ag) 1969. Crossed jambijas over crossed flags (= state emblem), dates. ℞ value, name of country	5.00	
2	2	Rials (Ag) 1969. Same type as No. 1	8.00	
3	5	Rials (Ag) 1969. Same type as No. 1	12.00	
4	7½	Riyals (Ag) 1970		30.00
5	10	Riyals (Ag) 1970		30.00
6	10	Riyals (Ag) 1970		30.00
7	15	Riyals (Ag) 1970		40.00
8	50	Riyals (Au) 1970		180.00
9	75	Riyals (Au) 1970		260.00
10	100	Riyals (Au) 1970		360.00
11	150	Riyals (Au) 1970		550.00
12	200	Riyals (Au) 1970		700.00
13	50	Dirhams (Cu–Ni) 1970. Value in Arabic, in circle. ℞ Berber falcon (Falco peregrinoides – Falconidae)	3.00	
14	2½	Riyals (Ag) 1970. Sheikh Saker. ℞ Berber falcon, value	10.00	
15	7½	Riyals (Ag) 1970. Type as No. 14	20.00	

COMMEMORATIVE ISSUE FOR THE FIRST ANNIVERSARY OF THE DEATH OF DWIGHT D. EISENHOWER

16	10	Riyals (Ag) 1970. Dwight D. Eisenhower (1890–1969), 34th President of the United States of America	26.00	

Area: 970 sq. mi. Population: 470,000.
French territory since 1643, the island of Réunion carried the name "Ile Bourbon" until 1848. In 1946 Réunion became a French Overseas Department.
Capital: Saint-Denis.

100 Centimes = 1 CFA Franc

		VF	XF
1 (8)	1 Franc (Al) 1948–. Head of Marianne, allegory of the French Republic	0.25	0.40
2 (9)	2 Francs (Al) 1948–	0.40	0.60

3 (10)	5 Francs (Al) 1955	0.60	1.00
4 (11)	10 Francs (Al–Br) 1955–1964	0.90	1.20
5 (12)	20 Francs (Al–Br) 1955–1964	1.00	1.50
6 (13)	50 Francs (Ni) 1962–	1.20	1.60
7 (14)	100 Francs (Ni) 1964–	1.80	2.50

Previous issues, see "Weltmünzkatalog 19. Jahrhundert" (World Coin Catalogue of the 19th Century)

Rhodesien　　　　　　　# Rhodesia　　　　　　　**Rhodésie**

Area: 150,333 sq. mi. Population: 5,500,000.

The territories of Northern and Southern Rhodesia were united under the administration of the British South Africa Company from 1889 to 1923. From 1953 to 1963 Southern Rhodesia together with Northern Rhodesia and Nyasaland belonged to the Central African Federation. October 1964 renaming of Southern Rhodesia as Rhodesia. On November 11, 1965 Rhodesia declared its independence and on March 2, 1970 became a republic.

Capital: Salisbury.

12 Pence = 1 Shilling, 10 Cents = 1 Shilling, 20 Shillings = 1 £;
since February 17, 1970: 100 Cents = 1 Rhodesian Dollar

			VF	XF
1 (A1)	3 Pence (Cu–Ni) 1968. ℞ 3 spear points		0.30	0.60
2 (1)	6 Pence = 5 Cents (Cu–Ni) 1964. Queen Elizabeth II. ℞ flame lily (Gloriosa sp. – Liliaceae)		0.50	0.80
3 (2)	1 Shilling = 10 Cents (Cu–Ni) 1964. ℞ coat of arms		1.00	1.60
4 (3)	2 Shillings = 20 Cents (Cu–Ni) 1964. ℞ large Zimbabwe bird		1.50	2.50

5 (4)	2½ Shillings = 25 Cents (Cu–Ni) 1964. ℞ Sable antelope (Hippotragus niger – Bovidae)		2.00	3.50

6 (A5) 10 Shillings (Au) 1966. ℞ sable antelope   160.00
7 (B5) 1 £ (Au) 1966. ℞ heraldic lion   350.00
8 (C5) 5 £ (Au) 1966. ℞ coat of arms   1200.00

CURRENCY REFORM (Decimal System):
100 Cents = 1 Rhodesian Dollar

		XF	Unc
9 (5)	½ Cent (Br) 1970–1972, 1975.	0.10	0.20

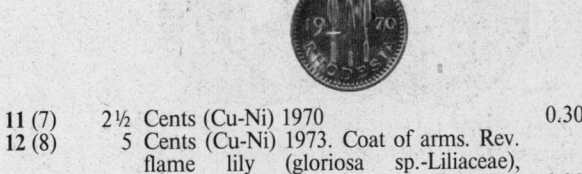

| **10** (6) | 1 Cent (Br) 1970–1976. | 0.10 | 0.20 |

| **11** (7) | 2½ Cents (Cu-Ni) 1970 | 0.30 | 0.50 |
| **12** (8) | 5 Cents (Cu-Ni) 1973. Coat of arms. Rev. flame lily (gloriosa sp.-Liliaceae), country name, date value | 0.30 | 0.50 |

13 (9)	5 Cents (Cu-Ni) 1975, 1976. Coat of arms, country name. Rev. flame lily, date, value	0.30	0.50
14 (10)	10 Cents (Cu-Ni) 1975, 1976.	0.50	1.00
15 (11)	20 Cents (Cu-Ni) 1975–1977	0.75	1.50
16 (12)	25 Cents (Cu-Ni) 1975–1977	1.00	2.00

Rhodesia and Nyasaland

In 1953 the colony of Southern Rhodesia and the protectorates of Northern Rhodesia and Nyasaland merged into the Central African Federation, which was dissolved again in 1963.

12 Pence = 1 Shilling, 2 Shillings = 1 Florin,
5 Shillings = 1 Crown, 20 Shillings = 1 £

ELISABETH II 1952–1963

		VF	XF
1 (1)	½ Penny (Br) 1955–1964. Giraffes (Giraffa camelopardalis – Giraffidae) and crown. ℞ value and ornamentations (center hole)	0.40	0.60

		VF	XF
2 (2)	1 Penny (Br) 1955–1963. African elephants (Loxodonta africana – Elephantidae) and crown. ℞ value and ornamentations (center hole)	0.50	0.80
3 (3)	3 Pence (Cu–Ni) 1955–1964. Elisabeth II, head right. ℞ flame lily (Gloriosa sp. – Liliaceae)	0.60	0.90
4 (4)	6 Pence (Cu–Ni) 1955–1963. ℞ lions (Panthera leo – Felidae)	1.10	1.60
5 (5)	1 Shilling (Cu–Ni) 1955–1957. ℞ antilope (Hippotragus niger – Bovidae)	2.00	3.00
6 (6)	2 Shillings (Cu–Ni) 1955–1957. ℞ African fish eagle (Haliaetus vocifer Accipitridae) with fish	3.50	6.50

			VF	XF
7 (7)	½ Crown (Cu–Ni) 1955–1957. ℞ coat of arms		7.50	10.50

			VF	XF
		from 1866 to 1881, King (Rege) of the country, as Carol I, from 1881 to 1914	15.00	25.00
14 (38)	5	Lei (Ag) 1906. Same type as No. 13	50.00	90.00
15 (39)	12½	Lei (Au) 1906. Portrait in uniform. ℞ crowned, double-headed eagle	170.00	250.00
16 (41)	20	Lei (Au) 1906. Same type as No. 13	280.00	320.00
17 (40)	25	Lei (Au) 1906. Same type as No. 15	350.00	450.00

18 (43)	50	Lei (Au) 1906. Carol I, portrait in uniform. ℞ Carol I on horseback	650.00	900.00
19 (42)	100	Lei (Au) 1906. Same type as No. 13	2000.00	2400.00
20 (44)	50	Bani (Ag) 1910–1914. Carol I, head left. ℞ crown above olive branch	3.00	4.50
21 (45)	1	Leu (Ag) 1910–1914. ℞ woman in national costume	4.00	6.50
22 (46)	2	Lei (Ag) 1910–1914. Same type as No. 21	5.50	9.00

FERDINAND I 1914–1927

23 (47)	25	Bani (Al) 1921. Eagle above name of country and date. ℞ value and crown (center hole)	0.80	1.50
24 (48)	50	Bani (Al) 1921. Same type as No. 23	1.20	2.00
25 (49)	1	Leu (Cu–Ni) 1924. Coat of arms and date. ℞ value in wreath	0.40	0.80
26 (50)	2	Lei (Cu–Ni) 1924. Same type as No. 25	0.80	1.50

COMMEMORATIVE COINS (4) FOR THE CORONATION OF FERDINAND I

27 (51)	20	Lei (Au) 1922. Ferdinand I, head with laurel wreath. ℞ crowned coat of arms with value	350.00	400.00
28 (52)	25	Lei (Au) 1922. Ferdinand I (1865–1927) in coronation robe. ℞ Queen Mary (1875–1938) in coronation robe	420.00	500.00
29 (53)	50	Lei (Au) 1922. Same type as No. 28	700.00	900.00
30 (54)	100	Lei (Au) 1922. Same type as No. 27	2000.00	2300.00

Rumänien   # Rumania   **Roumanie**
Romania

Area: 91,700 sq. mi. Population: 21,000,000.
The principalities of Moldavia and Wallachia which originated in the
14th century, came under Turkish suzerainty at the beginning of the
15th century. In 1881 Rumania was raised to the status of a kingdom,
after the two principalities had already had the opportunity of uniting
in 1859, which then assumed the name of Rumania on January 24, 1862.
Michael, the last king, had to abdicate in 1947; in 1948 the country
became a People's Republic.
Capital: Bukarest.

100 Bani = 1 Leu

		CAROL I 1881–1914	VF	XF
1 (24)	50	Bani (Ag) 1894–1901. Carol I (1839–1914), head left. ℞ value and date in wreath	3.50	5.50
2 (25)	1	Leu (Ag) 1894–1901. ℞ coat of arms, value and date	5.50	10.50
3 (26)	2	Lei (Ag) 1894–1901. Same type as No. 1	22.00	40.00
4 (23a)	5	Lei (Ag) 1901. Same type as No. 1	40.00	90.00
5 (29)	1	Ban (Cu) 1900	1.50	3.50
6 (30)	2	Bani (Cu) 1900	1.50	3.50
7 (31)	5	Bani (Cu–Ni) 1900. Crown and date in wreath. ℞ value	1.50	3.50
8 (32)	10	Bani (Cu–Ni) 1900. Same type as No. 7	2.00	4.50
9 (33)	20	Bani (Cu–Ni) 1900. Same type as No. 7	15.00	25.00
10 (34)	5	Bani (Cu–Ni) 1905–1906. Ribbon with name of country, crown above. ℞ value and date (center hole)	0.40	1.20
11 (35)	10	Bani (Cu–Ni) 1905–1906. Same type as No. 10	1.20	2.50
12 (36)	20	Bani (Cu–Ni) 1905–1906. Same type as No. 10	1.50	3.50

COMMEMORATIVE ISSUES (7) FOR THE 40th REGNAL ANNIVERSARY OF CAROL I

13 (37)	1	Leu (Ag) 1906. Karl Eitel Friedrich of Hohenzollern-Sigmaringen (1839–1914), Prince (Domnul) of Rumania

			VF	XF
31 (55)	5	Lei (Br) 1930. Michael I as a boy. ℞ coat of arms and value	1.20	2.00

32 (56)	20	Lei (Br) 1930. ℞ allegory of the unity of the country	5.50	9.00

CAROL II 1930–1940

33 (57)	1	Leu (Ni–Bra). Crown and date, surrounded by name of country and wreath		
		a) 1938, diameter: 21 mm (pattern)	10.00	15.00
		b) 1938–1941, diameter: 18 mm	0.40	1.20
34 (58)	10	Lei (Ni–Bra) 1930. Carol II (1893–1953), head left. ℞ crowned double-headed eagle and shield with monogram	1.20	2.50
35 (59)	20	Lei (Ni–Bra) 1930. Same type as No. 34	1.50	3.50
36 (60)	50	Lei (Ni) 1937–1938. Carol II in full-dress uniform. ℞ coat of arms in wreath	2.00	4.00
37 (62)	100	Lei (Ag) 1932. Carol II, head right. ℞ coat of arms in wreath	16.00	25.00
38 (61)	100	Lei (Ni) 1936–1938. Carol II, head left	2.00	3.50

39 (63)	250	Lei (Ag) 1935. Carol II, head left. ℞ crowned eagle with shield	22.00	40.00
40 (64)	250	Lei (Ag) 1939–1940. Carol II, head right. ℞ crowned coat of arms and wreath of wheat and grapes	12.00	20.00

COMMEMORATIVE ISSUES (4) FOR THE 100th BIRTHDAY OF CAROL I, ON APRIL 20, 1839

				VF	XF
41 (65)	20	Lei (Au) 1939. Carol II, head right. ℞ crowned coat of arms		900.00	1000.00
42 (66)	20	Lei (Au) 1939. ℞ heraldic eagle		500.00	600.00
43 (67)	100	Lei (Au) 1939. Same type as No. 41		4600.00	6000.00
44 (68)	100	Lei (Au) 1939. Angel with sword, and coat of arms		4600.00	6000.00

COMMEMORATIVE ISSUES (4) FOR THE 10th REGNAL ANNIVERSARY OF CAROL II

				VF	XF
45 (71)	20	Lei (Au) 1940. Carol II, head right. ℞ monogram with crown, surrounded by laurel wreath with heraldic ornamentation		350.00	400.00
46 (72)	20	Lei (Au) 1940. R crown above monogram, surrounded by chain		350.00	400.00
47 (A71)	100	Lei (Au) 1940. Same type as No. 45		2000.00	2500.00
48 (A72)	100	Lei (Au) 1940. Same type as No. 46		2600.00	2900.00

MICHAEL I 1940–1947

				VF	XF
49 (73)	2	Lei (Sn) 1941. Crown. ℞ value in wreath		2.00	4.00
50 (74)	5	Lei (Sn) 1942. ℞ value and ears of wheat		1.50	3.00
51 (75)	20	Lei (Sn) 1942–1944. ℞ value in wreath		2.00	3.00
52 (76)	100	Lei (Ni–St) 1943–1944. Michael I (1921–1970), head right. ℞ value in wreath, with crown above		1.00	2.50
53 (77)	200	Lei (Ag) 1942. ℞ coat of arms		4.00	5.00
54 (78)	250	Lei (Ag) 1941. Michael I, head left. ℞ crowned coat of arms and wreath, surrounded by wheat and grapes; edge inscription NIHIL SINE DEO (Nothing without God)		11.00	16.00
55 (78a)	250	Lei (Ag) 1941. Same type as No. 54, but edge inscription TOTUL PENTRU TARA		26.00	50.00
56 (79)	500	Lei (Ag) 1941. Stephan III the Great (Stefan cel Mare) (1433–1504), Prince of the Moldavia 1457–1504, kneeling, with model of church		20.00	30.00

COMMEMORATIVE ISSUE FOR THE REUNION WITH TRANSYLVANIA

				VF	XF
A56	20	Lei (Au) 1944. Heads of Prince Michael, King Ferdinand I and King Michael. ℞ 11 coat of arms		90.00	115.00
57 (81)	200	Lei (Bra) 1945. Michael I, head right. ℞ value and date in wreath, crown above		4.00	8.00
58 (80)	500	Lei (Ag) 1944. Michael I, head left. ℞ crowned coat of arms		5.00	8.00

			VF	XF
72 (93a)	2	Lei (Al) 1951–1952. Type as No. 70:		
		a) 1951	1.50	2.00
		b) 1952	2.50	5.00

73 (94)	5	Lei (Al) 1948–1951. Coat of arms of the People's Republic. ℞ value in wreath	2.00	4.00
74 (95)	20	Lei (Al) 1951. ℞ blacksmith with anvil in front of industrial plant	10.00	16.00

Change to gold currency on Januar 28, 1952

75 (96)	1	Ban (Al-Br) 1952. Coat of arms. Rev. value, date	0.25	0.50
76 (97)	3	Bani (Al-Br) 1952. Type as No. 75	0.80	1.50
77 (98)	5	Bani (Al-Br) 1952. Type as No. 75	1.00	2.50
78 (99)	10	Bani (Cu-Ni) 1952. Coat of arms. Rev. value in wreath	1.00	3.00

79 (100)	25	Bani (Cu-Ni) 1952. Type as No. 78	1.00	2.50
80 (96a)	1	Ban (Al-Br) 1953, 1954. Type as No. 75, but new coat of arms (star at top of arms)	0.80	1.50
81 (97a)	3	Bani (Al-Br) 1953, 1954. Type as No. 80	0.40	0.80
82 (98a)	5	Bani (Al-Br) 1953–1957. Type as No. 80	0.50	1.00
83 (99a)	10	Bani (Cu-Ni) 1953–1955. Type as No. 78, but new coat of arms (star at top of arms)	0.50	1.00
84 (100a)	25	Bani (Cu-Ni) 1953–1955. Type as No. 83	1.00	1.50

59 (82)	500 Lei (Bra) 1945. Same type as No. 58	6.00	9.00
60 (83)	500 Lei (Al) 1946. Michael I, head right. Ŗ value in wreath, with name of country above	3.00	5.00
61 (84)	2000 Lei (Bra) 1946. Ŗ crowned coat of arms	4.00	6.00

62 (85)	10000 Lei (Bra) 1947. Ŗ crowned shield, olive branches and value	4.00	7.00
63 (86)	25000 Lei (Ag) 1946. Same type as No. 62	5.00	10.00
64 (87)	100000 Lei (Ag) 1946. Ŗ Romania, allegory of the state with crowned coat of arms and dove of peace	12.00	25.00

CURRENCY REFORM of August 15, 1947:
20000 old Lei = 1 new Leu

65 (88)	50 Bani (Bra) 1947. Crown. Ŗ value	1.50	3.00
66 (89)	1 Leu (Bra) 1947. Crowned coat of arms. Ŗ value in wreath of wheat	2.00	4.00
67 (90)	2 Lei (Br) 1947. Same type as No. 66	2.50	4.50

| 68 (91) | 5 Lei (Al) 1947. Michael I, head right. Ŗ value and ears of wheat | 3.00 | 5.00 |

PEOPLE'S REPUBLIC
Republica Populara Romana since 1948

69 (92)	1 Leu (Al-Br) 1949-1951. Oil derrick in front of rising sun. Rev. value, date	1.50	3.00
70 (93)	2 Lei (Al-Br) 1950, 1951. Typical fruits of the country. Rev. value, date	1.50	3.00
71 (92a)	1 Leu (Al) 1951-1952. Type as No. 69:		
	a) 1951	1.50	2.00
	b) 1952	2.50	5.00

		VF	**XF**
85 (99b)	10 Bani (Cu-Ni) 1955, 1956. Type as No. 83, but country name ROMINA	0.40	0.80
86 (100b)	25 Bani (Cu-Ni) 1955. Type as No. 85	0.50	1.00
87 (101)	50 Bani (Cu-Ni) 1955, 1956. Type similar to No. 74	0.80	2.00

	VF	**XF**
15 Bani (Ni-St) 1960. Rev. value in wreath	0.30	0.60

		VF	**XF**
89 (104)	25 Bani (Ni-St) 1960. rev. value above tractor and ears of wheat	0.40	1.00
90 (102)	5 Bani (Ni-St) 1963. Coat of arms. Rev. value, date	0.15	0.40

		VF	**XF**
91 (105)	1 Leu (Ni-St) 1963. Rev. tractor in front of mountain landscape and rising sun	0.70	1.50

		VF	**XF**
92 (106)	3 Lei (Ni-St) 1963. Rev. oil refinery	0.90	1.70

				VF	XF
93 (107)	5	Bani (Ni-St) 1966. New coat of arms (with ROMANIA on ribbon in arms)		0.10	0.20
94 (108)	15	Bani (Ni-St) 1966. Type as No. 88, but new coat of arms		0.15	0.30
95 (109)	25	Bani (Ni-St) 1966. Rev. similar to No. 89		0.20	0.40
96 (110)	1	Leu (Ni-St) 1966. Rev. similar to No. 91		0.40	0.80
97 (111)	3	Lei (Ni-St) 1966. Rev. similar to No. 92		0.60	1.30

			VF	XF
98 (107a)	5	Bani (Al) 1975. Type as No. 93	0.10	0.20

			VF	XF
99 (108a)	15	Bani (Al) 1975. Type as No. 94	0.20	0.30

			VF	XF
100 (112)	5	Lei (Al) 1978	1.00	2.00

РОССИЯ - СССР

Area: 6,591,090 sq. mi. Population: 259,000,000.

Until February 1917 Russia was an empire ruled by a tsar and then a bourgeois republic. After the October Revolution of 1917, the Russian Soviet Federal Socialist Republic (RSFSR) was created. On December 30, 1922 the Union of Soviet Socialist Republics (USSR) was founded which consisted of the RSFSR, the T(ranscaucasian)SFSR, the U(krainian)SSR and the W(hite Russian)SSR. Later on the Usbek, Turkmen (1924) and Tadzhik SSR (1929) joined the Union. Further Union Republics originated 1940/41 out of the Baltic states and the Moldavian territory as well as Karelia, which, however, after World War II lost the status of an autonomous republic.
Capital: St. Petersburg (Leningrad), since 1922 Moscow.

100 Kopeks (КОПЕЙКИ) = 1 Rouble (РУБЛЬ)

NICOLAS II 1894–1917

The minor coins minted under Nicolas II exhibit in the main the same patterns as those of his predecessor Alexander III (1881–1894) and were struck in St. Petersburg practically without exception. The designation of this mint with С. П. Б. was omitted on the pieces between 1915 and 1917, perhaps because a part of the coinage was ordered to be struck in Osaka.

			VF	XF
1 (47)	¼ Kopek (Cu). Monogram of Nicholas II, between crown and laurel branches. ℞ value and date			
	a) 1894–1914, with mint mark		3.00	6.00
	b)1915–1916, without mint mark		6.00	10.00
2 (48)	½ Kopek (Cu) 1894–1916. Same type as No. 1			
	a) 1894–1914, with mint mark		3.00	6.00
	b) 1915–1916, without mint mark		4.00	7.50
3 (9)	1 Kopek (Cu). Crowned double-headed eagle. ℞ value in circle and wreath			
	a) 1894–1914, with mint mark		2.00	3.50
	b) 1915–1916, without mint mark		2.00	3.50

			VF	**XF**
4 (10)	2	Kopeks (Cu). Same type as No. 3		
		a) 1894–1914, with mint mark	2.00	3.50
		b) 1915–1916, without mint mark	2.00	3.50
5 (11)	3	Kopeks (Cu). Same type as No. 3		
		a) 1894–1914, with mint mark	2.00	3.50
		b) 1915–1916, without mint mark	2.00	3.50
6 (12)	5	Kopeks (Cu). Same type as No. 3		
		a) 1911–1912, with mint mark	3.50	6.00
		b) 1916, without mint mark	80.00	115.00
7 (19a)	5	Kopeks (Ag). Crowned double-headed eagle. ℞ value and date in wreath, crown above		
		a) 1897–1914, with mint mark	1.50	2.50
		b) 1915, without mint mark	1.50	2.50
8 (20a)	10	Kopeks (Ag). Same type as No. 7		
		a) 1895–1914, with mint mark	1.50	2.50
		b) 1915–1917, without mint mark	1.50	2.50
9 (21a)	15	Kopeks (Ag). Same type as No. 7		
		a) 1896–1914, with mint mark	2.50	4.00
		b) 1915–1917, without mint mark	2.50	4.00
10 (22a)	20	Kopeks (Ag). Same type as No. 7		
		a) 1901–1914, with mint mark	2.50	4.00
		b) 1914–1917, without mint mark	2.50	4.00
11 (57)	25	Kopeks (Ag). 1895–1901. Nicholas II (1868–1918), head left. ℞ crowned double-headed eagle	15.00	30.00
12 (58)	50	Kopeks (Ag) 1895–1914. Same type as No. 11	10.00	20.00

			VF	XF
13 (59)	1	Rouble (Ag). Same type as No. 11		
		a) 1895–1913	12.00	25.00
		b) 1914 (900 pieces), 1915 (600 pieces)	300.00	380.00
14 (62)	5	Roubles (Au) 1897–1911. Same type as No. 11	60.00	80.00
15 (63)	7½	Roubles (Au) 1897. Same type as No. 11	160.00	180.00
16 (64)	10	Roubles (Au) 1895–1911. Same type as No. 11	110.00	130.00

	VF	XF

17 (65) 15 Roubles (Au) 1897. Same type as No. 11 160.00 200.00
18 (A65) 25 Roubles (Au). Same type as No. 11:
   a) 1896 (300 pieces) 4500.00 9000.00
   b) 1908 (175 pieces) 5000.00 10000.00
19 (B65) 37½ Roubles with additional value 100 Franc as double currency (Au) 1902. Same type as No. 11 7500.00 9500.00

COMMEMORATIVE COIN FOR THE CENTENNIAL OF NAPOLEON'S DEFEAT

20 (68) 1 Rouble (Ag) 1912. Memorial legend. ℞ crowned double-headed eagle on St. George's shield, surrounded by six provincial arms 150.00 200.00

COMMEMORATIVE COIN FOR ALEXANDER III

21 (69) 1 Rouble (Ag) 1912. Alexander III (1845–1894), tsar 1881–1894. ℞ monument of the ruler 500.00 750.00

COMMEMORATIVE COIN FOR THE 300th ANNIVERSARY OF THE HOUSE OF ROMANOFF

22 (70) 1 Rouble(Ag) 1913. Nicholas II and Michael Feodorovich (1596–1645), first tsar of the Romanoff Dynasty, reigned 1613–1645. ℞ crowned double-headed eagle

	VF	**XF**
	20.00	35.00

COMMEMORATIVE COIN FOR THE 200th ANNIVERSARY OF THE NAVAL BATTLE OF GANGUT

23 (71) 1 Rouble (Ag) 1914. Peter I, the Great (1672–1725), portrait right. ℞ crowned double-headed eagle   1200.00   1500.00

RUSSIAN SOVIET FEDERAL SOCIALIST REPUBLIC
Name of country: РСФСР

24 (80) 10 Kopeks (Ag) 1921–1923. Arms of the Soviet Republic. Value in wreath   2.00   4.00

25 (81) 15 Kopeks (Ag) 1921–1923. Same type as No. 24   3.50   5.00

26 (82) 20 Kopeks (Ag) 1921–1923. Same type as No. 24   4.50   6.50

27 (83) 50 Kopeks (Ag) 1921–1922. Coat of arms. ℞ value in star, date below, all in circle and wreath   7.50   15.00

				VF	**XF**

28 (84) 1 Rouble (Ag) 1921-1922. Same type as No. 27 ...... 18.00 30.00

29 (85) 10 Roubles = Chervonetz (Au) 1923, 1925, 1975-1978. Sowing farmer. Rev. coat of arms. The issue of 1925 is a pattern piece:
a) 1923 ...... 280.00 360.00
b) 1925, pattern ...... –.– –.–
c) 1975–1980 ...... 110.00 125.00

UNION OF SOVIET SOCIALIST REPUBLICS
Name of country: CCCP

30 (75) ½ Kopek (Cu) 1925–1928. Name of country CCCP in circle. ℞ value spelt out 5.00 10.00

31 (76) 1 Kopek (Cu) 1924–1925. Coat of arms with new legend and name of country CCCP. ℞ value in wreath of wheat ears 2.50 4.00

32 (77) 2 Kopeks (Cu) 1924, 1925. Same type as No. 31. Year 1925 is very rare 4.00 6.00

33 (78) 3 Kopeks (Cu) 1924. Same type as No. 31 ...... 4.00 5.50

34 (79) 5 Kopeks (Cu) 1924. Same type as No. 31 ...... 6.00 8.00

35 (86) 10 Kopeks (Ag) 1924–1931. Same type as No. 31 ...... 1.80 2.50

36 (87) 15 Kopeks (Ag) 1924–1931. Same type as No. 31 ...... 2.50 4.00

37 (88) 20 Kopeks (Ag) 1924–1931. Same type as No. 31 ...... 2.50 4.00

38 (89) 50 Kopeks (Ag) 1924–1927. Blacksmith with anvil. ℞ coat of arms and value in letters 6.00 8.00

			VF	XF
39 (90)	1	Rouble (Ag) 1924. Workman and farmer in front of landscape and rising sun	12.00	20.00

			VF	XF
40 (91)	1	Kopek (Al–Br) 1926–1935. Coat of arms with new legend and name of country CCCP. ℞ value in wreath	0.40	0.80
41 (92)	2	Kopeks (Al–Br) 1926–1935. Same type as No. 40	0.80	1.20
42 (93)	3	Kopeks (Al–Br) 1926–1935. Same type as No. 40	0.40	0.80
43 (94)	5	Kopeks (Al–Br) 1926–1935. Same type as No. 40	0.80	1.50
44 (95)	10	Kopeks (Cu–Ni) 1931–1934. Coat of arms with new legend without name of country. ℞ workman, shield with value	0.40	0.80
45 (96)	15	Kopeks (Cu–Ni) 1931–1934. Same type as No. 44	0.60	1.20
46 (97)	20	Kopeks (Cu–Ni) 1931–1934. Same type as No. 44	0.80	1.20

Coins No. 47 to 74 can be distinguished by the number of ribbons on wreath around arms. The number of ribbons stands for the number of republics existing at the time of issue. Usually the coins have a rough rim, smooth rims are very rare and high in demand, and forgeries exist.

			VF	XF
47 (98)	1	Kopek (Al–Br) 1935–1936. Coat of arms with three ribbons on each side, name of country below, but without new legend. ℞ value and date in wreath	2.00	4.50

			VF	XF
48 (99)	2	Kopeks (Al–Br) 1935–1936. Same type as No. 47	1.50	4.00
49 (100)	3	Kopeks (Al–Br) 1935–1936. Same type as No. 47	2.50	4.50
50 (101)	5	Kopeks (Al–Br) 1935–1936. Same type as No. 47	4.00	7.50
51 (102)	10	Kopeks (Cu–Ni) 1935–1936. Coat of arms with three ribbons on each side. ℞ shield with value surrounded by ears of wheat, oak branches and date	0.40	0.80
52 (103)	15	Kopeks (Cu–Ni) 1935–1936. Same type as No. 51	1.00	1.50
53 (104)	20	Kopeks (Cu–Ni) 1935–1936. Same type as No. 51	1.20	1.80
54 (105)	1	Kopek (Al–Br) 1937–1946. Same type as No. 47, but coat of arms with five ribbons on each side	0.10	0.20
55 (106)	2	Kopeks (Al–Br) 1937–1946. Same type as No. 48, but coat of arms with five ribbons on each side	0.15	0.25
56 (107)	3	Kopeks (Al–Br) 1937–1946. Same type as No. 49, but coat of arms with five ribbons on each side	0.20	0.35
57 (108)	5	Kopeks (Al–Br) 1937–1946. Same type as No. 50, but coat of arms with five ribbons on each side	0.30	0.50
58 (109)	10	Kopeks (Cu–Ni) 1937–1946. Same type as No. 51, but coat of arms with five ribbons on each side	0.25	0.40
59 (110)	15	Kopeks (Cu–Ni) 1937–1946. Same type as No. 52, but coat of arms with five ribbons on each side	0.40	0.60

60 (111)	20	Kopeks (Cu–Ni) 1937–1946. Same type as No. 53, but coat of arms with five ribbons on each side	0.60	1.10
61 (112)	1	Kopek (Al–Br) 1948–1956. Same type as No. 47, but coat of arms with eight ribbons on left and seven on right side	0.15	0.25
62 (113)	2	Kopeks (Al–Br) 1948–1956. Same type as No. 48, but coat of arms with eight ribbons on left and seven on right side	0.20	0.40

			VF	**XF**
63 (114)	3	Kopeks (Al–Br) 1948–1956. Same type as No. 49, but coat of arms with eight ribbons on left and seven on right side	0.30	0.50
64 (115)	5	Kopeks (Al–Br) 1948–1956. Same type as No. 50, but coat of arms with eight ribbons on left and seven on right side	0.40	0.80
65 (116)	10	Kopeks (Cu–Ni) 1948–1956. Same type as No. 51, but coat of arms with eight ribbons on left and seven on right side	0.30	0.50
66 (117)	15	Kopeks (Cu–Ni) 1948–1956. Same type as No. 52, but coat of arms with eight ribbons on left and seven on right side	0.40	0.80
67 (118)	20	Kopeks (Cu–Ni) 1948–1956. Same type as No. 53, but coat of arms with eight ribbons on left and seven on right side	0.60	1.10
68 (119)	1	Kopek (Al–Br) 1957–1960. Same type as No. 47, but coat of arms with seven ribbons on each side	0.80	2.00
69 (120)	2	Kopeks (Al–Br) 1957–1960. Same type as No. 48, but coat of arms with seven ribbons on each side	0.80	2.00
70 (121)	3	Kopeks (Al–Br) 1957–1960. Same type as No. 49, but coat of arms with seven ribbons on each side	0.80	2.00
71 (122)	5	Kopeks (Al–Br) 1957–1960. Same type as No. 50, but coat of arms with seven ribbons on each side	1.20	2.60
72 (123)	10	Kopeks (Cu–Ni) 1957–1960. Same type as No. 51	0.50	0.80
73 (124)	15	Kopeks (Cu–Ni) 1957–1960. Same type as No. 52	0.60	1.20
74 (125)	20	Kopeks (Cu–Ni) 1957–1960. Same type as No. 53	0.80	1.50

CURRENCY REFORM
of January 1, 1961: 10 old Roubles = 1 new Rouble

75 (126)	1	Kopek (Bra) 1961–. State emblem. ℞ value and date in wreath	0.15	0.30
76 (127)	2	Kopeks (Bra) 1961–	0.15	0.30
77 (128)	3	Kopeks (Bra) 1961–	0.20	0.40
78 (129)	5	Kopeks (Bra) 1961–	0.30	0.60
79 (130)	10	Kopeks (Ni–Bra) 1961–	0.30	0.60

80 (131)	15	Kopeks (Ni–Bra) 1961–	0.40	0.75

		VF	XF
81 (132)	20 Kopeks (Ni–Bra) 1961–	0.40	0.80
82 (133)	50 Kopeks (Ni–Bra)		
	a) 1961, edge plain	1.50	2.50
	b) 1964–, edge with value in letters and date	0.80	1.50
83 (134)	1 Rouble (Ni–Bra)		
	a) 1961, edge plain	2.50	4.00
	b) 1964–, edge with value in letters and date	1.60	2.50

The 50 Kopeks, and the 1, 2, 3, and 5 Roubles pieces, bearing the same design as Nos. 82 and 83 (Ni–Bra) 1958, are pattern pieces. Other patterns are the 5 Kopeks (Al) 1953, with same obverse as No. 78, but reverse with value above oak branches and hammer and sickle, and 50 Kopeks (Br) 1953, identical with No. 82.

COMMEMORATIVE COIN FOR THE 20th ANNIVERSARY OF THE END OF WORLD WAR II

		VF	XF
84 (135)	1 Rouble (Ni–St) 1965. Berlin-Treptow: statue of soldier by E. Vouchetich. ℞ state emblem and value in letters	3.00	4.50

COMMEMORATIVE COINS (5) FOR THE 50th ANNIVERSARY OF THE OCTOBER REVOLUTION

		VF	XF
85 (136)	10 Kopeks (Ni–St) 1967. State emblem in circle of rays, dates. ℞ Moscow: monument	0.25	0.40

			VF	XF
86 (137)	15	Kopeks (Ni–St) 1967. Moscow: "laborer and female farm laborer", monument by Vera Muchina; dates. ℞ state emblem and value	0.40	0.60

87 (138)	20	Kopeks (Ni–St) 1967. State emblem, dates, legend "50 years of Soviet power". ℞ Small cruiser "Aurora"	0.50	0.80
88 (139)	50	Kopeks (Ni–St) 1967. Lenin statue in front of hammer and sickle. ℞ state emblem and value in letters	1.10	1.60

89 (140)	1	Rouble (Ni–St) 1967. Same type as No. 88	3.00	4.50

COMMEMORATIVE COIN FOR LENIN'S
100th BIRTHDAY

		XF	Unc
90 (141)	1 Rouble (Ni–St) 1970. Vladimir Ilyich Lenin (1870–1924), actually Ulyanov; Soviet Russian politician, leader of the world's proletariat. ℞ state emblem, value, memorial legend	2.00	3.00

30th ANNIVERSARY OF THE END OF WORLD WAR II

91 (142)	1 Rouble (German silver) 1975. Monument in Wolgograd	2.00	3.00

60th ANNIVERSARY OF THE OCTOBER REVOLUTION

92 (143)	1 Rouble (German silver) 1977. Bust of Lenin and small cruiser "Aurora". Rev. coat of arms, value	1.80	2.80

	XF	Unc
93 (144) 1 Rouble (German silver) 1977. Emblem of the Olympic games 1980. Rev. coat of arms, value	1.80	3.00

94　　　　　95

	Unc	Proof
94 (145) 5 Roubles (Ag) 1977. City view of Kiev	25.00	35.00
95 (146) 5 Roubles (Ag) 1977. City view of Leningrad	25.00	35.00

96　　　　　97

96 (147) 5 Roubles (Ag) 1977. City view of Minsk	25.00	35.00
97 (148) 5 Roubles (Ag) 1977. City view of Tallinn (Reval)	25.00	35.00

98   1977   99

				Unc	Proof
98 (149)	10 Roubles	(Ag) 1977. City view of Moscow		50.00	70.00
99 (150)	10 Roubles	(Ag) 1977. Map of Soviet Union		50.00	70.00
100 (A163)	100 Roubles	(Au) 1977. Globe and palm branch		300.00	350.00

101 (152)	150 Roubles	(Platinum) 1977. Olympic emblem		400.00	450.00

102 (153)	1 Rouble (German silver) 1978		3.00

1144   Russia

	Unc	Proof
103 (151) 100 Roubles (Au) 1978	320.00	370.00

	Unc	Proof
104 (162) 100 Roubles (Au) 1978	300.00	350.00
105 (154) 5 Roubles (Ag) 1978	20.00	30.00
106 (155) 5 Roubles (Ag) 1978	20.00	30.00
107 (158) 10 Roubles (Ag) 1978	35.00	45.00
108 (159) 10 Roubles (Ag) 1978	35.00	45.00
109 (160) 10 Roubles (Ag) 1978	35.00	45.00

110 111

	Unc	Proof
110 (156) 5 Roubles (Ag) 1978	20.00	30.00
111 (157) 5 Roubles (Ag) 1978	20.00	30.00

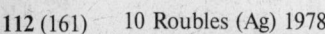

			Unc	Proof
112 (161)	10 Roubles (Ag) 1978		35.00	45.00

113 (168)	10 Roubles (Ag) 1978	35.00	45.00
114 (169)	10 Roubles (Ag) 1978	35.00	45.00

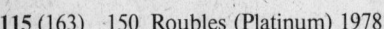

115 (163)	150 Roubles (Platinum) 1978	400.00	450.00

1146   Russia

	Unc	Proof
116 (173) 100 Roubles (Au) 1979	320.00	370.00
117 (174) 100 Roubles (Au) 1979	320.00	370.00

118 (164) 1 Roentgen (German silver) 1979	3.00
119 (165) 1 Rouble (German silver) 1979	3.00

120

121

120 (166) 5 Roubles (Ag) 1979	20.00	30.00
121 (167) 5 Roubles (Ag) 1979	20.00	30.00

122   123

	Unc	Proof
122 (170) 10 Roubles (Ag) 1979	35.00	55.00
123 (171) 10 Roubles (Ag) 1979	35.00	55.00

124 (172)   10 Roubles (Ag) 1979   35.00   55.00

125 (175)   150 Roubles   (Platinum)   1979.   Ancient
                 wrestlers   400.00   450.00

1148   **Russia**

			Unc	Proof
126 (176)	150	Roubles (Platinum) 1979	400.00	450.00
127 (186)	100	Roubles (Au) 1980	320.00	370.00
128 (177)	1	Rouble (German silver) 1980	3.00	
129 (178)	1	Rouble (German silver) 1980	3.00	
130 (181)	5	Roubles (Ag) 1980	20.00	30.00
131 (187)	10	Roubles (Ag) 1980	32.00	45.00
132 (183)	10	Roubles (Ag) 1980	32.00	45.00
133 (185)	10	Roubles (Ag) 1980	32.00	45.00
134 (182)	5	Roubles (Ag) 1980	20.00	30.00
135 (179)	5	Roubles (Ag) 1980	20.00	30.00
136 (180)	5	Roubles (Ag) 1980	20.00	30.00
137 (187)	150	Roubles Platinum) 1980	400.00	450.00

20th ANNIVERSARY OF MANNED SPACE FLIGHT

138 (188)   1 Rouble (German silver) 1981   3.50

RUSSO-BULGARIAN FRIENDSHIP

139   1 Rouble (German silver) 1981. Flags
                 above clasped hands   3.50

1 (1)   1 Rouble (Cu) 1918. Double-headed eagle
without crown. Legend, signifying the
Armawir Branch of the state bank as
issuer. ℞ value between branches

	VF	XF
1 Rouble (Cu) 1918	55.00	80.00

2 (2)   3 Roubles (Cu) 1918. Same type as No. 1

	VF	XF
a) diameter: 28 mm	90.00	120.00
b) diameter: 31 mm	160.00	180.00

3 (3)   5 Roubles (Cu) 1918. Same type as No. 1   140.00   160.00

The 1 Rouble piece is known with and without mint mark I. S.
(= Sadler) on the tail of the eagle. Pattern pieces: 3 Roubles (Ag),
10 Pieces, and 5 Roubles (Al).

KHWAREZM SOVIET PEOPLE'S REPUBLIC

			VF	XF
1 (1)	20	Roubles (Br) 1920–1921. Name of country and date (Mohammedan calendar 1338–1339) in Turkish. ℞ value in Russian and Turkish	52.00	75.00

			VF	XF
2 (2)	25	Roubles (Br) 1921. Similar type as No. 1	40.00	60.00
3 (3)	100	Roubles (Br) 1921. Similar type as No. 1	40.00	60.00

			VF	XF
4 (4)	500	Roubles (Br) 1921–1922. Similar type as No. 1	62.00	85.00

ISSUES FOR SPITSBERGEN

			VF	XF
1	10	Kopeks (Al–Br) 1946. Legend: Island of Spitsbergen in Russian, date. ℞ value and name of issuing authority ARKTIKUGOL in Cyrillic lettering	25.00	40.00
2	15	Kopeks (Al–Br) 1946. Same type as No. 1	25.00	40.00
3	20	Kopeks (Cu–Ni) 1946. Same type as No. 1	35.00	50.00
4	50	Kopeks (Cu–Ni) 1946. Same type as No. 1	35.00	50.00

Ruanda   # Rwanda   **République Rwandaise**

Area: 10,169 sq. mi. Population: 3,900,000.
A Republic in central equatorial Africa, that formerly belonged to
German East Africa, and later became part of the Belgian Trust Terri-
tory of Ruanda-Urundi. An independent republic since July 1, 1962,
Rwanda merged with Burundi under a monetary union, with the
Rwanda-Burundi Franc as the basic unit. Compare Burundi, Rwanda,
and Burundi (joint issues), and emissions prior to the independence,
also, check under Belgian Congo, years 1952 to 1960.
Capital: Kigali.

100 Centimes = 1 Rwanda Franc

			VF	XF
1 (1)	1 Franc (Cu–Ni) 1964, 1965. Gregoire Kayibanda (*1925), President. R coat of arms and value		0.30	0.80
2 (2)	5 Francs (Br) 1964		0.60	1.20
3 (3)	10 Francs (Cu–Ni) 1964		0.90	2.00

		Proof
4	10 Francs (Au) 1965	50.00
5	25 Francs (Au) 1965	125.00
6	50 Francs (Au) 1965	200.00
7	100 Francs (Au) 1965	350.00

ISSUE FOR THE FAO COIN PLAN

8 (4)   2 Francs (Al) 1970. Boy filling coffee

			VF	XF
		basket, symbol of the Rwanda Savings Bank. Motto: AUGMENTONS LA PRODUCTION. ℞ coat of arms, value	0.50	1.00
9 (5)	½	Franc (Al) 1970	0.20	0.40
10 (6)	1	Franc (Al) 1970. G. Kayibanda, head right. ℞ coat of arms, value	0.30	0.60

COMMEMORATIVE COIN FOR THE 10th ANNIVERSARY OF INDEPENDENCE AND THE FAO COIN PLAN

			XF	Unc
11 (7)	200	Francs (Cu–Ni) 1972. Scene of welcome on the occasion of the Declaration of Independence on 1st July 1962 in front of the national flag of Ruanda. ℞ agricultural worker cultivating rice	11.00	18.00
12 (8)	1	Franc (Al) 1974. Millet	0.30	0.80
13 (9)	5	Francs (Br) 1974. Branch of a coffee tree	0.40	1.80
14 (10)	10	Francs (Cu–Ni) 1974. Branch of a coffee tree	1.20	4.00

15 (11)	20	Francs (Bra) 1977	1.00	2.00
16 (12)	50	Francs (Bra) 1977	1.50	3.00

Rwanda and Burundi

Ruanda und Burundi   **Rwanda et Burundi**

The common administration of Ruanda-Urundi terminated with the
Declaration of Independence of 1st July 1962. Although on 22nd Sept.
1962 the Rwanda and Burundi Franc had been created as a new common
currency unit for the two states of Rwanda and Burundi (formerly
Urundi) which had now become independent, the existing economic
and monetary union was already cancelled on 30th Sept. 1964.

100 Centimes = 1 Rwanda and Burundi Franc

			XF	Unc
1 (1)	1	Franc (Bra) 1960–1961. Lion (Panthera leo – Felidae). ℞ value and name of country RWANDA * BURUNDI	0.60	1.20

St. Christopher-Nevis-Anguilla
St. Christopher-Nevis-Anguilla · Saint-Christophe-Nevis-Anguilla

Area: 168 sq. mi. Population: 65,000.
Group of islands in the Lesser Antilles. Member of the Caribbean Free Trade Area (CARIFTA). In 1967 Anguilla broke off relations with the neighboring islands, see also under Anguilla. St. Christopher-Nevis-Anguilla is united with the countries of Antigua, Barbados, Dominica, Grenada, Montserrat, St. Lucia and St. Vincent in the currency area of the East Caribbean Dollar. The issuing authority for the whole of the currency area is the East Caribbean Currency Authority with its seat in Bridgetown on the island of Barbados.
Capital: Basseterre on the island of St. Christopher (also known as St. Kitts).

100 Cents = 1 East Caribbean Dollar

COMMEMORATIVE ISSUE FOR THE INAUGURATION
OF THE CARIBBEAN DEVELOPMENT BANK AND THE FAO
COIN PLAN

		Unc	Proof
1 (3*)	4 Dollars (Cu–Ni) 1970. Coat of arms with shield supporters and helmet decoration. ℞ bananas, sugar cane, value	10.00	30.00

*This number refers to Yeoman's East Carribean Territories listings.

St. Helena

Area: 47 sq. mi. Population: 5,300.

St. Helena was discovered by the Portuguese on 21st May 1502 (the day of St. Helena). In 1588 the British were on the island, in 1633 the Dutch. The British East India Company were granted the Royal Charter in 1673 by the British King Charles II, permitting the this Company to occupy the island officially and to administer it. Since 1834 St. Helena is a Crown Colony.

Capital: Jamestown.

100 New Pence = 1 £

ELIZABETH II since 1952

COMMEMORATIVE COIN FOR THE TERCENTENARY OF THE GRANTING OF THE ROYAL CHARTER TO THE BRITISH EAST INDIA COMPANY

			Unc	Proof
1 (1)	25 Pence 1973. Elizabeth II facing right. R Sailing ship (17th entury):			
	a) (Ag)			30.00
	b) (Cu-Ni)		1.80	

25th ANNIVERSARY OF THE SILVER JUBILEE OF HER MAJESTY QUEEN ELIZABETH II

		Unc	Proof
2 (2)	25 Pence 1977:		
	a) (Ag)		45.00
	b) (Cu-Ni)	1.80	

25th ANNIVERSARY OF THE CORONATION OF HER MAJESTY QUEEN ELIZABETH II

		Unc	Proof
3 (3)	1 Crown 1978:		35.00
	a) (Ag)		35.00
	b) (Cu-Ni)	2.00	

80th BIRTHDAY OF QUEEN MOTHER

4 (4)	25 Pence 1980:		50.00
	a) (Ag)		50.00
	b) (Cu-Ni)	2.00	

WEDDING OF PRINCE CHARLES AND LADY DIANA

5	25 Pence 1981:		55.00
	a) (Ag)		55.00
	b) (Cu-Ni)	2.50	

St. Lucia

Area: 233 sq. mi. Population: 126,000.

An island in the group of the Lesser Antilles (Windward Islands). Discovered by Columbus in 1502, it became a British colony in 1814. On March 1, 1967 St. Lucia obtained internal autonomy; member of the Caribbean Free Trade Area (CARIFTA). St. Lucia is united with the countries of Antigua, Barbados, Dominica, Grenada, Montserrat, St. Christopher-Nevis-Anguilla and St. Vincent in the currency area of the East Caribbean Dollar. The issuing authority for the whole of the currency area is the East Caribbean Currency Authority in Bridgetown on the island of Barbados.

Capital: Castries.

100 Cents = 1 East Caribbean Dollar

COMMEMORATIVE ISSUE FOR THE INAUGURATION OF THE CARIBBEAN DEVELOPMENT BANK AND THE FAO COIN PLAN

		Unc	Proof
1 (7*)	4 Dollars (Cu–Ni) 1970. Coat of arms with shield supporters and helmet decoration. ℞ bananas, sugar cane, value	10.00	30.00

*This number refers to Yeoman's East Carribean Territories listings.

St. Pierre and Miquelon

Area: 96,5 sq. mi. Population: 6,000.
Island group south-west of Newfoundland, French territory.
Capital: St. Pierre.

$$100 \text{ Centimes} = 1 \text{ Franc}$$

			VF	XF
1 (1)	1	Franc (Al) 1948. Head of Marianne, allegory of the Republic of France. ℞ schooner	0.80	1.20

2 (2)	2	Francs (Al) 1948	0.80	1.20

St. Thomas and Prince Islands
St. Thomas und Prinzeninsel   **St. Thomas et Prince**

Area: 372 sq. mi. Population: 65,000.
The island discovered in 1470 on St. Thomas's Day (21st December)
was named after this day and the neighbouring island "Prince Island"
in honour of King Alfons V. At certain higher levels of administration,
Luanda in Angola was the competent authority, apart from which the
colony (since 1951 a province) had a large measure of autonomy. The
waterwheel in the coat of arms is the personal emblem of King Alfons V.
The Democratic Republic of Sao Tomé and Principe was declared on July 12,
1975.
Capital: São Tomé.

100 Centavos = 1 Escudo; 100 Centimos = 1 Dobra

		VF	XF
1 (1)	10 Centavos (Ni–Br) 1929. Head of Liberty. ℞ coat of arms in front of globe, value	3.50	5.50
2 (2)	20 Centavos (Ni–Br) 1929	4.00	7.00
3 (3)	50 Centavos (Ni–Br) 1928–1929		
	a) 1928	40.00	55.00
	b) 1929	6.00	10.00

		VF	XF
4 (4)	1 Escudo (Cu–Ni) 1939. Coat of arms with mural crown. ℞ value	4.00	9.00
5 (7)	2½ Escudos (Ag) 1939, 1948. ℞ coat of arms in front of cross of Jerusalem	6.00	9.00
6 (8)	5 Escudos (Ag) 1939, 1948	8.00	16.00
7 (9)	10 Escudos (Ag) 1939	22.00	40.00
8 (5)	50 Centavos (Ni–Br) 1948	5.00	10.00
9 (6)	1 Escudo (Ni–Br) 1948. Same type as No. 4	6.00	10.00
10 (10)	50 Centavos (Cu–Ni) 1951	4.00	6.00
11 (11)	1 Escudo (Cu–Ni) 1951	6.00	12.00
12 (12)	2½ Escudos (Ag) 1951	4.00	6.00

			VF	XF
13 (13)	5	Escudos (Ag) 1951. 25 mm dia.	6.50	10.00
14 (14)	10	Escudos (Ag) 1951	8.00	16.00
15 (15)	10	Centavos (Br) 1962	1.00	1.60

			VF	XF
16 (16)	20	Centavos (Br) 1962	1.00	1.50
17 (17)	50	Centavos (Br) 1962	0.80	1.20
18 (18)	1	Escudo (Br) 1962	1.00	1.50
19 (19)	2½	Escudos (Cu–Ni) 1962	1.50	2.50
20 (20)	5	Escudos (Ag) 1962. Type as No. 13, but 22 mm dia.	5.00	8.00

COMMEMORATIVE ISSUE FOR THE 5th CENTENARY OF THE DISCOVERY OF THE ISLANDS

			VF	XF
21 (21)	50	Escudos (Ag) 1970. Coat of arms (the revised city coat of arms of São Tomé and the city coat of arms of Santo Antonio do Principe, granted on 25th May 1954) above stylized waves. ℞ the 5 miniature shields from the coat of arms of Portugal, laid on the Cross of Jerusalem, value	8.00	12.00
22 (15a)	10	Centavos (Al) 1971	0.20	0.30
23 (16a)	20	Centavos (Br) 1971	0.20	0.40
24 (17a)	50	Centavos (Br) 1971	0.30	0.50
25 (20a)	5	Escudos (Cu–Ni) 1971	0.65	1.00
26 (A21)	10	Escudos (Cu–Ni) 1971	0.90	1.80
27 (B21)	20	Escudos (Cu–Ni) 1971	2.50	4.00

			XF	Unc
28 (22)	50	Centimos (Al-Br) 1977. Coat of arms, date. Rev. fish, value	0.10	0.20
29 (23)	1	Dobra (Al-Br) 1977. Cocoa beans on stem	0.15	0.30
30 (24)	2	Dobras (Cu-Ni) 1977. Goats	0.30	0.50
31 (25)	5	Dobras (Cu-Ni) 1977. Maize	0.40	0.70
32 (26)	10	Dobras (Cu-Ni) 1977. Chicken, eggs	0.80	1.50
33 (27)	20	Dobras (Cu-Ni) 1977. Fruits typical of the country	1.20	2.50

			Unc	Proof
34	250	Dobras (Ag) 1977. Friendship	20.00	25.00
35	250	Dobras (Ag) 1977. Folklore	20.00	25.00
36	250	Dobras (Ag) 1977. Globe	20.00	25.00
37	250	Dobras (Ag) 1977. Mother and child	20.00	25.00
38	250	Dobras (Ag)1977. We and the world	20.00	25.00
39	2500	Dobras (Au) 1977. Type as No. 34	110.00	130.00
40	2500	Dobras (Au) 1977. Type as No. 35	110.00	130.00
41	2500	Dobras (Au) 1977. Type as No. 36	110.00	130.00
42	2500	Dobras (Au) 1977. Type as No. 37	110.00	130.00
43	2500	Dobras (Au) 1977. Type as No. 38	110.00	130.00

St. Vincent

Area: 150 sq. mi. Population: 116,000.

Part of the Lesser Antilles; member of the Caribbean Free Trade Area (CARIFTA). On October 27, 1967 St. Vincent obtained internal autonomy. St. Vincent is united with the countries of Antigua, Barbados, Dominica, Grenada, Montserrat, St. Christopher-Nevis-Anguilla and St. Lucia in the currency area of the East Caribbean Dollar. The issuing authority for the whole of the currency area is the East Caribbean Currency Authority with its seat in Bridgetown on the island of Barbados.

Capital: Kingstown.

100 Cents = 1 East Caribbean Dollar

COMMEMORATIVE ISSUE FOR THE INAUGURATION OF THE CARIBBEAN DEVELOPMENT BANK AND THE FAO COIN PLAN

			Unc	Proof
1 (8*)	4 Dollars (Cu–Ni) 1970. Coat of arms.	Ŗ bananas, sugar cane, value	10.00	30.00

*This number refers to Yeoman's East Caribbean Territories listings.

El Salvador   # Salvador   **Salvador**

Republica de El Salvador

Area: 8,260 sq. mi. Population: 3,800,000.
The territory of the smallest republic of Central America was conquered
for Spain by Pedro Alvaredo, as early as 1526. After withdrawing from
the confederacy of the Central American States (Provincias Unidas del
Centro de América), the country declared its independence in 1841.
Capital: San Salvador.

8 Reales = 100 Centavos = 1 Peso, 100 Centavos = 1 Colón

REPUBLICA DEL SALVADOR

			VF	XF
1 (1)	1	Centavo (Cu-Ni) 1889-1913. Francisco Moraza'n y Quesada (1792-1842), military leader and national hero of the Honduras, President of the Republik of Central America 1829-1840. Head left. Ŗ value within wreath	3.00	5.00
2 (2)	3	Centavos (Cu-Ni) 1889-1913	3.00	6.00
3 (3)	50	Centavos (Ag) 1892-1894. Christopher Columbus (1451-1506), discoverer of the New World	12.00	25.00
4 (7)	1	Peso (Ag) 1892-1914	14.00	27.00
5 (15)	¼	Real (Cu) 1909. Old coat of arms. Ŗ value within wreath	40.00	80.00
6 (22)	5	Centavos (Ag) 1911. Old coat of arms. Ŗ value in wreath	4.00	7.50
7 (23)	10	Centavos (Ag) 1911. Same type as No. 6	4.00	6.50
8 (24)	25	Centavos (Ag) 1911. Same type as No. 6	6.50	10.50
9 (16)	1	Centavo (Cu–Ni) 1915–1936. Francisco Morazán, head left. Ŗ value within wreath	0.80	1.50
10 (17)	3	Centavos (Cu–Ni) 1915. Same type as No. 9	3.00	5.00
11 (18)	5	Centavos (Cu–Ni) 1915–1925. Same type as No. 9	0.60	1.20

REPUBLICA DE EL SALVADOR

12 (25)	5	Centavos (Ag) 1914. New coat of arms. Ŗ value within wreath	3.00	5.00
13 (26)	10	Centavos (Ag) 1914. Same type as No. 12	3.50	6.00

			VF	XF
14 (21)	10	Centavos (Cu-Ni) 1921-1972, 1977. Francisco Morazán. Rev. value within wreath		
A14 (21a)	10	Centavos (German silver) 1952. Same type as No. 14	0.40 0.50	0.70 0.90
15 (27)	25	Centavos (Ag) 1914. Same type as No. 12	5.50	9.00

COMMEMORATIVE ISSUES (2) FOR THE 4th CENTENNIAL OF THE FOUNDING OF SALVADOR

16 (30)	1	Colón (Ag) 1925. Alfonso Quiñónez Molina (1873–1950), President from 1914 to 1915, and 1923 to 1927, and Pedro Alvaredo (c. 1486–1541), Spanish Conquistador. ℞ coat of arms	200.00	300.00
17 (29)	20	Colónes (Au) 1925. Same type as No.16	3000.00	4000.00
18 (19)	1	Centavo (Cu–Ni) 1940. Francisco Morazán. ℞ value within wreath	2.50	5.00
19 (19a)	1	Centavo (Br) 1942–	0.15	0.25

20 (20)	5	Centavos (Cu-Ni) 1940-1976	0.30	0.60
A20 (20a)	5	Centavos (German silver) 1944, 1948, 1950, 1952. Same type as No. 20	0.40	0.80
21 (28)	25	Centavos (Ag) 1943–1944	3.50	5.50
22 (31)	25	Centavos (Ag) 1953. José Matias Delgado (1768–1833), President in 1823. ℞ value within wreath	1.50	3.00
23 (32)	50	Centavos (Ag) 1953	2.50	3.50
24 (33)	25	Centavos (Ni) 1970. Same type as No. 22	0.30	0.60
25 (34)	50	Centavos (Ni) 1970. Same type as No. 24	0.40	0.80

COMMEMORATIVE ISSUES (6) FOR THE 150th ANNIVERSARY OF INDEPENDENCE AND OF THE FIGHT FOR THE DIGNITY OF MAN

26	1	Colón (Ag) 1971. Coat of arms. Dr. José Simeón Cañas y Villacorta (1767–1838), priest, and one of the early contenders, fighting for the abolition of slavery. ℞ "La Fecundida" of Salvador Dali (*1904), surrealistic painter. Value	**Proof** 10.00

27	5	Colónes (Ag) 1971. Coat of arms. ℞ statue of liberty pillar. José Simeón Cañas y Villacorta. Value	15.00
28	25	Colónes (Au) 1971. Same type as No. 26	50.00
29	50	Colónes (Au) 1971. Same type as No. 27	90.00
30	100	Colónes (Au) 1971. Obverse like No. 26. ℞ map of América with special consideration given to Salvador	180.00
31	200	Colónes (Au) 1971. Obverse like No. 26. ℞ colonial church of Panchimalco	360.00

			XF	Unc
32 (19b)	1	Centavos (Bra) 1976. Type as No. 19	0.15	0.25
33 (A20)	2	Centavos (Bra) 1974. Type as No. 32	0.15	0.30
34 (B20)	3	Centavos (Bra) 1974. Type as No. 32	0.20	0.40
35 (20b)	5	Centavos (Ni-clad steel) 1975. Type as No. 32	0.35	0.70
36 (21b)	10	Centavos (Ni-clad steel) 1975. Type as No. 32	0.50	1.00

INTERAMERICAN BANKER'S CONFERENCE (2)

			Unc	Proof
37 (35)	25	Colónes (Ag) 1977	35.00	45.00
38 (36)	250	Colónes (Au) 1977	400.00	850.00

San Marino

Repubblica di San Marino

Area: 23 sq. mi. Population: 19,000.
This tiny republic, located south-west of Rimini, was, through the
establishment of a customs union, connected with Italy in 1862. The
independence is guaranteed by comity contracts.
Capital: San Marino.

100 Centesimi = 1 Lira; 1 Gold Escudo = 15,000 Lire

			VF	XF
1 (3)	50	Centesimi (Ag) 1898. Crowned coat of arms with "Tre Penne" in wreath. ℞ value in wreath	30.00	50.00
2 (4)	1	Lira (Ag) 1898–1906	35.00	70.00
3 (5)	2	Lire (Ag) 1898–1906	75.00	115.00
4 (6)	5	Lire (Ag) 1898. St. Marinus	190.00	285.00
5 (12)	10	Lire (Au) 1925. Tre Penne. ℞ St. Marinus	1200.00	1700.00

6 (13)	20 Lire (Au) 1925		1650.00	2100.00

7 (9)	5 Lire (Ag) 1931–1938. Head of Liberty with helmet. ℞ plough		16.00	25.00

			VF	XF
8 (10)	10	Lire (Ag) 1931–1938. Standing Liberty, half. R crowned coat of arms	25.00	36.00

			VF	XF
9 (11)	20	Lire (Ag) 1931–1938. St. Marinus. R three ostrich feathers above pinnacle, crown:		
		a) 1931–1933, 1935, 1936; 15 grams	120.00	170.00
		b) 1935; 20 grams	600.00	800.00
		c) 1937; 20 grams	400.00	520.00
		d) 1938; 20 grams	800.00	1000.00
10 (14)	5	Centesimi (Br) 1935–1938. Crowned coat of arms in wreath. R value	3.00	6.00
11 (15)	10	Centesimi (Br) 1935–1938	3.00	6.00
12 (16)	1	Lira (Al) 1972. Bust of St. Marinus	1.50	2.50
13 (17)	2	Lire (Al) 1972. Type similar to No. 12	1.50	2.50
14 (18)	5	Lire (Al) 1972. Type as No. 12	0.90	1.80
15 (19)	10	Lire (Al) 1972. Cow with suckling calf	0.50	1.00
16 (20)	20	Lire (Al–Bro) 1972. Garibaldi with woman	0.50	1.00
17 (21)	50	Lire (St) 1972. Saint Marinus and a woman	0.60	1.20

			VF	XF
18 (22)	100	Lire (St) 1972. Saint Marinus in a boat	1.00	2.00

			XF	Unc
19 (23)	500	Lire (Ag) 1972. Mother and child	9.00	12.00
20 (24)	1	Lira (Al) 1973. Arms, name of country, date. ℞ Girl with national flag, date, value	1.00	1.60
21 (25)	2	Lire (Al) 1973. ℞ pelican (Pelecanus sp. – Pelecanidae), feeding its young with the blood torn with its own beak from wounds in accordance with the Christian legend	1.00	1.60
22 (26)	5	Lire (Al) 1973. ℞ Heads of five men, stars as border	0.40	0.80
23 (27)	10	Lire (Al) 1973. ℞ Man with torch forcing back four-headed dragon with his shield	0.40	0.80
24 (28)	20	Lire (Al–Bro) 1973. ℞ man rescuing old man and child from the flames	0.40	0.80
25 (29)	50	Lire (St) 1973. ℞ girl with sword holding scales with three people in each scale pan	0.40	0.80
26 (30)	100	Lire (St) 1973. ℞ Ulysses while passing the Columns of Hercules	0.40	0.80
27 (31)	500	Lire (Ag) 1973. ℞ girl with dove	9.00	12.00
28 (32)	1	Lira (Al) 1974	1.00	1.60
29 (33)	2	Lire (Al) 1974	1.00	1.60
30 (34)	5	Lire (Al) 1974	0.40	0.80

ISSUE FOR THE FAO COIN PLAN

 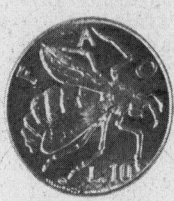

			XF	Unc
31 (35)	10	Lire (Al) 1974	0.60	1.00
32 (36)	20	Lire (St) 1974	0.40	0.70
33 (37)	50	Lire (St) 1974	0.40	0.70
34 (38)	100	Lire (St) 1974	0.40	0.80
35 (39)	500	Lire (Ag) 1974	8.00	11.00
36 (40)	1	Scudo (Au) 1974	Proof	70.00
37 (41)	2	Scudi (Au) 1974	Proof	115.00
38 (42)	1	Lira (Al) 1975	0.80	1.60
39 (43)	2	Lire (Al) 1975	0.80	1.60
40 (44)	5	Lire (Al) 1975	0.40	0.80
41 (45)	10	Lire (Al) 1975	0.40	0.80
42 (46)	20	Lire (Al-Br) 1975 (FAO issue)	0.50	1.00
43 (47)	50	Lire (St) 1975	0.40	0.80
44 (48)	100	Lire (St) 1975	0.40	0.80
45 (49)	500	Lire (Ag) 1975	9.00	12.00

OPENING OF NUMISMATIC AGENCY

			XF	Unc
46 (50)	500 Lire (Ag) 1975		10.50	16.00
47 (A41)	1 Scudo (Au) 1975		Proof	70.00
48 (B41)	2 Scudi (Au) 1975		Proof	115.00
49 (51)	1 Lira (Al) 1976		0.80	1.60
50 (52)	2 Lire (Al) 1976		0.80	1.60
51 (53)	5 Lire (Al) 1976 (FAO issue)		0.50	1.00
52 (54)	10 Lire (Al) 1976		0.20	0.40
53 (55)	20 Lire (Al-Br) 1976		0.25	0.50
54 (56)	50 Lire (St) 1976		0.80	1.50
55 (57)	100 Lire (St) 1976		0.90	1.80
56 (58)	500 Lire (Ag) 1976		9.00	12.00
57 (A60)	1 Scudo (Au) 1976		Proof	120.00
58 (B60)	2 Scudi (Au) 1976		Proof	180.00
59 (C60)	5 Scudi (Au) 1976		Proof	1200.00
60 (59)	500 Lire (Ag) 1976		12.00	20.00
61 (60)	1 Lira (Al) 1977 (FAO issue)		0.50	1.00
62 (61)	2 Lire (Al) 1977		0.50	1.00
63 (62)	5 Lire (Al) 1977		0.25	0.50
64 (63)	10 Lire (Al) 1977		0.15	0.30
65 (64)	20 Lire (Al-Br) 1977		0.20	0.40
66 (65)	50 Lire (St) 1977		0.20	0.40
67 (66)	100 Lire (St) 1977		0.30	0.60
68 (67)	100 Lire (St) 1977		0.30	0.60
69 (68)	500 Lire (Ag) 1977		9.00	12.00

600th ANNIVERSARY OF THE BIRTH OF F. BRUNELLESCO

70 (69)	1000 Lire (Ag) 1977. Filippo Brunellesco (1377-1446), architect and author	11.00	16.00

			Proof
71 (70)	1	Scudo (Au) 1977. Democrazia	70.00
72 (71)	2	Scudi (Au) 1977	120.00
73 (72)	5	Scudi (Au) 1977	380.00

150th ANNIVERSARY OF THE BIRTH OF LEO TOLSTOI

			Unc
74 (82)	1000	Lire (Ag) 1978. Leo Tolstoi (1828–1910), Russian writer	16.00

			Proof
75 (75)	1	Scudo (Au) 1978. Miss Liberta	80.00
76 (84)	2	Scudi (Au) 1978	125.00
77 (85)	10	Scudi (Au) 1978	1000.00

			XF	**Unc**
78 (73)	1	Lira (Al) 1978	0.60	0.80
79 (74)	2	Lire (Al) 1978	0.60	0.80
80 (75)	5	Lire (Al) 1978	0.20	0.40
81 (76)	10	Lire (Al) 1978	0.20	0.40

82 (77)	20	Lire (Al-Br) 1978	0.20	0.40
83 (78)	50	Lire (St) 1978	0.20	0.40
84 (79)	100	Lire (St) 1978 (FAO issue)	0.40	0.70

			XF	Unc
85 (80)	200 Lire (Al-Br) 1978		0.75	1.50
86 (81)	500 Lire (Ag) 1978		9.00	12.00

EUROPEAN UNITY

			Unc
87 (95)	1000 Lire (Ag) 1979		15.00

		Proof
88 (96)	1 Scudo (Au) 1979. PACE (Peace)	80.00
89 (97)	2 Scudi (Au) 1979	125.00
90 (A97)	5 Scudi (Au) 1979	400.00

		XF	Unc
91 (86)	1 Lira (Al) 1979	0.60	0.80
92 (87)	2 Lire (Al) 1979	0.60	0.80
93 (88)	5 Lire (Al) 1979	0.20	0.40
94 (89)	10 Lire (Al) 1979	0.20	0.40
95 (90)	20 Lire (Al-Br) 1979	0.20	0.40
96 (91)	50 Lire (St) 1979	0.40	0.80
97 (92)	100 Lire (St) 1979	0.60	1.00
98 (93)	200 Lire (Al-Br) 1979 (FAO issue)	0.80	2.00
99 (94)	500 Lire (Ag) 1979	9.00	12.00

1500th ANNIVERSARY OF THE BIRTH OF ST. BENEDICT

		Proof
100 (107)	1000 Lire (Ag) 1980	18.00

OLYMPIC GAMES 1980 IN MOSCOW (9)

		XF	Unc
101 (98)	1 Lira (Al) 1980	0.60	0.80
102 (99)	2 Lire (Al) 1980	0.60	0.80
103 (100)	5 Lire (Al) 1980	0.60	0.80
104 (101)	10 Lire (Al) 1980	0.60	0.80
105 (102)	20 Lire (Al-Br) 1980	0.60	0.80
106 (103)	50 Lire (St) 1980	0.60	0.80
107 (104)	100 Lire (St) 1980	0.70	1.20
108 (105)	200 Lire (Al-Br) 1980	0.90	2.20
109 (106)	500 Lire (Ag) 1980	10.00	14.00

		Proof
110 (108)	1 Scudo (Au) 1980	80.00
111 (109)	2 Scudi (Au) 1980	130.00
112 (110)	5 Scudi (Au) 1980	400.00

2000th ANNIVERSARY OF VIRGIL'S DEATH (3)

		XF	Unc
113 (112)	500 Lire (Ag) 1981		15.00
114 (113)	500 Lire (Ag) 1981		15.00
115 (114)	1000 Lire (Ag) 1981		28.00

Sarawak

Area: c. 47,000 sq. mi. Population: 862,000.

The Rajah of Sarawak, Sir Charles Johnson Brooke, formally placed his principality in 1888 under British protection. Due to the disastrous consequences of the Japanese occupation during World War II, the last rajah relinquished independence in favour of the colonial status in 1946. From 17th May 1946 until 1963 the country was a Crown Colony in Northwest Borneo. On 31st August 1963 Sarawak received self-government; thereupon it joined the Federation of Malaysia on 16th September of the same year. Together with Sabah it constitutes the section of East Malaysia.

Capital: Kuching.

Sarawak belonged to the currency area of the Straits-Dollar. The adoption of the Malaya-Dollar (1st April 1946) and subsequently of the Malaysia-Dollar is based on traditional economic and political interdependences.

100 Cents = 1 Straits Dollar

SIR CHARLES JOHNSON BROOKE 1868–1917

		VF	XF
1 (8)	1 Cent (Cu) 1892–1897. Sir Charles Johnson Brooke (1829–1917), raja of Sarawak, crossed flags. ℞ value in wreath (center hole)	4.00	6.50
2 (9)	5 Cents (Ag) 1900–1915. Sir Charles Johnson Brooke. ℞ value in circle of knotted cord	12.00	18.00
3 (10)	10 Cents (Ag) 1900–1915	15.00	20.00

4 (11)	20 Cents (Ag) 1900–1915	18.00	32.00
5 (12)	50 Cents (Ag) 1900–1906	35.00	52.00

		VF	XF
6 (13)	½ Cent (Br) 1933. Sir Charles Vyner Brooke (1874–1963), raja. ℞ value in wreath	2.00	3.00
7 (15)	1 Cent (Cu–Ni) 1920. Same type as No. 6	12.00	18.00

8 (14)	1 Cent (Br) 1927–1941. Same type as No. 6	1.50	2.50
9 (18)	5 Cents (Ag) 1920. ℞ value in circle of knotted string	55.00	80.00
10 (16)	5 Cents (Cu–Ni) 1920–1927. Same type as No. 6	3.00	4.50
11 (19)	10 Cents (Ag) 1920. Same type as No. 9	22.00	35.00
12 (17)	10 Cents (Cu–Ni) 1920–1934. Same type as No. 6	2.50	3.50
13 (20)	20 Cents (Ag) 1920–1927. Same type as No. 9	15.00	22.00
14 (21)	50 Cents (Ag) 1927. Same type as No. 9	22.00	35.00

Area: c. 800,000 sq. mi. Population: 8,500,000.
The ruler of the Wahhabis, Ibn Saud, united Asir and Hejaz with his
ancestral country, the Nejd, and in 1927 ordered to be proclaimed "King
of the Hejaz, the Nejd, and its dependent territories". Since September
20, 1932 the country's name is Saudi Arabia. After the end of the war
with the Yemen, the Nedjran was incorporated in 1934. Due to the
information, partly in dispute, concerning the location of the border
between Saudi Arabia and its neighboring countries, and thus of its
area, the figure concerning the latter can only be approximate.
Capital: Rijadh.

5 Halala = 1 Girsh, 20 Girsh = 1 Saudi Ryal,
40 Saudi Ryals = 1 Pound

ABDUL-AZIZ IBN ABDUL-RAHMAN AL-FAISAL AL-SAUD 1927–1953

			VF	XF
1 (1)	¼ Girsh (Cu) H-C 1343 (1925). Toughra. R value		8.00	12.00
2 (2)	½ Girsh (Cu) H-C 1343 (1925)		6.00	10.00
A2 (3)	¼ Girsh (Cu-Ni) H-C 1344–1348 (1926–1930)		5.00	10.00
B2 (4)	½ Girsh (Cu-Ni) H-C 1344–1348 (1926–1930)		6.50	12.00
3 (A3)	½ Girsh (Br) H-C 1344 (1926). Toughra. R value in circle, surrounded by new legend		3.60	8.00
4 (5)	1 Girsh (Cu–Ni) H-C 1344–1348 (1926–1930). New legend. R value above large date		8.00	12.50
5 (6)	¼ Girsh (Cu–Ni) H-C 1346–1356 (1928–1937). New legend. R value, date		2.50	5.00
6 (7)	½ Girsh (Cu–Ni) H-C 1346–1356 (1928–1937)		5.50	10.00
7 (8)	1 Girsh (Cu–Ni) H-C 1346–1356 (1928–1937)		6.00	10.00
8 (9)	1¼ Girsh (Cu–Ni) H-C 1356– (1937–). Same type as No. 5		0.50	1.00
9 (10)	½ Girsh (Cu–Ni) H-C 1356– (1937–). Same type as No. 6		0.50	1.00
10 (11)	1 Girsh (Cu–Ni) H-C 1356–1372 (1937–1953). Same type as No. 7		0.60	1.20

11 (12) ¼ Ryal (Ag) H-C 1346–1348 (1928–1930). Lettering in dotted circle, surrounded by legend. Crossed daggers, flanked by palm trees (state emblem), on lower edge. ℞ lettering and date in dotted circle, surrounded by legend, on lower edge small box with value, flanked by palm trees

12 (13) ½ Ryal (Ag) H-C 1346–1348 (1928–1930). Same type as No. 11

		VF	XF
11		35.00	55.00
12		60.00	100.00

13 (14) 1 Ryal (Ag) H-C 1346–1348 (1928–1930). Same type as No. 11 — 50.00 / 75.00

14 (18) ¼ Ryal (Ag) H-C 1354–1370 (1935–1951). Same type as No. 11, but smaller diameter — 4.00 / 6.50

15 (19) ½ Ryal (Ag) H-C 1354–1370 (1935–1951). Same type as No. 12, but smaller diameter — 6.00 / 10.00

16 (20) 1 Ryal (Ag) H-C 1354–1370 (1935–1951). Same type as No. 13, but smaller diameter — 8.00 / 12.00

17 (A21) ¼ Girsh (Cu–Ni) H-C 1365 (1946). No. 8 counterstamped "65" — 7.00 / 10.00

18 (B21) ½ Girsh (Cu–Ni) H-C 1365 (1946). No. 9 counterstamped "65" — 7.00 / 10.00

19 (C21) 1 Girsh (Cu–Ni) H-C 1365 (1946). No. 10 counterstamped "65" — 7.00 / 10.00

20 (23) 1 Pound (Au) H-C 1370 (1951). Same type as No. 11 — 80.00 / 100.00

				VF	XF
21 (30)	1	Halala (Br) H-C 1383 (1964). Coat of arms, surrounded by legend. ℞ value, date		0.10	0.25
22 (A23)	1	Girsh (Cu–Ni) H-C 1376– (1957–). Same type as No. 21		0.20	0.30
23 (24)	2	Girsh (Cu–Ni) H-C 1376– (1957–). Same type as No. 21		0.25	0.40

				VF	XF
24 (25)	4	Girsh (Cu–Ni) H-C 1376– (1957–). Same type as No. 21		0.40	0.80
25 (26)	¼	Ryal (Ag) H-C 1374 (1955). Same type as No. 14		2.00	4.00
26 (27)	½	Ryal (Ag) H-C 1374 (1955). Same type as No. 15		4.00	6.50

				VF	XF
27 (28)	1	Ryal (Ag) H-C 1374 (1955). Same type as No. 16		6.50	10.00

	VF	XF

28 (29) 1 Pound (Au) H-C 1377 (1957). Same type as No. 21   90.00   110.00

FAISAL 1964-1975
ISSUES (2) FOR THE FAO COIN PLAN

29 (A31) 25 Halala (Cu-Ni) H-C 1392 (1972). National coat of arms and the quotation from the Koran "Feed the poor and distressed". Rev. value   0.40   0.80

30 (31) 50 Halala = ½ Riyal (Cu-Ni) H-C 1392 (1972). Type as No. 29   0.70   1.40

31 (32) 5 Halala (Cu-Ni) H-C 1392 (1972). National coat of arms, Arabic inscription. R value, date   0.15   0.30

32 (33) 10 Halala (Cu-Ni) H-C 1392 (1972). Type as No. 31   0.20   0.35

33 (34) 25 Halala (Cu-Ni) H-C 1392 (1972). Type as No. 31   0.25   0.50

34 (35) 50 Halala (Cu-Ni) H-C 1392 (1972). Type as No. 31   0.30   0.60

			VF	XF
35 (39)	25	Halala (Cu-Ni) H-C 1397 (1976)	0.30	0.40
36 (40)	50	Halala (Cu-Ni) H-C 1397 (1976)	0.40	0.90
37 (41)	100	Halala (Cu-Ni) H-C 1398 (1978)	1.00	1.50

FOR THE FAO COIN PLAN (3)

38 (42)	5	Halala (Cu-Ni) H-C 1398 (1978)	0.30	0.40
39 (43)	10	Halala (Cu-Ni) H-C 1398 (1978)	0.45	0.75
40 (44)	1	Ryal (Cu-Ni) H-C 1398 (1978)	1.00	1.50

Senegal   # Senegal   Sénégal

Area: 76,084 sq. mi. Population: 4,200,000.
Formerly a part of French West Africa, Senegal became an autonomous
Republic in 1958, and entered into a federation with Mali, the former
French Sudan, in 1960. However, this alliance was a rather short one,
and upon its dissolution the country reached total independence.
Capital: Dakar.

100 Centimes = 1 CFA Franc

COMMEMORATIVE ISSUES (4) FOR THE 8th ANNIVERSARY OF INDEPENDENCE ON APRIL 4, 1960

			ST	Proof
1	10	Francs (Au) 1968. Coat of arms. ℞ value, date, inscription INDEPENDANCE 4 AVRIL 1960		60.00
2	25	Francs (Au) 1968		140.00
3	50	Francs (Au) 1968		280.00
4	100	Francs (Au) 1968		560.00

25th ANNIVERSARY OF THE EURAFRIQUE PROGRAM (6)

5	50	Francs (Ag) 1975. Leopold Sedar Senghor. Rev. Mercator's projections of North Africa and Europe; pirogue	30.00	35.00
6	150	Francs (Ag) 1975. Rev. Mercator's projections of North Africa and Europe; white pelican	90.00	100.00
7	250	Francs (Au) 1975. Rev. coat of arms	130.00	140.00
8	500	Francs (Au) 1975. Type as No. 7	200.00	225.00
9	1000	Francs (Au) 1975. Type as No. 7	400.00	425.00
10	2500	Francs (Au) 1975. Type as No. 7	950.00	1000.00

Serbia

СРБИЈА

In 1878 the Berlin Congress granted full independence to the Principality fo Serbia. In 1882 Prince Milan accepted the royal status. In the fall of 1918 the South Slavs of the Austro-Hungarian area and Montenegro united with Serbia, comprising the new kingdom. During World War II, from 1941 to 1944, Serbia became a separate state under German sovereignty. After this relatively short period under foreign government, the unity of the Yugoslavi state was restored.
Capital: Belgrade (Beograd).

100 Para (ПАРА) = 1 Dinar (ДИНАР)

PETER I 1903–1918

			VF	XF
1 (13)	2	Pare (Br) 1904. Crowned heraldic eagle. ℞ value	2.50	5.00
2 (14)	5	Para (Cu–Ni) 1904–1917	1.00	2.00
3 (15)	10	Para (Cu–Ni) 1912–1917	1.50	2.50

4 (16)	20	Para (Cu–Ni) 1912–1917	2.00	3.50
5 (19)	50	Para (Ag) 1904–1915. Peter I (1844–1921), head right. ℞ value in wreath with crown above	4.00	5.00
6 (20)	1	Dinar (Ag) 1904–1915	5.00	-6.50
7 (21)	2	Dinara (Ag) 1904–1917	8.00	10.50

COMMEMORATIVE ISSUE FOR THE CENTENNIAL OF THE REBELLION AGAINST TURKISH RULE AND FOR THE REINSTATEMENT OF THE HOUSE OF KARAGEORGEVICH

		VF	XF
8 (22)	5 Dinara (Ag) 1904. George Petrovich (Karageorge) 1766–1817, prince and national hero, and Peter I, head left. ℞ arms on mantle, dates 1804–1904	40.00	60.00
9 (23)	50 Para (Z) 1942. Heraldic eagle. ℞ value and date between ears of wheat	6.00	9.00

10 (24)	1 Dinar (Z) 1942	1.50	3.50
11 (25)	2 Dinara (Z) 1942	1.50	3.50
12 (26)	10 Dinara (Z) 1942	3.50	4.50

Seychellen   # Seychelles   **Seychelles**

Area: 156 sq. mi. Population: 60,000.
Island group in the Indian Ocean, discovered by the Portuguese during the
16th century; British territory since 1794. The Seychelles was granted limited
internal self-government in 1970, and attained independence on June 28, 1976.
Capital: Port Victoria.

100 Cents = 1 Rupee

			VF	XF
	GEORGE VI 1936–1952			
1 (1)	10	Cents (Cu–Ni) 1939–1944. George VI, crowned head, left. ℞ value (scalloped)	4.00	8.00
2 (2)	25	Cents (Ag) 1939–1944	5.00	10.00
3 (3)	½	Rupee (Ag) 1939	7.50	15.00
4 (4)	1	Rupee (Ag) 1939	6.00	12.00
5 (5)	1	Cent (Br) 1948. George VI, new legend KING GEORGE THE SIXTH. ℞ value in dotted circle	0.40	1.20
6 (6)	2	Cents (Br) 1948	0.50	1.20

			VF	XF
7 (7)	5	Cents (Br) 1948	0.60	1.50
8 (8)	10	Cents (Cu–Ni) 1951 (scalloped)	2.50	4.00
9 (9)	25	Cents (Cu–Ni) 1951	2.50	4.00

	ELIZABETH II since 1952			
10 (14)	1	Cent (Br) 1959–1969. Elizabeth II, crowned head, right. ℞ value	0.40	0.80
11 (15)	2	Cents (Br) 1959–1969	0.50	1.00
12 (16)	5	Cents (Br) 1964–1971	0.40	0.80

			VF	XF
13 (10)	10 Cents (Ni-Bra) 1953–1974		0.30	0.80
14 (11)	25 Cents (Cu-Ni) 1954–1974		0.50	1.00
15 (12)	½ Rupee (Cu-Ni) 1954–1974		0.60	1.20
16 (13)	1 Rupee (Cu-Ni) 1954–1974		1.00	2.00

ISSUES (2) FOR THE FAO COIN PLAN

		XF	Unc
17 (17)	1 Cent (Al) 1972. ℞ head of a cow	0.20	0.40

		XF	Unc
18 (18)	5 Cents (Al) 1972, 1975. Rev. head of cabbage (scalloped)	0.20	0.40

		Unc	Proof
19 (19)	5 Rupees 1972-1975:		
	a) (Cu-Ni), 1972, 1975	3.00	
	b) (Ag), 1972, 1974, 1975		70.00
20 (20)	10 Rupees 1974:		
	a) (Cu-Ni)	4.00	
	b) (Ag)		30.00

INDEPENDENCE

		Unc	Proof
21 (21)	1 Cent (Al) 1976. Profile of President Mancham. Rev. boueteur fish	0.20	2.00
22 (22)	5 Cents (Al) 1976. Rev. bourgeois fish	0.20	2.00
23 (23)	10 Cents (Ni-Bra) 1976. Rev. sailfish	0.40	2.50
24 (24)	25 Cents (Cu-Ni) 1976. Rev. black parrot	0.60	3.00
25 (25)	50 Cents (Cu-Ni) 1976. Rev. vanilla orchid	0.80	4.50
26 (26)	1 Rupee (Cu-Ni) 1976. Rev. triton conch shell	1.20	7.00
27 (27)	5 Rupees (Cu-Ni) 1976. Rev. coco-de-mer palm tree:		
	a) (Ag)		18.00
	b) (Cu-Ni)	2.00	
28 (28)	10 Rupees 1976. Turtle:		
	a) (Ag)		30.00
	b) (Cu-Ni)	4.00	
29 (29)	1000 Rupees (Au) 1976	320.00	450.00

25th ANNIVERSARY OF THE SILVER JUBILEE OF HER MAJESTY QUEEN ELIZABETH II

		Unc	Proof
30 (30)	25 Rupees (Ag) 1977. President Mancham. Rev. orb, commemorative inscription, value	20.00	30.00

		XF	Unc
31 (31)	1 Cent (Al) 1977		0.20
32 (32)	5 Cents (Al) 1977 (FAO issue)		0.40
33 (33)	10 Cents (Ni-Bra) 1977 (FAO issue)		0.40
34 (34)	25 Cents (Cu-Ni) 1977		0.60
35 (35)	50 Cents (Cu-Ni) 1977		0.80
36 (36)	1 Rupee (Cu-Ni) 1977		1.20
37 (37)	5 Rupees (Cu-Ni) 1977		2.00
38 (38)	10 Rupees (Cu-Ni) 1977		4.00

CONSERVATION COMMEMORATIVE (3)

		Unc	Proof
39 (39)	50 Rupees (Ag) 1977	35.00	40.00
40 (40)	100 Rupees (Ag) 1977	50.00	60.00
41 (41)	1500 Rupees (Au) 1977	600.00	900.00

INTERNATIONAL YEAR OF THE CHILD

42 (42)	50 Rupees (Ag)		55.00

FOR THE FAO COIN PLAN (2)

43	5 Cents (Al-Br) 1981		0.40
44	10 Cents (Al-Br) 1981		0.40

Area: 965 sq. mi. Population: 35,000.
The Sheikdom of Sharjah is one of the seven Trucial States in Pacified Oman. The enclaves of Dhiba, Kalba and Khor Fakkan belong administratively to Sharjah. Since December 2, 1971 Sharjah is a member state of the "United Arab Emirates" (UAE).

100 Naye Paise = 1 Rupee, 20 Piastre = 1 Rial,
since 1966: 100 Dirham = 1 Sharjah Riyal

SAKER BEN MOHAMMED AL KAISIMI until 1965

COMMEMORATIVE COIN FOR JOHN F. KENNEDY

		Unc	Proof
1	5 Rupees (Ag) 1964. John Fitzgerald Kennedy (1917–1963), 35th President of the United States of America. ℞ crossed flags (state emblem of the sheikdom)	12.00	

KHALED BEN MOHAMMED AL KAISIMI since 1965

2	1 Riyal (Ag) 1969–. Mona Lisa, also called La Gioconda, wife of the Marchese Francesco del Giocondo; after a painting by Leonardo da Vinci (1452–1519), Louvre, Paris. ℞ state emblem, name of country, value	15.00
3	2 Riyals (Ag) 1969–. Jules-Rimet cup between laurel branches in front of stylized globe. Football. Referring to the soccer world championship in Mexico City, 1970. ℞ like No. 2	30.00

| 4 | 5 Riyals (Ag) 1969–. Napoleon Bonaparte (1769–1821), Emperor of France 1804–1815. ℞ like No. 2 | **Proof** 40.00 |

5	10 Riyals (Ag) 1969–. Simón Bolivar (1783–1830), statesman and General, liberated South America from the Spanish. ℞ like No. 2	60.00
6	25 Riyals (Au) 1969–. Same type as No. 2	160.00
7	50 Riyals (Au) 1969–. Same type as No. 3	320.00
8	100 Riyals (Au) 1969–. Same type as No. 4	500.00
9	100 Riyals (Au) 1969–. Same type as No. 5	500.00
10	200 Riyals (Au) 1969–. Sheik Khaled Ben Mohammed Al Kaisimi (*1931). ℞ like No. 2	750.00

Sierra Leone   # Sierra Leone   **Sierra Leone**

Area: 27,925 sq. mi. Population: 3,500,000.
Formerly a British Crown Colony, Sierra Leone became an independent member of the Commonwealth of Nations on April 27, 1961. In April 1971, this West African country was proclaimed a Republic by Dr. Siaka Stevens.
Capital: Freetown.

100 Cents = 1 Leone, 50 Leone = 1 Golde

			XF	Unc
1 (1)	½ Cent (Br) 1964–. Sir Milton Margai (1895–1964), President of the Council and co-founder of the independent state. ℞ Bonga fish (Ethmalosa dorsalis – Clupeidae)		0.10	0.20
2 (2)	1 Cent (Br) 1964–. ℞ palm branches and fruit stalks (Elaeis guineensis – Palmae)		0.15	0.30

3 (3)	5 Cents (Cu–Ni) 1964–. ℞ kapok tree (Ceiba pentandra – Bombacaceae)		0.20	0.40

4 (4)	10 Cents (Cu–Ni) 1964–. ℞ value, surrounded by cocoa beans		0.30	0.60
5 (5)	20 Cents (Cu–Ni) 1964–. ℞ heraldic lion		0.50	0.90

6 (6)   1 Leone (Cu–Ni) 1964–. Coat of arms **Unc**   **Proof**
               with lions supporting shield   16.00

COMMEMORATIVE ISSUES (3) FOR THE
5th ANNIVERSARY OF THE INDEPENDENCE

7 (7)   ¼ Golde (Au) 1966. Lion's head (Pan-
               thera leo – Felidae). ℞ map   250.00   350.00
8 (8)   ½ Golde (Au) 1966. Same type as No. 7   650.00   800.00
9 (9)   1 Golde (Au) 1966. Same type as No. 7   1000.00   1200.00

COMMEMORATIVE ISSUE FOR THE FIRST ANNIVERSARY
OF THE REPUBLIC (19th April 1972)

10 (11)   50 Cents (Cu–Ni) 1972. Dr. Siaka Stevens,   **XF**   **Unc**
               head facing right; national motto. ℞
               national coat of arms, value   1.20   2.00

10th ANNIVERSARY OF THE BANK OF SIERRA LEONE

				Unc	Proof
11 (12)	1	Leone 1974. Rev. lion with mountains in background:			
		a) (Cu-Ni)		2.50	
		b) (Ag)			22.00

FAO REGIONAL CONFERENCE FOR AFRICA

12 (13)	2	Leones (Cu-Ni) 1976. Agricultural labour	4.00

O.A.U. SUMMIT CONFERENCE

			Unc	Proof
13 (20)	1	Leone 1980:		
		a) (Cu-Ni)	2.50	
		b) (Ag)		55.00
14 (21)	5	Golde (Au) 1980	400.00	600.00

Singapur # Singapore **Singapour**

Republic of Singapore

Area: 220 sq. mi. Population: 2,400,000.

Republic at the southern tip of the Malacca peninsula, consisting of the island of Singapore and a few small islands. Singapore became British in 1819 and until 1946 belonged to the Crown Colony of the Straits Settlements; from 1946–1957 a separate British Crown Colony, in 1957 internal self-government, in 1959 an autonomous state. From 1963 until August 8, 1965 Singapore was a part of Malaysia and has been independent since August 9, 1965. The Republic of Singapore is a member of the British Commonwealth.

Capital: Singapore.

100 Cents = 1 Singapore Dollar

			XF	Unc
1 (1)	1	Cent 1967–. Fountain in front of high-rise appartment building:		
		a) (Br) 1967-1975	0.05	0.10
		b) (Copper-clad steel) 1976–	0.05	0.10
2 (2)	5	Cents (Cu–Ni) 1967–. Great white egret (Casmerodius albus – Ardeidae)	0.05	0.15

3 (3)	10	Cents (Cu–Ni) 1967. Stylized great crowned seahorse (Hippocampus kuda – Syngnathidae)	0.10	0.25

4 (4)	20	Cents (Cu–Ni) 1967–. Swordfish (Xiphias gladius – Xiphiidae)	0.20	0.40
5 (5)	50	Cents (Cu–Ni) 1967–. Zebra fish (Pterois volitans – Scorpaenidae)	0.40	0.70

6 (6)   1 Dollar (Cu-Ni) 1967-. "Lion", Symbol of Singapore (Sanskrit = lion city). Rev. value:

	Unc	Proof
a) (Cu-Ni) 1967–	1.20	
b) (Ag) 1975–		40.00

COMMEMORATIVE ISSUE FOR THE 150th ANNIVERSARY OF THE CITY OF SINGAPORE

7 (7)   150 Dollar (Au) 1969. Shield with shield supporters. ℞ lighthouse, value   600.00   1500.00

ISSUE FOR THE FAO COIN PLAN

8 (8)   5 Cents (Al) 1971   0.30

9 (9)   10 Dollars (Ag) 1972. Coat of arms. R eagle, value   28.00   180.00

10 (9a)   10 Dollars (Ag) 1973, 1974. Type similar to No. 9. but the word »Singapore« in reserved position   26.00   65.00

FOR THE 7th SOUTH EAST ASIAN SPORTS GAMES IN SINGAPORE

			Unc	Proof
11 (10)	5 Dollars (Ag) 1973. National arms. ℞ emblem of the games above the National Stadium of Singapore		15.00	160.00

10th ANNIVERSARY OF THE REPUBLIC OF SINGAPORE (4)

12 (11)	10 Dollars (Ag) 1975. Steamship at quayside		16.00	50.00
13 (12)	100 Dollars (Au) 1975. High-rise buildings		150.00	175.00
14 (13)	250 Dollars (Au) 1975. four hands clasped together		380.00	450.00
15 (14)	500 Dollars (Au) 1975. Head of a lion		700.00	850.00

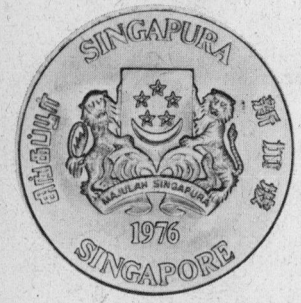

16 (15)	10 Dollars (Ag) 1976, 1977. Type as No. 12, but without commemorative inscription		16.00	25.00

10th ANNIVERSARY OF THE ASEAN PACT

17 (16)	10 Dollars (Ag) 1977		16.00	25.00
18 (17)	10 Dollars 1978–1980. Two communications satellite radio antenna:			
	a) (Ag) 1978, 1979		16.00	60.00
	b) (Cu-Ni) 1980		8.00	

INTERNATIONAL FINANCIAL CENTER

19 (18)	50 Dollars (Ag) 1980, 1981		40.00	80.00

YEAR OF THE ROOSTER

			Unc	Proof
20 (19)	10	Dollars 1981:		
		a) (Ag)		35.00
		b) (Cu-Ni)	9.00	
21	5	Dollars 1981. Changi Airport:		
		a) (Ag)		28.00
		b) (Cu-Ni)	4.50	

YEAR OF THE DOG

			Unc	Proof
22	10	Dollars 1982:		
		a) (Ag)		–.–
		b) (Cu-Ni)	9.00	
23	500	Dollars (Au) 1982		600.00

Slowakei

Slovakia
Slovensko

Slovaquie

An independent Slovakia arose in March 1939 which followed Germany
very closely in respect of foreign policy and the army. Since 1945
Slovakia is once more a state within the republic of Czechoslovakia.
Capital: Bratislava.

100 Halierov = 1 Koruna

			VF	XF
1 (S19b)	5	Halierov (Sn) 1942. Coat of arms, surrounded by name of country. ℞ value	10.00	18.00
2 (S20)	10	Halierov (Br) 1939, 1942. Coat of arms. ℞ castle of Pressburg (Bratislava)	1.20	2.00
3 (S21)	20	Halierov (Br) 1940–1942. Coat of arms. R Bishop's Castle, built on the identical spot where between 832/33 the first Christian church stood on Slovakian soil	2.00	3.00
4 (S22)	50	Halierov (Cu-Ni) 1940-1941. Coat of arms. Rev. plough:		
		a) 1940	25.00	50.00
		b) 1941	2.00	3.00
5 (S23)	1	Koruna (Cu–Ni) 1940–1942, 1944–1945. Coat of arms. ℞ ears of wheat	1.50	2.50

6 (S24)	5	Korun (Ni) 1939. Coat of arms. ℞ Andrej Hlinka (1864–1938), priest and leader of the Catholic autonomous Slovakian People's Party	2.50	3.50

COMMEMORATIVE ISSUE FOR THE ELECTION
OF TISO AS PRESIDENT

7 (S26) 20 Korun (Ag) 1939. Coat of arms. ℞
Dr. Jozef Tiso (1887–1947), President
1939–1945 12.50 20.00

8 (S27) 20 Korun (Ag) 1941. St. Cyrill (827–869)
and St. Methodius (815–885), propa-
gators of the Cyrillic alphabet 6.00 9.00
9 (S21a) 20 Halierov (Al) 1942, 1943. Type as No. 3 1.25 2.50
10 (S22b) 50 Halierov (Al) 1943, 1944. Type as No. 4 1.50 3.00
11 (S25) 10 Korun (Ag) 1944. Pribina (+861),
Slovakian Prince at the cornerstone
laying of the first Christian church on
Slovakian soil in Nitra (832). In the
background: priest with church model
and soldier with drawn sword 5.00 10.00

COMMEMORATIVE ISSUE FOR THE 5th ANNIVERSARY
OF THE SLOVAKIAN REPUBLIC

12 (S28) 50 Korun (Ag) 1944. Coat of arms. ℞
Dr. Jozef Tiso 5.50 10.00

Solomon Islands

Salomon (Iles)

Area: 11,500 sq. Population: 176.000.
The Solomon Islands, located in the Southwest Pacific east of Papua New Guinea, were discovered by the Spanish navigator Alvaro de Mendaña. The former British protectorate achieved self government in 1975 and full independence in 1978.
Capital: Honiara, on the island of Guadalcanal.

100 Cents = 1 Dollar

SELF GOVERNMENT COMMEMORATIVE (2)

		Proof
1	30 Dollars (Au and Ag) 1975. Coat of arms, name of country, value, fineness	80.00
2	100 Dollars (Au) 1975	—.—

FOR THE FAO COIN PLAN

		XF	Unc
3 (1)	1 Cent (Br) 1977. Bust right of the Queen, date. Rev. native food bowl	0.15	0.20
4 (2)	2 Cents (Br) 1977. Rev. eagle with spread wings and perched on a war club	0.15	0.20
5 (3)	5 Cents (Cu-Ni) 1977. Rev. native mask	0.15	0.30
6 (4)	10 Cents (Cu-Ni) 1977. Rev. a walking sea spirit	0.20	0.40
7 (5)	20 Cents (Cu-Ni) 1977. Rev. a traditional intricate design showing four monkeys in the center	0.35	0.60
8 (6)	1 Dollar (Cu-Ni) 1977. Rev. Nusu-Nusu head (war canoe figure head)	1.25	2.50

		Unc	Proof
9 (7)	5 Dollars 1977. Rev. Bokolo, an ornamental object fashioned from fossilized clam shell:		
	a) (Ag)		35.00
	b) (Cu-Ni)	25.00	

CORONATION JUBILEE

10 (8)   5 Dollars (Ag) 1978   25.00

ATTAINMENT OF SOVEREINGNTY

11 (9)   100 Dollars (Au) 1978   240.00
12 (10)   10 Dollars 1979:
              a) (Ag)   50.00
              b) (Cu-Ni)   25.00
13 (11) 100 Dollars (Au) 1980   80.00

Somalia **Somalia** Somalie

Area: 246,000 sq. mi. Population: 2,925,000.
The former protectorate of Italian Somaliland was united with Ethiopia in
1936 to form Italian East-Africa, and occupied by British troops in 1941.
After the withdrawal of the British troops, the territory came under
U. N. trusteeship and was administered by Italy from 1950 until its
independence on June 26, 1960. On July 1, 1960 British Somaliland
united with the republic as Somalia. A democratic republic since
October 21, 1969.
Capital: Mogadishu.

100 Centesimi = 1 Somalo,
since 1962: 100 Centesimi = 1 Somali Shilling (Scellino)

			VF	XF
1 (1)	1	Centesimo (Br) 1950. African elephant (Loxodonta africana – Elephantidae). ℞ value in circle	0.30	0.50
2 (2)	5	Centesimi (Br) 1950. Same type as No. 1	0.50	0.80

3 (3)	10	Centesimi (Br) 1950. Same type as No. 1	1.50	2.00
4 (4)	50	Centesimi (Ag) 1950. Crescents and star above lioness (Panthera leo – Felidae). ℞ value in dotted circle	6.00	9.00

5 (5)	1	Somalo (Ag) 1950. Same type as No. 4	5.00	8.00

NEW CURRENCY:
100 Centesimi = 1 Somali Shilling (Scellino)

COMMEMORATIVE ISSUES (5) FOR THE 5th ANNIVERSARY OF INDEPENDENCE, IN 1965

6		20 Shillings (Au) 1965. Aden Abdulla Osman (*1908), 1st President 1960–1967. ℞ coat of arms, value			**Proof** 60.00
7		50 Shillings (Au) 1965. Same type as No. 6			150.00
8		100 Shillings (Au) 1965. Same type as No. 6			250.00
9		200 Shillings (Au) 1965. Same type as No. 6			550.00
10		500 Shillings (Au) 1965. Same type as No. 6			1500.00
11 (6)		5 Centesimi (Br) 1967–. Coat of arms. ℞ denomination in English, Italian and Arabic	**XF** 0.15	**Unc** 0.20	
12 (7)		10 Centesimi (Br) 1967–. Same type as No. 11	0.20	0.40	
13 (8)		50 Centesimi (Cu–Ni) 1967–. Same type as No. 11	0.50	1.00	
14 (9)		1 Shilling (Cu–Ni) 1967–. Same type as No. 11	0.80	1.60	

DEMOCRATIC REPUBLIC

COMMEMORATIVE ISSUE FOR THE 2nd CONFERENCE OF THE FOOD AND AGRICULTURAL ORGANIZATION (FAO) OF THE UNITED NATIONS

15 (10)		5 Shillings (Cu–Ni) 1970. Coat of arms with leopards supporting the shield. ℞ ox (Bos primigenius taurus), sheep (Ovis ammon aries) and goat (Capra aegagrus hircus), all of the Bovidae family. Plants: corn (Zea mays) and genuine millet (Panicum miliaceum), both from the family of wheats – Gramineae. Bananas and grapefruits	2.50	3.50

			Proof
16	20	Shillings (Au) 1970. Coat of arms. ℞ model of an atom. Value	60.00
17	50	Shillings (Au) 1970. ℞ half-portrait of a man with censer. Value	150.00
18	100	Shillings (Au) 1970. ℞ Somali woman with bananas (Musa x paradisiaca – Musaceae), grapefruit (Citrus paradisi – Rutaceae), and cotton balls (Gossypium sp. – Malvaceae) in basket. Value	250.00

19	200	Shillings (Au) 1970. ℞ Dromedary (Camelus dromedarius – Camelidae), with heavy burden, pack-animal of the Somali nomads. Value	550.00
20	500	Shillings (Au) 1970. ℞ new parliament building in Mogadishu and map of Somalia. Value	1500.00

1st ANNIVERSARY OF THE REVOLUTION (3)

21	50	Shillings (Au) 1970. Ear of corn	150.00
22	100	Shillings (Au) 1970. Hand, helmet and rifle	250.00
23	200	Shilings (Au) 1970. Monument	550.00

ISSUES FOR THE FAO COIN PLAN (4)

			XF	Unc
24 (11)	5	Senti (Al) 1976. Coat of arms. Rev. fruits, value, date	0.15	0.30
25 (12)	10	Senti (Al) 1976. Rev. sheep, value, date	0.20	0.40
26 (13)	50	Senti (Cu-Ni) 1976. Type as No. 24	0.30	0.60
27 (14)	1	Shilling (Cu-Ni) 1976. Type as No. 25	0.60	1.20

			Unc	Proof
28 (15)	10	Shillings 1979:		
		a) (Ag)		45.00
		b) (Cu-Ni)	3.00	
29 (16)	10	Shillings 1979:		
		a) (Ag)		45.00
		b) (Cu-Ni)	3.00	
30 (17)	10	Shillings 1979:		
		a) (Ag)		45.00
		b) (Cu-Ni)	3.00	
31 (18)	10	Shillings 1979:		
		a) (Ag)		45.00
		b) (Cu-Ni)	3.00	
32 (19)	10	Shillings 1979:		
		a) (Ag)		45.00
		b) (Cu-Ni)	3.00	
33 (20)	1500	Shillings (Au) 1979		–.–
34 (21)	1500	Shillings (Au) 1979		–.–
35 (22)	1500	Shillings (Au) 1979		–.–
36 (23)	1500	Shillings (Au) 1979		–.–
37 (24)	1500	Shillings (Au) 1979		–.–

Südafrika   # South Africa   **Afrique du Sud**
Suid-Africa

Area: 472,736 sq. mi. (excl. S.W. Africa). Population: 24,000,000.
The Union of South Africa was formed on May 31, 1910 by the integration of the Cape Province which had already become British in 1814 and of Natal as well as the republics of the Orange Free State and the Transvaal captured in the Boer War. On May 31, 1961 the Union of South Africa left the British Commonwealth and since that time carries the title of the Republic of South Africa.
Capital: Pretoria.

12 Pence = 1 Shilling, 2 Shillings = 1 Florin,
20 Shillings = 1 £, since 1961: 100 Cents = 1 Rand

The currency area of the Rand also includes Southwest Africa (Namibia), Botswana (to 1976), Lesotho, Swaziland and Transkei.

GEORGE V 1910–1936

			VF	XF
1 (11)	¼	Penny (Br) 1923–1926. George V, crowned portrait left. ℞ 2 sparrows (Passer domesticus – Fringillidae) on acacia branches: compare Matthew 10, 29 = "Are not two sparrows sold for a farthing? And one of them shall not fall on the ground without your Father."	4.00	8.00
2 (11a)	¼	Penny (Br) 1928–1931. Same type as No. 1, but value instead of "¼ Penny ¼" only "¼ Penny"	4.00	7.00
3 (12)	½	Penny (Br) 1923–1926. ℞ »½ Penny ½«	9.00	18.00
4 (12a)	½	Penny (Br) 1928–1931. Same type as No. 3, but value instead of "½ Penny ½", only "½ Penny"	4.00	8.00
5 (13)	1	Penny (Br) 1923–1924. ℞ sailing vessel	3.00	4.00
6 (13a)	1	Penny (Br) 1926–1930. Same type as No. 5, but value instead of »1 Penny 1«, only »Penny«	2.00	4.50
7 (15)	3	Pence (Ag) 1923–1925. ℞ value in wreath	5.00	10.00
8 (17)	3	Pence (Ag) 1925–1930. ℞ Protea cynaroides – Proteaceae, surrounded by three brushwood bundles	5.00	10.00

				VF	XF

9 (16)   6 Pence (Ag) 1923–1924. ℞ value in wreath   8.00   16.00

10 (18)   6 Pence (Ag) 1925–1930. ℞ Protea cynaroides – Proteaceae   6.00   12.00

11 (19)   1 Shilling (Ag) 1923–1924. ℞ allegory of Hope   12.50   25.00

12 (19a)   1 Shilling (Ag) 1926–1930. Same type as No. 11, but value instead of "1 Shilling 1", only "Shilling"   10.50   21.00

13 (20)   1 Florin (Ag) 1923–1930. ℞ coat of arms   16.50   33.00

14 (21)   2½ Shillings (Ag) 1923–1925. ℞ crowned coat of arms   12.00   20.00

15 (21a)   2½ Shillings (Ag) 1926–1930. Same type as No. 14, but value instead of "2½ Shillings 2½", only "2½ Shillings"   10.00   20.00

16 (A21)   ½ Sovereign (Au) 1923–1926. George V. ℞ St. George fighting the dragon   90.00   105.00

17 (22)   1 Sovereign (Au) 1923–1932   120.00   150.00

There are many coins issued by Great Britain which appeared at the same time with identical designs. Coins No. 16 and 17 can only be distinguished from those by their mint mark SA.

18 (23)   ¼ Penny (Br) 1931–1936. ℞ sparrows. Value now "D" instead of "Penny"   4.50   9.00

19 (24)   ½ Penny (Br) 1931–1936. ℞ sailing vessel "Dromedaris"   5.00   10.00

20 (25)   1 Penny (Br) 1931–1936. ℞ sailing vessel   2.00   4.00

21 (26)   3 Pence (Ag) 1931–1936. ℞ Protea cynaroides – Proteaceae, surrounded by three bundles of brushwood   5.00   10.00

22 (27)   6 Pence (Ag) 1931–1936. ℞ Protea cynaroides – Proteaceae, surrounded by six bundles of brushwood   3.00   6.00

23 (28)   1 Shilling (Ag) 1931–1936. ℞ allegory of Hope   6.00   12.00

24 (29)   2 Shillings (Ag) 1931–1936. ℞ coat of arms   10.00   20.00

25 (30)   2½ Shillings (Ag) 1931–1936. ℞ crowned coat of arms   12.50   25.00

GEORGE VI 1936–1952

26 (31)   ¼ Penny (Br) 1937–1947. George VI, head left. ℞ sparrows   0.50   1.00

			VF	XF
27 (32)	½ Penny (Br) 1937–1947. ℞ sailing vessel		0.40	1.00
28 (33)	1 Penny (Br) 1937–1947. ℞ sailing vessel		0.60	1.20
29 (34)	3 Pence (Ag) 1937–1947. ℞ Protea cynaroides – Proteaceae, surrounded by three bundles of brushwood		0.70	1.50
30 (35)	6 Pence (Ag) 1937–1947		1.00	2.00
31 (36)	1 Shilling (Ag) 1937–1947. ℞ allegory of Hope		2.00	3.50
32 (37)	2 Shillings (Ag) 1937–1947. ℞ coat of arms		4.50	8.50
33 (38)	2½ Shillings (Ag) 1937–1947. ℞ crowned coat of arms		5.00	10.00

COMMEMORATIVE ISSUE FOR THE VISIT OF THE ROYAL FAMILY

			VF	XF
34 (39)	5 Shillings (Ag) 1947. ℞ Springbok (Antidorcas marsupialis – Bovidae)		12.00	18.00
35 (40)	¼ Penny (Br) 1948–1950. Same type as No. 26, but legend GEORGIUS SEXTUS REX		0.40	0.90
36 (41)	½ Penny (Br) 1948–1952		0.40	0.90
37 (42)	1 Penny (Br) 1948–1950		0.60	1.20
38 (43)	3 Pence (Ag) 1948–1952		0.65	1.30
39 (44)	6 Pence (Ag) 1948–1950		1.50	3.00
40 (45)	1 Shilling (Ag) 1948–1950		3.00	7.00
41 (45a)	1 Shilling (Ag) 1951–1952		3.00	6.00
42 (46)	2 Shillings (Ag) 1948–1950		10.00	15.00

			VF	XF
43 (47)	2½	Shillings (Ag) 1948–1950	20.00	30.00
44 (47a)	2½	Shillings (Ag) 1951–1952	5.00	10.00
45 (48)	5	Shillings (Ag) 1948–1950. ℞ Spring-bok	8.00	12.00
46 (57)	½	Sovereign (Au) 1952. ℞ Springbok	90.00	105.00
47 (58)	1	Sovereign (Au) 1952	125.00	140.00
48 (49)	¼	Penny (Br) 1951–1952	0.35	0.70
49 (50)	1	Penny (Br) 1951–1952	0.50	1.00
50 (51)	6	Pence (Ag) 1951–1952	1.00	2.00
51 (52)	2	Shillings (Ag) 1951–1952	3.50	6.00
52 (53)	5	Shillings (Ag) 1951	10.00	15.00

COMMEMORATIVE ISSUE FOR THE FOUNDING OF CAPE TOWN BY JAN VAN RIEBEECK (1619–1677)

			VF	XF
53 (56)	5	Shillings (Ag) 1952. ℞ sailing vessel in front of the Cape of Good Hope	9.00	12.50

ELIZABETH II 1952–1961

			VF	XF
54 (59)	¼	Penny (Br) 1953–1960. Elizabeth II, head right. ℞ sparrows	0.30	0.50
55 (60)	½	Penny (Br) 1953–1960. ℞ sailing vessel	0.40	0.60
56 (61)	1	Penny (Br) 1953–1960. ℞ sailing vessel	0.40	0.70
57 (62)	3	Pence (Ag) 1953–1960. ℞ Protea cynaroides – Proteaceae, surrounded by three bundles of brushwood	0.70	1.00
58 (63)	6	Pence (Ag) 1953–1960	1.00	2.00
59 (64)	1	Shilling (Ag) 1953–1960. ℞ allegory of Hope	2.00	3.00
60 (65)	2	Shillings (Ag) 1953–1960. ℞ coat of arms	3.00	6.00
61 (66)	2½	Shillings (Ag) 1953–1960. ℞ crowned coat of arms	4.00	6.50
62 (67)	5	Shillings (Ag) 1953–1959. Springbok	7.00	10.00
63 (68)	½	£ (Au) 1953–1960. Elizabeth II, head right. ℞ springbok	120.00	150.00
64 (69)	1	£ (Au) 1953–1960	150.00	180.00

COMMEMORATIVE ISSUE FOR THE 50th ANNIVERSARY OF THE SOUTH AFRICAN UNION

			VF	XF

65 (70)   5 Shillings (Ag) 1960. ℞ parliament building   10.00   15.00

REPUBLIC since 1961

NEW CURRENCY: 100 Cents = 1 Rand
Bilingual Legends

66 (71)   ½ Cent (Bra) 1961–1964. Jan Anthoniszoon van Riebeeck (1619–1677), Dutchman, founder of Cape Town, colonizer and governor of the Cape Colony. ℞ sparrows   0.25   0.40

67 (72)   1 Cent (Bra) 1961–1964. ℞ covered wagon from the Voortrekker time   0.25   0.50

68 (73)   2½ Cents (Ag) 1961–1964. ℞ Protea cynaroides – Proteaceae   1.20   2.40

69 (74)   5 Cents (Ag) 1961–1964. ℞ Protea cynaroides – Proteaceae, surrounded by five bundles of brushwood   0.80   1.20

70 (75)   10 Cents (Ag) 1961–1964. ℞ allegory of Hope   1.20   1.80

71 (76)   20 Cents (Ag) 1961–1964. ℞ coat of arms   2.00   3.00
72 (77)   50 Cents (Ag) 1961–1964. ℞ springbok   6.50   9.00
73 (78)   1 Rand (Au) 1961–1971. ℞ springbok   40.00   52.00

74 (79)   2 Rand (Au) 1961–1971. ℞ springbok   45.00   55.00

Name of country in English

75 (80)   1 Cent (Br) 1965–1969. ℞ sparrows   0.05   0.10
76 (81)   2 Cents (Br) 1965–1969. ℞ white-tailed gnu (Connochaetes taurinus – Bovidae)   0.05   0.10
77 (82)   5 Cents (Ni) 1965–1969. ℞ blue crane (Anthropoides paradisea – Gruidae)   0.10   0.20
78 (83)   10 Cents (Ni) 1965–1969. ℞ Aloe sp. – Liliaceae   0.15   0.30
79 (84)   20 Cents (Ni) 1965–1969. ℞ Protea cynaroides and Protea repens – Proteaceae   0.25   0.50

			VF	XF
80 (85)	50	Cents (Ni) 1965–1969. Jan van Rie-beeck. ℞ Zantedeschia elliottiana –Araceae; Strelitzia reginae – Musaceae and Agapanthus sp. – Liliaceae	0.50	1.00
81 (86)	1	Rand (Ag) 1965–1968. ℞ springbok Name of country in Afrikaans	7.50	10.00
82 (80a)	1	Cent (Br) 1965–1969	0.05	0.10
83 (81a)	2	Cents (Br) 1965–1969	0.05	0.10
84 (82a)	5	Cents (Ni) 1965–1969	0.10	0.20
85 (83a)	10	Cents (Ni) 1965–1969	0.15	0.30
86 (84a)	20	Cents (Ni) 1965–1969	0.25	0.50
87 (85a)	50	Cents (Ni) 1965–1969	0.50	1.00
88 (86a)	1	Rand (Ag) 1965–1968	7.50	10.00

COMMEMORATIVE ISSUES (2) FOR THE 1st ANNIVERSARY OF THE DEATH OF DR. H. F. VERWOERD

89 (87)	1	Rand (Ag) 1967. Dr. Hendrik Frensh Verwoerd (1901–1966), Prime Minister from 1958 to 1966. ℞ springbok; Calvin's motto: "SOLI DEO GLORIA", name of country in English	7.50	10.00
90 (87a)	1	Rand (Ag) 1967. Dr. Hendrik F. Verwoerd; name of country in Afrikaans	7.50	10.00
A90 (104)	1	Kruger Rand (Au) 1967– Name of country in English		*400.00*
91 (88)	1	Cent (Br) 1968. Charles Robert Swart (*1894), 1st President of the Republic of South Africa, from 1961 to 1967. ℞ sparrows	0.05	0.10

			VF	XF
92 (89)	2	Cents (Br) 1968. ℞ white-tailed gnu	0.05	0.10
93 (90)	5	Cents (Ni) 1968. ℞ blue crane	0.05	0.10
94 (91)	10	Cents (Ni) 1968. ℞ Aloe	0.10	0.20
95 (92)	20	Cents (Ni) 1968. ℞ Protea cynaroides and Protea repens – Proteaceae	0.25	0.50
96 (93)	50	Cents (Ni) 1968. ℞ Zantedeschia elliottiana – Araceae; Strelitzia and Agapanthus	0.50	1.00

Name of country in Afrikaans

			VF	XF
97 (88a)	1	Cent (Br) 1968	0.05	0.10
98 (89a)	2	Cent (Br) 1968	0.05	0.10
99 (90a)	5	Cents (Ni) 1968	0.05	0.10
100 (91a)	10	Cents (Ni) 1968	0.10	0.20
101 (92a)	20	Cents (Ni) 1968	0.25	0.50
102 (93a)	50	Cents (Ni) 1968	0.50	1.00
103 (94)	1	Rand (Ag) 1969. Dr. Theophilus Ebenhaezer Dönges, elected President. ℞ state emblem, value; name of country in English	7.50	10.00

			XF	Unc
104 (94a)	1	Rand (Ag) 1969. Same type as No. 103, but name of country in Afrikaans	7.50	10.00
105 (95)	½	Cent (Br) 1970–1975. Coat of arms with shield supporters, date, name of country in two languages. ℞ sparrows, value	0.05	0.10
106 (96)	1	Cent (Br) 1970–1975. Same type as No. 105	0.05	0.10
107 (97)	2	Cents (Br) 1970–1975. ℞ same type as No. 92	0.05	0.10
108 (98)	5	Cents (Ni) 1970–1975. ℞ same type as No. 93	0.15	0.30
109 (99)	10	Cents (Ni) 1970–1975. ℞ same type as No. 94	0.20	0.40
110 (100)	20	Cents (Ni) 1970–1975. ℞ same type as No. 95	0.30	0.60
111 (101)	50	Cents (Ni) 1970–1975. ℞ same type as No. 96	0.50	1.00
112 (102)	1	Rand (Ag) 1970–1975. ℞ springbok	7.50	10.00

COMMEMORATIVE ISSUE FOR THE 50th ANNIVERSARY OF THE PRETORIA MINT (1923–1973)

		Unc	Proof
113 (103)	1 Rand (Ag) 1974:		
	a) 1974	20.00	
	b) 1974, 1977, 1978		25.00

		XF	Unc
114 (105)	½ Cent (Br) 1976. Jacobus Johannes Fouché, President of the Republic of South Africa, from 1968 to 1974. Rev. sparrows	0.05	0.10
115 (106)	1 Cent (Br) 1976. Type as No. 114	0.05	0.10
116 (107)	2 Cents (Br) 1976. Rev. white-tailed gnu	0.05	0.10
117 (108)	5 Cents (Ni) 1976. Rev. blue crane	0.10	0.20
118 (109)	10 Cents (Ni) 1976. Rev. aloe	0.15	0.30
119 (110)	20 Cents (Ni) 1976. Rev. Protea cynaroides and Protea repens – Proteaceae)	0.20	0.40

120 (111)	50 Cents (Ni) 1976. Rev. Zantedeschia elliottiana– Araceae; Strelizia and Agapanthus	0.50	1.00

121 (102a)	1 Rand (Ni) 1977, 1978, 1980. Type as No. 112	1.00	2.00

			XF	Unc
122 (112)	½ Cent (Br) 1979		0.10	0.15
123 (113)	1 Cent (Br) 1979		0.15	0.25
124 (114)	2 Cents (Br) 1979		0.20	0.30

			XF	Unc
125 (115)	5 Cents (Ni) 1979		0.25	0.40
126 (116)	10 Cents (Ni) 1979		0.30	0.50
127 (117)	20 Cents (Ni) 1979		0.50	0.80
128 (118)	50 Cents (Ni) 1979		0.90	1.20
129 (119)	1 Rand (Ni) 1979		1.50	2.00

130 (120)	1/10 Kruger Rand (Au) 1980–		*45.00*
131 (121)	¼ Kruger Rand (Au) 1980–		*115.00*
132 (122)	½ Kruger Rand (Au) 1980–		*220.00*

South Arabia

Südarabische Föderation　　　　**Arabie du Sud (Fédération)**
Federation of South Arabia

Area: 61,890 sq. mi. Population: 1,250,000.
Several sultanates and emirates of the West Aden protectorate united
to form the South Arabian Federation in 1959/60. The Crown Colony of
Aden together with the islands of Sokotra and Abd-el-Kuri joined the
federation only in 1963.
Capital: Al Ittihad.

		1000 Fils = 1 Dinar	**VF**	**XF**
1 (1)	1	Fils (Al) 1964. Star. ℞ crossed daggers (jambijas)	0.30	0.80
2 (2)	5	Fils (Br) 1964	0.40	0.80
3 (3)	25	Fils (Cu–Ni) 1964. ℞ dhow, Arabian sailing vessel	0.60	1.50

4 (4)	50 Fils (Cu–Ni) 1964	0.90	1.80

Südrhodesien   # Southern Rhodesia   **Rhodésie du Sud**

In 1889 Southern and Northern Rhodesia were united under the administration of the British South African Company; since October 1st, 1923, the two territories are governed separately.
Capital: Salisbury.

12 Pence = 1 Shilling, 2 Shillings = 1 Florin,
5 Shillings = 1 Crown, 20 Shillings = 1 £

GEORGE V 1923–1936

			VF	XF
1 (1)	½	Penny (Cu–Ni) 1934–1936. Crown above stylized rose. ℞ value and ornamentations (center hole)	3.00	6.00

2 (2)	1	Penny (Cu–Ni) 1934–1936 (center hole)	2.00	3.00
3 (3)	3	Pence (Ag) 1932–1936. George V, crowned portrait, left. ℞ three spear tips	2.50	4.50
4 (4)	6	Pence (Ag) 1932–1936. ℞ crossed axes	3.50	6.00
5 (5)	1	Shilling (Ag) 1932–1936. ℞ large Zimbabwe bird (= soap stone sculpture)	6.00	10.50
6 (6)	2	Shillings (Ag) 1932–1936. ℞ sable antelope (Hippotragus niger – Bovidae)	12.00	16.00
7 (7)	½	Crown (Ag) 1932–1936. ℞ coat of arms	15.00	20.00

GEORGE VI 1936–1952

8 (8)	½	Penny (Cu–Ni) 1938–1939. Crown above stylized rose. ℞ value and ornamentations (center hole)	1.50	2.50
9 (9)	1	Penny (Cu–Ni) 1937–1942 (center hole)	1.50	3.00

			VF	XF
10 (8a)	½	Penny (Br) 1942–1944 (center hole)	0.60	1.20
11 (9a)	1	Penny (Br) 1942–1947 (center hole)	0.80	1.50
12 (12)	3	Pence (Ag) 1937. ℞ three spear tips	3.50	4.50
13 (13)	6	Pence (Ag) 1937. ℞ crossed axes	4.50	7.50
14 (14)	1	Shilling (Ag) 1937. ℞ large Zimbabwe bird	8.00	12.00
15 (15)	2	Shillings (Ag) 1937. ℞ sable antelope	12.00	25.00

			VF	XF
16 (16)	½	Crown (Ag) 1937. ℞ coat of arms	18.00	30.00
17 (17)	3	Pence. ℞ three spear tips		
		a) (Ag) 1939–1946	3.50	4.50
		b) (Cu–Ni) 1947	1.20	2.00
18 (18)	6	Pence. ℞ crossed axes		
		a) (Ag) 1939–1946	4.00	7.00
		b) (Cu–Ni) 1947	1.25	2.50
19 (19)	1	Shilling. ℞ large Zimbabwe bird		
		a) (Ag) 1939–1946	7.50	12.00
		b) (Cu–Ni) 1947	2.00	4.00
20 (20)	2	Shilling. ℞ sable antelope		
		a) (Ag) 1939–1946	12.00	18.00
		b) (Cu–Ni) 1947	4.00	7.00
21 (21)	½	Crown. ℞ coat of arms		
		a) (Ag) 1938–1946	16.00	22.00
		b) (Cu–Ni) 1947	5.00	7.50
22 (27)	½	Penny (Br) 1951–1952. Same type as No. 10, but with legend KING GEORGE THE SIXTH	0.60	1.20
23 (28)	1	Penny (Br) 1949–1952. Same type as No. 11, but with legend KING GEORGE THE SIXTH	1.00	1.50
24 (29)	3	Pence (Cu–Ni) 1948–1952	0.70	1.40
25 (30)	6	Pence (Cu–Ni) 1948–1952	0.80	1.60
26 (31)	1	Shilling (Cu–Ni) 1948–1952. ℞ large Zimbabwe bird	2.00	3.00
27 (32)	2	Shillings (Cu–Ni) 1948–1952	2.50	4.00
28 (33)	½	Crown (Cu–Ni) 1948–1952	4.50	7.50

COMMEMORATIVE COIN FOR THE
100th BIRTHDAY OF C. RHODES

			VF	XF
29 (34)		1 Crown (Ag) 1953. ℞ Cecil Rhodes (1853–1902), British South African chief economist and statesman, colonial pioneer, portrait above arms of Southern Rhodesia, Northern Rhodesia, and Nyasaland	22.00	32.00
30 (35)	$^1/_2$	Penny (Br) 1954. Crown above stylized rose. ℞ value with ornamentations (center hole)	2.00	3.00
31 (36)	1	Penny (Br) 1954	2.50	4.00
32 (37)	2	Shillings (Cu–Ni) 1954. Elizabeth II. ℞ sable antelope	10.00	15.00
33 (38)	$^1/_2$	Crown (Cu–Ni) 1954. ℞ coat of arms	12.00	18.00

Südjemen   # Southern Yemen   **Yemen du Sud**
Democratic Yemen

Area: 61,890 sq. mi. Population: 1,250,000.
Southern Yemen is the successor of the South Arabian Federation. The former Federation was transformed into a centrally governed state on 26th November 1967 by proclaiming the People's Republic. The old sultanates and emirates were replaced by 10 provinces with governors. On the occasion of the festivities for the third anniversary of independence, 1970, the designation of state "Democratic Yemen" was adopted, which meant the first step towards the aspired union with the Republic of Yemen.
Capital: Al Ittihad.

1000 Fils = 1 Southern Yemen Dinar;
since 1972: 1000 Fils = 1 Yemen Dinar

		VF	XF
1 (2)	5 Fils (Br) 1971. Star and name of the country, DEMOCRATIC YEMEN. ℞ crossed daggers, value, date	0.60	1.00

2 (3)	2½ Fils (Al) 1973	–.–	–.–
3 (4)	5 Fils (Al) 1973. Rev. cancer	–.–	–.–

4 (5)   25 Fils (Cu-Ni) 1976, 1977, 1979. Star and name of the country, PEOPLE'S DEMOCRATIC REPUBLIC OF YEMEN. Rev. dhow, Arabian sailing vessel   –.–   –.–

5 (6)   50 Fils (Cu-Ni) 1976, 1977, 1979. Type as No. 4   –.–   –.–
6 (7) 250 Fils (Cu-Ni) 1977   –.–   –.–
7 (8)   5 Dinars (Ag) 1977   –.–   –.–

South Korea
Taihan

Area: 38,452 sq. mi. Population: 32,200,000.
In the southern part of the country administered by Japan until 1945, the Republic of Korea was proclaimed on August 15, 1948. The border between North and South Korea is formed approximately by the 38th parallel. The dates on the coins correspond in part to Korean chronology. Capital: Seoul.

100 Hwan = 1 Won, since June 10, 1962: 100 Jeon = 1 Won

			VF	XF
1 (1)	10	Hwan (Bra) 4292–4294 (1959–1961). Rose of Sharon = hibiscus (Hibiscus syriacus – Malvaceae), national flower of South Korea. ℞ value and date	0.25	0.50
2 (2)	50	Hwan (Ni–Bra) 4292–4294 (1959–1961). Turtle boat, iron clad war vessel of Admiral Lee Shun-shin (1545–1598), appointed to ward off the Hideyoshi invasion from 1592 to 1598. ℞ value	0.40	0.80

| **3** (3) | 100 | Hwan (Cu–Ni) 4292 (1959). Syngman Rhee (1875–1965), President 1948–1960. ℞ phoenix, value | 0.70 | 1.40 |

			VF	XF
4 (4)	1	Won (Bra) 1966, 1967. Rose of Sharon. Rev. value	0.20	0.40
5 (4a)	1	Won (Al) 1968-1974. Same type as No. 4	0.10	0.20
6 (5)	5	Won (Br) 1966-1970. Turtle boat. R value	0.15	0.30
7 (5a)	5	Won (Bra) 1970-1972. Type as No. 6	0.15	0.40

			VF	XF
8 (6)	10	Won (Br) 1966–. Prabhuta-vatna-Stupa in Pulguksa, 8th century, great Silla dynasty. ℞ value	0.20	0.50
9 (6a)	10	Won (Bra) 1970-1974. Type as No. 8	0.15	0.40

			VF	XF
10 (7)	100	Won (Cu–Ni) 1970–. Admiral Lee Shun-shin. ℞ value, date	0.60	1.00

			Proof
11	50	Won (Ag) 1970–. Kwan Sun Yu (1904–1920) with national flag (Taegukki), girl student, fought for an independent Korea	7.00
12	100	Won (Ag) 1970–. Admiral Lee Shun-shin (also SUN SIN LEE) (1545–1598) and turtle boat	10.00
13	200	Won (Ag) 1970–. Seladon vase, porcelain, Koryo dynasty, 11th century	20.00
14	250	Won (Ag) 1970–. Tschang Hi Park (*1917), President since 1961. ℞ hibiscus flower between two phoenixes, state emblem, value	25.00

15	500	Won (Ag) 1970–. Kyongju: Bodhi-sattva from the Sokkuram (cave temple). ℞ state emblem surrounded by hibiscus branches, value	**Proof** 42.00
16	1000	Won (Ag) 1970–. Soldiers in front of fluttering South Korean and UN flags. Flags of the 16 countries supporting South Korea in the Korean war (1950–1953)	100.00
17	1000	Won (Au) 1970–. Seoul: Namdae-Mun (= Southern gate), built at the beginning of the Yi dynasty (1396)	85.00

18	2500	Won (Au) 1970–. Queen Sunduk (reign: 632–647), wearing the precious gold crown of the Silla dynasty	150.00
19	5000	Won (Au). Turtle boats of Admiral Lee Shun-shin. ℞ like No. 13	300.00
20	10000	Won (Au) 1970–. Same type as No. 12	600.00
21	20000	Won (Au) 1970–. Gold crown from the golden crown tomb in Kyongju, 5th to 6th century, of the Silla dynasty, today in Seoul, National Museum	1100.00
22	25000	Won (Au) 1970–. King Sedschong (1397–1450), creator of the Korean phonetic alphabet	1400.00

COMMEMORATIVE ISSUE FOR THE FAO COIN PLAN

			XF	**Unc**
23 (A7)	50	Won (Cu-Ni) 1972–1979. Rice. Rev. value, date	0.40	0.80

	30th ANNIVERSARY OF LIBERATION	XF	Unc
24 (8)	100 Won (Cu-Ni) 1975	1.00	2.00

WORLD SHOOTING CHAMPIONSHIPS 1978 (2)

		Unc	Proof
25 (9)	500 Won (Ni) 1978	6.00	40.00

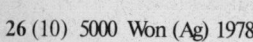

		Unc	Proof
26 (10)	5000 Won (Ag) 1978	60.00	160.00

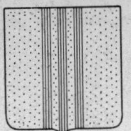

South Vietnam
Viet-Nam Cong Hoa

Area: 66,281 sq. mi. Population: 19,200,000.
After the coming into force of the armistice in Vietnam based on the
Geneva Indochina Agreement of 1954, the Republic of Vietnam was
formed south of the 17th parallel, when the Emperor Bao Dai had been
deposed in 1955. After a long conflict South Vietnam surrendered to North Vietnam
in 1975, and in 1976, both parts were united into the single socialist Republic of
Vietnam.

Capital: Saigon.

100 Xu or Su (= Cent) = 1 Dong (= Vietnam Piastre)

BAO DAI

			VF	XF
1 (1)	10	Su (Al–Bra) 1953. Vietnamese women. ℞ rice plant (Oryza sativa – Gramineae) and value	0.50	1.00
2 (2)	20	Su (Al–Bra) 1953. Same type as No. 1	0.50	1.00
3 (3)	50	Xu (Al–Br) 1953. Vietnamese women. ℞ sea dragon between value	1.20	2.40

REPUBLIC

4 (4)	50	Su (Al–Bra) 1960. Ngo Dinh Diem (1901–1963), President from 1955 to 1963. ℞ bamboo (belonging to the grass family, Gramineae), value	0.75	1.50

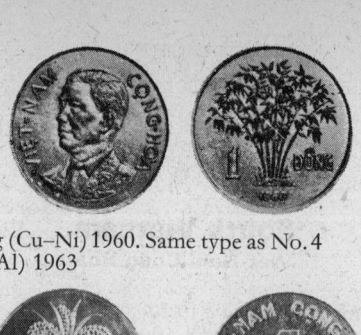

			VF	XF
5 (5)	1	Dong (Cu–Ni) 1960. Same type as No. 4	0.30	0.60
6 (6)	50	Xu (Al) 1963	0.30	0.60

7 (7)	1	Dong (Cu–Ni). Rice plant. ℞ value:		
		a) (Cu–Ni) 1964	0.15	0.30
		b) (Ni–St) 1971	0.20	0.40
8 (8)	5	Dong. (Scalloped)		
		a) (Cu–Ni) 1964	0.25	0.50
		b) (Ni–St) 1971	0.30	0.60
9 (9)	10	Dong:		
		a) (Cu–Ni) 1964	0.25	0.50
		b) (Ni–St) 1968–1970	0.20	0.40

10 (10)	20	Dong (Ni) 1968. Vietnamese woman in rice field. New legend NGAN-HANG QUOC-GIA VIET-NAM, date ℞ value	0.50	1.00

ISSUES (3) FOR THE FAO COIN PLAN

11 (12)	1	Dong (Al) 1971. Rice plant, date. ℞ value	0.25	0.50
12 (13)	10	Dong (Brass-clad-steel) 1974	0.30	0.60
13 (11)	20	Dong (Ni) 1968. Same type as No. 10 but with new legend CHIEN-DICH THE-GIOI CHONG NAN DOI	1.50	3.00

Spanien   # Spain   **Espagne**

Area: 194,232 sq. mi. Population: 34,300,000.
State on the Iberian peninsula including the Balearic and Canary Islands.
Capital: Madrid.

100 Centimos = 1 Peseta

ALFONSO XIII 1886–1931

			VF	XF
1 (87)	50 Centimos (Ag) 1896–1900. Alfonso XIII (1886–1941), first under regency of his mother, took over the reign in 1902; head left. ℞ crowned arms between pillars		4.00	10.00
2 (88)	1 Peseta (Ag) 1896–1901		4.50	12.00
3 (89)	5 Peseta (Ag) 1896–1899		15.00	28.00
4 (91)	20 Pesetas (Au) 1904. Alfonso XIII, portrait in uniform, right. ℞ mantled arms with crown		1700.00	2000.00
5 (96)	1 Centimo (Br) 1906. Alfonso XIII, portrait in uniform, right. ℞ crowned arms, value		3.00	4.50
6 (97)	2 Centimos (Br) 1904–1905		2.50	4.00
7 (92)	50 Centimos (Ag) 1904–1910. Alfonso XIII, head left. ℞ crowned arms between pillars		4.00	7.50
8 (94)	1 Peseta (Ag) 1902–1905		8.00	12.00

		VF	XF
9 (95)	2 Pesetas (Ag) 1905	12.00	22.00

			VF	**XF**
10 (98)	1	Centimo (Br) 1911–1913. Alfonso XIII, portrait in uniform, left. ℞ crowned arms, value	2.50	4.50
11 (99)	2	Centimos (Br) 1911–1912	2.50	4.50
12 (93)	50	Centimos (Ag) 1910	4.50	10.00
13 (100)	25	Centimos (Ni–Bra) 1925. Sailing vessel. ℞ value between branches, crown above	1.50	4.00
14 (101)	25	Centimos (Cu–Ni) 1927. Hammer, olive branch, crown. ℞ ears of wheat, value (center hole)	1.20	3.50
15 (102)	50	Centimos (Ag) 1926. Alfonso XIII, head left. ℞ crowned arms	4.50	11.00

REPUBLIC

16 (103)	5	Centimos (Fe) 1937. Head of Hispania. ℞ value in wreath	2.00	4.50
17 (107)	25	Centimos (Ni–Br) 1934. Hispania with olive branch. ℞ ears of wheat and olive branch in front of cog-wheel (center hole)	0.60	1.20
18 (104)	25	Centimos (Br) 1938. Intertwined chains. ℞ value (center hole)	2.00	4.00
19 (105)	50	Centimos (Br) 1937. Seated Hispania with olive branch. ℞ value	1.50	3.50

20 (108)	1	Peseta (Ag) 1933. Seated Hispania with olive branch. ℞ coat of arms with mural crown, between pillars	7.50	12.50
21 (106)	1	Peseta (Bra) 1937. Head of Hispania. ℞ bunch of grapes	0.60	1.50

NATIONAL GOVERNMENT

			VF	XF
22 (109)	25	Centimos (Cu–Ni) 1937. Name of country in sun rays, and emblem of the Falange "yoke and arrows" (= at the same time recalling the great national history). ℞ coat of arms, olive branch (center hole)	1.20	2.50
23 (110)	5	Centimos (Al) 1940–1953. Lancer. ℞ crowned coat of arms between Hercules pillars, with eagle above. The details on the arms illustrate the integration of the historic territories: castle = Castile, lion = León, poles = Aragon, net = Navarre, pomegranate = Granada	0.20	0.40
24 (111)	10	Centimos (Al) 1940–1953. Same type as No. 23	0.25	0.50
25 (112)	1	Peseta (Al–Br) 1944. Coat of arms. ℞ value surrounded by coat of arms	0.50	1.00

MONARCHY

Spain was converted to a monarchy on April 1, 1947, under a regency.

26 (115)	50	Centimos (Cu–Ni) 1949. Anchor, rope and steering wheel (symbolic of Spain as a seafaring nation). ℞ coat of arms, yoke and arrows. Arrows pointing down (center hole)	5.50	8.00
27 (116)	50	Centimos (Cu–Ni) 1949–. Same type as No. 26, but arrows pointing up (center hole)	0.25	0.40
28 (113)	1	Peseta (Al–Br) 1947–. Francisco Franco y Bahamonde (1892-1975). General and statesman, since 1938 with the title Caudillo. ℞ coat of arms	0.15	0.25
29 (114)	2½	Pesetas (Al–Br) 1953–	0.60	1.20
30 (117)	5	Pesetas (Cu–Ni) 1949–1952	2.50	6.00
31 (121)	10	Centimos (Al) 1959–. General Franco, head right. ℞ value, surrounded by olive leaves	0.10	0.20
32 (124)	50	Centimos (Al–Mg) 1966–. ℞ ear of wheat, value	0.10	0.20

Spain 1227

			VF	XF
33 (125)	1	Peseta (Al–Br) 1966–. ℞ coat of arms, value	0.10	0.20
34 (118)	5	Pesetas (Cu–Ni) 1957–. ℞ coat of arms in front of eagle	0.25	0.50

			VF	XF
35 (119)	25	Pesetas (Cu–Ni) 1957–	0.50	1.00
36 (120)	50	Pesetas (Cu–Ni) 1957–	1.30	2.60
37 (122)	100	Pesetas (Ag) 1966. ℞ crowned five-sectional coat of arms. Three crosses of the San Fernando Order, separating value, yoke, and arrows	10.00	12.50

JUAN CARLOS I since 1975

			XF	Unc
38 (126)	50	Centimos (Al) 1975 (76). Head left of the King, date. Rev. laurel branch	0.10	0.20
39 (127)	1	Peseta (Al–Br) 1975 (76). Rev. coat of arms	0.10	0.20
40 (128)	5	Pesetas (Cu–Ni) 1975 (76). Rev. coat of arms	0.25	0.50
41 (129)	25	Pesetas (Cu–Ni) 1975 (76). Rev. crown	0.55	1.10
42 (130)	50	Pesetas (Cu–Ni) 1975 (76). Type as No. 40	1.25	2.50
43 (131)	100	Pesetas (Cu–NI) 1975 (76). Rev. coat of arms	2.00	3.60
44	100	Pesetas (Au) 1977, 1978 (medallic issue)		600.00

WORLD SOCCER CHAMPIONSHIP GAMES 1982 IN SPAIN (6)

45 (132)	50	Centimos (Al) 1980	0.30	0.70

46 (133)	1	Peseta (Al-Br) 1980	0.40	0.80
47 (134)	5	Pesetas (Cu-Ni) 1980	0.50	1.00
48 (135)	25	Pesetas (Cu-Ni) 1980	0.60	1.25
49 (136)	50	Pesetas (Cu-Ni) 1980	0.90	2.00
50 (137)	100	Pesetas (Cu-Ni) 1980	2.00	3.20

ISSUES FOR VIZCAYA (EUZKADI)

During the time of the civil war the province of Vizcaya constituted an autonomous territory. Capital: Bilbao.

			VF	XF
1 (1)	1	Peseta (Ni) 1937. Head of Liberty right, new legend GOBIERNO DE EUZ-KADI. ℞ value and date in wreath	2.50	5.00
2 (2)	2	Pesetas (Ni) 1937	2.50	5.00

Area: 25,384 sq. mi. Population: 13,000,000.
Island in the Indian Ocean off the southern tip of India, Ceylon became
a sovereign member of the British Commonwealth on 4th February
1948. As of 22nd May 1972 Ceylon has declared itself a republic and
declared its former name, in Singhalese, to be Sri Lanka, the latter also
to be used exclusively on an international basis. Since 22nd May 1972
the monetary unit is called the Sri Lanka Rupee.
Capital: Colombo.

100 Cents = 1 Sri Lanka Rupee

		VF	XF
1 (1)	1 Cent (Al–Mg) 1973. Coat of arms. R value	0.05	0.10
2 (2)	2 Cents (Al–Mg) 1973	0.10	0.20
3 (3)	5 Cents (Ni–Me) 1973	0.15	0.30
4 (4)	10 Cents (Ni–Me) 1973	0.20	0.35
5 (5)	25 Cents (Cu–Ni) 1973	0.25	0.40
6 (6)	50 Cents (Cu–Ni) 1972	0.40	0.80

| **7** (7) | 1 Rupie (Cu–Ni) 1972 | 0.90 | 1.20 |

NON-ALIGNED NATIONS CONFERENCE 1976 (2)

| **8** (8) | 2 Rupees (Cu–Ni) 1976. Conference building | 1.00 | 1.60 |
| **9** (9) | 5 Rupees (Ni) 1976. Type as No. 8 | 1.50 | 3.00 |

INVESTITURE OF PRESIDENT JAYAWARDENE

| **10** (10) | 1 Rupee (Ni) 1978 | 0.60 | 1.00 |

Straits Settlements

Straits Settlements   **Établissements du Détroit**

Under the name of the "Straits Settlements" the British created in 1867 a Crown Colony out of smaller territories previously acquired around 1800 with the centre in the city of Singapore (= Lion City) situated on the Malayan peninsula purchased from the Sultan of Johore in 1824 by the British East India Company. On the Malayan peninsula only Penang and the town of Malacca were true components of the Straits Settlements. But the expansion in the direction of Siam by subordinating the Malayan princes under British rule or protection, extended the area of the Governor General far towards the North.
Capital: Singapore.
The Straits-Dollar was introduced on 25th June 1903 and was not only valid in the states of the Malayan peninsula, but also in British North Borneo, Brunei, the island of Labuan near Borneo, the Cocos Islands as well as on Christmas Island south of Java and in Sarawak. The Straits Dollar corresponded in fineness and weight to the up to then conventional Mexican Piaster.

100 Cents = 1 Straits Dollar

EDWARD VII 1901–1910

			VF	XF
1 (17)	¼	Cent (Cu) 1905–1908. Edward VII, crowned head, right. ℞ value in dotted circle	2.00	4.00
2 (18)	½	Cent (Cu) 1908	4.00	7.50
3 (19)	1	Cent (Cu) 1903–1908	2.50	4.50
4 (20)	5	Cents (Ag) 1902–1910	3.50	5.00
5 (21)	10	Cents (Ag) 1902–1910	4.00	6.00
6 (22)	20	Cents (Ag) 1902–1910	6.00	9.00
7 (23,24)	50	Cents (Ag)		
		a) 1902–1903	30.00	55.00
		b) 1907–1908, smaller diameter	9.00	15.00
8 (25)	1	Dollar (Ag) 1903–1904, 1907–1909. ℞ value, also in Malayan and Chinese		
		a) 1903–1904	15.00	30.00
		b) 1907–1909, smaller diameter	10.00	20.00

			VF	XF
9 (27)	¼	Cent (Cu) 1916. George V, crowned head, left. ℞ value	2.00	3.00
10 (28)	½	Cent (Cu) 1916	2.50	3.50
11 (29)	½	Cent (Br) 1932 (scalloped)	0.80	1.50
12 (30)	1	Cent (Br) 1919–1926	0.80	1.20
13 (31)	5	Cents (Cu–Ni) 1920	4.50	7.00
14 (32)	5	Cents (Ag) 1918–1935	2.50	3.50
15 (34)	10	Cents (Ag) 1916–1927	2.50	3.50
16 (35)	20	Cents (Ag) 1916–1935	3.50	5.50
17 (36)	50	Cents (Ag) 1920–1921	6.00	12.00

			VF	XF
18 (37)	1	Dollar (Ag) 1919–1920	18.00	22.00

For further issues see under **Malaya, Malaysia, North Borneo** and **Singapore**.

Sudan # Sudan **Soudan**
The Sudan

Area: 967,500 sq. mi. Population: 16,200,000.

The Anglo-Egyptian Condominium established over the Sudan on 19th January 1899 existed until its unilateral abrogation by Egypt on 18th October 1951. The present day Sudan Republic was declared independent with effect of 1st January 1956 and on 25th May 1969 declared a "Democratic Republic". With the introduction of the Sudanese Pound on 8th April 1957, the Egyptian Pound was superseded in circulation. Capital: Khartoum.

10 Millièmes = 1 Gersh (internationally called Piaster),
100 Gersh = 1 Sudanese Pound

			VF	XF
1 (34)	1 Millième (Br) 1956–. 'Flying postman' on dromedary (Camelus dromedarius-Camelidae). ℞ value		0.10	0.20
2 (35)	2 Millièmes (Br) 1956– (scalloped)		0.20	0.30
3 (36)	5 Millièmes (Br) 1956– (scalloped)		0.25	0.40
4 (37)	10 Millièmes (Br) 1956–		0.30	0.45
5 (38)	2 Piastres (Cu–Ni)			
	a) 1956. 17.5 mm dia.		1.00	1.50
	b) 1963–. 20 mm dia.		0.40	0.60

6 (39)	5 Piastres (Cu–Ni) 1956–		0.50	0.80
7 (40)	10 Piastres (Cu–Ni) 1956–		1.00	2.00
8 (41)	20 Piastres (Cu–Ni) 1967-1969; proof only			5.00

9 (42)   25 Piastres (Cu–Ni) 1968. Flying postman;   **Proof**
inscription FAO. ℞ value. The legend
reads 'Let us work together towards
providing food for all'   20.00

DEMOCRATIC REPUBLIC since 1969

10 (A43)   1 Millième (Br) 1970, 1971. Type as No. 1,
but inscription "Democratic Republic" added   2.00
11 (B43)   2 Millièmes (Br) 1970, 1971. Type as No. 10   2.00

12 (C43)   5 Millièmes (Br) 1970, 1971. Type as No. 10   2.00
13 (D43) 10 Millièmes (Br) 1970, 1971. Type as No. 10   2.00
14 (E43)   2 Piastres (Cu-Ni) 1970, 1971. Type as No. 10
20 mm dia.   2.20
15 (F43)   5 Piastres (Cu-Ni) 1970, 1971. Type as No. 10   2.50
16 (G43) 10 Piastres (Cu-Ni) 1970, 1971. Type as No. 10   4.00
17 (H43) 20 Piastres (Cu-Ni) 1970, 1971. Type as No. 10   15.00

COMMEMORATIVE COINS (5) FOR THE SECOND ANNIVERSARY OF THE REVOLUTION

18 (43)   5 Millièmes (Br) 1971. New state emblem   **XF**   **Unc**
(model of a secretary bird, Sagittarius
serpentarius – Sagittariidae) between
year dates. Legend. ℞ value between
cotton blossoms. Legend   0.15   0.30

			XF	Unc
19 (44)	10	Millièmes (Br) 1971. Same type as No. 11	0.20	0.40
20 (45)	2	Piastres (Cu–Ni) 1971. Same type as No. 11	0.25	0.50
21 (46)	5	Piastres (Cu–Ni) 1971. Same type as No. 11	0.40	0.80
22 (47)	10	Piastres (Cu–Ni) 1971. Same type as No. 11	0.80	1.50

ISSUES FOR THE FAO COIN PLAN (2)

 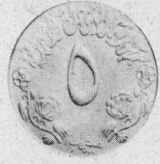

23 (48)	5	Millièmes (Br) 1972, 1973. New state emblem (model of a secretary bird. ℞ value, cotton, with inscription "Grow more food"	0.25	0.50

24 (49)	50	Piastres (Cu–Ni) 1972. ℞ man plough- ing with oxen, and inscription "Let us increase production"	4.00	5.00
25 (50)	5	Millièmes (Bra) 1975. Type similar to No. 18	0.15	0.30
26 (51)	10	Millièmes (Br) 1972. Type similar to No. 19 (scalloped)	0.20	0.40
27 (51a)	10	Millièmes (Bra) 1975. Type as No. 26 (scalloped)	0.20	0.40
28 (52)	2	Piastres (Cu–Ni) 1975. Type as No. 25	0.35	0.70
29 (53)	5	Piastres (Cu–Ni) 1975. Type as No. 25	0.40	0.80
30 (54)	10	Piastres (Cu–Ni) 1975. Type as No. 25	0.80	1.60

ISSUES FOR THE FAO COIN PLAN (5)

		XF	Unc
31 (58)	5 Millièmes (Bra) 1976. Coat of arms between ears. date. Rev. value between cotton	0.20	0.40
32 (59)	10 Milliémes (Bra) 1976. Type as No. 31 (scalloped)	0.25	0.50
33 (60)	2 Piastres (Cu-Ni) 1976. Type as No. 31	0.40	0.80
34 (61)	5 Piastres (Cu-Ni) 1976. Type as No. 31	0.55	1.10
35 (62)	10 Piastres (Cu-Ni) 1976. Type as No. 31	1.00	2.00

CONSERVATION COMMEMORATIVE (3)

		Unc	Proof
36 (55)	2½ Pounds (Ag) 1976	25.00	30.00
37 (56)	5 Pounds (Ag) 1976	50.00	60.00
38 (57)	100 Pounds (Au) 1976	600.00	900.00

20th ANNIVERSARY OF INDEPENDENCE

		XF	Unc
39 (63)	10 Millièmes (Bra) 1976	0.20	0.45
40 (64)	2 Piastres (Cu-Ni) 1976	0.30	0.50
41 (65)	5 Piastres (Cu-Ni) 1976	0.50	0.90
42 (66)	10 Piastres (Cu-Ni) 1976	0.70	1.50

ESTABLISHMENT OF ARAB COOPERATIVE

43 (67)	50 Piastres (Cu-Ni) 1976	3.00	4.00

Surinam
Suriname

Area: 55,143 sq. mi. Population: 420.000.
Surinam (Netherlands Guyana) was given the status of an autonomous
territory in 1948 and self-government in 1950. Since 1954 Surinam has been
an overseas territory of the Kingdom of the Netherlands. Full independence
was achieved on Nov. 25, 1975.
Capital: Paramaribo.

100 Cent = 1 Surinam Gulden

WILHELMINA 1890-1948

				VF	XF
1 (36a)	1	Cent (Bra) 1943. Type as No. 11 of the Netherlands, but mintmark P (= Philadelphia)		2.50	5.00
A1 (34a)	5	Cent (Cu-Ni) 1943. Type as No. 13 of the Netherlands		4.50	7.50
2 (43a)	10	Cent (Ag) 1942. Type as No. 20 of the Netherlands, but mintmark P		4.00	7.50
3 (44a)	25	Cent (Ag) 1942. Type as No. 21 of the Netherlands, but mintmark P		7.50	12.50

JULIANA 1948-1975

			VF	XF
4 (36b)	1 Cent (Br) 1957, 1959. 1960. Type as No. 11 of the Netherlands		1.20	3.50

			VF	XF
5 (2)	1 Cent (Br) 1962, 1966, 1970, 1972, 1973. Coat of arms. Rev. value, date		0.15	0.25

			VF	XF
6 (3)	5	Cent (Ni-Bra) 1962, 1966, 1971–1972. Type similar to No. 5 (square)	0.15	0.30
7 (4)	10	Cent (Cu-Ni) 1962, 1966, 1971-1973. Typ as No. 5	0.20	0.40
8 (5)	25	Cent (Cu-Ni) 1962, 1966, 1972, 1973. Typ as No. 5	0.50	1.00
9 (6)	1	Gulden (Ag) 1962, 1966. Juliana, Queen of the Netherlands:		
		a) 1962	6.00	11.00
		b) 1966	100.00	150.00

INDEPENDENCE

			XF	Unc
10 (2a)	1	Cent (Al) 1974–1979. Type as No. 5	0.05	0.10
11 (3a)	5	Cent (Al) 1976–. Type as No. 6	0.10	0.20

1st ANNIVERSARY OF INDEPENDENCE (3)

			Unc	Proof
12 (7)	10	Gulden (Ag) 1976	12.00	25.00
13 (8)	25	Gulden (Ag) 1976	28.00	40.00
14 (9)	100	Gulden (Au) 1976	120.00	160.00

Swasiland # Swaziland

Area: 6,704 sq. mi. Population: 422,000.
Belonging to the Ndwandwe group of the Zulus, the Swazi owe their
name to Chief Mswazi, head of the government in 1839. Swaziland
joined Transvaal in 1894, and became a British Protectorate in 1906.
Swaziland attained the right of self-government in April 1967, and its
independence on September 6, 1968.
Capital: Mbabane.

100 Cents = 1 Luhlanga, 25 Luhlanga = 1 Lilangeni;
since Sept. 6, 1974: 100 Cents = 1 Lilangeni (Plural: Emalangeni)

Swaziland belongs to the currency area of the South African Rand;
the Luhlanga corresponds to the Rand.

COMMEMORATIVE ISSUES (6) FOR INDEPENDENCE OF SEPTEMBER 6, 1968

		Proof
1	5 Cents (Ag) 1968. Sobhuza II, king since 1899. ℞ Swazi shield and spears (= state emblem), value in letters	5.00
2	10 Cents (Ag) 1968. Same type as No. 1	8.00
3	20 Cents (Ag) 1968. Same type as No. 1	15.00
4	50 Cents (Ag) 1968. Same type as No. 1	50.00

5	1 Luhlanga (Ag) 1968. Same type as No. 1		65.00
6	1 Lilangeni (Au) 1968. ℞ coat of arms with lion and elephant supporting shield		700.00

		XF	Unc
7 (1)	1 Cent (Br) 1974, 1979; ananas	0.15	0.25
8 (2)	2 Cents (Br) 1974, 1979; trees	0.15	0.30
9 (3)	5 Cents (Cu-Ni) 1974, 1975, 1979	0.25	0.50

			XF	Unc
10 (4)	10	Cents (Cu-Ni) 1974. sugar-cane	0.35	0.70
11 (5)	20	Cents (Cu-Ni) 1974	0.50	1.25
12 (6)	50	Cents (Cu-Ni) 1974	1.25	2.50
13 (7)	1	Lilangeni (Cu-Ni) 1974	2.10	4.20

75th ANNIVERSARY OF THE BIRTH OF KING SOBHUZA II
1st ISSUE (7)

			Proof
14	5	Emalangeni (Ag) 1974	25.00
15	7½	Emalangeni (Ag) 1974	40.00
16	15	Emalangeni (Ag) 1974	75.00
17 (8)	5	Emalangeni (Au) 1974	80.00
18 (9)	10	Emalangeni (Au) 1974	160.00
19 (10)	20	Emalangeni (Au) 1974	320.00
20 (11)	25	Emalangeni (Au) 1974	380.00

FOR THE FAO COIN PLAN (3)

			XF	Unc
21 (13)	1	Cent (Br) 1975. Type as No. 7, but inscription FOOD FOR ALL	0.15	0.30
22 (14)	2	Cents (Br) 1975. Type as No. 8, but inscription INCREASE EXPORTS	0.20	0.40
23 (15)	10	Cents (Cu-Ni) 1975. Type as No. 10, but inscription FOOD FOR ALL	0.35	0.70

75th ANNIVERSARY OF THE BIRTH OF KING SOBHUZA II
2st ISSUE (3)

			Unc	Proof
24	10	Emalangeni (Ag) 1975	25.00	30.00
25 (12)	50	Emalangeni (Au) 1975	90.00	110.00
26	100	Emalangeni (Au) 1975	180.00	225.00

INTERNATIONAL WOMEN'S YEAR 1975

27 (16)	1	Lilangeni (Cu-Ni) 1975	6.00

FOR THE COIN PLAN

28 (17)	1	Lilangeni (Cu-Ni) 1976	6.00

WORLD FOOD DAY (2)

29	20	Cents (Cu-Ni) 1981	1.00
30	1	Lilangeni (Cu-Ni) 1981	6.00

Schweden **Sweden** **Suède**
Sverige

Area: 173,629 sq. mi. Population: 8,100,000.
Kingdom on the eastern part of the peninsula of Scandinavia.
Capital: Stockholm.

100 Öre = 1 Krona

OSKAR II 1872-1907

			VF	XF
1 (14)	1	Öre (Br) 1877–1905. Crowned mono-gram. ℞ value and date, surrounded by three crowns	4.50	9.00
2 (15)	2	Öre (Br) 1877–1905	4.50	9.00
3 (16)	5	Öre (Br) 1889–1905	5.00	10.00
4 (27)	10	Öre (Ag) 1880–1904. ℞ value, date	5.00	10.00
5 (28)	25	Öre (Ag) 1880–1905	7.50	15.00
6 (29)	1	Krona (Ag) 1890–1904. Oskar II, (1829–1907), King of Norway 1872–1905 (abdicated), King of Sweden (1872–1907). ℞ crowned arms	18.00	35.00
7 (30)	2	Kronor (Ag) 1890–1904	25.00	50.00
8 (24a)	5	Kronor (Au) 1901. Oskar II, head right. ℞ value and crowns in wreath	130.00	170.00
9 (25b)	10	Kronor (Au) 1901	160.00	200.00

10 (26b)	20	Kronor (Au) 1900–1902	500.00	600.00
11 (32)	1	Öre (Br) 1906–1907. Legend SVERI-GES VAL	2.50	5.00
12 (33)	2	Öre (Br) 1906–1907. Same type as No. 11	3.00	6.00

			VF	**XF**
13 (34)	5 Öre (Br) 1906–1907. Same type as No. 11		2.60	5.50
14 (35)	10 Öre (Ag) 1907. Crowned monogram, three crowns, legends SVERIGES VAL. ℞ value in wreath		3.50	6.50
15 (36)	25 Öre (Ag) 1907. Same type as No. 14		4.00	8.00
16 (37)	50 Öre (Ag) 1906–1907. Same type as No. 14		6.00	12.00
17 (38)	1 Krona (Ag) 1906–1907. Oskar II, head left. ℞ crowned arms		10.00	20.00
18 (39)	2 Kronor (Ag) 1906–1907		20.00	40.00

COMMEMORATIVE ISSUE FOR THE GOLDEN WEDDING ANNIVERSARY

19 (40)	2 Kronor (Ag) 1907. Oskar II, and Queen Sofia. ℞ crowned arms		22.00	37.00

GUSTAF V 1907–1950

20 (44)	1 Öre (Br) 1909–1950. Crowned monogram. ℞ three crowns, value		0.60	1.20
21 (45)	2 Öre (Br) 1909–1950		0.60	1.20

22 (46)	5 Öre (Br) 1909–1950		1.20	1.60
23 (47)	10 Öre (Ag) 1909–1942. Crowned arms. ℞ value		1.20	2.50
24 (48)	25 Öre (Ag) 1910–1941. ℞ value in wreath		2.50	4.00

25 (49)	50 Öre (Ag) 1911–1939. ℞ value in wreath		4.00	6.50

			VF	XF
26 (50)	1	Krona (Ag) 1910–1942	4.00	6.50
27 (51)	2	Kronor (Ag) 1910–1940	7.00	12.00
28 (52)	1	Öre (Fe) 1917–1919. Same type as No. 20	5.00	8.00
29 (53)	2	Öre (Fe) 1917–1919. Same type as No. 21	10.50	16.00
30 (54)	5	Öre (Fe) 1917–1919. Same type as No. 22	25.00	42.00
31 (55)	10	Öre (Ni–Br) 1920–1947. Crowned monogram. ℞ value	0.80	1.50
32 (56)	25	Öre (Ni–Br) 1921-1947. Rev. value surrounded by ears of wheat	1.25	2.50
33 (57)	50	Öre (Ni–Br) 1920-1947	1.60	3.00

			VF	XF
34 (62)	5	Kronor (Au) 1920. Gustav V (1858–1950), head right. ℞ value, three crowns, branches	170.00	220.00
35 (63)	20	Kronor (Au) 1925. ℞ crowned coat of arms, date	900.00	1000.00

COMMEMORATIVE ISSUE FOR THE
400th ANNIVERSARY OF THE WAR OF LIBERATION
LED BY GUSTAF VASA

			VF	XF
36 (58)	2	Kronor (Ag) 1921. Gustaf Erikson Vasa (1496–1560), regent from 1521 to 1523, King from 1523 to 1560. ℞ crowned arms	20.00	35.00

COMMEMORATIVE ISSUE FOR THE 300th ANNIVERSARY
OF THE DEATH OF GUSTAF II ADOLF

			VF	XF
37 (59)	2 Kronor (Ag) 1932. Gustaf II Adolf (1594–1632), head with wreath, right. ℞ memorial legend on tablet		20.00	30.00

COMMEMORATIVE ISSUE FOR THE
500th ANNIVERSARY OF THE SWEDISH RIKSDAG

		VF	XF
38 (60)	5 Kronor (Ag) 1935. Gustaf V, head left. ℞ coat of arms	20.00	30.00

COMMEMORATIVE ISSUE FOR THE 300th ANNIVERSARY
OF THE FOUNDING OF THE COLONY NEW SWEDEN
ON THE DELAWARE RIVER, BY PETER MINUIT
(MINNEWIT)

39 (61)	2 Kronor (Ag) 1938. Gustaf V, head left. ℞ Calmare Nyckel, sailing vessel of the emigrants; crown	14.00	18.50
40 (69)	1 Öre (Fe) 1942–1950. Crowned monogram. ℞ three crowns, value	1.00	2.00
41 (70)	2 Öre (Fe) 1942–1950	1.50	3.00
42 (71)	5 Öre (Fe) 1942–1950	3.00	6.00
43 (64)	10 Öre (Ag) 1942–1950. Crown. ℞ value	1.50	2.50
44 (65)	25 Öre (Ag) 1942–1950	2.00	3.50
45 (66)	50 Öre (Ag) 1943–1950	3.00	4.50
46 (67)	1 Krona (Ag) 1942–1950. Gustaf V, head left. ℞ crowned arms	4.00	7.00
47 (68)	2 Kronor (Ag) 1942–1950	5.00	6.50

GUSTAF VI ADOLF 1950–1973

48 (72)	1 Öre (Br) 1952–1971. Crown above king's name. ℞ value	0.15	0.25
49 (73)	2 Öre (Br) 1952–1971	0.15	0.25

			VF	XF
50 (74)	5 Öre (Br) 1952–1971		0.20	0.40
51 (75)	10 Öre (Ag) 1952–1962. Crown. ℞ value		0.80	1.60
52 (76)	25 Öre (Ag) 1952–1961		1.20	2.00

		VF	XF
53 (77)	50 Öre (Ag) 1952–1961	1.80	3.50
54 (78)	1 Krona (Ag) 1952–1968. Gustaf VI Adolf, head left. ℞ crowned arms	1.80	3.50

		VF	XF
55 (79)	2 Kronor (Ag) 1952–1967	3.60	6.00
56 (80)	5 Kronor (Ag) 1954–1955, 1971	5.50	11.00

COMMEMORATIVE ISSUE FOR THE
70th BIRTHDAY OF THE KING

			VF	XF
57 (81)	5 Kronor (Ag) 1952. Gustaf VI, Adolf (1882–1973), head left. ℞ crowned monogram		45.00	75.00

COMMEMORATIVE ISSUE FOR THE 150th ANNIVERSARY OF THE SWEDISH CONSTITUTION REFORM

58 (82) 5 Kronor (Ag) 1959. Gustaf VI Adolf. ℞ constitutionalists, book with constitution on platform with state emblem   12.00   20.00

COMMEMORATIVE ISSUE FOR THE 80th BIRTHDAY OF THE KING

59 (86) 5 Kronor (Ag) 1962. Gustaf VI Adolf (* 1882), head left. ℞ Pallas Athena with Bird of Wisdom, the owl (little owl = Athene noctua – Strigidae), symbolic of the king's archeologic and scientific interests   75.00   120.00

60 (83) 10 Öre (Cu–Ni) 1962–1973. Crown above monogram. ℞ value   0.10   0.20

61 (84) 25 Öre (Cu–Ni) 1962–1973   0.15   0.30

			VF	XF
62 (85)	50	Öre (Cu–Ni) 1962–1973	0.30	0.60
63 (78a)	1	Krona (Cu–Ni) 1968–1973. Same type as No. 54	0.40	0.75
64 (79a)	2	Kronor (Cu–Ni) 1968–1971. Same type as No. 55	1.00	2.00

COMMEMORATIVE ISSUE FOR THE 100th ANNIVERSARY
OF THE CONSTITUTION REFORM AND THE
INTRODUCTION OF THE TWO-CHAMBER LEGISLATURE

65 (87)	5	Kronor (Ag) 1966. Gustaf VI Adolf. ℞ tablet with memorial legend, surrounded by laurel branches	5.50	8.50

66 (88)	5	Öre (Br) 1972, 1973. Three crowns, name of country. ℞ value, date	0.12	0.25

67 (89)	5	Kronor (Cu–Ni) 1972. Gustaf VI Adolf. ℞ crowned coat of arms, motto, value	1.50	2.50

		VF	XF
68 (90) 10 Kronor (Ag) 1972		9.00	15.00

CARL XVI GUSTAF 1973-

CONSTITUTIONAL REFORM

	XF	Unc.
69 (97) 50 Kronor (Ag) 1975. Three crowns, value Rev. raised hands, symbolic for the consent		40.00
70 (91) 5 Öre (Al-Br) 1976-. Crowned monogram, divided date. Rev. value, country name	0.12	0.20
71 (92) 10 Öre (Cu-Ni) 1976-	0.12	0.20
72 (93) 25 Öre (Cu-Ni) 1976-	0.15	0.25
73 (94) 50 Öre (Cu-Ni) 1976-	0.25	0.40
74 (95) 1 Krona (Cu-Ni) 1976-. Head left of the King, inscription CARL XVI GUSTAF SVERIGE, date. Rev. crowned coat of arms, inscription FÖR SVERIGE I TIDEN, value	0.40	0.60
75 (96) 5 Kronor (Cu-Ni) 1976-. Crowned monogram, curved SVERIGE and date. Rev. value	1.25	2.50

FOR THE WEDDING OF KING CARL XVI GUSTAV ON JUNE 6, 1976

76 (97) 50 Kronor (Ag) 1976. King Carl XVI Gustav and Queen Silvia		40.00

SWEDISH ROYAL SUCCESSION LAW

77 200 Kronor (Ag) 1980		40.00

Schweiz # Switzerland # **Suisse**
Helvetia

Area: 16,500 sq. mi. Population: 6,300,000.
The dissociation from the German Nation within the Holy Roman Empire which had already taken place in 1499 was only recognized in 1648. The original cantons of Uri, Schwyz and Unterwalden constituted the nucleus of an independent Switzerland. Strict neutrality is maintained, enabling numerous international organizations to set up their headquarters there.
Capital: Berne.

100 Rappen (Centimes) = 1 Franken (Franc)

The Cantons of Switzerland

* Appenzell-Ausserrhoden: In the case of Appenzell-Innerrhoden and of the whole canton the initials VR are omitted.

			VF	XF
1 (18)	1	Rappen (Br) 1850–1941. Swiss cross on shield, the whole within wreath. ℞ value in wreath		
		a) 1850–1895, 1897–1938, 1940, 1941	1.25	2.50
		b) 1896 (only 36 pieces struck)	–.–	–.–
		c) 1939	20.00	40.00
2 (19)	2	Rappen (Br) 1850–1941		
		a) 1850–1893, 1897–1941	0.75	1.50
		b) 1896 (only 20 pieces struck)	–.–	–.–
3 (20)	5	Rappen (Bi) 1850–1877		
		a) 1850–1851, 1872–1874, 1876–1877	20.00	40.00
		b) 1850, without mint mark	480.00	800.00
		c) 1851, mint mark BB	260.00	400.00
4 (21)	10	Rappen (Bi) 1850–1876	22.00	40.00
		a) 1850–1851, 1871, 1873, 1876	400.00	600.00
		b) 1875	18.00	36.00
5 (22)	20	Rappen (Bi) 1850–1859		
6 (26)	½	Franken (Ag) 1850, 1851. Seated figure of Helvetia. ℞ value within wreath	105.00	180.00
7 (27)	1	Franken (Ag) 1850–1861. Type as No. 6:		
		a) 1850, 1851, 1861	120.00	250.00
		b) 1857 (only 526 pieces struck)	–.–	–.–
		c) 1860	200.00	320.00
8 (28)	2	Franken (Ag) 1850–1863. Type as No. 6:		
		a) 1850, 1863	250.00	350.00
		b) 1857 (only 622 pieces struck)	–.–	–.–
		c) 1860, 1862	100.00	180.00

			VF	XF
9 (29)	5	Franken (Ag) 1850–1874. Type as No. 6:		
		a) 1850–1874	130.00	230.00
		b) 1873	600.00	1200.00
10 (23)	5	Rappen 1879–. Female head right. ℞ value within wreath		
		a) (Cu–Ni) 1879, 1887, 1889	26.00	60.00
		b) (Cu–Ni) 1880–1905	2.50	8.00
		c) (Cu–Ni) 1896 (only 16 pieces struck)	–.–	–.–

			VF	XF
	d) (Cu–Ni) 1906–1931, 1940, 1942–		0.05	0.10
	c) (Ni) 1932–1939, 1941		0.30	0.60
	f) (Al-Br) 1981–		0.05	0.10

11 (24) 10 Rappen 1879–. Type as No. 10:

a) (Cu–Ni) 1879	20.00	40.00
b) (Cu–Ni) 1880–1899	4.00	12.00
c) (Cu–Ni) 1896 (only 16 pieces struck)	–.–	–.–
d) (Cu–Ni) 1900–1931, 1940–	0.05	0.10
e) (Ni) 1932–1939	0.20	0.50

12 (25) 20 Rappen 1881–. Type as No. 10:

a) (Ni) 1881–1938	0.25	0.50
b) (Cu–Ni) 1939–	0.10	0.20

13 (30) ½ Franken (Ag) 1875–1967. Standing figure of Helvetia. ℞ value within wreath:

a) 1875–1894	40.00	90.00
b) 1896 (only 28 pieces struck)	–.–	–.–
c) 1898–1967	1.50	2.50
d) 1901	75.00	160.00

14 (31) 1 Franken (Ag) 1875–1967. Type as No. 13:

a) 1875–1880	75.00	150.00
b) 1886–1901	20.00	52.00
c) 1896 (only 28 pieces struck)	–.–	–.–
d) 1903–1967	2.50	4.00

			VF	**XF**
15 (32)	2 Franken (Ag) 1874–1967. Type as No. 13:			
	a) 1874–1894		25.00	50.00
	b) 1896 (only 20 pieces struck)		–.–	–.–
	c) 1901		225.00	1000.00
	d) 1903–1967		4.50	8.00

16 (33)	5 Franken (Ag) 1888–1916. Female head left. ℞ Swiss cross on shield, above with star, value, the whole within wreath:			
	a) 1888, 1900, 1916		600.00	1100.00
	b) 1889-1892, 1904, 1907-1909		125.00	220.00
	c) 1894, 1895		420.00	750.00
	d) 1896 (only 2000 pieces struck)		–.–	–.–
	e) 1912		1200.00	2400.00

17 (40) 20 Franken (Au) 1883–1896. Female head left. ℞ Swiss cross on shield, above with star, value, the whole within wreath:

	VF	XF
a) 1883–1896	110.00	125.00
b) 1888	7000.00	10000.00

18 (41)   20   Franken (Au) 1897–1949. Female bust left of "Vreneli". ℞ Swiss cross on shield, value, date:

a) 1897–1949	90.00	110.00
b) 1926	175.00	220.00

19 (42)   10   Franken (Au) 1911–1922

	a) 1911	260.00	340.00
	b) 1912–1922	80.00	100.00
20 (43)	100 Franken (Au) 1925. Type as No. 19	7000.00	10000.00
21 (23b)	5 Rappen (Bra) 1918. Type as No. 10	16.00	26.00
22 (24b)	10 Rappen (Bra) 1918–1919. Type as No. 11		
	a) 1918	25.00	30.00
	b) 1919	70.00	100.00
23 (34)	5 Franken (Ag) 1922, 1923. Bust of shepherd to right. ℞ Swiss cross on shield, value "5 Fr.", date. Diameter: 37 mm	65.00	90.00
24 (34a)	5 Franken (Ag) 1924–1928. Type as No. 23, but value "5 FR":		
	a) 1924	220.00	400.00
	b) 1925, 1926	80.00	160.00
	c) 1928	2600.00	4000.00
25 (36)	5 Franken (Ag) 1931–1967, 1969. Type as No. 24, but diameter: 31 mm:		
	a) 1931–1951	7.00	15.00
	b) 1952	45.00	90.00
	c) 1953–1967, 1969	7.00	12.00

COMMEMORATIVE MEDALS (2)
FOR THE RIFLEMENS MEETING IN FRIBOURG

		VF	XF
26 (44)	5 Franken (Ag) 1934. Standing soldier. ℞ crowned arms within wreath	35.00	60.00
27 (45)	100 Franken (Au) 1934	2500.00	2700.00

COMMEMORATIVE ISSUE FOR
THE CONFEDERATION ARMAMENT FUND

		VF	XF
28 (46)	5 Franken (Ag) 1936. Kneeling female figure with sword and dove held level. ℞ steel helmet above inscription within square	26.00	40.00

COMMEMORATIVE MEDALS (2)
FOR THE RIFLEMENS MEETING IN LUCERNE

29 (47)   5 Franken (Ag) 1939. Kneeling figure r.

	VF	XF
shooting. ℞ legend reading EINER FÜR ALLE, ALLE FÜR EINEN (One for all, all for one)	32.00	55.00
30 (48) 100 Franken (Au) 1939	700.00	800.00

COMMEMORATIVE ISSUE FOR THE 600th ANNIVERSARY OF THE BATTLE OF LAUPEN

31 (49)   5 Franken (Ag) 1939. Male figure facing. ℞ Swiss cross   265.00   420.00

COMMEMORATIVE MEDAL FOR THE SWISS NATIONAL EXPOSITION IN ZÜRICH

32 (50)   5 Franken (Ag) 1939. Agricultural scene, below which hands clasped. ℞ national arms over inscription   55.00   100.00

COMMEMORATIVE ISSUE FOR THE 650th ANNIVERSARY OF THE CONFEDERATION

33 (51)   5 Franken (Ag) 1941. Oath scene at the

			VF	XF
		Rütli. Three standing figures representing the original cantons of Uri, Schwyz and Unterwalden. ℞ inscription	40.00	75.00
34 (18a)	1	Rappen (Sn) 1942–1946. Type as No. 1	0.40	1.20
35 (19a)	2	Rappen (Sn) 1942–1946. Type as No. 2		
		a) 1942–1945	0.60	1.50
		b) 1946	16.00	25.00

COMMEMORATIVE ISSUE FOR THE 500th ANNIVERSARY OF THE BATTLE OF ST. JAKOB AN DER BIRS

			VF	XF
36 (52)	5	Franken (Ag) 1944. Warrior fighting. ℞ inscription	40.00	70.00

COMMEMORATIVE ISSUE FOR THE CENTENNIAL OF THE SWISS CONFEDERATION

			VF	XF
37 (53)	5	Franken (Ag) 1948. Group representing mother and child. ℞ inscription, Swiss cross	16.00	26.00
38	25	Franken (Au) 1955–1959. William Tell holding crossbow. ℞ value	–.–	–.–
39	50	Franken (Au) 1955–1959. Oath scene at the Rütli. Three standing figures representing the original cantons of Uri, Schwyz and Unterwalden. ℞ value	–.–	–.–

Coins Nos. 32 and 33 have not yet been issued.

			VF	XF
40 (54)	1	Rappen (Br) 1948–. Swiss cross. ℞ value and ear of corn	0.02	0.04

		VF	XF
41 (55)	2 Rappen (Br) 1948–1974, 1978	0.02	0.04

COMMEMORATIVE ISSUE FOR THE CENTENARY
OF THE RED CROSS

		VF	XF
42 (56)	5 Franken (Ag) 1963. Nurse standing and patient on stretcher, in form of cross. ℞ value	12.00	18.00
43 (30a)	½ Franken (Cu–Ni) 1968–. As No. 13	0.25	0.40
44 (31a)	1 Franken (Cu–Ni) 1968–. As No. 14	0.45	0.65
45 (32a)	2 Franken (Cu–Ni) 1968–. As No. 15	0.80	1.20
46 (36a)	5 Franken (Cu–Ni) 1968, 1970–. As No. 25	2.20	2.60

COMMEMORATIVE ISSUE FOR THE 100th ANNIVERSARY
OF THE REVISION OF THE CONSTITUTION
(29th May 1874)

		Unc	Proof
47 (57)	5 Franken (Cu–Ni) 1974	4.00	16.00

EUROPEAN MONUMENT PROTECTION YEAR

		Unc	Proof
48 (58)	5 Franken (Cu-Ni) 1975	4.00	18.00

49 (59) 500th ANNIVERSARY OF THE BATTLE OF MURTEN

	5 Franken (Cu-Ni) 1976	4.00	14.00

150th ANNIVERSARY OF THE DEATH OF J. H. PESTALOZZI

50 (60)	5 Franken (Cu-Ni) 1977	6.00	20.00

150th ANNIVERSARY OF THE BIRTH OF HENRY DUNANT

51 (61)	5 Franken (Cu-Ni) 1978	4.00	16.00

100th ANNIVERSARY OF THE BIRTH OF ALBERT EINSTEIN (2)

52 (62)	5 Franken (Cu-Ni) 1979. Portrait	6.00	60.00
53 (63)	5 Franken (Cu-Ni) 1979. Formula	4.00	45.00

HODLER COMMEMORATIVE

54 (64)	5 Franken (Cu-Ni) 1980. Ferdinand Hodler (1853–1918), painter	3.50	40.00

STANS CONVENTION OF 1481

55 (65)	5 Franken (Cu-Ni) 1981	3.50	20.00

Syria

Area: 12,234 sq. mi. Population: 6,600,000.
Following the collapse of the Ottoman Empire, Syria became a French Mandate, and later on, in 1944, independent. From 1958 to 1961 Syria belonged to the United Arab Republic.
Capital: Damascus.

100 Piastres = 1 Lira (£)

SYRIAN STATE 1920-1944

			VF	XF
1 (1)	½ Piastre (Cu–Ni) 1921. Value within wreath. ℞ value		2.50	4.00
2 (2)	2 Piastres (Al–Br) 1926		3.50	6.00
3 (3)	5 Piastres (Al–Br) 1926–1940		1.50	2.50
4 (4)	½ Piastre (Ni–Bra) 1935–1936		1.50	2.50
5 (5)	1 Piastre:			
	a) (Ni–Bra) 1929–1936		1.20	2.00
	b) (Sn) 1940		1.20	2.00
6 (6)	2½ Piastres (Al–Br) 1940		2.50	4.00
7 (7)	10 Piastres (Ag) 1929. Rosette design		6.00	11.00
8 (8)	25 Piastres (Ag) 1929–1938		11.00	16.00

9 (9)	50 Piastres (Ag) 1929–1937		16.00	20.00
10 (10)	1 Piastre (Bra) undated (1942)		2.50	4.00
11 (11)	2½ Piastres (Al) undated (1943)		2.50	4.00

SYRIAN REPUBLIC 1944-1958

12 (12)	2½ Piastres (Cu–Ni) 1948–1956. Coat of arms. ℞ value		0.40	0.80
13 (13)	5 Piastres (Cu–Ni) 1948–1956		0.40	0.80
14 (14)	10 Piastres (Cu–Ni) 1948–1956		0.40	0.80
15 (15)	25 Piastres (Ag) 1947		2.60	4.50
16 (16)	50 Piastres (Ag) 1947		3.50	6.50

			VF	XF
17 (17)	1	Lira (Ag) 1950	6.50	11.00
18 (18)	½	£ (Au) 1950. Coat of arms. ℞ legend in quadrangle	100.00	115.00
19 (19)	1	£ (Au) 1950	125.00	160.00

UNITED ARAB REPUBLIC 1958–1961

20 (21)	2½	Piastres (Al–Br) 1960. New coat of arms. ℞ value	0.20	0.40
21 (22)	5	Piastres (Al–Br) 1960	0.30	0.60
22 (23)	10	Piastres (Al–Br) 1960	0.40	0.80
23 (A19)	25	Piastres (Ag) 1958. ℞ value and ears of wheat, surrounded by cog-wheel	1.50	3.00
24 (B19)	50	Piastres (Ag) 1958	2.50	4.50

COMMEMORATIVE ISSUE FOR THE FOUNDING OF THE UNITED ARAB REPUBLIC ON MARCH 1, 1958

25 (20)	50	Piastres (Ag) 1959. Coat of arms. ℞ value, date, and commemorative legend	3.50	4.50

SYRIAN ARAB REPUBLIC since 1961

26 (24)	2½	Piastres (Al–Br) 1962–. Coat of arms of the Republic. ℞ value	0.10	0.20
27 (25)	5	Piastres (Al–Br) 1962–	0.15	0.25
28 (26)	10	Piastres (Al–Br) 1962–	0.30	0.45
29 (27)	25	Piastres (Ni) 1968	0.40	0.60
30 (28)	50	Piastres (Ni) 1968	0.60	0.90
31 (29)	1	Lira (Ni) 1968	1.00	1.40

				XF	Unc
32 (31)	5	Piastres (Bra) 1971. With design of olives and wheat and inscription "Food for All"		0.25	0.40

				XF	Unc
33 (30)	1	Lira (Ni) 1968. Coat of arms. ℞ pair of hands holding sign reading "Campaign against Hunger"; above five ears of wheat		1.20	2.00

COMMEMORATIVE ISSUES (3) FOR THE 25th ANNIVERSARY OF THE BAATH PARTY

34 (32)	25	Piastres (Ni) 1972. New coat of arms (without stars in the breast-shield), date. Rev. torch, value		0.40	0.60
35 (33)	50	Piastres (Ni) 1972. Type similar to No. 34		0.60	0.80
36 (34)	1	Lira (Ni) 1972. Type similar to No. 34		1.00	1.50
37 (35)	2½	Piastres (Bra) 1973. Type similar to No. 26 (without stars in the breast-shield)		0.10	0.15
38 (36)	5	Piastres (Al-Br) 1974. Type similar to No. 27 (without stars in the breast-shield)		0.12	0.20
39 (37)	10	Piastres (Al-Br) 1974. Type similar to No. 28 (without stars in the breast-shield)		0.25	0.40

			XF	**Unc**
40 (38)	25	Piastres (Ni) 1974. Type similar to No. 29 (without stars in the breast-shield)	0.35	0.50
41 (39)	50	Piastres (Ni) 1974. Type similar to No. 30 (without stars in the breast-shield)	0.50	0.75
42 (40)	1	Lira (Ni) 1974. Type similar to No. 31 (without stars in the breast-shield)	0.80	1.20

FOR THE FAO COIN PLAN (5)

43 (41)	5	Piastres (Bra) 1976. Rev. Euphrates Dam	0.10	0.15
44 (42)	10	Piastres (Bra) 1976. Type as No. 43	0.15	0.25
45 (43)	25	Piastres (Ni) 1976. Type as No. 43	0.20	0.40
46 (44)	50	Piastres (Ni) 1976. Type as No.43	0.30	0.60
47 (45)	1	Lira (Ni) 1976. Type as No. 43	0.40	0.80

RE-ELECTION OF HAFEZ AL-ASAD

48	1	Lira (Ni) 1978. Coat of arms. Rev. Portrait	1.00	1.50
49	5	Piastres (Bra) 1979	0.15	0.25
50	10	Piastres (Bra) 1979	0.15	0.25
51	25	Piastres (Ni) 1979	0.25	0.35
52	50	Piastres (Ni) 1979	0.40	0.55
53	1	Lira (Ni) 1979	0.60	0.80

Taiwan

Taiwan
Nationalist China

Formose

Area: 13,890 sq. mi. Population: 16,000,000.
From 1895 to 1942 Taiwan came under a governor general as a Japanese outlying possession. Since Taiwan had only temporarily been a part of the Japanese state, the return of the country to China took place in 1945. The Kuomintang government under Chiang Kai-shek retreated to the island in 1949 before the troops of Mao Tse-tung. On March 1, 1950 the Chinese Nationalist Republic was proclaimed.
Capital: Taipeh.

10 Cents = 1 Chiao, 100 Cents = 1 Taiwan Dollar

			VF	XF
1 (531)	1 Chiao (Br) 1949. Chiang Kai-shek (1886–1975), President. ℞ map of Formosa		0.30	0.50
2 (533)	1 Chiao (Al) 1955		0.15	0.25

3 (534)	2 Chiao (Al) 1950		0.20	0.40
4 (532)	5 Chiao (Ag) 1949		3.00	6.00
5 (535)	5 Chiao (Bra) 1954		0.20	0.40
6 (536)	1 Dollar (Ag) 1960. Plum blossom (Prunus sp. – Rosaceae). ℞ orchid (Dendrobium sp. – Orchidaceae)		0.50	0.90

COMMEMORATIVE ISSUES (6) FOR THE 100th BIRTHDAY OF DR. SUN YAT-SEN

7 (537)	5 Dollars (Cu–Ni) 1965. Dr. Sun Yat-sen (1866–1925). ℞ mausoleum in Nanking		1.50	2.50
8 (538)	10 Dollars (Cu–Ni) 1965. Same type as No. 7		2.00	3.00

			VF	XF
9 (539)	50	Dollars (Ag) 1965. Dr. Sun Yat-sen. ℞ sambar (Cervus = Rusa unicolor – Cervidae), with Manchurian crane above	10.00	12.50
10 (540)	100	Dollars (Ag) 1965. Same type as No. 9	12.00	16.00
11 (541)	1000	Dollars (Au) 1965. Dr. Sun Yat-sen, in profile. ℞ value between branches	–.–	–.–
12 (542)	2000	Dollars (Au) 1965. Same type as No. 11	–.–	–.–

COMMEMORATIVE ISSUES (2) FOR THE 80th BIRTHDAY OF CHIANG KAI-SHEK

13 (543)	1	Dollar (Cu–Ni) 1966. Chiang Kai-shek (1886-1975). ℞ value	0.60	0.80
14 (544)	2000	Dollars (Au) 1966. Chiang Kai-shek. ℞ Manchurian cranes (Grus japonensis – Gruidae), promising happiness and long life		450.00
15 (545)	1	Chiao (Al) 1967–. Orchid (Phalaenopsis sp. – Orchidaceae). ℞ value	0.12	0.20
16 (546)	5	Chiao (Al–Br) 1967. Orchid (Cattleya hybr. – Orchidaceae). ℞ value	0.30	0.60

COMMEMORATIVE ISSUE FOR THE FAO COIN PLAN AND FOR THE 24th ANNIVERSARY OF THE FAO
(16. 10. 1969)

17 (547)	1	Dollar (Cu–Ni) 1969. Plum blossom, surrounded by Chinese writing with implication toward the FAO campaign. ℞ female farm laborer and tractor; value	1.20	2.00

18 (548)	5	Dollars (Cu–Ni) 1970. Chiang Kai-shek, head left. ℞ value in circle of ornamentations	0.50	1.20

90th ANNIVERSARY OF THE BIRTH OF CHIANG-KAI-SHEK

		Unc
19 (549)	150 Dollars (Ag) 1976	15.00

Note: with the coinage appearing upon the occasion of the 60th birthday of the Republic in silver and gold, according the official information, these are medals.

70th ANNIVERSARY OF THE FOUNDING OF THE REPUBLIC OF CHINA (4)

20	½ Dollar (Al-Br) 1981	0.25	0.40

21	1 Dollar (Al-Br) 1981	0.35	0.50
22	5 Dollars (Cu-Ni) 1981	0.50	0.80

23	10 Dollars (Cu-Ni) 1981	1.50	2.50

Tansania # Tanzania # **Tanzanie**

Area: 363,700 sq. mi. Population: 17,000,000.
The Republic of Tanganyika and the People's Republic of Zanzibar
with Pemba united to form the United Republic of Tanganyika-Zanzibar
on April 26, 1964; renaming of the state designation in October of the
same year to Tanzania.
Capital: Dar-es-Salaam.

100 Senti (Cents) = 1 Tanzania Shilingi (Shilling)

			VF	XF
1 (1)	5 Senti (Br) 1966–. Julius Kambarage Nyerere (*1921), President of State. ℞ Indo-Pacific sailfish (Istiophorus gladius – Istiophoridae)		0.08	0.15

2 (2)	20 Senti (Ni–Bra) 1966–. ℞ ostrich (Struthio camelus – Struthionidae)	0.15	0.30
3 (3)	50 Senti (Cu–Ni) 1966–. ℞ Smith's red hare (Pronolagus crassicaudatus – Leporidae)	0.25	0.50
4 (4)	1 Shilingi (Cu–Ni) 1966–. ℞ Freedom torch	0.40	0.70

ISSUE FOR THE FAO COIN PLAN

5 (5a)	5 Shilingi (Cu–Ni) 1972, 1973. ℞ value in circle, surrounded with bananas, millet, maize and a zebu	1.25	2.50

COMMEMORATIVE ISSUE FOR THE 10th ANNIVERSARY OF THE INDEPENDENCE OF TANGANYIKA

6 (5)	5 Shilingi (Cu–Ni) 1971. Type as No. 5, but dates 1961–1971 behind the portrait	1.00	2.00

CONSERVATION COMMEMORATIVE (3)

			Unc	Proof
7 (6)	25	Shilingi (Ag) 1974. Rev. southern giraffe	30.00	35.00
8 (7)	50	Shilingi (Ag) 1974. Rev. black rhino	50.00	60.00
9 (8)	1500	Shilingi (Au) 1974. Rev. cheetah	650.00	700.00

10th ANNIVERSARY OF THE BANK OF TANZANIA

			XF	Unc
10 (9)	5	Shilingi (Cu-Ni) 1976. Building of the Bank of Tanzania	0.80	1.50
11 (11)	10	Senti (Bra) 1977, 1979	0.20	0.40

FAO REGIONAL CONFERENCE FOR AFRICA

12 (10)	5	Shilingi (Cu-Ni) 1978	1.00	1.50

20th ANNIVERSARY OF INDEPENDENCE (3)

			Unc	Proof
13	20	Shilingi (Ag) 1981	–.–	–.–
14	200	Shilingi (Ag) 1981	–.–	–.–
15	2000	Shilingi (Au) 1981	–.–	–.–

Thailand

Area: 198,247 sq. mi. Population: 45,000,000.
The Thai people originating from South China, pressed back the
Khmer and founded the kingdom of Sukothai. After changeable battles,
particularly also with the Burmese, Chao Phraya Chakri in 1782 founded
the Chakri Dynasty as King Rama I which has been governing until
the present day. In place of the old state designation of Siam, the name
of Thailand (Land of the Free People) is being used since 1939.
Capital: Bangkok.

64 Att = 8 Füang, 1 Füang = $^1/_8$ Baht, 1 Salüng = $^1/_4$ Baht,
1 Solot = $^1/_2$ Att = $^1/_{128}$ Baht, 1 Sio = 2 Att,
100 Satangs or Stangs = 1 Baht (Bat)

CHULALONGKORN (RAMA V) 1868–1910

			VF	XF
1 (21)	1 Solot (Br) 1887–1905. Rama V (1853–1910), portrait left. ℞ heavenly nymph with shield		2.50	3.00
2 (22)	1 Att (Br) 1887–1905		2.50	4.00
3 (23)	1 Sio (Br) 1887–1905		3.00	5.00
4 (32)	1 Füang (Ag) 1876–1908. Rama V, portrait left. ℞ coat of arms			
	a) 1876–1902 (undated)		3.00	4.00
	b) 1902–1908		6.00	8.00
5 (33)	1 Salüng (Ag) 1876–1908			
	a) 1876–1901 (undated)		8.00	12.00
	b) 1901–1908		10.00	15.00

6 (34)	1 Baht (Ag) 1878–1907			
	a) 1878–1900 (undated)		6.00	10.00
	b) 1901–1907		8.00	12.00

			VF	XF
7 (39)	1	Baht (Ag) 1908. Rama V, portrait left. R three-headed elephant	160.00	200.00
8 (35)	1	Satang (Br) 1908–1937. Common cobra (Naja naja – Elapidae or Elaphidae); (Sanskrit: naga). R kongchak, mythological weapon of the Hindu God Vishnu (a disc with very sharp teeth) (center hole)	0.40	0.60
9 (36)	5	Satangs (Ni) 1908–1937. Same as No. 8	0.50	0.80
10 (37)	10	Satangs (Ni) 1908–1937. Same as No. 8	0.50	0.80

VAJIRAVUDH (RAMA VI) 1910–1925

			VF	XF
11 (43)	1	Salüng (Ag) 1913, 1917–1919, 1924–1925. Rama VI (1881–1925), portrait right. R three-headed elephant	4.00	7.50
12 (44)	2	Salüng (Ag) 1913, 1919–1921	5.00	8.00

			VF	XF
13 (45)	1	Baht (Ag) 1913–1918	8.00	12.00

PRAJADHIPOK (RAMA VII) 1925–1935

			VF	XF
14 (48)	25	Satangs (Ag) 1929. Rama VII (1893–1941), portrait left. R Asiatic elephant (Elephas maximus – Elephantidae)	6.00	9.00
15 (49)	50	Satangs (Ag) 1929	8.00	12.00

ANANDA MAHIDOL (RAMA VIII) 1935–1946

			VF	XF
16 (50)	½	Satang (Br) 1937	0.40	0.60
17 (51)	1	Satang (Br) 1939	0.50	0.70
18 (54)	1	Satang (Br) 1941. Decorative design. R name of country, value (center hole)	0.60	1.00
19 (55)	5	Satangs (Ag) 1941	2.00	3.00
20 (56)	10	Satangs (Ag) 1941	3.00	5.00
21 (A56)	20	Satangs (Ag) 1942	6.00	8.00
22 (57)	1	Satang (Zn) 1942 (without center hole)	0.25	0.40
23 (58)	5	Satangs (Zn) 1942 (center hole)	0.50	0.80
24 (59)	10	Satangs (Zn) 1942 (center hole)	1.00	1.50

			VF	**XF**
		Value and date in Arabic numerals		
25 (60)	1	Satang (Zn) 1944 (without hole)	0.25	0.40
26 (61)	5	Satangs (Zn) 1944–1945 (with center hole)		
		a) 1944–1945, thick flan	0.50	0.80
		b) 1945, thin flan	0.60	1.00
27 (62)	10	Satangs (Zn) 1944–1945 (center hole)		
		a) 1944, thick flan	1.20	1.60
		b) 1945, thin flan	1.40	1.80

			VF	**XF**
28 (63)	20	Satangs (Zn) 1945	2.00	2.50
29 (64)	5	Satangs (Zn) 1946. Rama VIII (1925–1946), as child, portrait left. ℞ garuda, mythological bird	2.00	3.00
30 (65)	10	Satangs (Zn) 1946	2.50	3.50
31 (66)	25	Satangs (Zn) 1946	4.00	6.00
32 (67)	50	Satangs (Zn) 1946	9.00	12.00
33 (68)	5	Satangs (Zn) 1946. Rama VIII, portrait left	0.40	0.60
34 (69)	10	Satangs (Zn) 1946	0.50	0.80
35 (70)	25	Satangs (Zn) 1946	0.50	0.80
36 (71)	50	Satangs (Zn) 1946	0.90	1.20

PHUMIPHOL ADULYADET (RAMA IX) since 1946

			VF	**XF**
37 (72)	5	Satangs (Zn) 1950. Rama IX (*1927), in uniform decorated with one medal. ℞ coat of arms	0.25	0.40
38 (72a)	5	Satangs (Al–Br) 1950	0.25	0.40
39 (73)	10	Satangs (Zn) 1950	0.40	0.60
40 (73a)	10	Satangs (Al–Br) 1950	0.40	0.60
41 (76)	25	Satangs (Al–Br) 1950	0.50	0.80
42 (77)	50	Satangs (Al–Br) 1950	0.60	1.00
43 (78)	5	Satangs 1957. Rama IX in uniform decorated with three medals. ℞ coat of arms		
		a) (Al–Br)	0.10	0.20
		b) (Br)	0.10	0.20
44 (79)	10	Satangs 1957		
		a) (Al–Br)	0.20	0.40
		b) (Br)	0.35	0.50
45 (80)	25	Satangs (Al–Br) 1957	0.40	0.60
46 (81)	50	Satangs (Al–Br) 1957	0.55	0.80
47 (82)	1	Baht (Cu–Ni–St) 1957	1.50	2.00

			VF	XF
48 (83)	1	Baht (Cu–Ni) 1961. Rama IX and Queen Sirikit. ℞ coat of arms	1.20	2.00
49 (84)	1	Baht (Cu–Ni) 1962. Rama IX, legend, arranged in semicircle	1.00	1.50

COMMEMORATIVE ISSUES (2) FOR THE KING'S 36th BIRTHDAY

			VF	XF
50 (85)	1	Baht (Cu–Ni) 1963. Rama IX. ℞ royal insignia	0.60	1.20
51 (86)	20	Baht (Ag) 1963	10.50	14.00

COMMEMORATIVE ISSUE FOR THE 5th ASIAN GAMES FROM DECEMBER 9 TO DECEMBER 20, 1966, IN BANGKOK

			VF	XF
52 (87)	1	Baht (Cu–Ni) 1966. Rama IX and Queen Sirikit. ℞ emblem of the games, Motto: EVER ONWARD	0.60	0.80

COMMEMORATIVE ISSUES (3) FOR QUEEN SIRIKIT'S 36th BIRTHDAY, ON AUGUST 12, 1968

			Unc
53 (88)	150	Baht (Au) 1968. Queen Sirikit Kitiya-kara (*1932), portrait right. ℞ crowned monogram in wreath, value below	65.00
54 (89)	300	Baht (Au) 1968. Same type as No. 53	130.00
55 (90)	600	Baht (Au) 1968. Same type as No. 53	260.00

COMMEMORATIVE ISSUE FOR THE 6th ASIAN GAMES IN BANGKOK

			VF	XF
56 (91)	1	Baht (Cu–Ni) 1970. Similar to No. 52	0.40	0.60

COMMEMORATIVE ISSUES (3) FOR 25 YEARS OF REIGN
ON JUNE 9, 1971

			XF	Unc
57 (92)	10 Baht (Ag) 1971. Rama IX, bust right. Ɍ royal insignia		3.50	4.00

58 (93)	400 Baht (Au) 1971. Same type as No. 57		120.00
59 (94)	800 Baht (Au) 1971. Same type as No. 57		250.00

COMMEMORATIVE ISSUE FOR THE 20th ANNIVERSARY
OF THE WORLD FELLOWSHIP OF BUDDHISTS

60 (95)	50 Baht (Ag) 1971. Rama IX. Ɍ the bud-dhists wheel of the law (The Dhama-chakr)	15.00	20.00

COMMEMORATIVE ISSUE FOR THE 21st BIRTHDAY
OF CROWN PRINCE VAJIRALONGKORN

61 (97)	1 Baht (Cu–Ni) 1972	0.35	0.40
62 (98)	5 Baht (Cu–Ni) 1973	0.80	1.20

COMMEMORATIVE ISSUE FOR THE FAO COIN PLAN

63 (96)	1 Baht (Cu–Ni) 1973. Design shows the State Ploughing Ceremony, and ancient festival of Hindu origin which is now officially celebrated each year as a symbol government action for agricultural development. This coin was released on State Ploughing Day, 7 May 1973. The inscription reads 'FAO Thailand – With the improvement of agriculture the country prospers'	0.40	0.60

COMMEMORATIVE ISSUE FOR THE 25th ANNIVERSARY
OF THE WORLD HEALTH ORGANIZATION (WHO)

64 (99)	1 Baht (Cu–Ni) 1973. Ɍ Emblem of the WHO	0.30	0.50

100th ANNIVERSARY OF THE NATIONAL MUSEUM

65 (101)	50 Baht (Ag) 1974	7.50	11.50
66 (100)	1 Baht (Cu–Ni) 1974	0.25	0.40

		Unc	**Proof**

CONSERVATION COMMEMORATIVE (3)

			Unc	Proof
67 (102)	50 Baht (Ag) 1975. Rev. Sumatran rhino		30.00	40.00
68 (103)	100 Baht (Ag) 1975. Rev. Brow-antlered deer		35.00	50.00
69 (104)	2500 Baht (Au) 1975. Rev. whiteeyed river martin		650.00	900.00

8th ASIAN GAMES IN BANGKOK

			XF	Unc
70 (105)	1 Baht (Cu-Ni) 1975. Conjoined heads of the royal couple		0.25	0.40

100th ANNIVERSARY OF THE FINANCE MINISTRY

71 (106)	100 Baht (Ag) 1975		20.00	26.00

75th ANNIVERSARY OF THE BIRTH OF PRINCESS MOTHER (2)

72 (107)	1 Baht (Cu-Ni) 1976. Bust of Princess Mother. Rev. emblem		0.25	0.40
73 (108)	150 Baht (Ag) 1976. Type as No. 72		17.00	22.00

74 (110)	1 Baht (Cu-Ni) 1977. Head left of the King. Rev. royal barque		0.20	0.30

FOR THE FAO COIN PLAN (2)

75 (112)	1 Baht (Cu-Ni) 1977. Rice goddess		0.25	0.40
76 (113)	150 Baht (Ag) 1977. Elephants		17.00	22.00

GRADUATION OF PRINCESS SIRINTHORN (4)

		XF	Unc
77 (114)	1 Baht (Cu-Ni) 1977	0.25	0.40
78 (115)	10 Baht (Ni) 1977	0.80	1.30
79 (116)	150 Baht (Ag) 1977	17.00	22.00
80	2500 Baht (Au) 1977		220.00

WEDDING OF CROWN-PRINCE VIJIRALONGKORN (3)

81 (117)	10 Baht (Ni) 1977	0.80	1.30
82 (118)	150 Baht (Ag) 1977	17.00	22.00
83 (119)	2500 Baht (Au) 1977		220.00
84 (109)	25 Satangs (Bra) 1977	0.10	0.20

85 (111)	5 Baht (Cu-Ni) 1977; dia. 30 mm	0.60	0.9*

50th ANNIVERSARY OF THE BIRTH OF THE KING (2)

86 (120)	5 Baht (Cu-Ni) 1977	0.50	1.00
87 (122)	5000 Baht (Au) 1977		400.00

9th WORLD ORCHEED CONFERENCE IN BANGKOK

88 (123)	150 Baht (Ag) 1978. Bust of the King. Rev. orchid blossoms	18.00	22.00

INVESTITURE OF PRINCESS SIRINTHORN (3)

89 (124)	1 Baht (Cu-Ni) 1978	0.25	0.40
90 (125)	150 Baht (Ag) 1978	18.00	22.00
91 (126)	2500 Baht (Au) 1978		210.00

GRADUATION OF PRINCE VIJIRALONGKORN (3)

				XF	Unc
92 (127)	1	Baht (Cu-Ni) 1978		0.25	0.40
93 (128)	150	Baht (Ag) 1978		18.00	22.00
94 (129)	3000	Baht (Au) 1978			210.00

8th ASIAN GAMES (2)

95 (130)	1	Baht (Cu-Ni) 1978	0.25	0.40
96 (131)	5	Baht (Cu-Ni) 1978	0.60	1.00

ROYAL CRADLE CEREMONY (2)

97 (132)	5	Baht (Cu-Ni) 1979	0.60	1.00

98 (133)	200	Baht (Ag) 1979	20.00	25.00

GRADUATION OF PRINCESS CHULABHORN (3)

99 (134)	2	Baht (Cu-Ni) 1979	0.40	0.60
100 (135)	10	Baht (Cu-Ni) 1979	0.80	1.30
101 (136)	300	Baht (Ag) 1979	32.00	38.00

			XF	Unc
102 (137)	5	Baht (Cu-Ni) 1980	0.40	0.60
103 (138)	600	Baht (Ag) 1980		52.00
104 (139)	9000	Baht (Au) 1980		500.00

80th ANNIVERSARY OF THE BIRTH OF KING'S MOTHER (2)

105 (140)	5	Baht (Cu-Ni) 1980	0.40	0.60
106 (141)	10	Baht (Cu-Ni) 1980	0.80	1.30

KING RAMA VI BIRTH CENTENNIAL (2)

107 (142)	5	Baht (Cu-Ni) 1981	0.40	0.60
108 (143)	600	Baht (Ag) 1981		52.00

30th ANNIVERSARY OF THE WORLD FELLOWSHIP OF BUDDHISTS

109 (145)	10	Baht (Cu-Ni) 1981	1.50	2.50

RAMA VII CONSTITUTIONAL MONARCHY

110 (144)	5	Baht (Cu-Ni) 1981	0.40	0.90

KING RAMA IX ANNIVERSARY OF REIGN (3)

111 (146)	10	Baht (Cu-Ni) 1981	1.50	2.50
112 (147)	600	Baht (Ag) 1981		52.00
113 (148)	9000	Baht (Au) 1981		500.00

		XF	Unc

FOR THE FAO COIN PLAN

114	600 Baht (Ag) 1981		40.00

INTERNATIONAL YEAR OF THE CHILD (2)

115	600 Baht (Ag) 1981		55.00
116	9000 Baht (Au) 1981		480.00

200th ANNIVERSARY OF BANGKOK (3)

117	5 Baht (Cu-Ni) 1982		0.60
118	600 Baht (Ag) 1982		40.00
119	9000 Baht (Au) 1982		500.00

Tibet

Area: c. 471,700 sq. mi. Population: 1,280,000.

Since the reign of the Chinese Tang Dynasty (618 to 906), Tibet has been to a varying degree under the cultural and political influence of China. Under the Ching Dynasty (1644 to 1911) China was able to consolidate this influence considerably at first, but towards the end of the dynasty this influence, however, diminished very largely under the reign of weak emperors. After the supersession of the empire in China by the republic (1911/12), Tibet considered itself released from Chinese suzerainty. The independence of Tibet guaranteed in 1914 by Great Britain, India, and Russia was not acknowledged by China. For the purpose of counteracting increasing foreign influence in Tibet, the troops of the People's Republic of China occupied the country step by step in 1950 to 1951. Based upon the Peking agreements of May 23, 1951, Tibet was incorporated in the People's Republic of China as an autonomous region.

Capital: Lhasa.

10 Skarung = 1 Shokang, 15 Skarung = 1 Tangka
10 Shokang = 1 Srang, 3 Tangka = 1 Indian Rupee

			VF	XF
1 (1)	¼ Rupee (Ag) 1903 (undated). Portrait with cap, left ℞ name of province (Szechuan) in 4 Chinese letters, surrounded by leaf decorations. Rosette in center. Diameter: 19.5 mm. Several variations		32.00	40.00

Coins Nos. 1 to 4 were struck in the Chinese Province of Szechuan, for the frontier territory of Szechuan and Tibet. There are also gold strikes of Nos. 1, 2, and 3.

2 (2)	½ Rupee (Ag) 1903 (undated). Like No. 1, but diameter: 25.5 mm. Several variations		35.00	45.00

			VF	XF
3(3)	1	Rupee (Ag) 1903 (undated). Like No. 1, but diameter: 30 mm. Several variations	15.00	18.00
4	2½	Rupee (Ag) 1903 (undated). Like No. 1, but diameter: 38 mm	–.–	–.–

5(13)	1	Tangka (Ag) 18th century to 1948 (undated). Stylized lotus flower, surrounded by 8 Tibetan letter groups. ℞ Buddhist symbol in center, surrounded by 8 more symbols	5.00	8.00
6(4)	1	Skarung (Cu) (undated). Dragon in dotted circle and new legend in Tibetan letters ℞ name of country, denomination, and regnal era "Hsüan Tung" in 4 Chinese letters. In center stylized lotus flower in dotted circle	18.00	25.00
7(5)	1	Shokang (Ag) 1910 (?) (undated) Similar to No. 6	18.00	25.00
8(6)	2	Shokang (Ag) 1910 (?) (undated). Similar to No. 6	22.00	35.00
9	1	Shokang (Ag) 1908, 1909. Two squares in double circle. Tibetan letters between the squares. Buddhist symbol in center. 8 stars framing the double circle. ℞ In center two circles inside a double circle. Between the circles twice 8 dots. 8 groups of Tibetan letters constituting legend. Edge: 8 stars inside a double circle and in one outer circle	65.00	90.00

			VF	XF
10 (8)	5	Shokang (Ag) 1908, 1909 (?). Similar to No. 9, but 16 stars in outer circle	20.00	30.00
11 (9)	1	Srang (Ag) 1908 Similar to No. 9, but 24 stars in outer circle	160.00	220.00
12	5	Shokang (Ag) 1908–1912. Stylized flower in center, surrounded by 8 Tibetan letter groups. ℞ Buddhist symbol in center, surrounded by 8 more symbols	–.–	–.–
13	1	Tael (Ag) 1908 (undated). 8 Chinese letters and denomination. ℞ name of country and value in 4 Chinese letters	–.–	–.–
14 (10)	2½	Skarung (Cu) 1909. Lion in circle and 8 Tibetan letter groups. ℞ in center Buddhist symbol in double circle. Legend in Tibetan letters	12.00	16.00
15 (A10)	5	Skarung (Cu) 1909	12.00	16.00
16 (11)	7½	Skarung (Cu) 1909	20.00	26.00
17 (12)	1	Srang (Ag) 1909. Stylized lion in circle, surrounded by 8 Tibetan letter groups. ℞ in center Buddhist symbol in circle, surrounded by legend in Tibetan letters. All surrounded by 8 Buddhist symbols	385.00	450.00
18 (14)	1	Tangka (Ag) 1910. Obverse similar to No. 9, but dotted circle instead of stars around the edge. ℞ in center a stylized flower with 8 petals, surrounded by one dotted and one regular circle	6.00	9.00
19 (16)	2½	Skarung (Cu) 1914–1916. Lion in circle and 8 Tibetan letter groups. ℞ double circle in center, surrounded by two groups of 8 dots each, all surrounded by one dotted and one regular circle. Legend in Tibetan letters	4.00	6.00
20 (17)	5	Skarung (Cu) 1913–1918. Obverse similar to No. 19. ℞ stylized flower in double circle and legend in Tibetan letters	3.50	5.00
21 (18)	5	Shokang (Ag) 1914–1918. Stylized lion in circle, surrounded by 8 Tibetan letter groups. ℞ in center Buddhist symbol in circle, surrounded by legend in Tibetan letters (date and value). All surrounded by 8 Buddhist symbols	11.00	16.00
22 (22)	20	Srang (Au) 1917–1920. Stylized lion and Tibetan letters (date) in circle. Surrounded by 8 Buddhist symbols. ℞ in center stylized flower in circle. Legend in Tibetan letters, name of country, value	620.00	800.00
23 (A19)	2½	Skarung (Cu) 1918–1919. Stylized lion and legend in Tibetan letters. ℞ in		

center a Buddhist symbol, surrounded
by Tibetan letters and arabesques.
(Scalloped)

	VF	XF
	35.00	48.00

24 (19) 5 Skarung (Cu) 1918–1925. Stylized lion
and legend in Tibetan letters. ℞ Tibet-
an letters in circular design, legend in
Tibetan letters 2.60 4.00

25 (20) 7½ Skarung (Cu) 1918–1925. Stylized lion
in dotted circle and legend in Tibetan
letters. ℞ in center 3 curved lines in
circle, surrounded by 8 dots in dotted
circle. Legend in Tibetan letters. (Scalloped) 2.60 4.00

26 (21) 1 Shokang (Cu) 1918–1922. Lion in circle
and legend in 8 Tibetan letter groups.
℞ Tibetan letters in one regular and one
dotted circle. Legend in Tibetan letters 3.50 5.00

27 (21a) 1 Shokang (Cu) 1923–1928. Similar to
No. 26, but lettering variety 4.00 6.50

27a (32a) 5 Shokang (Ag) 1930. Diameter 24 mm -.- -.-

28 (23)   1 Shokang (Cu) 1932–1938. Stylized lion, sun, and clouds in circle. Legend in Tibetan letters. ℞ Tibetan letters and arabesques in circle. Legend in Tibetan letters and 5 rosettes

	VF	XF
	2.50	3.50

29 (24)   1½ Srang (Ag) 1935–1937. Stylized lion, 5 mountain peaks, two suns, and clouds in circle. In legend 4 Tibetan letter groups, and 4 Buddhist symbols. ℞ arabesques in circle. Legend in Tibetan letters, and Buddhist symbols

6.00	8.00

30 (25)   3 Srang (Ag) 1933, 1934 (?). Stylized lion and clouds in circle. In legend 4 Tibetan letter groups, and 4 Buddhist symbols. ℞ Tibetan letters, value, and arabesques in circle. Legend in 3 Tibetan letter groups, and 3 Buddhist symbols

12.00	16.00

			VF	XF
31 (26)	3	Srang (Ag) 1935–1938. Stylized lion, 5 mountain peaks, 2 suns, and clouds in circle. In legend 4 Tibetan letter groups, and 4 Buddhist symbols. ℞ arabesques in circle. In legend 4 Tibetan letter groups, date, 2 rosettes with 8 petals, and 2 Buddhist symbols	12.00	16.00
32 (27)	3	Shokang (Cu) 1946. Stylized lion, 5 mountain peaks, and 2 suns in circle. In legend 4 Tibetan letter groups, and 4 Buddhist symbols. ℞ Tibetan letters and arabesques in circle. Legend in Tibetan letters and 6 Buddhist symbols	7.50	10.50
33	1	Tangka (Ag) 1946–1948 (undated). In center Yin-Yang symbol in 2 circles. In legend 8 Tibetan letter groups. ℞ arabesques in circle, surrounded by 8 Buddhist symbols	9.00	12.00

			VF	XF
34 (28)	5	Shokang (Cu) 1947–1949. Lion, 3 mountain peaks, 2 suns, and clouds. ℞ Tibetan letters in circle surrounded by 8 Tibetan letter groups	2.60	4.00
35 (28a)	5	Shokang (Cu) 1950–1951. Like No. 34, but sun and moon instead of 2 suns	3.50	5.00

				VF	XF

36 (29) 10 Srang (Ag) 1948, 1949. Lion with 3 mountain peaks and 2 suns in circle. In legend 8 Tibetan letter groups, name of country. ℞ Buddhist symbols and Tibetan letters, date, value in circle. In legend 8 Tibetan letter groups, name of country   **18.00**   **25.00**

37 (29a) 10 Srang (Ag) 1950, 1951. Like No. 36, but sun and moon instead of 2 suns   **18.00**   **25.00**

38 (30) 10 Srang (Ag) 1950, 1951. Lion, 3 mountain peaks, and 2 suns in circle. In legend 8 Tibetan letter groups. ℞ 3 lines of Tibetan letters in circle. In legend 8 Tibetan letter groups   **18.00**   **25.00**

Area: 6,970 sq. mi. Population: 574,000.
While the western part, including the village of Kupang, belonged to Indonesia
since 1947, the north-eastern part of the island of Timor remained Portuguese.
In 1952 Portugal changed the colony into an Overseas Province. In 1976
Portuguese Timor was annexed by Indonesia.
Capital: Dili.

100 Avos = 1 Pataca; since 1958: 100 Centavos = 1 Escudo

			VF	XF
1 (1)	10	Avos (Br) 1945–1951. Cross. ℞ value	7.50	11.00
2 (2)	20	Avos (Ni–Br) 1945. Head of Liberty. ℞ coat of arms in wreath and value	40.00	55.00
3 (3)	50	Avos (Ag) 1945–1951. Coat of arms on cross. ℞ value	18.00	26.00

NEW CURRENCY: 100 Centavos = 1 Escudo

			VF	XF
4 (4)	10	Centavos (Br) 1958. Coat of arms with mural crown. ℞ value	4.00	8.00
5 (5)	30	Centavos (Br) 1958	2.00	4.00
6 (6)	60	Centavos (Cu–Ni) 1958	2.50	4.00
7 (7)	1	Escudo (Cu–Ni) 1958	2.50	4.00
8 (8)	3	Escudos (Ag) 1958	4.50	7.50
9 (9)	6	Escudos (Ag) 1958	7.50	11.00
10 (10)	10	Escudos (Ag) 1964	8.00	12.00
11 (12)	20	Centavos (Br) 1970. Coat of arms with mural crown. ℞ value	0.40	0.80
12 (13)	50	Centavos (Br) 1970. Same type as No. 11	0.40	0.80
13 (14)	1	Escudo (Br) 1970. Same type as No. 11	1.20	2.50
14 (15)	2,50	Escudos (Cu–Ni) 1970	1.20	2.50
15 (16)	5	Escudos (Cu–Ni) 1970	1.60	2.80
16 (17)	10	Escudos (Cu–Ni) 1970	2.50	4.00

Area: 20,000 sq. mi. Population: 2,100,000.

The former German protectorate was occupied by the British and French in August 1914 and in 1920 partitioned as a mandate between Great Britain and France under the League of Nations. The British part which was incorporated in the Gold Coast, also remained, after a plebiscite in 1957, with that state which had become independent under the name of Ghana. The French part received limited autonomy in 1957 and became independent on April 27, 1960.

Capital: Lomé.

100 Centimes = 1 Franc

			VF	XF
1 (1)	50	Centimes (Al–Br) 1924–1926. Laureate head of Marianne, symbol of the French Republic. ℞ value and palm leaves	4.00	8.00
2 (2)	1	Franc (Al–Br) 1924–1925	5.00	10.00
3 (3)	2	Francs (Al–Br) 1924–1925	8.00	15.00
4 (4)	1	Franc (Al) 1948. ℞ slender-horned gazelle (Gazella leptoceros – Bovidae)	4.00	6.50

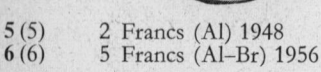

5 (5)	2	Francs (Al) 1948	6.00	10.00
6 (6)	5	Francs (Al–Br) 1956	2.50	3.50

			Proof
7	2500	Francs (Ag) 1977	35.00
8	5000	Francs (Ag) 1977	70.00
9	10000	Francs (Au) 1977	130.00
10	25000	Francs (Au) 1977	300.00
11	50000	Francs (Au) 1977	600.00

Tokelau Islands

Area: 4 sq. mi. Population: 2,000.
Tokelau or Union Islands located in the South Pacific. The group, a New Zealand Territory, consists of Atafu, Fakaofo and Nikunono.

100 Cents = 1 Dollar

			Unc	Proof
1 (1)	1	Tala 1978:		
		a) (Ag)		45.00
		b) (Cu-Ni)	10.00	
2 (2)	1	Tala 1979:		
		a) (Ag)		38.00
		b) (Cu-Ni)	6.00	
3 (3)	1	Tala 1980:		
		a) (Ag)		38.00
		b) (Cu-Ni)	6.00	

Tonga
Friendly Islands

Area: 270 sq. mi. Population: 92,000.
The Tonga Islands (Friendly Islands) united as a kingdom in 1845, were under British protection since 1900. The first king of the united island realm was George Tupou I (1845–1893). On June 4, 1970 the Polynesian kingdom became independent.
Capital: Nuku'alofa.

1 Koula = 16 British Pounds; since 1967: 100 Seniti = 1 Pa'anga (Tonga Dollar), 100 Pa'anga = 1 Hau

SALOTE TUPOU III 1918–1965

			Proof
1 (1)	¼ Koula (Au) 1962. Salote Tupou III (1900–1965), head right. ℞ coat of arms		200.00
2 (2)	½ Koula (Au) 1962. Salote Tupou III, standing		400.00
3 (3)	1 Koula (Au) 1962		800.00

TAUFA'AHAU TUPOU IV since 1965

CURRENCY REFORM (Decimal System):
100 Seniti = 1 Pa'anga, 100 Pa'anga = 1 Hau

			XF	Unc
4 (4)	1 Seniti (Br) 1967. Salote Tupou III, head right. ℞ giant tortoise (family Testudinidae)		0.20	0.40
5 (5)	2 Seniti (Br) 1967. ℞ giant tortoise		0.30	0.50
6 (6)	5 Seniti (Cu–Ni) 1967. ℞ value in wreath		0.30	0.60
7 (7)	10 Seniti (Cu–Ni) 1967		0.50	0.90
8 (8)	20 Seniti (Cu–Ni) 1967. Coat of arms		0.90	1.20
9 (9)	50 Seniti (Cu–Ni) 1967		1.20	2.00

				XF	Unc
10 (10)	1	Pa'anga (Cu–Ni) 1967		3.50	4.50

COMMEMORATIVE ISSUES (7) FOR THE CORONATION OF TAUFA'AHAU TUPOU IV ON 4th JULY, 1967

				XF	Unc
11 (11)	20	Seniti (Cu–Ni) 1967. Taufa'ahau Tupou IV, head right, memorial legend, edge decor: crowns. R coat of arms		2.00	4.00
12 (12)	50	Seniti (Cu–Ni) 1967		3.00	6.00
13 (13)	1	Pa'anga (Cu–Ni) 1967		3.50	7.00
14 (14)	2	Pa'anga (Cu–Ni) 1967		4.50	9.00
15 (15)	¼	Hau (Pd) 1967			250.00
16 (16)	½	Hau (Pd) 1967			500.00
17 (17)	1	Hau (Pd) 1967			1000.00
18 (18)	1	Seniti (Br) 1968. Taufa'ahau Tupou IV, head right. R giant tortoise		0.15	0.30
19 (19)	2	Seniti (Br) 1968, 1974. R giant tortoise		0.20	0.40
20 (20)	5	Seniti (Cu–Ni) 1968, 1974. R value between leaves		0.25	0.50
21 (21)	10	Seniti (Cu–Ni) 1968, 1974		0.40	0.70
22 (22)	20	Seniti (Cu–Ni) 1968, 1974. R coat of arms		0.60	0.90
23 (23)	50	Seniti (Cu–Ni) 1968		0.85	1.50
24 (24)	1	Pa'anga (Cu–Ni) 1968		1.50	3.50
25 (25)	2	Pa'anga (Cu–Ni) 1968		3.00	6.00

COMMEMORATIVE ISSUES (7) FOR THE 50th BIRTHDAY OF TAUFA'AHAU TUPOU IV

			Proof
26 (11a)	20	Seniti (Cu–Ni). Type as No. 11, but with countermark 1918/monogram/TT IV/1968	6.00
27 (12a)	50	Seniti (Cu–Ni). Type as No. 12, but countermark as No. 26	10.00
28 (13a)	1	Pa'anga (Cu–Ni). Type as No. 13, but with countermark as No. 26	15.00
29 (14a)	2	Pa'anga (Cu–Ni). Type as No. 14, but with countermark as No. 26	40.00
30 (5a)	¼	Hau (Pd). Type as No. 15, but with countermark as No. 26	200.00
31 (6a)	½	Hau (Pd). Type as No. 16, but with countermark as No. 26	400.00

32(7a) 1 Hau (Pd). Type as No. 17, but with   **Proof**
countermark as No. 26   **800.00**

COMMEMORATIVE ISSUES (2) FOR THE FIRST SCIENTIFIC OIL SEARCH IN TONGA

                                                     Unc

33 (24a) 1 Pa'anga (Cu–Ni, gilded). Type as No. 24,
but with countermark OIL SEARCH
1969 and oil derrick left and right side
of date   **10.00**
34(25a) 2 Pa'anga (Cu–Ni, gilded). Type as No.
25, but with countermark as No. 33   **20.00**

COMMEMORATIVE ISSUES (2) FOR JOINING THE BRITISH COMMONWEALTH

35(24b) 1 Pa'anga (Cu–Ni). Type as No. 24,
but with countermark COMMON-
WEALTH MEMBER 1970 left and
right side of date   **10.00**
36(25b) 2 Pa'anga (Cu–Ni). Type as No. 25, but
with countermark as No. 35   **20.00**

COMMEMORATIVE ISSUES (2) FOR THE 5th ANNIVERSARY OF THE DEATH OF QUEEN SALOTE TUPOU III

37(9a) 50 Seniti (Cu–Ni) 1970. Type as No. 9, but
with countermark   **10.00**
38(10a) 1 Pa'anga (Cu–Ni) 1970. Type as No. 10,
but with countermark   **20.00**

COMMEMORATIVE ISSUES (2) FOR INVESTITURE 1971

39(24c) 1 Pa'anga (Cu–Ni, gilded). Type as No.
24, but with countermark INVESTI-
TURE 1971   **10.00**
40(25a) 2 Pa'anga (Cu–Ni, gilded). Type as No.
25, but with countermark as No. 39   **20.00**

		XF	Unc
41 (18a)	1 Seniti (Bra) 1974. Type as No. 18	0.10	0.20
42 (23a)	50 Seniti (Cu-Ni) 1974. Type as No. 23 (12-sided)	0.80	1.50

FOR THE FAO COIN PLAN (8)

43 (26)	1 Seniti (Br) 1975	0.10	0.20
44 (27)	2 Seniti (Br) 1975	0.10	0.20
45 (28)	5 Seniti (Cu-Ni) 1975	0.15	0.30
46 (29)	10 Seniti (Cu-Ni) 1975	0.25	0.50
47 (30)	20 Seniti (Cu-Ni) 1975	0.45	0.90
48 (31)	50 Seniti (Cu-Ni) 1975	0.70	1.40
49 (32)	1 Pa'anga (Cu-Ni) 1975	2.00	4.00
50 (33)	2 Pa'anga (Cu-Ni) 1975	3.50	7.50

CONSTITUTION CENTENNIAL (7)

51 (34)	5 Pa'anga (Ag) 1975	22.00
52 (35)	10 Pa'anga (Ag) 1975	40.00
53 (36)	20 Pa'anga (Ag) 1975	150.00
54 (37)	25 Pa'anga (Au) 1975	100.00
55 (38)	50 Pa'anga (Au) 1975	200.00
56 (39)	75 Pa'anga (Au) 1975	300.00
57 (40)	100 Pa'anga (Au) 1975	500.00

FOR THE FAO COIN PLAN

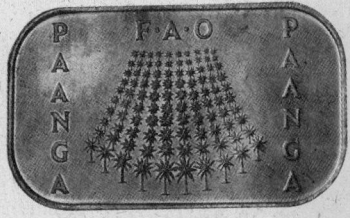

		XF	Unc
58 (41)	1 Pa'anga (Cu-Ni) 1977	1.60	3.00

			Unc	Proof
59 (42)	1	Pa'anga 1978. Type as No. 58, but DIAMOND-BIRTHDAY/1918–1978« added:		
		a) (Ag)		22.00
		b) (Cu-Ni)	3.00	
60 (43)	2	Pa'anga 1978. Type as No. 50, but »DIAMOND-BIRTHDAY/1918–1978« added:		
		a) (Ag)		80.00
		b) (Cu-Ni)	6.00	

FOR THE FAO COIN PLAN (2)

			Unc	Proof
61 (44)	1	Pa'anga 1979. Type as No. 58, but »DECADE OF PROGRESS 1969–1979« added. Rev. inscription »F.A.O. TECHNICAL/COOPERATION PROGRAMME« added:		
		a) (Ag)		75.00
		b) (Cu-Ni)	7.00	
62 (45)	2	Pa'anga 1979:		
		a) (Ag)		40.00
		b) (Cu-Ni)	7.00	

FAO COIN PLAN AND RURAL WOMEN'S ADVANCEMENT (4)

			Unc	Proof
63 (46)	1	Pa'anga 1980. Head of Salote Tupou III. Rev. woman in front of a cabin:		
		a) (Ag)		50.00
		b) (Cu-Ni)	4.00	
64 (47)	2	Pa'anga 1980. Type as No. 62, but without »DECADE . . .«:		
		a) (Ag)		70.00
		b) (Cu-Ni)	8.00	
65 (48)	10	Pa'anga (Au) 1980. Feminal symbol on dove		60.00
66 (49)	20	Pa'anga (Au) 1980. Feminal symbol on dove		100.00

Transvaal
Zuid Afrikaansche Republiek
Südafrikanische Republik   République Sudafricaine (Transvaal)

Boers dissatisfied with British rule in the Cape Colony, migrated via Natal into the deserted areas north of the Waal river and founded in 1852 the "South African Republic" by the integration of the smaller Free States of Potschefstroom, Zoutpansberg and Lyndenburg, which was called "Transvaal" abroad and from the British aspect due to is geographical position. Great Britain which had immediately recognized this republic, occupied its area from 1877 to 1881, but again recognized its independence in 1881. In the treaty of 27th February 1884 Great Britain alse recognized the name "South African Republic". The Boer War which broke out in 1899 ended on 31st May 1902 with the recognition of the annexation by Great Britain on the part of the Boers. After administering the Transvaal for several years as a Crown Colony, it was integrated as a province of the newly formed Union of South Africa in 1910, whose further development towards the sovereign republic has very strongly been determined by the Boer element of the province of Transvaal.

Capital: Pretoria.

12 Pence = 1 Shilling, 20 Shillings = 1 Pound (Pond)

With the law of 1891 the Pond was declared as the chief gold coin and on a par with the British gold sovereign.

PAUL KRÜGER 1883–1902

		VF	XF
1 (1)	1 Penny (Br) 1891–1898. Paul Krüger (1825–1904), called Ohm Krüger, President of the Republic. ℞ devided coat of arms	4.00	10.00
2 (2)	3 Pence (Ag) 1892–1897. ℞ value in wreath	8.00	12.50
3 (3)	6 Pence (Ag) 1891–1897	7.00	10.00

			VF	XF
4 (4)	1	Shilling (Ag) 1892–1897	10.00	18.00
5 (5)	2	Shillings (Ag) 1892–1897. ℞ coat of arms	12.50	20.00
6 (6)	2½	Shillings (Ag) 1892–1897	15.00	22.00
7 (7)	5	Shillings (Ag) 1892. ℞ covered wagon with one shaft (bottom section of coat of arms)	175.00	200.00
8 (7a)	5	Shillings (Ag) 1892. ℞ covered wagon with two shafts (bottom section of coat of arms)	250.00	360.00
9 (8)	½	£ (Au) 1893–1897. ℞ covered wagon with one shaft	140.00	160.00
10 (8a)	½	£ (Au) 1892. ℞ covered wagon with two shafts	150.00	170.00

			VF	XF
11 (9)	1	£ (Au) 1892–1900. ℞ covered wagon with one shaft	160.00	180.00
12 (9a)	1	£ (Au) 1892. ℞ covered wagon with two shafts	170.00	190.00
13 (10)	1	Pond (Au) 1902. ZAR, abbreviation of the name of the country, date. ℞ value in letters	*1400.00*	*1600.00*

Trinidad and Tobago

Trinidad und Tobago   **Trinité et Tobago**

Area: 1980 sq. mi. Population: 1,100,000.
The island of Trinidad was discovered by Christopher Columbus in
1498. Until captured by the British, Trinidad was a Spanish possession. Together with Tobago, Trinidad has formed an independent state
within the British Commonwealth since August 31, 1962.
Capital: Port of Spain.

100 Cents = 1 Trinidad Tobago Dollar

			XF	Unc
1 (1)	1 Cent (Br) 1966–1973. Coat of arms; crest: hummingbird (Polytmus guain-numbi – Trochilidae). R value		0.05	0.10
2 (2)	5 Cents (Br) 1966–1973. Same type as No. 1		0.10	0.20
3 (3)	10 Cents (Cu-Ni) 1966–1973. Same type as No. 1		0.15	0.30
4 (4)	25 Cents (Cu-Ni) 1966–1973. Same type as No. 1		0.30	0.60
5 (5)	50 Cents (Cu-Ni) 1966–1971. Same type as No. 1		0.50	1.00

			Unc	Proof
6 (6)	1 Dollar (Cu-Ni) 1970, 1971. Same type as No. 1:			
	a) 1970			25.00
	b) 1971		4.00	8.00

ISSUE FOR THE FAO COIN PLAN

			XF	Unc
7 (7)	1 Dollar (Ni) 1969. Coat of arms, name of country, date. R value, cocoa beans on a branch (Theobroma cacao – Sterculiaceae), motto: FOOD FOR ALL		4.00	10.00

			Unc	Proof
8 (8)	5	Dollars 1971-1975. Rev. red-tailed guan (Ortalis ruficauda - Cracidae), national bird of Tobago, called the "Cocrico"		
		a) (Ag) 1971, 1973-1975		35.00
		b) (Cu-Ni) 1974, 1975	10.00	

COMMEMORATIVE ISSUES (8) FOR THE 10th ANNIVERSARY OF INDEPENDENCE

			Unc	Proof
9 (9)	1	Cent (Bro) 1972. Type as No. 1, but with additional commemorative legend	0.20	1.00
10 (10)	5	Cents (Bro) 1972. Type as No. 9	0.25	1.10
11 (11)	10	Cents (Cu-Ni) 1972. Type as No. 9	0.50	1.50
12 (12)	25	Cents (Cu-Ni) 1972. Type as No. 9	0.80	2.00
13 (13)	50	Cents (Cu-Ni) 1972. Type as No. 9	1.50	2.50
14 (14)	1	Dollar (Cu-Ni) 1972	4.50	9.00
15 (15)	5	Dollars (Ag) 1972. Type as No. 8, but with additional commemorative legend	28.00	30.00
16 (16)	10	Dollars (Ag) 1972. R map of the islands	32.00	36.00
17 (9a)	1	Cent (Br) 1973. Type as No. 9, but without commemorative inscription	1.00	2.00
18 (21)	50	Cents (Cu-Ni) 1973-1976. Rev. Drums of a steel band, called »pans«	1.40	2.50
19 (22)	1	Dollar (Cu-Ni) 1973-1975	3.50	6.00
20 (23)	10	Dollars 1973-1975. Type as No. 16, but without commemorative inscription:		
		a) (Ag) 1973-1975	32.00	35.00
		b) (Cu-Ni) 1974, 1975	15.00	28.00
21 (17)	1	Cent (Br) 1974, 1975	0.20	1.00
22 (18)	5	Cents (Br) 1974, 1975	0.25	1.00
23 (19)	10	Cents (Cu-Ni) 1974, 1975	0.50	1.20
24 (20)	25	Cents (Cu-Ni) 1974, 1975	0.80	2.00
25 (24)	100	Dollars (Au) 1976		80.00
26 (17a)	1	Cent (Br) 1976-1980. Type as No. 17, but inscription »Republic of . . .«	0.10	1.00
27 (18a)	5	Cents (Br) 1976-1980	0.20	1.50
28 (19a)	10	Cents (Cu-Ni) 1976-1980	0.40	1.50
29 (20a)	25	Cents (Cu-Ni) 1976-1980	1.00	2.50
30 (21a)	50	Cents (Cu-Ni) 1976-1980	1.30	4.00
31 (22a)	1	Dollar (Cu-Ni) 1976-1980	7.00	8.00
32 (8)	5	Dollars 1976-1980:		
		a) (Y 8b) (Ag)		30.00
		b) (Y 8c) (Cu-Ni)	40.00	
33 (23)	10	Dollars 1976-1980:		
		a) (Y 23b) (Ag)		35.00
		b) (Y 23c) (Cu-Ni)	50.00	
34 (7a)	1	Dollar (Cu-Ni) 1979. FAO issue	6.00	
35 (25)	25	Dollars (Ag) 1980. Development Bank		30.00

Tristan da Cunha

Area: 45sq. mi. Population: 300.
Tristan da Cunha is midway between Africa, South America and Antarctica
and 1,320 miles from St. Helena of which it became a dependency in 1938.
It is a volcano (which last erupted in 1961) rising to a height of 6,760 feet above
the Atlantic. Up to now, the circulating coinage has been British. Tristan da
Cunha has also used South African currency up to 1961.

100 Pence = 1 £

ELIZABETH II since 1952

25th ANNIVERSARY OF THE SILVER JUBILEE OF HER MAJESTY QUEEN ELIZABETH II

			Unc	Proof
1 (1)	25 Pence 1977:			
	a) (Ag)			40.00
	b) (Cu-Ni)		3.00	

25th ANNIVERSARY OF THE CORONATION OF HER MAJESTY QUEEN ELIZABETH II

2 (2)	1 Crown 1978:			
	a) (Ag)			35.00
	b) (Cu-Ni)		3.00	

80th BIRTHDAY OF QUEEN MOTHER

3 (3)	1 Crown 1980:			
	a) (Ag)			30.00
	b) (Cu-Ni)		2.50	

WEDDING OF PRINCE CHARLES AND LADY DIANA

4 (4)	1 Crown 1981:			
	a) (Ag)			30.00
	b) (Cu-Ni)		3.00	

Tunesien   # Tunisia   **Tunisie**

Al Djoumhouria Attanusia

Area: 48,000 sq. mi. Population: 5,300,000.
In 1881 Tunisia became a French protectorate and in 1946 an associated state of the French Union. Since 1956 the country has been independent. In the following year, after Bey Mohammed Lamine had been deposed, the country became a republic.
Capital: Tunis.

100 Centimes = 1 Tunisian Franc, 1000 Millimes = 1 Tunisian Dinar

ALI BAI 1882–1902

			VF	XF
1 (11)	1	Centime (Br) 1891. Arabic legend between branches. ℞ name of country and denomination in French; date	4.00	6.00
2 (12)	2	Centimes (Br) 1891. Type as No. 1	4.00	6.00
3 (13)	5	Centimes (Br) 1891–1893. Type as No. 1	1.50	2.00
4 (14)	10	Centimes (Br) 1891–1893. Type as No. 1	1.50	2.50

			VF	XF
5 (15)	50	Centimes (Ag) 1891–1902:		
		a) 1891	4.00	6.00
		b) 1892–1902	40.00	55.00
6 (16)	1	Franc (Ag) 1891–1902. Type as No. 5:		
		a) 1891–1892	5.50	10.00
		b) 1893–1902	80.00	110.00
7 (17)	2	Francs (Ag) 1891–1902. Type as No. 5:		
		a) 1891–1892	8.00	12.00
		b) 1893–1902	120.00	160.00

			VF	XF
8 (18)	10	Francs (Au) 1891–1902. Type as No. 5:		
		a) 1891	65.00	80.00
		b) 1892–1902	300.00	400.00
9 (19)	20	Francs (Au) 1891–1902. Type as No. 5:		
		a) 1891–1892, 1897–1901	110.00	120.00
		b) 1893	140.00	160.00
		c) 1894–1896, 1902	520.00	650.00

MOHAMMED AL HADI BEI 1902–1906

			VF	XF
10 (20)	5	Centimes (Br) 1903–1904. Type as No. 3	1.50	2.60
11 (21)	10	Centimes (Br) 1903–1904. Type as No. 4	4.00	6.50
12 (22)	50	Centimes (Ag) 1903–1906. Type as No. 5	40.00	55.00
13 (23)	1	Franc (Ag) 1903–1906. Type as No. 6:		
		a) 1903, 1905, 1906	70.00	90.00
		b) 1904	4.50	6.50
14 (24)	2	Francs (Ag) 1903–1906. Type as No. 7:		
		a) 1903, 1905, 1906	120.00	160.00
		b) 1904	8.00	12.00
15 (25)	10	Francs (Au) 1903–1906. Type as No. 8	300.00	400.00
16 (26)	20	Francs (Au) 1903–1906. Type as No. 9:		
		a) 1903–1904	120.00	140.00
		b) 1905–1906	520.00	650.00

MOHAMMED EN-NACEUR BEI 1906–1922

			VF	XF
17 (27)	5	Centimes (Br) 1907–1917. Type as No. 3	1.70	2.50
18 (28)	10	Centimes (Br) 1907–1917. Type as No. 4	2.60	4.00
19 (29)	50	Centimes (Ag) 1907–1921. Type as No. 5:		
		a) 1907, 1912, 1914–1917	3.50	5.00
		b) 1908–1911, 1913, 1918–1921	36.00	55.00
20 (30)	1	Franc (Ag) 1907–1921. Type as No. 6:		
		a) 1907–1908, 1911–1912, 1914–1918	4.00	6.00
		b) 1909–1910, 1913, 1919–1921	80.00	110.00
21 (31)	2	Francs (Ag) 1907–1921. Type as No. 7:		
		a) 1907, 1909–1910, 1913, 1917–1921	120.00	160.00
		b) 1908, 1911–1912, 1914–1916	6.50	9.00
22 (32)	10	Francs (Au) 1907–1921. Type as No. 8:		
		a) 1907	550.00	600.00
		b) 1908–1921	250.00	320.00
23 (33)	20	Francs (Au) 1907–1921. Type as No. 9:		
		a) 1907, 1909–1921	550.00	600.00
		b) 1908	400.00	500.00

24 (34)	5	Centimes (Cu–Ni) 1918–1920. Arabic

			VF	XF

legend. ℞ French legend. Date between branches. Diameter 19 mm, 3 g (with hole) — VF 0.40 — XF 0.80

25 (34a) 5 Centimes (Cu–Ni) 1920. Type as No 24, but diameter 17 mm and weight 2 g (with hole) — 1.50 — 2.50

26 (35) 10 Centimes (Cu–Ni) 1918–1920. Type as No. 24 (with hole) — 0.40 — 0.80

27 (36) 25 Centimes (Cu–Ni) 1918–1920. Type as No. 24 (with hole):
a) 1918 — 2.50 — 4.00
b) 1919–1920 — 1.20 — 1.60

MOHAMMED AL-HABIB BEI 1922–1929

28 (41) 50 Centimes (Ag) 1922–1928. Type as No. 6 — 35.00 — 48.00

29 (42) 1 Franc (Ag) 1922–1928. Type as No. 6 — 75.00 — 100.00

30 (43) 2 Francs (Ag) 1922–1928. Type as No. 7 — 110.00 — 130.00

31 (44) 10 Francs (Au) 1922–1928. Type as No. 8 — 280.00 — 400.00

32 (45) 20 Francs (Au) 1922–1928. Type as No. 9 — 400.00 — 500.00

33 (40) 10 Centimes (Ni–Br) 1926. Type as No. 26 (with hole) — 1.20 — 2.00

AHMED BEI 1929–1942

34 (46) 5 Centimes (Cu–Ni) 1931, 1933, 1938. Type as No. 25 — 0.40 — 0.80

35 (47) 10 Centimes (Cu–Ni) 1931, 1933, 1938. Type as No. 26 (with hole) — 0.80 — 1.20

36 (48) 25 Centimes (Cu–Ni) 1931, 1933, 1938. Type as No. 27 — 1.50 — 2.00

37 (37) 50 Centimes (Al–Bro) 1921, 1926, 1933, 1941, 1945. Date between tied laurel branches, above name of country in French. ℞ value between palm branches, above BON POUR — 0.40 — 0.80

38 (38) 1 Franc (Al–Bro) 1921, 1926, 1941, 1945. Type as No. 37 — 0.70 — 1.20

39 (39) 2 Francs (Al–Bro) 1921, 1924, 1926, 1941, 1945. Type as No. 37 — 1.00 — 2.00

			VF	XF
40 (49)	10	Francs (Ag) 1930–1934:		
		a) 1930, 1932, 1934	26.00	40.00
		b) 1931, 1933	85.00	115.00
41 (50)	20	Francs (Ag) 1930–1934. Type as No. 40:		
		a) 1930, 1932, 1934	35.00	55.00
		b) 1931, 1933	250.00	320.00

42 (57)	100	Francs (Au) 1930–1937	135.00	160.00

43	100	Francs (Au) 1938–1942. Type as No. 42, but large date in place of value	400.00	520.00

44 (51)	5	Francs (Ag) AH 1353, 1355 (1934, 1936)	4.00	6.50
45 (52)	10	Francs (Ag) AH 1353–1356 (1934–1938). Type as No. 44:		
		a) AH 1353 (1934)	6.00	9.00
		b) AH 1354–1356 (1936–1938)	80.00	120.00

		VF	XF
46 (53)	20 Francs (Ag) AH 1353–1356 (1934–1938). Type as No. 44:		
	a) AH 1353 (1934)	10.00	15.00
	b) AH 1354–1356 (1936–1938)	260.00	300.00

47 (54)	5 Francs (Ag) 1939	4.00	6.50
48 (55)	10 Francs (Ag) 1939–1942. Type as No. 47:		
	a) 1939	8.00	12.00
	b) 1940–1942	80.00	110.00
49 (56)	20 Francs (Ag) 1939–1942. Type as No. 47:		
	a) 1939	16.00	26.00
	b) 1940–1942	260.00	300.00
50 (58)	10 Centimes (Sn) 1941–1942 (with hole)	0.40	0.80
51 (59)	20 Centimes (Sn) 1942	2.50	4.00

MOHAMMED AL MONCEF BEI 1942–1943

52	100 Francs (Au) 1943. Type as No. 43	–.–	–.–

MOHAMMED LAMINE BEI 1943–1957

53 (60)	10 Centimes (Sn) 1945	25.00	40.00
54 (61)	20 Centimes (Sn) 1945. Type as No. 51	27.00	45.00

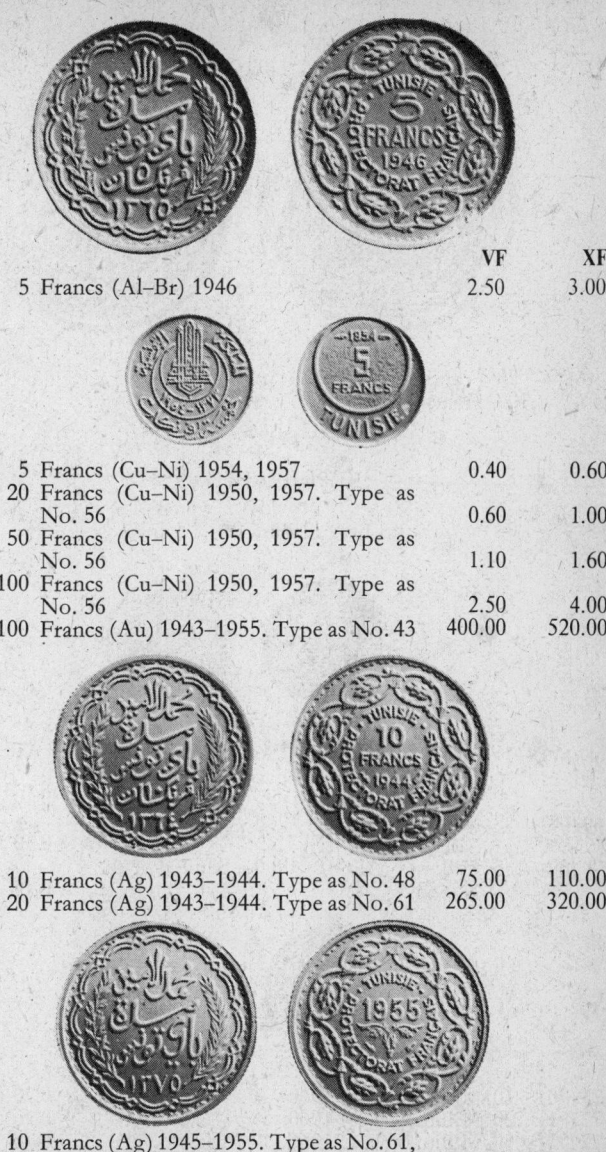

			VF	**XF**
55 (62)	5	Francs (Al–Br) 1946	2.50	3.00

56 (63)	5	Francs (Cu–Ni) 1954, 1957	0.40	0.60
57 (64)	20	Francs (Cu–Ni) 1950, 1957. Type as No. 56	0.60	1.00
58 (65)	50	Francs (Cu–Ni) 1950, 1957. Type as No. 56	1.10	1.60
59 (66)	100	Francs (Cu–Ni) 1950, 1957. Type as No. 56	2.50	4.00
60	100	Francs (Au) 1943–1955. Type as No. 43	400.00	520.00

61	10	Francs (Ag) 1943–1944. Type as No. 48	75.00	110.00
62	20	Francs (Ag) 1943–1944. Type as No. 61	265.00	320.00

| **63** | 10 | Francs (Ag) 1945–1955. Type as No. 61, but large date in place of value | 40.00 | 55.00 |

			VF	XF
64	20	Francs (Ag) 1945–1955. Type as No. 63	75.00	110.00
65	10	Francs (Ag) 1956. Legend ROYAUME DE TUNISIE	–.–	–.–

66	20	Francs (Ag) 1956. Type as No. 65	–.–	–.–
67	100	Francs (Au) 1956	–.–	–.–

REPUBLIC since 1957

1000 Millimes = 1 Dinar

			XF	Unc
68 (67)	1 Millime (Al–Mg) 1960–. Cork oak (Quercus suber – Fagaceae). ℞ value in wreath	0.10	0.15
69 (68)	2 Millimes (Al–Mg) 1960–. Same type as No. 33	0.10	0.20
70 (69)	5 Millimes (Al–Mg) 1960–. Same type as No. 33	0.15	0.30

			XF	Unc
71 (70)	10	Millimes (Bra) 1960–	0.20	0.40
72 (71)	20	Millimes (Bra) 1960. Type as No. 71	0.40	0.70
73 (72)	50	Millimes (Bra) 1960. Type as No. 71	0.70	1.10
74 (73)	100	Millimes (Bra) 1960. Type as No. 71	1.10	1.60

	XF	Unc
75 (74) ½ Dinar (Cu–Ni) 1968–	1.50	2.50

COMMEMORATIVE ISSUES (5) FOR THE 10th ANNIVERSARY OF THE REPUBLIC

		Proof
76	2 Dinars (Au) 1967. Habib Ibn Ali Bour-guiba (*1903), President since 1957. ℞ Kairuan, minaret of the Grand Mosque	50.00
77	5 Dinars (Au) 1967. Same type as No. 76	100.00
78	10 Dinars (Au) 1967. Same type as No. 76	200.00
79	20 Dinars (Au) 1967. Same type as No. 76	450.00
80	40 Dinars (Au) 1967. Same type as No. 76	800.00

COMMEMORATIVE ISSUES (10) FOR THE HISTORY OF TUNISIA

81   1 Dinar (Ag) 1969. President Bourguiba.
      ℞ Phoenician sailing vessel with oars.
      On the sail is the symbol of Tanit, the

patron goddess of Carthage, also ruler of the moon and goddess of fertility; reference to the Phoenicians who colonized the North African coast, founded Carthage in 814 B. C., and maintained a fleet as early as 650 B. C. Carthage became center of the Empire in 332 B. C. when Alexander the Great drove the Phoenicians to the western areas of the Mediterranean. Following there were the three Punic Wars against the rising Roman power

82   1 Dinar (Ag) 1969. ℞ Venus. Goddess of horticulture. Originates partly from the Punic goddess Aphrodite, from Mount Eryx in northern Sicily, which was for a time stronghold of the Carthaginian Empire. During the Second Punic War Venus became a patron goddess of Rome, and Carthage finally had to renounce northwestern Sicily. Venus, shown with the Ribbon of Love, is also the goddess of beauty. According to mythology, she sprang from the foam of the sea. Her son was Aeneas (see No. 87)

83   1 Dinar (Ag) 1969. ℞ Neptune, in vessel, drawn by four sea-horses. He is accompanied by a Triton (merman) on his left, and a mermaid on his right. While Venus was the goddess of fertility, Neptune (Greek: Poseidon) was the god of the seas, responsible for successful seafaring and fishing, (see the attributes in his hands), and therefore much respected by the Mediterranean people

30.00

30.00

30.00

84   1 Dinar (Ag) 1969. ℞ Hannibal (246–183

B. C.), son of Hamilcar Barca. Next to
his father, he was the most successful
Carthaginian commander. Hero of the
Second Punic War, he became, only
25 years old, the Commander-in-Chief
in Spain. In Spain in 219 B. C. he conquered the Roman stronghold of Sag-
untum and thus began the Second
Punic War (218–201 B. C.). The coin
pictures Hannibal leading his troops
(50,000 men, 9,000 horsemen, and 37
war elephants) over the Pyrenees and
the Alps towards Italy. This resulted in
the most crushing defeat ever suffered
by Rome (battle of Cannae). In 211
B. C., after years of fighting, Hannibal
finally approached Rome. Since a rea-
sonable peace treaty could not be
realized, Hannibal finally had to leave
Italy in 203 B. C. Following the decisive
battle at Zama (202 B. C.), Carthage
lost her predominance in the western
Mediterranean region

Proof

30.00

85   1 Dinar (Ag) 1969. ℞ Masinissa (after
        240–148 B. C.) Berber Prince and King
        of East Numidia. Supported the Car-
        thaginians in their fight against the Ro-
        mans in Spain. After the year 206 B. C.
        he sided with Rome, and united East
        and West Numidia in 201 B. C., thus
        becoming Carthage's principal oppo-
        nent. His cavalry conquered large Car-
        thaginian territories, thus causing the
        Third Punic War (149–146 B. C.), and
        the destruction of Carthage. Coin de-
        sign: Masinissa's profile, Numidian
        horseman, and map of Greater Numi-

dia which extended from Mauretania to Cyrenaica and included Carthage, the later Roman Province of Africa, today's Tunisia (see No. 86)

86   1 Dinar (Ag) 1969. ℞ Jugurtha. Jugurtha above map of Numidia. A scale behind his portrait shows a Numidian coin balancing the Capitoline she-wolf, the emblem of Rome. (The coin pictures a horse in front of a palm tree, symbolic of stock-farming and fruit growing). The adopted son of Micipsa (who is a son of the obove mentioned Masinissa), outwitted Micipsa's own sons, taking their inheritances as well as their lives. When he defeated the Italic people he became a danger to the Romans, a fact that led to the so-called Juguthine War (111–105 B.C.). His successful briberies among leading Romans culminated in his exclamation, "Oh venal city (Roma), how soon you shall be lost, if you will find a buyer."

30.00

87   1 Dinar (Ag) 1969. ℞ Vergilius. Publius

Vergilius Marco (70–19 B. C.), greatest Roman poet of the Augustan times. Also called Virgil. Pictured between Clio, the muse of history, and Melpomene, the muse of vocal music, Virgil is writing his National Epos, the Aeneid. Since Aeneas is considered the ancestor of the Romans, the poem tells the story from the Trojan War to the founding of Rome. The first chapter is about a storm that brought Aeneas' fleet after a seven year odyssey, to the Court of Queen Dido, the legendary founder of Carthage. The four-volume educational poem " Georgica" made Virgil famous in Africa, which was at that time the granary of Rome. It deals with the art of agriculture, the cultivation of trees, stock-raising, and bee-keeping. The design on the coin is modelled after and 2nd century Roman floor mosaic from Hadrumetum (Sousse), today in the Bardo Museum, Tunis ... 30.00

88 1 Dinar (Ag) 1969. ℞ Sbeitla – Sufetula. A portal with three arches built at former Roman Sufetula in honor of Emperor Antoninus Pius (150 A. D.). View of the ruins of the three Capitoline Temples near the Forum ... 30.00

89 1 Dinar (Ag) 1969. ℞ El Djem – Thysdrus. Amphitheatre. Because of its dimensions, the African Romans called it Colosseum. It was built around 240 A. D., in what is today El Djem (Roman: Thysdrus) by the emperors Gordianus I and III. Measuring 485 × 400 feet, with an arena of 214 × 124 feet. It seats approx. 35,000 people. As the second largest amphitheatre of the Roman Empire it is a silent witness of North African wealth. ... 30.00

90 1 Dinar (Ag) 1969. ℞ St. Augustinus. St. Aurelius Augustinus was one of the Latin ecclesiastical teachers of ancient times. Born in Tagaste (Numidia) in 354 A. D., he was Bishop in Hippo Regius/Bône, today's Annaba (Algeria) from 396 until his death in 430. As teacher of rhetoric in Carthage and Tagaste he founded the Augustinian philosophy, a sort of Christian Platonism, also known as Neo-Platonism.

Therefore, the bishop is portrayed on the coin sitting behind his desk in front of a bust of Plato. In the background are the ruins of the early Christian Basilica of St. Cyprian at Carthage, excavated in 1915

Proof

30.00

COMMEMORATIVE ISSUE FOR THE 2nd CONFERENCE OF THE FOOD AND AGRICULTURAL ORGANIZATION (FAO) OF THE UNITED NATIONS

			XF	Unc
91 (75)	1 Dinar (Ag) 1970		8.00	12.00

20th ANNIVERSARY OF INDEPENDENCE

			Unc
92 (76)	5 Dinars (Ag) 1976		40.00

FOR THE FAO COIN PLAN (2)

93 (77)	½ Dinar (Cu-Ni) 1976		5.00
94 (78)	1 Dinar (Cu-Ni) 1976		10.00

Türkei	**Turkey**	Turquie
	Türkiye Cümhuriyeti	

Area: 296,108 sq. mi. Population: 37,000,000.
From the nucleus of the once powerful Ottoman Empire, the modern Turkish state originated after the collapse as a sequel of World War I on October 29, 1923. Mustafa Kemal Pasha (Atatürk) was at the head of the National Turks during the time of the struggle for independence from 1919 to 1923. As the country's president, Kemal Pasha championed vigorously reforms and created a state on the lines of a Western pattern. Mustapha Kemal Pasha was given the surname of Atatürk (= Father of the Turks).
Capital: Ankara.

40 Para = 1 Piastre, 100 Piastres = 1 Lira or Pound,
100 Kurus = 1 Lira

			VF	XF
1 (43)	5	Para (Ni) 1910–1914 Toughra. ℞ value	0.80	1.50
2 (44)	10	Para (Ni) 1910–1915	0.80	1.50
3 (45)	20	Para (Ni) 1910–1914	0.80	1.50
4 (46)	40	Para (Ni) 1911–1913	1.50	2.50
5 (47)	1	Piastre (Ag) 1909–1911. Toughra, surrounded by stars	2.50	4.00
6 (48)	2	Piastres (Ag) 1909–1914	3.50	4.50
7 (49)	5	Piastres (Ag) 1909–1915	5.50	8.00
8 (50)	10	Piastres (Ag) 1909–1915	16.00	26.00
9 (51)	20	Piastres (Ag) 1916–1918	40.00	60.00
10 (F51)	12½	Piastres (Au) H-C 1327 (1909). Toughra, surrounded by stars and olive branches		160.00
11 (53)	25	Piastres (Au) H-C 1327 (1909)	52.00	65.00
12 (54)	50	Piastres (Au) H-C 1327 (1909)	85.00	105.00
13 (55)	100	Piastres (Au) H-C 1327 (1909)	100.00	120.00
14 (56)	250	Piastres (Au) H-C 1327 (1909)	620.00	800.00
15 (57)	500	Piastres (Au) H-C 1327 (1909)	800.00	1150.00
16 (58)	40	Para (Cu–Ni) 1921	2.00	3.00
17 (59)	2	Piastres (Ag) 1918–1919		250.00
18 (60)	5	Piastres (Ag) 1918–1919		260.00
19 (61)	10	Piastres (Ag) 1918–1919		300.00
20 (62)	20	Piastres (Ag) 1918–1919		250.00
21 (63)	25	Piastres (Au) 1919–1921	60.00	105.00
22 (64)	50	Piastres (Au) 1919–1921	220.00	260.00
23 (65)	100	Piastres (Au) 1919–1921	140.00	160.00
24 (66)	250	Piastres (Au) 1919–1921	120.00	140.00

			VF	XF
25 (67)	500	Piastres (Au) 1919–1921	1200.00	1550.00

Numbers 26–69 omitted.

REPUBLIC since 1923

			VF	XF
70 (68)	100	Para (Al–Br) H-C 1340–1342 (1922–1924). Ear of wheat. ℞ oak branch, value, state emblem above	6.00	12.00
71 (69)	5	Piastres (Al–Br) H-C 1340–1341 (1922–1923)	3.00	5.00
72 (70)	10	Piastres (Al–Br) H-C 1340–1341 (1922–1923)	3.00	5.50
73 (71)	25	Piastres (Ni) H-C 1341 (1923)	7.50	12.00
74 (68a)	100	Para (Al–Br) 1926	8.00	12.00
75 (69a)	5	Piastres (Al-Br) 1926	3.50	6.00
76 (70a)	10	Piastres (Al-Br) 1926	3.00	4.50
77 (71a)	25	Piastres (Ni) 1928	6.00	12.00
78 (72)	25	Piastres (Au) 1926–1929	80.00	120.00
79 (73)	50	Piastres (Au) 1926–1928	90.00	120.00
80 (74)	100	Piastres (Au) 1926–1928	300.00	400.00
81 (75)	250	Piastres (Au) 1926–1928	600.00	800.00

			VF	XF
82 (76)	500	Piastres (Au) 1926–1929	600.00	800.00
83 (77)	25	Piastres (Au) 1927–1928	120.00	160.00
84 (78)	50	Piastres (Au) 1927–1928. Same type as No. 83	170.00	220.00

		VF	XF
85 (79)	100 Piastres (Au) 1927–1928. Same type as No. 39	270.00	300.00
86 (80)	250 Piastres (Au) 1927–1928. Same type as No. 39	420.00	520.00
87 (81)	500 Piastres (Au) 1927–1928. Same type as No. 39	600.00	900.00

NEW CURRENCY: 100 Kurus = 1 Lira

		VF	XF
88 (82)	100 Kurus (Ag) 1934. Mustafa Kemal (1881–1938), called Atatürk (= Father of the Turks), 1st President 1923–1938. ℞ crescent and star (state emblem) and value	18.00	30.00
89 (83)	25 Kurus (Ag) 1935–1937. ℞ ear of wheat and value	5.00	10.00
90 (84)	50 Kurus (Ag) 1935–1937	8.00	13.00
91 (85)	1 Lira (Ag) 1937–1939	12.00	18.00
92 (87)	1 Kurus (Cu–Ni) 1936–1937	8.00	13.00
93 (88)	5 Kurus (Cu–Ni) 1935–1943	2.50	4.50
94 (89)	10 Kurus (Cu–Ni) 1935–1940	2.50	4.00
95 (90)	1 Kurus (Cu–Ni) 1938–1944	1.50	3.00
96 (91)	10 Para (Al–Br) 1940–1942	1.50	3.00
97 (92)	25 Kurus (Ni–Br) 1944–1946	2.50	4.00
98 (100)	25 Piastres (Au) 1943–. Head of Atatürk. Rev. Writing surrounded by wreath and 2 figures when added provide the exact year of minting, e.g. 1923 + 20 = 1943. No value; dia. 14.75 mm	22.00	25.00
99 (101)	50 Piastres (Au) 1943–. Type as No. 98; dia. 18 mm	35.00	48.00
100 (102)	100 Piastres (Au) 1943–. Type as No. 98; dia. 22 mm	90.00	100.00
101 (103)	250 Piastres (Au) 1943–. Type as No. 98; dia. 27.2 mm	190.00	210.00
102 (104)	500 Piastres (Au) 1943–. Type as No. 98; dia. 35 mm	400.00	450.00

			VF	XF
103	25	Piastres (Au) 1938–. Head of Atatürk in circle of stars and ornaments. Rev. Writing and year in circle of stars and ornaments. No value; dia. 18 mm	25.00	28.00
104	50	Piastres (Au) 1938–. Type as No. 103; dia. 22.5 mm	48.00	55.00
105	100	Piastres (Au) 1938–. Type as No. 103; dia. 31 mm	90.00	100.00
106	250	Piastres (Au) 1938–. Type as No. 103; dia. 43.5 mm	220.00	250.00
107	500	Piastres (Au) 1938–. Type as No. 103; dia. 46.5 mm	410.00	460.00
108 (86)	1	Lira (Ag) 1940–1941. Ismet Inönü (1884–1973), 2nd President 1938–1950	10.00	18.00
109 (A99)	25	Piastres (Au) 1943–1949. Head of Ismet Inönü. Rev. Writing surrounded by wreath and 2 figures, their addition provides the exact year of minting, e.g. 1923 + 20 = 1943. No value; dia. dia. 14.75 mm	30.00	40.00
110 (B99)	50	Piastres (Au) 1943–1950. Type as No. 109; dia. 18 mm	50.00	60.00
111 (C99)	100	Piastres (Au) 1943–1950. Type as No. 109; dia. 22 mm	95.00	105.00
112 (D99)	250	Piastres (Au) 1943–1947. Type as No. 109; dia. 27.2 mm	220.00	260.00
113 (E99)	500	Piastres (Au) 1943–1948. Type as No. 109; dia. 35 mm	400.00	450.00

LUXURY STRIKES (5)

114	25	Piastres (Au) 1943–1949. Head of Ismet Inönü in circle of stars and ornaments. Rev. Writing and year in circle of stars and ornaments. No value; dia. 18 mm	90.00	120.00
115	50	Piastres (Au) 1943–1949. Type as No. 114; dia. 22.5 mm	130.00	150.00
116	100	Piastres (Au) 1943–1950. Type as No. 114; dia. 31 mm	130.00	150.00
117	250	Piastres (Au) 1943–1950. Type as No. 114; dia. 43.5 mm	250.00	270.00
118	500	Piastres (Au) 1943–1948. Type as No. 114; dia. 46.5 mm	500.00	600.00
119 (A92)	½	Kurus (Bra) 1948		450.00
120 (93)	1	Kurus (Bra) 1947–1951	0.20	0.40
121 (94)	2½	Kurus (Bra) 1948–1951	0.80	1.60
122 (95)	5	Kurus (Bra) 1949–1957	0.80	1.60
123 (96)	10	Kurus (Bra) 1949–1956	1.20	2.50
124 (97)	25	Kurus (Bra) 1948–1956	1.20	2.50
125 (98)	50	Kurus (Ag) 1947–1948	5.00	7.00

			VF	XF
126 (99)	1	Lira (Ag) 1947–1948	5.00	8.00
127 (110)	1	Lira (Cu–Ni) 1957. Mustafa Kemal, called Atatürk. ℞ value in wreath	1.60	3.00
128 (111)	5	Kurus (Br) 1958–1968	0.20	0.40
129 (112)	10	Kurus (Br) 1958–1968	0.25	0.50
130 (113)	25	Kurus (St) 1959–1966. Peasant woman	0.40	0.60
131 (114)	1	Lira (St) 1959–1967. Atatürk	0.50	0.80
132 (115)	2½	Lira (St) 1960–. Atatürk in uniform:		
		a) 1960–1968; 12 gm.	0.80	2.00
		b) 1969–; 9 gm.	0.40	0.80

			VF	XF
133 (116)	10	Lira (Ag) 1960–. Atatürk. ℞ emblem of the National Unity Committee and date May 27, 1960 = the day when General Cemal Gürsel came to power	10.50	16.00
134 (117)	1	Kurus (Bra) 1961 1963. Olive branch	0.25	0.35
135 (117a)	1	Kurus (Br) 1963–1974	0.10	0.20
136 (111a)	5	Kurus (Br) 1969–1973. Same type as No. 128, but reduced weight	0.10	0.20
137 (112a)	10	Kurus (Br) 1969–1973. Same type as No. 129	0.10	0.20
138 (113a)	25	Kurus (St) 1966–1978. Same type as No. 130	0.30	0.50
139 (114a)	1	Lira (St) 1967–1979. Same type as No. 131, but lower weight	0.30	0.50

ISSUES (2) FOR THE FAO COIN PLAN

			XF	Unc
140	10	Kurus (Br) 1971–1974. Atatürk on tractor (symbolical for progress). R Ears of wheat (Triticum aestivum – Gramineae), value, date:		
		a) (Y A118) 1971, 1972; 3.40 gm.	0.35	0.50
		b) (Y A118a) 1974; 2.75 gm.	2.50	6.00

Turkey 1315

141 (118) 2½ Lira (St) 1970. Atatürk at wheel of tractor. Motto: "The plough is superior to the sword". ℞ value and date between tied ears of wheat and laurel branches

	XF	Unc
	0.80	1.20

COMMEMORATIVE ISSUE FOR THE 50th ANNIVERSARY OF THE TURKISH PARLIAMENT

142 (119) 25 Lira (Ag) 1970. Atatürk. ℞ Parliament building in Ankara, value

	XF	Unc
	12.00	16.00

143 (A113) 50 Kurus (Ac) 1971–1977. Turkish woman in national costume. R value

	XF	Unc
	0.16	0.35

COMMEMORATIVE ISSUE FOR THE 900th ANNIVERSARY OF THE VICTORY OF THE SELJUKS OVER THE BYZANTINES

144 (120) 50 Lira (Ag) 1971. Alparslan (reigned

	Unc	Proof

from 1063 to 1073), was victorious at Manzikert on Lake Wan over the Byzantines led by Romanos IV. ℞ Asia Minor with marking of the battle-field 15.00 35.00

COMMEMORATIVE ISSUE FOR THE 50th ANNIVERSARY OF KEMAL ATATÜRK'S ENTRY INTO SMYRNA

145 (121) 50 Lira (Ag) 1972. Equestrian statue of Atatürk. ℞ scene of battle   15.00   35.00

50th ANNIVERSARY OF THE REPUBLIC (3)

	XF	Unc
146 (122) 50 Lira (Ag) 1973		12.00
147 (123) 100 Lira (Ag) 1973. Type as No. 146		22.00

148 (124) 500 Lira (Au) 1973. Type similar to No. 146		140.00
149 (111b) 5 Kurus (Br) 1974. Type as No. 136; 1.35 gr.	0.10	0.30

	XF	Unc
150 (112b) 10 Kurus (Br) 1974. Type as No. 137; 2.5 gr.	0.10	0.30
151 (125) 5 Lira (St) 1974–1979. Atatürk on horseback	0.80	1.20
152 (117b) 1 Kurus (Al) 1975–1977. Type as No. 134	0.05	0.10
153 (111b) 5 Kurus (Al) 1975–1977. Type as No. 128	0.05	0.15
154 (112b) 10 Kurus (Al) 1975–1977. Type as No. 129	0.10	0.20

FOR THE FAO COIN PLAN (2)

		XF	Unc
155 (126) 5 Kurus (Al) 1975. Anatolic bride		0.25	0.40
156 10 Kurus (Al) 1975, 1976. Type as No. 140		0.40	0.60

FOR THE FAO COIN PLAN (3)

		XF	Unc
157 (128) 5 Kurus (Al) 1976		0.25	0.40
158 (129) 10 Kurus (Al) 1976		0.25	0.40

		XF	Unc
159 (127) 5 Lira (St) 1976		1.00	1.50

FOR THE FAO COIN PLAN (3)

		XF	Unc
160 2½ Lira (St) 1977		0.80	1.20
161 5 Lira (St) 1977		1.20	2.00
162 50 Lira (Ag) 1977		10.00	16.00

WORLD SOCCER CHAMPIONSHIP GAMES IN ARGENTINA 1978

		Unc	Proof
163	150 Lira (Ag) 1978	25.00	80.00

705th ANNIVERSARY OF THE DEATH OF MEVLANA (3)

164	200 Lira (Ag) 1978. Mevlana Jelal ed-Din Rumi (1207–1273), mystic poet	15.00	20.00
165	500 Lira (Au) 1978 (900 pieces)		300.00
166	1000 Lira (Au) 1978 (450 pieces)		650.00

FOR THE FAO COIN PLAN (8)

		XF	Unc
167	50 Kurus (St) 1978. Type as No. 159	0.20	0.40
168	1 Lira (St) 1978. Type as No. 159	0.40	0.60
169	2½ Lira (St) 1978. Type as No. 159	0.50	1.00
170	5 Lira (St) 1978. Type as No. 141	1.00	1.50
171	150 Lira (Ag) 1978. Type as No. 141	16.00	20.00

172   150 Lira (Ag) 1978. Type as No. 171, but
        edge inscription FAO and arabesques   30.00

173   500 Lira (Au) 1978. Mother and child   300.00
174   1000 Lira (Au) 1978. Anatolic bride   500.00

FOR THE FAO COIN PLAN (9)

		XF	Unc
175	1 Kurus (Br) 1979. Anatolic bride. Rev. olive branch	0.50	1.00
176	1 Kurus (Al) 1979. Type as No. 175	0.50	1.00

		XF	Unc
177	50 Kurus (St) 1979. Type as No. 141	0.50	1.00
178	1 Lira (St) 1979. Type as No. 141	0.50	1.00
179	2½ Lira (St) 1979. Anatolic bride. Rev. value	0.50	1.00
180	5 Lira (St) 1979. Type as No. 179	0.90	1.50
181	150 Lira (Ag) 1979. Type as No. 179	10.00	12.00

		Proof
182	500 Lira (Au) 1979. Anatolic bride	300.00
183	1000 Lire (Au) 1979. Mother and child	500.00

1320   **Turkey**

		XF	Unc
184	5 Kurus (Br) 1980. Fishermen within a flounder. Rev. oak branch	0.40	0.80
185	10 Kurus (Br) 1980. Anatolic bride. Rev. corn-ears	0.40	0.80
186	50 Kurus (St) 1980. Anatolic bride. Rev. value in wreath	0.40	0.80
187	1 Lira (St) 1980. Type as No. 186	0.40	0.80
188	2½ Lira (St) 1980. Fishermen within a flounder. Rev. value in wreath	0.50	1.00
189	5 Lira (St) 1980. Type as No. 188	1.00	1.50
190	500 Lira (Ag) 1980. Mother and child		15.00
191	500 Lira (Au) 1980. Type as No. 190	Proof	300.00

Turks and Caicos Islands

Turks- und Caicos-Inseln   **Turks et Caicos (Iles des)**

Area: 166 sq. mi. Population: 8000.
The Turks and Caicos Islands form the southeastern group of the Bahamas.

12 Pence = 1 Shilling, 20 Shillings = 1 £

			Unc	Proof
1 (1)	1	Crown (Cu–Ni) 1969. Elizabeth II. ℞ coat of arms with heraldic designs: queen conch (Strombus gigas – Strombidae), lobster (Palinurus argus – Palinuridae), Turks's head cactus (Melocactus communis – Cactaceae); helmet decoration: brown pelican (Pelecanus occidentalis – Pelecanidae); shield supporters: red flamingos (Phoenicopterus ruber ruber – Phoenicopteridae)	4.00	15.00

100th ANNIVERSARY OF THE BIRTH OF SIR WINSTON CHURCHILL (3)

			Unc	Proof
2 (2)	20	Crowns (Ag) 1974. Bust of Sir Winston Churchill	30.00	45.00
3 (3)	50	Crowns (Au) 1974. Type as No. 2	80.00	110.00
4 (4)	100	Crowns (Au) 1974. Type as No. 2	150.00	220.00
5 (6)	5	Crowns (Ag) 1975–1977	15.00	20.00
6 (9)	25	Crowns (Au) 1975, 1976. Rev. coat of arms:		
		a) 1975; 17 mm dia.	70.00	50.00
		b) 1976, 1977; 19 mm dia.	45.00	50.00

			Unc	Proof
7 (5)	1	Crown (Cu-Ni) 1975–1977. Rev. map	4.00	8.00
8 (7)	10	Crowns (Ag) 1975. Two spacecraft in orbit	35.00	45.00
9 (8)	20	Crowns (Ag) 1975. Christopher Columbus	40.00	50.00
10 (10)	50	Crowns (Au) 1975. Type as No. 9	150.00	125.00
11 (11)	100	Crowns (Au) 1975. Type as No. 8	200.00	200.00

BICENTENARY OF AMERICAN INDEPENDENCE (2)

			Unc	Proof
12 (12)	20	Crowns (Ag) 1976. King George III and George Washington	40.00	50.00
13 (13)	50	Crowns (Au) 1976. Type as No. 12	150.00	140.00
14 (14)	10	Crowns (Ag) 1976, 1977. Rev. salt windmill	35.00	40.00

QUEEN VICTORIA COMMEMORATIVE (3)

			Unc	Proof
15 (15)	20	Crowns (Ag) 1976. Four portraits of Queen Victoria	40.00	50.00
16 (16)	50	Crowns (Ag) 1976. Type as No. 15	65.00	80.00
17 (17)	100	Crowns (Au) 1976. Type as No. 15	200.00	220.00

25th ANNIVERSARY OF THE SILVER JUBILEE OF HER MAJESTY

QUEEN ELIZABETH II (2)

			Unc	Proof
18 (18)	25	Crowns (Ag) 1977	50.00	75.00
19 (19)	50	Crowns (Au) 1977	100.00	120.00

GEORGE III PORTRAITS

			Unc	Proof
20 (20)	20	Crowns (Ag) 1977	40.00	50.00
21 (21)	50	Crowns (Ag) 1977	70.00	75.00
22 (22)	100	Crowns (Au) 1977	200.00	220.00

11th COMMONWEALTH GAMES (2)

			Unc	Proof
23 (23)	20	Crowns (Ag) 1978	40.00	
24 (24)	100	Crowns (Au) 1978	220.00	

25th ANNIVERSARY OF CORONATION (20)

		Proof
25 (25)	25 Crowns (Ag) 1978. The lion of England	50.00
26 (26)	25 Crowns (Ag) 1978. The griffin of Edward III	50.00
27 (27)	25 Crowns (Ag) 1978. The red dragon of Wales	50.00
28 (28)	25 Crowns (Ag) 1978. The white greyhound of Richmond	50.00
29 (29)	25 Crowns (Ag) 1978. The unicorn of Scotland	50.00
30 (30)	25 Crowns (Ag) 1978. The white horse of Hanover	50.00
31 (31)	25 Crowns (Ag) 1978. The black bull of Clarence	50.00
32 (32)	25 Crowns (Ag) 1978. The yale of Beaufort	50.00
33 (33)	25 Crowns (Ag) 1978. The falcon of the Plantagenets	50.00
34 (34)	25 Crowns (Ag) 1978. The white lion of Mortimer	50.00
35 (35)	50 Crowns (Au) 1978. Type as No. 25	120.00
36 (36)	50 Crowns (Au) 1978. Type as No. 26	120.00
37 (37)	50 Crowns (Au) 1978. Type as No. 27	120.00
38 (38)	50 Crowns (Au) 1978. Type as No. 28	120.00
39 (39)	50 Crowns (Au) 1978. Type as No. 29	120.00
40 (40)	50 Crowns (Au) 1978. Type as No. 30	120.00
41 (41)	50 Crowns (Au) 1978. Type as No. 31	120.00
42 (42)	50 Crowns (Au) 1978. Type as No. 32	120.00
43 (43)	50 Crowns (Au) 1978. Type as No. 33	120.00
44 (44)	50 Crowns (Au) 1978. Type as No. 34	120.00

10th ANNIVERSARY OF INVESTITURE OF CHARLES AS PRINCE OF WALES (2)

		Proof
45 (45)	10 Crowns (Ag) 1979	50.00
46 (46)	100 Crowns (Au) 1979	250.00

LORD MOUNTBATTEN (4)

47 (47)	5 Crowns (Ag) 1980:	
	a) normal thickness	25.00
	b) Piéfort	100.00
48 (48)	10 Crowns (Ag) 1980:	
	a) normal thickness	40.00
	b) Piéfort	140.00

				Proof
49 (49)	20	Crowns (Ag) 1980:		
		a) normal thickness		45.00
		b) Piéfort		180.00
50 (50)	100	Crowns (Au) 1980:		
		a) normal thickness		350.00
		b) Piéfort		1200.00

WEDDING OF PRINCE CHARLES AND LADY DIANA

51 (51)	100	Crowns (Au) 1981. Conjoined heads	250.00

Tuwa   # Tuva   **Touva**

Area: 65,800 sq. mi. Population: 192,000.
This country, also known by the name of Tannu Tuva, used to belong
as the northern part of Mongolia to the Chinese, later to the Czarist
sphere of influence, and in September 1921 became the independent
Tuvin Aratic Republic (TAR = People's Republic Tuva). Since October 11, 1944, Tuva is an autonomous region within the association of
states within the Soviet Union.
Capital: Kyzyl.

100 KΘPEJEH (= Kopeks) = 1 AKSA (= Rouble)

				VF	**XF**
1 (1)	1	KΘPEJEH (Al) 1934. Designation of state in a circle inscription in Tuvinian-Latin letters. ℞ value and date		40.00	60.00
2 (2)	2	KΘPEJEH (Al) 1934. Type as No. 1		40.00	60.00
3 (3)	3	KΘPEJEH (Al) 1934. Type as No. 1		40.00	60.00
4 (4)	5	KΘPEJEH (Al) 1934. Type as No. 1		40.00	60.00
5 (5)	10	KΘPEJEH (Cu–Ni) 1934. Type as No. 1		40.00	60.00
6 (6)	15	KΘPEJEH (Cu–Ni) 1934. Type as No. 1		50.00	70.00
7 (7)	20	KΘPEJEH (Cu–Ni) 1934. Type as No. 1		50.00	65.00

Tuvalu

Area: 10 sq. mi. Population: 7,000.

In October 1975, the nine Ellice Islands (formerly a part of the Gilbert and Ellice Colony) gained self government and became British Dependency of Tuvalu.
Capital: Funafuti.

100 Cents = 1 Dollar

			Unc	Proof
1 (1)	1 Cent (Br) 1976. Bust right of the Queen. Rev.		0.15	1.00
2 (2)	2 Cents (Br) 1976		0.20	1.00
3 (3)	5 Cents (Cu-Ni) 1976		0.40	1.50
4 (4)	10 Cents (Cu-Ni) 1976. Rev. crab		0.50	2.00
5 (5)	20 Cents (Cu-Ni) 1976. Rev. flying fish		0.80	2.50
6 (6)	50 Cents (Cu-Ni) 1976. Rev. octopus		1.50	3.00
7 (7)	1 Dollar (Cu-Ni) 1976. Rev. sea-turtle		4.00	5.00
8 (8)	5 Dollars (Ag) 1976. Rev. outrigger canoe			40.00
9 (9)	50 Dollars (Au) 1976. Rev. native's hut			300.00

1th ANNIVERSARY OF INDEPENDENCE

10 (10)	10 Dollars 1979. Two-masted sailing vessel »Rebecca«:		
	a) .925 silver		60.00
	b) .500 silver	30.00	

80th BIRTHDAY OF QUEEN MOTHER

11 (11)	10 Dollars 1980. Portrait of Queen Mother:		
	a) .925 silver		40.00
	b) .500 silver	25.00	

WEDDING OF PRINCE CHARLES AND LADY DIANA

12 (12)	5 Dollars (Ag) 1981	65.00

DUKE OF EDINBURGH'S AWARD

13 (13)	10 Dollars (Ag) 1981	30.00

Uganda # Uganda **Ouganda**

Area: 93,981 sq. mi. Population: 14,000,000.
This former British protectorate in East Africa became an independent
republic within the framework of the British Commonwealth on October 9, 1962.
Capital: Kampala.

100 Cents = 1 Uganda Shilling

			XF	Unc
1 (1)	5	Cents (Br) 1966. Value in letters. ℞ numeral of value between elephant's tusks	0.10	0.20
2 (2)	10	Cents (Br) 1966. Same type as No. 1	0.15	0.30
3 (3)	20	Cents (Br) 1966. Same type as No. 1	0.25	0.40
4 (4)	50	Cents (Cu–Ni) 1966. Coat of arms. ℞ eastern crowned crane (Balearica pavonina gibberifrons – Balearicidae) and mountains	0.30	0.50
5 (5)	1	Shilling (Cu–Ni) 1966	0.40	1.00

6 (6)	2	Shillings (Cu–Ni) 1966	0.90	1.50

7 (7) 5 Shillings (Cu–Ni) 1968. On the left of the coat of arms a southern Uganda buffon's kob (Adenota kob thomasi – Bovidae), supporting the shield, coffee branch below (Coffea arabica – Rubiaceae), on the right the shield is supported by an eastern crowned crane, below cotton plant. (Gossypium sp. – Malvaceae). ℞ cattle: cow with calf. Legend reads "Produce more food – FAO Coin Plan"

	Unc	Proof
	4.00	12.00

COMMEMORATIVE COINS (10) FOR THE VISIT OF POPE PAUL VI TO KAMPALA, ON JULY 31, 1969

8 2 Shillings (Ag) 1969–. Portrait of Pope Paul VI, right, with cap; papal arms; martyr shrine. ℞ coat of arms, value

12.00

9

11

9	5	Shillings (Ag) 1969–. Eastern crowned crane and hippopotamus in African landscape. ℞ like No. 8	**Proof** 22.00
10	10	Shillings (Ag) 1969–. Martyr shrine in Namugongo near Kampala, built in honour of the 22 Uganda martyrs (1885/87). ℞ like No. 8	35.00
11	20	Shillings (Ag) 1969–. Pope Paul VI, in blessing gesture. Map of Africa and Southern Europe, with itinerary Rome – Libya – Sudan – Kampala. ℞ like No. 8	55.00
12	25	Shillings (Ag) 1969–. Pope Paul VI in front of stylized globe, marking the Pope's visits during the past pontificate: Jerusalem 1964, Bombay 1964, New York 1965, Fatima 1967, Constantinople 1967, Bogotá 1968, Geneva 1969, Kampala 1969. ℞ like No. 8	**Proof** 75.00
13	30	Shillings (Ag) 1969–. Same type as No. 8	90.00
14	50	Shillings (Au) 1969–. Same type as No. 10	120.00
15	100	Shillings (Au) 1969–. Same type as No. 11	240.00
16	500	Shillings (Au) 1969–. Same type as No. 12	1000.00
17	1000	Shillings (Au) 1969–. Same type as No. 8	1750.00
			Unc
18 (8)	5	Shillings (Cu–Ni) 1972. Same type as No. 4 (heptagonal)	–.–

Umm Al Kiwain   # Umm al Qiwain   **Oumm Al Qiwain**

Area: 290 sq. mi. Population: 3700.
The Sheikdom of Umm al Qiwain is one of the seven Trucial States in
Pacified Oman. Since December 2, 1971 Umm al Qiwain is a member
state of the "United Arab Emirates" (UAE).
Capital: Umm al Qiwain.

100 Dirham = 1 Umm al Qiwain Riyal

			Proof
1	1	Riyal (Ag) 1970. Old cannon. ℞ state emblem, value	8.00
2	2	Riyals (Ag) 1970. Portuguese fort of the 19th century, and cannon. ℞ like No. 1	10.00

3	5	Riyals (Ag) 1970. Gazelle (Gazella gazella – Bovidae). ℞ like No. 1	18.00
4	10	Riyals (Ag) 1970. Abu Simbel, seated statues of Rameses II from the northern facade of the Great Rock Temple (19th Dynasty, c. 1250 B. C.). ℞ like No. 1	30.00
5	25	Riyals (Au) 1970. Same type as No. 1	60.00
6	50	Riyals (Au) 1970. Same type as No. 2	120.00
7	100	Riyals (Au) 1970. Same type as No. 3	250.00
8	200	Riyals (Au) 1970. Sheik Ahmed Ben Rashid Al Maalla. ℞ like No. 1	500.00

United Arab Emirates

Vereinigte Arabische Emirate   **Émirats Arabes Unis**

The sheikdoms of Abu Dhabi, Ajman, Dubai, Fujairah, Sharjah and
Umm al Qaiwain proclaimed the Federation of Arab Emirates on 2nd
December 1971. The residence of Sheikh Sajed bin Sultan in Abu Dhabi
was declared the provisional capital. By mid-February 1972 the seventh
Gulf sheikdom, Ras al Khaimah, joined the federation.

100 Fils = 1 Dirham

COMMEMORATIVE ISSUES (2) FOR THE FAO COIN PLAN

		XF	Unc
1 (1)	1 Fils (Br) 1973. Date palms (Phoenix dactylifera – Palmae) with legend "Increase Food Production"	0.30	0.60

2 (2)	5 Fils (Br) 1973. Mata Hari fish (Lethrinus nebulosus – Lithrinidae) with legend "Cleaner seas, more food for mankind"	0.30	0.60
3 (3)	10 Fils (Ni–Bra) 1973. Arab dhow	0.40	0.60
4 (4)	25 Fils (Cu–Ni) 1973. Arab dune gazelle (Gazella leptoceros – Bovidae)	0.50	0.80
5 (5)	50 Fils (Cu–Ni) 1973. Oil derricks	0.80	1.20
6 (6)	1 Dirham (Cu–Ni) 1973. Jug	1.00	2.00

INTERNATIONAL YEAR OF THE CHILD (2)

		Proof
7 (7)	50 Dirhams (Ag) 1980	40.00
8 (8)	750 Dirhams (Au) 1980	800.00

United States of America

Vereinigte Staaten von Amerika   **États-Unis d'Amérique**

Area: 3,619,615 aq. mi. Population: 216,000,000.
The United States of America are a presidential republic in accordance with the Federal Constitution of 1787.
Capital: Washington, D.C.

> 10 Cents = 1 Dime, 25 Cents = Quarter Dollar,
> 50 Cents = Half Dollar, 100 Cents = 1 Dollar,
> 10 Dollars = 1 Eagle

Mints and mintmarks:

CC = Carson City, Nevada. 1870-1893.
D = Denver, Colorado. 1906 to date.
O = New Orleans, Louisiana. 1838-1909.
P   = Philadelphia, Pennsylvania. 1793 to date. Coins struck at Philadelphia
     (with some exceptions) do not carry a mintmark.
S   = San Francisco, California. 1854 to date.
L   = the initial of the engraver, Longacre.

1 (2b)   1 Cent (Br) 1864–1909. Head of Red Indian squaw with plumes. ℞ denomination in words, surrounded by laurel wreath and escutcheon:

	Mintage	Fine	VF	XF
1864	39,233,714	8.00	16.00	65.00
1864 L		40.00	90.00	140.00
1865	35,429,286	6.00	15.00	30.00
1866	9,826,500	25.00	50.00	85.00
1867	9,821,000	25.00	50.00	85.00
1868	10,266,500	25.00	50.00	85.00
1869/8	6,420,000	165.00	300.00	460.00
1869		50.00	85.00	150.00
1870	5,275,000	35.00	60.00	110.00
1871	3,929,500	40.00	76.00	110.00
1872	4,042,000	60.00	100.00	160.00
1873	11,676,500	12.00	20.00	45.00
1874	14,187,500	10.00	18.00	40.00
1875	13,528,000	10.00	20.00	40.00
1876	7,944,000	18.00	30.00	50.00
1877	852,500	350.00	600.00	900.00
1878	5,799,850	22.00	42.00	56.00
1879	16,231,200	7.00	14.00	20.00
1880	38,964,955	3.00	5.00	12.00
1881	39,211,575	2.50	5.00	12.00
1882	38,581,100	2.50	5.00	12.00
1883	45,589,109	2.50	5.00	12.00
1884	23,261,742	4.00	9.00	18.00
1885	11,765,384	7.00	14.00	30.00
1886	17,654,290	5.00	10.00	22.00
1887	45,226,483	2.00	4.00	10.00
1888	37,494,414	2.00	4.00	10.00
1889	48,869,361	2.00	4.00	10.00
1890	57,182,854	2.00	4.00	10.00
1891	47,072,350	2.00	4.00	10.00
1892	37,649,832	2.00	4.00	10.00
1893	46,642,195	2.00	4.00	10.00
1894	16,752,132	4.00	8.00	20.00
1895	38,343,636	1.50	3.00	6.00
1896	39,057,293	1.50	3.00	6.00
1897	50,466,330	1.50	3.00	6.00
1898	49,823,079	1.50	3.00	6.00
1899	53,600,031	1.50	3.00	6.00
1900	66,833,764	1.50	3.00	6.00
1901	79,611,143	1.50	3.00	6.00
1902	87,376,722	1.50	3.00	6.00
1903	85,094,493	1.50	3.00	6.00
1904	61,328,015	1.50	3.00	6.00
1905	80,719,163	1.50	3.00	6.00
1906	96,022,255	1.50	3.00	6.00
1907	108,138,618	1.50	3.00	6.00
1908	32,327,987	1.50	3.00	6.00
1908 S	1,115,000	16.00	30.00	45.00
1909	14,370,645	2.00	4.00	9.00
1909 S	309,000	160.00	220.00	285.00

2 (14) 5 Cents (Cu–Ni) 1883–1913. Head of the
Goddess of Liberty facing left. ℞
Roman numeral in laurel wreath, name
of country, coin designation CENTS
at bottom:

	Mintage	Fine	VF	XF
1883 NC	5,479,519	4.00	7.00	12.00
1883 WC	16,032,983	15.00	22.00	40.00
1884	11,273,942	18.00	26.00	45.00
1885	1,476,490	450.00	600.00	900.00
1886	3,330,290	90.00	130.00	220.00
1887	15,263,652	15.00	22.00	40.00
1888	10,720,483	17.00	24.00	42.00
1889	15,881,361	18.00	26.00	45.00
1890	16,259,272	18.00	26.00	45.00
1891	16,834,350	18.00	26.00	45.00
1892	11,699,642	18.00	26.00	45.00
1893	13,370,195	18.00	26.00	45.00
1894	5,413,132	20.00	35.00	70.00
1895	9,979,884	22.00	28.00	46.00
1896	8,842,920	22.00	28.00	46.00
1897	20,428,735	4.00	8.00	22.00
1898	12,532,087	4.00	9.00	24.00
1899	26,029,031	3.00	8.00	25.00
1900	27,255,995	3.00	8.00	25.00
1901	26,480,213	3.00	8.00	25.00
1902	31,480,579	3.00	8.00	25.00
1903	28,006,725	3.00	8.00	25.00
1904	21,404,984	3.00	9.00	28.00
1905	29,827,276	3.00	8.00	25.00
1906	38,613,725	2.50	7.00	22.00
1907	39,214,800	2.50	7.00	22.00
1908	22,686,177	2.50	7.00	22.00
1909	11,590,526	3.00	8.00	24.00
1910	30,169,353	2.50	7.00	22.00
1911	39,559,372	2.50	7.00	22.00
1912	26,236,714	2.50	7.00	22.00
1912 D	8,474,000	10.00	20.00	55.00
1912 S	238,000	60.00	110.00	260.00
1913	only 5 pieces known.			

3 (15) 1 Dime (Ag) 1892–1916. Laurel-wreathed head of the Goddess of Liberty facing right. ℞ denomination in words in wreath:

	without mintmark		D		O		S	
1892	15.00	35.00			20.00	40.00	80.00	130.00
1893	20.00	45.00			60.00	90.00	35.00	60.00
1894	35.00	65.00			130.00	220.00	–.–	–.–
1895	180.00	300.00			380.00	550.00	65.00	100.00
1896	40.00	65.00			160.00	220.00	150.00	200.00
1897	17.00	35.00			140.00	200.00	50.00	80.00
1898	15.00	32.00			45.00	80.00	20.00	45.00
1899	12.00	28.00			35.00	60.00	30.00	50.00
1900	15.00	35.00			40.00	75.00	16.00	35.00
1901	15.00	35.00			22.00	50.00	170.00	260.00
1902	15.00	32.00			20.00	42.00	35.00	60.00
1903	15.00	32.00			20.00	42.00	130.00	220.00
1904	16.00	35.00					125.00	190.00
1905	15.00	30.00			35.00	60.00	20.00	40.00
1906	12.00	30.00	20.00	42.00	30.00	50.00	20.00	40.00
1907	12.00	30.00	20.00	40.00	20.00	40.00	20.00	40.00
1908	15.00	32.00	15.00	32.00	30.00	50.00	22.00	42.00
1909	15.00	32.00	40.00	65.00	22.00	45.00	48.00	70.00
1910	15.00	32.00	20.00	40.00			25.00	45.00
1911	12.00	28.00	12.00	28.00			20.00	40.00
1912	12.00	28.00	12.00	28.00			20.00	40.00
1913	12.00	28.00					80.00	155.00
1914	12.00	28.00	12.00	28.00			20.00	40.00
1915	18.00	40.00					25.00	50.00
1916	12.00	28.00					17.00	36.00

4 (16) Quarter Dollar (Ag) 1892–1916. Laurel-wreathed head of the Goddess of Liberty facing right. ℞ state coat of arms of the Union and thirteen stars, symbolizing the thirteen original States:

	without mintmark		D		O		S	
1892	36.00	70.00			40.00	75.00	75.00	130.00
1893	40.00	75.00			40.00	75.00	60.00	110.00
1894	32.00	68.00			50.00	90.00	45.00	85.00
1895	36.00	70.00			45.00	85.00	65.00	110.00
1896	36.00	70.00			70.00	130.00	800.00	1300.00
1897	32.00	65.00			30.00	60.00	70.00	120.00
1898	35.00	70.00			45.00	85.00	42.00	80.00
1899	30.00	65.00			45.00	85.00	55.00	100.00
1900	35.00	70.00			60.00	115.00	36.00	70.00
1901	35.00	70.00			100.00	180.00	2400.00	3600.00
1902	30.00	65.00			45.00	80.00	60.00	100.00
1903	35.00	70.00			45.00	80.00	65.00	110.00
1904	35.00	70.00			65.00	110.00		
1905	35.00	70.00			68.00	115.00	45.00	82.00
1906	42.00	75.00	45.00	85.00	52.00	90.00		
1907	35.00	70.00	45.00	85.00	40.00	72.00	45.00	82.00
1908	35.00	70.00	32.00	70.00	32.00	70.00	60.00	110.00
1909	30.00	70.00	30.00	70.00	90.00	170.00	35.00	75.00
1910	38.00	75.00	45.00	85.00			45.00	92.00
1911	35.00	72.00	60.00	110.00			45.00	90.00
1912	40.00	78.00					1000.00	1700.00
1913	140.00	380.00	45.00	100.00			80.00	175.00
1914	30.00	65.00	30.00	65.00			50.00	100.00
1915	30.00	65.00	30.00	65.00				
1916	35.00	68.00	30.00	65.00				

5 (17)   Half Dollar (Ag) 1892–1915. Laurel-wreathed head of the Goddess of Liberty facing right. ℞ state coat of arms of the Union and thirteen stars:

1892	75.00	180.00			280.00	460.00	280.00	380.00
1893	90.00	180.00			110.00	250.00	250.00	350.00
1894	95.00	190.00			100.00	240.00	70.00	170.00
1895	80.00	175.00			90.00	190.00	120.00	240.00
1896	100.00	210.00			130.00	290.00	190.00	360.00
1897	70.00	150.00			180.00	390.00	170.00	375.00
1898	60.00	125.00			150.00	340.00	70.00	140.00
1899	60.00	130.00			80.00	180.00	65.00	130.00
1900	65.00	140.00			80.00	180.00	65.00	130.00
1901	60.00	130.00			120.00	280.00	175.00	380.00
1902	70.00	150.00			70.00	150.00	100.00	200.00
1903	75.00	165.00			100.00	200.00	65.00	145.00
1904	60.00	130.00			120.00	250.00	150.00	300.00
1905	100.00	210.00			130.00	285.00	65.00	140.00
1906	60.00	130.00	60.00	130.00	60.00	130.00	65.00	140.00
1907	60.00	130.00	60.00	130.00	60.00	130.00	65.00	140.00

	without mintmark		D		O		S	
1908	90.00	210.00	60.00	130.00	60.00	130.00	70.00	150.00
1909	60.00	130.00			85.00	200.00	60.00	130.00
1910	100.00	250.00					60.00	130.00
1911	70.00	145.00	80.00	190.00			65.00	140.00
1912	60.00	130.00	60.00	130.00			60.00	130.00
1913	180.00	350.00	80.00	170.00			80.00	175.00
1914	185.00	370.00					65.00	140.00
1915	150.00	340.00	60.00	130.00			60.00	130.00

6 (18)   1 Dollar (Ag) 1878-1921. Head of Liberty,
Morgan type:

	without mintmark		CC		O		S	
1878	20.00	30.00	35.00	42.00			18.00	22.00
1879	15.00	20.00	70.00	180.00	15.00	20.00	15.00	20.00
1880	14.00	19.00	50.00	75.00	14.00	19.00	15.00	20.00
1881	14.00	19.00	80.00	100.00	14.00	19.00	14.00	19.00
1882	14.00	19.00	35.00	40.00	14.00	19.00	14.00	19.00
1883	14.00	19.00	35.00	40.00	14.00	19.00	14.00	20.00
1884	14.00	19.00	40.00	50.00	14.00	19.00	15.00	25.00
1885	14.00	19.00	150.00	190.00	14.00	19.00	20.00	28.00
1886	14.00	19.00			14.00	19.00	35.00	50.00
1887	14.00	19.00			14.00	19.00	20.00	28.00
1888	14.00	19.00			14.00	19.00	50.00	65.00
1889	14.00	19.00	400.00	800.00	14.00	19.00	48.00	60.00
1890	14.00	19.00	35.00	48.00	15.00	22.00	22.00	30.00
1891	20.00	24.00	35.00	48.00	20.00	24.00	22.00	28.00
1892	22.00	28.00	55.00	90.00	22.00	28.00	75.00	175.00
1893	60.00	100.00	180.00	400.00	130.00	280.00	2200.00	4000.00
1894	300.00	500.00			28.00	40.00	70.00	125.00
1895	Proof	–.–			150.00	320.00	180.00	540.00
1896	14.00	19.00			15.00	20.00	60.00	120.00

	without mintmark		CC		O		S	
1897	14.00	19.00			18.00	26.00	20.00	28.
1898	14.00	19.00			14.00	19.00	20.00	28.
1899	65.00	90.00			14.00	18.00	30.00	40.
1900	14.00	19.00			14.00	19.00	18.00	26.
1901	40.00	50.00			14.00	18.00	30.00	40.
1902	18.00	26.00			14.00	18.00	80.00	125.
1903	18.00	26.00			250.00	340.00	60.00	150.
1904	19.00	28.00			14.00	18.00	50.00	120.
1921	14.00	18.00					14.00	18.
1921 D	14.00	18.00						

7 (22)   2½ Dollars (Au) 1840-1907. Head of Liberty
with diadem. Rev. state coat of arms:

	without mintmark		C		D		O	
1840	225.00	280.00	360.00	550.00	680.00	900.00	220.00	280.
1841	28000.00 36000.00		340.00	480.00	800.00	1200.00		
1842	500.00	700.00	320.00	500.00	700.00	1000.00	200.00	275.
1843	220.00	270.00	400.00	550.00	680.00	900.00	200.00	275.
1844	400.00	550.00	300.00	450.00	500.00	800.00		
1845	200.00	275.00			500.00	800.00	700.00	1000.
1846	200.00	275.00	500.00	750.00	450.00	680.00	200.00	275.
1847	200.00	275.00	300.00	450.00	450.00	680.00	200.00	275.
1848	600.00	900.00	320.00	500.00	700.00	950.00		
1849	200.00	270.00	320.00	500.00	680.00	900.00		
1850	200.00	270.00	320.00	500.00	680.00	900.00	200.00	270.
1851	200.00	270.00	280.00	420.00	680.00	900.00	200.00	270.
1852	200.00	270.00	300.00	460.00	900.00	1300.00	200.00	270.
1853	200.00	270.00			700.00	1000.00		
1854	200.00	270.00	360.00	520.00	3600.00	5000.00	200.00	270.
S	22000.00	29000.00						
1855	200.00	270.00	900.00	1200.00	3500.00	5000.00		
1856	200.00	270.00	380.00	480.00	5000.00	8000.00		
S	200.00	270.00					220.00	285.
1857	200.00	270.00			950.00	1400.00	200.00	280.
S	200.00	270.00						
1858	200.00	270.00	300.00	460.00				

	without mintmark		C/D		S	
1859	210.00	280.00	D: 950.00	1300.00	210.00	280.00
1860	210.00	280.00	C: 380.00	550.00	210.00	280.00
1861	160.00	200.00			210.00	280.00
1862	210.00	280.00			220.00	320.00
1863	–.–	–.–			210.00	280.00
1864	1400.00	1800.00				
1865	1200.00	1700.00			210.00	280.00
1866	350.00	500.00			210.00	280.00
1867	280.00	420.00			210.00	280.00
1868	270.00	370.00			220.00	290.00
1869	220.00	290.00			200.00	270.00
1870	210.00	280.00			200.00	270.00
1871	210.00	280.00			200.00	270.00
1872	280.00	360.00			200.00	270.00
1873	160.00	200.00			200.00	270.00
1874	230.00	300.00				
1875	3500.00	5000.00			200.00	270.00
1876	250.00	320.00			230.00	300.00
1877	400.00	650.00			170.00	200.00
1878	170.00	200.00			170.00	200.00
1879	170.00	200.00			170.00	200.00
1880	240.00	300.00				
1881	1100.00	1600.00				
1882	210.00	280.00				
1883	250.00	360.00				
1884	250.00	360.00				
1885	950.00	1400.00				
1886	180.00	280.00				
1887	170.00	200.00				
1888	165.00	200.00				
1889	165.00	200.00				
1890	165.00	200.00				
1891	165.00	200.00				
1892	220.00	350.00				
1893	165.00	200.00				
1894	210.00	280.00				
1895	165.00	200.00				
1896	165.00	200.00				
1897	165.00	200.00				
1898	165.00	200.00				
1899	165.00	200.00				
1900	165.00	200.00				
1901	165.00	200.00				
1903	165.00	200.00				
1904	165.00	200.00				
1905	165.00	200.00				
1906	165.00	200.00				
1907	165.00	200.00				

8 (23a)   5 Dollars (Au) 1866-1908. Head of Liberty
          facing left. Rev. state coat of arms and
          motto: IN GOD WE TRUST:

	without mintmark		CC		S	
1866	400.00	650.00			320.00	480.00
1867	400.00	650.00			240.00	350.00
1868	350.00	500.00			170.00	260.00
1869	780.00	1200.00			250.00	390.00
1870	480.00	700.00	2600.00	4000.00	230.00	300.00
1871	400.00	550.00	500.00	750.00	260.00	320.00
1872	850.00	1200.00	850.00	1200.00	190.00	250.00
1873	185.00	200.00	1000.00	1400.00	215.00	300.00
1874	385.00	560.00	650.00	850.00	220.00	300.00
1875	–.–	–.–	850.00	1200.00	520.00	700.00
1876	865.00	1200.00	760.00	1000.00		2000.00
1877	850.00	1250.00	1000.00	1400.00	180.00	200.00
1878	180.00	200.00	1850.00	2600.00	180.00	200.00
1879	180.00	200.00	350.00	560.00	180.00	200.00
1880	180.00	200.00	250.00	400.00	180.00	200.00
1881	180.00	200.00	260.00	400.00	180.00	200.00
1882	180.00	200.00	285.00	450.00	180.00	200.00
1883	180.00	200.00	240.00	360.00	180.00	200.00
1884	180.00	200.00	260.00	380.00	180.00	200.00
1885	180.00	200.00			180.00	200.00
1886	180.00	200.00			180.00	200.00
1887	Proof	–.–			200.00	270.00
1888	180.00	200.00			175.00	195.00
1889	270.00	360.00				
1890	280.00	440.00	200.00	280.00		
1891	180.00	200.00	190.00	220.00		
1892	180.00	200.00	200.00	280.00	180.00	200.00
O	700.00	1000.00				
1893	180.00	200.00	200.00	300.00	180.00	200.00
O	195.00	260.00				
1894	180.00	200.00			180.00	200.00
O	240.00	350.00				
1895	180.00	200.00			180.00	200.00
1896	180.00	200.00			180.00	200.00
1897	180.00	200.00			180.00	200.00
1898	180.00	200.00			180.00	200.00
1899	180.00	200.00			180.00	200.00
1900	180.00	200.00			180.00	200.00

	without mintmark		CC	D		S	
1901	180.00	200.00				180.00	200.00
1902	180.00	200.00				180.00	200.00
1903	180.00	200.00				180.00	200.00
1904	180.00	200.00				180.00	200.00
1905	180.00	200.00				180.00	200.00
1906	180.00	200.00		180.00	200.00	180.00	200.00
1907	180.00	200.00		180.00	200.00		
1908	180.00	200.00					

9 (24a)　10 Dollars (Au) 1866-1907. Head of Liberty facing left. Rev. state coat of arms and motto: IN GOD WE TRUST:

	without mintmark		CC		O		S	
1866	450.00	720.00					360.00	500.00
1867	400.00	660.00					400.00	600.00
1868	250.00	320.00					360.00	500.00
1869	1400.00	2000.00					400.00	600.00
1870	450.00	700.00	2000.00	3000.00			360.00	500.00
1871	1200.00 2000.00		800.00 1400.00				320.00	475.00
1872	1100.00 1700.00		700.00 1000.00				300.00	460.00
1873	2500.00 3600.00		1500.00 2400.00				300.00	460.00
1874	250.00	320.00	500.00	850.00			360.00	500.00
1875	–.–	–.–	800.00	1200.00				
1876	2400.00 3200.00		1000.00 1500.00				500.00	800.00
1877	2600.00 3500.00		1300.00 2000.00				280.00	360.00
1878	220.00	300.00	1200.00 1800.00				220.00	300.00
1879	220.00	300.00	5000.00 7500.00		2200.00 3000.00		220.00	300.00
1880	220.00	300.00	270.00	360.00	360.00	500.00	220.00	300.00
1881	220.00	300.00	240.00	380.00	240.00	380.00	220.00	300.00
1882	220.00	300.00	300.00	520.00	220.00	300.00	220.00	300.00

	without mintmark		CC		O		S	
1883	220.00	300.00	250.00	360.00	3600.00 5000.00		220.00	300.00
1884	220.00	300.00	225.00	400.00			220.00	300.00
1885	220.00	300.00					220.00	300.00
1886	220.00	300.00					220.00	300.00
1887	220.00	300.00					220.00	300.00
1888	220.00	300.00			220.00	300.00	220.00	300.00
1889	400.00	640.00					220.00	300.00
1890	220.00	300.00	220.00	300.00				
1891	220.00	300.00	240.00	320.00				
1892	220.00	300.00	260.00	400.00	220.00	300.00	220.00	300.00
1893	220.00	300.00	340.00	350.00	220.00	300.00	220.00	300.00
1894	220.00	300.00			220.00	300.00	220.00	300.00
1895	220.00	300.00			220.00	300.00	220.00	300.00
1896	220.00	300.00					220.00	300.00
1897	220.00	300.00			220.00	300.00	220.00	300.00
1898	220.00	300.00					220.00	300.00
1899	220.00	300.00			220.00	300.00	220.00	300.00
1900	220.00	300.00					220.00	300.00
1901	220.00	300.00			220.00	300.00	220.00	300.00
1902	220.00	300.00					220.00	300.00
1903	220.00	300.00			220.00	300.00	220.00	300.00
1904	220.00	300.00			220.00	300.00		
1905	220.00	300.00					220.00	300.00
1906	220.00	300.00			220.00	300.00	220.00	300.00
1906 D	220.00	300.00						
1907	220.00	300.00					220.00	300.00
1907 D	220.00	300.00						

10 (25) 20 Dollars (Au) 1866-1907. Head of Liberty facing left. Rev. state coat of arms and motto: IN GOD WE TRUST:

	without mintmark		CC		O		S	
1866	600.00	700.00					600.00	700.00
1867	600.00	700.00					600.00	700.00
1868	600.00	700.00					600.00	700.00
1869	600.00	700.00					600.00	700.00
1870	600.00	700.00	16000.00	24000.00			600.00	700.00
1871	600.00	700.00	1500.00	2400.00			600.00	700.00
1872	600.00	700.00	700.00	1000.00			600.00	700.00
1873	600.00	700.00	750.00	1200.00			600.00	700.00
1874	600.00	700.00	650.00	800.00			600.00	700.00
1875	600.00	700.00	600.00	700.00			600.00	700.00
1876	600.00	700.00	600.00	700.00			600.00	700.00
1877	580.00	675.00	650.00	800.00			580.00	675.00
1878	580.00	675.00	700.00	840.00			580.00	675.00
1879	580.00	675.00	900.00	1300.00	2800.00	4000.00	580.00	675.00
1880	580.00	675.00					580.00	675.00
1881	3000.00	5400.00					580.00	675.00
1882	8500.00	12000.00	600.00	750.00			580.00	675.00
1883	–.–	–.–	600.00	720.00			580.00	675.00
1884	–.–	–.–	550.00	660.00			550.00	660.00
1885	5000.00	7800.00	800.00	1100.00			550.00	660.00
1886	6000.00	10000.00						
1887	18000.00	30000.00 proofs only					540.00	650.00
1888	540.00	650.00					540.00	650.00
1889	540.00	650.00	650.00	800.00			540.00	650.00
1890	540.00	650.00	650.00	800.00			540.00	650.00
1891	2200.00	3400.00	1300.00	2000.00			540.00	650.00
1892	1250.00	1800.00	650.00	800.00			540.00	650.00
1893	540.00	650.00	650.00	800.00			540.00	650.00
1894	540.00	650.00					540.00	650.00
1895	540.00	650.00					540.00	650.00
1896	540.00	650.00					540.00	650.00
1897	540.00	650.00					540.00	650.00
1898	540.00	650.00					540.00	650.00
1899	540.00	650.00					540.00	650.00
1900	540.00	650.00					540.00	650.00
1901	540.00	650.00					540.00	650.00

	without mintmark		D		S	
1902	540.00	650.00			540.00	650.00
1903	540.00	650.00			540.00	650.00
1904	540.00	650.00			540.00	650.00
1905	540.00	650.00			540.00	650.00
1906	540.00	650.00	540.00	650.00	540.00	650.00
1907	540.00	650.00	540.00	650.00	540.00	650.00

COMMEMORATIVE ISSUE FOR LAFAYETTE

11 (C2) 1 Dollar (Ag) 1900. Double portrait: George Washington and Marie Joseph Paul Roch Yves Gilbert Motier, Marquis de Lafayette (1757–1834), French Liberal and friend of Washington, supported the American battle of independence against Britain. ℞ equestrian statue of Lafayette in Paris (1900), a gift of the American people   **VF** 400.00   **XF** 600.00

COMMEMORATIVE ISSUES (2) FOR THE LOUISIANA PURCHASE IN THE YEAR 1803

12 (C59) 1 Dollar (Au) 1903. Thomas Jefferson (1743–1826), 3rd President. ℞ denomination, date, laurel wreath   400.00   480.00

13 (C60) 1 Dollar (Au) 1903. William McKinley (1843–1901), 25th President 1897–1901. ℞ denomination, date, laurel wreath

	VF	XF
	400.00	480.00

COMMEMORATIVE ISSUE FOR THE EXPOSITION UPON THE OCCASION OF THE 100th ANNIVERSARY OF DESPATCHING THE LEWIS AND CLARK EXPEDITION FOR THE EXPLORATION OF THE LOUISIANA TERRITORY PURCHASED FROM FRANCE IN 1803

14 (C58) 1 Dollar (Au) 1904–1905. Captain Meriwether Lewis (1774–1809). R Lt. William Clark (1770–1838):

a) 1904	900.00	1100.00
b) 1905	900.00	1100.00

15 (26) 1 Cent (Br) 1909–1958. Abraham Lincoln (1809–1865), 16th President 1861–1865. ℞ denomination in words between ears of corn:

	900.00	1100.00

	without mintmark		D		S	
1909	0.70	1.40			60.00	85.00
1910	0.75	1.50			10.00	18.00
1911	2.00	4.00	10.00	18.00	18.00	30.00
1912	3.00	6.00	11.00	21.00	15.00	25.00
1913	3.50	7.00	10.00	18.00	12.00	20.00
1914	4.00	8.00	180.00	300.00	15.00	25.00
1915	12.00	25.00	6.00	12.00	12.00	20.00
1916	1.00	2.00	3.50	7.00	3.50	7.00
1917	1.00	2.00	3.00	6.00	3.00	6.00
1918	1.00	2.00	3.00	6.00	3.00	6.00
1919	1.00	2.00	2.60	5.50	1.50	3.00
1920	1.00	2.00	2.00	4.00	2.00	4.00
1921	2.00	4.00			6.00	12.00
1922	300.00	500.00	8.00	16.00		
1923	1.00	2.00			7.50	14.00
1924	1.75	3.50	15.00	35.00	3.50	7.00
1925	1.00	2.00	2.00	4.00	2.00	4.00
1926	1.00	2.00	1.50	3.00	6.00	12.00
1927	1.00	2.00	1.30	3.00	2.00	4.00
1928	0.80	1.60	0.80	2.00	1.20	2.50
1929	0.60	1.20	0.60	1.20	0.60	1.20
1930	0.50	1.00	0.50	1.00	0.50	1.00
1931	0.50	1.00	3.50	7.00	30.00	50.00
1932	1.50	3.00	1.50	3.00		
1933	1.00	2.00	2.00	4.00		
1934	0.25	0.50	0.60	1.20		

	without mintmark		D		S	
1935	0.20	0.40	0.20	0.40	0.25	0.50
1936	0.15	0.30	0.20	0.40	0.25	0.50
1937	0.15	0.30	0.15	0.30	0.20	0.40
1938	0.15	0.30	0.30	0.60	0.35	0.70
1939	0.10	0.20	0.40	0.80	0.20	0.40
1940	0.10	0.20	0.10	0.20	0.10	0.20
1941	0.10	0.20	0.10	0.20	0.15	0.30
1942	0.10	0.20	0.10	0.20	0.20	0.40
1944	0.10	0.20	0.10	0.20	0.10	0.20
1945	0.10	0.20	0.10	0.20	0.10	0.20
1946	0.10	0.20	0.10	0.20	0.10	0.20
1947	0.10	0.20	0.10	0.20	0.10	0.20
1948	0.10	0.20	0.10	0.20	0.30	1.00
1949	0.10	0.20	0.10	0.20	0.50	2.50
1950	0.10	0.20	0.10	0.20	0.10	0.20
1951	0.10	0.20	0.10	0.20	0.10	0.20
1952	0.10	0.20	0.10	0.20	0.10	0.20
1953	0.05	0.10	0.05	0.10	0.10	0.20
1954	0.15	0.30	0.05	0.10	0.10	0.20
1955	0.05	0.10	0.05	0.10	0.10	0.20
1956	0.10	0.20	0.10	0.20		
1957	0.10	0.20	0.10	0.20		
1958	0.10	0.20	0.10	0.20		

16 (27) 5 Cents (Cu-Ni) 1913. Head of Read Indian facing right. Rev. bison (Bison bison – Bovidae), on a mound (Mound Type):

	Mintage	Fine	VF	XF
1913	30,993,520	4.00	7.00	12.00
1913 D	5,337,000	8.00	12.00	20.00
1913 S	2,105,000	12.00	22.00	40.00

17 (27a) 5 Cents (Cu-Ni) 1913–1938. Type as No. 16, but bison on a level (Line Type):

	without mintmark		D		S	
1913	6.00	10.00	65.00	95.00	85.00	120.00
1914	7.00	14.00	70.00	100.00	18.00	32.00
1915	6.00	12.00	30.00	55.00	40.00	75.00
1916	3.00	6.00	20.00	35.00	16.00	30.00
1917	5.00	10.00	35.00	75.00	32.00	55.00
1918	6.00	12.50	35.00	75.00	35.00	80.00
1919	4.00	8.00	65.00	100.00	38.00	80.00
1920	3.50	8.00	65.00	100.00	30.00	80.00
1921	7.00	15.00			90.00	200.00
1923	3.00	6.00			25.00	55.00
1924	4.00	9.00	45.00	70.00	90.00	200.00
1925	3.00	10.00	50.00	85.00	20.00	40.00
1926	2.50	5.00	40.00	90.00	80.00	260.00
1927	2.50	5.00	12.00	30.00	20.00	55.00
1928	2.00	4.00	4.00	10.00	5.00	10.00
1929	2.00	4.00	3.00	10.00	2.00	6.00
1930	2.00	4.00			3.00	7.00
1931					5.50	12.00
1934	1.50	4.00	2.50	5.00		
1935	1.00	2.00	1.50	3.00	1.00	2.00
1936	0.70	1.50	1.00	2.00	1.00	2.00
1937	0.70	1.50	0.80	2.00	1.00	1.60
1938			0.80	1.60		

18 (28) 1 Dime (Ag) 1916–1945. Head of figure of Liberty with winged helmet; due to the similarity with the messenger of the gods, however, generally designated as "Mercury Dime". Rev. fasces:

	without mintmark		D		S	
1916	5.00	9.00	1500.00	2000.00	5.00	12.00
1917	4.00	8.00	11.00	25.00	4.00	8.00
1918	9.00	20.00	8.50	18.00	6.00	12.00
1919	4.00	8.00	16.00	32.00	16.50	33.00
1920	3.00	6.00	5.00	12.00	6.00	12.00
1921	150.00	470.00				

	without mintmark		D		S	
1923	2.00	5.00			10.00	20.00
1924	4.00	7.00	8.00	16.00	7.00	15.00
1925	3.00	6.00	26.00	60.00	8.50	17.00
1926	3.00	5.00	7.50	15.00	33.00	80.00
1927	2.00	4.00	16.00	32.00	7.00	15.00
1928	2.00	4.00	15.00	30.00	6.00	12.00
1929	2.00	4.00	4.00	8.00	2.00	4.00
1930	2.00	4.00			5.50	12.00
1931	3.00	6.00	15.00	30.00	5.00	10.00
1934	1.00	2.00	2.00	4.00		
1935	1.00	2.00	3.00	6.00	1.00	3.00
1936	1.00	2.00	2.00	4.00	2.00	4.00
1937	1.00	2.00	1.00	2.00	1.00	2.00
1938	1.00	2.00	1.00	2.00	1.00	3.00
1939	1.00	2.00	1.00	2.00	1.00	2.00
1940	1.00	2.00	1.00	2.00	1.00	2.00
1941	1.00	2.00	1.00	2.00	1.00	2.00
1942	1.00	2.00	1.00	2.00	1.00	2.00
1943	0.50	1.00	1.00	2.00	1.00	2.00
1944	0.50	1.00	1.00	2.00	1.00	2.00
1945	0.50	1.00	1.00	2.00	1.00	2.00

19 (29) Quarter Dollar (Ag) 1916–1917. Standing figure of Liberty. ℞ Bald Eagle (National bird = Haliaetus leucocephalus - Accipitridae):

	Mintage		
a) 1916	52,000	3000.00	4000.00
b) 1917	8,792,000	30.00	70.00
c) 1917 D	1,509,200	65.00	150.00
d) 1917 S	1,952,000	55.00	140.00

20 (29a) Quarter Dollar (Ag) 1917–1930. Type as No. 19, ℞ however with differing arrangement of wording and three stars underneath the Bald Eagle:

	without mintmark		D		S	
1917	30.00	70.00	60.00	120.00	60.00	120.00
1918	30.00	70.00	50.00	100.00	35.00	70.00
1919	45.00	80.00	160.00	260.00	120.00	200.00
1920	20.00	45.00	80.00	140.00	30.00	70.00
1921	150.00	225.00				
1923	20.00	50.00			180.00	300.00
1924	20.00	50.00	65.00	115.00	32.00	60.00
1925	15.00	30.00				
1926	15.00	30.00	30.00	70.00	30.00	75.00
1927	15.00	30.00	40.00	85.00	220.00	550.00
1928	15.00	30.00	22.00	50.00	20.00	46.00
1929	15.00	30.00	18.00	45.00	20.00	48.00
1930	15.00	30.00			20.00	50.00

21 (30) Half Dollar (Ag) 1916–1947. Walking figure of Liberty in front of rising sun. Rev. Bald Eagle:

	Mintmark on obverse					
	without mintmark		D		S	
1916	100.00	200.00	60.00	130.00	200.00	320.00
1917			70.00	140.00	120.00	285.00
	Mintmark on reverse					
1917	15.00	30.00	40.00	100.00	20.00	42.00
1918	50.00	125.00	55.00	135.00	20.00	42.00
1919	90.00	280.00	120.00	350.00	90.00	320.00
1920	18.00	45.00	90.00	120.00	40.00	100.00
1921	400.00	1000.00	500.00	1250.00	250.00	1100.00
1923					40.00	120.00
1927					25.00	70.00
1928					30.00	90.00
1929			18.00	55.00	20.00	50.00
1933					18.00	40.00

Year	without mintmark		D		S	
1934	10.00	20.00	15.00	35.00	13.00	26.00
1935	10.00	20.00	15.00	35.00	10.00	30.00
1936	10.00	18.00	10.00	28.00	10.00	28.00
1937	10.00	18.00	15.00	35.00	10.00	28.00
1938	10.00	18.00	40.00	100.00		
1939	10.00	18.00	10.00	18.00	10.00	22.00
1940	10.00	18.00			10.00	20.00
1941	8.00	12.00	8.00	12.00	10.00	15.00
1942	8.00	12.00	8.00	12.00	9.00	14.00
1943	8.00	12.00	8.00	12.00	8.00	12.00
1944	8.00	12.00	8.00	12.00	8.00	12.00
1945	8.00	12.00	8.00	12.00	8.00	12.00
1946	8.00	12.00	8.00	12.00	8.00	12.00
1947	8.00	12.00	8.00	12.00		

22 (31) 1 Dollar (Ag) 1921–1935. Peace type, head of Liberty with halo. ℞ seated eagle with motto: E PLURIBUS UNUM:

Year	without mintmark		D		S	
1921	40.00	65.00				
1922	16.00	20.00	16.00	20.00	16.00	20.00
1923	16.00	20.00	16.00	25.00	16.00	20.00
1924	16.00	20.00			20.00	35.00
1925	16.00	20.00			20.00	30.00
1926	18.00	24.00	18.00	24.00	18.00	24.00
1927	30.00	40.00	20.00	32.00	20.00	30.00
1928	125.00	200.00			20.00	28.00
1934	25.00	35.00	20.00	28.00	40.00	140.00
1935	20.00	28.00			20.00	28.00

23 (32) 2½ Dollars (Au) 1908–1929. Head of Red Indian. ℞ Golden Eagle (Aquila chrysaëtos – Accipitridae). Incused legend:

	without mintmark		D	
1908	120.00	180.00		
1909	120.00	180.00		
1910	120.00	180.00		
1911	120.00	180.00	850.00	1500.00
1912	120.00	180.00		
1913	120.00	180.00		
1914	120.00	180.00	120.00	180.00
1915	120.00	180.00		
1925			120.00	180.00
1926	120.00	180.00		
1927	120.00	180.00		
1928	120.00	180.00		
1929	120.00	180.00		

24 (33) 5 Dollars (Au) 1908-1929. Head of Red Indian facing left. Rev. Golden Eagle:

	without mintmark		D		O		S	
1908	200.00	250.00	200.00	250.00			350.00	600.00
1909	200.00	250.00	200.00	250.00	420.00	1000.00	220.00	265.00
1910	220.00	265.00	220.00	265.00			220.00	270.00
1911	200.00	250.00	300.00	500.00			220.00	265.00
1912	200.00	250.00					200.00	250.00
1913	200.00	250.00					280.00	400.00
1914	200.00	250.00	200.00	250.00			210.00	265.00
1915	200.00	250.00					250.00	350.00
1916							200.00	250.00
1929	2000.00	3600.00						

25 (34) 10 Dollars (Au) 1907-1908. Head of Liberty with Red Indian ceremonial head dress. Rev. Golden Eagle:

a) 1907	400.00	500.00
b) 1908	450.00	550.00
c) 1908 D	400.00	500.00

26 (34a) 10 Dollars (Au) 1908-1933. Type as No. 25, but with motto: IN GOD WE TRUST:

	without mintmark		D		S	
1908	400.00	450.00	400.00	450.00	500.00	800.00
1909	400.00	450.00	400.00	450.00	400.00	450.00
1910	400.00	450.00	400.00	450.00	400.00	450.00
1911	400.00	450.00	750.00	1000.00	500.00	720.00
1912	400.00	450.00			400.00	480.00
1913	400.00	450.00			550.00	900.00
1914	400.00	450.00	400.00	450.00	400.00	450.00
1915	400.00	450.00			400.00	450.00
1916					400.00	450.00
1920					8000.00	14500.00
1926	400.00	450.00				
1930					3000.00	4600.00
1932	400.00	450.00				
1933	10000.00	18000.00				

		VF	XF
27 (35)	20 Dollars (Au) 1907. Standing figure of Liberty. ℞ Golden Eagle in flight in front of rising sun, date in Roman numerals	2500.00	4000.00

28 (35a) 20 Dollars (Au) 1907–1908. Type as No. 27, but date in Arabic numerals   VF 650.00   XF 720.00

29 (35b) 20 Dollars (Au) 1908-1932. Type as No. 28, motto: IN GOD WE TRUST:

	without mintmark		D		S	
1908	500.00	650.00	500.00	650.00	700.00	1100.00
1909	500.00	650.00	500.00	650.00	600.00	750.00
1910	500.00	650.00	500.00	650.00	500.00	650.00
1911	500.00	650.00	500.00	650.00	500.00	650.00
1912	500.00	650.00				
1913	500.00	650.00	500.00	650.00	500.00	750.00
1914	500.00	650.00	500.00	650.00	500.00	650.00
1915	500.00	650.00			500.00	650.00
1916					500.00	650.00
1920	500.00	650.00			4000.00	7500.00
1921	8000.00	16000.00				
1922	500.00	650.00			550.00	800.00
1923	500.00	650.00	550.00	850.00		
1924	500.00	650.00	550.00	850.00	550.00	850.00
1925	500.00	650.00	700.00	1000.00	700.00	1000.00
1926	500.00	650.00	780.00	11000.00	700.00	1000.00
1927	500.00	650.00	95000.00	165000.00	3600.00	6000.00
1928	500.00	650.00				
1929	1800.00	3200.00				
1930					5000.00	8500.00
1931	3600.00	6500.00	3200.00	6200.00		
1932	4500.00	8000.00				

COMMEMORATIVE ISSUES (5) UPON THE OCCASION OF THE PANAMA-PACIFIC EXPOSITION OF 1915 IN SAN FRANCISCO FOR THE OPENING OF THE PANAMA CANAL

		VF	XF
30 (C39)	Half Dollar (Ag) 1915. "Columbia" strewing flowers with small angel child and horn of plenty; in the background, rising sun over Golden Gate Bay. ℞ eagle with USA coat of arms between oak and laurel leaves	220.00	300.00

31 (C62)	1 Dollar (Au) 1915. Portrait of a Panama Canal worker. ℞ denomination in words. Two bottle-nosed dolphins or porpoises, symbolizing the two oceans	320.00	400.00

			VF	XF
32 (C63)	2½	Dollars (Au) 1915. "Columbia" on sea-horse. ℞ eagle with raised wings on column with motto: E PLURIBUS UNUM	1200.00	1500.00
33 (C65)	50	Dollars (Au) 1915. Head of Minerva. ℞ Great Horned Owl (Bubo virginianus – Strigidae) on pine branch; in the 8 corners: bottle-nosed dolphins or porpoises; octagonal	12000.00	16000.00
34 (C64)	50	Dollars (Au) 1915. Type as No. 33, but circular and without the bottle-nosed dolphins	17000.00	20000.00

COMMEMORATIVE ISSUE FOR WILLIAM MCKINLEY

35 (C61)	1	Dollar (Au) 1916–1917. William McKinley (1843–1901), 25th President, head facing left. ℞ McKinley-shrine in Niles, Ohio	350.00	400.00

COMMEMORATIVE ISSUE FOR THE 100th ANNIVERSARY OF THE STATE OF ILLINOIS

36 (C28)		Half Dollar (Ag) 1918. Abraham Lincoln (1809–1865), 16th President. Head facing right. ℞ eagle of the coat of arms, escutcheon, rising sun (seal of the State of Illinois)	60.00	80.00

COMMEMORATIVE ISSUE 100 YEARS OF MAINE

37 (C31)   Half Dollar (Ag) 1920. Coat of arms of the State of Maine, above the motto DIRIGO (I show the way). ℞ legend in wreath of fir branches with cones attached

VF **XF**

75.00 110.00

COMMEMORATIVE ISSUE FOR THE 300th ANNIVERSARY OF THE LANDING OF THE PILGRIM FATHERS ON THE CAPE COD PENINSULA, MASSACHUSETTS, ON DECEMBER 22, 1620

38 (C40)   Half Dollar (Ag) 1920–1921. Portrait of Bradford, the first governor (1589–1657). ℞ "Mayflower"

a) 1920   40.00   65.00
b) 1921, with date in the field of the obv.   45.00   85.00

COMMEMORATIVE ISSUE 100 YEARS OF ALABAMA (1819–1919)

39 (C4)   Half Dollar (Ag) 1921. William Wyatt

Bibb (1781–1820), doctor, first governor, and Thomas Erby Kilby (1865–1943), governor in 1920. ℞ large eagle on escutcheon

		VF	XF
a) with 2 x 2 (22nd State of the Union)		180.00	250.00
b) without 2 x 2		100.00	130.00

COMMEMORATIVE ISSUE 100 YEARS OF MISSOURI

40 (C34) Half Dollar (Ag) 1921. Forest runner of the early 19th century with racoon fur cap. ℞ Red Indians and forest runners of the times

	VF	XF
a) with 2 * 4 (24th State of the Union)	450.00	800.00
b) without 2 * 4	300.00	500.00

COMMEMORATIVE ISSUES (2) FOR THE 100th BIRTHDAY OF ULYSSES S. GRANT

41 (C22) Half Dollar (Ag) 1922. Ulysses Simpson Grant (1822–1885), 18th President 1869 – 1877. ℞ block house under trees – birthplace of Grant in Point Pleasant, Ohio

	VF	XF
a) with star	360.00	500.00
b) without star	55.00	90.00

42 (C56) 1 Dollar (Au) 1922. Type as No. 41

	VF	XF
a) with star	480.00	600.00
b) without star	580.00	700.00

COMMEMORATIVE ISSUE FOR THE 100th ANNIVERSARY OF THE PROCLAMATION OF THE MONROE DOCTRINE

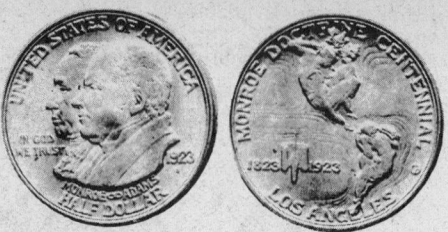

43 (C35) Half Dollar (Ag) 1923. Double portrait: James Monroe (1758–1831), 5th President from 1817 to 1825; in accordance with the doctrine named after him, European powers were to be prevented from exercising their influence on the political affairs of the states of the two Americas under the call of "America for the Americans", and John Quincy Adams (1767–1848), 6th President, who took a decisive part in formulating the Monroe Doctrine. ℞ two female figures, representing North and South America

	VF	XF
	25.00	40.00

COMMEMORATIVE ISSUE FOR THE 300th ANNIVERSARY OF THE LANDING OF THE HUGENOTS AND WALLOONS IN AMERICA

44 (C25) Half Dollar (Ag) 1924. Gaspard de Coligny (1519–1572), French admiral and leader of the Hugenots and William I of Orange, called the Silent (1533–1584), stadholder of the Netherlands. Both personalities bear no relation to the cause of this commemoration; as representatives and martyrs of the Protestant faith, their portraits were chosen symbolically. ℞ emigrants' ship the "Nieu Nederland"

	60.00	90.00

COMMEMORATIVE ISSUE FOR THE 75th ANNIVERSARY
OF THE ENTRY OF CALIFORNIA
INTO THE UNION AS A FEDERAL STATE

			VF	XF
45 (C11)	Half Dollar (Ag) 1925. Gold washer of 1849. ℞ striding grizzly bear (Ursus arctos – Ursidae), state symbol		60.00	105.00

COMMEMORATIVE ISSUE FOR THE 150th ANNIVERSARY
OF THE BATTLE OF LEXINGTON AND CONCORD

46 (C27)	Half Dollar (Ag) 1925. The "Minute Man", volunteer of the American Revolution, after a bronze statue by Daniel Chester French in Concord. ℞ "Old Belfry" in Lexington		40.00	60.00

COMMEMORATIVE ISSUE FOR THE PROJECTED
STONE MOUNTAIN MEMORIAL IN GEORGIA IN HONOR
OF THE CONFEDERATE ARMY

47 (C48) Half Dollar (Ag) 1925. Equestrian statues of Generals Robert Edward Lee (1807–1870) and Thomas "Stonewall" Jackson (1824–1863). ℞ Bald Eagle with outspread wings on mountain top. The Stone Mountain is situated some 15 miles east of Atlanta, Georgia and represents the largest block of massive granite on the North American continent. The projected memorial is being hewn out of rock on the north-east side of the mountain as the "largest sculpture in the world". Work commenced in 1920, was abandoned in 1930 and only recommenced in recent times

VF **28.00** XF **40.00**

COMMEMORATIVE ISSUE 100 YEARS OF FORT VANCOUVER

48 (C50) Half Dollar (Ag) 1925. John McLoughlin (1784–1857), doctor, explorer, agent of the Hudson Bay Company for the District of Columbia, leader of the first settlers on the Oregon Trail towards the Far Northwest, built Fort Vancouver on the Columbia River in 1825. ℞ forest runner of the early 19th century with levelled rifle, in the background high mountain landscape and Fort Vancouver **180.00** **275.00**

COMMEMORATIVE ISSUE FOR THE OREGON TRAIL

49 (C38) Half Dollar (Ag) 1926–1939. Mountain

	VF	XF

Red Indian with plumes, gazing towards the East, in front of a map of the USA. ℞ Conestoga Wagon drawn by oxen on its way to the Far Northwest. The 2000 miles long Oregon Trail, leading from East to West through the North-American Continent, was of decisive importance for the settlement of the Far Northwest during the 19th century   70.00 105.00

COMMEMORATIVE ISSUES (2) FOR THE 150th ANNIVERSARY OF THE SIGNING OF THE DECLARATION OF INDEPENDENCE

50 (C46) Half Dollar (Ag) 1926. George Washington (1732–1799), 1st President and Calvin Coolidge (1872–1933), 30th President. ℞ cracked Freedom Bell (Liberty Bell) in the Independence Hall in Philadelphia, Pa.   35.00 55.00

51 (C66) 2½ Dollars (Au) 1926. Goddess of Liberty, standing, with torch and scroll. ℞ Independence Hall of the Union in Philadelphia, Pa.   300.00 360.00

COMMEMORATIVE ISSUE FOR THE 150 YEARS
OF VERMONT AND THE BATTLE OF BENNINGTON

		VF	XF
52 (C51)	Half Dollar (Ag) 1927. Ira Allen (1751–1814), politician, founder of Vermont. ℞ puma (Puma concolor – Felidae)		
		115.00	160.00

COMMEMORATIVE ISSUE FOR THE REDISCOVERY
OF HAWAII BY CAPTAIN JAMES COOK 150 YEARS AGO

53 (C23) Half Dollar (Ag) 1928. James Cook (1728–1779), British world circumnavigator. ℞ Hawaii island chief in festive garb; to the left village near Diamond Hill on Waikiki Beach, to the right coconut palm tree
1100.00   1400.00

54 (37) 5 Cents (Cu–Ni) 1938–1965. Thomas Jefferson (1743–1826), 3rd President 1801–1809. ℞ "Monticello", Thomas Jefferson's residence:

	without mintmark		D		S	
1938	0.25	0.50	1.20	2.40	1.80	3.60
1939	0.25	0.25	5.00	10.00	1.00	2.00
1940	0.15	0.30	0.20	0.40	0.30	0.60
1941	0.15	0.30	0.15	0.30	0.20	0.40
1942	0.20	0.40	1.20	2.50		
1946	0.05	0.10	0.15	0.30	0.20	0.40
1947	0.10	0.20	0.10	0.20	0.15	0.30
1948	0.10	0.20	0.20	0.40	0.20	0.40
1949	0.10	0.20	0.15	0.30	0.35	0.70
1950	0.30	0.60	5.00	10.00		
1951	0.10	0.20	0.10	0.20	0.40	0.80
1952	0.10	0.20	0.30	0.60	0.10	0.20
1953	0.10	0.20	0.10	0.20	0.15	0.30
1954	0.05	0.10	0.05	0.10	0.10	0.20
1955	0.20	0.40	0.05	0.10		
1956	0.05	0.10	0.05	0.10		
1957	0.05	0.10	0.05	0.10		
1958	0.05	0.10	0.05	0.10		
1959	0.05	0.10	0.05	0.10		
1960	0.05	0.10	0.05	0.10		
1961	0.05	0.10	0.05	0.10		
1962	0.05	0.10	0.05	0.10		
1963	0.05	0.10	0.05	0.10		
1964	0.05	0.10	0.05	0.10		
1965	0.05	0.10				

55 (39) Quarter Dollar (Ag) 1932-1964. George
Washington (1732-1799), 1st President
1789-1797. Rev. Bald Eagle:

	without mintmark		D		S	
1932	7.00	10.00	100.00	170.00	80.00	125.00
1934	7.00	10.00	10.00	20.00		
1935	6.00	10.00	10.00	20.00	7.00	12.00
1936	6.00	10.00	16.00	35.00	6.00	10.00
1937	6.00	10.00	7.00	11.00	10.00	20.00
1938	10.00	16.00			7.00	13.00
1939	7.00	10.00	8.00	11.00	8.00	11.00
1940	7.00	10.00	9.00	14.00	7.00	10.00
1941	2.00	4.00	2.00	4.00	2.00	4.00
1942	2.00	3.00	2.00	3.00	2.00	3.00
1943	2.00	3.00	2.00	3.00	2.00	3.00
1944	2.00	3.00	2.00	3.00	2.00	3.00
1945	2.00	3.00	2.00	3.00	2.00	3.00
1946	2.00	3.00	2.00	3.00	2.00	3.00
1947	2.00	3.00	2.00	3.00	2.00	3.00
1948	2.00	3.00	2.00	3.00	2.00	3.00
1949	2.00	3.00	2.00	3.00		
1950	2.00	3.00	2.00	3.00	2.00	3.00
1951	2.00	3.00	2.00	3.00	2.00	3.00
1952	2.00	3.00	2.00	3.00	2.00	3.00
1953	2.00	3.00	2.00	3.00	2.00	3.00
1954	2.00	3.00	2.00	3.00	2.00	3.00
1955	2.00	3.00	2.00	3.00		
1956	2.00	3.00	2.00	3.00		
1957	2.00	3.00	2.00	3.00		
1958	2.00	3.00	2.00	3.00		
1959	2.00	3.00	2.00	3.00		
1960	2.00	3.00	2.00	3.00		
1961	2.00	3.00	2.00	3.00		
1962	2.00	3.00	2.00	3.00		
1963	2.00	3.00	2.00	3.00		
1964	2.00	3.00	2.00	3.00		

COMMEMORATIVE ISSUE FOR THE 200th BIRTHDAY OF DANIEL BOONE

56 (C9)   Half Dollar (Ag) 1934–1938. Daniel Boone (1734–1820), most famous American forest runner, entered world literature as the hero of a novel, Nat Bumppo (Leather Stocking) by James Fenimore Cooper. ℞ Daniel Boone parleying with the Shawnee Chief "Black Fish"

	VF	XF
a) 1934–1938	60.00	80.00
b) 1935, also with supplementary date "1934" on ℞ (see illustration)	75.00	105.00

COMMEMORATIVE ISSUE FOR THE 300th ANNIVERSARY OF THE FOUNDING OF MARYLAND

57 (C32)   Half Dollar (Ag) 1934. Cecil Calvert (1580–1632), the later Lord Baltimore, founder of the colony. ℞ coat of arms of Maryland   90.00   120.00

COMMEMORATIVE ISSUE FOR THE CENTENARY
OF THE FOUNDING OF THE REPUBLIC OF TEXAS

58 (C49) Half Dollar (Ag) 1934–1938. Eagle in front of five-peaked star; this star was the distinctive sign of the Republic of Texas. ℞ kneeling guardian angel above the mission station "Alamo" between portraits of Sam Houston (1793–1863), political and military leader on the road to independence, 1st President of the Republic, later US senator and Governor of Texas, and Stephan Austin (1793–1836), co-founder of the Republic, distinguished politician and colonizer; above flags. Texas seceded from Mexico in 1835 and became an independent republic; as late as 1845 Texas joined the Union as the 28th State

	VF	XF
	75.00	110.00

COMMEMORATIVE ISSUE FOR THE CENTENARY
OF THE STATE OF ARKANSAS

59 (C7) Half Dollar (Ag) 1935–1939. Double por-

trait: Red Indian chief of 1836 and
young American woman of 1936. ℞
eagle in front of Arkansas emblem

	VF	XF
	60.00	90.00

COMMEMORATIVE ISSUE FOR THE 300th ANNIVERSARY OF THE FOUNDING OF THE COLONY OF CONNECTICUT

60 (C17) Half Dollar (Ag) 1935. "The Charter
Oak", underneath which the first colonists were handed the Charter, at one
time also served as a hideout; destroyed
by lightning in 1856. ℞ eagle   160.00   200.00

COMMEMORATIVE ISSUE 150 YEARS OF HUDSON, N. Y.

61 (C24) Half Dollar (Ag) 1935. The "Half Moon",
sailing ship of the explorer and dis-
coverer Hendrick Hudson. ℞ Neptune
with trident, astride a bottle-nosed dolphin or porpoise (Tursiops truncatus –
Delphinidae) = the seal of the town of
Hudson   550.00   950.00

COMMEMORATIVE ISSUE FOR THE CALIFORNIA-PACIFIC EXPOSITION IN SAN DIEGO

62 (C45) Half Dollar (Ag) 1935–1936. Seated female figure with spear and grizzly bear, coat of arms of the State of California. ℞ observation tower and cupola of the California Hall at the exposition; Gulf States of the Union

	VF	XF
	75.00	110.00

COMMEMORATIVE ISSUE 400 YEARS OF THE "OLD SPANISH TRAIL"

63 (C47) Half Dollar (Ag) 1935. Emblem of the leader of the expedition, Cabeza de Vaca ("Cow's Head"). De Vaca was one of the four survivors who after eight years of traveling on foot reached the West Coast of the Continent from Florida. ℞ Yucca tree with map of the Gulf States and route taken by the expedition

600.00	900.00

COMMEMORATIVE ISSUE FOR THE 250th ANNIVERSARY OF THE GRANTING OF THE FREEDOM OF THE CITY TO ALBANY, N. Y.

		VF	XF
64 (C5)	Half Dollar (Ag) 1936. Canadian (American) beaver (Castor fiber canadensis – Castoridae), gnawing a maple branch. ℞ Governor Thomas Dongan of New York granting the freedom of the city; handing the document to Peter Schuyler, the first mayor of Albany and his Secretary Robert Livingston	175.00	220.00

COMMEMORATIVE ISSUE FOR THE OPENING OF THE BAY BRIDGE BETWEEN SAN FRANCISCO AND OAKLAND

| **65** (C8) | Half Dollar (Ag) 1936. Grizzly bear (Ursus arctos – Ursidae). ℞ Oakland Bay Bridge with historical "Ferry Tower" in the foreground | 35.00 | 75.00 |

COMMEMORATIVE ISSUE 100 YEARS OF BRIDGEPORT, CONNECTICUT

| **66** (C10) | Half Dollar (Ag) 1936. P. T. Barnum (1810–1891), circus king and prominent citizen of Bridgeport. ℞ stylized eagle | 105.00 | 150.00 |

COMMEMORATIVE ISSUE 50 YEARS OF THE MUSIC
CENTER CINCINNATI, OHIO

		VF	XF
67 (C12)	Half Dollar (Ag) 1936. Stephen Collins Foster (1826–1864), interpreter of American folk songs (Oh! Suzanna). ℞ kneeling female figure with lyre, as allegory of music	270.00	400.00

COMMEMORATIVE ISSUE 100 YEARS
OF CLEVELAND, OHIO, AND JUBILEE EXPOSITION

68 (C13)	Half Dollar (Ag) 1936. Moses Cleaveland (1754–1806), general, city founder. ℞ map of the Great Lakes region, with the nine largest cities marked by stars and a circle based on Cleveland	45.00	75.00

COMMEMORATIVE ISSUE 150 YEARS OF COLUMBIA, S. C.

69 (C14)	Half Dollar (Ag) 1936. Goddess of Justice with sword and balance between the old (1786) and new (1936) State Capitol. ℞ palm (emblem of the State)	160.00	270.00

COMMEMORATIVE ISSUE FOR
THE 300th ANNIVERSARY OF THE LANDING
OF THE SWEDES IN DELAWARE BAY IN 1638

		VF	XF
70 (C18)	Half Dollar (Ag) 1936. The "Kalmar Nyckel", Swedish emigrants' ship. ℞ "Old Swedes' Church" in Wilmington, erected at the point of landing	150.00	270.00

COMMEMORATIVE ISSUE 100 YEARS OF ELGIN, ILLINOIS

71 (C19)	Half Dollar (Ag) 1936. Idealized head of a pioneer. ℞ pioneer family, group taken from a monument in Elgin. The date 1673 has no relation to the occasion of the anniversary, but designates the year in which the explorers Louis Jolyet and Jacques Marquette (1637-1675) set foot in the territory of Illinois for the first time	120.00	200.00

COMMEMORATIVE ISSUE FOR THE BATTLE OF GETTYSBURG, PA., IN 1863

72 (C20)	Half Dollar (Ag) 1936. Double portrait: soldier of the Confederate States and soldier of the Union army. ℞ fasces between the coat of arms of the Union and the Confederation	150.00	200.00

COMMEMORATIVE ISSUE FOR THE JUBILEE OF THE FIRST COLONIZATION OF LONG ISLAND 300 YEARS AGO

		VF	XF
73 (C29)	Half Dollar (Ag) 1936. Dutch colonist and Red Indian. ℞ Dutch merchantman	45.00	70.00

COMMEMORATIVE ISSUE 150 YEARS OF LYNCHBURG, VIRGINIA

		VF	XF
74 (C30)	Half Dollar (Ag) 1936. Portrait: Senator Carter Glass (1858–1946). ℞ standing figure of Liberty with the old Town Hall of Lynchburg in the background	120.00	190.00

COMMEMORATIVE ISSUE 200 YEARS OF NORFOLK, VIRGINIA

75 (C37)   Half Dollar (Ag) 1936. Seal of the city of

Norfolk with a sailing ship as center piece. ℞ the Mace, granted the city in 1753

	VF	XF
	175.00	270.00

COMMEMORATIVE ISSUE FOR THE TERCENTENARY OF THE FOUNDING OF PROVIDENCE, RHODE ISLAND

76 (C42) Half Dollar (Ag) 1936. Founder of the town and colony, Roger Williams (1604–1684), landing from a canoe and being received by Red Indians. ℞ coat of arms of the Colony of Rhode Island: "Hope" inscribed above an anchor   65.00   100.00

COMMEMORATIVE ISSUE FOR THE ARKANSAS CENTENARY

77 (C7) Half Dollar (Ag) 1936. Senator Joseph T. Robinson (1872–1937). ℞ same as No. 59   55.00   95.00

COMMEMORATIVE ISSUE FOR THE CENTENARY OF WISCONSIN TERRITORY

78 (C54) Half Dollar (Ag) 1936. Seal of the Terri-

		VF	XF
tory (arm with pick axe). ℞ American badger (Taxidae taxus – Mustelidae) on tree trunk		115.00	175.00

COMMEMORATIVE ISSUE FOR THE TERCENTENARY OF YORK COUNTY, MAINE

79 (C55)   Half Dollar (Ag) 1936. Seal of York County, Maine. ℞ Brown's Garrison (fort on the Red Indian frontier), situated on the Saco river   115.00   175.00

COMMEMORATIVE ISSUE FOR THE 75th ANNIVERSARY OF THE BATTLE OF ANTIETAM CREEK, MARYLAND SEPTEMBER 17, 1862

80 (C6)   Half Dollar (Ag) 1937. Double portrait of generals McClellan (1826–1885) (Union) and Lee (Confederation). ℞ Burnside Bridge, fought over, strategically important point in this battle   220.00   275.00

COMMEMORATIVE ISSUE FOR THE 350th ANNIVERSARY OF THE SETTLING OF ROANOKE ISLAND, N. C.

			VF	**XF**

81 (C43) Half Dollar (Ag) 1937. Sir Walter Raleigh (1552–1618), seafarer, explorer, writer, founded the first settlement of whites in 1584 on the Roanoke Island, extending in front of what was to be North Carolina. ℞ Eleanor Dare holding her daughter Virginia in her arms, the first white child to be born in America 90.00 130.00

COMMEMORATIVE ISSUE FOR THE 250th ANNIVERSARY
OF THE FOUNDING OF
NEW ROCHELLE, N. Y. BY THE HUGENOTS

82 (C36) Half Dollar (Ag) 1938. The Hugenots acquired the land for their settlement from Lord John Pell; the contract of sale provided for a fattened calf to be given away each year on a certain day. J. Pell with a calf is represented on the obverse. ℞ stylized lily, part of the State coat of arms 250.00 350.00

83 (26a) 1 Cent (Sn-St) 1943. Abraham Lincoln (1809-1965), 16th President. Rev. value between ears of corn:
a) 1943 0.15 0.30
b) 1943 D 0.15 0.30
c) 1943 S 0.15 0.30

84 (37a) 5 Cents (Bi) 1942-1945. Thomas Jefferson (1743-1826), 3rd President. Rev. Monticello, Jefferson's residence:

	D		P		S	
1942			1.60	3.20	0.70	1.50
1943	0.80	2.00	0.70	1.40	0.50	1.20
1944	0.50	1.20	0.50	1.20	0.50	1.20
1945	0.50	1.50	0.50	1.00	0.50	1.00

85 (38)　1　Dime (Ag) 1946-1964. Franklin Delano
Roosevelt (1882-1945), 32nd President
1933-1945. Rev. torch between branches:

	without mintmark		D		S	
1946	0.70	1.20	0.70	1.20	0.70	1.20
1947	0.70	1.20	0.90	2.00	0.70	1.20
1948	0.70	1.20	0.90	2.00	0.70	1.20
1949	2.00	4.00	0.90	2.00	2.50	5.00
1950	0.70	1.20	0.70	1.20	1.50	2.50
1951	0.70	1.20	0.70	1.20	0.90	2.00
1952	0.70	1.20	0.70	1.20	0.90	2.00
1953	0.70	1.20	0.70	1.20	0.70	1.20
1954	0.70	1.20	0.70	1.20	0.70	1.20
1955	1.00	2.00	0.80	1.50	0.70	1.20
1956	0.70	1.20	0.70	1.20		
1957	0.70	1.20	0.70	1.20		
1958	0.70	1.20	0.70	1.20		
1959	0.70	1.20	0.70	1.20		
1960	0.70	1.20	0.70	1.20		
1961	0.70	1.20	0.70	1.20		
1962	0.70	1.20	0.70	1.20		
1963	0.70	1.20	0.70	1.20		
1964	0.70	1.20	0.70	1.20		

86 (40)　Half Dollar (Ag) 1948–1963. Benjamin
Franklin (1706–1790), diplomat, scien-
tist, inventor and writer. ℞ Liberty
Bell:

	without mintmark		D		S	
1948	4.00	8.00	4.00	8.00		
1949	7.00	10.00	8.00	11.00	10.00	20.00
1950	4.00	9.00	4.00	9.00		
1951	4.00	9.00	4.50	8.00	3.00	6.00
1952	4.00	7.00	4.00	7.00	4.00	7.00
1953	4.00	7.00	4.00	7.00	4.00	7.00
1954	4.00	6.50	4.00	6.50	4.00	6.50
1955	4.00	6.50				
1956	4.00	6.50				
1957	3.50	6.00	3.50	6.00		
1958	3.50	6.00	3.50	6.00		
1959	3.50	6.00	3.50	6.00		
1960	3.50	6.00	3.50	6.00		
1961	3.50	6.00	3.50	6.00		
1962	3.50	6.00	3.50	6.00		
1963	3.50	6.00	3.50	6.00		

COMMEMORATIVE ISSUE FOR THE CENTENARY OF THE STATE OF IOWA

		VF	XF
87 (C26)	Half Dollar (Ag) 1946. Coat of arms Eagle (State Seal). ℞ Old State Capitol in Iowa City	45.00	60.00

88 (C52) Half Dollar (Ag) 1946–1951. Booker Taliaferro Washington (1856–1915), born a negro slave, pedagogue, reformer of the educational system for colored people. R Tuskagee College, and birthplace of B. T. Washington in Virginia and inscription: FROM SLAVE CABIN TO HALL OF FAME

	VF	XF
	10.00	15.00

COMMEMORATIVE ISSUE FOR WASHINGTON AND CARVER

89 (C53) Half Dollar (Ag) 1951–1954. Double portrait: Booker T. Washington and George Washington Carver (1864–1943), biologist, chemist and philantropist. R map of the USA — 10.00 14.00

90 (36) 1 Cent (Br) 1959-. Abraham Lincoln. Rev. Hall of Remembrance:

	without mintmark		D		S
1959	0.05	0.10	0.05	0.10	
1960	0.05	0.10	0.05	0.10	
1961	0.05	0.10	0.05	0.10	
1962	0.05	0.10	0.05	0.10	
1963	0.05	0.10	0.05	0.10	
1964	0.05	0.10	0.05	0.10	
1965	0.05	0.10			

	without mintmark		D		S	
1966	0.05	0.10				
1967	0.05	0.10				
1968	0.05	0.10	0.05	0.10	0.05	0.10
1969	0.05	0.10	0.05	0.10	0.05	0.10
1970	0.05	0.10	0.05	0.10	0.05	0.10
1971	0.05	0.10	0.05	0.10	0.05	0.10
1972	0.05	0.10	0.05	0.10	0.05	0.10
1973	0.05	0.10	0.05	0.10	0.05	0.10
1974	0.05	0.10	0.05	0.10	0.05	0.10
1975	0.05	0.10	0.05	0.10	Proof	
1976	0.05	0.10	0.05	0.10	Proof	
1977	0.05	0.10	0.05	0.10	Proof	
1978	0.05	0.10	0.05	0.10	Proof	
1979	0.05	0.10	0.05	0.10	Proof	
1980	0.05	0.10	0.05	0.10	Proof	
1981	0.05	0.10	0.05	0.10	Proof	

91 5 Cents (St, Cu-Ni plated) 1966-. Thomas Jefferson. Rev. Monticello:

	without mintmark		D		S	
1966	0.05	0.10				
1967	0.05	0.10				
1968			0.05	0.10	0.05	0.10
1969			0.05	0.10	0.05	0.10
1970			0.05	0.10	0.05	0.10
1971	0.05	0.10	0.05	0.10	Proof	
1972	0.05	0.10	0.05	0.10	Proof	
1973	0.05	0.10	0.05	0.10	Proof	
1974	0.05	0.10	0.05	0.10	Proof	
1975	0.05	0.10	0.05	0.10	Proof	
1976	0.05	0.10	0.05	0.10	Proof	
1977	0.05	0.10	0.05	0.10	Proof	
1978	0.05	0.10	0.05	0.10	Proof	
1979	0.05	0.10	0.05	0.10	Proof	
1980	0.05	0.10	0.05	0.10	Proof	
1981	0.05	0.10	0.05	0.10	Proof	

92 1 Dime (St, Cu-Ni plated) 1965-. Franklin Delano Roosevelt. Rev. torch between branches:

	without mintmark		D		S	
1965	0.10	0.20				
1966	0.10	0.20				
1967	0.10	0.20				
1968	0.10	0.20	0.10	0.20	Proof	
1969	0.10	0.20	0.10	0.20	Proof	
1970	0.10	0.20	0.10	0.20	Proof	
1971	0.10	0.20	0.10	0.20	Proof	

	without mintmark		D		S
1972	0.10	0.20	0.10	0.20	Proof
1973	0.10	0.20	0.10	0.20	Proof
1974	0.10	0.20	0.10	0.20	Proof
1975	0.10	0.20	0.10	0.20	Proof
1976	0.10	0.20	0.10	0.20	Proof
1977	0.10	0.20	0.10	0.20	Proof
1978	0.10	0.20	0.10	0.20	Proof
1979	0.10	0.20	0.10	0.20	Proof
1980	0.10	0.20	0.10	0.20	Proof
1981	0.10	0.20	0.10	0.20	Proof

93   Quarter Dollar (St, Cu-Ni plated) 1965-. George Washington. Rev. Bald Eagle:

	without mintmark		D		S
1965	0.25	0.40			
1966	0.25	0.50			
1967	0.25	0.50			
1968	0.30	0.60	0.40	0.90	Proof
1969	0.30	0.50	0.40	1.00	Proof
1970	0.30	0.50	0.30	0.50	Proof
1971	0.30	0.50	0.30	0.50	Proof
1972	0.30	0.50	0.30	0.50	Proof
1973	0.25	0.40	0.25	0.45	Proof
1974	0.25	0.40	0.25	0.40	Proof
1977	0.25	0.40	0.25	0.40	Proof
1978	0.25	0.40	0.25	0.40	Proof
1979	0.25	0.40	0.25	0.40	Proof
1980	0.25	0.40	0.25	0.40	Proof
1981	0.25	0.40	0.25	0.40	Proof

94 (41)   Half Dollar. John Fitzgerald Kennedy (1917-1963), 35th President 1961-1963. Rev. Great Seal of the USA:

	without mintmark		D		S
	Silver Coinage				
1964	5.00	6.00	5.00	6.00	
	Silver Clad Coinage (Clad 40% Silver)				
1965	0.80	2.00			
1966	0.80	2.00			
1967	0.80	2.00			
1968			0.70	1.80	Proof
1969			0.70	1.80	Proof
1970			10.00	20.00	Proof
	Cupro-Nickel Clad Copper				
1971	0.60	1.00	0.60	1.00	Proof
1972	0.60	1.00	0.60	1.00	Proof
1973	0.60	1.00	0.60	1.00	Proof
1974	0.60	0.90	0.60	0.90	Proof
1977	0.60	0.90	0.60	0.90	Proof
1978	0.60	0.90	0.60	0.90	Proof
1979	0.60	0.90	0.60	0.90	Proof
1980	0.60	0.90	0.60	0.90	Proof
1981	0.60	0.90	0.60	0.90	Proof

95 (A48)   1 Dollar 1971–. Dwight Eisenhower (1890–1969), 34th President from 1953 to 1961. ℞ Bald Eagle with olive branch in his fangs, gliding down on to moonscape; in the lunar sky the (waning) Earth. Representation following the emblem of spaceship "Apollo 11", with which humans landed for the first time on the moon on July 21, 1969

	without mintmark		D		S	
Silver Clad Coinage (Clad 40% Silver)						
1971			6.00		7.00	
1972			6.00		7.00	
1973			6.00		7.00	
1974			6.00		7.00	
Cupro-Nickel Clad Copper						
1971	1.50	2.50	2.00	3.00		
1972	1.50	2.50	1.40	1.80		
1973	9.00	14.00	9.00	14.00	Proof	
1974	1.50	2.00	1.50	2.00	Proof	
1977	1.50	2.00	1.50	2.00	Proof	
1978	1.50	2.00	1.50	2.00	Proof	

BICENTENARY OF AMERICAN INDEPENDENCE (3)

96 (67)   Quarter Dollar 1976. George Washington. Rev. drummer:

	without mintmark		D		S	
Clad Metal	0.30	0.50	0.30	0.50	Proof:	2.00
.400 Silver					Proof:	4.00

97 (68)   Half Dollar 1976. John Fitzgerald Kennedy. Rev. Independence Hall:

	without mintmark		D		S	
.400 Silver					5.00	8.00
Clad Metal	0.70	1.00	0.70	1.00	Proof: 2.00	

98 (69)   1 Dollar 1976. Dwight David Eisenhower. Rev. Liberty Bell:

	without mintmark		D		S	
.400 Silver					Proof: 14.00	
Clad Metal	1.50	2.00	1.50	2.00	Proof: 5.00	

99   1 Dollar (Cu-Ni) 1979–. Susan B. Anthony (1820–1906), suffragette   1.25   1.50

Uruguay

Republica Oriental del Uruguay

Area: 72,180 sq. mi. Population: 3,000,000.
The Republic of Uruguay extends to the North of the Rio de la Plata
(River Plate) between the river Uruguay and the Atlantic Ocean.
Capital: Montevideo.

100 Centésimos = 1 Peso

			VF	XF
1 (15)	1	Centésimo (Cu–Ni) 1901, 1909, 1924, 1936. Sun. ℞ value in wreath	0.80	1.60
2 (16)	2	Centésimos (Cu–Ni) 1901, 1909, 1924, 1936, 1941	0.80	1.20
3 (17)	5	Centésimos (Cu–Ni) 1901, 1909, 1924, 1936, 1941	0.80	1.20
4 (20)	20	Centésimos (Ag) 1920. José Artigas (1764–1850), General, fighter for independence; Dictator from 1813 to 1820. ℞ coat of arms	6.00	10.50
5 (22)	50	Centésimos (Ag) 1916–1917	9.00	15.00
6 (23)	1	Peso (Ag) 1917	45.00	85.00

COMMEMORATIVE ISSUES (3) FOR THE CENTENNIAL OF THE CONSTITUTION

7 (18)	10	Centésimos (Al–Br) 1930. Head of Liberty. ℞ puma (Puma concolor – Felidae), value, and memorial legend	4.00	8.00

8 (21)	20	Centésimos (Ag) 1930. Allegory of the Republic and shield with memorial legend. ℞ ears of wheat, value	6.00	10.50

			VF	XF
9 (24)	5	Pesos (Au) 1930. José Artigas, head right. ℞ laurel branches, rays of the rising sun, memorial legend, value	175.00	200.00
10 (16a)	2	Centésimos (Br) 1943, 1944, 1945, 1946, 1947, 1948, 1949, 1951. Same type as No. 2	0.40	0.60
11 (17a)	5	Centésimos (Br) 1944, 1946, 1947, 1948, 1949, 1951. Same type as No. 3	0.50	0.80
12 (19)	10	Centésimos (Al–Br) 1936. Same type as No. 7, but without memorial legend	4.50	8.00
13 (25)	20	Centésimos (Ag) 1942. Head of Liberty, right. ℞ ears of wheat	3.50	6.00
14 (26)	50	Centésimos (Ag) 1943. ℞ value	4.00	7.00
15 (27)	1	Peso (Ag) 1942. José Artigas, head right. ℞ puma	8.00	12.00
16 (28)	1	Centésimo (Cu–Ni) 1953. José Artigas. ℞ value in wreath	0.25	0.40
17 (29)	2	Centésimos (Cu–Ni) 1953	0.25	0.40
18 (30)	5	Centésimos (Cu–Ni) 1953	0.25	0.40
19 (31)	10	Centésimos (Cu–Ni) 1953–1959	0.40	0.65
20 (32)	20	Centésimos (Ag) 1954. ℞ five ears of wheat	2.00	4.00
21 (33)	2	Centésimos (Ni–Bra) 1960. José Artigas. ℞ value in wreath	0.20	0.30
22 (34)	5	Centésimos (Ni–Bra) 1960	0.25	0.40
23 (35)	10	Centésimos (Ni–Bra) 1960	0.25	0.40
24 (36)	25	Centésimos (Cu–Ni) 1960. ℞ coat of arms	0.40	0.60
25 (37)	50	Centésimos (Cu–Ni) 1960	0.50	0.80
26 (38)	1	Peso (Cu–Ni) 1960	0.80	1.20

			VF	XF
27 (39)	10	Pesos (Ag) 1961. Gaucho, head right. ℞ value in wreath, memorial legend	7.00	12.00
28 (40)	20	Centésimos (Al) 1965. José Artigas. ℞ value in wreath	0.15	0.25
29 (41)	50	Centésimos (Al) 1965	0.20	0.30
30 (42)	1	Peso (Al–Br) 1965. ℞ coat of arms	0.30	0.50
31 (43)	5	Pesos (Al–Br) 1965	0.50	0.80

32 (44)	10	Pesos (Al–Br) 1965	1.00	1.50
33 (45)	1	Peso (Al–Br) 1968. José Artigas. ℞ ceibo (Erythrina crista-galli – Leguminosae) = national flower; value	0.10	0.20
34 (46)	5	Pesos (Al–Br) 1968. Same type as No. 33	0.20	0.40

35 (47)	10	Pesos (Al–Br) 1968. Same type as No. 33	0.35	0.60

	VF	XF
36 (48) 1 Peso (Al–Br) 1969. Sun, date. ℞ ceibo	0.10	0.20
37 (49) 5 Pesos (Al–Br) 1969. Same type as No. 36	0.25	0.40

	VF	XF
38 (50) 10 Pesos (Al–Br) 1969. Same type as No. 36	0.40	0.60
39 (51) 20 Pesos (Cu–Ni) 1970. Coat of arms. ℞ ears of wheat, value	0.45	0.80

	VF	XF
40 (52) 50 Pesos (Cu–Ni) 1970. Same type as No. 39	0.70	1.20

ISSUE FOR THE FAO COIN PLAN

	XF	Unc
41 (53) 1000 Pesos (Ag) 1969. Man, nature and agriculture, by Uruguayan sculptor Francisco Matta Vilaró. Legend reads "FAO – Fiat Panis". ℞ sun with twelve rays, value. Gold and copper trial strikes also known!	16.00	25.00

COMMEMORATIVE ISSUE FOR THE 100th BIRTHDAY OF J. E. RODO

42 (54) 50 Pesos (Cu–Ni) 1971. José Enrique

Rodó (1871–1917), philosopher and writer. Gold and copper trial strikes also known!

	VF	XF
	0.80	1.50

			VF	XF
43 (A53)	100 Pesos (Cu–Ni) 1973. Bust of José Artigas. ℞ value, date		0.70	1.10

CURRENCY REFORM: 1000 Old Pesos = New Peso

			VF	XF
44 (59)	5 Nuevo Pesos (Al-Br) 1975		3.00	6.50
45 (A55)	1 Centésimo (Al) 1977		0.12	0.25
46 (B55)	2 Centésimos (Al) 1977		0.12	0.25
47 (C55)	5 Centésimos (Al) 1977		0.12	0.25
48 (55)	10 Centésimos (Al-Br) 1976		0.15	0.30
49 (56)	20 Centésimos (Al-Br) 1976		0.20	0.40
50 (57)	50 Centésimos (Al-Br) 1976		0.40	0.70
51 (58)	1 Nuevo Peso (Al-Br) 1976		0.70	1.25

250th ANNIVERSARY OF THE FOUNDING OF MONTEVIDEO

			VF	XF
52 (60)	5 Nuevo Pesos (Al-Br) 1976		3.00	6.50
53 (61)	1 Peso (Cu-Ni) 1980		0.30	0.60
54 (62)	5 Pesos (Cu-Ni) 1980		0.70	1.50
55 (63)	10 Pesos (Cu-Ni) 1980		1.00	2.00

Vatican City
Stato della Città del Vaticano

Area: 109 acres. Population: 1025.
The Vatican City not only possesses its own railway station and a radio transmitter, but also has currency and postal privileges. In the Lateran Treaty of February 11, 1929, ratified on June 7, 1929, the sovereignty of the Pope over the Vatican City with the Vatican enclaves was recognized by Italy. In the Vatican City there are also the Vatican Collections (Collection of Antiquities, Vatican Library, Vatican Archives, Vatican Picture Gallery).

100 Centesimi = 1 Vatican Lira

POPE PIUS XI 1922–1939

			VF	XF
1 (1)	5 Centesimi (Br) 1929–1937. Coat of arms. ℞ olive branch:			
		a) 1929	26.00	42.00
		b) 1930–1937	6.50	9.00
2 (2)	10 Centesimi (Br) 1929–1938. ℞ St. Peter, portrait right:			
		a) 1929	20.00	35.00
		b) 1930–1937	6.00	9.00
3 (3)	20 Centesimi (Ni) 1929–1937. ℞ St. Paul, portrait left:			
		a) 1929	20.00	35.00
		b) 1930–1937	3.00	4.50
4 (4)	50 Centesimi (Ni) 1929–1937. ℞ Archangel Michael:			
		a) 1929	20.00	35.00
		b) 1930–1937	3.50	5.50

			VF	XF
5 (5)	1 Lira (Ni) 1929–1937. ℞ Virgin Mary:			
		a) 1929	20.00	35.00
		b) 1930–1937	4.00	6.50

		VF	**XF**
6 (6)	2 Lire (Ni) 1929–1937. ℞ Virgin Mary:		
	a) 1929	25.00	36.00
	b) 1930–1937	6.50	9.00
7 (7)	5 Lire (Ag) 1929–1937. Pius XI, Ratti (1857–1939), portrait right. ℞ St. Peter in a boat:		
	a) 1929	26.00	40.00
	b) 1930–1937	12.00	16.00

		VF	**XF**
8 (8)	10 Lire (Ag) 1929–1937. ℞ sitting Madonna with child:		
	a) 1929	30.00	50.00
	b) 1930–1937	15.00	18.00

		VF	**XF**
9 (9)	100 Lire (Au). Rev. standing Christ:		
	a) 1929, 1931–1935, diameter 23.5 mm	350.00	400.00
	b) 1930, diameter 23.5 mm	1000.00	1200.00
	c) 1936, diameter 20.5 mm	400.00	460.00
	d) 1937, diameter 20.5 mm	3200.00	4000.00
	e) 1938, diameter 20.5 mm	–.–	–.–

SEDE VACANTE 1939

		VF	**XF**
10 (20)	5 Lire (Ag) 1939. Coat of arms of Cardinal Pacelli. ℞ dove	12.00	16.00

		VF	**XF**
11 (21)	10 Lire (Ag) 1939. Same type as No. 10	16.00	22.00

			VF	XF
12 (22)	5	Centesimi (Br) 1939–1941. Coat of arms. ℞ olive branch	7.50	11.50
13 (23)	10	Centesimi (Br) 1939–1941. ℞ St. Peter, portrait right	7.50	11.50
14 (24)	20	Centesimi. ℞ St. Paul, portrait left		
		a) (Ni) 1939	8.00	12.00
		b) (St) 1940–1941	1.60	3.00
15 (25)	50	Centesimi. ℞ Archangel Michael		
		a) (Ni) 1939	5.50	8.00
		b) (St) 1940–1941	1.60	2.80
16 (26)	1	Lira. ℞ Virgin Mary		
		a) (Ni) 1939	8.00	12.00
		b) (St) 1940–1941	2.50	3.50
17 (27)	2	Lire. ℞ Virgin Mary		
		a) (Ni) 1939	10.00	13.00
		b) (St) 1940–1941	2.50	3.50
18 (28)	5	Lire (Ag) 1939–1941. Pius XII, Pacelli (1876–1958), portrait left. ℞ St. Peter in boat	10.00	15.00
19 (29)	10	Lire (Ag) 1939–1941. ℞ seated Madonna with child	75.00	105.00

			VF	XF
20 (30)	100	Lire (Au) 1939–1941. ℞ standing Christ	350.00	500.00
21 (31)	5	Centesimi (Bra) 1942–1946. ℞ dove	75.00	120.00
22 (32)	10	Centesimi (Bra) 1942–1946. ℞ dove	62.00	80.00
23 (33)	20	Centesimi (St) 1942–1946. Coat of arms. ℞ Justice	2.00	3.00
24 (34)	50	Centesimi (St) 1942–1946. Same type as No. 23	2.00	3.00
25 (35)	1	Lira (St) 1942–1946. Same type as No. 23	2.00	3.00
26 (40)	1	Lira (Al) 1947–1949. Same type as No. 23	15.00	18.50
27 (36)	2	Lire (St) 1942–1946. Same type as No. 23	3.00	4.00

			VF	XF
28 (41)	2	Lire (Al) 1947–1949. Same type as No. 23	12.00	26.00

				VF	XF

29 (37)	5 Lire (Ag) 1942–1946. ℞ Caritas	70.00	90.00
30 (42)	5 Lire (Al) 1947–1949. Same type as No. 29	10.00	12.50
31 (38)	10 Lire (Ag) 1942–1946. Same type as No. 29	120.00	145.00
32 (43)	10 Lire (Al) 1947–1949. Same type as No. 29	10.00	13.00
33 (39)	100 Lire (Au) 1942–1949. Same type as No. 29	325.00	400.00

COMMEMORATIVE ISSUE (5) FOR THE HOLY YEAR

34 (44)	1 Lira (Al) 1950. Coat of arms. ℞ Holy Portal	6.00	9.00
35 (45)	2 Lire (Al) 1950. Pius XII, portrait right. ℞ peace dove in front of St. Peter's Cathedral	6.00	9.00
36 (46)	5 Lire (Al) 1950. Pius XII, portrait left. ℞ procession	4.00	5.00
37 (47)	10 Lire (Al) 1950. Same type as No. 38	6.00	8.00

38 (48)	100 Lire (Au) 1950. The Pope's portrait with tiara. ℞ Pius XII opening Holy Portal	250.00	320.00
39 (49)	1 Lira (Al) 1951–1958. Coat of arms. ℞ Temperantia	1.00	2.00
40 (50)	2 Lire (Al) 1951–1958. Same type as No. 41	1.00	2.00
41 (51)	5 Lire (Al) 1951–1958. ℞ Justitia	1.00	2.00
42 (52)	10 Lire (Al) 1951–1958. ℞ Prudentia	1.00	2.00
43 (A52)	20 Lire (Al–Br) 1957–1958	2.50	3.50
44 (54)	50 Lire (St) 1955–1958. ℞ Spes	1.60	2.80
45 (55)	100 Lire (St) 1955–1958. Fides	2.60	3.50
46 (53)	100 Lire (Au) 1951–1956. ℞ Caritas	550.00	700.00
47 (A53)	100 Lire (Au) 1957–1958. ℞ coat of arms	400.00	520.00

COMMEMORATIVE ISSUE FOR THE 20th ANNIVERSARY OF THE PONTIFICATE

48 (56)	500 Lire (Ag) 1958. Pius XII, portrait left. ℞ coat of arms	36.00	55.00

SEDE VACANTE 1958

			VF	**XF**

49 (57) 500 Lire (Ag) 1958. Dove. ℞ coat of arms   15.00   20.00

POPE JOHN XXIII 1958–1963

50 (58)   1 Lira (Al) 1959–1962. Coat of arms. ℞
           Temperantia   9.00   12.00
51 (59)   2 Lire (Al) 1959–1962. Rev. Fortitudo   9.00   12.00

52 (60)   5 Lire (Al) 1959–1962. John XXIII,
           Roncalli (1881–1963), portrait right.
           ℞ Justitia   6.00   9.00
53 (61) 10 Lire (Al) 1959–1962. Rev. Prudentia   4.00   6.50
54 (62) 20 Lire (Al–Br) 1959–1962. ℞ Caritas   3.50   5.00
55 (63) 50 Lire (St) 1959–1962. ℞ Spes   1.20   1.60
56 (64) 100 Lire (St) 1959–1962. ℞ Fides   1.50   2.00
57 (66) 100 Lire (Au) 1959. ℞ coat of arms   1200.00   1600.00

58 (65) 500 Lire (Ag) 1959–1962. ℞ coat of arms:
         a) 1959, 1961–1962   22.00   32.00
         b) 1960   120.00   160.00

COMMEMORATIVE ISSUES (8) FOR THE 2nd ECUMENICAL COUNCIL OF THE VATICAN

		VF	XF
59 (67) 1 Lira (Al) 1962. Coat of arms. ℞ dove, symbolizing the Holy Ghost		2.60	4.50
60 (68) 2 Lire (Al) 1962		2.60	4.50
61 (69) 5 Lire (Al) 1962		1.80	3.50
62 (70) 10 Lire (Al) 1962		0.80	1.50
63 (71) 20 Lire (Al) 1962		0.80	1.50
64 (72) 50 Lire (St) 1962. ℞ John XXIII, head of the Council		0.80	1.50
65 (73) 100 Lire (St) 1962. Same type as No. 64		1.20	1.80

		VF	XF
66 (74) 500 Lire (Ag) 1962. Same type as No. 64		22.00	30.00

SEDE VACANTE 1963

		VF	XF
67 (75) 500 Lire (Ag) 1963. Coat of arms. ℞ dove		8.00	10.00

POPE PAUL VI 1963-1978

		VF	XF
68 (76) 1 Lira (Al) 1963–1965. Coat of arms. ℞ Temperantia		4.00	5.00
69 (77) 2 Lire (Al) 1963–1965. Coat of arms. ℞ Fortitudo		4.00	5.00
70 (78) 5 Lire (Al) 1963–1965. Paul XI, Montini (1963-1978), portrait right. R. Justitia		2.00	3.00
71 (79) 10 Lire (Al) 1963–1965. ℞ Prudentia		2.00	3.00
72 (80) 20 Lire (Al–Br) 1963–1965. ℞ Caritas		1.20	1.60
73 (81) 50 Lire (St) 1963–1965. ℞ Spes		0.80	1.20
74 (82) 100 Lire (St) 1963–1965. Fides		0.40	1.20
75 (83) 500 Lire (Ag) 1963–1965. ℞ coat of arms		16.00	20.00
76 (84) 1 Lira (Al) 1966. 4th year of the pontificate. Head of Paul VI, left, with cappa and miter. ℞ shepherd, carrying a lamb on his back: "I am the Good Shepherd", John 10, 2, motto of Pope Paul VI		1.00	2.00
77 (85) 2 Lire (Al) 1966. Same type as No. 76		1.00	2.00
78 (86) 5 Lire (Al) 1966. Same type as No. 76		0.80	1.20
79 (87) 10 Lire (Al) 1966. Same type as No. 76		0.40	0.80
80 (88) 20 Lire (Al–Br) 1966. Same type as No. 76		0.80	1.20
81 (89) 50 Lire (St) 1966. Same type as No. 76		0.40	0.80
82 (90) 100 Lire (St) 1966. Same type as No. 76		0.40	0.80
83 (91) 500 Lire (Ag) 1966. Same type as No. 76		12.00	16.00

			VF	XF
84 (92)	1	Lira (Al) 1967. Coat of arms of Pope Paul VI. ℞ crossed keys above Holy Sword in front of rising sun	1.20	2.00

85 (93)	2	Lire (Al) 1967. Coat of arms of Pope Paul VI. ℞ tiara (symbol of the educational, pastoral and ministerial duties of the pope) above upside-down cross with ropes (allegory of St. Peter's crucification with head down – John 21, 18); key on right and left side of cross connected with ropes and tiara bows	1.20	2.00

86 (94)	5	Lire (Al) 1967. Portrait of the Pope, right, with pileolus (cap) and mozzetta (short-hooded cape) and stole. ℞ St. Peter's key and sword in front of rising sun (sword as St. Paul's instrument of torture – 1900th anniversary of his martyrdom)	0.80	1.20
87 (95)	10	Lire (Al) 1967. Portrait of the Pope, left. ℞ like No. 85	0.40	0.80
88 (96)	20	Lire (Al–Br) 1967. Portrait of the Pope, right. ℞ sword in front of rising sun between the Saints Peter to the left and Paul to the right; crossed keys symbolizing the papal banning and redeeming power, as a direct successor to St. Peter – Matthew 16, 19 (1900th anniversary of the martyrdom of St. Peter and St. Paul)	0.40	0.80
89 (97)	50	Lire (St) 1967. Portrait of the Pope, right. ℞ Damascus Hour: conversion of Saulus – apostle 9, 3 to 4; Saulus on horseback	0.40	0.80
90 (98)	100	Lire (St) 1967. Portrait of the Pope, left. ℞ the Pope holding the highest		

	VF	**XF**

ecclesiastical professorial chair, giving
an ex-cathedra explanation ... 0.40 ... 0.80

91 (99) 500 Lire (Ag) 1967. Portrait of the Pope,
left. ℞ like No. 88 ... 14.00 ... 20.00

COMMEMORATIVE ISSUES (8)
FOR THE 6th ANNIVERSARY OF THE PONTIFICATE AND FOR THE FAO COIN PLAN

92 (100) 1 Lira (Al) 1968. Portrait of the Pope
with pileolus and mozzetta. ℞ wheat
in form of a cross, in front of sun, symbolizing the fertility in Christian faith ... 1.20 ... 2.00

93 (101) 2 Lire (Al) 1968. R Feeding of the Five
Thousand ... 1.20 ... 2.00

94 (102) 5 Lire (Al) 1968. ℞ Our Lady of the
Harvest ... 1.20 ... 2.00

95 (103) 10 Lire (Al) 1968. Same type as No. 93 ... 0.40 ... 0.80
96 (104) 20 Lire (Br) 1968. Same type as No. 92 ... 0.40 ... 0.80
97 (105) 50 Lire (St) 1968. Same type as No. 94 ... 0.40 ... 0.80
98 (106) 100 Lire (St) 1968. Same type as No. 93 ... 0.40 ... 0.80
99 (107) 500 Lire (Ag) 1968. Same type as No. 92 ... 14.00 ... 20.00

COMMEMORATIVE ISSUES (8) FOR THE 7th ANNIVERSARY
OF THE PONTIFICATE

			VF	XF
100 (108)	1	Lira (Al) 1969. Pope Paul VI, with miter. ℞ angel	1.00	2.00
101 (109)	2	Lire (Al) 1969	1.00	2.00
102 (110)	5	Lire (Al) 1969	0.80	1.20
103 (111)	10	Lire (Al) 1969	0.40	0.80
104 (112)	20	Lire (Al–Br) 1969	0.40	0.80
105 (113)	50	Lire (St) 1969	0.20	0.40
106 (114)	100	Lire (St) 1969	0.30	0.60

			VF	XF
107 (115)	500	Lire (Ag) 1969	10.00	13.00

COMMEMORATIVE ISSUES (8) FOR THE
8th to 15th ANNIVERSARY OF THE PONTIFICATE

			VF	XF
108 (116)	1	Lira (Al) 1970-1977. Coat of arms of Pope Paul VI. Rev. palm leaf (date palm-Phoenix dactylifera - Palmae)	0.80	1.20
109 (117)	2	Lire (Al) 1970-1977. Rev. lamb (Ovis ammon aries - Bovidae)	0.80	1.20
110 (118)	5	Lire (Al) 1970-1977. Rev. pelican (Pelecanus sp. - Pelicanidae), according to Christian legend it feeds it's young ones with the blood drawn from the self-inflicted chest wounds	0.40	0.60
111 (119)	10	Lire (Al) 1970-1977. Rev. fish	0.40	0.60
112 (120)	20	Lire (Al-Br) 1970-1977. Rev. red deer (Cervus elaphus - Cervidae)	0.30	0.40
113 (121)	50	Lire (St) 1970-1976. Rev. olive branch (Olea europaea - Oleaceae)	0.20	0.30
114 (122)	100	Lire (St) 1970-1977. Rev. domestic pigeon (Columba livia domestica - Columbidae) and olive branch	0.20	0.30
115 (123)	500	Lire (Ag) 1970-1976. Rev. grape (Vitis vinifera - Vitaceae) and ear of barley (Hordeum sp. - Gramineae)	9.00	12.00

HOLY YEAR 1975 (8)	XF	Unc
116 (124) 1 Lira (Al) 1975	1.00	2.00
117 (125) 2 Lire (Al) 1975	1.00	2.00
118 (126) 5 Lire (Al) 1975	0.50	1.00
119 (127) 10 Lire (Al) 1975	0.50	1.00
120 (128) 20 Lire (Al-Br) 1975	0.80	1.50
121 (129) 50 Lire (St) 1975	0.80	1.50
122 (130) 100 Lire (St) 1975	0.80	1.50
123 (131) 500 Lire (Ag) 1975	13.00	20.00
124 (A121) 50 Lire (St) 1977	1.00	1.50

125 (132) 500 Lire (Ag) 1977	11.00	16.00

16th ANNIVERSARY OF THE PONTIFICATE (7)

126 (133) 5 Lire (Al) 1978	0.50	1.00
127 (134) 10 Lire (Al) 1978	0.50	1.00
128 (135) 20 Lire (Al-Br) 1978	0.60	1.00
129 (136) 50 Lire (St) 1978	0.90	1.50
130 (137) 100 Lire (St) 1978	1.00	2.00
131 (138) 200 Lire (Al-Br) 1978	1.50	2.50
132 (139) 500 Lire (Ag) 1978	12.00	15.00

SEDE VACANTE 1978 (I)

133 (140) 500 Lire (Ag) 1978	15.00	18.00

POPE JOHN PAUL I 1978

		XF	Unc
134 (142) 1000 Lire (Ag) 1978		25.00	28.00

SEDE VACANTE 1978 (II)

		XF	Unc
135 (141) 500 Lire (Ag) 1978		15.00	18.00

POPE JOHN PAUL II since 1978

			XF	Unc
136 (143)	10 Lire (Al) 1979–1980		0.50	1.00
137 (144)	20 Lire (Al-Br) 1979–1980		0.60	1.00
138 (145)	50 Lire (St) 1979–1980		0.90	1.50
139 (146)	100 Lire (St) 1979–1980		1.00	2.00
140 (147)	200 Lire (Al-Br) 1979–1980		1.50	2.50
141 (148)	500 Lire (Ag) 1979–1980		12.00	15.00

Venezuela **Vénézuéla**

Venezuela

Area: 352,150 sq. mi. Population: 11,500,000.
Republic in northern South America.
Capital: Caracas.

100 Centavos (Centimos) = 1 Bolívar

ESTADOS UNIDOS DE VENEZUELA

				VF	XF
1 (25)	1	Centavo (Cu–Ni) 1876–1877. Coat of arms. ℞ value in wreath		4.00	6.00
2 (26)	2½	Centavos (Cu–Ni) 1876–1877		5.00	10.00
3 (27)	5	Centimos (Cu–Ni) 1896–1938		0.60	1.00
4 (28)	12½	Centimos (Cu–Ni) 1896–1938		0.60	1.60
5 (19)	⅕	Bolivar (Ag) 1879. Simón Bolívar (1783–1830), liberated South America from the Spanish government. ℞ coat of arms		160.00	250.00
6 (20)	¼	Bolivar (Ag) 1894–1948		1.20	2.50
7 (21)	½	Bolivar (Ag) 1879–1936		2.50	4.00
8 (22)	1	Bolivar (Ag) 1879–1936		3.50	5.00
9 (23)	2	Bolivares (Ag) 1879–1936		6.00	8.00

10 (24)	5	Bolivares (Ag) 1879–1936	15.00	20.00
11 (31)	10	Bolivares (Au) 1930	90.00	110.00
12 (32)	20	Bolivares (Au) 1879–1912	140.00	180.00
13 (17)	25	Bolivares (Au) 1875	265.00	320.00
14 (33)	100	Bolivares (Au) 1886–1889	520.00	580.00

Further gold pieces, 5, 50, and 100 Bolivares, with the date 1875 are
extremely rare pattern pieces.

			VF	XF
15 (29)	5	Centimos (Bra) 1944. Coat of arms. ℞ value in wreath	2.80	4.00
16 (29a)	5	Centimos (Cu–Ni) 1945–1948	0.25	0.50
17 (30)	12½	Centimos (Bra) 1944	12.00	22.00
18 (30a)	12½	Centimos (Cu–Ni) 1945–1948	0.30	0.60
19 (21a)	½	Bolivar (Ag) 1944–1946. Same type as No. 7	2.00	3.00
20 (22a)	1	Bolivar (Ag) 1945. Same type as No. 8	4.00	6.00
21 (23a)	2	Bolivares (Ag) 1945. Same type as No. 9	5.50	7.00

REPUBLICA DE VENEZUELA

			VF	XF
22 (38)	5	Centimos. Coat of arms. ℞ value in wreath		
		a) (Cu–Ni) 1958	0.20	0.30
		b) (Ni) 1964	0.10	0.20
23 (39)	12½	Centimos (Cu–Ni) 1958	0.20	0.30

			VF	XF
24 (35)	25	Centimos (Ag) 1954	0.80	1.20
25 (35a)	25	Centimos (Ag) 1960. Same type as No. 24, but narrow shield	0.80	1.20
26 (40)	25	Centimos (Ni) 1965–	0.20	0.40
27 (36)	50	Centimos (Ag) 1954	1.60	2.60
28 (36a)	50	Centimos (Ag) 1960. Same type as No. 27, but narrow shield	1.60	2.60
29 (41)	50	Centimos (Ni) 1965–	0.40	0.60
30 (37)	1	Bolivar (Ag) 1954	3.00	4.50

			VF	XF
31 (37a)	1	Bolivar (Ag) 1960–1965. Same type as No. 30, but Bolívar's head slightly altered	3.00	4.00
32 (42)	1	Bolivar (Ni) 1967–	0.60	9.00
33 (A37)	2	Bolivares (Ag) 1960–1965	5.00	7.00
34 (43)	2	Bolivares (Ni) 1967–	1.00	1.80

35 (A40) 10 Centimos (Cu–Ni) 1971. National coat of arms, name of country, date. ℞ denomination between laurel branches tied underneath

	XF	Unc
	0.20	0.30

COMMEMORATIVE ISSUE FOR SIMON BOLIVAR

			XF	Unc
36 (45)	10	Bolivar (Ag) 1973	20.00	28.00
37 (44)	5	Bolivar (Ni) 1973. Type as No. 31	2.00	3.00
38 (49)	5	Centimos (Cooper-clad steel) 1974, 1976. 1977. Coat of arms, date. Rev. value	0.10	0.20

CONSERVATION COMMEMORATIVE (3)

			Unc	Proof
39 (46)	25	Bolivares (Ag) 1975	30.00	35.00
40 (47)	50	Bolivares (Ag) 1975	50.00	60.00
41 (48)	1000	Bolivares (Au) 1975	600.00	750.00

NATIONALIZATION OF OIL INDUSTRY

42 (54)	500	Bolivares (Au) 1975		–.–

			XF	Unc
43 (50)	25	Centimos (Ni) 1977–:		
		a) 1977; 26.8 gm., 1.18 mm thick	0.15	0.30
		b) 1978; 26.5 gm., 1.07 mm thick	0.15	0.30
44 (52)	1	Bolivar (Ni) 1977	0.50	1.00
45 (53)	5	Bolivar (Ni) 1977, 1978	1.80	2.50

150th ANNIVERSARY OF INDEPENDENCE (2)

46 (55)	75	Bolivares (Ag) 1980		35.00
47 (56)	100	Bolivares (Ag) 1980		45.00

West African States

Westafrikanische Staaten   Afrique de l'Ouest

The West African Monetary Union (UMOA) within the Franc Area
comprises the states of Dahomey (now Benin), Jvory Coast, Mauritania (up
to June 1973), Niger, Upper Volta, Senegal and Togo.

100 Centimes = 1 CFA Franc

				XF	Unc
1 (1)	1	Franc (Al) 1961–. Dune gazelle (Gazella leptoceros – Bovidae). ℞ gold weight of the Ashanti, 17th to 18th century between value		0.20	0.40
2 (2)	5	Francs (Al–Br) 1960–		0.50	0.80
3 (3)	10	Francs (Al–Br) 1959–		0.60	1.20
4 (A3)	25	Francs (Al–Br) 1970. Dune gazelle. ℞ Ashanti gold weight between value		1.00	1.60

ISSUE FOR THE FAO COIN PLAN

				XF	Unc
5 (5)	50	Francs (Cu–Ni) 1972. ℞ rice, millet, groundnuts, cocoa and coffee. Value and date		0.60	1.20
6 (4)	100	Francs (Ni) 1967–. Ashanti gold weight. ℞ value		1.60	2.50

COMMEMORATIVE ISSUE FOR THE 10th ANNIVERSARY OF THE WEST AFRICAN MONETARY UNION

				Unc	Proof
7 (6)	500	Francs (Ag) 1972		35.00	50.00

				XF	Unc
8 (7)	1	Franc (Cu–Ni) 1976–1978. Obv. as No. 6. Rev. value, date, inscription UNION MONETAIRE OUEST AFRICAINE		0.20	0.30
9 (8)	25	Francs (Al–Br) 1980		0.80	1.20

Western Samoa

Area: 1,133 sq. mi. Population: 156,000.
Group of islands in the Pacific with Savaii, Upolu, Manong and Apolima.
The former German protectorate came under New Zealand administration as a League of Nations mandate in 1919 and from 1946–1962 under
UN trusteeship. Since January 1, 1962 Western Samoa is an independent
chiefs aristocracy.
Capital: Apia, on the island of Upolu.

100 Sene = 1 Tala (Dollar)

MALIETOA TANUMAFILI since 1963

			XF	Unc
1 (1)	1	Sene (Br) 1967. Malietoa Tanumafili II. Head of State. ℞ value in wreath	0.10	0.20
2 (2)	2	Sene (Br) 1967	0.15	0.30
3 (3)	5	Sene (Cu–Ni) 1967	0.20	0.40
4 (4)	10	Sene (Cu–Ni) 1967	0.40	0.70
5 (5)	20	Sene (Cu–Ni) 1967	0.50	1.00
6 (6)	50	Sene (Cu–Ni) 1967, but with scroll	1.20	1.80

7 (7)	1 Tala (Cu–Ni) 1967. Type as No. 6		2.50	4.00

COMMEMORATIVE ISSUE FOR THE 75th ANNIVERSARY OF STEVENSON'S DEATH

				Unc	Proof
8 (8)	1 Tala (Cu–Ni) 1969. Robert Louis Stevenson (1850–1894), writer. Best known publication: "Treasure Island". He lived for many years in Vailima, Samoa, where he is also laid to rest. ℞ coat of arms, value			6.00	140.00

COMMEMORATIVE ISSUE FOR JAMES COOK

9 (9)	1 Tala (Cu–Ni) 1970. James Cook (1728–1779), British circumnavigator	6.00	70.00

COMMEMORATIVE ISSUE FOR THE VISIT OF POPE PAUL VI IN SAMOA ON NOVEMBER 29, 1970

10 (10)	1 Tala (Cu–Ni) 1970	6.00	80.00

COMMEMORATIVE ISSUE FOR THE 250th ANNIVERSARY OF THE DISCOVERY OF SAMOA BY JACOB ROGGEVEEN (JUNE 14, 1722)

11 (11)	1 Tala (Cu–Ni) 1972	6.00	110.00

COMMEMORATIVE ISSUE FOR THE 10th BRITISH EMPIRE AND COMMONWEALTH GAMES IN CHRISTCHURCH, NEW ZEALAND (24. 1.–2. 2. 1974)

			Unc	Proof
12 (12)	1 Tala 1974. Boxer, functional legend, date. Rev. national coat of arms, name of coutry, value:			
		a) (Ag)		200.00
		b) (Cu-Ni)	5.00	

			XF	Unc
13 (13)	1 Sene (Br) 1974		0.10	0.15
14 (14)	2 Sene (Br) 1974		0.15	0.25
15 (15)	5 Sene (Cu-Ni) 1974		0.20	0.30
16 (16)	10 Sene (Cu-Ni) 1974		0.35	0.50
17 (17)	20 Sene (Cu-Ni) 1974		0.45	0.80
18 (18)	50 Sene (Cu-Ni) 1974		1.20	1.80
19 (19)	1 Tala (Cu-Ni) 1974		1.80	3.50

BICENTENARY OF AMERICAN INDEPENDENCE (2)

			Unc	Proof
20 (20)	1 Tala 1976:			
		a) (Ag)		100.00
		b) (Cu-Ni)	4.00	
21 (21)	100 Tala (Au) 1976			260.00

OLYMPIC GAMES 1976 IN MONTREAL (2)

22 (22)	1 Tala 1976:			
		a) (Ag)		45.00
		b) (Cu-Ni)	4.00	
23 (23)	100 Tala (Au) 1976			260.00

25th ANNIVERSARY OF THE SILVER JUBILEE OF HER MAJESTY QUEEN ELIZABETH II (2)

24 (24)	1 Tala 1977:			
		a) (Ag)		50.00
		b) (Cu-Ni)	6.00	
25 (25)	100 Tala (Au) 1977			260.00

LINDBERGH COMMEMORATIVE (2)

26 (26)	1 Tala 1977:			
		a) (Ag)		40.00
		b) (Cu-Ni)	6.00	
27 (27)	100 Tala (Au) 1977			220.00

50th ANNIVERSARY OF THE FIRST TRANS PACIFIC FLIGHT (2)

		Unc	Proof
28 (28)	1 Tala 1978:		
	a) (Ag)		40.00
	b) (Cu-Ni)	6.00	
29 (29)	100 Tala (Au) 1978		220.00

COMMONWEALTH GAMES (2)

30 (30)	1 Tala 1978:		
	a) (Ag)		40.00
	b) (Cu-Ni)	6.00	
31 (31)	100 Tala (Au) 1978		220.00

200th ANNIVERSARY OF THE DEATH OF JAMES COOK (3)

32 (32)	1 Tala 1979:		
	a) (Ag)		30.00
	b) (Cu-Ni)	6.00	
33 (33)	10 Tala (Ag) 1979	30.00	50.00
34 (34)	100 Tala (Au) 1977		400.00

OLYMPIC GAMES 1980 IN MOSCOW (3)

35 (35)	1 Tala (Cu-Ni) 1980	6.00	
36 (36)	10 Tala (Ag) 1980	30.00	50.00
37 (37)	100 Tala (Au) 1980		400.00

FOR THE FAO COIN PLAN (2)

38 (38)	1 Tala (Cu-Ni) 1980	5.00	
39 (39)	10 Tala (Ag) 1980		50.00

GOVERNOR WILHELM SOLF (3)

40 (40)	1 Tala (Cu-Ni) 1980	5.00	
41 (41)	10 Tala (Ag) 1980	30.00	50.00
42 (42)	100 Tala (Au) 1980		270.00

WEDDING OF PRINCE CHARLES AND LADY DIANA (3)

43	1 Tala (Cu-Ni) 1981	5.00	
44	10 Tala (Ag) 1981	30.00	50.00
45	100 Tala (Au) 1981		270.00

Area: 61,890 sq. mi. Population: 6,000,000.
The Imamate, under Osman governorship since 1517, obtained its independence in 1918. On September 27, 1962, upon the death of Imam Ahmed, his son and successor, Mohammed el-Badr was deposed a few days after his accession by a coup d'etat of the army, and the republic was proclaimed. The Imam who had excaped, however, succeeded in rallying devoted tribal warriors and to keep parts of the impassable hill country under his control.
Capital: San'a and Taiz.

2 Halala = 1 Bogash, 40 Bogash = 1 Imadi;
since 1962: 40 Bogash = 1 Riyal

YAHYA BIN MOHAMMED HAMID AL-DIN 1918–1948

			VF	XF
1 (1)	½ Halala (Br) A.H. 1342–1346 (1924–1928). Legend and crescent. ℞ legend		8.00	16.00
2 (2)	1 Halala (Br) A.H. 1322–1361 (1904–1944)		2.00	4.50
3 (3)	1 Bogash (Br) A.H. 1341–1367 (1923–1948)		2.50	5.00
4 (4)	1/20 Imadi (Ag) A.H. 1337–1366 (1919–1948)		8.00	12.00
5 (5)	1/10 Imadi (Ag) A.H. 1337–1366 (1919–1948)		5.50	8.00
6 (8)	⅛ Imadi (Ag) A.H. 1339 (1920)		130.00	220.00

			VF	XF
7 (6)	¼ Imadi (Ag) A.H. 1344–1366 (1926–1948)		6.50	10.50
8 (7)	1 Imadi (Ag) A.H. 1344 (1926)		16.00	28.00

AHMED HAMID AL-DIN 1948–1962

			VF	XF
9 (11)	1 Halala. Legend and crescent. ℞ legend			
	a) (Br) A.H. 1368–1381 (1949–1962)		1.50	2.50
	b) (Al) A.H. 1374–1378 (1955–1959)		0.80	1.60

				VF	XF
10 (12)	1	Bogash			
		a) (Br) A.H. 1368–1379 (1949–1960)		2.00	3.00
		b) (Al) A.H. 1374–1376 (1955–1957)		0.80	2.00

			VF	XF
11 (13)	¹/₁₆	Imadi (Ag) A.H. 1367–1374 (1948–1955). Pentagon	4.00	6.50
12 (14)	¹/₈	Imadi (Ag) A.H. 1367–1380 (1948–1961)	4.00	6.00
13 (15)	¼	Imadi (Ag) A.H. 1367–1377 (1948–1958)	5.00	8.00
14 (16)	½	Imadi (Ag) A.H. 1367–1379 (1948–1960)	8.00	16.00
15 (17)	1	Imadi (Ag) A.H. 1367–1380 (1948–1961)	16.00	22.00
16 (G15)	¼	Imadi (Au) A.H. 1370–1377 (1951–1958). Crescent and legend. ℞ legend	180.00	240.00
17 (G16)	½	Imadi (Au) A.H. 1370 (1951)	300.00	360.00
18 (G17)	1	Imadi (Au) A.H. 1377 (1958)	720.00	840.00

			VF	XF
19 (18)	1	Halala (Al) no date (1956)	1.20	2.50
20 (19)	1	Bogash (Al) no date (1956)	1.60	3.50

REPUBLIC since 1962

			VF	XF
21 (20)	1	Halala (Br) A.H. 1382 (1963). Hand holding torch	0.80	1.20
22 (21)	1	Halala (Br) A.H. 1382 (1963). Flag with star in circle	1.50	2.50
23 (32)	½	Bogash (Br) A.H. 1382 (1963). Flag with star in circle	2.80	5.00
24 (22)	1	Bogash (Bra) A.H. 1382 (1963)	1.50	2.50
25 (23)	¹/₂₀	Riyal (Ag) A.H. 1382 (1963)	2.00	3.50
26 (24)	¹/₁₀	Riyal (Ag) A.H. 1382 (1963)	2.50	4.00
27 (25)	¹/₅	Riyal (Ag) A.H. 1382 (1963)	4.00	6.00

		VF	**XF**

28 (A25) ¼ Riyal (Ag) A.H. 1382 (1963) 8.00 12.00

29 (26) ½ Bogash (Al–Br) A.H. 1382 (1963).
Coffee plant (Coffea arabica – Rubiaceae), branch 0.40 0.60

30 (27) 1 Bogash (Al–Br) A.H. 1382 (1963) 0.50 0.80
31 (A27) 2 Bogash (Al–Br) A.H. 1382 (1963) 0.80 1.50
32 (28) 5 Bogash (Ag) A.H. 1382 (1963) 1.60 3.20
33 (29) 10 Bogash (Ag) A.H. 1382 (1963) 2.50 4.00
34 (30) 20 Bogash (Ag) A.H. 1382 (1963) 5.00 8.00

35 (31) 1 Riyal (Ag) A.H. 1382 (1963). Coffee
plant, branch 9.00 12.00

COMMEMORATIVE ISSUES (10) FOR THE 1st MANNED MOON LANDING ON JULY 20, 1969, AND IN MEMORY OF QADHI MOHAMMED MAHMUD AZZUBAIRI

36 1 Riyal (Ag) 1969. Man riding on drome-

dary. ℞ state emblem, value, date, name
of country

37   2 Riyals (Ag) 1969. Lion's head. ℞ like
       No. 36

20.00

38   2 Riyals (Ag) 1969. Cape Kennedy: take-
       off of "Apollo 11" on July 16, 1969. ℞
       like No. 36

30.00

39   2 Riyals (Ag) 1969. US moon research
       programme, 3rd section "manned

		landing". Apollo programme. Astronauts examining the ground, moon capsule "Apollo 11" and date of the landing, July 20, 1969. Globe. ℞ like No. 36	**Proof**
			30.00
40	5	Riyals (Au) 1969. Head of falcon. ℞ like No. 36	36.00
41	10	Riyals (Au) 1969. Arabian slender-horned gazelles. ℞ like No. 36	85.00
42	20	Riyals (Au) 1969. Same type as No. 36	160.00
43	20	Riyals (Au) 1969. Same type as No. 39	200.00
44	30	Riyals (Au) 1969. Qadhi Mohammed Mahmud Azzubairi, fighter for independence	260.00
45	50	Riyals (Au) 1969. Lion. ℞ like No. 36	550.00

			XF	**Unc**
46 (33)	1	Fils (Al) 1974. Coat of arms. Rev. value, date	0.15	0.25
47 (34)	5	Fils (Bra) 1974. Type as No. 46	0.25	0.40
48 (35)	10	Fils (Bra) 1974. Type as No. 46	0.30	0.60
49 (36)	25	Fils (Cu-Ni) 1974. Type as No. 46	0.40	0.80
50 (37)	50	Fils (Cu-Ni) 1974. Type as No. 46	0.50	1.00
51 (42)	1	Rial (Cu-Ni) 1976. Type as No. 46	2.00	3.50

FOR THE FAO COIN PLAN (6)

			XF	**Unc**
52 (43)	1	Fils (Al) 1978	0.15	0.25
53 (38)	5	Fils (Bra) 1974	0.25	0.40
54 (39)	10	Fils (Bra) 1974	0.30	0.60
55 (40)	25	Fils (Cu-Ni) 1974	0.40	0.80
56 (41)	50	Fils (Cu-Ni) 1974	0.50	1.00

			XF	**Proof**
57 (44)	1	Rial (Cu-Ni) 1978	3.00	4.00

			Unc	**Proof**
58	2½	Riyals (Ag) 1975. Oil Exploration	20.00	30.00
59	5	Riyals (Ag) 1975. Mona Lisa	25.00	30.00
60	15	Riyals (Ag) 1975. Jerusalem	50.00	60.00
61	20	Riyals (Au) 1975. Mosque	70.00	90.00
62	25	Riyals (Au) 1975. Oil Exploration	100.00	130.00
63	50	Riyals (Au) 1975. Mona Lisa	200.00	225.00
64	100	Riyals (Au) 1975. Jerusalem	380.00	400.00

OLYMPIC GAMES 1976 IN MONTREAL (2)

			Unc	**Proof**
65	10	Riyals (Ag) 1975	35.00	40.00
66	75	Riyals (Au) 1975	250.00	350.00

Yugoslavia

Area: 98,740 sq. mi. Population: 21,000,000.
Alexander as Regent united Serbia, Croatia and Slovenia to form a kingdom on December 1, 1918, which has been named Yugoslavia since 1929. On November 29, 1943 the Federal Republic of Yugoslavia was created which was transformed into a Federal People's Republic on November 29, 1945.
Capital: Belgrade (Beograd).

100 Para = 1 Dinar

PETER I 1918–1921

			VF	XF
1 (1)	5	Para (Sn) 1920. Crowned arms. ℞ value	8.00	18.00
2 (2)	10	Para (Sn) 1920. Same type as No. 1	4.00	7.50
3 (3)	25	Para (Ni–Br) 1920	1.50	4.00

ALEXANDER I 1921–1934

			VF	XF
4 (4)	50	Para (Ni–Br) 1925. Alexander I (1888–1934), Regent 1918–1921, King 1921–1934. ℞ value in wreath, crown above above	0.80	2.00
5 (5)	1	Dinar (Ni–Br) 1925. Same type as No. 4	1.00	2.00
6 (6)	2	Dinara (Ni–Br) 1925. Same type as No. 4	2.50	3.50
7 (7)	10	Dinara (Ag) 1931. Alexander I, head left. ℞ crowned heraldic eagle	4.00	8.00
8 (8)	20	Dinara (Ag) 1931. Same type as No. 7	10.50	20.00
9 (9)	50	Dinara (Ag) 1932. Same type as No. 7	32.00	70.00

			VF	XF
10 (10)	20	Dinara (Au) 1925. Same type as No. 4	220.00	250.00
11 (A11)	1	Dukat (Au) 1931–1934	110.00	130.00
12 (12)	4	Dukats (Au) 1931–1933	900.00	1200.00

PETER II 1934–1945

			VF	XF
13 (13)	25	Para (Br) 1938. Wreath, crown above. ℞ value (center hole)	2.50	4.50
14 (14)	50	Para (Al–Br) 1938. Crown. ℞ value	1.00	1.50
15 (15)	1	Dinar (Al–Br) 1938	1.00	1.50

			VF	XF
16	2	Dinara (Al-Br) 1938		
		a) (Y 16) large crown (see illustration)	1.00	1.50
		b) (Y 17) small crown	5.00	15.00
17 (18)	10	Dinara (Ni) 1938. Peter II (1923–1970), head right	1.00	2.50
18 (19)	20	Dinara (Ag) 1938. Peter II, head left	4.00	6.00

			VF	XF
19 (20)	50	Dinara (Ag) 1938. Peter II, head right	6.00	12.00

PEOPLE'S REPUBLIC since 1945

			VF	XF
20 (21)	50	Para (Sn) 1945. Coat of arms of the People's Republic. ℞ value	1.20	3.00
21 (22)	1	Dinar (Sn) 1945	0.80	2.50
22 (23)	2	Dinara (Sn) 1945	1.20	2.50
23 (24)	5	Dinara (Sn) 1945	1.50	2.80
24 (25)	50	Para (Al) 1953. Coat of arms, new legend FEDERATIVNA NARODNA REPUBLIKA JUGOSLAVIJA. ℞ value	0.10	0.20
25 (26)	1	Dinar (Al) 1953. Cyrillic legend	0.10	0.25
26 (27)	2	Dinara (Al) 1953	0.15	0.30
27 (28)	5	Dinara (Al) 1953. Cyrillic legend	0.25	0.40

				VF	XF
28 (29)	10	Dinara (Al–Br) 1955. Coat of arms. ℞ female farm worker with sheaf of wheat		0.20	0.40
29 (30)	20	Dinara (Al–Br) 1955. ℞ factory worker, section of a cog-wheel, symbolizing the industrialization		0.30	0.60
30 (31)	50	Dinara (Al-Br) 1955. ℞ male and female worker, section of cog-wheel, and ear of wheat		0.50	1.00
31 (32)	1	Dinar (Al) 1963. Coat of arms, new legend SOCIJALISTIKA FEDERATIVNA REPUBLIKA JUGOSLAVIJA. ℞ value		0.10	0.20
32 (33)	2	Dinara (Al) 1963		0.15	0.25
33 (34)	5	Dinara (Al) 1963		0.20	0.35
34 (35)	10	Dinara (Al–Br) 1963		0.20	0.40
35 (A35)	20	Dinara (Al–Br) 1963		0.30	0.60
36 (B35)	50	Dinara (Al–Br) 1963		0.40	0.75

CURRENCY REFORM: 100 old Dinara = 1 new Dinar

37 (36)	5	Para (Al–Br) 1965		0.15	0.30

38 (37)	1	Dinar (Cu-Ni) 1965		0.50	1.00
39 (38)	5	Para (Al-Br) 1965, 1972–1975, 1979. Coat of arms. New legend SFR JUGOSLAVIJA		0.05	0.10
40 (39)	10	Para (Al-Br) 1965–1980		0.10	0.20
41 (40)	20	Para (Al-Br) 1965–1980		0.15	0.30
42 (41)	50	Para (Al-Br) 1965–1980		0.30	0.60

43 (42)	1	Dinar (Cu–Ni) 1968		0.40	0.80

COMMEMORATIVE ISSUES (6) FOR THE 25th ANNIVERSARY OF THE YUGOSLAV FEDERATED REPUBLIC

44 (48)   20 Dinara (Ag) 1968. Monument in Jaice, Bosnia. ℞ state emblem, value, name of country   **Proof**

                                                                  25.00

45 (49)   50 Dinara (Ag) 1968. Josip Broz Tito (*1892), President since 1953. ℞ like No. 44   55.00

46 (50)   100 Dinara (Au) 1968. Same type as No. 44   160.00

47 (51)   200 Dinara (Au) 1968. Same type as No. 45   400.00

48 (52)   500 Dinara (Au) 1968. Same type as No. 44   1100.00

49 (53)   1000 Dinara (Au) 1968. Same type as No. 45   1800.00

COMMEMORATIVE ISSUES (2) FOR THE FAO COIN PLAN

50 (43)   2 Dinara (Cu–Ni) 1970. State emblem. ℞ value in circular inscription, date, and FIAT PANIS above. FAO between ears of wheat

                                          XF   **Unc**

                                          0.60   1.00

51 (44)   5 Dinara (Cu–Ni) 1970. Same type as No. 50   1.00   1.80

			XF	Unc
52 (A45)	1	Dinar (Cu-Ni) 1973–1980	0.20	0.40
53 (45)	2	Dinara (Cu-Ni) 1971–1980. Type as No. 52	0.20	0.40
54 (46)	5	Dinara (Cu-Ni) 1971–1976, 1979. Type as No. 52	0.30	0.60
55 (A47)	10	Dinara (Cu-Ni) 1976–1979. Type as No. 52	0.50	1.00

30th ANNIVERSARY OF THE END OF WORLD WAR II

56 (47)	5	Dinara (Cu-Ni) 1975. Type as No. 54, but commemorative legend	0.60	1.20

FOR THE FAO COIN PLAN (2)

57 (54)	1	Dinar (Cu-Ni) 1976. Type as No. 50	0.20	0.40
58 (55)	10	Dinara (Cu-Ni) 1976. Type as No. 50	0.80	1.60

85th ANNIVERSARY OF THE BIRTH OF J. B. TITO

59 (56)	200	Dinara (Ag) 1977		22.00

8th MEDITERRANEAN GAMES AT SPLIT 1979 (11)

			Proof
60 (57)	100	Dinara (Ag) 1978	20.00
61 (58)	150	Dinara (Ag) 1978	30.00
62 (59)	200	Dinara (Ag) 1978	40.00
63 (60)	250	Dinara (Ag) 1978	50.00
64 (61)	300	Dinara (Ag) 1978	60.00
65 (62)	350	Dinara (Ag) 1978	70.00
66 (63)	400	Dinara (Ag) 1978	80.00
67 (64)	1500	Dinara (Au) 1978	250.00
68 (65)	2000	Dinara (Au) 1978	320.00
69 (66)	2500	Dinara (Au) 1978	400.00
70 (67)	5000	Dinara (Au) 1978	800.00

VUKOVAR CONGRESS (3)

			Unc	Proof
71 (68)	500	Dinara (Ag) 1980		25.00
72 (69)	1000	Dinara (Ag) 1980		50.00
73 (70)	1500	Dinara (Ag) 1980		75.00

TITO'S DEATH

			Unc	Proof
74 (71)	1000	Dinara (Ag) 1980	40.00	50.00

WORLD TABLE TENNIS CHAMPIONSHIP GAMES 1981 (3)

			Proof
75 (72)	500	Dinara (Ag) 1981	25.00
76 (73)	1000	Dinara (Ag) 1981	50.00
77 (74)	1500	Dinara (Ag) 1981	75.00

Saire   # Zaire   **République du Zaïre**

Area: 902,080 sq. mi. Population: 30,000,000.
The new name of Zaire was adopted by Congo (Kinshasa) on October 27, 1971.
Capital: Kinshasa.

100 Sengi = 1 Likuta, 100 Makuta = 1 Zaire
(Makuta = plural of Likuta)

			XF	Unc
1 (3)	5	Makuta (Cu-Ni) 1977. Bust of President Mobuto. Rev. value	0.60	1.00
2 (4)	10	Makuta (Cu-Ni) 1973, 1975. Bust of President Mobuto. Rev. coat of arms, value, date	1.00	1.50
3 (5)	20	Makuta (Cu-Ni) 1973, 1976. Bust of President Mobuto. Rev. arm holding torch	1.20	2.00

CONSERVATION COMMEMORATIVE (3)

			Unc	Proof
4 (8)	2.50	Zaires (Ag) 1975	30.00	35.00
5 (9)	5	Zaires (Ag) 1975	50.00	60.00
6 (10)	100	Zaires (Au) 175	600.00	750.00

Sambia   # Zambia   **Zambia**

Area: c. 288,130 sq. mi. Population: 5,000,000.
The former Northern Rhodesia was a part of the Central African Union with the designation of Rhodesia and Nyasaland from 1953 to 1963. Under the name of Zambia the country became independent on October 24, 1964. The Republic of Zambia is a member of the British Commonwealth.
Capital: Lusaka.

12 Pence = 1 Shilling, 20 Shillings = 1 £,
since January 16, 1968: 100 Ngwee = 1 Kwacha

		XF	Unc
1 (1)	6 Pence (Ni–Bra) 1964. Coat of arms. ℞ morning glory flower (Ipomoea sp. – Convolvulaceae)	0.60	1.00
2 (2)	1 Shilling (Ni–Bra) 1964. ℞ crowned hornbill (Tockus = Lophoceros alboterminatus – Bucerotidae)	1.20	2.00
3 (3)	2 Shillings (Ni–Bra) 1964. ℞ bohor reedbuck (Redunca redunca – Bovidae)	1.80	3.50

COMMEMORATIVE ISSUE FOR THE FIRST ANNIVERSARY OF INDEPENDENCE

		Unc	Proof
4 (4)	5 Shillings (Ni) 1965. Kenneth David Kaunda (*1924), President of State. ℞ coat of arms	7.00	12.00

			XF	Unc
5 (5)	1	Penny (Br) 1966 (center hole)	0.50	0.80
6 (6)	6	Pence (Cu–Ni) 1966. Kenneth David Kaunda. ℞ morning glory flower	0.40	0.80
7 (7)	1	Shilling (Cu–Ni) 1966. Crowned hornbill	0.70	1.20
8 (8)	2	Shillings (Cu–Ni) 1966. ℞ bohor reedbuck	1.50	3.00

NEW CURRENCY (Decimal System): 100 Ngwee = 1 Kwacha

9 (9)	1	Ngwee (Br) 1968. ℞ aardvark (Orycteropus afer – Orycteropidae)	0.15	0.25

10 (10)	2	Ngwee (Br) 1968. ℞ martial eagle (Polemaëtus bellicosus – Accipitridae)	0.20	0.30

11 (11)	5	Ngwee (Cu–Ni) 1968. ℞ morning glory flower	0.30	0.50

			XF	Unc
12 (12)	10 Ngwee (Cu–Ni) 1968. ℞ crowned hornbill		0.50	0.90

			XF	Unc
13 (13)	20 Ngwee (Cu–Ni) 1968. ℞ bohor reed-buck		0.80	1.80

ISSUE FOR THE FAO COIN PLAN

			XF	Unc
14 (14)	50 Ngwee (Cu-Ni) 1969. Kenneth David Kaunda, head right. R maize (Zea mays – Gramineae)		2.00	3.50
15 (15)	50 Ngwee (Cu–Ni) 1972		2.50	4.00

SECOND REPUBLIC 13th DECEMBER 1972

			XF	Unc
16 (16)	50 Ngwee (Cu-Ni) 1972		2.50	4.00

10th ANNIVERSARY OF INDEPENDENCE

			Unc	Proof
17 (17)	1 Kwacha (Ag) 1974			40.00

CONSERVATION COMMEMORATIVE (3)

			Unc	Proof
18 (18)	5 Kwacha (Ag) 1979		30.00	35.00
19 (19)	10 Kwacha (Ag) 1979		50.00	60.00
20 (20)	200 Kwacha (Au) 1979		600.00	750.00

Area: 640 sq. mi. Population: 330,000.

A Portuguese rule over this island lasting 150 years, during which the town of Zanzibar was founded, ended with its recapture by the Arabs from Oman. The Imam of Muscat, Seyyid Said, became Sultan in Zanzibar in 1833, transferred his main seat there in 1840 and extended his rule to the East African coastal strip from Lindi beyond Kilwa in the south, then Mombasa in the north as far as Lamu and Mogadishu. After his death in 1856, the Sultanate of Zanzibar separated from the Imamate in Muscat, but remained in the same dynasty with a common ruling regarding the succession to the throne. The agreement between the German Reich and Great Britain regarding the delimitation of their mutual interests in the so-called Heligoland/Zanzibar Treaty of 1890 robbed the Sultan of his influence over the African coast, but left him the Island of Pemba and placed him under the protection of British rule. The independence granted the Sultanate on 10th December 1963 lasted only one month. Since 12th January 1964 Zanzibar is a republic which united on 27th April 1964 with Tanganyika to form the United Republic of Tanganyika-Zanzibar – since 3rd November 1964 known as Tanzania.

Capital: Zanzibar.

100 Cents = 1 Rupee

ALI BEN HAMOUD 1902–1911

			VF	XF
1 (8)	1 Cent (Br) 1908. Arabic legend. ℞ cocos palm (Cocos nucifera-Palmae)		160.00	200.00

			VF	XF
2 (9)	10 Cents (Br) 1908		200.00	250.00
3 (10)	20 Cents (Ni) 1908		250.00	300.00

Previous issues, see "Weltmünzkatalog 19. Jahrhundert" (World Coin Catalogue of the 19th Century)

Zimbabwe

Simbabwe   **Zimbabwe**

Area: 150,333 sq. mi. Population 7,000,000.
The name of Zimbabwe was adopted by this new country on April 18, 1980.
(cf. Rhodesia, Rhodesia and Nyasaland, Southern Rhodesia).
Capital: Salisbury.

100 Cents = 1 Dollar

			XF	Unc
1 (1)	1	Cent (Br) 1980	0.30	0.50
2 (2)	5	Cents (Cu-Ni) 1980	0.40	1.00
3 (3)	10	Cents (Cu-Ni) 1980	0.50	1.20
4 (4)	20	Cents (Cu-Ni) 1980	0.80	1.50
5 (5)	50	Cents (Cu-Ni) 1980	1.00	2.00
6 (6)	1	Dollar (Cu-Ni) 1980	2.00	3.00